€ 58.

THE WESTERN GREEKS

THE WESTERN GREEKS
Classical Civilization in the Western Mediterranean

Giovanni Pugliese Carratelli

With 1,600 illustrations, 600 in colour

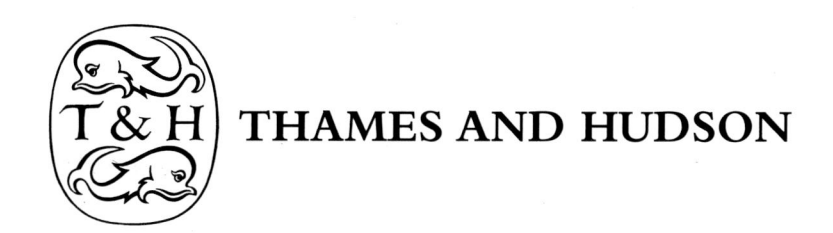

THAMES AND HUDSON

First Published in Great Britain in 1996 by
Thames and Hudson Ltd, London

Copyright © 1996 RCS Libri & Grandi Opere S.p.A.

Any copy of this book issued by the publisher is sold subject to the condition that it shall not by way of trade or otherwise be lent, resold, hired out or otherwise circulated without the publisher's prior consent in any form of binding or cover than that in which it is published and without a similar condition including these words being imposed on a subsequent purchaser

All Rights Reserved. No part of this publication may be reproduced or transmitted in any form or by any means, electronic or mechanical, including photocopy, recording or any other information storage and retrieval system, without prior permission in writing from the publisher

British Library Cataloguing-in-Publication Data

A catalogue record for this book is available from the British Library

ISBN 0-500-23726-3

Printed and bound in Italy

The theme of the fourteenth exhibition at Palazzo Grassi is *The Western Greeks*. With the benefit of experience acquired in the course of ten years of activity, it will constitute a valuable addition to the series of exhibitions devoted to the great civilizations of the past that have been of lasting significance for Europe as we know it today.

In the first place, my heartfelt thanks must go to the Minister for the Cultural Assets, who participated in the organization of the exhibition and decided that it should be included in the program of events devoted to Magna Graecia. Without his support, the exhibition would not have been able to present such a splendid range of exhibits, nor could it have made such an important contribution to scholarship.

Then I would like to thank those who helped to get the exhibition off the ground: not only the staff at Palazzo Grassi, therefore, but also Mario Serio, Director General of the Ministry for the Cultural and Environmental Assets, Antonino Scimemi, Director General for the Cultural Assets of Sicily, the members of the Exhibition Committee – first and foremost, Giovanni Pugliese Carratelli, and also Angelo Bottini, Dieter Mertens, and those who have designed the exhibition itself, especially Gae Aulenti and Pierluigi Cerri.

From the outset, it has been the policy of Palazzo Grassi to combine special skills and knowledge of differing kinds, in the firm belief that a successful exhibition is not merely a collection of objects, however beautiful they may be, or a series of attractive installations. On the contrary, it should be a cultural product that is able to communicate ideas to the public, stimulating the minds and according with the taste of those who are interested in the particular theme.

Because Palazzo Grassi has always taken this course, it has received ample recognition for its role on an international level. This is demonstrated by the readiness with which leading cultural institutions throughout the world have agreed to collaborate – and this has been particularly true on this occasion.

I hope that those who visit the exhibition and read the catalogue will appreciate the hard work that has gone into the organization of this extremely complex project, which is but one of various cultural events sponsored by Fiat. Moreover, I am convinced that the demand for culture in our society reflects a desire for self-improvement and a thirst for knowledge that should be fostered by those who are in a position to do so, whatever their roles and responsibilities may be.

Giovanni Agnelli

PALAZZO GRASSI

Comitato Amici
di Palazzo Grassi

President
Feliciano Benvenuti

Vice-President
Marella Agnelli

Vice-President
Giuseppe Donegà

Director of Cultural Programs
Paolo Viti

Director of the Administration
Pasquale Bonagura

President
Susanna Agnelli

Committee
Marella Agnelli
Umberto Agnelli
Mirella Barracco
Vittore Branca
Cristiana Brandolini D'Adda
Francesco Cingano
Attilio Codognato
Giancarlo Ferro
Gianluigi Gabetti
Knud W. Jensen
Michel Laclotte
Giancarlo Ligabue
Pietro Marzotto
Thomas Messer
Philippe de Montebello
Sabatino Moscati
Giovanni Nuvoletti Perdomini
Richard E. Oldenburg
Giuseppe Panza di Biumo
Alfonso Emilio Pérez Sánchez
Claude Pompidou
Maurice Rheims
Cesare Romiti
Norman Rosenthal
Guido Rossi
Francesco Valcanover
Mario Valeri Manera
Bruno Zevi

Secretary
Paolo Viti

Palazzo Grassi S.p.A.
San Samuele 3231, Venezia

The Western Greeks testifies to Palazzo Grassi's efforts to bring together and present the masterpieces that resulted from the transplantation of Greek culture to foreign soil.

The works of art presented in the exhibition speak for themselves. They need no explanations, as they emanate the vibrant expressiveness of the Classical ideal, an ideal that has remained fundamental to all western civilization.

This art has always been the primeval source of western aesthetics, both yesterday and today, owing to the purity of its forms and its figurative plasticity. These creations are the outcome of a process of progressive perfection, a striving to achieve the sublime. That achievement, however, drew on a formidable background of civilization and theoretical culture, and such are the values that we take in – unconsciously and instinctively – as we admire each exhibit, and proceed, filled with marvel and anticipation at the new archaeological finds, along the corridors of history. This ever-unfolding story of humanity continues to be a part of modern man, not merely because of his affinities with the Greek colonists of the western Mediterranean, but because the foundations of today's mentality and morality lay on the Greek heritage. The fundamental canons of both individual and collective ethics descend from Greek culture and continue to permeate our own.

Today's inhabitants of the Greek colonial lands of Italy are the product of other civilizations as well – both Roman and "barbarian" – making ours a complex culture, in which the individual has varied origins and multiple frames of reference. And yet the civilization represented in *The Western Greeks* is the pivot, the very core of our cultural references. Each of these works of art is an ancestor, a "parent", in the etymological sense.

While we have become used to much simplification and hurried superficiality, this exhibition and the studies that preceded it, manage instead to penetrate all that lies behind each exhibit and the vast world to which it refers. That background includes the Greek colonists' inquiries into philosophy and the physical world, and the spiritual foundations of the *polis*, which help shed light on these exceptional works of art. A kind of luminous aura surrounds each exhibit, urging the visitor to penetrate beyond the extraordinary exterior and discover the pulsing interior of the civilization that the Greek settlers brought with them to the West. The task of this catalogue is to serve as a guide to that civilization.

Feliciano Benvenuti

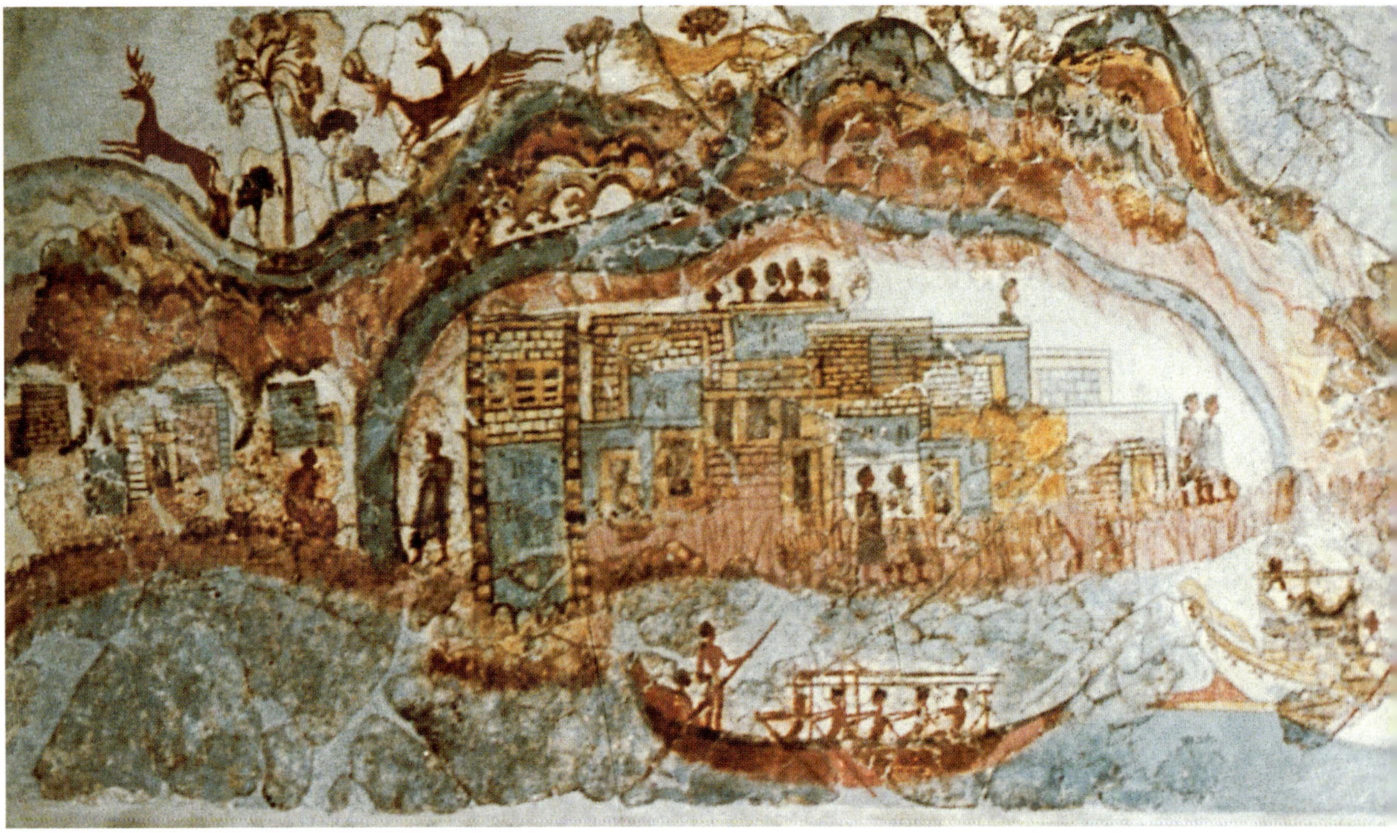

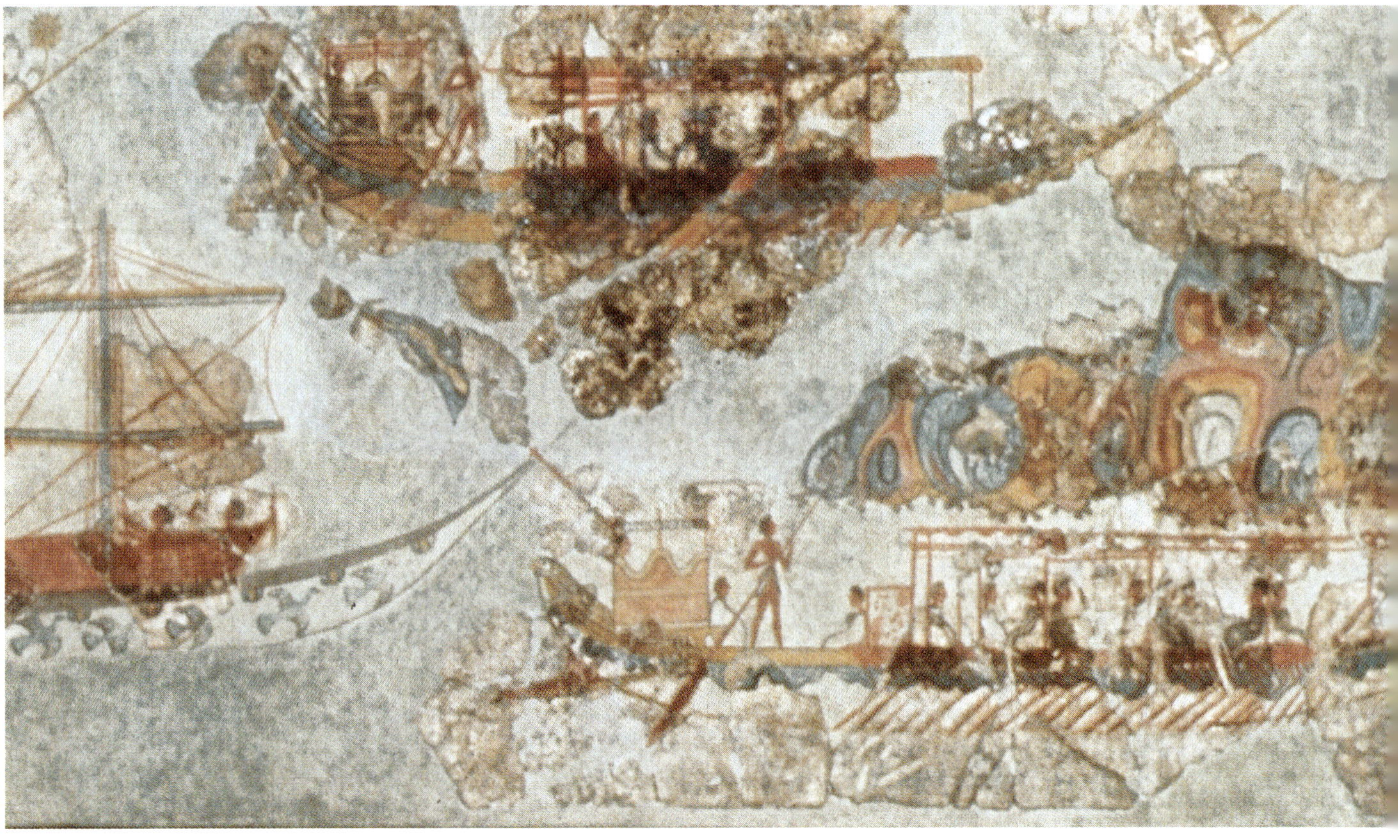

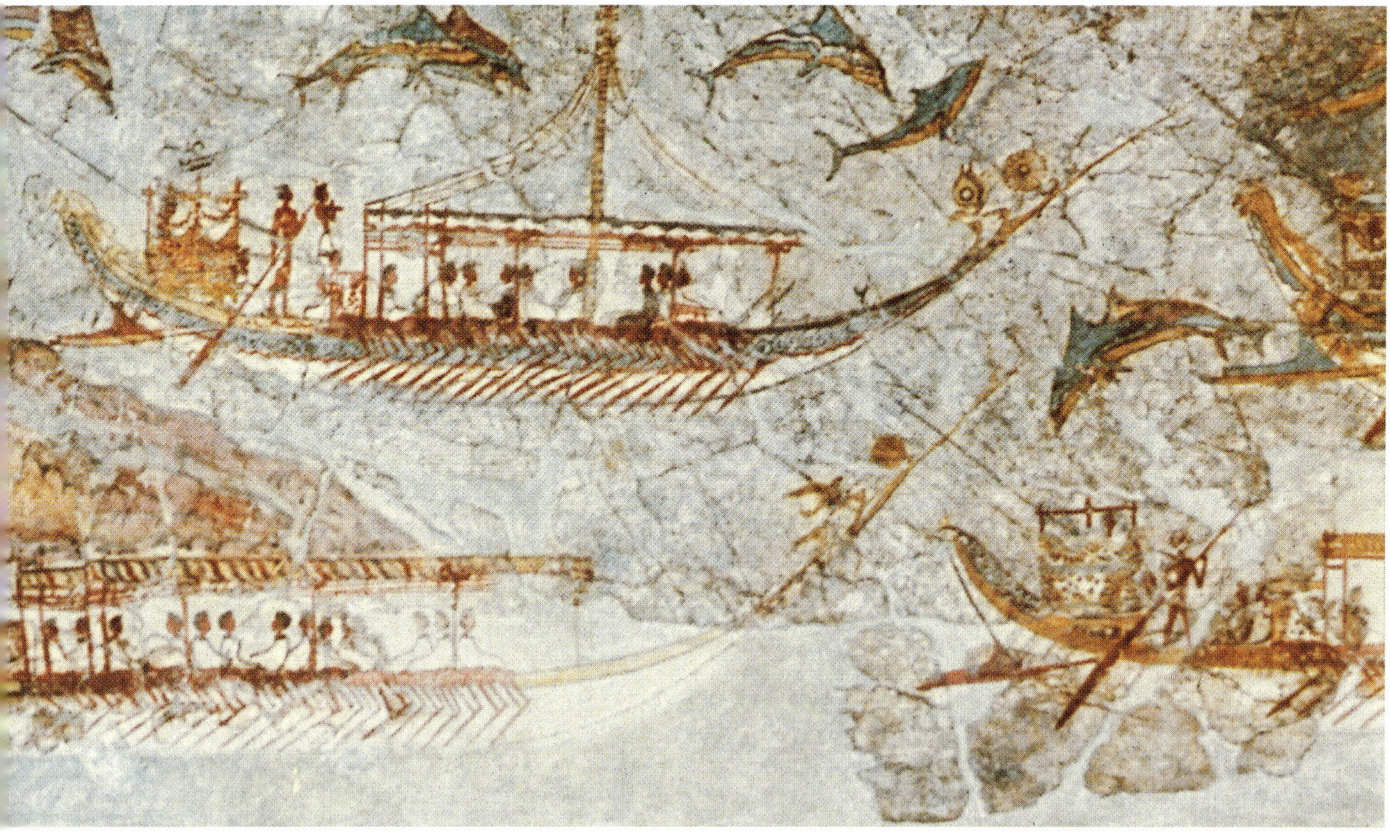

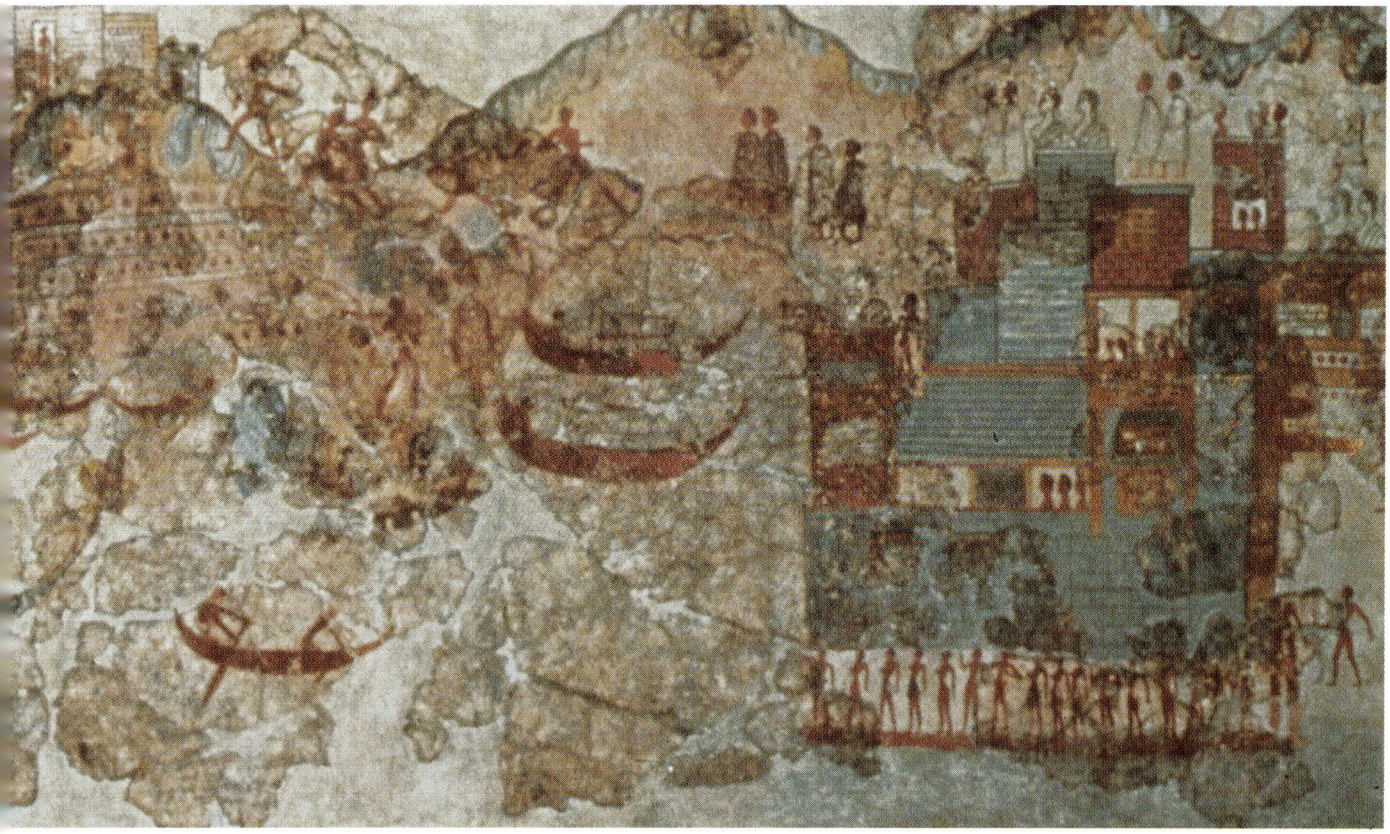

With the patronage of
the President of the Italian Republic

and with the endorsement of
the Accademia Nazionale dei Lincei, Rome

This book was published
on the occasion of the exhibition
THE WESTERN GREEKS
Palazzo Grassi, San Samuele 3231, Venice
March-December 1996

Honorary Committee

The Prime Minister
Lamberto Dini

The Minister of Foreign Affairs
Susanna Agnelli

*The Minister for Cultural
and Environmental Assets*
Antonio Paolucci

The Minister of Education
Giancarlo Lombardi

*The Minister of University
Scientific and Technological Research*
Giorgio Salvini

The President of the Regione Veneto
Giancarlo Galan

The Lord Mayor of Venice
Massimo Cacciari

The Ambassador of Greece
Evangelos Frangulis

*The President of the Papal
Commission for the Cultural
Assets of the Church*
Francesco Marchisano

*The President of the Regione
Sicilia*
Matteo Graziano

*The President of the Regione
Basilicata*
Angelo Raffaele Dinardo

*The President of the Regione
Calabria*
Giuseppe Domenico Nisticò

*The President of the Regione
Campania*
Antonio Rastrelli

*The President of the Regione
Puglia*
Salvatore Distaso

*The President of the Accademia
Nazionale dei Lincei*
Sabatino Moscati

*The Regional Councillor
of the Departments of Cultural
and Environmental Assets
and of Education*
Leonardo Pandolfo

*The Director General
of the Regional Department
of Cultural and Environmental
Assets and of Education
of the Regione Siciliana*
Antonino Scimemi

*The President of the Consiglio
Nazionale delle Ricerche*
Enrico Garaci

*The President of the Province
of Venice*
Luigino Busatto

*The Chancellor of the Università
degli Studi di Venezia*
Paolo Costa

*The Chancellor of the Istituto
Universitario di Architettura
di Venezia*
Marino Folin

*The President of the Pontificia
Accademia Romana di Archeologia*
Victor Saxer

*Director, Department
of Information and Publishing
Presidency, Council of Ministers*
Stefano Parisi

*The Director General
of Cultural Relations Ministry
of Foreign Affairs*
Michelangelo Jacobucci

*The Director General
of the Defense of the Land Ministry
of Public Works*
Francesco Sisinni

*The Director General of University
Education of Scientific
and Technological Research
Ministry of Education*
Giovanni D'Addona

*The Director General of Cultural
Exchange Ministry of Education*
Antonio Augenti

*The Director General of the
Central Office for Archaeological,
Architectural Artistic and Historic
Assets of Ministry of Cultural
and Environmental Assets*
Mario Serio

*The Director General of Library
Assets and Cultural Institutes
Ministry of Cultural
and Environmental Assets*
Francesco Sicilia

*The Director General
of the Central Office
for Environmental and Landscape
Assets Ministry of Cultural
and Environmental Assets*
Giuseppe Proietti

Exhibition Committee

Giovanni Pugliese Carratelli
President

Giuseppe Andreassi
Nicola Bonacasa
Angelo Bottini
Stefano De Caro
Ernesto De Miro
Antonino Di Vita
Giovanni Gorini
Pietro Giovanni Guzzo
Elena Lattanzi
Alain Pasquier
Carlos Picon
Giovanni Rizza
Giuliana Tocco
Vincenzo Tusa
Dyfri Williams

Coordinator
Angelo Bottini

Secretary
Elisabetta Setari

*Coordinator for architecture
and urban studies*
Dieter Mertens

*Coordinator of the exhibitions
on the Western Greeks*
Pietro Giovanni Guzzo

Executive Committee

*Director General of the Central
Office for Archaeological,
Architectural
Artistic and Historic Assets
Ministry of Cultural
and Environmental Assets*
Mario Serio

*Director General of the Regional
Department of Cultural
and Environmental Assets
and of Education
of the Regione Siciliana*
Antonino Scimemi

*Director of the Cultural Programs
of Palazzo Grassi and of Gruppo Fiat*
Paolo Viti

The Exhibition Committee
would like to draw the public's
attention to the Ministerial Decree
No. 13 (12/01/1989), signed
by the then minister, Alberto
Ronchey, which set up the
National Committee with the task
of elaborating the program
of cultural projects designed to
illustrate aspects of the
civilization of Magna Graecia, of
Greek Sicily and of the
Greek areas in Africa, Provence,
the Iberian peninsula
and its spread throughout Italy
and Roman Europe.

The Exhibition Committee
would like to extend their thanks
to Professor Giorgio Gullini
and to Professor Attilio Stazio for
their contributions in the early
phase of the project.

This exhibition is the representation of a journey. This journey, which is certainly the most momentous in the history of our civilization because of its successful outcome and the important consequences for the future that derived from it, is the one that brought the Greeks to Italy and the West between the eighth and the sixth centuries before the birth of Christ. Right through the thirty-six rooms of Palazzo Grassi, like a vivid atlas that accompanies us along the way, the panels designed by Pier Luigi Cerri recount the modality and chronology of the journey. This extraordinary adventure is documented by the materials displayed: brought together here from the museums of Italy and the rest of the world, they have been chosen both for what they represent and their intrinsic value. I have been favorably impressed by the way Gae Aulenti has, wherever possible, avoided filters and screens, thus permitting the exhibits to be illuminated by natural light. This is not only "to allow everyone to perceive the radiance of the Grand Canal and the views of surrounding urban space" as the exhibition designer writes, but also, I might add, because this light is the light of Venice, and Venice is a splendid metaphor for the journey. In fact, this city has always been a point of departure and arrival. It is the historical queen of those "wine-dark seas" that the Greeks crossed a thousand years before the winged lion of St. Mark alighted on its lagoon. Thus, the light that filters though the windows of Palazzo Grassi fraternizes, so to speak, with the magnificent works on show, bathing them with great familiarity, almost as if from force of habit.

I have spoken of the "magnificent" works displayed in Palazzo Grassi and, once in a while, this adjective does not seem to be overblown. In the introduction, Angelo Bottini, the co-ordinator of the exhibition project on behalf of the Ministry for the Cultural and Environmental Assets, does well to remind us that "the most beautiful works have been chosen". Maintaining this level of excellence with over a thousand exhibits and in thirty-six rooms is no mean feat. I am well aware of the sheer hard work that the preparation of this splendid display of loans has required — and Paolo Viti, whose skill and patience have been indispensable to the exhibition organization, is even more conscious of this than me. I am fully aware of just how much painstaking negotiation has been necessary; how many journeys and inspections have been made; how many technical checks and guarantees have been requested and obtained; and how much restoration work has been planned, funded, and carried out. I am also aware how much all this has cost in purely financial terms. Yet it had to be done. If it is true, as Bottini writes, that one of the insights of the Greek mind was that of considering the aesthetic dimension as a fundamental component of the human experience, then the exhibition must take place under the banner of pure beauty, without compromise or confusion. This is an exhibition that beauty justifies and makes eloquent, because the primacy of beauty is the distinctive trait of Greek civilization. If this was intended to be the overriding objective of the exhibition at Palazzo Grassi, then I must say that it has come up to expectations.

It should be said at once that the exhibition is, to all intents and purposes, a child of the Ministry. Palazzo Grassi administration has provided the venue, taken care of the exhibition installation, funded the restoration work, and arranged the loans; it has borne the entire burden of its organization, promotion, and finance. It has done a great deal, therefore, and naturally it has carried out its task with its proverbial efficiency. It has done it with the modern "corporate culture" that is allied to the institutions and is respectful of the expertise of the specialists who have made the successes of the last few years possible, for example the superb exhibition devoted to the architecture of the Renaissance. But political responsibility for the exhibition, together with the management and control of the academic policy are wholly the responsibility of the Ministry of the Cultural Assets. This exhibition was, in fact, created by a decree of my predecessor, Alberto Ronchey, while the preliminary organization was the task of Directors General Francesco Sisinni and Mario Serio. From the outset, and to a growing extent in the course of the last year, it has involved superintendents and museum directors, restorers, and experts in the state administration. In this respect, the contribution of the Sicilian offices and museums has been of fundamental importance for the quality and quantity of their loans, their willingness to collaborate, and their total agreement with the line of research followed. I say this with particular satisfaction (and my heartfelt thanks go to the Director General, Antonino Scimemi) as a minister who has neither administrative powers nor managerial responsibilities regarding the archaeological heritage of the autonomous region of Sicily. Nonetheless, I have noticed that, on this occasion, the higher interests of culture manage to overcome bureaucratic compartmentalization. The appointment of Giovanni Pugliese Carratelli, the doyen of the archaeologists specializing in this field, as chairman of the Exhibition Committee has been a fortunate choice since, at an international level, his name is closely linked to the considerable prestige of the Italian school of archaeology. But the specialists of the Italian Archaeological Agency have collaborated with Pugliese Carratelli, working with a true team spirit in total accord with his scholarly approach and methodological choices. It is on occasions such as these that the remarkable human resources and the specialist skills present in the state administration come to the fore. In fact, if the Ministry had not thrown the weight of its peripheral organization, scholarship, and vast reserves of experience, behind this enterprise, we would have neither the main exhibition in Venice, nor the series of subsidiary exhibitions coordinated by Pier Giovanni Guzzo and organized directly by the local Archaeological Agencies all over southern Italy. Including such significant places as Policoro, Paestum, Naples, Taranto, and Sibari, these present thousands of exhibits illustrated by the more than 1,500 pages of the catalogues published by Electa Napoli. Thus, for the first time, the Greek presence in Italy is closely examined in all its various aspects: its artefacts, its cults, its social and political structure, and its relations, often of an osmotic nature, with the pre-existing native cultures. We should, therefore, be proud of an undertaking that I consider exemplary not only for the thoroughness of the research and its aesthetic appeal, but also because it demonstrates that relations between the public and private sectors can function excellently when they are based on respect for the contributions of one's colleagues, openness when dealing with others, and steadfastness of principle.

The exhibition that seeks to elucidate the most important journey in history is being held in Venice, therefore. At the meeting place of the *poleis* and the *nomos* – the independent community of free men and the secular law that governed them – the migration from Greece to the coasts of Italy and the West marked the dawn of modern civilization, under the banner of beauty and scientific thought. All this will be explained to the citizens of the world in the year 1996 in Palazzo Grassi. And, amidst the turmoil of the end of the second millennium, when renascent barbarism rears its ugly head, an exhibition like this – which permits the moving spirit of our destiny as free men to emerge in all its splendor – conveys an important message of serenity that augurs well for our future.

Antonio Paolucci
Minister for the Cultural and Environmental Assets

The Western Greeks: the title evokes a historical period during which, in the first millennium B.C., the Mediterranean world was transformed in the space of a few centuries. In fact, for the Mediterranean, then the whole of Europe and – thanks to Alexander – central Asia, this marked the beginning of a new era, with a series of outstanding intellectual and ethical achievements. And when we consider the events that immediately preceded the first episode, the foundation of *poleis* in the West from the eighth to the sixth centuries, we have the impression that not only the peoples of the Greek peninsula and the Aegean Islands, but also those of the seaboard of the eastern Mediterranean, from Anatolia to Egypt, opened up the western seas for the Greeks. In fact, the ships of those seeking raw materials, merchants, and craftsmen, and also of adventurers, whether they be Aegeans, Anatolians, Syrians, and Phoenicians, had long plied this part of the Mediterranean. And the routes they opened up, and the information they gathered, allowed the Greek colonial expeditions to be organized. Until not very long ago, the theory favored by modern historians was that Greek expansion toward both Asia Minor and Italy and Sicily was the result of upheavals in the homeland due to the lack of adequate food supplies. Although more recent, better informed writers do not deny that the impetus given by the need to resolve these social problems was an important factor, they also focus their attention on the inevitable conflict of powers caused by the dissolution of the "Mycenaean" monarchies, which were similar to the Near Eastern monarchies invested with sacred authority. When the turmoil in the Greek world between the Trojan War and the Dorian invasion led to the brilliant invention of the *polis* (a community of freemen governed by a law that had been unanimously determined), the Greek nation was able to resume its place in international trade in the Mediterranean. It was then that it became necessary for the mercantile *poleis* to ensure that the routes on which their livelihood depended posed no obstacles to seafarers. And here the Greeks were quite different from all the other peoples of the eastern Mediterranean, because they discovered lands with which the others only became acquainted at a later date and as result of their contacts with the Greeks. For the latter – who, more than any other people, had already shown themselves willing to accept and rework the intellectual achievements of foreign cultures – freedom from submission to traditional canons, the result of their independence, gave them both the courage to attempt new experiences and the desire not to repress impulses of the intellect and imagination.

For the Greeks who came to the West, this courage and desire had an even greater freedom to express themselves. The members of the aristocracies of the cities, who were necessarily the promoters and leaders of the *apoikiai* (colonial venture), did not feel themselves to be bound, as they were in their homeland, by either the traditions of the nobility or the authority of the priestly colleges of the great sanctuaries that existed there. It is significant that the first expressions of scientific thought were produced in colonial areas – Asian Ionia, Italy and Sicily – and that philosophers and artists of Ionia found a more favorable atmosphere for their speculation and teaching in the Italiot and Siceliot *poleis*, where they were less influenced by the ancient cultures of Asia and Egypt.

In order to elucidate this character of the *poleis* in the West, it has been felt desirable to supplement the introductory part of this catalogue, consisting of essays on the most important aspects of that very special civilization, with a number of chapters dedicated to the forms of culture common to the whole Greek world, such as dialects, writing, political institutions, and forms of artistic expression, about which our schools generally provide very scanty information in comparison with what they teach us about literature and philosophy. Thus, in their quest for beauty, typical of every culture, the Greeks continued to produce new works of art with an intensity that was rarely equalled by the other cultures of the ancient world.

Naturally the exhibition has had to focus on artistic and technical creation. However, while it was being organized, the problem arose of how the other forms of culture, such as literature, philosophy, experimental science, should be presented. Because they reached great heights in the Greek world, they cannot be ignored by those who wish not only to get a complete picture of this civilization, but also understand its unique power to investigate and teach. Much more than their mercantile skills – with which the Phoenician and Etruscan traders were certainly no less endowed than their Greek competitors – it was their remarkable humanity and intellectual richness, an inexhaustible tendency to propound problems and the related *historia* (knowing by inquiry), and the way that theoretical invention took precedence over praxis that gave the Greeks their unparalleled capacity to fascinate and influence the other nations. The fragility of written documents has not permitted literary, philosophical, and scientific works to survive in contemporary versions, but only in copies that are the last link in the long chain created in the ancient book workshops and medieval monastic and lay scriptoria. And it is to manuscripts produced there that we now have recourse in order to present together both the works and one stage of their transmission through time. The Biblioteca Marciana in Venice is privileged to house a collection of Greek *codices* acquired in the fifteenth century by one of the exponents of European humanism, Cardinal Bessarion. As well as complete texts, this collection comprises precious exemplars of works that have saved, in fragmentary quotations, verses by Italiot, Siceliot, and Cyrenaican poets, writings by philosophers, mathematicians, and astronomers, and records of the historical events and the social development of the *poleis* in the West. Thus, the outstanding heritage that this civilization constituted for posterity is reflected in the parchments and folios that have for centuries enlightened other poets, thinkers, and scientists, just as the legacy of artists who worked in Magna Graecia and Sicily is revealed to expert eyes in the Late Antique and medieval works of art produced in the West that had been colonized by the Greeks.

Hence, this vital heritage is given greater immediacy. Not only is European civilization founded on it, but it also takes a whole host of forms: the eternal stimulus of the architectural projects of the great sanctuaries of Italy and Sicily; the friezes of their temples; wall- and vase-painting; the works of such poets as Stesichorus and Ibycus, Leonidas and Nossis; the reconstructions of Italiot, Siceliot and Massaliot historians; the political and metaphysical doctrines of Pythagoras and Parmenides; the cosmologies of Pythagoras and Empedocles; Archimedes' "inventions"; the medical research of Alcmaeon and the schools of Croton and Velia. And colonial Hellenism, the vehicle for the diffusion of Greek civilization in the West, was also of fundamental importance to the development of Rome from an Italic city to a special form of state that an erudite disciple of Aristotle, Heraclides Ponticus, perceived as a Greek *polis*.

Giovanni Pugliese Carratelli

The organizers of the exhibition entitled *The Western Greeks* hope that it will constitute an event of exceptional importance, both for the advancement of scholarship and for culture in the widest possible sense. That this is indeed the case is indicated by the fact that the exhibition was born of a decision of the Ministry for the Cultural and Environmental Assets, which, in addition to the principal exhibition in Palazzo Grassi, and in furtherance of a decision made by former Minister Alberto Ronchey, has organized a series of supplementary exhibitions that involve the whole of southern Italy, from Naples to Sicily. While the other exhibitions will offer an in-depth analysis of a wide range of specific subjects, presenting new research and critical reappraisals, the one in Venice will seek to offer the most complete picture ever attempted of Greek civilization in the West, with particular reference to the Italian peninsula and Sicily. It will not only consider the evidence relating to the Greeks themselves, but also that regarding the fascinating phenomenon of the acculturation of the native peoples, which caused this colonial venture to be both the initial stage and the formative nucleus of the entire civilization of Europe as we know it today.

The organization of the exhibition has necessitated a lengthy process of selection that has sought to reconcile the requirements of exhaustiveness with the safeguarding of the most delicate exhibits, while the problems relating to their display in Palazzo Grassi have also had to be addressed. A few facts and figures are in order here: nearly a thousand requests for loans have been made, and they regard a very large number of pieces, given that many of them are for groups and not individual artefacts. These requests have been sent to almost all the Archaeological Agencies and museums in southern Italy, Sicily (which has contributed about a third of the total), and Sardinia, as well as many museums and collections in the rest of Italy. In addition, museums in the following countries have collaborated: Germany, the United States, Great Britain, France, Libya, Spain, Greece, Switzerland, Vatican City, the Netherlands, Denmark, and Austria.

The exhibition is divided into three sections.

The first one, of an introductory nature, illustrates contrasting themes: the metahistorical one of the voyages of the Greeks to the West, seen through various myths, then that of the first contacts between the Greeks and the native peoples of Italy, from the arrival of the Mycenaeans to the resumption of relations between the ninth and eighth centuries B.C.

The second section, the main body of the exhibition, is devoted to what this civilization has produced and the archaeological research that has brought this to light. There is a carefully selected range of objects that have a high intrinsic value: thus there are those that may be defined as "monuments". This comprises the artefacts made by craftsmen – in the widest sense of the term as it was used by the ancients, including activities that we would now describe as "artistic" – produced in the period extending from the eighth to the second centuries B.C., interspersed by a selection of historical "documents" of fundamental importance, consisting of the principal epigraphic evidence still extant.

The third section refers, albeit very succinctly, to the Greek presence in the rest of the West – that is, the areas to the north and west of Magna Graecia.

In order to be consistent with this structure, a minor role has been assigned to what is merely of documentary interest, so that the everyday life of the western Greeks has not been taken into consideration; there are not, therefore, sections devoted to such themes as "the home" or "sport", or even "war". On the other hand, reference has been made to those events, and aspects of social behavior (conviviality, athletics, funerary rites, theater, religion), as a result of which many specialized products were developed and distinctive forms were created for many objects.

In quite a number of cases, these objects are finds from recent excavations, or they are ones that have not hitherto been publicly displayed in a manner appropriate to their importance. They include grave goods from Campania and Sicily; the painted slabs from a Lucanian tomb at Paestum; part of the cargo of the ancient ship that sank off Gela; recently discovered examples of architectural terra-cottas from Naxos; arms found among the large number of votive offerings in the deposit in the Scrimbia area at Hipponium; the splendid bearded head in bronze that has been returned to Italy by the Antikenmuseum of Basel (this probably came from the wreck at Porticello, near Reggio Calabria).

Without doubt, those who have lent these finds have shown their desire to contribute to making the exhibition at Palazzo Grassi an occasion – an unrepeatable one, at least in the short term – for assembling a large part of the material creations on which archaeologists base themselves in the reconstruction of the cultural vicissitudes of the western Greeks. The only real limit has been one of transportability.

The exhibition will also provide an opportunity to examine some of the objects more closely – for instance, it will be possible to see the "Ludovisi Throne" next to the "Boston Throne" for the first time.

Nevertheless, as far as possible, the choice of the exhibits has been based on aesthetic criteria. Although the displays do not merely consist of a sequence of styles, personages, and objects, the most beautiful works have been chosen in an attempt to exemplify one of the most important insights of the Greek mind, that of considering the aesthetic dimension to be a fundamental component of the human experience, so that, of all the perceptive faculties, pride of place was offered to the visual one.

It is simply not possible to illustrate many of the aspects of the theme by means of displays; this is due either to their immaterial nature, or the dimensions of the objects in question, or else because they consist of entities that are not in any way transportable. It has, therefore, been decided to publish an exhibition guide that will have the task of providing information relating to the overall development of Greek civilization in the West. It will also tell the story of the city planning and architecture of this period through photographs of the sites and monuments, proposals for reconstruction, and plans. These are the work of the various generations of architects, draftspeople, and scholars who have permitted the subject to be analyzed in depth from the eighteenth century onwards.

Angelo Bottini

Lenders

Agrigento, Museo Archeologico Regionale
Aidone, Museo Archeologico Nazionale
Athens, Ministry of Culture
  National Archaeological Museum
  Olympia, National Archaeological Museum
Bari, Museo Archeologico della Provincia
Basel, Antikenmuseum Basel und Sammlung Ludwig
  Bequest of Frederick M. Watkins
Berlin, Staatliche Museen zu Berlin, Antikensammlung
Bern, Bernisches Historisches Museum
Boston, Museum of Fine Arts, H.L. Pierce Fund
Cagliari, Museo Archeologico Nazionale
Cambridge, Arthur M. Sackler Museum, Harvard University Art
  Museums
Catania, Istituto di Archeologia dell'Università
Catania, Museo Civico di Castello Ursino
Cefalù, Museo della Fondazione Culturale Mandralisca
Comune di Castelvetrano
Comune di Ozieri
Copenhagen, Ny Carlsberg Glyptotek
Cosenza, Museo Civico Archeologico
Egnazia, Museo Archeologico Nazionale
Florence, Museo Archeologico Nazionale
  Gabinetto di Numismatica
Gela, Museo Archeologico Regionale
Kansas City, Missouri, The Nelson-Atkins Museum of Art
  (Purchase: Nelson Trust) 33-3/4
Karlsruhe, Badisches Landesmuseum
Lecce, Museo Provinciale "Sigismondo Castromediano"
Leiden, Rijksmuseum van Oudheden
Lipari, Museo Archeologico Regionale
Locri, Antiquarium
London, British Museum, Department of Coins and Medals
London, British Museum, Department of Greek and Roman Antiquities
Lucera, Museo Civico "G. Fiorelli"
Madrid, Museo Arqueológico Naciónal
Malibu, California, Collection of the J. Paul Getty Museum,
  Gift of Malcolm Wiener
Marianopoli, Museo Archeologico
Marseilles, Musée d'Histoire
Matera, Museo Archeologico Nazionale "D. Ridola"
Melfi, Museo Archeologico Nazionale del Melfese
Messina, Museo Interdisciplinare Regionale
Messina, Soprintendenza per i Beni Culturali ed Ambientali
Metaponto, Museo Archeologico Nazionale
Munich, Staatlichen Antikensammlungen und Glyptothek München
Mozia, Museo Giuseppe Whitaker
Naples, Museo Archeologico Nazionale

Naples, Soprintendenza Archeologica delle Province di Napoli e Caserta
Naxos, Museo Archeologico
New York, The Metropolitan Museum of Art, Rogers Fund
  and Fletcher Fund
Padua, Soprintendenza Archeologica per il Veneto
Paestum, Museo Archeologico Nazionale
Palermo, Museo Archeologico Regionale "A. Salinas"
Palermo, Soprintendenza per i Beni Culturali ed Ambientali
Paris, Bibliothèque Nationale de France, Cabinet des Médailles
Paris, Musée du Louvre, Département des Antiquités Grecques
  Etrusques et Romaines
Policoro, Museo Archeologico Nazionale della Siritide
Pontecagnano, Museo Archeologico Nazionale dell'Agro Picentino
Potenza, Museo Archeologico Provinciale
Potenza, Soprintendenza Archeologica della Basilicata
Reggio Calabria, Museo Archeologico Nazionale
Roccagloriosa, Deposito Ufficio Scavi
Rome, Musei Capitolini
Rome, Soprintendenza Archeologica per l'Etruria Meridionale
  - Museo Nazionale di Villa Giulia
Rome, Soprintendenza Archeologica di Roma
Rome, Soprintendenza Archeologica per il Lazio
Salerno, Direzione dei Musei Provinciali del Salernitano
Salerno, Soprintendenza Archeologica
Sassari, Museo Archeologico Nazionale "G.A. Sanna"
Segesta, Magazzini di Casa Barbaro
Sezione Archeologica in deposito presso il Museo Civico Ietino
  di San Cipirello
Sibari, Museo Archeologico Nazionale della Sibaritide
Siena, Museo Archeologico Nazionale
Syracuse, Museo Archeologico Regionale "P. Orsi"
Syracuse, Soprintendenza per i Beni Culturali ed Ambientali
Syracuse, Soprintendenza per i Beni Culturali ed Ambientali in deposito
  presso il Museo Civico di Noto
Syracuse, Soprintendenza per i Beni Culturali ed Ambientali
Sorrento, Museo Correale di Terranova
Taranto, Museo Archeologico Nazionale
Trieste, Civici Musei di Storia ed Arte
Tripoli, The Department of Antiquities, El Saraya El-Hamra
Vatican City, Musei e Gallerie della Biblioteca Apostolica Vaticana
Vatican City, Musei Vaticani
Velia, Acropoli, Cappella Palatina
Velia, Deposito Ufficio Scavi
Venice, Museo Archeologico Nazionale
Vibo Valentia, Museo Archeologico Statale "V. Capialbi"
Vienna, Kunsthistorisches Museum, Antikensammlung

and of all those who wish to remain anonymous.

Installations   Catalogue

Project and Coordination
Gae Aulenti
with
Francesca Fenaroli

Graphic Design
Pierluigi Cerri
with
Olivier Maupas
Dario Zannier
Michele Rebessi

Lighting
Piero Castiglioni

Press Relations
Vladimiro Dan

The Istituto Centrale per il Restauro
has directed the restoration projects with the collaboration of
Maria Costanza Laurenti
Mario Micheli
Ciro Nastri
Carlo Usai

Editorial Director
Mario Andreose

Graphic Design
Pierluigi Cerri
with
Carla Parodi
Roberta Giudice

Coordinating Editor
Simonetta Rasponi

Editorial Staff
Andrew Ellis
Gianna Lonza
Franca Cucciardi

*Coordination
of Catalogue Files*
Gilda L'Arab

Iconographic Research
Evelina Rossetti
Carla Viazzoli

Coordination
Carla Bonacina
Milena Bongi

Production Staff
Italo Cisilino
Sergio Daniotti
Rino Pasta
Carla Regonesi
Enrico Vida

Secretary
Luisa Gandolfi

Contents

First Part

25   Aegean Thalassocracy
     Christos G. Doumas
29   The Prehistoric Background: the Minoan-Mycenaean
     Civilization
     Vincenzo La Rosa
37   From the Minoic Syllabary to the Greek Alphabet
     Pietro Militello
43   The Genesis of the Greek Alphabet
     Giovanni Garbini
47   Greek Forms of Political Structure
     Filippo Càssola
55   A Profile of Archaic Greek Sculpture
     Carlos A. Picon
63   A Profile of Classical Greek Sculpture
     Alain Pasquier
75   An Outline of Hellenistic Sculpture
     Bernard Andreae
85   Greek Pottery and the Role of Athens
     Dyfri Williams
99   A Survey of Greek Wall-Painting
     Agnès Rouveret
109 The First Contacts between the Minoan-Mycenaean
     and the Western Mediterranean Worlds
     Lucia Vagnetti
117 Relations between Cyprus and the West
     in the Precolonial Period
     David Ridgway
121 The Phoenicians in the Western Mediterranean
     (through to the Fifth Century B.C.)
     Giovanni Garbini
133 Navigation and Ships in the Age of Greek Colonization
     Patrice Pomey
141 An Outline of the Political History of the Greeks in the West
     Giovanni Pugliese Carratelli
177 The Metropolises of the Western Greek Colonies
     Michail Sakellariou
189 The Greek Colonization of the West: Dialects
     Renato Arena
201 Maritime Communications
     Francesco Prontera
209 The Colonial Experience in the Greek Mythology
     Bruno d'Agostino
215 The Constitutions of the Western Greek States:
     Cyrenaica, Magna Graecia, Greek Sicily, and the Poleis
     of the Massaliot Area
     Franco Sartori
223 The Western Greeks: Coinage
     Giovanni Gorini
233 City and Countryside
     Emanuele Greco
243 Urban Planning in Magna Graecia
     Dieter Mertens-Emanuele Greco
263 Urban Planning in Ancient Sicily
     Antonio Di Vita
309 Town Planning in Ancient Cyrenaica
     Lidiano Bacchielli
315 Greek Architecture in the West
     Dieter Mertens
347 Greek Military Architecture in the West
     Henri Tréziny
353 Housing and Workshop Construction in the City
     Marcella Barra Bagnasco

361 Agricultural Settlements
     Joseph C. Carter
369 Sculpture in Magna Graecia
     Claude Rolley
399 Siceliot Sculpture in the Archaic Period
     Giovanni Rizza
413 Greek Sculpture in Sicily in the Classical Period
     Ernesto De Miro
421 Sculpture and Coroplastics in Sicily
     in the Hellenistic-Roman Age
     Nicola Bonacasa
437 Sculpture in Greek Cyrenaica
     Luigi Beschi
443 Southern Italian and Sicilian Vases
     Margot Schmidt
457 Wall-Painting in Magna Graecia
     Angelo Pontrandolfo
471 The Jewelry of the Western Greeks
     Pier Giovanni Guzzo
481 Cults and Religious Doctrines of the Western Greeks
     Gianfranco Maddoli
499 Literary Culture in Magna Graecia and Sicily
     Marcello Gigante
511 The Literary History of Cyrenaica
     Valeria Gigante Lanzara
515 Philosophy in the Western Greek World
     Maria Michela Sassi
523 The Impact of the Greek Colonists on the non-Hellenic
     Inhabitants of Sicily
     Vincenzo La Rosa
533 The Impact of the Greek Colonies on the Indigenous Peoples
     of Campania
     Bruno d'Agostino
541 The Impact of the Greek Colonies on the Indigenous Peoples
     of Lucania
     Angelo Bottini
549 The Impact of the Greek Colonies on the Indigenous Peoples
     of Apulia
     Ettore M. de Juliis
555 The Greeks in the Po Valley
     Pier Giovanni Guzzo
559 The Encounter with the Bruttii
     Pier Giovanni Guzzo
563 The Greeks in Sardinia
     Carlo Tronchetti
567 The Encounter with the Etruscans
     Mario Torelli
577 The Greeks in Gaul and Corsica
     Michel Bats
585 The Greek and Celtic Worlds: a Meeting of Two Cultures
     Venceslas Kruta
591 Greek Influence on Italic Art
     Antonio Giuliano
607 Greek Artists in Republican Rome: a Short History of Sculpture
     Eugenio La Rocca
627 The Legacy of the Western Greeks in the Art of Late Antiquity
     and the Middle Ages
     Raffaella Farioli Campanati

Second Part

635 Catalogue of Works on Exhibit
     Bibliography
     Index of Names

cover
Clay plaque with a Gorgon
from the *temenos*
of the Athenaion of Syracuse
570-550 B.C.
Syracuse
Museo Archeologico Regionale
Cat. 56

previous pages
"The Naval Campaign"
details of the fresco at Thera
16th cent. B.C.
Athens, Ministry of Culture
National Archaeological Museum

First Part

Christos G. Doumas   Aegean Thalassocracy

The watery divide between Asia and Europe, the Aegean Sea, sown with countless islands, challenged man to adventure as soon as he came in contact with it. Aegean society was passing through the last phases of its hunting and gathering stage when, in the ninth millennium B.C., daring fishermen trusted their rafts, and from their home in the Franchthi Cave in the Argolid, floated in the open sea to catch tunny fish. Borne by the currents and northerly winds, they came to the island of Melos, where they discovered obsidian, the volcanic glass which abounded on the island, an ideal raw material for making sharp tools. They took some obsidian back to their cave and there made microlithic tools. This is not an improbable scenario, for in a Mesolithic stratum of the Franchthi Cave twentieth-century archaeologists discovered these tools along with bones of tunny, a fish that can only be caught in deep waters. This discovery constitutes the oldest testimony for the use of Melian obsidian on the Greek mainland, and consequently for the earliest voyage in the Aegean.

Indeed it would not be too extravagant a claim that tunny fish and obsidian were the main motives for the origins of navigation in the Aegean. For as soon as people became familiar with the qualities of obsidian its trade began, as is attested by its wide distribution, already in the seventh millennium B.C., from Macedon to Crete and from the coasts of Asia Minor to the Ionian Islands.

Thenceforth, and until the end of the Bronze Age, the end of the second millennium B.C., Melian obsidian was one of the most traded commodities in the Aegean region.

A new impetus for maritime activities came with the permanent settlement of the Cyclades around the middle of the fifth millenium B.C. The intensification of the obsidian trade, perhaps the cause and effect of this permanent settlement, resulted in the creation of trading stations and distribution centers. The Late Neolithic (fourth millennium B.C.) settlement on the islet of Saliagos between Paros and Antiparos, and the extensive Early Bronze Age coastal conurbation of Manika near Chalcis, in the northern part of the Euboian gulf, appear to have been important centers of this kind.

Whereas archaeological evidence for seafaring in the Stone Age Aegean is largely indirect, the testimony for the Early Bronze Age is both direct and concrete. As early as the third millennium B.C. representations of seagoing vessels appear in the archaeological record showing a quite high development in shipbuilding and, consequently, in seafaring. And it does not seem to be accidental that these depictions of ships are known from the Cyclades.

Oared ships are depicted on a group of Early Bronze Age vases, known by their conventional name as "frying-pan" vessels. They come from the island of Syros and their principal decoration, restricted to the exterior of their "underside," consists of one or two incised ships surrounded by impressed spirals, possibly evoking the waves of the sea. The type of vessel depicted on these "frying-pan" vessels, with a low prow and a high stern, is also known from rock engravings on the island on Naxos. From the same island come a group of lead models of ships of the same type reported as found in an Early Cycladic grave. On a pottery sherd from Phylakopi on Melos the greater part of a ship is incised along with a human figure in outline. The importance of this sherd is that the ship it depicts is equipped with a rudder. On another pottery sherd from Orchomenos in Boeotia, also dated to the third millennium B.C., the ship is depicted with two vertical incisions which could be interpreted as masts. All these monuments, despite their small size, constitute an eloquent testimony to the development of shipbuilding in the Aegean during the Early Bronze Age.

The limitations of the islands in natural resources meant that their inhabitants had to rely on the nearby coastal zones of the mainland for their subsistence. This was an important motive for the continuing development and improvement of the means of sea transport. Besides, being frugal and inventive, the islanders managed not only to survive on their rocks but also to develop methods and techniques in order to exploit their natural resources to the full. This is the reason why the most advanced technology in the Aegean in the Bronze Age is found on the islands. Obsidian, marble, millstone, emery, and pumice were not only exploited at home but were also exported to the surrounding areas, either as raw materials or as artifacts and works of art, obviously in exchange for goods of a more perishable nature of which the islanders had need. The role of trade in the Early Bronze Age Aegean Islands is also reflected in the pattern of settlement. The scattered small villages, which constituted the norm in the early phases of the third millennium B.C., gradually disappeared and large harbor towns developed, such as Poliochni in Lemnos, Phylakopi in Melos, Ayia Irini in Kea, Akrotiri in Thera.

Contacts with the outside world enabled the islanders to come across new ideas and technological developments. It is not surprising, therefore, that metallurgy, a technological innovation at the beginning of the third millennium B.C., spread more rapidly in the islands and was further advanced locally. The case of Lemnos, in a key position on the crossroad between the Aegean and the Black Sea, is very characteristic. It is on that island that urbanization was first manifested in the Aegean region and Poliochni, on its east coast can be considered the most ancient city in Europe. The importance of metallurgy for Lemnos is not only evident from the archaeological data but is also echoed in a number of ancient Greek myths. The voyage of the Argonauts is associated with Lemnos and so is the godsmith of the ancient Greeks, Hephaestus, who had his smithy on that island. Further south in the Cyclades the earliest mining activities are attested on the island of Siphnos, where a gallery of the third milleninium B.C. has been located.

With such a technological background it is not at all surprising that the islanders maintained their leading role in seafaring and trade during the Middle Bronze Age too (first half of the second millennium B.C.). Depictions of ships on a quite large variety of monuments are frequent, but the miniature frieze from the West House at Akrotiri on Thera constitutes the best source of information about Middle Bronze Age Aegean ships, their construction, their rigging, their capacity, their propulsion. Large sailing vessels could now cross not only the Aegean but also the entire Mediterranean. And indeed imports from Egypt, Syria, and Palestine recovered in the ruins of Akrotiri bear witness to the role of this harbor town as an international trading station. The cosmopolitan character of Akrotiri is not only recorded in its material wealth but is also reflected in the "bourgeois" mentality of its inhabitants, who vied with each other in decorating their residences with wall-paintings depicting exotic landscapes and animals. The artistic vocabulary of the Theran artists conforms with the conventions characteristic of the art of Egypt and Mesopotamia.

It has often been argued that the control of the seas during the Bronze Age in the Aegean was in the hands of Crete. It is true that Thucydides talks about King Minos as the ruler of the sea. It is also true that both Thucydides and Herodotus tell us that King Minos manned his ships with crews from the islands, for these were the real mariners, these were the "pirates" of the Aegean.

The author of the present text has argued elsewhere that Crete culturally is not an island; it is a self-sufficient landmass surrounded by water. Its inhabitants were never forced to launch into maritime adventures for their survival. And when the agricultural surplus led to the centralization of authority and to the palace economy, at the beginning of the second millennium B.C., Crete needed the means to export this surplus. It did not need to build a fleet since the ships were readily available in the nearby Cyclades. The masters of the sea, the pirates of Thucydides, could undertake the transport of its produce. The affluence which characterizes the island communities of this period can only be understood as a consequence of maritime entrepreneurial activities, and their best client could only be Crete. As an economic power, Crete could have conquered the Cyclades, but it could not secure the services of the islanders unless it negotiated terms with them. And this, it seems, it did. The colonization of the islands by King Minos and the establishment of his sons as their rulers, according to Thucydides, can now be understood as the sending of ambassadors (agents) who would guarantee the services of the islanders. And these emissaries would surely be drawn from the aristocratic ranks of Minoan society, those closest to King Minos, perhaps his sons.

During the Late Bronze Age the islands kept their primary role in maritime affairs and it seems that they contributed to the emergence of the Mycenaean "empire." They may also have contributed to the decline of the Minoan civilization by shifting their services toward the rulers of the Greek mainland, if the latter offered better terms. Otherwise it is difficult to understand the rapid rise of the Mycenaeans from farmers and shepherds to seafarers and merchants.

The Aegean islanders never stopped being the masters of the seas. With the collapse of the Mycenaean palaces, around the twelfth century B.C., perhaps because of insurrections, certain of the overthrown rulers migrated with their followers to the east Mediterranean. Some of them colonized Cyprus and others settled along the coast of Syria and Palestine. Intense archaeological work in these regions now recognizes in those known from the written sources as Sea Peoples, a branch of which were the Philistines, these Mycenaean refugees. Such a massive movement of people could not have been achieved without the centuries-long experience and the skills of the islanders in seafaring, a skill which was never lost. For even after the collapse of the Mycenaean world it is the islands which took the lead in the formation of what is known as the Greek World.

During the first half of the third millennium B.C. each island developed independently into a center of art, culture, and education. Lemnos, Thasos, Samothrace, Lesbos, Chios, Samos, Cos, Rhodes, Delos, Tenos, Ceos, Melos, Paros, Naxos, Thera, each developed international contacts and traded with the entire Mediterranean world as is witnessed by the archaeological records. Each of these islands be-

opposite
Bowl with a ship, from Syros
proto-Cycladic II
2800-2300 B.C.
Athens
National Archaeological Museum

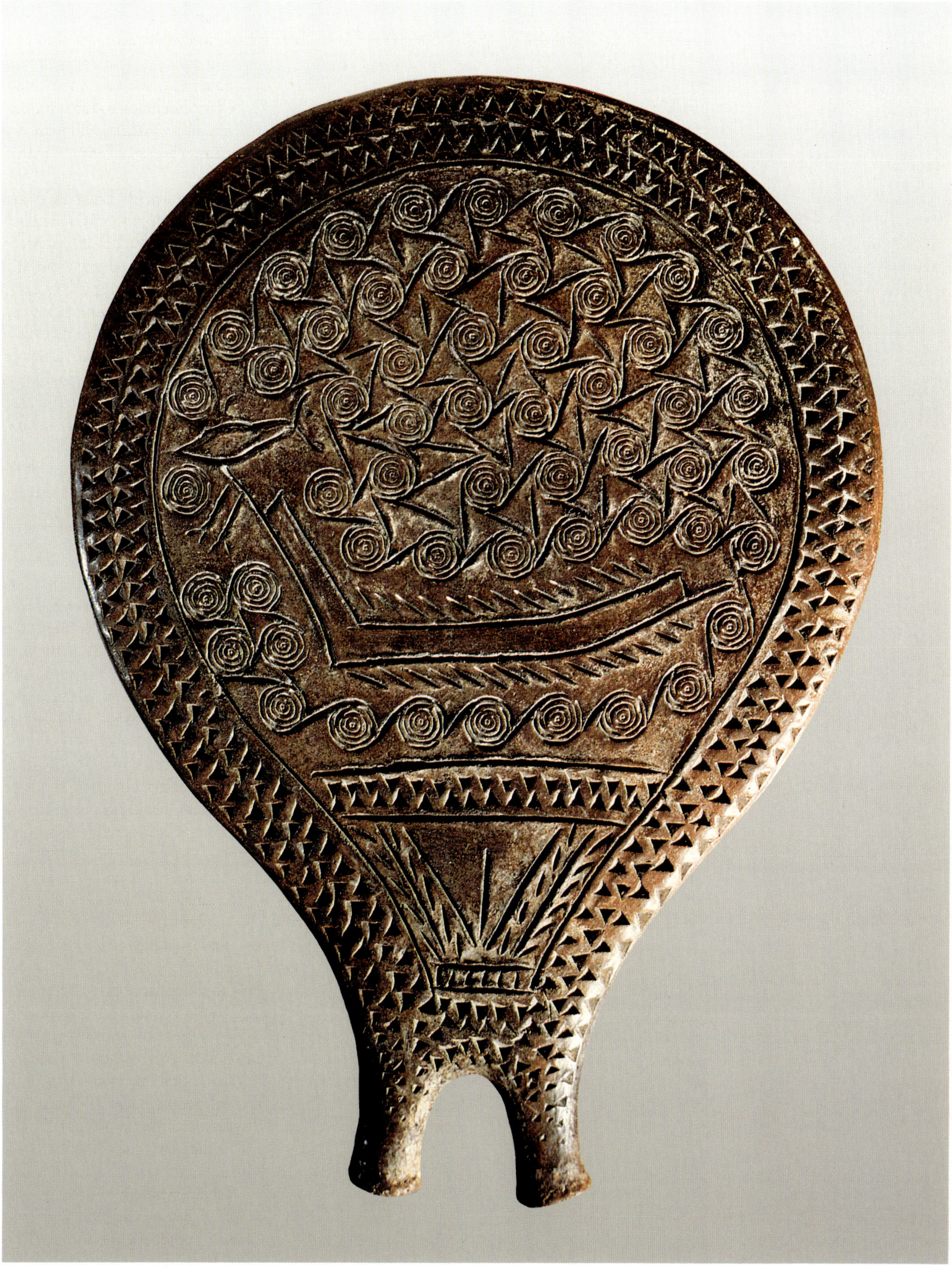

Aegean Thalassocracy

Examples of weights for scales
from Akrotiri
ca. 160 B.C.
Athens
National Archaeological Museum

Rhytion, libation vessel
ostrich egg imported from
Syria and pottery
from Akrotiri
ca. 160 B.C.
Athens
National Archaeological Museum

came famous for their sanctuaries, their schools of art, their philosophers, their poets. Perhaps it is not fortuitous that the first Greek city to mint coins was on an island: Aegina.

The islanders' strong ties with the sea have always constituted their strength. This is also apparent in more recent times when political and economic conditions had changed a great deal since antiquity. For example, during the 400-year Ottoman occupation of Greece, the small islands, because of the scarcity of cultivable land, were not settled by Muslim populations, as occurred on the mainland, in Crete, and in the major islands. The Sublime Porte only demanded from them, as tribute, experts to man her ships. By developing their trading activities, the islanders from the smaller islands managed to acquire such wealth and to create such fleets that, during the 1821 War of Independence, it was they who managed not only to fight the Ottoman fleet but also to cover most of the expenses of the eight-year war. And today, in the capitalist system of the twentieth century, it is thanks to the islanders that Greece can claim third place in international shipping.

Vincenzo La Rosa   The Prehistoric Background: the Minoan-Mycenaean Civilization

Ruins of the palace of Cnossos
Crete
detail of the northern entrance
16th-15th cent. B.C.

The single most important phenomenon in the Aegean world during the Middle Bronze Age is the appearance of the Cretan Palaces, whose history is branded by a series of earthquakes. The emergence of these structures was a complex process, and came about in a chapter in which both the economy and the population of certain zones of this large island were on the rise: the growing farmer groups of Early Minoan tradition, the specialist craftsmen who are well-documented for Middle Minoan IA, the important cultural input of Mesopotamian and Egyptian building typologies, together kindled the emergence about the new type of architecture of an interests system based on the collection and redistribution of produce and goods. In spite of the apparent chronological congruence, the destruction of Troy V or the arrival of the Hatti (Hittites) in their historical area, in no way diminish the sheer peculiarity of what was evolving on Crete: the new political structures that had developed in the Late Bronze Age were without comparisons elsewhere in the Aegean, as the palaces of the fortified citadels in Mainland Greece were architecturally and functionally quite different (and first appeared, probably, only in the fifteenth century B.C.).

The most traumatic event during the Late Bronze Age was undoubtedly the eruption of the volcan on the island of Thera (modern Santorini), followed by the explosion and collapse of its cone, as well as by tidal waves. The latest proposed chronological data based on peak acidity readings in the glaciers of Greenland and effects of freezing detectable from the pines in California (caused by climatic changes following volcanic activity) would seem to endorse the theory that the eruption took place in the second half of the seventeenth century B.C. That date, however, clashes with the pottery finds of Late Minoan IA, which have turned up in excavated destruction layers of the island's settlement Akrotiri. It is generally agreed, however, that the demise of the Second Palaces on Crete, was not directly caused by the same Thera's eruption that covered the Akrotiri settlement. On the other hand, layers of pure ash and pumice found recently in the excavations at Trianda on Rhodes, in the Serraglio and the compound cataclysms on Cos, and at Mochlos on Crete itself, attest to the effect of the eruption which are reckoned to have been felt as far as the southeastern extremes of the Mediterranean and around the Dead Sea.

The eruption of Thera is tied to the so-called Minoan thalassocracy, which might best be defined as a kind of trade control in the waters of the Aegean, a basically non-political setup whose purpose was to ensure safe passage for Minoan merchant vessels plying the seaways. Ch. Doumas recently claimed that this trade activity was mainly Cycladic, given the abundance of such finds in the archaeological layer marking the destruction of Akrotiri (including the superb figured wall decorations). The third economic force in the region during this same lapse of time honored its warrior-princes with the splendid funerary goods of Shaft Grave Circles A and B at Mycenae, and was an authentic warrior oligarchy. The establishment of Myce-

The Throne Room
in the palace of Cnossos
Crete

naean interests gave rise to a regular trade route through the Tyrrhenian Sea, presaging the "discovery" of the West that would lead to the *apoikiai*, or colonies, recorded in Greek historical times. The event that marked and decanted the close of the Late Bronze Age is the Mycenaean conquest of Knossos (usually fixed at around the middle of the fifteenth century B.C.). The Cretan model was most likely the one – albeit adapted to the Mycenaean sociopolitical structures – for the original fortified palaces (including the purely "garrison" settlement of Gla in Boeotia), a type of building that was exclusive to the continent.

After an interim period of turmoil, the dissolution of the Mycenaean citadels was followed by a new order. Between the two wars waged by the Sea Peoples with Egypt (the first in the fifth year of Pharaoh Merneptah's rule in around 1230 B.C.; the second under Ramses III, toward 1190 B.C.), there is indeed evidence for the destruction of the citadels of Mycenae and Tiryns and the burning of the palace at Pylos (usually fixed at the close of the thirteenth century B.C.). In a series of tablets unearthed in this building, which offer clues as to the specific system by which the territory was organized (a system that apparently involved a decidedly small group of people, nonetheless), some scholars detect telltale signs of the impending threat. This same period also witnessed the dissolution of the Hittite empire. The real causes of the collapse of Mycenaean power are still strongly debated, however. Some suggest mass migration or invasions from outside (perhaps by the Sea Peoples, or the Dorians); others attribute the end to natural causes (earthquakes, changes of climate, followed by drought, and so forth); yet others see internal conflicts and disorder as the likely cause. The end of the Palatial system, however, did not trigger the disappearance of Mycenaean civilization, though mass deportation and displacement undoubtedly accompanied the fall of the Mycenaean reigns. Evidence for a subsequent destructive calamity in the late twelfth century B.C. occurs in Mycenae, Tiryns, and Lefkandi.

For the articulation of a Mycenaean kingdom, the most explicit testimony remains the archives in the palace at Pylos (*pu-ro*), whose tablets contain records of seventeen place-names divided into two provinces (the

Fresco of the procession
from the great southern *propylaia*
of the palace of Cnossos
1500 B.C.
Heraklion, Archaeological Museum

Krater with relief flowers
from the palace of Phaestus
Crete
Middle Minoan II
18th cent. B.C.
Heraklion, Archaeological Museum

Blue bird among flowers
detail of the frescoes
of the palace of Cnossos
ca. 1500 B.C.
Heraklion, Archaeological Museum

The Prehistoric Background: the Minoan-Mycenaean Civilization

The fisherman
detail of the frescoes of Thera
ca. 15th cent. B.C.
Athens
National Archaeological Museum

The Prehistoric Background: the Minoan-Mycenaean Civilization

capital of the "ulterior" one was *re-u-ko-to-ro*). The fieldwork of the Minnesota Messenia Expedition (second half of the 1960s) substantially confirmed the hierarchical organization of Pylos' surrounding territories in the Mycenaean age, and proposed a set of dimensional types for the settlements. It has not been so easy to envisage the situation in Argolis, owing to the existence of several power centers in a relatively restricted area. Renfrew's Early State Module attributes equality of status among the main cities: Mycenae, Tiryns, Midea, and Argos. Chadwick and Binliff, however, advocate Mycenae's superiority, as sanctioned by Homer's *epos* (whose "Catalogue of Ships," while not offering an exact profile of the political situation nor of the power relationships and territorial setup of Mycenaean Greece, may well reflect the situation). Another aspect of the Palatial culture worth studying is the general question of crafts specializations. In Cretan spheres, the high level of workmanship in pottery production even in the Proto-Palatial period (not to mention the glyptics and sphragistics skills, stone vases, and scribes) is explained by the basic organization of labor supported by the palaces. The trend shows signs of consolidation toward Late Minoan, during which specific professional skills are noticeable in the field of architecture (the design of buildings, the organization of building yards, the figured fresco walls' work). Specialized artisans were also responsible for manufacturing the assorted weapons: the development of different types of fighting gear offers clues on the combat techniques and the kind of arms that were in use (as noted from the inquiry of I. Kilian Dirlmeier on the grave goods of the Shaft Grave Circles A and B at Mycenae). The parade armor interred with the Lord of Dendra, the galloping chariot on the *stelai* in Circle A, the procession of warriors on the homonymous *Warrior Vase* found in a house just south of the above grave circle – all these finds propose different iconographies of the some subject in chronological succession.

The face of power
Given that for many of the contexts on the Minoan-Mycenaean world little is yet known about just how social status was qualified and what the power insignia were the material evidence allows us little more than guesswork. The emergence of recognizable elites in the Mainland can be detected as early as Early Helladic II in the House of the Tiles at Lerna (Argolis), with its elaborate system of storerooms and stocktaking for produce, has been interpreted as a public administration building, where there are signs of a landowning class that carefully managed the accumulation of resources. The tumulus-type of tomb (such as those at Nidri, almost coeval with the House of the Tiles) may be associated with some form of social rank tied to the warrior(-hunter?) figure, complete with dagger bow and arrows of the kind documented as far east as Vrana-Marathon also for the Middle Helladic. Much clearer are the warrior oligarchies exemplified by the Shaft Grave Circles A and B of Mycenae, who were responsible for the emergence of Proto-Mycenaean civilization. The subsequent stage is represented by the *wa-na-ka* or full-fledged princely ruler, who occupied the top of the Palatial pyramid-shaped political system in the golden days of the Mycenaean civilization. In such a context, class divisions are an inevitability.
On Crete, the circular tombs in Messara dating to the Early Minoan period may be linked to social grouping based on kin systems, whose leaders were undoubtedly ranked according to the yield of their lands and the raising of livestock. The Red House (Early Minoan IIB) at Vasiliki has yielded no clay stamps or seals,

Cretan gold pendant
from the Aegaen Treasure
ca. 1700-1600 B.C.
London, British Museum
Department of Greek
and Roman Antiquities

Bronze Mycenaean dagger
with gold and silver inlays
scene of a lion hunt
16th cent. B.C.
Athens
National Archaeological Museum

Terra-cotta Mycenaean vase
with octopus decoration
London, British Museum
Department of Greek
and Roman Antiquities

Long-stemmed terra-cotta
Mycenaean cup
London, British Museum
Department of Greek
and Roman Antiquities

and yet even here it is acceptable to infer the presence of landowning power groups similar to those of the House of the Tiles at Lerna. Clues of a similar trend can be seen in the isolated oval house at Chamezi (Middle Minoan IA). With the Middle Bronze Age, the island's social structures began to diverge from those of the mainland: the Proto-Palatial oligarchies (with their indispensable administration and bureaucratic phalanx) supervised the stockpiling and redistribution of goods, which, in the course of time, ceased to be merely agricultural. By the start of the Neo-Palatial times, the interests of the palaces became even more diversified and controls over the land even more systematic; for this the authorities now involved sacred matters and began to run the sanctuaries. The reigning oligarchy at this point was probably presided by a monarchical figure, perhaps with some religious connotations (which Sir A. Evans equated with "priest-kings" at the time). When the Mycenaeans overran Knossos, in the Throne Room sat a mainland type of *wa-na-ka*, who brought the political structure in line with those elsewhere in the Aegean, after a hiatus through the Middle and the beginning of the Late Bronze Age.

In the Cyclades there is little or no discernible differentiation between classes in the socio-political structure. The spread of obsidian imported from Melos and Yali presupposes that even in Neolithic times the society was made up of seafarers and traders. The considerable degree of mobility of the islanders probably determined the creation of Cycladic nuclei on the shores of Attica (Tzepi of Marathon, and A. Kosmas), Euboea (Manika) or of Crete (A. Photià) in Early Cycladic II. The Admiral of the Fleet, who according to some scholars is represented by the fresco of the Miniature Frieze found in a princely residence in Akrotiri, may attest to the existence of political structures, just prior to the catastrophe. The supposition that this figure was of Mycenaean "nationality" (R. Laffineaur) clashes with the prevailing opinion of Minoan control of the Aegean seaways during the Late Minoan I period; the "middle-class" label put forward by Doumas, who considered that the trade-oriented structure typical of the Cyclades prevailed here, is more tenable.

In Cyprus, for the earliest phases, the numerous little models of a religious nature found in the tombs at Vounoi (dating to Early Cypriot II), suggest an emphasis on religious matters, and hence a specific priesthood running the sanctuaries and religious functions. From the Late Cypriot II period onward, the defense walls and buildings in the centers of Enkomi and Kytion, together with the high quality of certain finds, are convincing evidence for the existence of specific power groups probably linked to the extraction, working and commercialization of the metals (copper), perhaps under the aegis of a religious structure (Knapp). The inevitable encounter with the Semitic maritime forces may have given a boost to the mobility and penetration of Cypriot goods trade (as testified by pottery and bronze vessels brought to light in Sicily). The widespread popularity of certain types of Mycenaean wares of the thirteenth-century "pictorial style" may be explained by the arrival to the island of groups of potters of Mainland Greek extraction. As for the so-called Achaean colonization of the island through the collapse of the kingdoms (together with a second episode probably in the eleventh century B.C.), the archaeological evidence affords no clues whatever on the sociopolitical setup.

Contemporary accounts

Some idea of Minoan (or more generally Aegean) trading with other powers in the Mediterranean can be gleaned from a series of wall-paintings in the tombs of ancient Thebes in Egypt, which give more authoritative account than the individual products of material culture. The scenes featuring the Keftiu (the inhabitants of Crete) in the tombs of certain dignitaries (Senmut, User-Amon, Rekhmira, Menkheperreseneb, alive from the beginning to the third quarter of the fifteenth century B.C.) testify that at a certain point the Egyptians' relations with their Cretan trade partners were extended to include Mycenaean merchants (indicated as hailing from the "islands in the middle of the sea"); this substitution has been inferred from the alterations and changes made to the Keftiu skirt on the wall paintings. Among the place-names listed in the inscriptions from certain statue plinths in the temple of Amenhophis III at Qurna (late fifteenth century B.C.), names of Mycenaean localities alternate with those of Minoan origin. A passage from the *Admonitions*, a sort of prophetic text, of which a fourteenth-century version exists, though some scholars claim that the original dates from the First Intermediate period (late third to early second millennium B.C.), notes the interruption of trade relations with the Keftiu, who supplied the necessary scented oils used for embalming corpses; the reasons for this interruption are given as natural calamities.

The Egyptian list of the so-called Sea Peoples include the *Eqwesh*, who have been identified with the *Ahhiyawa* mentioned in Hittite documents, in turn linked (though not unanimously) to the Greek ethnic Achaioi (who may relate to the place-name in locative case *a-ka-wi-ja-de* inscribed on a tablet in Linear B found at Knossos). A recent proposal by Bryce suggests that the *Ahhiyawa* belonged to a Mycenaean kingdom in Mainland Greece, with an outpost at Miletus that served as a form of anti-Hittite station. The con-

Gold signet-rings
scenes of hunting and fighting
from Tomb IV of Grave-Circle A
Mycenae
16th cent. B.C.
Athens
National Archaeological Museum

trasts between the Hittites and the Mycenaeans are supposed to be the basis for the Trojan saga. A putative Hittite embargo on Mycenaean trade seems to be substantiated by the scarcity of respective imported artifacts in the two spheres, besides the well-known decree by Tudhaliyas IV to Sausgamuwa, king of Amurru, by which trading with the Assyrians – and hence indirectly with the *Ahhiyawa* – was prohibited (Cline). Among the Sea Peoples the Peleshet are also included, probably of Cretan stock, assuming their identification with the Philistines of the Bible is correct (Jeremiah 47: 2, 4). The only written document that vouches for trade relations between Ugarit and Crete is one recording the tax exemption enjoyed by the ship of the wealthy *tamkaru* (merchant) by the name of Sinaranu: "when it docks in from Crete". The exemption was conceded by King Ammistamru II in the second half of the thirteenth century B.C.
Scholars are generally agreed over the identification of Cyprus with the *Alashiya* cited in Hittite and Ugaritic documents, as well as in the letters of Amarna: one of these notes that the king of that realm had a commitment to supply the pharaoh with a yearly quantity of copper.
A reference to Cypriot metal (*alum*) can be found perhaps in a Linear B tablet from Pylos, where it is cited thus: *ku-pi-ri-jo tu-ru-pte-ri-ja*.

Myths and traditions of the Greek era
The attribution of Crete as the birthplace of the god Zeus and the site of his tomb by the Greeks was probably an expression of their historical memory for the early Crete's extraordinary preeminence. The tradition that has been linked to Minos – even indirectly – is fairly manifold (Herodotus III. 122; Thucydides I. 4 and I. 9; Bacchylides I. 22ff; Pindar, *Paeans* IV. 27–44), commonly known as the legends of the thalassocracy (compiled in Huxley's volume *Minoan in Greek Sources*, 1968), is also considered to be a later Athenian reworking to justify the predominance of the city during the Delian-Attic alliance (Starr). Some of these legends encompass events beyond the Cyclades, about which the most signal piece of news that can be correlated with archaeological evidence is Thucydides' account of the first inhabitants, the Carians (Thucydides I. 4 and 8). Utterly nebulous, however, remains the Platonic tradition concerning Atlantis, which some have rather unsuccessfully attempted to identify with the island of Thera or with Crete itself (*Crito* 113c–121c; *Timaeus* 24e–25d). The eruption of Thera and the ensuing tidal waves the seaquake unleashed are cited in several passages by Apollonius of Rhodes (*Argonautica* IV. 1537ff; 1694–1701); further mention comes in Diodorus (V. 57, 8), who refers to the tidal waves that reached the island of Rhodes. Some have even hazarded identifying the cataclysms subsequent to the eruption with the series of disasters unleashed by Jehovah upon the pharaoh for his impeding the exodus of the Jews from Egypt. Ancient legends have also been cited with regard to the origins of Mycenaean culture: the story of Danaus and of the Danaidai from Egypt for the emergence of the towns in the Argolid, aided by the wealth offered to the mercenaries by the Kings Hyksos; that of the Semite figure Cadmus, to justify the events about Thebes (on the Cadmeia citadel). But it is Homer's epics that confer on Mycenaean Greece its literary consecration with the Trojan War and the *Nostoi*. Besides the various philological issues of Homer's work, an archaeological question has steadily emerged by which attempts have been made to establish to what extent Homer's musings on Mycenaean Greece (architecture, types of material evidence, ideology, customs, religious beliefs, and so on) are mingled with facts of more recent date from the Iron Age. And it is certainly significant that, in the second of the two epic poems (the *Odyssey*), the island of Crete features as a remote, almost inaccessible land and hence fits in with the lies of Odysseus: whereas in the *Iliad* Idomeneus piloted eighty ships to the *ekatompolis* island, in the *Odyssey* the king of Ithaca unharmfully hid his true identity by telling Penelope that he is Aëtion, the brother of Idomeneus, and that the shipwrecked Ulysses was his guest at Amnisus. Another dilemma yet to be solved involves the archaeological endorsement of the tradition linked to the formation itself of the Greek people, implicating the Dorian invasion and the debated return of the Heraclidae to the Peloponnese. The substantial continuity of the material evidence, and the uninterrupted

opposite
The Lion Gate
of the acropolis of Mycenae
ca. 13th cent. B.C.

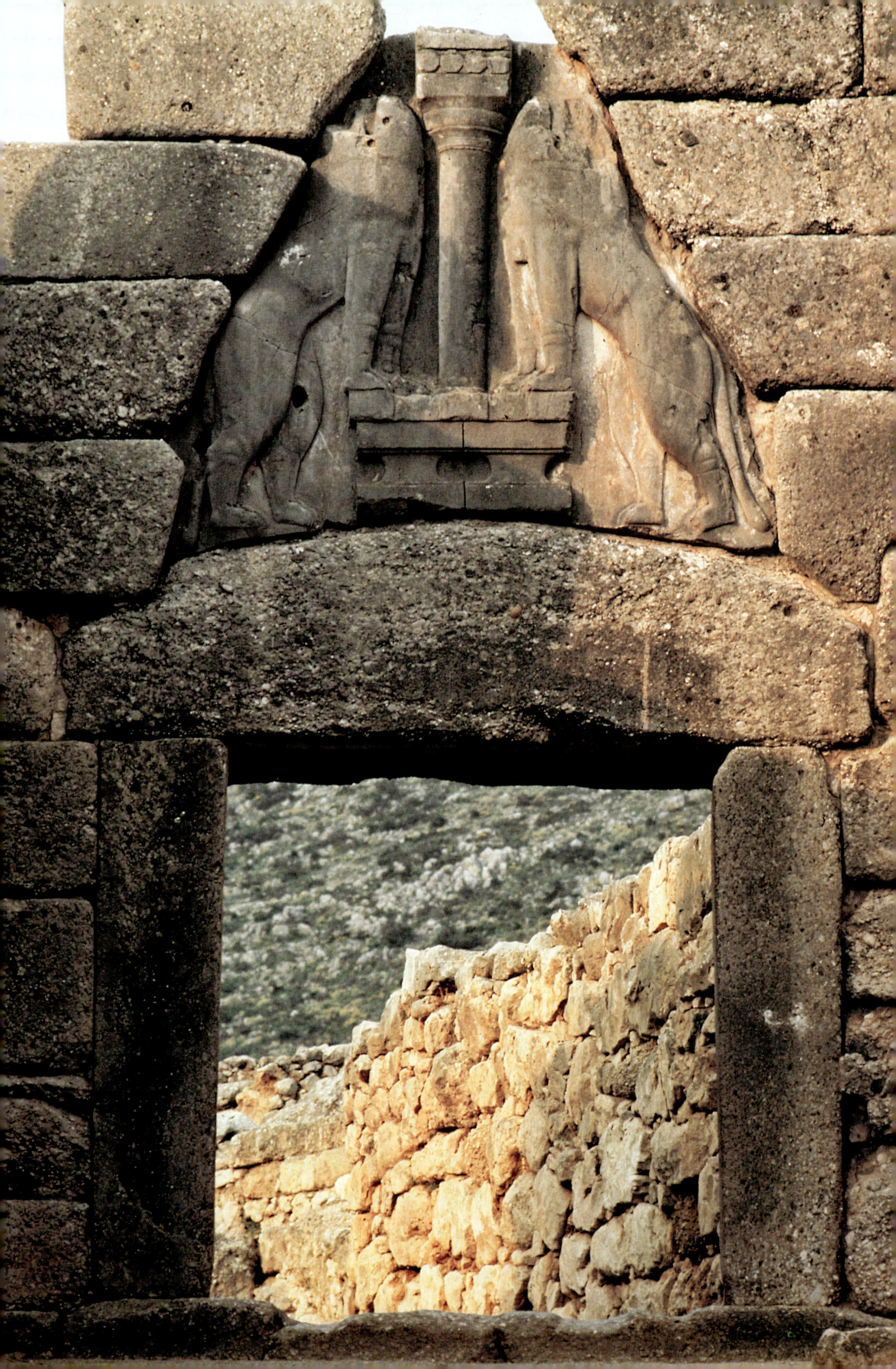

Detail of the Megaron
Palace of Nestor, Pylos
13th cent. B.C.

records of certain Mycenaean settlements leave little margin for individual elements of typological novelty in the transition from the Bronze to the Iron Age. Given the generalized recourse to that literary tradition, one can only admit the insufficiency of archaeological data: excavation levels and stratigraphical sequences may record the passage of invader populations, but they are as yet without name or face.

The historical legacy
In the long term, it is opportune to tackle the issue of the strong anthropological and cultural models that the three main civilizations may have communicated to the Greek *poleis*, namely, the Cretan, Peloponnesian, and Cycladic cultural models. The Minoan "functionary" (and his Mycenaean successor) represents the original figure behind the bureaucratic machinery that made the city-state work. The mobility and lively business of the Cycladic-type of merchant seaman, whose experience would be enhanced by that of the Cypriot and Phoenician traders, may have provided the backbone of the commercial activity of Athens, giving added force and efficacy to its triremes. The Mycenaean warrior-prince, who in the *pelopeion* of Olympia or the *ampheion* of Thebes already enjoyed the status of hero, may have supplied the standard by which the ruling classes judged themselves (thanks also to the Homeric *epos*), through to the age of the tyrant rulers – a spirit that probably died away with the advent of purely representative magistracies such as those of the archon.
An emblematic case of the complexity of these historical processes can be found in the case of Athens. Scant remnants on the southern slopes of the Acropolis testify to the practice of tumulus burials in Meso-Helladic times. A dominant social group did not emerge until the political structures of the Argolid had achieved greater consolidation; the *tholos* tomb never became popular (and indeed its presence throughout Attica is only recorded at Thorikos, Marathon, and Menidi); the "cyclopean" defense wall did not arrive until the end of Late Helladic IIIB, when the other fortified citadels began to disintegrate. In the Greek world, however, the *polis* of Athens, at the peak of its superb vases of the Geometric period, rapidly became the major focus, a primacy curtailed only by the disastrous pillage of the Persians: but in order to conquer the Acropolis, the armies of Mardonius were obliged to tear down the very walls built by the Mycenaean *wa-na-ka*.

Bibliography
An exhaustive bibliography on the subject is R. Treuil-P. Darque-J.C. Poursat-G. Touchais, 1989.
General references: P. Warren-V. Hankey, 1989; *Transition...*, 1989; *L'habitat...*, 1990; S.A. Immerwahr, 1990; G. Hiesel, 1990; J. Vanschoonwinkel, 1991; *La transizione...*, 1991; *Bronze...*, 1991; G.J. Younger, 1991; *Eikon...*, 1992; E. Borgna, 1992; P. Cassola Guida, M. Zucconi Galli Fonseca, 1992; *Agriculture...*, 1992; *La civiltà micenea...*, 1992; N. Marinatos, 1993; P.A. Mountjoy, 1993; O. Dickinson, 1994; *The Role...*, 1995; *La Crète...* (Actes de la Table Ronde, Athens, March 1991), forthcoming; *Atti del II Congresso Internazionale di Micenologia* (Rome-Naples, October 1991), forthcoming.

Pietro Militello   From the Minoic Syllabary to the Greek Alphabet

Aegean scripts: the discovery

When in the spring of 1893 Sir Arthur Evans arrived in Crete, it was widespread opinion that the pre-Homeric world had enjoyed no form of written language whatever. This conviction dated back to the studies carried out in the seventeenth century by the abbot D'Aubinac. Subsequently sanctioned by Vico and by Wolf, the father of Homeric philology, this belief held sway even after Heinrich Schliemann's discoveries in the 1870s and 1880s forced scholars to acknowledge the existence of a flourishing culture – denominated "Mycenaean" from the eponymous site of Mycenae in the Argolid – whose extraordinary material evidence testified to a level of civilization that could hardly be deemed "prehistoric."

Evans' research, however, stemmed from a diametrically opposite premise. His discovery of certain signs scored into a seal in the Ashmolean Museum, Oxford, had convinced him of the possibility of the existence of one or more "pre-Phoenician" scripts (a term by which he referred to the pre-Homeric world) and that these scripts were in use on the island of Crete in the third and second millenniums. The excavation of the Palace of Minos at Cnossos, started in 1900, confirmed the supposition, and even enabled a distinction to be made of three different writing systems: hieroglyphs (a form of pictogram), Linear A (so named for its more schematic and simplified representation of hieroglyphic writing), and Linear B (similar but successive to Linear A). The Linear A script soon proved to be closely related to the Cypro-Minoan syllabary discovered in Cyprus and Ugarit (modern Ras Shamra, Syria).

While hieroglyphics, Linear A, and Cypro-Minoan continue to defy interpretation to this day, the Linear B script was brilliantly deciphered in the early 1950s by an enterprising British architect and code-breaker, Michael Ventris. A subsequent article by his colleague John Chadwick, "Evidence for Greek Dialect in the Mycenaean Archives," published in 1953, explored the linguistics and philology of what Ventris had intuited earlier, and marked the birth of Mycenaeology as a separate branch of inquiry into antiquity.

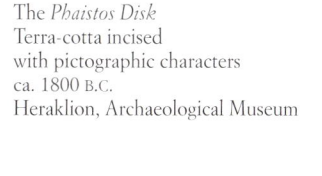

The *Phaistos Disk*
Terra-cotta incised
with pictographic characters
ca. 1800 B.C.
Heraklion, Archaeological Museum

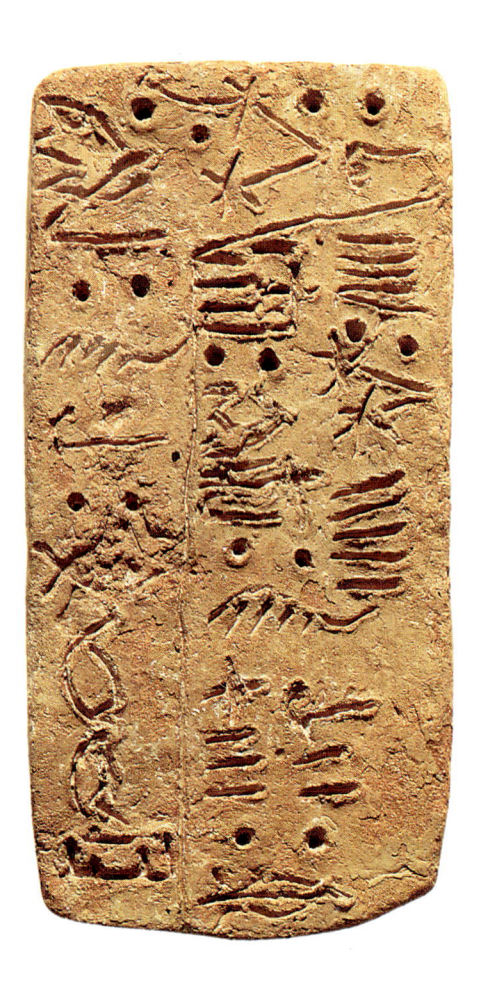

Minoan tablet with Linear A script
ca. 1700 B.C.
Heraklion, Archaeological Museum

Minoan tablet with Linear B script
from Pylos
ca. 1400 B.C.
Athens
National Archaeological Museum

Aegean scripts: evolution
However, the process that led to the adoption and elaboration of several different forms of script – first in Crete and subsequently on Mainland Greece – was not quite as straightforward as Evans had at first supposed. In fact, only a few stages of this long and complex path of development are illustrated by archaeological evidence. Nothing is yet known, for example, about the genesis of written language in the Aegean: the formal independence of the various Aegean syllabaries from other systems of notation affords no clues of possible introduction from outside (Egypt or Anatolia, for instance). Nor can any light be shed on possible links between the first occurrences of hieroglyphs or Linear A, and earlier types of annotation represented by potters' stamps or seal-impressions (impressed clay markers for sealing receptacles or doors). It is not possible, moreover, to fix the exact date within this development process of the "Archanes script" (2200–1900 B.C.), a set of characters found on a number of Early Minoan II to Middle Minoan I seals disinterred in the Archanes necropolis.
One undisputed point is that the first positive epigraphic evidence dates to Proto-Palatial Minoan, that is, to what archaeologists have come to term Middle Minoan II (1800–1700 B.C.). To this period belong around twenty texts in characters scratched on clay tablets found in the Mu Quarter at Mallia, and a substantial group of tablets and seal-impressions found in Chambers 25 and LI at Phaestus; the latter are scored with Linear A glyphs. In the successive phase (MM III, 1700–1600 B.C.), this type of script is used for the archives at Cnossos, Mallia, and Phaestus, and also for various sacred inscriptions in the "Hilltop Sanctuaries." The growing spread of Linear A did not prevent the use of pictographic writing, however, and both types of script have turned up in Room III8 in the palace at Mallia. The contemporary use of two types of scripts has not been convincingly explained as yet, and the question is further complicated by certain inscriptions of difficult classification, such as the one on an ax from Arkalochori, and on an altar at Mallia. Belonging to this category is the long spiral seal-impression text of the famous *Phaistos Disk*: many of the signs it bears have no comparable examples elsewhere in Cretan scripts; for this reason scholars argue that the piece in question may have come from elsewhere, from Anatolia or Egypt.

The widespread disparity in types of writing that prevails throughout MM III tends to dwindle in Late Minoan I (1600–1450 B.C.), during which Linear A begins to show up everywhere, not only throughout Crete itself but also in the islands of the Aegean (Melos, Thera, Ceos, Cythera). In this same lapse of time, galvanized by new contacts with the Minoan world, a new complex civilization began to take shape on Mainland Greece, a culture that takes its name from its best-known city, Mycenae. It was perhaps at this point, or in the immediately ensuing phase, that Minoan scribes on the continent, or Mycenaean invaders on Crete, began to develop Linear B. Although the new script has many features in common with its precursor, it can be distinguished by certain specific formal and graphical features. For at least two centuries thereafter, during LH IIIA and IIIB (Late Helladic, synonymous with Mycenaean: 1400–1200 B.C.), Linear B became the standard administrative script for the Mycenaean palatial powers. Although it was less diffuse than Linear A, the new script has turned up on archaeological sites at Cnossos, Pylos, Thebes, Tiryns, Mycenae, and Cydonia (modern Khaniá, Greece).

Upon the demise of the Helladic citadels around 1200 B.C., traces of written evidence cease to appear in Crete, but also in Greece. It is almost certain that reading and writing skills in the Aegean world in the Bronze Age petered out with the end of the palaces, and for the entire period known as the Greek Dark Ages (1200–800 B.C.), though some scholars attribute this gap to a lack of extant material evidence. Undoubtedly, as regards Aegean syllabaries, the link between the second and first millenniums is to be found a little further afield, in Cyprus. Here, or in Mainland Ugarit (Syria) around 1600 B.C. a glyph system known as "Cypro-Minoan" was developed, under the influence of Linear A and cuneiform script. To date, at least four variants emerged during the period spanning from the sixteenth to the eleventh centuries B.C. These spawned the Cypriot syllabary in use until as late as the second century B.C. The necropolis of Palaepaphos-Skales has yielded two inscriptions dated to the eleventh century B.C., one on a metal cup in Cypro-Minoan script in an unknown language; the other on a bronze *obelos* (skewer) in Greek written in the Cypriot syllabary; this site has therefore provided the link between the Bronze Age and the Iron Age.

The evidence

Spanning almost a millennium, the Aegean scripts provide a substantial corpus of material evidence, which however pales in comparison with the Hittite and Assyrian archives. They are similar to each other in their basic concept, and adopt a syllabary with around eighty basic glyphs and several dozen additional signs, including ideograms and modifiers; that said, the material evidence for each differs in terms of quantity and physiognomy.

Of the 270 extant inscriptions in Cretan hieroglyphics, 150 occur on seals, and the others on vases and archival documents. The latter class constitutes eighty-nine percent of the examples of Linear A script (1,427 specimens in all); the remaining examples are found on vases – in clay, stone, or metal – and small objects such as rings and pins. The "bureaucratic" epigraphs are predominantly in Linear B script, a category in which of some five thousands texts, ninety-nine percent are purely administrational. The evidence in Cypro-Minoan constitutes a less homogeneous group: the circa one hundred specimens are found on tablets, copper bars, silver cups, seals, and curious clay spheres or cylinders. Common to all these writing systems is the use of clay tablets for keeping records. This kind of support, widely used in the Near East, was usually a rectangular piece of clay, sometimes modeled over a framework of sticks, of variable dimensions depending on the length of the text to be taken down. Their production was entrusted to assistants of between nine and twelve years of age (as attested by the analysis of the handprints on the tablets). In Cypriot spheres the "document" was generally kiln-fired with the Syrian or Mesopotamian method, whereas in Crete and Mycenae it was usually sun-baked. The glyphs were scored into the surface with a stylus which, as evidenced by some bone specimens from Tiryns, was pointed at one end and flattened like a spatula at the other, for erasing mistakes. The tablet changed shape in the course of time: the "bar" or "blade" type of tablet – sometimes with a hole so it could be hung up – is typically found in the hieroglyphic deposits of Middle Minoan II, gradually becoming more akin to the Linear A epigraph tables from Phaestus; in Middle Minoan III and Late Minoan I the tablet's shape steadily became a flat rectangle, occasionally with smoothed edges, approximately 12 by 6 centimeters long and 1 centimeter thick; in some cases it was written on both sides (referred to as "opisthographic," from the Greek *opisthen* meaning "behind" or "at the back"). By Late Helladic (1400–1200 B.C.), the one-page tablet had reached a considerable size (the largest measures 27 by 14 centimeters), and a new long and narrow type was introduced, known as the "palm leaf" type, enabling one or two lines of writing. At the same time, the page layout became

Impressed seals
1450 B.C.
Florence, Museo Archeologico

far more systematic, with columns like inventories and incised lines to separate one line of text from the next; capital letters were introduced to emphasize the more important terms. For the purpose of stock-taking and accounting, the palace administrators also used a small clay tool to ensure that the goods concerned were not tampered with in any way (like the seal-impressions mentioned earlier), and to facilitate transactions or redistribution by means of tokens (such as roundels). For this type of "written" document, where the message was generally limited to a brief phrase or countermark, the script system vied with the non-alphabetic notation of seals, which could be more easily read by people not in the administration.

The types and places in which such evidence has turned up, together with the detailed palaeographic studies and even the analysis of finger- and hand-prints, have made it possible to reconstruct how the scribes elaborated and recorded information on goods movement and trade.

Information on production was gathered directly from the manufacturing workshops and warehouses, either directly or via seal-impressions "wheel" seals, and subsequently jotted onto small writing tablets by a scribe. This information was then sent off to the appropriate office – such as those at Cnossos identified as being specifically for managing livestock, wool products, or manpower; subsequently, the data were transcribed onto larger documents ready for the archives. It seems that the accounts were inventoried at the end of each year, as suggested by the records of deficits for previous and current years. This final stocktaking operation was carried out in special departments, full-fledged offices usually located in upper stories (and hence no longer identifiable in terms of their architectural form). In the cases of Chamber XVI at Zakros (Late Minoan I, ca. 1450 B.C.), and in Chambers 7–8 at Pylos (Late Helladic IIIB, ca. 1200 B.C.), the archives were installed on the ground story and we therefore know how they were laid out. They consisted of a set of small rooms with appropriate installations like chests or cabinets in which the tablets were filed away according to subject.

In the case of both Linear A and Linear B, the identity of those who actually wrote on the tablet records is so far unknown. Unlike in Anatolia, Syria, Mesopotomia, and Egypt, here the profession of scribe did not exist. Some seventy-five different "hands" have been attributed with a total of 2,444 epigraphs of Cnossos; similarly, the forty-five different authors accredited with the 1,478 tablets of Pylos authored around thirty each. Whereas the twenty-four Linear A scribes of Hagia Triada only wrote around three or four epigraphs each – too few for them to be comparable to today's typists or secretaries. This impression is confirmed by the content of the Linear B texts, in which no document is signed, and no one qualified as a "scribe" as such; the inevitable conclusion is that the tablets were written by those in charge of a given operation. In fact, the Aegean syllabary is a relative simple system, compared to the cuneiform or Pharaonic scripts with their system of several hundred or even several thousand signs.

Linear B
Linear B is a syllabic system of writing that accompanies the standard set of signs with ideograms and additional signs known as determinatives (denoting semantic class). The signs therefore do not represent individual phonemes, but syllables (open syllables, to be exact) comprising a single vowel or consonant and an accompanying vowel. This structure, which was probably borrowed straight from Linear A and the kind of spoken language it aims to represent, proved very awkward for transcribing Mycenaean Greek, an Indo-European language in which the syllables are often closed, and in which most terminate in a consonant. When he had to transcribe a closed syllable, the Linear B scribe was obliged to omit the closing consonant, or attach a so-called quiescent vowel, that is, use the corresponding sign for the syllable containing the consonant he needed to express, with the same vowel as that of the ensuing syllable. A further drawback was the lack of signs for fricative, soft, or medium consonants (except dentals), or liquid or rotated.
The representation of Mycenaean Greek with Linear B was therefore rather approximate, and such terms as *doelos* (servant) and *chalkeus* (bronzeworker) become *do-e-lo*, *ka-ke-u* respectively, while the place-name Cnossos is written *ko-no-so*. The inevitable pitfalls of the system provided fuel for the detractors of Michael Ventris' work on deciphering the script, which nonetheless enabled the interpretation of most of the texts in Linear B so far discovered.

The contents of the Linear B documents
The successful decipherment of Linear B carried out by Ventris confirmed what many had supposed for years: that the extant documents are basically financial records, lists of varying length detailing foodstuffs, livestock, weaponry, manpower rosters, records of gifts to the deities, garrisons, and the redistribution of raw materials to craftsmen. The nature of this evidence provides us with specific information regarding economic and administrative operations, the number of oxen owned by a given person, the quantity of corn or oil produced, the pattern of the various fiscal departments of the palaces. Furthermore, the close hermeneutic study of the texts has shed light on many other aspects of Late Helladic culture, making it possible to reconstruct the basic geography of the kingdom of Pylos; distinguish the Minoan substratum of the population of Cnossos; detect the presence of certain dialect differences between scribes in Messenia, and even discern the dynamics of the social climbing that took place among high-ranking people in the Palace of Minos. Most information garnered through this study of Linear B material relates to the political hierarchy. The absolute head of the palace itself was the *wa-na-ka* (king), under whom served the *ra-wa-ke-ta* (people's leaders), and the *e-qe-ta* (companions); the decentralization of the various district authorities was in the hands of the *ko-re-te-re* (governors), *po-ro-ko-re-te-re* (vice-governors), and *qa-si-re-we* (group heads). There is frequent mention of the *i-je-re-u* (priesthood, always singular), and of deities among which certain names appear that – assuming the translation is correct – went on to be fundamentally important for Greek religion in the Classical era: *Di-we* (Zeus), *A-ta-na* (Athena), *Po-se-da* (Poseidon), and *Di-wo-nu-so* (Dionysus).
While the list of terms successfully deciphered are many, so are those which have yet to be interpreted. There are no epic or religious poems, no juridical texts, no literary compositions, and nothing has survived that resembles the Egyptian medical subscriptions, or narratives such as the Gilgamesh epic. The diffusion of this kind of literature may have still been oral. But there is a surprising lack of documents covering questions of diplomacy or international treaties, such as those of the Hittite and Egyptian registrars. It remains to be seen whether this culture's literary output or, at any event, some form of non-economic documentation, was ever put into written form. This may have been recorded on perishable materials such as leather or parchment. The use of this kind of writing support is indicated by the impressions left by rolls of some kind on several seal-impressions at Zakros, and by the rather sinuous shapes of certain signs in Linear B, which suggest that they were previously executed in ink, as attested by certain vase inscriptions. And yet we cannot overlook the absence of Linear B documents of "minor" literary production, such as acclamations, dedications, maledictions – the kind of extra material which sheds light on the general level of reading and writing skills of a given culture. While no real problem for reproducing bureaucratic phraseology, the basic imprecision of this particular type of script would have produced innumerable impediments to the proper expression of a poetic or more articulated discourse.

Cup with hunting scene
inscription in the Cypriot syllabary
7th cent. B.C.
Nicosia, Cyprus Museum

Conclusion
As an expression of Minoan Palatial culture, Aegean scripts disappear with the demise of the Mycenaean citadels toward the end of the thirteenth century B.C. The exception was Cyprus, where links with the centers of power had been weaker, and it was here that these scripts remained in current use. While for some aspects of the Mycenaean world there is a suggestion of possible continuity with the Greek culture of the first millennium, as regards scripts and writing the answer is clear, and the rupture between the graphical systems of the two civilizations could not have been more total. The new alphabetic system, borrowed from the Phoenician script, differed structurally and formally from the Aegean syllabaries. Moreover, it had a more penetrating and long-lasting effect on the society that used it as a mode of expression: its very phonetic nature allowed for a far more faithful representation of words and thought, fostering the emergence of that "culture of the written word" which was to have such overwhelming importance for the entire western world.

The Minoan and Mycenaean systems were in a different class. They were marginal to the great revolution that brought about the development of writing in the Near East. While the Aegean syllabaries failed to penetrate the Cretan and Helladic societies, and did not enjoy the wide diffusion of their coeval cuneiform and hieroglyphic counterparts, they nonetheless played a crucial role in the birth and growth of the palaces which characterized the civilizations of the Aegean in the Bronze Age; they are also responsible for having fostered the diffusion of written tradition toward the western end of the Mediterranean basin, thereby inspiring the vase-makers stamps of the potters on the Lipari Islands off the coast of Mylae, Sicily, during that phase of intense exchange and contact between the Helladic world and the Italic world, the first chapter of the ensuing Greek colonization drive across to the West.

Bibliography
A useful guide is the issue of *La Parola del Passato* that deals with Aegaean scripts ("Dal sillabario..." in *La Parola del Passato*, 31, 1976), as well as the more recent work by L. Godart, 1992. In the specific field of Linear B and Mycenaean civilization, see the second revised edition of the volume edited by G. Maddoli with essays by the main experts in this field. We also note the wide account by A. HEUBECK, 1977, and the concise essays, although complete and bibliographically updated, in *Les civilisations egéennes* 1989. On the Mycenaean world in Linear B documents see S. HILLER-O. PANAGL, 1986; on the technique of tablet-making and on writing tools see L. GODART, 1988, pp. 245-250.

Giovanni Garbini The Genesis of the Greek Alphabet

The genesis of the Greek alphabet poses a set of problems which, given the fairly detailed information provided by Herodotus, combined with certain inherent features of the alphabet itself, would otherwise make discussion unnecessary: we have all the essential data to reach a fairly swift conclusion. The problem is that Herodotus was actually expressing a personal view based on his own inquiry, and lacked certain crucial facts.

For one, he had no precise chronological reference, and here and there his geographical locations are unclear. This lack of data hardly justifies the sheer breadth of current discussion on the issue, which arises from the fact that the Greek alphabet is of Semitic origin. This means that the Greek question has been encumbered – without any real reason – with many unsolved problems that have obscured our understanding of the birth of the Semitic alphabet, and has been further complicated by ongoing ideological positions that accompany research into the origins of the latter – a particularly challenging and attractive field for scholars. Given this framework, even a summary description of the background to current studies is not called for, as it has been done numerous times of late. It would be more useful instead to take a brief look at the two basic positions into which scholarly research has

Reconstruction of the ʿIzbet Ṣarṭah *ostrakon* ca. 11th cent. B.C.

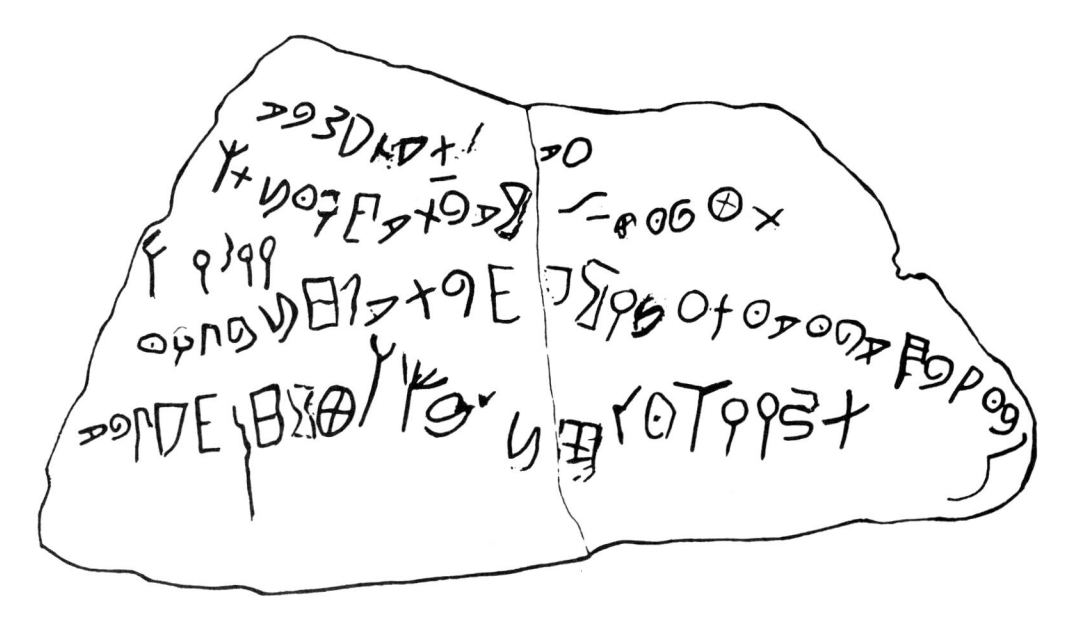

become polarized, though there are many scholars who prefer a balanced view to avoid aligning themselves with either of the two "positions" outlined below.

Common to both positions is the rejection of Herodotus' account, and greater faith in the evidence gained from modern archaeology. As a consequence, each fresh discovery tends to spark new hypotheses and rekindle debate.

The "western" group, which considers the structure of the Greek alphabet as being directly modeled on the Phoenician's, is concerned with identifying the precise time and place in which these two peoples met, and hence the moment that fostered the birth of the Greek alphabet. Chronologically speaking, this first group is not prepared to accept a date before the first half of the eighth century B.C. As regards the place of exchange, this has regularly been shifted to a new location each time some new particularly significant find is made: after Al Mina on the Syrian coast, the seat of a supposed Greek colony, the candidacy was successively assigned to Cyprus, Crete, Rhodes, and Anatolia. At present, each archaeologist seems to abide by his or her particular preference.

On the other side, the "eastern" group follows a more complex line of argument, by which the transmission of the alphabet to the Greeks is thought to be merely a secondary (albeit ever-present) aspect of the current dominant claim that the written alphabet used in Palestine predates that of the Phoenicians, thereby denying the primacy which classical tradition (with some slight oscillations) has regularly accorded to the latter. Scholars are constantly searching for ever-earlier inscriptions in Palestine (as excavations are not possible in Lebanon) to thereby provide an earlier date for the transmission of this alphabet to the Greeks; by this reckoning, the Greeks supposedly received the alphabet from the Canaanites, not the Phoenicians.

The hypothesized date of the eleventh century B.C. for the birth of the Greek alphabet has received

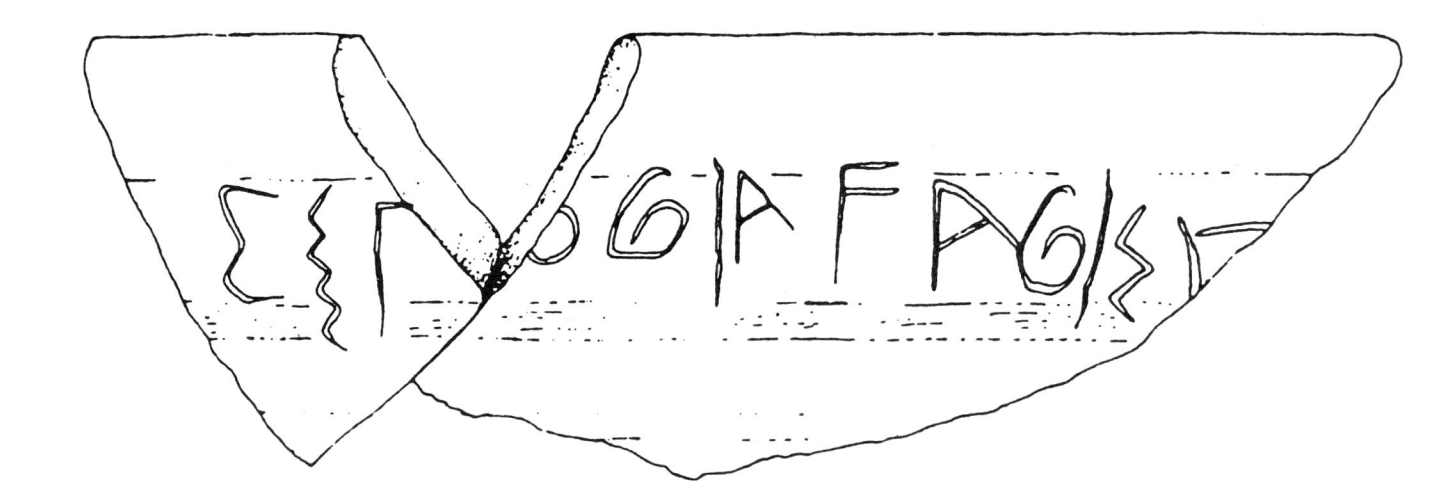

Reconstruction of the Philistine inscription on an *ostrakon* from Qubur el-Walaydah south of Gaza, southern Palestine 11th-10th cent. B.C. Written in fully developed Canaanite script it is surprisingly similar to the Greek alphabet
The text reads from right to left:
ŠMPʼL / ʼYʼL / Š
The first two words are Phoenician names

wide acceptance, though some scholars have set the date back to as early as the fifteenth century B.C. It is worth noting the criteria upon which these epigraphists base their work. The *ostrakon* of 'Izbet Ṣarṭah (Israel), one of the texts most frequently used as proof, was unearthed in an archaeological level dated to the twelfth-eleventh century B.C., but the date of the sherd has been assigned to 1200 B.C. for "paleographic" reasons. The real knowledge in this sector has however been revealed by the bilingual Assyro-Aramaean inscription on a statue discovered at Tell Fekheriyeh (Syria) not long ago. On the basis of paleographic data, this Aramaean text was dated to the eleventh century B.C.; but a global study of the monument has since postdated it to the ninth or perhaps eighth century B.C.

The clearest illustration of the birth of the Greek alphabet can be found in the passage by the Greek historian Herodotus (V. 58) already referred to; this can then be compared against the archaeological data in our possession. "These Phoenicians who came with Cadmus," writes Herodotus, "when they established themselves in this country introduced many new notions among the Greeks, and the alphabet notation in particular, which in my opinion the Greeks did not possess beforehand. Firstly, they were the letters that the Phoenicious used up to now. Then, as time passed, as spoken language changed so did the forms of the letters. The Greeks who at the time mostly lived around the lands of the Cadmeians were Ionians; these learned the letters [of the alphabet] from the Phoenicians and adopted them, modifying their shapes slightly, and in using them called them Phoenician letters, given that the Phoenicians had indeed introduced them to Greece."

Wherever it has been possible to check up on Herodotus' details, they have invariably proved accurate. The name Cadmus (*kadmos* is a Phoenician word *qadmon* that means antique) is of Phoenician origin; likewise, Greek script from the archaic period bears a striking likeness in most of its signs to early first-millennium Phoenician. The differences that arise are due to those slight modifications discussed by Herodotus. Further to this is the order in which the Greek alphabet came to be systematized, together with the names of the letters: these are virtually all identical to the Semitic set. In particular, the terms *iota* and *rho* are typically Phoenician for the presence of the vowel "o" (where in other Semitic languages it would be "a"). The Phoenician origins of the Greek writing are therefore undeniable.

The date is another question, however. Herodotus avoided the issue, but some inferences can safely be made. The earliest Greek inscriptions so far discovered date to the second half of the eighth century B.C. Given the ample scale of the excavations carried out in over a century of archaeological activity, it is unlikely that much earlier examples will come to light. If some kind of link exists between the introduction of writing and the start of the dating system based on the Olympiads (776 B.C.), then the suggestion that the Greek alphabet was born between the end of the ninth and early eighth century is tenable. This corresponds with the second of those transformations mentioned by Herodotus, namely, the one effected by the Ionians, which was preceded by the transformation brought about by the Cadmeians themselves as they dropped the Phoenician language in favor of Greek. This was the moment in which the decisive shift from consonantal Phoenician writing to a true alphabetic writing, in which vowels were also represented, took place. At this point we are most likely well into the ninth century, which puts the arrival of Cadmus in Boeotia to late tenth–early ninth century B.C. This arrival, which has long been regarded as mere legend, fits in plausibly with this geographical and chronological context. Archaeological research at numerous sites on the Aegean has revealed a host of eastern goods dating through the ninth century. Since the modern alternative propositions are no more than vague hypotheses, it is perhaps more viable – at least until proof to the contrary is forthcoming – to give credence to Herodotus when he discusses Cadmus and the events related to him, that is, that the Greek alphabet came into existence in an Ionian context. Doubts inevitably remain, however, where Herodotus talks of the "surrounding regions," by which he may either have meant Boeotia itself, or the island of Euboea, or some other not far-off location: these areas are known to have been frequented by eastern peoples of varying provenance.

This, then, is the core problem with regard to the origin of the Greek alphabet: Herodotus writes of the Phoenicians, but the term *phoinikes* in the Greek tongue covered a wider range of meanings than its derivative does today. The Phoenician alphabet was used by a variety of different peoples who expressed themselves directly in Phoenician or some close dialect, a category that comprises the Israelites, the Moabites, the Ammonites, and the Philistines. The other Semitic language at the time was Aramaean, spoken by the Aramaeans of Syria and Anatolia. The use of Phoenician names for the letters of the alphabet themselves is not a decisive argument: even in later periods the Aramaeans continued to use the Phoenician names for the letters of the alphabet. At present, there is no precise solution to this complex historical and cultural situation. When outlining the various changes undergone by the alphabet, Herodotus himself shows that the situation is a complex one.

One aspect of the question that has not yet been thoroughly assessed is the nature of the Greek names for the letters of the alphabet. The ending in *-a* of most of the letters may be of Greek origin; the question is, then, why such ending is not *-ē*, as one legitimately expects in the Ionian dialect. Looking at the Semitic languages, we find an excellent explanation in the grammatical determinate state of the Aramaean language, indicating the presence of the article. If this is true, letter names such as *alpha* and *beta* are probably the Aramaean forms of the Phoenician names *alph* and *bet*: the Aramaeans, whose presence in Euboea is documented through the ninth century B.C. (such as the inscription

Fragmentary Phoenician
inscription on a cup
from Citium, Cyprus
clay with white slip
9th cent. B.C.
Nicosia, Cyprus Museum

The Genesis of the Greek Alphabet

Philistine *ostrakon*
recording an agreement
from Tell Qasile
8th cent. B.C.
Jerusalem, Museon Israel

found in the Temple of Apollo in Eretria), must therefore have influenced the development of the Greek alphabet. They were the only people in the early centuries of the first millennium B.C. to add indications of the vowel sounds in their written language. While Cadmus was not an Aramaean, perhaps those who suggested the changes to the Ionians were.

The discussion does not end here, however. One of the archaeological documents that is frequently referred to in terms of the transmission of the Semitic alphabet to the Greeks is the *ostrakon* of 'Izbet Ṣarṭah, mentioned earlier. This potsherd abecedary has to be dated approximately to the eleventh century B.C. With its left-to-right script, and certain signs closely resembling those of the Greeks, this text (in an as yet unidentified language, but with a full alphabet at the end) has to be classified as Philistine, and predates the other well-known Philistine *ostrakon* of Qubur el-Walaydah (south of Gaza). Of slightly later date, the latter inscription is also left-to-right, the two surviving names written on the *ostrakon* are decidedly Phoenician: by 1000 B.C. the Philistines had been deeply influenced by Phoenician culture. What makes the Qubur el-Walaydah *ostrakon* important to the discussion here is a series of anomalies in the Phoenician script: one of them is most striking, the signs for *aleph* and *shin* have been turned through ninety degrees, foreshadowing the Greek letters *alpha* and *sigma*.

There is no point in accrediting these inscriptions with more than they actually mean. It is nonetheless important to bear in mind that in Palestine in the eleventh–tenth century B.C. the resident population was noticeably Phoenician in culture, with extensive experience of seafaring, and wrote in a form of Phoenician closely resembling the script that appeared subsequently in Greece. The Cretan origin of the Philistines, and their evolved trade activity across the Aegean, offer further important features for the current debate: it would not be then surprising to discover one day that Cadmus was a Phoenician of distant Cretan descent who actually came from Palestine.

Bibliography
G. Pugliese Carratelli, in *La Parola del Passato*, 1976, pp. 5-15; B.S.J. Isserlin, in *Phoinikeia Grammata*, 1991, pp. 283-291.

Filippo Càssola Greek Forms of Political Structure

In the Late Bronze Age (1600–1200 B.C.), known also as the Mycenaean age due to the major role played by the kingdom of Mycenae, Greece was divided into various states whose sovereigns bore the title of *wanax*. They lived in great palaces built on high places and surrounded by huge defensive walls.

Numerous officials dealing with the administration of the state lived in the palace with the *wanax* and his family. A large part of the economy was run by the king, who distributed raw materials (bronze, textiles) to the craftsmen and established the quantities of finished products that they were to manufacture and deliver to the palace. Agriculture and cattle breeding were also under the control of the palace, but the rural communities (*damoi*) enjoyed a certain degree of independence. Each one was headed by a local notable, the *basileus*, who was assisted by a *gerusia*, or council of elders (*gerontes*). It is not yet clear whether the *basileis* were appointed by the king or if the office was hereditary.

A part of the arable land was reserved for the *wanax*, for the top administrators, and for the temples. The rest was run by the *damoi*, who distributed the single farms among private individuals (the latter appear to have been the beneficiaries of a concession, rather than the actual owners of the farm).

Greece was devastated in the twelfth and eleventh centuries by a series of raids and invasions. The last onslaught was the invasion by the Dorians, a people of Greek origin, coming from Macedon and Epirus, but who had only hovered on the fringe of the growing Mycenaean civilization. The long crisis led to the fall of the ancient dynasties, and to the dissolution of the administrative structures run from the palaces. The rural communities survived however, with their *basileis* and councils of elders. In the long run, the new arrivals ended up adopting the traditional structures in force in the occupied territories. For example, the division of the land into *damoi* can be found both in Attica, which remained more or less unaffected by the invasion (the classical form of *demoi* developed at a later date), and in the Dorian Elis, where the original title of the Dorian leaders, *archagetas* (he who guides the way, leads), was slowly substituted throughout the entire Dorian sphere of influence by the term *basileus*. In the period following the invasion, known as the Hellenic Middle Ages or Dark Age (1100–900 B.C.), nearly all the regimes in Greece were monarchic, where the throne was handed down dynastically. Some of these survived up to the seventh century (Thera) or to the start of the fifth (Argos). The Battiad dynasty ruled over Cyrene, a colony of Thera founded in 630, from the beginning to the latter half of the fifth century. Sparta was a special case, where power was shared between two dynasties, and in spite of constant friction between the two, the structure lasted up to the Hellenistic age.

It is possible that the kings of various Dorian states descended directly and without any interruption from the captains who led the conquest. New states arose in the greater part of Greece from the aggregation of the old rural communities: one of the local *basileis* would subordinate the others and concentrate power into his own hands. The royal title would be limited to him and his heirs. Homer confirms this (*Iliad* II. 284–285) when he observes: "Many leaders is not a good thing; there should be only one head (*koiranos*), only one king (*basileus*)." The *Odyssey* describes a phase of this development. Alcinous on the island of the Phaeacians and Ulysses in Ithaca are without doubt the supreme authority, but Alcinous is flanked by twelve notables who share with him the title of *basileus* (VIII. 390–391), and there are even more *basileis* at Ithaca, who are Ulysses' rivals (I. 394–396). The supremacy of the king is a fact which is not sanctioned by a specific title. The poet simply says that Ulysses' stock is "more royal" than the others (XV. 533–534). Homer certainly based his story on reality, but not on the reality of his time (eighth century) which was characterized by the decline of the monarchy. He preferred the period of transition when one *basileus* was rising above his compeers.

We are unable to reconstruct the process which led to the creation of the *polis*, but we do know that this had been concluded by the eighth century. It is better to use the Greek word *polis* rather than the conventional translation "city-state", which is misleading. It suggests that the state is enclosed within the city walls, while it usually included cultivated land which could have been very extensive. Sometimes, as in Sparta, there was not even a real urban nucleus. The modern term is useful only as far as indicating that the state has just one political center, comprising the seats of the magistrates in office, the public square (*agora*) where the people hold their assemblies, and the most important temples, especially that of the divinity whose task it is to protect the city (*polias*). The *polis* was first and foremost a community. We talk of Argos, Athens and Thebes, but the Greeks preferred saying "the Argives, the Athenians, the Thebans". Each community had its own particular characteristics (institutions, cults, calendar, dialect, and alphabet) different from those of neighboring states, and none was prepared to give them up. This was the origin of the well-known particularism of the *poleis*, who were jealous of their independence whatever their size.

Political rights were not always distributed equally among all the citizens. Very often there were privileges belonging to the descendants of noble families (aristocratic regimes), or based on riches (timocracy). Every citizen could exercise his own rights, as many or as few as he was entitled to, in the assembly. The idea of delegating legislative power to representatives elected by the people, typical of modern parliamentary systems, was

Greek Forms of Political Structure

Mycenaean vase with warriors
ca. 12th cent. B.C.
Athens
National Archaeological Museum

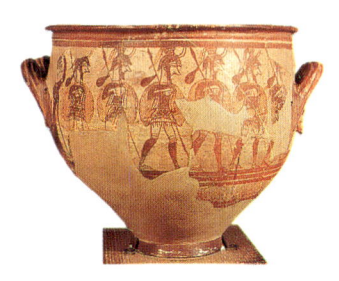

practically unheard-of. This fact was a further incentive towards the defense of the state's independence. It would be impossible to maintain the direct relations between citizens and the holders of executive power in an overlarge state. The territory belonging to Athens with its 2,500 square kilometers (about the size of the modern province of Venice) was already excessively large according to Greek standards, because the inhabitants of the *demoi* on the borders had to cover dozens of kilometers to come to the assembly. A typical symptom of Greek particularism is the independence of the colonies. Right from the time of its foundation, each colony became a new *polis*, or sovereign state, which was tied to the old country only in terms of friendship (economic links were possible, but were not always the case). The only exception were Corinth's colonies which considered themselves close to the mother country and which remained faithful to it for centuries.

The state had very light-weight administrative structures. It therefore delegated a part of its tasks to the smaller groups forming the population, such as the *phylai* (tribes) and the *phratriai* (clans). The latter held and updated the lists of the citizens – each head of a family had to present his children to the *phratria* in order to establish their belonging to the *polis*. The mobilization of the army was the *phylai*'s responsibility.

In the course of its long history the *polis* saw a succession, or better, an alternation, of regimes: monarchies, aristocracies, timocracies and democracies. The presence of a monarchy was not incompatible with the citizens' active participation in the life of the community. In the *Iliad*, even though Troy was the "city of King Priam" (VII. 296), it was the Trojans who chose Theano as the high priestess of Athena (VI. 388); and the Achaean army camp included an *agora* where assemblies and trials were held, and where there were the altars of the gods (XI. 806–808). In the *Odyssey*, an old Ithacan remarks that the popular assembly had not met since Ulysses left for the war (II. 25–27): this suggests that the meetings were a normal activity when the king was present.

The Mycenaean monarchy of the *wanax* fell under pressure from external forces. The new monarchy of the *basileus* disappeared gradually due to internal factors in the majority of the Greek states. Between the ninth

Plate with Menelaus and Hector
fighting over the body of Euphorbus
terra-cotta
ca. 600 B.C.
London, British Museum
Department of Greek
and Roman Antiquities

Detail of the Chigi vase
Corinthian krater
scene of soldiers fighting
7th cent. B.C.
Rome, Museo Nazionale
di Villa Giulia

Marble fragment
with Greek horseman
end 5th cent. B.C.
New York
Metropolitan Museum of Art

and eighth centuries, population increase and a slight recovery of the economic activities made the community's life increasingly complex and obliged the king to choose some aides, selected naturally from among the aristocracy, to whom he delegated a part of his tasks. The nobles took advantage of the situation to concentrate more and more power in their hands, until the *basileus* only exercised a priestly role. In some states certain functions remained the hereditary privilege of a single family so that the old dynasties continued to exist, even though they were deprived of authority. In others, such as Athens, where the new offices were elective, it seemed logical to make the *basileus* subject to election. Consequently, he became a magistrate like the others. In Archaic societies, power was in the hands of warriors; and a man must buy his own weapons in order to enter the army. During the Hellenic Middle Ages, the nobles had the greatest possibilities of arming themselves. They fought on horseback (and for this reason the word "cavalier" is a synonym of "nobleman") and sometimes on foot, as hoplites or heavily armed foot soldiers. A middle class developed between the eighth and the seventh centuries, whose members (land-owners, shipowners, craftsmen) were in a position to procure themselves weapons and to take part as hoplites in the defense of the state. They could therefore demand to have a share in political power, and they did so. The word *demos*, or *damos*, which literally meant a territory and all its inhabitants, was used to indicate the people in opposition to the nobles. In some *poleis*, the *demos* succeeded in affirming their rights, as from the start of the sixth century, but it was only during the fifth century that the term democracy ("the *demos* in power") could be used. Other concepts at least partially equivalent were *isonomia* (isonomy, equality of political rights for all citizens) and *isegoria* (equal rights to speech).

The evolution of democracy was not always straightforward and easy. During the fairly common conflicts between the heads of the noble families of the aristocracy, it was quite usual for one of the contenders to ally himself with the *demos* in order to defeat his rivals and create personal power (seventh or sixth centuries; in Sicily, this form of rule lasted until the fourth century). The new monarchs were given the certainly un-Greek title of tyrant. The word first only meant that their authority was unlawful since it was not based on the hereditary dynasty. Later on, following certain episodes, "tyrant" acquired the sense of blood-thirsty oppressor, hated by his subjects. Nearly all the tyrannies were overthrown by an insurrection – sometimes supported by Sparta – after two or three generations. In some *poleis* the aristocracy returned to power, as in Corinth; in others, the crisis led to the introduction of democracy, as in Athens after the expulsion of the Pisistratids (508 B.C.), and at Syracuse after the end of the Deinomenids' rule (465 B.C.).

A rapid glance at the institutions of the *poleis* reveals their considerable homogeneity. For example, nearly everywhere there was a popular assembly (*ekklesia*, or *halia*) and a restricted council (*boule*, or *gerusia*). In nearly all cases the most important magistracies were collegial. Nevertheless, the right of access to the assembly, the way in which members of the restricted council and the magistrates were chosen, as well as the relations be-

Greek Forms of Political Structure

Bronze statuette of a hoplite
ca. 530 B.C.
Sibari, Museo Nazionale
Archeologico della Sibaritide
Cat. 46/I

tween these institutions, vary according to the states and the epochs. Knowledge of these conditions is necessary in order to understand whether the regime of a *polis* could be called aristocratic, timocratic or democratic. Naturally, these definitions allow for a whole series of variations, from moderate forms to very radical ones. For the sake of simplicity we will consider first of all the Athenian constitution of the fifth and fourth centuries, and then consider the (few) characteristics in common and the (many) differences to be found in the other constitutions compared to the original chosen as a model.

The regime in Athens was a radical democracy. The popular assembly (*ekklesia*) included all free men over twenty. It met at fixed dates, and was the only seat of deliberative power in the legislative field, as far as war and peace were concerned, and for interstate treaties. It could sack incompetent or dishonest magistrates. All the proposals made by the magistrates or the council were discussed freely, amended or rejected. Even judicial power, except for exceptionally serious crimes, was in the hands of the people. Every year six thousand citizens, of at least thirty years of age, were drawn by lots to constitute the judges' list. Further lots established the various courts which accounted for 200 to 500 members, and sometimes even 1,000 or 1,500. In the mid-fifth century, Pericles introduced a compensation of two obols a day to encourage average Athenians to accept these responsibilities. Cleon raised the amount to three obols in 424. These were, however, modest sums of money, because a worker's daily wage was one drachma, or six obols. It appealed most of all to the older citizens (according to Aristophanes, the comic poet, a typical juryman was old and run-down) and the unemployed.

The council (*boule*) was composed of 500 members (*bouleutai*) drawn from lots among the citizens over thirty years of age. The radicals believed that the elective system was incompatible with the ideal of equality, and feared that it might reintroduce the aristocratic regime. Fifty *buleutai* were drawn by lots from each of the ten tribes. The year was divided up into ten periods (*prytaneiai*) of thirty-six days on average, and during each period the *bouleutai* of one tribe carried out their duties in the name of the whole council. As compensation, they received one drachma a day. The fifty councilors in office were known as *prytaneis* (the first). Every day, in turn, one of them presided the meeting. The *boule* did not have the power to take any decisions. Its task was that of preparing the agenda of the assembly, as well as formulating, together with the magistrates, the proposals the people would have debated. This task made them very influential from the political point of view, and the *boule* became the most important institution of the state. The president of the *prytaneis* was more or less the head of the republic. There were never more than thirty thousand citizens over thirty. The *bouleutai* totaled 500 a year. Nobody could be a *bouleutes* more than twice. During a *pritania*, thirty-six *prytaneia* out of fifty assumed the presidency. It is clear therefore that every Athenian had a good chance of entering the *boule* at least once during his lifetime, and a fair possibility of becoming head of state for one day.

There was another council called the *Areopagus* from the place where it met (the Hill of Ares). It was composed of retired high magistrates who were members for life (an unusual event for Athens). Up to the sixth century it exercised very wide powers: for example, it acted as a watchdog over the magistrates in office so that it ran all the political activity; it also judged the greater part of the trials. The *Areopagus* was stripped of its preroga-

Embossed bronze shield
detail
599-575 B.C.
Bari, Museo Archeologico
Cat. 118/I

tives by the democrats. These rights were distributed among the *boule*, the *ekklesia* and the popular courts. In the fifth century its jurisdiction was limited to crimes of willful murder, violence and false testimony.

The highest judicial body, in theory, was that of the nine archons (*archontes*). One of them, known simply as "the archon" without any further titles, prepared the civil cases for trial by the popular courts, and organized the tragic plays which were so important in the social and religious life of Athens. He was a highly respected figure because his name was used to date official documents. The *polemarchos* had once been the commander in chief of the army, but in the Classical period, his powers were limited to preparing the cases concerning foreigners resident in Athens. The *basileus* had inherited the sacral role of the former kings. Lastly, the six *thesmothetai* administered the courts' activities and distributed the trials among them.

In the past, the archonship was limited to the richest citizens, but in the fifth century the qualification regarding a certain level of property ownership was lowered and then abolished. Up until the year 486 B.C. the office was elective. After this date a mixed system was introduced: the archons were drawn by lots from 500 elected citizens. In the end, they were simply drawn by lots. This was the way in which the principle of equality could be respected in this case too. The only branch in which specific competence was considered necessary was that of the military offices which therefore continued to be elective. Every year the people voted for ten commanders, the *strategoi*, one for each tribe, who were formally subordinate to the *polemarchos*, but who ended up depriving him of his authority and became the supreme commanders of the army. Over time, the *strategoi* – who were chosen on the basis of the esteem they won, and represented the political majority – acquired great authority among the citizens. The office of *strategos* became the apex of a political career. The leadership of Pericles was based on his being a *strategos* from 443 to 430 B.C.

The popular assembly had the power to banish from Athens for a period of ten years, without any trial, any politician considered a danger to the democracy. The votes were expressed by writing the name of the person on a potsherd (*ostrakon*), and that is the reason why the procedure was called ostracism. This decision, which was not a sentence but a safety measure, should not be confused with exile, which presupposed a crime and was therefore usually combined with the confiscation of property.

Very often it has been suggested that the uncompromising defense of equality among all the free men, nobles and plebeians, rich and poor, is in flagrant contradiction with the existence of slavery. However, it does not make sense to criticize a *polis* for an institution which was common to the greater part of the ancient world and not unknown in this one. Rather, we should keep in mind that in Greece slaves were treated better than in Rome, and in Athens better than in the rest of Greece. An anonymous reactionary Athenian writer protested because the law forbade the beating of slaves, and he complained that it was impossible to distinguish slaves from citizens by their appearance and how they dressed, and that sometimes the slaves were even well-off (*The Constitution of Athens* I. 10–11). Some Greek *poleis* introduced democracy before Athens (for example, Chios); others were influenced by Athens and adopted a democratic regime (Samos), but aristocratic and timocratic regimes were very common. In Sparta the right to vote was limited by age (electors had to be over thirty) and by property ownership. The tendency to concentrate landed property in few hands led to a situation where the numbers of citizens with the right to vote decreased from 9,000 in Archaic period, to 1,000 in the fourth century, and to 700 (or, according to a second interpretation, to only 100) in the third century B.C. In some of the colonies of Magna Graecia, the number of citizens who could take part in the assembly was fixed by law at 1,000, such as at Locri (Lokroi), where the selection was based on the fact of belonging to noble families, at Rhegium (Rhegion), where it was based on riches, and at Croton (Kroton).

Ostrakon incised
with the name of Themistocles
471 B.C.
Athens, Museum of the Agora

Bronze tablet documenting a loan
made by the Sanctuary of Zeus
to the *polis* of Locri
for the contribution to the king
350–250 B.C.
Reggio Calabria, Museo Nazionale

In various *poleis*, the assembly was not called on regular occasions, but only when the magistrates or the council considered it necessary. It could neither debate nor amend the proposals, but only accept them completely or reject them. According to Aristotle, the assembly had no power whatsoever in the Cretan *poleis*: it was obliged to accept all the proposals presented (*Politics*, 1272. 10–12). Popular courts were few and far between outside Athens (they existed in Cyrene in the Hellenistic period).

In Sparta, the council was made up of thirty members: the two kings and twenty-eight elders (minimum age, sixty) elected for one year by the people. It could ignore the opinions of the assembly and dissolve it if it proved to be too independent. In Massalia, the council comprised 600 members, but these were designated by cooptation. They were members for life and had to belong to the nobler families, so that the constitution of Massalia was considered a perfect example of aristocracy.

The titles of the magistrates varied from one *polis* to another. Archons (heads), ephors (overseers), demiurges (workers for the people) and *cosmoi* (orderers). Likewise the numbers of them varied, as well as their powers and tasks. The five ephors in Sparta chaired the assembly, acted as judges in civil cases, and verified the activity of the other magistrates and the kings themselves. Usually the public offices were elective in both aristocratic and timocratic regimes as in the democratic ones. The Athenian system of drawing lots was limited to only a few cases: in Syracuse (Syrakousai), toward the end of the fifth century, and in Tarentum (Taras), in the fourth. Syracuse was the only *polis* to imitate the Athenian institution of ostracism, but the period of banishment abroad of individuals considered dangerous or undesirable was reduced to five years. The vote was written on an olive leaf, and was therefore known as "petalism."

As we have said, particularism was a very strong tendency in the Greek world. All the same, it was often counterbalanced by other factors that implied, or imposed on the *poleis*, a total or partial renunciation of their independence. The foregoing was total when a synechism, or fusion, of several *poleis* was involved. Literally, the term indicates the confluence of all the citizens in the same place, which did not always occur. Rhodes was founded in 408 when Ialysus, Camirus, and Lindus united in one state to oppose the power of Athens. The three ancient and glorious *poleis* each transferred a part of their populations to the new city, but they were not abandoned: in fact, they survived as considerably important urban centers. The synechism in Megalopolis came closer to the literal sense. The "large *polis*" was set up in Arcadia in 370 as a bastion against Spartan encroachment. The inhabitants of about forty smaller *poleis* and villages moved or were forced to move to Megalopolis, leaving many of them completely deserted.

Several states often formed alliances (symmachies). Some of these unions lasted a certain period of time, also because one of the members was stronger than the others and imposed, in its own interests, the continuation of the coalition (hegemonic symmachies). The oldest of these alliances was the Peloponnesian League, led by Sparta (sixth–fifth centuries B.C.). Then there were the two leagues, one in the fifth and the other in the fourth century B.C., that were proposed and piloted by Athens, and the Boeotian League dominated by Thebes (fifth–fourth centuries). The members of these leagues agreed to collaborate on foreign policy. A series of rebellions broke out every time the hegemonic power tried to intervene in the domestic policy of its allies, leading to the dissolution of the symmachy.

Less far from the spirit of the *polis*, and therefore more lasting, were a few leagues that grew up around a sanctuary that the members ran collegially. Cohesion was favored both by the religious ties and by the common interests (the large sanctuaries were enormously wealthy and active centers of the economic life, thanks to pil-

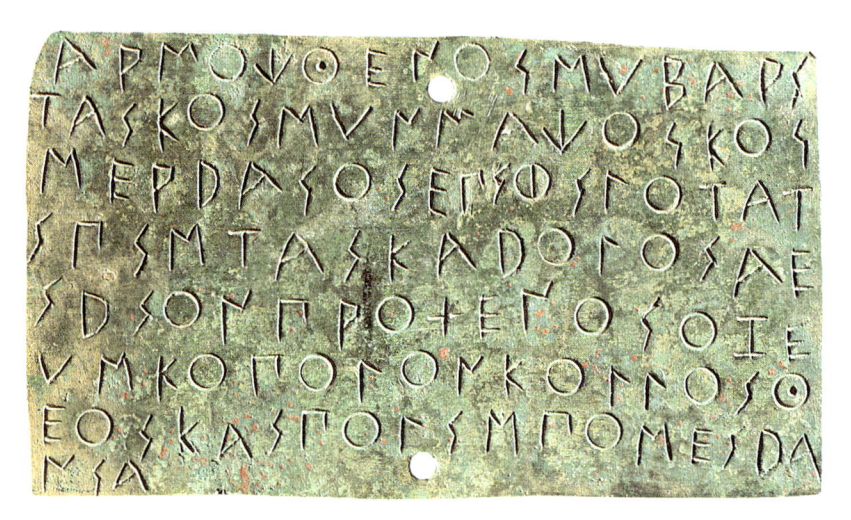

Bronze tablet registering the alliance between Sybarites and Serdaioi
550-525 B.C.
Olympia, Archaeological Museum
Cat. 71

grimages, feast days, markets, and fairs). The most famous of these was the Pileo-Delphic Amphictyony, which had two centers: the Temple of Demeter at Anthili and that of Apollo at Delphi. The name means "the league of neighbors" (*amphictiones*), and the first community was actually composed of the peoples living around Anthili. Later on, nearly all the most important states joined it. In some parts of Greece the *polis* developed only in a later period, or failed to achieve real independence due to a lack of sufficient vitality. In these areas, particularly solid regional unity was established (or perhaps continued to survive).

The Thessalian League in northern Greece was founded as early as the eighth century. It was governed by an oligarchy which in turn elected a commander of the army for life. The commander, or *tagos*, was flanked by a college of tetrarchs (the rulers of the four regions comprising Thessaly). In spite of the quarrels between the main families, some of which tried to make the office of *tagos* hereditary, the Thessalians succeeded in forcing the neighboring peoples to accept their supremacy and in controlling the Pileo-Delphic Amphictyony until at least the fifth century.

The Aetolian League and the Achaean League acquired power and prestige in the fourth century, and, in the Hellenistic age, they became the strongest states in Greece, spreading far beyond their original regions. Even though the two leagues had always been rivals, their structures were remarkably similar. Both organizations were inspired by democratic principles and excluded the delegation of powers to elected representatives. Decisions were therefore taken by an assembly which, in theory, was open to all the citizens of the member *poleis*. Year by year, the assembly elected the magistrates. There was also a council whose task it was to present proposals. However, real participation became more and more difficult as the territory of the league expanded, because the poor could not afford to leave their work, or to pay for their journey. The assembly was transformed as a result into the privilege of a wealthy minority. This was even more true of the council, whose members were not compensated. In reality, the two bodies functioned as timocratic regimes.

It is worth noting that, besides the right of citizenship in the individual *poleis*, there was also a common citizenship within the league. Consequently, in contrast with Greek tradition, citizens from one *polis* in the league could marry legitimately and own property in the others. For these reasons, this kind of league can be compared to today's federal state.

Bibliography
On the *polis* in general:
G. GLOTZ, 1928; S. ACCAME, 1941; F. SARTORI, 1953; M. SORDI, 1958; L. MORETTI, 1962; V. EHRENBERG, 1965; L.A. STELLA, 1965; C. MOSSÉ, 1967; J.A.O. LARSEN, 1968; R. MEIGGS, 1972; G. PUGLIESE CARRATELLI, in *Scritti...*, 1976, pp. 135-158; idem, in *op.cit.*, pp. 395-411; A.M. SNODGRASS, in *Opus* V, 1976, pp. 7-22; D. ROUSSEL, 1976; M. MOGGI, I, 1976; F.W. WALBANK, in *Scripta classica Israelica* III, 1976-77, pp. 27-51; G. MADDOLI, 1977; C. AMPOLO, 1980; G. CAMASSA, in *Storia delle idee...*, I, 1982, pp. 3-126; P. CARLIER, 1984; F. DE POLIGNAC, 1984; E. MEYER, 1990; D. STOCKTON, 1990; D. MUSTI *et. al.*, *La transizione...*, 1991, pp. 15-33; M. NAFISSI, 1991; K. TAUSEND, 1992.

Carlos A. Picon

A Profile of Archaic Greek Sculpture

The conventional chronological limits of the Archaic style in Greek sculpture (ca. 660–480 B.C.) are based on two historical events, the conquest and unification of Egypt before 653 B.C. by the Pharaoh Psammetichos I, who employed eastern Greek and Carian mercenaries to defeat the Assyrian invaders, and the Persian destruction of the Athenian Acropolis in 480 B.C. The validity of these historical correlations and chronological boundaries is open to discussion, but the approximate dates may be retained as a convenient framework for the study of Archaic sculpture. It should be stressed, however, that other manifestations of Greek art during the Archaic period, such as architecture or vase-painting, require different chronological brackets.

Monumental marble sculpture first appears in Greece around the middle of the seventh century B.C. in the Aegean Islands, notably Samos and the Cyclades, where supplies of marble were readily available. No single source of inspiration can fully explain the first sculptural creations, revolutionary as they are. They differ markedly from the artistic achievements of other ancient Mediterranean and Near Eastern cultures, yet direct influence from Egypt is both crucial and undeniable. To be sure, there is a considerable Greek legacy that has firm associations with various regions of the ancient world: the long Geometric sculptural tradition in terra-cotta and bronze; the Orientalizing styles in Crete and Mainland Greece during the eighth century B.C., a product of contacts with the Near East, specifically Syria and the neo-Hittite kingdoms; and finally the decorative Daedalic style of the seventh century B.C. This movement, somewhat misleadingly named after the legendary Cretan artisan Daedalus, likewise has its origins in the Syro-Phoenician world.

Marble statue of Artemis
with dedication by Nikandre
640-630 B.C.
Athens
National Archaeological Museum

The *Auxerre Goddess*
clay statue found in Crete
mid-7th cent. B.C.
Paris, Musée du Louvre
Département des Antiquités
Grecques, Etrusques et Romaines

Marble head of *kouros*
from the Dipylon necropolis
ca. 600 B.C.
Athens
National Archaeological Museum

The Daedalic style is best represented in Crete, though in fact it flourished throughout the Greek world. None of these antecedents prepare us for the advent of monumental Archaic sculpture in marble. Individual details certainly hark back to earlier traditions, such as the Daedalic-looking heads of some of the first Archaic marble figures, or the enigmatic Daedalic belt worn by a number of the early island *kouroi* (youths), perhaps as a characterization of Apollo. The new Archaic style, however, owes more to Egypt and its long tradition of colossal sculpture in hard stone than to any Greek or eastern antecedents that have no true followings in terms of artistic production. Yet it has recently been argued that the quarrying techniques used by the Greeks were borrowed from the neo-Hittite civilizations of Asia Minor and the northern Levant.

Two important traits that set apart the beginning of the Archaic style from the Daedalic creations are the use of marble rather than the softer limestone, and the monumental scale of the sculptures, often over life-size if not colossal. To grasp the difference in approach and monumentality, one only has to contrast the inscribed marble *kore* (maiden) from Delos dedicated by Nikandre, with the roughly contemporary Daedalic statuette known as the *Auxerre Goddess*. The Nikandre stands 1.75 meters high, plank-like and rigid. Dated to about 640–630 B.C., it is the earliest *kore* to have survived fairly complete; only portions of her arms and the metal objects they held are missing. Several early *kouroi* from Delos, Thasos, Samos, and Sounion stood well over three meters, and the famous fragments of the marble Apollo dedicated by the Naxians in Delos attest to a figure that originally measured about nine or ten meters in height. Both the technique of carving such large monolithic blocks of marble, as well as the use of a grid to magnify the human proportions on to the block, could have been adopted by the Greeks from the Egyptians, even if the quarrying methods in Greece seem to have direct links with the Near East.

The motivation(s) that led to these colossal figures, however, is more difficult to fathom. It has been suggested that the widespread cult of Apollo in the later seventh century provided the impetus to depict the god in an entirely new guise, with one foot advanced as if walking or striding. Yet not every monumental male statue of this early period can represent Apollo, even if many can be associated one way or another with this god. The early sculptures all seem to be commemorative, that is, votive or funerary in function, and in fact the purpose to which they were put varied from region to region. Be that as it may, the *kouros* remained one of the quintessential sculptural types throughout the Greek world for well over one hundred and fifty years, down to the end of the Archaic period. Enormous at first, the *kouroi* gradually diminish in scale, and by the later sixth century natural size is more the norm.

Given the Greek political structure of independent city-states (*poleis*) in the Archaic period, a system which encouraged and thrived on interstate rivalry, one wonders to what extent did religious pride and political competitiveness determine or affect the initial spread and subsequent uniformity of the various Archaic sculptural types. As we shall see shortly, regional styles play an increasingly important role in the history of this period, yet one of the hallmarks of Archaic sculpture is the degree of artistic coherency that sets apart these works from the products of those same foreign cultures that sparked its formation. The Greeks absorbed and transformed a wide variety of foreign elements to create a stylistic language that is instantly recognizable and uniquely different.

Who were these Archaic sculptors? We learn little from the ancient literary sources, and here it is well worth remembering that the Romans had no great appetite for Archaic sculpture, probably because of its relative anonymity. Even if the Archaistic style flourished during the early Roman Empire, as it certainly did, the fact remains that the Romans produced very few, if any, faithful copies of Archaic Greek originals. This stands in sharp contrast to the mass production of copies after Classical creations: some anonymous, others by Greek masters evidently held in great esteem at least by the Romans. The inscribed sculptors' signatures that have survived give us an occasional glimpse into their world. The earliest extant inscription is of Euthykartides from Naxos, who signs an unusually shaped and elaborately decorated *kouros* base in Delos. The artist states that he also dedicated the monument, which has been dated to the second half of the seventh century B.C. Another monument from Delos seems to confirm what we already know from literary sources and inscriptions from every period, namely the existence of families of sculptors, the craft handed down from father to son. This is the winged marble *Nike* (ca. 550 B.C.) in Athens which probably belongs with a fragmentary inscribed base found near the statue naming Archermus, Micciades, and Melas. The Roman historian Pliny the Elder and other ancient authors refer to them as a Chian family of sculptors.

Every inscription provides precious new evidence, but they are far and few between, most of them coming from Athens and its territory. It is not known why some sculptors (the minority) chose to sign

A Profile of Archaic Greek Sculpture

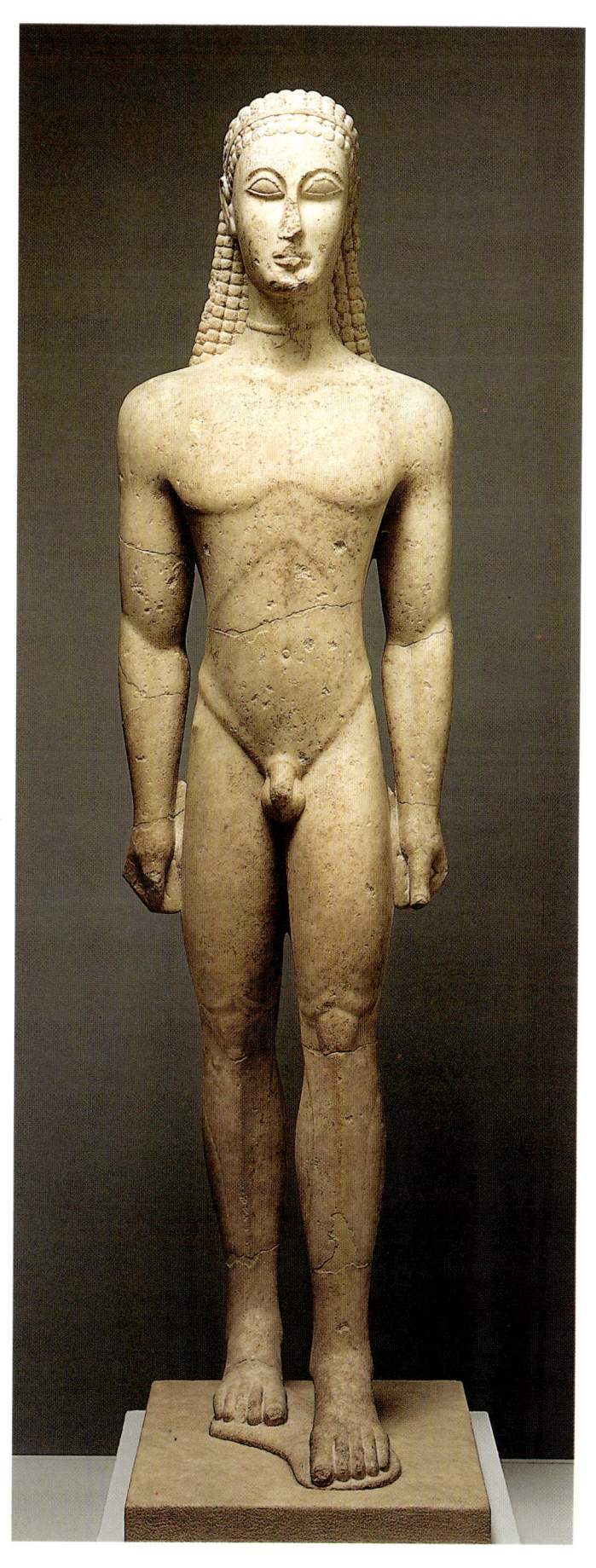

Marble statue of winged *Nike*
from Delos
ca. 550 B.C.
Athens
National Archaeological Museum

The *New York kouros*
marble
ca. 600 B.C.
New York, The Metropolitan
Museum of Art
Fletcher Fund, 1932

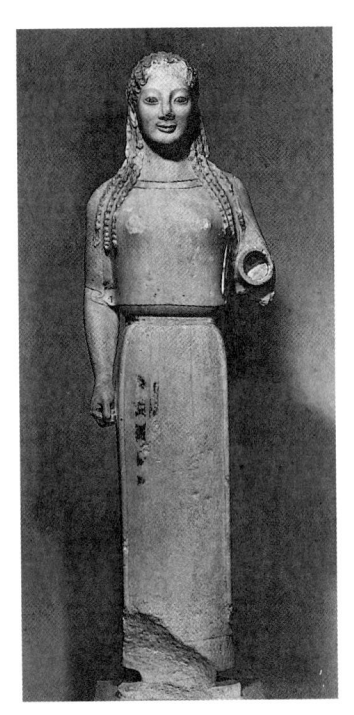

The *Peplos Kore*
marble
from the Acropolis, Athens
540-530 B.C.
Athens, Akropolis Museum

Seated Athena
by the sculptor Endoios
from the Acropolis, Athens
530-520 B.C.
Athens, Akropolis Museum

opposite
The *Rampin Rider*
marble statue
from the Acropolis, Athens
ca. 550 B.C.
Paris, Musée du Louvre
Département des Antiquités
Grecques, Etrusques et Romaines

their works; no logical pattern emerges, and it surely is not a matter of survival, geography, or of the quality or function of the monument. Oddly enough, only one instance of a sculptor's signature is certain in all of the architectural sculpture from the Archaic period, on the north frieze of the Siphnian Treasury at Delphi.

The extant signatures, especially those from Athens, have encouraged some scholars to attribute stylistically related works to individual hands, such as Endoios, Antenor, or Aristion of Paros; others speak of workshops or of masters. Yet Archaic sculpture remains largely anonymous, its history impossible to chronicle on the basis of artistic personalities alone. The wealth of surviving material is best surveyed by examining sculptural types chronologically, noting geographical trends as well as patterns of distribution, and by observing regional styles rather than individuals hands.

We have already encountered the two prime Archaic sculptural types, *kouroi* and *korai*, both of which served the same variety of functions. The nudity of the former (never with *korai*) can easily be taken for granted, but it remains a significant trait which must have had specific connotations in antiquity. After all, statues of standing draped or semi-draped men are not that uncommon. The so-called *Ilissus Kouros* from Athens wears a short mantle over his shoulders, and the heavily draped male is one of the predominant sculptural types in eastern Greece, where the traditional nude *kouroi* also abound. Perhaps the nudity of these figures is an indication of young age, a sign of the eternal youthfulness of the gods as well as of the heroized dead whom these sculptures commemorate.

Compared to the Cyclades and Samos, the Attic production of *kouroi* starts somewhat late, about 600 B.C., with the so-called *Dipylon Head* and the *New York kouros* (shown here after recent cleaning). After this date regional schools begin to emerge more clearly. Attic works tend to dominate our view of Archaic sculpture, thanks to the wealth of material recovered from the cemeteries in the city and in the countryside (witness the *kouros* from Anavyssos) as well as the quantity of dedications and architectural sculpture from the Athenian Acropolis. On the other hand, there is relatively little Attic sculpture that is not of high artistic merit, which is not always the case with some provincial centers. One thinks of the Ptoan Sanctuary of Apollo in Boeotia, for instance, where the local style can be somewhat crude and inorganic, even if the extant remains are considerable. The site has yielded evidence for nearly one hundred and twenty *kouroi*.

There is no space here even for a quick survey of the architectural and votive sculpture in limestone and marble from the Acropolis in Athens. Suffice it to point to the great variety of dedications, from the ambitious *Rampin Rider* (one of a pair possibly depicting the Dioskouroi or Dioscuri), to the serenely sober *Peplos Kore* or the dainty small maiden associated with a column bearing the signature of Archermus of Chios, whom we have already encountered. This last monument may serve as a timely reminder of several important points: the extent to which all Archaic sculpture in stone and terracotta was richly painted; the decorative quality of this style which may appear artificial to modern eyes; the fact that many of these dedications stood atop columns or pedestals which were often inscribed; and the presence of itinerant sculptors, not only in Athens but also at every major sanctuary in the mainland, if not throughout the Greek world.

Seated figures constitute yet another notable sculptural type, represented on the Acropolis by statues of deities (associated with the sculptor Endoios), as well as of mortals traditionally identified as scribes or treasurers of Athena, but quite possibly meant to depict secretaries of a cult; one of these "scribes" has recently been seen to join the *Fauvel Head* in the Louvre, furnishing us with a striking example of the kind of generic portraiture attempted in this period.

The seated type is amply represented in eastern Greece, and this leads us to the other great center of Archaic sculpture in the sixth century B.C., the island of Samos, close to the coast of Asia Minor. The venerable Sanctuary of Hera on the southern coast of the island has yielded one of the most remarkable sculptural groups of the period, the *Geneleos Group*. It consists of six large marble statues: a seated female at left inscribed with the name Phileia and bearing the artist's signature "Geneleos made us," four standing figures, and a corpulent reclining draped male who completes the group at the other end. The reclining man is the dedicator of the group. We may note that his pose as a banqueter is encountered in monumental sculpture only in the East.

Samos may appear atypically rich in Archaic marble sculpture, and in fact new finds continue to surprise us, witness the magnificent colossal inscribed *kouros* (about five meters high) unearthed only a few years ago. Yet the relative dearth of material in other eastern Greek sites is deceptive, partly attributable to the chance of survival. The sanctuaries at Samos, Ephesos, and Didyma all boasted massive Ionic temples in a scale and of a lavishness not encountered on the mainland. These enormous

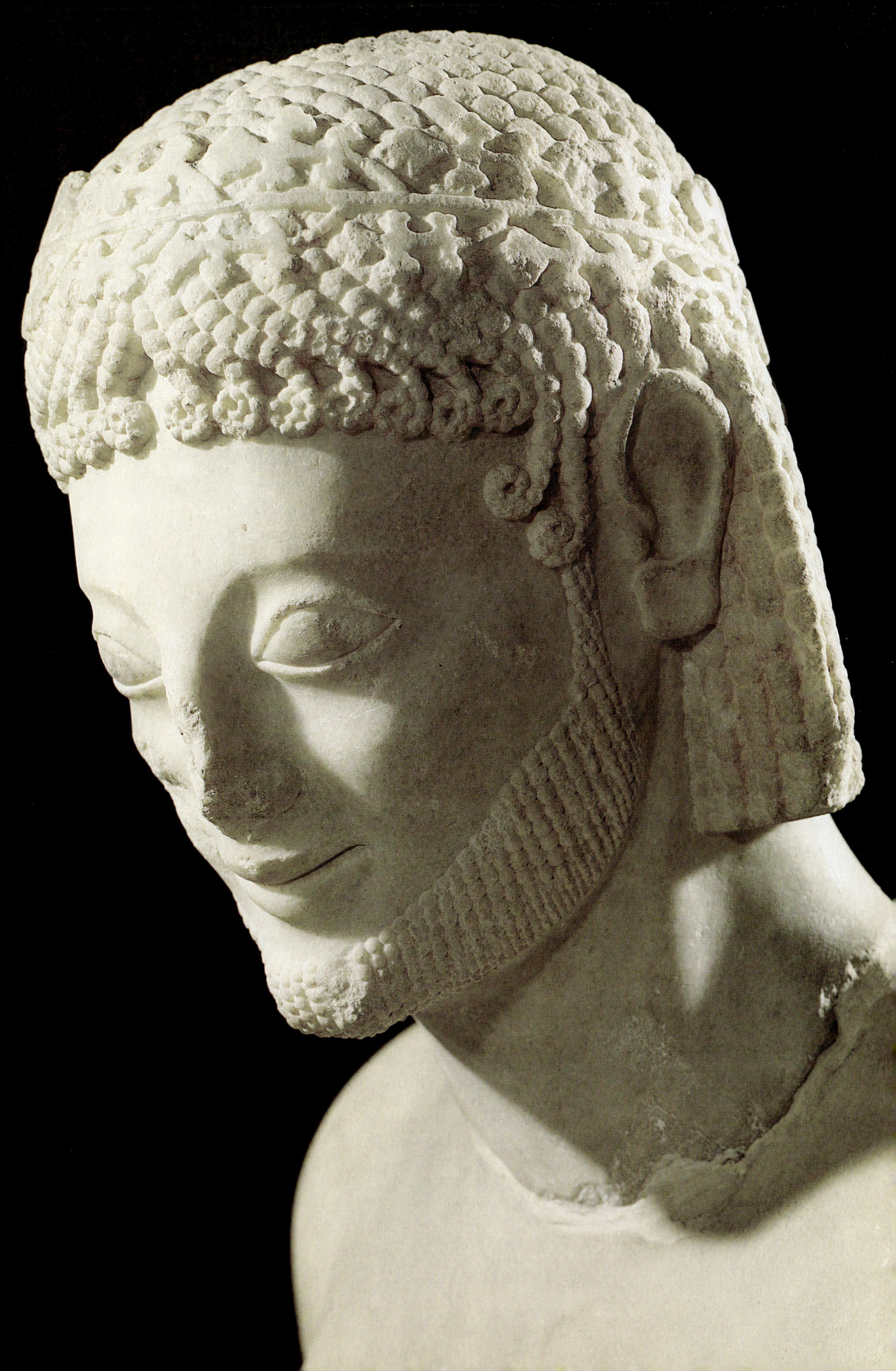

A Profile of Archaic Greek Sculpture

Reclining figure
from the *Geneleos Group*
marble
550-540 B.C.
Samos, Archaeological Museum

Column drum relief
from the Temple of Apollo at Didyma
marble
550-530 B.C.
Berlin
Staatliche Museen zu Berlin Preussischer Kulturbesitz, Antikensammlung

The *Sleeping Head*
relief from the Temple of Artemis at Ephesus
marble
6th cent. B.C.
London, British Museum, Department of Greek and Roman Antiquities

structures took generations to build, not unlike European medieval cathedrals. Apart from their forests of columns and unroofed *cellae*, these buildings are distinguished by the staggering variety and quantity of architectural sculpture, sadly preserved for the most part in tantalizing fragments often of exquisite quality.

The continuous carved frieze was an eastern Greek invention, under Oriental inspiration. At Samos it appears along the bottom or the top of the *cella* walls, in a distinctive technique of horizontal superimposed courses. The *artemision* at Ephesus and the Temple of Apollo at Didyma both feature decorated column drums carved with life-size figures and animals in high relief. The Ephesian ones are the more elaborate, including even a horse and rider curving around the drum. A marble parapet carved with elaborate narrative scenes serves as a gutter around the roof of the *artemision*, and the *didymaion* includes winged gorgons and mighty reclining lions at the corners of the entablature. The celebrated *Sleeping Head* from Ephesus preserves a vertical joint-surface at left, suggesting it comes from one of the massive carved pedestals (composed of several blocks) that embellished the west end of the temple. Here we see the fleshy and softly rounded features so typical of the eastern Greek production.

That eastern Greek sculptors were in much demand elsewhere seems obvious and, in any case, polit-

West pediment
Temple of Artemis at Corfu
limestone
ca. 580 B.C.
Corfu, Archaeological Museum

ical events at home must have encouraged some artists to seek employment elsewhere. Mainland Greece apart, there are definite stylistic links between eastern Greece and Magna Graecia, and the presence of eastern architectural features (carved wall friezes, decorated column drums) is amply attested in those regions as well. Even Syracuse, Corinthian in origin, has yielded an entire great Ionic temple patterned after the Ephesian *artemision*. Finally, a truly exceptional find of exquisite chryselephantine sculptures in purely eastern Greek style was recovered at Delphi, buried under the Sacred Way leading up to the Temple of Apollo. Though sadly fragmentary, they furnish the best evidence for work in this most lavish of all techniques. Sculpture in ivory and precious metals was held in the greatest esteem throughout antiquity, to judge from our literary sources.

A word must be said about architectural sculpture in Mainland Greece. The first major stone pediment appears at Corfu, on the Temple of Artemis (ca. 580 B.C.). This vast limestone monument, with its formidable central Gorgon, rivals any of the early pediments from the Athenian Acropolis if not in terms of quality or design, certainly in terms of scale. The large number of limestone pediments from the Acropolis seems somewhat surprising, given the relatively limited distribution of this kind of architectural decoration during the Archaic period. Figured *akroteria* and carved metopes have a wider pattern of distribution during this period, and here one must take into account the quantity of important evidence from two of the great pan-Hellenic sanctuaries, Olympia and Delphi. At Delphi, the small but lavishly decorated Siphnian Treasury surely takes pride of place. Not only is the treasury one of the few firmly dated monuments in the entire Archaic period (ca. 525 B.C.), it also exemplifies the confluence of different artistic trends that has aptly been termed the "International Style." Moreover, the continuous carved frieze encircling the building shows Archaic narrative at its best, its masterful depictions drawn from the rich world of Greek mythology.

It is easy to forget that, by this time, the predominant medium for the finest sculpture in the round was bronze, not marble, and that bronzes not only dominated the market, but also influenced the contemporary marble production. At least half of the late Archaic dedications on the Athenian Acropolis were made of bronze. I illustrate one of the very few that has survived, the head of a bearded warrior, its helmet now missing. The sober, simplified sharp features, which bring to mind the pedimental marble sculptures from Aegina, herald the new early Classical style of the fifth century B.C. There are other miraculous survivals of bronze statuary from the late Archaic period, such as the serene *Piraeus Apollo*, which came to light in recent years together with other Greek bronzes dating to later pe-

A Profile of Archaic Greek Sculpture

Apollo, Artemis, and a giant
detail of the Siphnian Treasury
at Delphi
marble
ca. 525 B.C.
Delphi, Archaeological Museum

The *Piraeus Apollo*
bronze
ca. 530-520 B.C.
Athens, Piraeus Museum

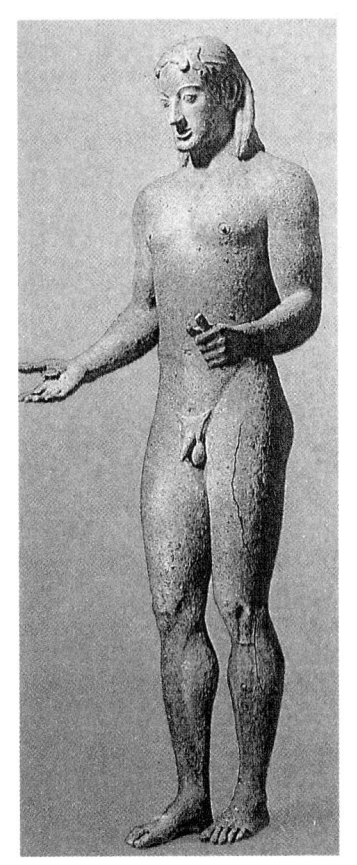

riods. Yet the tradition of exquisite sculpture in marble was never to die in ancient Greece. We have not had occasion in this essay to explore the rich world of funerary or votive sculpture in relief. The enigmatic late Archaic *stele* of a nude, helmeted youth in Athens, surely a funerary monument, typifies much of the flavor and youthful vitality of the period. This is not an ambitious monument, nevertheless it conveys some of the best qualities of Archaic Greek sculpture: a strong schematic rendering, painstaking finish of surface, idealized beauty coupled with delicate ornament, and an element of timelessness that could only have pleased the gods.

Bibliography
J. BOARDMAN, 1933; C.M. ROBERTSON, 1975; B.S. RIDGWAY, 1977 (second edition: 1993); J. BOARDMAN, 1978; A. STEWART, 1990.

Funeral *stele* of helmeted youth
marble
ca. 510 B.C.
Athens
National Archaeological Museum

Alain Pasquier   A Profile of Classical Greek Sculpture

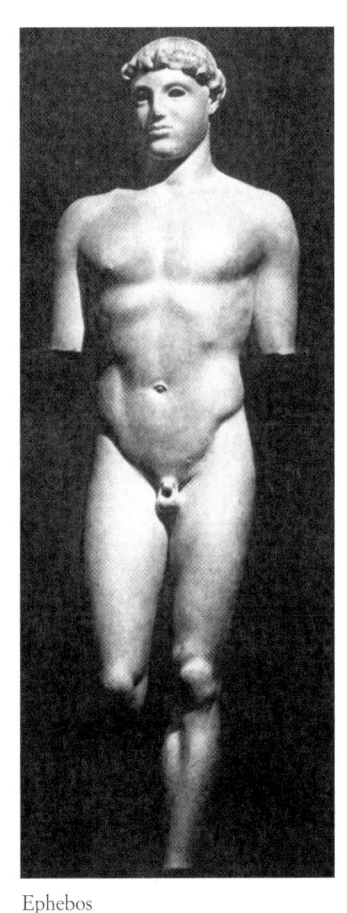

When the Athenians abandoned their city because of the Persian invaders, they did not merely leave behind their houses but they also left behind – and this time definitively – a form of art that had remained unaltered for 150 years. In fact, from the beginning of the fifth century Archaic art continued to develop variations on themes that had been conceived in the seventh century, perpetuating that decorative spirit that was its fundamental merit. In a universe in which many intellectual activities had enlarged the horizons of knowledge, the shock of the war with the Medes caused the edifice of religious customs that had conditioned artists to vacillate. Piously buried in the land of the Acropolis, the last *korai*, outraged by the Barbarians, belonged to a race that was close to extinction. The votive offering of Euthydicus already demonstrates how, under a covering of tradition, a new project was taking form that established a relationship between the statue and the outside world that was thitherto unknown. The *kouros* gave up its place to the youth and the athlete. The statue of a youth attributed to Critius' chisel, despite its delicacy and grace, announced a real, authentic revolution: the body, finally obeying the laws of nature, balances on the hips, whilst the skeleton and the muscles that move it are subject to the laws of gravity. Movement, which is best highlighted by the technique of full-relief bronze, either animates an anatomy that is no longer either conventional or arbitrary, as expressed in simple subjects like the *Discobolos*, or it combines loose figures inside more complex evocations in which the gestures respond and balance each other. This is what happened, for example, with the Tyrannicides, who with their assault did not merely proclaim the end of tyranny but also the irreversible decline of purely paratactical groups of concepts.

The great architectural complexes, at Aegina and later at Olympia, confirm with their evolution this transition that moves from stylized plastic works of art to a realistic approach. The whole is no longer considered to be simply the sum of the parts, but rather of another nature. The detail is significant only inside the unity of the composition both for singular figures, in relation to the body that is no longer a simple machine, and for the creation of building pediments with multiple figures, within activity that is no longer limited to balancing the movement of graceful puppets but now adopts real people whose behavior and physiognomy simultaneously project sensations and sentiments, *pathos* and *ethos*.

The decision to represent part of a legend or mythological episode derived from this new and ardent interest for spirituality (as exemplified by the painter Polygnotus of Thasos), as by then the development of an action was less interesting than its preparation or consequences. The *Centauromachy* of the Temple of Olympia seems to perpetuate the Archaic mixture with its themes, but it is dominated by the majestic figure of Apollo, who endows it with a completely different meaning – the omnipotence of the divine gesture expresses the imminence and the necessity of the return of order. The simplicity of the shape focuses the interest back to the essentials. The billowing folds that enlivened Archaic garments give way to the vast shrouds of the *peplos* and powerful bodies covered by thick cloth, like that of Athena on the metope in Olympia. Sometimes a smile spreads sweetly over the faces, now the countenances expressed austerity, as in the case of the *Blond Ephebos*, whose thoughtful expression reflects deep emotions. This gravity, this

Ephebos
attributed to ritius
marble
beginning 5th cent. B.C.
Athens, Akropolis Museum

Detail of the statue of Apollo
from the west pediment
of the Temple of Zeus, Olympia
ca. mid-5th cent. B.C.
Olympia, Archaeological Museum

Kore by Euthydicus
detail
end 6th cent. B.C.
Athens, Akropolis Museum

Blonde ephebos
ca. 480 B.C.
Athens
Akropolis Museum

A Profile of Classical Greek Sculpture

Bronze Zeus
480-470 B.C.
Athens
National Archaeological Museum

The philosopher of Porticello
bronze
460-440 B.C.
Reggio Calabria
Museo Archeologico Nazionale
Cat. 9

severe aspect, to reuse terms that today identify the style of this generation of artists, pervades the features of all Grecian faces from Cyrene to Pharsalus, from Paros to Tarentum. The entire Hellenic civilization was touched by this phenomenon, even if here and there we can occasionally appreciate personal responses elaborated by cities or regions to the common impulse. Severe-style sculpture symbolized man's new role within the *kosmos*, but the return to sobriety was not the consequence of scrupulous wisdom since this generation of sculptors showed itself to be very bold. In fact, was it not an audacious creator who produced the *Paros Nike* which, completely overturning the traditional scheme, suggests in such a vigorous and persuasive way, the real flight of a figure, who, nevertheless, is still in contact with the ground that supports him? Likewise, was it not a bold artist who, though inspired by the dictates of a cult, introduced the sensual presence of a completely nude flute-player (a figure that had never before been seen in Greek sculpture), into a representation of the birth of Aphrodite in the *Ludovisi Throne*? The splendid statue from Motya, which still poses questions for researchers, is another example of emancipation. If we concentrate on the face, its chronological context is unquestionably the Severe style. The almost immodest prominence of the hips in the body, whose delicately gathered clothes reveal powerful and, at the same time, fluid muscles, expresses the incredible independence of a master whose genius was many genera-

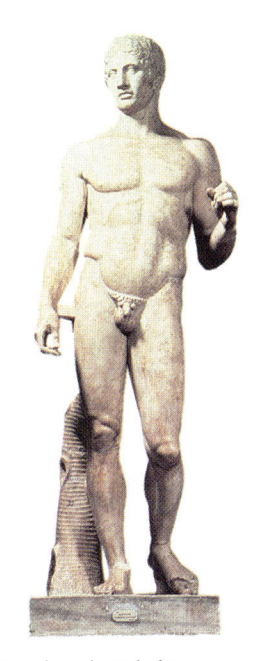

Doryphorus by Polyclitus
Roman copy
original dated mid-5th cent. B.C.
Naples
Museo Nazionale Archeologico

Athena Parthenos
roman copy
known as the *Varvakeion*
of the colossal statue by Phidias
mid-5th cent. B.C.
Athens
National Archaeological Museum

tions ahead of its time. As regards the bronze "philosopher's" head from Porticello, this confirms what the inscribed herm copy of a Themistocles portrait, in Ostia, had already suggested (despite the uncertainty arising from its being a Roman copy): the explicit desire of certain artists of the period to represent the individual's personal features, while keeping within the bounds of aesthetics essentially based on idealized beauty. If one thinks of the success that the sculptured portrait subsequently had in the Greek world, the reawakening of interest in the specificity of faces must be considered as being very important. The works of art rightly considered to be most representative of Greek sculpture – such as the fabulous warrior figures found off the coast of Riace, Italy, and the Artemisium Zeus – were also created in bronze, although with a more generalized concept of physical beauty. The Zeus is precisely a clear demonstration of the happy marriage between strength and self-control, movement and balance, beauty and good, that classical Hellenism desired. Statue A of the Riace warriors above all demonstrates how the refinement of an extremely adroit technique lends itself to molding the simplest of subjects, a nude man, erect, immobile, with the result that an effect of realism freely accompanies the harmony of the motif. The radiant pride, the virile self-assurance of these splendid bodies, glorifies the human form, making it the goal of all the spiritual achievements of Greek civilization.

The successive Early Classical period is of paramount importance not only for the history of Greek sculpture, but also for the history of art in general, at least as far as western art is concerned. Notwithstanding its importance, this period lasted barely a generation. Moreover, those characteristic works of the period's statuary, namely the bronzes unanimously considered to be masterpieces of sculpture, completely disappeared as they were melted down to retrieve their metal. Their beauty can be judged indirectly from the surviving copies and imitations, namely the coeval statuettes that adopted the true canons on a reduced scale, and the life-size marble copies which the Romans – spellbound by the works of art discovered by their legions as they progressively subjugated the Greek *poleis* – made in large numbers for shrines, palaces, villas, and gardens.

Polyclitus (Polykleitos), the sculptor from Argos who worked in Athens, was one of those artists whose importance we can appreciate thanks to ancient texts and to the Roman copies of his work, which reveal the sculptor's extraordinary inventive powers. An examination of the copies reliably attributed to Polyclitus clearly demonstrates that Early Classical sculpture took, above all, the idea of an idealized statuary from the vast experience of the so-called Severe style. The first attempts at realism and the study of movement temporarily disappear, at least from official art. Polyclitus in fact devoted himself almost exclusively to studying the rhythm and balance of the male nude form in erect and immobile poses. Every new version, from the Discophorus to Diadumenus, hoped to offer even more satisfying representations of this same theme. However, the satisfaction was not confined to the eye, which delighted in the discovery that the unfettered leg and the slightly raised heel endowed the composition with a dynamism that was able to animate even an immobile body with perpetual force. This discovery, like the *contrapposto* arrangement of the body and legs marked the introduction of the aesthetic program that lay at the center of the universe of values underlying Greek thinking, and grafted it with the principles of order, balance, and reason. The *Doryphorus*, one of Polyclitus' most sublime creations, is not the only fruit of an ever more precise and subtle faculty of observation of the anatomy of a young athlete: it is the culmination of a complex set of calculations of proportion. The width of a finger is in harmonic relation to the height of the whole body, and hence provides a perfect illustration of the sculptor's book, the *Canon*, in which he described the rules for the perfect representation of the human body. The *Doryphorus* is more an ideal figure than true representation of a spear-carrier; it is a paradigm without defect representing the Athlete as part of an ideal set. Nothing can be added or removed, the figure relies on its perfection and its face is the image of Reason.

It is very difficult to establish with any precision the attribution of the statues of Phidias, that other great name at the summit of classicism. Its worth has been highly acclaimed in literature, from ancient times up to the present day, as a symbol of the classic style that was produced in Athens and even possibly in all Greek art. The *Kassel Apollo*, which the present author considers to be original, clearly demonstrates the distance that separates it from the athletes of Polyclitus. The bands of muscle swathing the torsos of these athletes were very different from the technique adopted by Phidias, who endowed his human figures with a majestic sense of volume, while conserving the suppleness of the limbs and sensitivity in the modeling of form. If we accept the traditional reconstruction of Phidias' career we notice the large variety of subjects on which he worked and, unfortunately, we regretfully acknowledge that there survives only a faint echo of the two great chryselephantine statues that consecrated his fame, namely the Zeus from the temple at Olympia, and the Athena Parthenos. It is frustrating not being able to experience

A Profile of Classical Greek Sculpture

Detail of the *Centauromachy*
on a metope of the Parthenon
second half of 5th cent. B.C.
London, British Museum, Department
of Greek and Roman Antiquities

firsthand the skill with which Pericles' friend Phidias managed to conserve the sense of composure and the restrained wisdom (the nucleus of the Classical *ethos*) in the execution of these two masterpieces, which were splendidly decorated almost to the point of being gaudy and were situated at the end of the *naos* in their respective temples, the Temple of Zeus (Olympia), and the Temple of Athena Parthenos (the Parthenon). The fundamental role that Phidias played in the decoration of the Parthenon sheds important light on his art as a whole. With its 92 metopes, its continuous frieze comprising 350 figures, and two pediments, this immense work, completed in only fifteen years, saw the united efforts of all the marble-carving talent that the Greeks possessed. The variety of technique, which is discernible to the observant eye, testifies to the presence of many different artists, some of whom noticeably still comply with the Severe style, while others show bursts of inspiration that open up unexplored avenues of expression. However, if we first examine the metopes, then the frieze, and finally the two pediments, we see that despite this variety, from the start the execution of the work has a uniformity which was progressively reinforced as work proceeded. The careful according of methods and styles, and likewise the spurts of evolution in the forms are undoubtedly the handiwork of the master Phidias who, by supplying plans, designs, and models, undoubtedly gave the sculptors full indications as to the results they were to achieve. In the Athenian Acropolis, thanks to the impetus of the Attic master, Early Classical sculpture passed in less than twenty years from the somewhat fixed rigidity of certain scenes of the *Centauromachy* on the metopes on the southern side, to the *Assembly of the Gods* present at the birth of Athena, on the eastern pediments. In this last example the female figures, who are generally believed to be the goddesses Aphrodite and Dione, are astonishingly natural with their rippling robes and drapery, so skillfully rendered that it is difficult to identify the means used to create these effects. Athens is once again glorified in the frieze depicting the Panathenaic Way, where it is represented in a manner which today we probably consider more direct and complete, since the city's past and present are reunited here. In this reunion we find the summation of the most important phenomena of the history of Greek sculpture, and once again it is important to stress how brief the period was, to emphasize therefore the intensity and the decisiveness of the artistic developments linked to it. And what finer symbol could there be of the intimate fusion of ethical-philosophical values with politics and artistic creation than the portrait of the Athenian statesman Pericles, undoubtedly by Cresilas, who has sculpted an ideal commander for an ideal city rather than portraying the likeness of Xanthippe's son.

The sculptures that can be dated to the period after the death of Pericles and of Phidias' consequent fall from grace during the grim years of the Peloponnesian War, contain a different mixture of aesthetic trends, many of which continue the stylistic evolution seen in the Parthenon marbles; others, however, mark a break in style and even betray a change of direction. In Athens one can already detect the return to favor of the Ionic style and of its sense of decoration. For example, the construction of the Erechtheum, and later, the Temple of Athena Nike, which, though expressions of traditional Greek religion, testified to a new direction that was probably influenced by shifts in the political situation. Yet the reliefs decorating Athenian funeral *stelai* after 430 B.C. betray close links with the figures in the Parthenon frieze; the artists who carved these *stelai* was undoubtedly members of the immense workshop directed by Phidias.

The Nemesis of Rhamnus
by Agoracritus
ca. 430 B.C.
Copenhagen, Ny Carlsberg
Glyptothek

Aphrodite and Dione
detail of east pediment
of the Parthenon
440-430 B.C.
London, British Museum
Department of Greek
and Roman Antiquities

Among the fellow artists and pupils of the master, Alcamenes and Agoracritus have attracted particular attention. The personal style of the latter is no longer obscure as he was reliably identified as the author of a famous work, the cult statue of *Nemesis* from the temple at Rhamnus. The written sources traditionally speak of a close affinity between Agoracritus and Phidias, a view that is endorsed by the statue, as far as the underlying spirit is concerned, although the drapery tends to multiply the effect of the surfaces much more than that of the *Athena Parthenos*. As for Alcamenes, if we accept the conventional and, in places, very hypothetical reconstruction, of his undoubtedly glorious career, it seems to be more conservative in the way he often evokes the Archaic style and was very much inclined to portray female subjects, a custom that is widespread in all forms of art. The serenity begins to weaken. The group of *Procne and Itys*, attributed to Alcamenes, demonstrates how the *peplophorai* or *peplos*-figures of the Parthenon were animated by a dramatic tension that was expressed by the movement, however slight, of the drapery. Must we, and in fact, can we recognize the hand of these two master-sculptors in some Caryatids of the Erechtheum (fig. 19)? Whatever one's conclusions, it must be acknowledged that these *peplophorai*, which would seem to come from the procession of the Ergastinai or *peplos*-weavers, the ornamental elegance of the hair and the jewels, of which the copies in Villa Adriana give us some idea. This somewhat ostentatious lavishness and the agitated movement of the material on the *apoptygma* of the *peplos*, confirms the difference in respect to the Parthenon figures, and announces the onset of mannerism in Greek sculpture. At this point the garments begin to swirl around the female figures, to enhance the movement, to cling to the plump bodies and reveal more than they cover. One of the earliest statues that belong to this new manner is the *Victory* at Olympia, which stood in front of the facade of the Temple of Zeus on a ten-meter-high pillar. This monument was astonishingly original and alarmingly innovative; history records with a certain precision that it was made in 420 B.C. In it we discover a careful study of a body that is naturally suspended in the air thanks to the beating of the outspread wings, and is wrapped in voluminous drapery that seems to offer a paradigm for the divine revelation. Here the grace of the apparition and the robust constitution of the messenger of the gods are effortlessly married and their figures, now nude,

Bust of Pericles
copy of the original by Cresilas
ca. 440-430 B.C.
London, British Museum
Department of Greek
and Roman Antiquities

Procne and Itys
attributed to Alcamenes
ca. 430 B.C.
Athens, Akropolis Museum

Nike unlacing her sandal
fragment of the balustrade
of the Temple of Athena Nike
on the Acropolis
end 5th cent. B.C.
Athens, Akropolis Museum

The Victory of Olympia
by Paeonius of Mende
ca. 420 B.C.
Olympia, Archaeological Musem

now clad in waves of an almost ethereal drapery, are expressed in a full, smooth plasticity. It is true that the Iris and the Amphitrite of the western pediments in the Parthenon already foretell this new plasticity, but the *Victory* cannot be considered merely heir to them. The origins and craftsmanship of the artist who created and signed the *Victory*, Paeonius of Mende, without doubt influenced this tendency in a decisive manner. The so-called "rich" style became widespread at the end of the century. Its extreme lavishness, both calm and composed in its opulence and torturous in its sumptuous fury, is consecrated in the balustrade reliefs in the Athena Nike temple on the Athenian Acropolis. The Victory figures carved by several different artists, many of whom were very talented, spread their feathered wings, intent on different religious acts, while Athena in person officiates: there is a peculiar irony in this plethora of Victory figures on the Acropolis, created in the very decade in which Athens was to suffer irremediable defeat. The subtle artistry brings out the many facets of a refined illusory vision, so distilled that it mattered little if there was an imbalance between reality and artistic expression, between background and form,

Flute player
detail of the Ludovisi throne
marble
ca. 460-450 B.C.
Rome, Museo Nazionale Romano
Cat. 189

an imbalance that the Parthenon so miraculously merges. Human artifice, sublime artifice, triumphed and the seductive but unreal garments that cling to the body of Victory from head to foot seem to mirror the brilliant, artificial reasoning of the contemporary Sophists.

This regression into mannerism, whose capricious expressions returned to favor with neo-Atticism, did not survive long after the paroxysmic events of the end of the century. At the dawn of the fourth century B.C. the frieze in the temple at Bassae reproposed the same confusion of drapery, extolling movement, and manifestly reproposed some of the formulas and motifs of the Parthenon artists. However, the entire work is redolent of the provincial accents of Peloponnesian sculpture, and is sometimes marred by strident effect grafted onto almost trivial experiences, like the marked tension of the drapery hampering the forward movement of one of the Amazons, or the bite inflicted by a Centaur on the neck of a young Lapith. This discordant interruption of the Classical continuum heralded a return to a more realistic vein. Hence the Discophorus attributed to Naucydes abandons the invisible covering that isolated Polyclitus' athletes from their abstract perfection, and the figure's gesture reintegrates space and time.

In the transition to the following century, the Greek sculptors encountered a new aspect of reality, namely the diversity of the Barbarian or non-Hellenic populations who strove to imitate their achievements. The Nereid monument in Xanthus, Lycia, associated the ostensibly Grecian figures of the Nereids with other scenes of sieges or surrender drawn from the local repertoire. The introduction of new subject matter, albeit for outside commissions, was food for thought for artists who were deeply attached to forms of an ideal type. This may have heralded the return of greater attention to the peculiarities of human form. It is symptomatic that the figure of Socrates, which demanded a completely different set of skills from the artist (the philosopher's outward appearance was reportedly as repulsive as his soul was beautiful), signaled a turning point and a significant shift in values. At any event, the beginning of the fourth century B.C. saw the emergence of renewed interest in transposing mood and emotion to sculpture. This reawakening – albeit hesitant – can be observed in the vast series of Attic *stelai*, and much more eloquently in certain architectural decorations, and in particular those of the Temple of Asclepius at Epidaurus. The pain and distress that marks the face of Priam on the "Ilioupersis" pediments (relating the *Iliad* saga), is one of the strongest representations of both physical and moral anguish known in Greek art. As for the figures from the same group that are fighting or prostrate, the exasperation of the postures powerfully expresses the vehemence of passions that are more and more liberally expressed, and with increasing frequency.

Is it therefore correct to continue using the term "classical" for a type of sculpture whose spirit is so far removed from the canons of the impassiveness of Cresilas' statue of Pericles? The return to a more "sensitive" expression perhaps justifies describing the new sculpture as a form of "romanticism", as recently suggested. Any reply must be cautious. The group, by the Athenian Cephisodotus, which includes Irene carrying the infant Plutus, would not really belong to this category, even if the subject, in a sign of the preoccupation for the new times, is showered with affection, were it not for the fact that the composition conserves a composure and an overall balance characteristic of Early Classical style. The same thing can also be said of the sculpture of a monument that is emblematic of the fourth century, the famous Mausoleum of Halicarnassus. What little remains today of the incredible abundance and concentration of the decoration executed by the most famous sculptors of the age – Timotheus, Bryaxis, Leochares, and Scopas – aided by their workshop, nonetheless allows us to appreciate how much of Classical idealization endures here in certain parts of the *Amazonomachy* frieze. On this building, constructed for a Barbarian prince and decorated by Greek artisans, the clear and regular rhythm, the melodious plasticity binding the figures, almost as if they were dancers performing skillful and perfectly synchronized steps in a ballet, are perpetuated and strong contrast the sense of confused violence that pervades the Bassae frieze.

If we examine all the works of art attributable to the sculptor Scopas, we can see the gradual reassertion of human emotion over self-control, of passion over overt reason, and the relegation of civilian values in favor of individual aspiration. We are tempted to attribute one of the most inspired sections of the *Amazonomachy* at Halicarnassus to the Parian master-sculptor Scopas, namely the one in which the vibrant tension of the body of one warrior has caused his legs to be exposed as far as the hip. Although this particular detail is striking, it in no way breaks the syntax of the frieze. Tradition tends to attribute a statue of a maenad to Scopas, a work much praised by Callistratus. The *Dresden Maenad* is very probably related to the said work; the position is identical to that of the relief Amazon, though the effect is much more intense, with the figure staggering in strong *contrapposto*, her body taut and head twisted backward in the throes of a spasm that completely distort the features – the complete antithesis of the Classical ideal. Pathos, or human yearning, another theme of Scopas' sculptures, attempts to bring out dissatisfaction and imbalance, whereas the *Doryphoros* signified perfect equilibrium and a type of ataraxia or utter peace of mind. As for the faces, it is thanks to the surviving fragments of the pediments from the temple at Tegea in Arcadia that we have been able to discover the vigorous features of the

Amazonomachy
from the frieze
on the Mausoleum of Halicarnassus
4th cent. B.C.
London, British Museum, Department
of Greek and Roman Antiquities

Dancing maenad
Roman copy
original attributed to Scopas
330 B.C.
Dresden, Staatliche
Kunstsammlungen

opposite
The Cnidian Aphrodite
by Praxiteles
mid-4th cent. B.C.
Roman copy
Vatican City
Musei Vaticani

Leaning satyr
by Praxiteles
ca. 330 B.C.
Roman copy
Rome, Musei Capitolini

square jaw and the deep-set eyes, raised to the sky in a pitiful expression that is a mixture of energy and alarm, challenge and terror. Once seen they are hard to forget.

The same ambiguity of combined Classical and anti-Classical expression can be found in works attributed to the Attic master Praxiteles, son of Cephisodotus. His, however, is an ambiguity devoid of emotional transport, an ambivalence expressed in "half-tones." The world of Praxiteles is fascinating, as can be seen in the smooth body of the amiable *Leaning Satyr* whose pouring movement is modulated by a *contrapposto* arrangement prolonged by the imaginary jet of wine flowing from the jug; the figure is in perpetual movement, and could easily be among the Classical repertoire. And yet, the subtle play of the boy's muscles under the taut skin seem to comply with the rules of Polyclitus. Equally fascinating is the delicate figure of Apollo in the *Sauroctonus* or "Lizard-Slayer," possibly a reference to the god's fight with the mythical dragon Python. The body seems to fluctuate between infancy and adolescence, and the features of the face shift from male to female; the effect is full of mystery, a mystery which, though subtle, does not easily concur with that sense of emotionless Reason. Maybe it is exactly this sensation of mystery that is the cause of the awed thrill that ran through the worshipers of the *Cnidian Aphrodite* in the temple at Cnidos, which the artist pictured completely naked and is said to have been inspired by his companion and model, the courtesan Phryne. Prefigured in the nude bust of the Venus at Arles, which is undoubtedly a copy of an original by the master, the earlier goddess' nudity is not supposed to be *picant* but an intense revelation of the force "exercised by the goddess of love," the *Cnidian Aphrodite* (first of the great sculptures) disconcerted its first viewers before becoming widely accepted as a model. There is another characteristic that imperceptibly marks a distance (albeit substantial) in the works of Praxiteles from the Classical universe, in which the human figure triumphs unrivaled in art, and that is the modest but undeniable intrusion of the natural world, exemplified by the bush where Apollo sees the running lizard, and by the tree trunk on which the *Leaning Satyr* rests his weight. In the country landscape that the satyr figure evokes, with his enigmatic, barely suggested smile, his idle, unfocused gaze, the sensual abandon of his pose, jointly express the unique, muted Praxitelean harmony that allows us to appreciate undisturbed many otherwise unperceived inflections. In this case too, the visual notes peculiar to the artist were propagated for a long time, right up to the period of Hellenistic and Roman sculpture.

Lysippus – the third outstandingly talented sculptor in this quarter-century of great contrasts and opposition – was the first to lead sculpture to a completely renovated idea of heroism. Thanks to Lysippus, the sculptures of athletes in bronze reappeared, though now they had a curious lack of stability that makes it impossible to distinguish between the "free" leg and the one on which the body rests. The body became more slender, with less muscle, though more powerful. Nothing remains of Polyclitus' *Canon*, apart from that formal abstraction which made the *Doryphoros* aloof from the world. Agias the

A Profile of Classical Greek Sculpture

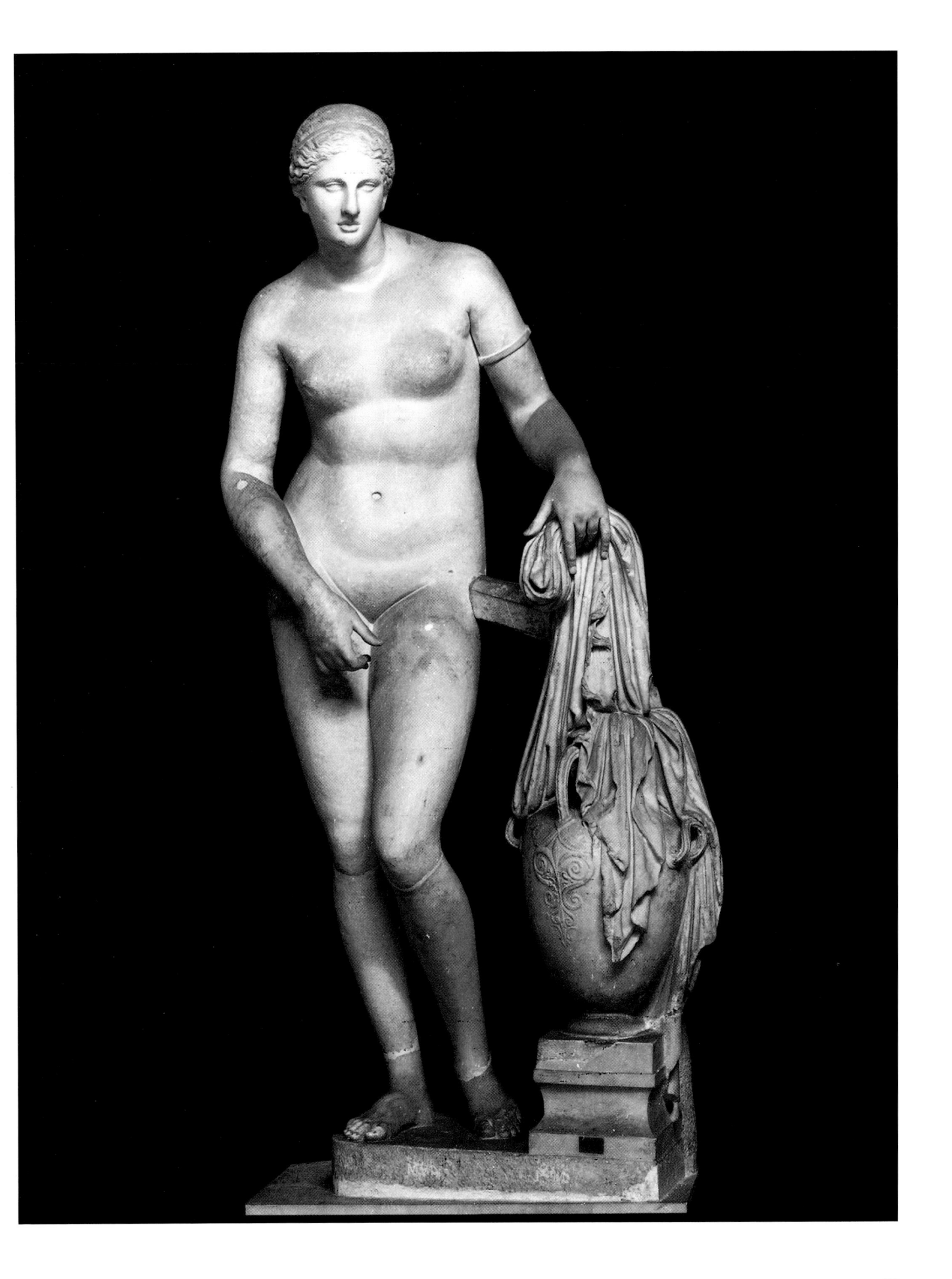

A Profile of Classical Greek Sculpture

The Farnese Heracles
by Lysippus
3rd cent. B.C.
Chieti, Museo Nazionale Archeologico

Apoxyomenos, by Lysippus
Roman copy
Vatican City, Musei Vaticani

Portrait of Alexander
by Lysippus
Roman copy
Paris, Musée du Louvre
Département des Antiquités
Grecques, Etrusques et Romaines

boxer-wrestler, with his ears swollen from blows, summons his strength for the imminent fight; the moment of respite is caught in a precise instant in the flow of time. As for the sculptor's treatment of space, the tense arm of the athlete using his strigil in the *Apoxyomenus* shows greater exploration of the third dimension and expands the figure, inducing us to walk round it to appreciate the multiple viewing angles. From the small but formidable Eros drawing his bow, his gaze focused on the distance, to the stout *Farnese Heracles* (which we must walk round in order to discover the three apples from the Garden of Hesperides in the palm of his hand, the reason for his tiredness), Lysippus is an innovator who constantly searches for the *kairos*, the moment the artist must know how to capture, when all the conditions necessary for obtaining the desired result converge. This concept tormented Lysippus so much that he carved an allegorical figure to stand outside his house: the *kairos*, the favored but transitory instant, is portrayed as a winged genius represented in swift flight, holding a razor on whose blade balances a pair of scales. Whoever wants to seize him by the hair must do so immediately, as his shaved head will not allow a second chance. At any event, the moment Lysippus so admirably portrayed was the transition from the Greece of the cities to the Greece of the Hellenistic domains, in which the qualities of the individual, of the exceptional being, imposed itself over those of the collectivity. By creating numerous effigies of Alexander the Great, whose face, like the soul of the Greek world, altered with each new military exploit (with numerous official copies faithful to the model), this consummate artist of the Sicyon school ushered in a new era, in which sculptural art would be radically affected by the personal destinies of the new deified, heroized protagonists of world history, and by the expansion of Hellenism as far as the border with China.

Bernard Andreae An Outline of Hellenistic Sculpture

The Belvedere Torso
1st cent. B.C.
Vatican City
Museo Pio Clementino

The Laocoön Group
from a bronze original
of ca. 140 B.C.
Vatican City
Museo Pio Clementino

When asked today to pin down a definition of the imposing, unmistakable, and constantly evolving style of sculptural art in the period between the death of Alexander the Great and the twilight of the Hellenistic world (marked by the Battle of Actium), scholars seek a weighty formula that encompasses all the many peculiarities of this art. Inevitably, the term "Baroque" springs to mind. It is easy enough, in fact, to demonstrate that the precursors of modern Baroque, Michelangelo and Raphael, were directly influenced by the masters of the aforesaid period. The *Belvedere Torso*, the *Laocoön* group, the *Farnese Bull* – all sculpted in the Hellenistic style – were recognized models for Michelangelo. Similarly, in his last work, the *Battle of Constantine*, which foretells the advent of the Baroque, Raphael was paying homage to that great Hellenistic sculptor and painter, Phyromachus of Athens. The concept of Baroque therefore indicates a form of art that developed and asserted itself after Lysippus. But it comprises only a part of this form of art expression, and not the complexity of the historico-artistic process that unfolded in the course of those three hundred years. This phenomenon is well identified by Droyssen's formula, which aptly expresses the act of capturing the faculties of emotion and passion in all their profundity, violence, and convulsiveness, but also manages to encapsulate the outcome of this evolution of form. Hellenistic art, and sculpture in particular, does not stem from a predetermined form, but from the Classical ideal, whose development in diverse directions is anticipated by it.

The early critics of art were aware of all this, and noted that the generation of artists that followed Lysippus imitated more than the *costantia*, the *elegantia* of the father, and was more inclined toward a *iucundo* than an *austero* expression (Pliny, *Naturalis Historia*, XXXIV.66). The fact that Hellenic art was acknowledged to be in constant elevation is convincingly illustrated by a work by Eutychides, a pupil of Lysippus, whose work marked an epoch. His statue of Eurotas was defined as "more flowing than liquid." Though the original is regrettably lost, an idea of this flux can be seen in the replica of Orontes,

An Outline of Hellenistic Sculpture

Tyche of Antioch
3rd cent. B.C.
Florence
Museo Archeologico Nazionale

An Outline of Hellenistic Sculpture

Bronze bust of Seleucus I
beginning 3rd cent. B.C.
Naples, Museo
Archeologico Nazionale

Demosthenes
marble statue by Polyeuctus
280 B.C.
Copenhagen, Ny Carlsberg
Glyptothek

pictured swimming, in the Tyche and Antiochus group. While there is only a hint of fluidity, one cannot mistake the powerful arm of the river god. In the seated Tyche, we not only find a representation of a goddess – the goddess of felicity, under whose spell the entire period seems to have indelibly fallen – but also an invention of body and drapery which would serve as a pivotal example for the new epoch that this work heralded. The movement of the exuberant bodily forms of this figure, more robust than elegant, are emphasized by the drapery, which somehow seems to move in an opposite direction. The upper part of the body is almost constrained by the heavy, oblique folds while the mobility of the legs is facilitated by the soft cloth of the chiton, and portrayed with emphasis by the oscillating folds between the upper and lower part of the body. The strange antagonism between the body's movement and the motion implied by the clothing, whose forms are underlined by the lavishness of the material and by a form of representation no longer based on standardized rectangular movements but those provoked by physical torsion and bearing – this antagonism is the salient feature of Hellenistic sculpture, a feature that become tangible in this landmark work from the first period of the *diadochoi*.

The work, which is known exclusively through Roman copies and coin dies, was commissioned by one of the most signal *diadochoi*, Seleucus I, shortly after the foundation of Antioch in 301 B.C. The portrait of Seleucus himself, which has come down to us via a bronze bust found at Herculaneum which must have been sculpted in the early third century, evinces, compared to the fourth-century likenesses, all the features of a Hellenistic portrait of a sovereign. Instead of the features being smooth, the facial traits are heavily scored into the material. The head is crowned with thick curls gathered by a broad royal headband in a rear tail with twists of hair close to the scalp and a crown of sickle-like curls. A deep crease cuts right across the top of his forehead. The upper part is oblique to the profile and only delicately convex under the fringe; whereas the lower part is swollen above the bridge of the nose, which is slightly curved and descends to slightly sunken cheeks. The bone formation above the eyes

77

is full and fleshy, and the eyebrows form a single, sinuous path across the face. The eyes themselves are deep-set, and the lower lids emphasized by the tension of the flesh covering the cheekbones.

The nasal cartilage is slightly heavy and curved toward the base. The distance between the bridge of the nose and the corner of the eye is considerable, making the nose more prominent and accentuated. The mouth is large, the lips fleshy; the chin expresses energy and the two grooves on either side of the mouth evince a certain tension within the facial muscles. The handling is quite different from the serenity of Classical portraiture, and is informed with a sense of weight, force, and mobility, not to mention the emotive and passionate inner tautness which the Hellenistic artists sought to express.

Similar stylistic expression can likewise be observed in the portraits of the Ptolemies, the Antigonids, the Attalids, and other statesmen, the poets and philosophers of the period datable to between the statue of *Demosthenes* by Polyeuctus of 280 B.C., or the seated statue of *Menander* of the sons of Praxiteles, of Cephisdotus, and Timarchus early that century, up until the *Poseidon* from Apamea, who died in 45 B.C. These portraits give an articulate picture of the development of Hellenistic art over a period of 300 years.

A pre-Hellenistic period can be discerned until around 230 B.C.; full Hellenistic lasted through 150 B.C., and Late Hellenistic until around 80 B.C., which trailed through 30 B.C., while in the late Republican period one sees the onset of Roman art. Besides the works cited above, the extraordinary works of the pre-Hellenistic period include the seated *Menander*, the statue of *Demosthenes*, the *Capitoline Aphrodite*, the *Themis* of Chairestratos at Athens, the *Priene Nike* in Berlin, the Dionysus figure from the *Thrasyllus' Monument* in London, the *Epicurus* completed in 270 B.C., the statues from the Mausoleum of Antiochus II at Belevi, Smyrna, together with the *Aphrodite* of Doidalsas, to which one must add the *Antium Girl*. The common feature of all these works is their "withheld" energy, an energy that never quite breaks the surface and yet is unextinguished, as are those of the later Hellenistic phase.

A monument marking the advent of the new era, dated to before the year 223, is the Attalid Gallic monument at the fortress of Pergamum. A group of naked combatants of gigantic dimensions with superbly carved torsos lay variously crushed around the figure of their chieftain, whose heroic form thrusts upward in their midst, his scornful gaze turned on the approaching foe. Recognizing that all is lost, he slays his wife, who slips lifeless from his grip, and then turns his sword on himself, his right arm raised high above his head, inserting the blade into the flesh between the throat and the breastbone. His superb physique is twisted about as he takes a last seething look at the enemy before eluding them forever. This twisting of the head and fierce gaze was a leitmotif of the period, and an excellent example can be seen in is the *Menelaus*, who single-handedly essays to recover Patrocles' body from the clutches of his enemies; another is the formidable warrior turning his imperious head in another direction; or the figure of Attalus II in the bronze sculpture of the Hellenistic soldier in the Museo Nazionale delle Terme, Rome, dated around 175 B.C., thereby completing the spiral that encircles his body from the left foot to the right finger hooked around his lance. It is this rather brusque movement of the head – as also seen in the *Aphrodite* on the Campidoglio, timidly returning the stare of an onlooker – that best illustrates the sense of the period, rather than a simple turning of the head.

Figures from the Middle Hellenistic period are always more restive than pensive in mood. In the main work of the period – the grand frieze of the Great Altar of Pergamum – nearly all the one hundred figures are in violent tension and pictured in a fatal situation. It is worth comparing these battling figures with the disputes of the gods for the Attic kingdom in the west pediment of the Parthenon, from which the master of the east frieze of Pergamum took his cue, transforming the concept to suit his personal style. Even the diverging compositional lines containing the figures of Poseidon and Athena represents a kind of explosion of the accumulated tension that continues up to the pediment enclosing all the figures of the inhabitants of Athens, each one garbed in superb attire, while they look on at the gods' dispute over their own lands. Poseidon strikes the ground with his trident and releases a fountain of salt water; Athena causes an olive to sprout from the earth.

The substantial difference between the pediment of the Parthenon and the Pergamum frieze does not, however, lie entirely in the competition on the one hand, and the bloody struggle on the other, but in the sheer nobility of the forms portrayed. The clothes are transformed into fluttering drapery, the figures' muscles into tense muscular tissue, sweeping gestures become violent. The memory of the images of the gods in the Pergamum tympanum also has a significant counterpart in the east frieze of the Great Altar at Pergamum, namely in the votive offering for the victory of King Eumenes II over the Gauls in 166 B.C. In this war Eumenes fell and his life was spared by a miracle or by the intervention of the gods.

Maiden of Anzio
marble
3rd cent. B.C.
Rome, Museo Nazionale Romano

An Outline of Hellenistic Sculpture

Crouching Aphrodite by Doedalsas
Roman copy
3rd cent. B.C.
Rome
Museo Nazionale Romano

The Capitoline Aphrodite
Roman copy
3rd cent. B.C.
Rome, Musei Capitolini

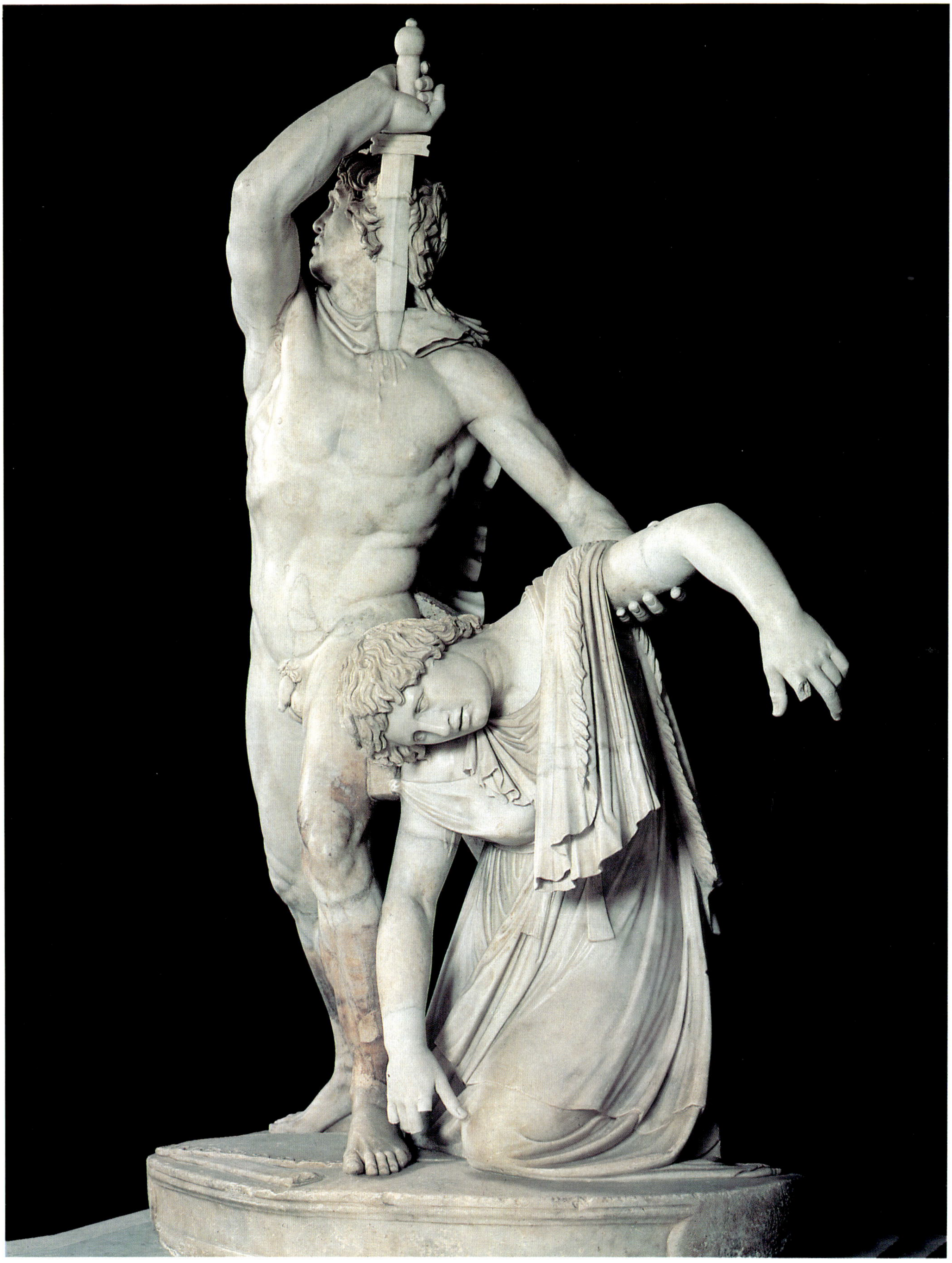

Dying Gaul
3rd cent. B.C.
Rome, Musei Capitolini

opposite
Gaul slaying himself
from the Donarium of Attalus I
at Pergamum
marble copy
from an original bronze
second half 3rd cent. B.C.
Rome, Museo Nazionale Romano

For this benevolent intercession of the gods, who had pacified the giants, Eumenes personally consecrated the Great Altar, and had the portraits of Zeus and Athena made which visitors to the Athenian Acropolis may still see today. On the south wall of the Acropolis Eumenes II and Attalus II commissioned the scene of a votive ritual to be sculpted by Phyromachos, who had a lasting influence on the style of the Great Altar, together with three other masters named Eisogonos, Stratonicos, and Antigonos comprising over 120 figures, by which posterity can witness the crushing defeat of the Gauls, or, as Pausanias put it, their *phtora* or annihilation.

When viewed unobstructed from a distance, the groups of combatants aligned on the walls of the Acropolis offer a striking impression of battle under way. This annihilation of the Gauls was part of the interminable struggle of Greek culture for supremacy which, despite its superiority, was under constant threat from the barbarians everywhere, who are represented in the metopes of the Parthenon.

In the same way that the inhabitants of Pergamum, in their day, spared their *ethnos* from Gallic incursion, just as the gods had had to rid themselves of the Giants, the Athenians of the Amazons, and the Greeks of the Persians. Only a few figures in the gigantic *Anathema* have come down to us in Roman copies, including only one securely attributable to Phyromachos, namely the *Dying Giant* in Naples. Be that as it may, no less than three (perhaps five) authenticated works by this famous Hellenic sculptor are presently known, as related by the writers of antiquity. The three autograph works – namely the portrait of the Cynic philosopher *Antisthenes*, the famous *Asclepius* of Pergamum, and the *Dying Giant* of the Athenian Acropolis – enable us to follow the master's stylistic development from the earlier second century, although in one direction only. His recourse to Classical models of the fifth and particularly of the fourth century is evident.

The *Antisthenes*, which seems to have been modeled on those of *Socrates*, *Plato*, *Epicurus*, and *Zeno* in terms of their idealized portraiture, nonetheless introduces a new startling realistic approach, with its deeply scored lines and toothless mouth.

The entire work demonstrates the peculiarity of Hellenistic portraits, as described in the treatment of *Seleucus I*: the characteristic division of the hair clinging to the skull and the crown of curls gathered above the forehead, the somewhat heavily cast traits of the faces, the prominent nose, and the deep cavity of the eyes. The references to the *Epicurus* portrait are especially evident in the handling of the eye, which is typical of third-century art in general. The artist's mark is particularly noticeable in the handling of the hair. As is usual for fourth-century works, the hair does not conform with the natural shape of the head but lies haphazardly, with a life of its own that does not match the smooth oval suggested by the skull itself, but instead seems to stress a contrast between scalp and hair.

The disorderliness of these ungovernable locks is captured in masterly fashion. The sculptor seems to have taken his cue from a bald head, which he has then clad with a mane of hair, each lock treated separately, just as if they were pushing out of the scalp. At all events, as for all Hellenistic sculpture,

An Outline of Hellenistic Sculpture

Detail of the east frieze
of the Great Altar of Zeus
at Pergamum
with Athena crowned by Nike
while fighting Alkyoneus
Berlin, Staatliche Museen
zu Berlin Preussischer
Kulturbesitz, Antikensammlung

the hair on the head seems to be a separate entity. It is not modeled together with the body or bust, as it was in the Classical period: in Hellenistic art the hair is treated as a kind of counterpoint to the body, like clothing. If we now look at the stylistic development of hair in the *Antisthenes*, the *Asclepius*, and the *Dying Giant* from the Attalid monument, we can quite clearly follow the increasingly accentuated language of forms applied. It is in constant evolution, and seems to reach a peak in the savage though artistically executed mane of flaming locks sported by the Giant.

The culmination of this process can be seen in the Great Altar at Pergamum, which was erected under the immediate influence of Phyromachos.

The sculptures of the Great Altar were commissioned by Pergamum's monarchy, and were fostered by the dominant style of the period, particular the styles known as Attic and Rhodian, which induced the artists to contrive a sort of fusion of the two traditions.

The works are renowned for two remarkable figures in particular, the so-called *Nike* of Samothrace (ca. 190 B.C.) and the *Scylla* group from Sperlonga, which is a Roman copy of a national Rhodian monument dedicated to victory and to the fallen combatants in the battle against the pirate in the second and third Macedonian wars. The Samothracian *Nike* (who represents Victory) can be dated to around 180 B.C., and anyway to before 168 B.C., that is, before work on the Great Altar of Pergamum began

Dead giant
from the Small Donarium
at Pergamum
3rd cent. B.C.
Naples
Museo Archeologico Nazionale

An Outline of Hellenistic Sculpture

The Victory from Samothrace
ca. 190 B.C.
marble
Paris, Musée du Louvre
Département des Antiquités
Grecques, Etrusques et Romaines

Portrait of Antisthenes
first half 2nd cent. B.C.
Vatican City, Musei Vaticani

in 166 B.C., which drew considerable inspiration from this extraordinary figure. This composition – originally a group work of some complexity – represents the climax of an artistic genre which has an incomparable significance for the Hellenistic period, namely national monuments with figures in the round representing with dramatic immediacy the culminating moment of a tragic episode, thereby transmitting a political message of considerable import. The typical example of this kind of group composition is the *Laocoön* in the Vatican. The group continues to be considered Rhodian in origin, when in fact – in light of findings at Sperlonga – it is a Roman copy of a Rhodian workshop piece after an original Pergamene bronze dating from around 140 B.C. This sculpture is a masterpiece of the group genre characteristic of the Late Hellenistic period, to whose preliminary phase it belongs. The genesis of the group composition is indicative of the peculiarity of Late Hellenistic sculpture: the individual figures of the group draw on figures of an earlier date; the figure of the father is reminiscent of the Giant Alcyoneus being destroyed by Athena in the Great Altar frieze. Like his counterpart, the Trojan priest Laocoön is wracked with *hubris*, and is defeated by an invisible Athena, as denoted by the unnatural position of his head. Athena's giant serpents finish off the job. The younger of the two sons is suspended like the dying *Niobid* in Dresden crushed in the coils of the giant serpent. He expires from *hubris*, like the figure in the *Niobe*. The elder son is pictured in virtually the same pose of the fleeing wineskin-carrier from the *Blinding of Polyphemus* group at Sperlonga, and like his counterpart he seems able to flee the situation. The mastery of the *Laocoön* group lies in the seamless fusion of figures borrowed from the models of antiquity and transposed to a new compositional structure, and in the perfect command of anatomy and the mechanics of human movement.

However, we should not be misled into thinking that the creativity of Late Hellenistic art depends on its completeness; it delved into Classicist feeling and a lively imitation of nature.

The *Laocoön* group, which to some extent was concluded by another group from Pergamum, harbingered a new epoch of extraordinary promise. This latter work comprises an almost picturesque background before which, like Heracles, Mithridates VI of Pontus essays to free the Greek people from Roman slavery; the figure is bound in chains to a rock like Prometheus. The stylistic means are once more those of the Great Altar, though the piece lacks the sheer grandeur and interior cogency of the Pergamene masterpiece. What subsequently became the purpose of Greek art, that is, to recreate matter and nature's space, was achieved in the Post-Hellenistic period, and with this the artistic cycle – which was to remain a permanent gauge and reference point – came to an end.

Dyfri Williams

Greek Pottery and the Role of Athens

The making of pottery, that is the creation of utensils from fired clay, is one of man's oldest and most widespread crafts. All manner of things could be stored in pottery, both wet and dry, food could be prepared and cooked in it, and people could eat and drink from it. For all of antiquity and, indeed, right up until the twentieth century of our own era it has been the all-purpose material.

On the Greek peninsula the craft of pottery-making goes back as early as about 6000 B.C. From the center of Athens, however, although a small Middle Neolithic habitation has been found on the south slope of the Acropolis, little dates before the Late Neolithic period, which is represented by a local, undecorated Red Burnished ware that probably belongs around to 3000 B.C. or soon after. Elsewhere in Greece, once Neolithic potters could achieve a smooth surface, they soon began to experiment with painted decoration as well as the use of clay slips. It was, however, only in about 2000 B.C., at the start of the Middle Bronze Age, that potters first regularly used a fast-rotating wheel, a radical advance in technology that enabled them to articulate the clay in a much more sophisticated manner. It seems likely that Neolithic and Early Bronze Age pottery was produced in the household and for the household: its makers and users being the womenfolk. The employment of the fast wheel coincides with the development of a palace-based society, especially on Crete, and it is, therefore, quite plausible to assume that palace patronage gave a particular stimulus to this technological advance. It is also to this time that the earliest preserved examples of clay potters' discs belong. Pottery production, however, was not completely under palace control, for there were also many rural centers of production.

During the Middle Bronze Age the main pace of change and development was set on Crete with the creation of the first palaces. Minoan, that is Cretan, influence on the pottery perhaps first permeated the mainland from the Cretan colony on Cythera via Laconia. Minoan-style pottery was adopted in the Argolid, the growing center of power in southern Greece, but it also spread to coastal Attica, appearing alongside the more traditional, monochrome and matte-painted Middle Helladic wares. Athens itself, situated inland, seems to have been rather introverted.

The gradual rise in wealth on the mainland around the middle of the second millennium B.C. is well exemplified by the finds in the Shaft Graves at Mycenae and the square built-tomb at Peristeria in Messenia. This growing prosperity may have been the result of various factors, including the intensification of trade with Crete, the Cyclades, and Anatolia, but in Attica the exploitation of the metal resources (lead, silver, and copper) at Laurion in southern Attica probably also played a role. Following the destructions of the palaces on Crete in about 1460 B.C., the island's influence on the mainland was greatly reduced: indeed, the current began to turn in the opposite direction.

At Athens there was a consequent growth. Imported pottery and local imitations are discernible. In addition, there developed during this period a wheel-made hard-fired pottery coated only with an orange wash that was then burnished to a high luster (Acropolis Burnished Ware). This local fabric has been found right across Attica, as well as on the island of Ceos and at Corinth. It belongs to the second half of the fifteenth century B.C. and the early part of the fourteenth century.

The balance of power finally shifted from Crete to the mainland not long after 1400 B.C. Society was dominated by small states centered around palaces, and the Linear B tablets found in the later destruction debris of the palaces give an idea of the extent of palace control and bureaucracy. At Athens all that has remained are traces of some five terraces, on which the palace was built atop the Acropolis, and the fortification wall, built somewhat later, with its secret descent to a fountain house.

Mycenaean pottery was now mass-produced, extremely homogeneous and of very high technical quality with decoration in a fine lustrous slip. The decorative motifs were drawn from the marine and plant worlds, but were severely stylized. It is very difficult to isolate local variations without the aid of scientific analysis of the clay, although sometimes a local preference for particular motifs can be distinguished. A pictorial style, however, developed in the fourteenth century B.C., especially on the broad field of the krater. These kraters seem to have been made in the Argolid, probably at Berbati, for export to Cyprus and the Near East. The impetus for this style may have come from wall-paintings, but no close parallels have yet been found. In the thirteenth century B.C. the number of production centers increased and the kraters were now made for local use as well as export.

Around 1200 B.C. the palaces on the Greek mainland were destroyed, never to be rebuilt. The consequent fragmentation of Mycenaean culture led to an initial loss of quality in the production of pottery and then to an increase in local variations. In general, the decoration became very linear and uninspired, while monochrome vessels became more common. By the end of the twelfth century, however, a number of easily recognizable local styles had appeared. The Close Style, produced in the Argolid, employed motifs such as birds, animals and fish, surrounded by a huge variety of closely-packed

Mycenaean stemmed goblet
ca. 1400 B.C.
London, British Museum
Department of Greek
and Roman Antiquities

Sub-Mycenaean stirrup-jar
made in Attica
1110-1050 B.C.
London, British Museum
Department of Greek
and Roman Antiquities

Greek Pottery and the Role of Athens

Proto-Geometric
amphora
made in Athens
975-950 B.C.
London, British Museum
Department of Greek
and Roman Antiquities

Proto-Geometric *pyxis*
made in Athens
950-900 B.C.
London, British Museum
Department of Greek
and Roman Antiquities

filling ornaments. At Mycenae appeared the Granary Style, a loose, linear style and in the Dodecanese an Octopus Style. The Pictorial Style continued, produced at a number of centers, including Athens. From the middle of the eleventh century B.C. there was a further, gradual decline in the fashioning and in the decoration of pottery, as well as a diminution in the variety of shapes produced. This final, Bronze Age phase, known as sub-Mycenaean, forms a bridge to what is called proto-geometric.

It is at Athens, toward the end of the eleventh century B.C., that we can first observe an awakening from the sub-Mycenaean slumber and the birth of the proto-geometric period. The production techniques seem to have improved, for the clay appears more carefully prepared, and the slip is more lustrous as a result of more thorough refining and a higher firing temperature. In general, new shapes appear, while the old shapes tighten their contours. The dark-on-light scheme of the Mycenaean period is gradually replaced by an overall dark-ground scheme punctuated by bands or panels of decoration. There are new decorative motifs, including sets of circles and semicircles, which were rendered with geometrical exactness thanks to a new technical device, an Athenian invention, the multiple brush fitted to one arm of a compass.

Other complex motifs, including cross-hatched diamonds and checker, also appear, often framed by or combined with dog-tooth, zigzag or groups of opposed diagonals. It was during the tenth century that the first attempts at figured drawing were attempted: some small horses on Athenian pieces and two archers on a tiny *oinochoe* from Lefkandi on Euboea.

The clarity of shape and decoration suggests a new self-respect among the potters of Athens that grew in the coming centuries, while it can now be seen that Athenian pottery began to be attractive to both distant buyers and potters, for it is to be found from northern Greece to Miletus in the east and Crete in the south. Indeed, if the claim of Critius, the fifth-century poet and politician, that Athens "invented the potter's wheel and the offspring of clay and kiln, pottery so famous and useful about the house" were to reflect a historical moment then it would have to be the beginning of the tenth century. Around about 900 B.C. there was a change in the repertoire of decorative motifs, for the large circular motifs are replaced by two new rectilinear motifs, the meander and the battlement, often in rectangular panels. But there was also another dramatic change, for Athenian Early Geometric pottery (900–850 B.C.) is suddenly found no further afield than its immediate neighbors. This was probably once again a period of isolation for both Athens and Attica.

Middle Geometric *oinochoe*
made in Athens
800-760 B.C.
London, British Museum
Department of Greek
and Roman Antiquities

Early Geometric *oinochoe*
made in Athens
900-850 B.C.
London, British Museum
Department of Greek
and Roman Antiquities

It was not to last, however, for a number of tombs around the middle of the ninth century B.C. reveal an immense resurgence in wealth, as measured by the presence of gold jewelry and foreign trinkets in them. The vases that accompanied these aristocratic burials are of consummate quality. Some are of monumental splendor and served as grave markers above ground: the belly-handled *amphorae* over the tombs of women, the pedestaled kraters over the men's. The pottery of this Middle Geometric period (850–760 B.C.) was settled and harmonious. The decoration began to cover more and more of the vessel and some shapes were remodeled. The number of birds and small animals, such as horses, stags and dogs, that appear next to the complex abstract designs increased. In addition, there is an isolated example of a mourning woman to be found above the handle of one the pedestaled kraters. Some of these particularly large vessels, both *amphorae* and kraters, were exported to Crete, Cyprus, and even Hama on the Orontes, perhaps as part of a gift-exchange system. By the end of the period Attic fashions had become a *koine* across almost the whole Aegean and, indeed, the circulation of Athenian pottery now reached its highest point until the sixth century B.C.

Around 770 B.C. Athens entered a new phase of artistic revolution. The most important change was the sudden development of ambitious figured scenes. The painting used on these vases was essentially conceptual – the artist drew what he knew to be there rather than what he could actually see. Each part of the body was given its most diagnostic view – head in profile, chest frontal and triangular (female breasts project from the sides), and legs in profile with prominent buttocks and calves. The subjects are mourning around the funeral bier, processions of warriors and chariots, and fight scenes, both on land and on sea.

These are concentrated on monumental grave monuments, well over one meter high and are combined with the most meticulous geometric patterns. Of the thirty-five or more known, some twenty-one are the work of one master and his close associates, active in a single workshop, the so-called Dipylon workshop. These must have been special commissions placed by aristocratic families. On some the work of more than one hand has been distinguished, perhaps the result of the scale of the vase, the complexity of the decoration, and the need to finish the commission in time for the third day when the body had to be buried.

With such narrative scenes from reality as funerals and battles attempts at mythological narrative also slowly developed among the successors of this first identifiable Athenian potter's workshop during

Late Geometric spouted krater
730-720 B.C.
London, British Museum
Department of Greek
and Roman Antiquities

the second half of the eighth century. The subjects of such scenes are not always easy to distinguish – perhaps the artists were reluctant to give up the generalized approach to narrative. One clear mythological scene, however, is to be found on a large spouted-krater in London.

The front is dominated by a huge oared ship, with two rows of oarsmen, one row either side rather than a two-decker. In front a man is leading a woman onto the boat, most probably Theseus and Ariadne – she is holding the wreath of light with which, according to some versions of the story, she lit Theseus' path through the Labyrinth.

The second half of the eighth century B.C. was a period of ferment and as new ideas and new motifs shook the old rigidity of geometric patterning, so too did the Athenian-dominated *koine* give way as the regional schools rapidly asserted their independence. Indeed, one of these schools, that of Corinth, began to rise to pre-eminence, no doubt supported by the fineness of its clay and the high quality of the potting that its craftsmen achieved. From about 730 B.C. there was a general dispersal of wealth from Athens into the Attic countryside, which may reflect a move away from maritime and commercial interests toward agriculture.

If Athens was the dominant force in the world of Greek pottery for much of the eighth century B.C., then the seventh century belonged to Corinth. The city may well have taken on a new aggressive commercialism at this time; certainly it is then that its potters achieved great quality, immense productivity, and wide distribution. Some of its potters even emigrated to Italy to work on Pithekoussai (modern Ischia) and in nearby Campania. Under such stimuli not only did the iconographic range of Corinthian vase-painters suddenly burgeon but a new technique was also developed, that of scratching with a fine point through the black glaze, which, when combined with added color in the form of a purplish red, is now known as black-figure. At Athens there was continuity from the Late Geometric tradition and a similar reluctance to accept the new incised technique from Corinth, although some adventurous artists began adding a good deal of white. The range of subjects represented on Athenian vases is somewhat contracted and exports became rare: Early proto-Attic has been found only on Aegina and in Boeotia.

By the middle of the seventh century B.C., however, there were some changes. Potters once again produced large shapes as tomb markers, added red began to be used together with some tentative incision and the painting was also much more disciplined. There was much borrowing from Corinth, but there remained something large and spontaneous about the style. The last quarter of the century saw the final adoption of the black-figure technique as pioneered by Corinth and Athenian pottery began to be exported again, at least as far as Etruria, as a fragment by the Nettos Painter from Cerveteri indicates. It is to the seventh century B.C. that the first evidence of a kiln in the Agora at Athens can be attributed, as well as a workshop deposit.

The sixth century B.C. reveals an immense growth in the pottery industry at Athens. The scene was set by the reforms of Solon, which were both constitutional and economic. It is from now on that we can begin to attribute, on the basis of style, vases to various painters with a good degree of confidence. The early first quarter of the century was dominated by the Gorgon Painter, whose style shows considerable power and control. At this time there also seem to have been workshops scattered elsewhere in Attica and neighboring areas, often in close proximity either to a sanctuary, such as that of Demeter at Eleusis, or a wealthy cemetery area, such as that at Vari. In addition, there were imitators and even Athenian emigrant potters in Boeotia. Following on from the Gorgon Painter came about six recognizable pupils, the most famous of whom was Sophilus, the first Athenian vase-painter to have left his name, a fact that is no doubt suggestive of the growing importance and self-confidence of the Athenian vase-painting tradition. One notable development at this time was the abandonment of large vases that served as funerary markers. This probably reflects a change in burial customs, but vase-painters' products continued to have a role in the cemetery, at least for the sixth century, for then began a series of funeral plaques that must have been attached to the exterior of built-tombs. Potters and painters, however, now produced a series of large and elaborate vessels for the symposium, especially kraters and *dinoi*. There is still a good deal of influence from Corinth, especially in the animal friezes, but their arrangement is much more subtle in the hands of the Athenian painters.

In the second quarter of the sixth century B.C., the time of the great potters and painters, Clitias, Ergotimos, Nearchus, and the early years of Lydos, the preserved vases suggest, roughly speaking, a doubling in the numbers of painters at work, with two large specialist groups arising, the Tyrrhenian *amphorae*, most of which were exported to Etruria, hence their name, and the so-called Siana cups. This is also the time when Panathenaic prize *amphorae* began to be made – they were required in substantial numbers for the quadrennial games, more than 1,400 – and they were decorated with the figure of Athena on one side and a representation of the relevant event on the other. By contrast, the rural groups of painters seem to have disappeared, probably drawn into the great urban center that Athens was fast becoming under the rule of Pisistratus.

With the increase in the number and variety of signatures we can now begin to deduce something more about these Athenian craftsmen. Firstly, three very early fragmentary Panathenaic *amphorae* record the potter's name in the form Hyperides son of Androgenes. This inclusion of the patronymic was the normal way in the sixth century B.C. of showing one's citizenhood, since the use of demotics seems only to have come in with Cleisthenes at the end of the sixth century, when it was officially sanctioned, and even then was only slowly adopted. By contrast the name of Lydos, especially in the

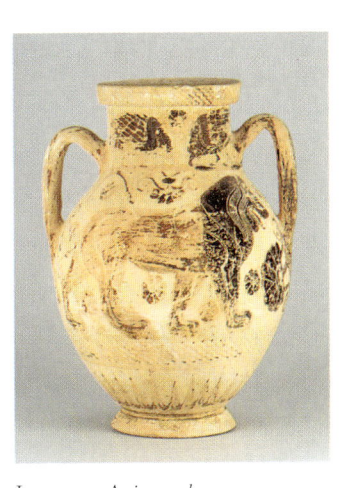

Late proto-Attic *amphora*
attributed to the Nettos Painter
620-610 B.C.
London, British Museum
Department of Greek
and Roman Antiquities

Middle proto-Attic krater
ca. 650 B.C.
London, British Museum
Department of Greek
and Roman Antiquities

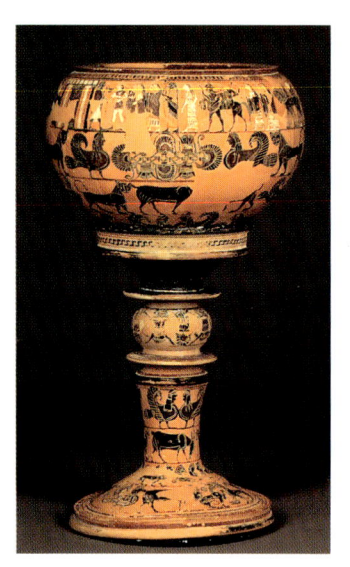

Athenian black-figure *dinos*
and stand
signed by Sophilos as painter
ca. 580 B.C.
London, British Museum
Department of Greek
and Roman Antiquities

opposite
Athenian black-figure *amphora*
signed by Execias
ca. 530 B.C.
Vatican City, Museo Etrusco

manner in which he writes it – *ho ludos*, the Lydian – together with his mistakes in writing, suggests not only a foreign origin, but also possibly a slave or metic status. His name, in fact, reminds one of Strabo's comment that "the Athenians would either name their slaves after the peoples from whom they were imported, like 'Lydos' or 'Syros,' or give them names which were common in those countries, like 'Manes' or 'Midas' for a Phrygian, or 'Tibios' for a Paphlagonian." If we consider every craftsman who signed with a foreign ethnic a slave, which may well not be correct in any case, it would still represent less than seven percent of the total known signatures. Of Strabo's other formation of a slave's name, one immediately thinks of the late-fifth-century potter, Midas, but other possible candidates are few.

Schools of black-figure pottery occurred in a number of parts of the Greek world during the sixth century B.C. In Greece itself, that in Laconia was the most competent and attractive. In Italy the immense quantities of imported vases were further supplemented by various local centers of production, especially in Etruria and Campania, as well as in southern Italy (the so-called Chalcidian). The eastern Greek fabrics are, in general, both more conservative and more diverse, but small amounts of black-figure with figured decoration are known from a number of centers, notably Samos and Chios.

At Athens the third quarter of the sixth century B.C. was dominated by two major artists, Amasis and Execias. Amasis signed as potter on a wide variety of shapes. With one exception these are all painted by the same anonymous artist, whom we call the Amasis Painter. Amasis might at first be taken as a slave with a Greek version of the popular Egyptian name A-ahmes, but a group of late signatures that take the form "Cleophrades son of Amasis" make this unlikely, for one cannot imagine an Egyptian slave having a son called Cleophrades, who then proclaimed his paternity with such pride. If Amasis was, then, a citizen, one must assume that he was given the name of a foreign king, much as a rich Athenian youth during the Pisistratid period was also given the Lydian royal name Kroisos (Croesus). The great Execias, a younger contemporary of Amasis, signed both as potter and painter. He seems to have begun as a potter and then went on to develop his talent by painting some or perhaps all of his vases as well. His potting is crisp and clear, while his painting reveals him to have been a master of speaking form and contour, as well as incision. The renderings of his chosen themes are filled with great psychological insight and intensity.

It is during this period, and until about 440 B.C., that Athenian vase-painters sometimes wrote the praises of a youth on their vases, whether in the form *Leagros kalos* ("Leagros [is] beautiful"), or in the vaguer and more common formula, *ho pais kalos* ("The boy [is] beautiful"). The objects of such attention seem to have been chiefly of the uppermost class and as such they can offer some help in the relative dating of vases, and even, on occasion, in the search for absolute dating. In the last quarter of the sixth century a change may be observed, for females were also first praised in this way on vases. They, however, must belong to a different class of society than the *kaloi*, for they were surely courtesans – *hetairai* – whether involved in erotic or sympotic scenes or even at fountain-houses. These *kalos* and *kale* names were, therefore, little more than fashionable references to contemporary young beauties, whose names were on the lips of all in the gossip-ridden Agora.

Alongside Amasis and Execias was the series of Little Master cups that grew out of Ergotimos' Gordion cups. These wonderfully potted cups with their miniature decoration bear a plethora of signatures and lively exhortations. There are some twenty-eight signatures of potters but only four of painters, a fact which, when it is combined with the frequently reduced level of decoration, seems to suggest that the potters were the leading figures in the group. What is immediately clear from a number of signatures is the way that the craft of potting was being passed from father to son, for one finds Eucheiros son of Ergotimos, and even a son of Eucheiros – a third generation potter it would seem. This was surely the normal pattern at Athens, a family business, perhaps amplified in the more successful establishments around the Agora by the use of slaves and metics, the technological mysteries being passed down through the sons.

One of the potters of Little Master cups was Nikosthenes. He was clearly an adventurous potter, for he has left his own signature on some 130 or more vases. He seems, in fact, to have been a real entrepreneur, his special neck-*amphorae* and *kyathoi* deliberately imitating Etruscan shapes for the Etruscan market. He also appears to have got his painters, not always it must be admitted the best, to experiment with a number of new techniques, in particular white ground and super-posed color, the so-called Six technique. It is possible, therefore, that he was also the force behind the invention of the red-figure technique, in which the color scheme was reversed so that the figures were left in the reserved red clay and the backgrounds painted black.

Greek Pottery and the Role of Athens

Greek Pottery and the Role of Athens

Athenian red-figure *calyx-krater* signed by Euxitheos as potter and Euphronius as painter
ca. 510 B.C.
New York, The Metropolitan Museum of Art
Purchase, Bequest of Joseph H. Durkee Gift of Darius Ogden Mills and Gift of C. Ruxton Love, by exchange 1972

The invention of red-figure in about 530–520 B.C. is, however, usually connected with the potter Andocides. A metrical inscription on the base of a dedication from the Acropolis that once supported a bronze statue reads [M]*nesiades kerameus me kai Andokides anetheken*. It is possible that this inscription was made at the time of the transfer of the ownership or direction of the business from Mnesiades to Andocides, or that it in some way records the merging of two smaller operations into one larger workshop. From this period there was, indeed, an immense mushrooming of activity and personnel that must be reflected in the sheer number of pottery workshops as well as in their sizes. One may now also observe the sharing of a particular vase between two painters, a sure sign of increased demand, since painting would clearly be the slower of the two stages prior to firing, and an indication of the increased physical size of some workshops. This phenomenon seems to occur first in the circle of Andocides, where the Andocides and Lysippides Painters shared so-called bilingual vases, one side black-figure, the other red-figure, and Psiax may have decorated the rim of an *amphora* otherwise decorated by the Andocides Painter. Such sharing, however, is also to be found among the members of the next group of artists, the so-called Pioneers. It came to a peak, it would seem, in the second quarter of the fifth century B.C. in a workshop that specialized in the production of red-figured cups, the workshop of some twenty recognized painters that included the Penthesilea Painter.

Greek Pottery and the Role of Athens

Of the Pioneers, the names of seven painters and some dozen potters are known. Three of the most important Pioneer painters, however, also signed as potters: Euphronius, Phintias, and Euthymides. In each case these *epoiesen* signatures belong later than the *egraphsen* signatures. Of these three painters who turned to potting, it would seem that only Euphronius made a success of it. His *epoiesen* signatures go on until the 470s B.C. This pattern of turning from painting to potting, when set alongside the evidence of the Little Master cups, strongly suggests that what seems obvious is true, namely that the potter was the most important member of the workshop. The case of Execias would seem to be different, but it does nothing to counter such a suggestion, for he did not give up potting.

The Pioneers also indulged in a good many references to each other on their vases. Thus, there are many toasts between artists and one apparent challenge on an *amphora* by Euthymides – *os oudepote Euphronios* ("as never Euphronius"). In addition, three of the painters have left "portraits" of each other. It seems clear that such references to potters and painters amid the *jeunesse dorée* should be considered as little more than jokes. There is evidence that Euphronius, like Mnesiades and Andocides, was prosperous enough to make an elaborate dedication on the Athenian Acropolis: it probably belongs to the moment when he turned from painting to potting, perhaps thanking Athena for good health as well as wealth during a long career. This sort of evidence, however, does not mean that he, or any of his companions, could really have entered the world of the wealthy aristocracy. Euphronius might have witnessed the fall of the Pisistratids, the birth of Athenian democracy under Cleisthenes and, indeed, the defeat of the Persians, but it did not make him one of the elite.

The Pioneers have been given their name as a result of a pioneering interest in the representation of the human form, especially as it moves and turns in space. These painters had totally mastered their technique and could paint whatever they wished. Their observation of minute details of the human anatomy and their careful delineation, as shown particularly by the painter Euphronius, are really remarkable.

The time of the successors of the Pioneers is usually referred to as the Late Archaic period (500–475 B.C.). These successors divide into two main streams, those who specialized in the production of drinking vessels, cups and *skyphoi*, and those who concentrated on large shapes, such as kraters and *amphorae*. The former seem to depend on Euphronius' workshop, although they soon spread out into other new establishments. The first main figure here is Onesimos, who remained with Euphronius and whose tradition passed down through the Antiphon Painter, to the Pistoxenos Painter and ultimately on to the busy Penthesilean workshop, which was still active after the middle of the century. Others, especially Douris, Makron, and the Brygos Painter, moved on to work for other potters, namely Python, Hieron, and Brygos. The potters for whom the painters of larger vessels, the pot-painters, such as the Berlin Painter and the Cleophrades Painter, who perhaps owed more initially to the work of Euthymides than to Euphronius, sadly remain, like the painters themselves, anonymous. Has the reason for this anything to do with the fact that the guests at the symposium actually held the cups and therefore might have been expected to read the signatures, while the larger sympotic vessels were pre-

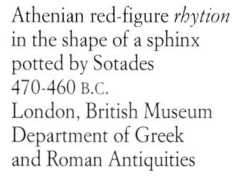

Athenian red-figure *rhyton* in the shape of a sphinx potted by Sotades
470-460 B.C.
London, British Museum
Department of Greek and Roman Antiquities

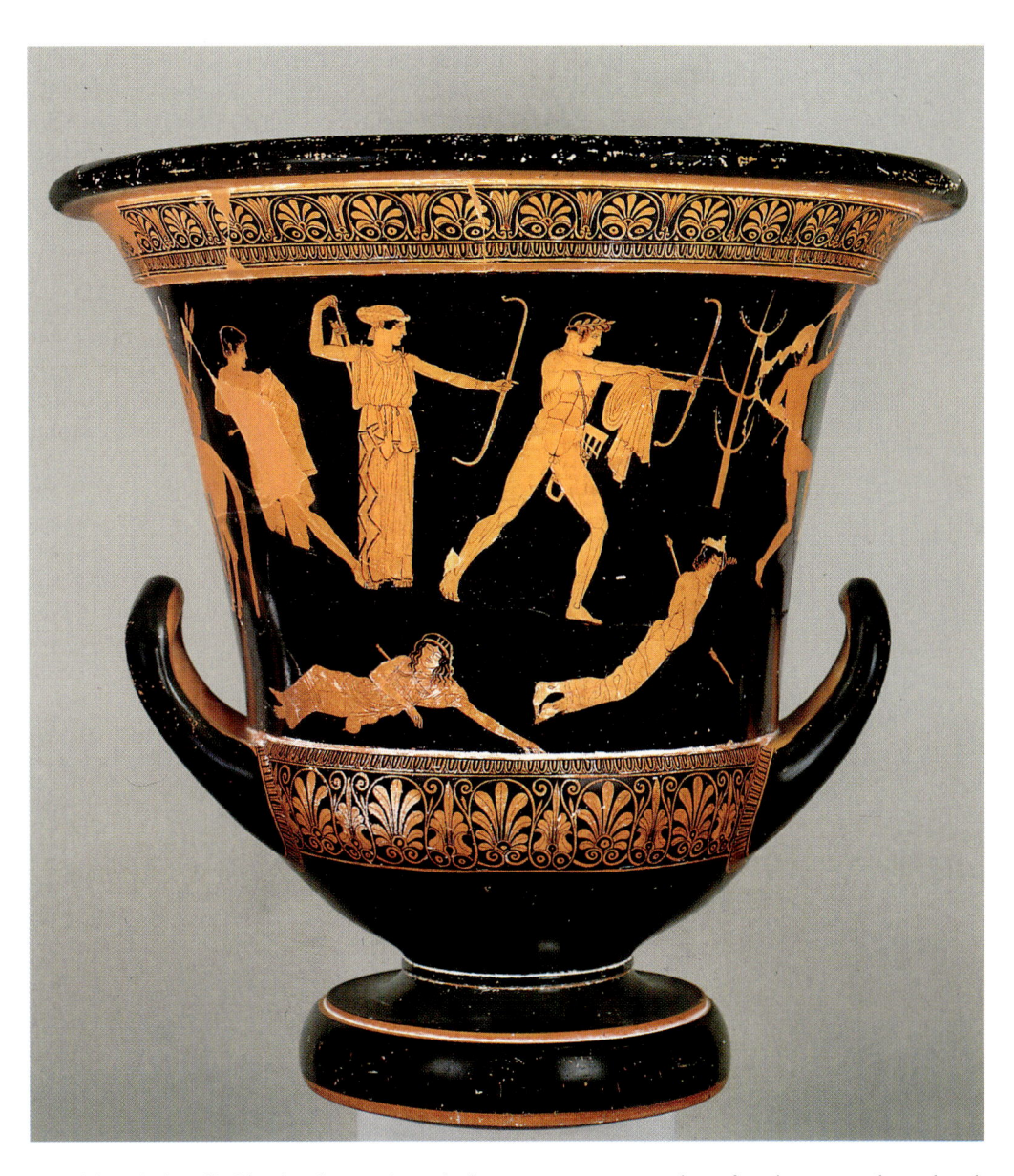

Athenian red-figure *calyx-krater*
attributed
to the Niobid Painter
ca. 450 B.C.
Paris, Musée du Louvre
Département
des Antiquités Grecques
Etrusques et Romaines

sumably only handled by the slaves? As with the cup-painters a number of traditions can be isolated. One of the most important is the one that derives from the Berlin Painter, for it continues until the end of the third quarter of the century. The finest of these Late Archaic pot-painters built upon the inventions of their teachers, the Pioneers, and some produced real *tours de force*, employing an immense degree of foreshortening. There were also some experiments of their own, particularly with the shading of inanimate objects, such as shields and jugs.

The next generation, the Early Classical period (ca. 475–450 B.C.), saw something of the same divisions continue but signatures, both of painters and potters, became much rarer. One special type of vase, the "plastic" vase, in which both regular potting and a mold-formed section were combined, became particularly popular at this period. The most famous potter of this class of object was Sotades, although others have left their signatures too, namely Charinos, Proklees, and Midas (he signed as *ho Midas*, and was probably a slave of the second type referred to by Strabo). The quality of the mold-made part of these vessels is regularly far in excess of normal terra-cottas of the period. The relatively high number of potters' signatures is probably related to the success and importance of the fashion for this sort of vessel, as well as its function.

It is in the same generation that a particularly important new development may be observed on some of the larger vases, especially kraters, the breaking up of the regular single ground level into a number of small, separate ground-lines spread up and down the field in an attempt to add a feeling of space and depth to the picture. This scheme matches the detailed account in Pausanias' *Description of Greece* (second century A.D.) of two works by the wall-painter Polygnotus in a building at Delphi that dated to 470–460 B.C. This suggests a direct borrowing by vase-painters from the world of large-scale painting. The earliest exponent of this on vases seems to be the Niobid Painter and from him stems a long and important tradition of painters of monumental vessels; to them belongs at least one vase-painter with the name Polygnotus.

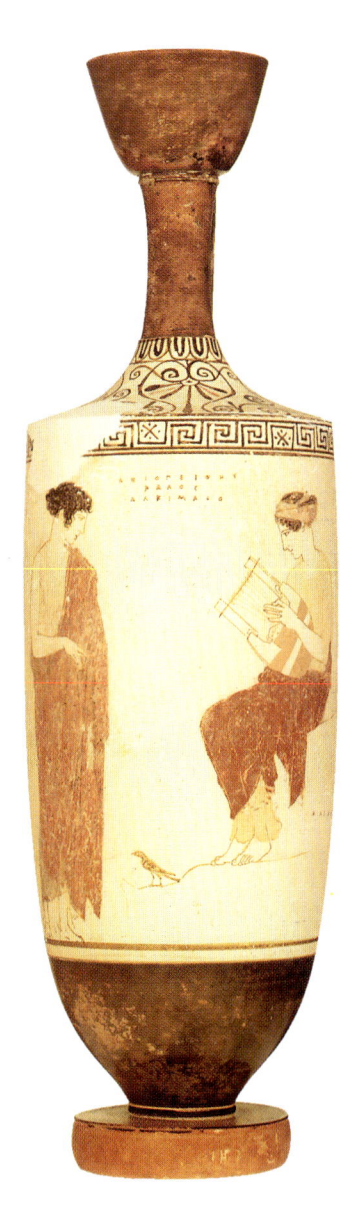

It is possible that the sack of Athens and the virtually single-handed defeat of the Persians by the Athenians did have an effect on the history of vase-painting, but it is difficult to identify just what it was. It is not that, as might have been imagined, the fighting wiped out a generation of such craftsmen, for, as far as one can judge, the craftsmen soon began work again – indeed, given the destruction wrought by the Persians, business must have been rather good. It is possible, however, that a new sense of self-confidence in the population may have led to a turning away from elaborate mythological scenes peopled by heroes and a wish for contemporary Athenians to see themselves on their vases. The trend for borrowing ideas and scenes from free painting had probably already begun in the first quarter of the fifth century, but it intensified in the 470s and 460s and was eventually to lead to the decline in Athenian vase-painting.

Following the defeat of the Persians Athens slowly turned her leadership of the allies into a maritime Empire. This was made reality by the transfer of the treasury to Athens in 454 B.C. It is the years following this, a period of great public wealth and stability that we think of as the high point of the Classical period, the time of Pericles' great building program that included the Parthenon. It is perhaps the work of the Achilles Painter that typifies this moment. He was the last pupil of the Berlin Painter and, together with his own pupil the Phiale Painter, represents one of the great traditions of fifth-century vase-painting. Both painters decorated a variety of shapes and both worked in red-figure and white-ground (the Achilles Painter also produced black-figured Panathenaic prize *amphorae*, as his teacher had done before him).

The white-ground technique, which originated in the later sixth century, had initially been used on a variety of shapes, but the most important proved to be the *lekythos*, a shape designed to hold sweet smelling oil and one that was regularly associated with burials. The Achilles Painter's earliest *lekythoi* have soft brown dilute glaze contours and a small range of added colors – purplish reds, blacks and a brighter white for the flesh of women. Soon after the middle of the century the painters began to experiment with matte colors in a wider variety of shades that were not to be so permanent – indeed, drapery done with washes of color has often faded completely leaving little but a misleading brown contour of the figure below. The Achilles Painter's women have a pure classical mood and style that match the Parthenon sculptures. They are imbued with the grace and confidence that one naturally attributes to the wives and womenfolk of rich and powerful Periclean Athens – tall, serene and beautiful, like Olympian goddesses.

The red-figure technique had been invented at Athens and it was translated to or imitated in a number of other centers. It is likely that its introduction to southern Italy just after the middle of the fifth century was the result of emigrants participating in the foundation of Thurii, a Panhellenic colony instituted by Pericles in 443 B.C. (see essay by Margot Schmidt). By contrast, the simultaneous appearance of the technique in Etruria seems rather to have been the result of imitation. At the end of the century the rise of a school based at Falerii was also most probably dependent on emigration from Athens in the bad years after the Peloponnesian War. In Greece itself, there were also smaller-scale productions of red-figure in Boeotia and Laconia, at Corinth, Olympia and Eretria, and in Crete. Of all these other red-figure fabrics it is only those of the Greek cities of southern Italy that are of any significance.

The last quarter of the fifth century B.C. saw further experiments with the white-ground technique on *lekythoi*. Matte red and black began to be used for the contours of the figures and other objects, while the palette of additional colors, often very fugitive, was increased to include green, blue, and mauve. In the realm of red-figure we can observe two main traditions, the first continues the monumental style that may be traced back through the Kleophon Painter to the Polygnotan Group: here belong artists such as the Dinos Painter, Polion, and the Nicias Painter, a painter who worked for a potter, an Athenian citizen, named Nicias, who signed as Nicias son of Hermokles of the deme of Anaphlystos. This tradition in fact continues on into the early fourth century by which time it has essentially merged with the second, richer style, that of the Meidias Painter and his followers.

The last decades of the fifth century B.C. had seen Athens brought to its knees by the Peloponnesian War. The city soon began to recover economically but political power had moved elsewhere in

White ground *lekythos*
attributed to the Achilles Painter
ca. 440 B.C.
Munich, Staatlichen
Antikensammlungen
und Glyptothek München

opposite
Athenian red-figure *pelike*
attributed to the Marsyas Painter
ca. 360 B.C.
London, British Museum
Department of Greek
and Roman Antiquities

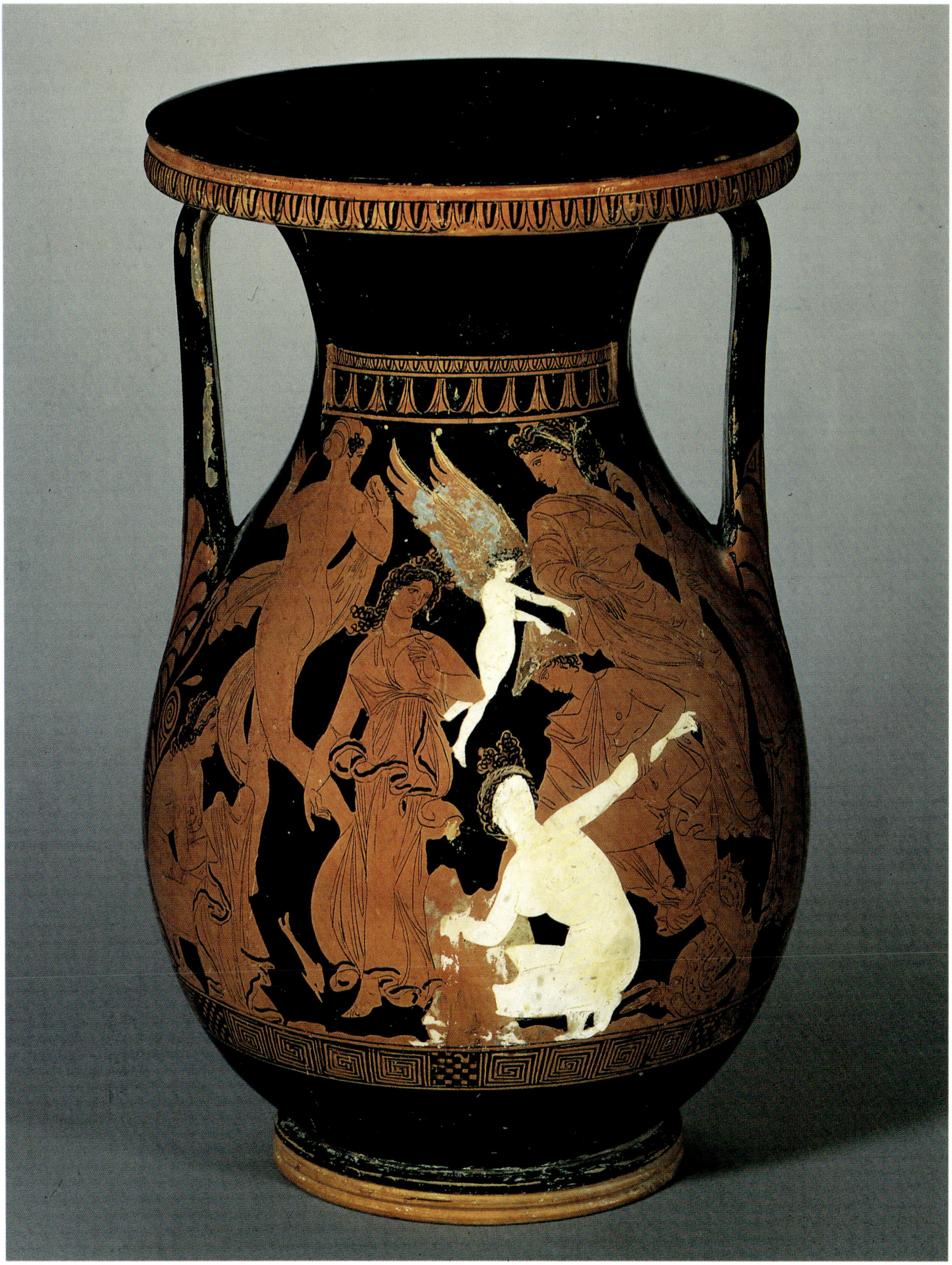

Greece, first to Sparta, later to Thebes and finally to Macedon. In the second quarter of the fourth century B.C. a second rich style of vase-painting developed, sometimes known as the Kertsch style because most of the best pieces were exported to the rich Bosporan city of Penticapaeum (or Pentikapaion), modern Kertsch. The outstanding artists were the Marsyas Painter and the Eleusinian Painter. They painted not only *pelikai*, *lekanides*, and nuptial *lebetes*, but also, as has now been recognized, black-figured Panathenaic *amphorae*. These Panathenaic *amphorae*, which had since early in the fourth century borne the name of the presiding magistrate, are a great aid to the unraveling of the final decades of figure-painted pottery in Athens. The end must have come between 320 and 310 B.C. This was neither the end of figured painting on vases elsewhere in Greece or Italy, nor the end of pottery produced in Athens itself, but it marks a momentous change. At Athens all-black vases had been produced as a specific line since the sixth century B.C. In the fifth century most decoration was done under the glaze in the form of simple stamped or impressed decoration. In the fourth century, however, there was a fashion for large black vessels decorated with designs in raised clay that were then gilded: the most common motifs are those taken from the world of jewelry, namely wreaths and necklaces. From the latest examples of this style that replaced the gilding with orangey yellow paint derive the so-called West Slope pottery with its much more elaborate decoration, often in the form of checkered patterns, squares and floral chains. From about 220 B.C. there began at Athens a series of footless, mold-made bowls with relief decoration, the so-called Megarian bowls, but by the middle of the second century it is clear that Athens was no longer an important center for pottery production: the Hellenistic *koine* had taken over and other centers, especially in Ionia, began to lead the way. The real future, however, was to be in the West where the Italian potters took up the idea of mold-made pottery. With the beginning of the production of Roman fine pottery and its export all over Europe, Africa and the Near East, the end of this survey of Athenian pottery must end.

By way of conclusion, it is interesting to consider an important nexus of evidence from the latter part of the fourth century. A tombstone, found near Athens, and to be dated about 330 B.C., bears, in addition to the name of the deceased, Bakchios son of Amphis[tratos?] the elegiac poem: "Of those who blend earth, water, fire into one art, Bakchios was judged by all Hellas first, for natural gifts; and in every contest appointed by the city he won the crown." With this epitaph has been combined a decree of the senate and people of Ephesus dating to about 320 B.C. awarding citizenship of Ephesus to the Athenians Kittos and Bakchios, sons of Bakchios, and their descendants, since they have undertaken to provide the black pottery for the city, and the *hydria* for the goddess, at the price established by law, for as long as they remain in the city.

The signature of a Bakchios is known from two Panathenaic prize *amphorae*, one from the Kerameikos, the other from Lindos, which have been dated to 375/4 B.C. He is presumably the Bakchios who died in Athens in about 330 B.C. His sons Kittos and Bakchios thereupon emigrated to Ephesus, perhaps because the pottery trade was already in decline at Athens. Another Kittos has left his name as potter on a Panathenaic that may be dated to 367/6 B.C. This cannot, therefore, be one of the emigrants, but it is probably a member of the same family, perhaps the brother of our first Bakchios.

This precious evidence provides insights into various aspects of the world of potters: it hints at competitions for some public contracts, probably for the production of Panathenaic prize *amphorae*, and records the actual placing of others for black-glazed pottery; it gives clear indications of citizen status; and it emphasizes the mobility of craftsmen.

Bibliography
J.D. BEAZLEY, 1951; S.A. IMMERWAHR, 1971; R.M. COOK, 1972; V.R. D'A. DESBOROUGH, 1972; J. BOARDMAN, 1974; J. BOARDMAN,1975; J.N. COLDSTREAM, 1977; D. WILLIAMS, 1985; J. BOARDMAN,1989; T. RASMUSSEN and N. SPIVEY (eds), 1991; B.A. SPARKES, 1991; P.A. MOUNTJOY, 1993; O. DICKINSON, 1994; M. ROBERTSON, 1994.

Agnès Rouveret A Survey of Greek Wall-Painting

According to the antique sources, painting developed into a fully autonomous art in the course of the fifth century B.C., when it ceased to be a mere sub-category of architecture and sculpture. In the period following that of the founding masters (Polygnotus and Micon) who, just after the Persian Wars, had secured Athenian predominance in the field by establishing a tradition of monumental wall-painting particularly suited to the celebration of victory by way of battle scenes and mythicizing pictorial rhetoric, the majority of the technical developments resulting from researches on colors, harmonies and shading methods (Apollodorus of Athens) and the representation of three-dimensional space (the treatise on perspectival stage design by Agatharcus of Samos) took place between the chronological parentheses of the Peloponnesian War and the epoch of Philip, Alexander, and their immediate successors. Emblematic pairs of painters mark the two extremes of this "golden age" of Greek painting. With Zeuxis and Parrhasius, counterparts in the art of painting of the Sophists in the field of literature, the figure of the artist was thrust into the foreground. A century later, the contrasting careers of Apelles and Protogenes, emphasize the new importance of the courts, near the cities, for the artists' lives and realizations. If we are to trust the antique sources – which, admittedly, often reach us through the filter of Latin authors – this period of intense formal and technical invention gave rise to independent "schools", bringing prestige to the cities which had fostered them: Athens had Apollodorus, Euphranor and Nicias while Thebes had Nicomachus and his students, Aristeides and Philoxenus of Eretria. Particularly outstanding was the long line of erudite painters working in Sicyon (Eupompus, Pamphylus, Melanthius, Pausias), who secured for painting the status of a true liberal art. It was from this milieu that the figure of Apelles emerged, and it was the example of Eupompus that led Lysippus to his vocation.

In looking back on the earliest phases of monumental Greek painting, through the prism of written sources, we do not encounter wall-painting as the primary affirmation of the great painting. Though some texts do mention frescoes, such as those executed by Polygnotus at Plataea and Thespiae, archaeological sources confirm that the paintings of Polygnotus and Micon were done instead on large wooden panels which were then affixed to a wall. The expansion of painting and the consequent development of connoisseurship, as witnessed by certain remarks of Aristotle, conspired to favor the notion of the portable picture which lent itself to collecting. Thus we see Aratus winning the favor of Ptolemy III by assembling for him a collection of the prized paintings of the Sicyonian school. Athenaeus describes in *The Learned Banquet* (V. 196e) how such works had been incorporated into the decorations for the banquet tent of Ptolemy II. Another example of their importance can be seen in the early practice of copying paintings for domestic decoration, as can be seen by the example of the pebble mosaics from

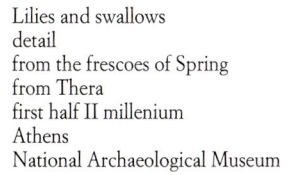

Lilies and swallows
detail
from the frescoes of Spring
from Thera
first half II millenium
Athens
National Archaeological Museum

Blue monkeys
detail of a fresco
from Thera
first half II millenium
Athens
National Archaeological Museum

Pella of the late fourth century B.C. The phenomenon continues with the Roman conquest: following the sieges of Syracuse and, to an even greater extent, Corinth, paintings were carried by the victors in triumph along with other precious spoils of war. This is why the antique accounts tend to valorize these portable works rather than wall-paintings, except in cases where the latter were venerated relics of the past. Indeed, Vitruvius (*On Architecture* II. 8. 9) and Pliny the Elder (*Natural History* XXXV. 154 and 173) cite numerous examples of wall-paintings being detached and set in wooden frames so as to facilitate their decorative utility. The visit to the *pinakotheke*, or picture gallery, is a recurrent theme in literature from the Hellenistic period onward. A reflection of what these galleries must have looked like is found in the *trompe-l'oeil* frescoes of the Villa Farnesina in Rome, perhaps once a residence of Agrippa.

Today, with the evidence of the "grotesques" brought to light in the Renaissance, the frescoes of Pompeii and Herculaneum, and the countless number of discoveries made since the beginning of this century, our knowledge of ancient painting has come to be based largely on wall decorations or on objects such as votive images and funerary *stelai* which used stone or terra-cotta as their support. Surviving examples of wooden panel paintings are either rare (i.e., the Archaic panels of Pitsà in the Peloponnese) or part of an homogeneous and well-circumscribed whole (the Fayûm portraits from Egypt). After a first period of rather important discoveries and publications during the first two decades of this century (the various *stelai* of Pagasae-Demetrias (Volos), Sidon, Thebes, and Alexandria; the funerary paintings found in southern Russia, southern Italy and Etruria; the domestic decorations of Delos, etc.), the late 1950s saw the start of an extraordinary renewal of archaeological efforts which have added greatly to the available documentation. The discoveries range from the Archaic to the Hellenistic periods – the frescoes of Lycia; the "Tomb of the Diver" at Paestum (Greek Poseidonia); Etruscan, Campanian, Lucanian, and Apulian funerary paintings; Alexandrian *stelai* and mosaics; Thracian and Macedonian tombs. Sophisticated techniques for the analysis of pictorial materials, of restoration and photography have revolutionized our conception of the "document" itself, in a field where its conservation is vested with particular import. Unlike written theoretical documents, which are often prescriptive or necessarily reduced to the mere enumeration of the subjects and authors of renowned works, archaeological research offers a more

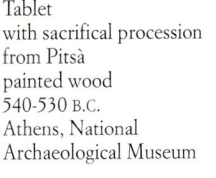

Tablet
with sacrifical procession
from Pitsà
painted wood
540-530 B.C.
Athens, National
Archaeological Museum

varied and concrete range of materials, capable of revealing new paths of study. Above all, it allows us to re-evaluate the periods and cultures which the written tradition has all but ignored. Only Egypt is mentioned by the Greco-Latin sources as a civilization in which a pictorial tradition had developed. They say nothing of Minoan painting, for example, and are silent on the subject of Mycenaean frescoes, the first manifestation of Greek painting.

Linked to the Minoan tradition, although with a character distinctly their own, the paintings found on the island of Thera (preserved, as at Pompeii and Herculaneum, thanks to a volcanic eruption) attest to the existence as early as the first half of the second millennium B.C. of complex decorative programs which brought together diverse representational techniques – imitation of veined marbling; naturalistic landscapes graced by lilies, swallows, blue monkeys, dolphins and antelopes; figures captured in characteristic poses, such as the fisherman with his catch, the boxer, women harvesting saffron. One can already detect the contrast between the candid treatment of female bodies, articulated by supple and subtle contours, and the

Fishing scene
detail
from the Tomb
Hunting and Fishing
ca. 530-520 B.C.
Tarquinia

Girls playing knucklebones
monochrome on a marble slab
by Ercolano
1st cent. B.C.
original dated
end 5th cent. B.C.
Naples
Museo Archeologico Nazionale

more indistinct ochre silhouette given to male forms. In the miniature frieze that decorates Room 5 of Thera's so-called West House, the landscape becomes a veritable historical compendium describing the movements of armies, a shipwreck, processions of dignitaries on parade in front of a city thronged with spectators. In Room 4 of the same house we find illusionistic representations of a ship's rails serving as the principal motif of the wall decoration, anticipating the *trompe-l'oeil* tradition.

Archaic painting is scarcely mentioned in contemporary accounts. One must wait until the Roman era to find evidence of an archaizing taste for earlier painting, most often celebrated by scholars of the antique in their researche of their own origins. Thanks to Pliny the Elder and Athenagoras, a Christian apologist of the second century, we have a record of the earliest periods of Greek painting and clay modelling, a record that is probably based on Hellenistic sources. It takes the form of fictionalized anecdotes concerning the art of "shadow painting" (*skiagraphia*), whereby the contours of the shadow cast by a man or animal upon a surface was traced and subsequently filled in with details and areas of flat color, at first monochromatic and later polychromatic. It is clear, however, that such a practice is a species of *a posteriori* construction, even if it is based on the observation of Archaic paintings. While these shadow paintings have been lost, a number of funerary paintings survive from various cultures situated in the periphery of the principal Greek cities, in which the practice of decorating the interior of the tombs with figural scenes was not in use. Thus we can observe the evolution of pictorial techniques, as soon as the seventh century B.C., in the wall decorations of some tombs at Veii and Caere (modern Cerveteri) in Etruria. These frescoes illustrate a hybrid artistic production, whereby techniques of representation derived from the Greek world are adapted to the exigencies of local aristocracies. Whenever it is possible to compare contemporary pictorial programs from different regions, we can see all the more clearly the coexistence of shared stylistic traits as practiced by the artists themselves, and the diversity of contents, often apparent in the compositional principles used, which characterize the intentions and values of the patrons. Significant discoveries in Asia Minor are particularly illuminating in this regard: the funerary decorations at Kizilbel and Karaburun in Lycia, and those found in the houses of Gordium in Phrygia allow us to evaluate with maximum precision the impact of Ionian models on Etruscan painting (i.e., the frescoes at Tarquinia, the painted terra-cotta slabs from Cerveteri) from the period between 540 and the end of the century, at which time the encroachment of the Persians caused a great number of artists to flee from the cities of Asia Minor toward the West. In the Tomb of Hunting and Fishing at Tarquinia, a pictorial-rhetorical *chiasmus* is engaged to organize the motifs of the two funerary chambers, pairing the themes of the banquet and the dance with scenes of hunting and fishing. In the boundless landscape that sprawls across the lower walls of the second chamber we can perhaps see a link with the scarce written testimony regarding archaic Ionian painting, the only instance in which such representations are mentioned at all. Similarly, according to

Mosiac with stag-hunting scene
firmato da Gnosis
end 4th cent. B.C.
Pella, Archaeological Museum

Herodotus (*Histories*, IV. 88), the architect Mandrocles, in the *heraion* of Samos, dedicated a painting to the subject of Darius and his army crossing the bridge he had built over the Bosporus. Though the tomb of Kizilbel does in fact include a painting of a sea voyage, it is the Etruscan monument that has always exemplified with the greatest clarity a distinctive feature of Ionian painting – the evocation of the landscape – which most likely developed as a result of contact with the eastern monarchies.

The earliest decades of the fifth century give us the chance to compare the banquet scenes of the Etruscan tombs with those of the Lycian tomb at Karaburun and the *symposion* depicted in the Tomb of the Diver at Paestum. The latter, an exceptional witness to the pictorial art of western Magna Graecia, creates a rebounding effect through its very conception, a result of the Greek city's relationship to the bordering cultures of Campania and Etruria, wherein the practice of funerary painting was widespread. Its importance depends not so much on its technique as on the depths of its meanings, achieved through an extraordinary economy of means. Indeed, the two artists responsible for this work betray, in both the treatment of color and mastery of drawing, a less refined technique than that which we find in the Lycian tomb or in any of its Etruscan counterparts. Yet few images in the lexicon of Lycian or Etruscan painting, which are aimed above all at celebrating the power and magnificence of the defunct, can rival the expressiveness, the sense of "disquieting strangeness" that we see in the pair of lovers in the *symposion*, or in the famed figure of the diver himself.

These monuments bring us to the threshold of the Classical period, from which no Greek originals have come down to us, apart from a number of funerary *stelai* and Macedonian funerary paintings. From the middle of the fifth century and throughout the first half of the fourth, the documentation still consists for the most part of ceramics and of Hellenistic and Roman imitations and copies, such as the paintings on marble at

A Survey of Greek Wall-Painting

The rape of Persephone by Hades
detail
from the Persephone Tomb
in the "large tumulus"
at Vergina in Macedonia
350 B.C.

Herculaneum. Often the most significant documents, such as the white-ground *lekythoi* or the engraved *stelai* of Thebes, tell us more about the art of drawing than that of color – which is appropriate insofar as virtuosity in drawing is a major feature of the Classical experience. Indeed, the texts mention monochromes on white grounds executed by Zeuxis. The only written fragment explicitly attributed to the founders of Hellenistic art criticism, Xenocrates and Antigonus of Carystus (Pliny the Elder, *Natural History* XXXV. 67) analyzes the use of line in defining contours in the work of Parrhasius. Also rather significant is Pliny's anecdote (*Natural History* XXXV. 81–83) concerning the "signatures" of Apelles and Protogenes, executed through the use of an ever finer and more subtle line. In describing one such "painting," the naturalist writes, "I saw it before [the fire in which it was destroyed]: its vast surface carried nothing but lines which were nearly invisible to the eye, appearing almost empty in the company of other masterpieces by various artists, but for precisely this reason it attracted one's attention, and was more worthy of esteem than any other work." Pliny additionally observed that unfinished paintings provoke stronger responses because in them "one sees the traces of the drawing, the very thoughts of the artist" (*Natural History* XXXV. 145).

All of this notwithstanding, Classical painting did in fact undergo a profound transformation, with the development of the technique of chiaroscuro, in both the representation of space and the expression of color. These developments permit us to define the Classical period as a breakthrough of sorts, the passage from a representational mode that can be called "archaic" – the kind of painting introduced in the past, in Egypt, and in Crete, from which Greek culture did not yet break away – to the "naturalistic" mode of representation which gave the pictorial arts of the West its first form and its first theorists.

The contribution of Macedonian funerary painting resides in its having provided a contemporary reflection of the full flowering of Greek painting proper, executed as it was for princes and kings, the noblest of clientele. In this case it becomes both possible and relevant to establish a direct connection between that which we have learned from texts and from archaeological sources. From the fifth century on, Macedonian rulers displayed a strong adherence to Greek culture, particularly that of Athens. The court of King Archelaus attracted artists and writers such as Euripides and the poet Agathon. Zeuxis, at the end of a career that took him from South Italy and Sicily (from whence he probably came) to Athens and Asia Minor, decorated the king's palace and gave him a painting depicting the god Pan as a present. This decisive patronage of the Macedonian kings which followed the trajectory of their own political ascendancy was carried on by Alexander the Great after his conquest of the eastern Mediterranean basin. Meanwhile, the Macedonian aristocracy continued to maintain the custom, foreign to the Greek cities, of burying their dead beneath conspicuous funerary mounds, a practice to which we owe from the last century onward the discovery of monumental tombs dating from the fourth–third century B.C. Such tombs are characterized by facades decorated with false architecture, accompanied in some instances by figural decorations, and in others found within the burial chambers themselves. A number of cist tombs have survived which contain decorated marble furnishings, such as thrones and beds. Despite the fact that such paintings were executed on stone supports, we are nonetheless struck by the variety of pictorial techniques in use at this time. We can conclude that, from the end of the fourth century B.C. onward, Greek painters had at their disposal a range of expressive means which we find codified and, in effect, preserved in Hellenistic painting. As such, the pictorial decorations of the so-called Tomb of Persephone and those of the Tomb of Philip II, discovered in 1977, beneath an enormous burial mound, some 110 meters wide known as the "Great Tumulus" in present-day Vergina (formerly Aegae, the ancient capital of the Macedonian kings), bear markedly different stylistic traits.

In the first tomb, depicting the rape of Persephone by Hades, the painting is distinguished by a rapidity of

Hunting scene
detail
from the painted decoration
on the front
of Philip II's tomb
in the "large tumulus" at Vergina
340-330 B.C.

execution, underscored by the quick strokes and incisions of the preparatory drawing which lays out the basic volumes of the faces and figures. We see a contrast between the rendering of characters such as the mourning Demeter, the Fates and Hermes, conceived essentially in terms of drawing, with nervous contours that stand out against the white ground, and the lively oppositions of color in the draperies of Persephone and the nymph Cyane. The most remarkable visual effect is created by the face of Hades, constructed entirely of juxtaposed brush strokes of different colors which provide an impression of blurred indistinctness, particularly in the figure's glazed stare, a most appropriate characterization for the god of the invisible. The attribution of the frescoes to the workshop of Nicomachus of Thebes proposed by Manolis Andronikos, who discovered the tomb, has been definitively confirmed by Paolo Moreno on the basis of their proximity to the mosaic from the House of the Faun at Pompeii depicting the battle between Darius and Alexander, which by common consent is taken to be a copy of a painting executed for King Cassander by Philoxenus of Eretria, a pupil of Nicomachus. Indeed, Philoxenus was renowned for the rapidity of his technique, which the antique sources refer to as his art of "abbreviation." In this regard he even surpassed his master, also celebrated for his painterly efficiency. It is not insignificant that Nicomachus is recorded as having used this gift to execute a funerary monument in the course of just a few days. In *The Rape of Persephone*, the painter capitalizes on the limits inherent in the fresco technique so as to accentuate the violence inherent in the subject.

Another style entirely distinguishes the hunting scene that adorns the facade of the second tomb, discovered at the same burial site, inviolate – the royal sepulcher of Philip II, who was murdered in 336 B.C. The technique is at once telling: we are not dealing here with a simple fresco, for the painter continued to work even after the *intonaco* had dried, re-wetting the surface in order to tighten up the colors and details, thereby approaching the technique of easel painting. The carefully planned composition creates an effect of perpetual movement while at the same time causing the figure at the center of the frieze, a young knight wearing a crown whose features allow us to identify him as Alexander the Great, to stand out. There are in all four different hunting scenes depicted here, organized in terms of the two central scenes of the boar and the lion hunt, both focused upon the actual slaying of the animal, and the two lateral scenes of the deer hunt, on the left, and the bear hunt on the right, which depict the hunters engaged in other activities, such as the pursuit of a wounded animal. This compositional conceit creates the impression of a broken narrative that operates from either side of the depicted scene. Furthermore, the core of the composition – the lion hunt, in which the principal figures are Alexander the Great and his father Philip II – is displaced slightly to the right. Another noteworthy aspect of the work, signaling a precocious development of the art of landscape painting, is the importance given to the natural setting. We are no longer looking at a cursory, symbolic suggestion of a setting, as in the Tomb of the Diver. In the painting from Vergina, the landscape is highly particularized; on the left, a sparse, sacred wood surrounds a votive column, while on the right, a somber forest and a rocky outcropping serve as a

Sarcophagus of the Amazons
details
from Tarquinia
4th cent. B.C.
Florence
Museo Archeologico Nazionale

framing device for the powerfully dramatized image of the deceased king, thus creating an atmosphere that underscores the action represented. Though functioning in part as dynastic propaganda – the young Alexander, through his participation in the royal hunt, is designated as his father's legitimate successor – the Vergina frieze, like the mosaic of *The Battle of Alexander and Darius*, is an eloquent exemplar of the principles of Classical painting as dictated by Aristotle: a painting is above all a dramatic narrative, which captures the crucial moment in which the characters are unveiled.

From a technical point of view, however, an image more strictly faithful to Classical norms is the one which adorns the back of the marble throne discovered in the Tomb of Eurydice, also at Aegae, which depicts the epiphany of the gods of the Underworld. The fact that it is an imitation of a painting is underlined by the rich molding in the form of a scroll which functions as a frame. In addition to the use of precious materials such as gold leaf in certain parts of the decoration, one notices the exceptional refinement of the modeling, particularly in the musculature of the horses. These horses are akin to such animal figures to be found in works by artists from the region of Taras (modern Taranto), of which the marble Sarcophagus of the Amazons, discovered at Tarquinia but of Italiot manufacture, is an exemple.

Indeed, the techniques of painting on marble, which was practiced by even the greatest artists – Nicias, for example – are closest to those of easel painting as described in the written sources. These same techniques were also used on different types of stone supports. As such, we are not without a good number of surviving works, beginning with the *stelai* discovered at the Great Tumulus of Vergina, and to which we can add the metopes of a tomb discovered at Cyrene in the nineteenth century, now in the Louvre. Also of great importance are the results of the work by a French and German research team on the *stelai* of Pagasae-Demetrias, in Thessaly. These paintings, executed *a tempera* with the brush, utilize an albumen-based binder instead of the wax that characterizes encaustic painting, a technique described in

Reconstruction of the facade
of the tomb
at Lefkadia, Macedonia

the antique texts which is still today a source of controversy and conjecture. These paintings result from the overlapping and blending of colors over a preparatory layer in which drawn contours give form to the figures. Not even in the tomb paintings of Cyrene does the encaustic technique appear for the rendering of figures, though the red used for the architectural elements is in fact a vermilion bound with wax.

The Tomb of the Last Judgment at Lefkadia perhaps gives us a glimpse into the techniques of *trompe-l'oeil* painting, designated by the ancient authors – Plato in particular – by the name *skiagraphia*, though the use of the term had evolved since first being used for the aforementioned shadow painting of the Archaic period. The aim of *skiagraphia* was to trick the senses, and it probably grew out of experiments in the field of theatrical set design. Plato censures this aspect of the art of his own time, seeing it as a perversion of the painter's art, a transgression of the perfection that should be the goal of any good artisan. In the Lefkadia tomb, whose entire architectural facade is set upon a *trompe-l'oeil* executed in stucco and paint, some of the figures depicted in the lower intercolumniation of the monument – especially that of Rhadamanthys, one of the judges who welcomes the dead, led by Hermes, to Hades – are rendered by means of fine strokes of unblended color which, in their juxtaposed proximity, are blended instead by the eye. The painter has explicitly avoided smooth chromatic gradations, taking into account the distance of the image from the viewer, thus creating the illusion of relief by playing on the optical fusion of unmixed and partially overlapping colors.

Having focused thus far on figural painting, we cannot forget the fundamental importance of wall decoration, whether residential or funerary, for the history of the tradition of architectural ornamentation which would result in the so-called First and Second Styles of the Roman era. The funerary painting of the fourth–third century B.C. is particularly rich, and is distributed throughout the eastern Mediterranean basin, from Alexandria to Apulia, from southern Russia to Macedon to Thrace.

It is by emphasizing this point that we would like to conclude this survey: the extraordinary diffusion of the new techniques of representation and of new iconographies, fruit of the researches and the creations of Classical Greek painting. One of the more immediate reasons for this was the power and effectiveness of the images themselves, made so through the mastery of light effects and the representation of bodies in three-dimensional space. Perfectly in step with these kinds of artistic developments, the social force of

A Survey of Greek Wall-Painting

Women bearing offerings and *quadriga*
detail of the frescoes
of the cupola
of a tomb
Kazanlăk (Bulgaria)
end 4th cent. B.C.

Funerary *stele*
with Macedonian horseman
end 4th cent. B.C.
Alessandria, Greco-Roman Museum

aristocratic self-celebration – among the more important themes in funerary painting – helped to cultivate the art of the portrait, the symbolic objects of social status. And thus we find the image of the heroic knight, its form varying in accordance with the peculiarities of a given culture, appearing in the tombs of Thrace, in the necropolis of Spinazzo (near Paestum), or on the facade of Hypogeum 1 at the necropolis of Mustafa Pasha in Alexandria. By studying the type of client for whom a monument was created, we can distinguish various stages in the progressive popularization of certain motifs, from the tombs, for example, of the Macedonian officers to the *stelai* of the mercenaries. Again, we must not forget the elegance and refinement of non-figural, decorative painting as exemplified by the vegetal motifs favored since the dawn of domestic luxury, whose forms made their way into every aspect of artistic production.

A final point which seems worthy of note: the importance of the contribution of the western Greeks to the development of painting at the threshold of the Hellenistic period, thanks to the influence of great cities like Tarentum, Neapolis, and Syracuse, as well as to the ability of the local aristocracies – Apulians, Lucanians, Campanians, Etruscans – to absorb and avail themselves of this common patrimony at a time when the expansion of the Romans made it possible for all the expressive resources of these new visual languages to come together, a process that is perhaps best embodied in the emblematic figure of Fabius Pictor, painter and aristocrat.

Bibliography
A. ADRIANI, in "Annuaire du Musée Gréco-Romain", 1933/34-1934/35, 1936; F. TINÈ BERTOCCHI, 1964; PH. PETSAS, 1966; M. NAPOLI, 1970; F. VILLARD, in *Grèce Archaïque*, 1968 (ed. it. *La Grecia arcaica*, 1969); *Grèce Classique*, 1969 (ed. it. *La Grecia classica*, 1970); *Grèce Hellénistique*, 1970 (ed. it. *La Grecia ellenistica*, 1971); M.J. MELLINK, in "Mélanges Mansel", 1, 1974, pp. 537-547; M.J. MELLINK, in "Mélanges Mansel", 1, 1974, pp. 537-547; L. BACCHIELLI, in "Quaderni di Archeologia della Libia", 8, 1976, pp. 355-383; V.J. BRUNO, 1977; M.J. MELLINK, Atti del X Congresso Internazionale di Archeologia Classica, 1978, pp. 805-809; P. MORENO, *La conquista...* in "Storia e civiltà dei Greci", 4, 1979, pp. 631-676; *La pittura in Macedonia...*, in "Storia e civiltà dei Greci", 6, 1979, pp. 703-721; *La pittura tra classicità...*, in "Storia e civiltà dei Greci", 6, 1979, pp. 458-520; R. BIANCHI BANDINELLI, 1980; F. COARELLI, in "Nuove ricerche e studi...", 1983, pp. 547-557; *Lettura ed interpretazione della produzione pittorica...*, in "DArch", 1983.2 e 1984.1, ripubblicato con il titolo *Ricerche di Pittura Ellenistica*, in "Quaderni dei Dialoghi di Archeologia", I, 1985; A. REINACH, in "Recueil Milliet", 1921, ripubblicato, 1985; M. ANDRONIKOS, 1987; V. VON GRAEVE-B. HELLY, in "PACT", 17-1.2, 1987, pp. 17-33; P. MORENO, 1987; A. ROUVERET, B.E.F.A.R. 274, 1989; *Pittura Etrusca...*, 1989; G. PUGLIESE CARRATELLI, 1990; M. TORELLI, in *Magna Grecia, Epiro e Macedonia*, Atti del XXIV Convegno di Studi sulla Magna Grecia (1984), 1990, pp. 399-410; CHR. DOUMAS, 1992; A. PONTRANDOLFO-A. ROUVERET, 1992; R. GINOUVÈS ET AL., 1993; S.G. MILLER, 1993; J. VALEVA, in "Functional and Spatial Analysis...", 1993, pp. 119-126; M. ANDRONIKOS, 1994; I. SCHEIBLER, 1994; *L'Italie méridionale...*, Atti della tavola rotonda, 1994 (forthcoming); I. BALDASSARRE-A. ROUVERET, in "Céramique et peinture...", 1995 (forthcoming).

Lucia Vagnetti

The First Contacts between the Minoan-Mycenaean and the Western Mediterranean Worlds

Detail of the wall inside a thermal *tholos* at Lipari

Any historical and archaeological survey of the western Greeks should include an examination – however brief – of the questions and information arising from regular contact between Greece and the central-western Mediterranean during the second millennium B.C.

Indeed, since prehistoric times the Aegean peoples had intense and enduring relations with the peoples who inhabited neighboring regions and even more distant lands. The geographic situation of Greece, thrust into the sea and characterized by heavy territorial fragmentation, certainly contributed in part to this tendency; on the other hand, raw materials were so scarce that it was often necessary to seek them elsewhere, even at great distance. Naturally, this phenomenon reached its greatest expansion and intensity, with complex economic developments, during the Late Bronze Age (second half of the second millennium).

Crete, when the palatial culture had reached the height of its splendor (ca. 1700–1500 B.C.), had intense relations with Egypt, Cyprus, the eastern islands of the Aegean, and the shores of Asia Minor. In the same period, the Greek peninsula, characterized by the advanced stages of the so-called Middle Helladic culture, seems to have been less projected toward the overseas world and substantially outside of the international trade and communications network of which Crete was so much a part. The cultural shift on the Greek peninsula from its Middle Helladic roots to a material culture and socioeconomic organization that were typically Mycenaean seems to have been a gradual process that occurred unevenly in time and space.

The first areas to be affected were the leading centers in the Argolid and Messenia, which were soon joined by the neighboring regions, Laconia, Attica, and Boeotia.

The period during which the Mycenaean civilization took form and consolidated probably lasted a century and a half, over which time rather complex intercultural relations became established, whereby the Mycenaeans showed a marked interest in the surrounding areas, at first in a selective way, and then increasingly systematically, in the end embracing a vast geographical area.

The study of Mycenaean relations with the central-western Mediterranean peoples cannot omit an overview of long-distance trade in the Late Bronze Age, in which the Mycenaeans without a doubt played a leading role.

Archaeological elements datable to the early stages in the Mycenaean civilization (sixteenth-fifteenth centuries B.C.) first appear alongside elements of Minoan origin (later replacing them) in the islands of the Aegean, along the Aegean coast of Anatolia, on Cyprus, on the Levantine coast, and in Egypt. As far as the central-western Mediterranean is concerned, unlike what happened in the eastern areas, interconnections during the Mycenaean age do not appear to have been preceded by contacts in Minoan times. Thus, it is highly significant that the earliest archaeological evidence of Mycenaean origin in Italy, belongs to the formative phase of that civilization and appears in greater quantities than elements of the same period discovered in the East.

From the point of view of distribution, the finds datable to the sixteenth and fifteenth centuries B.C., (almost exclusively pottery) are mainly concentrated in the archipelagos of the southern Tyrrhenian, in particular on the Aeolian Islands (Lipari and Filicudi) and the Phlegraean Islands (Ischia and Vivara), with a few scattered traces along the southern Italian coast, from the Gargano to Ionian Calabria. Only recently has this data been joined by preliminary reports of Aegean-type materials of such early date found in southern Sicily as well.

An extraordinary architectural monument on the island of Lipari, recently identified and cleaned, might belong to this phase. It is a small, *tholos*-type structure, in many respects quite similar to Mycenaean *tholoi*, outfitted as a thermal stove heated by a hot water spring with outstanding healing powers. The presence in the deepest layers of prehistoric materials contemporary to the proto-Mycenaean phase (Capo Graziano culture) seems to indicate clearly that the structure took its inspiration from Aegean models.

Toward the close of the fifteenth century B.C., and even more so in the following century, the political and economic power and the Mycenaean palatial organization were fully consolidated. Archaeological, epigraphic, and textual evidence all offer proof of this, clearly indicating that of Rhodes and Crete, two key regions in the area under consideration, entered into the Mycenaean orbit. Anatolia, Cyprus, the Levant, and Egypt are densely dotted with Mycenaean archaeological evidence, which is also abundant in the central Mediterranean, but in the latter, there are major shifts in the main areas of activity. Interest in the Phlegraean Islands, where archaeological documentation dates no later than the start of the fourteenth century B.C., seems to have waned, while it seems to have remained alive for the Aeolian archipelago, with only some changes that seem to follow the evolution of the island settle-

The First Contacts between the Minoan-Mycenaean and the Western Mediterranean Worlds

Prehistoric huts
on the acropolis at Lipari

Single-handled cup
from the acropolis at Lipari
Mycenaean I-II (1500-1425 B.C.)
Lipari
Museo Archeologico Regionale Eoliano

ments. In fact, the large settlement area of Lipari continued to flourish, while that of Filicudi ceased to exist, perhaps having been replaced by that of Panarea, wose position was more favorable for links with the Italian peninsula.

Most of the finds in Sicily date from the fourteenth and the early thirteenth centuries. They are largely concentrated in the native cemeteries of the Syracuse area, among which that of Thapsos is outstanding in importance and rich in Mycenaean artifacts. The Cypriot and Maltese pottery found alongside the Mycenaean objects gives a tangible idea of the variety of trade carried on in that highly important site. The settlement of Thapsos brought to light over the past twenty years has various building stages that show its transformation from an indigenous-type settlement made up of round huts, presumably contemporary to the fourteenth-century graves, to a planned settlement made up of multi-roomed rectangular structures opening onto a paved square the exact dating of which has not yet been defined.

Recent excavations at the Cannatello settlement east of Agrigento and just inland of the coast have brought to light plentiful Mycenaean and Cypriot pottery of the same period, a meaningful complement to the Aegean and Cypriot elements already identified in various sites along the Platani River Valley.

As far as the Italian peninsula is concerned, most of our data concerning these phases is concentrated in the south – especially Apulia, Basilicata and northern Ionian Calabria – where we know of a few

Grave goods from Tomb D
in the necropolis of Thapsos
Mycenaean III A 22
Syracuse
Museo Archeologico Regionale
Cat. 19

The First Contacts between the Minoan-Mycenaean and the Western Mediterranean Worlds

Mycenaean jug
from the necropolis of Thapsos
Mycenaean III A
Syracuse
Museo Archeologico Regionale

Mycenaean female figurine
from Scoglio del Tonno
1375-1300 B.C.
Taranto, Museo Nazionale
Cat. 16

dozen settlements, chiefly along the coast or just inland of it, that have yielded a number of Aegean and Mycenaean artifacts.

The most important center in terms of direct relations with the Mycenaean citadels seems to be the Scoglio del Tonno settlement situated at the mouth of the Mare Piccolo at modern Taranto, one of the most extraordinary natural inlets of the Mediterranean for its size and safety. Such topographic circumstances are all the more meaningful when compared to those of the main lagoon-harbors in the eastern Mediterranean and the northern coast of Africa, such as Tel Abu Hawam and Marsa Matruch, which were used by the Mycenaeans as landing points in the same period in which they periodically visited the shores of Apulia. The Scoglio del Tonno is also one of the rare sites in southern Italy that have yielded abundant materials as early as the fourteenth century, while those found in most of the other fairly well-explored sites seem to be primarily datable to the thirteenth century and after.

It is worth noting here that our knowledge of Mycenaean-age harbors and mooring points is unfortunately quite limited and fragmentary because the strategically situated settlements have continued to be inhabited over the centuries; this fact makes it practically impossible to explore them thoroughly and thus to obtain information that would shed light on various aspects of the trade relations between the Aegean and Italy.

But, although the research of the past fifteen years has not adequately met the problem of ports of call, it has brought to light a series of settlements just inland of the Ionian coast of Basilicata and northern Calabria which have provided data that shed new light on the quality of relations between the Aegean and the Italian peninsula, especially from the thirteenth century.

The best-documented case at present is that of the Sybaris area, a region characterized by the plain of the Crati River (ancient Crathis) and the surrounding hills. Since 1979 this area has been the focus of systematic protohistoric study and excavations, in particular at the sites of Broglio di Trebisacce and Torre Mordillo, situated respectively north and south of the Crathis.

The plentiful Aegean-type pottery was once believed to have been all imported ware, but upon closer examination it showed technological and typological peculiarities that suggested it was imitation. Confirmation in this respect was offered by a sweeping archaeometric research campaign.

In addition to the Aegean-type pottery, two classes of specialized pottery traceable to the Aegean tradition have been identified at both Broglio and Torre Mordillo. These are the fine gray, wheel-made wares that recall in technique the Minyan Ware of the Middle Helladic period, and a class of large containers made of refined clay, the so-called *dolia* with rope decoration inspired by the characteristic Aegean *pithoi*, mainly, but not exclusively, used for the storage of foodstuffs. These classes, too, should be considered of local or regional manufacture in light of archaeological considerations as well as archaeometric analysis.

The data from the Sybaris area raise the question of the organization of crafts production and the processes of acculturation that led to the specialized production of Aegean-inspired pottery in a setting that continued to make pottery for most everyday needs from unrefined clay, without the aid of the wheel, unpainted and fired using unsophisticated methods. The most widely accepted theory at present suggests the presence, at least at the beginning, of itinerant craftsmen of Aegean origin and training who circulated in both contexts, similarly to what we know occurred with metalsmiths.

As far as Aegean-type, but locally produced, painted ware is concerned, a site just inland of the coast and of the greatest importance (although it is only known through preliminary reports) is that of Termitito in Basilicata, situated in the valley of the Cavone. The extraordinary abundance and variety of Aegean-type finds – our knowledge of which, however, is thus far limited and of a preliminary nature – make it a key point for understanding the questions surrounding the "Italo-Mycenaean" workshops

Italo-Mycenaean chalice
from Termitito
13th-12th cent. B.C.
Policoro, Museo Nazionale
Archeologico della Siritide

Italo-Mycenaean *amphora*
from Broglio di Trebisacce
13th-12th cent. B.C.
Sibari, Museo Nazionale
Archeologico della Sibaritide

and, especially, their differentiation in the various regional areas and the possible domestic circulation of their products.

The panorama of our data in recent years has broadened and been enriched considerably, thanks also to a series of discoveries in Sardinia. Up to a very few years ago, possible Aegean relations with the large island were more theoretical than documented. In the opinion of some scholars, the *tholos*-type vaults of the inner chambers of some nuragic towers, suggestively similar to examples of Mycenaean funerary architecture, supported legends that link the mythical architect Daedalus with the island. Recent, in-depth debate shows how divided scholars are over the subject, though today most uphold the independence of the two phenomena.

As far as movable materials are concerned, the only evidence that in the past could reasonably be taken into consideration were the famous copper ox-hide ingots found on the island as early as the last century. The discovery of some fragments of Mycenaean pottery in the northeastern coastal zone (the Orosei\ territory) and, above all, the excavation at the Antigori *nuraghe* near Cagliari, where a large quantity of Mycenaean pottery has been brought to light, has helped to provide relative and absolute chronological links for the native materials, until recently of uncertain date.

At Antigori, alongside a remarkable quantity of thirteenth-century pottery imported from the Peloponnese, Crete and Cyprus, it is possible to identify imitations that show less careful craftsmanship than the "Italo-Mycenaean" ware of the Sybaris area or other sites in southern Italy. Recent research in the Arrubiu *nuraghe* at Orroli has brought to light a small Mycenaean vase of Peloponnesian provenance, datable to the fourteenth century, that seems to be the earliest piece of pottery found so far on the island. This would confirm the similar dating proposed for an important fragment of a small ivory head with a boar's tusk helmet, belonging to a well-known type of Mycenaean warrior, found at Decimoputzu in southern Sardinia.

The evidence from Sardinia takes on an even broader significance if compared with the very recent discovery of Mycenaean pottery on the Iberian peninsula, consisting of two small fragments, presumably from the Argolid, found at the protohistoric site of Llanete de los Moros in the upper Guadalquivir Valley, probably datable to the late fourteenth or the thirteenth century. Though rather scanty as far as evidence goes, they do suggest the existence of a port of some importance for foreign trade. Even if we cannot bar the possibility that ships from the eastern Mediterranean occasionally reached the Iberian shores, it would be more prudent to attribute the presence of the Llanete de los Moros fragments to trade between the Iberian peninsula and areas of the central Mediterranean that had frequent contacts with the Mycenaeans. An excellent candidate for this role would be Sardinia, whose relations with the Iberian peninsula are thoroughly documented for much of the Bronze Age. During the thirteenth century the powerful and well-equipped citadels of Mycenae, Tiryns, Thebes, and Gla were destroyed one after another and almost everywhere immediately reconstructed. Toward 1200 B.C. a further wave of destruction struck the Argolid citadels, the palace at Pylos, and many other centers. Even though some sites, such as Tiryns, Mycenae, and Argos, were built again and remained long active through the twelfth to eleventh centuries, the consequences of the destruction were irreversible as far as the political and socio-economic Palace-system was concerned. The debate over the causes of this event, and the subsequent disappearance of the centralized kind of economy that had characterized Greece in the Late Bronze Age, is still very much alive and we are still far from identifying a solution that is fully acceptable from all points of view. The blame has been variously laid on the Dorians, the so-called Sea Peoples, and interior social upheavals. More recently, these traditional hypotheses have been flanked by others based on the direct observation of data from archaeological surveys and digs, carried out with sophisticated modern techniques. It seems highly probable that the destruction of the palaces was caused by a series of disastrous earthquakes and consequent fires. This may have been followed by a period of famine that made the centralized, redistributive Palace economy unfeasible and ineffective and had inevitable repercussions on the trade networks. Thus, after the destruction of the palaces due to natural events, the end of the Mycenaean civilization came about gradually, in the form of a slow slump and recession that lasted about a century. During this time, non-palatial forms of Mycenaean life continued on a smaller scale, as demonstrated by recent excavations at the southern citadel of Tiryns, but also with a seeming concentration of the survivors in a few centers, in a sort of synechism. The centripetal movement probably went hand in hand with a centrifugal movement of some groups of people who shifted to the peripheral areas. This background information is necessary to sketch out the last stages of Mycenaean contacts with the outside world and to understand some of the processes of change that they foreshadow.

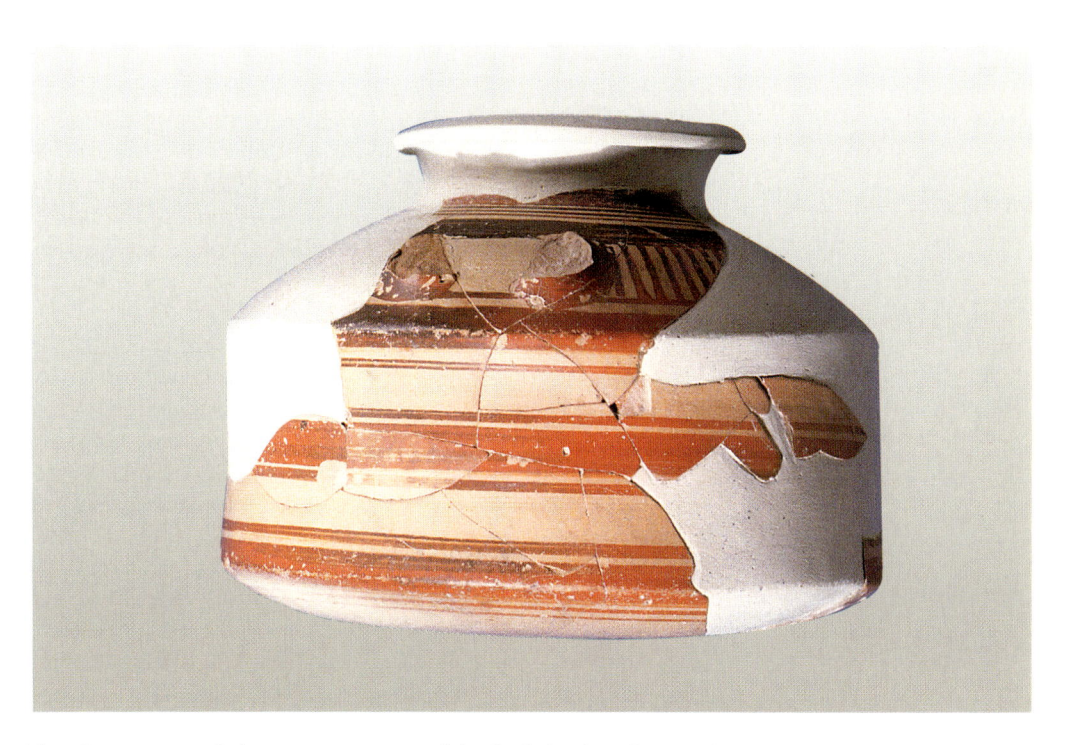

Angular painted *alabastron*
from Nuraghe Arrubiu di Orroli
Middle Bronze Age, 1400 B.C.
Sassari
Museo Archeologico "G.A. Sanna"
Cat. 18

The destruction of the Mycenaean citadels doubtlessly influenced relations with the West, even though archaeological evidence suggests no immediate breaks. On the other hand, as already demonstrated, the emergence of locally made pottery technologically and stylistically inspired by Aegean wares in various parts of southern Italy and Sardinia dates back to as early as the thirteenth century and gained momentum and diffusion in a second phase, when importation of Aegean pottery tapered off considerably, without, however, disappearing entirely. It may be assumed that Aegean-type pottery made in southern Italy was distributed along the interior trade routes of the Italian peninsula to peripheral regions, such as the Lazio area (Casale Nuovo) and the eastern Po Valley (Frettesina, Fondo Paviani, Villabartolomea).

In Sicily, already by the end of the thirteenth century but especially during the twelfth century, after importation from the Aegean had ground to a halt, a similar series of phenomena may be observed; in the sphere of Pantalica culture, the potter's wheel was introduced and a number of clay and metal forms inspired by the Aegean repertory were adopted, although no class of painted pottery of Mycenaean derivation emerged. The eastern Mediterranean influence in the architecture of some dwellings and funerary structures is striking.

As for Sardinia, just one fragment of imported ware from this phase has been found at Antigori, and we have still not been able to make a detailed analysis of the possible chronological distinction between the thirteenth and twelfth centuries for locally produced pottery. On the other hand, of particular interest in Sardinia is the rich array of metal goods that show very close links with Cypriot craftsmanship, for both the great abundance of ox-hide ingots scattered throughout the island and the use of special tools, clearly Cypriot in type and suited to metalcraft, as well as for the broad diffusion of rare status objects, such as the Cypriot tripods, known on the island through both imports and imitation.

Little evidence of the Cypriot presence has been found in southern Italy and it is known in Sicily almost exclusively through the fourteenth- and thirteenth-century pottery discovered in the Thapsos graves and recently at Cannatello. A few Cypriot metal items have also been found at Pantalica and in the district of Agrigento (ancient Acragas). Thus, the situation in Sardinia seems to be unique. In fact, it seems plausible that the kind of relationship that developed with the island hinged on its readily available resources and by its possible role as intermediary in supplying metals from further-away places; tin in particular was sought after as a necessary component of bronze. The rich deposits of tin in some of the westernmost parts of the island are well known, and the diffusion of the mineral has often been linked to the distribution of Atlantic-type crafts articles also found in Sardinia. Tin of western provenance took on increasing importance after 1200 B.C., given the destruction of Ugarit, the main port for the arrival and distribution of eastern tin.

This fact might explain the presence of such a strong Cypriot component in Sardinian metallurgy in the Final Bronze Age, echoed in the middle Tyrrhenian area of the Italian peninsula opposite, where alongside bronzes of Sardinian origin there were probably also introduced the well-known Cypriot bronzes of Piediluco-Contigliano.

To complete this overview, it should be noted that the most recent discoveries and studies have greatly narrowed the scope of the question of possible Mycenaean colonies, making it clear that there are no settlements of Mycenaean foundation or culture, nor are there any exclusively Mycenaean graves in the territories of historical colonization; there are only cases of more or less massive integrations into pre-existing local contexts.

In substance, the presently available evidence suggests, instead of settlements, systematic movements of small nuclei of residents in a predominantly, though not exclusively, east-west direction and a significant exchange of craft know-how, very probably thanks to the itinerant potters, bronzesmiths and maybe even master builders, especially in the advanced stages of the Late and Final Bronze Ages.

It seems better to describe such a context as the "precolonial phase" than that of "precolonization," reserving the latter term exclusively for the events that characterize the few decades between the ninth and eighth centuries on the eve of the foundation of the colonies. And we must make a net distinction between the political, economic and social realities in the Aegean that led to the Bronze Age interconnectins (the Palace) and those of the Age of Colonization (the *polis*).

Both the memory of the Bronze Age connections and the knowledge of the routes and territories were kept alive, especially in the Cypriot and Levantine spheres where groups of Mycenaeans probably put down new roots after the destruction of the palaces. This may have been a significant factor in the renewal of regular westward travel between the ninth and eighth centuries by the Greeks and Phoenicians, just before the foundation of the colonies.

Bibliography
W. TAYLOUR, 1958; F. BIANCOFIORE, 1967; L. VAGNETTI (ed.), *Magna Grecia...,* 1982; *Magna Grecia...* Proceedings of the 22nd Conference for the Study of Magna Graecia (Taranto, October 1982), 1983; F. LO SCHIAVO, E. MACNAMARA, L. VAGNETTI, PBSR, 53, 1985, pp. 1-70; M. MARAZZI, S. TUSA, L. VAGNETTI (eds.), *Traffici micenei nel Mediterraneo...* Proceedings of the Conference held in Palermo (May and December 1984), 1986; M. BALMUTH (ed.), *Studies in Sardinian Archaeology III,* 1986), BAR 387, 1987; F. LO SCHIAVO, E. MACNAMARA, L. VAGNETTI, "Late Cypriot Imports to Italy and Their Influence on Local Bronzework," PBSR, 53, pp. 1–70.

On the Lipari *tholos*
L. BERNABÒ BREA, M. CAVALIER, P. BELLI, *Studi Micenei ed Egeo-Anatolici*, XXVIII, 1990, pp. 7–78.

On the recent finds on the Iberian peninsula
J.C. MARTIN DE LA CRUZ, et al., in *Prähistorische Zeitschrift*, 65, 1990, pp. 49–52; idem, in *Seminari 1990...,* 1991, pp. 85–103.

Archaeometric studies on pottery
L. VAGNETTI, R.E. JONES, in *Problems in Greek Prehistory*, 1988, pp. 335–348; R.E. JONES, L. VAGNETTI, *Bronze Age Trade in the Mediterranean*, 1991, pp. 127–147.

David Ridgway   Relations between Cyprus and the West in the Precolonial Period

The Greek colonization of southern Italy and Sicily was achieved in different ways and for different reasons by a number of independent city-states from the second half of the eighth century B.C. onwards. It was preceded by a precolonial period, the essentially commercial nature of which was determined in turn by a series of phenomena that had for long affected a significantly wider area of the West. Given the inevitable predilection for the Greek point of view displayed by all ancient and most modern commentators on colonial matters, these earlier activities, in which precolonial Greeks joined at a comparatively late stage, have traditionally been assessed in terms of the awakening (ca. 850 B.C.) and subsequent renaissance (ca. 770 B.C. onwards) of Greece after the period of relative isolation that followed the demise of Mycenaean long-distance trade. In fact, it is becoming increasingly clear at the time of writing that the ninth-century Greek entrepreneurs, emerging from their Dark Age, cannot themselves be credited to any real extent with the reactivation and coordination of pan-Mediterranean commerce and contact. No less significantly for the future of Greece and for the diffusion and transmission to us of its genius, they rather re-established profitable relationships with areas of both the East and the West that had been well known to their Mycenaean predecessors, and had in the meantime never lost touch with each other. The Age that had been Dark in Greece had clearly not been so everywhere else, in other words; and the first stage of the major Greek expansion to the West, culminating in the establishment ca. 760 B.C. of the unique precolonial Euboean *emporion* of Pithekoussai (Ischia) in the Bay of Naples, was made possible by the revival around a century earlier of Greek participation in an East–West network of trade and culture that had been operating without a break since the Bronze Age.

In recent years, archaeological evidence, much of it frankly less than aesthetically pleasing in appearance, has accumulated from properly excavated contexts to suggest that this network owed the greater part of its continuing success to the long-standing exchange between some sectors of ideas, raw materials, services and technical skills. Economically and socially, and indeed culturally, the effect of these "invisible exports" went deeper and lasted longer than the attractive luxury goods from the Levant that were deposed in certain tenth- and ninth-century graves at Athens, Cnossos, and Lefkandi. It might even be supposed that the latter were in some sense made possible by the former, and thus amount to trace elements – readily identifiable in the archaeological record – of the less glamorous un-

Copper "oxhide-shaped" ingot
with incisions
II-I millennium B.C.
from Ozieri, Bisarcio district
Ozieri, Civico Museo Archeologico
Cat. 17

derlying processes that were at work in the wider world. However this may be, nothing less than an authentic axis has been defined, along which advanced metallurgical techniques – and, surely, personnel qualified to apply and teach them – were transmitted from Cyprus to Sardinia, where they were employed extensively throughout the four centuries of the local Late Bronze Age (ca. 1300–900 B.C.). Indeed, the earliest known piece of worked iron in the Western Mediterranean occurs in the Nuraghe Antigori (Sarroch), in stratigraphical association with a fragment of Late Cypriot II base ring ware (earlier than 1200 B.C.). Iron is rare in Cyprus: the search for it, and the processing of it *in loco* by resident Cypriot specialists and their local pupils, could well have provided an ideal technological context for the early introduction to Sardinia of the lost wax method of casting bronze, already available in the Levant and indispensable to the production of many local Sardinian types – not least the evocative category of human and animal figurines (and miniature boats) known as *bronzetti nuragici*, a number of which are now known to come from contexts that are demonstrably earlier than 900 B.C.

Three other artifact categories afford typological comparison between Cyprus and Sardinia (and in the West *only* Sardinia) that are both striking and instructive. The massive bronze double axes from various Sardinian sites find their closest parallels in the twelfth-century Enkomi hoards. The individual types in the remarkable Sardinian "kits" of smithing tools – all otherwise unknown not only in the West but also in Greece – are represented in firmly Late Cypriot III contexts (ca. 1200–1050 B.C.) in what is clearly their country of origin; so too are the *comparanda* for an imported bronze tripod stand (cast by the lost wax method), dated to the first half of the eleventh century and now in a private collection in Oristano. In addition, Cyprus and Sardinia both figure prominently on all distribution maps of copper ingots of the patently international ox-hide shape. Metallographic and other analyses have been combined to suggest a single source for more than seventy such ingots occurring in the range ca. 1500–900 B.C. on no fewer than eighteen sites in Sardinia.

Whether the single source of the substantial quantity of copper encountered in this form in Sardinia was Cyprus (as strongly suggested in some quarters) or Sardinia itself (which would be more logical) is not particularly important for the purposes of the present essay. There is rather more food for thought in the fact that the currency of an international ingot type seems to have been prolonged in Sardinia to a period substantially later than 1050 B.C. regarded with good reason as the round date after which the export of recognizably Cypriot artifacts to the West virtually ceased. This does not mean that Sardinia was in any sense cut off from the outside world. On the contrary, nuragic pottery (which is unlikely to have been exported for its own sake) has been found in post-1050 contexts on Lipari

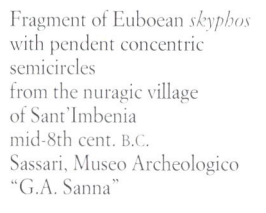

Fragment of Euboean *skyphos*
with pendent concentric
semicircles
from the nuragic village
of Sant'Imbenia
mid-8th cent. B.C.
Sassari, Museo Archeologico
"G.A. Sanna"

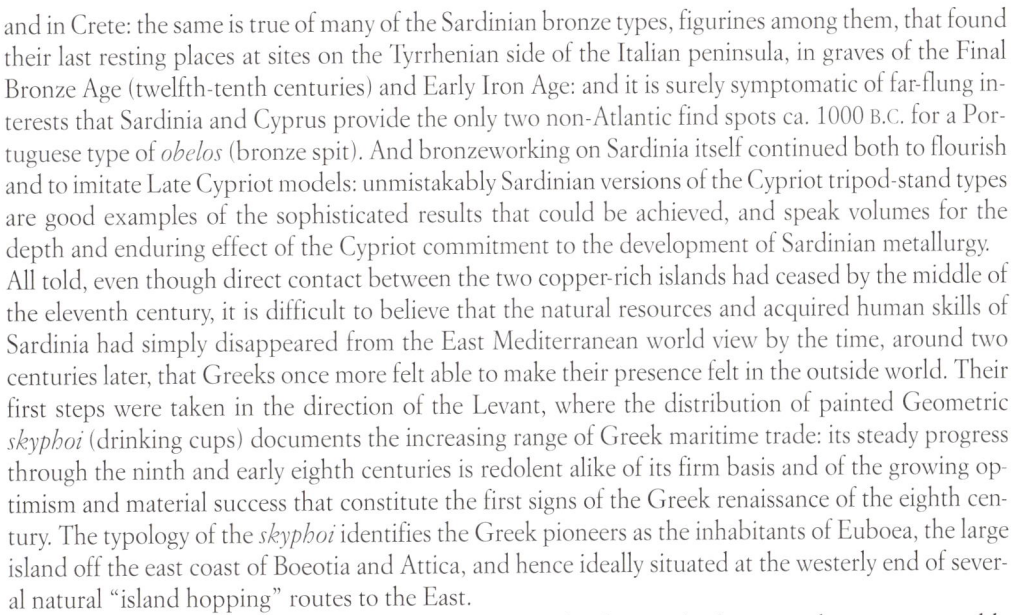

Relations between Cyprus and the West in the Precolonial Period

and in Crete: the same is true of many of the Sardinian bronze types, figurines among them, that found their last resting places at sites on the Tyrrhenian side of the Italian peninsula, in graves of the Final Bronze Age (twelfth-tenth centuries) and Early Iron Age: and it is surely symptomatic of far-flung interests that Sardinia and Cyprus provide the only two non-Atlantic find spots ca. 1000 B.C. for a Portuguese type of *obelos* (bronze spit). And bronzeworking on Sardinia itself continued both to flourish and to imitate Late Cypriot models: unmistakably Sardinian versions of the Cypriot tripod-stand types are good examples of the sophisticated results that could be achieved, and speak volumes for the depth and enduring effect of the Cypriot commitment to the development of Sardinian metallurgy.

All told, even though direct contact between the two copper-rich islands had ceased by the middle of the eleventh century, it is difficult to believe that the natural resources and acquired human skills of Sardinia had simply disappeared from the East Mediterranean world view by the time, around two centuries later, that Greeks once more felt able to make their presence felt in the outside world. Their first steps were taken in the direction of the Levant, where the distribution of painted Geometric *skyphoi* (drinking cups) documents the increasing range of Greek maritime trade: its steady progress through the ninth and early eighth centuries is redolent alike of its firm basis and of the growing optimism and material success that constitute the first signs of the Greek renaissance of the eighth century. The typology of the *skyphoi* identifies the Greek pioneers as the inhabitants of Euboea, the large island off the east coast of Boeotia and Attica, and hence ideally situated at the westerly end of several natural "island hopping" routes to the East.

Cyprus was reached at an early stage in the sequence of Euboean *skyphos* types that may reasonably be taken to symbolize the passing of the Greek Dark Age. It was not long before a few specimens of one type (decorated with instantly recognizable painted pendent concentric semicircles) reached three different areas of the West: eastern Sicily, not far from the site of the future Chalcidian colony of Leontini, southern Etruria, in the native Early Iron Age (Villanovan) cemeteries of Veii (Isola Farnese, Rome); and Sardinia, in the nuragic village of Sant'Imbenia, overlooking the Baia di Porto Conte (Alghero). Of these areas, the first two have long been recognized as interesting for one reason or another to the precolonial pioneers from the Aegean. In particular, the native Iron Age cemeteries of Tyrrhenian Italy (notably Veii, sixteen kilometers north of Rome, and Capua, pre-Hellenic Cumae and Pontecagnano in Campania) have yielded a number of imported and locally imitated "precolonial *skyphoi*" of various types. They have traditionally been seen as the trace elements left in the indigenous archaeological record by technologically ambitious Euboean "visitors" (or prospectors) prior to their exploitation of the ores – supposedly unappreciated locally, and hence previously untapped – in the *Colline Metallifere* of modern Tuscany (where, incidentally, precolonial *skyphoi* are conspicuous by their absence…) and to their consequent establishment of the precolonial *emporion* of Pithekoussai. As mentioned above, however, it is now known that the native society of northwest Etruria had already been penetrated as early as the Final Bronze Age by individuals, some of them probably of high social rank, whose grave goods included bronze artifacts brought from Sardinia. Much current speculation centres on the question of whether these nuragic pieces reached Etruria as a result of (dynastic?) marriage, sale, or gift: whatever the answer, the Sardinian connection is plain – and so too is the decided preference for the metal-rich area of the Italian peninsula. This being the case, it already seemed likely that the first mutually profitable exploration of Etruria's mineral resources was planned no further away than Sardinia, and that Euboeans joined – or tried to join – in the business of exploitation at a comparatively late stage. How is this hypothesis affected by the precolonial Euboean ceramic material recently found for the first time in Sardinia itself?

The remarkable discovery of a Euboean pendent semicircle *skyphos* at Sant'Imbenia was made as recently as 1990; excavation continues at the site, and no more than a brief preliminary notice has been published. From this, we learn that the find is part of a coherent non-funerary context that extends to all the other precolonial Euboean *skyphos* types attested in southern Etruria and Campania, Phoenician plates and other forms, and *amphorae* (of types that also find good parallels in Tyrrhenian Italy); one of the latter contained a hoard (ca. 44 kilos) of plano-convex copper ingots. As for the pendent semicircle *skyphos* itself, a preliminary opinion has been expressed that it is close to certain specimens found (but not necessarily made) in Cyprus; and it is slightly earlier in the sequence than the other Western examples of its type. At the time of writing, then, the oldest known piece of Euboean (or any kind of post-Mycenaean Greek) painted pottery in the West seems to come not from a Villanovan cemetery in southern Etruria (Veii), as has reasonably been supposed hitherto, but from a nuragic village on the northwest coast of Sardinia that was clearly a nodal point of international contact.

Fragment of Euboean cup
with chevrons
from the nuragic village
of Sant'Imbenia
mid-8th cent. B.C.
Sassari, Museo Archeologico
"G.A. Sanna"

Fragment of Euboean cup
with chevrons
from the nuragic village
of Sant'Imbenia
mid-8th cent. B.C.
Sassari, Museo Archeologico
"G.A. Sanna"

Further discussion of this new evidence will be possible when its acquisition and presentation are complete. For the moment, we may tentatively conclude that the occurrence on the same site of copper ingots and Euboean precolonial ceramic types confirms some kind of connection between metallurgy and the earliest stage yet attested of the Euboean relationship with the West. That this confirmation should come from Sardinia is surely not a coincidence. Cyprus, as we have seen, was reached by Euboean pioneers very soon after the end of the Greek Dark Age. There if anywhere traditions of Sardinian metal resources will have survived, for onward transmission to foreign visitors; there too, and at the same time (not long after ca. 850 B.C.), Phoenicians were taking their first steps towards the West by establishing their first overseas base, Kition, which ensured access for Tyre to the rich copper deposits of Tamassos. In the circumstances, it is hardly surprising that it is so difficult to disentangle the early Phoenician and Euboean initiatives in the West. Competition between the experienced navigators from Tyre and the newcomers from Eretria and Chalcis would have been so unequal as to seem unlikely. Perhaps we should do better to reflect on the degree of emulation that caused the Euboeans to establish their own first overseas base, Pithekoussai, in precisely the same kind of geographical situation as that notoriously preferred by the Phoenicians for their dealings with the native communities of Sicily ("headlands and small islands off the coast": Thucydides, VI. 2).

Bibliography
H.G. NIEMEYER, in "Jahrbuch... Mainz" 31, 1984, pp. 3-94; F. LO SCHIAVO, E. MACNAMARA, L. VAGNETTI, in "Papers of the British School at Rome", 53, 1985, pp. 1-71; L. VAGNETTI, F. LO SCHIAVO, in *Early Society in Cyprus*, 1989, pp. 217-243; S. BAFICO, in "Archeo" 74, April 1991, p. 18; D. RIDGWAY, 1992.

Giovanni Garbini The Phoenicians in the Western Mediterranean
(through to the Fifth Century B.C.)

Phoenician inscription
on a *stele*
from Nora, Sardinia
9th-8th cent. B.C.
Cagliari
Museo Archeologico Nazionale

The migration and settlement of peoples of eastern origin on the western shores of the Mediterranean Sea was a regular occurrence, and began in prehistoric times. The Mediterranean basin, and particularly its western shores, was a natural destination for the movements of ethnic groups that periodically migrated from the southwest section of the Euro-Asiatic continent. Such migrations were caused each time by different reasons, and issued from centers of various kinds, even remote, generating waves that invariably broke on the shores around the Strait of Gibraltar. The history of the Phoenicians in the West, a history that developed in the first millennium B.C., is one of the most significant examples of this type of ethnic movement. The Phoenician colonization drive, which took place in parallel with Greek expansion, introduced to these new settlement areas (North Africa, western Sicily, southwest Sardinia, southern Spain) an authentic urban culture with the foundation of the first towns, much the same as the Greeks were doing in the south of the Italian peninsula and on the east coast of Sicily. Greek and Phoenician expansion in the West was basically a uniform phenomenon, despite the differences in the type of development and the contingent causes that induced it. The need to seek new territories in which to expand was evidently one of the roots in both cases. To today's way of thinking, which is conditioned by a "traditional" view of the Greek world and its influences, it seems obvious to make a distinction between Greek colonization – which profoundly affected Etruscan and Roman cultures – and Phoenician colonization, whose influence on the Italian peninsula was basically marginal. The picture changes if we take the point of view of the western Mediterranean peoples observing the arrival of foreigners from some unclear provenance in the Orient. For the Italics, Siculi, Elymi, Sardi, Libyans, and Iberians, the appearance of new colonists signaled the disintegration of the existing balance of relations and the onset of a period of contrasts, irrespective of whether the intruders were Hellenes or Sidonians. In order to fully assess a historic event it is essential to pinpoint its temporal context. A satisfactory date for the arrival of the Phoenicians in the West is not yet forthcoming. Classical authors, such as Pliny (*Natural History* XVI. 216; XIX. 63) and Velleius Paterculus (I. 2) fixed the foundation of the first colonies in Utica, Cadiz, and Lixus (modern Larache) in Morocco to the twelfth century B.C.; for Carthage, however, sources based on Timaeus set the foundation date to around 814 B.C. These dates, which were considered tenable until the end of the last century, were first refuted by historians and subsequently by archaeological research which, in the best of cases, has not been able to go beyond the first half of the eighth century B.C. Since 1950 various attempts have been made to reconcile the contrasts between the literary sources (besides the classical texts there are those of the Old Testament) and the archaeological evidence by making a distinction between authentic colonization – which took place not before the second half of the eighth century B.C. – and earlier visits to the areas in question for strictly commercial purposes. Such activity is endorsed by archaeological evidence in the form of objects imported from the Levant or imitated in the West; the dates in question take us to the eleventh century B.C. In the 1980s the term "precolonization" was used, albeit for a limited period, to indicate the earliest phase of Phoenician presence in the West. The term is misleading and quite inappropriate, as the areas that were later settled do not coincide with those in which the Phoenicians previously conducted their trade. There are two quite distinct phenomena in question: on the one hand, we have the colonization process, which covers the last decades of the eighth century B.C. and the early seventh; and on the other, evidence of trading activity that predates settlement, with characteristics and players of a different nature. It is mistaken to consider them in reference to each other, or to uncritically accept the dates of the authors of antiquity, or those of the Bible (even less reliable).

A further source of historical confusion is the simplistic superimposing of the currently accepted definition of "Phoenician" to what the Greeks termed *phoinikes*. Today's Phoenicians were given their definition about the middle of this century, in reference to the people who in the first millennium B.C. inhabited the coastal towns and cities of modern Lebanon (Aradus, Byblos, Berytus, Sidon, Tyre), while the term *phoinikes* for the Greeks meant not only this ethnic group (called by both the Greeks and by themselves as Sidonians) but also the inhabitants of the coastal towns both north and south of the Lebanese coast, including those of Anatolia. The outcome of this misleading identification is that in many modern essays – and those that deal with the West in particular – the term "Phoenician" comprises also the Philistines of Palestine (who throughout the first millennium B.C. spoke and wrote almost exclusively in the Phoenician tongue), together with the Semites of Syria, the Aramaeans, whose writing in the first centuries of the first millennium B.C. was identical to Phoenician, though they spoke quite differently. These distinctions, which are irrelevant to the Greeks and have been largely overlooked by modern scholars, are useful for understanding the historical dynamics of the eastern expansion across the Mediterranean. From the fourteenth century B.C. on the western Mediterranean experienced ex-

Steatite scarab
with religious scene
and hieroglyphic
and Phoenician inscription
5th-4th cent. B.C.
Sant'Antioco, Biggio Collection

Amphora for transport
from Sulcis
8th cent. B.C.
Sant'Antioco, Museo Comunale

Phoenician *amphora*
for transport
from Carthage
6th-5th cent. B.C.
Carthage, Museum

tensive and frequent trade contacts with eastern peoples who exported their luxury goods (wine, oil, perfumes), usually stored in "Mycenaean" vases, whose production – contrary to the opinion of certain archaeologists – was not exclusive to the Mycenaeans but actually shared among many other groups, including the Aegeans and Anatolians, who practiced this form of trade and for whom writers tend to borrow the Egyptian expression the "Sea Peoples." These peoples comprised the Mycenaeans, and more generally all the Achaean peoples, though by no means exclusively. The activities of "Mycenaean" (i.e., Aegeo-Anatolian) elements in the Mediterranean intensified in the thirteenth century B.C., particularly in the second half, though in this period it took on different connotations, namely, the strictly commercial link gradually became more colonial and lasting, albeit still on limited scale, owing to the deep ethnic, political, and economic upheavals that shook the Aegean and the eastern Mediterranean basin from the mid-thirteenth century B.C. to the early part of the twelfth. It was in this way that in the "time of the Trojan War" (a distorted reflection of those dramatic events) the "Mycenaean" Sea Peoples established themselves in Palestine (Philistines, Tjeker, and Danaoi) and along the Anatolian coastlands (other Danaoi, Teresh at Tarsus), in Sicily (Sheqelesh), in Etruria (other Teresh), and in Sardinia (Sherdana). For around two centuries the new peoples succeeded in preserving their ethnic identity in terms of both language and material culture, before becoming assimilated with the indigenous cultures. This process, by which the Philistines became "Phoenician", was not substantially different from that which took place elsewhere. This explains the disappearance of "Mycenaean" wares, a fact that is elsewhere seen (in Helleno-centric terms) as the petering out of "Mycenaean" trade links.

The dire economic aftermath of the upheavals that so radically transformed the eastern Mediterranean in 1200 B.C. lasted almost two centuries. The upturn did not come until well into the eleventh century, and it was in this scenario of new political balances that the economy finally began to pick up, kindled by the quest for new sources of raw materials and new trade outlets. Given the situation, it seems only natural that the first peoples to ply the former trader routes of the Sea Peoples were indeed their descendants, not least the Philistines and the Tjeker tribes of Palestine. Both the Egyptian text *The Adventures of Wenamun* and Hebrew tradition credit these two with considerable trading prowess as early as the eleventh century B.C. It can be reliably inferred from this that their seafaring

*The Phoenicians in the Western Mediterranean
(through to the Fifth Century B.C.)*

activity was never entirely interrupted. It is fairly likely that the Bible account by which the Philistines held a kind of monopoly on iron in the eleventh-tenth centuries B.C. is reliable (1 Samuel 13: 19–21). When coupled with another item of information, this fact becomes even more cogent: in a particularly iron-rich area of northern Sardinia (echoed in such modern place-names as Montiferro, meaning "iron mount") there was also a town known at the time as Macompsisa (modern Macomer), whose root *maqom* means "market" in Phoenician; the meaning behind the last half of the word has not yet been deciphered. The curious thing is that there is no Phoenician settlement there, and that the Phoenicians never in fact reached this far inland, unless perhaps after the Carthaginian conquest. It therefore seems fairly certain that the town's name Macompsisa stems from trade activity that was linguistically Phoenician and was established before the arrival of the Phoenicians themselves in Sardinia, at a later date. One might suppose, therefore, that the Philistines discovered iron at Macompsisa, with which they manufactured metal tools that they sold to the Israelites. That underlying "oriental" slant of the nuragic statuettes with their Phoenician subject, typical to the La Nurra area (Sardinia), started in the ninth century B.C.; the ancient cultural affinity and historically documented exchange between the Peleshet and Sherdana, who had fought side-by-side against Egypt, offered the basis of the trade relations that sprang up so early between Philistines and Sardinians.

While, as indeed seems to be the case, the first eastern traders to frequent Sardinia were Philistines (without creating proper settlements, but dwelling, like the natives, in *nuraghi*), there are no clues enabling us to assign a precise provenance for the Levantine presence in eastern Sicily over the tenth–ninth centuries B.C. This activity is characterized by the introduction of iron, and suggests a stable settlement rather than just a trading outpost. As for ethnic groups that developed enduring relations with the chiefs of the abundant silver mines in the lower Guadalquivir in Spain, they most certainly hailed from Tyre (see also Justin, XLIV. 5. 1–2). The most evolved culture of Tartessus and perhaps a greater turnover of trade enabled the Tyre merchants to set up more enduring outposts in Iberia than the Philistines did in Sardinia. The foundation of Gades (modern Cadiz) dates to well in the eighth century, however (ca. 770 B.C.). Oddly, the name missing from this overview of trading posts of a fairly substantial nature is Etruria, the region with most abundant metal seams, and most easily reached by the oriental navigators, who undoubtedly knew they could find there members of their related tribe, the Teresh. There can be

Phoenician silver coins
made by the Sicilian mint
obverse and reverse
ca. 320-300 B.C.
Tunis, Bardaw Museum

Amphora for transport
from Monte Sirai
6th-5th cent. B.C.
Cagliari
Museo Archeologico Nazionale

The Phoenicians in the Western Mediterranean
(through to the Fifth Century B.C.)

only one explanation for utter lack of oriental undertones or imports from the Levant: the way was barred by the Etruscan fleets. This is the oldest manifestation of the Etruscan thalassocracy mentioned by Livy (V. 33. 7). Exactly why the Etruscans set up such a naval barrier is impossible to say, though some kind of accord with the Sardinians is a possibility (whose little votive ships have turned up in Etruscan tombs), or perhaps with the Philistines in Sardinia, who reached the island from the west. The situation changed toward 770 B.C., when the Etruscans – possibly yielding to the increasing pressures – consented the Greek and oriental merchants to open an *emporion* at Pithekoussai on the Isle of Ischia off the west coast of Italy, level with their southern frontier. Here, some decades later, inscriptions testify to the presence not only of Greeks from Euboea, but also Semites from Syria and the central and southern coasts. From the scattered evidence, however, it is unclear whether the latter group was Phoenician or Philistine; as for the former, an inscription and several characteristic Syrian seals picturing a lyre-player indicate that they were Aramaeans. These are another, somewhat unexpected, presence with which historians studying the Mediterranean basin will have to familiarize themselves, given the results of epigraphic studies made in the last ten years; it was the Aramaeans, who trafficked eastern goods around the Aegean in the ninth and eighth centuries B.C., having close links with the powerful kingdom of Damascus. In the last decades of the eighth century B.C. a change occurred which brought a radical reorganization of cultural presences in the western reaches of the Mediterranean. What had thitherto been a prevalently commercial movement, with the occasional sprouting of slightly larger settlement nuclei here and there, was transformed into a major colonization drive, lasting through most of the ensuing century. This wave of emigration stemmed prevalently from the coasts of Lebanon and its sibling, Cyprus. This was the period that saw the emergence of Selinus, Panormus, Motya in Sicily; Caralis, Nora, Bithia, Sulcis, and Tharros in Sardinia; Sexi (modern Almuñécar), Mezquitilla-Chorreras, Toscanos, Malaka (Malaga) in southern Spain; Carthage and Utica in Tunisia. The Phoenician migration effort – which must have been dramatic considering the rather meager population in the homeland – seems to have been catalyzed by a variety of causes which, moreover, we can only guess at. As for the precise provenance of the colonists, we are completely in the dark, except for Kart-Hadasht (Carthage), which became the new Tyrian "capital." The frequent claim that all or most of the Phoenician colonies in the West were of Tyrian origin is not borne out by the evidence. On the contrary, recent studies on the subject observe that not only are imported Phoenician items rare in the ancient Phoenician colonies, but that the colonial vase production is distinctly different in shape from that of the parent lands, such that it may even be modeled on pottery used by the Phoenicians residing in Egypt (A. Ciasca).

Remains of a nuragic village
at Su Muru Mannu, near Tharros
15th-8th cent. B.C.

The Phoenicians in the Western Mediterranean
(through to the Fifth Century B.C.)

Remains of a Punic settlement
at Tharros
9th-8th cent. B.C.

Remains of Punic cisterns found at Tharros

The surge in the population in the colonial centers that can be observed in the first decades of the seventh century was probably provoked by the arrival of "refugees" who fled Phoenicia after Assyrian forces under Esarhaddon (680–669 B.C.) tore through the homeland. Whereas for the early phases of colonization, a variety of theories have been put forward. The least likely cause is environmental (desertification of the land) coupled with overpopulation: these phenomena (which have yet to be ratified) are out of phase, as they must have taken place several hundred years before the eighth century B.C., and if such were the case, it is not clear why only some cities along the coast suffered from the widespread situation of hardship. More recently there has been suggestion of a form of colonization that reflected the economic thrust of Tyre, which was basically allied with Assyria. Besides the aforementioned fact that the major Phoenician cities were virtually extraneous to the wave of migration, it is hard to reconcile the picture of Phoenicia as a major political and economic power with the utterly modest dimensions of the early colonial settlements, sited in regions that were not previously in the network of trade routes. One of the least improbable causes is the hardship in Phoenicia caused by the Assyrian expansion under Tiglathpileser III (745–727 B.C.), upon which a great number of people sought refuge elsewhere.
Another point worth bearing in mind is the perfect chronological overlap of the Phoenician and Greek colonization drives, which both began around 725 B.C. with the dwindling commercial clout of Pithekoussai. This event marks the close of the Archaic period of trade in the western Mediterranean. The year 725 B.C. also marks the estimated date for the Euboean foundation of Cumae (Kyme), the first in the chain of Greek colonies West of an invisible line that ran from the northeast of Sardinia down to the *Arae Philaenorum* on the Libyan coast. Indeed, it can hardly be a coincidence that all the Phoenician colonies lie west of that line. This frontier delimiting the "colonial" zones, which foreshadows the geometrical frontiers of the European colonies in Africa, is too precise to be a question of chance. It is reasonable to infer that an understanding was reached between the Greeks and the Phoenicians, enabling the latter to keep their seaways through the Mediterranean free.
We know nothing of the earlier events of the colonies, which for simplicity we will refer to as "Phoenician," despite the proven existence of other ethnic input (Philistine in Cadiz and Tharros, perhaps Aramaean at Soluntum). Their activity was largely tied to trade across the Mediterranean, and there was no expansionist intention, even though problems with local inhabitants cannot be ruled out. This period of calm lasted throughout the seventh century B.C., until it was abruptly curtailed by the Greeks, who, not content with their complex internal wranglings, began to cast their nets wider. Toward the year 631 B.C. the foundation of Cyrene respected that invisible truce line between Greek and Phoenician spheres of activity. Whatever agreement there had been was broken by the Phocaeans in around 600 B.C. with

The Phoenicians in the Western Mediterranean
(through to the Fifth Century B.C.)

Phoenician umbonate
medallion pendents
and aedicule medallion
found at Tharros
7th-6th cent. B.C.
Cagliari
Museo Archeologico Nazionale

Phoenician gold bracelet
with winged scarab
found at Tharros
7th-6th cent. B.C.
Cagliari
Museo Archeologico Nazionale

the foundation of Massalia (Marseilles, France). The new seaport became a focus of Greek expansion toward the areas under Phoenician control. New Greek colonies sprang up at Nicaea (Nice), Rhode, Emporiae, and Maenaca (near Malaga), bringing the enterprising Greeks of Asia Minor into direct contact with the mines of Tartessus, which yielded them enormous lucre thanks to their fellowship with the legendary Arganthonius. What is not made explicit by Herodotus (I. 163–167), to whom we owe this piece of information, was the final outcome of the Massaliot policy as revealed by archaeological inquiry: between 600 B.C. and 550 B.C. all the Phoenician colonies east of Gibraltar met their end, together with the culture of Tartessus. With Spain laid waste, and new waves of refugees pouring in from Asia Minor, the Phocaeans turned their attention to the Mediterranean islands. Midway through the sixth century B.C. they founded a new colony, Alalia (modern Aleria, on the east coast of Corsica). It is no coincidence that it was in this period that the people of Tharros built the city's defense wall.
The Phocaeans were not the only ones to shatter the harmony in the Mediterranean. Toward the year 580 B.C. another Greek kinsman, Pentathlon, attempted to establish a way station at Lilybaeum, right opposite the Motyan colony, but was routed by the Elymi, the colony's protectors (Diodorus Siculus, V. 9; Thucydides, VI. 2. 6); in this case too, the city of Motya decided to erect a screen of defense.
It was in this general state of affairs that the power that was Carthage emerged. The very name of the city (Kart-Hadasht in Phoenician, meaning "new capital") alludes openly at the intended political role which the homeland capital Tyre entrusted to its new outpost, though that role did not last long –

Punic houses at Nora

The Phoenicians in the Western Mediterranean
(through to the Fifth Century B.C.)

Ruins of the Phoenician colony
at Motya (Mozia), Sicily

Punic votive *stele* from Mozia
6th-5th cent. B.C.
Mozia, Museo Whitaker

there was no need. Diodorus' claim (V. 16. 2–3) that the people of Carthage founded Ibiza in 654 B.C. has since been contradicted by archaeological finds. Ibiza was in fact founded midway through the seventh century by colonists from Cadiz. The Carthaginians did not reach the island until 540 B.C. or thereabouts. The fact that the Phoenicians were unable to deter the foundation of Massalia (Marseilles) nor curb its expansion along the western coast of the Mediterranean is strong evidence against any Carthaginian presence in the area.

A major change in circumstances took place in around 550 B.C., however. The Carthaginian reply to Phocaean presence in Iberia was the *de facto* annexation of the island of Ibiza, which lay in a strategic vantage point over traffic toward Spain and Sardinia (Tharros). When the Massaliots subsequently founded Alalia, Carthage quickly allied itself with the Etruscans, and the naval battle that ensued forced the Phocaeans to abandon Corsica (535 B.C.). In order to circumvent any further Greek attacks on Sicilian soil, the Carthaginians swarmed into the island, and thereby achieved a dual goal of creating a bastion against the Greek forces (the first to feel the effects was Dorieus in 510 B.C.; see Diodorus Siculus, X. 18. 6), and of annexing all the Phoenician colonies. The situation was polarized even further with the annexing of the Phoenician colonies in Sardinia, though the first attempts failed. On this account our only reference source is the Latin historian Justin (XVIII. 7. 1), and there is still much discussion as to whether it was the indigenous or the Phoenician colonists whom the Carthaginians fought. Given the overall political picture, there can be no doubt that Carthage hoped to subjugate the colonies, which at first managed to cling to their independence (thanks to Sardinian aid). This is amply confirmed by evidence found at the temple of Antas (situated near Iglesias, Sardinia), founded in the second half of the sixth century B.C., in which the national deity Sardus Pater was worshipped alongside Sid, the lord of Sidon, whom the Phoenicians dubbed *babi* (father) in the vernacular of Sardinia.

Until now, Carthage has been quoted somewhat generically. Actually, the sense of political cohesion that prevailed during this period was the work of a historical figure who goes by the name of "Malchus" in Justin's account (XVIII. 7) of Sicilian and Sardinian exploits; the name is misleading, however, and was coined by a modern philologist who was unaware that the name Malchus is of Aramaean origin, not

The Phoenicians in the Western Mediterranean
(through to the Fifth Century B.C.)

Punic-Roman Temple
of the Sardus Pater
at Antas, Sardinia

The Phoenicians in the Western Mediterranean
(through to the Fifth Century B.C.)

Remains of the Punic necropolis at Puig des Molins, Ibiza

Phoenician bronze male statue found at Gades (Cadiz)
7th cent. B.C.
Cadiz, Museo de Cádiz

Phoenician. The written source from which Pompeius Trogus drew his material is unfairly hostile toward the exploits of this Carthaginian general; many modern historians, in fact, prefer to attribute his deeds to his successor, Mago, who nonetheless successfully subdued the Sardinian colonies and, apparently, created the structural basis for the upcoming empire of Carthage. At the close of the sixth century a new political reality began to take shape in the western Mediterranean: the once independent Phoenician way stations began to coalesce into a single, uniform entity of federative stamp under the aegis of Carthage. This naval empire came into existence as a direct reaction to Greek imperialist encroachment. Nor was it without its own expansionist ambitions: it quickly burgeoned through the creation of a dense network of colonies (many of which are, regrettably, as yet undocumented), establishing a dominion stretching westward along the North African shores from Tripolitania to Morocco. Meanwhile in Sardinia, the Phoenician colonists pushed ever further inland. Only Spain, where the ancient colony at Cadiz continued to flourish, seems to have been spared this tightening of Phoenician dominion.

As for foreign policy, the long-standing Phoenician alliance with the Etruscans continued to provide an effective curtain against Greek ascendancy. The renowned inscribed plates of Pyrgi bear out the close links between Caere (Cerveteri) and Carthage around 500 B.C.: the very place-name Punicum testified to previous Carthaginian activity in one of the Etruscan city's harbors. In 509 B.C., moreover, Carthage drew up its first treaty with Rome, a new and growing power in the Tyrrhenian, vying with that of the Etruscans. That treaty seems to invalidate the claim of Pompeius Trogus regarding the ancient confederation between Massalia and a Rome ruled by Etruscan monarchs (Justin, XLIII. 5. 3). The Etruscans and Romans were fickle allies, however, and Carthage was unable to ward off the Greek encroachment alone. Toward 520 B.C. the Etruscans were defeated by Cumaeans and Latini at Aricia (now Ariccia); less than fifty years later, crushed at Cumae, they were driven out of Campania altogether. Furthermore, Carthage suffered defeat at the hands of the Massaliots on numerous occasions (Thucydides, I. 130); the drubbing they received at Artemisium in Spain in 490 B.C. (according to S. Mazzarino) led to the acknowledgment of Massaliot eparchy as far as the *mastia* of Tarsis (cf. Justin, XLIII. 5. 2). In 480 B.C. the Carthaginians once again suffered a terrible defeat, this time at the hands of the Syracusans at Himera. Interior struggles, however, impeded the Greeks from exploiting their victory, and Carthage managed to keep its hold on western Sicily, where in 409 B.C. it even took back territories. But in 397 B.C. Motya was razed by the forces of the tyrant Dionysius of Syracuse. Our chronicle of events terminates here, though the history of the Phoenicians in the West continued. The Greeks never quite managed to overrule Carthage, which only later fell to Rome. Furthermore,

The Phoenicians in the Western Mediterranean
(through to the Fifth Century B.C.)

Proto-Aeolian capital
found at Gades (Cadiz)
7th cent. B.C.
Cadiz, Museo de Cádiz

Phoenician bronze male statuette
found at Gades (Cadiz)
7th cent. B.C.
Cadiz, Museo de Cádiz

Phoenician incense burner
found at Gades (Cadiz)
7th cent. B.C.
Cadiz, Museo de Cádiz

The Phoenicians in the Western Mediterranean
(through to the Fifth Century B.C.)

Attic black-figure *amphora*
found at Tharros
6th cent. B.C.
Cagliari, Museo Archeologico
Nazionale

western Phoenician culture continued to prosper long after 146 B.C., a culture that Carthage had endowed with its own stamp, imposing its Punic models. While the Greeks had failed to achieve political supremacy over the Carthaginians, the cultural fallout was considerable, and although the fifth century witnessed the wars between the two peoples, the Punic world was increasingly influenced by the structure of Greek civilization. The effects of Hellenization may be most noticeable in the figurative arts, but the transformation of the internal political setup was far-reaching (albeit not total), and likewise of the religious ideology, particularly as concerns eschatological concepts. Despite everything, the Phoenician identity endured long, even in the West, and only began to wane upon the arrival of new ideas and new Semitic peoples from the Orient i.e. Christianity and the trabs.

Bibliography
GENERAL REFERENCES
E. ACQUARO-M.E. AUBET-M.H. FANTAR, 1933; *Phönizier im Western...*, 1982 (= Madrider Beiträge, 8); *Fenici e Arabi...*, 1983; *Momenti precoloniali...*, 1988.
SPECIFIC ISSUES
S. MAZZARINO, 1947, pp. 8-20; A. CIASCA, in *Kokalos*, 34-35 (1988-89) [1992], pp. 75-88.

Patrice Pomey

Navigation and Ships in the Age of Greek Colonization

When the first Greek settlers left familiar shores in the course of the eighth century B.C. for the remote western Mediterranean coast, they already had a great deal of experience in the field of navigation. Although at that time their knowledge was essentially limited to the eastern Mediterranean, even there this involved crossing the open sea, far out of sight of the shore and more a challenging experience than the relatively easy traversal of the Otranto Channel. From a strictly technical point of view, the only problem the penetration of the western basin presented was that of venturing into a sea where few had firsthand knowledge of such hazards as shoals and sandbanks.

The Greek colonists were preceded by merchant seamen from the eastern Mediterranean basin, in particular Mycenaeans and Phoenicians. In the meantime, the farthest coast, now the Gulf of Lyons and the Gulf of Genoa, was separated by the Etruscan world and hence remained relatively unexplored. This coast was also the last to receive Greek settlers – more than a century and a half after the first settlements in Magna Graecia. The credit was entirely due to the Phocaeans, whose abilities as discoverers are praised by Herodotus (*History* I. 163–167). This faraway sea had already been frequented, however, by Etruscan sailors; it is also possible that the Phocaeans were preceded, as archaeology finds tend to suggest, by solitary Greek merchants whose experiences were undoubtedly a later source of guidance.

The ancient techniques of navigation appear very primitive to today's way of thinking, given the total absence of any type of instrumentation or nautical charts. More than a science, navigation in antiquity was an art based on the ability to interpret natural phenomena. However, it was an art so well suited to the geographic peculiarities of the Mediterranean that it remained unaltered for the entire period of antiquity, and

Krater by Aristonothos
scene of a naval battle between
a war galley with one row of oarsmen
and a flat ram
and a merchant ship with one mast
and a rounded hull
first half 7th cent B.C.
Rome, Musei Capitolini
Cat. 6

Henri Tréziny's reconstruction
from fragments
of a geometric decoration
of a war galley
with one row of oarsmen
and no bridge
from Megara Hyblaea
end Geometric period

even after it was only slightly improved. A closed sea divided into basins that are well defined by important headlands and numerous islands, the Mediterranean lent itself to coastal navigation with intervals of open-sea crossings of a few days, not months. For this reason the need to use navigation instruments or nautical charts was never an imperative, and it is significant that the use of compasses and pilot's books from the thirteenth and fourteenth centuries onward did not in the least change the habits derived from antiquity. Without maps or instruments, navigation was based on a sound knowledge of the area and of the natural elements. We are told so frequently by the written sources that it was a good captain who "knew the descriptions of the coasts, the movement of the stars and the science of the winds," that it has become a *topos* of ancient literature: all the art of the ancient navigators is summed up in these words. As a result of the shape of the Mediterranean every sea voyage began and finished with a large tract of coastal navigation, with all the attendant risks. It was essential to have a good knowledge of the rocks and the shallows, of the headlands that were difficult to round, and of the currents, just as it was vital to know the important landmarks and the distances that separated them, the places for anchoring and for taking shelter, as well as the places where it was possible to stock up with water and other supplies. We are reminded of this, together with other examples, by the Scylla and Charybdis myths, of the sinister fame of Cap Malée (Malea) and the proverb "when you round Cape Malea, forget the home you left behind you" (Strabo, VIII. 6. 20). This knowledge was based on the experiences handed down from generation to generation, first orally and then in written form, in the famous *periploi*, which have been compared to modern-day pilot's books. The oldest of these documents to have survived date to the fourth century B.C., though they presuppose the existence of other written works from previous ages. We do not know if the first Greek settlers were able to benefit from these works, but very probably they profited from information handed down by sailors who came before them. This would explain why the first settlements, founded by the Chalcidians, were

Navigation and Ships in the Age of Greek Colonization

Reconstruction of the decoration
of a Late Geometric *krater*
from Pithekoussai
with a scene of a shipwreck

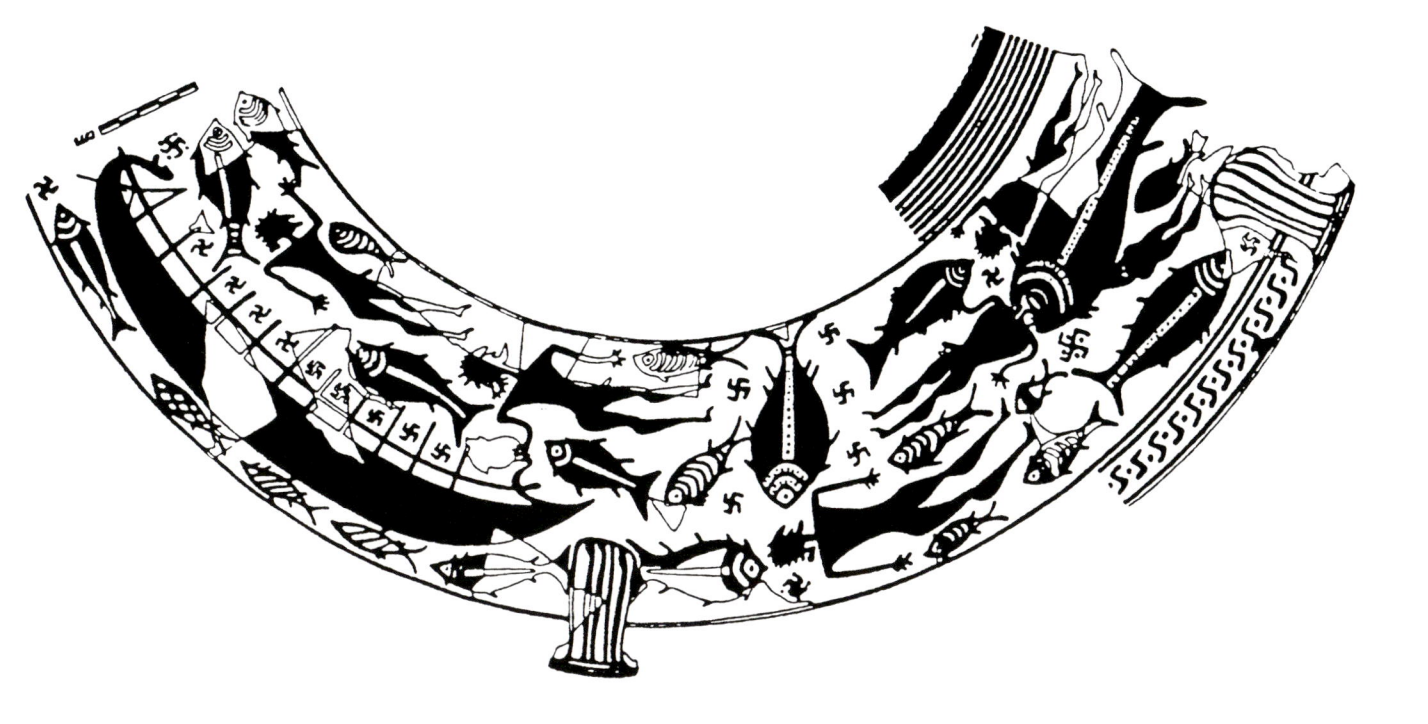

Shipwreck scene
on a Late Geometric *krater*
from Pithekoussai
the small ship has
neither a forecastle
nor a poop deck
last quarter 8th cent. B.C.
Lacco Ameno, Antiquarium
Cat. 5

135

Navigation and Ships in the Age of Greek Colonization

Geometric *krater* from Thebes
one of the earliest pictures
of a ship with two rows of oars
end 8th cent. B.C.
Toronto, Royal Ontario Museum
University of Toronto

initially situated in places such as Pithekoussai on the island of Ischia in the Tyrrhenian Sea (founded 770 B.C.), and a little later at Cumae on the mainland, opposite, rather than in the nearer Gulf of Taranto or in Sicily. On the other hand it is possible that they handed down the new knowledge to their successors. Any discussion of the progress in navigation in ancient times must take account of the ever-widening knowledge of the coasts, resulting in improved navigational conditions that favored the regularity of trade. However, despite the importance of coastal navigation, the time had come when it was necessary to abandon small coastal vessels in order to confront open-sea crossings; these were quite long and the captain had only himself to count on when deciding the course. In the absence of navigational instruments, he had to rely on the system of "reckoning," which consisted in evaluating as best he could the course followed and the distance covered. It was here that a good knowledge of the stars came into play. By day the course could be studied in relation to the sun, whose position was known at dawn, at sunset, and when it was at its zenith. Since night navigation was necessary on certain routes – as documented by many texts, from Homer onward, depicting the helmsman keeping a lonely watch on the bridge – by night the route was plotted in relation to the position of the stars and to the movement of the constellations. As for the distance covered, or the speed of the ship in relation to the length of time passed, estimates were based entirely on the experience of the captain and on a sound knowledge of the characteristics of the vessel in relation to the different "tacks," according to the strength and direction of the wind and the sea conditions. Obviously this type of navigation was anything but precise, but in the Mediterranean the reduced distances limited the consequences. When the ship approached dry land in a fairly spacious area, the captain completed the voyage using coastal navigation. The instrument that was fundamentally important in this phase was the sounding line, which was used for measuring underkeel depths. Lastly, the sail, being the principal means of propulsion for ancient ships (including those equipped with oars, since the use of these was limited to particular circumstances) meant that a good knowledge of the winds was also paramount. The direction of the great seasonal winds, like the famous Etesian winds of the eastern basin, the peculiarities of local winds, like the Mistral on the coast of Provence, the regularity of off-shore and solar wind, all determined the seasons for navigation, influenced the course, and indicated the time for departing, for resting, for weighing anchor, and for entering port.

Given the total dependence on meteorological conditions, in ancient times sailors distinguished the bad seasons as the periods in which the atmospheric instability, the frequency of storms and covered skies prevented them from making important voyages. We know from Hesiod (*Works and Days*, 663–665, 678–684) that the most favorable weather for navigation was during a brief period in spring, however full of risks, and in the good season that lasted from approximately mid-July to mid-September. In any case there were always many dangers, as witnessed in the adventures of Ulysses in the *Odyssey*. It is true that Colaeus the Samian was the first Greek to reach Tartessus in the seventh century, but only because of a long storm that blew him off course from his original destination of Egypt. Seven centuries later Saint Peter encountered the same dangers on his way from Rome to Caesarea, and seventeen centuries after him Chateaubriand, en route from Alexandria to Tunis, suffered the same difficulties. Navigation in the Mediterranean during the time of sailing ships was for a long time subject to unexpected events, in spite of maps and instruments.

The Phocaeans "were the first Greeks to undertake long-distance navigation; ... they did not navigate in round ships but in pentecounters." Apart from this passage from Herodotus (*History* I. 163), we have no other evidence about the ships used by the Greek navy at the time of the colonization of the western Mediterranean. By emphasizing that the Phocaeans did not use round ships but rather pentecounters, Herodotus seems to be suggesting that the other Greeks used merchant ships. However, was he referring to the contemporaries of the Phocaeans who founded Massalia (modern Marseilles) in 600 B.C., or to the predecessors of the eighth and seventh centuries? The distinction between round merchant ships and long war ships dates back at least to the middle of the second millennium B.C. The choice of merchant sailing ships for the task of colonization would in fact be justified by their capacity to carry cargo, and by their seaworthiness, even if their total dependence on wind and their lack of speed could prove to be worrying handicaps in expeditions where the unexpected was always present, not to mention the threat of pirates. The use of mixed-propulsion merchant galleys (i.e., with oars and sails) was possibly a good compromise, but unfortunately we do not have sufficient elements to throw light on a problem which cannot be reduced to a simple question of alternatives, given the extraordinary diversification of the Greek colonization phenomenon.

On the other hand, iconography offers numerous illustrations of long ships fitted with a ram, forecastle, and bow rake. From the illustration of older ships we can infer that the galleys were equipped with a line of oars that required twenty, thirty, or fifty oarsmen, depending on the vessel's importance. These light ships

Attic black-figure *dinos*
signed by Execias
penteconter
with two rows of oarsmen
but only the upper row working
550-530 B.C.
Rome
Museo Nazionale di Villa Giulia

without a bridge and with a limited capacity were transformed toward the end of the eighth century into more powerful vessels. The period between the eighth and the seventh century, in fact, seems to have been one of great activity and of profound change in ship construction; iconographically this is represented by the appearance of the bireme, with two tiers of oars. Thucydides (I. 13–14), who highlighted this strengthening of the Greek navy, ascribes a predominant role in this evolution – which was definitely affected by colonization – to the Corinthians, and in particular to Ameinocles, their famous naval engineer. Until the appearance of the trireme, the backbone of the Greek war navy was made up of penteconters, alongside smaller ships. As its etymology suggests, the term penteconter originally referred to a ship with one row of fifty oarsmen, but it was later applied to the most imposing class of ships – the monoremes and biremes – whose crews sometimes boasted over fifty oarsmen. The Phocaean penteconters in the late seventh and early sixth centuries must have been the most developed and important. Their excellent sails were strong enough and ideal for the sea so that the ships could be used for long-range expeditions and, according to the testimony of Herodotus (*History* I. 164), they had a notably large capacity for carrying cargo. In fact, when the Phocaeans abandoned their city around 540 because of the threat from the Persians, they set sail on their penteconters for Alalia in Corsica, taking with them "women, children, furniture and statues of the Gods … and other offerings, except for the bronze and marble objects and the paintings," as well as their provisions, all of which represented a considerable volume of cargo for a ship with oars. These ships were replaced during the course of the sixth century by the trireme, although we do not know the exact date, and Thucydides (I. 13–14) attributed its introduction to the Corinthians. Triremes came progressively into use, but it was not until the second half of the sixth century that sizable fleets of these new vessels began to appear, including the fleet of Syrakousai (modern Syracuse). The trireme was the result of a lengthy evolutionary process, and remained for a long time at the pinnacle of Greek naval art.

As far as merchant ships are concerned, the iconography is much less generous with us, even if they must have been regularly employed in the western Mediterranean before eventually registering a massive presence around 675 B.C., during the second Greek colonization. Alongside the round, sail-propelled ships, with rounded hulls, high bulwarks, and bulging sides suitable for carrying large cargoes, we find mixed-propulsion merchant ships with a smaller tonnage, but quicker and more agile. We will ignore inquiring into the tonnage of the biggest of these ships, which were considerably different in dimensions and characteristics. These ships, like the ships with oars where the sail was the usual means of propulsion, were fitted with a central mast rigged with guys and shrouds and carrying a square sail that was perpendicular to the axis of the ship. A yard, raised by means of a halyard, supported the canvas, and lateral jibs made it possible to align the ship to the wind's direction. However, there is no trace of any ties for balancing the yards and regulating the inclination, although these were used on Egyptian and Minoan ships and they reappeared in the Hellenic era. The most important characteristic, which is often portrayed, is

Attic black-figure *oinochoe*
small merchant ship
with oarsmen and sails
ca. 510 B.C.
The Hague, Rijksmuseum Meermanno
Westreenianum Museum
van het Boek

represented by a series of hemp ropes that ran from the bottom to the top on the front part of the sail, before descending to the rear of the ship, where they were secured. These were the brails that made it possible to shorten the sail, by raising it up like a Venetian blind, depending on the wind strength. Simple but complete in its essential elements, the ancient square sail rigging was particularly suitable for tacking with the wind in the stern or the three-quarters, but it also presented a good deal of flexibility of use that made it possible to vary the sail area in order to adapt it to the direction of the wind. For example, by giving it a triangular shape – using a maneuver described by Aristotle (*Mechanical Problems* 851b), which seems to have been the origin of the Latin sail – it was possible, if not to sail against the wind then at least to sail close to the wind in an acceptable way for the length of time necessary to round a headland or to reach port or safe moorage.

All of the ships of the time had the same type of steering equipment, consisting of two rudders fixed to the two sides of the stern. Thanks to the large blade on the rudders and to the possibility of rotating them on their axis, these were authentic rudders, a counterbalanced, sensitive, precise, and efficient device. The

Attic black-figure cup
with merchant ship
under assault
from a pirate ship
clearly distinguishable
by the brails on the sails
ca. 510 B.C.
London, British Museum
Department of Greek
and Roman Antiquities

Remains of a Greek merchant ship
and boat abandoned
in the port of Massalia
at the end of 6th cent. B.C.
Marseilles
excavations in Place Jules Verne

ancient lateral rudder, far from constituting an obstacle to navigation and to marine development, revealed itself to be extremely suited to the conditions present in the Mediterranean and in particular to coastal navigation which, more so than long voyages, required a particularly sensitive rudder.

Recently two exceptional archaeological discoveries at Gela in Sicily and at Massalia have revealed the wrecks of two Greek merchant ships and a boat that date back to the end of the sixth and the beginning of the fifth century B.C. The two ships are 15 meters long and 4–5 meters wide, with a cargo capacity in the order of 15 tons. They have small keels and light frameworks with relatively rounded hulls and thin, elongated extremities. The most notable thing, however, is the construction technique. The ship from Gela and the boat from Massalia are in fact entirely assembled by means of rope, using the archaic "stitching" technique, as related in texts of that era by Homer (*Iliad* II. 135) and Aeschylus (*Supplications* 134–135). These confirmed the use of this technique that had been suggested by the more fragmented remains of the sixth-century wrecks found off the coast of Giglio, Italy, and at Bon-Porté, France. The Massaliot ship, however, has a mixed construction where the new assembly technique requiring tenons and mortises – which later became the usual type of construction in the Mediterranean until the end of antiquity – is found alongside a form of binding that is still abundantly present in some parts. We are therefore dealing with a transitional type of ship, which throws crucial light on the evolution of naval construction techniques at the end of the sixth century B.C. Even if they were light and agile, these vessels must have possessed good nautical characteristics that enabled them to navigate throughout the Mediterranean.

As can be seen, only a general picture of the navigational conditions at the time of the Greek colonizations is possible, since there are many aspects still to be clarified about the effective reality of expeditions that lasted for almost two centuries, and whose range was without precedent. The different types of ships used, their construction, and the tonnage remain largely unknown. The discovery of a few wrecks – even more important because of their rarity – has begun to lift the veil on some aspects of naval construction at the end of the sixth century, but we hope that other discoveries will bit by bit shed light on those ships of the eighth and seventh centuries that were the instruments of one of the greatest human and naval adventures in the Mediterranean.

Bibliography
C. Torr, 1964; J.S. Morrison-R.T. Williams, 1968; L. Casson, 1971; J. Rougé, 1975; H. Treziny, MEFRA, 92, 1980-81, pp. 17-34; P. Pomey, in B.A.R., 1985, pp. 35-47; L. Basch, 1987; L. Casson, 1991; J.-P. Morel, in Etudes Massaliètes, 3, 1992, pp. 15-25; P. Pomey-L. Long, in Etudes Massaliètes, 3, 1992, pp. 189-198; P. Pomey-A. Hesnard, in *Le temps des découvertes...*, 1993, pp. 59-62.

Giovanni Pugliese Carratelli   An Outline of the Political History of the Greeks in the West

The foundation of the colonial poleis

The foundation of the Greek colonial *poleis* (cities) in Italy and Sicily marked the conclusion of a long period in which contacts occurred between the Greeks who came from the Aegean and Anatolian areas, and the Balkan Peninsula, in search of raw materials and markets, and the autochthonous peoples of southern Italy and Sicily. These contacts, which became increasingly frequent over the centuries (at least, after the middle of the second millennium B.C.), allowed the Greeks to discover the numerous coastal ports and the fertile lands of Italy and Sicily. This rapidly created an atmosphere that was favorable not only to commerce, but also to the founding of trading settlements. Meanwhile the Mycenaean – and later Hellenic – culture conveyed by adventurous merchants and craftsmen to the interior of the Italian Peninsula and Sicily began to have a growing influence on the indigenous communities, stimulating not only the importation of the products of the Greek and eastern craftsmen, but also the imitation of these and, as a result, notable progress in the local crafts. Their advanced culture was certainly of great benefit to the Greeks in their expansion, which was at first mercantile, then colonial. Thus, the Italian and Sicilian *poleis* developed rapidly from both the territorial and the economic points of view. Generally speaking, the coexistence that was soon established with the non-Greek peoples, even where the occupation of land by the settlers had given rise to conflict, did not undergo serious interruptions. Indeed, it was consolidated by the absorption of native workers into the subordinate population of the *poleis*; the admission of members of the native aristocracies into the ruling class; and the adoption of the language, lifestyle and art of the Greeks by the natives. However, the possibility the indigenous religions had any influence on the settlers must be ruled out, especially in view of the fact that their religious beliefs constituted an inviolable bond with their homeland.

The success of the Greek colonization was even more remarkable when it is compared with the much less appreciable and enduring effects of Phoenician mercantile expansion and Carthaginian colonization. Not only was it the result of the incomparable splendor and creative vigor of the Greek civilization, but it was also due to a particular aptitude of the Aegean peoples for coming into contact with – and understanding – the most varied cultures. This was a sign of a freedom of thought and a natural bent for learning that was able to reconcile the attention paid to innovation with sagacious respect for their own traditions and those of others. It was no coincidence that the policy of colonial expansion was initiated by the aristocratic *poleis* and that its promoters and executors belonged – as is confirmed by the names of the *oikistai*, the leaders of the colonial expeditions – to the class that had been able to enrich its culture with study and journeys. Thanks to their political and military experience, only the *aristoi*, the nobles, were able to prepare and lead expeditions overseas; to give political form to the mass of settlers, who were extremely varied, both as regards their social origin and their occupations (often they included citizens of *poleis* other than the metropolis that was promoting the colonization); and found and defend the new settlements. Naturally, the colonial ventures (*apoikiai*) were supported by their respective metropolises, frequently because they solved their social and economic problems by reducing the surplus in the workforce. However, none of the earliest *apoikiai* appear to have been undertaken directly by the metropolitan governments. Thucydides, in fact, explicitly attributes (I. 12. 2) the first colonial settlements in the Aegean area to nobles who had been defeated in the internal struggles following the return of the kings from the long Panhellenic war against Troy and the clash with those who had taken their places at home. For the western colonies, he uses a phrase (I. 12. 4 "Hellas … sent colonial expeditions"), the vagueness of which seems to be inappropriate for political acts.

Although the ancient historians refer to episodic conflicts between the colonial *poleis* and the indigenous peoples, they pay more attention to the struggle for hegemony between the different *poleis*. Notable interruptions in the coexistence between Greeks and natives occurred later, when it was not only the military strength that began to decline, but also the culture and institutions of the Italian and Sicilian *poleis*. Conversely, confederations of indigenous communities formed that were armed in the Greek manner, while mercenary troops settled permanently, especially in Sicily, and behaved as if they were independent communities. And, although the majority of the non-Greek peoples maintained their traditions and institutions, the Greek influence was of fundamental importance for them. It suggested new forms of organization and, in many cases, helped to promote the development of a national consciousness (as happened during the fourth century in the case of the Lucani and Bruttii).

From what has been said, it is clear that the choice of the sites for the colonies was anything but accidental, and was directed toward precise objectives on the basis of certain information regarding the characteristics of the natives, the available resources, and the opportunities for development. Particularly significant is the case of the oldest Greek colony in the West, Cumae "in Opicia" (that is, in Campania), which was the farthest from the homeland of the promoters of the venture, Chalcis in Euboea.

overleaf
The colonial expansion of the Greeks in the Mediterranean
8th-6th cent. B.C.

An Outline of the Political History of the Greeks in the West

Greek colonial expansion in the Mediterranean (VIII-VI cent. B.C.)

- 🟡 Greek colonies
- 🔴 *Phoenician colonies*
- 🟩 Other towns and cities
- 🔷 Emporia

0 100 200 300
km

An Outline of the Political History of the Greeks in the West

View of the acropolis of Cumae
the first Greek colony in the West

Although citizens of other *poleis* were allowed to participate in the expeditions organized by one *polis*, the nucleus was homogeneous and the *polis* from which they came was recognized as the metropolis (mother-city) of the colony. In some cases, one of the founders of the colony (*oikistai*) came from a *polis* that was different from that of the majority of the colonists. Obviously, these included craftsmen, merchants, farmers, and servants. Frequently, the founders of a colony, or their descendants, pressed for a new contingent of colonists in order to give a new lease of life to the *polis*. For instance, Cyrene was founded about 630 B.C. by Theraeans; to these, between 580 and 570, were added Peloponnesians, Cretans, and inhabitants of the Aegean Islands (as we know from Herodotus, IV. 161) – among the latter were Rhodians (Blinkenberg, *Lindos* II, p. 167ff. and *Tituli Camirenses* 105).

In Libya (as the Greeks called the north coast of Africa to the west of Egypt) there was a vast, fertile plateau stretching out into the sea that was easily accessible from the port of Barca. This area attracted the Greeks of the Aegean because it constituted a Greek nucleus that had great potential for development: situated on the route usually taken by the Greek and Phoenician ships sailing from the Aegean, Anatolian, and Syrian areas to the West, it marked the point at which this turned toward the southern coast of Crete (the close relation between the latter and Cyrenaica later formed the basis of the Roman province of *Creta et Cyrenae*). This explains why members of the Theraean aristocracy decided to found a colony in that area, since their island was a way station on the sea routes between the Cretan ports and those of Euboea and beyond. The isolation of the group of *poleis* of Cyrenaica favored the long duration of a dynasty (until 456) in which the names Battus (the Libyan title of the king assumed by one Aristotle, founder of Cyrene) and Arcesilas alternated. Royal power was limited by a reformer, Demonax of Mantinea, designated by the priests of Delphi in the mid-sixth century.

It is easy to see why the first expedition of Greek colonists to the West chose the Bay of Naples as its destination: it was the most convenient base from which to expand trade toward the western Mediterranean. The Aegean and Levantine seafarers could take two main routes to the lands further west – Sardinia and Corsica, the Ligurian coast, and the Rhône valley, the Balearic Islands and the Iberian Peninsula – in order to find new markets and land routes into the interior, and to obtain supplies of precious minerals, such as obsidian, alum, lead, and copper. One route, after the perils of the Strait of Messina had been overcome, skirted the Aeolian Islands and followed the Tyrrhenian coast, where there was the most attractive harbor in the huge Bay of Naples, the islands of which – Ischia (Pithekoussai), Prochyte, and Vivara – had, since the Mycenaean era, provided convenient sites for workshops and trading settlements for Aegean and "Phoenician" (Levantine) merchants and artisans. The other route, which was also risky, due to the shallows in the Libyan Syrtis, passed through the Sicilian Channel and went round Sicily to reach Sardinia.

The Euboean colonies

The Rhodians claimed to have sailed across the western Mediterranean as far as Iberia before the Olympian games were established, and to have founded Parthenope in the Bay of Naples. They probably built a warehouse on the island of Megaris (occupied much later on by the *Castrum Lucullanum* and the Castel dell'Ovo) and instituted the cult of Aphrodite Euploia, the goddess of seafaring, on the hill opposite, the modern name of which, Echia, seems to be associated with her. However, the most authoritative Greek historians indicated Cumae as the first colonial *polis* in the West. Around 750 B.C. its founders came from various *poleis* of Euboea, especially Chalcis; but, rather than from the small Euboean Cyme, its name derived from the large Aeolian *polis* of the same name on the seaboard of Asia Minor. It is likely that citizens of this city joined up with Chalcidians and Eretrians in the colonization of the Phlegraean Fields. Evidence of the latter's relations with the territories of the northeast Mediterranean, especially Mysia, is provided by a historical place-name of the Cumaean area, Teuthras. The participation of the Asian Cumaeans in the foundation of the Phlegraean colony is also indicated by the prestige that the cult of an oracular Apollo had there. The priestess of this was a Sibyl, another sign of the links with Anatolia: an authoritative tradition, in fact, associated it with Erythrae, founded in Asian Ionia by the homonymous Boeotian city, and the same applies to the Sibyl and the *Sibylline Books* that, from the age of the Tarquins onward, were consulted in Rome in times of trouble.

The position of Cumae was particularly important, because, from its territory, the Euboeans controlled both the bay (with their ports at Puteoli and Neapolis, and the island of Ischia) and the sea route to the mouth of the Tiber, the island of Elba and the bay of Populonia opposite this – that is, the area occupied by the people known as the Tyrrhenoi (Etruscans), whose links with Anatolia are evident and are attested by ancient traditions. The aspiration of the Euboean trading cities to dominate the sea traffic is also demonstrated by the Cumaean occupation of the site where Zancle was later founded; from this, privateers controlled the busiest access to the eastern Tyrrhenian. An even more significant indication of this plan of theirs was provided by the foundation in about 735 B.C. of the first Greek colony in Sicily, at Naxos, on Capo Schisò, near

Remains of the Greek colony of Naxos

the Strait of Messina. The founders were Chalcidians under Thucles (by tradition, he was of Athenian origin); but the name of the new *polis*, which was derived from that of an island in the Cyclades, is significant. In the Archaic period, the Naxians of the Aegean were preeminent on Delos, the island sacred to Apollo, which had become the religious center of all the Ionian peoples. The founders of the Sicilian colony immediately proclaimed their ties with the famous Aegean sanctuary by dedicating an altar to Apollo Archegetes even before they began to build the town itself.

This episode is important because it demonstrates that, during the first stage of the colonization of the West, the Delian Apollo – linked by the history of the sanctuary to Crete at the time of Minos and the adventures of Theseus – was the spiritual leader of the colonial movement. And the latter, through its Euboean initiators, among whom ancient Aegean, Boeotian, and Anatolian traditions survived, was related to the expansion of Minoan and Mycenaean trade and culture. It was only in a more recent period that an almost ritual function as a guide for the foundation of colonies was attributed to the Pythian Sanctuary of Apollo. Thanks to his great erudition, Virgil was well aware of the prestige that the Aegean oracle had acquired before the Peloponnesian Greeks decided in favor of the sanctuary at Pytho (Delphi).

The foundation of Naxos was followed a few years later by that of another Euboean colony, Zancle, (ca. 730?). That this occurred with the approval of Cumae in Italy is demonstrated by the presence of a founder from Cumae (certainly the one in Campania) together with a Chalcidian. In order to establish control of the straits, the Chalcidians of Zancle invited their fellow countrymen to come to the West to found a colony on the mainland side of them, at Rhegium. The participants in this foundation included Messenian nobles that had dissociated themselves from their compatriots who, during the festivities held jointly by Messenians and Laconians in the Sanctuary of Artemis Limnatis, had violated Laconian virgins. Some of these exiles belonged to an ancient royal family of Messenia, as may be deduced from an account handed down by Antiochus of Syracuse and other Greek historians in southern Italy and Sicily, according to whom, until the time of Anaxilas, Rhegium had always been governed by nobles of Messenian stock. In fact, the name Anaxilas is composed of words typical of the "Mycenaean" dynastic language (ἄναξ, λαοί).

Peloponnesian and Achaean colonies
Hence the protagonists of the first stage of the colonization were the Ionian *poleis* of the homeland. Rather like the Etruscans, who had brought technical and cultural traditions from the Aegean coast of Anatolia to central Italy, they probably followed routes established by seafarers from the eastern Mediterranean. However, the colonies founded by Greeks from the Peloponnese multiplied on the Ionian coast of Italy and in eastern Sicily. For instance, around 735 B.C. Syracuse was founded by Corinthians; from the island of Ortygia, it dominated two good harbors, thus according with the maritime vocation of the metropolis, which was also evident in its other important colony of Corcyra (Corfu). Colonists arrived in southeast Sicily around 728 B.C. from another city with a great Aegean tradition, Megara, which was as interested in the western seas as it was in the Euxine Sea (Black Sea) – the Greeks were attracted to the latter by the grain-growing plains of the Crimea, as well as by the mineral deposits of Colchis. For a short time they coexisted with the Chalcidians from Naxos who had founded the city of Leontini in the same period, possibly in order to check Syracusan expansion toward the Straits of Messina. But an irresolvable conflict with the Chalcidians obliged the Megarian colonists to leave Leontini. In the first place, they sought their own site on the peninsula of Thapsos, which had already been visited by the Mycenaeans, but this was too close to Syracuse for the latter to permit the enterprising Megarians to set up their own *polis* there. Moreover, for some time the Megarians had maintained good relations with the native Sicels. This is demonstrated by the support that was readily offered to the exiles by the Sicel king, Hyblon, whose name indicates that he was heir to the traditions of the Sicans, the inhabitants of the area before the Sicel invasion.

That the Sicans were accustomed to having dealings with the visitors coming from the Aegean coast of Asia Minor may be deduced from various circumstances that appear to be a consequences of this: the existence of Sicilian communities with the name of Hybla (among which one was famous for its seers), namesakes of the Carian Hybla of Samos, the seat of an oracle; the generosity of King Hyblon toward the Megarians, to whom he granted a site near to the coast, where Megara Hyblaea was founded; and, above all, the rapid growth of Selinus, the city that the Megarians built about a century after the foundation of the Hyblaean colony on the southwest coast of the island, in an area dominated by the Sicans near to that of the Elymi, but distant from most of the other Greek colonies. Unlike Selinus, which became one of the most magnificent Sicilian *poleis*, Megara Hyblaea did not have a large amount of space at its disposal; thus, around 484 B.C. it was absorbed by Syracuse, which dominated it to the south.

Aerial view
of the archaeological remains
at Selinunte

Ruins of the temples at Selinunte

In the late eighth and early seventh centuries B.C. groups of colonists came from Peloponnesian Achaea, where Greeks similar to the Dorians had vanquished the ancient inhabitants of Ionian descent, resulting in the foundation of the colonies in Asia Minor that constituted the twelve Ionian towns (as recounted in Herodotus). They settled in various parts of the "instep" of the Ionian coast of southern Italy, in fertile areas at the seaward ends of river valleys. The first Achaean colony, founded about 720 B.C., was Sybaris, on the Crathis River. The name of the *polis* is that of a spring near the town of Bura in Achaea, but it is also that of the capital of Colchis, so it is not certain that it was imported by the Achaean colonists. The founder of Sybaris was called Wis (Ϝις, transcribed as Οἶς by the literary sources), and he came from Helice. The colonists came from the latter city, and Bura and Aegium (three of the sixteen Achaean districts); in addition there were Troezenians (from the Argolid) and Locrians. Aristotle (*Politics* V. 2.10) informs us that the Troezenians were expelled by the Sybarites, but does not tell us why or when this happened. The participation of the Locrians was mentioned by Nicander, the erudite poet of the third century B.C. from Colophon, who was a priest of Apollo at Claros: he linked the name of the city to that of a spring near Crisa, on the border of Phocis with Western Locris. Solinus stated that Sybaris was founded by Troezenians and Sagaris, son of Aias the Lesser. Further west, near Capo Colonna, on which a famous sanctuary dedicated to Hera Lacinia stood, other Achaeans founded Croton about 708 B.C. This *Heraion* became the main sanctuary of the new *polis*: its distance from the city suggests that it may have been a center for Hellenic religion that was established before the foundation of the colony. If this were the case, it would be evidence of the arrival of Greeks in the area before the colonial period.

Extramural sanctuaries and religions in the poleis
Similar cases occurred in other Italiot *poleis* with important extramural sanctuaries located nearby, such as the temple dedicated to Athena on the Sorrento peninsula or the *Heraion* near Poseidonia (Paestum). Traditions alive in the sanctuaries themselves ascribed their founding to mythical characters (Odysseus for the Athena temple in the Bay of Naples, Jason for the *Heraion* at the mouth of the Sele River), but this meant that these centers of Greek religion were precedent to the founding of the nearby *poleis*, whose founders were often guided in their choice of sites by them. Naturally, for their own *poleis*, the colonists claimed the respected remains of a remote Hellenic presence that served to favor good relations with the natives. It is well known from the historical sources that the first thing the Greeks did – in their trading settlements, too

– was to establish their religion: this was the case in Naucratis, where, as Herodotus recounts (II. 178), in the mid-sixth century B.C. the merchants allowed to trade in the Nile Delta by the pharaoh Amasis immediately founded the sanctuaries of their numerous deities. And Thucydides noted that the dedication of an altar to Apollo Archegetes was the first step taken by the founders of Naxos in Sicily. Since it would have been inconceivable for the Greek colonists – for whom the religion of their homeland was a sacred and inviolable heritage, as well as being the strongest bond with their metropolis – to adopt native religions, the distance of the great sanctuaries of a colonial *polis* from the town itself can only be convincingly explained by the fact that these important religious sites were pre-colonial in origin. The thesis that the sanctuaries were constructed by the various *poleis* to mark the extent of their territories, or to facilitate contact and trade with the natives, may easily be countered by the argument that the Greek religious sites would serve no purpose in political relations with the neighboring native peoples. Furthermore, the distance of these sanctuaries from the towns hardly seems sufficient to indicate territorial expansion of an extent that would be justified by their size. In any case, most of them are located in places (the end of a promontory in the case of the Athena temple on the Sorrento peninsula and the Temple of Hera near Croton, at a river mouth in the case of the *Heraion* at Poseidonia) in which their supposed symbolic function would be pointless. Nor would this justify the splendor of the sacred buildings and the works of art that adorned them, which were inspired by religious and mythical traditions that were valid for the Greeks, but certainly not for the other peoples: typical examples are the themes of the friezes on the Archaic treasury of the Sele. The thesis is also countered by the existence of large sanctuaries that are not linked to a *polis*, such as the temple of Apollo Alaios on the Crimisa promontory (Punta Alice) between Croton and Sybaris, and the Athena temple at Punta della Campanella. Lastly, it is not possible to ignore the traditions rooted in the sanctuaries themselves, which are, of course, expressed in mythical form. The prestige that they conferred reflected on the *poleis* that took possession of the sanctuaries and made use of them in their relationships with other *poleis*; in them were housed signs of the veneration of the traditions (as has been supposed for the Archaic treasury of the *Heraion* near the mouth of the Sele, attributed to Siris). The legend of Heracles, the founder of Croton, and the public cult of Helen and Achilles may possibly be linked to the myths concerning the temple of Hera Lacinia: the historic founder was an Achaean (perhaps of Cretan origin), Myskellos of Rhypes, who is attributed with the plan to found a colony on the site of Sybaris before the one at Croton, although it was thwarted by a response of the Pythian Apollo. Of the various oracles connected with Myskellos' venture, one, quoted by Diodorus (VIII. 17), is particularly interesting, because it outlines, as if it were a logbook, the route from Rhypes to the West: Mount Taphios and Chalcis in the "sacred land of the Curetes" (that is, Aetolia), the Echinades Islands, and then directly to the mouth of the Esaro on the Italian coast between the Crimisa promontory and the site of the Temple of Hera Lacinia, Capo Colonna.

The other colonies of the Ionian coast. Epic traditions and historical memories
About 706 B.C. the Laconian colony Tarentum (Taras) was founded at a point providing excellent shelter for ships in the "instep" of the Ionian coastline at the eastern extremity of the Italian peninsula, where the Mes-

Heraion at the mouth of the Sele River near Paestum

Metaponto, ruins of the Temple of Hera known as the "Tavole Palatine"

Female figurine
found in the extramural sanctuary
at San Biagio alla Venella
525-500 B.C.
Metaponto, Museo
Archeologico Nazionale
Cat. 81/VI

sapii lived. Its founders came from an ancient sacred town of the Spartan state, Amyclae, but they were not Spartans, because they were of illegitimate birth, as two historians quoted by Strabo (VI. 3.2f.), Antiochus of Syracuse and Ephorus of Cyme, stated. According to Antiochus, in fact, these colonists were born of Lacedaemonians (Spartans) who had been reduced to the status of helots because they did not fight in the war against the Messenians; Ephorus, on the other hand, asserted that they were the product of liaisons of their Spartan mothers with helots. Known as *Partheniai* (that is, born of unwed women), they did not, therefore, have the same civil rights as the Spartans. Their leader in the colonial venture was Phalanthus, who, according to Antiochus, was encouraged by a Pythian oracle to go to that part of Italy "to become the scourge of the Iapygi." Here Phalanthus and his comrades were welcomed by the descendants of the Cretans who, during the return voyage to their island from the disastrous expedition to Minos in Sicania (central Sicily), settled among the Messapii. In fact, the site of Tarentum and the nearby port of Satyrion have yielded a great deal of evidence of contacts between the Messapii and the Mycenaean world. The designation *Partheniai* is of particular interest because it indicates that the colonists were only linked to the Lacedaemonians by blood ties through the female line. Details of the tradition regarding their bonds with the cult of Hyacinthus, the major god of Amyclae, whose cult had been absorbed by that of Apollo Hyakinthios, seem to suggest that the *Partheniai* were Laconians of pre-Dorian origin who had rebelled against their inferior status in Spartan society.

Not far from Tarentum, another colonial *polis* boasted Mycenaean origins. This was Metapontum, the name of which resembles that of a district of the Mycenaean kingdom of Messenian Pylos. The existence of a heroic cult (*enagismós*) of the Neleidai, the Pylian dynasts, was adduced (Strabo, VI. 1.15) as confirmation of the tradition that linked an earlier Metapontum with the *nostoi* (the eventful journeys of the Greek heroes returning home from Troy) and proclaimed that the founders of the city were Nestor and his comrades. This is referred to by Bacchylides, who, in an *epinicion* (XI) in honor of a victor from Metapontum in the Pythian games, mentions both the myth of Proetus mad daughters cured by Artemis Hemera at Lysoi (a sacred site in Arcadia that probably formed part of the Mycenaean kingdom of Pylos in the thirteenth century B.C.) and the introduction of the cult of Artemis to Metapontum. Here her sanctuary was probably the one dedicated to Zeus Aglaios as well as to a goddess – as is shown by the votive figurines – near the health-giving spring of modern San Biagio. Although the assertion that the city of Pylian origin had been destroyed by a "Samnite" attack appears to be anachronistic, it cannot be excluded that, by tradition, Oenotrians from areas of the interior that were later settled by the Lucanians were referred to by this ethnic; alternatively, it may relate to one of the early forays of the Italics toward the Ionian coast.

Just as the recollections of the contacts of the peoples of Italy and Sicily with the pre-Hellenic and early Greek world were tinged with *epos*, the traditions relating to contacts with the peoples of Asia Minor depicted the Trojans and Mysians as the protagonists of journeys to the West. In this case, too, it would be prudent not to exclude the existence of a historical basis for the legendary form that memory had assumed. This is the case with the Elymians, a people in western Sicily that Thucydides (VI. 2.3) stated was composed of Trojans and Phocians, and also with Siris, a Magna Grecian city to the west of Metapontum that, according to Antiochus (in Strabo, VI. 1.14), was founded by Trojan exiles and then occupied by the Chones (a people from the Ionian coast of Italy who were linked to the Chaones of the nearby region of Epirus), probably in the first half of the seventh century B.C. The vicissitudes of Siris are particularly interesting, not only because of its supposed Trojan origins – for which the cult of Athena Ilias was cited as proof – but also due to a pious invention in which the strength of the "Trojan" tradition was evident; the series of occupations of the area round Siris by the Ionians and Achaeans after the Chonic period; and, lastly, the links between Siris and the nearby *poleis* of Metapontum and Tarentum. After the intervention of the Chones, Ionians came to Siris from Colophon in Asia Minor (where the Neleidai had arrived from Pylos after the crisis in which the "Mycenaean" kingdoms dissolved), and took the city from the Chones. The suggestion that the city's name was changed to Polieion is not entirely convincing because, in the tradition relating to subsequent events, the *polis* was still called Siris. Possibly the name Polieion replaced the one that the Chones had given to the acropolis they had occupied (and Polieion might also be the site of the tutelary gods of the *polis*). The Ionian conquerors were merciless, and pursued the vanquished into the temple of Athena, dragging those who had sought refuge there from the holy *cella*. It was then that, according to the legend, the eyes of the *xoanon* (sacred image) closed, repeating the miracle caused by Aias in the temple of Athena at Troy, when the Locrian hero did not hesitate to assault Cassandra, and the sacred image averted its gaze from the sacrilege.

An echo of the memory of Aias and his misdeed at Troy was also to be found in another Italiot city, Locri Epizephyrii. Founded about 670, this was quite unique due to the character of its religion and the archaic nature of its institutions. It was already a matter for debate in antiquity whether its founders had come from Opuntian (western) Locris or from Ozolian (eastern) Locris. But the tradition relating to the social status of

Remains of the Achaean colony of Sybaris

Incused silver stater from Sybaris with retrorse bull
silver
ca. 540-510 B.C.
Reggio Calabria, Museo Nazionale

the first colonists is of greater importance than this controversy. According to Aristotle, their ancestors were the illegitimate children of women belonging to the noble families of the Hundred Houses who had committed adultery with servants while their husbands were away fighting for the Spartans during the Messenian war. In the third century B.C., Timaeus denied the validity of Aristotle's assertion, but Polybius (who in XII. 5f. described the main points of the dispute very precisely) stated that he had learned from the testimony of the Italian Locrians, his contemporaries, that the tradition accepted by Aristotle was based on the truth. The nobility of the Hundred Houses has been erroneously identified by modern scholars with the nobility of the whole of Locri. It is evident, however, that the term *hekaton oikiai* (hundred houses) does not refer to the large Locrian *gene* (stocks), but the hundred families of a single *genos*. This is certainly the *genos* of the Aianteioi, which was founded by Aias, the sacrilegious hero, and originally lived in the city of Naryka in Opuntian Locris. For centuries it had been obliged by the enduring strength of the sacred law to expiate the impiety of its founder by sending two virgins every year to serve the goddess in the sanctuary of Athena of Ilium. In fact, although it was expiatory, this custom was cause for pride for the Aianteioi, and even the illegitimate ancestry of the noblewomen of this *genos* was of particular significance in the conservative, religious milieu of a city famous both in Magna Graecia and elsewhere for its cults that were largely chthonic and mystical in character.

Sirites, Locrians, and Troezenians on the Tyrrhenian coast
A close sacred bond therefore linked Siris with Locri. The former's strength became evident when the two cities had to face the coalition of the Achaean *poleis* of Italy. For these – especially for Sybaris and Croton, devoted to commerce with both East and West – the Chalcidian hegemony over the Strait of Messina was a hindrance to their participation in the Tyrrhenian trade. For this reason, during the fourth century, both of them sought to obtain direct communication with the Tyrrhenian coast by overland routes. Croton, which, around 650 B.C. had already founded Caulonia near Punta di Stilo (almost as if it wished to check any Locrian plans to expand to the east at the Sagras River), thanks to the foundation of Scylacium, obtained control of the routes crossing the mountainous isthmus that formed the narrowest point of the peninsula. And where these reached the Tyrrhenian, in the plain of the Lametos (now Lamato or Amato), it built Terina, the importance of which as a trading center is indicated by the name "Terineo" given to the Lamentinus Sinus (Bay of Sant'Eufemia). Although Sybaris did not found any colonies, it strengthened its relations with a major city, Poseidonia (Paestum), founded around 700 B.C. by the Troezenians who had helped to found Sybaris together with its Achaean promoters, but had subsequently been driven away. While this was considered by the Italiot historians to be an injustice on the part of the Sybarites that was expiated by the destruction of their city (Aristotle, *Politics* V. 3.1303a), this event did not appear to disturb relations between Paestum and Sybaris for long, possibly because the Troezenian exiles from Sybaris were given shelter in the

Aerial view of the temples at Paestum

teikhos (warehouse) that other Sybarites had built near the mouth of the Silarus (Sele), probably near a native village. The name of this, Paestum, which re-emerged after the Lucanian conquest of the *polis*, immediately brings to mind Phaestus in Crete Παιστός / φαιστός. Possibly, in order to favor pilgrimages to their sanctuaries, the Locrians had also founded two colonies at Medma and Hipponium, native villages on the Tyrrhenian coast between the Strait of Messina and Terina.

Rhodians and Cretans in Sicily. Rivalry between the poleis *and the first conflicts with the Carthaginians*
In Sicily, the large number of Euboean *poleis* included Leontini, probably founded in order to mark the limit to Syracusan expansion to the north, and Catana, between Mount Etna and the sea, which was intended to keep the Sicel communities that crowded the lower slopes of Etna in check. Around 688 a colony of Rhodians (that is, Greeks from the Southern Sporades) and Cretans was added to these. The name Lindioi given to the fortified nucleus of Gela, the new *polis*, was a clear sign of the preeminent role in the foundation played by Rhodians, especially those from Lindos, the site of the pan-Rhodian sanctuary of Athena. The Geloans extended their dominion to vast plains suitable for the cultivation of grain and horse-breeding.
The rapid economic and political growth of Gela induced the Syracusans to exclude it from the southeastern corner of the island by the foundation of two colonies serving as garrisons in the Anapos Valley, at Acrae (ca. 660) and at Casmenae (ca. 640). More decisive was the founding around 600 of an important colony, Camarina, on the south coast between the Hipparis and the Oanis. This soon became independent and acquired considerable prestige among the Sicels, so that it rivaled its metropolis in the region, and even came into conflict with Syracuse around the middle of the sixth century. In accordance with the age-old Corinthian vocation, the Syracusans aspired to play a leading role in the Greek sea trade in the West. With the foundation of Camarina, they showed that they were interested in the Sicilian Channel, which provided an alternative route to the Tyrrhenian and the western Mediterranean that avoided the Strait of Messina. In this

respect, the Syracusans' designs were in competition with those of the Geloans and the Megarians. Around 628 the latter, who were more enterprising, had hastened to found Selinus, prompting the Geloans to found, about 580, Acragas, midway between Gela and Selinus. Situated between two rivers, it was four kilometers from the sea, so that, as Polybius observed, the new city had "all the advantages of a sea-town." In order to halt the Geloan and Acragantine advance toward the west, the Selinuntines colonized an old port at the mouth of the Halykos, Heraclea Minoa: this was an outlet for the Sican area of which the King Cocalus had been the overlord. In his palace, the Cretan king Minos met his death, according to the Cretan tradition recorded at Praisos by Herodotus (VII. 170f.).

Together with the Syracusans, the Geloans and Acragantines were the main protagonists of the history of the Greeks in the West from the mid-sixth to the mid-fifth centuries. In fact, it was in Acragas that the tyrant Phalaris (ca. 570–555) began the first attempt to form a single monarchical state, with the search for a port on the Tyrrhenian, of vital importance for the Acragantine economy, which necessarily involved an attack on the most immediate enemies of the Greeks in Sicily, the Carthaginians, who had possessions in the west of the island. In the early sixth century, the Geloan tyrant Hippocrates attempted to bring eastern Sicily under his rule and to get control of the Strait of Messina. In Syracuse, however, Gelon and Hieron (sons of Deinomenes) pursued Hippocrates' schemes with a broader political vision and greater success, and, in Acragas, Theron repeated Phalaris' attempt to conquer an outlet onto the Tyrrhenian at Himera. This city was founded about 649 by the Zanclaeans on the north coast of Sicily, between the Himeras (now called Imera Settentrionale or Fiume Grande) and the Torto, with the evident aim of countering any Carthaginian plans to expand their territory.

Conflicting aspirations to hegemony of the western Mediterranean poleis

Toward the middle of the sixth century the political and cultural life of the western Mediterranean was dominated – as far as Magna Graecia and Sicily were concerned – by power struggles between the main *poleis*. These were provoked by plans for territorial expansion and active participation in international trade, in which competition between Greeks, Carthaginians, and Etruscans was accentuated. And in the Greek area, economic and political development was matched by extraordinary progress in philosophy, science, technology, and the arts. In eastern Sicily, tension increased between the Dorian *poleis* (principally Rhodian Gela and Acragas, and Corinthian Syracuse) and the Ionian ones, which were anxious to defend their hegemony of the Strait of Messina; obviously, this was not due to the origins of their founders, but to the conflict of interests existing at that time. In the western part of the island, on the other hand, Selinus rapidly increased the volume of its trade, and enjoyed great prestige among the non-Greek peoples who surrounded it. But, using their territories as a base, the Carthaginians of Sicily joined forces with their fellow countrymen in North Africa and the Etruscan cities in an attempt to hinder Greek sea trade.

Inevitably, events in the eastern Mediterranean had repercussions in the western part of the sea: as early as the end of the seventh century, the war between the two main *poleis* of Euboea, Chalcis and Eretria, for possession of the Lelantine Plain, the richest area of their island, had resulted in the defeat of Eretria. During this conflict various *poleis* had allied themselves with one or other of these cities: Samos and the Thessalians with Chalcis, and Miletus with Eretria; and it is likely that the effects of the dispute were felt throughout the West. The Persian conquest of Asia Minor, however, had more immediate and serious consequences in the West: when, in 546, Cyrus' armies, having occupied the kingdom of Lydia, reached the coast with its numerous Greek *poleis*, most of these surrendered to the Persians. But the citizens of the Ionian city of Phocaea did not wish to submit to the "barbarian" conqueror, and the majority of them preferred to leave their city and move further west, where around 600 B.C. their colonists had founded an important trading *polis*, Massalia (Marseilles), near the mouth of the Rhône; this was soon followed by other smaller towns on the Ligurian and Spanish coasts.

The Phocaeans, who were particularly enterprising traders and built fast cargo ships, had, more than anyone else, been able to take advantage of the discovery, made by the Samian navigator Colaeus, of a pan-Iberian trading settlement at Tartessus at the mouth of the Baetis (Guadalquivir) that was not yet open to international commerce. The Phocaeans made friends with the king of Tartessus, Arganthonius, and he contributed generously to their defense against the Persian menace. But, when it was clear that any resistance was in vain, most of the Phocaeans decided to emigrate to a trading settlement of theirs, Alalia, founded about 560 on the north-eastern coast of Corsica. From this base, they disturbed the trade of the Etruscan cities, situated not far distant across the Tyrrhenian Sea, so that, around 540, the Etruscans decided to join forces with the Carthaginians against Alalia. Although the Phocaeans were able to repel the enemy ships, their losses of men and ships were such that they found it necessary to abandon Corsica. And, judging by

Velia (Elea), view and detail of the archaeological remains

the total silence of the most authoritative historians, Massalia and the other Phocaean colonies in this area remained totally extraneous to their conduct and the resulting conflict: evidently they were on good terms with both the Etruscans and Carthaginians. Thus, together with the Massaliots' policy of non-intervention, there was the fact that the Phocaeans of Alalia, forced to find another site, headed for Magna Graecia, where, with the aid of the Rhegians and, above all, of the Paestans, they acquired a village in the Oenotrian area, between Paestum and Pyxus (a trading settlement founded by Siris), and founded their own *polis*, which kept the Oenotrian name, Velia (Hyele, then Grecized as Elea).

Serious conflicts in Magna Graecia. The demise of Siris and Sybaris
Meanwhile, events were taking a turn for the worse in Magna Graecia, where the Achaean *poleis* Sybaris and Croton, apart from trade, also engaged in agriculture (this was particularly important for Metapontum). Thus, they had become trading partners with the leading cities of the Aegean: Sybaris with Corinth and Miletus, and Croton with Samos. However, the activity of Siris, which was linked to Colophon, disturbed these Aegean cities and their western partners. It is probable that the presence of the Phocaeans – whose good relations with Colophon are indicated by the arrival of the philosopher Xenophanes at Elea – was a matter of serious concern to the two Achaean *poleis* on the Ionian coast, as they were particularly interested in the Tyrrhenian trade. In this respect, the tradition (attested by Timaeus in Athenaeus, XII, 520 B.C.) of trading relations between Sybaris and the Etruscans is significant. Between 540 and 538 Sybaris and Croton, together with Metapontum (the proximity of Siris was an even greater obstacle to the expansion of this city) attacked Siris and obliterated it. The record of events in Magna Graecia in this period is extremely fragmentary, but, from what happened during the period between the demise of Sybaris and that of Siris, it is evident that relations between the Italiots were extremely unstable, especially due to the effects of civil wars. There was a sequel to the war against Siris in the conflict between Croton and Locri Epizephyrii: a long-standing community of interests, probably nurtured by religious bonds, had induced the Locrians to support Siris. The Crotoniates, however, wanted to punish them for this, encouraged by the belief that they now had an opportunity to conquer at least part of the Locrian territory. The boundary of this with Croton was

Detail of the remains of Caulonia

marked by the Sagras River, and on the banks of this the two armies met. Against all the odds, the Locrians won: in fact, on the basis of the historical fact of a request for aid sent to Sparta, possibly through Tarentum – to which the Spartans are alleged to have replied with an exhortation to invoke the assistance of the Dioscuri (or else they sent images of Castor and Pollux) – the legend of the presence of the two gods on the side of the Locrians during the battle was born. Certainly, this epiphany was fitting for the city possessing the temple that was, as Diodorus put it (XXVII. 4), "the most illustrious of the sanctuaries in Italy."

The defeat humiliated the Crotoniates, who made a recovery a few years later, thanks, above all, to the work of Pythagoras, an exile from Samos oppressed by the tyranny of Polycrates and his brothers that had begun in 538. The foundation of the school of Pythagoras, the beneficial influence that his religious and ethical doctrine (identifiable with Orphism) had on Crotoniate society, the political leadership assumed by Pythagoras, and the remarkable development of the study of mathematics, astronomy, nature, and medicine, gave new vigor to the Crotoniates. The effects were seen a few years later in their victory over the Sybarites, which marked the end of rivalry that had declined during the war against Siris, but had become intense once again due to the addition of an ideological conflict to the extenuated conflict of interests. Sybaris had appeared to be very powerful, especially as it had lavished its citizenship on the native peoples of the region, forming a ring of twenty-five smaller towns dependent on it, and it had made military alliances with four native peoples. Moreover, in order to maintain its presence on the Tyrrhenian, it had strengthened its old friendship with Paestum: thanks to its links with the Phocaeans of Elea, this city could expect solidarity to be shown with itself and the Italian *poleis* with which it was on good terms.

Regarding this relationship of the Paestans with Sybaris, a treaty of eternal friendship between the Sybarites and the Serdaioi is documented: the text of this, written on a bronze plaque, was deposited at the Panhellenic sanctuary of Olympia. The guarantors of this pact were declared to be Zeus, Apollo, and the other gods, as well as "the *polis* Poseidonia." The identity of the Serdaioi is uncertain, although they minted coins based on Paestan types. Thus, the majority of scholars believe that the Serdaioi, who are not mentioned in the extant historical writing, were a non-Greek people of Magna Graecia. This is not contradicted by the suggestion that they may be associated with Sardinia (as the ethnic seems to imply), since a tradition mentioned by Diodorus (V. 15) states that the Thespiadai, Greek colonists in Sardinia, emigrated from the island to Italy, "close to Cumae" – in other words, in an area on the Tyrrhenian where it is likely that the Paestans would have had an intermediary role.

The wealth and prestige of Sybaris were not, however, matched by its military power, because, convinced as they were of their invulnerability, the Sybarites led a life of ease and comfort that was in sharp contrast with the strict discipline imposed in Croton by the Pythagoreans. Further weakening of Sybaris was caused by the acquisition of the Sirite territory and the internal struggles for the distribution of the new lands. It was in this difficult situation, moreover, that the Sybarites requested the Achaeans of the Peloponnese to increase the population of Metapontum, which had been weakened by the incursion of a native people (described as "Samnites"), rather than found a new city in the territory formerly occupied by Siris. Strabo (VI. 1.15) gives a clear explanation for this: since two territories were available, and that of Metapontum was closer to Tarentum – the Achaeans wanted to slow down the latter's expansion toward the west (the only direction possible that would have avoided a clash with the Messapii) – the new colonists decided it was preferable to settle at Metapontum, which urgently needed fresh blood. Thus, effective defense was provided for the area of Siris, which could be divided between Metapontum and Sybaris (obviously this would get the lion's share). All this explains why both Metapontum and Croton wanted to free themselves of the power that threatened both *poleis*. The Crotoniates, now the strongest, took action: about 510 Sybaris was conquered, its public buildings were destroyed, its citizens had to leave, and another famous Italian *polis* was no more. A deep impression must have been made on the Greeks: it is known that the Milesians wanted to observe public mourning. It is also worth noting that the destruction of Sybaris coincided with the fall of the monarchy in Rome. In view of the pro-Hellenic leanings of the Tarquins and the friendship of Tarquinius Superbus with Aristodemus, the tyrant of Cumae, it is likely that there was a link between the two events. Certainly, the disappearance of the two great *poleis* upset the balance of power in the Italiot and Siceliot areas, and, more generally, in the whole of the western Mediterranean.

The Siceliot tyrants
It hardly seems to be a coincidence that one of the first steps taken by the republican government in Rome was the signing of a treaty with Carthage, the text of which, translated into Greek, is found in Polybius (III. 22). The document indicates that the Romans, who had been busy extending their rule over Latium for some time and were already engaged in trade on a large scale in the western seas, were anxious to tackle an emergency. Moreover, it is probable that a similar concern for the repercussions of events in Magna Graecia and in Sicily, where there was a danger of anti-Greek initiatives by the Carthaginians, was related to the rise of the tyranny in Gela. Everywhere, especially in Sicily, the existence of high political tension favored unitary and authoritarian solutions, such as tyranny; and the *poleis* of the south coast of the island were most vulnerable to Carthaginian attack.

The first tyrant of Gela was Cleander (ca. 505); he was succeeded by his brother Hippocrates, who between 498 and 493 conquered Sicel and Greek territories in eastern Sicily, with the evident aim of bringing the Strait of Messina under his control. In fact, he took possession of Zancle; as governor, he installed Scythes, an important personage from Cos, perhaps in the belief that the high esteem in which he was held by the Persian king would be beneficial to the relations of Gela with Asia Minor, where the Ionian revolt was coming to an end. But, in order to fully control the straits, it was necessary to get possession of both Rhegium and Zancle. To this end, the tyrant of Rhegium, Anaxilas, decided to seize Zancle from Hippocrates by taking advantage of the arrival of numerous Samians who, after the defeat of the Ionians at Lade in 494, had left their homeland in order to found a colony on the north coast of Sicily at Kale Akte. Anaxilas, however, persuaded them to take Zancle during the absence of Scythes, who, together with Hippocrates, was engaged in a difficult war against the Sicels in the area round Etna. The Geloan tyrant decided the time was now ripe for an agreement with the Samians, thus managing to maintain a degree of control over Zancle, where Scythes, who had returned to Cos, was replaced by his son Cadmus. Shortly afterward, Hippocrates met his death while he was besieging Hybla Geleatis.

A revolt by the Geloans against Hippocrates' sons was crushed by the cavalry-commander, Gelon, the son of Deinomenes. He belonged to an influential family from Tilos, in the Dodecanese, in which there was a hereditary priesthood of a cult – probably mystic – of chthonic gods. Thanks to his priestly authority, one of Gelon's ancestors, Telines, had already managed to crush a rebellion in Gela. The prestige of his family and his military experience allowed Deinomenes' son to succeed Hippocrates. Meanwhile, taking advantage of these disorders, Anaxilas had occupied Zancle, changing its name, in honor of his homeland (Messenia), into Messana. He expelled the Samians and Cadmus, thus obtaining the longed-for possession of the straits; he protected their northern access against the Etruscans with a fort at Scylla. The need to reinforce his dominion over the areas conquered by Hippocrates and to pursue the latter's political and military designs – but more systematically and in a broader perspective – momentarily distracted Gelon from a war against Anaxilas and focused his attention on Syracuse, the largest Siceliot port. This had been one of the objectives

Stater of the Serdaioi
with Dionysus
and a branch of a grape vine
ca. 480 B.C.
Paris, Bibliothèque Nationale
de France
Cabinet des Médailles

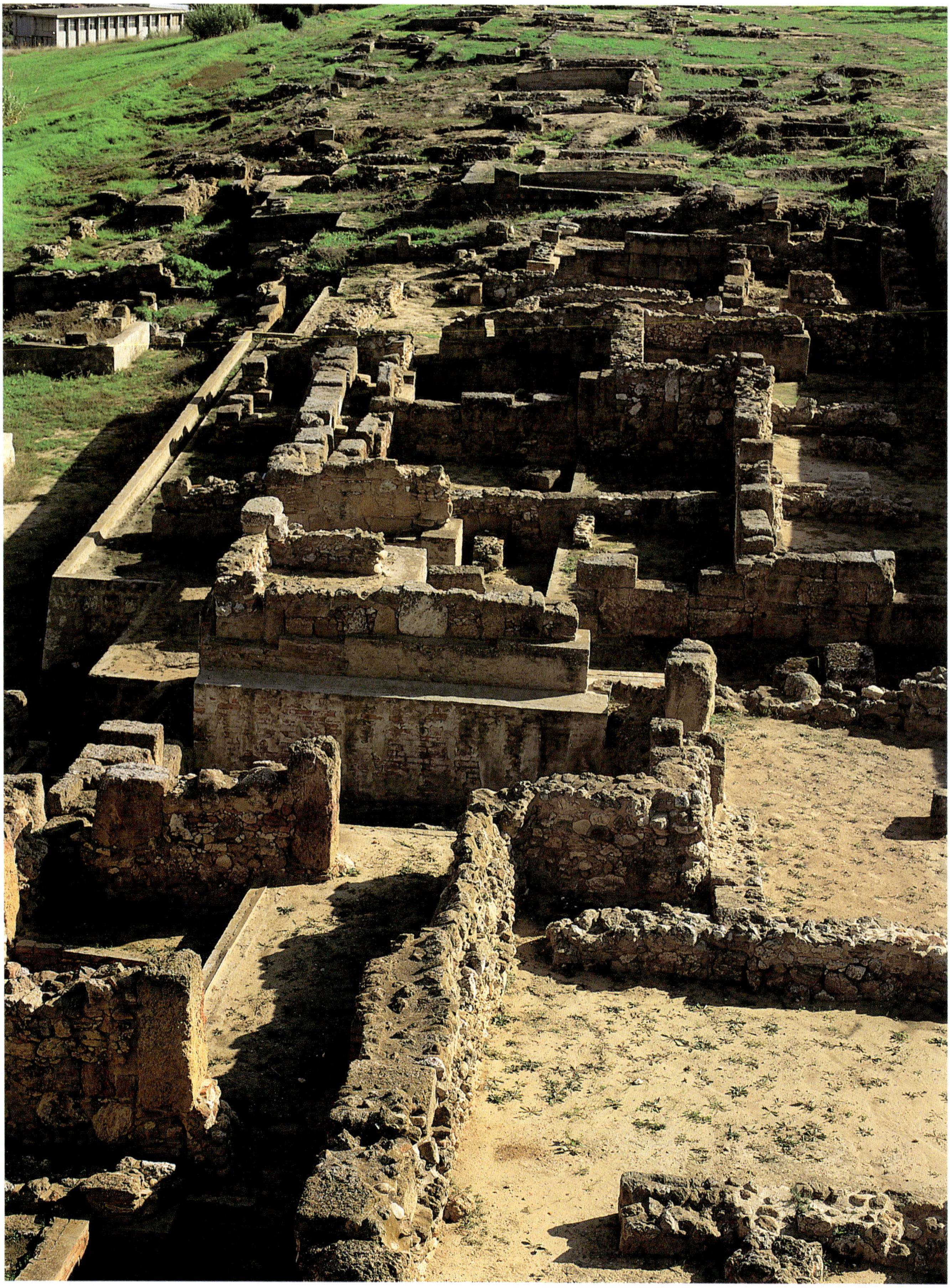

opposite
View of part of the ruins of Gela

Syracuse
the archaeological area

of Hippocrates, who, in 492, had defeated the Syracusans on the Helorus River. However, due to the intervention of Corinth and Corcyra, he had been obliged to make do with the territory of Camarina, and had refounded the city, the political life of which had declined notably after an unsuccessful conflict with its metropolis in 553.

In 485 Gelon managed to enter Syracuse, assuming the role of mediator in a bitter conflict between the aristocratic class known as the *gamoroi* (land-owners), and the democrats, who were supported by the mass of serfs of Sicel or Sican origin (the *Kyllyrioi* or *Killikyrioi*). This crisis favored the designs of Gelon, who, thanks to his military power, became the ruler of the city. He was responsible for making it the center of a great state that extended from Gela to Naxos, including, from 485 onward, the isolated city of Megara Hyblaea; this had been weakened by civil strife that had exiled the aristocrats, who found asylum in Selinus. The Megarian aristocracy had supported the Syracusans in the war against Camarina: now Gelon, who had designated his brother Hieron as ruler of Gela, removed all the inhabitants of Camarina to Syracuse (after its refoundation in 492 by Hippocrates, they were mostly of Geloan origin) and destroyed their city. He permitted the wealthy citizens of Megara – the ones who had offered resistance earlier – to move to Syracuse, while he reduced the common people to slavery, and had them deported from Sicily. The same fate awaited the population of Euboea, a colony founded by the Chalcidians of Leontini. Apart from the increase in the population and the cynical reduction in the numbers of the lower classes, Gelon instituted a trained army and built a large fleet; this was to meet the requirements not only of the already intense Syracusan trade, but also of future military operations that were to be expected after the constitution of his large state in eastern

Remains at Camarina

Agrigento
the archaeological remains
including the colossus

opposite
The temple of Concordia
at Agrigento

Sicily. Naturally, this was cause for considerable concern for Anaxilas, as well as for the Etruscans and Carthaginians, whose ships had been plundered by a skillful admiral, Dionysius of Phocaea. Formerly commander of the Ionian fleet, he had risen against Darius of Persia, and, after the defeat at Lade, had taken refuge with his ships in the Aeolian Islands. His activity confirms the historical authenticity of a tradition that attributed the initiative for an agreement with the Carthaginians to Darius at the time of his expedition against Athens and Eretria in 490. On the other hand, that the Greek West formed part of the political horizon of the Persian king is indicated by the episode, related by Herodotus (III. 134–137), when Persian emissaries were sent to the West to inquire about the political situation. They were headed by the Crotoniate physician Democedes, who stood high in the favor of Darius and his queen, Atossa: after having been taken prisoner with other courtiers of Polycrates of Samos, he was able to demonstrate his superiority over the king's Egyptian physicians.

Perhaps the rapid and unexpected conclusion at Marathon of the punitive expedition of the Persians against Athens restrained the Carthaginians from waging war against the Greeks in the West. But the opportunity arose again when Xerxes decided to intervene forcibly in Greece; while the negotiations between Persia and Carthage were in progress, the Greeks, who had confederated against the formidable adversary, sought the aid of the tyrant of Syracuse, now that the fame of his military and naval power had spread far and wide. Naturally, it is difficult to imagine that a decisive conflict like the one that was brewing would not involve both the Greeks in Italy and Sicily and the Carthaginians, who could not remain indifferent to the political ascent of the Siceliot states, or the dangers incurred by their Sicilian possessions and their hegemony over trade in the Mediterranean lying to the west of the Tyrrhenian. Gela and Syracuse had now been joined by Acragas, where the tyrant was Theron, a descendant of the Emmenidai, a Theraean family that had migrated in the second half of the seventh century to Telos, and thence to Sicily with the founders of Gela. The friendly relations that probably existed between the Deinomenidai and the Emmenidai were strengthened by their common interests, since both the Syracusan tyrant and the Acragantine one endeavored to be preeminent among the Siceliot states in order to defend their political independence and trading interests from the ever-present threat of the Carthaginians and Etruscans.

The extent to which Carthage strove to maintain its position in Sicily was evident in the early sixth century, when a war between the Elymians of Segesta and the Selinuntines aided by a Cnidian noble, Pentathlus, the founder of a Greek colony at Lilybaeum in territory controlled by Carthaginians, had provoked the intervention of a Carthaginian army commanded by Malchus to support the Carthaginian garrisons in western Sicily. About 575 Pentathlus and his Rhodian and Cnidian companions had been expelled from Lilybaeum

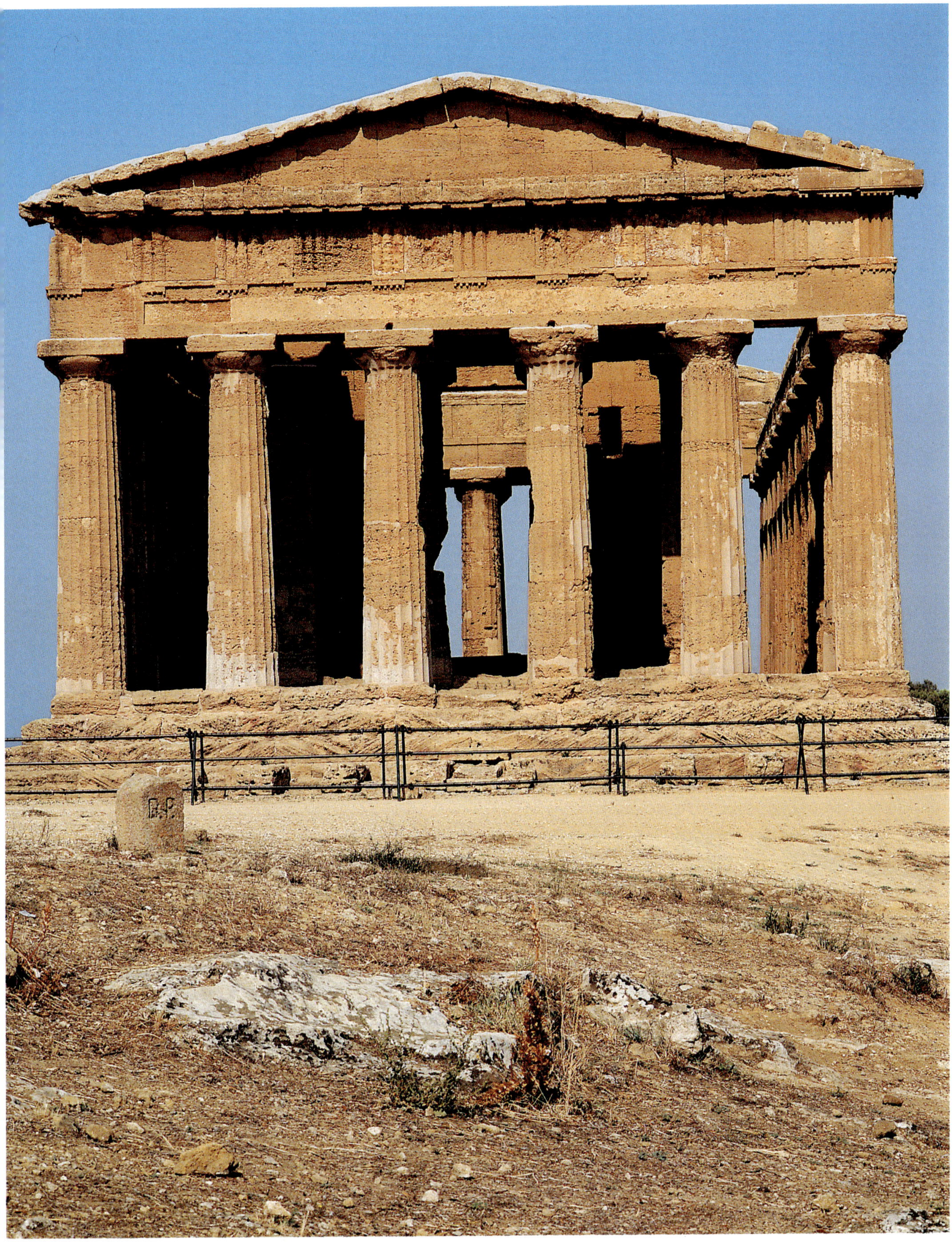

and had moved to Lipara in the Aeolian Islands, where the coexistence of the Greeks with the native population, who had been dedicated seafarers for centuries, was governed by an unusual collectivist system. Toward the end of the same century, a Spartan prince, Dorieus, had founded a colony, Heraclea, near Eryx, a promontory famous for an ancient sanctuary of the Aegean Aphrodite. However, the Carthaginians and the Elymians immediately joined forces in order to destroy Heraclea: Carthage could not abide any foreign interference in its total control of the Sicilian Channel, one of the two main routes between the eastern and western Mediterranean.

From the outset of colonization, these vital requirements of the Carthaginians had certainly not escaped the attention of the Siceliot leaders. But it was Gelon who, following in Hippocrates' footsteps, was first able to counter them effectively. In 491 when he was still tyrant of Gela, he established excellent relations with Rome, donating grain for a *frumentatio* (charitable distribution of corn): he thus showed that he was fully conscious of the role that Rome could play in limiting the Etruscan hegemony of the Tyrrhenian. He also strengthened his links with Acragas, forming a military alliance with Theron, whose designs on Himera were compatible with the policy of the Syracusan state: indeed, they helped to check any further expansion of Carthaginian power toward the West. And, in order to strengthen the alliance, Gelon married Theron's daughter, Damareta.

The first conflict between Siceliotes and Carthaginians and Etruscans
At the beginning of the fifth century the crisis arrived in both the East and West; and, once again, the Persian plans to subject Greece converged with those of the Carthaginians, for whom, in any case, it was worth supporting the great power whose Mediterranean dominions now extended from Asia Minor to Egypt. Faced with this difficult, complex situation, Gelon acted with great caution. Aware that the war would inevitably spread to the West, he replied to the request for aid that the Panhellenic congress held at Isthmus sent to him, and to the Cretans and other western Greek states, with the proposal – which was not accept-

The remains of Himera

Decadrachma Demareteion
with a *quadriga*
and the nymph Arethusa
from Syracuse
ca. 480-471 B.C.
Paris, Bibliothèque Nationale
de France
Cabinet des Médailles

ed – that he should be entrusted with the supreme command. Moreover, he sent Cadmus to cruise in Greek waters as confirmation of Syracuse's friendship in case the Persians should be victorious.

In this climate, the antagonism between Syracuse and Rhegium soon came to a head: Anaxilas and his father-in-law, Terillus, the tyrant of Himera threatened by Theron, urged the Carthaginians to intervene against Syracuse and Acragas. The Carthaginians had in fact already prepared large forces to attack the two main Siceliot states at the same time as the Persian offensive in the Aegean. And the pressure of Anaxilas and Terillus directed the operations along the north coast of the island toward the Strait of Messina. In the year 480 a large Carthaginian land and sea force attacked: the first battle, which took place near Himera, was won by the Syracusans and Acragantines. They routed the Carthaginians, whose defeat was aggravated by the death of their commander, Hamilcar, an important member of the Carthaginian aristocracy.

Such was the enthusiasm for this Greek victory over the "barbarians" of the West that, by tradition, the victory of Himera was considered to have taken place on the same day as the equally decisive one at Salamis (or else on the day of Thermopylae, thus linking in a fascinating rhetorical contrast "a glorious victory and a glorious defeat"). Realistically, the Carthaginians did not attempt to repeat the attack, and made peace with Gelon; he imposed the building of two temples (one of which was in Carthaginian territory) in which, guaranteed by the gods, the treaty documents were to be kept, and abstention from human sacrifice (for different reasons, tradition also attributed this prohibition to Darius). Terillus lost Himera, and Anaxilas, who had not taken part in the military operations, was obliged to accept terms that, naturally enough, safeguarded the interests of Syracuse and Acragas.

Geron died about two years after the victory at Himera; he was succeeded by his brother, Hieron, who married Damareta and appointed his brother Polyzelus ruler of Gela. In furtherance of his predecessor's policy, Hieron did not neglect the other side of the straits. In fact, he intervened to defend the Locrians – to whom he was also linked by the hereditary role (indicated by his full name of Hieronymos) of priest of the chthonic gods – against an attempt at conquest by Anaxilas, who was now aware that the death of Gelon had not reduced Syracusan vigilance over Italian affairs. Further confirmation was provided by Hieron when he intervened in favor of the surviving Sybarites who, when they attempted to reoccupy the site of their city, were faced with the implacable hostility of the Crotoniates. In fact, after the defeat of Sybaris, there had been violent disputes in Croton, culminating in the expulsion of Pythagoras, who fled to Metapontum after a vain attempt to find refuge in Locri.

Meanwhile, there was a deterioration in relations between Hieron and Polyzelus; the latter was suspected of conspiring, together with his father-in-law, Theron, to usurp his brother as ruler of the Syracusan state. However, in 474 Hieron's prestige was boosted throughout the Greek world thanks to his great victory off Cumae over the fleet of the Etruscan states, which were seeking to take possession of the Bay of Naples, an area of vital commercial and strategic importance that had long been coveted by the Etruscans of the Tyrrhenian, Capua, and the Gulf of Salerno. Their designs were definitively thwarted by Hieron's victory, and Syracuse replaced Cumae as the guardian of Hellenism on the northern borders of Magna Graecia. It was not only solidarity with the oldest Italian *polis*, which was no longer able to assume the role that it had played until the time of the Aristodemus' rule – when it had repulsed in 524 the attack of an alliance of Etruscans from the Adriatic coast, Umbrians, and Daunians – that obliged Hieron to intervene, but also the position that Syracuse had now taken in the Tyrrhenian. In order to ensure that there was a vigilant presence in the bay, a Syracusan garrison was placed on Ischia, at the entrance to the bay, and the city of Parthenope, which was now expanded, became totally independent and was given the name of Neapolis, fulfilling the function that Cumae could no longer perform.

The collapse of the tyrannies in Sicily. Ducetius and the Sicels
On the death of Hieron, who, even more than Gelon, had patronized the letters and arts, and, like his brother, had frequently participated in the Panhellenic games at Olympia and Delphi, Thrasybulus, the last of the Deinomenids, became the ruler of Syracuse. But neither he, nor Thrasydaeus, who succeeded his father, Theron, in Acragas, had the mettle of their predecessors, and both ruled only for a short time. In Rhegium, Anaxilas' minister, Micythus, had ruled in his capacity as guardian of the tyrant's children from 476 to 467 B.C.; furthermore, in 461 a popular uprising overthrew the tyranny. Thus, all the Siceliot cities had regained their independence: Messana was once again called Zancle; and the former inhabitants of Catana returned to their city – together with those of Naxos, they had been compelled by Hieron to move to Leontini, while their city received five thousand Peloponnesians, evidently mercenaries, and the same number of Syracusans, and was called Aetna. In 461 the Catanaeans also returned to their city, restored its former name, and expelled the mercenaries, who occupied a Sicel town, Inessa, calling this Aetna. In other *poleis*, too, the new

Heraclea Minoa

democratic governments deprived the mercenaries who had settled there during the period of the tyrannies of their civil rights, obliging them to return the dwellings they had occupied to the inhabitants who had returned from exile.

The influx of mercenaries in the service of the tyrants continued to create problems not only for many Sicilian *poleis*, but also for many native communities, the sites of which were forcibly occupied by the mercenaries. The latter were usually less culturally developed than the Sicels and Sicans, who, during their prolonged contact with the Greeks, had assimilated more refined institutions and customs. An indication of this was, in particular, the career of a Sicel chief, Ducetius, who, after collaborating with the Syracusans and, during the siege of Aetna, leading a Sicel army he had raised himself, promoted the foundation, on the Greek model, of a confederation of Sicel towns around the Sanctuary of the Palici, the twin gods of a volcanic lake near Menaenum, his home town. Thus, the leader managed to establish a Sicel state that Hellenized towns such as Inessa and Morgantina joined. About 450 Ducetius decided he could expand his state at the expense of Acragas, perhaps believing that the demise of the closely linked dynasties of the Deinomenidai and the Emmenidai was of little import to the Syracusans, with whom he was on excellent terms. But the spirit of Hellenic solidarity and the concern for the ascent of a Sicel leader prevailed, and the Syracusans came to the aid of the Acragantines: Ducetius was defeated in a battle at Nomai. He surrendered to the Syracusans, presenting himself as a suppliant at the altar of the *agora*. He was then exiled to Corinth; yet, despite his banishment from Sicily, he returned five years later with the support of the Corinthians and, probably, the assent of the Syracusans, to found a new colony at Kale Akte. This would in fact have offered Syracuse – which did not yet control the straits – a longed-for outlet to the Tyrrhenian. However, Ducetius' death in 440 led to the failure of this plan; and the attempt to constitute a unified Sicel state was not repeated.

Athens and Magna Graecia. The foundation of Thurii and Heraclea
Athens, which had favored sea routes since the age of Themistocles, had, since that time, looked westward, especially toward Italy. When the Spartans opposed Themistocles' clever plan to engage the Persians in a naval battle in the Saronic Gulf, Themistocles threatened that he would persuade his fellow-citizens, who had already been evacuated from Athens, to offer no resistance to the invader and emigrate to Siris in Italy. As Themistocles declared in Herodotus' account (VIII. 62), "this has been ours since ancient times, and the oracles have pronounced that we must colonize it." Whatever may have been the source of this statement, which is not lacking in contradiction, it is evident that the memory of the settlers from Colophon present at

Siris was still alive in Athens, and reference was made to this in the arguments of those advocating a more incisive Athenian presence in the West. In this regard, Athens was also encouraged by its rivalry with Corinth, which, for its sea traffic with the West, availed itself of two naval stations, Corcyra and, above all, Syracuse. So far, Athens, which had not participated in the colonization of the West, had only had direct relations with a Hellenized Elymian city, Segesta; this had requested a treaty of alliance in 458, when it was at war with Selinus.

The chance for firm intervention in the West was provided in 448 by an episode that occurred during the long conflict between Croton and the surviving Sybarites, who were very attached to their ancestral city. In 453 with the aid of Poseidonia (Paestum) and Laus (a Sybarite colony on the Tyrrhenian), they had founded a new Sybaris; however, in 448 the Crotoniates compelled them to abandon it. This was when the Sybarites invited Athens and Sparta to participate in the foundation of a new city on the site of the old one. Although Sparta was not in the least interested in a colonial venture in the West, Pericles saw this as an excellent opportunity for direct intervention in Italy. In 445 he sent ten fully equipped ships under the command of Lampon, an authoritative seer, and Xenocrates; he also sent heralds to all the *poleis* of the Peloponnese, with which Athens had recently made the Thirty Years' Peace, to announce that whosoever wished

Heraclea Minoa
the Greek theater

Heraclea Minoa
the archaeological area
with detail of a Greek column

could take part in the colonial venture promoted by Athens. Many accepted, and the Athenian and Peloponnesian colonists, together with the Sybarites, founded the new city where the remains of the old one still existed, but they gave it a new name, Thurioi (from the name of a nearby spring, Thuria), in order to avoid causing further resentment on the part of the Crotoniates. The Sybarites, who had been reluctant to accept the change of name of the *polis*, did not get on well with the new settlers, because the former demanded privileges that were unacceptable to the latter. After a bloody conflict with the new colonists, the Sybarites left Thurii and founded another Sybaris on the Traeis River, without provoking a reaction from the Crotoniates this time, perhaps because it was enough for the latter that their old rivals did not rebuild their city in its original form (and the firm opposition to its rebirth on the first site seems to suggest that its destruction was accompanied by deprecatory rites, and this would explain the presence of Lampon). The inhabitants of Thurii requested, therefore, that other Greeks should be sent, and distributed the land equitably: this had been one of the causes of the dispute with the Sybarites. The constitution of the *polis* was drawn up by a philosopher friend of Pericles, Protagoras of Abdera, in accordance with the democratic principles that were also respected in the planning of the new city by the architect Hippodamus of Miletus, who was responsible for the city plan of Piraeus. Its citizens included men of culture, one of whom, Herodotus of Halicarnassus, wrote the final draft of his history in Italy, as is indicated by the *incipit* of this ("the history of Herodotus of Thurii"). There was also a famous Spartan *strategos*, Cleandridas, who had left his homeland after being accused of corruption.

Evidently, Thurii had to face problems concerning its relations with other Italian *poleis*: there was friction with Terina, Croton's colony on the *Lametinus Sinus* (Bay of Sant'Eufemia), where Thurii also sought an outlet to the Tyrrhenian; and a more serious conflict with Tarentum, which, after it had finally checked the frequent incursions of Iapygians and Peucetii, endeavored to expand its territory westward, to where the destruction of Sybaris had made available the area assigned to this *polis* in the division of the territory of Siris with Metapontum. Naturally, Thurii was also interested in this; after inconclusive clashes, the inhabitants of Thurii and Tarentum agreed to share the disputed land. However, Tarentum, politically and militarily the stronger of the two, tended to dominate the area, as is demonstrated by the foundation of one of its colonies, Heraclea, not far from the site of Siris.

This foundation, which for the Tarentine aristocracy resolved urgent problems resulting from an increase in population, boosted the prestige of the Laconian *polis* among the Italiotes, who now felt the repercussions of the Peloponnesian War. During the decline of Croton's power – evidence of which is the minting of coinage by Pandosia (an Oenotrian city incorporated into the Sybarite state and then, after 510, into that of Croton) and Caulonia – the Locrians, backed by Tarentum and Sparta, attempted to bring the colonies of Medma and Hipponium under their control once again, thereby coming into conflict with Rhegium, which had been hostile to Locri for some time and was no longer restrained by the fear of Syracusan intervention. In 433 Rhegium had concluded a treaty of alliance with Athens, and, in 427 the Athenians helped it to invade part of the Locrian territory. However, this occupation did not last long: in 425 the Locrians aided the Syracusans, who were striving to bring the straits under their control. But a grave threat was now hanging over Magna Graecia: the Sabelli were spreading southward from the mountainous areas of central Italy, while Sicily was preparing for the predictable involvement of the island in the conflict between Athens and Sparta.

First of all, the Samnite invasion of Campania overwhelmed Etruscan Capua in 424 and Greek Cumae in 421; further south, in Magna Graecia, another Sabellian group, the Lucanians, became a nation, and one of Philoctetes' cities, Petelia (between the Crimisa promontory [Punta Alice] and Capo Colonna), was described as the metropolis of this new Italic confederation. Within this, another nation, that of the Bruttii, asserted its independence: less advanced culturally, it comprised Samnite conquerors and native peoples of the southern tip of Italy, such as the Chones of Epirote origin. Thurii was one of the first cities to be subjected to attack by the Lucanians, who were attracted by the fertile plains and the rich cities of the coast. Early in the century, the Lucanians conquered Poseidonia and the former Sybarite colonies of Laus, Pyxus, and Scidrus; the very name "Poseidonia" disappeared, and was substituted by the pre-Hellenic "Paistom"; and in that same century Aristoxenus of Tarentum very effectively expressed the grief with which the Italiotes subject to the "barbarians" mourned the defunct Hellenic institutions. Neapolis (with Ischia), where many Cumaeans had taken refuge, managed to preserve its Grecism in its language and institutions, but was obliged to receive many Samnites as its citizens. Possibly because of the limited extent of its territory and the difficulty of land access, Elea also remained immune from attack. The impending danger meant that greater unity of the Italiotes was of vital importance: at the beginning of the fourth century, Thurii, Metapontum, and Elea joined a league formed at the end of the previous century by Croton, Sybaris (the one on the Traeis River), and Caulonia. There is, however, no evidence that Rhegium, Tarentum, or the city most exposed to the Lucanian offensive, Heraclea, joined.

Athenian intervention in Sicily. The war between Athens and Syracuse

In the last quarter of the fifth century events in Sicily became more complex and violent: its *poleis*, in fact, could not remain mere spectators of the great conflict that had involved many of their metropolises (Corinth and Megara on Sparta's side, and bellicose Euboea on that of Athens), and had already reached Magna Graecia and Sicily. In 433 Rhegium and Leontini had formed an alliance with Athens. Syracuse, however, which had always paid attention to events on the Straits of Messina, showed its preference for the Peloponnesians by promising aid to Corinth; it was supported by the other *poleis* of Dorian origin, except for Acragas and Camarina. The latter, which was always distrustful of its metropolis, joined the pro-Athenian group comprising the Ionian *poleis* of Leontini, Catana, and Naxos. In 426, Leontini, after being attacked by Syracuse, asked Athens for help. Its envoy, the orator Gorgias, was able to describe the advantages that would be derived by intervening in favor of Leontini so convincingly that a squadron of twenty ships was dispatched to Sicily to persuade the Syracusans to be more prudent. One of the first consequences was that Zancle decided to side with Athens. These events played an important part in the decisions of a conference of the Sicilian *poleis* that took place at Gela in 424. On this occasion, in fact, approval was given to the proposal of the Syracusan Hermocrates to avoid involving the island in political disputes that did not regard it, and to prevent non-Sicilian forces from intervening in the political affairs of the Sicilian Greeks.

Essentially, this vote favored the plans of the leading power, Syracuse, to secure the hegemony of the island. Thus, the only opportunity for intervention that remained for Athens – now convinced of the need to concern itself with Sicily, and apparently freer to take action after the peace made with Sparta in 421 – offered

An Outline of the Political History of the Greeks in the West

Leontini, view and detail
of the archaeological area

by its alliance with the isolated city of Segesta. This appealed to Athens in 415, after a political dispute with the neighboring city of Selinus and an invasion by the latter of its territory. In vain, Segesta had requested intervention by Syracuse and Acragas, and even the Carthaginians of the nearby territories. Finally, with the agreement of Leontini and other Sicilian *poleis* that, although they had accepted the decision taken at Gela, feared Syracusan hegemony, it directed Athens' attention to the danger constituted by the power of Syracuse, which, naturally, was favorable to Corinth and Sparta. In reality, the Athenian intervention in Sicily was the continuation of the war against Sparta – transposed to the West. The outstanding events in a conflict that was decisive for all the states involved in it were: the great expedition of 415, and the dissent and mistakes that accompanied its very costly preparation and execution; the divisions between the Sicilian and Italian *poleis* and the disappointments that Athens had to face; the long siege of Syracuse; the second expedition of 413 (when Sparta had started hostilities again); Corinthian and Spartan intervention in favor of Syracuse; and, finally, the tragic defeat of Athens. As Thucydides wrote, they had taken part "against Sicily and for Sicily: some to conquer it, others to defend it, not in the name of justice, nor even for their common origins, but rather due to a concurrence of circumstances, either to gain advantage, or for necessity."

Athens suffered irreparable damage, and all its designs for hegemony of both the Aegean and the western seas came to naught. But the Syracusan victors were also exhausted, as were the Siceliotes and Italiotes overwhelmed by the war, in which the Sicilian unity sanctioned at Gela dissolved; in the long antagonism between Athens and Sparta, the same happened with regard to the Hellenic unity that had been victorious against the Persians. Carthage decided that the time was ripe for further forceful military intervention in Sicily. Apart from their constant hostility towards the Greeks, the Carthaginians were still anxious to wreak vengeance for the defeat of Himera. Evidence of this is provided by the route followed by the land and sea forces that in 409 left Carthage under the command of Hannibal, a descendent of the Hamilcar who had perished at Himera. The first objective was the flourishing city of Selinus, which was sacked and destroyed. The same fate awaited Himera, where three thousand Greeks were sacrificed during an expiatory rite on the site where Hamilcar had immolated himself to the gods of his nation. The end of Himera had immediate repercussions in Syracuse, from which an expedition was dispatched in aid of the Himeraeans: its commander, the demagogue Diocles, was a poor strategist, and against him and the other demagogues the wrath of the Syracusans was unleashed. They did not, however, revoke the exile of an expert politician and *strategos* such as Hermocrates, who had organized the resistance against the Athenians, but was subsequently opposed by the democratic party. When, confident of the reaction of his fellow citizens against Diocles' failure, he returned to the *agora* of Syracuse, he met his death at the hands of democrats who accused him of aspiring to become a tyrant.

The tyranny of Dionysius I

However, one of Hermocrates' adherents certainly was aiming at tyranny: this was Dionysius, who managed to win over the popular assembly in the dramatic climate following the destruction of Acragas by a new

Segesta, view of the theater

Segesta, the archaeological area
with the Doric temple

Carthaginian expedition that left Carthage under the command of Hannibal (he died of plague during the siege of Acragas) and Himilco. It was now clear that the Carthaginians intended to destroy the major Greek cities, and Dionysius was able to take advantage of the Carthaginian threat. Following the example of Gelon, he managed to get himself elected as a *strategos* with full powers, and then he expanded the bodyguard assigned to him by the popular assembly by adding mercenaries. He thus paved the way for tyranny; and the variations in his ambiguous political and military conduct may be explained in the light of this constant objective. In fact, when he was commander-in-chief of the army sent by Syracuse in aid of Gela, which was besieged by Himilco, he decided to abandon the city – although it had withstood the siege so far, and had received the help of the Italiote troops – and he evacuated all the inhabitants to Syracuse. He took similar measures in Camarina, which had not yet been attacked by the Carthaginians. A revolt by the knights, the social class that was not responsive to demagogy, was unsuccessful, and the ascendancy that Dionysius continued to have over the lower classes permitted him to conclude a treaty with Himilco recognizing Carthaginian hegemony of all western Sicily, including the areas inhabited by Sicans, as far as Acragas and Thermae Himeraeae. Gela and Camarina were declared to be tributaries of Carthage, while Leontini and Messana remained independent, as did the Sicels. The Syracusans were described as being subjects of Dionysius, who was, therefore, recognized by the Carthaginians as the only ruler of the city (Diodorus, XIII. 114).

Like the majority of tyrants, Dionysius considered the climate of war to be the one most favorable to his autocratic designs. And it suited Carthage that there was only one counterpart in the choice of war or peace. The treaty gave Dionysius the opportunity for the pause he needed in order to make Syracuse a power that was able to impose its dominion over Greek Sicily, and to drive the Carthaginians out of the island. In parallel with his political activity, there were military preparations. The isle of Ortygia, where Dionysius had his headquarters, was fortified and the small port became an arsenal. Then the ruler of Syracuse began military operations, in violation of the clause of the treaty signed with Himilco: it was a calculated risk, because it was unlikely that Carthage, after bearing the heavy financial burden of the two previous expeditions, could immediately intervene in Sicily with large forces. While Dionysius was engaged in besieging the Sicel town of Erbessus, the Syracusan troops rebelled against him. But the tyrant, who returned to Ortygia and was himself besieged there, secretly enlisted twelve thousand Campanian mercenaries who had come to Sicily during the war against Himilco; with these he rapidly raised the siege. With the tyrant's approval, the Campanians seized an Elymian city, Entella, and made it the first Italic colony in Sicily. Naturally, tyrants preferred to recruit mercenaries rather than expand their city's armies, and this was also the case with Diony-

Taormina, the Theater

sius. In 404, having occupied Catana and Naxos, he sold their inhabitants into slavery, and made Catana the stronghold of the Campanian mercenaries, while, after its destruction, the territory of Naxos was ceded to the Sicels. Having seen the treatment meted out to the latter city, the inhabitants of Leontini were relieved to be asked to move to Syracuse as citizens. With the buildings on the Euryalus plateau, Syracuse acquired the largest fortress existing at the time; a major boost was given to the manufacture of siege-machinery, and the fleet was expanded and equipped with all the latest technical innovations.

At was at this point that the tyrant was able to put into effect his plans to drive the Carthaginians out of the island and attack their territories. In 398 he conquered the fortified island of Motya, and sacked it before abandoning it to the Sicels. In the following year, he continued the military operations with blockades of Segesta and Entella. An expedition commanded by Himilco reconquered Motya, but the island was then abandoned and a city on the coast, Lilybaeum was fortified. Himilco then advanced toward Syracuse; but first he destroyed Messana, and moved the Sicels – to whom Dionysius had given the site of Naxos, the first Greek colony in Sicily – to Tauromenium, a city he founded on the heights above Naxos. He then laid siege to Syracuse, where Dionysius, who isolated himself on Ortygia, did not react to the incursions of the Carthaginians and their sacrilegious treatment of the extramural sanctuaries, and braved the disapproval of the Syracusans as he waited for the summer. When this arrived, the miasmas from the marshes where the besieging army was camped favored the outbreak of epidemics that decimated Himilco's troops and obliged him to abandon his mercenaries, while most of the Carthaginian ships were sunk.

In 396 Dionysius was able to make good use of the interval which, once again, preceded the preparation of a new Carthaginian expedition: he rebuilt Messana, bringing colonists there from Locri Epizephyrii and Medma; he founded a new city, Tyndaris; he subjugated Morgantina, Cephaloedium, and Enna; and he made alliances with the tyrants of Agyrion and Centuripae. And, although he did not manage to occupy Tauromenium, he conquered Soloeis, near Panormus: the Carthaginians had to act immediately, and war broke out again. And once more, Dionysius – and the most important of the Sicilian tyrants allied with him, Agyris – prevailed. The peace treaty sanctioned the limitation of the Carthaginian territory to the northwestern corner of the island and the recognition of Dionysius' hegemony over the Sicels; at Tauromenium, the latter were replaced by mercenaries. The changed situation was cause for concern for the Rhegians, who feared that Dionysius' successes would lead to a revival of Syracusan aspirations to control the Strait of Messina. Thus, they attempted to create difficulties for the tyrant on the Sicilian side of the straits: here they founded Mylae, which received the exiles from Naxos and Catana. But the new city was seized by the Messenians, who exiled the inhabitants.

In Italy, Dionysius could count on the longstanding friendship of the Locrians with Syracuse, an alliance that had always protected them against Rhegium. And, in fact, now that the designs of the tyrant on Magna Graecia were quite clear, the Italiote League had to intervene in defense of Rhegium. At first, the Syracusan fleet, which sailed from Locri, and was technically superior and more experienced than the League's squadron of sixty ships, had the upper hand; but a desperate sortie by the Rhegians and a sudden storm caused many of the Syracusan ships to run aground, and, for the moment, Rhegium was safe. The next steps taken by Dionysius showed his hostility to the league of the Italiotes: he attempted to weaken their resistance to the extension of his dominion to the other side of the straits by forming an alliance with the Lucanians.

In 389 the Lucanian confederates attacked Thurii, the army of which was lured by a sham retreat of the enemy into a plain surrounded by heights occupied by the Lucanians. The inhabitants of Thurii who survived the massacre were saved by Leptines, Dionysius' brother, who was cruising with the Syracusan fleet off the coast: but this show of Greek solidarity cost him the command of the fleet. Once again, Dionysius attacked Rhegium; and, after his victory, he imposed heavy tribute on the Rhegians and obliged them to hand over all their ships, as well as hostages. Then he destroyed Caulonia, and transferred its inhabitants to Syracuse as citizens, annexing its territory to Locri; the same fate awaited Hipponium. The next year, a revolt by the Rhegians against new taxes was followed by an exhausting siege, and the survivors were taken to Syracuse, where only those who were able to pay a ransom were saved from being sold into slavery. Now that he had become lord of the straits, Dionysius occupied Scylacium, a Crotoniate colony on the Ionian coast of the isthmus between the *Lametinus Sinus* (Bay of Sant'Eufemia) and the *Scylleticus Sinus* (Bay of Squillace); but the Lucanians and other native peoples thwarted his plans to close the isthmus with a wall.

The Carthaginians were able to profit by Italiotes resentment at the domination of Dionysius: they forged a military alliance with the Italiote League around 383, and began a war against the tyrant. Although it lasted about five years, only some episodes of this conflict are known, such as the battles to liberate the Sanctuary of Hera Lacinia, which had been plundered and occupied by the tyrant's mercenaries, and the Carthaginian conquest of Hipponium, which was restored to its former inhabitants.

overleaf
The theater at Syracuse

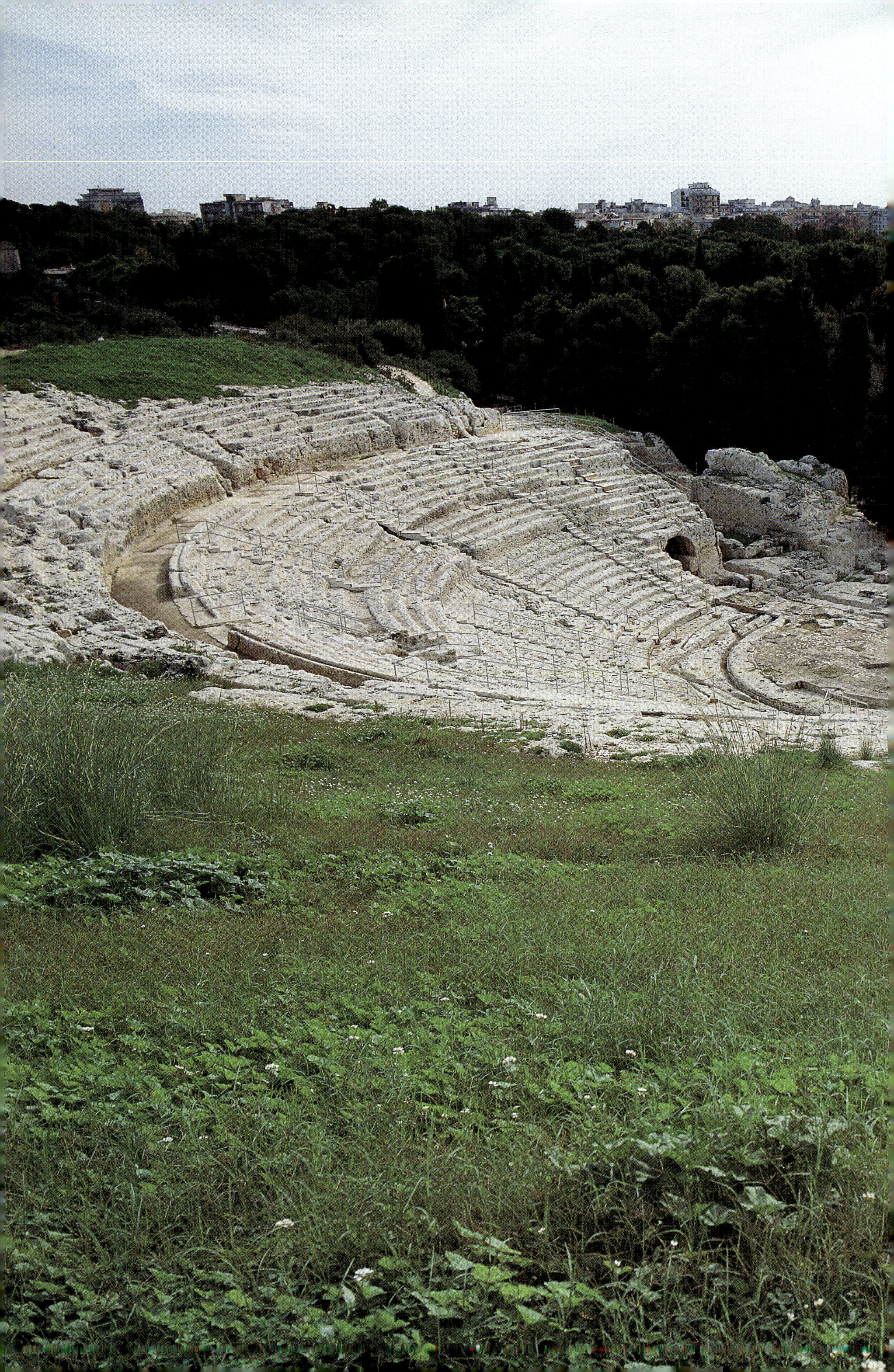

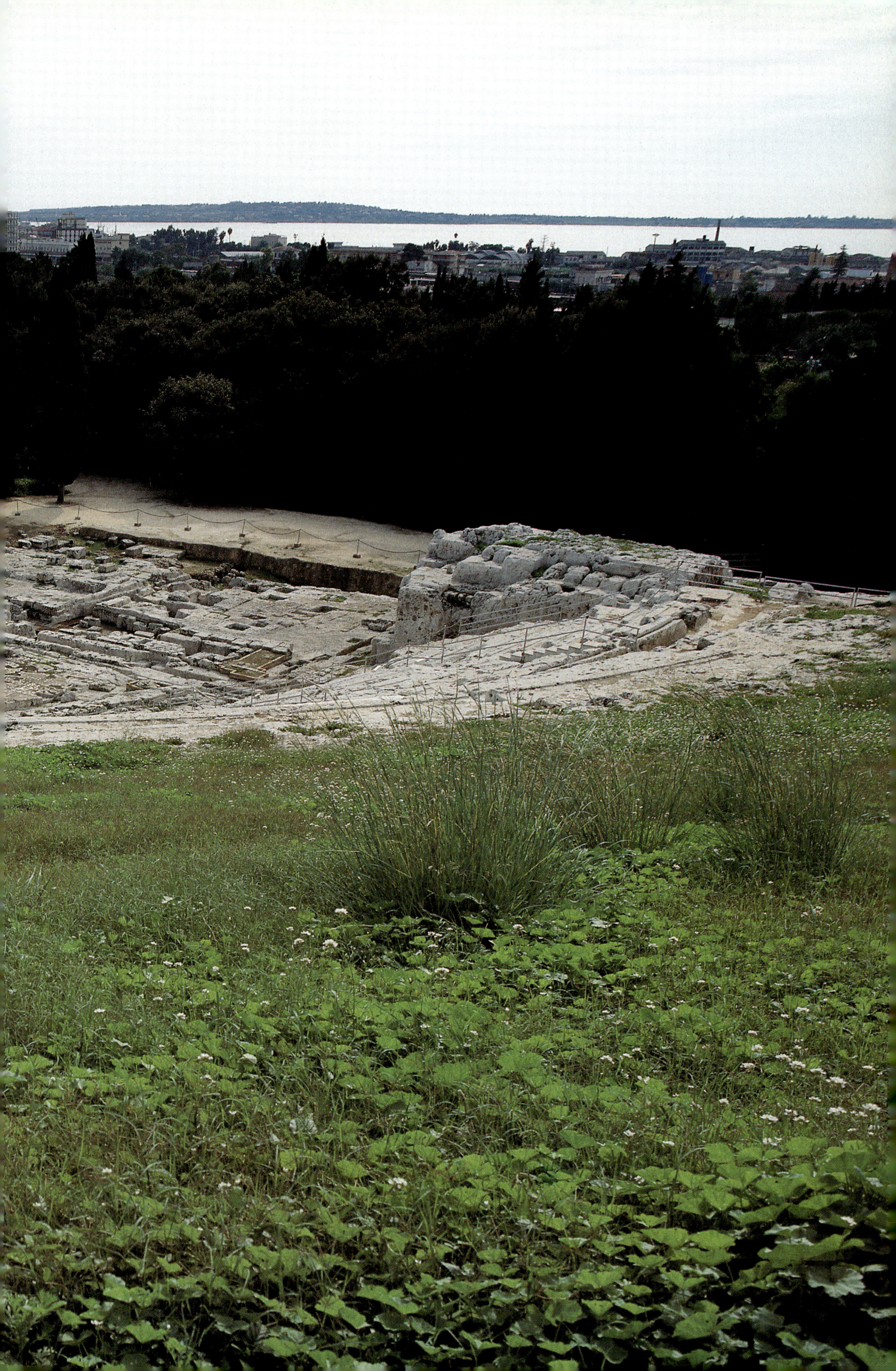

At the same time, Carthage started the war in Sicily again: in 375 the Carthaginians reconquered Thermae Himeraeae and Selinus, and, once more, the Halykos River marked the eastern border of Carthaginian territory. This was invaded again in 368 by Dionysius, who reoccupied Selinus, Eryx, and Drepanum, and laid siege to Lilybaeum; but a part of his fleet was captured by the Carthaginians. Finally, in this year, the terrible tyrant suddenly died; in 393, in Athens he had been designated "ruler (*archon*) of Sicily," but he had maintained the Syracusan constitution, as may be deduced from the treaty with Athens (in which mention is made of magistrates [*archontes*] and the council [*boule*] of Syracuse).

Dionysius II and Plato. The role of Timoleon
Plato had met Dion, a young brother of the tyrant's wife, at Syracuse in 388 during his first journey to the West. On this occasion a firm friendship based on common ideals formed between the Syracusan and the Athenian. Plato personally experienced the harsh cruelty of Dionysius, and it was only by chance that he escaped the captivity or death that the tyrant had in store for him. When Dionysius was succeeded by his son bearing his name, Dion was certain that the youth was different from his father and was animated by a sincere interest in philosophy. He informed Plato of his conviction, and the latter, now sixty years of age, returned to Syracuse in 366, after the conclusion of the peace treaty negotiated by Dion between Dionysius II and the Carthaginians. The philosopher and the munificent politician hoped that a genuine philosophical disposition would induce the young ruler to replace tyranny with a just government, confirming the political doctrines that had been discussed in the Academy by Plato and his followers. But soon Dionysius II revealed that, in reality, he preferred to model himself on his father, rather than the Athenian philosopher. Nonetheless, he availed himself of the latter in order to create good relations with Tarentum, which had then attained great authority thanks to the wise rule of Archytas and the other Pythagoreans. This city had, in fact, a vital role to play in the development of the policy of colonial and commercial expansion in the Adriatic that had been initiated by his father. This renewed vigor on the part of the Tarentines is the best confirmation of the observation made by Polybius (II. 39) with regard to the anti-Pythagorean insurrection, the harbinger of which had been the revolt by Cylon in Croton at the end of the sixth century. By the middle of the fifth century, it had spread to all the Italian *poleis*: "In the years in which, in the region then called Magna Graecia, the colleges of the Pythagoreans were burnt down, and this was followed by general devastation – as was natural, since the most eminent citizens of every state had suddenly been exterminated – it came to pass that, in the Greek cities there, massacres, civil troubles, and all manner of disorder were rife." Nonetheless, the basic tenet of Pythagorean politics, the balance of forces, had no influence whatever on the Syracusan tyrant; Plato soon realized that he was totally lacking in any inclination towards philosophy, and resembled the type defined as *tyrannos* by historical sources. But, for Magna Graecia, especially for the Italiotes League, the Pythagorean interlude at Tarentum was a period of renaissance, and the seat of the assemblies of the league was moved from the sanctuary of Hera Lacinia to Tarentine Heraclea. An agreement between the Italiotes was now even more necessary than it had been before, because they were increasingly threatened by the pressure of the Lucani and, in the middle of the century, the Bruttii – who had also formed a confederation with its center at Cosentia, not far from Pandosia (traditionally, the seat of the Oenotrian kings). In fact, in 344 the Bruttians occupied Terina and attacked Thurii.
Meanwhile, Dionysius II's power was waning; he had banished Dion, and had so far refused to recall him, despite Plato's entreaties. For the third time the philosopher visited Syracuse, and having come into conflict with the tyrant, whose true nature was now exposed, he only escaped imprisonment (or even assassination) thanks to the determined intervention of the Tarentine rulers, who sent a ship to rescue him from Syracuse. Dion then decided to lead an armed expedition to Sicily against Dionysius: the eventful voyage was followed by clashes with the garrison on Ortygia, where the tyrant had retreated, and friction with the Syracusans, who were timorous and irresolute. Finally, after Dionysius had fled to Locri, the suspicion that Dion aspired to tyranny spread: one of his companions, the Athenian Callippus, who had attended the Academy and had been initiated into the Eleusinian mysteries, had Dion murdered and proclaimed himself ruler in 354 B.C.
After Callippus, who, in turn, was killed by mercenaries, two of Dionysius' sons came to power. The tyrant, whose conduct had also made the Locrians hostile to him and his family, in 346 had reoccupied Syracuse by surprise. In order to free themselves of him for good, the now dispirited Syracusans turned to one of the tyrants who, in the nearby cities, throve on the permanent state of war and the ever-present Carthaginian threat: Hicetas, the ruler of Leontini, who, with other Siceliotes, requested the intervention of the Corinthians. In 345, the latter responded to the appeal by sending Timoleon, a fellow citizen of theirs who had distinguished himself for his attachment to freedom, at the head of a small army. It was then that Hicetas' ambitious designs were revealed: he attempted to hinder Timoleon's mission, and even to cause his death. However, nei-

ther his intrigues with the Sicels, nor the arrival of land and sea forces sent by the Carthaginians in support of Hicetas managed to stop the Corinthian, who obliged first Dionysius, then Hicetas, to leave Syracuse.

The balanced constitution that Timoleon gave to the Sicilian *poleis*, which were no longer accustomed to these institutions, marked a renaissance of the traditions of Greek civilization, which were seriously threatened – as Plato had so lucidly foreseen (*Letter* 8. 353e) by "the tyrannical power of the Phoenicians or Opicians" (in other words, the Oscans, with an evident allusion to the threat constituted by the Campanian mercenaries at the service of either the tyrants or Carthage). Faced with this Hellenic revival, the Carthaginians decided to deal a deathblow to the Sicilian *poleis*, and prepared a huge expedition commanded by Hamilcar and Hasdrubal. According to their plans, once their troops had landed at Lilybaeum they would rapidly reach Syracuse. But Timoleon forestalled the Carthaginians: with inferior forces, he attacked them south of Entella, on the west bank of the Crimesus River. Having won a decisive victory, he hastened back to the eastern part of the island, where Mamercus, a Campanian who had become tyrant of Catana, and Hicetas, who had returned to Leontini, now threatened Syracuse. They, too, were vanquished by Timoleon, and then put to death, together with Hippon, the tyrant of Messana. Colonists arrived from Greece to inject new blood into the Siceliot cities, now on the decline, while Timoleon made peace with Carthage, which undertook not to change the borders of its territories and to avoid supporting tyrants in the future.

Intervention by the Epirot princes in Magna Graecia and Sicily. The reign of Agathocles

The wars and the violent disputes, the rebellion of native forces reinvigorated by long contact with Greek civilization, the political decay determined by the tyrannies, and the growing influx of mercenaries had, however, demoralized the majority of the Sicilian *poleis*. And the Italian *poleis*, which felt the effect of events in Sicily, and were exposed to the attacks of the Lucanians and Bruttians, were hardly more fortunate. Indeed, the whole of the Mediterranean area was undergoing profound political and religious transformation, especially under the pressure from Alexander the Great and the new forces, political and otherwise, that resulted from the formation of his empire and its subsequent break-up.

Clear evidence of the decline of the Italiotes and Siceliotes is provided both by the repeated requests for assistance made to Epirot monarchs (Alexander the Molossian in 333, Pyrrhus in 280), and the establishment of a type of Hellenistic monarchy, such as that of Pyrrhus' father-in-law, Agathocles, a Syracusan from Rhegium (between 316 and 289, with the assumption of the title of *basileus* in 304), of which Dionysius I's tyranny can be considered to be the precursor. Agathocles, who became tyrant following the now familiar pattern (*strategos* and "guardian of the peace," then *strategos* with full powers and "protector of the state"), had to deal with similar problems to those facing other Syracusan tyrants: first and foremost, the endless conflict with the Carthaginians. In this, he was responsible for a major strategic innovation, because he unexpectedly transferred the military operations to Africa, after having made an agreement with Ophellas, the governor of Cyrene on behalf of Ptolemy I, and then – possibly at the expense of Ophellas – with the king of Egypt himself.

Agathocles' death in 289 resulted in the dissolution of his kingdom, which also included a number of Italiot cities (from 299 onward, Croton). An expert politician, and well aware of the risks of a dynastic succession, the king restored democracy to Syracuse on his deathbed. But he left a tyrant's legacy: bereavement and material and moral misery, as well as the presence of numerous mercenaries, who, when not enlisted, devoted themselves to plundering the land. This is what happened at Messana, where the Mamertines ("sons of Mars") treacherously seized the city after it had welcomed them, and killed or expelled the able-bodied men, sharing out their property, the womenfolk and children among themselves. From Messana they carried out raids on the southeastern part of the island, which both Syracuse and Carthage coveted. In fact, these two powers were indifferent to the destruction of Gela by the Mamertines around 282, and the removal of the Geloans, by the tyrant Phintias of Acragas, to a new city further west, which was duly called Phintias of the Geloans (Licata). But the success of a Syracusan intervention against Acragas in 280 immediately provoked a Carthaginian expedition, which arrived as far as Syracuse. Against the twofold threat of the Mamertines and the Carthaginians, the Syracusans invoked the intervention of King Pyrrhus, who had sailed from Greece to Italy to assist the Tarentines against Rome.

In fact, due to the rise of Rome as a Mediterranean power, the conquest of Magna Graecia inevitably became a primary objective: the second Samnite War had been an unequivocal sign of this, with Roman intervention in defense of the Greek city of Neapolis in 327, and the subsequent conclusion of the *foedus Neapolitanum* that gave Rome the effective dominion of the Bay of Naples. Rome then focused its attention on Tarentum, the leading Italian *polis*, which was suspected of collaboration with the Samnites. Its military power had now declined, and on various occasions the Tarentine government turned to Sparta (from where King

Tetradrachm of Agathocles
obverse: head of Kore-Persephone
reverse: Nike crowning a trophy
silver
310-304 B.C.
Syracuse, Museo
Archeologico Regionale

Acrotatus had come in 314 in an attempt to free Syracuse from the rule of Agathocles, and Cleonymus in 303 to defend them against the Lucanians), and to Epirus. The *poleis*, now at a low ebb, were no longer able to resolve their frequent military problems with their own resources. Moreover, their situation was worsened by the new methods of warfare, which required larger armies and more complex and expensive equipment. Pyrrhus' intervention was not decisive in either Italy or in Sicily, where his authoritarian temperament and his manifest ambitions aroused the suspicions of the Sicelian *poleis* and neutralized the goodwill that his victory over the Mamertines and Carthaginians had generated hitherto. Thus he returned to Italy in 275, and – amidst the now chronic disorientation of the Greeks in Sicily – a Syracusan, Hieron, who had distinguished himself in the conflicts with the Carthaginians, now appeared.

The reign of Hieron. The Roman conquest of Magna Graecia and Sicily
The ascent of Hieron II in the city of his birth followed the classic model, beginning with his election as *strategos* with full powers about 375. Having married a daughter of one of the great Syracusan families (the one to which Philistus, admiral of Dionysius I and II and historian, belonged), Hieron proved himself to be an excellent politician and military commander, putting an end to the war with Carthage and turning his attention to the equally threatening Mamertines. As a result of his military successes, his soldiers proclaimed him king (*basileus*), and, in accordance with the Greek custom, he wore the royal crown, which Agathocles had spurned.

In 264 war broke out between Carthage and Rome. At the time, Hieron was allied with the age-old adversaries of the Siceliotes, but it soon became clear that, in the situation then existing in Sicily, and since it was impossible for Syracuse to recover its former prestige, it was fitting that Rome should play a major role in the island. In particular, it was a power that had much closer affinities with the Greeks than Carthage, and it was able to keep the Campanians in check. Moreover, the friendship with the Syracusan king suited the Romans, since he ensured them vital supplies, good harbors, and technical support for the fleet, which were all indispensable for the war in Sicily. The First Punic War ended in 241, with a treaty that confirmed that the Carthaginians would evacuate the island. Hieron's kingdom, which had excellent relations with the Ptolemies of Egypt, was guaranteed independence; and limited autonomy was conceded to a number of cities. For instance, decrees relating to Camarina and Phintias of the Geloans have been discovered on Cos; in these, they responded to a request made in 242 to recognize the *asylia* (inviolability) of the Sanctuary of Asclepius on Cos. Meanwhile, Messana was declared a *civitas foederata* (confederate state).

Hieron's friendship with Rome lasted until his death in 215; but during the Second Punic War a number of Sicilian cities believed they could regain full independence with the aid, however hazardous this may have been, of the Carthaginians: and Hieron, the second son and successor of Hieron II, followed suit (and Hieron II's first son, Gelon, who preceded him to the grave, also seems to have shown a preference for Carthage). So it was that Syracuse came to suffer the same fate as the other *poleis*: in 211, after a siege lasting nearly two years, Marcus Claudius Marcellus entered the city – which, despite ingenious machines, Archimedes had defended to no avail – and the kingdom of Syracuse was absorbed into the first of the Roman provinces.

The decline of Syracuse and Greek Sicily was preceded by that of Tarentum and Magna Graecia. When Pyrrhus returned to Epirus, leaving a garrison at Tarentum commanded by his son, Helenus, as a pledge for his return to Italy, Rome had already won over Thurii and Heraclea, and there were strong pro-Roman parties in Croton and Locri. Neapolis and Elea had always been loyal to Rome, which, in any case, was their only defense against the Samnites and the mercenaries. Paestum (Poseidonia) was made a Latin colony in 273. Finally, in the spring of 272, Tarentum was obliged to surrender to Lucius Papirius Cursor. But, wisely, the Romans offered generous terms, and did not treat the last defenders of Italiote independence as vanquished enemies, but as *socii* (allies). The territories of the old *poleis* became part of the *ager publicus populi Romani* (public domains of the Roman people), and Roman colonists were settled there. In the cities, the aristocracy generally sought to maintain its privileged status by winning the favor of the Roman authorities. Thus, they adopted the Latin language, further weakening the traditions of Greek civilization that were expressed in their way of speaking; in fact, Plato had feared the disappearance of this due to the massive influx of Oscan mercenaries into Sicily. Until Late Antiquity, however, Neapolis, successor to the oldest Greek colony in the West, Elea, closely linked to its Ionian past, and Rhegium were resolute guardians of the Hellenic heritage.

Michail Sakellariou   The Metropolises of the Western Greek Colonies

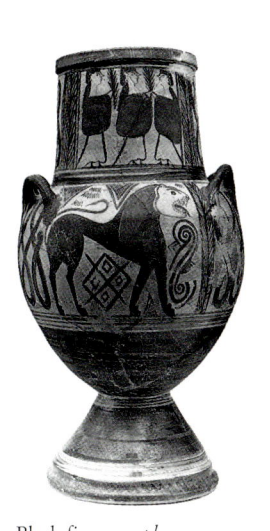

Black-figure *amphora*
from Eretria
8th-7th cent. B.C.
Athens
National Archaeological Museum

Chalcidian black-figure *hydria*
with facing sphinxes
ca. 530-520 B.C.
Taranto, Museo Nazionale
Cat. 134/V

The *Odyssey* places the turbulent adventures of Ulysses in the lands and seas to the west and south of Greece, with a scenario of storms and gales, shipwrecks, encounters with savages, monsters, hostile deities and the descent to the Underworld. The descriptions of the natural phenomena probably echoed the experiences of the sailors who had begun to cross the Ionian Sea at the start of the eighth century B.C., braving the Strait of Messina to reach the Tyrrhenian Sea. The other tales describe the mental excitement of the navigators who risked their lives facing the violence of the elements and strange tribes in far-off waters and on foreign shores. They were the first members of a community to penetrate far into the unknown, surviving the dangers of nature and overcoming the fear of the supernatural. Resolute and unyielding in their exertions, they were driven on by an unquenchable thirst for new experiences. Four centuries had gone by since the last Mycenaean Greek mariners had sailed to the lands beyond the Ionian Sea. Four centuries that had seen upheavals and transformations. The Greek peoples who settled on the ruins of the Mycenaean world were more backward from the technological, social, and cultural points of view compared to their predecessors, but they were exceptionally creative. In the eighth century B.C. the more advanced Greek communities began trading overseas, eastward and westward. New techniques were developed, and the artistic and intellectual life flourished in the newly established city-states. During the next two centuries, when the Greeks were experiencing the great period of Archaic art and lyric poetry and laying the foundations of science and philosophy, colonial expansion became widespread. At the same time, however, they were tormented by social unrest, political instability and war.

Greek colonial expansion covered the coasts of the Mediterranean and of the Pontus Euxinus with innumerable city-states. But there was not a similarly large number of metropolises (mother cities) for two reasons. On the one hand, some metropolises set up many colonies, on the other, some colonies founded their own.

The growth of the colonization movements is tied to questions regarding the mother cities. They usually derived from particular social problems such as an increase in the number of the propertyless, or famine. Later on they were linked to the procurement of raw materials, to acquiring supplies along the maritime routes, to the forced exile of a defeated people or of one threatened by a foreign enemy, and so forth. In some ways colonization had a positive influence on the economy of the metropolises. For some of them it solved a population problem regarding the excessive numbers of the poor, and contributed to the development of commerce and craftwork (see the paragraph on Corinth, below). A considerable number of the landless took to craftwork or offered their services for a salary. At the same time, the number of slaves increased. Working in the city, craftsmen, laborers, and slaves consumed foodstuffs they did not produce. This led to an increase in the demand for agricultural products and cattle-breeding and, naturally, their prices rose likewise. Small landowners did not gain from these changes because they did not harvest enough to sell an excess on the market. Rather, they were worse off, because loans became more expensive. No brake could be put on this tendency, which hit the small landowners, as long as the aristocracy remained in power.

We will now examine the individual metropolises of the Greek colonies in the West.

The cities in Euboea
The metropolises of the oldest Greek colonies in the western Mediterranean, Pithekoussai (ca. 770 B.C.) on the island of Ischia, and Cumae (Cyme, 757 B.C.) in Campania, were two city-states in Euboea, Chalcis and Eretria. The first was the most active mother city in the eighth century B.C., and also founded Naxos (734 B.C.) and Zancle (730/725 B.C.) in Sicily as well as Rhegium (Rhegion, 720/715 B.C.) in Calabria. At Cumae, native settlers from Cyme in Euboea, and Greeks from the coast of Boeotia in front of Eretria, lived together with colonists from Chalcis and Eretria. At Naxos, emigrants from Chalcis founded the colony together with another group from the island of Naxos in the Aegean. The colonial expansion of Chalcis and Eretria is the better-known part of the history of the two cities in the eighth century. Before founding Pithekoussai and Cumae, they had set up an emporium at Al Mina on the coast of Syria (ca. 800 B.C.) to attract supplies of bronze for the two Euboean cities' workshops. The demand for even greater amounts of bronze stimulated them to found Pithekoussai and Cumae. These colonial settlements would never have survived without their rural populations. Historical sources neither provide the information nor give any suggestions as to whether the metropolises of Euboea had attempted to solve a problem of overpopulation by setting up their colonies. Contrariwise, we know from the sources that the settlement in Rhegium was due to a famine which had impoverished Chalcis.

Chalcidian black-figure *amphora*
end 5th cent. B.C.
New York
The Metropolitan Museum
of Art, Rogers Fund
Cat. 134/I

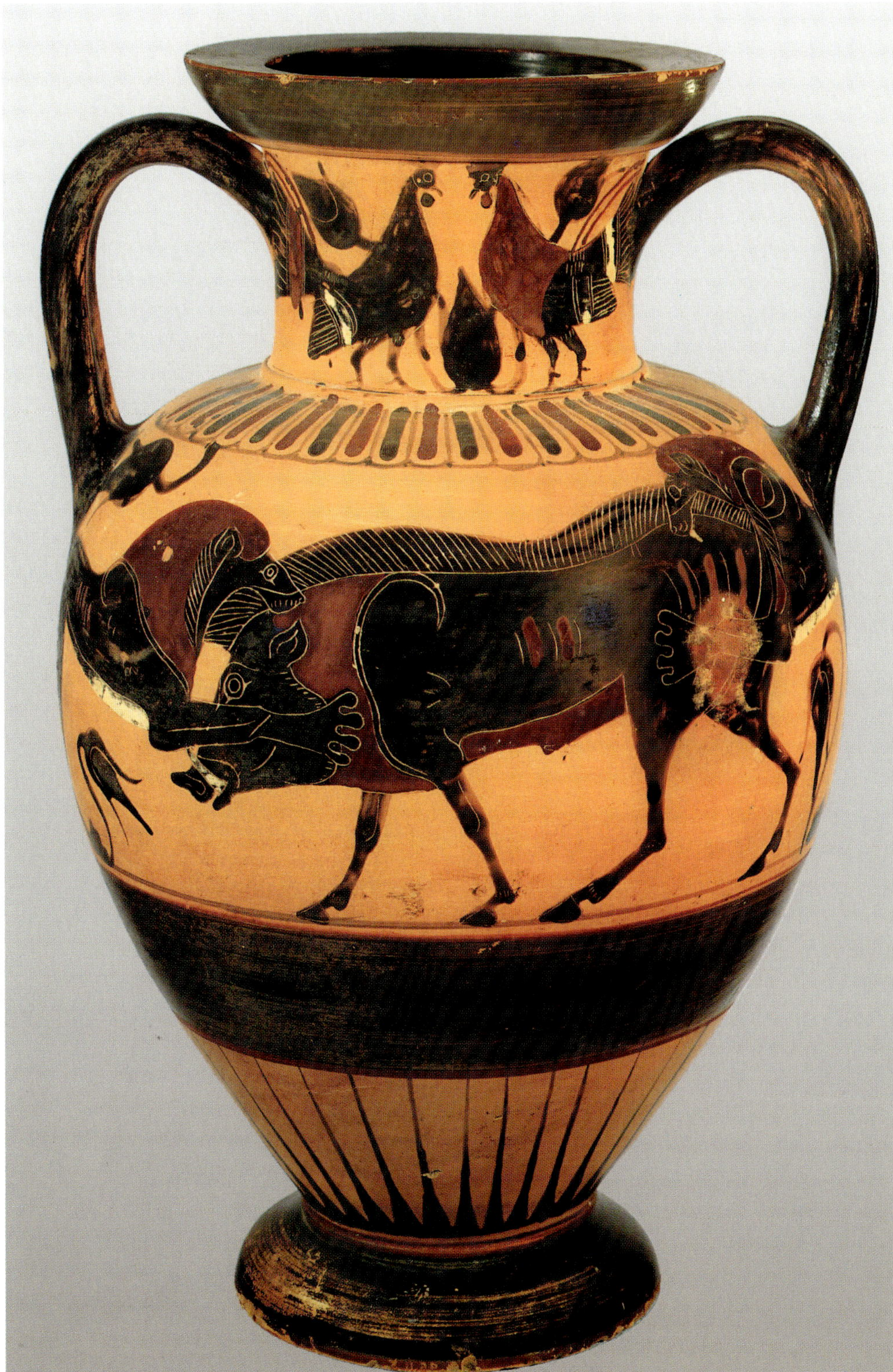

Eliminating the excess population in Chalcis seems also to have been the reason for sending colonists to Naxos and to Zancle, as well as to the peninsula on the northern Aegean which adopted the name of Chalcidice. Chalcis also took into consideration the need to protect her communications with the Tyrrhenian Sea when choosing the opposite shores of the Strait of Messina for founding two of her colonies.

The political history of the cities of Chalcis and Eretria during the eighth century is practically unknown. One source refers to Eretria possessing sovereignty over the islands of Ceos, Andros and Tenos among others. Some modern historians date back to the end of the eighth century the famous Lelantine War which broke out because of the conflicting claims of both cities to the plain separating them, and which turned into a large-scale war involving many Greek powers. Other historians observe, quite rightly, that the extent of the war presupposes complex interests and an exceptionally advanced network of relations between states for the eighth century B.C. All the same, the destruction of an important town, Lefkandi, near Eretria, during the decade from 720 to 710, belongs to the period of the limited conflict before the outbreak of the great war.

There are no other references to emigration from Chalcis after the founding of Rhegium. The clash between the two cities of Chalcis and Eretria during the Lelantine War led to the economic and political decline of both of them. This was, however, also partly due to competition from Corinth.

Corinth

At the end of the ninth century, Corinth founded a small colony on the island of Ithaca which served as a supply base for ships en route to and from Illyria where they bought metals. The discovery of Corinthian vases dating from the mid-eighth century B.C. in Etruria shows that the Corinthians became interested in the metal ores to be found on the Italian peninsula shortly after the Euboeans. After a brief period of closer contacts with the west which allowed the Corinthians to discover the best places for establishing colonies, they founded Syracuse (733 B.C.).

Corinth was situated in a very advantageous position compared to any other Greek city. It had two ports: Cenchreae on the Saronic Gulf, and Lechaeum, on the Gulf of Corinth. Thanks to Lechaeum, boats sailing from Corinth to the Ionian or the Tyrrhenian seas made much shorter voyages than those starting from Chalcis or from other places further east in the Aegean which had to round the Peloponnese. Through Cenchreae, the Corinthians communicated with the ports of the Aegean. Moreover, they also transported goods coming from the west overland from Lechaeum to Cenchreae, and vice versa, those shipped from the east. The original border between Corinth and Megaris lay in the narrowest part

Krater by Eurythios
Corinthian black-figure vase
end 7th cent. B.C.
Paris
Musée du Louvre, Département
des Antiquités
Grecques, Etrusques et Romaines

Etrusco-Corinthian *kotyle*
by the Bad Wolf Painter
beginning 6th cent. B.C.
Pontecagnano, Museo Nazionale
dell'Agro Picentino
Cat. 136

Corinthian *pyxis*
ca. 640-630 B.C.
Rome, Museo Nazionale
di Villa Giulia

of the Isthmus where the canal slices through it today. This meant that both of the ports were in danger if the Megarians were on bad terms with the Corinthians. Around 735 B.C., the Corinthians drove the Megarians back further east, but they did not succeed in holding their new territories for long. The boundary was established once and for all to the advantage of Corinth in the seventh century B.C.

Corinth developed considerably during the second half of the eighth century B.C. Corinthian potters outgrew the influence of Athens and Argos and created their own mature Geometric style. From then on, Corinthian earthenware spread throughout the Aegean and its design was widely imitated. About 725 B.C. the Corinthians were the first to give up the geometric style and to absorb the oriental influence. They were also famous for their metalworking techniques and made remarkable progress in shipbuilding. The four boats, for example, commissioned by the Samians from a Corinthian shipyard in 704 B.C., created a lasting impression. Corinth began to prosper. An echo of this prosperity rings even in the lines of the *Iliad* where the word αφνειος (rich, opulent) is used to define the city and one of its inhabitants. During the same period, Corinth was one of the Greek cities that could boast its own epic poet: Eumelus, who was author of the *Corinthiaca*, relating the mythical history of his fatherland, and of *Titanomachia* and other poems. Eumelus was a member of the Bacchiad family, of royal descent.

After the mid-eighth century B.C., the Bacchiads imposed the abolishment of the royal right to inheritance and substituted it with an annual elective office, the *prytanis* (ruler). Only the members of the Bacchiad family had the right to vote and to be candidates. Then they went even further in their political exclusiveness by forbidding marriages outside their family. In the meanwhile, the population rose at a faster rate than the economy could account for. Colonization therefore became necessary to send small property owners, landless agricultural workers, and the malcontent nobles away from Corinth. The sources reveal that many of the colonists who went to Syracuse came from a town called Tenea, but the originator, Archias, was a Bacchiad. Corcyra was founded at the same time as Syracuse. Corinthian trade with other cities increased from the mid-seventh century. In about 650 B.C., Corinthian earthenware entered the markets in Rhodes even though local pottery was almost as good. Corinthian vases also started arriving at Al Mina in Syria at about this time. New aesthetic influences arrived together with the goods that Corinthian merchants brought from the east, renewing and intensifying the oriental style decorations typical of Corinthian ceramic motifs. Corinthian pottery spread to the Milesian colonies in the Propontis and the Pontus Euxinus. Corinthian trade flows were

Middle Corinthian globular *aryballos*
first half 6th cent. B.C.
Palermo, Museo Archeologico
Regionale "A. Salinas"

even greater to the west. All their products, especially the earthenware, were sought after not only by other Greeks, but by Carthaginians and Etruscans who acquired them through Syracuse. Boats on the return voyage to Corinth brought back products from the colonies and the emporiums of the Carthaginians and Etruscans. Some of these products were then distributed by Corinthian merchants to other Greek cities. It was the Corinthian ceramists who discovered the various types of clay roof tiles that could line and roof the Archaic temples. Corinth was also famous for metalworking techniques and bacame one of the foremost producers of weapons.

In spite of all this activity, the number of landless agricultural workers continued to increase and the social climate worsened. Meantime Corcyra, a Corinthian colony, began to compete with its mother city, and over the years commercial rivalry turned into open hostility. In 660 B.C. the Corcyrans defeated the Corinthians in a naval battle. The Bacchiad regime was overthrown by Cypselus, who established an individual leadership, the tyranny. Cypselus ruled from 620 to 590 B.C. Under his rule and that of his successor, Periander (590–550 B.C.), colonies were founded on Leucas, at Anactorium (ca. 600 B.C.), and at Ambracia (ca. 625 B.C.) on the Greek coast of the Ionian Sea, on the Illyrian coast (Apollonia, ca. 600 B.C.), and Potidaea on the Chalcidice peninsula. The exiled Bacchiads joined the Corcyrans to set up Epidamnus on the Illyrian coast (ca. 620 B.C.) and together became much more of a danger to the Corinthians on the Sicilian and Illyrian sea routes. The increased demand for earthenware products from Corinth forced the potters to increase their quantities at the expense of quality. From 575 B.C. onward Corinthian pottery diminished progressively on all its markets until it disappeared around 550 B.C. It only remained for some time further on the Syracusan market.

The tyranny survived for a few years after the death of Cypselus, and was then superseded by a moderate oligarchy. During the same period, Corinth joined the Peloponnesian League that Sparta had founded. Corinth's domestic affairs and its position in the Greek world became stabilized. It was a very important commercial power and a leading naval force. Syracuse and the other colonies were a vitally important part of its commercial interests. It was to clash first with Corcyra and later with Athens in defending its trade routes to Sicily and its rank as a sea power.

Megara

Megara Hyblaea was established in 727 B.C. by a group of Megarians who came to Sicily shortly after the colonists from Chalcis had founded Naxos in 734 B.C. These Megarians were probably refugees fleeing from the lands occupied by Corinthians. No other episodes in the history of Megara during the eighth century have come to light. After Megara Hyblaea, the Megarians founded other colonies, but not in the West. They built settlements in the Propontis (Selymbria and Astacus), in the Bosporus (Chalcedon and Byzantium) and in the Pontus Euxinus (Mesembria).

There were no quarrels between Megara and its colony in Sicily, or with the other ones, neither did it interfere in their affairs. For this reason we will end here the description of the events concerning the history of the city.

Achaea

Achaea was a poor and backward region at the time the emigrants left to found the new colonies of Croton and Sybaris (ca. 710 B.C.), Metapontum (690/680 B.C.) and Caulonia (675/650 B.C.). The sources offer us a rather approximate description of the political system of the Achaeans. The region was divided up into independent zones (μερεα, according to Herodotus) and these zones were linked in a confederacy (κοινόν). The colonists of Croton mostly came from the area of Ripe (in Achaea) while those settling in Sybaris emigrated from three towns, Helice, Bura, and Aegae. There is also literary evidence that colonists also arrived in Sybaris from Troezen, a city in Argolis. It appears that the Achaeans had been forced to leave their homelands and emigrate to Italy due to the insufficiency of agriculture. Later on, Achaea played an important role in Greek history during the period of the Achaean *koinon* (early third century B.C.).

Western and Eastern Locris

Locri (Lokroi Epizephyrioi) was founded (679 or 673 B.C.) by Locrians who had settled near Zephyrion. Locrian was the name given to a Greek *ethnos*, or population. A part of them lived in Western Locris whose southern territories reached the Gulf of Corinth, and the other part in Eastern Locris, which stretched to the northern Euboean Gulf. The two Locrises had neither common borders nor political unity, but this did not prevent the Locrians from keeping in contact and working together for common aims. The information about the colonists who settled in Italy is not precise but it can be inferred that emigrants from both Locrises reached the shores of the Gulf of Corinth for the purpose of sailing to Italy. The traditions concerning the social status of the colony's founders and the reasons for the colonization are contradictory and, in fact, were elaborated at a later date. They do not offer any useful information about the actual situation in the two Locrises, which were to remain for a considerable time in the shades of history.

Messenian refugees

At the end of the twenty-year-long first Messenian War (most likely from 735 to 715 B.C.) Messenia was overrun by the Spartans. Many Messenians fled the region to avoid falling into slavery. Some of these sailed to Italy and took part in colonizing Rhegium together with the emigrants from Chalcis, and Metapontum with the Achaeans.

Zancle was occupied by Samian refugees after 494 B.C. (see below). Anaxilas, the tyrant of Rhegium, drove out the Samians in 486 B.C., and replaced them with Messenians, a part of whom might have been descendants of the ancient Messenians of Rhegium whereas the others were refugees who had escaped overseas recently from the defeated and subjected mother country. This was when Zancle changed its name to Messana (Messina).

Sparta

The Spartans faced the overpopulation problem by occupying new territories and distributing the fertile districts to Spartan citizens using a work force of helots. Laconia was occupied by the Spartans until halfway through the eighth century B.C., and Messenia in about 715 B.C., after the first Messenian War. At that time, there were nine thousand Spartan citizens and each one of them satisfied his own needs from a plot of land. Before this, the Spartans had set up a regime with two kings, a *gerusia* composed of twenty-eight elders and an *ekklesia* of the *demos* which was limited to the owners of a plot of land. The kings and the elders presented proposals to the *ekklesia* for its approval. The assembly had the right to reject, but not to modify them.

In about 710 B.C., a problem arose over the distribution of the plots of land and the concession of political rights to a group of young men whom the sources called *partheniai*. During the first Messenian War, according to the sources, wives and daughters of Spartans had illegitimate children from both citizens and helots. When these youngsters became of age they claimed political rights and land. Moreover, since their demands were rejected, they organized a conspiracy but were discovered. After this, the *partheniai* were authorized to emigrate and found a colony, and they built Tarentum (Taras, 708/706 B.C.). The name *partheniai* and their definition as illegitimate children is subject to considerable debate. It is however likely that they really were illegitimate children of Spartans and that they claimed a right to the same political, economic, and social position as Spartan citizens. This hypothesis is reinforced by the fact that after the first Messenian War, the two kings of Sparta agreed to circumscribe the habit of the popular assembly of modifying the proposals presented by the council of elders and by the kings. On the other hand, however, one of the kings, Polydorus, seemed to be in sympathy with the people, whereas the other one, Theopompus, is mentioned as heading the opposite faction. Polydorus was assassinated by an aristocrat. Far from being punished, his murderer was held in honor. Only a long time later was Polydorus given his due. It is therefore quite likely that after Polydorus' murder, the measures that had been taken in favor of the *partheniai*, or that were at least on the books, were revoked, and for this reason they attempted the *coup d'état*.

Rhodes

The island of Rhodes was separated into three city-states: Lindus, Ialysus, and Camirus. Lindus founded a colony in Sicily called Gela in 688. Cnidos colonized one of the Aeoliae Insulae (Lipari) in about 580–576, and in the same period, Rhodians set up colonies on the Italian Adriatic coast, in the Balearic Islands and on the Iberian peninsula.

Before taking the West into consideration, Rhodian merchants, following in the footsteps of the Euboeans, had been the most active traders with Al Mina in Syria since 700 B.C. They had lost, however, their trade with Tarsus which had been razed by the Assyrians in 696. However, in the same years that they were colonizing Gela, they predominated in the Aegean mercantile world, trading with Cyprus and the ports of the eastern Mediterranean (controlled by foreign peoples) to such an extent that they even founded Phaselis on the coast of Pamphylia to protect their sea routes to the east. In the Aegean Sea

Rhodian *oinochoe*
9th-8th cent. B.C.
London, British Museum
Department of Greek
and Roman Antiquities

The Metropolises of the Western Greek Colonies

Rhodian cup with birds
8th-7th cent. B.C.
Heidelberg
Archäologisches Institut
der Universität

Rhodian jug
perhaps from Vulci
650-640 B.C.
Rome, Museo Nazionale
di Villa Giulia

185

Black-figure *stamnos*
scenes of flying birds
made in Gela
second half 7th cent. B.C.
Gela
Museo Archeologico Regionale
Cat. 24

they traded with Samos, the Cyclades, after 650 B.C., and with Corinth. Vases from Rhodes and other countries, thrown in potteries in the eastern Aegean, were transported to the West by Rhodian merchant ships after 640 B.C. The quality of Rhodian ceramics was nearly on a par with Corinthian earthenware.

Crete
The Cretans also took part in colonization, joining the Rhodians in founding two colonies in 688 B.C.: Gela and Phaselis (see above). Crete's relations with the other Greeks slowly became sporadic, but did not come to an end. Good quality products continued to be manufactured by Cretan workshops in all the branches of the arts and crafts. During this period, the hereditary kings were substituted by a limited number of people from among whom leaders were chosen to rule one year. Both the groups and the leaders were called *kosmoi*, from the word *kosmos*, meaning "order", "organization".

Thera
The history of the island of Thera is completely unknown up until the mid-seventh century B.C. At that time, events took place which preceded the colonization of Cyrene, and others which involved this same operation (about 630 B.C.). Herodotus' account of it and a marvelous epigraph of the fourth century B.C., found in Cyrene, not only reveal the typical setup but create the whole atmosphere. The oracle of Apollo at Delphi repeatedly ordered the Therans to found colonies in Libya, but they did not obey straightaway. Some time later, an expeditionary force was sent to explore the territory. Following this, it was decided that every family had to send one young man away from Thera, and any others could volunteer to go. Any of the ones drawn by lots who disobeyed would have been sentenced to death. If the colonization failed within a period of five years, the emigrants could return to Thera and their former properties would revert to them. The arrangements proceeded with maledictions against those who did not comply, and with magic rites. Figures of men were modeled from wax and then burnt before the whole population with the warning: "Those who break their oaths and their descendants will burn and melt like this!" So few emigrants presented themselves on the day of departure that they left in two boats of fifty oarsmen each. They never reached Libya, but landed at Plataea. Disappointed by their results, they abandoned the settlements and set sail for Thera, but the inhabitants refused to allow them ashore. The colonists were therefore forced to return to Plataea. Only two years later did they dare land on the mainland where they founded Cyrene. Similar events and experiences must have occurred in the other Greek cities as well in Archaic times, where problems of overpopulation and a limited production of foodstuffs forced them to found colonies.

The Metropolises of the Western Greek Colonies

Fragment of *kantharos*
geometric decoration
from Samos
9th-8th cent. B.C.
Samos, Museum

Cities in Ionia
Miletus, Samos, Chios, and other cities in Ionia benefited from the trade routes between inland Asia Minor and the Aegean and from those along the coasts of Asia Minor. The Milesians, the Samians, and the Chians founded colonies on the Thracian coasts of the Aegean and in the Propontis. The Milesians also built dozens of colonies in the Pontus Euxinus area. The mother cities in Ionia supplied many merchant ships sailing the Aegean with grain, animals, salted foodstuffs, metals, and slaves.
In the year 638 B.C. a Samian boat sailing from Libya to Egypt was driven in the opposite direction by a westerly gale, and beyond the Pillars of Hercules where it finally found shelter at the city of Tartessus, in southwestern Spain. It carried a load of silver on the journey back to Samos, which was sold for a fortune. The Samians, however, did not express much interest in keeping up trade with Tartessus. Phocaea, and not Samos, was, in fact, the first of the Ionian cities to trade with the West. This city was the northernmost one of the Ionian group, and the nearest to Thrace, to the Hellespont, and the Propontis. However, when it decided to found some colonies, all the best places in these regions were already occupied. Therefore, after founding Lampsacus (modern Lapseki) in the Hellespont, it turned toward the western Mediterranean. Phocaean navigators set up a sea route between Tartessus and the Aegean. The voyages from Phocaea to Tartessus and vice versa were extraordinarily long and highly risky. The Phocaeans set up various stages along the way for supplies and repairs. Some of these developed into colonies such as Massalia (Marseilles) at the mouth of the Rhône (ca. 600), Maenaca in Spain (ca. 600), and Alalia in Corsica (565/560). The history of Phocaea at that time is unknown. However, we do know that Phocaea was a small city. Twenty years later, the Phocaeans emigrated to escape a foreign enemy. This was when the Persians occupied Ionia. The Persian satrap Mazare overran Priene and subjugated part of its inhabitants. Later on, Magnesia on the Maeander River was sacked and the surrounding plain ravaged. The next satrap, Harpa-

Ionian cup known as
the Bird Catcher Cup
from Caere
530-520 B.C.
Paris, Musée du Louvre
Département
des Antiquités Grecques
Etrusques et Romaines

Krater from Chios
close to the Rhodian style
with imaginary animals
and decorative motifs
end 7th cent. B.C.
Würzburg
Martin von Wagner Museum

gus, started from Phocaea. After laying siege to the city, he sent a message to the Phocaeans saying that he would withdraw his troops without causing any harm to them if they accepted to demolish one rampart and to hand over to him symbolically one building within the city. The Phocaeans asked for a day's truce to consider his offer, and used it to launch their ships and to cast off for Chios with all their families and belongings, and all the transportable statues and ex-votos of their sanctuaries. The Persians then entered an empty city. The Phocaeans decided to sail towards Corsica where they had already founded Alalia. They sank a piece of iron in the sea and swore that they would only return to their mother country when the iron floated up again, and cursed all those who would not emigrate. In spite of this, more than half the citizens did not have the heart to leave the mother country and its customs, and so turned back. The others went to Alalia.

Inhabitants of another Ionian city, Colophon, founded some colonies to escape the danger of invasion by a foreign army from Lindus in 600 B.C. The emigrants built Siris. Colophon possessed rich agricultural land and did not need to trade overseas, or to found colonies for either commercial reasons or to send landless citizens away.

Samos succeeded in avoiding the Persian yoke for several years, but from 538(?) to 522 it bore the tyranny of Polycrates who exiled the aristocrats opposing him and put restraints and economic burdens on those who remained. Samian exiles and fugitives founded Dicaearchia (Pozzuoli, 531 or 526) in southern Italy. Pythagoras, the philosopher, was one of them.

After the destruction of the Ionian rebel fleet by the Persians, near the island of Lade, a group comprising mostly Samians, some Milesians, and various other Ionians, sailed for Italy. They lived like pirates until the Samians settled at Zancle. They were however driven away from this colony in about 486 B.C.

Samian culture flourished in the Archaic period, but this had nothing to do with the above-mentioned departures of its citizens. Throughout its history, Samos never suffered from any repercussions from its colonies.

The Greek Colonization of the West: Dialects

The Greek colonization of the West was a complex, widespread phenomenon involving economic and cultural issues which, beginning in the eighth century B.C., principally affected Sicily and southern Italy. It was the result of colonial expeditions organized by a given *polis* in Mainland Greece, to which on occasion people from other *poleis* were admitted. The colonies inevitably reflected the customs and traditions of the mainland polis of origin, especially as regards the alphabet and the spoken idiom. From this point of view, linguistically the colonies can be grouped into Ionic and Doric. The Ionic category includes those colonies founded by Euboean cities, in particular Cumae, Naxos, Leontini, Catana, Zancle, and Himera in Sicily; and Rhegium in Calabria. From Asiatic Ionia the colonists set sail from Colophon to found Siris, from Phocaea to found Massalia (modern Marseilles); the Phocaeans also survived the battle of Alalia (in Corsica) and went on to found Elea in Campania. Also in the Doric group we find Syracuse, founded by the Corinthians, Megara Hyblaea and Selinus founded by the Megarians of Isthmia, Gela and Acragas founded by the Rhodians and Cretans. Achaea founded the colonies of Sybaris, Croton, and Metapontum; Sparta founded Tarentum, and the colonists of Ozolian Locris the new town of Locri Epizephyrii. Lastly, Thera (modern Santorini) sent settlers to found Cyrene. The populations speaking Aeolic dialects (Thessalians, Aeolians of Asia Minor, Arcadians, and Cypriots) appear not to have been involved in the migratory trends discussed here.

The Ionian Colonies

Ionic. The Ionic dialect includes the language spoken in Asiatic Ionia, in the Cyclades, and in Euboea (Attic is an offshoot); it stands out from all the other Greek dialects above all for the evolution of the ancient $\bar{a}$ and $\bar{e}$, that conflate into the ancient $\bar{e}$, represented graphically by the sign Ⱶ (H in more recent graphics), whence the Doric ΔΙΚΑ, which corresponds to the Ionic ΔΙΚΗ, meaning "justice". In Cycladic, however, the results were originally kept distinct from each other: the ancient *e* was represented as $\bar{e}$ was represented as E, while the new $\bar{e}$ (derived from $\bar{a}$) was indicated by the sign Ⱶ (an attempt to differentiate the two results can be noticed in Euboea also, and in the colony of Rhegium, witness ΔΕΜΟΦΑΝΗ as against the Doric ΔΑΜΟΦΑΝΕΣ. The group ηο (in which η represents the cursive form of H) from the earlier $\bar{a}$ο turns into εω via quantitative *metathesis*, witness Doric λᾱοφόρος: and Ionic λεωφόρος meaning "frequented by the people". Another peculiarity is assibilation of the voiceless dental (τ, ϑ) before ι, a feature that has precedents in the Mycenaean dialect, witness the Ionic δίδωσι with respect to the Doric δίδωτι meaning "[he] gives".

The *digamma* (Ϝ = semivocalic *u̯*) disappeared quite early, leaving only slight traces (mostly as an indication of a transitional sound, such as δύϜō "due"). The analogical influence of the singular of the article ὁ, ἡ (= *ho, hē*) brought about the substitution of τοί, ταί (original forms of the nominative plural of the masculine and feminine of the article, conserved in Doric) with οἱ, αἱ. A typical Ionic feature in both Asia and the Cyclades (though the phenomenon affects contiguous Doric areas: Rhodes, Cos, Crete, Thera, and the Argolid) is the compensatory lengthening of the preceding short vowel after the disappearance of the *digamma* in the groups ϱϜ, λϜ, νϜ, whence κούϱη (da Ϝ *κοϱϜ ᾱ) = Attic κόϱη meaning "girl/maiden", with ου marking the long closed *o*. Later, in Ionic the identity of the singular nominative of masculine stems in -*a*, that is, -ης, and the nominative singular of the masculine stems in the sibilant -ης bring about a certain contamination between the two declensions: Τηλεφάνεω in lieu of the regular Τηλεφάνεος, being the genitive of Τηλεφάνης. In Asia, the Ionic idiom, as spoken in the colonies founded by Colophon and Phocaea, presents the phenomenon of *psilosis*, i.e., the elimination of the initial aspiration (whence the availability of the sign Ⱶ, H, which corresponds elsewhere to *h*, to indicate a vocalic value), witness το̄ϱμοκϱάτεος in the Ionic form on the *stele* from Sigeum (modern Yenisehir, Turkey), as compared with τō *h*εϱμοκϱάτōς in its Attic version. This is the area, moreover, of the ancient adoption of the sign of ὦ μέγα. The Ionic dialect kept the original pronunciation of υ (= *u*) as against the palatalization typical of the Attic language (= *ü*).

The Euboean Colonies

Pithekoussai–Cumae. From the first half of the eighth century B.C. comes the earliest written document so far discovered, which attests to the presence of mainland Greeks at Pithekoussai on the island of Ischia. According to Strabo (v. 247) the island was the site of the very first settlement of Eretrians and Chalcidians in Magna Graecia. The remains of an *amphora* bear an inscription drawn with a confident hand from right to left: Μιμαλ(λ)όν (one of the denominations of the female Bacchante), beneath which a less skilled hand has written indications of ownership, though of this only the words]ονος ἐμί remain. Several Late Geometric *skyphoi* bear inscriptions running on several lines (once again right-to-left); the second and third lines are contrived to form hexameters. Several gaps make it impossible to restore the full text: Νέστοϱος: [...]:

The Greek Colonization of the West: Dialects

Table of Greek and Archaic alphabets

Phonetic value of selected signs

- *a* 8 : h (rough breathing), ē
  - 15 : z
- *b* 8 : ē
- *c* 8 : h
  - 25 : kh
- *d* 8 : h
  - 25 : kh (χ)
- *e* 8 : ē
  - 15 : khs (χσ, ξ)
  - 25 : kh
  - 26 : phs (φσ, ψ)
- *f* 8 : h
  - 15 : khs (z)
  - 25 : kh
  - 26 : phs
- *g* 8 : h
  - 25 : khs
  - 26 : kh
- *h* 8 : h
  - 26 : kh
- *i* 8 : h
  - 15 : š
  - 25 : kh
  - 26 : f
- *l* 3 : c, g
  - 8 : h
  - 25 : x

The signs of the two Etruscan alphabets (*h*, *i*) are written right-to-left

This table is a reproduction with some slight adjustments of the one that accompanies the chapter (p. 350, Abb. 19) by A. Rehm e G. Klattenbach "Entstehung und Frühentwicklung der Schriften des griechisch-italischen Kreizes" in *Allgemeine Grundlagen der Archäologie* (ed. U. Hausman), C. Beck, Munich, 1969. For a more ample discussion, especially on the local alphabets of *poleis* in the West, see L.H. Jeffery *The Local Scripts of Archaic Greece*, Clarendon Press, Oxford, 1961 and M. Guarducci, *Epigrafia Greca*, I, 2nd ed., Istituto Poligrafico e Zecca dello Stato, Rome, 1995.

	a – Thera	b – Crete	c – Dipylon oichnoe	d – Attica	e – Ionia and Asia	f – Corinth	g – Western Greeks	h – Etruria (Massaliot alphabet)	i – Etruria (classical period)	l – Early Rome
1	A	A	⊳A	A	A	AA	A	A	A	A
2	⌐B	⌐B	(B)	BB	B	⊔⌒	B	B	—	
3	Γ	Λ	(ΛΛ)	Λ	⌐Γ	<C	CΛΓ	⌐	))	C
4	Δ	Δ	Δ	Δ	Δ	Δ	ΔD	⌐	—	D
5	⋌E	⋌E	⋌	⋌E	⋌E	B⋌	⋌E	⋰	⋰E	E
6	—	⌐F	—	—	—	⋌⋌F	CF	⋰	⋰	
7	—	I	I	I	I	I	I	I	≠	
8	⊟	⊟	⊟	⊟H	⊟H	⊟	⊟H	⊟	⊟	⊟
9	⊗⊕	⊗⊕	⊗	⊗⊕	⊗⊕	⊗	⊗⊕	⊗	⊗	—
10	ʃʃ	S	ʃ(I)	I	I	ξεʃ	I	I	I	I
11	K	K	K	K	K	K	K	⊁	⊁	K
12	Λ	Λ	Γ(L)	L	ΛΛ	Λ	LΛ	⌐	⌐	L
13	M	M	M	MM	M	MM	MM	⋎	⋎	⋎
14	⋀⋁	N	N	⋀⋁⋀⋁	⋀⋁	⋀⋁ N	N	⋎	⋎	⋎
15	⧧	—	—	⊥	⊥	—	⊞	⋈	—	
16	O	O	O	O	O	O	O	O	—	O
17	ΓΓ	ΓC	ΓΓ(Γ)	ΓΓ	Γ	Γ	Γ	⌐	⌐	Γ
18	M	M	—	—	—	MM	—	M	M	—
19	Ϙ	Φ	Ϙ	Ϙ	Ϙ	Ϙ	Ϙ	Ϙ	Ϙ	Ϙ
20	P	PP	P(P)	PPRD	PPD	PPR	RP	⟜	⟜⌐	P
21	—	—	ʃ(ξ)	ʃ	εξ	—	ʃʃ	ʃ	ʃ	ʃʃ
22	T	T	T	T	T	T	┼T	T	┼	T
23	V Y	V Y	V(Y⋎)	V Y	V Υ	V⋎Y	V Y	⋎	V	V
24	—	—	Φ	ΦΦ	Φ	ΦΦ	ΦΦ	Φ	Φ	—
25	—	—	X	X +	X	X +	X +	X	⋁⋁	+
26	—	—	—	⋁Υ	Ψ	⋁Y	Ψ	Ψ	8	—
27	—	—	—	Ω	—	—	—	—	—	—

εὔποτ[ον]: ποτ ἔριον / ℎος δ' ἄν τόδε πίεσι: ποτερί[ō]: αὐτίκα κε͂νον / ℎίμερος: ℎαιρ ἔσει: καλλιστε[φάν]ō: 'Αφροδίτες "Nestor had a fine drinking cup, but anyone who drinks from this cup will soon be struck with desire for fair-crowned Aphrodite."

It has been observed that there is no other evidence of archaic compositions with such perfect alignment and order: the expression εὔποτον ποτέριον "fine cup from which to drink" may have influenced another inscription from Pithekoussai, of which only the fragment]ευποτε π[. remains. Also from Ischia, painted from right to left is one of the earliest known artist's signatures, though also badly mutilated:]ινος μ' ἐποίεσε[meaning "[…]inos made me." From the last quarter of the eighth century we find θεō ("of the deity"), a right-to-left inscription on an *amphora* from the so-called Nestor Tomb. From these and other items of archaeological evidence there is a clear relationship between the written tradition of Pithekoussai and that of Cumae on the mainland opposite, the first true Greek colony in the West, which was settled by inhabitants of Ischia together with groups of people sent from Euboea. The first written document from Cumae is a right-to-left graffito on an *aryballos* of Protocorinthian manufacture, dated to the second quarter of the seventh century: Ταταίες ἐμὶ λ/έqυθος· ℎος δ' ἄν με κλέφσ/ει θυφλὸς ἔσται ("I am the ampoule of Tataies; whosoever steals me will go blind"). On a bronze *sors* from the early sixth century we find an inscription running in a right-to-left spiral: ℎέρε͂ οὐκ ἐα̃ι ἐπιμαντεύεσθαι ("Hera does not allow the making of prophecies"). Evidence of Hera cult worship has been confirmed elsewhere by right-to-left-spiral graffiti on potsherds.

A great many inscriptions have turned up in chamber tombs: most of these are engraved on the inner tomb walls. Some consist simply in the name of the deceased (Κριτοβ/όλες "of Critobolos"), whereas others assume a slightly more complex formula: Δε̄μοχ/άριδός /ἐ̄μι τō/[…] ("I am of Demochares. [son] of […]"). Yet others seem to give a warning: ℎυπὺ τε͂ι κλίνει τούτει λε͂νος ℎυπύ ("beneath this [chamber] tomb is a sarcophagus"; late sixth-century); or οὐ θέμις ἐν/τοῦθα κεῖσθ/αι με̃ τὸν βε/βαχχευμέ/νον ("in this place it is not allowed to deposit deceased persons who are not initiated into the Bacchic rites"; 450 B.C.). From the close of the sixth century we have a bronze *lebes* bearing a "speaking" inscription: ἐπὶ τοῖς 'Ονομάστō τō Φειδίλεο ἄθλοις ἐθέθε̄ν ("I was offered as a prize for the funeral games in honor of Onomastos [son] of Pheidileos").

Zancle. Originally founded as a way station by pirates from Cumae in 755 B.C. and subsequently colonized by Perieres of Cumae and Cratemenes of Chalcis, Zancle has yielded drachmas (of 515 B.C. or later) bearing the word Δάνκλε̄, a fragment of an inscribed bronze plaque (barely legible) and dedications to Olympia: Δανκλαῖοι Ῥε̄γίνōν ("the Zanclaeans [from the spoils] of the [defeated] Rhegians" (500–490 B.C.). From the period following the refoundation of Zancle by Anaxilas of Rhegium, who in 488 B.C. renamed the town Μεσσέ̄νε̄, (Messene), we have some dedications to Zeus Olympius: Δὺ ['Ολ]υν[π]ίōι Μεσσέ̄νιοι Λοκ[ρōν] "to Zeus Olympios the inhabitants of Messene from the spoils) of the (conquered) Locrians" and Μεσσέ̄νιοι Μυλαίōν "the inhabitants of Messene (from the spoils) of Mylae", in addition to tetradrachms with the legend Μεσσενίōν, which in 460–430 B.C. was replaced by the entirely Doric form Μεσσανίōν.

The earliest written evidence from the subcolony Himera – which was founded in 648 B.C. and destroyed in 476 by the tyrant Thrasydaeus, who then repopulated it with people of Dorian stock – comprises a set of graffiti on vases naming the owners in the genitive form: Λύκō ("of Lykos"; note that the *qoppa* has been abandoned), Χαρίνō("of Charinos"). A metrical dedication, etched in a spiral on the foot of a vessel, datable to the end of the sixth century, betrays certain epic overtones (*Hymn to Hera* 3): Ζε̄νὸς ἐριγδούποιο κόρει γλαυκōπι Ἀθέ̄νει/Θρίπυλος εὐξάμενος τέ̄νδ' ἀνέθεκε θεα̃ι ("To Athena glaucopis, daughter of the thunderous Zeus, Thripylos dedicates this [cup?], having promised it to the goddess"). Another inscription, Σίξας, this time on a rectangular lead plaque with a perforation at each corner, is datable to the later sixth century. Dating from the decade 482–472 B.C. is a set of drachmas bearing the right-to-left-spiral inscription: ℎιμερα(ίōν). Another lead plaque, which was probably reused in the second quarter of the fifth century, is inscribed with a legend in which a slingman is connoted by his name, his family name, and even the name of the commander under whom he served, recalling the former's duties: Εὐōπίδας ℎίαλ(λ)ε / Διεύχες: λοχᾱγὸς / Δαῖτις ("Dieuches Euopidas pitched; [his] commander [was] Dactis"). Both here and in the mid-fifth-century dedication to Ergoteles at Olympia one notes the evident transition to the Doric usage.

Rhegium. The foundation of the colony took place during the First Messenian War (end eighth century) prompted by the people of Zancle, who appointed Antimnestos as the *oikistes* or founder (οἰκιστής) for the original group of settlers; an important contingent of the population was however made up of Messenian exiles, a descendant of whom, Anaxilas, subsequently rose to the position of tyrant and governed the city. Evidence of the Archaic period comes in the form of inscriptions painted on fragments of clay lids of the Chalcidian type (the pottery seems to be attributable to Rhegium); a name worth noting from these examples is

The Nestor Cup
Rhodian Late Geometric *kotyle*
with Euboic inscription
last quarter 8th cent. B.C.
Ischia, Museo
Archeologico di Pitecusa
Cat. 21

Reconstruction
of the metric inscription
on the Nestor Cup
(Buchner, Russo 1955)

that of the centaur Μάρφσος. The most ancient coins, moreover, datable to between the sixth and fifth centuries B.C., bear the right-to-left-spiral legend Ρ̄εγίνōν ("of the Rhegians"). On a fragment of a bronze *lebes* datable to 475–450 B.C. one can make out the remains of a dedication to Heracles: hε̄ρακλέος Ρ̄εγίνυ (= Ρηγίνου) ("of Rhegian Heracles"). On three clay projectiles of the same period (styled in imitation of *glandes missiles*) are inscribed the name and patronymic of the dedicator; of particular interest is the one bearing the writing Δε̄μ(ο)φάνης Θράρυος ("Demophanes [son] of Thrarys"), owing to the distinction between the two letters ē (of different origin) and for the rhotacism of intervocalic σ (Θράσυος > Θράρυος) a distinction that foreshadows similar developments in the homeland.

Naxos. Founded in the year 734 B.C. by the Chalcidians of Euboea under the leadership of Theocles, in historical times the polis of Naxos vaunted a splendid altar to the Ἀρχηγέτης "founder" Apollo Archegetes, erected outside the city walls. An inscribed *cippus* seems to confirm the existence of a group of settlers from the island of Naxos in the Cyclades. The *polis* was destroyed in 403 B.C. by the tyrant Dionysius of Syracuse. Among the documents of special interest are the coin inscriptions (550–530 B.C.): Ναξίōν and the graffito Ἀρχ(υ)κλε̃ς ("Archicles," a proper name) on the base of a small cup (500 B.C.). Dating to the late fifth–early fourth century is the graffito on the base of a small black-painted cup: Εὐδράμōν ("Eudramon," a proper name) and likewise the acclamatory inscription: Τιτταβὸ· φίλη ("Darling Tittabo"); also in this category are the various graffiti on clay projectiles bearing indications of the family name (Ἑρμῶνδαι), the proper name (Ὀνομόστατος) and the patronymic (Ἐπαμέ(νο)νος). In the latter specimens the writing betrays a tendency toward Milesian usage, with the adoption of η and ω. As regards the subcolonies Leontini and Catana, the only surviving written evidence is found on coins, which tend to indicate the ethnic group Λεοντίνōν and the toponym Κατάνε̄ (first half of the fifth century B.C.).

Fragment of Late Geometric krater with potter's signature
last quarter 8th cent. B.C.
Ischia, Museo
Archeologico di Pitecusa
Cat. 22

The Ionian Colonies

Siris. The authors of antiquity state that Siris was an Ionian colony founded in the seventh century by exiles of Colophon who fled the onslaught of King Gyges of Lydia. The *apoikia* or settlement did not flourish for long: a century or so later it was conquered by the Achaean coalition forces. From the early period of Siris' existence we have an inscription: : Ἰσοδίκης ἐμί ("I belong to Isodice") on a loom weight, dating to the earlier seventh century. Nearby, from an evidently short-lived Greek settlement of probable Ionian foundation sited on the Incoronata hillside near Metapontum (Bay of Taranto), we have a fine cup with a graffito inscription that is almost cursive in script: Πύρρō ὄλπ(η) ("cup of Pyrrhos").

Massalia. Massalia (modern Marseilles) was a seaboard settlement in Ligurian territory, founded around 600 B.C. by colonists from Phocaea. It engaged in busy trade with Gaul in the interior, and with Spain, challenging Carthage's hegemony, and successfully dominating most of the western reaches of the Mediterranean basin. Written evidence of this *polis* can be found in the Ionic alphabet on a stele at Delphi for Apellis, son of Demone (datable to the early fifth century): Ἀπέλλι/ος τō Δή/μωνος Μ/ασσαλι/ήτεο. From Antipolis (modern Antibes), an entrepôt founded to stave off the Liguri, we have a metrical dedication to Aphrodite (450–425 B.C.): Τέρπων εἰμὶ θεᾶς θεράπων/σεμνῆς Ἀφροδίτης/τοῖς δὲ καταστήσασι Κύπρις/χάριν ἀνταποδοίη ("I am Terpone, minister of the hallowed Aphrodite, Cypris returns the favor to those who erected me").

The Dorian Colonies

Doric. The Doric dialects differ from the Ionic by having retained: 1) the long ᾱ; 2) the *digamma* (Ϝ), e.g., in Ϝ οῖνος; 3) the voiceless dental (τ) and voiceless dental aspirate (θ) before the ι (τι, θι); 4) the form of the nominative masculine and feminine plural of the article (τοί, ταί).
Other distinguishing features include: a) the ending of the first person plural of the active voice -μες (elsewhere -μεν); b) the formation (albeit not generalized) in -ξ- of the future and of the aorist of verbs in -ζω (δείπνιξεν); c) the contraction of ᾱ+ŏ into ᾱ (genitive singular Πυρρίᾱ, Σōμροτίδᾱ; genitive plural Κλευλ(λ)ιδᾶν); and of α+ε into ē (τιμε̄τō from τιμαέτō); d) τῆνος meaning "that" in lieu of (ἐ)κεῖνος; e) *h*ιαρός meaning "sacred" as against the Ionic-Attic (*h*)ιερός; f) the numerals πρᾶτος (Ionic πρῶτος) meaning "first", τέτορες (Ionic τέσσαρες) meaning "four", *Ϝ ίκατι (Ionic εἴκοσι) meaning "twenty"; g) the conjunction αἰ "if" compared to the Ionic εἰ; and the modal particle κα, Ionic ἄν.
Within the Doric group of dialects there are further subdivisions:
A) Doric dialects in the strict sense (southern Doric), including Laconic, Messenian, Elean, Rhodian, Cretan, and Cyrenaic, with their open timbre due to the contraction and compensatory lengthening: ἠμί (=ē̜*mí*)

The Greek Colonization of the West: Dialects

Silver tetradrachma from Himera
ca. 470-450 B.C.
Naples, Soprintendenza archeologica
delle Province di Napoli e Salerno

meaning "[I] am" from *es-mi (Ionic εἰμί with ει = ẹ̄), Γοργίππω (Ionic-Attic, Doric *mitior* Γοργίππου), Πύρρω = Πύρρου.

The transition of ε to ι before ο, α is frequent: Ἀριστοφάνιος for Ἀριστοφάνεος.

B) Northern Doric dialects (or from the northwest), including Megarian, Corinthian, and perhaps Achaean. Among these special attention should be paid to the closed timbre resulting from the compensatory lengthening and contraction: εἰμί ("[I] am").

Dorian colonies in Magna Graecia

The Achaean colonies (Sybaris, Croton, Metapontum)

Sybaris. The Achaean settlements along the seaboard of southern Italy were established on fertile coastland from Tarentum right across the Gulf of Taranto. The first of these colonies, Sybaris, was founded in the last quarter of the eighth century; from here a few years later the inhabitants set up a new subcolony, Poseidonia (Paestum). The new *polis* was destroyed by Croton first in 510 and again in 448 after having been refounded by the Poseidonians in 453 B.C. The extant written documents include several coin legends dating from the later sixth century: Συβαρίτας (right-to-left inscription). From the district of Sybaris comes a bronze plaque of the late seventh–early sixth century bearing a right-to-left-spiral inscription whose meaning is still partly under discussion: Δο. Κλεόμροτος/ὁ ΔεξιλάϜο ἀνέθεκ·/Ὀλυνπίαι νικάσας/Ϝίσο(μ) μᾶκός τε πάχος τε/τἀθάναι ἀϜέθλōν/εὐξάμενος δεκάταν ("Do. Cleombrotos [son] of Dexilaos, having won at Olympia, dedicated a life-size statue of himself, having vowed to Athena a tenth of the prizes"; the alternative translation runs "having won at Olympia against men of equal height and strength, following the dedication etc."). What is notable here is the absence of the rough breathing (in the article ὁ), the retention of the *digamma* (Ϝ), the absence of the *epenthesis* (β in Κλεόμροτος; whereas in Classical Greek: Κλεόμβροτος), the assimilation of the final -ν with the initial μ in Ϝίσομ (against the tendency to generalize the spelling with ν even before the labial). The last two lines form a pentameter. On a silver tessera of unknown provenance we have a boustrophedic inscription, i.e., written "as the ox plows" ἈριστέϜις ἀνέθēκε (first half of the sixth century) meaning "Aristeuis [female given name] dedicated [me]." Another inscription bears witness to the female proper name Ῥεγά, inscribed on a loom weight: Ῥεγᾶς ἐ̄μι meaning "I belong to Regas"; the piece is from the same epoch (on other clay pyramids dating from the late sixth–early fifth century we find the simple nominative: Τιμṓ, Χιṓ).

Silver tetradrachma
from the Messana mint
493-480 B.C.
Syracuse
Soprintendenza per i Beni
Culturali e Ambientali
Gabinetto di Numismatica

Poseidonia (Paestum). Datable to the second half of the sixth century are some dedications found in the temple area; a silver plaque bears the inscription: τᾶς hḗρας hιαρόν. Ϝρονφιτοξαμιν ("[I am] sacred to Hera"), τᾶς θεō̃ ἐ̄μι hιαρόν ("I am sacred to the goddess"), τᾶς θεō̃ τ(ᾶ)ς παιδός ἐ̄μι ("sono della dea παῖς"), τō̃ Διὸς ξείνō (read: ξενίō) "of Zeus protector of guests". The Nymphaeum yielded an small *amphora* (?) bearing the graffito: τᾶς νύνφας ἐ̄μὶ hια[ρόν] ("I am sacred to the Nymph"). The earliest inscription carved into

The Greek Colonization of the West: Dialects

Bronze *lamina*
with Archaic inscription
beginning 6th cent. B.C.
Sibari, Museo
Nazionale Archeologico della Sibaritide
Cat. 46/III

a somewhat crude *stele* (or *cippus*?) found near the Basilica temple seems to date back only as far as mid-sixth century; the inscription runs right to left, and includes the name: Χίρōνος "of Chiron". Dating from the second half of the sixth century is a set of coins bearing the legend Ποσ(ειδανιάτας), sometimes accompanied by Ϝ υς (it could be a river name, or the name of the founder of Sybaris, the mother-city of Paestum).

Croton. Founded at the end of the eighth century on the southernmost tip of the Gulf of Taranto, Croton gradually extended its dominion toward the north and south, taking over other settlements and *poleis* such as Terina, Petelia, Cremissa, Temesa, and Pandosia, where the Greeks lived side-by-side with the native inhabitants. The minting of coins began in the second half of the sixth century with the issue of *incusi* bearing the Delphic tripod emblem and the ethnic initials *qρο*; the use of the *qoppa* in these inscriptions remained until 450 B.C. Among the other written documents worth mentioning is the inscription on a block of the *temenos* of Hera Lacinia datable to the second half of the sixth century: hἕρας ἐλευθέρια by which the dedicators – the ἐλεύθεροι, or attending freedmen – note their offerings to the goddess. Belonging to the start of the fifth century we have the dedication inscribed into a piece of a ship's anchor: τō Διὸς/τō Μελιχίō/ΦάϜ (υ)λλος hέζατο (= hέσσατο) ("of Zeus Meilichios; Phayullo laid [this]; the dedicator, who was a worthy discus-thrower, took part in the Battle of Salamis with his own vessel").

Incused stater from Poseidonia
silver
530-510 B.C.
Naples, Soprintendenza archeologica
delle Province di Napoli e Salerno

195

Stater from Croton and Temesa
silver
ca. post 450 B.C.
Naples, Santangelo Collection

Metapontum. The foundation of the colony of Metapontum – promoted apparently by Sybaris to block the southward expansion of the Tarentines – dates to the early years of the seventh century. The coinage (second half of the sixth century) bears the symbol of the corn-ear and the wording: Μετα(πόντιον); in the first quarter of the fifth century one notes the appearance of the legend Ἀχελōίō ἄεθλον ("prize for the races of Acheloos"), celebrating the games in honor of the river of that name. Among the many dedications that have come to light – and especially those to Apollo – one in particular stands out, an elaborate metrical dedication addressing Heracles (second half of the sixth century), incised *boustrophedon* on the four faces of a clay model obelisk: Χαῖρε Ϝ ἄναξ hε̄ρακλες/ὅ τοι κεραμεύς μ'ἀνέθε̄κε/Νικόμαχος μ'ἐπόε̄·/δὸς δέ Ϝ 'ἰν ἀνθρō̃ποις/δόξαν ἔχε̄ν ἀγαθ(ά)ν ("Hail, Ϝ ἄναξ Heracles! I was dedicated by the potter; Nicomachos made me. May his name be known among men"; the name Nicomachos is no doubt that of the potter).

Among the distinctive phonetic features of the Achaean inscriptions, one notes:

a) the conservation of the *digamma* (ṷ) above all in the initial position: Ϝέργō̄ν, Ϝ ἄναξ, Ϝ ίσō(μ), Ϝ οικίαν, Ϝ(έ); as an internal part of a word it is present throughout the Archaic period: ἀϜέθλον, ἈριστεϜίς, ΛαϜῖνος; but it is soon omitted (in ΦάϜ(υ)λλος the purely graphic omission of υ seems to be linked to the concern for resuscitating the Ϝ, which is etymologically justified in a proper name,

b) the use of ζ with a different value from that in Ionic-Attic (to which in Doric corresponds moreover δ-, -δδ-) stems from τέζαρα of Metapontum (= τέσσαρα) and from hέζατο of Croton (= hέσσατο),

c) the assibilation in the dental of the name of the subcolony Ποσειδανία (*Poseidonia*, originally an adjective referring to πόλις, *polis*, meaning "city") compared to the conservation of τ in the Doric variant Ποτιδαία *Potidaia*. This seems to shed light on the non-Doric component that emerges from certain morphological facts, such as: 1) the form of the article οἱ (an Ionic-Attic innovation) as against the Doric τοί; 2) the nominative Ἀχιλ(λ)ές on a *pinax* fragment datable to the first half of the sixth century (though the appellative κεραμεύς seems to be a "normal" outcome); 3) the numeral τέζαρα (= Ionic τέσσαρα meaning "four") as against the Doric τέτορα.

Locri Epizephyrii

Between 680 and 670 B.C. under the guidance of Euanthes and with the help of Syracuse – and perhaps even Tarentum – a new settlement was founded on the headland of Capo Zefirio. It is not clear whether the colonists were Ozolae (West Locrians) or Opuntii (East Locrians) from Mainland Greece. The fact remains, however, that the alphabet in use in the new colony Locri Epizephyrii was identical to that of Ozolian Locris. According to Ephorus, the city was the birthplace of Zaleucus, the author of the first written set of laws. In the seventh century further colonies were founded: Hipponium, Medma, and Mataurus on the Tyrrhenian. Except for a graffito on seventh/sixth-century sherd bearing a written form for the name Cybele: -]ς ϙυβάλας and for a fragmentary bronze plate with the remains of a text concerning instructions about property and ownership, most of the other inscriptions come from the Sanctuary of Persephone. One of these (early fifth century) runs: Φρασιάδας ἀνέθε̄κε τᾶι θ[ε]ō̃ι ("Phrasiadas dedicated [this] to the goddess"); from the second quarter of the century comes the dedication on a *cippus*: Οἰνιάδας/καὶ Εὐκέ/λαδος/καὶ Χείμ/αρος/ἀνέθε̄κ/αν τᾶι θ/εō̃ι ("Oiniadas and Eucelados and Cheimaros dedicated [this] to the goddess"). Other inscriptions that refer to religious practices can be found on several *skyphoi*, reading: hιαραὶ

Clay column with Greek epigraph made by the potter Nicomaco
6th cent. B.C.
Naples
Museo Archeologico Nazionale
Cat. 100

τᾶς Ἀφροδίτας ("sacred to Aphrodite"). The two subcolonies Hipponium and Medma are associated to Locri in an *en pointillé* dedication on a bronze plaque from Olympia (later sixth century): τοὶ Ϝ ειπονιε͂[ς] ἀ[ν]έθ[εκαν ἀπὸ]/τον ϙροτονια[ταν]/καὶ Μεδμαῖοι καὶ Λ[οϙροί] ("the citizens of Hipponium and Medma and Locri dedicated [this] from the spoils of the Crotonians").

Tarentum. The only colony in the West of Spartan foundation, Taras or Tarentum, was settled at the close of the eighth century. Among the earliest documentary evidence we have a "speaking" inscription on an Attic eye-*kylix* (540–530 B.C.): Μελο͂σας·ἐμὶ·νικατε͂ριον·ξαίνοσα·τὰς κόρας·ἐνίκε͂ ("I am the prize for the victory of Melosas; carding [wool] he triumphed over the maidens"). In this inscription one notes the use of a point as a word-divider, the absence of the *qoppa*, a feature in which Tarentum adapts to the customs of the motherland. Belonging to the second half of the sixth century are the earliest extant coins, with an *incuso* as for Achaean mintage, with a right-to-left inscription: Τάρας (Taras). Produced at the end of the century is clay die bearing numerals from one to six incised on the faces: κύ(βος), δύο, τρία, τέτο(ρα), πέν(τε), Ϝ έξ. From the same period comes a bronze plinth with the incised legend: Πόλυλ(λ)ος ἀνέθε͂κ(ε)ν/Εὐ(ō)πίδας ἐποίε͂ ("Polyl[l]os dedicated [this], Euopidas made it"); in this case there is an uncustomary use of the ν (ephelkystikon) typical of the Ionic-Attic tradition. Dating to 443–433 B.C. are the dedications on three spear-butts (σαυρωτῆρες) found at Olympia: σκῦλα ἀπὸ Θουρίον Ταραν/τίνοι ἀνέθεκαν Δὶι Ὀλυ/μπίōι δεκάταν ("The Tarentines dedicated to Zeus Olympius one tenth of the spoils of Thurii"). Another document of signal importance is the *Tabulae Heracleenses*, found at Heraclea (a subcolony of Tarentum and Thurii), which contains various elements of apparent pre-Doric formation, such as κοθαρός, ἀνεπιγρόφως in the place of καθαρός, ἀνεπιγράφως. Among the more important phonetic features is the retention of the initial *digamma* (Ϝ-, in use as late as 300 B.C.): Ϝ έξ, Ϝ άριχος, Ϝ οινιο͂ν together with the retention and conservation of θ, σ, ζ, thereby ignoring the evolution that was taking place in the homeland (> σ, h, δ).

Doric colonies in Sicily

Megara Hyblaea and Selinus. Megara Hyblaea was founded in the year 727 B.C. by colonists from Megara Nysea under the leadership of the *oikistes* Lamis, whereas the foundation of the subcolony Selinus dates to a century earlier. In 483/2 Megara fell under the power of nearby Syracuse; while Selinus was overrun by the Carthaginians in 408 B.C. The alphabet in use does not correspond entirely with that used in the homeland: it lacks the characteristic form of the *epsilon*, which is similar to that of the Corinthian alphabet (Β), a point of particular interest is the somewhat peculiar *beta* (ᴎ). A fair amount of the documents stem from the necropolis; the deceased is usually indicated with the genitive (sometimes accompanied by the patronymic) after which there is frequently the word ΕΙΜΙ ("[I] am"), given us: Καλ(λ)ιστέος : εἰμί ("I belong to Kallistes"; 500 B.C.), Καλ(λ)ιόψ[ιός]/εἰμι ("I belong to Kal[l]iop[si]" 500 B.C.), τᾶς hαγία θ/υγατρός εἰμι/Καπρογόνō ("I belong to the daughter of Hagia, Kaprogono"; early fifth century). In some rare cases the sepulchral function of a *stele* is underlined with the wording σᾶμα meaning "sepulcher," as in the examples: Μαρύλο͂ τόδε σᾶμα ("This [is] the sepulcher of Marylos"; 500 B.C.), and, Θεσ(σ)άλο͂ τόδε σᾶμα το͂[---]/hυιο͂ ("This [is] the sepulcher of Thes[s]alos, son of..." early fifth century). The most intriguing of these epitaphs concerns a physician. The legend runs right-to-left on the right leg of a marble *kouros* (mid-sixth century): Σōμροτίδα:το͂ hιατρο͂:το͂ Μανδροκλέος ("[Sepulcher] of the physician Somrotidas, [son] of Mandrocles"). The name is a conspicuous one, in which "the study and practice of the medical profession was probably hereditary." The initial aspiration in the form hιατρός is without comparison. Among the other inscriptions found, those particularly worth mentioning include the metrical dedication on a votive *stele* (early fifth century): Φιντύλος hοὑγρίτο͂ τὰν στάλαν τάνδ' ἀνέθε͂κε ("Phintylos [son] of Eucritos dedicated this *stele*"); the (Φιντύλος stands for Φιλτύλος stands for λτ to ντ or through dissimilation of the two λ-λ; another item of note is the hοὑγρίτο͂ instead of hοὑκρίτο͂) and lastly the graffito on the foot of a *kylix* found at Gela (500 B.C.): Πανχάρεός εἰμι/καὶ το͂ν φίλōν ϙοινά εἰμι ("I belong to Panchareos and am shared among friends").
At Selinus, the form ΕΙΜΙ appears alongside ΕΜΙ (perhaps through influence from Acragas), giving: Ἀριστογείτο͂ ἐ/μὶ: το͂ Ἀρκαδίōνος./hος hυπὸ Μοτύ/Ϝ αι: ἀπέθανε 500 B.C.) "I belong to Aristogeiton [son] of Arcadion, who died at Motya"); Ἐπιχάρμō εἰμι το͂ Μ/νασανδρίδα 475–450 B.C. ("I belong to Epicharmos [son] of Mnasandridas"); here again, the epitaphs contain the indication σᾶμα meaning "sepulcher", as in: [σᾶ]μά εἰμ/ι Μύσϙō το͂/Μενεπτο/[λέμō] late seventh century ("I am the sepulcher of Myscos [son] of Menepto[lemos?]"). A set of epitaphs (550–540 B.C.) present the exclamation of condolence οἴμοι, which itself defines the series as sepulchral inscriptions: οἴμοι /ο͂ Λυκίσκε (Alas, O Lyciscos"), and οἴμοι ὀ͂ρχέδ[α]μ/ε hο Πυθέα Σελινόντιος ("Alas, O Archedamos [son] of Pythea of Selinus").

Stater from Tarentum
silver
ca. 510 B.C.
Naples, Santangelo Collection

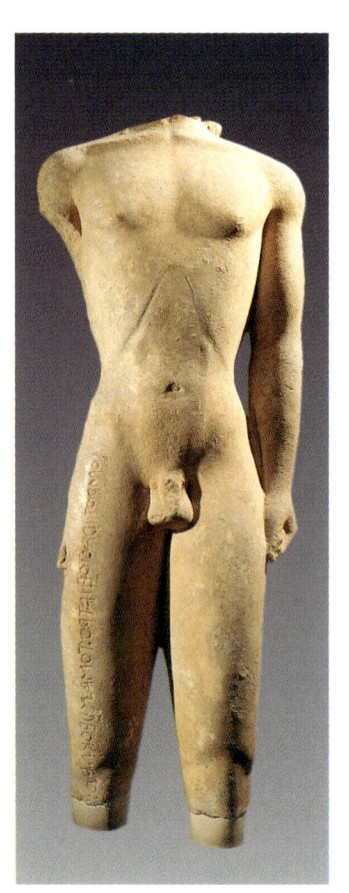

Whereas one detects a slight redundancy or emphasis in the formulation Ἀγασία ἐμ/ὶ τὸ σᾶμα τ/ō Καρία· οἴμοι (550–500 B.C.) ("I am the sepulcher of Agasias [son] of Carias. Alas"). In addition to the dedications to Heracles, Hecate, and Malophoros (Demeter), a group of other inscriptions are of interest, including one that appears on a ἀργοὶ λίθοι from the Sanctuary of Zeus Meilichios (550–450 B.C.): hε[ῦ]ρις hέ/σ(σ)α/το Μειλι/χίōι ("Heuris offered up to Meilichios"). Some of these stones, which represent aniconic portraits of the deity in question, bear nothing more than the name of the dedicator, sometimes in the nominative case: Αἰνέας, Εὐμαΐδας, and sometimes in the genitive: Λυϙοφρο/νίδα ("of Lycophronidas"); occasionally a variant crops up, as in Σōταίρ/ō εἰμί ("I belong to Sotairos"). Among the official documents belonging to this city, mention should be made of the long votive inscription in which the Seluntines acclaim their victory thanks to their particular favor with the gods. Among the other, "private" documents is an important metrical inscription etched onto a *lekythos*: Ἀριστοκλείας ἐμὶ τᾶς καλᾶς καλά·/haύτα δ' ἐμά·Πίθαϙος αἰτέσας ἔχει 550–525 B.C. ("I, beautiful [vessel] belong to the gracious Aristocleias"; to this the dedicator adds, "she is mine. Pythacos owns it, having requested it."). Among the *defixiones* (a dozen curses inscribed into lead plaques, of which one is unusually long), the oldest (sixth–fifth century) runs thus: --]κōι hότ(ι) κα λείēι ἀτέλε/στα καὶ ἔργα καὶ ἔπεα ἔ[σ/τ]αι·καὶ Σικανᾶι ἀτέλε/στα καὶ ἔργα καὶ ἔπε[α hό/τ]ι κα λείēι ("to …, whatever he [she?] might wish, and their actions and words will be in vain. Likewise at Sicana may their actions and words have no effect, whatever they so wish").

Linguistic peculiarities abound, however, as one can see in the dialect at Megara Hyblaea, where the form EIMI ([I] am") is alternated at Selinus with EMI (= ἠμί?), the reason for this may be the influence of nearby Acragas. The first form, EIMI, with its initial diphthong (as against the usual result of compensatory lengthening) is found throughout the Attic language, even in the earliest documents. Similarly, the term Εὐμενίδō, hερμιō differs from written evidence in general to the genitive singular in -ᾱ and seems more compatible with Attic. Come what may, the dialect spoken in Acragas must have influenced the usage of variations like Ἀριστοφάνιος for Ἀριστοφάνεος in contrast with the general retention of εο in this area.

Gela and Acragas. The former of these two colonies was founded in 688 B.C. by Antiphemos of Rhodes and Entymos of Crete. The relatively weak influence of Rhodian on the language, however, is clear from the eth-

Headless marble *kouros*
with inscription on the right leg
ca. 550 B.C.
Syracuse
Museo Archeologico Regionale
Cat. 75

Herm of Zeus Meilichius
with inscription
mid 5th cent. B.C.
Palermo, Museo Archeologico
Regionale "A. Salinas"
Cat. 95/I

Bronze helmet
with Doric Greek inscription
found at Olympia
ca. 474 B.C.
London, British Museum
Department of Greek
and Roman Antiquities
Cat. 157

nic Λίνδιοι, Lindioi, the term used for the fortress (Lindus was the name of a city-state on Rhodes); the toponym Γέλα (Gela) is linked to the local river name Γέλας. Thwarted in their eastern expansion by the puissant Syracusans, the Geloans pushed westward. In 580 B.C. they founded Acragas. Continuing their expansion, in the interior they came into contact with the Chalcidians of Leontini. Toward the end of the century, the city-state's oligarchic government became a tyranny, under which Gela rose to great splendor and set its sights on the conquest of the entire eastern section of Sicily. In the year 485 B.C. Syracuse was brought to heel, and most of the population of Gela transferred thereto. In 460, once the tyranny came to an end, the Geloans were able to return to their homeland – a series of events that are reflected at linguistic level. As for Acragas itself, the subcolony began its period of expansion under the tyranny of Phalaris. Under its next tyrant, Theron, the *polis* reached the height of its grandeur, assisted by the Syracusan tyrant Gelon in the Battle of Himera (480 B.C.), in which the Carthaginians were crushed and annihilated.

As regards the alphabet, there are certain discrepancies between that in use in Gela and that of the homeland, Rhodes. This is particularly noticeable in the use of the *chet* (H) indicating exclusively an aspiration at the beginning of the word. Among the various dedications that have come to light, of particular interest is the metrical inscription (variously integrated) of Pantares at Olympia (525 B.C.) on a bronze plate: Πανταρες μ'ἀνέθεκ[ε] Μενεκράτιος Διὸ[ς ἆθλον]/τὸ Γελοαίō ("Pantares [son] of Menecrates of Gela dedicated me, prize in the competition [in honor] of Zeus"); another plate dedicated to Hera, inscribed on the foot of a *lekythos* (550–500 B.C.) with the word: *h*έρα, (Hera); the one with the *oikistes* Antiphemos, etched into the foot of an Attic *kylix* (500 B.C.): Μνασιθάλες ἀνέθεκε Ἀντιφάμοι. On a fragment of an Attic *pyxis* the artist has inscribed a dedication to Thesmophoros (475–450 B.C.): hιαρὰ Θεσμοφόρō·/ἐκ τᾶς Δικαιōς σκανᾶς ("[I am] sacred to Thesmophoros; [I come] from the tent of Dikaios").

On a sepulchral stone we find a metrical *boustrophedon* inscription (550-500 B.C.): ΠασιάδαϜ ο τὸ/σᾶμα·Κράτες ἐποίε ("The sepulcher [belongs] to Pasiadas; Crates made it"). On a *hydria* a series of painted captions (500 B.C.) declares Geloos' love for Akkas: Γελōιος/Ἀκ(κ)ας /ἔραται ("Geloos loves Akkas"). Another inscription with an amorous theme (whose meaning is not entirely clear) is the graffito inside an Attic *kylix*: τοῦτον τὸν σφύφον Πόρϙος ἀποδίδοτι ἐς τὸν θίασον τōν π[ᾱõ]ν(?)· /αἰ δ'ἐφίλε Φρύναν, οὐκ ἄλλος κ'ἆγε/ho δὲ γράψας τὸν ἀννέμο(ν)τα πυγίξει ("Porcos returns this *skyphos* to the *thiasos* of the [...?]. If he loved Phryne, another would not take her [as a wife]. He who writes will fuck the reader"). Recently, a repository in the sanctuary of the local deity of Camarina has yielded a group of bronze plates bearing anthroponyms, patronymics, and indications of the: φράτρα of ownership. The pieces were part of an archive.

Among the more important linguistic phenomena we should remember:
1) the lengthening of the vowel after the disappearance of the digamma in the following consonantal groups: νϜ, ρϜ, λϜ, whence Ξηνιάδα, Ξήνιππος, and so forth from ΞενϜ-, (c.f., the Attic Ξένιππος);

2) the presence of irregular genitive forms: ΠασιάδαϜο ("of Pasiadas"), Ἀδεινίαυ ("of Adeinias"), compared to the normal termination in -ᾱ (from -ᾱο) of the genitive singular of the masculine themes in -ᾱ, 3) the sporadic use of the Aeolic termination -εσσι of the dative plural of themes ending in a consonant (a quirk found also at Selinus): μέτ᾽ ἀνδρέσι μέτε γυναίκεσσι ("for neither women nor men") in which ἀνδρέσι seems to be a form of compromise with regard to the customary ἀνδράσι.

Syracuse. A colony of Corinth founded by the *oikistes* Archias in the year 73 B.C., Syracuse regrettably offers little epigraphic material. A fragment of a Protocorinthian *pyxis* from the first quarter of the seventh century bears the remains of an engraved inscription apparently written in the ancient alphabet of the homeland: παρβ[--]/[Δ]άνκλας(?) ε·[--]; in the sixth century, however, a less characterized model was in use. The earliest coins (530–520 B.C.) bear the legend Συραϙο/σίōν ("of the Syracusans"). While in 500 B.C. the *qoppa* makes way for the *kappa*, in certain other types of document the letter lasted a while longer. Dating to the sixth century is the inscription cut into the western step of the Temple of Apollo: Κλεομ[--]ε̄ς: ἐποίε̄σε τō̄πέλ(λ)ōνι: ho Κνιδιείδα: κε̄πία[λ]ε στύλεια: καλὰ ἐϜ ἔργα ("Cleom[enes?] [son] of Cnidieidas paid homage to Apollo and erected the columns; a fine job"). Dating to the end of the sixth century is the epigraph incised into a *cippus* in the necropolis of the Archaic period: Ἀλέξιος τὸ σᾱμα ("The sepulcher [belongs to] Alessi"). From the fifth century we have several dedications made by the Deinomenids (Gelon, Hieron, Polyzelus) at Olympia and Delphi: an Etruscan helmet at Olympia conserves the record of the Battle of Cumae (474 B.C.): hιάρōν ὁ Δεινομένεος καὶ τοὶ Συρακόσιοι/τοῖ Δὶ Τυρ(ρ)άν᾽ ἀπὸ Κύμας ("Hieron [son] of Deinomenes, and the Syracusans [offered up] to Zeus the spoils of the Tyrrhenians [Etruscans] [brought] from the victory of Cumae").

Cyrene. In the wake of overpopulation and bouts of famine, a part of the inhabitants of Thera (Santorini) were forced to leave the island and look for more suitable location. Following the advice of the Delphic oracle, they beached first at the island of Plataea, off the Libyan coast. Subsequently, in 631 B.C., under the guidance of a certain Aristoteles (who assumed the royal Libyan title of "Battus"), they occupied the area opposite, around the Cyre spring sacred to Apollo. Under Battus II the city attracted new waves of colonists from various different areas of Mainland Greece.

Documentation covering the preceding period is very scarce. For the early sixth century, however, we have a fragment of a dedication to Olympia that retains the initial part of the ethnic: ϙυρα[ναῖοι] (on the coinage minted at the end of the century the *qoppa* has disappeared altogether). On a fragment of Laconian cup (575 B.C.) we find a crudely inscribed ἀρχαῖος ἀ[-- ("the ancient ..."). Of greater interest perhaps is the metrical inscription running "as the ox plows" on a tufo *stele* (likewise dating to the earlier sixth century):]?Ἰσόνος στάλα[ν]/ἔστασαν ἑταῖροι ("The company laid the *stele* of Isone"). What one notices immediately here is the lack of the aspiration in ἑταῖροι, parallels of this variation can be seen in Thera, IG xii 3. 450b). On the rim of a plate from the *apollonion* in Cyrene we find the dedication to the deity (early sixth century) τō̄ Ἀπόλλōνός ἐ̓μι ("I belong to Apollo"). Dating to the second half of the century, when the *san* (M) had been replaced by *sigma* (Σ) and the *iota* interrupted with the vertical slash, we have a set of dedications, including a curious right-to-left-spiral one to Ὀφέλει (=Ἐφιάλτῃ) ("to the nightmare"). Another inscription, this time on the foot of a beaker (sixth–fifth century) reads: τō̄πόλλōνος : δεκάτα ("tenth of Apollo"). Also from the Apollo sanctuary comes a dedication on a *stele* from the early fifth century: Αἰγλάνορ μ᾽ἀνέθε̄κεhὸ̄ντιπάτρō δεκάταν ("Aiglanor [son] of Antipatros dedicated me as a tenth"). Dating to after 400 B.C. come certain examples of writing of some length, such as the *lex sacra* relating to the oracle of Apollo. The language in which these articles are drafted is a peculiar composite one, with "Aeolisms" such as (πεδά for μετά, -νσ- instead of -ισ-); moreover, there is no lack of reminders of Delphi, such as (ἐντόφιον "funeral gift", where the Delphic counterpart is ἐντοφήια "funeral rites", and the form of the participle χρείμενος). Other peculiarities worth observing are: 1) the ν falls without the compensatory lengthening of the preceding vowel in the termination of the accusative plural -νς (by the same development as that seen in the case of): ἀνθρώπος (accusative plural); 2) in place of βούλομαι an apophonic, phonetic variant appears δήλομαι "I wish"; 3) the feminine participles κατίασσα, ἔκασσα retain the ancient formation in -*ntjă*, where elsewhere it is normalized to (κατιοῦσα, ἑκοῦσα).

Tetradrachma from Syracuse
silver
ca. 500-480 B.C.
Naples, Soprintendenza archeologica delle Province di Napoli e Salerno

Bibliography

Inscription collections: *Corpus Inscriptionum Graecarum* I-IV, 1828-1877; H. ROEHL, 1882; *Sammlung griechischer Dialektinschriften*, 1884; *Inscriptiones Graecae* XIV, 1890; H. ROEHL, 1907; E. SCHWYZER, 1923.
Grammar creatises: F. BECHTEL, 1921-1924; E. SCHWYZER, 1939; C.D. BUCK, 1955; V. PISANI, 1973.
Epigraphy creatises: L. JEFFERY, 1961 (new edition by A. Johnston in 1990); M. GUARDUCCI, I-IV, 1967-1978.
General works: J. BÉRARD, 1957; AA.VV., *Magna Grecia*, I-IV, 1985-1988.

Francesco Prontera   Maritime Communications

Greek emigration and the foundation of new cities in southern Italy and Sicily (as well as in Provence and Catalonia later on) brought about a new and lasting drive to communications between the Aegean Sea and the western Mediterranean. These communications have already been well documented by archaeological discoveries concerning the Late Bronze Age (sixteenth to thirteenth centuries B.C.), but it was the "colonization" in the historic age (eighth to seventh centuries B.C.) that created the conditions necessary to revive and strengthen the maritime network, disrupted by the crisis of the Mycenaean civilization. This colonization as well as the Greek and Phoenician-Punic commerce in the West led to the discovery that the Mediterranean was a great sea surrounded by the three continents of the ancient inhabited world and that it had a passage to the ocean. The Greeks invented the term "inner sea" to distinguish it from the "outer sea," beyond the Pillars of Hercules, a sea that (perhaps) circled the whole of the inhabited world. This denomination was completely foreign to the ancient Egyptian, Mesopotamian, and Anatolian civilizations which knew only the eastern sectors of the Mediterranean, and therefore could never have had any idea about its overall shape. The maritime communications with the colonial world provide an explanation for the oldest Greek description of the inhabited world, the *Periegesis*, or "journey round the world" by the Milesian logographer Hecataeus (ca. 500 B.C.), written as a clockwise itinerary along the coasts of the inner sea. Two different kinds of evidence can be considered when examining the question of the maritime routes between the Aegean and the western Mediterranean seas: manufactured products unearthed in archaeological excavations (and more recently, in submarine sites) and the ancient literary tradition. The maps indicating the distribution of Greek pottery exported to the West (usually discovered in necropolis) provide a synoptic view of both the places of production and the sites of finds. Since the pottery was part of the load carried on cargo ships, its unperishable nature makes it concrete evidence of the transport of manufactured products. However, these maps are of no help in isolating the intermediate ports of call along the transmarine routes. Moreover, there is a danger of classifying the sites which reveal similar types of ceramics as links of the same chain, or stopping places along a single route. This would be an illusory simplification. The most discerning archaeologists are aware of the problem and rightly advise against transfering the identity of an item (Euboic, Corinthian, or Attic pottery) to the identity of the merchants (Euboeans, Corinthians, or Athenians). Added to this, there is the question of the archaeological evidence differing in terms of space and time due to its fortuitous character and the considerable gaps still existing. Much caution therefore is understandably necessary when tracing the lines of the maritime network on the maps that illustrate the distribution of Mycenaean, Greek or Etruscan pottery exported to the West in the various different epochs. The ancient literary evidence is equally fragmentary and dissimilar. It usually provides information about the circumstances that led to foundation of new cities, about the origins of the colonists and the names of the founders, but it rarely documents the early voyages of exploration, the routes followed and the ports of call along the way. The Italic, Siceliot, and Etruscan cities all had varying degrees of com-

Map of the principal maritime routes during the colonial period

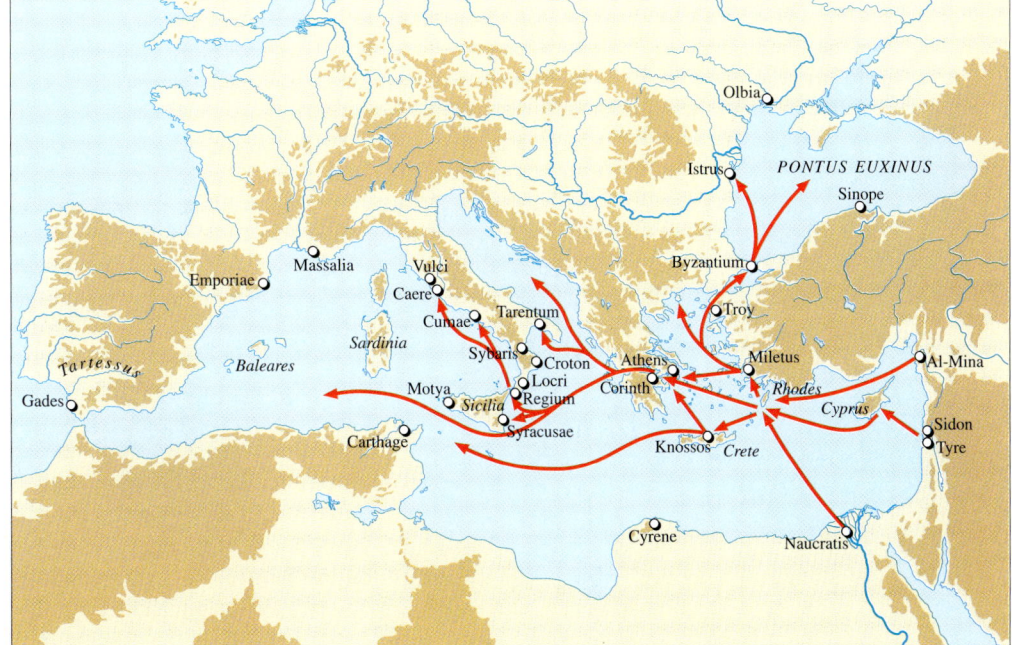

Maritime Communications

Fragment of a votive
model war galley
end 6th-beginning 5th cent. B.C.
Lipari, Museo
Archeologico Regionale Eoliano
Cat. 4

opposite
Cup by Execias
with Dionysus on a sailing boat
540-530 B.C.
Munich, Staatlichen
Antikensammlungen und Glyptothek
München

mercial relations with the centers of the Aegean and eastern Mediterranean, but very little is known about how the transmarine routes actually functioned. The terms of the question raised by G. Columba in an article published in the *Archivio Storico Siciliano* in 1889, over a hundred years ago, are equally appropriate today: "The first question that springs to mind when studying the history of the Greek colonies in southern Italy and Sicily is naturally the following: what were the communications between Greece proper and these other countries and in what way did they take place? Unluckily for us, an answer is delayed by the fact that the information in our possession is too disconnected and partial. What is worse, it regards different epochs and therefore cannot all be used, nor in the same way." Archaeological documentation has increased enormously since the time when G. Columba was making his observations, but the utilization of literary sources still creates the same difficulties today. Ancient historians were interested in navigation because of the military and political functions of the navy (Thucydides, I. 13–14; Polybius, I. 20–21). Accounts, which can be read in Herodotus, of the long voyages of the Phocaeans (I. 163) who had discovered the Adriatic Sea, Etruria and the region of Tartessus beyond the Pillars of Hercules (the southern valley of the Guadalquivir), or of the adventurous arrival of Colaeus, the Samian merchant, at Tartessus (IV. 152), do not give any details about the real structure of the maritime communications between the Aegean and the western Mediterranean in the Archaic age. The literary documentation of the Classical age (fifth to fourth centuries B.C.) contains fewer gaps and therefore enables us to elaborate some reasonable hypotheses concerning the intermediate ports of call along the commercial routes. But before we examine these, we should make a brief introduction.

A progressive and irreversible separation of roles took place in the navy during the course of the seventh century B.C., with the creation of military and merchant fleets, which can be observed in the construction of the vessels. The war vessels, on the one hand, were long and narrow galleys with a ram, propelled chiefly by oars, while the sails served only as extra power when the winds were favorable. On the other hand, the merchant ships, driven only by sails, were of a rounder shape more suited to the dangers of long voyages on the high seas. There is no trace of this distinction in Homer's world, where the same ship transports wares and warriors who are also the oarsmen. The building of sailing cargo ships doubtlessly brought with it improved techniques in navigation over long distances. The route taken by a merchant ship was therefore much more subject to the prevailing winds than that taken by a warship, which could count, to a certain extent, on the strength of its oarsmen for movement. The meteorological and geographical conditions (the availability of ports, and sheltered moorage) were bound to influence the routes used for maritime transport which was active mostly during a brief period (roughly from the end of May to mid-September) and which petered out throughout the rest of the year.

Maritime Communications

Maritime Communications

Bas-relief showing ship
with three rows of oars
4th cent. B.C.
Athens, Akropolis Museum

The seasonal characteristics of trade overseas was already well-known to Hesiod (ca. 700 B.C.). However, even within the favorable season, attention had to be paid to the quirks of the local meteorological situation in the various sectors of the Mediterranean. In the Aegean Sea, for example, strong north-northwesterly winds prevailed from July to early September. They were called the Etesian winds by the ancient Greeks, and are now known locally as the *meltemia* (a word of Turkish origin). These winds can be a hazard to navigation along the routes between Crete and the Peloponnese. Being forced to drop anchor for days on end until the winds changed direction, or being blown off course were normal events in antiquity.

With these premises in mind, we can now try to establish a few stages and stopping places along the commercial routes between the Aegean and the colonial world to the west.

"When you double Cape Malea, forget your home." The proverb, which was still well-known in Strabo's time (VIII. 6. 20), implies the difficulties of sailing through the turbulent waters of the promontory. Once round the cape, it was a point of no return for mariners who entered the Strait of Cythera, leaving the Aegean Sea behind them.

The troublesome circumnavigation of the Peloponnese as far as the Gulf of Patras could be avoided by transporting the ships over the Isthmus of Corinth, along rails lying on a paved road (*diolkos*), whose remains have been brought to light by archaeologists. There is very little certain information about how this form of land transport worked and how its traffic was regulated. Corinth does have two ports however, one on the Saronic Gulf (Cenchreae), the other on the Gulf of Corinth (Lechaeum) so that it clearly was in a privileged position for communications with the West.

The western coast of Messenia offers two good natural harbors, at Mothone and the wide bay of Pylos (Navarino). Other landings exist along the shallow and marshy coasts of the Gulf of Kiparissia (Trifilia), marked by the mouths of the Neda and Alpheus rivers. From here to the Strait of Otranto, first the Ionian Islands – Zacynthus, Cephallenia, and Leucadia – and then, the long, narrow stretch of sea separating Corcyra (Corfu) from the coast of Epirus, allowed the ancients to navigate without ever losing sight of land, and, if necessary, provided various possibilities for sheltered anchorage. The crossing to the Salentina Peninsula can be undertaken from the northern coast of Corfu, or ships can run further north to the bay of Valona, sheltered by the island of Saseno and by the promontory of the Acroceraunia mountains (a conspicuous landmark for navigators of the past, which anyone traveling on the ferry from Corfu to Brindisi will have noticed, when visibility is good, towering over the Albanian coast as the boat leaves the strait). The Strait of Otranto is narrower here, and measures as little as seventy kilometers. This is the gateway to the Adriatic Sea and its width was estimated by the ancient marine geographers (as 500 stades from the Acroceraunia promontory to Otranto according to the *Periplus* of Scylax; as 400, according to Strabo).

The cargo boats sailing for the commercial ports in the delta of the Po River (Adria and Spina) to buy grain and metals, sailed up the Adriatic along the Dalmatian coast, perhaps as far as Zadar where they crossed over to the Conero coast (the ports of Numana and Ancona) and from there up the western shores of the Adriatic. The boats on the route for the Greek cities in the Gulf of Taranto and eastern Sicily, or further on to the ports of the Tyrrhenian Sea, sailed along the Ionian coast as far as the Strait of Messina (we do not know whether the crossing from Capo Leuca to the Lacinian headland (Capo Colonna, south of Croton) which Strabo mentions in the Augustan Age, was already the practice in Classical times).

This is in all likelihood the route taken by Greek emigrants to southern Italy and Sicily, as some anecdotes about the intermediate stages of the colonists' voyages suggest. It was also the route taken by the great Athenian expedition to Sicily (415–413 B.C.), whose stages we know about thanks to Thucydides' fairly detailed description. Cabotage with the sole crossing of the Strait of Otranto seems to be the natural route of Aegean trade toward Magna Graecia and the Tyrrhenian Sea, even though the advantages of having land nearly always in sight have sometimes been overrated. An expedition, like the Athenian one, given the diplomatic and strategic implications (the search for safe ports in the territories under the control of the Italiot cities) and the periodic needs to procure supplies (horses were even transported on some ships), could have only chosen the coastal route, just as Xerxes' fleet invading Greece did in 480 B.C. Furthemore, a military fleet can count on the propulsive force of its oars, whereas the navigation of a merchant ship along a coast is certainly less direct and continual than the tracing of routes constantly parallel to the shore would suggest.

With an eye on the map, we will now return back to the mouth of the Gulf of Patras where the route running round the Peloponnese meets the one coming from the Gulf of Corinth. Could the cargo boats have steered directly across the Ionian Sea for the ports of eastern Sicily (Syracuse) or toward the Tyrrhenian, thus avoiding the circumnavigation along the coast of Epirus and southern Italy? Several factors support an affirmative answer.

Long crossings were certainly not a novelty of Roman-Hellenistic nautical history, even though in this period there was a great improvement in the construction of cargo boats, making them larger and better equipped to face the high seas. Without going back to the transmarine communications of the Greek Bronze Age, proved by archaeological discoveries, we can recall Homer's knowledge of direct navigation from Crete to Egypt, favored by the north winds (*Odyssey* XIV. 246ff.). More certain information can be gleaned from the ancient tradition about Greek colonization in Africa. The circumstances surrounding the foundation of Cyrene by emigrants from Thera in about 631 B.C. (Herodotus, IV. 151) in fact show that at the height of the Archaic age the crossing from Crete to the Cyrenaica was nothing out of the ordinary. This is also true, in the Classical age, of communications between the Peloponnese and Sicily as a few precious literary documents reveal.

Thucydides makes a clear distinction between the waters of the "Ionic Gulf" (the Strait of Otranto) subject to cabotage between Greece and Sicily, and those of the "Sicilian Sea," which is marked by direct routes, and stretches as far as Cythera (IV. 53). As in other examples deriving from the ancient marine terminology, the extension of the *Sikelikon pelagos* as far as the shores of the Aegean must be due to the fact that it is crossed by those actually going to Sicily. However, if this is the case, it is hard to imagine the long circumnavigation along the coasts of Messenia and Elis, across the mouth of the Gulf of Patras, north to the Straits of Corfu and of Otranto, and then down the coasts of the Ionian to the Strait of Messina. If, as seems more reasonable, the name is believed to derive from the experience of the high-sea routes, these must have been more frequent than they would appear to have been from the few known episodes regarding this period described in ancient literature.

As we know from Plutarch (*Parallel Lives* [Dion] XXV) in 357 B.C., a convoy, including two cargo ships, sailed from the island of Zacynthus and arrived near Cape Pachynus (Capo Passero, Sicily) after twelve days on the high seas. When estimating the distance between the Peloponnese and Sicily, toward the end of the fourth century B.C., the points of reference are the mouth of the Alpheus River (which flows into the sea slightly south of Zacynthus) and Syracuse. The surprising position of Cape Pachynus in Hellenistic cartography is worth investigating. Although no original documents have survived, we can make a convincing reconstruction of the geometric setup. According to Strabo, who probably relied on Eratosthenes' calculations as a source, Cape Pachynus lies on almost the same latitude as the Strait of Messina, so that the eastern coast of Sicily is only slightly off the

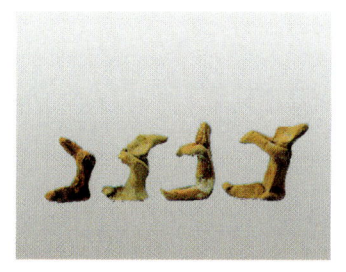

Clay model of a boat
and four oarsmen
ca. mid-3rd century B.C.
Milazzo, Deposito Archeologico
Cat. 3

Clay prow-shaped consoles
second half 2nd cent. B.C.
Segesta, Magazzini di Case Barbaro
Cat. 2

east–west course, pointing to the north instead of the east. The main parallel of Rhodes (36°N), the so-called *diaphragma*, along which Hellenistic geographers tried to establish the length of the inhabited world, passes through the Mediterranean Sea from the southern tips of the Peloponnese and then touches Cape Pachynus *before* crossing the Strait of Messina. Therefore, when calculating the distance between the Peloponnese and Sicily, it is Cape Pachynus that must be considered as the most eastern point of the triangular-shaped island, while Cape Lilybaeum provides the most southern end, pointing toward the Gulf of Carthage. Such distortions in the representation of Sicily, traces of which could still be found in Ptolemaic maps (second century A.D.), in all likelihood reflect the longstanding experience of the maritime communications: from the western tip of the island and Africa, between the eastern coast (Syracuse) and the Peloponnese.

Naturally it is impossible to imagine that the route was directed straight toward the fixed destination. Once the "Sicilian Sea" had been crossed, the cargo ship, reached its goal only after navigating along the coast. The same considerations are true of the routes leading to the Tyrrhenian Sea. The merchant ship, not wanting to undergo the long circumnavigation of western Greece and the Gulf of Taranto, with all its meteorological problems and the limits to maneuver and astronomical seafaring, ended up setting anchor along a fairly large spread of coast which could range highly approximately from the Gulf of Squillace to the coasts of Mount Etna.

Both the coastal and the high-seas routes, leading to the ports of the Tyrrhenian, merge at the Strait of Messina. The circumnavigation of the Calabrian point demands two sharp changes of direction within a space of twenty nautical miles. For a cargo ship, sailing before the wind or with cross winds, the coast between the Heracleum promontory (Capo Spartivento) and Leucopetra (Capo dell'Armi)

Southern Italy and Sicily
as drawn by Strabo
(*Geography*, V-VI
F. Lasserre, ed., Paris 1967)

opposite
Ulysses and the Sirens
detail of decoration
on a Greek vase
3rd cent. B.C.
Berlin, Staatliche Museen
zu Berlin Preussischer Kulturbesitz
Antikensammlung

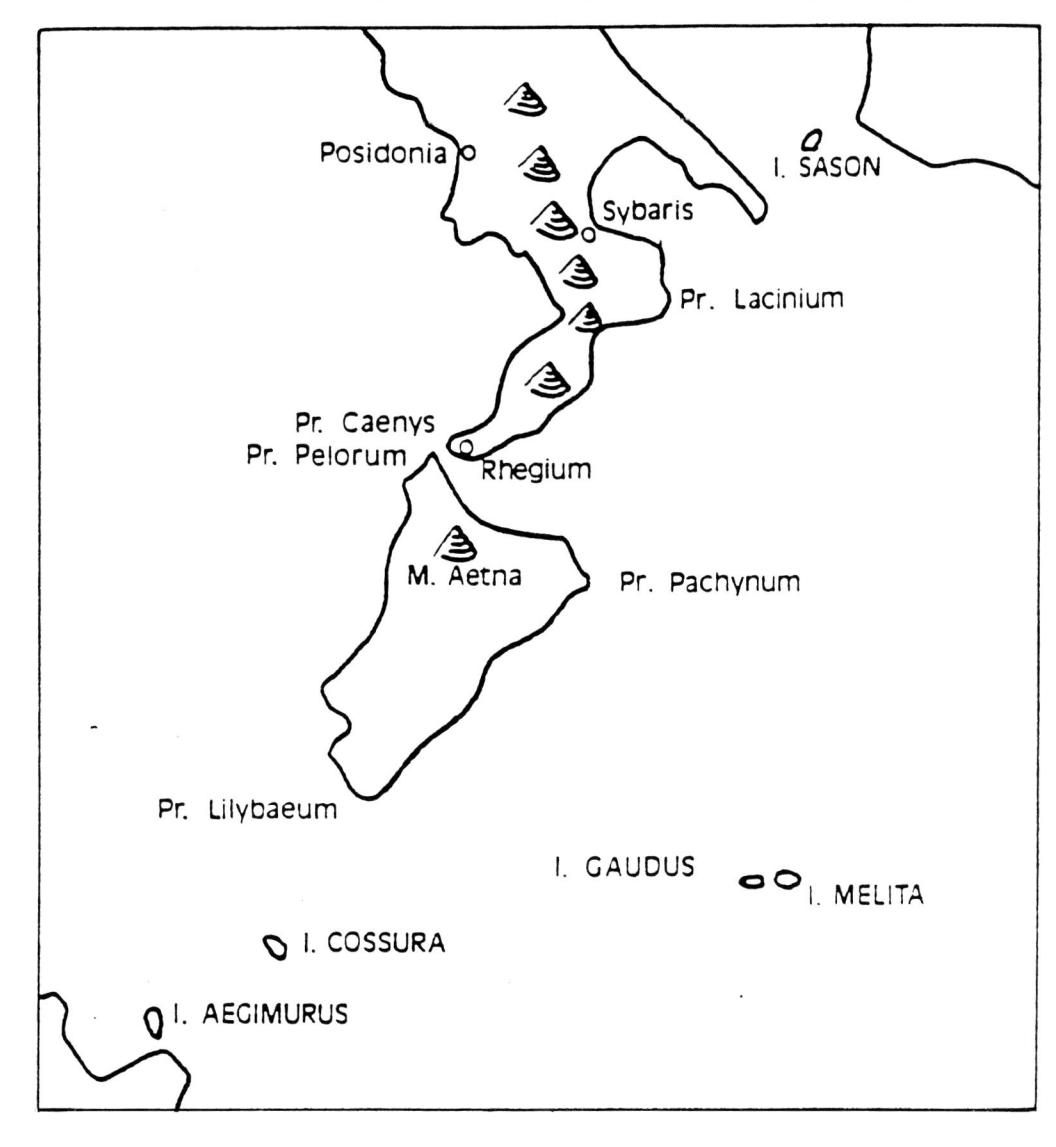

Maritime Communications

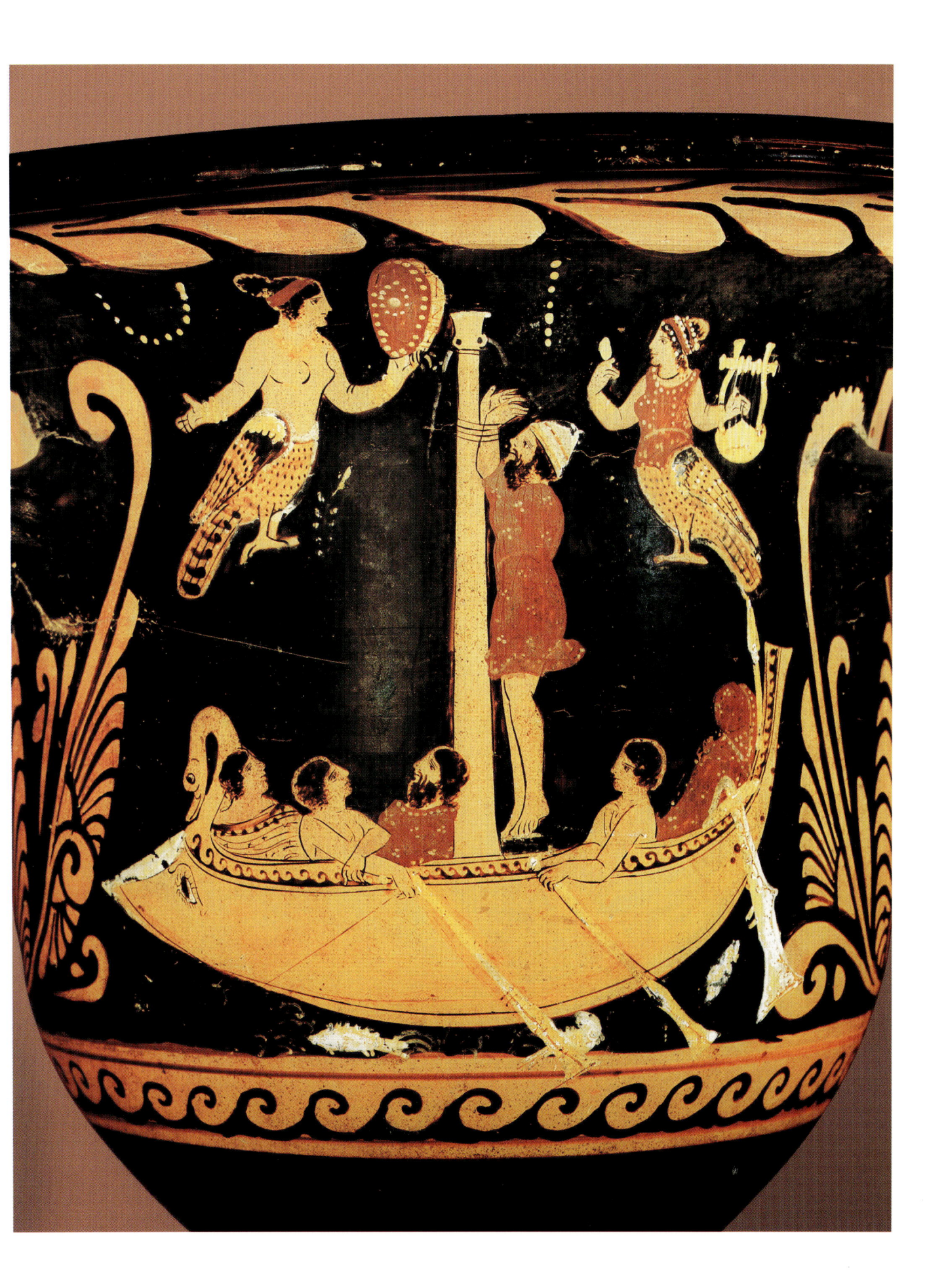

is the most difficult for navigation, and it may be forced to deviate towards the Sicilian coast before crossing the strait. Scholars have been particularly interested in the bay that opens up between Cape Taormina and Cape Schisò where Naxos, the first Greek colony in Sicily, was founded (Thucydides, IV. 3). I find it hard to agree with Columba that the very choice of the site was due to the fact that Naxos was the first landing place on the island for ships arriving from Greece. It is much more likely that the bay of Taormina was a suitable sheltering place while waiting for favorable winds, for boats rounding Leucopetra that were pushed by prevailing winds towards the Sicilian coast.

In conclusion, brief mention must be made of the trade routes in the Strait of Messina which the Euboeans – the founders of the oldest Greek colony in the West at Pithekoussai (Ischia) – thought they recognized as the legendary setting of Ulysses' dramatic adventures between Scylla and Charybdis. Modern portolanos offer the following advice to yachtsmen before crossing the strait: "Wait for the best time for crossing on the basis of the currents and countercurrents." (H. M. Denham, *The Tyrrhenian Sea. A Sea-Guide to its Coasts and Islands*, Italian translation, Milan 1979, p. 191).

If we set aside the echoes of the Homeric myth in ancient literature, we cannot find any indication of how the cargo boats really crossed from the Ionian Sea to the Tyrrhenian and vice versa. The alternating currents were however studied by the great Eratosthenes, who was the first to give a fairly precise description of the phenomenon and its causes. He observed that the current changed direction twice every day and twice every night (every six hours, as in fact it does). It was known as the current that descends (toward the Ionian) and the current that runs out (toward the Tyrrhenian). Today they are known locally as the "rema scendente" and "rema montante," or descending and ascending thrusts. Eratosthenes compared them to the ebb and flow of the ocean tide (Strabo, I. 3. 11).

Long before scientists took any interest in it, the alternate movement of the waters was well-known to the founders of Messana and Rhegium, and naturally the mariners sailing toward the west would have learnt the same practical instructions to be read in modern portolanos. If the "rema montante" was then known as the current that runs out, as Eratosthenes declares, it was obviously used by navigators to exit the Ionian Sea and to enter the Tyrrhenian.

Bibliography
G. VALLET, 1963, pp. 117-135; P. JANNI, 1984; L. CASSON, N.J. 1986², cap. XII; *Lo Stretto crocevia...*, 1993; M. GRAS, 1995; *La Magna Grecia...*, 1996.

Bruno d'Agostino

The Colonial Experience in Greek Mythology

Hesiod, who wrote his poem describing the origins of the gods and mythological beings when Greece was just beginning to embark on her colonial adventure, reveals his knowledge of the existence of the Tyrrhenians (*Theogony* 1011–1016). How does he explain the presence of other peoples outside the Greek world? It is quite obvious to Hesiod that they descend from Odysseus, the Greek hero, whose destiny drew him to wander overseas, far from the "bread-eaters," and thus, to encounter people with very different customs from the Greeks. Agrius, who corresponds perhaps to Faunus, and Latinus, the leaders of the Tyrrhenians, were the fruits of Odysseus' love affair with Circe. They live "far away, in the midst of the sacred islands."

When Hesiod was writing the poem, after the long dark age following the end of the Mycenaean voyages, the discovery of the West had already taken place. Following the example of the Phoenicians, ships sailing from Euboea, the large island in front of Athens, and from the Cyclades, had reached the two known ends of the earth: to the west, beyond Sicily, Campania and Etruria, as far as Tartessus in Iberia; to the east, the coasts of northern Syria and the mouth of the Orontes. Why then did Hesiod refer to the Tyrrhenians in mythological terms? In reality, the urge to explore was restricted to the private initiative of individual merchants and ship-owners. Only such travelers possessed a still vague knowledge of those distant lands. The few ports of call seemed more like coves of pirates.

This world disappeared rapidly when the first colonial cities were founded: Cumae in Campania, Megara Hyblaea and Syracuse in Sicily. However, its brief existence had a profound influence on the creation of the geography and mythological history of the West.

The mythological tales, which were invented to account for these experiences, go back to a model preceding the *Odyssey*. The poem attributed to Eumelus of Corinth tells the story of Jason's voyage with the Argonauts, and unfolds a generation before the Trojan War. The journey from Iolcus in Thessaly to the Black Sea, which was already known to Hesiod, was undertaken to bring back the fabled Golden Fleece; the expedition was followed by a never-ending return journey, the subject of continual new episodes, until, in Hellenic times, it involved the greater part of the known world. Jason's voyage was linked to the spreading of the worship of Hera, and, in the West, to the founding of the great Archaic sanctuary at the mouth of the Sele River.

The task of discovering the West is assigned first and foremost to Heracles and Odysseus, the two heroes whose lives lie on the borderline between the civilized and barbarian worlds. While their function is similar, their destinies are very different. Heracles will become an immortal, accepted by the gods on Mount Olympus. Odysseus, on the other hand, rejects the offer of immortality offered to him by Circe, because this would condemn him to a definitive exile from his own world. His preference for his mortal condition is, in fact, a choice to entrust his fame to posterity, to recollection. In his passage, Odysseus does not transform the places he comes to, but links them as stepping stones on a journey suspended between imagination and reality, much as the tales of shipwrecks punctuate the epic account of the discovery of America.

The *Odyssey* is not a real description of a voyage. Certainly, its stages correspond to actual places, which can be rediscovered – with greater or lesser probability – in the light of later experiences. The most thorough attempt, in this direction, was that of V. Bérard in the first thirty years of this century. But in the poem, these stages are handed down as moments in a human experience: an equal number of crucial encounters between the hero and his destiny. While unreliable as a "history of the discovery," the *Odyssey* is highly effective in illustrating how the experience of the discovery was felt and absorbed by the minds of the people of the time.

The various trials are, therefore, of an emblematic nature, as already suggested above regarding Circe. However, the episode that struck the ancients most of all, ever since the sixth century B.C., is that of the Sirens. The two mythical creatures have birdlike bodies and an irresistibly seductive song, but their faces are those of women. The notes of their song offer a foreknowledge forbidden to men. If Odysseus was to learn – while he is still alive – his destiny as a hero, it would be like cheating himself that he had already run his course, and he would have fallen into a state of timeless forgetfulness, equivalent to death. He counters the trickery of the Sirens with his own: he will listen to the song while he is tied to the mast of his boat, and his sailors' ears will be plugged with beeswax. He will thus be able to resist the enchantment, and the Sirens, now defeated, will commit suicide, throwing themselves down on the boat. The struggle between memory and oblivion, the risk of forgetting and being forgotten, ever present, weigh heavily on the mariner, and that is why "it is a fearful thing to die among the waves (Hesiod, *Works and Days* 687).

Unlike Odysseus, Heracles transforms deeply the places to which he goes. He is a cultural hero whose

Circe offers Odysseus
the drugged potion
detail from the decoration
on a *skyphos*
600-500 B.C.
Oxford, Ashmolean Museum

passage brings civilization and hence the basis of the *polis*. He also brings the institution of sacrifice. Of all his feats, the one which best symbolizes his function is the theft of the cattle belonging to Geryon, the three-bodied monster.

Geryon lives in the far West, on an island on the other side of the ocean called Erythia, where his herdsman Eurytion tends his immortal cattle. Heracles does not know how to get to the island which is on the other side of the ocean where the sun sets. So he tricks the Sun, Helius, into lending him the goblet in which he makes his daily voyage.

When he reaches the island, he kills Geryon, and takes the herd of immortal cattle with him as he journeys back to the East, introducing them into the human world. These animals are closely linked to the labor of man, and are the privileged victims of the sacrifice to the gods of Olympus. The passage of the cows marks the birth of cities and sanctuaries, the introduction of a correct kind of sacrifice, and the end of human sacrifice. The genesis of civilization, however, is nearly always the reparation of an act of violence: first and foremost, the murder of Geryon.

This is the structure of the myth, which serves to explain the discovery of the West and of its acceptance in the civilized world inhabited by the Greeks. The pattern was enriched in time by the addition of new implications. The coming of Heracles to Rome was built along the lines of the story of Geryon, and concluded with the foundation of the Ara Maxima cult in the Forum Boarium. However, in this case, the tables are turned. This time, the cattle is stolen from Heracles by Cacus, a three-bodied monster, who lives on the slopes of Mount Palatine and in the stagnant marshes of

opposite
Corinthian black-figure *aryballos* with Odysseus and the Sirens
575-550 B.C.
Boston, Museum of Fine Arts
Cat. 11

right
reconstruction of the decoration

the Velabrum. The hero kills the monster, regains possession of the cattle, and introduces both the cult and sacrifice.

Other episodes have been added that can be explained in terms of the hegemonic ambitions of Cumae and the other Euboean cities of the peninsula, such as the battle and defeat of the Giants in the Phlegraean Plain, the tales of the foundation of Locri Epizephyrii and the sanctuary of Hera Lacinia (Capo Colonna, Croton).

Other myths of discovery and colonization are linked to the adventures of the various Homeric veterans of Troy (Diomedes, Philotectes, Epeius). The Cretan version involving King Minos and his craftsman Daedalus is particularly interesting. King Minos was a guest of the Sicilian king, Cocalus, in the city of Camicus, and was deceived and killed by the latter. While the myth of King Minos is limited to Sicily and Apulia, where his followers will settle after his death, that of Daedalus is more widespread. His flight from King Minos will bring him to Cumae where he makes the doors of the temple of Apollo, and then as far as the "Electrides Islands, which are to be found in the inner gulf of the Adriatic Sea" (Pseudo-Aristotle, 836 A-B, *De Mirabilibus Auscultationibus* 81). The discovery of a *Golden Pendant* (dated to the second quarter of the fifth century) at Spina, and a *stele* (last quarter of the same century) in a burial-ground in the Giardini Margherita, Bologna, prove that this tradition was well-rooted in the Po Valley.

The act of giving a Greek identity to the barbarian peoples with whom they came into contact corresponded, for the Greeks, to a deeply felt need. In order to understand their motives, it is worthwhile examining the traditions that propose giving the various peoples inhabiting the peninsula an Arcadian origin. Arcadians are called the oldest inhabitants of Latium. Aeneas meets their king, Evander, at the end of his travels. Two sons of the Arcadian king, Lycaon, are Oenotrus, founder of the population of the ancient Basilicata, and Iapygia, ancestor of the peoples of Apulia. The assimilation of these peoples with the Arcadias was certainly stimulated by some basic analogies: the pastoral economy, the lack of cities and the form of village life. However, the presentation of the new world as an offshoot of the Greek world depended clearly on other incentives. It allowed a Greek to imagine a new reality

The Colonial Experience in Greek Mythology

The Colonial Experience in Greek Mythology

Chalcidian black-figure *amphora*
with Heracles fighting Geryon
ca. 540 B.C.
Paris, Bibliothèque Nationale
de France, Cabinet des Médailles
Cat. 12

The Colonial Experience in Greek Mythology

The Colonial Experience in Greek Mythology

Attic red-figure cup
with Heracles in Helios' goblet
ca. 480 B.C.
Vatican City
Museo Gregoriano Etrusco
Cat. 14

which was otherwise inconceivable, and to establish relations with the peoples who lived there. The latter must needs be inserted into the order of things, and the only possible solution was the creation of a genealogical relationship or a common ancestry, such as that provided by Hesiod, the oldest example, where Agrius and Latinus were the sons of Odysseus and Circe. The assimilation of the unknown was the only way of saving a stranger from a state of total and utterly irreversible difference.

Bibliography
Recent bibliography on these subjects is in C. JACOB, 1991. On the *Odissey*, see V. BÉRARD. On Heracles' labors, see C. BONNET-C. JOURDAN-ANNEQUIN, 1992. On the Argonauts, see M. VOJATZI, 1982; M. LLINARES GARCÍA, in Gèrion 5, 1987, pp. 15-42; F. VIANN, in CRAI 1987, pp. 249-262.

Franco Sartori

The Constitutions of the Western Greek States
Cyrenaica, Magna Graecia, Greek Sicily, and the Poleis in the Massaliot Area

Any attempt to construct a homogeneous outline of the constitutions in the Mediterranean regions to the west of the Greek peninsula, and likewise in the regions of the ancient Hellenic world, is destined to come up against insoluble problems. The original particularism of the founding cities (the *metropoleis*) was not only reproduced in their colonies, but, as the years passed and the single colonies were affected by historical events that did not involve the mother country, their constitutions slowly became more and more dissimilar to the original schema established by the founding city at the time of the settlement. This does not mean, however, that, in the first stage at least, the new city was not generally modeled along the lines of the metropolitan structure, and therefore knowledge of the institutions of the metropolis could not be of some use to modern scholars undertaking this research. Nevertheless, a comparative examination of the constitutional documents of the mother countries and the colonies shows sufficiently clearly that the colonies acquired autonomous constitutional forms that were sometimes the opposite of those of the *metropoleis*. This affirmation concerns the Italiot and Siceliot colonies in particular, about which Robert Cohen wrote sixty years ago, that being "too eager for independence and too proud of their prosperity, they lived such a different life from that of the metropolis that they failed... to fulfill their obligations... Their egoism prevented them from serving the Hellenic cause as they should have done" – a judgment that was certainly harsh from the political point of view, but suitable as far as constitutional questions were concerned.

The important Dorian colony of Cyrene, which composed the so-called Pentapolis with its sub-colonies, Barca, Ptolemais, Taucheira, and Euhesperides, conformed considerably to its metropolis Thera in the three centuries following its foundation in 631 B.C. Like Thera, Cyrene was governed as a monarchy by the Battiad dynasty, whose power was only limited toward the mid-sixth century by Demonax of Mantinea following an order from the Delphic oracle. A democratic constitution was then introduced which subdivided the citizens into three tribes (Theraeans and Perioeci, Peloponnesians, Cretans). After the end of the monarchy in 456 B.C., the sovereign authority became the assembly of the so-called Ten Thousand, which, according to one recent opinion, was responsible during the fourth century for rewriting the "founders' oath" and incorporating in it the constitutional principles that had been preeminent when the Theran colony was established in the seventh century. It has also been suggested that the revision (surviving in an epigraphic text) reveals a certain influence of the doctrine of the Platonic Academy, whose exponent in Cyrene between 363 and 361 was the Athenian Chabrias.

Other Cyrenaic epigraphs of the fourth century include lists of officials and magistrates. Some rather interesting ones are the accounts of the *damiorgoi* or *damiergoi* (demiurges) who were introduced in that century and continued to exist for the next two. These reveal information about financial transactions, especially about expenses for sacrifices, a frequent item in a city whose intense religious life is confirmed by the monumental remains and numerous inscriptions referring to priests, priestesses, other cultic offices, ceremonies, oracles, omens, thanksgivings, and sacrifices.

A fundamental chapter in the history of Cyrene and its territory was its annexing to Egypt by Ptolemy I Soter. The first result was a constitutional reform, documented by a famous and long studied inscription known as the "Diagram of Cyrene." In all probability, this inscription dates back to 322 or 321 B.C. as the attribution to the time of Ptolemy III Euergetes, proposed by some scholars, seems to be unsubstantiated. The Diagram opens with the definition of which groups of people comprise the citizens. Immediately after, it establishes what is the *politeuma*, or the collective organ of local sovereignty, and here turns back to the concept of the Ten Thousand, thus creating two categories with differing qualifications: the upper had full political rights, the lower was in a subordinate position. The *politeuma* was formed according to precise criteria, in some cases implying property assessment by a college of sixty *timeteres* (fiscal officials dealing with taxable properties) chosen from among the Ten Thousand by the assembly of the hundred and one *gerontes* (whose members had to be over fifty years of age) who in turn were selected by Ptolemy at the time the reform was introduced. Later on, following the eventual death or dismissal of any of its members, new *gerontes*, citizens over fifty, could be elected by the Ten Thousand. The *gerontes* could not hold any other office of the magistracy, except the one responsible for strategy in time of war. The priests of Apollo were chosen from among them excepting those who had already been priests.

Even though this name immediately recalls the well-known Spartan Gerousia, or Council of Elders, the Cyrenaic *gerontes* were not the equivalent of a senate or city council which appears in the Diagram under the name of *boule*. This was formed of five hundred members for a two-year term, half of whom were renewed in the third year by sortition among the over-fifties. The over-forties could only be taken into consideration if there were not enough candidates over fifty. The *gerontes* were therefore a body of elders with limited but important tasks, as is proved by the fact that Ptolemy himself chose them the first time – and obviously aimed at establishing a political instrument that would remain faithful to him, and capable of influencing the composition and renewal of the *politeuma* which governed the life of the city and its surrounding territory. As a whole, however, the *gerontes*, *boule*, and *politeuma* comprised a kind of tricameral structure, analogous to others elsewhere in the Greek world.

The Diagram also lists: one *strategos*, who is Ptolemy himself, aided by another five military commanders who

Inscribed *stele*
with the oath of the founders
4th cent. B.C.
Cyrene, Archaeological Museum
Cat. 419

The Constitutions of the Western Greek States
Cyrenaica, Magna Graecia, Greek Sicily, and the *Poleis* in the Massaliot Area

Inscribed bronze tablet
recording a loan
made by the Sanctuary of Zeus
to the *polis* of Locri
350-250 B.C.
Reggio Calabria, Museo Nazionale
Cat. 346/I

have never held the office before and who are at least fifty years old; nine *nomophylakes* (guardians of the law) who have never held the office before and who satisfy the age requirements (perhaps fifty years old) which remain unknown due to a gap in the epigraphic text; and five ephors (inspectors) who are at least fifty years old. Further paragraphs deal with the judicial procedures, the incompatibility between certain professions and the magistracies, the crimes and offenses and their relative punishments, as well as a series of cases concerning the economic sector with the solutions laid down by the law.

The Diagram ends with the names of all the people in office at the time of writing, who are mentioned with the title of *archai*. At the head of the list there is a priest (dedicated to the cult of Apollo), followed by the *strategoi* (twelve, of the earlier structure?), *nomophylakes* and ephors and it finishes with five *nomothetes* (legislators) who were probably the authors of the text of the Diagram.

The next epigraphic material, mostly belonging to the Roman period, corroborated the constitutional schema expressed in the Diagram and made some aspects clearer, such as eponymy being linked to a priest when it was not attached to the king of Egypt or of Cyrene itself, as well as adding complementary information on institutions. We will just mention here that the local administration was under the authority of the king in the Lagidic period, and under that of the prince, represented by his Egyptian prefect, during the Roman Empire, each one with its respective government and administrative offices.

There are numerous references to sacred offices, involving probable interferences in the city's administrative life, such as in the case of the *hieromnemones* or archivists and business managers of the sanctuaries. Other magistracies recur frequently: the *polianomoi* (urban police functionaries), the *sitonai* (responsible for the purchase and distribution of grain), the treasurers (responsible for the public revenue). Then there were those who supervised the education of the young in the ephebic institution and the gymnasium: *ephebarchoi*, *paidonomoi*, *gymnasiarchoi*, *akademarchoi*, *dekadarchai*, *triakatiarchai*, *epistatai* and, lastly, *aporytiazontes* (whose function remains unclear).

The constitutional systems elaborated throughout the centuries in *Megale Hellas*, or Magna Graecia of the ancient literary tradition, present a much more complex situation. The aforementioned particularism of the Hellenic colonies, plus changes in internal and external political affairs, the varying economic priorities of the single cities, their position on the coast along major or minor sea routes, the strategic importance of this or that center and, lastly, the unhomogeneous character of the documentary evidence, that is to say, information that is sometimes sufficient, sometimes scarce, make the task of arriving at a statement that would reflect the multiplicity of the phenomena particularly arduous, when it would be better to study the cities, one by one. Moreover, we should keep in mind the, at least initial, difference between the centers of Ionian origin (those in Campania, and the one case in Lucania) and the more widely spread centers of Dorian origin. Lastly, we should not forget that many documents date back to the Magna Graecia that had become Roman politically, where the traditionally Greek institutions gradually gave way to more markedly Roman ones (with few exceptions, such as Neapolis and Chalcidian Rhegium), and Latin ended up prevailing over Greek. Against this background, we can now illustrate the most interesting characteristics of the constitutions. Like the model established by the metropolis, the entire population of the city was called the *demos* or *damos*, whatever kind of regime was in power whether it was a monarchy (rare), a tyranny, an aristocracy, an oligarchy, a timocracy or a democracy. The civic body was often composed, especially in the most important cities, of tribes whose division could have been handed down from the original system, such as that of the Hylleis, the Dymanes, and the Pamphyloi in Dorian territory, but which could also appear under other guises. Sometimes, such as, for example, at Heraclea (Herakleia) on the Siris River and at Locri (Lokroi Epizephyrioi), there existed further subdivisions indicated by abbreviations which qualified as ethnic groups, family groups, places of origin or places of residence.

The body politic, with real powers in truly democratic regimes, or with variously limited powers in other cases, was the assembly, called *ekklesia* or *(h)alia*, or even, antonomastically, the plain *demos* or *damos*. The term *(h)alia*, typical of the Dorian sphere (although outside southern Italy and Sicily the word *apella* occurs) was sometimes but not always known at Heraclea on the Siris River, as *katakletos*, which suggests an extraordinary or enlarged assembly, and this fact has stimulated a hypothesis regarding the presence of some signs of democracy in this traditionally oligarchical institution.

An inscription found at Reggio Calabria (Chalcidian Rhegium) dating to the end of the second century or to the beginning of the first century B.C., mentions a not better identified assembly known as the *eskletos* together with the *(h)alia* and the *boula*. The existence of the assembly of the township, almost certainly going back to the time of the foundation of the single settlements, is proved by the archaeological recognition of buildings where it was held (*ekklestiasteria*, or assembly halls) in Metapontum (sixth century) and Paestum (fifth century), and also by literary sources from the sixth to the fourth centuries regarding Croton, Cumae, and Rhegium for example.

Since the calling of an assembly at short intervals created obvious difficulties even for cities of limited dimensions as were many of the ancient settlements compared to the towns we know today, especially considering that the citizens were spread throughout the territory as they were mostly involved in raising crops and food animals, it soon became necessary to create a smaller assembly, which could be defined as a senate or council, but which was then known as a *boule* or *boula*, or even *bola* as in Locri. According to a literary source, there was a *gerousia* in Locri in its earliest period, that is to say, a council of elders, of which the *bola* – documented in a now well-known group of bronze tablets from the sanctuary of Zeus Olympius, datable to the fourth or third centuries – could be considered a distant continuation.

Some data from the documents, however, give rise to a much debated question regarding the assembly and the council of the citizens. A body of citizens called a *synkletos* was active at Neapolis, Elea (Hyele), Croton and in the Sicilian *polis* of Acragas, alongside the *demos* or *damos*. Various scholars have interpreted it as a tacit noun indicating a council or assembly, and it is generally identified with one or other of these two bodies, and in Roman times it refers doubtlessly to a council of the citizens or even to the senate in Rome. Another hypothesis is that this was a third collective body, called on special occasions for specific tasks, and it could have been a trace, with suitable modifications, of an ancient aristocratic or oligarchic institution, similar to the Thousand of Rhegium or to the Thousand of Locri, or the six hundred *timouchoi* in Massalia, a city whose constitution was perhaps comparable to that of Elea, given their common Phocaean origins. The existence of a third assembly, between the council and the assembly of the citizens, would mean that the cities of Magna Graecia and Sicily had a tricameral structure as was probably the case of Cyrene (above). Lastly, a *proskletos* is mentioned in Neapolis during the Roman period. Was this the same council or just a section of it or a committee? Or could it have been an extraordinary assembly? The Italiot magistracies are characterized by their variety. Differences in terminology and chronological difficulties make their analysis and systematization laborious. The very word *archon* raises doubts, since it could be used in a general sense, meaning magistrate, or in a specific sense to indicate a well-defined public office in the civil or even military services, when it did not indicate, as in Rhegium, the president of a craftsmen's association. From two decrees dated 242 B.C., one issued in Neapolis and the other in Elea, it appears that the archons were responsible together with the *synkletos* and *demos* in Neapolis and with just the *demos* in Elea for their publication. In these cases the archons were exercising not just a general power, and this was confirmed in Neapolis by epigraphic texts deriving from the later Roman period. In other places (Vaglio in Lucania, and Volcei, neither a markedly Greek environment) the Greek terminology should be considered as just a way of making a non-Greek title, such as *med(d)ikia* – the highest magistrate among the Sabellian ethnic groups – comprehensible to a Greek-speaking people.

A certain similarity is however to be found in the constitutions of the group of the so-called Achaean colonies: Croton, and its subcolonies, Crimisa, Petelia, Terina, Scylacium, and Caulonia. At the head of each city there was a *prytanis* and a *damiourgos* (in Attica, *demiourgos*). The demiurge was the eponymous official, perhaps because this had been the highest office in ancient times. Valerius Maximus, the Latin writer, recalled a senate of one thousand members which was probably a limited form of assembly. Some testamentary tablets of the fifth century

The Constitutions of the Western Greek States
Cyrenaica, Magna Graecia, Greek Sicily, and the *Poleis* in the Massaliot Area

opposite
Tabulae Heracleenses
with texts of two reports
on sacred ground
bronze
end 4th-beginning 3rd cent. B.C.
Naples
Museo Archeologico Nazionale
Cat. 272

mention *proxenoi*, who should be understood as simply being witnesses and not the protectors of foreign guests. References to the Greek constitution of Cumae (Kyme) in Campania can be found in occasional and general information concerning *strategoi* at the time of Aristodemus the Malacus (late sixth–early fifth century), and *hoi en telei* (magistrates) as well as a *boule* in an atmosphere of tension between aristocrats and the people. There is much better information about Neapolis, a Cumaean colony, where, at least originally, the highest office was that of the demarchy, which can be inferred from a comment of Strabo and which is confirmed by the fact that centuries later it still existed and was actually conferred as an honorary title upon the emperors, Titus and Hadrian. After the demarchy there came the archonship which in one of the aforementioned decrees of 242 B.C. appears as the only magistracy together with the *synkletos* and the *demos* – a sign of the possible decline of the demarchy as an office holding real power. There are also documents referring to antarchons in the Roman age, who are now usually considered as pro-magistrates or prefects substituting the normal top magistrates of a city with a Roman administration, but there are also epigraphic references to the same in other Greek cities. Documents also nominate *agoranomoi*, whose role overseeing the market was known all over the Greek world (and in Roman times they were identified with the *aediles*), and the much debated *laukelarchoi*, recently suggested to be aides to the demarchs in selecting and summoning the *boule*. Like many other cities, Neapolis had various minor magistrates, civil servants and numerous priests.

The freedom of choice of constitutional solutions in the colonies compared to the *metropoleis* is evident in the case of the *strategoi* known in Tarentum (Taras, of Spartan origin) during the life of Architas, philosopher, scientist, and statesman, who was in fact a *strategos* with maximum power for a decade toward the mid-fourth century. The office of *strategos* was unknown in Sparta and therefore Tarentum was not faithful to the metropolitan model whereas Heraclea on the Siris River, a Tarentine colony, remained loyal to it. Its eponymous magistracy, the ephorship, was a Spartan institution, as illustrated in the epigraphic evidence, especially in two famous large bronze tablets. These include two reports of a college of (*h*)*oristai* (border surveyors: five in the first and three of them in the second) about the recovery of sacred grounds usurped by individuals, as well as a contract for rent of agricultural land, elaborated in the city's name together with two *polianomoi*. There is no mention of a council, but it could hardly not have existed. Sovereignty lay with the aforementioned (*h*)*alia*. As well as the (*h*)*oristai* and the *polianomoi* there are *sitagertai*, magistrates responsible for the harvesting and storage of grain crops.

Strategoi existed at Croton, Rhegium, and in Thurii, the Panhellenic colony founded in two stages, from 445 to 443, under the leadership of Pericles. Here the *strategoi* receive an appellative "after five years," which means they cannot be re-elected after a brief pause. Alongside them, there are the *symbouloi*, magistrates who appear elsewhere in oligarchies. The limit on the re-election of the *strategoi* could perhaps be interpreted as the introduction of a touch of democracy.

The aforesaid tablets in the sanctuary of Zeus Olympius provide us with a satisfactory survey of the constitution of Locri between the fourth and third centuries – a period which could be reduced to a more precise date, 280–276 B.C., if the anonymous king recorded in some of them could be identified as Pyrrhus, the lord of the city in those years, rather than a local magistrate. Before the tablets were discovered scholars only knew that in ancient times Locri had had as its supreme magistrate and moderator of the city's life a *kosmopolis*, that its *gerousia* was a collective body composed of the aristocracy of the so-called Hundred Houses, its assembly was the meeting of the Thousand, from which the lowest classes were excluded, and its magistrates were the not better identified archons and *nomophylakes*. The structure emanating from the texts of the tablets seems to have rejected by then the conservatism that had already reigned for over two hundred years when Demosthenes was alive, i.e., from the first decades of the sixth century.

At the beginning of the tablets, immediately after the abbreviation representing all the anthroponyms, is the indication of the eponymous official, without his specific title. Was he a priest or a magistrate, the ideal perpetuator of the ancient *kosmopolis*? Afterwards, without a precise order, come three *hiaromnamones* or *hieromnemones*, with both religious and magisterial tasks regarding the treasury or the grain harvest; three *proboloi proarchontes*, who were perhaps the coordinators of the work of the *bola*; three *prodikoi* whose responsibilities were unclear, but perhaps concerned judicial procedures; three polemarchs without military prerogatives, but involved in the financial operations published in the tablets because these were for the construction of defensive works; three *logisteres*, public auditors; three *episkeuasteres*, responsible for the building or renovation of cultic equipment; three *toichiopoioi*, supervisors of building sites; three *epistatai*, a general term which means supervisor or overseer. There are archons as well, to be understood in the normal sense of magistrates. Obviously there are also the *bola* and *damos* and sacred offices, such as treasurers, male cultic officials and perhaps female ones, and scribes. A phratry works within the sanctuary, run by twelve *ph(r)atarchoi*, each one given the appellative of *prostatas* (in the Attic language, *prostates*) who is president for one month. Reasons of space prevent us from examining the very interesting mechanism regulating the financial administration of the sanctuary.

The Constitutions of the Western Greek States
Cyrenaica, Magna Graecia, Greek Sicily, and the *Poleis* in the Massaliot Area

The common heritage of the Ionian world did not produce constitutional similarities in Neapolis and Rhegium. Tradition in the latter city evokes a semi-legendary legislation handed down by Charondas of Catana and an assembly of the Thousand of timocratic derivation, which could have been the forerunner of the aforementioned *eskletos* dating to the late Roman period. There is much debate about the interpretation to be given to the term *hegemones*, which in Strabo refers to the primitive constitution. Were these founders of the colony or real magistrates? Whatever the case, Anaxilas the tyrant overrode the timocratic assembly of the Thousand in 494 B.C., with more than likely constitutional changes, which were surely followed by others at the end of the tyranny in 461, following the expulsion of Anaxilas' sons and successors. Diodorus Siculus mentions *strategoi* in 399, which was perhaps a sign of a democratic regime. In the second century or certainly before acquiring Roman citizenship in 90 B.C., the city appears to have been run by three collective bodies: the *halia*, the *eskletos* and the *bula*, the latter presided over by a *prostates*. A *prytanis* was the eponymous official. Other titles of offices, including *prytaneis* and archons, are still written in Greek, but seem to refer not to civic offices, but rather to sacred institutions or professional colleges. We should note all the same, the persistence of Greek traditions and terms right into the Roman age, as is proved also by the gymnasiarchy. However we cannot ignore that the city gradually ended up conforming to the Roman municipal structure.

The constitutional history of the *poleis* in Sicily is more complex than that of the Greek cities in Italy because of the variety of solutions adopted in communities open to a wide range of ethnic and economic interaction and competition, which helps to explain the frequent recurrence of personal forms of power extending beyond the confines of the single cities. The epigraphic and numismatic evidence and literary tradition provide with greater or lesser authority the individual leaders who appeared on the scene for at least five centuries starting from the seventh B.C., with unequivocal titles: kings, dynasts, rulers (*aisymnetai*), and especially tyrants. Sometimes the same person is recorded with more than one of these appellatives. The first of the series were Panaetius of Leontini and Pollis of Syracuse, who were followed by a whole list of names, some famous and some almost unknown: Phalaris, Alcamenes, and Alcander of Acragas; Theron of Selinus (if he did exist), Cleander and Hippocrates of Gela; Gelon I and Hieron I of Gela and then of Syracuse; Polyzelus and Thrasybulus of Syracuse; Theron and Thrasydaeus of Acragas; Terillus of Himera; Scythes and Micythus of Zancle; Archonides I and Archonides II of Herbita; Dionysius I, Dionysius II, Callippus, Hipparinus and Nisaeus of Syracuse; Agyris and Apolloniades of Agyrium; Hicetas of Leontini; Andromachus of Tauromenium; Mamercus of Catana; Agathocles of Syracuse; Tyndarion of Tauromenium; Phintias of Acragas; Heracleides of Leontini; Hieron II, Gelon II and Hieronymus of Syracuse. Other names could be added to the list, even that of Pyrrhus who was honored as king of Syracuse for a short time. The origin of these personal powers lay on the whole in the struggle of the people against aristocracies and oligarchies, but there were a few different cases. Personal government obviously brought changes *ipso facto* from the constitutional point of view, even though very often the city's administrative bodies conserved their traditional schema. More concrete changes took place in the passage from oligarchic to democratic regimes or vice versa, especially due to the authority of the lawmakers, such as the aforementioned Charondas of Catana whose basically conservative principles were to have an influence, according to tradition, on the constitutions of some of the Chalcidian cities in the west, or Diocles of Syracuse, a democratic legislator in 412, or Timoleon the Corinthian invited to Syracuse in 345 to lead the struggle against the tyranny and author of reforms from 343 to 338 that were partly inspired by Diocles' laws.

In spite of the dispersive panorama arising from the autonomist particularism of the Greek cities in Sicily, and the fragmentary character of the documents, sometimes chronologically uncertain, and in part deriving from events in Roman times, it is possible to isolate some institutions as constitutional elements of a non-episodic nature. Even centers of non-Greek origins, such as those in the Punic and Elymian areas of Sicily, or insular centers, like Lipara and Melita (Malta), should be considered here because their constitutions slowly became more and more Hellenized.

Evidence reveals that in some cities there was a division of the population into tribes (*phylai*) divided in turn into phratries led by phratriarchs that, at least originally, grouped together consanguineous families. It is also most likely that in all the centers founded by the Dorians, separated into the three tribes of the Hylleis, Dymanes, and Pamphyloi, there was a ternary system for some magisterial or sacred colleges, sometimes with the inclusion of multiples of three. This could also be the case of the *triakades* in Syracuse, Acrae, and Camarina, if they are to be interpreted as groups of thirty families for religious purposes. But this cannot be true of the *eikades* of Camarina again and of Morgantina, which were based on the number twenty. The need to distinguish individuals by means of abbreviations in front of their names, as mentioned above for the cities of Magna Graecia, was also felt in Acrae, Alaisa (Halaesa), Camarina, and Syracuse, as recent studies have corroborated, even though they used a variety of solutions.

Like the majority of the Greek cities, for those in Sicily the year is indicated by the eponymous official, sometimes without a specific title, other times meaning a priestly office (*hierothytas* or *hierothytes*, *hierapolos*) and occasionally perhaps an archon. In Syracuse the eponymous official could at first have been a *prytanis* whom Timoleon substituted with the *amphipolos* of Zeus Olympius, whose dignity was defined as *arche* by Diodorus Siculus, which means that the office of *amphipolia* was also a magistracy of a very high order. An *amphipolos*, this time of the goddesses Paides, is documented in Acrae, the Syracusan colony.

The civic structure was expressed on a political level in an assembly which in non-democratic regimes had mostly only formal powers. This was known by the names of *halia*, *damos*, or *demos*, *ekklesia* and *syllogos*, right into the Roman age. What was usually called the *bola*, *bula* or *bule* was a council or senate with a consultative and sometimes decision-making role. The problem of the *synkletos* arises again in Acragas, Alaisa (Halaesa), Centuripae, Melita and Syracuse. In particular, an epigraph found at Magnesia ad Maeandrum leads us to believe that it was separate from the council, which was definitely not the case in Roman Agrigentum, where the *synkletos* was composed of one hundred and ten members with functions typical of a *boule* under the presidency of the *hierothytas*. An *eskletos* is described in Hesychius' lexicon as a "meeting of the eminent" personages of Syracuse, and this brings to mind the Six Hundred of the hoplitic census in the constitution of Timoleon, reduced to a private association by Agathocles in 319. When the tyranny of Thrasydaeus of Acragas was overthrown in 471, the timocratic body of the Thousand lasted for only three years, and was abolished in the democratic reform introduced by Empedocles, the philosopher. Again in Acragas, an epigraphic mention of a *synedrion* appears to have referred to the *halia* mentioned in the same context.

There were numerous kinds of magistrates recorded by the sources, but unfortunately we cannot deal with them here, city by city, which would have been the most practical solution. The title of *prytanis* recurs to indicate Pollis or Hieron I in Syracuse, but could also have been used at Lipara and Tauromenium. *Prostatai* and *paraprostatai* as presidents of the council or assembly are known in the Hellenistic-Roman age in some cities, and together with this office we should mention, in connection with the activity of the council, the *probouloi* at Alaisa and perhaps at Tauromenium. The abbreviation *pr* in the epigraphic texts could refer to one of these offices, but it has also been interpreted as indicating a *proagoros*, the highest magistrate in Catana and Tyndaris at the time of Cicero, but also present in Syracuse during the time of Timoleon, and in Acragas in the second century B.C. The abbreviation has also been attributed to the word *praktor*, the collector of tributes and incomes from state and sacred property. As far as the archonship is concerned, the terminological ambiguity, whether it was a general term or a specific office, is valid in Sicily too. The specific role was true of Entella at the time of Agathocles, and of Acrae and Melita later on. In particular, this was the case of Syracuse where under Diocles' reforms the archons were chosen by sortition and chaired the assembly instead of the *strategoi*, the only magistracy that remained elective. Over time, the number of Syracusan *strategoi* are recorded as varying from three to twenty-five, and they could not be reelected except after at least a one-year period. Some of them became absolute rulers (autocratic *strategoi*) and sometimes this became a passage towards a tyranny. The authority of the office of *strategos* was reduced by Timoleon and increased by Hieron II. Tradition relates that Phalaris was an autocratic *strategos* in Acragas. A long list of pairs of "after five years" *strategoi*, similar to those in Thurii, referred to Tauromenium in the third century B.C. Other *strategoi* are mentioned by literary sources for the fourth century in Lipara and for the third in Messana. The latter case, however, concerned a Roman official who found refuge in the city then in the hands of the Mamertines, which suggests an example of Oscan *med(d)ikia*. In Gela, the same epigraphic text that speaks of the eponymous *hierapolos*, includes a high magistrate in office one year known as the *kateniausios* and a college of thirty magistrates or functionaries with undefined powers.

Hiaromnamones or *hieromnemones* with a priestly role and lay responsibilities regarding the temple's finances, were mentioned in inscriptions at Aluntium (now San Marco d'Alunzo), Entella, Gela, Segesta, and Tauromenium, dating back to between the fourth and second centuries. In the first two cities they were also the eponymous officials, as they were also from perhaps the fourth century at Issa (Lissa), the Syracusan colony on the Adriatic coast, which was first administered by a governor (*eparchos*) nominated by Dionysius I.

The sources record *nomothetai* or reformers in Syracuse at the time of Diocles. Nearly sixty years later, in 355 B.C., Dion's reform project laid down a plural sovereignty, flanked by thirty-five *nomophylakes*, guardians of the law. A brief survey of the historical documentation of the cities, especially the epigraphic material, reveals many other offices: the *agoranomoi*, the *polianomoi*, and the *laurarchoi* who perhaps supervised the quarters of the city, and lastly, the *gynaikonomoi* who watched over the morality of the women, but perhaps also over that of the men. In the military sector there were polemarchs and *phrourarchoi*; in the judicial branch, judges, *synallakteres*, and *ampochoi* dealt with justice and the fulfillment of obligations. Confiscation and controls on measures in the financial sector were the responsibility of treasurers (there are important reports on this relating to Tauromenium), *logisteres* (probable) public auditors, *poleteres* and *akribazontes*. The grain stores were run by *agertai*, *sitonai*, and *sito-*

Silver coin of Hieron II
obv. portraits of his wife
and her name and title:
Filistide Basilissa
rev. quadriga driven by a Nike
269-215 B.C.
Syracuse
Museo Archeologico Regionale

phylakes appearing in Tauromenian epigraphic documentation, which also brought to light the gymnasiarchy to be found in other cities as well.

The sacerdotal world was well-represented in Greek Sicily, but was in fact separate from the constitutional field. We will also exclude here mention of the minor officials, except for the *grammateis* who were responsible for writing the acts of the councils and assemblies.

The most significant achievement of Greek expansion in the western Mediterranean was Massalia, which was founded toward 600 B.C., by colonists from Ionian Phocaea, and which, in turn, became a metropolis and protector of other colonies of the same kind along the Provençal coast, in the area of the lower Rhône valley and on the coasts of Languedoc and Iberia. The main characteristic of the Massaliot constitution is its considerable faithfulness to the original oligarchical structure which, according to a tradition noted by Aristotle, underwent only the slightest of changes in a hundred or so years, in any case before the beginning of the fifth century B.C. The modifications concerned the access to positions of government which had initially been limited to the wealthy heads of families operating chiefly in commerce and trade. First, their eldest sons and, later, younger ones could take part, and in the end, this right was extended to people outside the privileged civic group (*politeuma*) as long as they were sufficiently propertied. This was then a timocracy in power in a community which both Cicero and Valerius Maximus approved of for its morality and customs. Strabo gives a clear picture of the constitution which was probably the structure of the Massaliot state in his lifetime, and which was perhaps reformed sometime between the end of the fourth and beginning of the third centuries. The community appears to be organized in a *synedrion* (senate) of six hundred members known as *timouchoi* coopted for life among those who had sons and were citizens for at least three generations. A limited group of fifteen members (the verb used by Strabo suggests that they are *prostatai*) dealt with day-to-day business. Among the fifteen (whom Julius Caesar also mentioned in his *De Bello Gallico*) there are three with supreme powers and perhaps one of the three is more powerful than the other two. Together the three possess executive power. Unfortunately there is no information about the constitutional characteristics of the cities in Massalia's sphere of influence. Nevertheless, the *episcopus Nicaensium*, a magistrate (*duumvir* also *quinquennalis*) of Roman Massalia held a "bishopric" in Nicaea which could have been the survivor of an office established in the preexisting Greek city of Massaliot origin.

Bibliography

On Greek Cyrenaica: F. CHAMOUX, 1953, pp. 104-114, 138-142; A.A. KWAPONG, in *Africa in...*, 1969, pp. 101-109; S. DUŠANIĆ, in *Chiron*, 8, 1978, pp. 55-76; A. LARONDE, 1987, pp. 85-128, 249-256, 424-425; G. PUGLIESE CARRATELLI, in *Cirene e i Libyi...*, 1987, pp. 25-28; A. LARONDE, in B. GENTILI, *Cirene: storia...*, 1990, pp. 35-50. Quite useful is *Lessico...* by S.M. MARENGO, 1991, especially at pp. 562-570.

On both Magna Graecia and Sicily: *Bibliografia topografica...*, I, 1977-XI, 1992; F. CORDANO, 1986, pp. 124-137; R.K. SHERK, in *Zeitschrift...*, 96, 1993, pp. 267-276; F. GHINATTI, "Autenticazione...", in *Sileno*, 19, 1993, pp. 57-69 e "Ancora...", ivi, 20, 1994, pp. 53-69; N. LURAGHI, 1994.

On Magna Graecia: the concise and substantial contributions of C. AMPOLO, G. PUGLIESE CARRATELLI, F. COSTABILE, in *Magna Grecia...*, 1987, pp. 89-114. A partial updating is by G. DE SENSI SESTITO, *La Calabria...*, e G. CAMASSA, in *Storia della Calabria*, I, 1988, pp. 230-232, 630-649 (bibliography at pp. 293-294, 655-656); E. MIRANDA, I, 1990, pp. 47-74 and II, 1995, pp. 42-43; R. ULANO, in *Rendiconti...*, 123, 1989, pp. 123-129; G. DE SENSI SESTITO, in *Miscellanea...*, 8, 1990-91, pp. 25-34; R. FUDA, R. VAN COMPERNOLLE, F. COSTABILE, in *Polis...*, 1992, pp. 203-228; M. GIRONE, in *Annali...*, 35-36, 1992-93, pp. 261-269 and in *Miscellanea...*, 18, 1994, pp. 81-87; M. MOGGI, in *L'incidenza...*, I, 1995, pp. 391-399 (with various bibliographical references). Besides, the *Atti dei Convegni di studi sulla Magna Grecia*, which have been held annually since 1961 in Taranto under different titles, are to be considered.

On Greek Sicily: it is still to be hoped for a global work on the constitutions of the many cities based on principles that are at the same time analytical and comparative, capable of combining the monographic quality of W. HÜTTL's (1929) and the systematic trait of G. BUSOLT's(-H. SWOBODA), I, 1920. The number of articles on this subject is so wide that we cannot list them. Let's just mention the review *Kokalos*, released for the first time in 1955 thanks to the initiative of Eugenio Manni. It often contains studies regarding, either directly or indirectly, constitutional problems (a partial collection of mine bearing the title *Storia costituzionale della Sicilia antica* is in the issue 26-27, 1980-81, pp. 263-284; also useful are the periodical historical and epigraphic reviews). S. CONSOLO LANGHER, in *Helikon* 9-10, 1969-70, pp. 107-143; G. MANGANARO, in *Agrigento...*, 1992, pp. 207-218; F. CORDANO, *Le tessere...*, 1992 and *La città...*, in *La Parola del Passato* 49, 1994, pp. 418-426. Of course constitutional themes are dealt with in essays on specific periods, events, and matters, as well as in studies about some outstanding personalities (such as Phalaris, the Emmenids and Deinomenids, Dionysius the Elder and the Younger, Timoleon, Agathocles, Pyrrhus, Hieron II) and in general treatises. Among them E. GABBA-G. VALLET, 1980, with the essays by G. MADDOLI (*Il VI e V secolo a.C.*, pp. 1-102), M. SORDI (*Il IV e III secolo...*, pp. 207-208), S. CONSOLO LANGHER (*La Sicilia dalla scomparsa...*, pp. 289-342), G. DE SENSI SESTITO (*La Sicilia dal 289...*, pp. 343-370), G. MANGANARO (*La provincia romana*, pp. 411-462).

On the Massaliot area: M. CLERC, I, 1927, pp. 424-434; E. LEPORE, in *La Parola del Passato*, 25, 1970, pp. 44-48, reprinted in *Colonie greche...*, 1989, pp. 124-126; M. CLAVEL-LÉVÊQUE, 1977, pp. 79-84, 115-124; M. BATS-G. BERTUCCHI-G. CONGÈS-H. TRÉZINY, in *Études Massaliètes*, 3, 1992; particularly notable are the essays by E. SANMARTÍ-GREGO (*Massalia et Emporion...*, especially at p. 38) e C. GUYOT-ROUGEMONT e G. ROUGEMONT (*Marseille antique...*, especially at pp. 47-48).

Giovanni Gorini

The Western Greeks: Coinage

Greek coinage came into being between the late seventh and early sixth century B.C. in Ionian Asia Minor and the process that saw the emergence of coins made of precious metal stamped with the badge or device of the issuing authority, was a complex, intermittent one, parts of which are still unclear. Notwithstanding the discrepancies between literary sources, archaeological evidence, and the reconstructions of today's scholars, one element remains clear: in the beginning coinage was not adopted for commercial reasons but was used within the *polis* for all kinds of internal transactions, such as for mercenary activity, war damages, tolls, federal contributions, tributes, and taxes. The Phoenicians – a trading people *par excellence* – did not begin using coinage until a much later date, preferring their custom of "silent bartering" to the use of coins (Herodotus, IV.96.1–3).

When it was introduced, coinage lead to the establishment in the Greek world of a new type of "occult" wealth (Plato, *Republic* VIII.548a-c), a form of wealth that was unprecedented and structurally different from what the Greeks had known theretofore, namely their land, their flocks or herds of livestock. Such property was understood by all. Characteristically, coinage was not in fact adopted by the great Egyptian, Assyrian, and Babylonian kingdoms, and was not adopted in the Persian kingdom until a much later date. From the psychological and moral points of view, the introduction of coinage was something of a shock to the population, the effect of which can be seen in the poems of Theognis and Solon. It is no coincidence that coinage was first introduced at the end of the seventh century in Ionia, a region that lay between the Greek world on one side, and the Lydian kingdom and Persian Empire on the other. This area was the site of the first wave of Greek colonists and the melting-pot that produced new social structures within the different communities, where a gradual identification and selection of roles and functions among the citizenry evolved, and consequently those very functions that led to the "discovery" and use of coinage.

Herodotus (I.94) is a fundamental source on the social developments of the Lydians – the first to issue both gold and silver coins. In the space of two or three generations, Lydian coinage had begun to circulate throughout Mainland Greece with a range of sophisticated and elegant coin types. Up to this time coins had had an irregular, globular shape with a simple square incuse on the reverse left by the die that helped prevent the blank from slipping when it was being struck; soon, however, this method was abandoned and two-sided coins were produced, much the same as those in circulation today. Among the well-known types are those bearing the Aegina turtle, the Corinthian "Pegasus," or the Athenian owl, to name but a few of the most common and widely circulated ancient coins from Mainland Greece.

A further confirmation of the theory that in their early stages coins were not produced in order to simplify commercial trade, either inside or outside the *polis*, is the discovery throughout the Mediterranean basin, from Tarentum to Asyut (Egypt), of large *thesauroi* or hoards created in Archaic times that document the types of coinage not in circulation but destined for storing in treasuries or for smelting.

One of the principal reasons why coins were adopted and were so quickly used in the Greek world, from the cities of the homeland to the western colonies, was that they symbolized the autonomy of the *polis* and the issuing authority. This concept of a close relationship between coinage and the issuing *polis* can also be seen in the way coins were often minted according to a separate standard: in Athens the stater was divided into two drachmas, into three in Corinth and Magna Graecia, and into five in Macedon. The adoption of a "canting" type bearing the symbol of the city (Plutarch, III.399f), is a typical characteristic of the method of tying the coinage with the *polis*. Examples of this system include the seal (*foca*) of Phocaea, the *selinon* (wild celery) of Selinus, the rose of Rhodes, and the sickle (*zanklon* in Greek) of Zancle; alternatively the coins bore the portrait of the eponymous divinity of the *polis* such as Athena for Athens, Poseidon for Poseidonia (Paestum), and Taras for Tarentum.

A result of all this was the effective monopoly of coinage by the *polis*, through special magistrates (as evidenced by the monetary agreement between Phocaea and Mytilene) and an endorsement system, which also checked the quality of the metal. In Athens these controllers were known as the *dokimastes*. Within the *polis* the quality of coinage was guaranteed by legislation; whereas outside it tended to be accepted at face value because of its prestige and intrinsic value.

Hoarding, a phenomenon that affected coinage down through history, was virtually unknown in the period before 500 B.C. (6 hoards in continental Greece, 4 in Macedon and Thrace, 14 in Asia Minor, 1 in the Levant, 8 in Egypt, 1 in Persia, 6 in Magna Graecia, and 3 in Sicily), compared with the Classical and Hellenistic periods. For the latter period the phenomenon was much more common and is very well documented, which in itself was a sign that the circulation of coinage was

Incused stater with retrorse bull
from Sybaris
silver
530-510 B.C.
Naples
Museo Archeologico Nazionale

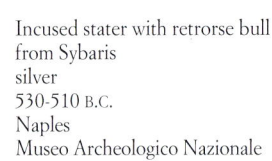

Incused stater with tripod
from Croton
silver
ca. 530-510 B.C.
Naples
Museo Archeologico Nazionale

more widespread and that it was in general use among the different levels of the citizenry. However, *thesauroi* are also evidence of a growing interest in coinage as an article worth hoarding, a means of accumulating personal wealth. Apart from supplying us with an often reliable picture of the type of coinage that was present in a particular area or "market" during a specific period of history, the composition of these *thesauroi* is also a useful means of determining the relative and absolute chronology of the coinage present. Thanks to research carried out on the "sequence of coin types," it is possible to reconstruct the likely order in which the coins from a given mint were issued and – accepting the limits imposed by chance and imprecise information – to establish the mint's production volume. It is also possible, using non-destructive analysis techniques, to determine the metal content (silver, for example) and its origin, namely the supply source for the *polis*. In this sense it is worth noting the special significance of the presence of silver coinage (before the Hellenistic age, special gold issues were always used by the *polis* in moments of crisis) in the overall picture of the Greek economy, so long as the traditional agrarian and servile or slave labor values lasted, as many historians of Greek economy have amply illustrated.

The transmission of coinage from Mainland Greece to Magna Graecia and Sicily came about swiftly, following the routes taken by the western colonists as they settled along the shores of the Mediterranean, like "ants or frogs around a pond" (Plato, *Phaedrus* 109b). In fact the oldest examples of western Greek coinage in Magna Graecia date from the end of the sixth century B.C. Here the Greeks came into contact with an existing form of Italian trade based on the barter of bronze ingots and rings, often contained within a larger one, like those found in the necropolis at Suessula (Naples), which date to the seventh/sixth century B.C. Initially, only the major colonial centers introduced a monetary system. However, even if these colonies tended to use social models and politico-religious structures similar to those in their respective mother-countries, the coinage they developed was one of the most fascinating and artistically valid in the ancient world. Although the technical solutions adopted were inspired by types from Mainland Greece (Corinth) and Asia Minor (Ionia), for reasons as yet in debate, they were independent and quite unique. While initially the coins all bore the square incuse on the reverse, and were rather thick and irregularly shaped, in Magna Graecia the coins became thinner but larger in diameter, and involved a special "reverse incuse" technology that was developed with the same obverse type produced on the reverse of the coins. The reasons for this are obscure though some scholars believe it to be associated with a monetary association (of Pythagorean stamp); in fact such types bear strong stylistic links with the Rhodian and Milesian world, from which one could infer that an independent, local evolution developed in the absence of close technological relations with the centers that produced the very first coins. The cities which issued this type of coinage and adopted a single weight standard of Corinthian origin with a 7.8–8 gram stater and 2.6 gram thirds, were Sybaris, with a retrorse bull type; Croton, with Apollo's sacred tripod; Metapontum, with an ear of barley; Caulonia, with an Apollo banishing the plague; Tarentum, with Phalanthus riding a dolphin; Rhegium, with a bull; and Zancle, with a leaping dolphin in a harbor. Only Poseidonia (Paestum), with a Poseidon caught in the act of throwing a trident, strayed from this weight standard, with a 7.5 gram stater composed of two drachmas. There were also coins issued by less important towns, like Siris (Sirino), Pixunte, Palinurus, Molp[a], Laus, Amin[ei], and So[ntia], and others issued by towns under the influence of the dominions of Croton and Sybaris. In these last two cases the customary image of a Sybarite bull with the name of the "subordinate" city or the Croton tripod was on the obverse of the coins, while the reverse bore the device of the subjugated or "allied" city, as in the case of the helmet of Temesa or the eagle of Hipponium, which possibly document the relationship between the hegemonic city and others that were subjects of it.

The Western Greeks: Coinage

Incused stater with barley-ear
from Metaponto
silver
ca. 530-510 B.C.
Naples
Museo Archeologico Nazionale

Incused stater with Apollo
male figure and stag
from Caulonia
silver
ca. 530-510 B.C.
Naples
Museo Archeologico Nazionale

Incused stater with naked
standing Poseidon and trident
silver
ca. 530-510 B.C.
Naples
Museo Archeologico Nazionale

Chronologically, incuse coinage is divided into three separate periods characterized by large, medium and thin coin-blanks. The first phase, the large coin-blank, came to an end in approximately 510 B.C. with the destruction of Sybaris. This was followed by the medium coin-blank phase which lasted in Caulonia, Croton, and Metapontum until approximately 480/470 B.C., and finally the thinner coin-blank phase, which for some mints, like those of Metapontum and Croton, lasted until approximately 440 B.C.

Among the two-sided coins attributed to the Magna Graecia area (though Sardinia and the Illyrian region have also been suggested as alternatives), worth noting are those of the Serdaioi tribes that date back to around 480 B.C. and can be associated with a fragment of an inscription from Olympia which mentions this population in connection with Sybaris, possibly even before the ruinous siege of 510 B.C. Of the cities of Magna Graecia a special place is reserved for Elea (Hyele) and Cumae (Kyme). The former, a Phocaean colony and seat of the famous philosophical school of the Eleatics, did not follow the reverse incuse technique, but instead was inspired by the typology of the mother-country with a lion devouring its prey and a square incuse on the reverse. These coins found their way West, merging with those of Massalia, which had an identical typological and composition. The latter, a colony set up by Chalcis and Eretria, minted coins of various weight while the reverse remained essentially the same with the constant presence of a mussel, a symbol of the sea-faring vocation of the Greek colonists.

In the fifth and fourth centuries B.C. two-sided coins of Magna Graecia were more variegated and composite, with staters and sometimes double staters (Thurii and Metapontum) that portrayed the typology of the issuing *polis*, with references on the reverse to Zeus Olympius and sometimes to a local deity. Although fractional denominations became more popular with the passing of time, the silver stater and didrachm emerge as the most widely circulated and readily hoarded small denominations, which is evidence of the growing importance of the liberating function of coins, especially in centers like those in Magna Graecia which were by then open to traffic and trade with the entire Mediterranean. Among the various cities, Heraclea issued a series of *dioboloi* with Heracles strangling the Nemean lion; these were widely circulated and adopted by other mints in the area, possibly in connection with the Italiot League, in at least two gold issues that confirm, after the experience of Philip II of Macedon, how gold coins, based on the Attic standard, spread throughout the Greek world, including the western regions. This was followed by Croton's subcolony Terina, with the eponymous nymph on the obverse and a seated Nike on the reverse, attributable to an Attic sculptor whose style has close affinities with the author of the reliefs in the Nike temple in the Athenian Acropolis. The Neapolis and the other Campanian mints produced staters depicting Nike crowning a half man half bull figure; these were in circulation throughout the whole of Magna Graecia. Locri Epizephyrii, which was one of the few mints in the Greek world to initially reject minted coinage. This choice, which Locri shared with Sparta, was possibly made in accordance with the rigid clauses of Zaleucus' legislative code, although the city permitted the circulation of "foreign" coinage in its territory since it did not introduce its own coins until the earlier fourth century, after which they circulated in its colonies Medma and Hipponium. Among other mints, those of Metapontum, Croton, Paestum, and above all Tarentum continued with substantial issues of silver coins until the advent of Romanization. Characteristic of the Tarentine issues was the "horsemen" series of legends, bearing the badges or devices of monetary magistrates and ephors or *strategoi*; such details make these coins objects of undoubted historical value and also attest to donations to a sanctuary; in some cases they show evidence of interference, such as markings scored into one of the faces. Apart from a few exceptions, gold coins were very rare, unlike the later bronze coins which were destined in the Hellenistic era to become the standard currency of the western *polis*. The coins issued by Rhegium have a special significance since the city had close links with events taking place in other cities on the Strait of Messina, especially during the tyranny of Anaxilas (494–476 B.C.), with an issue of coins bearing the image of a calf (*vitello*) on one side, symbolizing Italy (then known as Vitelia or Vitalia meaning the "land of calves"); the reverse bore a Samian lion. Subsequently, the coinage evolved along the lines of what was being produced in the other mints in the area, until Roman influence became predominant.

The evolution of the western Greeks in the fourth and third centuries was strongly influenced by their interactions with the indigenous populations. In the areas now known as Campania, Apulia, Lucania, and Calabria much of the coinage issued was inspired by Greek models. These include those of the Brettii in silver and bronze; of Ceglie and Suessa in Campania; of Arpi in Apulia, whose didrachmas bore the name of Dasios, a local chief; and those of Canusium bearing a face that was

The Western Greeks: Coinage

Didrachma from Cumae
obverse: head of a woman
reverse: shell on a barley grain
silver
ca. 420-380 B.C.
Naples, Museo
Archeologico Nazionale

Didrachma from Velia
obverse: head of Athena
reverse: flying Nike
and lion walking to the left
silver
4th-3rd cent. B.C.
Naples, Museo
Archeologico Nazionale

Third of a stater from Metaponto
obverse: helmeted head
of the hero Leucippus
reverse: two barley-ears
with at the center οι
gold
post 350 B.C.
Syracuse, Soprintendenza
per i Beni Culturali e Ambientali
Gabinetto di Numismatica

Didrachma from Neapolis
obverse: head of a woman
reverse: half man-half bull figure
silver
ca. 450-430 B.C.
Naples
Museo Archeologico Nazionale

Stater from Tarentum
obverse: horseman
reverse: Taras on a dolphin
silver
ca. 334-330 B.C.
Naples
Museo Archeologico Nazionale

Stater from Tarentum
obverse: winged head of Hera
reverse: horseman
gold
340-334 B.C.
Taranto, Museo Nazionale

probably that of Diomedes. While the language, typology, and style of these coins were reminiscent of Greek examples, their design was sometimes affected by the local cultural substratum and the types included indigenous names and divinities.

As far as Sicilian coinage is concerned, we will follow the tripartition proposed by Publius Statius. In the first area, Naxos, there circulated a Chalcidian drachma bearing an image of Dionysus and a bunch of grapes, and others with an inebriated satyr; Zancle and Himera issued a type bearing a cockerel – a bird sacred to Asclepius – and on the reverse a hen and sundry designs. The second area was dominated by a set of didrachmas: in southwest Sicily and Acragas (eagle and crab), Selinus (*selinon* or wild celery), Camarina (helmet and greaves), and Gela (horsemen and a *protoma* of an anthropomorphic bull); these last two mints used a typology that included warlike elements which possibly referred either to the mercenaries who were paid with these coins or to the land owners (*gamoroi*) who were the holders of power. The tetradrachma was currency in the third area, the eastern part of the island, comprising mints such as Syracuse, Leontini, and Aetna/Catana which either produced coins of identical type to those of the island's capital Syracuse, or used the latter's coinage directly.

The Syracusan mint was one of the oldest and most productive in all of the western Greek territories. It began its production with a series of types designed with horses, wheels, and the nymph Arethusa, who was particularly venerated on Ortygia owing to its freshwater spring enclosed within the island's fort. The introduction of the decadrachma, a splendid silver coin with the image of the nymph Arethusa surrounded by four dolphins on the obverse and a *quadriga* crowned by a winged Nike on the reverse, was a key moment in the evolution of both Syracusan and Sicilian coinage. According to traditional theory, the coin took its name of *demareteion* from Demarete, wife of the tyrant Gelon, and it dates back to 480 B.C. However for some years now, after the date of the Athens decadrachma was readjusted to 468 B.C. following the discovery of a hoards in Turkey, the dating of the two decadrachmas has been revised and the Syracusan one is now thought to belong to approximately 460 B.C., as suggested by Kraay in 1969. Naturally once this new dating was accepted it influenced the chronological ordering of parallel monetary series and of other issues in that period, while remaining a reference point in the reconstruction of the different phases of minting in the western Greek territories. Another fundamental stage in the evolution of Syracusan minting was the period under the tyrant Dionysius I (430-367 B.C.), when a considerable number of decadrachmas were produced by some of the most prestigious engravers who had the privilege of "signing" coins. These "signatures," always in minute but nonetheless often legible characters, can be seen on the scroll held by the winged Victory, on the hair of the nymph Arethusa, or in the neck or other parts of the body. Such types are universally recognized masterpieces of art and are among the most beautiful coins produced by the western Greeks. The monetary evidence bears witness to the artistic genius of numerous engravers, such as Evenetus, Euclid, Eumenes, Frigillus, and Cimon, who were mainly active in Syracuse, as well as Aristoxenus and Doxenus who, along with other engravers whose names are only known by the first two or three letters, were active in Magna Graecia.

Dionysius I was also notable for his monetary reforms and for the introduction of a bronze drachma (with the head of Athena on the obverse and two dolphins and a starfish on the reverse), with a fiduciary value based on Plato's *Letter VII*. These coins signaled another step in the evolution of the concept of coinage by creating "fiduciary" money which, despite experiencing various vicissitudes, has lasted right up until modern times. At the same time, there was a period of Syracusan expansion in the eastern Adriatic with the founding of colonies at Pharos and Issus at the beginning of the fourth

The Western Greeks: Coinage

Tetradrachma from Agrigento
obverse: standing eagle
reverse: crab
silver
550-450 B.C.
Syracuse, Soprintendenza
per i Beni Culturali e Ambientali
Gabinetto di Numismatica

Silver drachma
from the Himera mint
obverse: cock
reverse: square incuse
silver
ante 482 B.C.
Syracuse, Soprintendenza
per i Beni Culturali e
Ambientali, Gabinetto di Numismatica

Tetradrachma from Leontinoi
with auriga
obverse: crowned by Nike
reverse: head of Apollo
and lion at the bottom
silver
ca. 480-470 B.C.
Naples
Museo Archeologico Nazionale

The Western Greeks: Coinage

Tetradrachma from Camarina
obverse: Athena crowned by a Nike
driving a quadriga
and two amphorae at the bottom
reverse: head of Heracles
silver
415-405 B.C.
Syracuse, Soprintendenza
per i Beni Culturali e Ambientali
Gabinetto di Numismatica

Auriol type obol
obverse: head of divinity
reverse: square incuse
silver
520-460 B.C.
London, British Museum
Department of Coins and Medals

Heavy drachma from Massalia
obverse: head of Artemis
reverse: walking lion
silver
370-360 B.C.
London, British Museum
Department of Coins and Medals

Light drachma from Massalia
obverse: head of Artemis
with arc and quiver
reverse: walking lion
silver
210-50 B.C.
London, British Museum
Department of Coins and Medals

Tetradrachma from Cyrene
obverse: plant of Silphium perfoliatum
reverse: head of Zeus Ammon
silver
ca. 430-390 B.C.
London, British Museum
Department of Coins and Medals

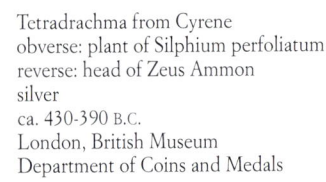

Tetrobol from Cyrene
obverse: young horseman
reverse: plant of Silphium perfoliatum
gold
308-277 B.C.
London, British Museum
Department of Coins and Medals

century B.C. The former minted silver and bronze coins based on Syracusan models, while the latter, after an initial phase of minting coins based on the Syracusan coinage of the Dionysian age, only issued bronze coins. In front of these colonies on the Italian coast there was the Ancona mint, which from the beginning of the third century B.C. issued bronze coinage with the characteristic *ankon*.

In the extreme west the Phocaean Greeks penetrated as far as Massalia (Marseilles), firstly with *auriol* coins, then with the heavy drachma of the first half of the fourth century B.C., then the light drachma, and finally the very common *obolos*. Massaliot coins were in use from Provence to Catalonia and as far as Liguria, and they were later used as the prototypes which inspired the proto-historic population of northern Italy when they began using their own coins between the third and first centuries B.C., thus contributing to a late Grecism in the West.

Finally, to complete the picture of Greek expansion in the West, we must not forget the Mediterranean shores of North Africa, where the main focus of circulation was Cyrenaica. Here the first issues from Cyrene initially involved stamping a new type on Athenian coins, using the same weight standard, confirming the close links between the two *poleis*. The first phase consisted of square incuse coins that subsequently evolved into coins which on one side depicted a Zeus Ammon and on the other a silphium, an extinct medicinal plant that was widely used in the ancient world and whose production contributed to the fortune of Cyrene. Completing this prolific coin production, in the third century B.C. valuable gold coins were issued in connection with those of the Ptolemies of Egypt.

To conclude, the history of Greek coinage and, in particular, western Greek coinage, was a fragmentary rather than a unitary history that reflects the complexity of Greek society and the different colonial components. It furthermore reflects the type of relations the Greeks had with the non-Greek population with which they came into contact. It is therefore necessary to recognize and analyze the different components of the coinage of the western Greeks, from the religious factors (traditional and local cults), to the economic factors (monetary areas, weight systems, and circulation). To these we must also add the different social realities (mixed marriages, and indigenous integration), and political factors (constitutional changes, foreign invasions, and the dissemination of various types of ideologies). All of these elements must be considered, mint by mint, monetary area by monetary area, in order to better understand the innovative significance that the introduction and spread of coinage had on the evolution of the societies that experienced this phenomenon in antiquity.

Bibliography
As to the problem connected to the birth of coinage see: N. PARISE, 1992.
On Greek coinage in Archaic and Classical times, as well as on its main issues see: C. KRAAY, 1969; M. THOMPSON, O. MORKHOLM, C.M. KRAAY, 1973; C. KRAAY, 1976.
On incused coins of Magna Graecia see: G. GORINI, 1975; N. PARISE, in *Storia della Calabria...*, 1987, pp. 307-321.
On Magna Graecia's coinage in general see: A. STAZIO, in *Megale Hellas*, 1983, pp. 105-169; *La monetazione...*, 20-24 aprile 1980, 1986.
On coinage in Sicily see: A. STAZIO, in *Sikanie*, 1985, pp. 79-122; S. GARRAFFO, in *Sikanie*, 1985, pp. 261-276; C. ARNOLD-BIUCCHI, 1990; M. CACCAMO CALTABIANO, 1993.
On Marseilles see: C. BRENOT, in *De Phocée à Massalia*, 1981, pp. 17-54.

City and Countryside

Emanuele Greco

As has been evident now for some time, whoever wishes to study the urban entity in all its complexity must stand back and obtain an overall view of the articulation of urban spaces (within the walls or, when this is lacking, within the corona of necropolises), together with the organization of the surrounding territory.

This is particularly applicable in the case of the Greek colonies, which were created in answer to the dearth of farmland and hence the need for indispensable crop cultivation for the survival of the ever more numerous communities hemmed into their restrictive places of origin. In the final analysis, however, it applies to Greek towns and cities in general, from the earliest phases of development to the Late Geometric period and through the Classical period.

In this perspective, the colonial installations in Magna Graecia and Sicily have offered major insights in the study of the Greek *chora* (territory), especially since the first breakthrough studies made after World War II, accompanied by "pioneering" research efforts in this field. It should be noted that while the study of the western colonial world gave a major impetus to the definition of the more macroscopic aspects of territorial organization around Greek townships, the innumerable surveys being carried out today on the agrarian landscapes of continental Greece, the islands, and Asia Minor, while they undoubtedly secure much new information, they systematically ignore the results of research carried out in the West. As a result, many problems that were encountered as long as forty years ago in Magna Graecia and Sicily are posited as if they were utterly new.

The delay, therefore, with which scholars have begun to occupy themselves with questions of agrarian culture is quite surprising. And yet, in the past the major focuses of study were the sanctuaries and acropolises – certainly richer in their yield of objects of superb artistic value or craftsmanship (and tend to shower more fame on their finder than on the anonymous artisan who crafted them); but this line of action is in keeping with the cultural demands of each society, as it looks back upon past glories.

Today the outlook has broadened considerably, now that the majority of scholars agree on the need for a historical view that embraces antiquity in its entirety, with less concern for what is beautiful or otherwise; in this respect, such objects as mills for extracting olive oil or granary millstones can hardly be termed "artistic," whereas their historical value is beyond question.

One of the first aspects of the problem concerns the distribution of indigenous dwelling units at the time of the arrival of the Greek colonists.

Elsewhere in this volume the reader will find a more detailed essay on this specific topic: here we are more concerned that the Greek standards of territorial organization imported by the first colonists had an imperative basis, namely, that the foundation of a *polis* presupposed the acquisition of a piece of land of an established size that would insure the survival of the population – and in this sense presupposing also the complete sovereignty of the new political entity, with the elimination of any special rights of those who previously occupied the site. This elimination is not equivalent to physical suppression. There are many documented cases in which the local populations survived in occupied Greek territories (perhaps serving their new lords?), and even, one supposes, cases of integration in the colony.

As a first stage of study, it is crucial to take account of how the colony's population is arranged. Tarentum (Greek Taras) offers an excellent though quite unique example of distribution. Since the end of the last century, much intense excavation work has been carried out in the modern city, yielding large quantities of archaeological material, particularly in the bountiful necropolises.

The layout of Tarentum's cemeteries reveal a sudden enlargement of the city toward the east in the middle period of the fifth century B.C. Compared against changes in the population of the neighboring countryside, the mechanisms of the phenomenon become clearer: the growth of the city corresponds to a substantial drop in the agrarian population. By studying the fossils from excavation (usually in the necropolises) we can tentatively reconstruct the situation that preceded the phase of urban expansion.

From the first days of the colony's foundation at the end of the eighth century B.C. (a chronology that is endorsed by literary tradition and material evidence), certain groups of inhabitants farmed large tracts of land lying west and east of the principal nucleus, which was much smaller than in the later Classical period. The Archaic town in fact nestled on the tip of the promontory (where the "old city" currently stands) and stretched eastward, inland along the promon-

City and Countryside

Map of Tarentum and its territory
1) Masseria Follerato
2) Masseria Minerva
3) Masseria Torrata
4) Mottola
5) Ponte di Lemme
6) Bellavista
7) Leucaspide
8) Gravinola
9) Statte
10) Accetta grande
11) Accetta piccola
12) Amastuola
13) Crispiano
14) Punta del Tonno
15) Salina piccola
16) Salina grande
17) Romanelli
18) Cimino
19) Casino Galeone
20) Casino Fiore
21) Masseria la Cattiva
22) Calabrese
23) Capo San Vito
24) Lama
25) Amendulo
26) Leporano
27) Saturo
28) P. Baracca
29) Pulsano
30) Lizzano
31) Monacizzo
32) Torricella
33) Masseria Agliano
34) Faggiano
35) Roccaforzata
36) Masseria Minerva
37) San Marzano di San Giuseppe
38) Masseria Niviera
39) Misicuro
40) Masseria Vicentino (on the edge of the *chora* of Tarentum)
41) Monteiasi
42) Montemesola
43) Monte Salete
44) Masseria Mutata
45) Francavilla Fontana
46) Ceglie Messapico

♦ Sanctuaries
7th-6th cent. B.C.

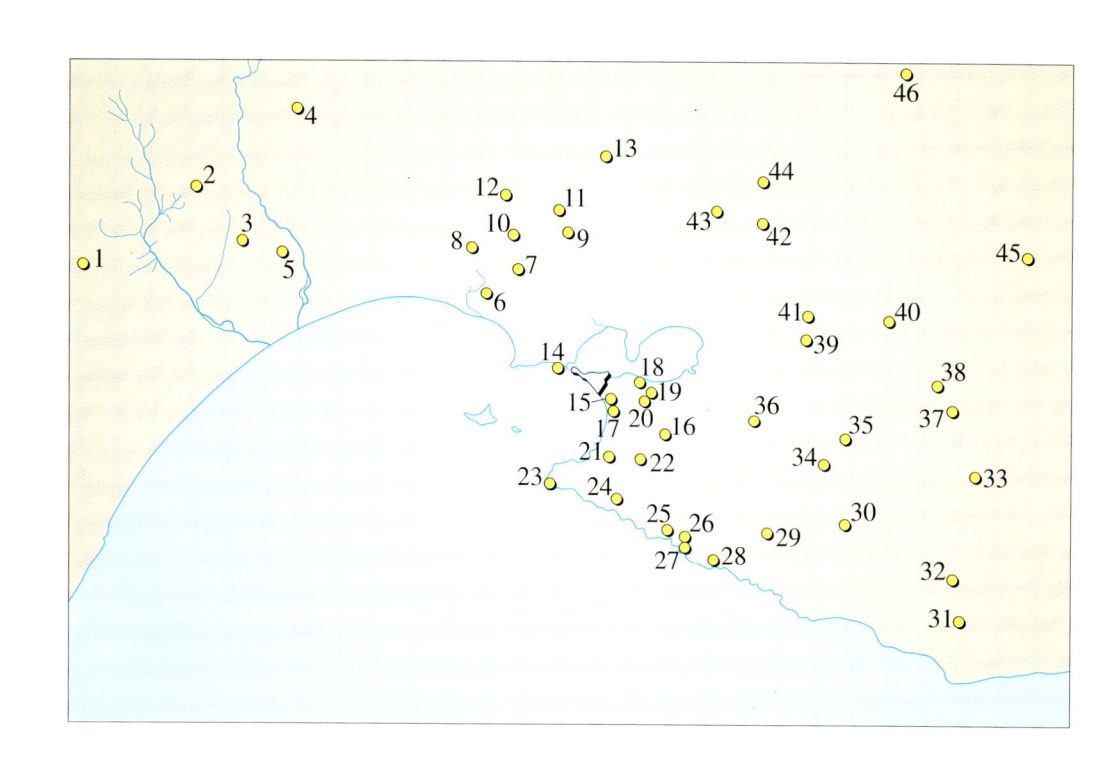

tory. An undetermined quota of the population lived in scattered hamlets in the surrounding countryside.
What at first seemed fairly clear from studies of the distribution and chronology of the burial grounds (from the seventh to the end of the sixth century B.C.) has now been resoundingly confirmed by the discovery of one of those hamlets, in the Amastuola quarter, near Crispiano, north-northwest of the city, where excavations directed by the local Soprintendenza have brought to light the first traces of the Archaic-period dwelling units, relative to the hamlet of the seventh-sixth century B.C.
The full data have yet to be published before it will be possible to know firsthand the features of the context of this remarkable discovery, which will undoubtedly throw light on how Greek farming villages worked in the Archaic period. Like the other sites already investigated at tomb level, Amastuola was also abandoned over the seventh to the sixth century B.C.
These findings contribute to some degree to understanding the layout of Tarentum, which became a major seaport, complete with an *agora* and sanctuaries; while the surrounding territories were dotted with full-fledged villages (and not just isolated clusters of farmsteads), through to the so-called crisis period of the fifth century B.C., when the exodus from the countryside to the town caused the latter's layout to be completely reworked.
Another quite distinct case from the others, thanks also to recent studies, is the town of Sybaris, where one can observe a phenomenon with implications which are quite startling on several accounts, namely the survival of the indigenous peoples – as can be noted from certain cultural and organizational characteristics of the village-type communities that lived in the orbit of the growing Achaean colony.
Two groups of observatories can be identified to date: on the one hand are the remains (in some cases clues only, as no proper excavation work is yet done; in others, as in the case of Francavilla Marittima, more articulate evidence has turned up, thanks to systematic excavations carried out under P. Zancani Montuoro) of sanctuaries or areas of worship that afford concrete evidence of the way in which the colonists gradually allocated the territory around them; on the other hand, evidence of indigenous survival has turned up in more recent digs at both Francavilla and Amendolara, along the northern fringe of the Sybaritic enclave.
But let us proceed in order. Before the migrant colonists put in anchor here, the hill known as Timpone della Motta (Francavilla Marittima) was occupied by a large village populated by locals, and included a necropolis of its own. The site is renowned for its abundant yield of metal grave goods, particularly specimens in bronze.

The Greek settlers took over the crown of the hill, where they established a sanctuary dedicated to Athena (as testified by the inscription by the Olympian artist Cleombrotos), a monument of which substantial remains have survived, together with a good quantity of votives delineating the history of the city of Sybaris, from its foundation at the end of the eighth century B.C., to its destruction in 510 B.C. — a history that spanned a good 210 years, according to tradition.

The process by which the indigenous tribes were overruled is eloquently epitomized by the replacement of their village with the religious enclave of the newcomers. The dwellings that have been brought to light on the hill slopes suggest a Greek plan, though it is as yet unclear whether these are villages or scattered farmsteads (rather less like in Archaic times); the coeval tombs (seventh–sixth century B.C.) bear witness to the continuation of some indigenous funeral practices.

Seen alongside the yields from the excavations at Amendolara (where, at the start of the sixth century B.C. the village relative to these indigenous burials, the land was redeveloped with a Greek-style layout of parallel streets), we can infer that the territorial patterns used in Sybaris (together with the traditional accounts of the city's size, the ease with which the council accorded citizenship, the abundance of land to be shared out, and the sizable population at the time of the city's destruction) were fairly unusual: alongside the observance of sovereignty over the city's lands, the Sybarites seemed nonetheless to have encouraged the local population to maintain their villages.

Tarentum, view of the peninsula
area of the first settlement
bottom left
site of the temple

Bronze statuette of a woman
found in the Sanctuary
of Athena on the uplands
of Motta di Francavilla Marittima
575-550 B.C.
Sibari, Museo Nazionale
Archeologico della Sibaritide
Cat. 46/II

These, one may assume, were politically under the control of the Greek city, despite enjoying a certain degree of formal autonomy.

Notwithstanding the specifics of the case, the case of Sybaris introduces one of the macroscopic issues regarding territorial patterns of use in the Greek colonies: the so-called Achaean model, which takes the name of the parent region, Achaea, in the north of the Peloponnese, the homeland of the founders of Sybaris, Croton, and Metapontum, to which we should add Paestum (Greek Poseidonia), a sibling colony of Sybaris.

In brief, one might define the characteristic features of this city's development over time, without omitting to observe that the common feature linking them (at least initially) lies in the similar social structure of the colonial contingent, without there being any necessary bond between ethnic origins and social organization.

In the first place, there is evidence that in at least three cases concomitant with the city's foundation, the Achaean colony founded the extramural sanctuary of Hera, the patron deity, lady of Argos, closely tied to the land and the processes of nature and of humankind. She is the mother goddess, armed protectress of order amid the *polis* and its surrounding farmlands.

Irrespective of the question of their origins, the Hera sanctuaries at Croton (Capo Colonna-Lacinio), Metapontum (on the Bradano River, home of the "Tavole Palatine" temple), Paestum (on the bank of the Sele River, two miles east of the estuary) were founded together with the city itself, as if to affirm that the establishment of a new community is unthinkable without also defining the territory over which it commands, and without putting it immediately under the aegis of the Achaeans' supreme tutelary deity.

The map shows, moreover, that the colonists tended to locate the Hera sanctuaries on the outskirts of their territory, as if to display to those arriving from without that the act of occupying, possessing, and exploiting such lands was sanctioned by the gods.

There is less certainty, however, as regards the use of the farmlands in the period between the city's foundation through the end of the fifth century B.C.

The issue that comes to the fore at this point – an issue of considerable importance – concerns the Greek "lifestyle" both at home and in their colonies. Briefly, in numerous instances, literary tradition denotes that the Greek city consisted of a community of villages, a supposition frequently endorsed by modern scholarship.

At this point it is essential to make an important distinction in terminology. The term "city" is taken to mean the community of citizens occupying a physical space (living nuclei plus surrounding unbuilt land) in ways that differ highly from one geographical area to another. This is the reason why when we say city we refer to the political community as a whole, without immediately connoting the physical implications of the term.

During the Archaic period, the typical city of continental Greece was essentially a political center (acropolis, sanctuary of the patron deity, *agora*, crafts workshops, and so forth), constituting the hub of a territorial system prevalently characterized by a network of villages (*kata komas*).

This prevalence does not, of course, rule out the existence of alternative forms of dwelling fabric, such as the single-family farm, though it seems certain that the size of this type of accommodation remained contained until later in the Classical period (and particularly before the Late Classical and Hellenistic periods).

What is most striking is the macroscopic difference between the organization of the *chora* (territory) in the homeland and that of the colonies; through our observations of the Achaean urban territories, which have been studied more closely than others (particularly at Metapontum, with the remnants of the ancient farm divisions revealed through aerial surveys), the dominant trend throughout the Archaic period was the concentration of most of the population in the built-up area, which in the space of a mere two generations rapidly became a sizable urban conglomeration.

The Greek *chora* was punctuated by large places of worship, together with small shrines or *sacella* (dedicated to Hera or Demeter, the "ladies" of the earth); these were probably located at the junctions of the roads that crisscrossed the farmland. Research is still in its infancy as regards these phenomena, and any deeper analysis is as yet impossible.

However, it is evident that the population in the colonies consisted of a kind of farmer-citizen who commuted to his urban home after the day's work in the fields. Here, despite the exis-

Map of Sibari and its territory

● settlements of the whole 7th cent.
○ settlements of the second half of the 8th cent.
◆ Greek imports of before 720
◇ settlements between 8th and 7th cent.
★ settlements of 7th cent.

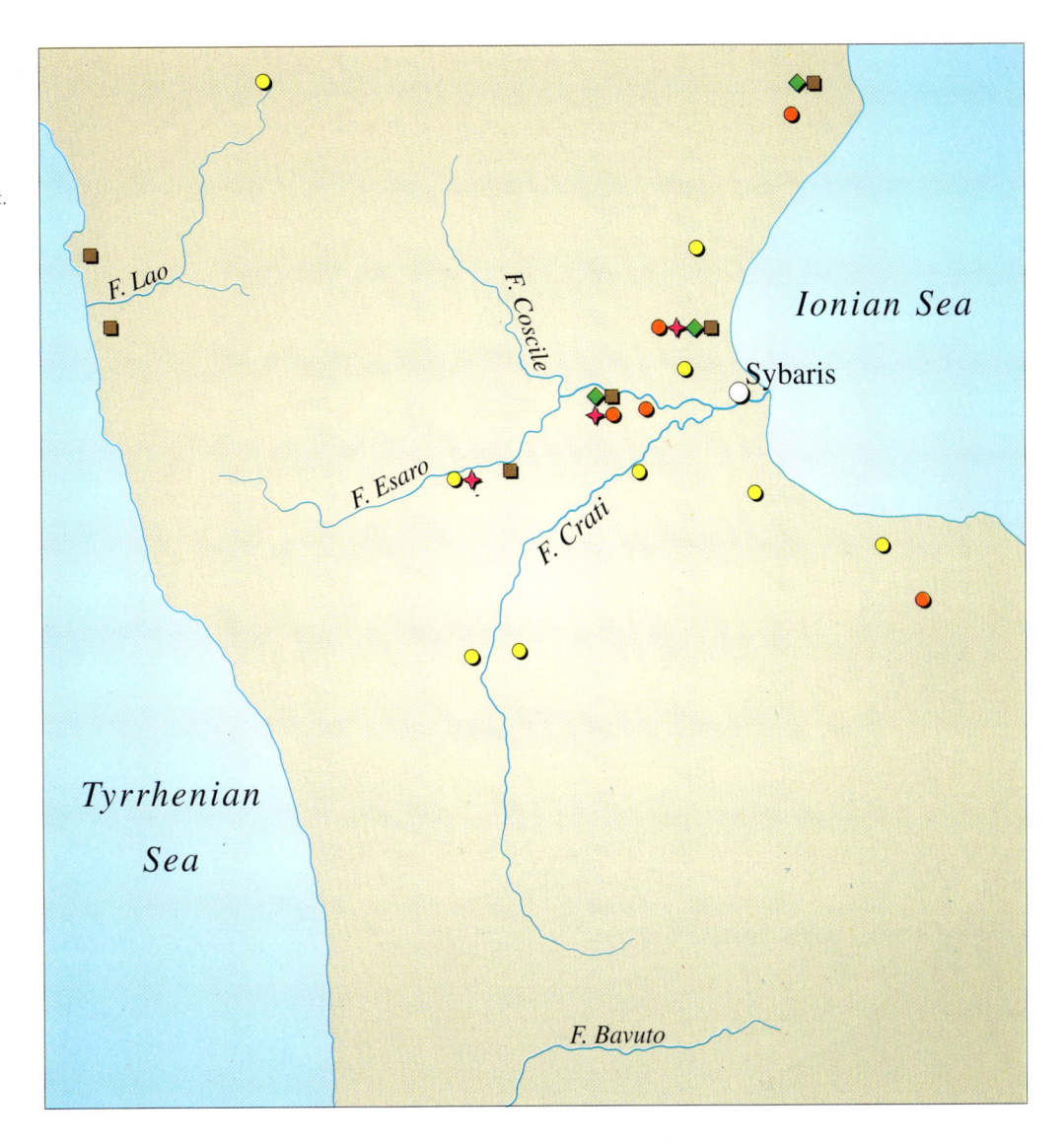

tence in certain cases of small installations, probably for storing farm equipment or huts for servant workers, the lack of true residential fabric testifies to the presence of cereal farming (which imposes limited seasonal rhythms as regards residence on the farmlands); at any event, it confirms that the population resided in the town, at least in the cases where the urban fabric was reasonably close at hand.

One of the most remarkable cases in this respect is the colonial city of Locri. The written sources have enabled the identification of the city's markedly conservative makeup, a society based on a rigid territorial oligarchy.

The Locrians entrusted the gods to define the arrangement of the land (which was [formerly] achieved with the "sacred enclave" of the temple structures, sacred areas, and *sacella*, along a route that was later marked approximately by the defensive walls); but besides certain remnants of indigenous nuclei dating from the first years of the new colony – correctly interpreted as a "reservoir" of manual labor – there are no signs whatever of farms or villages in the *chora*; the limited ownership of this land, in fact, triggered internal imbalances that were righted by the foundation of further colonial stations on the Tyrrhenian coast (Medma, Hipponium, and undoubtedly also Metaurus).

In the case of two other colonies, Siris and Cumae, data so far gathered afford a completely different situation.

Siris, founded in the first half of the seventh century B.C., was short-lived as an independent *polis*; it is very likely that before it was actually founded by inhabitants of Colophon who fled

View of Capo Colonna
site of the Temple of Hera

the dominion of the Lydian usurper Gyges, it was frequented by Greek traders from Asia Minor who were already on friendly terms with the indigenous populations; the permanence of the settlement fabric is superbly testified by the structures at Incoronata near modern Metaponto and Santa Maria d'Anglona; these are datable to the transition from late eighth to early seventh century B.C.

Clues of the introduction of a new form of territorial structure – albeit negative as the *argumentum ex absentia* – can be noted only from the last quarter of the seventh century B.C., when all trace of the indigenous villages seems to disappear.

We have no idea, however, how the colonists actually organized themselves in this sense, whether they proceeded with a straightforward exploitation of the land or a continuation of the site's original role as an *emporion*, by concentrating both residential fabric and economic activity on the coast itself. At any event, the untimely destruction of Siris (shortly before 580 B.C.) at the hands of the Achaean alliance of Metapontum, Croton, and Sybaris prevented the city from developing and assuming a more readily definable physiognomy; the administration of the territories seems to have been taken over by Sybaris at this point, though this is indicated exclusively by the coinage.

Cumae poses a quite different case: the earliest Greek colony in the western world, also offers the most complex and problematic case of colonial organization yet encountered. As is well-documented, the Eretrians and Chalcidians founded Pithekoussai (Ischia) midway through the eighth century B.C. Not less than a quarter-century later the natives of Chalcis and Kyme in Mainland Greece founded a new colony, Cumae, on the mainland opposite the island of Ischia. This new town did not involve a transfer of the same people, as many scholars have implied (basing their opinion on Livy, VIII. 22. 5, who makes the improbable claim that the foundation process took place in "two stages").

Current archaeological research in Pithekoussai (brilliantly illustrated recently by G. Buchner and David Ridgway, together with a host of very recent finds) shed light on the very early Greek colony, whose (apparent) "anomaly" lies in its sheer antiquity.

Undoubtedly, our knowledge of Cumae is still very scant indeed, but the pre-Hellenic necropolises and the sparse data from the archaeological digs at the acropolis confirm that Cumae was in fact founded after Pithekoussai.

What we know about the latter seems to suggest that in the course of the seventh century B.C. the island colony was gradually "absorbed," as it were, by its mainland counterpart: at the peak of the Archaic period, Pithekoussai became effectively part of Cumae's *chora*. It therefore never minted its own coinage (coin production only began in the late sixth century B.C.), nor are there any literary references to acts of foundation nor names of *oikistai* (founders).

The plain of Metaponto

Cumae's "aggressive" political outlook meant that it not only took over rule of the island colony, but also (during the seventh and sixth centuries) a chain of *epineia* or way stations at Pozzuoli (before the colonists of Samos founded Dicaearchia in 531 B.C.), Misenum, Parthenope (later renamed Palaepolis, after the foundation of Neapolis). The dense network of settlements stretching from Cumae to the central part of the Bay of Naples guaranteed the colony full political control over the coastline and rule over the seaways plied by merchant traffic through the Tyrrhenian. This lasted until the direct clash with the Etruscans, especially the second battle of Cumae (474 B.C.) after which crisis set in: Ischia fell – first to the Syracusans, and then shortly after to the recently founded Neapolis, the rising power of the bay.

The years stretching from the mid-fifth to the mid-fourth century B.C. have been notoriously attributed as a chapter of dire crisis. Actually, it was a period of intense metamorphosis for Archaic Greek society – and even more so for the indigenous populations of Campania, Iapygia, and Lucania. Archaeological evidence for this particular phase of history is almost completely lacking, and hence we are without any direct clues as to changes in modes of territorial organization.

This silence is spectacularly broken by a subsequent explosion in the mid-fourth century B.C. – lasting through the advent of Romanization – of a phenomenon that one can now consider typical of the entire Mediterranean basin: the land surrounding the *poleis* suddenly became

City and Countryside

The *chora* of Metapontum
detail of the ancient topography
(Carter 1990)

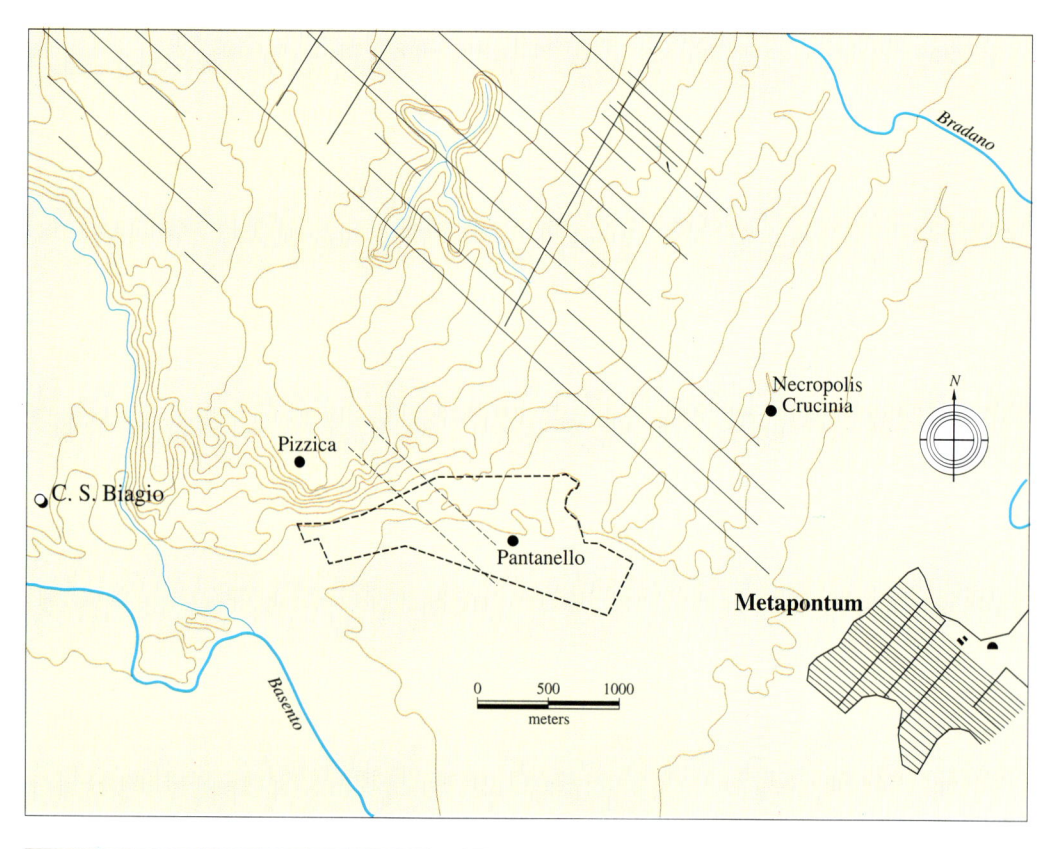

Paestum
distribution of the rural
settlements over the territory
in the 6th and 7th cents. B.C.
(Greco 1979)

Paestum
distribution of the rural
settlements over the territory
in the 4th cent. B.C.
(Greco 1979)

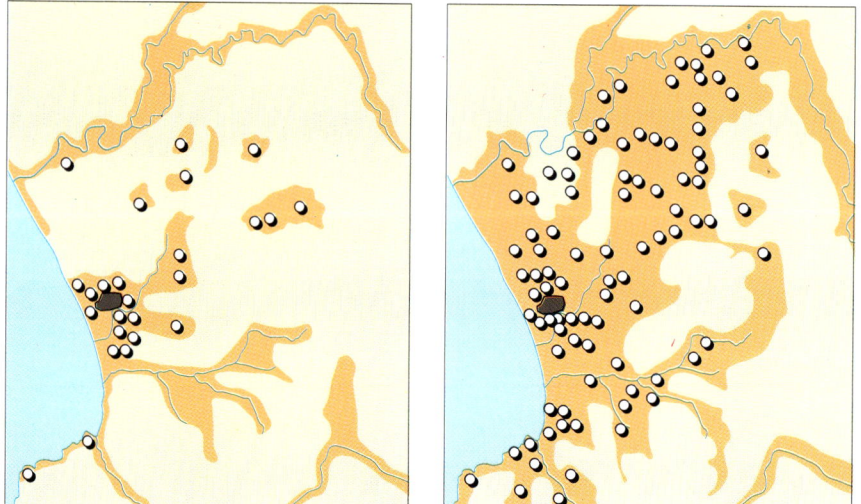

densely populated with farms. This applies equally to the river plains and the hillsides (olive groves, vineyards, fruit trees?).

Almost everywhere in Magna Graecia, now the dominant dwelling configuration was a single-family farm with its allocated lands. Further proof of the radical change in habitation patterns, the dead were now buried alongside the farmhouses (the practice of burying in the urban necropolis as well as at the farm is an essential indicator of the more even distribution of the population between city and countryside).

Evidence for the application of the agrarian village format can be found at Heraclea (Herakleia), and may be also inferred from the mention in the *Tabulae Heraclaensis* of two such villages (Pandosia and Cene), and not least from archaeological surveys of the surface strata.

In summary, the change in the fabric of the society itself (with new land allocations) was undoubtedly accompanied by substantial transformations of the crops and farming.

Those same *Tabulae*, datable to between the fourth and third centuries B.C., offer an outstanding testament and thereby allow us to conclude this brief overview of land use and territorial management in the Greek West: taking advantage of a moment of turmoil, certain private citizens took unauthorized possession of the sacred land inside the enclaves of Dionysus and Athena Polias. It seems that, at the time, protest was in vain. Later, however, the situation reversed, as the city imposed upon the lawbreakers to bend to the law. The land was measured out, divided into lots, and reassigned to tenant farmers.
No better guide than land-use to illustrate the conflicts, contradictions, shifting makeup of society, and economic perspectives of antiquity.

Bibliography
As to the Ionic area see the detailed collection of data in M. OSANNA, 1992, of invaluable importance are the works by E. LEPORE, in "Atti...", 1968, pp. 29-66 and by G. VALLET, ivi, pp. 67-142; E. LEPORE, in *Problèmes...*, 1973, pp. 15-47; D. MUSTI, in *Storia e civiltà dei Greci*, VI, 1979, pp. 523-568; E. GRECO, 1993², focuses this problem at pp. 311-319.
As to the situation in Sicily, beside Vallet's article mentioned above, see: A. DI VITA, in "Kokalos", II, 1956, pp. 177 ff.; IDEM, in "Kokalos", XXXIII, 1987, pp. 77 ff.; AA.VV., *La Sicilia antica* (edited by E. Gabba and G. Vallet); E. DE MIRO, in *Sikanie*, 1985, pp. 563 ff.
On Taranto see: E. GRECO, in "AION ArchStAn", III (1981), pp. 139 ff.; the recent findings at Amas-

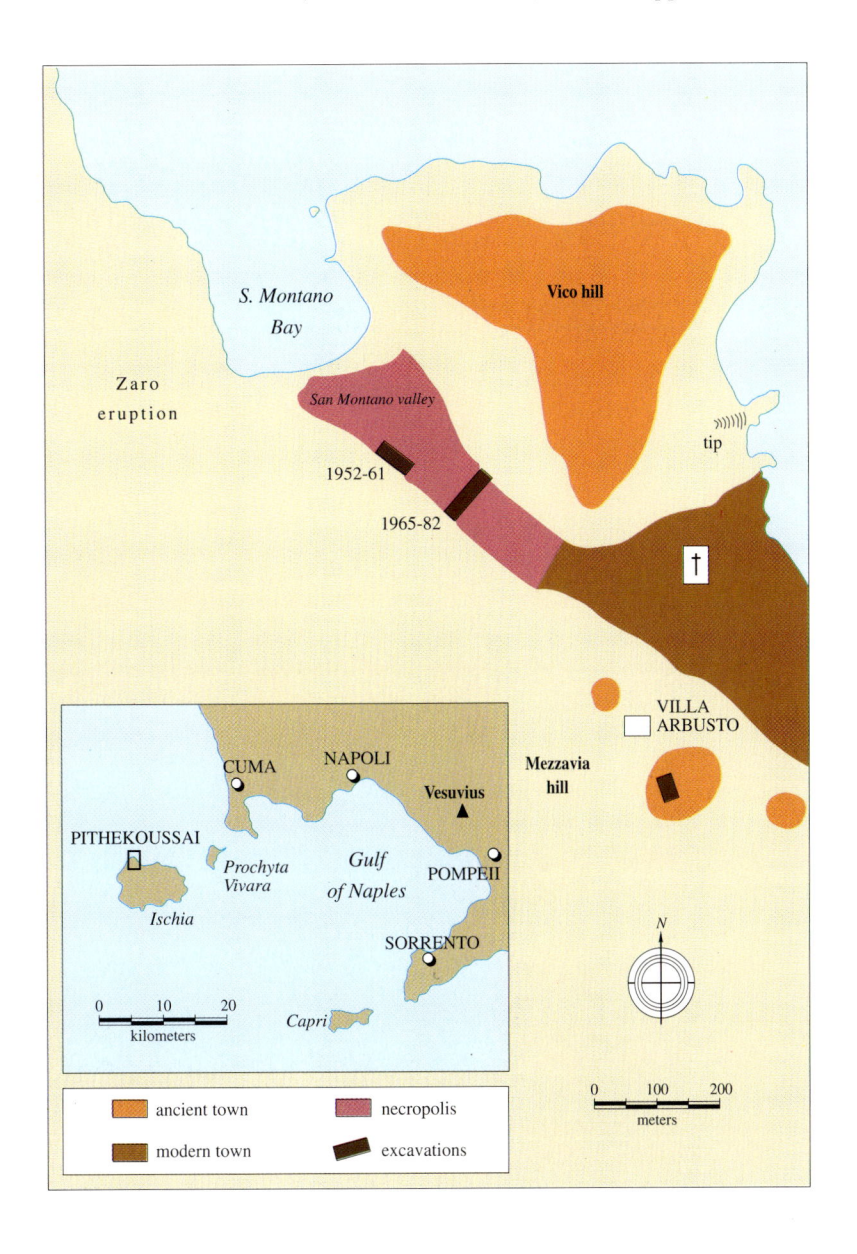

Map of the archaeological sites of Ischia and the Gulf of Naples (Ridgway)

tuola (Crispiano) are to be credited to G. Maruggi (Soprintendenza Archeologica della Puglia) who communicated about them at a seminary on *L'edilizia domestica in Magna Grecia* organized by the Università di Lecce in June 1992 (1996).
On Sibari see E. GRECO, in "Atti..." 1992, 1994, pp. 459-485.
On extramural sanctuaries see: G. PUGLIESE CARRATELLI, in *Magna Grecia*, III, 1989, pp. 149-158; E. GRECO, in *Magna Grecia*, IV, 1990, pp. 159 ff.
On Himera: D. ASHERI, in "Rivista di Filol. e istr. class." 1973, 4, pp. 457 ff.; *Himera III*, 1988.
On Gela a recent general work is that by G. FIORENTINI, 1985.
On Siris and Metapontum see *Siritide e Metapontino...*, 1991 (1996); on the Metapontian *chora* see D. ADAMESTEANU-C. VATIN, in "CRAI" 1976, pp. 110 ff.; J.C. CARTER, 1990.
On Euboean colonization on the Gulf of Naples see the monumental work about the excavations at Ischia in G. BUCHNER-D.RIDGWAY, 1993.
On Heraclea's Greek tablets: F. COARELLI, in *Siritide e Metapontino...*, 1991 (1996).

Dieter Mertens
Emanuele Greco

Urban Planning in Magna Graecia

In its broadest sense the science of planning both the urban fabric and its outlying agricultural land (*chora*), urban planning is without doubt the most tangible outward manifestation of the specifics of the colonial condition. Planning is the expression of a programmed and systematic process of occupation of new territory, so organized that it can be later developed in an independent and continuous manner. The examples which prove this for the period of the foundation itself are few, most notably Megara and Syracuse in Sicily, where the characteristic regular pattern of distribution appears in geometrical groundplots within a pre-established area designated for future expansion. Yet the overall picture offered by the currently available data seems to confirm the general opinion that the process behind the formation of the colonial cities – in contrast to developments in Mainland Greece – complied with an explicit set of priorities, albeit allowing for the characteristics of each locality. It is equally clear, moreover, that the principal objective of the Greek emigrants was to found settlements which would depend economically the methodical exploitation of the ample farming areas along the coasts of southern Italy. Given the nature of their society, which contrasted with that of the native inhabitants of the land, this was the only basis upon which the Greeks could guarantee development, prosperity, and longevity.

The first stage of settlements: Pithekoussai–Cumae, Incoronata–Metapontum

While the coastal lands (and to some extent deeper inland tracts of southern Italy) had been known to navigators in the Mycenaean era, after the so-called Dark Age the Greeks needed first to renew contact by setting up provisional trading stations for exchanges with the local inhabitants. The earliest and best-known of these Greek settlements is Pithekoussai, founded in ca. 750 B.C. on what is now Ischia off the coast of Campania. Pithekoussai seems to have had all the characteristics of an *emporion*, thanks to the uncommon capacity of its inhabitants to establish trade relations with 60th the mineral-rich lands of Etruria and the ports of the East. However, it cannot be ruled out that Pithekoussai may have been the first attempt in the Early Archaic period at establishing a full-fledged colony; the experiment was subsequently repeated in a more complex form on the mainland opposite, at Kyme (Cumae). This settlement is still mostly unexcavated, known from random architectural details (mostly architectural terra-cottas) rather than from any monumental structures as such; it was the springboard for the occupation by Euboean colonists of much of Campania, as far down the coast as Parthenope/Neapolis on the part of Euboean colonists. The natural talent of the Chalcidian Greeks for occupying sites of strategic relevance to their trade routes is exemplified by the foundation of Rhegion (Rhegium) and Zankle (modern Messina), which were all founded in fairly quick succession in the second half of the eighth century B.C.

The foundation of the Achaean colony of Metapontion (Metapontum) was more modest and circumscribed, despite the fact that this locality also seems to fit in neatly with the general evolution of Greek colonial expansion. The Greek geographer and historian Strabo in fact claims that the first Achaean colony, Sybaris, guided the new arrivals to the preassigned sites in a bid to curb the expansion of the adjacent Laconian colony of Taras (Tarentum). Research carried out in the last ten years, with the spectacular finds effected by Piero Orlandini at Incoronata, poses one of the most troublesome dilemmas of interpretation regarding the settlement dynamics of Greek colonies of the Archaic period.

From the eighth century the Incoronata hilltop had been home to a thriving Iron Age settlement, whose native inhabitants came into contact with Greek merchants in the course of the seventh century; it may even be that a number of the latter actually settled in the native community. What is significant, however, is that the village met an abrupt end (toward 630 B.C.), just as Metapontum was being founded, as if to denote a fundamental incompatibility between the budding Greek colony and territorial occupation not under its control.

The spatial definition of the colony.

It is worth stressing that at Metapontum both the identification and delimitation of the future urban area, and the definition and organization of the *chora* (the territory upon which the colony's economy depended), occur together and are part and parcel of a single design. To judge from the archaeological evidence, it seems that one of the first things the new colonists actually undertook was to stake out and protect the ample arable zones stretching inland. This procedure is borne out by votive finds of early date on the borders of the *chora* and in the sanctuaries of the hinterland, particularly those dedicated to Zeus, Athena, and Artemis at San Biagio.

The extraordinary importance of this last sanctuary lies in the rich figurative decoration of its oldest

The Temple of Hera at Metaponto from the northeast with the Bradano River in the foreground

temple, which illustrates scenes of the Greek worship of Athena; such images were an unmistakable message of the compactness and cultural superiority of the Greek colonists.

It seems that the sanctuaries surrounding the agrarian areas, like some *ceinture sacrée* (Martin), performed a crucial role in the constitution of the entire colony. The large sanctuary sited on the northeast border of the *chora* of Metapontum, on the banks of the Bradano River, bordering Iapygia and hence areas under Tarentum's influence, was of interest not only to Metapontum. Endowed in the sixth century with a large peripteral temple, this sacred enclosure dedicated to Hera (the most important deity in the pantheon of Magna Graecia) is together with the *Heraion* on the Sele River and its counterpart at Capo Colonna (the Lacinian promontory), one of the three great Hera temples of regional importance. Similarly, the famous *Heraion* on the Sele limited and protected Paestum (Greek Poseidonia) on the frontier with the Etruscan part of modern Campania; while the Capo Colonna *Heraion* marked the limit of the dominion of Croton, the southernmost of the Achaean colonies. At the height of the Archaic period, these three sanctuaries were the only monumental extramural temples in the whole of Magna Graecia. Fountains and springs lying within the *chora* also tend to serve as natural focuses of cultural aggregation, such as the plentiful spring near Pantanello, or the *nymphaeum* in the sanctuary at San Biagio. As mentioned above, the definition and structuring of the *chora* at Metapontum by means of religious sites is not an isolated case. For her sister city Paestum, the hillfort on the promontory of Agropoli south of the Paestan plain was evidently the first settlement of the colonists from Sybaris; this view has been recently endorsed by the discovery of significant traces of a large Archaic temple on the site of the Medieval castle. It must have been from here that the colonists from sybaris set out to found Paestum itself in the fertile plain; the site they chose lay on a distinct platform of sedimentary limestone shielded to the south by the Salso River and to the west by a lagoon that afforded excellent moorage. To the north, on the left bank of the Sele River – a natural frontier of Etruscan expansion in Campania – they erected the above-mentioned monumental sanctuary to Hera. As at the San Biagio sanctuary near Metapontum, these temples were adorned with figured scenes of a markedly propagandistic nature, including metopes depicting the heroic feats of Heracles, symbolic guarantor of Greekness in the face of non-Greek enemies. The pattern of outlying temples at Paestum is complemented by a wide ring of smaller sacred sites established near or along the roads leading into the interior, or along the foot of the hills and possessing plentiful springs, like the sanctuary at Capo del Fiume.

Without listing all the examples available, the basic pattern is nonetheless generally viable for all the large colonies, and particularly for those founded by the Achaeans. At Sybaris there is a similar chain of sacred sites encircling a plain, including the most famous of all, the *Athenaion* at Motta di Francavilla Marittima al Mare to the north[a], and the area of Croton stretches from the *Heraion* at Capo Colonna in the south, to the much older Sanctuary of Apollo Alaios at Punta Alice in the Crimisa district. Undoubtedly, this somewhat ideal picture of the "sacred protection" of the colonial area is probably not valid in all cases, and is less applicable in areas where the native inhabitants were more culturally advanced and socially compact. Above all, the colonies founded toward the end of the Archaic period found themselves having to deal with neighbors that were less complacent about Greek occupation. A prime example is the last major colony, Phocaean Elea (Velia), which had to defend its territory in a more concrete way with the use of military outposts, such as the one at Moio della Civitella.

The economic basis of the colonies
As noted above, it is now generally held that the commercial potential of the early colonies was somewhat limited. Natural features, such as the splendid harbor at Tarentum were not fully exploited until a later and much more advanced stage in the colony's evolution. In many cases, river inlets or lagoon formations were enough to guarantee safe moorage for the Greeks' vessels. On the other hand, the inland courses of the rivers, toward the valleys, created natural channels of communication with the native populations and with the other colonial cities along either the Ionian or the Tyrrhenian coasts.
The most thoroughly documented of these, with full details on its settlements, is the territory between Metapontum and Paestum along the Basento and Sele. In any case, the base of the colonies economy and the real reason for their being there in the first place was the systematic exploitation of the farmland around the urban sites themselves. On occasion, these *chorai* were, as evinced by the natural conformation and the pattern of the sanctuaries mentioned above, so extensive (e.g., Metapontum, Sybaris, and Croton) that they could not be managed by the residents of the urban settlements alone. One can presume that in many cases the *chora* itself had a stable population of farmers cultivating the land. Such an arrangement is suggested by the existence of the rural sanctuaries which, besides serving as monumental symbols for the entire colony, must have fulfilled specific daily functions for the rural population.
This hypothesis is amply borne out by recent studies carried out in the territories of Metapontum and

Ruins of the Sanctuary of Athena on Motta di Francavilla Marittima with the plain of Sibari in the distance

Croto. In the Metapontine hinterland in particular, joint studies undertaken by archaeologists, geologists, topographers, and paleontologists of various nationalities have included a thorough study of the aerial survey photographs, then an extensive field surveys of the terrain, as well as individual excavations; these joint efforts have yielded an astonishing mass of useful field data for interpreting farming methods, animal husbandry, hunting, and the exploitation of forests in the course of the colony's history.

According to this new information, first in the alluvial plains along the river courses, and subsequently in the hilly country up to twelve to fourteen kilometers, from the coastline certain areas were parceled out systematically and regularly, with roads and conduits for irrigation. The parallel system of causeways and channels, ca. 195-240 m. a part, were arranged in various large systems according to the morphology of the terrain. It is more difficult to ascertain the position of the transverse roads, and hence the true dimensions of the groundplots accorded to each household. Nonetheless, the identification of a vast number of farm sites and neighboring burial grounds (another confirmation of the stable presence of settlers in the *chora*) enables us to reconstruct a hypothetical grid for the plot dimensions. So far around 1,500 sites have been identified in the Metapontum area, each affording a cultivated area of 18.5 hectares – a fairly large unit that would have required the assigned family to engage extra hands to maintain it properly.

The overall picture must, however, be interpreted in terms of its historical evolution. In the Archaic period preference was given to the flatter land along the rivers, until the progressive rising of the water table forced the colonists to occupy higher ground in the hills. Around one thousand farms are attested during the colony's heyday in the second half of the fourth century B.C. The farm buildings and walls were constructed with river stones, mudbrick, and tiled roofs; their layout is very compact, almost square, with a series of rooms apparently without a courtyard.

Abundant finds of seeds, pollen, and animal bones have provided accurate clues as to the kind of farming undertaken, and to the species of animals (both domestic and wild), and hence the principal factors of diet, forage, and even the production of farm goods for retail.

On the basis of this data one can infer that Greek occupation not only triggered a radical transformation of the way in which the land was exploited relative to precolonial farming methods, but above all marked a considerable improvement on the techniques of cultivation, particularly with the introduction of crop rotation. Besides cereals, the preferred crops – amply documented by the Metapontine coinage and the famous Delphic votive offering of the "golden ear of wheat" – were legumes (broad beans, chickpeas, vetch, peas, lentils), plus olives and grapes, together with a mixture of for-

Diagram of the division
into agricultural plots
in the *chora* of Metapontum
(from De Siena-Carter)

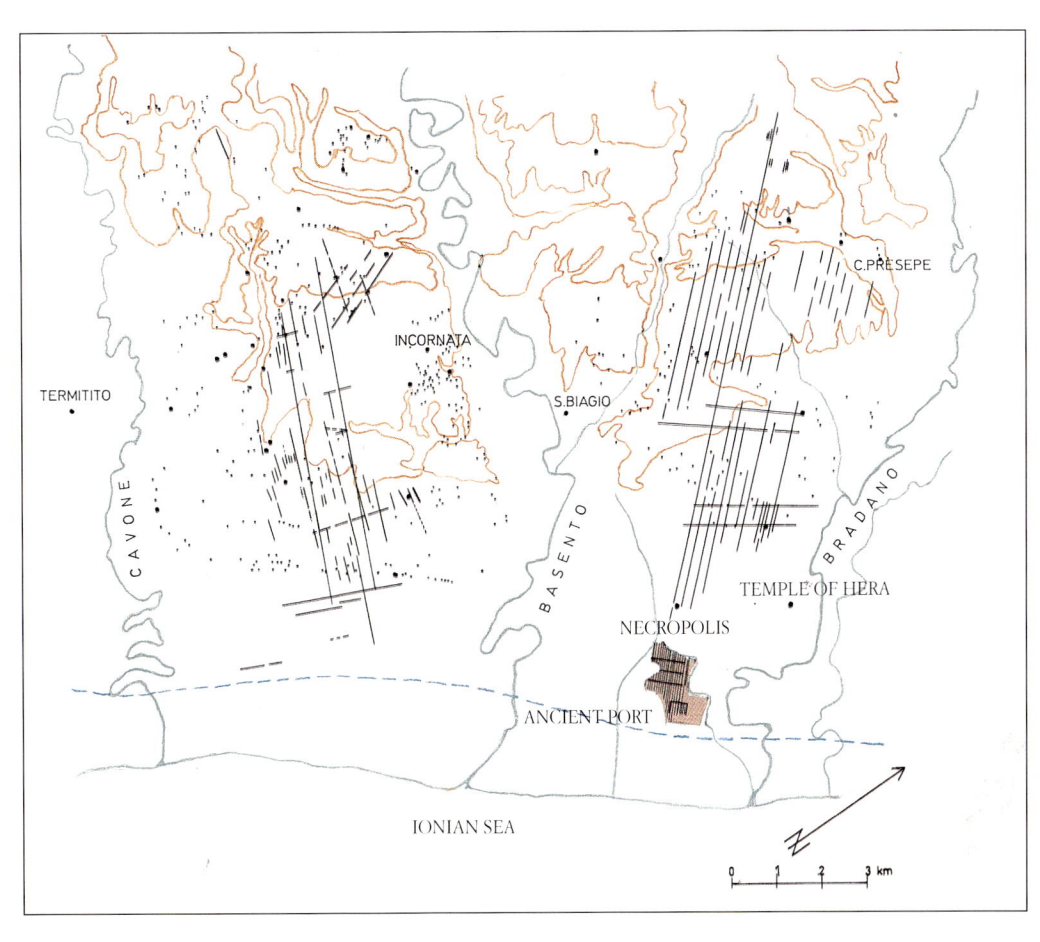

Reconstruction of the division
into agricultural plots
in the *chora* of Metapontum
the dots indicate the farms
existing between 350-300 B.C.
(from Carter)

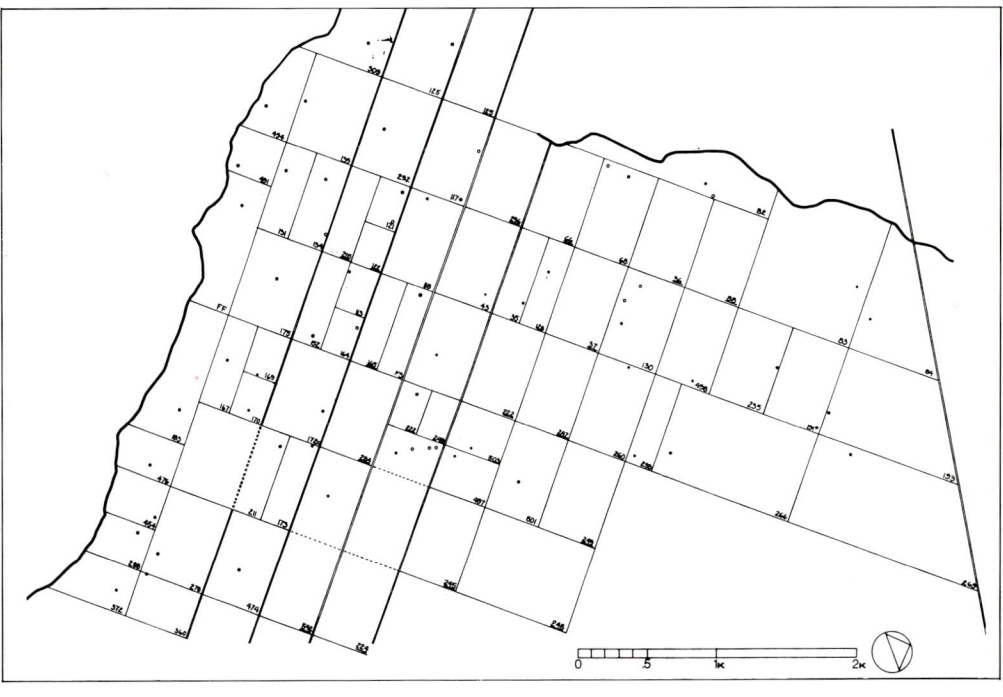

age, lucern (*Medica sativa*), oats, and rye. The changes in crop types during the colonial period, and in the combination of crops (for instance, cereals plus olives), and above all the decision to alternate cultivation with periods of abandonment, can be accurately followed by analyzing pollen deposits in the various stratified level, which are dated with conventional archaeological methods; such analyses furnish significant information on the history of occupation and farming practice. The range of forage plants sheds light on the kind of animal husbandry that took place. The masses of animal bones, moreover, supply a detailed picture of the prominent role played by, both livestock and wild animals in the colony's economy. In addition to these archaeological data, another important source of information is the well-known bronze inscription known as the Tabulae Heracleenses, which bear witness to the economic situation in the second half of the fourth century. The bronze tablets detail the legal redistribution of land of varying quality (and hence suitable for different types of planting) from vineyards to woodland, extending from the fertile alluvial beds and along the bed of the Akiris (the Agri River) that were run by the sanctuaries of Athena and Dionysus. Besides the use of these tracts of land, the requisite infrastructure to define and make them accessible, the tablets give information on how the institutions were financed – in this case the sanctuaries.

Division and organization of the urban area
Metapontum offers one of the few examples of the initial definition and articulation of the urban space. An area with an irregular border defined by the shoreline and the bends of two rivers (Basento and Bradano) offering a fairly extensive area (ca. 150 hectares) is separated from the *chora* via a simple, almost rectilinear wall between the two rivers. Only at a later stage, apparently, the fortification was closed with earthworks along the rivers and the sea. The vast area thus defined was parceled up into large zones for different functions; initially, this division may have consisted of an area for public functions (sanctuaries and *agora*) and one for residential structures. The division seems to have been constituted by a straight line running northwest–southeast, i.e., from the hinterland to the sea. This line was probably the main road leading from the shore (moorage) to the interior *chora*, and seems to have generated the entire complex and regular grid of the urban fabric. For one or two generations after the foundation of the town in the second half of the seventh century B.C., this pattern seems to have amply satisfied their needs, given that the area was only sparsely inhabited, with large open spaces (perhaps even unusable owing to drainage problems), and with scattered hut-type dwellings. The lack of burials around the first hut-houses confirms the fundamental urban character of this area

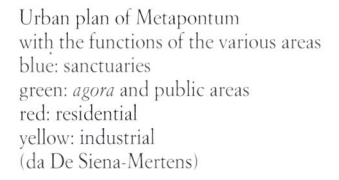

Urban plan of Metapontum
with the functions of the various areas
blue: sanctuaries
green: *agora* and public areas
red: residential
yellow: industrial
(da De Siena-Mertens)

Urban Planning in Magna Graecia

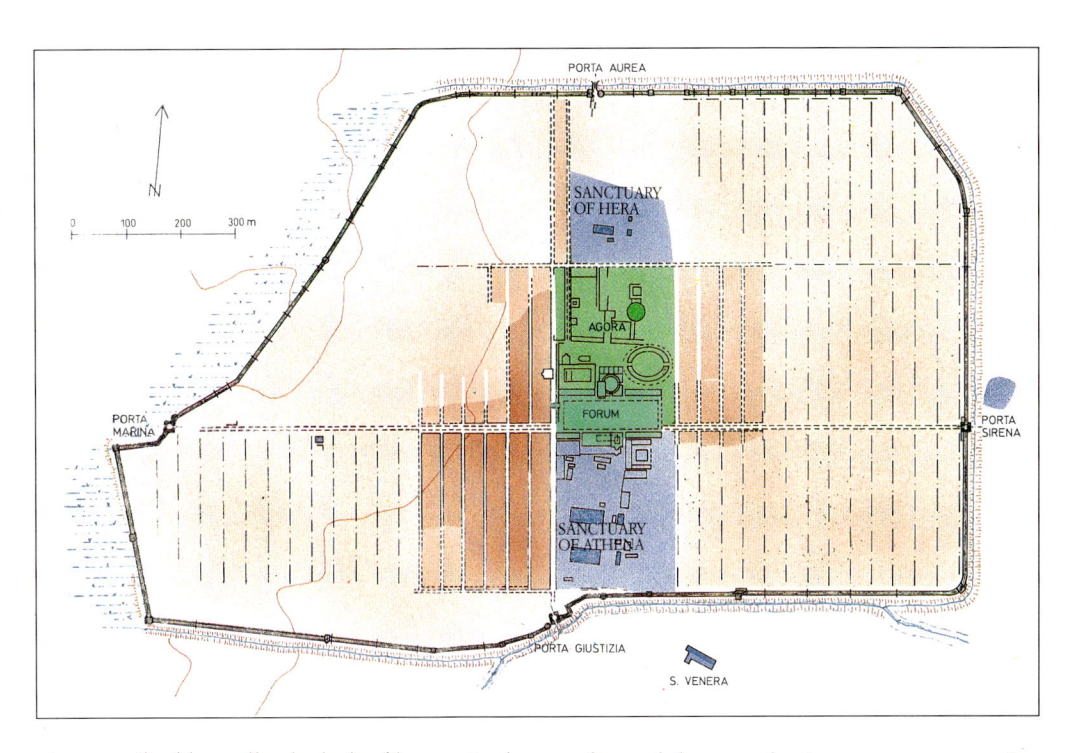

Urban plan of Poseidonia with the functions of the main areas (from Greco-Theodorescu)

circumscribed by walls; the lack of houses in the zone beyond the central axis seems to suggest that this land had a different status, or was designated as sacred.

Such forms of division of the urban area into large zones with separate functions – an arrangement established at the time of foundation – seems to have been an axiom of colonial urban planning. At Poseidonia too in the urban area defined along its western half by the natural contours of a limestone platform, a broad band of land that cut through the city in a north–south direction was earmarked for the town's sanctuaries and the *agora*. Here too, the main north–south artery linking the city gates (perhaps maintained in Roman times) forms the dividing line between public functions and residential area. Our knowledge, however, is still insufficient to establish the existence of any general rule for the marking out of the two main areas. Some criteria have come to light, however, as regards location choices for the sanctuaries. At Taras, the two main sanctuaries were located on the westernmost point and on the isthmus with the mainland and appear to define the peninsula as a kind of acropolis, while the *agora* is located on what is now the mainland; this scheme is confirmed by written sources. But the sizable area between these two sanctuaries was also occupied (see Syracuse for a similar topographical situation) by a well-planned residential fabric. Rather than an acropolis, the site must have been the first settlement nucleus of the colony that was distinct from the quarters located on the present-day mainland (perhaps also at a social level).

Actually, a full-fledged acropolis is nowhere to be seen in the colonial cities. Although Elea, whose lofty promontory is crowned by a temple whose remains lie hidden beneath the foundations of the medieval castle, seems to offer the necessary topographical premises, the temple was initially dovetailed into the residential fabric of distinctive houses built of polygonal masonry. The crest of the promontory, running east, was instead set aside for the sanctuaries. Given their close bond with the city walls, the sanctuaries must have served less as places of worship for their respective residential quarters, than as part of a *ceinture sacrée* encircling the town, just as might happen in the *chora* (see above).

This phenomenon is particularly evident in the case of Lokroi Epizephyrioi. The town covers an extensive area (230 hectares) encompassed by the fourth-century defensive walls, and comprises two halves of different morphology. The first is flat coastland, defined on one side by the sea and on two others by bounding streams on the northeast and southwest (the Gerace and the Portigliola); the northwest half is composed of fairly steep hilly land divided into three crests by two deep gorges.

The boundary between the flatter area and the hillside is marked out by an almost straight causeway whose modern-day name "dromos" is most likely a relic of one of the more important ancient arteries. As for the sanctuaries, this markedly differentiated area seems to be girt by a series of key shrines that

Urban Planning in Magna Graecia

Reconstruction of the urban
plan of Tarentum
(E. Lippolis)

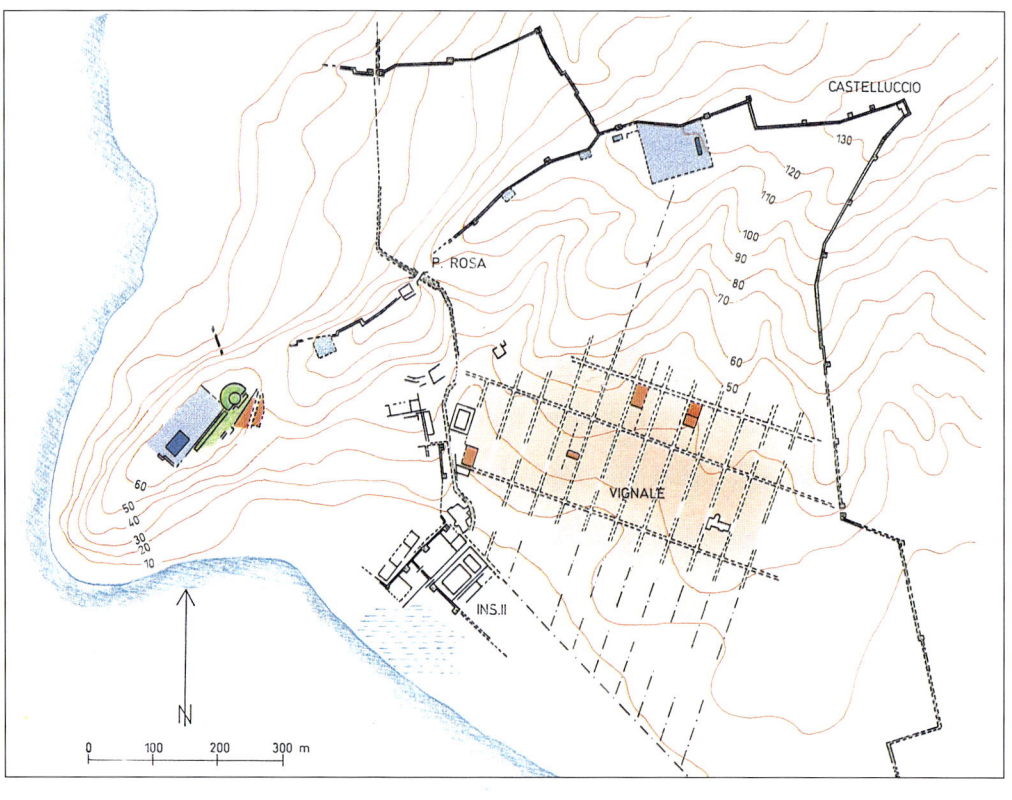

Urban plan of Elea (Velia)
with the function of the main areas
(da Krinzinger)

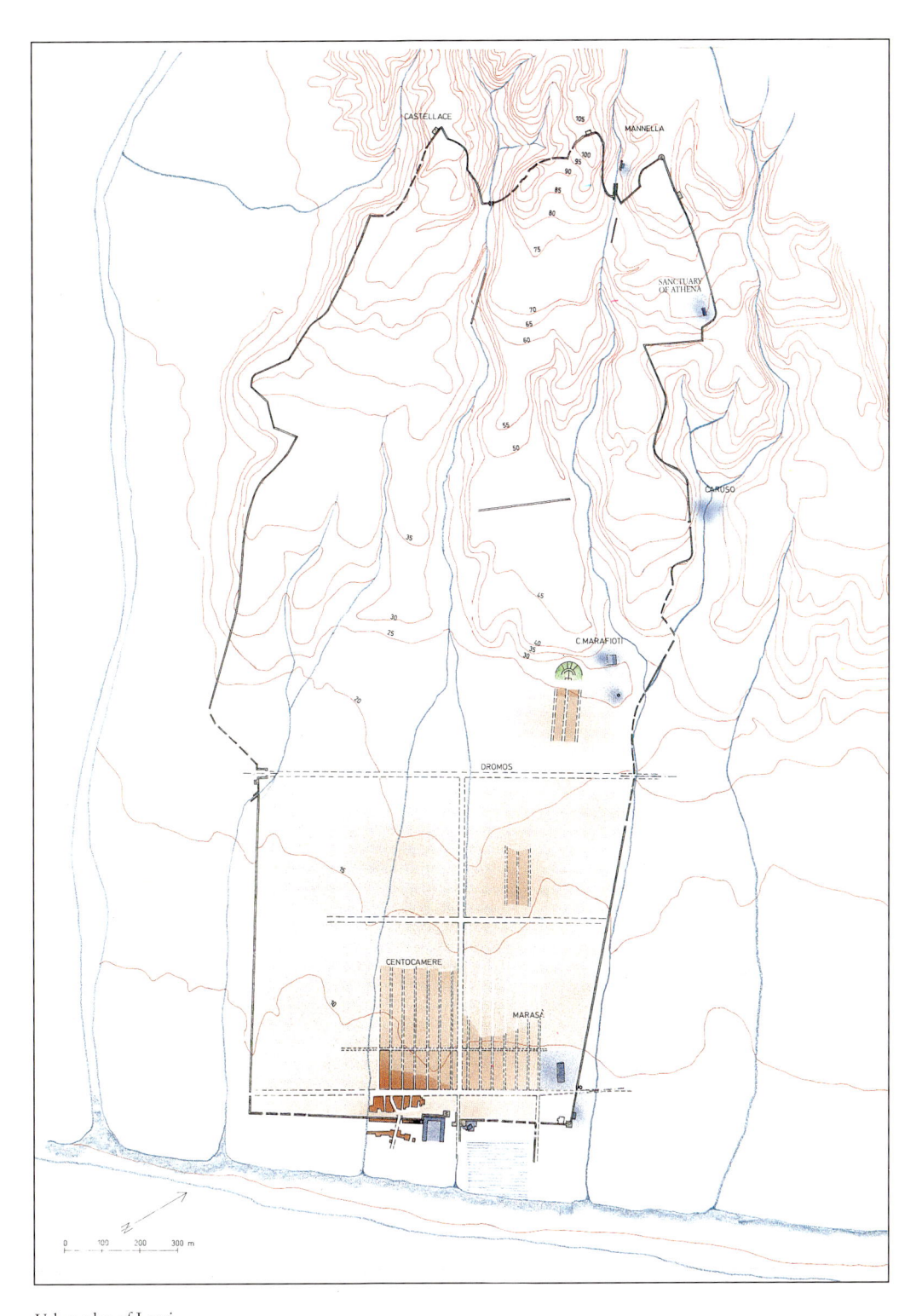

Urban plan of Locri
with the functions
of the main areas
(from Barra-Bagnasco)

neatly prefigure both the internal and external course of the later defensive walls. This fact is particularly noticeable along the main stretch of the eastern stretch of the wall.

The sanctuary in the Marasà quarter – undoubtedly the most important within the urban enclosure, and located not far from the northeast corner of the town – is also part of this sweeping sacred *ceinture*. Of a quite different category is the sanctuary in the U-shaped *stoa* complex, and in the nearby Temple of Aphrodite; both lie immediately outside the walls, which here form the most conspicuous identified tract of the ancient defense works at Locri, near the beach, and hence part and parcel of the harbor system. A similar hypothesis has been proposed for the urban sanctuary at Caulonia, represented by the Doric temple of the Classical period, which occupies a similar setting near the shoreline, albeit within the *ceinture*.

Road layouts and the monumentalization of public sites
Rising prosperity, growing populations, the general economic situation, along with, suitable political conditions, led the *poleis* of Magna Graecia from around the mid-sixth century to bestow more precise and concrete form on the basic urban layout, which until then had been limited to the road arrangements outlined above. It seems certain that the basic procedures stemmed from experience acquired in the parceling of land, starting from the early days of colonization itself. The principle is the regular division of space according to strict geometric patterns, initially reflected not so much in built-up housing lots as in a precise street grid; this served both as a system of division and as a network of thoroughfares and conduits for the water supply and drainage. According to the earliest documents of Siceliot settlements, such as Megara Hyblaea or its subcolony Selinus, the early form of spatial division was based on the road grid. This served as the pattern for the streets themselves, while the *insulae*, or housing blocks, filled the gaps between the streets. Actually, given the ample extra space available to the early colonists, the lots were rarely fully occupied by houses, and hence could not be seen as architectural units conceived as such.

As for the streets, they were from the very start laid out with different widths according to their importance, and were constructed with different techniques and services (earthen, pebble, stone pavements; water channels). The basic distinction is in width: a few wider *plateiai* are intersected perpendicularly at regular intervals by narrower *stenopoi*, creating a regular grid. The *stenopoi* created long narrow blocks about one-hundred feet in width.

There is good reason to believe that at least the pattern of the major arteries belongs to the phase of monumental urbanization of the sixth century B.C. And once again it is Metapontum that yields the most valuable information in this respect, while excavation has yet to offer confirmation of the pre-existence of arteries earlier than the fifth and fourth centuries, without any doubt the general relationship between the street grid, the defensive system, and the principal sanctuaries sheds important light.

As noted above, the early *plateia* separates the sacred area from the residential quarter, and links the urban area with the necropolis and the *chora*, traversing the oldest sections of wall through one of the city gates (Porta Settembrini, the northwest gate), built here when the walls were first laid out. From this we can infer that the causeway running northwest–southeast was decisive for the subsequent pattern of the entire street grid.

The orientation of the first monumental structures in the sanctuary enclave does not follow the street pattern at all; the buildings were all oriented more or less to the east, presumably for religious reasons. This type of layout changes shortly after mid-sixth century with the construction of two peripteral temples, the main shrines of the *polis*, which mark a breach with the old pattern and instead lie parallel to each other and to the main artery, and are hence aligned with the general urban layout. To conform to this new plan, construction on a major temple (A I) was interrupted and a new one (A II) started in its place, oriented differently.

This was an extraordinary decision: the former religious alignment of the temples was abandoned and instead they were adapted to the rationalized grid of the town as a whole, rather than the other way round. The explanation lies in the fact that the temples were not simply focuses of religious activity, but the most conspicuous landmarks of the entire *polis*, offering a monumental ratification of the urban plan, which might otherwise have been abstract and less easily perceived. The temples therefore became the town's most prominent monuments, acting as guarantors of the order imposed on the town. It is significant, furthermore, that some generations later the strict and severe link between the sacred monuments and the urban plan was once more forsaken when from the first half of the fifth

Urban Planning in Magna Graecia

Plan of the urban sanctuary
and of the *agora* of Metapontum
reconstruction
(Mertens
disegno Schützenberger)

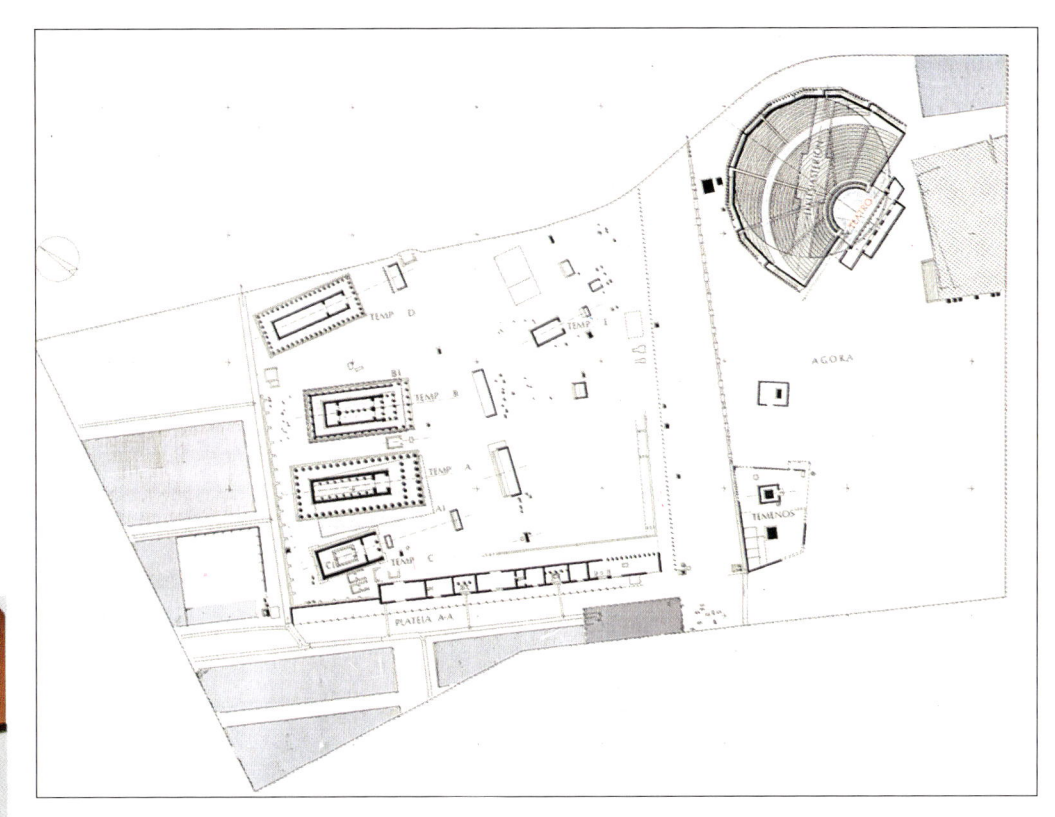

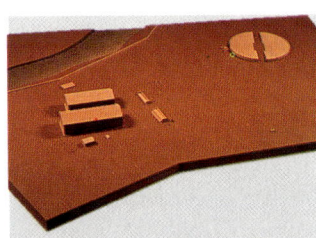

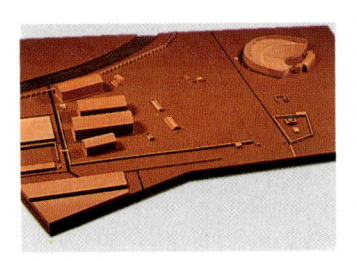

Model of the urban sanctuary
and of the *agora*
of Metapontum
(Mertens)

Plan of the phases of development
of the urban sanctuary
and of the *agora* of Metapontum
(Mertens
disegno Schützenberger)

- end 7th cent. B.C.
- first half 6th cent. B.C.
- second half 6th cent. B.C.
- first half 5th cent. B.C.
- end 4th cent. B.C.
- 3rd cent. B.C.

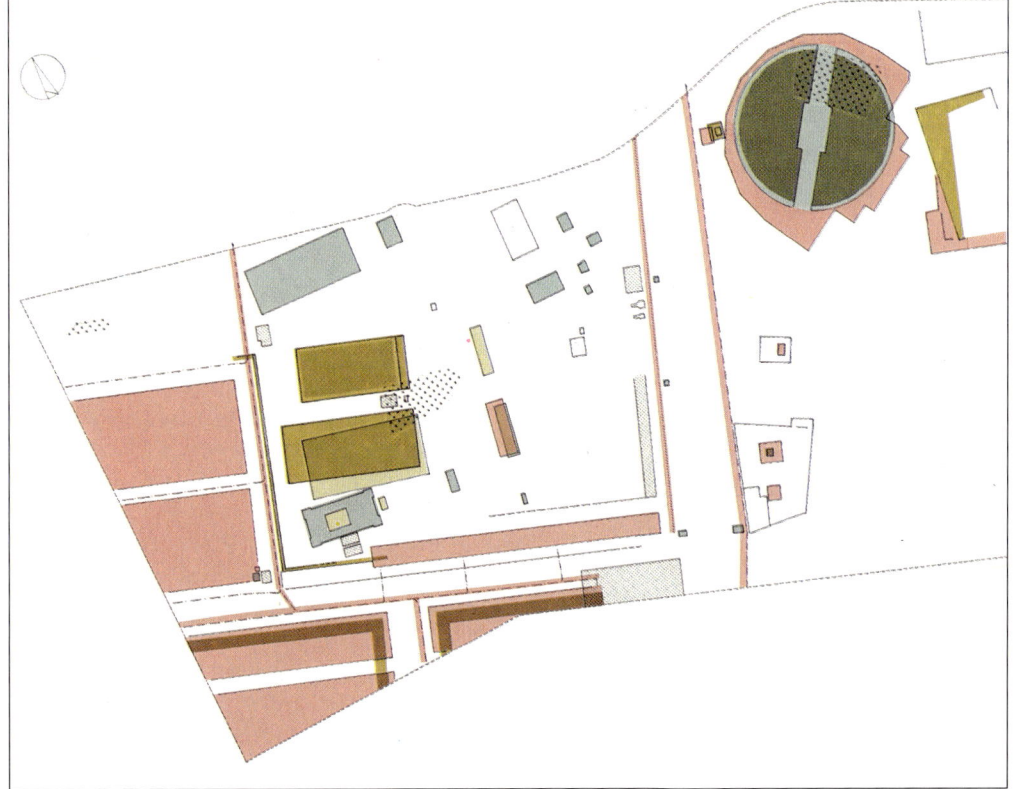

century – starting with the Ionic temple in the southern sector of the town – new monuments were again oriented strictly according to religious needs.

Given such rigid and binding planning concepts, one can only wonder about the underlying political structures, and, in the sphere of urban planning, about the buildings in which such decisions were made. Once again, Metapontum provides some vital clues.

The extensive space assigned at the time of foundation for the public, religious, and administrative functions was divided into two separate areas: an urban sanctuary and an *agora*. The dividing line created in the major reworking of the town plan in the fourth century B.C. consisted of a long straight row of stone blocks known as *horoi*, offering a kind of monumental endorsement of an existing demarcation. In the sixth century the broad open area of the *agora* was equipped with a set of inscribed *horoi* marking off a specific area; one of these *cippi*, known as the *horos* of Zeus Agoraios, has survived.

From the very first phase of colonization, just this area was the site of a highly significant monument for public meetings. In its various rebuildings this monument remained a fixed feature for planning and architecture in Metapontum until the demise of the *polis*. In its first form, it consisted of wooden bleachers (*ikoia*), which was destroyed by fire around 600 B.C. and rebuilt with a more robust structure around the mid-sixth century. The original was built on a circular plan (diameter 62 meters) with two opposing sets of seating tiers separated by a central access corridor, and the seating supported on an earthen embankment contained on the outside by a solid wall; at the center a rectangular open area provided an *orchestra* or *bema* for the orators. In the first quarter of the fifth century, the entire construction was reworked with the same underlying plan, but given a more monumental frame with the substitution in stone of most of the tiers resting on the embankment.

This type of monument, of which examples can be found at Acragas (Agrigentum) and Paestum, was defined somewhat generically as an *ekklesiasterion*, meaning a public gathering place. The one in question, which once accommodated between 7,000 and 8,000 people, is by far the largest and oldest monument of this kind in the whole of the Greek world. As to its specific functions, besides accommodating public gatherings of a political nature, it may have hosted dancing and athletic events linked to the veneration of the deity to whom the entire area was dedicated. The complete lack of textual confirmation or analogous structures means that interpretations as to its true function can only be guesswork. But there is no doubt that this grandiose monument provides a significant visual counter-balance, as it were, to the large temples of the urban sanctuary, which were built during the same period. To judge from its great size, one can infer that the political meetings held in the *ekklesiasterion* were attended not only by members of the local citizenry but by people from all over the Metapontine region, including the rural areas. It may have been the place where the decision was taken – or put forward as a proposal – to undertake the major overhaul of the town plan and erect the main temples; it may also have been here that the distribution scheme for new farmlands of the *chora* was decided. As such, the *ekklesiasterion* seems to have been created to meet certain specific needs of a large colonial town, which may explain why nothing similar has turned up in the Greek homeland. This is a paramount example of the colonial capacity for inventiveness and innovation, a capacity that is most clearly expressed in the major monuments of colonial architecture.

Although for the time being there are no comparable structures in other *poleis* in Magna Graecia to confirm this conclusion, a similar monument at Paestum offers a few interesting clues. The actual street network of the Greek *polis* is still little known, but the research carried out by a mixed Italian and French team has located the *agora* in a large central area contained between the southern sanctuary (dedicated to Hera, and perhaps also to Zeus) and that of the north (Athena); this formed an extensive zone reserved for public functions (see above). At the center of this area, which extends from the imaginary axis linking the south and north gates and a line lying east of the modern museum (see discussion of the city limits), a circular monument has come to light. Though of much smaller dimensions (with a capacity of 900 to 1,400 spectators), it closely resembles the structure in Metapontum, and is datable to the first quarter of the fifth century B.C. In this case too, the building must have been meant to receive assemblies for the administrative bodies of the town, that is, it was a *bouleuterion* or an *ekklesiasterion* for a town with a smaller population. Paestum offers yet another monument of outstanding significance for the social and political structure of the colonial *polis*, namely the underground sacellum which, to judge from its elaborate contents, was a kind of cenotaph: this has been interpreted as the *heroon* or hero cult of the *oikistes* or founder of the colony.

The most important elements in the question of the earliest street grid at Paestum are nonetheless the main monuments of the Archaic period, and the great temples in particular. Given the analogy with Metapontum, it is presumed that for Paestum too, the fixed orientation of the three main temples (given also the great distance between the two temples of the *Heraion* and the *Athenaion*) can only be explained by some kind of planning pattern based on an axis running through the north and south gates, to which presumably there was a second perpendicular axis running to the west city gate. But, as in Metapontum, there is no monumental evidence to verify that these axes were indeed the main thoroughfares. There are no clues, moreover, as to the internal subdivisions within this very approximate arrangement.

While the town plan of Sybaris in the Archaic period is still completely buried beneath the mud of the Crathis River and by the overbuilding of later settlements, the fourth in the series of Achaean cities, Croton, affords a glimpse here and there of its elements, despite the considerable hurdles to proper archaeological research imposed by the modern city. The ancient city was spread over a vast area during the second half of the fourth century, the period of the city's maximum expansion (excavators estimate some 618 hectares judging from the current 13-kilometer course of the city walls), and thus Croton seems to have been by far the largest and most extensive city of all Magna Graecia. However, its dimensions arouse a certain perplexity. To the south, the city is delimited by the steep castle-topped hill which, together with the examples of Cumae (Kyme) and Elea (Hyele), suggests most convincingly an acropolis, and also by the Esaro River, which bisects the city.

Archaeological research done in the area has revealed three areas – the foot of the castle hill (Via Tedeschi and Via Firenze), and the areas either side of the river (the Via Castro district, and the Collina della Batteria district) – in which a regular town plan is observable (apparently with several monumental features) dating to the early sixth century. The plan is based on a set of parallel streets with three different orientations; all three, however, seem to have a common point of convergence in the plain either side of the estuary of the Esaro River. In the convergence point of these systems south of the river it seems there was some sort of a public precinct. Other fragmentary observations include two orders of streets, one 8.8 m wide (one example), and *stenopoi* measuring around 5 meters in width, about 35 meters apart; the length of the individual blocks was about 300 meters. This *strigae* system seems to have remained basically unaltered throughout the town's history, even when in the fourth century after a long period of stagnation much of the town was rebuilt.

The particular conditions posed by modern Croton have not yet made it possible to identify major structures of the scale of the temples of Paestum or Metapontum, serving as monumental markers of the urban system. However, bearing in mind the prototype at Metapontum, we can presume the existence of a large public gathering place, as mentioned in the written sources. The monumental potential of Croton can be inferred in any case from the great Archaic Temple to Hera, which predates the pre-Classical temple at Capo Colonna.

As described above, the ground plan of Locri is clearer: the sweeping plain slopes gently down from the foot of the hills to the shore, defined by a valley on either side, making for a simpler plan. Even the basic problem of drainage would have prompted a solution comprising a series of parallel *stenopoi* perpendicular to the shoreline; these streets would be linked by *plateiai*, or avenues, parallel to the shoreline. The main artery has been successfully excavated in part, and it is also implied by the arrangement of the important gate in the Parapezza quarter, near the urban sanctuary; the *plateia* on higher ground may have followed the course of the so-called "dromo" in use today.

It has not yet been feasible to ascertain the number of intermediate *plateiai*, though an estimate can be made on the basis of the distance of around 810 meters separating the main *plateiai*.

The form of the *insulae*, or blocks, and streets currently visible in the Centocamere quarter stems from the last phase of the city's prosperity (the second half of the fourth century B.C.). Leading off from the major *plateiai* 14 meters wide are the *stenopoi* measuring between 4 and 4.5 meters wide; these delimit blocks of between 27.5 to 28 meters in width. Stratigraphic analysis of the terrain has yielded data on the urban pattern at least from the mid-sixth century, throwing light therefore on the continuity found elsewhere in all the other cities so far examined. Only the broad strip between the Centocamere *plateia* and the city walls seems to have been left vacant in the Archaic period, and not actually developed until the fourth century and later, and then in a haphazard fashion.

The area marked out for public functions, namely the town's *agora*, is as yet unidentified. In the sixth century B.C. the middle of the broad strip between the *plateia* and the shore saw the construction of the U-shaped *stoa*, which is held to be a Sanctuary of Aphrodite – basically a house of "sacred prostitution" – and was linked to the harbor functions and hence to the trade activities apparently undertaken in this band of terrain embracing the shoreline. A problem remains, however:

while the walls in the Centocamere quarter separate this quarter from the city proper, a large stretch of wall sloping off to the beach seems to suggest that this area too was somehow part of the city's defensive system.

A separate case can be seen in Tarentum, the only colony established by the Laconians, in which the ponderous relics of Magna Graecia's oldest stone temple afford a glimpse of the splendor attained in the Late Archaic period. Compared to other examples, however, here we lack sufficient evidence to attribute the temple as evidence for a well planned and spacious city. To judge from the archaeological data so far available, it seems as though the Archaic city was concentrated (most likely with a far higher building density than those of the *poleis* examined above) on the narrow peninsula, which offered a mere 18 hectares of developable land, defended by a wall no more than 2 kilometers long. A fortified ditch in place of the present canal may have marked the boundary with the mainland, where there may have originally been a vacant area suitable for staging the kind of functions held in an *agora*.

Besides this, the peninsula itself seems to be based on a strict grid layout comprising transverse *stenopoi* linked up by an east–west artery running along the crest of the peninsula; this *stenopos* determines the orientation of the sanctuaries and in particular the alignment of the major temple attributed to Poseidon. Parallel to this on the other side of the *plateia* there may have stood another sanctuary; and recent excavation appears to suggest the existence of a large temple on the westernmost tip of the peninsula as well.

This layout is conspicuously similar to that of the island of Ortygia in Syracuse, the only truly comparable case, and this likeness bears out the hypothesis expressed above.

The restricted space occupied by the first settlement nucleus before the establishment of the colony proper, does not mean, however, that it involved merely the utilization of the geography for port and commercial functions alone. There is evidence to suggest that the Laconian settlers went about exploiting the surrounding farmland in a different way from other colonists. The site of Satyrion (modern Porto Saturo), which was founded at the same time as Tarentum, offers insights into the way the land was gradually occupied; despite the close contact with their Messapic neighbors, the Laconians set up scattered settlement nuclei across the land. It was only in a later phase that demographic and functional concentration took place, focusing on the *polis* of Tarentum itself. The way and period in which this unfolded are still being debated amid considerable doubt. One fact is clear: in time the necropolis occupied an increasing amount of land on the terra firma. Thus said, it is nonetheless possible that the necropolis in question was already patterned on a system of land parceling and road layout, very much as if it were part of an actual urbanization program.

After the mid-fifth century the scheme of the town (which had meanwhile begun to spread over the mainland as well) was given a new monumental pattern with the inclusion of a robust defensive wall eleven kilometers long, arranged in two branches at an angle to each other within the triangular area contained between the two harbors, and thereafter running along the coast to the eastern fortifications of the initial colonial settlement. In this way the entire urban network was turned into an acropolis (later defined as such in the written sources) embracing the main sanctuaries and probably the residences of the families of original colonists. The area once occupied by the necropolis received the bulk of the city's housing, together with the various public areas and monumental structures. The way in which this took place, and especially its unusual relationship with the necropolis (an exceptional fact underscored by the early sources) still pose many problems, which should be resolved as soon as a proper ground-plan of the city has been pieced together from all the available new data.

The various hypotheses put forward so far are based on observations made by writers of antiquity (mainly regarding monuments and public spaces) and on a very limited quantity of monumental remains, including several stretches of ancient streets. For the most part, these are actually remnants of the last wide-scale rebuilding of the colony, effected by the Romans in the year 123 B.C. This situation is reminiscent of what took place in Paestum and Thurii-Copiae (see also the case of Naples below). And just as in those cases, particularly in the second, there is reason to believe that the Roman colonists largely adopted the orientation of their predecessors. To judge from the last collation of all the available data, the town plan is highly regular (even excessively so), though this regularity has certain quite distinct characteristics from that adopted for the Archaic cities discussed above, and seems to indicate the presence of substantial change.

The new conception of city in the Classical age
In none of the cases discussed so far has it been possible to obtain a reliable picture of urban struc-

Aerial view of Naples
the plan of the Greek *neapolis*
is still identifiable

ture as a whole, though several basic features have been demonstrated:
– very large spaces envisaged for the urban complex; these are in turn fairly well circumscribed and reserved within the boundaries of the entire colonial territory (or more precisely, normally situated on the seashore, along the boundaries);
– elementary zoning schemes applied to the area: normally in the form of bisection into a residential zone and a public zone; given the simple bisection of the available area, the public zone is often on the edge of the overall space;
– organization of space, particularly the residential area, prevalently with a wide mesh of *plateiai*, together with long narrow blocks separated and made accessible by rows of *stenopoi* or narrower alleys;
– special emphasis on the public zones (especially the sanctuaries) with large important monuments symbolizing the cultural identity of the colonial community;
– considerable inventiveness in creating new building types to suit the changing needs of each colony.

From the first quarter of the fifth century the Greek cities of the West begin to transform themselves, as a consequence of a growing complexity of social and political relationships within the colonies, which by this point had reached a state of consolidation; furthermore, the rapport between a city and its surrounding territory was more differentiated; and above all the urban population had undergone considerable growth. Indications of these changes in certain Siciliot cities are more macroscopic and all-encompassing: here the era of the first tyrants and the subsequent restoration had made the Archaic urban structures obsolete. The most telling examples are the more heavily restructured townships, such as Himera, Naxos, and Camarina. These and similar *poleis* responded to the shifting needs with highly rational town plans: the new and fundamental element consists in the apportionment of the residential terrain into building lots based on a fixed grid partitioned by a network of streets that follow strictly functional criteria. Some of the features of the Archaic layout, it is true, are maintained, such as the slightly elongated *insulae* (and hence the general *strigae*-based arrangement), together with the differentiation between the wide *plateiai* avenues and the narrower *stenopoi*. But the overall scheme is more rigorous: the dimensions of the housing blocks are defined with clarity and exact proportions (following a standard 1:5 to 1:4 throughout all the *poleis*); the streets also follow a clear hierarchy, their widths varying according to specific functions.

This underlying concept is particularly well established in Magna Graecia. A later town such as Neapolis (Naples) was carefully planned on a virgin territory not far from the previous settlement effort, Paleopolis (Parthenope).

Although only a few stretches of the city walls remain of the Greek *polis* founded in the second quarter of the fifth century, much of the original town plan has survived to our own age owing to the complex process of overbuilding; it is therefore one of the most powerful and monumental testaments to the binding force of the rational town plan: assuming that history has allowed for some continuity (as in this exceptional case), without dramatic moments of total destruction.

The restructuring operations carried out over the centuries entailed a composite rise in the ground level of around six to seven meters; regrettably, there is no evidence of the precise width of the *insulae* defined by the streets. Nevertheless, within the area circumscribed by the old walls one can detect a general distribution consisting in twenty blocks measuring 35 meters wide, and cut through by *stenopoi* 3 meters wide arranged perpendicularly to the slope of the hill above the sea. Three *plateiai*, one above, one along the middle, and a lower one, probably around 6 meters wide (20 feet), 13 meters (50 feet), and 6 meters (20 feet) respectively, laid out at an equal distance of around 150 meters, cut across the *strigae* at right-angles; in this way they form regular housing blocks measuring 38 by 190 meters (130 by 650 feet), and hence at a ratio of 1:5.

More or less central to the urban area partitioned in this way lies a large unclaimed tract of land between the upper and lower *plateiai*, estimated at approximately six blocks in breadth. This area is cut down the middle by the central *plateia* (now Via dei Tribunali). The slope of the land has given rise to two quite distinct ground levels. This was so in the Roman period, in which the most significant monuments (the theater, the *odeum*, the Temple of the Dioscuri, and the monumental area below San Lorenzo, the *tabernae*) are the most concrete evidence for the specifically public use of the area in question, or at least a part of it, as an *agora*. In this hypothesis, the bisection of the territory by the middle *plateia* may also have helped to mark off a division into different functions, possibly political, cultural, religious, and commercial. The public zone, which can be measured in terms of a specific number of parcels of the entire urban area, establishes a precise relationship with the overall plan, reflecting the set of needs formulated on the experience of the Archaic period. Like the new invention of the *insula* as a modular element based on neat and uncomplicated proportions, the entire layout of the city's fabric is now conditioned by the idea of a studied interdependence between the functional components. But like the *insulae*, in their still somewhat elongated shape these components are derived from the long Archaic *strigae*; and the definition of the public areas in the fundamental simplicity of their design, reveal their dependence on the simple spatial economy established earlier in the Archaic period.

In order to endorse what has been discussed so far, namely, that there are precise functional links between the various urban areas, established via the proportions assigned to each type of space, we now need to make a new decisive step forward: the building volume itself must increase at a rate that forces this very form of articulation. The temple by itself, despite its impressive size and elaborate decorative features, can no longer embody the city's corporate identity. The blocks themselves must be built up in full, rather than merely represent a pattern of division: they too must become three-dimensional, like the temple. This is in fact exactly what began to take place in all the *poleis*. In the absence of material evidence in Naples, we can refer to the Sicilian towns of Himera, Naxos, and even the monumental case of Selinus in the Classical period; in Magna Graecia something on these lines only emerges in the Vignale quarter in Elea. Archaeological confirmation is as yet scarce, but the idea is fairly clear: as the city (distinguishing itself clearly from its *chora*) becomes increasingly an organism that is not only planned out but actually constructed in a material sense, and therefore more intensively used, the more urgent it becomes to establish a clear differentiation of the various functional sectors.

At this point it is fundamental to understand the contribution made by the planner-philosopher Hippodamus of Miletus to the discussion of colonial urban planning, although it is unduly generic and has long concealed the real origins and complex evolution of the practice of city design. It is no longer

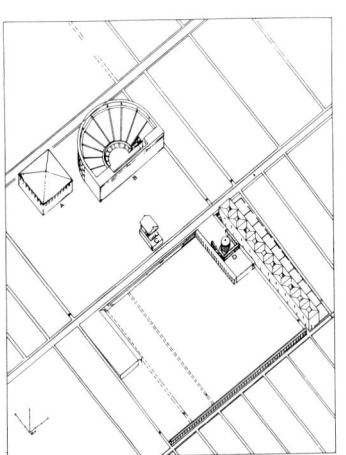

Axonometric reconstruction of the area of the *agora* of Neapolis (from Greco)

the phenomenology of the city in itself that concerns us in the debate over Hippodamus' ideas, but his specific contribution to the question of the compositional elements of the Greek *polis* with regard to the political, social, and economic needs as they were gradually established in the course of the fifth century, and particularly in Attica. Without straying too far into this complex discussion, it is worth underlining this last aspect, that is, the need to assess Hippodamus' thought in the immediate milieu in which this planner-philosopher actually participated in the discussion under way. By this we intend to verify the Milesian planner's contribution – which is often judged to have far-reaching and absolute validity – in proportion to the limited sphere of interests in which he operated. As for the western Greek cities, with their particular legacy of urban planning experiences (as noted above in the case of the newly founded towns in Sicily and Magna Graecia from the first half of the fifth century), the new contribution could be applied, therefore, only to situations in which such conditions prevailed.

The best illustration of Hippodamus' theories in application is Thurii, the new Panhellenic colony founded in 444 B.C. on the site of earlier *polis* of Sybaris.

There are three basic features to take into account:
– the Panhellenic nature of the new city, and hence the special interest of Athens during the period of its foundation;
– the mention of the name of Hippodamus, though the specifics of his involvement are by no means certain;
– the importance of the outstanding monumentality of the new town plan, as described by Diodorus Siculus (XII. 10. 12. 19. 9. 2–5). According to Diodorus, the urban area was subdivided into a wide mesh of four *plateiai* laid in one direction and three in the other; each of these seven *plateiai* was assigned a name that has survived to the present (Herakleia, Aphrodisia, Olympia, Dionysias; Heroa, Thuria, Thurina). Nevertheless, there is nothing new about this idea of conceiving a large

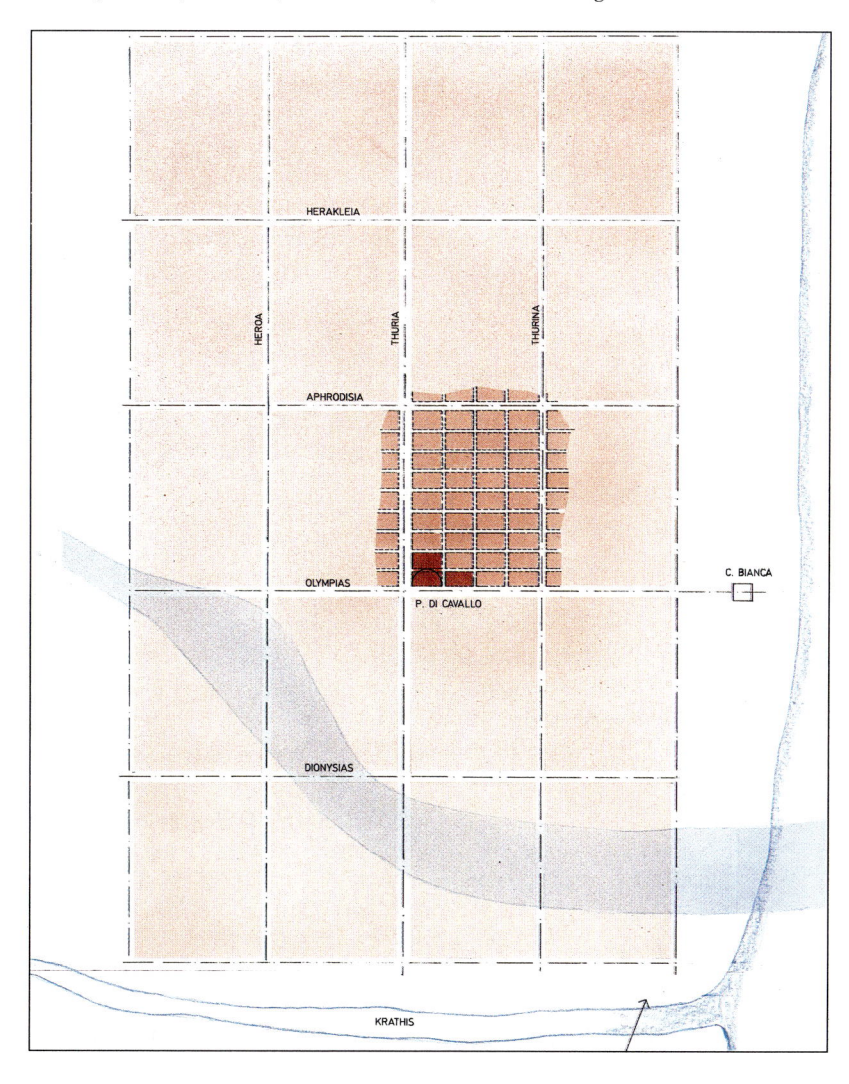

Schema of Thurii according to Diodorus
Diod. Sic. 12. 10. 7
(Mertens)

grid composed of two sets of large parallel avenues that intersect at right-angles and were perhaps ranked by size.

A similar arrangement can be seen in the Sicilian sites of Megara and Syracuse (to some extent), and in more monumental form at Selinus. On the peninsula, however, evidence of the system has not been conclusively found as yet, though both Metapontum and Paestum tend to show signs of a similar organization. It is surprising, therefore, not to find it at Neapolis or at Locri. And though Thurii, where archaeological excavations have fully confirmed Diodorus' descriptions, is for the time being the only positive case of the application of Hippodamus' system of the *plateiai* hierarchy, the fact remains that if the urban scheme were realized in this way, it must have had parallels elsewhere.

According to a new hypothesis (recently sanctioned), the *strigae* layout was replaced by a decidedly more modern arrangement. It looks as if the large neighborhoods carved out by the *plateiai* were in fact subdivided by a more close-knit system of *stenopoi* streets, so as to form *insulae* whose sides were not much longer than their ends. The schema proposed first by Vallet, and then seconded by Belvedere, shows a ratio of 1:2 for the individual blocks, suggesting a ratified planning module, at least as regards the internal organization of the main blocks established by the *plateiai*.

The new hypothesis suggests that the overall urban scheme was accomplished in two stages: 1) the arrangement of principal grid measuring 1,000 by 1,200 feet per unit, followed by a choice of width for the *plateiai*; and 2) the subdivision of the undeveloped areas between the *plateiai* into a grid based on a ratio of 1:2 (i.e., 116 by 232 feet per unit), followed by the choice of the width of the *stenopoi*.

If this basic ground-plan is confirmed by excavation, a new feature comes into play, namely the articulation of the developable area in compliance with more evolved criteria of planning the street systems, generating housing blocks that, once physically built upon, would provide a set of volumetric units with better proportions, conceived along the lines of the aesthetic rules which in this same period influenced the design of the principal temples – albeit in a much more complex fashion, of course. Owing to the lack of other hard data, our speculations must end here. There is absolutely no evidence to facilitate any judgments about far more important features, namely the situation and pattern of the public zones and hence their links with the overall distributive scheme outlined above. Consequently, any notion of the relationship between Thurii's urban blueprint and the modern planning taking place in the Greek homeland (and hence on the Hippodamian system) is bound to remain pure guesswork.

As regards the innovation described above, Thurii is not the only example. A few years later, in 440–430 B.C., it seems that in Tarentum, the only *polis* actually flourishing during the second half of the fifth century, a new and very wide scale reorganization of the urban fabric was brought into play. In the third quarter of the fifth century a new street system was introduced in the wide expanse circumscribed by the defensive walls, and with the streets a new pattern of *insulae*, comprising a remarkable close-knit reticular system within a set of large hierarchical *plateiai*.

Recently, E. Lippolis has put forward a new hypothesis, largely based on the monuments of the later Roman period (much like the situation in Naples), by which there was a notably differentiated arrangement of the public areas: while the old city clustered on the tip of the western peninsula was treated increasingly as an acropolis with its imposing monuments, the "new" town was endowed with more than one specific public area, partly located in the heart of the new street grid (i.e., residential grid) and partly on the border near the sea, perhaps coinciding with an undeveloped zone that had been assigned to public functions since the Archaic period.

A particularly significant example of this new system of spatial subdivision could be expected from a later colony, Heraclea, founded jointly as a subcolony on the site of the destroyed *polis* of Siris by colonists from Tarentum and Thurii around 433 B.C.; the urban fabric of Heraclea developed particularly in the course of the third century. Although confirmation is still awaited from the excavations, the new settlement on the southern plain, with its rigorously straight defensive walls arranged at right-angles, seems to comply abundantly with the new planning rule. Aerial surveys have shown up the pattern of distribution – in all probability built with a system of streets and housing blocks – based on a strict network of units (measuring 55 by 175 meters). This system seems, furthermore, to have influenced the organization of the flat terrain surrounding the city walls).

The new urban scheme on the long, narrow hillside to the south (Collina del Castello) on which the earlier settlement stood has been investigated in greater depth through the excavation of two of the residential quarters. Given the geography, with its long and narrow elevation, the urban pattern hinges on a central *plateia* (10 meters in breadth) that follows the gradient with two slight changes in direc-

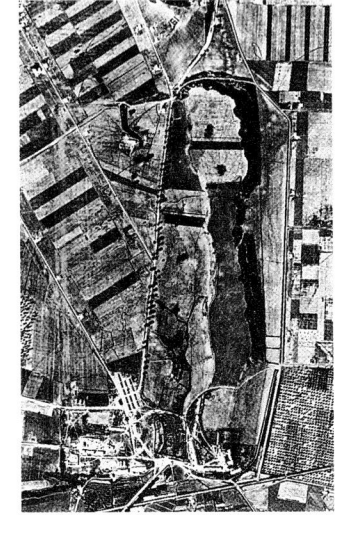

Aerial view of Heraclea

The Pink Gateway
at Elea (Velia)
seen from the south

tion; the *stenopoi* are laid orthogonally to this at a distance averaging 41 meters (creating blocks 35.8–36.8 meters wide, with the *stenopoi* around 4.8 meters wide).

Some scholars have interpreted the slight irregularities of the pattern (which could have been remedied without any great difficulty) as the outcome of adapting the scheme to accommodate surviving features of the Archaic *polis*. Excavation work on the Collina del Castello has in fact brought to light evidence of a certain continuity of living activities, even after the destruction of Siris and up until the foundation of the new settlement.

In the valley between the two hills there seems to have been an area marked off for public activities (apparently from the Archaic period onward), with an emphasis on religious practices. The whereabouts of the *agora* is still being debated: there are good reasons for locating the site in the ample clearing on the Castello hillside; alternatively, another space on the southern hill seems to have been omitted from the zoning scheme. Lastly, the easternmost tip of the bluff to the north was quite possibly the site of the acropolis. Also to be taken into account are the terraces built into the steep inclines facing the central valley; these were created to accommodate urban features linking the hills to the valley, and evince an overall pattern of a more complex and differentiated nature.

These are indications of a certain sensibility for the dramatic effects of landscape and setting, a characteristic of the more evolved Hellenistic brand of urban planning. The only case, however, in which this concept has been undeniably applied in the Greek cities on the mainland is Elea. Recent archaeological fieldwork has revealed that the acropolis hill appears to have been reworked in the Late Hellenistic period with ample terraces endowed with *stoai* and a theater; everything culminates in a peripteral temple in accomplished Ionic style. A better-known feature is the slightly curved avenue that affords spectacular linkage between the complex harbor facilities and the monumental Porta Rosa, the renowned road linking the two main urban neighborhoods across the crest of the acropolis. This is the most extensive and successful realization of modern urban planning in the West, whose only parallels in Asia Minor are Pergamum and the like.

The later development and, in some respects, consolidation of this well-ordered and deliberately planned vision of the urban fabric, laid out on major thoroughfares that determine the building pattern, can be observed more clearly in some recently investigated cases, e.g., Laos, one of Sybaris' subcolonies, completely overrun by Lucanians and rebuilt in the second half of the fourth century. Formally speaking, the town's layout evidently follows the Greek principles of regular distribution with a large *plateia* running north–south (ca. 13.5 meters wide) intersected every 96 meters with an east–west street around 5 meters wide; however, the domestic structures built in the grid so formed consists of very large houses (700–800 sq.m) with rooms and service areas arranged around a spacious inner court. This fact is of special interest because it enables us to observe the adaptation of the Greek urban form to the social structures of the Lucanian township, whose society pivoted on extensive family groups.

In the final analysis, the transformation in the Roman age of the surviving *poleis* in Magna Graecia took place largely within the framework of the existing urban scheme. This is observable in the cases of present-day Naples and Taranto, and is confirmed by excavations at Thurii-Copiae. The only extensively investigated colonial *polis* remains Paestum founded in 273 B.C., which enables us to assess the way and extent to which the Romans intervened with the original Greek-Lucanian fabric. The Romans in fact conserved – or even restored – the ancient Greek temples and adopted the basic grid based on the *strigae* in the rebuilding of the residential quarters (and perhaps in the enlargement schemes in the east section of town). What they did change, however, and radically, were the structures in the public area – the forum and all the political and economic buildings, the new places of worship for their own deities, and the amphitheater – in order to adapt the town to the needs of the new civic structure, following the model established by Rome itself.

Bibliograhy
On the Greek *polis*: E. Lepore, in *Modelli di città*, 1987, pp. 87-108 on the colonial city, idem, 1989; *La cité...*, in *Opus* VI-VIII, 1987-89; summoning up the research on the colonial city of Magna Graecia: D. Mertens, in *Megale Hellas*, Atti Taranto, XXI, 1981, 1982, pp. 97-141; E. Greco, *Atti Taranto*, XXVIII, 1988, 1990, pp. 305-328.
Histories of Greek urban planning: R. Martin, II, 1974; E. Greco, M. Torelli, 1983; W. Hoepfner-E.L. Schwandner, 1986.
On the relation between mother cities and colonies in terms of urban planning: R. Martin, in *Architecture...*, Ecole Française de Rome 1983, pp. 9-41; *Apoikia* (*AION ArchStAnt* N.S. 1, 1994).
On Megara Hyblea as a fossil guide to Greek urban planning in the Archaic period G. Vallet, F. Villard, P. Auberson, 1976.
On Tarentum: see E. Greco, in *AION ArchStAnt* 1981, pp. 139-157.
On Sybaris: E. Greco, in *Atti Taranto* XXXII, 1992, pp. 459-485.
On Metapontum: D. Mertens, *Metaponto. Il teatro-ekklesiasterion*, in *Bd'A* 16 (1982), pp. 1-60; idem, *Metapont...*, in *AA* 1985, pp. 645-671; on Poseidonia: E. Greco, D. Theodorescu, 1983; E. Greco, D. Theodorescu, in *Poseidonia-Paestum*, Atti del XXVII Conv. di Taranto, 1987, 1992, pp. 471-540.
On *Dios agora* a Metaponto: see D. Adamesteanu, in *ParPass* 1979, pp. 296-312; *SEG* XXIX 1979, 955; F.G. Lo Porto, in "Xenia" XVI, 1988, p. 15.
R. Martin's important article is in *Problèmes...*, 1973, pp. 97-112.
On Neapolis: E. Greco, in *Neapolis, Atti del XXV Conv. di Taranto 1985*, 1986, pp. 187-219.
On Thurii: O. Belvedere, in *Xenia*, 14, 1987, pp. 11 ff.; E. Greco, *Atti del Convegno di Acquasparta 1994*, forthcoming.
On Heraclea: L. Giardino, 1992, pp. 136 ff.
On Laos: E. Greco, S. Luppino, A. Schnapp, 1989.
Some questions on urban planning transformations, in Roman times: I. Baldassarre, in *Neapolis, Atti Taranto* XXV, 1985, 1986, pp. 221-231; E. Greco, D. Theodorescu, 1987.

Introduction

In order to delve significantly deeper into the world of colonial urban planning than is currently allowed by the available archaeological evidence, we would do well to direct our attention toward a recent study by one of the more renowned specialists on the subject, a historian who has for many years concerned himself with the long-term and perpetually complex issue of the Greek city. I refer to the fundamental opus by M. B. Sakellariou, *The Polis-state. Definition and Origin* (Athens, 1989) which, though markedly classificatory, offers far more insights than its title suggests, and makes it finally possible to disentangle the innumerable meanings and interpretations that the antique sources and modern scholars have proposed for the word *polis*. In the course of his monumental study, Sakellariou delineates the distinctions between *polis* as "settlement" (this being the true sense of the word *polis*, through often erroneously translated as "city"), *polis* as "community" (related to *settlement*) and *polis* as state (related in turn to *community*); the author also includes a great deal of information on the colonization of the western Mediterranean basin in the eighth–seventh centuries B.C. But it is the overall picture that induces us to consider the phenomenon of colonial urban planning from a point of view that has not been fully explored until now. From the mid-eighth to the mid-seventh century B.C. droves of Greek peoples disembarked upon the shores of southern Italy and Sicily from widely disparate parts of the Greek world (Euboea, Cyclades Megaris, Corinthia, Achaea, Western Locris, Crete, Rhodes), peoples that can be grouped into pre-political *ethne* (such as the Achaean colonists) or confederations of "parties" μέρη (*mere*), as yet not grouped into *poleis* or city-states (the Megarians), or as having just formed a *polis*, such as Corinth (the Syracusans).

So much for the geopolitical aspect of the migration; as for the matter of urban structure, we must remind ourselves that at the moment when the first colonists left Greece around 750 B.C. there did not exist as yet in any of their respective homelands a coherent, consistent model upon which they might have based the urban and political organization of the sibling colonies. Not even Corinth, despite its rudimentary state structures, had attained in the mid-eighth century B.C. a unified settlement pattern, its own settlement being constituted at the time by a group of geographically proximate villages the κατὰ κύμας οἰκεῖν (*katá kōmos oikeín*), which Thucydides, III. 94. 4, held to be a true manifestation of *ethnos*).

Generally speaking, despite their being demographically sizable and ecnomically prosperous (thanks to agricultural activity and a well-developed maritime trade), none of the towns of Mainland Greece from which the first colonists set sail for the West in the second half of the eighth century had achieved a proper state structure in political terms, nor had they really even begun to form a community identity in urban planning terms.

The ships of the first colonists were open vessels, that is, uncovered or partly covered by a bridge; they carried from thirty to fifty oarsmen (triconters and pentaconters) with a shallow draught that made them unsuitable for transporting heavy cargo. These early colonists, prompted to leave the homeland by the natural urge to improve their lot – and in some cases by social upheavals in zones where the rise to power of certain *gene* entailed the disenfranchisement of other tribal groups – were certainly not all propertyless. They converged from many different areas of Mainland Greece, each group led by an *oikistes* or founder. The *oikistes* made it his business to know where they were going. He was a person who possessed the knowledge and the means to organize such an expedition, and the authority to keep his charges under control, and not least the charisma to spark the neo-colonists' fantasies of conquest on foreign soil. Irrespective of whether these men were of aristocratic extraction (and hence the only members of the upper classes present among the expedition), or small landowners, or propertyless tenants, once aboard their westbound ships they were on their own, totally independent of their birthplaces insofar as they left everything behind. And it was in this moment of transition, during the voyage itself, that a state of socioeconomic equality ἰσο μοιρία (*isomoiria*) among the voyagers was attained. Even the groups with some prior experience of state structure (as pointed out by Sakellariou) developed into classless communities in which each individual had the right to his own slice of the conquered territory κλῆρος (*kléros*), regardless of whether he was formerly a landowner or a humble tenant. The new arrivals to southern Italy and Sicily could not really have done other than form such prepolitical societies, naturally geared to the distribution of land, to the exploitation of resources, and to self-defense. Theirs were societies as yet without state structures, which only the eventual emergence of class distinctions would necessitate.

The conditions that gave rise to these colonial *poleis* (meaning at first "inhabited centers," later "states") were therefore quite different from the formative processes of the "evolutionary type" (Martin) which lay behind the *poleis*-settlements in Mainland Greece, such that the establishment of the *polis*-state occurred more rapidly in the colonies than in the motherland. The continuous influx of souls to the new colonies ἔποικοι (*épaikai*) and the progressive assimilation or subjugation of the indigenous populations into servitude were fundamental factors in the development of the colonies, the communities of which became, over a relatively long period of time, increasingly characterized by a minority of large landowners who controlled ever greater numbers of tenants and slaves, while the small landowners evolved into a sort of intermediate class (Sakellariou). These are among the premonitory signals that herald the formation of the *polis*-state in the colonial territories, a process in which the key role would be played by the *polis*-settlement, from which both the state and all the communities contained therein would derive their name.

Insomuch as urbanization did not necessarily implicate the creation of the *polis*-state (and indeed there were *poleis*-states such as Sparta that never recognized citizenship), in the colonies of Magna Graecia and Sicily, the creation of the *polis*-state with an advanced political organization and a high degree of cohesion among the various groups of the community seems to have gone hand in hand with the creation of urban centers made up of a regular building fabric, in which not only the divisions between public and private spaces were made clear, but where residential, communal, and monumental zones were harmonically interwoven according to a precise global plan and an articulate program of community life.

By way of demonstration, the best-known examples – Megara Hyblaea, Selinus, and Himera – show that after only two or three generations the constitution of the state effectively coincided with the actualization of the true "city" (here, Sakellariou rightly rejects the equation of the *polis* with the city, and the *polis*-state with the European city-state, while I trust "city" to be the best term for rendering the concept of the mature colonial settlement).

Archaeologists have succeeded in identifying these first two phases in the evolution of the colonial cities – in the long run the most important phases – namely the original colonial settlement layouts and the subsequent "city" layouts of the new colonial states. Logically, these are expressions of two entirely different situations. The first was the work of the proto-colonists, who brought with them a minimal political and urban experience, members of a community composed of familial clans, completely independent of the homeland. Theirs was a new community that was largely egalitarian, dynamic, unburdened by preconceptions, though nonetheless subject to undeniable necessities. Among such necessities, one was to become immediately self-sufficient in terms of food supplies and military strength and another one to resist (we should recall that, for better of for worse, territories had to be conquered and thereafter defended) against the indigenous populations, although these were impeded by somewhat backward combat techniques and a less-evolved material culture.

The second, on the other hand, seems to have been the fruit of the conquests and battles which, in the space of two or three generations, had profoundly changed not only the makeup of the original contingent, but also the entire social structure of the community that emerged. The product of the new shared wealth was put to use to establish a full-fledged city within the bounds of the new territorial organism. Together with the defensive, religious, and administrative functions of the original settlement, this new focus became a hub of the trade operations, crafts production, and especially the cultural activities (*paideia* of the city), becoming more outspokenly political with each new articulation, with the scope of achieving equality as a form of civil justice, the ἰσονομία (*isonomía*).

The upshot was a new "geometry of organized space" (Lepore) that was probably applied with the consensus of the community as a whole, though fostered by the tax-paying classes which successfully asserted themselves, a stratum of society which in Sicily in the seventh and early sixth centuries emerged as the landowning aristocracy, partly metamorphosing into the wealthy merchant class, and thereafter into the tyrannical dynasties.

After this somewhat general perspective of the situation, we can now proceed to examine some of the more significant *poleis*-cities of Greek Sicily, bearing in mind that it is impossible to recount the history of "colonial planning, but rather of the many specific urban patterns of the colonies, for the adaptability and flexibility of the environmental conditions (from the topography to the level of political maturity) which each one possessed" (Lepore).

Despite this, some constants can be detected in the various proto-colonial settlements along the Sicilian seaboard.

The new arrivals were keen to occupy the fertile, well-irrigated terrain along the coast, land that would amply fulfill their future needs (see Aeschylus, *Promethens* 371 (Loeb) "...the level fields of Sicily, land of four fruits"). Thus they dedicated them to their patron deities, the protectors of their undertaking, thereby construing a link with religious practices in the homeland communities that they had abandoned forever. It goes without saying that territory of this kind, often of considerable extension, would not have interfered with the equable apportionment of the land and the cultivation of the fields, which was the

Urban Planning in Ancient Sicily

fundamental reason for having set off to found a colony in the first place. Other spaces were assigned to community activities in the heart of the zone of cultivable groundplots upon which each colonist would build a home for himself and his family. This central public space was the *agora*, a place for community gatherings and for exercising the trade activity of the individual or the community, and the place in which the *heroon* or shrine to the *oikistes* was often later erected. Further over the colonists built the necropolis on terrain that was considered not immediately essential for the burgeoning colony's survival. The protection of the new community involved establishing defense lines at some distance from the built-up area, albeit affording suitable natural defense or easily fortifiable features; the Greeks are known for their accomplished ability to adapt their needs to the geography of the land. The original settlements were generally installed on promontories or headlands that could be easily defended, with ample plains behind them protected by mountainous rises; in other cases they settled on flat countryside, though always on

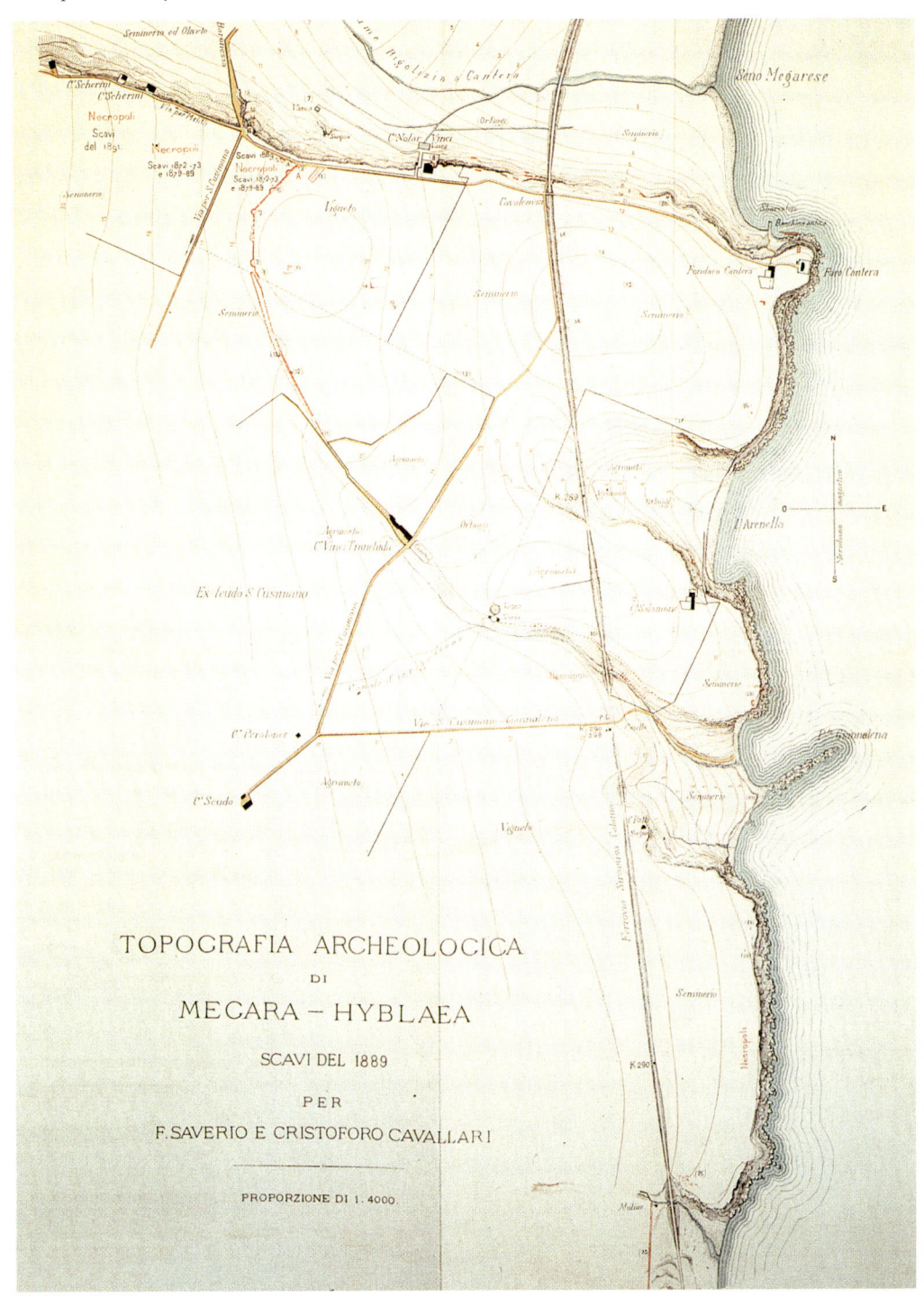

Map of Megara Hyblaea with the sites of recent excavations in the reconstruction by Francesco Saverio and Cristoforo Cavallari, 1889

rivers, which offered a natural line of defense and a constant source of fresh water, together with a navigable route to the interior and a workable river port.

The area occupied from the outset was always vast, sometimes covering over one hundred hectares. This was approximately the area that the second and third generations of colonists would mark out with an orthogonal grid of avenues and smaller streets, with housing plots of perfectly equal width.

From the Foundations to the City

Megara Hyblaea

Thanks to the fieldwork carried out by the École Française, Rome, the port town of Megara Hyblaea on the Augusta bay provides an excellent picture of the makeup of the typical Siceliot colony.

The site lies on a level plateau, well supplied with water, overlooking the sea toward the east, and bordered to the north by the Cantera River and west and south by a gushing stream, the San Cusmano, whose course fostered the development of the settlement into an arc of a circle. The unoccupied plain was given over to the incoming Greeks by the Sicel king, Hyblon, and is divided into two parts by a deep glade leading down to the sea, and must have had a somewhat thin surface stratum of soil. This notwithstanding, the land was suitable for agriculture, both extensive and intensive (grape vines perhaps?), as attested by the constant farming vocation of the Archaic city and its layout, concealed beneath the layers of the Hellenistic city, which also seems to have had close bonds with the land, as testified by the farmsteads of the second and first centuries B.C. and those of the Late Imperial period. This area of around sixty hectares received the survivors gathered under the *oikistes* Lamis, the intrepid kinsman of the mainland Megarians, who were among the first to set forth to conquer the lands of the West. These pioneers actually arrived shortly after the mid-eighth century with Theokles, who, buffeted by the strong Sicilian coastal winds, revealed the presence of the island to the mainland Greeks and who, according to Ephorus, after failing to galvanize his Athenian kinsmen into action, soon after his return home organized an expedition party made up of Euboeans, Ionians, and Dorians – the bulk of whom were more specifically of Megarian stock. Thus united they set sail for Sicily. It is unsure whether Lamis traveled together with Theokles or, as Thucydides claims, came with a different group of Megarians a few years later; the fact is that the founders of Megara Hyblaea made more traversals across the waters of the Mediterranean than other colonists of the West. Their numbers were such, however, that they were in no position to impose themselves on the natives; it is unlikely, moreover, that these adventurous travelers had time to devise a form of township different from the structure with which they were acquainted in the homeland. Once they reached Sicily and finally took possession of the land of their dreams, the Megarians were only in a position to section up the land into farm-type

Megara Hyblaea: the area of the *agora* toward mid 6th cent. B.C.
red: 8th cent. houses

Megara Hyblaea
Plan and view
axonometric
reconstruction
of the 8th-6th cent. houses

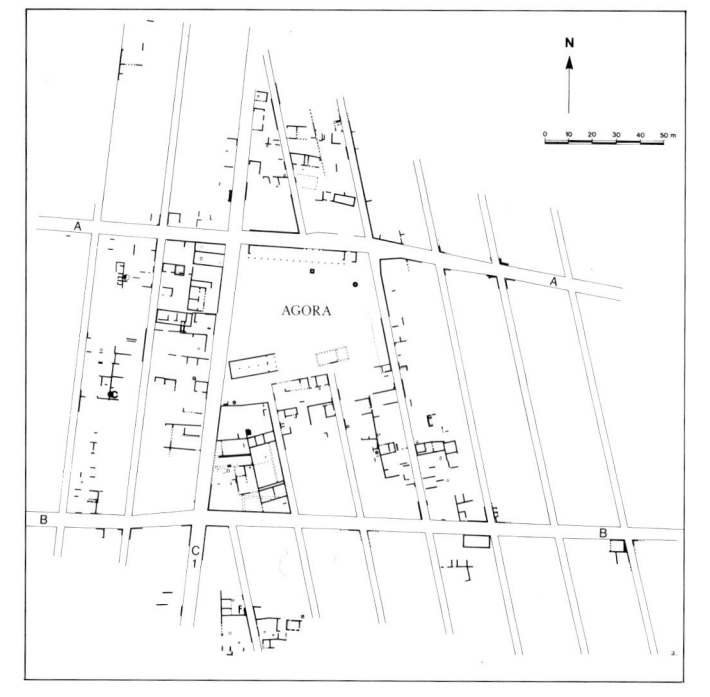

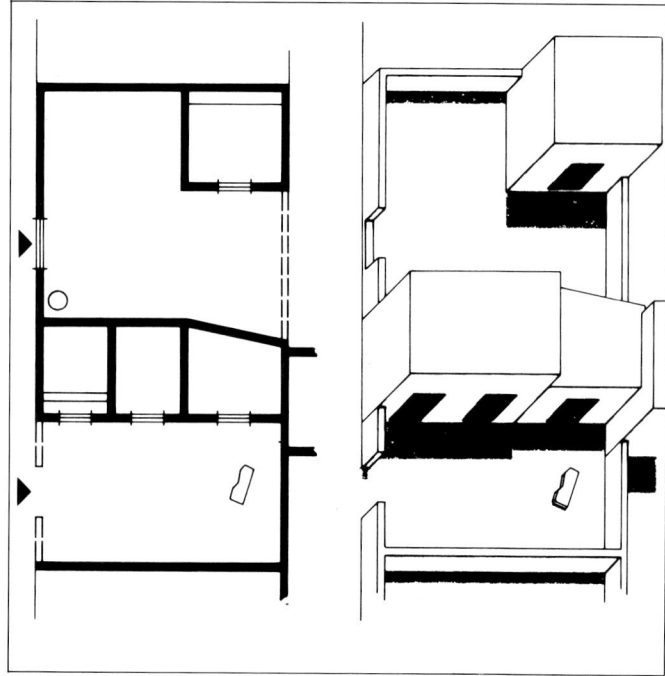

lots. Despite this, they staked out a special area to implant an entirely new urban nucleus with a regular layout: a flat piece of land free of previous settlement structures, reasonable relations with the local Sicel population occupying the upland that blocked the coastal plain two kilometers away, and with the Chalcidians of Leontini to the north, and the Corinthians at Syracuse to the south. The latter turned out to be dangerous neighbors, but at the end of the eighth century they posed no immediate threat. The Megarians, therefore, who were hardly numerous (or there would be no reason for the lack of eighth-century tombs in an area that has been so thoroughly explored by archaeologists), settled on both ends of the plateau, north and south of the central depression. Such a strategy shows the settlers to be judicious about establishing a defensible position between the Ionio, the Cantera (the ancient Alabon), and the San Cusmano, and that they did not proceed to construct an organism that could be defined as "urban." The novelty of this enterprise – which derives from the very essence of the colonization in question – is that the immediate aim of the first Megarians seems to have been to occupy the land and share it out equably, each unit large enough to offer adequate sustenance for a family. As for the question of just how much land was allotted to each, and in what way it was divided up, the archaeologists G. Vallet, F. Villard, and P. Auberson have attempted exhaustive replies with each successive update of their fieldwork. With irreproachable methodology they have shown that in the two nuclei in the excavated areas in the eastern section of the north plateau, and in the three that have turned up in the remaining north and south plateaus, there appears to have been five neighborhoods that reflect "de l'origine ou du statut" of the various colonial groupings, and above all the outcome of the five villages that subsequently amalgamated to form Megara of Greece. The archaeologists have shown that the dimensional unit used to sharing out the terrain was a groundplot of 12 meters (i.e., 40 feet of 0.3 meters) and that the *insulae* took up two groundplots, a shared alley (later a wall) of 0.45 meters wide together with the borders (these too became walls at a later date) along the streets, which were set parallel to each other. They have shown that from the very outset the colonists envisaged a multiple street grid – the two main causeways running east–west (i.e., from shore to plateau) and the minor streets running north–south, which can be defined as "farm to farm" roads – excepting street C1, which formed the urban axis for the road to Leontini in one direction, and to Syracuse in the other; the program also included the vast undeveloped space for community gatherings toward the north where the two excavated zoned areas meet, one lying skewed twenty-one degrees to the other.
In other words, from the moment the Megarians took possession of the land they staked out the areas that were to remain common ground, applying a simple and ostensible geometrical structure to their ideal of egalitarian possession of the land, and likewise to the houses they built upon the plots. These were of uniform design, all having a single squarish room measuring between 15 to 25 square meters. Each dwelling faced south onto a space which – to apply to the eighth century the known perimeter of groundplots datable to the mid-seventh century – must have had an average surface area of 120 square meters. The French team, whose book *Megara Hyblaea* showed them still favorable to the idea of the *oikopeda* or developable urban plot (and hence part of a specifically urban grid), later began to sanction an interpretation of the excavated units as "agrarian." Basically, we know nothing of the lengthwise division of these twelve-meter-wide groundplots; as noted above, by forecasting from data regarding the colony's foundation, Vallet has hypothesized that in two or three generations there was an urban area that formed the basis of the γεώπεδον (*gheopodon*), that is, the city garden or, put another way, a small rural house with kitchen garden, in contrast with the *kleros*, or authentic agricultural allotment, that first provided a means of sustenance and goods for exchange, and then a source of wealth.
The French team's reconstruction is undoubtedly reliable ("il ne s'est pas agi, au départ, d'un phénomène urbain, mais d'un phénomène de répartition de lots e de division des éspaces"), and offers the clearest picture yet of the vital chapter of establishing the first settlement, though some of the data, to my mind, are liable to a different interpretation.
It should be noted that the section explored by Vallet and Villard covers an area of three hectares out of sixty-one, a fact that the excavators indeed are anxious to point out. This means, furthermore, that the orientation of the blocks of the groundplots (civil neighborhoods) can be not only those five so far recognized or glimpsed; it is moreover prudent to resist the temptation – at least for the time being – to link this figure five with the original villages in the homeland region of Megaris, from which Greek Megara was formed by the process of *synoikismos*. The main goal of the *oikistes*, as Vallet has rightly pointed out, was to create a relative unity, a certain cohesion among the different kin groups that followed him in the conquest not only of new lands but also of a new community identity. Naturally, this does not exclude that the different orientations of the groundplots could reflect some kind of attribution to a particular *phratria*, or a specific *genos*.

Whatever the case, there is no doubt that where two groups of these lots met, each one 25 meters wide, and each one more or less parallel to the sea, an area of 2,370 square meters was left free; this was doubtless for public use, given that the only remains unearthed in such areas dating to before the mid-seventh century are two underground pits for storing grain – a cogent testimony to the existence of primitive community structures. The fact that in the seventh century this particular area became the *agora*, with temples for the gods and *stoai* for mortals, shows that it was considered the most central part of the zoning program, set in the very heart of the city's two main causeways. It is also likely that similar clearings were created where the different orientations of the single plots had given rise to odd patches of irregular-shaped land, which were common property before the land parceling took place, before becoming ideal points in which to install places for worship or for public gatherings of the various *phratriai* and *gene*. I therefore agree with my French colleagues that the initial scheme of land parceling included sizable vacant lots which, like single γεώπεδα (*ghheopeda*) would later be filled by constructions when, three generations later, Megara seems to have reached the size of a *polis*-state with sufficient affluence and population to prompt the creation of a subcolony to alleviate the territorial needs, namely Selinus. What I cannot agree with is the suggestion that the pattern of land division was at the time of foundation a form of "urban" zoning scheme (according to Vallet, in fact, we will never know exactly what the first *kleroi*, the earliest farm lots in Megara were actually like).

Given that the presence of remains attributable to the first colonists can be traced in the sixth-century walls, enclosing an area of sixty hectares, if we accept the hypothesis of a garden-city (or, better, a farm-plot-city) as suggested by the French team, with plots of 120 meters square each, this would mean that the first settlement consisted of 5,000 plots, even assigning forty percent of the space to religious and community facilities (the *agora* actually occupies a mere ten percent of the area excavated so far, and the streets take up only a little more room). Three thousand plots means at least the same number of dwellings, and at least 5,000–6,000 inhabitants, a substantial number, and too high not only for Lamis and his fellow adventurers, but even for the first generation of colonists. This is why I reckon it is acceptable to suggest a variant (albeit with caution) by which the eighth-century houses unearthed near the tract of land which was undoubtedly the most important community area from the start could be part of the one of the housing nuclei that coagulated around the deliberately vacant areas where the bands of *kleroi* met. This would soon have led to the creation in the new homeland of the well-known pattern of clusters of dwellings in which those who were at the general service of the community as a whole resided – the craftsmen, whose houses were usually grouped near the *agora* itself. In other words, we can safely affirm that the archaeological digs at Megara Hyblaea carried out by Vallet and Villard afford a glimpse of the original farmland parceling scheme of the occupied area, and that, except for the clustering of houses around the community spaces, the groundplots in the eighth century must have been larger than the supposed 120-150 square meters noted for the civil dwelling units midway through the seventh century and later. It is unlikely that the sixty-one hectares of the area that was subsequently built up were enough on their own to provided adequate sustenance for the first settlers. The minimum for three people has been calculated at 2.3 hectares; whereas fifty *pletri* (4.4 hectares) seem to have been the minimum allotment for the *kleroi* of the fifth and fourth centuries B.C.; we must moreover suppose that the proto-colonists were able to immediately take possession of more far-flung plots of land as well, in proportion to their number, of which we know nothing as yet. In this framework it seems viable that the "urban lots" (the γεώπεδα, *ghheopeda*) were educed directly from the original *kleroi* aligned along the main urban causeways, which were considered essential for communication with the land outside the zoning area, and doubtless provided the original blueprint the settlers applied to their new land. This predetermination of the main thoroughfares, the public spaces, and the careful parceling of the land, was new to the Greek world, and in the course of a few generations it came to represent the "voluntary" type of city so well outlined by Martin.

It would, of course, be expecting too much of the *oikistes* Lamis and his companions to have also made the plan for Megara symmetrical, maintaining a parallel and orthogonal grid, or to have created a conceptually "urban" fabric; this lay outside their experience. However, the first major step was already accomplished, namely that an agrarian type of colonization required the geometrical parceling of the land, a factor that would never have reached Mainland Greece if it had not been for the colonies, as I pointed out some time ago in conclusion of a reassessment of the available data on the urban planning to the *poleis* of Magna Graecia and Sicily. Today the model posed by Megara Hyblaea can only be a point of departure to delineate the origin and development of the urban apparatus of the Siceliot *poleis*, but it should be noted that the moment we move slightly to the south to the same eastern coast of the island, to Syracuse, the situation is quite different.

Urban Planning in Ancient Sicily

Aerial view of Syracuse from the south
showing the urban grid
that still follows the main axis
of the Greek city

Aerial view of Syracuse
with the medieval layout
of Ortygia that repeats the plan
of the Archaic Greek city

Plan of Syracuse showing the ancient
extraurban axis
one of the main arteries
of the Hellenistic quarters
on the mainland

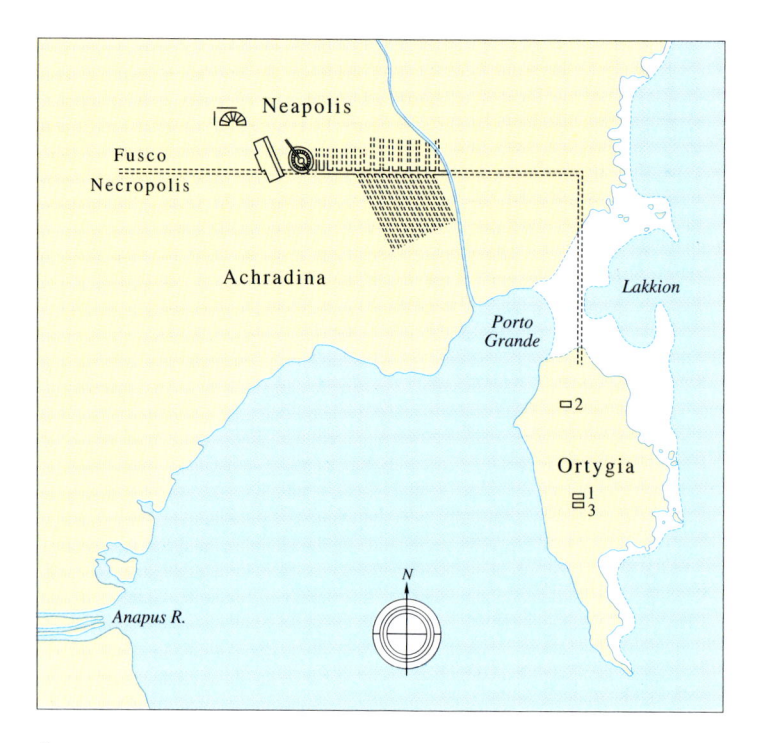

Syracuse

The pattern underlying the urban fabric of the most ancient Syracuse is a *kata komas* system, i.e., an agglomeration of villages; though not exactly a Panhellenic colony (Manni), Syracuse undoubtedly enjoyed a larger population than nearby Megara Hyblaea. Here the colonists were guided to their destination by Archias, probably a member of the powerful Bacchiad family of Corinth. The colonists settled on the small island of Ortygia and along the mainland alongside, spreading as far as little more than half a kilometer from the Fusco necropolis, the oldest of Syracuse's burial grounds, which was deliberately set outside the original settlement area. The arrival of the Greeks at Ortygia was traumatic for the indigenous inhabitants, the Sicels, who were either slain or expelled from the territory forthwith. Greek expansion along the mainland bridgehead toward the south was rapid indeed, and was spurred by a growing population swelled by continuous waves of new arrivals. But, as in the previous case, the first settlers to reach Syracuse cannot have numbered that many to have occupied the over one hundred hectares of urban fabric offered by Ortygia and mainland Achradina, where evidence of the first Greek occupation has come to light.

It therefore looks likely that the dwellings unearthed by Pelagatti in the area later occupied by the Ionic temple and in the Prefettura area were part of one of the nuclei in which the first settlers installed themselves; these nuclei, according to the most recent discoveries (the Voza digs, south of Via del Consiglio Regionale), seem to have been of considerable extension, and nonetheless closer together than those at Megara Hyblaea. As Orsi so rightly noted, from the start the backbone ridge of Ortygia offered the most natural axis traversing the entire islet north to south, linking up these nuclei with those of the mainland (Achradina); the same basic logic was followed at Tarentum, Gela, and Selinus.

Perpendicular to this backbone ran a set of *stenopoi*, or transverse streets, some of which may also have been natural pathways; witness *stenopos* 13, the only street excavated for a considerable stretch, on which are aligned the earliest houses of the beaten street datable to 700 B.C. These east–west streets ended up becoming the lesser axes of the city (varying between 2.5 and 3 meters wide), which seems to have been organized in parallel *insulae* of twenty-three to twenty-five meters wide. The vacant space for gatherings, the oldest *agora* of the island, according to a brilliant and highly credible suggestion of Pelagatti (which to my mind is endorsed by the presence nearby of early seventh-century pottery workshops), must have occupied the area behind the unfinished Ionic temple and the neighboring Temple of the Deinomenids, the *Athenaion*, sloping down toward the sea from today's Piazza Duomo.

On the main axis – which S. L. Agnello has correctly identified with the current route of Via Dione and Via Roma – lie the sacred *temene* first of the *Apollonion* and then of the *Athenaion*, areas dedicated to the tutelary deities of the colonists (if not from the start, from a very early stage certainly).

The eighth-century houses disclosed during the present excavation work are similar in design to those of Megara Hyblaea. Once again they are small one-room dwellings (ten-fifteen square meters) on a square

Syracuse
the street scheme of ancient Ortygia
— ancient streets
- - - probable ancient streets
— medieval streets
over ancient streets

1. Ionic temple - *Artemision*
2. *Apollonion*
3. *Athenaion*
4. Excavations at the prefecture
5. Sperduta
6. Wells near via Gelone (today via Veneto)
7. Banco di Sicilia, traces of northsouth artery
8. Cassa di Risparmio V.E., *Koreion*
9. Piazza S. Giuseppe, *temenos*
10. Credito Italiano
11. City walls and gate
12. Graziella
13. Giudecca
14. Old archaeological museum

A. Via Resa libera
B. Via Mirabella
C. Via Maestranza
D. Ronco I alla Giudecca
E. Via Dione and, continuing south, Via Roma
F. Via Cavour

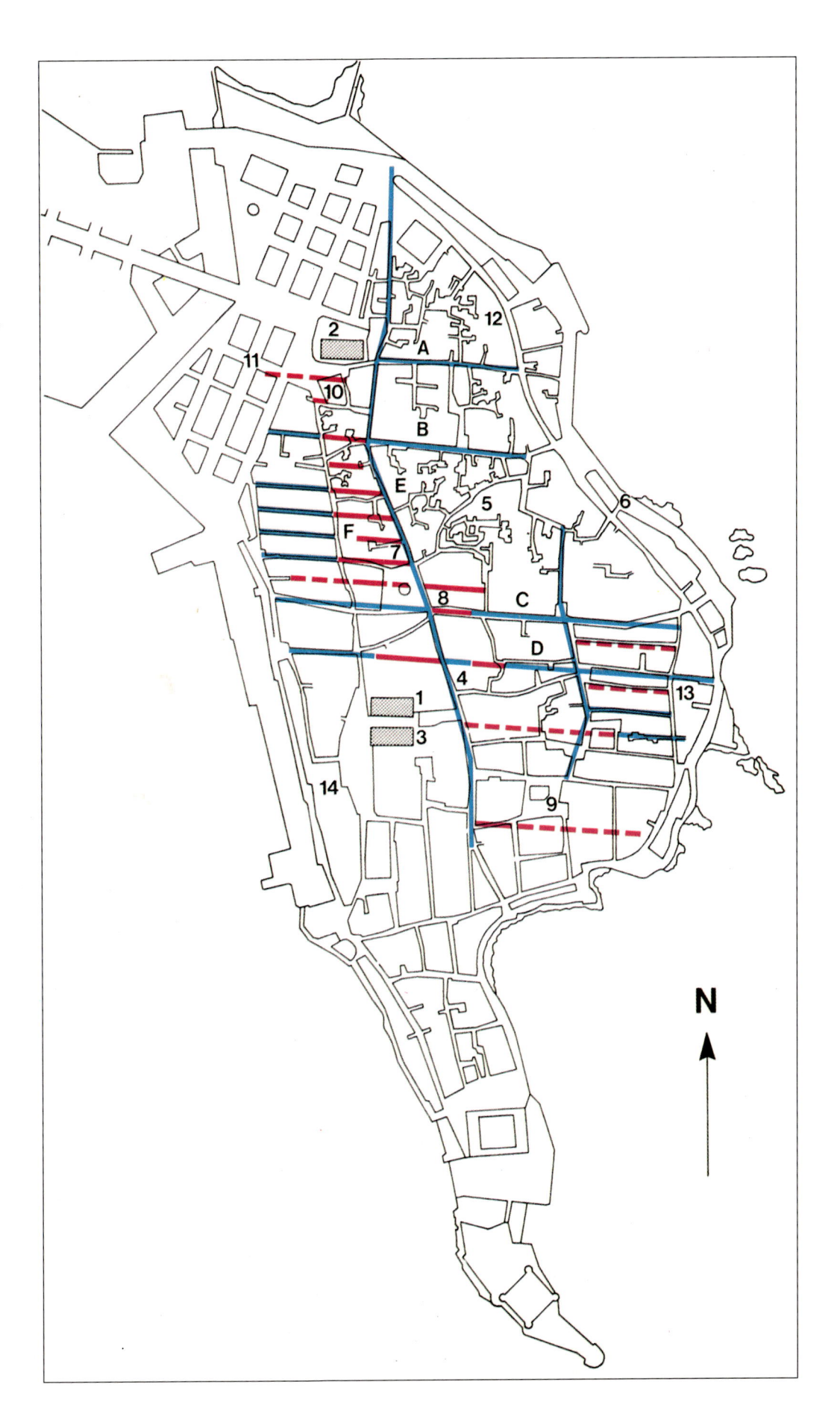

or oblong plan, the only layout adopted throughout the Siceliot colonies, linked perhaps to the growing practice of using mudbrick as the main building material for the walls, laid on a stone foundation of small and medium dimensions. The dwellings are open on the south side to a small yard, and line the streets that ran from the spinal ridge west to today's Porto Grande; like those of Megara, they seem to be increased in size by duplication. They ran along an abundant water table, attested by numerous wells; in fact these wells and the natural pathways crisscrossing Ortygia probably determined the original sites of the dwelling nuclei on the islet, where, in the limited patches of excavated ground, the individual houses are noticeably closer together, more clustered than those of Megara Hyblaea, with their surrounding "kitchen gardens." In my opinion, as in Megara, here the empty spaces between the living nuclei (the forthcoming residential quarters) were divided up into garden plots from the start, as a means of nourishing the family, though this situation lasted only for the first few decades of the life of the budding colony, which was in rapid transformation. In conclusion, the archaeological evidence at Megara and Syracuse seems to suggest that the birth of the Siceliot towns did not immediately trigger a new type of urban scheme with respect to that in Mainland Greece, which excavations and written sources testify were still well-articulated κατὰ κώμας (*kata komas*), in agglomerates linked by streets which largely followed the natural and most logical routes, and were separated by ample stretches of farmable land.

Moreover, the act of colonization with the conquest of large tracts of territory to be parceled out and organized involved a type of urban program that was unseen in the *metropoleis* of Mainland Greece, which had grown through the natural processes of coagulation and anyway on pre-existing features that seriously conditioned development. In the West this programming affected as much the land to be shared out as cultivable *kleroi*, as the land to be apportioned for residential fabric to be installed near the spaces earmarked for community functions. The constant dilation of the *chora* of the burgeoning colony made it possible to assign more and more *kleroi* in increasingly far-flung places, and to reappropriate those of the original urban fabric, without becoming embroiled in the repeated expropriation of the older housing stock. As for the initial burial grounds, unlike what took place in Pithekoussai (Ischia), there does not seem to have been any real pattern, though they were planned like the areas dedicated to the gods and those reserved for men from the first days of settlement. At Syracuse, and likewise at Megara Hyblaea (albeit with less evidence, as the earliest burials have not yet been detected), from the start the tombs were sited as in the homeland along the streets that led out into the *chora*, and were set up in an area outside the parceled fields upon which the first colonists had settled. At Megara they were sited near the road to Syracuse, south of and outside the southern plain, beyond the San Cusmano; whereas in Syracuse the Fusco necropolis was confined west of the Achradina built-up area on the mainland, agglomerated along the original territorial expansion lines toward the west and south. This placement of the necropolis was carefully deliberated, on a slight rise of barely five meters above the Lysimeleia plain, and easily accessed from Achradina or the sea, and hence by the "islanders" of Ortygia.

If we take account of the extremely early foundation date for Helorus, the stronghold and gateway to the Syracusan *chora* on the south, we must conclude that by the end of the eighth century Syracuse already vaunted a set of consolidated institutions, an efficient organization and network of citizens to sustain such a swift and important acquisition of territory. On the other hand, the presence in excavation layers for the seventh century of Corinthian, Argive, Rhodian, and Etruscan wares, and above all the foundation of Acrae, Casmenae, and Camarina – which assured the mother colony Syracuse at the start of the sixth century if not the possession the supremacy over the whole of southeastern Sicily – attest to the astonishing magnetic power that this ancient Corinthian *apoikia* exercised over the entire Greek world (and not least over the local indigenous population) throughout the seventh century B.C.

Naturally, all this could not remain without repercussions on the city's physical layout. Although we are familiar with a mere handful of sections, there are clues to indicate that on Ortygia as in Achradina – more or less in the areas marked out by Drögenmüller – the original groundplots became authentic dwelling *strigae* along streets which, as elsewhere in the Archaic world, took account of the lie of the terrain, and on Ortygia (a main north–south axis plus the east–west *stenopoi*) as in Achradina, these seem to comply with a farsighted program of expansion.

On the basis of the most recent excavation work, we can affirm that, at least in Achradina in the fourth and third centuries B.C., the layout consisted of a set of northwest–southeast axes whose alignment, to my mind, was derived from a previous street that ran between the Latomia del Paradiso and the Latomia di Santa Venera, where the rock is scored with numerous deep ruts worn by the passage of carts and crossing the Epipolae plateau led directly to the coast, level with today's Scala Greca (the Hexapylon) and thence toward Megara Hyblaea and Leontini.

Syracuse
the ancient street scheme identified in the eastern part of Achradina

There seems to be no doubt that this was the main thoroughfare leading northward out of the city, given the precocious territorial expansion of Syracuse (such a roadway would furthermore justify the orientation of the Altar of Hieron); similarly, the present street grid of modern Syracuse pivots on Corso Gelone, and conserves more or less the same itinerary, having the same objective of providing the swiftest route to the north coast without crossing the plateau bordered on the south by the Latomie dei Cappuccini and on the north by the San Panagia quarry.

If we follow on the map the southward route, it can be reasonably identified with the *via strata et conglareata* (i.e., of crushed brick) of which Orsi found the eastern roadbed in 1908 at the northeast corner of Piazzale Marconi (where "the rotunda preceding the station ... intersects with the carriageway for Catania"), i.e., in the area (on its western border) of the great *agora* which by the seventh century B.C. must have already been the fulcrum of the layout of Achradina.

Orsi's roadbed stands 1.4 meters below the level of the plateau, and as he pointed out in *Notizie Scavi* in 1909, it formed part of that "grandiose paved causeway which (for ca. 15 meters) is still visible today in the Piazza d'Armi, intersecting sharply with Corso Umberto I; it proceeded in a straight line toward the group of suburban monuments of the Amphitheater and the Ara Massima (Altar of Hieron)"; basically it ran northwest, perfectly aligned with the Altar of Hieron, parallel with the streets identified this decade by Voza in the eastern part of the Achradina. This shows that all the streets of Achradina ran for at least 400–500 meters from the *agora*, aligned northwest–southeast, parallel with the main concourse thirteen meters wide and paved with slabs which, starting at the *agora* led off to the opposite coast. Orsi dated this street, which was paved in a particularly durable type of sandstone, to the Roman-Byzantine era; he surmised, however, that at a deeper level the *via conglareata* might feasibly be attributed to the Greeks themselves, given the discovery of tiny shards of Archaic material in the gravel bed in which the heavy slabs of the roadbed were laid, and because of the fact that "it was unlikely that the main causeway leading to the monuments had undergone alterations to its path, only to its structure."

Toward the south, the Achradina *agora* was cut through (or delimited?) by an important east–west artery, which Voza identified in the early 1970s, together with four building phases in which the earliest "directly superimposed on the base rock," upon which the first archaeological layer dates to the last quarter of the eighth century B.C. Vestiges of sixth-century houses, the Hellenistic paving of the *agora*, the artery, and paving beneath the present Corso Umberto were brought to light in the same years.

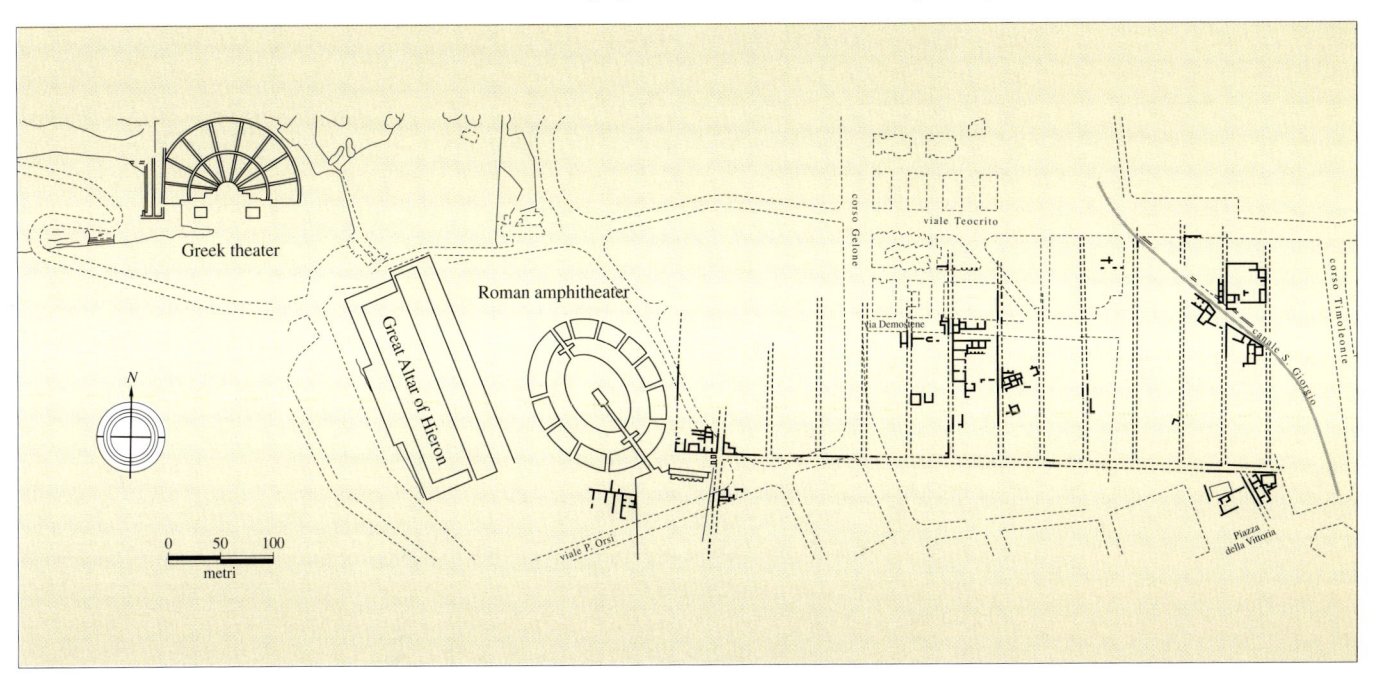

The very early date for the expansion of the Achradina district over the plain, which ascends very gently to the north, is furthermore attested by remains of walling dated in association with potsherds from late eighth–early seventh century B.C. found midway along Corso Gelone, and above all from the necropolises a which, starting from the west from Viale Orsi–Via Cavallari (with tombs dating to the later eighth century) through the Giardino Spagna and Piazza della Vittoria, led to Santa Lucia. The discoveries involve hundreds of burials ranging from the mid-seventh century through to the end of the sixth, and occupy from east to west a rocky shelf with marked changes in level (in the Giardino Spagna in 1937–38 Cultrera unearthed graves cut into the rock face as far as five meters from the normal ground level), a geography that evidently made the area unsuitable for urbanization and involved considerable undertaking to make it level when (not before Timoleon) a regular residential quarter was built over the earlier cemetery.

Dating from the late fifth century, a very long street (ca. 400 meters running from the amphitheater to Viale Cadorna) measuring a good five meters wide was brought to light by Voza in Piazza della Vittoria; the causeway traversed this band of burials, linking up Achradina in the north with the *Lakkion*, or small eastern port, and the Fusco necropolis; it is possible, however, that this causeway already existed (at least as a transitable route) from around 540 B.C. when Strabo (I. 3. 18) cites Ibycus, saying that a strip of blocks formed a bridge between Ortygia and the terra firma at their nearest point.

Furthermore, before 75 B.C., when Cicero was *quaestor* in Sicily, this section of stone blocks was substituted for what the orator (*Against Verres*, IV. 117) defines as a small *angustus* bridge, which may well have rested upon the base course that ran the antique route of the north coast, today under water but duly investigated in 1981, between the Santa Lucia imbarcadero and the north jetty of the present smaller harbor facility. This jetty is datable to the first century A.D., and one can presume that another jetty stood at the tip of the island, marking the point where first a section of boulders lay (later a bridge proper) uniting the island of Ortygia with the mainland.

This point was noted by the Cavallaris as long ago as 1883 in their *Atlante*, and investigated later in depth in the 1960s by P. Gargallo and G. Kapitän just west of the modern piers erected to protect the smaller harbor, which in antiquity must have looked much like a *cothon* at the end of the harbor, with the *Lakkion* or little eastern harbor behind it.

It has correctly been pointed out by the authors of *Sicilia antica* (I. 3), that the north–south spine of Ortygia flows toward this very point, and that it logically continued in the street plan of Achradina via a north–south concourse (as suggested by Cnidos) and with a northwest–southeast artery parallel to the street grid ascertained for the west-central part of the quarter – a hypothesis with which I concur more readily. This street must have met up with the long artery bound for the Fusco quarter, a stretch of which was brought to light by Voza in Piazza della Vittoria; this street must have run outside the residential sector, but later became a major artery during the urbanization of the Tyche and Neapolis quarters.

By this stage we are in the era of Timoleon and Hieron, which will be discussed later. The scarcity of the remains of *insulae* divided by north–south streets five meters wide – which can perhaps be associated archaeologically with the fifth-century potsherds unearthed once again by Voza in the area of the Neapolis, which he reckoned to belong to a "suburban" area – makes it extremely difficult to extrapolate dates that add something new to the hypothetical delineations of the quarter based on authors of antiquity – descriptions that have been examined in great detail by Drögenmüller.

Casmenae: a colony of Syracuse on the Hyblaean Hills
Despite their inevitable similarities, the processes involved in the foundation of Megara and Syracuse are in many ways starkly different. Such differences are determined by factors (in the first place chorographic and economic, but also political and cultural in the broad sense) which make each colony a case on its own. The significance of these diversities becomes increasingly ostensible during the process of stabilization and growth of each *apoikia*. As noted above, the utter fascination that Syracuse exercised over those who stayed in Mainland Greece was lacking in the case of Megara Hyblaea, whose *chora* was limited in comparison. The coast, which from the Lysimeleia marshlands just opposite Ortygia sloped down toward Capo Passero, soon came under Syracusan control, at least the southern half as testified by the foundation of Helorus at the end of the eighth century B.C. at the mouth of the Tellaro. The land was flat to a depth of a dozen or so kilometers and around thirty down to Helorus, well-served by freshwater springs and fertile soil, and able to sustain a considerable number of colonists, assuming it was sufficiently protected against the Sicels of the nearby Hyblaean Hills.

Relations with the latter were not always conflicting, but the rapidly growing colony and the potential threat of the easternmost Sicel townships on the Hyblaean Hills (such as Pantalica in the north and Monte Finocchito in the south) meant that the conquest of the plateau was centermost to the aims of the Syracusans, the sons and grandsons of the founders of the original *apoikia*. As noted above, we now know that after two or three generations (between seventy and one hundred years) the colonies were capable of handling strong outward expansion, boosted by a accrual of substantial economic resources and by a population growth that matched the attraction of the city's immense wealth. While the foundation of Helorus assured Syracuse the dominion of the nearby coastal plain, it also allowed for expansion toward

Acrae, the theater
built in the time of Hieron II

Gela, remains of the dwellings on the acropolis

the Vindicari and Pachino plains. The establishment of a subcolony at Acrae (Akrai) in 664 B.C. shows that, through the terraced tablelands of Canicattini Bagni, Syracuse had successfully created a bridgehead in the most plentiful stretch of the Hyblaean plateau and above all had managed to effectively curb anyone wishing to spread out into the coastal plain, which was at this point under the dominion of the *polis*-state of Greek Syrakousai.

When in 1956 I came to the conclusion that Monte Casale was in fact Thucydides' second subcolony, Casmenae (Kasmenai), it seemed defensible to propose that Syracuse had a definite expansionist program, conceived in the second half of the seventh century B.C. and concluded fifty years after, with the foundation of Camarina. Casmenae was the intermediate stage in this expansion, whereas with Camarina, which rebelled against the mother-city a mere two generations after its establishment, Syracuse was extending its sphere of command as far as the Dirillo River (in antiquity, the "river of Acrille"). On the fertile plains west of this river (one of the most important in Sicily) the Rhodians and Cretans planted their roots in the early seventh century, creating Gela and blocking the Euboean penetration effort northward along the Dirillo, starting with Licodia Eubea. Where with the foundation of Acrae the Syracusans were attempting primarily to dilate their sovereignty over a part of the neighboring plateau for agricultural reasons – and to forestall any attempt by the local tribes to hamper their own occupation of the coastal plains – with the foundation of Casmenae (which acted as a wedge penetrating the Hyblaean plateau) they essayed to maneuver northward, round the backs of the Sicels of powerful Hybla, so as to cut themselves a pathway toward the plain between the Dirillo and Hyblaeans Hills at the foot of modern Chiaramonte Gulfi. Here, the sixth century (if not almost contemporary with the founding of Camarina) saw the foundation of the new *apoikia* named Akrillai (perhaps established by the people of Acrae). With Camarina to the south and Akrillai to the extreme north, the plainlands east of the Dirillo were safely in Syracusan hands. And whether or not different aims were originally in sight – Acrae for defense and farming development, Casmenae as a military stronghold, and Camarina as a thriving colony – it cannot be ruled out that these flourishing settlements did not eventually become elements in a premeditated design that gradually crystallized over time: Syracuse was bent on extending its sovereignty over a well-defined physical area, comprising the whole of southeast Sicily, swallowing up the strongest nucleus of the Sicels ensconced between the plateau overlooking the Comiso and Ispica plain, namely the area revolving on the *polis* of Hybla. For centuries this was to remain the heart of the great state of Syracuse.

Despite its singular connotations as a "military" settlement, Casmenae offers the finest example so far discovered (and not only in Sicily) of a city planned and built from scratch in the mid-seventh century B.C. Since this center arose specifically as a stronghold having a strategic and highly defensible location within the plainlands, which were enclosed by the deep valleys of the modern rivers Irminio, Tellaro, and Anapo, it has always seemed to me logical to suppose that its construction took place quite suddenly, according to a precise design.

The urban fabric pivots on a series of parallel streets roughly 3.1 to 3.5 meters in breadth, laid out to guarantee the most efficient division of the plain from north to south, delimiting not only the housing *insulae* but also marking off the sacred area for the seventh-century temple, that interlock perfectly with the urban fabric. Casmenae's remarkable feature lies in its lack of either *plateiai* or proper east–west transverse streets; the street blocks are therefore marked off at the south section by tight alleyways. According to digs carried out in Monte Casale by Voza, the houses are inserted in sets of four in blocks roughly twenty-five meters long, divided midway along a north–south axis by an *ambitus* or a wall. Generally each abode is composed of three rooms on the south side giving onto a wide yard; the units are all the same, like the *insulae* in which they are contained.

Casmenae, also planned in advance but with elementary vertical strips and virtually no monumental buildings in the public area (though in the westernmost tip there are traces of a temple and relative *temenos* with a wealth of votive weaponry), bears a likeness to the town plan (albeit heavily overbuilt) of seventh-century Smyrna with its *insulae* lining north–south streets that run the length of the promontory. One might therefore infer that this was still an elementary planning experience common to Greek colonists of both East and West, or even a case of transposition to an urban area of the system of parceling farmable land (witness the *chora* of Metapontum), if Megara Hyblaea did not give us other clues.

Today we know a little more: the moment the Syracusan subcolony came into being on the headland of Monte Lauro, at least for its central areas the Megarian *apoikia* already had the prepared monumental layout that was to remain unaltered until the city's destruction in 483 B.C.

Megara Hyblaea and Casmenae, therefore, offer insights into the development of spatial organization in the Greek colonies in the mid-seventh century B.C., and a closer study of the two cases suggests that the two urban plans were apposite ways of addressing a quite different set of needs. On the one hand we have Megara, a community of some substance, which expands and augments its public spaces, endowing them with monuments and revolutionizing its relationship with the surrounding *chora*, even though the burgeoning *polis* swallows up some of the pre-existing structures of the earlier land parceling scheme. On the other hand we have a colony which, despite its sizable population and self-sufficiency, could be defined as "military" in nature, completely preordained – perhaps even in the very number of inhabitants, its functions, and natural geographical location – to a limited development, with the monumental community enclosures reduced to a bare minimum, a settlement conceived and realized according to principles of equality (ἰσομοιρία, isomoiria).

The city without *plateiai* (and hence without *hippeis*) seems almost the fruit of hoplitism, a widespread

Gela: profile of the hill
with a map
of the settlements
A. Acropolis
B. Archaic city
C. Medieval city
D. Archaic necropolis
E. Classical necropolis and then western Hellenistic quarters
F. Hellenistic necropolis

Reconstruction of the urban plan of the acropolis
Excavations
1953-1960
1973-1976:
— 7th cent. B.C. phase
······ 6th cent. B.C. phase
— 5th cent. B.C. phase
— 4th cent. B.C. phase

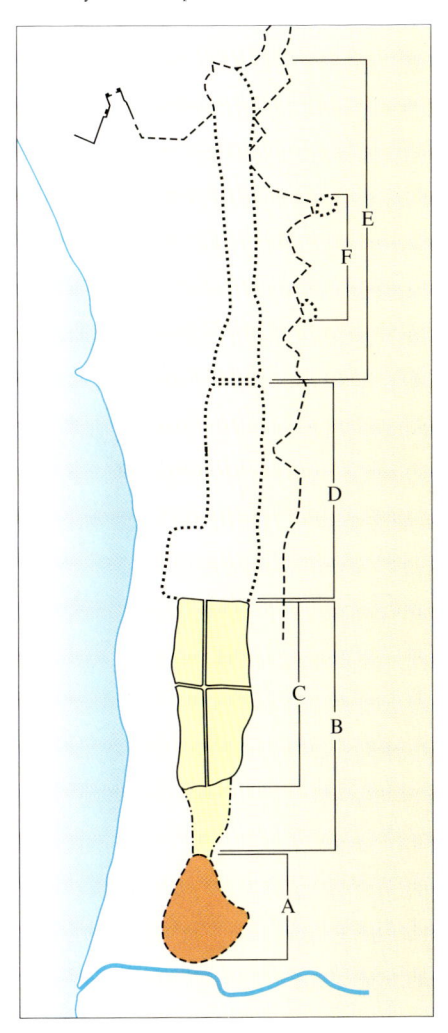

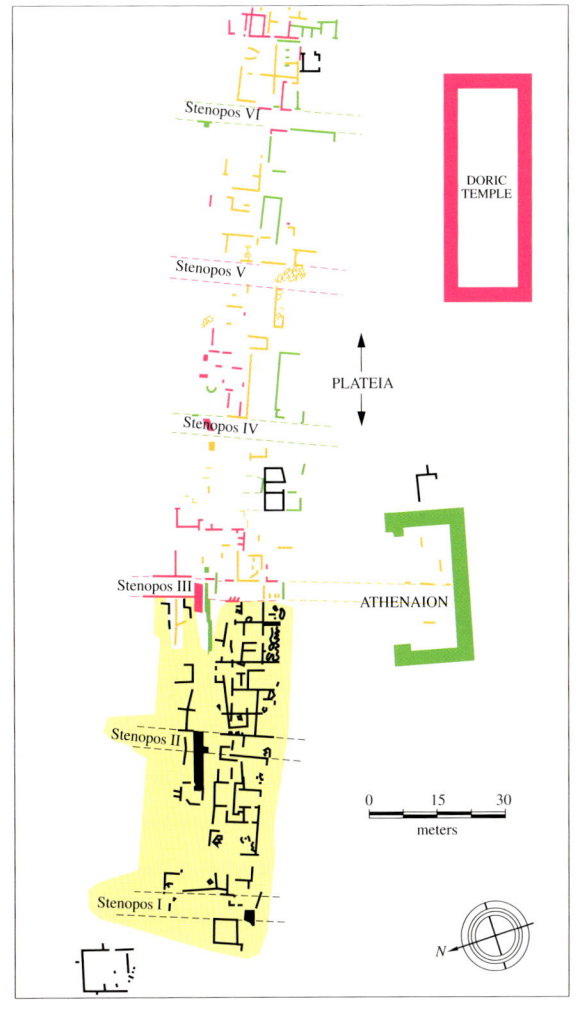

phenomenon in the Greek world in the seventh century; the peculiar ground plan can be explained by the function for which the settlement was created in the first place, a function underlined by the powerful encircling wall along the north–south axis on the eastern part of the plain, which rises slightly above ground-level, a sort of redoubt for a last defense. The streets all running north–south, moreover, allowed for a very narrow *chemin de ronde* along the defensive wall; the streets were so numerous that they covered the entire circuit, allowing the inhabitants to swiftly reach any part of the wall under attack; and should the invaders manage to trespass beyond the wall, this network offered an excellent means of splitting the enemy up and containing them in a particular street.

The singular nature of the city allows us to affirm that Casmenae is the only colonial site in Sicily that permits a sufficiently credible estimate of its population. This is because, given its task as a fortress-colony, it was built to house all its inhabitants within the walls, with regularly distributed houses in an even, continuous pattern. The invaluable town plan drawn up by Rosario Carta enables a detailed reading of the building fabric as a whole, and the excavations carried out by Voza have brought to light detailed information on the specifics of the living units. The city-walls ran a circuit of approximately 3,400 meters, enclosing an area of between 55 and 60 hectares. The building fabric of this area consisted of at least 42 bands of housing blocks (*strigae*), running NNW–SSE, measuring 25 meters wide and averaging 400 in length. Given that each *insula* was 25 meters square, a *striga* commanded 16 housing blocks, making that 672 for the plateau overall. Since each block contained four dwellings, we have a total of 2,688 houses of 156 square meters each, a surface that afforded enough space and an allotment for four people; by comparison, Olynthus and Himera offered 290 and 256 square meters respectively, for eight free citizens plus their various vassals (Travlos has attributed six people per unit for Classical Athens). Considering that in a "military" colony the areas earmarked for monumental architecture had to be limited in number and size, I would say that, allowing a detraction of thirty percent for these (and for the occasional east–west alleyway between the *insulae*), this were an acceptable figure. In conclusion, there remain 1,882 houses which, multiplied by 4 inhabitants each gives a population of 7,528 individuals. This sum is endorsed by significant comparisons for the ratio between total surface area and number of inhabitants, and is strikingly close to the figure at which Orsi arrived regarding Megara Hyblaea, to which he attributed a population of around 8,000. The two colonies are very similar, as Megara has a circuit of wall running 3,407 meters enclosing 61 hectares. It goes without saying that such estimates are only approximations – at least as regards Casmenae in the sixth century, when the *insulae* appear to have been fully occupied.

Casmenae, plan

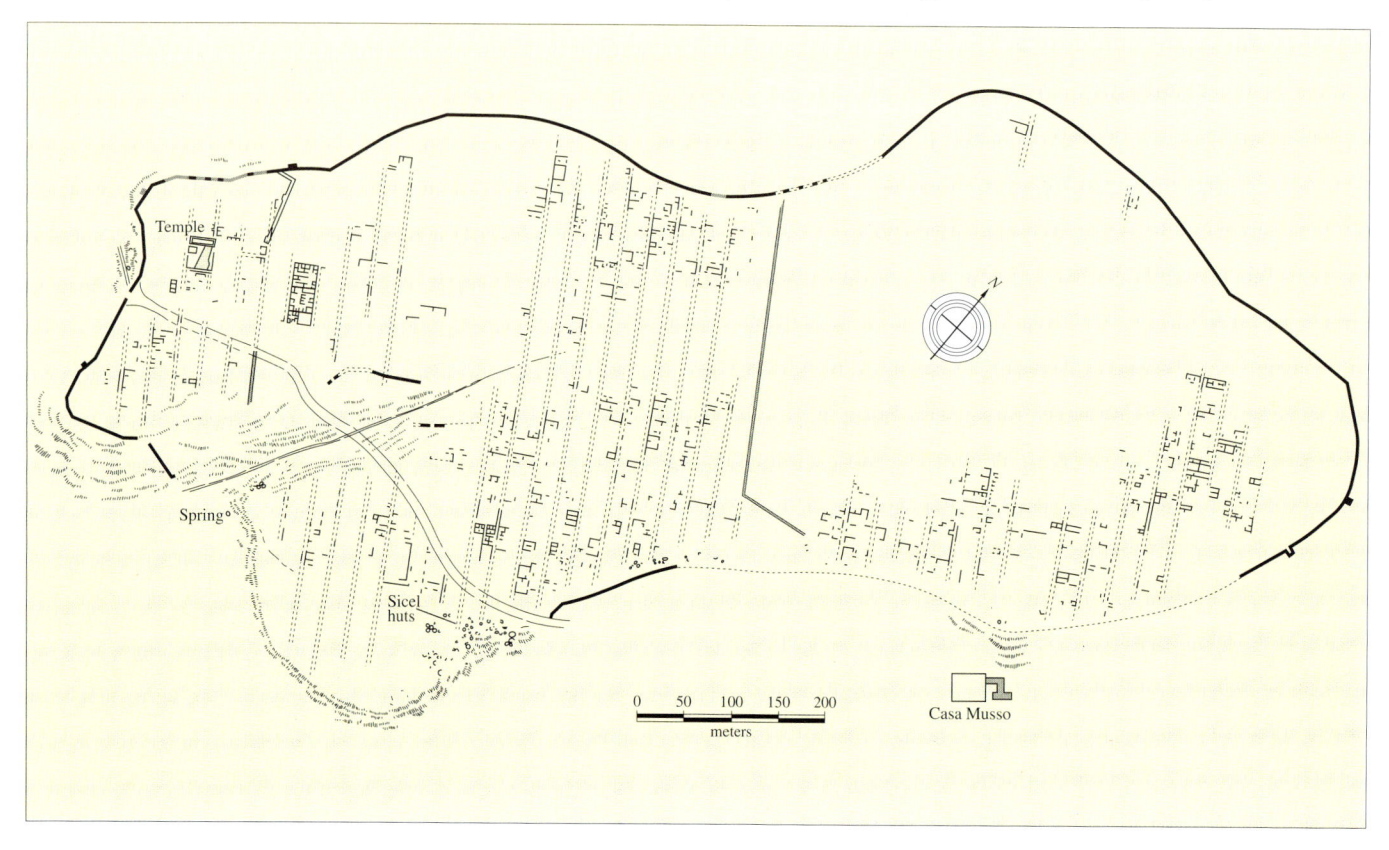

Urban Planning in Ancient Sicily

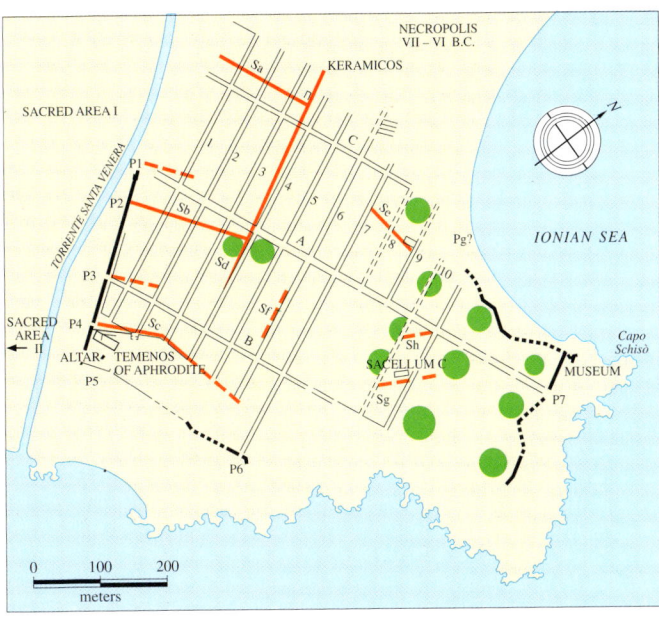

The peninsula of Naxos viewed from the west

Naxos: urban plan 5th cent. B.C. lying over the Archaic phases (in red)
A-B-C   *Plateiai*
from 1 to 10   Blocks
P 1-2-etc.   Gates
● Remains of 8th cent. B.C.
Sa-b-c-d-e   Streets 7th-6th cent. B.C.
Sf-g-h   Hypothetical Streets 7th-6th cent. B.C.
——— Short course of the walls
······· Supposed course of the walls

To wind up, more than any other western colony, Casmenae provides an excellent yardstick for the thorny and unresolved question of the true population of the ancient colonial cities, and is further confirmed by the contrasting results of fieldwork carried out by Asheri in Himera.

Other seventh-century cities: Naxos, Gela, Selinus, Himera
In the case of these four *apoikiai*, the choice of site was typical of the Siceliot settlements, namely hilly ground near a river large enough to enable the creation of a port and afford a means of natural defense. Of the four cities, only Naxos, the oldest and most "sacred" of Sicily's *poleis* owing to its altar to Apollo Archegetes, remained strangely contained, even in its heyday. The eighth-century settlement that occupied the easternmost tip of the spur between Santa Venera and Capo Schisò covered an area no larger than ten hectares. The only house so far identified is a single-room unit with a ledge; the foundations of dwellings and *sacella* continued in the ensuing century to be composed of pebbles and rough-hewn lava stone, with walls most likely made of mudbrick (brick also seems to have been used for the acropolis of Gela in the early seventh century, though it must be said that evidence of the use of this material on the island is very scarce). At Naxos only two streets (Sh, Sg) can be dated to the eighth century, and seem to suggest a settlement oriented along a northeast–southwest axis, parallel with the shoreline in order to make the best use of the contours of the large terracing which descended evenly toward the sea from the Larunchi and Saluzzo peaks.

It is not until the mid-seventh century that Naxos and Gela yield useful evidence as regards their urban fabric; while for the younger *apoikiai* of Selinus and Himera we have to wait another few decades.

Each of these colonial settlements followed its own individual course of development, as is to be expected. Nonetheless it is possible to pinpoint a set of important constants in their setup as regards the seventh century B.C. The main sacred enclaves delimited by a *peribolos*, although generally aligned to the street grid and houses, were sited in such a way as not to hamper the development of the fabric, and hence slightly displaced from the residential nuclei; this pattern is repeated at Naxos and Gela, Selinus and Himera. Moreover, both the chthonian sanctuaries (Gela, Selinus) and the shrines of the gods who protected the town (as Enuó at Naxos) are situated beyond the rivers separating the urban area from the outlying *chora*, though still very close to the city; the quarter of the potters, whose kilns were the cause of countless hazardous fires, tended to be sited on the outer rim of the built-up area (to the west in Gela, north in Naxos), and these were followed by the necropolises.

In these *apoikiai*, as in other colonies across Sicily, only at the close of the century and mainly in the course of the sixth, the *sacella* that filled the ancient *temene* gave rise to full-fledged temple buildings. Consequently, the original *temene* were often enlarged, though not relocated and therefore tended to occupy the same site for several centuries. The building in Naxos presumed to be an *aphrodision* and the cult buildings to the west of Santa Venera have shed much light on the matter; the pattern recurs in Gela, Selinus, and Himera. As for data on the physical planning of the city, Gela reveals that the *sacel-*

la occupying the acropolis, together with the residential quarter extending westward from it, were aligned on the main natural axis of the hill that runs parallel with the shoreline, marking off the southern border of the fertile Geloan farmlands.

This tillage is so close-by that the original settlement must have been urban rather than agrarian from the outset. The Cretan and Rhodian colonists of the early settlement in 689 B.C. found the area inhabited by the Lindioi (or the Ialysci), who had preceded them by a few decades, their dwellings scattered across the land between the Dirillo to the east and the westernmost point of the Geloan hillside.

The seventh-century *apoikia* of Naxos has yielded a great many more clues, and its structure has been carefully traced out by Paola Pelagatti. The area covered around forty hectares, and, like Megara Hyblaea, the township seems to have been divided up into quarters aligned differently from those in the western sector (which are of more recent construction) and older, eastern sector (whose pattern may have been affected by pre-existing structures). In the western sector, streets Sa Sb (3 meters wide) lie at approximately ninety degrees and at fairly constant intervals along a long street (Sd) which, starting from south–southeast, seems to slice through the ledges leading toward the low hills to the north. At the point where it emerged from the built-up area, archaeological digs have revealed the sixth-century potters' quarter; whereas in the south the artery Sd seems to have bordered the original *temenos* dedicated to Aphrodite, delimited by a *peribolos* in polygonal blocks and solid enough to be used for the walling that encircled the city in the sixth century. Remains of another important north–south concourse (the road to the neighboring colony of Zancle) have come to light slightly further east (Sp) and a third street (3.5 meters wide) has been disclosed in the southern half, where there is evidence of two different alignments, of which the northeast–southwest route was laid on an eighth-century roadbed. It is possible that the community areas lay at the meeting point between these differently aligned quarters; our knowledge of the "public" fabric, however, is for the time being limited to a few *sacella*, whose foundations were obliterated by fifth-century house-building. Within the walls the town endured a mere few decades, as the Syracusan tyrant Hieron deported all the inhabitants in the year 476 B.C.

This concludes the rapid overview of the urban situation in Sicily in the second half of the seventh century. In the one hundred years that elapsed since the foundation of Syracuse and Megara Hyblaea, the physical expression of the very concept of "city" seems to have come a long way; it is no surprise, therefore, that from the early decades of the sixth century the terrain was subjected to programmed development that included detailed schemes for sizable urban complexes which in turn allowed for future development: for Early Archaic times Selinus provides the most signal example – though it is not the only one, as suggested by the latest excavations at Himera.

The Archaic City

Selinus.
The first generations. Although the parallels with distant Megara Nisaea are vague, we know for certain that the new colony of Selinus was founded at the joint wish of the Megarians of Greece and those of Sicily, under the leadership of the *oikistes* by the name of Pammilus. The year was 651–650 and Diodorus' chronology is sanctioned by archaeological evidence that has ruled out Thucydides' date of 628 B.C. The colonists' choice of site was undoubtedly influenced strongly by the advantageous conditions of the basin with its three low rises separated by two rivers, the Selinos to the west and the Cothon (modern Cottone) to the east, which enabled the settlers to construct two harbors (a small river port, plus a more open one on the eastern rise); between them stood a ridge composed of the Manuzza and so-called acropolis hills, though the hill became the acropolis only after the town's destruction in 409 B.C. The latter hill, extending for around 9.5 hectares, ends with a seaward crag to the south and continues toward the north up through a narrow isthmus to the Manuzza plateau, which splays out to twice the width as it stretches out of sight toward the north. If for no other reason than for defense, from the very first settlement the two hills must have been completely occupied as far as the northern border of Manuzza. Moreover, the first encampments must have been sparse and, given the jutting spur, the occupation of the land was not of the agrarian type, unlike at Megara Hyblaea: good tillable land was within easy reach, and the two harbors quickly became the focus of busy trade activity.

Together with the extensive fertile territory the settlers had conquered, the ports contributed significantly to the extraordinary growth and wealth of Selinus. The town, which grew also thanks to the fact that first the Phoenician port of Motya and then Carthage itself took advantage of its presence as a center of primary importance for trade between the Greek world and the West, remained faithful to its mer-

Urban Planning in Ancient Sicily

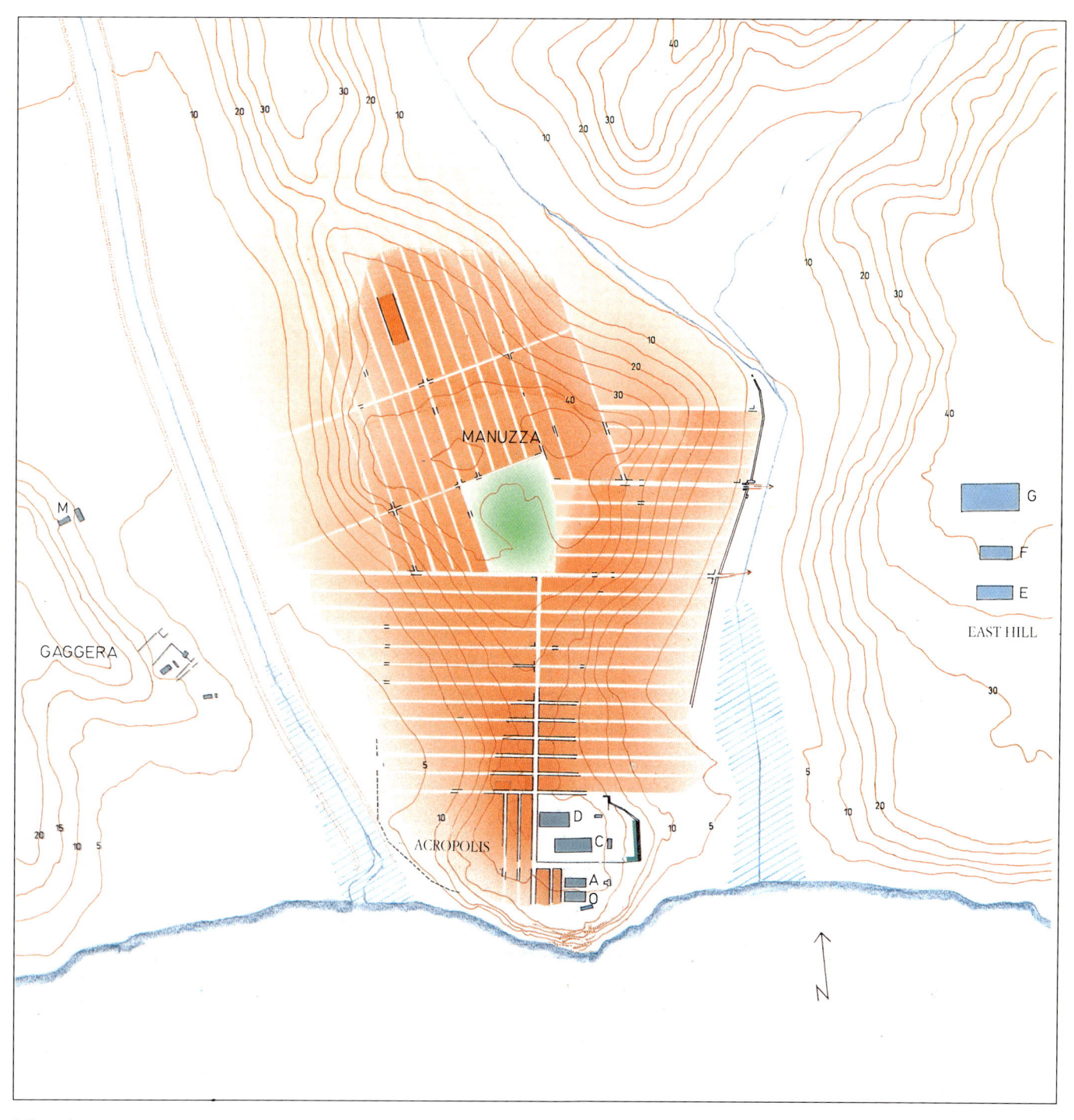

Selinus plan
by Dieter Mertens
on the basis of data
from recent excavations

cantile interests until 480 B.C., the year in which the Greek areas of the island were under greatest threat, and only when this powerful and restive commercial partner seriously upset the balance of power – guaranteed by the Carthaginians in the western tip of the island – was the fate of Selinus decreed.

By the close of the seventh century Selinus appears to have already reached the extension that the sixth- and fifth-century *polis* would come to occupy. Beyond the western port, the Malophoros sanctuary – the first of a series of temples erected on the west bank of the Selinos – had already welcomed the oldest *megaron*; on the other side, the east hill saw the construction of Temple E1, the precursor of the temple reconstructed by the Bovio-Marconi excavation team in the 1960s.

The availability not only of financial reserves but of manpower and also advanced solutions to technical problems (such as expert stoneworking and the large tiles in Corinthian style of Temple E1), were to rank Selinus among the Siceliot townships with the richest legacy of experimentation in temple architecture. The seventh-century houses were compact, the walls built of aggregate laid on a base of large blocks in rows of different heights; in some cases, as at Megara, the walls were made of rubble (with a form of cement binder) and clad in slabs. There are also examples of walling involving a texture of small stones between blocks set on end, such as those found by Gullini on the east hill in the excavations for Temple E1, a technique characteristic of nearby Punico-Phoenician spheres. The dwellings at Manuzza (and undoubtedly those on the acropolis hill which with Manuzza accommodate the bulk of seventh-century Selinus) seem to have been interspliced with large empty spaces, though oriented on the natural alignments of the two hills, which are not parallel.

At the intersection of these two axes, at the southeast fringe of Manuzza there was a necropolis of small rock-cut graves for ashes (which has yielded material from the first half of the seventh century) that was without doubt utilized by the inhabitants of both hills. After the end of the seventh century B.C. the population carried out their burials on the Galera knoll to the north, and on the Manicalunga, beyond the Temple of Demeter Malophoros; the very early necropolis of Manuzza was probably gradually obliterated.

The temenos *of the* poliouchoi *gods and the emergence of the organized township*
At the start of the sixth century the ancient residential fabric on the two hillsides was subjected to a thorough renewal program, an undertaking that can be closely followed via the first major restructuring of the ancient sacred enclave of the necropolis. The hill has two natural axes, one running north–south, the other east–west, which at the foot of the hill joined the two harbor complexes. These two roadways were vital to the development of the housing on the acropolis, though the east–west axis has been mistakenly contested as an urban causeway, and its existence even doubted.

To my mind, this ancient natural route actually denoted a kind of primeval distinction on the hill between that which belonged to the sacred sphere and that which was civilian – it is wholly logical that the most ancient dwellings (those of the *oikistes* Pammilus and his companions) were built on the two southernmost mounds of the acropolis, which were later terraced in the fifth century to make room for Temples A and O. The two mounds in question were decently exposed and surrounded on three sides by sea and rivers, and easily accessed from the river port; each time excavation work has been undertaken in these areas, new evidence of non-public buildings has come to light.

Conversely, the area at the center of the hill north of this natural axis was quickly assigned to receive religious structures. Starting in the late seventh and early sixth centuries B.C. construction was undertaken on at least four *sacella*, or small temple buildings, and their presence shows that the entire area was dedicated to the tutelary deities, probably from the very foundation of the *apoikia*. These *sacella* may have been equipped with separate sacred enclosures; there can be no doubt that from the early decades of the sixth century this sacred enclave was augmented and encircled by a single *peribolos* or retaining wall.

As in the south, the northern sector of the sacred area seems to have been closed off by an important roadway that followed the course of another natural route between the two rivers; testifying to this path is a dwelling from the mid-seventh century and directly associable to this route (excavated by Fourmont). The route is denominated Street *f*, and later served as the spine for the urban development of the northern sector of the acropolis and in Manuzza. Toward the west the large *temenos* must have been linked up to the north–south axis, which in early Archaic times seems to have been positioned a little more to the west than it did subsequently. The construction of these features meant that when they wanted to renew and increase the number of religious buildings and associated structures built by the first and second generations of colonists, the Selinuntines were forced to terrace the hillslopes looking east. Basically, in 580–570 B.C. two terraces were built, perhaps linked by a stepped walkway, thereby amplifying the primitive sacred enclave toward the east; the wall of the *peribolos* was shifted to a lower point on this same side, along the road which, coming from the direction of the Cothon port, crossed the east–west axis at its easternmost point, and was limited on the north side for a good 150 meters by the *peribolos* of the newly built *temenos*.

The development of this *temenos* was not an isolated episode at either architectural or urbanistic level. It was effectively part of a far-reaching and carefully planned program that evinces considerable attention to the contours of the land, to the legacy of existing features, and to the development needs of a community in rapid growth. Basically, in the period 580–570 B.C. the settlement's inhabitants drew up a blueprint for a full-fledged city – a city of extraordinary articulation and size for those of the Greek world which have reached posterity – establishing an urban pattern which, on the basis of current knowledge, seems to have been designed around a basic rectangle 32.5 meters wide (i.e., 100 feet of 0.325 meters) comprising the *insula* of 90 feet plus an interaxis of 10 feet. From excavation work carried out on the northern and central areas of Manuzza, we can infer the optimal length of the street blocks planned and applied to the land by Selinus' chief *geometres* or town planner.

The basic *insula* is estimated to have had a ratio of 1:6 between its length and width (29.25 by 175.5 meters) within a module of 600 feet (195 meters) including 6 *insulae* and the streets dividing them (Rallo, Di Grazia).

We might say that the town planner marked out twelve bands for residential building stock in the southern sector in which the acropolis and South-Manuzza stand – with its almost north–south alignment (6.2°E) – multiplying the street grid northward via a set of parallels to the two causeways that marked off the sacred area in an east–west direction and hinged with the north–south axis, which was transformed into a major artery of around 9 meters wide. The *insulae* extended from east-to-west between the two harbor complexes, and the first module of 600 feet and the later module toward the north seem to have been boxed in with streets (from 0 to 6) which, being already extant in the last quarter of the seventh or early sixth century, were probably natural pathways of antique use. Together with the southern Street *f*, these may have prompted the basic module 600 feet wide for the overall urban pattern. The *insulae* – on average 29 meters wide, and as yet of undetermined length – with the relative streets (i.e., the narrower *stenopoi* of 3.5 meters, and the *plateiai* of approximately twice the width, such as *f* and 6) met at right-angles, from one side to the other on the north–south artery.

To the North of Street 6 along the Cothon River, where the valley splays out slightly, the recent excavations conducted by Mertens enable us to reconstruct five further bands of *insulae* parallel to the previous set, closed off at the north by a third main artery around 8.5 meters wide, and therefore as broad as the Manuzza causeway, though slightly less so than the main acropolis thoroughfare. This street proceeded from a monumental double portal on the Cothon and led to the intersection of the Manuzza system and that of the acropolis, in an area that is gradually being confirmed as the *agora*.

This additional imposing causeway (north of which Mertens reckons there to be at least four *strigae*) greatly enhances our knowledge of the urban plan of Archaic Selinus. In places, this scheme seems to be no longer oriented on the main converging thoroughfares that crossed respectively the acropolis and south Manuzza, and north Manuzza, but also on a third important axis running east–west. All three of these main axes – of equal importance – seem to start in a large clearing generated by them, the *agora*, a junction point for separate systems of urban fabric that complied with the lie of the land and were hence markedly different from each other. The new axis disclosed by Mertens allowed linkage between the *agora* and the terrace of the eastern temple group (its extension seems to cut off Temple G at the north) behind the harbor, which certainly did not reach this point; on the other hand it provided the backbone of the quarters inside the walls (and perhaps even those outside) which are now known to have completely occupied the eastern slopes of Manuzza, and at least a portion of the Cothon Valley bottom.

As for the Manuzza plateau, once again in perfect conformity with the contours of the site, the "generating" element of the urban layout is the causeway that cut through everything from the northwestern tip of the settlement to the acropolis hill.

Here the NNW–SSE orientation of the tableland (382.87°) imposed the construction of new *insulae* aligned differently, and in fact the excavations have shown that the *plateia 0* (zero by Rallo's system), measuring 8.5 meters wide and in use from the first half of the sixth century, cut across the hill from its northernmost point (which led out in a westerly direction, without descending the steep slopes toward the valley) reaching the southern section of the plateau. Here it was not possible to extend it beyond Street 6, which the French team's fieldwork has shown to be the limit of the acropolis–south-Manuzza system; this is the termination point of the westernmost *stenopoi*, four of which ran parallel west of *plateia* 0. East of this *plateia* at least six *insulae* have come to light beyond which there looks to have been another three, served by streets once again oriented NNW–SSE, cut into the rock of the plateau slopes; according to Mertens, two of these were between 6.0 and 6.5 meters wide, instead of the customary width of ca. 3.3 meters of the others. This would entail a layout arranged on 4–5–4 long parallel *strigae*.

As for the major thoroughfare *0* in north Manuzza, it is likely that it ran into *plateia 6* of the acropolis–south Manuzza system, delimiting the west side of the presumed *agora* area. Actually, the architects of new Selinus must have taken into account the fact that the two *plateiai* of north Manuzza and the acropolis constituted the support structure of the town plan they had devised, given that their angle of incidence was 23.33°, and that once they reached the same level they would delimit a trapezium. Now this junction, which was an essential feature in such a sweeping urban scheme, had perforce to be assigned to public functions, given that its very situation made it a select area for both the plateau residents and those living near the port. It had always been so for the early systems composed of residential quarters with diverse alignments (witness Megara Hyblaea) and it is likely that the northernmost street of the acropolis–south Manuzza borough, namely *plateia 6*, marked off the southern border of Selinus' *agora* (de La Genière). Furthermore, since Schubring's work in 1865 the *agora* has often been located in the southern section of Manuzza; on the basis of current data it is quite probable that it occupied the area bordered to the west by *plateia 0*, to the north by the basic *stenopos* of the north Manuzza system, and to the south by Street *6* of the acropolis–south Manuzza system. Toward the east this area, on fairly even ground, must have extended at least as far as the rock-cut graves of the earliest necropolis; this was destroyed to lay the foundations of Punic houses(?), which therefore occupied a vacant area that had not been built upon before the year 409 B.C.

In the process of applying the preset building pattern to the terrain, the primary axes of the system were laid with great care; the same cannot be said for the individual *insulae*, nor for the streets. In either case the dimensions are not consistent. Similarly, the *plateiai* vary in breadth from 6–6.75 meters for the minor ones, to the 8.5–9.4 meters for the three main ones – and not in proportion to the widths of the *stenopoi* (3.8–3.49 meters for the east–west *stenopoi* of the acropolis, and 3.8–3.3 for those of north Manuzza).

During this phase of the town's development (ca. 580–570) the roadbeds themselves were composed of a gravel and grit foundation covered with a reddish sand; here and there was added a beaten reddish earth infill, sometimes with rock made level with a layer of marlstone or clayey earth duly compacted to create a uniform road surface.

Given the strong incline of the land, these streets were equipped (in some cases probably from the outset) with gutters either side and were "humped" (as was the main *plateia 0* of Manuzza). In the second half of the fifth century B.C. all the vehicular streets were overlaid with a proper bed of cobbles or, in some case, of cut slabs.

In conclusion, by the end of the first quarter of the sixth century, Selinus had already equipped itself with the broad-mesh street scheme (covering a good 100 hectares) on which the city developed until its destruction. There are reasons to suppose that this pattern was not merely a street grid composed around a set of parallel *strigae* that would progressively be filled in with public buildings and housing stock; the town plan seems also to have comprised a definitive blueprint for the areas reserved for worship (for the east hill and for the Malophoros sanctuary) and the definition of the community spaces such as the *agora* and the southern section of the acropolis, and special concessionary areas for private building. Around the two rivers, moreover, both within and without the defensive walls – which recent fieldwork by Mertens and certain ancient sources (Polyaenus, I. 28, II. 10; Plutarch, *Moralia*. Αποφ. Λακ. (*Apoft. Lak.*, *Areus*, 2) attest to have enclosed the urban area from the mid-sixth century – must have gradually attracted the commercial activities and those linked to the maintenance of the fleet of triremes with which Selinus was soon to arm itself (Thucydides, VI. 20. 2ff). The transition from a residential fabric ordered around preset axes (at times imposed by the terrain) to a fabric programmed to cover broad carriageways which, making ample use of those innate axes, became the spinal network of an overall system designed to last long into the future (presupposing a constant growth rate of the political community) is indicative of how advanced the Greek colonial *geometrai* were in the concept of planned growth – and how important the means of mapping it onto the land – in the more prosperous Greek *poleis* in Sicily in the early sixth century.

The monumental phase (ca. 560–460)

This phase in Selinus and its distant rival Acragas (modern Agrigento) is exemplary for a proper understanding of the transition of urban planning toward monumentalization. It should be clear that this phase as much as the previous one presupposed solid economic development and a growing political leverage. It is worth recalling, however, that from the second quarter-century through the end of the sixth century Seli-

The *temenos* of the Malophoros
of Selinus
left, the walls
center, the *propylaeum*
higher up, the altar
and beyond, the *megaron*

Urban Planning in Ancient Sicily

nus was run by tyrants (Theron, Peithagoras, Euryleon), and that the considerable public and private fortunes that the authors of antiquity attributed to Selinus probably derived not only from the exploitation of the fertile terrain but also from the systematic trading of its products and from the sheer variety and quantity of business which its geographical position and a virtually constant pro-Phoenician and pro-Punic outlook (significantly illustrated by the silver ingots found recently in a late-sixth-century repository) permitted Selinus in the sixth and fifth centuries B.C. This combination of factors favored the ongoing monumentalization of the acropolis, a program that pivoted on the ancient *temenos* and was perhaps furthered by an episode a violent destruction that seems to have hit the *polis* shortly before mid-sixth century.

Around 560 B.C. the acropolis saw the start of a new program of public works, which included the reinforcement of the north–south artery and the east section (*f–f2*) of Street *f* with the addition of a solid roadbed that remained a unique feature linked to the transport of the immense blocks of stone used for Temple C; these blocks came from the quarries at Cusa slightly further north. The last episode of these public works was the creation of the monumental terraces that obliterated the eastern shelves of the *temenos*; these had already been terraced and were now buried under the huge mound of sand which only a major retaining system could safely bear up. The highly original design took the form of an enormous perimeter wall 9.8 meters high and pyramidal in section, stepped on either side (23 on the east face), with a base of 17 meters; the wall followed the contours of the hillside at a height of 14 meters, extending approximately 75 meters from north to south, and then curving toward northwest for a further 50 meters or so. The boldness and magnificence of the device was unparalleled in the entire Greek world.

As with the previous *peribolos*, the new *temenos* was erected south on the main southern causeway through the acropolis, the eastern stretch of which in this phase assumed the appearance of a grand flight of steps; while to the east the stepped rampart (as for the Early Archaic *peribolos*) was aligned with one of the main roadways bearing traffic to and from the western section of the harbor.

There is no doubt that Temple C was the monumental focus of this construction activity: before it the artificial terracing was made to slope gently in order to make the peak of the temple level with the top of the stepped rampart, which otherwise lay a few meters lower; this was done by adjusting the heights of the two naves of the *stoa* with the level at which the terrace concluded.

The stepped rampart did not, however, create terracing of the hillside as far as Street *f–f2*, as it was thought until the recent Tusa excavations; instead it left unaffected the northeast corner. Here a second terrace was created, smaller and lower than the other, enabling a saving in the costly job of infilling the ledges; this was the terrace upon which the Punic dwellings were scattered at various levels, as revealed by the Tusa excavations. The terrace appears to have been closed off at the southeast and southwest by a massive, remarkably high retaining wall that ran from the stepped rampart in a southwest direction, twenty-nine meters above the bend in the wall itself. As with the stepped rampart, this retaining wall seems to have been built from the sandstone blocks of the acropolis, and in the first stretch stood the northwest wall of a two-section *stoa*.

A few decades later the second stretch (northwest–southeast) of this original retaining wall was partially obliterated and replaced by a solid wall of enormous blocks of limestone quarried from Cusa, which was linked up to an equally massive terracing wall running toward the north for around thirty meters and then swerved sharply to the west to align itself with the Street *f–f2*, effectively delimiting the same; in this

The acropolis of Selinus
temenos of Temple C
I phase, ca. 650-560 B.C.
—— existing course
═══ certain course
===== hypothetical course

The acropolis of Selinus
temenos of Temple C
II phase
ca. 560 - beginning 5th cent. B.C.

Acropolis of Selinus
temenos of Temple C
III phase
beginning 5th cent. - 409 B.C.

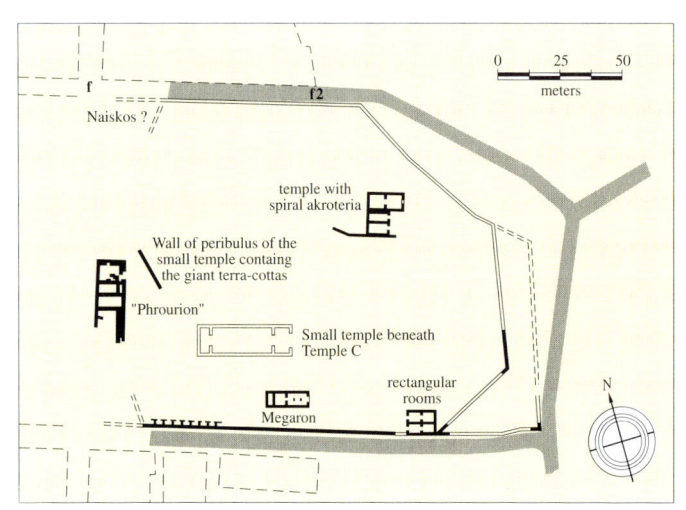

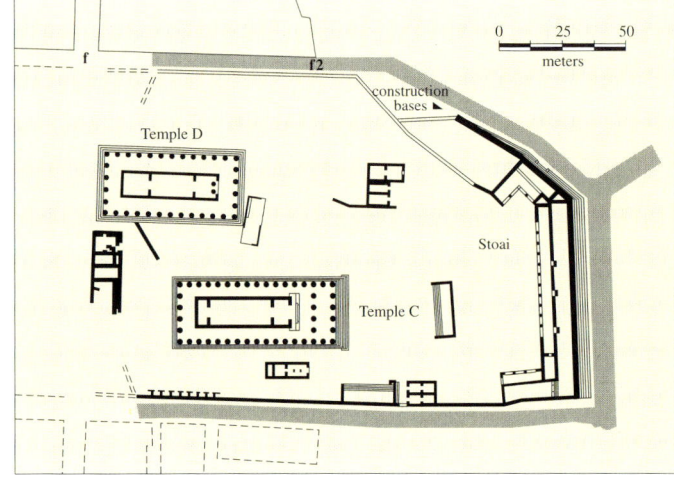

Selinus
south side of Temple C

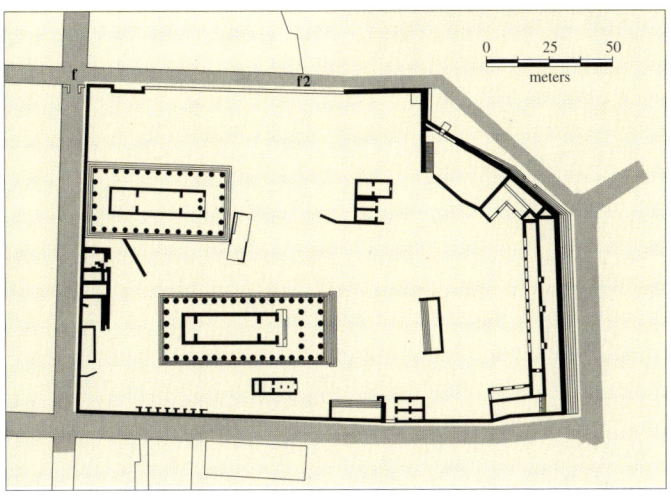

way it filled in the hill at the northeast corner, effectively enlarging the *temenos*, which had meanwhile been enhanced by Temple D. In this further phase of development of the sacred enclave, the lower terrace of the previous stage was modified in terms of size and appearance most of all, it was closed off in the east, toward the road that ran around the base of the stepped rampart, and a high screen inset with an elegant tapering gateway (h. 2.32 meters by 1.2 in width). Coming from the direction of the Cothon harbor via several low steps one reached the other gateway that had since become a kind of monumental entrance hall to the sacred *temenos*. In fact a long flight of steps was inserted along the east wall of the new artificial corner of the *temenos* and made to ascend to the height of the latter.

This flight of at least twenty-one steps was built in Punic times (originally it seems to have been equipped with landings of 1.8 by 1.6 meters), and led to a terrace set lower than the Temples C and D, channeling visitors directly to the heart of the *temenos* so that, as with the south entrance, they could appreciate the soaring mass of Temple C on one side and the imposing altar on the other.

Regarding this last modification – which afforded extra space and introduced a new monumental feature to the oldest and most revered *temenos* of Selinus (and dates to the fifth century, perhaps to the first decades, when work on rectifying the opposite, northwest corner of the *temenos* was undertaken, making it lie in line with the main north–south artery) – it is evident that the last part of the alterations to be completed was the tapered gateway. This gateway (which is in no way part of the defensive systems of the Archaic, Classical, or post-Classical periods) was accessed from an important stepped platform enclosed in side walls, and was blocked up with pieces of the same wall when the height of this was raised to transform it into a proper defensive wall (a project probably undertaken by Hermocrates).

With this monumental screen the second phase on the *temenos* of Temples C and D was complete, a phase of work that began in 560 B.C. and continued for almost a century, enriching Selinus with some of most superb architectural compositions, while providing a crucial focal point of everyday life in the *polis*.

This rings particularly true when one realizes that from the fifth century two new temples, A and 0, enclosed in their own perimeter wall, were combined with Temples C and D to give the entire southern sector of the acropolis hill an outstanding and utterly unique monumental configuration and sacred significance. The sacred enclave was far from being a mere *pendant* to the east hill, on which in the meantime Temples F, G, and E had been erected, without considerations of space but in preassigned areas that took account of the pattern of the built-up fabric. These new temples were also set parallel to one another, and oriented east–west; together with their counterparts on the acropolis hill and those (or other public monuments) which we can suppose stood on the east coast of Manuzza, they formed a magnificent sequence dominating the east port and the outlying quarters; the nearest in resemblance to this complex of sacred architecture can be found in Acragas, which is guarded over by its superb crown of majestic sacred buildings.

These public monuments were virtually matched in scale by a surge of private building. From the sixth century – reaching a peak at the start of the fifth – numerous houses were built; the materials used included either rough boulders or shaped isodomic blocks. This building boom comprises many of the houses on the acropolis (which were perhaps already in ruins, however, by the mid-sixth century, together with the Archaic *temenos* and the north Manuzza neighborhood, which seems to have been the focus of an extensive renewal scheme during the second half of the sixth century), together with some of the many dwellings being put up to fill the *stenopoi* leading down to the harbors. This phenomenon was not limited to Selinus – witness the building programs of Acragas (Diodorus, XIII.83–84; Diogenes Laertius, VIII.63). But in the case of Selinus it is well documented archaeologically; moreover, recently Mertens has proposed that the restructuring of the Archaic-period housing was imposed by public administrators following a "redistribution of property." The *insulae* were reorganized into equal lots of dwellings of 220 square meters apiece (Mertens reckons as many as 900 such lots spanned from the Selinos to the Cothon); besides the risk of attributing close ratios between housing module and an egalitarian structure to society (especially in a so highly organized *polis*), there is no evidence that these dwellings sprang up in such a brief lapse of time and, furthermore, as much before as after the battle of Himera 480 B.C., in which the Syracusan tyrant Gelon scored a crushing victory over the Carthaginians, Selinus seems to have safely avoided political and institutional upheavals and radical economic problems, as public and private wealth continued to increase unchecked.

To recapitulate, at Selinus the Megarian subcolonists installed themselves immediately on the three hills close by the shore, choosing elevated ground that enabled them to make best use of the two natural harbors and the intervening ridge formed by the Manuzza and acropolis hills. The eastern eminence and the western hill were quickly ascribed sacred status for temple sites, the first dedicated to the celestial gods, the second to the chthonian deities; whereas, from the outset the tutelary deities were assigned the hub

Selinus
aerial view of Temple E

of the acropolis. South of this, and separated by a natural east–west axis, we should look for the homes of the first colonists, dappling the southernmost ledges of those ample, sunlit slopes overlooking the river estuaries. Soon enough these ridges became entirely built up – for obvious reasons of defense – while the original residential quarter became aligned to the main natural axes and the necropolis of the first colonists spread out over the southeast flank of the Manuzza hillside.

In the first decades of the sixth century Selinus – by this time rich and powerful (and probably governed by an oligarchic regime) – set forth upon a highly ambitious urban planning scheme starting with the principal thoroughfares prompted by the geography of the terrain and based on a modular system of orthogonal land parcels. Of all the Archaic systems so far known to posterity, the urban pattern of Selinus is the most revealing in terms of its compositional elements, and best enables us to follow its complex development, showing that the experiences of Megara Hyblaea, Casmenae, and Naxos had borne fruit. It hardly comes as a surprise, however, that such experiences in planning (though soon to be common across the Greek world) found a fertile seedbed for experimentation in the colonies of the West, where expropriation and subsequent rectifications were far easier to put into effect than in the ancient cities of Mainland Greece or Asia Minor, where large public fortunes and political forces ruled the day.

The basic framework of Selinus' grandiose urban program seems to have been complete by 570 B.C.; there may have also been some natural cataclysm to speed things up, such as a quake. Ten years later work was taken in hand again and this time with special attention to the monumental development of the *polis* on the acropolis, the west hill, and in the enclave dedicated to Demeter Malophoros.

Before mid-fifth century the city had assumed the configuration it would keep until the ruinous assault of the Carthaginians, who swiftly overpowered the city's antiquated and unmanned defensive wall. The urban plan evinces a system of *strigae* rather than the layout type devised by Hippodamus with its simple, functional scheme – however rigid and lacking in aesthetic features. Instead, the town was animated by "relational spaces" of some importance, rich in vistas and monumental compositions. Despite the utter lack of archaeological data on the public buildings of the Manuzza plateau, one need only recall the Temples C, D, A, and O, which served as a brilliant visual and conceptual counterpoint to the superb temples that were being erected on the border of the east hill. At the time of the city's destruction, this entire area between the east hill and the Malophoros zone were completely urbanized, given that the area between the hill quarters and those down by the harbor had been filled in.

After Hannibal razed the city in 409 B.C., the first reoccupation program took place under Hermocrates, then Dionysius, and then (after 367 B.C.) the Punic peoples reoccupied the acropolis, and then part of Manuzza (the acropolis could hardly have contained Hermocrates' population of 6,000); and yet there are no signs of further planning exploits. The dwellings and public areas were sited wherever needs dictated. Despite this, the year 250 B.C. saw Selinus as a modest Punic way station within the Carthaginian *epikrateia*, but not so abundant in population or so important to be worth defending against the encroaching Romans.

Himera

Excavation work carried out in the last few years has quite revolutionized our knowledge of the built-up area of ancient Himera which, in the course of its development, became more comparable with the system of Selinus, even in terms of chronology. My earlier supposition was that at Himera the installation of the first colonists, who had their sights on the coastal plains, was sited on the mouth of the Himera River; this suggestion was confirmed by the excavations conducted by Rosalia Camerata Scovazzo, Nunzio Allegro, and Stefano Vassallo at the foot of the Himeran hills in the Bonfornello plain, starting west of the so-called Temple of Victory on the left bank of the Himera.

The stratigraphic surveys conducted in this area have revealed the presence of walls with a base of cobbles of small and medium dimensions, occasionally rough-hewn, and elevations in mudbrick (in some cases the entire structure is in mudbrick); such structures can be dated to within the seventh century B.C., and were evidently destroyed before midway through the ensuing century. The chambers to which the vestiges of wall refer (together with remnants of flooring in whitish clay) are not apparently all oriented in the same way, though some are aligned with the regular residential sector (NNO–SSE) which, shortly before or after the mid-sixth century, involved leveling the earlier housing stock, supposedly somewhat sparsely scattered over the lowland, as they seem to have been also on the east slopes and the plateau of the Himera hillside. Evidence in the east quarter for the very first colonial encampment is scarce: the remains of four dwellings with storage cisterns for grain, destroyed and filled in around 580–570 B.C. when these ledges were terraced to make room for a properly programmed residential zone. On the plateau, which stretches from south to north, covering a limited area (approximately 20 hectares), the excavations of Palermo University – directed by Achille Adriani in the first stages, and subsequently by Nicola Bonacasa – have disclosed a mere few scattered single-room units of which remains some evidence of paving in a double layer of cobbles laid in an earth binder; in the opinion of Bonacasa, these units are part of a farmhouse-type division of the land. The sacred enclave of the tutelary deity, Athena, was given a key position overlooking the sea, but in the northeast corner of the plateau so as not to interfere with the groundplots of the first colonists; in this way the sacred area and the urban fabric could grow together unimpeded. West of the *temenos* an area that remained undeveloped must have been allocated for community use from the start; Bonacasa has in fact suggested that this vacant area was the upper *agora*.

In the second quarter of the sixth century – in perfect parallel with Selinus of which the Chalcidian colony for its date of foundation (648 B.C.) and the scope it was to fulfill constitutes a singular counteweight on the northern coast of the island – Himera carried out a thorough and coherent program of urban planning. As at Selinus, the natural features provided the skeleton for the new urban structure. This time, however, it was built with an eye far into the future. On the hill, instead of the previous northeast–southwest alignment attested by the earliest of the sacred buildings (Temple A), the architects favored a central axis running north–south, 6.2 meters wide, that afforded a better division of the narrow

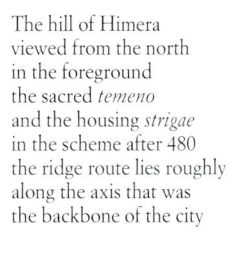

The hill of Himera viewed from the north in the foreground the sacred *temeno* and the housing *strigae* in the scheme after 480 the ridge route lies roughly along the axis that was the backbone of the city

Himera
plan of the city
in the 5th cent. B.C.

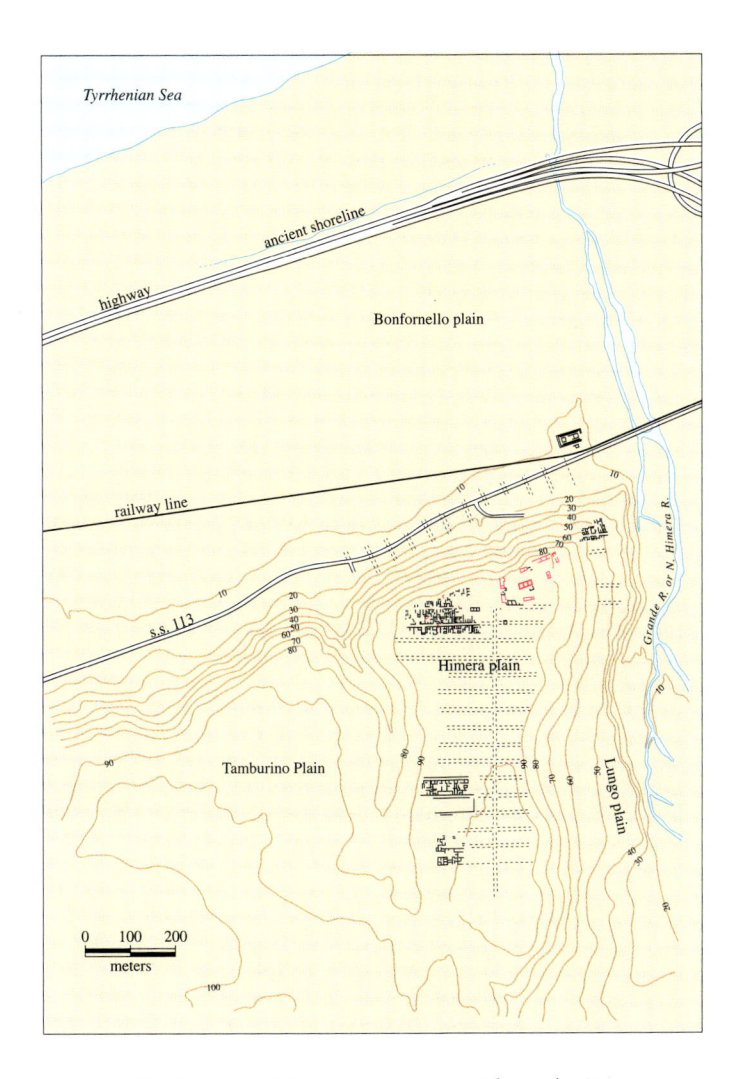

plateau, allowing a set of housing *strigae* on either side. Sixteen east–west streets lying parallel with each other and the coast – from 5.6 to 6 meters wide – divided up the entire plateau, forming housing *strigae* 32 meters wide and considerably long (some reaching 196 meters). As at Selinus, the city was programmed to expand along the flanks of the plateau (the east quarter below was aligned with the upper *strigae*); furthermore, the planners radically altered the orientation of the housing blocks, setting them along streets running NNW–SSE in the great port quarter at the foot of the tall mount, which has proved to be the most important living nucleus of the sixth and fifth centuries. Here the shoreline and the path of the northern part of the Himera River determined the main axes of alignment, and excavations have brought to light remnants of an artisans' quarter denoting a fairly high tenor of life, with rooms grouped around spacious cobbled courtyards (some partially roofed), and with *androneṣ*, the special rooms in which the menfolk entertained their guests.

Besides having located the northern border of the residential fabric (apparently defended by a wall) lying very close to the shore, the latest excavations have enabled the archaeologists to reconstruct an urban system based on eleven (though possibly seventeen) *strigae* 40.5–41 meters wide, flanked by streets 6–6.3 meters wide running perpendicular to the shoreline (three have so far been identified) and intersected by narrow *ambitus* (0.5 meters) that suggest, at least for some sectors, dwellings measuring 20 by 20 meters. The fieldworkers have since speculated the presence of *plateiai* parallel to the NNW–SSE streets and of others lying transversely (though this has yet to be verified).

To judge from current data, this system is datable to shortly after the system established on the plateau, or of the houses built on terraced land in the east quarter. For this reason it seems defensible to infer that the system was a single scheme, datable to between 575 and 550 B.C. and implemented piecemeal on the land in the space of a century (Allegro and Vassallo). The fact that the *insulae* are much broader than those of the tableau is a point to consider; however, as with the alignment, the extra width of the area to be occupied and hence the width of the *insulae* may well have been determined by the morphological

Urban Planning in Ancient Sicily

The promontory of Camarina
viewed from the south
the ruins of the Temple of Athena
lie between the River Ippari
to the north, and the River Oanis
running through the town

Camarina
plan of the area of the *agora*

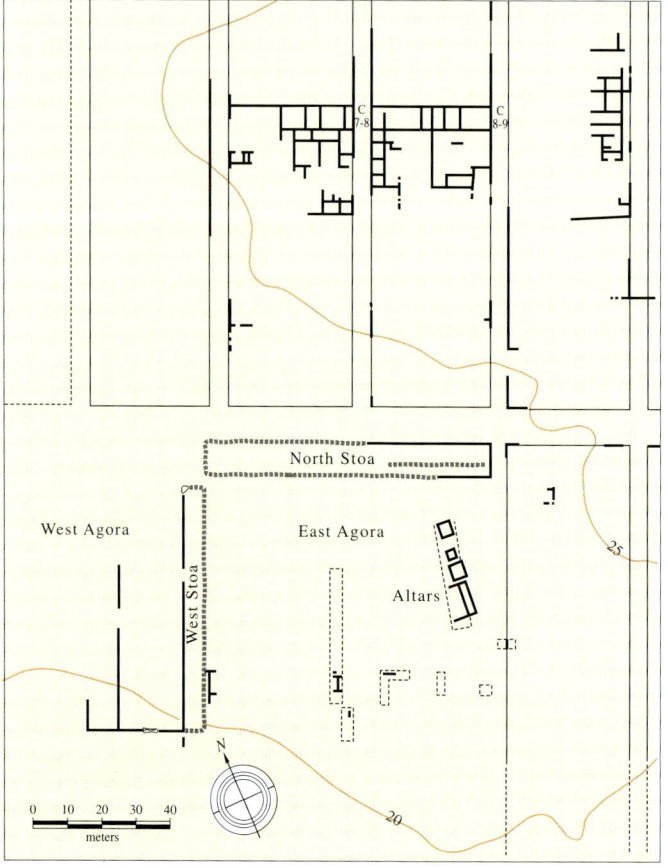

conditions; equally possible, it could have been influenced by socioeconomic factors that are best explained by the presence of a busy harbor facility on the river below.

Be that as it may, the fundamental fact gleaned from this latest stint of fieldwork is that not after 480 B.C., but a mere two or three generations after its foundation, Himera in the second quarter of the sixth century attempted to keep apace with Selinus, and endowed itself with a new territorial urban system, reoccupying, terracing, leveling areas that had so far been only sparsely occupied since the foundation. Imposing public works were planned (the *peribolos* of the old Athena *temenos* was rebuilt and the enclave endowed with new buildings), indicative of a political outlook geared to the future. As I hypothesized for Selinus around 560 B.C., Himera was probably wrecked by a natural disaster that facilitated a program of reconstruction that the city maintained until 409 B.C. The excavations suggest a city far larger than was formerly imagined (12,000–16,000 inhabitants), with an extension calculable at ca. 80 hectares, either equal to or slightly less than that of Selinus. The important difference from Selinus, however, is that in 476 B.C. the oldest section of the town was resettled by 10,000 colonists of Dorian extraction sent by the tyrant Theron of Acragas (who a few years before 480 had expelled from Himera the pro-Punic Terillus, provoking the intervention of Carthage). Despite the apparent redistribution of terrain in the Himera *chora*, the urban fabric betrays no overall alterations. It may be, therefore, that these new inhabitants were responsible for the dwellings brought to light by the Istituto Archeologico, Palermo.

In the "north quarter" at least, the *strigae* are delineated by the ancient east–west streets and traversed in the same direction by a long median passageway (*ambitus*) and in a north–south direction by a set of *ambitus* so narrow that they can only have served as conduits for carrying away water; the elevation of the walls is once more in mudbrick, and the roof in tiles in terra-cotta. This "north quarter" with its rigid scheme of housing lots is not so noticeably different from Hieron's Naxos, whose orthogonal street system seems to pivot on the *insula* as a fixed modular element, within which all the buildings – be they public or private – are duly inserted. I will discuss this question below, after giving a picture of two other townships, Camarina and Acragas, which came into being shortly after Selinus and Himera established their ultimate system.

Camarina

There can be no doubt that, from certain aspects, Camarina is the colonial settlement that most closely resembles Selinus, and not surprisingly they were both secondary settlements, whose layout was undoubtedly precluded by a careful study and choice of site.

First and foremost, the actual site is a "promontory" above the sea, with two hills limited at their foot by rivers, the Oanis and the Hipparis, the latter of which was suitable for the installation of a port-canal. Consequently, we also find at Camarina a long natural axis that followed the ridge of the headland, a line that would become the pivot of the entire urban layout from the settlement's foundation, though it did not actually determine the orientation of the very first houses. These occupied the area closest to the shore, and were followed further inland by the sacred enclave, shut off from the private fabric by a *temenos*, which was awarded the highest point of the promontory. This development is an exact parallel to my suppositions regarding first-generation Selinus, and, like at Selinus, apart from this elementary zoning – the areas reserved for the living, for the gods, for the community activities, and for the dead –, its pattern did not constitute a system that can reliably be classified as urban.

The system of occupancy of the broad area of at least 150 hectares was not of a strictly urban type, even though Camarina was a secondary colony (like Selinus, Himera, and Acragas) of numerical importance and involved consolidated kinship groups. In fact the situation of the Rifriscolaro necropolis, coeval with the first encampments and aligned (as at Naxos, Syracuse, and Megara Hyblaea) with the dominant route out to the *chora*, shows how the colonists were ranged haphazardly over the promontory and the two hills behind it, though there was a greater concentration of dwellings on the seaward side. At least in Classical times, therefore, here stood the *agora*, though one can assume that it occupied the same site (an area that has yielded no housing remains, moreover) from the dawn of the colony's foundation at the hands of Daskon and Menekolos at the start of the sixth century B.C. (599–598 B.C. according to Thucydides). The area was exposed to the south, near the moorage (later a harbor) at the mouth of the Hipparis and furthermore this particular stretch of land was devoid of humus and hence unsuitable for cultivation, and in a position to not impede the division of the land into *kleroi*, or allotments.

On the other hand, the walls which toward the mid-sixth century encircled the headland and hills with a full seven-kilometer circuit seem to advocate an original "agrarian" setup for the settlement; while the farms of recent discovery east of the Archaic necropolis (Rifriscolaro), whose nearest burials lie a mere hundred meters from the wall, show how, outside the circuit of the walls, only from the mid-fifth century did Camarina assume a preordered assignation of land to be cultivated. The fields seem to have been regularly divided up, to a distance of four kilometers from the town, with alignments and intervals that take their cue from the town's own pattern.

This parceling scheme can be attributed to the Geloan refoundation of the *apoikia* in 461 B.C., and it is likely that only then did the layout shift from a series of scattered housing nuclei to an organic urban structure filling most of the enclosed area and become organized around *insulae* delineated by an orthogonal grid. What is puzzling is the skewed position of the Temple of Athena (which may have been decided by an existing *naos* of earlier date) and that of the large building unearthed in the *quadrivium* of *plateia* C with the transverse Street 43-44: it seems that the Timoleontian layout of the fourth century reiterates the earlier fifth-century system (in a general sense at least) and that this was pivoted on the cardinal southeast–northwest axis and on Street A, slightly further south and also parallel. In this period it may be that the *agora* was already in use which, limited by the *plateiai* B and A, gave southward onto the sea at the tip of the spur.

Attempts have been made to precisely equate the urban scheme brought to light in recent excavations at Camarina with the post-461 setup, thereby making the colony – like Naxos and Himera – a model of Siceliot urban planning in the "age of tyrants," with Theron recolonizing the settlement of Himera in 476 and Hieron the new *ktistis* of Naxos in the same lapse of time (Belvedere 1987). The archaeological data, furthermore, throw little light on the question, and only Naxos can truly hold the title of "tyrant's city" attributed by Paola Pelagatti. According to the most recent studies on Himera, it appears that the city's sixth-century layout remained basically unaltered in terms of orientation, the width of the *insulae* and the streets, and their ratios) from the transferal of the Dorian colonists sent by Theron; whereas in Camarina, the *polis* with which we are familiar is pure Timoleontian; of the fifth-century city only scattered remains have come to light in not more than five or six excavation sections (Di Stefano 1993), sufficient perhaps for a hypothetical reconstruction which, however, could prove well-founded only as regards the general layout and not the relationships between the several constituent parts of the fabric.

Acragas

To my mind the first installation at Acragas, the most famous Siceliot subcolony, consisted of scattered dwellings, or grouped houses, or clusters of houses within a zoning scheme. This does not mean, of course, that trade beyond the seas was not a major factor of the economy and development of these colonies of southern Sicily – as amply testified by the thousand or more *amphorae* from all over the Mediterranean reutilized as *enchytrismoi* in the necropolises in sixth-century Camarina. In the sixth century their ports seem to have been particularly busy; moreover, Acragas' *emporion*, discovered six kilometers south of today's city at Montelusa, then on the estuary of the confluence of the Akragas and the Hypsas, seems to have quickly become a highly efficient station. The immense wealth (and consequent political force) accrued by Acragas by the mid-sixth century under the tyranny of Phalaris was above all tied to the fertility of the farmlands between the two rivers on which the first colonists from Gela (and perhaps directly from Rhodes) installed themselves; the rivers provided excellent irrigation by means of a system attested at Camarina that would be practiced far and wide in Greek Sicily.

The area taken over by the *oikistai* Aristonoüs and Pistilus in around 580 B.C. was a glade gently sloping toward the sea, clearly marked on either side by the two rivers and protected to the north by the sharp crag which forms the Rupe Atenea, once the site of the acropolis, and to the south by the long hill of temples. Approximately 450 hectares in which there are no burials and no *temene* for the gods, except the one at San Nicola, almost central in the valley 123 meters above sea level, were soon destined to become the focus of community and political life. While the *bouleuterion* and *ekklesiasterion* are the work of the recolonization effort of Timoleon, it is likely that a community space existed in this area from either the Archaic or Classical period. At least in an early stage of development, this may have been the monumental L-shaped *stoa* erected toward the close of the sixth century on the north slopes of the hill, and of the clearing onto which this building gave; alternatively it may be that the clearing accommodated a *bouleuterion* of Classical construction.

The valley was girded by a massive enclosure wall as early as the later sixth century, but was not treated to a rational and grandiose process of urbanization until fifty years later. This is reflected in the city gates, which are clearly oriented to the routes to and from the *chora* rather than to the urban grid. The gods were assigned the banks that were unsuitable for agriculture, given the rocky peaks, which were effective in emphasizing the small *sacella* and temples which from mid-century began to sprout on the south hill, complete with *temene*, between Villa Aurea, Colimbetra, and the spur northwest of this, conveniently close to Gates IV and V. Immediately outside the curtain wall, and built close alongside, we find a cluster of later sixth-century coroplast workshops; the necropolis coeval with the foundation of the *apoikia* has been excavated just 300 meters from Gate VI and extended westward.

From the end of the sixth century the *sacella* on the hill were gradually converted into temples, and the valley – which varies from 70 to 190 meters above sea level – was gradually urbanized according to a complex program of building to which Acragas, despite dreadful moments of destruction and the ravages of time, clung until late antiquity. Ernesto De Miro has provided a reliable survey of the *per strigas* system of the town, arranged on six east–west *plateiai* 7 meters wide (though the second and fourth are considerably wider) and on numerous north–south *stenopoi*, identified from aerial surveys by G. Schmidt in the 1950s, a system that dates to the close of the sixth century. Thanks to an ambitious program of land consolidation, the *insulae* in the lower part of the valley began to vaunt those mansions which justified Empedocles' aphorism on his kinsmen who "devoted themselves to luxury as if there were no tomorrow, but built as if they would live forever" (Diogenes Laertius, VIII.63).

At this time Gate II of Gela and the southeastern quarters were linked via an artery twelve meters wide that ran in a straight line to the complex of ancient sanctuaries near Gate V; perpendicular to this *plateia* – practically the backbone of the entire system – ran a set of *stenopoi* 5.5 meters wide; furthermore, aligned with the *plateia* stood one of the three largest temples of the Greek world, the *olympieion* dedicated to Zeus Olympus in thanks for Gelon's crushing victory over the Carthaginians at Himera of 480. This triumph was largely the merit of the tyrants of Syracuse and Acragas, and had a decisive influence in every sphere of the subsequent development of Greek Sicily, from the political and economic sphere, to the cultural and artistic sphere. East of the *Olympieion*, south and north of the *plateia* bordering it – on the first two of the massive terraces over which the town gradually spread as it climbed the hill – stood two large *agorai* (the upper one of which was later occupied by an Augustan *gymnasium*); while, after 480 B.C., the thousands of slaves and the immense riches snatched from the Carthaginians enabled the Acragantines to complete the complex water conduits designed by the engineer Phaeax (Diodorus, XI. 25. 3–4). A series of underground canals were engineered for channeling and distributing the water from the Rupe Atenea and Girgenti hills throughout the urban area; according to Giulio Schmidt, this system comprised twen-

Acragas: aerial view from the south of Temple A or the Temple of Hercules

ty-three separate branches, for a total length of 14,600 meters. The conduits ran at the base or in the walls of galleries cut into the rock or constructed (in the case of clayey terrain), up to two meters high and one wide; these conduits channeled the residue waters from the *kolymbethra*, or lake, with its rich stock of fish, swans, and bird-life at the southwestern border of the town. In the mid-fifth century Acragas must have been one of the most populated and prosperous *poleis* in the entire Hellenic world (Diogenes Laertius, VIII. 63; Pindar, *Olympian* II. 20. 96. 170; *Pythian*. VI. 6. 46; Diodorus, XIII. 90. 3).

Basically at Acragas we can witness a further consolidation and refinement of urbanistic principles which had been effected in Selinus six or seven decades earlier; whereas the growing emphasis on the *insula* in the construction of the *polis* seems to have been favored by the fact that here the existing sacred areas were on the hills on either side of the valley, which accommodated the superb *polis* programmed at the end of the sixth century. The San Nicola mount served as the political and physical hub of the urban system.

Some decades later this system was reworked and applied by Hippodamus of Miletus to Piraeus (the port of Athens), to Thurii, and to Rhodes. The system eventually assumed his name.

Town planning in Sicily of the 5th–6th centuries: from Naxos to Tyrdans
Once the impending threat of Punic invasion was over, after 480 B.C. the Siceliot towns and cities passed into the hands of the "liberating" tyrants who, with their Dorian blood, began to tailor the recolonization of the ancient Chalcidian *apoikiai* to their own interests – first by deporting the inhabitants. Traces of this mass deportation are most evident in Naxos, whose population was transferred to Leontini in 476 by Hieron of Syracuse.

The written sources (Diodorus, XI. 76. 4) talk of a redistribution of land, which presumably entailed canceling all prior private ownership and in some cases may even have meant a total restructuring of the built-up area or the addition of new residential quarters.

Fifteen years later, around 460 B.C., when the Deinomenid and Emmenid tyrannies had come to an end, with or without violence, the exiles returned to the towns from which they had been expelled; this would perforce have involved further changes in ownership and new adjustments, particularly in the *chora*, but evidence of this process in the urban fabric is still lacking. In fact, it is difficult to establish which changes belong to the efforts of the *tyrannoi* and which to the renewal of democracy.

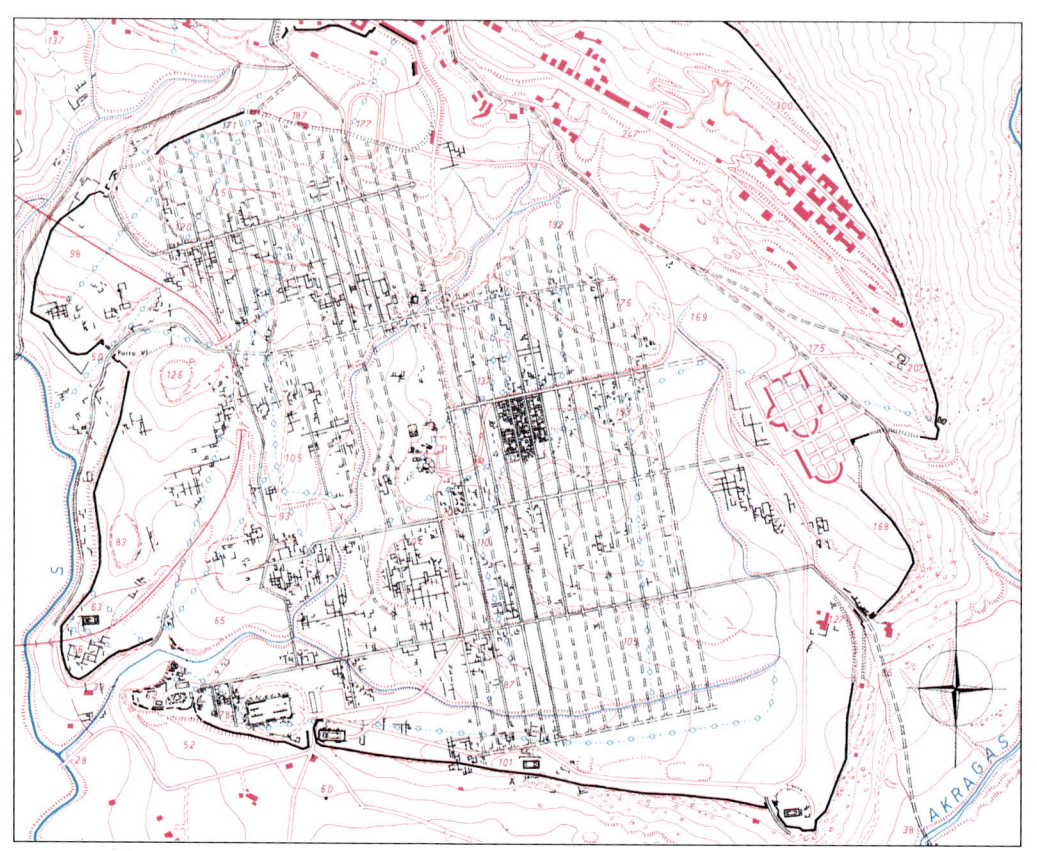

Acragas: plan of the ancient city as to 1984
— walls: certain course
∷∷∷∷ walls: supposed course
═══ streets: certain course
═ ═ ═ streets: supposed course
— — — ancient aqueducts

Acragas: plan of the Hellenistic Roman quarter
1. House of the gazelle
2. House of the swastika
3. Square
4. House of the peristyle
5. House of the hoard
6. House of the mill
7. House of the abstract maestro
8. House of the Dionysus
9. House of the *cryptoporticus*
10. House of the Aphrodites
11. *Tabernae*
12. House of the rhomboid mosaic
13. House of the atrium *in antis*
14. House of the hypostyle cistern
15. House of the athlete
16. House of the portico
17. House of the *pelte*
18. House of the veiled woman

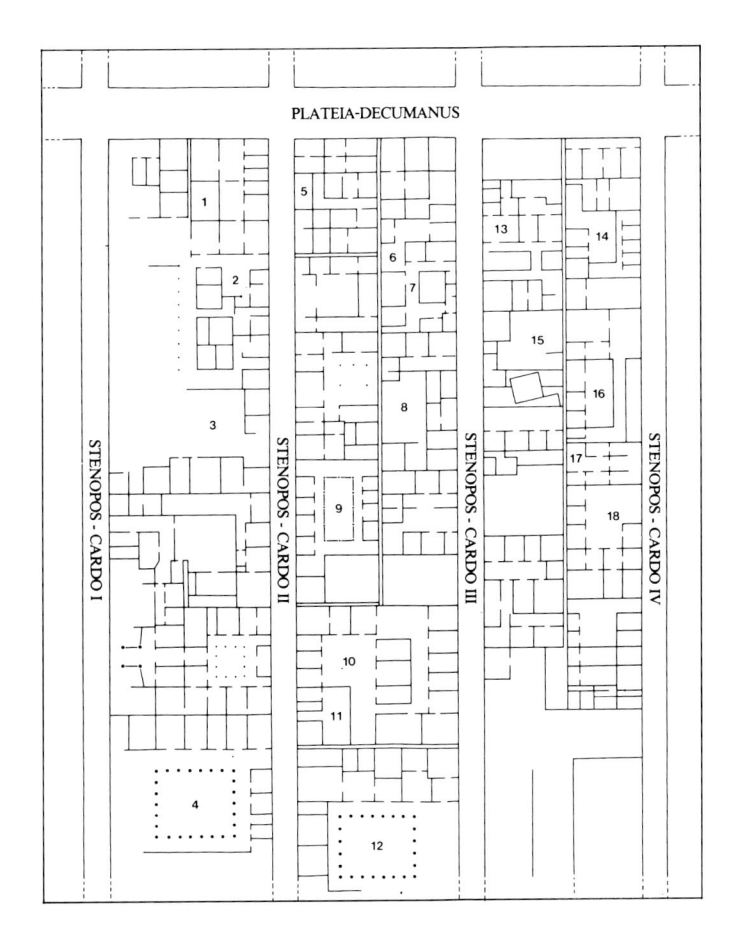

Naxos

In many respects, Naxos betrays a unitary program of building on the ruins of the Archaic city in the early decades of the fifth century, and since in 403 B.C. the city was razed permanently by another Syracusan tyrant, Dionysius I, it is possible to detect in the forced partitioning of the built-up area the advanced stage of planning that had been reached in Sicily by the time of the tyrants Hieron and Theron (and, in Magna Graecia, witness Neapolis).

The situation is more legible for Syracuse, home of the Deinomenids and the most puissant military and economic city-state of Sicily in the fifth century. Here, the complex series of expulsions, reaccommodation of deported citizens and mercenaries, the return of exiles (Herodotus, VII. 156; Diodorus, XI. 72. 3) must have had a keen influence on the makeup of the urban fabric, and yet reliable traces of these upheavals have not yet been disclosed, although a planned level of later date (fourth–third centuries) glimpsed between the northernmost rim of Achradina and Tyche seems to be an extension of the planning schemes undertaken in Syracuse under the tyrants (Belvedere, 1990). At Naxos, which was rebuilt from the foundations by Hieron – probably to garrison his mercenaries – a standard *insula* (39 meters wide composed of 4 housing units 9 meters wide, separated by an *ambitus*, and 156–158 meters long) seems to have formed the basis of the grid. This rigidly regular scheme pivots on three *plateiai* running east–west that rationally section up the peninsula, plus a set of minor north–south streets.

The Aphrodite *temenos* was not incorporated in this somewhat unyielding Hippodamian setup, and there are residues of the primeval tendency to emphasize certain natural axes: the *plateia* that halves the rectangle of the peninsula is wider than the others (9.5 meters against 6.5); likewise the *stenopos* that traces the ancient Syracuse–Zancle route is 6.5 meters wide instead of the 5 of the other *stenopoi* running parallel to it. Be that as it may, the city of the "tyrants" – as Pelagatti meaningfully described it – rests on a true *per strigas* plan, built, moreover, with the authoritarian intention of allocating the new inhabitants by building groundplots of equal size. One peculiar feature is the set of quadrangular base courses situated at the northwest corner of each *insula*, projecting into the *plateiai*. They are proof that the entire plan was built outright, imposed by a strong political power with economic means, and these are likely to have been small altars whose lanterns helped illuminate the *quadrivii* on feast days.

Hence, more explicitly than any of its counterparts, Naxos affords a paradigmatic vision of the stage of

Naxos, remains of the Greek colony

advancement achieved by town planning in early fifth-century Sicily. Although similar experiences (determined by analogous circumstances) have appeared in the Greek *poleis* of Asia Minor, there can be little doubt that in the first decades of the fifth century the western colonies provided the homeland with brilliant models of planning science. Without going into the thorny issue of the reconstruction program of Hippodamus, who was an adopted Athenian of Ionian stock, it is important to realize that he must have taken account of these models. And when some years later in the mid-fourth century the Corinthian-born tyrant Timoleon braced himself to physically and morally rebuild the Siceliot towns, he decided to apply the ancient *per strigas* system – with its rational integration of fairly standard components (*stenopoi, plateiai, insulae*) – to most of them, although influences of the new ideas introduced by Hippodamus are detectable here and there.

The practical form of town planning advocated by Hippodamus, with its geometrical blueprint of "juxtaposed planes, extended surfaces, continuations of lines" (Martin), characterized furthermore by ease and speed of execution and a philosophical egalitarianism, but whose overly rigid modular repetition fails to take account of the morphology of the site, was ultimately lacking in imagination and engendered a monotony that was not attenuated by the cumbrous *agorai* at the heart of the system, nor by the community buildings inserted into this geometric scheme. Only in the Hellenistic capitals was Hippodamus' scientific layout enlivened by a renewed appreciation of monuments; from the fourth century, moreover, urban planning came to be affected by the precepts of Hippocrates' philosophy of medicine.

The principles of Hippodamian urban planning – which spread throughout the Greek world between the fifth and the fourth centuries owing to the constant interchange of ideas between Mainland Greece, Asia Minor, and the West, providing a common language albeit with different accents – were developed and applied in Sicily, though they did not supplant the established way of building towns, from which it is likely that Hippodamus himself took his cue.

It has been shown, however, that the new theories of Hippodamus regarded a quite different reality from that in which the ancient *poleis* had originally developed (Belvedere, 1987). They were geared to creating large-scale towns from scratch, of which Piraeus, Thurii, and Rhodes are examples – towns instituted by strong economic and political powers and programmed to be as functional as possible for their inhabitants. In such cities the most evident novelty on the terrain (Rhodes, for instance) is the multiplication of the *plateiai* and *stenopoi* and by the consequent contraction of the lengths of the *insulae* (creating an optimal ratio of 1:2), so as to favor the rapid traversal from one side of the broad fabric to the other. To return to fifth-century Sicily, the element linking the development from the last of the *apoikiai* founded in the sixth century to the *poleis* of Timoleon is provided (excluding Camarina for now) by Naxos, by the early and mid-fifth-century layouts of Gela and Morgantina. Morgantina's planning is most likely datable (at least the project) to the refoundation drive led by Ducetius from 459 to 449 B.C. and the regular *insulae* covered the hillsides around the central glade (running 125 meters east–west and 250 north–south) where the townsfolk erected the *agora*, at the time merely an undeveloped area of medium dimensions that was later widened and adorned with monumental constructions between mid-fourth century and the era of Hieron II.

For the first half of the fourth century this link was best represented by the Dionysian subcolony of Tyndaris, which is laid out upon three broad causeways parallel to the shoreline, intersected at 90 degrees every 30 meters by *stenopoi* that rapidly descend the rocky headland on which the citadel was built. The *insulae*, lying perpendicular therefore to the sea, were 78 meters long, and the most important monuments – the theater, the so-called *basilica*, the *agora* – were arranged at the head of the highest of these *plateia* causeways; the position was excellent, and was perfectly inserted in the grid of the exquisitely regular Hippodamian layout which survived intact through to imperial times.

The Siceliot cities between Timoleon and Hieron II

Of the Timoleontian cities of Sicily, the best-known is undoubtedly Camarina, given that it was destroyed a hundred years after its refoundation and was only minimally involved in the ensuing reconstruction program.

But before discussing Camarina, we should give a rapid glance at Heraclea Minoa, and once again at Acragas and Gela.

Heraclea Minoa

Heraclea Minoa, founded by the inhabitants of Selinus, was perpetually fought-over due to its ideal strategic position on the estuary of the Platani (the ancient Halykos). The first contender was Acragas, but subsequently it drew the attention of the Carthaginians, the Syracusans, and finally the Romans. Excavation work has revealed that the fourth–third-century town was planned with *insulae* running east–west on the natural shelves that descended toward the sea and the Platani, following a Hippodamian scheme by which the theater was given a superb panoramic position. In these *insulae* a layer of well-built homesteads has come to light, above which more modest dwellings were later built in the second and first centuries B.C. The city walls – as was customary for this kind of *polis* – followed the natural contours of defense, and were rebuilt when a serious landslide within the chalky hill decreed the abandonment of the eastern quarters, leaving room to reconstruct the walls alongside the later built-up area.

Acragas

As for Acragas, after its destruction by Carthage in the year 406 B.C., the city did not reacquire its former glory until the advent of Timoleon in the mid-fourth century.

Having restored the defensive walls, the old urban pattern was resumed in which the construction of an imposing *ekklesiasterion* to accommodate 3,000 people, plus the resurrection of the *bouleuterion* disclosed by excavation work – buildings which served as part of the democratic order imposed by the Corinthian-born tyrant on the Siceliot *poleis* – emphasizing the crucial value of the San Nicola ridge as the epicenter of the new city's political and urbanistic activity.

Recently E. De Miro has discerned in Acragas' urban planning (and monumental architecture) of the Proto-Hellenistic period the reflection of the direct relations between Sicily and Asia Minor via the principles elaborated by the Milesian school of planning, of which Hippodamus was the most eminent exponent. De Miro has managed to identify traces of functional diversification in the Late Archaic and Classical layers of the city's fabric, namely, the two lower terraces, the *agorai*, the third (central) terrace, the core of the community, the dwellings reserved for the upper classes, and the urbanistic junction between the eastern quarters and those of the northwestern sector of the town, together with the upper quarters for the lower classes and craftsmen.

This new functional distinction, and the arrangement of terraces strikingly accentuated by flights of steps and a "rigorous application of the orthogonal system to the sloping ground" (a feature already present in pre-406 Acragas), are planning principles that crop up in the same decades in the newly founded Camarina, for instance, and show how the urban model advocated by Hippodamus had quickly become currency throughout the Greek world. However, Acragas and Camarina (as De Miro has duly pointed out) were simply resuscitated *poleis* and the conditions imposed by the earlier layout – and by inveterate cultural traditions and entrenched customs – make direct comparisons with coeval *poleis* in Asia Minor impossible.

Repopulated by the Romans after the bitter events of the Second Punic War, Acragas (renamed Agrigentum) may have lost its freedom but it conserved for long centuries to come the outline of its Classical layout. This can be seen in the residential *strigae* dating to Late Hellenistic and Roman times, relics of which have been brought to light at the foot of San Nicola; to the north the ancient *plateia* IV became the Roman *decumanus*, remaining the foremost thoroughfare for both urban and extraurban traffic (leading to Gates I and VI). Eleven meters wide, the *decumanus* was marked off by the half-width *cardines* (formerly the *stenopoi*) running north–south, creating street blocks 35 meters wide and a good 280 meters long, complying with the traditional system of Siceliot town construction. These street blocks are divided by long perpendicular *ambitus* and – perhaps in conformity with the more numerous system advanced by Hippodamus, by a set of east–west *ambitus*.

Until the late fourth and early fifth century A.D. the city maintained its scheme of zoning, and the twenty dwellings brought to light at the foot of the San Nicola hill have provided one of the most significant examples of dwellings in Siceliot cities of the Hellenistic-Roman period.

Gela

Timoleon's refounded colony Gela spread lavishly westward outside its Archaic and Classical boundaries and was girded by powerful defensive outworks, a section of which, with hewn blocks below and mud-

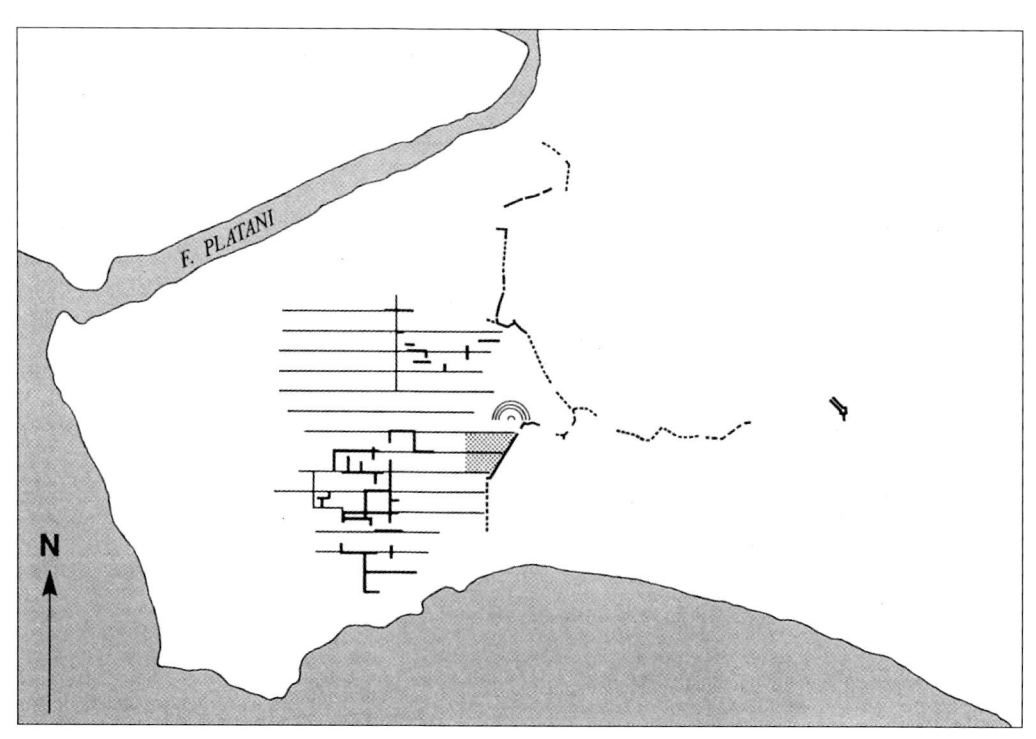

Heraclea Minoa, plan of the Timoleontian-Hellenistic city

Remains at Heraclea Minoa

bricks above, was found by Griffo at Capo Soprano. In the last few years, moreover, Graziella Fiorentini and Ernesto De Miro have brought to light the stratigraphic sequence of the acropolis buildings; in their last phase these constructions were raised during Timoleon's reign. However, it is at Camarina that the terrain has permitted greater exploration, revealing an extensive Timoleontian town plan.

Camarina

Timoleon's Camarina – as described by Pindar in the fifth century – likewise accommodated a composite kind of community. The Geloan foundation in 461 B.C. is attested by the discovery of 158 small lead *tesserae* deposited in the Temple of Athena (Cordano, 1992), which testify to a Dorian system of constitution (fifteen *phratriai*, traditionally divided into three tribes) albeit with some Athenian inflexions, though a study of the names on the pieces make it clear that the populace was of mixed stock.

This situation inevitably also recurred in the fourth century, given that a significant quota of Timoleon's colonists were from Mainland Greece, with which Camarina had moreover entertained direct and intensive links throughout the fifth century, particularly through Athens, to which the Siceliot colony had remained a faithful ally. (It is significant that a good third of the Attic vases in the Museo Archeologico, Syracuse, were found in Camarina.)

The cultural legacy of the new settlers most likely included "new" ideas and experiences regarding urban planning – indeed, those canvassed by Hippodamus – and echoes of these can be discerned in the Timoleontian layers of the town brought to light by modern excavation work.

The town was enlarged (Diodorus, XVI. 82. 2) and in truth areas within the Archaic walls that had always been vacant now appear to be occupied (the southeastern slopes, all or part of the so-called Heracles' Rise, and the bluff of the Lauretta houses to the northeast); this implies that fourth-century Camarina covered a greater area with a more complex layout than the settlement abandoned in 405 B.C., which means that we should be cautious about extrapolating information on the earlier town setup.

Aerial view of Camarina with the modern road running almost parallel to the ancient routes

The Timoleontian layout pivots on five *plateiai* (four of which have been reliably pinpointed) which, like the two (or three) of the preceding systems, ran parallel north and south of Street *B*. In the fifth century this street had provided a kind of backbone for the residential fabric, traversing the narrow "spur" in a southeast–northwest direction between the Hipparis and Oanis, taking account of the geographical layout and avoiding the actual peak of the elevation. It was probably only at this stage that the fabric was continued over Heracles' Rise; here and across the other *plateiai* (10 meters wide) ran a host of *stenopoi* (4.5–5.0 meters wide) with a mean ratio of approximately 1:2. The *insulae* thus marked out by this grid were of strictly equal widths (135–138 meters) with a ratio never in excess of 1:4 – lower, therefore, than those found in other Siceliot street plans in the fifth century B.C.

Furthermore, in many cities of the same period – from Priene in Ionia to the Hellenized Punic settlement of Soluntum – the *stenopoi* climb from the two rivers to the crest of the hill, tackling various abrupt changes of ground level but without diverging from the perpendicular plan of the *plateiai*, thereby creating "a geometrical subdivision without reference to either site or terrain" (Martin). What is involved here is the application of a set of standards (an inflexible layout, a greatly facilitated street pattern, a further reduction of the traditional length of the *insulae*, which are now conceived by the planner as *oikopeda*) which reflect principles inferred from the design of Hippodamus' *megalopoleis*. The fact that the main thoroughfare, Street *B*, is extended only in this phase toward the southeast, and does not yield when it meets Heracles' Rise is further proof: in medieval and modern times the street grid has always bypassed the hill from the north.

A solid north–south wall from the Hipparis to the Oanis divided the headland from the rest of the residential fabric, since the area stretching from the *temenos* of Athena toward the shore – an area that comprised the *agora*, with large warehouses and doubtless also the town's main public buildings – constituted a veritable acropolis. The restored temple of the town's tutelary deity Athena – which may have been enhanced at this point with a series of pedimental decorations – remained enclosed with the *peribolos* of the Archaic sacred enclave; the western tract of this enclosure has been identified in the space of two and a half *insulae* delimited respectively in the north and south by *plateiai* C and B, on which the *propylaion*, or monumental gateway, to the enclave stood.

Nine street blocks further down, this *plateia* marked off the north flank of the *agora*, which in the fifth century may have been squared off on the south side by *plateia* A (the southernmost, if we discard the street that ran straight behind the city wall and, like the *plateiai*, was around ten meters wide).

In the early phases of Camarina, the *agora* occupied an ample space corresponding to the southwest corner of the promontory. As noted above, this scheme was for practical purposes, and down the centuries the *agora* was never moved – not even when it became slightly peripheral with respect to the town's effective growth; one can infer the existence, nonetheless, of other community spaces within the town's eastern sector.

There can be little doubt that in Timoleon's Camarina the *agora* was carefully ensconced by the modular street plan, where it occupied at least three *insulae* (perhaps even four), proceeding westward from *stenopos* 8/9. It is also possible, to my mind, that by comparison with what we have observed at Syracuse itself and in Morgantina, the monumental systematization of the area came about in a later stage, under Agathocles, or perhaps even at the start of Hieron II's reign.

A *stoa* 10.5 meters wide and more or less 80 long, aligned on *plateia* B, closed off the square at the north, and gave onto the south with a galleried building 3.3 meters deep that comprised 34 square pillars framing 17 units; on the west side, at the height of *stenopos* 6/7, a second *stoa* 66 meters long separated this politico-religious *agora* (as attested by the three square bases and a rectangular altar) from the one on the west, which was of more strictly commercial nature.

The commercial destination of this latter *agora* is also testified by the fact that in the southern section of the west *stoa* – which both separated and joined the two *agorai* as it gave onto both (toward the west with a broad gateway) – fieldworkers have found an extraordinary underground repository of Greco-Italian *amphorae* datable to late fourth–early third century B.C.; in addition to this, in the water 45 meters from the tip where the second *agora* was situated, researchers have found six thick square lead plaques whose symbols and inscriptions imply them to be sample-weights (multiples, and sub-multiples of the *leitra* standard), a system in use in the Hellenistic period in Camarina. In all likelihood these were kept in an *agoranomeion*, possibly located right on the water's edge (Di Stefano, 1994).

Camarina: Timoleontian plan
capital letters indicate
the *plateiai*
numbers indicate the blocks
a. Area of the docks - b. Tower
c. Gela Gate - d. Cloaca - e. Kiln
f. House of the altar
g. Eastern quarter
h. Temple of Athena - i. Tower
j. *Quadrivium* - k. Hyblaea Gate
l. Rifriscolaro Archaic necropolis
m. Hill of Heracles
n. Street 6th cent. B.C.
o. Area of the Sanctuary of Demeter
p. House of the inscription
q. House of the merchant
r. Unascertained course
   of the urban walls
s. Urban walls - t. Gate
u. Tower - v. Kiln
w. Passo Marinato Classical necropolis
z. Defense wall 4th cent. B.C.

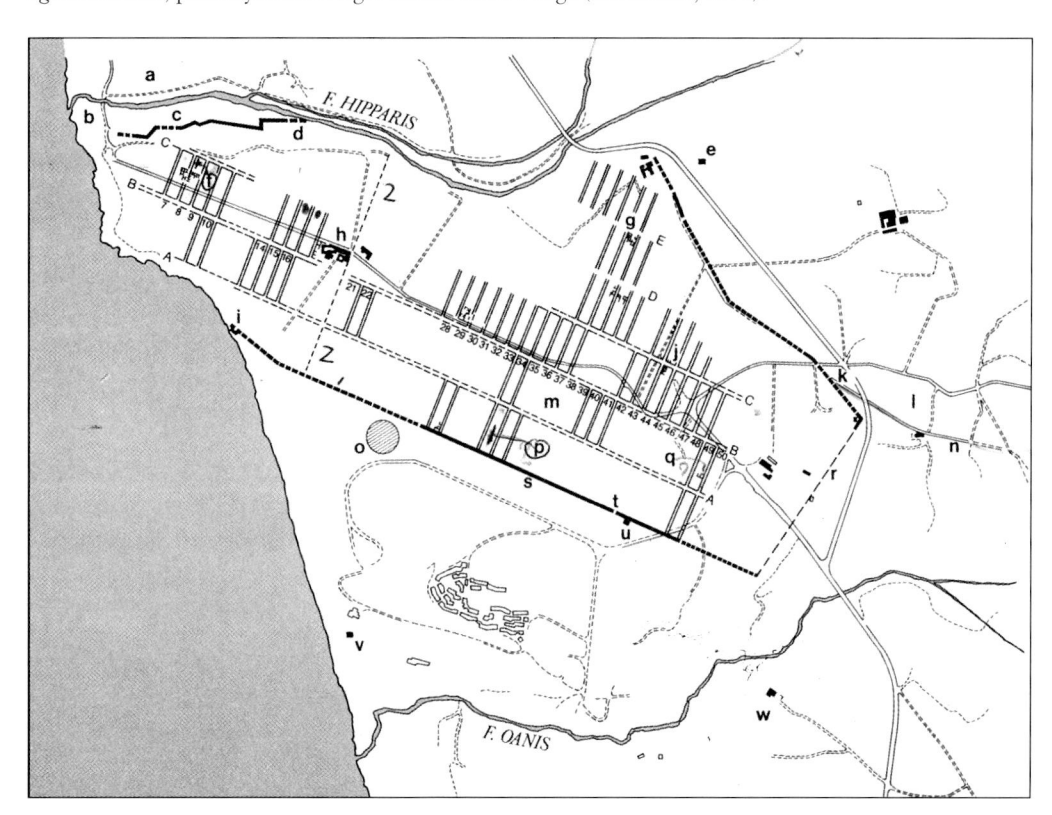

The dominant features noted here were the integration of the ancient *agora* area in the new urban fabric (three or four *insulae* wide and one long, giving a ratio of 1:1), its probable enlargement (reaching an estimated surface area of 20,000 square meters), the specialization of the functions envisaged in the new scheme of the town and the spectacular monumentalization of an *agora* which, despite its rather outlying position, was still considered the key community focus, according to Hippodamus' model. However, ancient practical motives, pre-existing features, cultural stratification (and perhaps rites of worship), together played a fundamental role in causing this decentralized site, and lead to the conclusion that the grandiose *agora* of Timoleon's Camarina is not strictly referable to the Hippodamian model.

If we now look at the residential fabric itself, a set of highly informative tablets inscribed with deeds of sale for land inform us that, like those of the fifth century, the new settlers transferred to Camarina by order of Timoleon were divided into the original three Dorian tribes, and each tribal group occupied its own sector of the town. Furthermore, it has been reliably established by recent excavation work that the dwellings of the farmers were in the northeast quarter, nearest the fields where they worked each day. Each *insula* was divided perpendicularly by an *ambitus* a half-meter wide, creating two blocks 17 meters wide containing ten dwellings of approximately 220 square meters apiece. As in Casmenae three centuries earlier, these blocks were composed of three to four rooms giving onto a courtyard on the south, including the kitchen; the artisans' houses, which stood this side of those of the farmers, were equipped with rooms on two sides of the court. The southern quarter – which the inscribed tablets locate near the sanctuary of Gaia and Persephone – was ascribed a different system. Workshops were situated here, one of which was sold, together with the abode alongside, for the sum forty Siceliot silver talents.

In conclusion, having resuscitated the fifth-century scheme of the town, the Camarina of Timoleon took its cue from the sixth-century layout inasmuch as it adapted itself to the lie of the terrain; with the advent of recolonization, however, the town was enlarged and restructured with uniform geometrical precision. Within this uniformity a major role was played by the thoroughfare B, the natural causeway across the promontory; this remained the main artery on which later urban schemes would pivot. It ran in a straight line for around 2.5 kilometers, affording the town with a kind of "processional" high-street which, in imitation of the *dromos* of Alexandria, became the constitutive element of all the Hellenistic metropolises structured around the *strigae* system, and together with the *agorai*, constituted the heart and soul of the life of the township.

Syracuse

In the case of Syracuse it was Cicero who, after praising the monuments that graced the Achradina district, noted the *strigae* of dwelling units as "partes quae una via lata perpetua multisque transversis divisae privatis aedificiis continentur" (*Against Verres*, IV.119). This said "via lata perpetua" could well

Morgantina: general plan of the *agora* and the west hill with the potters' workshops

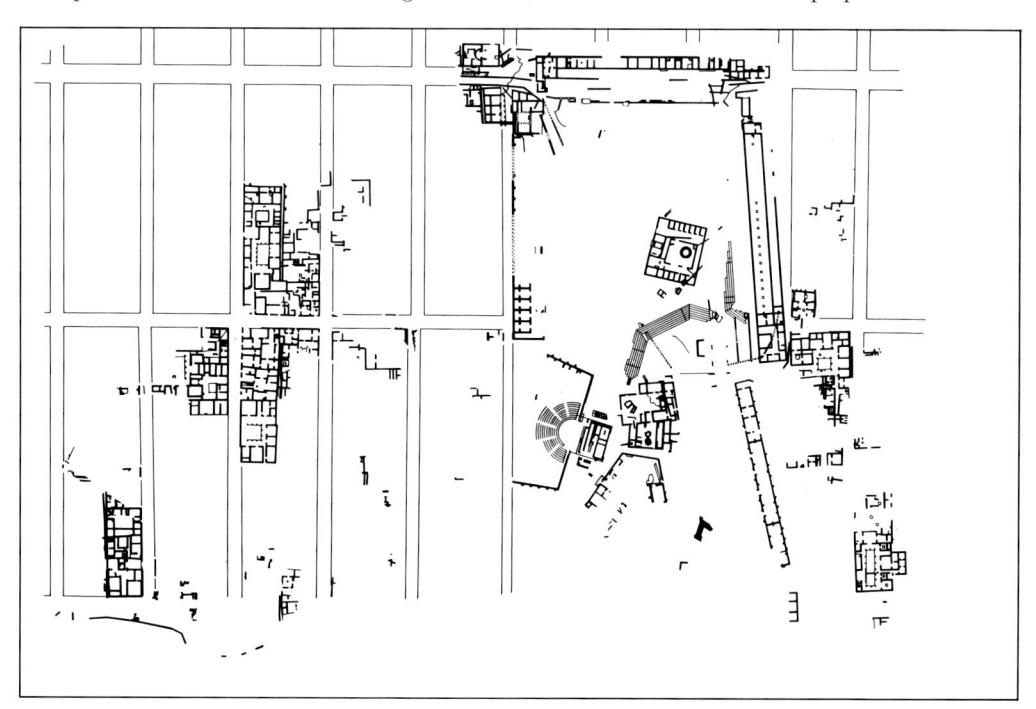

Morgantina, central area of the city in the Hellenistic phase

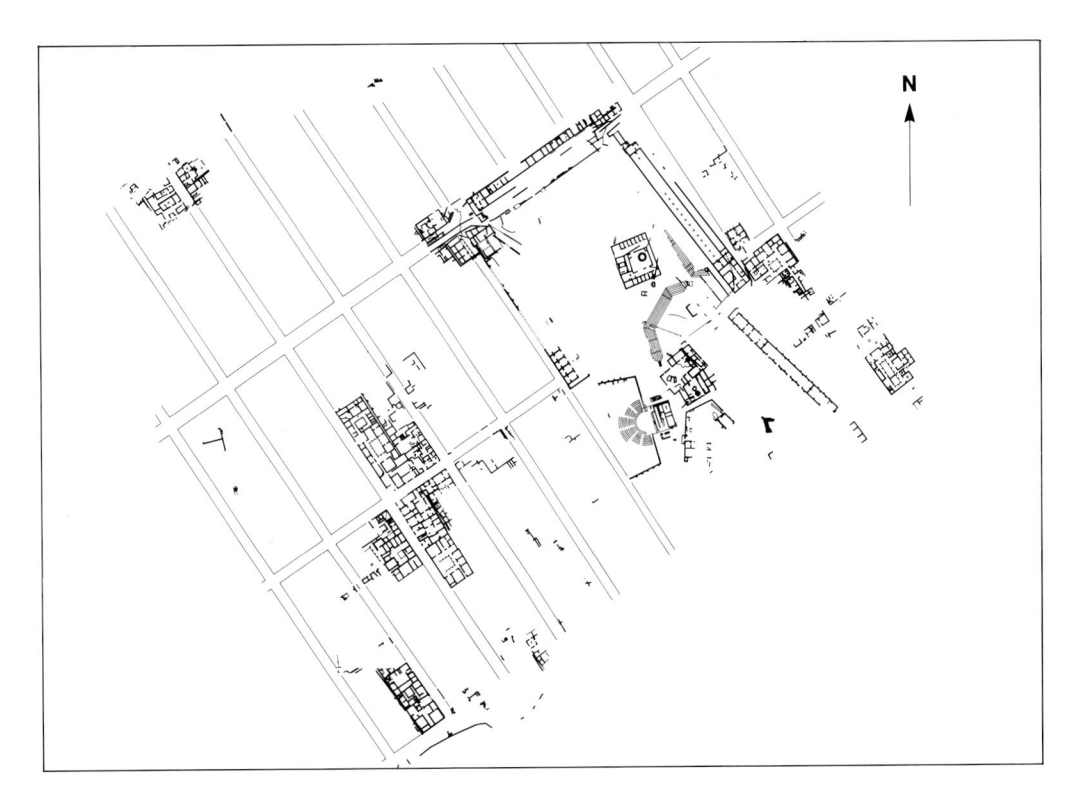

have been (as Torelli has already advocated) the one 13 meters wide – i.e., the one witnessed perhaps by Orsi at the border of the early *agora* of Achradina running northwest–southeast. It was not, however, the only such causeway in Hellenistic Syracuse. Refounded by Timoleon as the capital of the kingdom, Syracuse subsequently enjoyed the attention of Agathocles at the close of the fourth century B.C., and later of Hieron in the third. The city grew to an immense scale on the mainland and, as discussed above, from the late fifth century a thoroughfare cut off Achradina at the north between today's Viale Cadorna (but perhaps between Santa Lucia) and the Fusco hill. In the last few decades, the archaeologist Giuseppe Voza has been racing against the encroaching urban sprawl to recoup a series of rectangular *insulae* lying parallel, 38 meters wide and delimited by north–south *stenopoi* 3 meters wide (though Cultrera had previously noted a street 4.86 meters wide), lying at ninety degrees to this unusually long *plateia* along which lies the south wall of the *thesmophorion* of Piazza della Vittoria, which is estimated to exist from between late fifth to mid-fourth century B.C. Voza's fieldwork has been set in relation to the excavations made by Orsi, and particularly to those of Cultrera in Giardino Spagna. To my mind, this street was already an important urban thoroughfare in Archaic and Classical times, and this may explain its rather reduced width of only 5 meters; however, it should be pointed out that its existence has so far been proved archaeologically from the Hellenistic period onward. The *insulae* linked to this thoroughfare on the south side are all apparently oriented northwest–southeast, and it is likely that this (as I have attempted to show above) was the alignment of the residential sector of Achradina from the first layout of the burgeoning settlement: "An urban layout converging toward the shoreline around Ortygia" (Voza).

While the regularly drawn *insulae* north of the thoroughfare – particularly in Tyche – have reliably been dated to the Hellenistic period, the date for those aligned northwest–southeast in the section above the necropolis is as yet uncertain; at least in the vicinity of the *thesmophorion* (given that the *stenopos* traversing it cut through the north wall of the *temenos* to reach the east–west *plateia*) the earliest date possible is the reign of Timoleon.

Actually, excavations of the *insulae* investigated by Voza have not reached beyond the Hellenistic-Roman layers. In short, it is possible that by the fifth century the geometric regularity of Achradina's layout of parallel northwest–southeast streets had already reached the important east–west thoroughfare brought to light by Voza in Piazza della Vittoria; but a systematic occupation on either side is documented only from the second half of the fourth century, at the earliest. There is no doubt, moreover, that, even in the exact correspondence of the dimensions, the *insulae* in the north were part of an urban plan of later date, probably in the time of Hieron.

It is acknowledged that in the course of his long period of supremacy Hieron saw not only to enlarg-

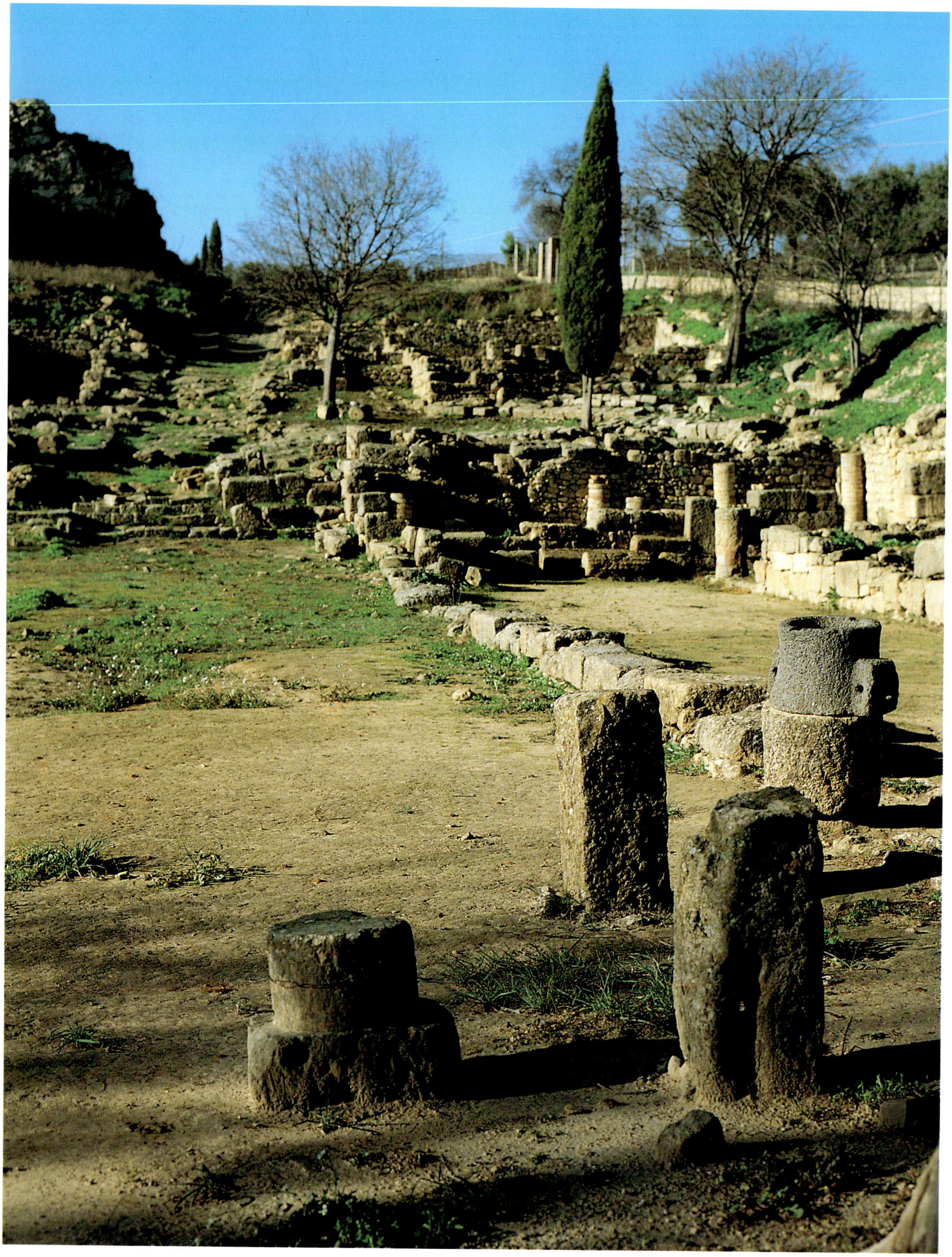

opposite
View of Morgantina from the north

ing the city with new residential quarters, but also to erecting monuments on such a scale that the city of Syracuse quickly became one of the most sumptuous *poleis* in the entire Hellenistic world. Witnesses to this fabulous project are the theater and the famous Altar, both of which are enclosed in monumental *stoai*. These buildings were devised to provide a "background for a dynamic space," to quote Malcom Bell III, whose dating of most of the monuments of the Morgantina *agora* to the period of Hieron II has been rightly acknowledged as correct, while it also sheds some light (albeit indirectly) on Hieron's Syracuse.

Morgantina was redeveloped by architects of Hieron who created the artificial division of the *agora* into two terraces, the upper one of which is upheld by the grandiose stairway of the *ekklesiasterion*, by the use of long, free-flowing *stoai* as a backdrop, and by the orientation of the *agora* as a whole toward an open, distant space. These features show the planners' skills in applying a "scenographic" vein to urban planning, which many other Greek *poleis* in the East had already adopted – notably Rhodes, Halicarnassus, and Pergamum. On the basis of these principles we have to imagine the last monumental phase of Syracuse under the last Siceliot *basileus*. This is the city illustrated by Cicero in his clipped prose: of Achradina, for instance, he recalled a gigantic forum, a *prytaneion* full of works of art, an imposing *curia*, a Temple to Jupiter, and magnificent arcaded buildings. While Polybius (VIII. 3. 2) mentions the Σκυτική (*Skytike*) or stoa of the cobblers situated near the shore at the time of the assault of the Romans.

Despite the pillage perpetrated by Verres, it is the urban layout of a Hellenistic city, still opulent, whose monuments, culture, and magnificence rivaled its counterpart on the coast of Africa opposite, Alexandria, the city built by Alexander the Great's architect Deinocrates of Rhodes. Cicero aptly pictured the appearance which the Hellenistic capital of Hieron II had assumed: a Syracuse which the foolishness of its last governors and the fury of Rome had reduced to provincial thraldom.

Bibliography
The most important bibliography up to 1983-84 is contained in the appendix to the chapter "L'urbanistica" that I wrote for *Sikanie. Storia e civiltà della Sicilia greca* (series *Antica madre*, VIII) 1985, pp. 412-414.

General information
A number of essays on the Greek city and colonization have been published over the last decade. I will mention only those works where further useful bibliography can be found: R.J. MARCHESE, 1983; W. LESCHHORN, 1984; FR. DE POLIGNAC, 1984; H. VAN EFFENTERRE, 1985; M.A. LEVI, 1981; F. CORDANO, 1986; M.B. SAKELLARIOU, 1989; E. LEPORE, 1989; J.P. DESCOEUDRES, 1990; N. CUSUMANO, 1994.
Lastly, *Opus* has devoted the 1987-89, VI-VII issues to *La cité antique? A partir de l'œuvre de M.J. Finley*, while *Kokalos* XXX-XXXI, 1984-85 (1987), XXXIV-XXXV, 1988-89 (1992) and XXXVIII, 1992 (1995) issues contain severla important contributions on colonization, as well as update information on excavations and findings.
There are several articles regarding either directly or indirectly, town planning in the Greek colonies of southern Italy and Sicily, published in a number of works. Among them see particularly: *Magna Grecia*, 1990; *Lo stile severo...*, 1990; *La transizione...*, 1991; *Princípi e forme...*, 1993.
Sicilia dal cielo. Le città antiche, 1994, is worth mentioning for its wide collection of a new set of photographs.
Of course, also refer to the topographycal entries of BTCG whose thirteenth volume was published in 1994 (last entry *Pisa*) and the following articles: O. BELVEDERE, in *Xenia*, 14, 1987, pp. 5-20; D. THEODORESCU, in *Atti* XXVII, 1987 (1988), pp. 501-540; L. KARLSSON, in *Opuscola romana*, XVII, 1989, pp. 77-89; A. DI VITA, in *Greek Colonists: a Native Populations*, 1990, pp. 343-363; N. KOZLOSKAIA, in *Le Pont Euxin vu par les Grecs*, 1990, pp. 37-50; G. MANGANARO, 4, 1990, pp. 127-174; N. LURAGHI, in *Hesperìa*, 2, 1992, pp. 41-62; C. ZOPPI, in *Rend. Acc.*, n.s. LXII, 1991-92 (1992), pp. 157-187; A. WASOWICZ, *Modèles de l'amenagement...*, in *Territoires des cités grecques* (table ronde Ecole Française d'Athènes 31 octobre/3 novembre 1991) forthcoming; idem, *École d'urbanisme...*, in *Riv. di Topografia antica* II, 1992, pp. 9-22; M. BELL III, in *Eius Virtutis Studiosi...*, 1993, pp. 327-341; A. BULTRIGHINI, in *Rivista di Filologia e Istruzione Classica* 121, 1993, pp. 67-71; M. LOMBARDO, in *Hesperìa*, 3, 1993, pp. 161-188.
Important reference works are: *Le dessin...*, 1985; I. MALKIN, 1987; L. GALLO, Salerno 1994.
As to the individual *poleis*, beside vol. I, 3 of *La Sicilia antica* edited by E. Gabba and G. Vallet published in F. Coarelli, M. Torelli, *Sicilia*, 1984, and in addition to the bibliography published in *Sikanie, op. cit.*, I will especially mention:

Acragas
E. DE MIRO, in *Quaderni dell'Istituto di Archeologia*, 3, 1988, pp. 63-72; idem, 1994, especially pp. 21-49.

Camarina
A.J. PARKER, in *Sic. Arch.*, 30, 1976, pp. 25 ff. (a port at the mouth of the Ippari River); C. AMPOLO, in *La Parola del Passato*, 224, 1985, pp. 331-336; F. CORDANO, 1992; G. DI STEFANO, *Camarina...*, 1993; idem in *Archeologia viva*, XIII, 45, May-June 1994, pp. 46-49.

Gela
C. Raccuia, in *Kokalos*, XXXVIII, 1992, pp. 273-302.

Himera
N. Allegro-S. Vassallo, in *Kokalos*, XXXVIII, 1992, pp. 79-150, and other bibliography.

Naxos
M. Guarducci, in *MEFRA*, 97, 1985, pp. 7-34.
Naxos..., in *Not. Sc.* 1984-85 (1988), pp. 253-497; M.C. Lentini, S. Garraffo, *Il tesoretto...*, Istituto Italiano Numismatica, 1995, pp. 3 ff.

C. Parisi-Presicce, in *Archeologia Classica*, XXXVI, 1984 (1987), pp. 19-132; J. De la Genière-J. Rougetet, in *Rendiconti Lincei*, XL, 1986, pp. 289-297; A. Di Vita, *Selinunte...*, in *Annuario Atene*, LXII, 1984 (1988), pp. 7-62; idem., *Le fortificazioni...*, in *Annuario Atene*, LXII, 1984 (1988), pp. 69-79; A. Rallo, in *Annuario Atene*, LXII, 1984 (1988), pp. 81-91; D. Mertens, in *Römische Mitteilungen*, 96, 1989, pp. 87-154; idem, *L'architettura...*, in *Sicilia op. cit.*, pp. 75 ff., and an updated-to-1990 map of 1990; idem, in *Studi...*, 1993, pp. 131-138; H.P. Isler, *Les nécropoles...*, in *Nécropoles...*, Napoli 1994, pp. 165-168;
and also: A. Carbè, *Note sulla monetazione di Selinunte...*, *RIN* 1986, pp. 3-20. As to a storeroom with silver ingots at Selinus: C. Arnold-Biucchi, L. Beer-Tobey, N.M. Waggoner, in *American Numismatic Society, Museum Notes*, 33, 1988, pp. 1-35; A. Tusa Cutroni, in *Kokalos*, XXXIV-XXXV, 1988-89, p. 397; G. Manganaro, in *ASNP*, s. III, XX, 1990, p. 427.

Syracuse
Both the *Atlante* by F.S. Cavallari, A. Holm and L. Cavallari, 1883 (with an Appendix published in 1891) and the numerous excavation reports published by P. Orsi *Notizie Scavi* (especially *NS* 1891, pp. 391 ff.; 1909, pp. 338-340; 1925, pp. 177, 309, 313 ff., 319 ff.) and by Cultrera in *N.S.* 1943, pp. 33-42, 124-126 (Giardino Spagna) are still useful references. As to the Hellenistic-Roman *kerameion* see S. Agnello in *Archivio Storico Siracusano* 1972-73, pp. 91 ff.; as to the debatable definition of Syracuse's borders: H.P. Drögenmüller, *Syrakus*, Heidelberg 1969.
The knowledge of the city's topography has greatly advanced since the Sixties, and the relative bibliography is contained in *Sikanie, op. cit.*, up to 1983-84, and in the issues of *Kokalos* published subsequently.
As to the delimitation of *Lakkian* and the passage between Ortygia and Achradina the data provided by underwater research are essential: G. Kapitän, *Sul Lakkion...*, in *Archivio Storico Siracusano* XIII-XIV, 1967-68, pp. 167-180 (and previous bibliography); G. Voza, in *Kokalos*, XXX-XXXI, 1984-85, pp. 674 ff.

Lidiano Bacchielli   Town Planning in Ancient Cyrenaica

In ancient times Cyrenaica was virtually a sort of "island" in the Mediterranean, as if it were detached from the rest of the African continent by the desert sands, and from Greece by water; to reach it one inevitably passed through Crete. The region was a guaranteed attraction even before the foundation of Cyrene (ca. 630 B.C.): this fact is demonstrated by recent studies and excavation work, which has revealed traces of Aegean populations who traveled there for purposes of trade as early as the fourteenth century B.C.; later Cretan and Samian literary sources confirm this influx.

The first city to be founded in the region was Cyrene itself, built on a plateau in eastern Libya. It was founded by colonists from Thera, and Herodotus relates their first movements. They were led by a certain Battus, who had been assigned to the task by Apollo of Delphi. The colonists, who can have been little more than a hundred in number, took possession of the land on the island of Plataea, just below Crete. After an interval of two years or more they sailed to the continent, to Aziris, which can be identified in the estuary of the Wadi Khalij. Neither of the two locations have revealed structures that can be directly attributed to these early garrisons, but the passage of the colonists is endorsed by finds made on the hillsides above the *wadi* (water course), including fragments of pottery datable to 675–650 B.C. But the site failed to satisfy in full the expectations of the colonists, particularly the future needs linked to the arrival from Greece of reinforcements; several years later, in fact, the Greeks abandoned the area and were led by the Libyans to a more fertile region, with good rainfall, where lore held that "the sky was pierced."

It was here that the foundations of Cyrene were laid. The first settlement site can be identified in the westernmost tip of a calcareous spur (the future site of the acropolis), which rises east of the Jabal, delimited and screened on the other sides by wadis, prompting Pindar to describe the city as "nestled on a candid breast". Aerial photographs have helped pinpoint in the acropolis area a small circuit of

The hill of the acropolis of Cyrene

Aerial view of the settlement of Cyrene

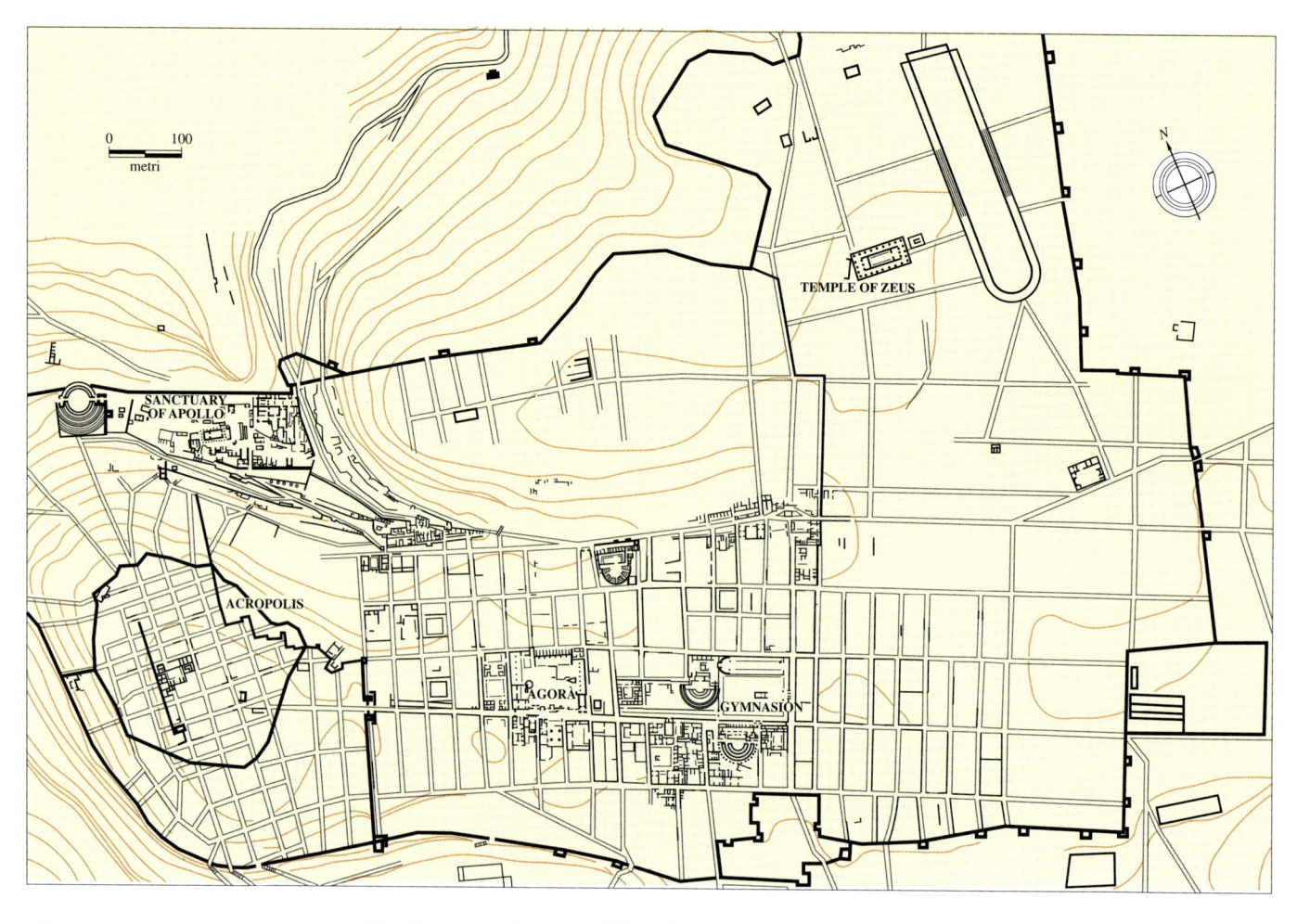

Urban plan of Cyrene

wall, otherwise no longer visible today. Its many-sided circuit flows with the contours of the upper esplanade, delimiting an area of around 300 by 250 meters. The photographs have shown a grid of small rectangular blocks (20.05 by 35.3 meters), squared off by an orthogonal network of streets arranged along the main north–south and east–west axes. The few buildings and tracts of original wall discovered in the course of excavations comply with this same orientation. The compact formation of housing blocks corresponds significantly with the earliest cases of town planning, and the layout of the acropolis could date to within a few decades of the township's foundation.

At the southeast part of the original nucleus lies a broad straight causeway that crosses the breadth of the southern hillside, reminiscent of an arrangement found also on Thera (modern Santorini), the homeland. The first stretch of this causeway – as far as the western rim of the *agora* – coincides with part of the course of the *skyrota*, a street that Pindar recalls as having been traced out by Battus the founder for the processions in honor of Apollo. The street, he says, was "laid with gravel, flat and straight, and rang with the sound of horses' hoofs." Where it met the *agora* quarter, the *skyrota* veered off toward the north, in the direction of the Wadi Bu Turquia before turning westward once more and terminating in the Sanctuary of Apollo. The monuments that rise along this route testify to the force of aggregation of the cult worship and religious ceremonies, according to those principles of urban organization that are characteristic of the old cities of Greece. Along the *skyrota*, for example, stands the Temple to the Dioscuri, while at the point where the causeway reaches the summit of the esplanade stand the first monuments erected for the *agora*: including the Sanctuary of Apollo and an L-shaped flight of steps opening onto the sacred concourse, enabling bystanders to spectate at the celebrations in honor of the deity.

But complementing these principles of urban layout, there are certain elements that constitute a novelty in the Greek world. One such feature is the deliberate configuration of the public areas assigned to civilian and community activities; another characteristic is the partitioning of specific areas into plots of cultivable land in an arrangement that stretched as far as the eastern border of the *agora*. The plots in the north are rectangular, while those flanking the main causeway tend to be trapezium-shaped which, though not an ideal shape for construction lots, establish the pattern for the subsequent urbanization of the zone. Small variations to this basic lattice of land plots are noticeable, however, east of the *agora* in particular. And while the older buildings of the plaza (those dating from the late seventh to early sixth century B.C.) are perfectly aligned to the *skyrota*, and to its continuation toward the nub of the calcareous spur, the eastern boundary of the enclosure of the *Oikos* of Opheles\Opheltes (dating to shortly after 550 B.C.) emulates the variations in direction subsequently applied to the non-aligned streets. The development of the *agora* quarter is related to the arrival of new settlers who began to flow into Cyrene in response to promises of land assignations around 560 B.C., together with the reforms introduced by Demonax of Mantinea, who had been called into to placate the unrest which the new arrivals had triggered amid the existing sociopolitical fabric.

It is likely that the urban expansion was accompanied by a respective enlargement of the circuit of defense works, especially since the eastern sector, closest to the base of the spur, afforded inadequate defense. There are no visible traces left of these walls, nor have excavations been carried out to verify their position and course. Corroboration for their existence can be found in Herodotus who, in his narrative of the Persian expeditions in around 515 B.C. against Barce, notes that upon their return journey the Cyrenaics opened the city gates to troops, led them through the city and allowed them to set up camp on the southern hillock dedicated to Zeus Lykaios (Lycaeus). Evidently, the circumstances and scope of the episode recounted – the crossing of Cyrene on their Barce–Egypt itinerary – rules out that the walls mentioned by Herodotus were those of the acropolis, because its physical conformation cuts it off from the rest of the plateau.

A third phase of urban development can be noticed in the eastern slope of the hill, site of both the acropolis and the *agora*. This sector's development dates largely to the mid-second century B.C. and is

View of the *agora* and of the acropolis of Cyrene

Cyrene: the Gymnasion and the ridgeway

the result of a deliberate, regular planning that has obliterated the preceding building fabric (from the late sixth century B.C. and after), imposing a new axis to the building pattern. In correspondence with the Hellenistic *Gymnasion* and the area immediately east of this, the spatial arrangement is based on a grid system of rectangular units arranged orthogonally along the main causeway over the hill. Placed on this grid are certain monuments constructed in the second half of the second century B.C., such as the *Gymnasion* whose sheer magnitude, public function, and royal commissioning make it the fulcrum of this particular phase of urban expansion. The accommodation of the *insulae* to the circuit of the city walls – particularly noticeable in the southern section of the east side – suggests that the definition of the urban layout coincided with the planning of the enclosure walls. The new walls encircled the known city in its entirety, with a perimeter of around five and one-half kilometers in length. It was erected in the most favorable points, blockading the rim of the escarpments, and following the rises in the plateau. The square towers were added principally to the sections on flatter terrain.

For the other areas of the town, the urban structure is less immediately perceivable, as excavation activity has been concentrated mainly around the principal monuments; such information must therefore be inferred from aerial photography. On the north hill, in the zone that could be termed the *Olympieion*, it appears that the basic orientation was established by the Temple of Zeus; in the zone further in the central valley, the building fabric is arranged around a median east–west axis, which is not straight but articulated in various segments in compliance with the contours of the terrain. The north–south thoroughfares conform with this orthogonal grid, creating irregular *insulae* in the resulting gaps.

For the last two zones described above, given the scarcity of indications discernible from the aerial surveys, one can only infer the existence of partial urbanization.

In conclusion, it should be stressed that the building layout of Cyrene is composed of unhomogeneous

Cyrene
ruins of Hellenistic walls

patterns without interruption. As noted earlier, the phenomenon is in part attributable to the fact that development took place in phases. But alongside this explanation, one should also undoubtedly note the fact that the street grid seems to have been applied section by section, and modeled systematically to the contours of the land.

The history of the plans and development of the other towns and cities of Cyrenaica have reached us in a highly fragmentary form. At Barce, which was founded in 560 B.C. by a breakaway group of dissident Cyrenaic colonists, the successive layers of development have tended to completely obliterate the evidence of what went before.

Cradled in a sweeping bay, Cyrene's coastal outlet Apollonia dates back to the late seventh century and early sixth B.C. By the late Hellenistic period the seaport had matured into an independent city in its own right, and was the focus of extensive applied planning and monumental construction. The full identification of the town plan, however, is seriously impeded by the later Byzantine developments, which began to envelope the past glories of the city midway through the fifth century A.D., when Apollonia achieved the status of capital of *Libya Superior*. Nevertheless, there is scattered evidence of a regular grid-like layout, with several *plateiai* (main thoroughfares) in the east–west direction, together with smaller streets along the north–south axis. More easily interpretable features, however, have survived of the defense works which in the second century B.C. girdled the coastal peaks upon which the town was perched. The southern tract of the walls follows the geography of the land and is arranged in rack fashion. Square towers were erected to overlook the breaches, and posterns built to facilitate forays out of the enclave. A limb of the town actually lies outside the walls (a scheme apparently devised to secure the protection of the port facilities, and extending out along the quay, which divides the port neatly in two).

The foundation of Ptolemais dates to the mid-third century B.C., at a key point in the restoration of Lagid power throughout Cyrenaica. But the roadstead over which the town looms was a port of call long before, in the Archaic period, serving as a way station for Barce. Right from the town's foundation, a perfectly regular street grid was traced out between the Jabal massifs and the sea. On either side the town was flanked by wadis, but the line of natural defense was reinforced by a ponderous curtain wall. The *insulae* were marked out in Ptolemaic feet (100 by 500) and measure 36.5 by 182.5 meters: they are intersected by streets along the cardinal axes in both directions, with two much broader concourses lying along the north–south direction, starting from the harbor itself, endorsing the town's strictly commercial character.

Taucheira, another seaport town just west of Ptolemais, was founded around 625 B.C. The archaeological finds made in the area corroborate the evidence that the city enjoyed a period of particular importance not long after its foundation, and particularly in the Late Roman and Byzantine periods. The lack of a systematic program of excavations renders it impossible to speculate on the town planning with any confidence, though traces of several *plateiai* crossing the town in an east–west direction have come to light; these are intersected by a network of smaller streets arranged orthogonally. Those in the northern sector of the town lead straight down to the harbor, which was documented by underwater surveys in 1972. As with Ptolemais, the construction of the urban fabric seems to stem from the reconquest of Cyrenaica by Ptolemy III, who renamed the city Arsinoe.

The westernmost city of Cyrenaica was Euhesperides, which stood on the site of modern Benghazi

Ptolemais: remains of walls at the Taucheira Gate

Urban plan of Euhesperides

and was probably founded by the Cyrenaics at the start of the sixth century B.C. The first settlement grew on a rise in the land embraced on the south flank by a lagoon. Very little has survived of the actual constructions, but aerial surveys have enabled the identification of part of the city grid, with a network of small streets on a similar plan to that of the acropolis at Cyrene. In the fourth century B.C. the city was extended toward the south, spreading out over land reclaimed from the lagoon. This enlargement may coincide with the arrival in Euhesperides of new colonists from Messenia, who had been summoned to help deal with the attacks of Libyan tribes from the Sirte region. In 414 B.C. these tribes had managed to besiege the city. The new quarter was arranged in two sectors, to which a regular planning pattern was applied, though, as in Cyrene, this takes account of the geography of the terrain. The difference in orientation between the street grid on the lower sections of the hillside and that of the former lagoon land is neatly resolved by the creation of an open space, identified as the *agora* or marketplace, which is fed by a concourse of much larger dimensions than all the other east–west streets. Dating to the same period of urban expansion is the construction of the city walls, long tracts of which have been discovered along the southern flank of the city: these are enhanced by jutting towers arranged at regular intervals along the curtain.

The silting up of the lagoon and the loss of the port functions spelled the eventual abandonment of Euhesperides, which took place so rapidly, however, that one can only infer some political decision. Midway through the third century B.C. Euhesperides was simply supplanted by Berenice, founded on new ground three kilometers up the coast, upon the wish of Ptolemy III. Berenice was built closer to the shore, taking over the port functions formerly enjoyed by its neighbor Euhesperides. Excavations have revealed traces of a suburb, as the city was in fact encompassed by a sturdy wall, completing the natural geographical defenses offered by the lagoon behind it. The street grid of this new town was designed on an orthogonal plan.

Bibliography
S. STUCCHI, 1967; S. STUCCHI, 1975; B. JONES, in *Cyrenaica...*, 1985, pp. 27-41; J. LLOYD, in *Cyrenaica...*, 1985, pp. 49-66; L. BACCHIELLI, in *Cirene...*, 1990, pp. 5-33.

Greek Architecture in the West

Urban planning and architecture – respectively the organization of space and the physical realization of the new habitat – have always played a critical and decisive role in the great colonial movements down through history. In the Greek case, while adapting themselves to the new reality, both planning and architecture underwent transformations with respect to the models of Mainland Greece, while nonetheless retaining the fundamental features of their original culture.

The scope of the present essay is to propose a brief historical outline of the salient moments of western Greek colonial architecture, highlighting some of the more important features that firmly distinguish colonial architecture from that of the Greek mother country – features which, in hindsight, seem at least partly to return in other far more recent colonial experiences (admitting, of course, the profound differences that distinguish the Greek colonial movements from the great trends of modern times).

Premises and Origins

The chronology

Unlike most other arts or forms of craft production, the models and examples of the practice of building cannot be transmitted from place to place in physical form. The knowledge of architecture which the colonists took with them consisted of abstract concepts, mental blueprints, functional notions, and firsthand experience of the various technological solutions. Their knowledge depended upon the projects they had already worked on in the homeland. Consequently, the more elaborate and extensive was their experience of architecture at home, the more expert and equipped with ideas, specific models, and technological know-how were the master builders in the colonies. This means that the premises for the transmission of concrete and well-defined architectural concepts from Mainland Greece must have changed considerably during the two-hundred-year history of colonial development. While the first settlements of the later eighth century emerged in a phase in which the Greek metropolises and their architecture were still not yet fully developed, the last colony, Elea (Hyele), was founded around the year 540 B.C. by Phocaea, a city that had evolved a sophisticated style of monumental architecture, with all the relative technological apparatus. Once the right economic and technical conditions had been met, the early colonies developed a quite independent form of architecture that was less tied to the prototypes being formed over the same period in the Greek metropolises.

Environmental and economic conditions in the new colonial territories

The first phase of establishing an *apoikia* or colonial settlement in domains far from the homeland was conditioned by a need for security and an acceptable level of economic sustenance to insure the colony's survival. Given the lack of resources for the construction of large-scale architectural works of a public or private nature, the continuation of the building types that were evolving in the colonists' homeland was inevitably suspended. It has been calculated that it took at least one generation if not more before a colony was actually able to undertake building and planning of any consistency. The initial settlement phase of the earlier colonies is in fact represented by crude house-building (examples at Megara Hyblaea, Naxos, and Syracuse). In time the colonists adjusted to their new surroundings, particularly as regards the availability of building materials and the respective techniques of preparing them. The Achaean settlers, for example, from the mountainous regions of the Peloponnese found themselves in quite alien conditions in their new habitat in the broad flood plains along the Ionian coast of southern Italy, and were consequently obliged to develop new technologies based primarily on the use of clay – for both wall-building (mudbrick) and for the decorative features (terra-cotta antefixes, etc.).

It is fascinating to observe the extent to which the incoming colonists adopted techniques already in use by the indigenous population, nonetheless managing to create functional ground plans of a purely Greek kind (as in the case of Francavilla Marittima). Later the colonists were to develop a rich, individual style of their own, decorated throughout with figured and ornamental terra-cotta details.

A far less drastic change of environment greeted the pioneers of the great Dorian colonies of Syracuse, Megara Hyblaea, and the latter's offshoot Selinus. Here they found a supply of an excellent limestone similar to the *poros* used in central Greece. The very first houses built on a straightforward square or rectangular plan were constructed from stone found on-site, and were therefore quite unlike the hut-houses of the Achaean colonists, which consisted of curved ground plans, their foundations partially sunk into the terrain, making them very much like the houses of their indigenous neighbors.

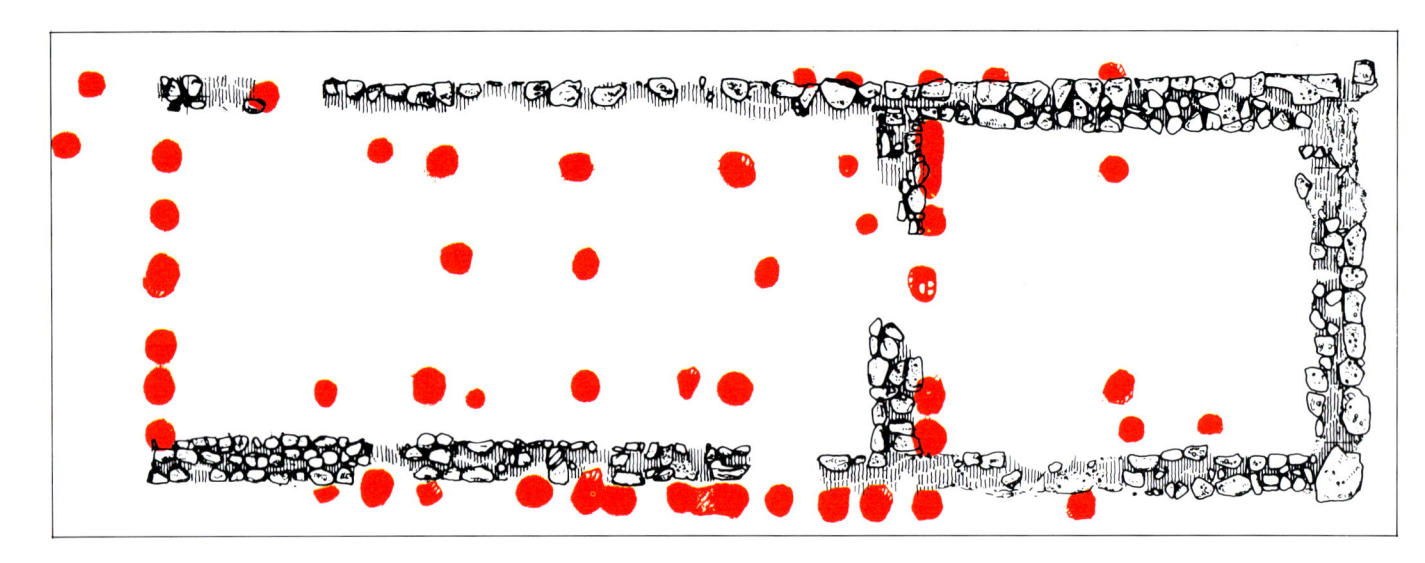

Francavilla Marittima temple "Building III" in red, Phase I (7th cent.) *megaron* facing east built with timber lacing in black, Phase II (6th cent.) reconstruction with stone bases mudbrick walls and polychrome terra-cottas (Mertens drawing Schützenberger)

This fact illustrates the importance of the relationship established with the native populations that inhabited the area prior to colonization, though there is no general pattern and each case has to be evaluated separately. At any event, when the colonies began to face more complex and enterprising projects such as monumental temples, the areas under Greek control from which the building material could be procured were evidently quite extensive.

Space availability and management

The primary objective of the foundation of most of the *apoikiai* was to occupy and control an area of sufficient size to guarantee a proper economic base; this meant establishing certain priorities in the building program. The colonists first had to settle urgently a set of planning guidelines and to make sure that the complied buildings with them, rather than viceversa, as happened in many cities in the homelands. The most well-known example so far is Megara Hyblaea, which illustrates the way in which the rudimentary single-room dwellings erected at the time of the foundation are perfectly aligned with the overall well-planned scheme of land-parceling of the urban space that was adopted with admirable precision. This scheme not only complied with the principle of equal distribution of the *oikopeda* or family lots among the individual colonists, but also guaranteed from the outset the proper functioning of community life through a set of fundamental measures, namely the division between common public spaces and those for private use, and the differentiation of streets according to their practical importance in the life of the city. Functionality was in fact the rule for the subsequent architectural realization of the colony in the West.

The composition and constitution of the city

From the arrival of the first colonists, the composition of the township was in perpetual flux. As the population grew with each wave of new arrivals from the cities of Mainland Greece, there was also an inflow of local natives from the hinterland, though the true entity of their presence is difficult to assess. More important and more widely documented are the changes in the composition of the population through the influx of colonists from areas of Mainland Greece other than that of the founding city. Another major factor is the abrupt migration of large numbers of people (sometimes the entire population of a town) owing to war, social unrest, or other difficult circumstances. Basically, the community of most colonial towns was prone to much more far-reaching changes than those in Mainland Greece, and such factors inevitably affected the pace of city building and the stylistic characteristics of the architecture of the growing *polis*.

The same applies to the internal changes due to each town's diverse constitutional setup. Take for example the *poleis* of the great tyrants, with their outward display of wealth and splendor and their consequent rife instability leading, in some cases, to catastrophe. Be that as it may, the frequent availability of substantial human resources (prisoners of war, unengaged mercenaries), who were often employed on ambitious building schemes, was a crucial factor in the programming of city construction, and the ability to organize and coordinate such masses of laborers must have influenced the general way in which the *polis* was conceived.

The first architectural projects in the context of the nascent polis

The colonial *polis* with its regular building fabric is part of a similarly organized land system known as the *chora* or territory. In many ways, in fact, the *polis* is only the nucleus of the *chora*. The land parceling schemes (i.e., Metapontum and the *Tabulae Heracleenses*, a veritable essay in town planning) conform to regulatory standards similar to those underlying the organization of the *polis* itself, and viceversa. Later, the area within the city walls was to include further types of regulation of a more articulated and concrete nature, needed to cope with the increasingly close-knit and intense network of functions. But the *chora* also had its points of aggregation, such as sanctuaries and freshwater springs, either within or on its boundaries.

The first architectural projects were contrived to satisfy this variety of functions, each building according to its specifics. The dwelling unit is basically the standard cell of this system of land parceling, whether it lies within the *polis* itself or further out in the *chora*. The original one-room unit was progressively enhanced with secondary structures tailored to the needs of the household, following a set of tried-and-tested typologies, all inserted within the boundaries of the preset building lot; the pattern was only altered by the increase or decrease in personal wealth of the family in question.

In nearly all cases, however, even through long periods of the town's history, urban development obeyed the fundamental division between public space (the streets) and private space (the housing

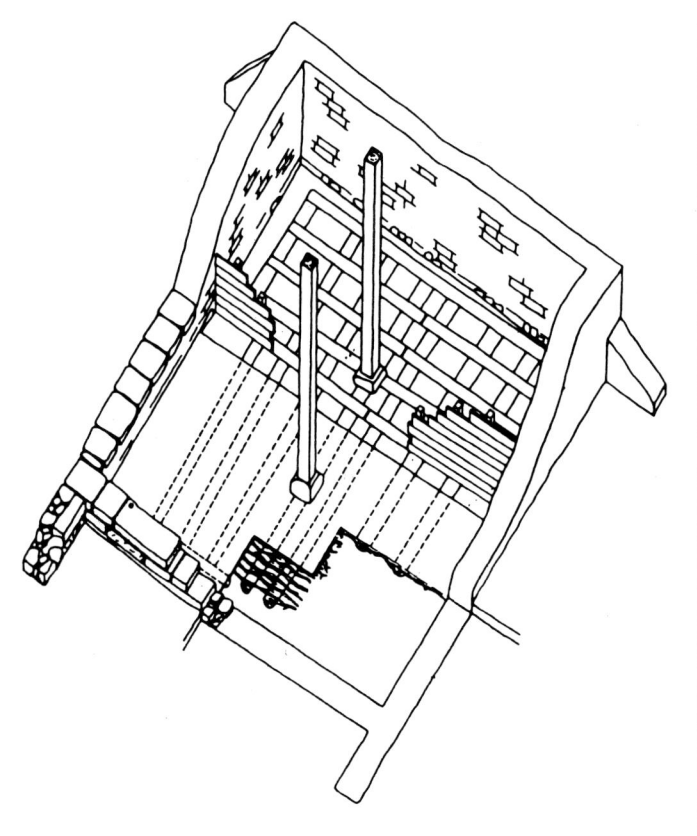

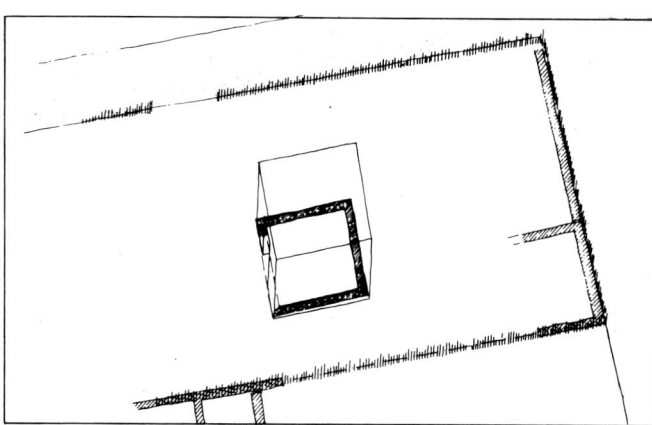

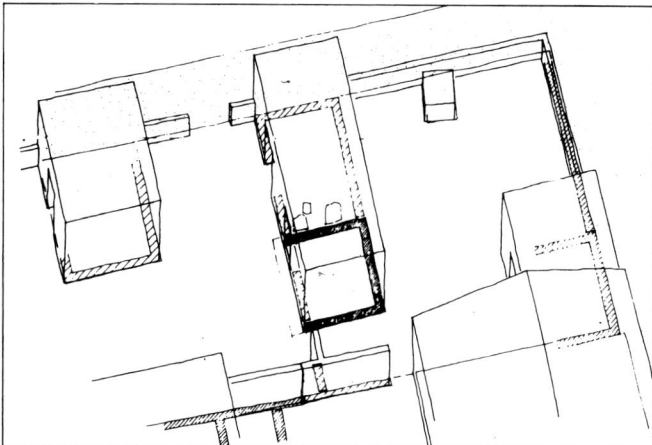

Elea (Velia) house built of mudbricks
beginning 5th cent. B.C.
(Krinzinger)

Megara Hyblaea Archaic
one-room house built of stone
inside the *oikopedon*
8th cent. B.C.
(Vallet, Villard, Auberson)

Megara Hyblaea enlargement
to the house in the 7th cent. B.C.
(Vallet, Villard, Auberson)

Megara Hyblaea Archaic *agora*
(Vallet, Villard, Auberson)

blocks composed of the *oikopeda*). In the end, during the city's main period of development, the blocks become completely occupied, constituting a large uninterrupted built-up grid in which the order and distributional scheme of the city is composed. The schemes for the public monuments were less conditioned by the immediate practical necessities. Among these, some were conceived to give form and distinction to the central public spaces and to accommodate the basic institutions. An example of such organization is the *agora* at Megara Hyblaea, which shows us that during the seventh century B.C. such needs gave rise to appropriate building types: the *agora* is bordered on two sides by arcaded structures – the *stoai* – which delimit and highlight the town's most important civic facility. The *stoai* created the space for public activities such as commerce and meetings. In this period, on another side of the *agora* stood a group of administrative buildings, such as the *estiatorion*, the hall for the political banquets, and in some cases the *prytaneion*, the main administration building. One final observation about the *agora* at Megara: it conserves the evidence of one of the last, rather than the first public monument of the Greek colonial town, and this is the *heroon*, a shrine consecrated to the *oikistes* (the hero-founder of the *polis*), situated at the town's most important intersection.

This curious monument, of which the only parallel is the *heroon* in the *agora* at Paestum (Greek Poseidonia), introduces the idea of the hallowed place, the temple, which is undoubtedly the most significant building type of the Greek world and also the most representative. This building type was destined to become increasingly vital to the fabric of the community as a whole. From the outset, the temple was devised to stand out immediately in the town's fabric, and especially to distinguish itself from the dwelling, from whose basic plan the *oikos* was nonetheless derived.

In Greece as in the colonies, even the most primitive forms of temples stood out for their oblong ground plan and their physical isolation, for their dimensions (which soon increased drastically) and decorations, and not least for the technical efforts that went into their design.

Before dealing with the question of the early evolution of temple architecture, it is appropriate to observe that, at least for the most renowned example (Megara), not only the temples but also the major public buildings – the *stoai*, the *estiatorion*, the *heroon* – differ from house design owing to the decision to use well-fashioned blocks of stone. This and the superlative workmanship of the execution were the first steps taken in the ambitions plan of monumentalizing the communities' most important buildings.

The First Phase of Monumentalization (Early Sixth century B.C)

The demonstration of Greek superiority
Their forms of worship and the conspicuous presence of their deities provided the colonists from Mainland Greece with the basic symbol for their coexistence with (and superiority over) the indige-

Poseidonia (Paestum) *heroon* of the founder

Metapontum: clay figured frieze of the extra-urban sanctuary of San Biagio (Mertens, Horn drawing Schützenberger)

Metapontum: clay figured frieze of the urban sanctuary Sacellum C (Mertens, Horn drawing Schützenberger)

nous populations around them. The first sanctuaries were not only erected as vital hubs of daily life at the heart of the settlement; they were also built at the boundaries of the occupied lands, and with this they had the dual function of affording sacred protection of the recently acquired land, and of persuading the surrounding natives of Greek prowess and power. The monumental dimensions of the temple architecture of the western Greeks has its roots, therefore, in its origins. There are basically three paths that led to this result: the careful choice and skillful preparation of the stone (where available), the abundant decorative features, and the absolute dimensions of the finished building.

At Selinus, a subcolony founded by the Megarians, the oldest temples in the extra-urban sanctuaries (in the Gaggera district) were erected in the first quarter of the sixth century B.C. entirely of excellently carved stone blocks of quasi-isodomic shape, and were given no added decoration. The only recognizable architectural feature is the unadorned cornices. The extensive use of large-format squared stone blocks is one of the decisive features of this particular type of monument.

Elsewhere, in the fertile flood plains, such as Metapontum, the situation was strikingly different, however. The complete lack of building stone meant that the only way to distinguish the religious architecture was its rich array of ornament. In this area, greater attention was paid to elaborate figural or ornamental decoration of the terra-cotta details. The fact that motifs could be so easily reproduced by molds led to an abundance of embellishment.

Of special importance in this respect is the first of the temples of this kind, namely the one sited in the sanctuary at the boundary of the *chora*, in the San Biagio district. The temple was decorated with a highly elaborate figured frieze that illustrated the realistic departure for war of a heroic warrior figure, probably Achilles.

This fact is crucial for understanding the true function of the early religious monuments in the colonies. They stood as points of reference of immense significance for the identity of the individual and as a cultural landmark for the entire community from within and from without.

In other cases, as in the friezes of Temple C, built in the first quarter of the sixth century in the urban sanctuary of Metapontum, the reliefs portray the salient moments of the religious practices themselves. The fact that elements of the same frieze – cast from the same mold even – have also turned up at Siris and Sybaris (and hence from identical temples of the same cult) is indicative of the extent to which the Hellenic cults helped bind and unify the western Greek world despite the complexity and extension of the existing native society.

This formative role of architecture and particularly its decorative features, with their accessible, easily interpreted narratives, was vital for a long time through the Archaic period, and especially in the sphere of the Achaean colonies. Another site, this time on the frontier with southern Campania, which was under growing Etruscan influence (similar to the circumstances of Selinus, the westernmost outpost of the Greeks before the start of Carthaginian territory), is that of the *heraion* or Sanctuary of Hera

Aegina: reconstruction
of the Temple of Aphaea I
(Schwandner)

at the mouth of the Sele River, just north of modern Paestum where there is an even more monumental elaboration of the concept of "communicative" architecture. In the first temple dedicated to Hera, the process by which the fronton of stone was being transformed into something new and more expressive is strikingly evident: the images of the famous metopes reveal a vividly expressive account of the feats of Heracles. The style is highly sculptural, and furthermore does not involve only the figured compositions, but numerous (albeit more abstract) non-figural decorative elements, such as the moldings with their elaborate floral motifs. In these colonies in fact the architects soon developed a complex system of rich and abundant ornament that included stylistic elements not found in other zones of the Greek world – elements that seem at first sight to be of Dorian origin mingle with others of an equally generic Ionian stamp, making impossible any precise determination of their place of origin.

The first elements of a "colonial style"
To grasp the significance of this phenomenon it is worth reflecting a moment: before the period in question, and that is in the first half of the sixth century B.C., certain decisive and definitive steps took place in Mainland Greece in the evolution of monumental temple architecture. In the seventh century – a period of adjustment and formation for most colonies (see above) – the concept of the grand peripteral temple began to take hold (as exemplified by Isthmia, Corinth, Thermos, Argos, and Eretria), with the preliminary introduction of the architectural orders, at least the Doric order (Thermos, Olympia). But most of the monuments, and especially their peristasis – and hence the basic elements of which the orders would be composed – were still made from timber and terra-cotta. It was not until the first decades of the sixth century that the transition to stone for the external orders was finally made – comprising the columns, capitals, and entablatures. This transition heralded the start of radical alterations to the basic proportions of the various compositional elements; indeed, the early monuments (of which the oldest temple to Aphaea at Aegina, and the *artemision* in Corfu are representative), with their somewhat ungainly and unbalanced proportions, demonstrate the novelty of the phenomenon.

At the same time, the Ionic order was still the object of experimentation, and seems to have been developed at first in two main directions: one native to the islands of the Aegean, and one in the main *poleis* in Asia Minor. The Ionic order was basically more prone to variations in proportion, and also in the compositional standards and decoration, consequently, never quite reached a stable, canonical formula throughout the whole of the Archaic period as had been the case of the Doric order. From this overview we can infer that, despite the economic ascent experienced by the colonies, they were still unable to establish any fixed and predefined models for temple architecture. This is particularly applicable in the case of the major temples of regionwide importance; in the primary cities to which the colonists referred, i.e., Delphi and Olympia, there were no temples from which to deduce a standard: the *heraion* in Olympia, built around the year 600 B.C., was still largely constructed from timber; likewise in Delphi for this period there are no traces of important stone artifacts. The notion of an "original temple" (Urtempel) or prototype, as has long been suggested for these centers, is therefore untenable.

Greek Architecture in the West

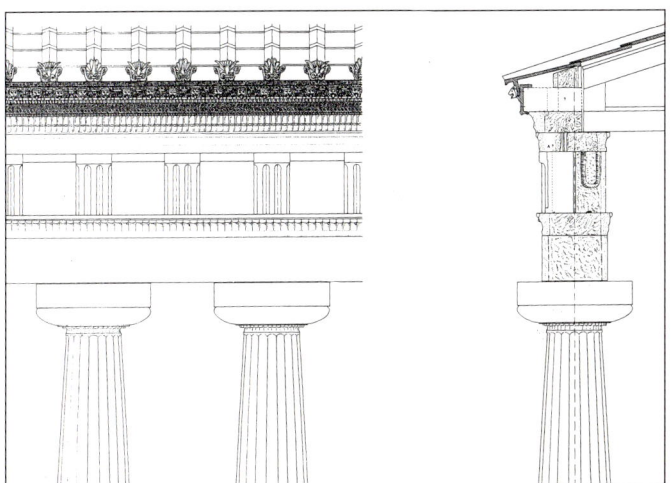

Paestum: Temple of Hera ("the Basilica") viewed from the north-east

Paestum: Temple of Hera reconstruction of the entablature in the Dorio-Achaean style (Mertens drawing Schützenberger)

Paestum: Temple of Hera reconstruction viewed from the north-east (Mertens drawing Schützenberger)

Paestum: Remple of Athena viewed from the north-west

Paestum: Temple of Athena mature example of the Dorio-Achaean style reconstruction of the facade (Krauss)

Paestum: Temple of Athena Ionic colonnade of the *pronaos* (Krauss)

This situation would seem to account for the diversity and lack of balance in colonial architecture at the time when the colonies are ready and willing to tackle the important step toward a proper form of monumental architecture that would do justice as a representation of their culture.
In the colonies of Achaean foundation – and hence of the Peloponnese, which were still relatively little urbanized – we find that peculiar interpenetration of proto-Doric and proto-Ionic elements, suggesting a "colonial style" of sorts that has been labeled variously as "Achaean" or "Dorico-Achaean" (or elsewhere "Ionian Sea Style").
During the phase of "standardization" of the architectural elements, this style – which is based on the colonists' previous experiences of architectural standards in Greece (and particularly in the central Peloponnese) – developed rapidly in the colonies of Magna Graecia and became apparent in the major monuments built in stone.
The most important and most sublime representation of this particular architectural concept is the so-called Basilica at Paestum. The other Achaean *poleis* of Metapontum, Sybaris, and Croton (each one with its own specifics) also took part in this gradual elaboration of architectural forms, and shared a striking variability in the attempt to establish a common formula. Still at the close of the sixth century B.C., with the *athenaion* at Paestum and the *heraion* at the mouth of the Sele River, this particular style was to bring about some striking results in the use of the two emerging orders; however, the stasis in evolution would subsequently be overcome with the final acceptance of the two primary orders, Doric and Ionic, in a true canonical form.

The Archaic Period in Sicily

The monumentalization of the Dorian colonies: the birth of a colonial prototype
The development of architectural forms in the chief Dorian colonies of Sicily – Syracuse, Megara, Selinus, Gela, and Acragas – seems to have been more consonant with the evolution of the greatest centers of the mother land. It should be noted immediately, however, that evidence for the first phase of monumentalization in the early sixth century in the respective metropolises of Mainland Greece (Corinth, Megara, Rhodes) is extremely scarce, and it is impossible to establish any direct links between the metropolises and their colonies. For the time being one can only postulate that the metropolises harbored a creative potential that in some way came to the surface in the new colonial environment. Otherwise it is hard to explain the vast difference from the coeval colonies of Ionian (i.e., Euboean) foundation, which even later failed to develop their own style of monumental architecture. This postulate, however, is also for the time being purely speculative. As noted earlier, the first *megara*

Syracuse: Temple of Apollo viewed from the north

to be constructed entirely in stone marked the beginning of the colonies' approach to their own monumental architecture, without actually drawing on recognizable models from the homeland.

Soon the colonists would take the second step in their progress toward the peripteral temple. Undoubtedly, the primary typology would be based on the above-mentioned Greek peripteral temples of the seventh century B.C. But the first temple of this type erected in the West, the Temple of Apollo in Syracuse, and the first entirely in stone, demonstrates this new quality with an intensity and forcefulness unheard of in Mainland Greece. The massive, close-set monolithic columns are striking expression of self-esteem and a demonstration of ability that is typical of a young colony, proud of its progress. Given its importance, the monument's completion was appropriately celebrated with a large inscription along the stylobate on the temple's main facade. The master-builders seem to have been so stimulated by their labors that they either completely failed to calculate, or they overlooked, the serious consequences that the new arrangement of the colonnade would have on the orders. It was no longer possible to coordinate the members of the heavy entablature with the rhythm of the columns. The overall picture that emerges is one of a true prototype without any previous example or pattern. Any reference to one of the early monumental temples of Greece is to be excluded, and would result in dire anachronisms: an architect with any foreknowledge of the *artemision* in Corfu, the oldest stone temple in the homeland (and hence often considered the model for the great temples of the West), taking into account furthermore the strategic role of Corfu as a stepping stone between Greece and the colonies – an architect would have at least respected the primary rules that this model embodied, and would have employed the technical expedients (smoothing of contact surfaces, pulley systems) adopted in Corfu; that are absent from the Syracusan temple.

Moreover, like all true prototypes, the ground plan of the temple actually marks a decisive breach with developments under way in the homeland, thereby establishing a fundamental blueprint that would become almost obligatory throughout Sicily. The distinguishing features of the Archaic temple in Sicily are its frontal emphasis, its extension along a central axis, and its unaccustomed spaciousness. The double colonnade at the front and the *adyton* or inner sanctuary at the back of the *naos*, constitute the two principal features of Archaic colonial temple architecture.

The Temple of Apollo erected at Syracuse would therefore seem to be the forerunner of the entire set of temples built in the first half of the sixth century B.C. It is followed by the Temple of Zeus (in the *olympieion*), situated outside the city walls; the only distinguishing feature of this temple with respect to its precursor is the attempt to remedy the dissonance created among the orders by means of wider intercolumniation (and hence a further indication of the unwitting error perpetrated with the Temple of Apollo). Also belonging to the first phase of Doric temple construction in Sicily was the Temple of Athena, again at Syracuse, together with the large and splendid temple at Megara Hyblaea, and the first of the group in the *athenaion* in Gela – all documented by precious stone architectural fragments which also provide definitive proof that the whole of the Doric order was how built of this material.

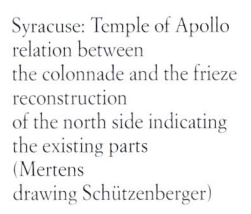

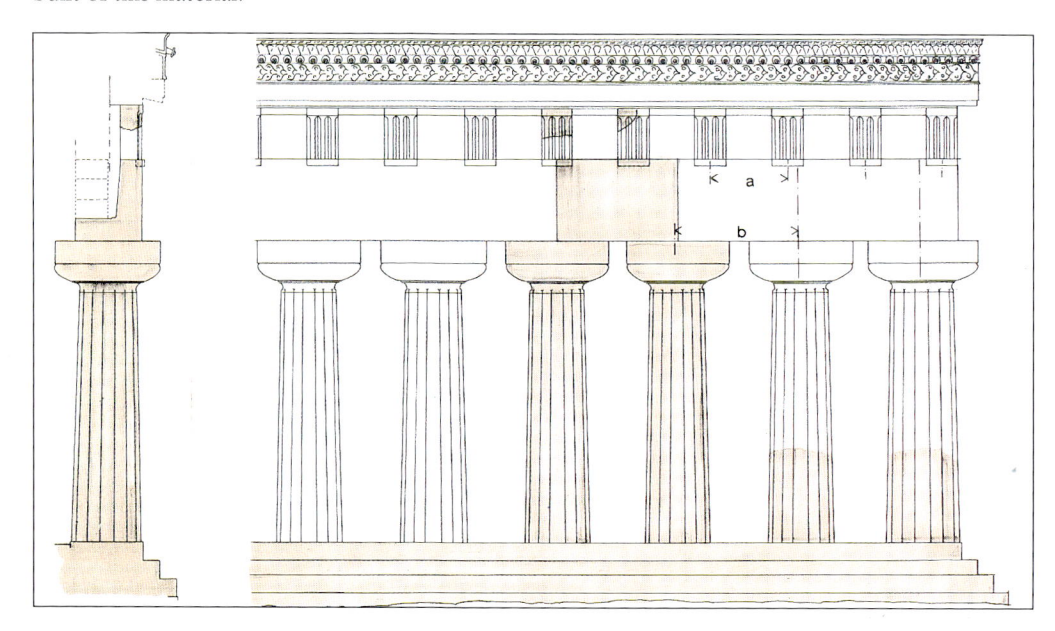

Syracuse: Temple of Apollo
relation between
the colonnade and the frieze
reconstruction
of the north side indicating
the existing parts
(Mertens
drawing Schützenberger)

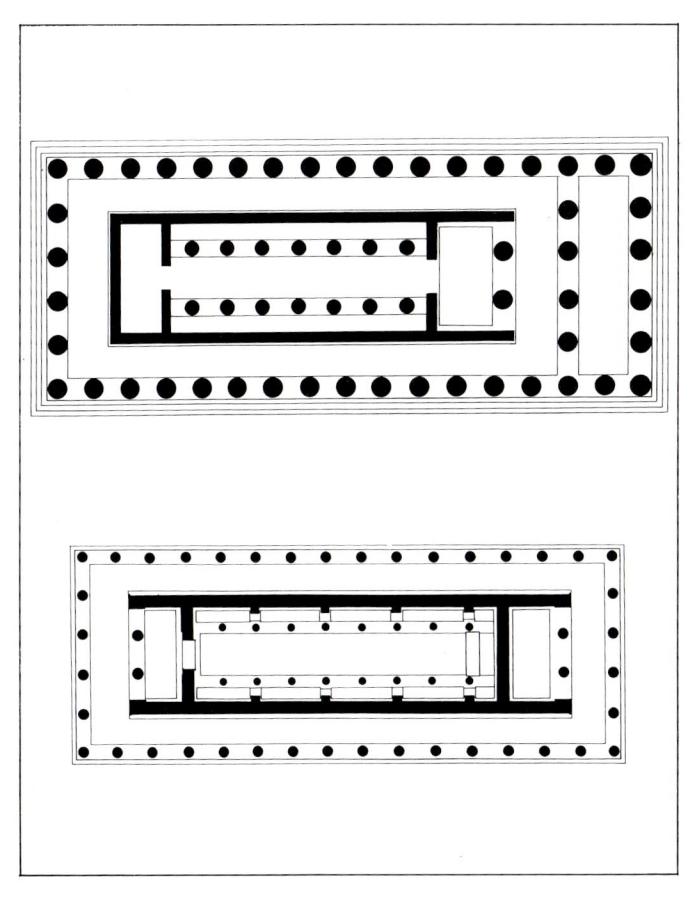

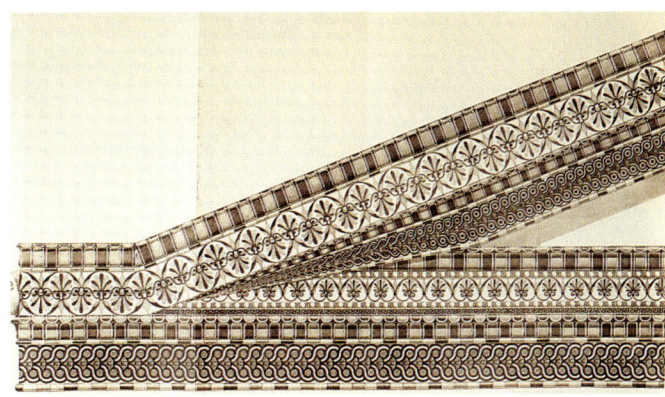

The Early-Archais temples in Greece and the West plans of the Temple of Hera at Olympia (above) and the Temple of Apollo at Syracuse (right) (Mertens drawing Schützenberger)

Siceliot architectural terra-cottas from the Geloan Treasury at Olympia (Doerpfeld)

Siceliot architectural terra-cottas from Temple C at Selinus (Gabrici)

There is little documentation except for the main *geison*, or strongly protruding cornice, that crowns the order itself and creates a link with the massive planes of the roof; hence the importance of the surviving terra-cotta fragments, whose most important centers of production and marketing were in the main Dorian *poleis* (Syracuse and Gela). Among the broad range of styles is a prevalent type classified as "Siceliot"; this is composed of two elements: the cladding, whose structural origins may lie in an early strategy for protecting the timber beam-ends, though this supposition is yet to be proved definitively. (Thanks to the decorative potential of this element, whose flat plane carries various geometrical ornaments, the cladding remained an integral part of the crown of the order, even when the timber elements were replaced with stone ones.) The second, upper element extends from the border tile and usually has a large, tall cyma, also bearing a rich polychrome decoration pierced by long tubular downsponts. The cyma is sometimes replaced with a rich array of relief lotus and palmette motifs, which are occasionally perforated to facilitate the drainage of rainwater.

This blueprint for the great peripteral temple of Siceliot creation, whose main structural and ornamental features are sketched out briefly here, was developed through the sixth century in a series of monuments of which those of the Selinus school are splendid examples.

The master-builders of Selinus

In one of the earlier, still rather contained monuments, the Archaic-period Temple Y (also known as the Temple of the Small Metopes, owing to six small metopes in the Museo Archaeologico, Palermo), the Selinuntine craftsmen directed their efforts toward developing the examples left by master-builders of eastern Sicily, and hence of the metropolis of Megara in Mainland Greece. In the rather squat columns such as those of the *apolloneion* in Syracuse (albeit with considerably more elegant capitals), and in the proportion of the entablature coordinated with the interaxis of the columns, one can observe the intense debate under way regarding the temple models. For the first time – at least as regards the main proportions of the monument – comparisons can be made with one of the temples of the homeland, namely the Temple of Aphaea at Aegina. If we overlook some of the stylistic phenomena ascribable to the prevailing colonial circumstances, such as the generous size of the individual formal elements, one notices in the ratio between the squat but well-spaced columns and the high entab-

Greek Architecture in the West

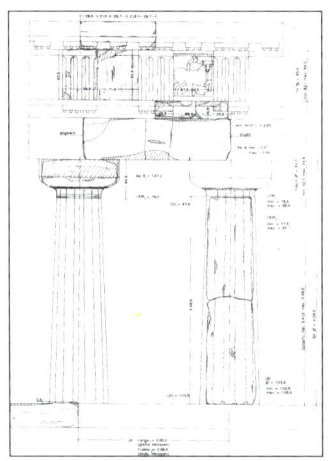

Temple Y, the "temple of the small metopes" at Selinus reconstruction of the intercolumniation (Mertens drawing Schüzenberger)

Temple C at Selinus viewed from the north

The Archaic plan of Temple C at Selinus compared to the plan of the Temple of Himera built in the 5th cent. (Mertens drawing Schützenberger)

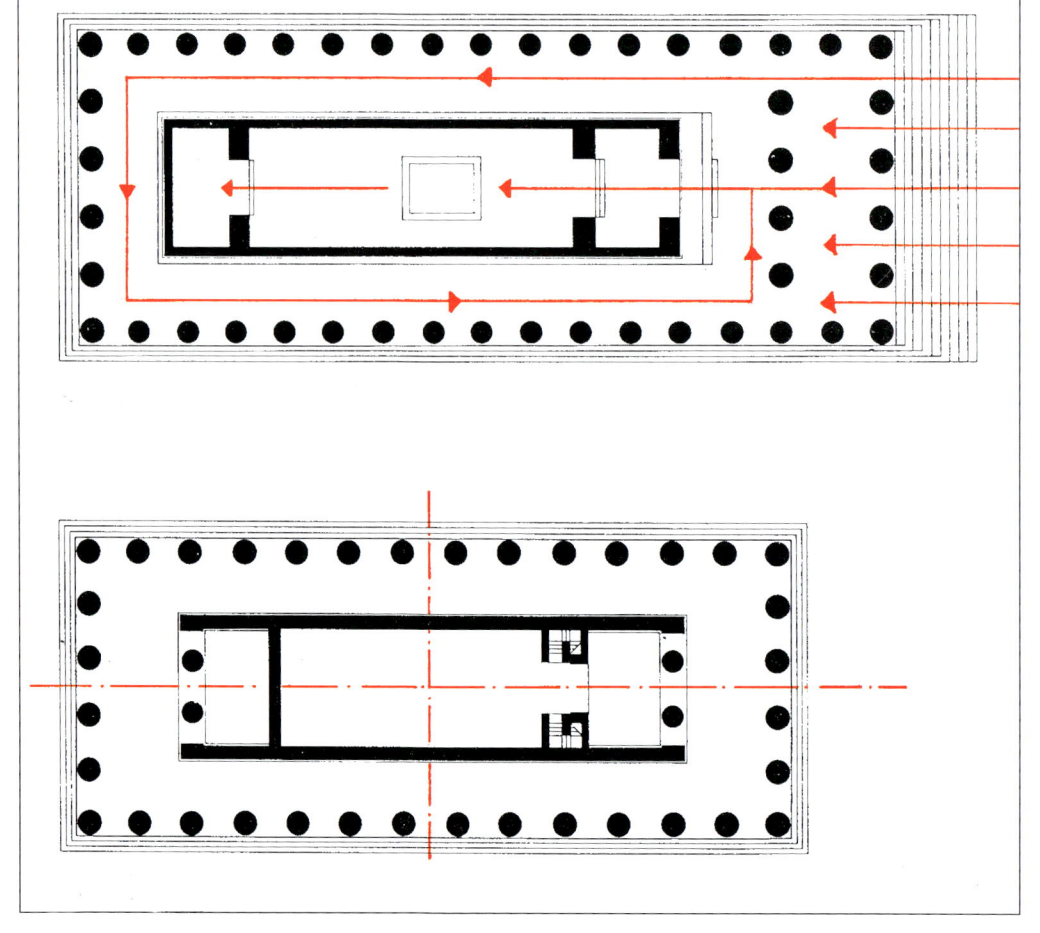

lature a tendency to show off the stone, while trying to master the new medium. Seen as a whole – the individual forms, the proportions, the style of the figured metopes – the two temples seem fairly similar in absolute chronological terms, as Temple Y slightly predates the Aegina temple (around 570 B.C.). This also confirms indirectly not only the framework for the first generation of temples in eastern Sicily during the period in which stone was thoroughly mastered, but also that the entire Siceliot evolution developed in parallel with that of the homeland.

Like in a sample-book, Temple Y contains all the premises for the coming glorious phase of peripteral temple-building at Selinus, a phase that began around mid-century or shortly thereafter, with Temple C, the majestic principal temple of the acropolis. This monument expresses the essence of the Siceliot temple; it is heavily conditioned by its layout, which in turn seems to respond cogently to the functional needs of the rites performed in it. Otherwise there would be no explanation for the striking spatial arrangement. The inviting entrance steps spread the full width of the front, the vast first hall of the *propteron*, the spacious *peristasis* to allow for solemn processions, and lastly the long *cella* (that could be reached through the wide doorway of the *pronaos*, down to the end of the *adyton*, or inner shrine) for the statue of the cult set in the utter of gloom at the end of the *naos*. What an enormous difference from the Mainland Greek temples, that were balanced on both back and fronts, remaining inaccessible to the majority of the faithful, and what a logical consequence of the elaboration of a basic concept which we had noted in the first monumental temple of Sicily, namely that of the *apolloneion* at Syracuse.

The main lines of development in Sicily in the later sixth century B.C.
The spatial arrangement of a wide *peristasis* and a long deep *naos* – clearly dictated by functional requirements – became a constant in the Archaic temples of the western Greeks. The functional equivalence between *naos* and peristasis can be further underlined for a unusual device: in some temples the *peristasis* is actually closed off toward the exterior by high partitions (Temple F, Selinus) or by walls even, articulated on the exterior by engaged half-columns (Temple B, Metapontum; the *olympieion*, Acragas).

Assuming this priority of the functional aspects in the layout of the temples, the architectural elements shared with the homeland temples begin to appear with increasing regularity in the basic proportions and formal criteria: the ratio of length to width, which is immediately perceivable in the number of columns along the flanks, begins to be more balanced, as testified by Temples D and F at Selinus, or the *athenaion* at Paestum, and the so-called Tavole Palatine (*heraion*) at Metapontum: the design for the latter can only be interpreted as a deliberate response to the larger sanctuary within the city walls.

At the same time one notices an evolution in the way the elements of the facade are related, at least in Sicily, while in Magna Graecia the architects continued for some time yet to follow the rules of their own style, as described above. The columns became taller, the shafts less massive, and a purer relationship among the components of the entablature was gradually established. Only in the general voluminousness of the individual forms, particularly as regards the somewhat bulky, stout capitals, and in the predilection for an abundance of polychrome terra-cotta decorative work, continues to manifest itself as that characteristic expressiveness of the western world.

The climax of the outstanding ability of the colonies at the peak of their development – the end of the Archaic and start of the Classical periods – is represented by the two colossal temples of Selinus (Temple G) and the *olympieion* or Temple to Zeus Olympus at Acragas (Roman Agrigentum).

But this is not all. If these monuments are properly interpreted, their intentions are far more ambitious than may seem at first. In its faithful repetition of the basic ground plan borrowed from the *apolloneion* at Didyma near Miletus, the dipteral (or pseudo-dipteral?) scheme, the spacious prostylar hall of the *pronaos*, and above all the central sanctum in the form of a hypaethral *sekos*, that is, open to the sky and with a *naiskos* (isolated mini-temple) for housing the cult statue – the great Selinuntine temple, with all probability also an *apolloneion*, seems to be as crucial to temple design in the West as the *apolloneion* at Didyma was for Asia Minor. What a daring gesture is the Olympieion at Acragas, if the atlantes really represent the conquest of Carthage, crushed in the battle at Himera (as convincingly argued by Drerup)!

But here we should pause to reflect.

By referring simultaneously to these two colossal monuments of western Greece, we have unwittingly subscribed to an idea of continuity of development that is not actually traceable. Before analyzing

Metapontum: Temple of Hera of the "Tavole Palatine" outside the walls viewed from the south

The colossal temples: Temple G at Selinus viewed from the east

The colossal temples: reconstruction of the Temple of Olympian Zeus at Acragas (Agrigento) (Prado)

the transition (which are actually elusive and discontinuous) to the Classical period of the fifth century, it will be useful to see the temples in their broader context.

At any event, the other temples also evince a keen sense of ambition – not only in their absolute dimensions (they too were built to monumental scale) but also in their position with respect to the urban plan as a whole. It is interesting to note, for example, that the main temples at Metapontum, Paestum, Syracuse, and the eastern hill of Selinus, are all perfectly parallel to each other, and form large compact ensembles of architectural masses, the monumental and representational effect of which basically supersedes that of the two colossal monuments. The evolution of the urban sanctuary at Metapontum in terms of the city layout has shown without a shadow of a doubt that Temples A and B, with their identical orientation, comply with the street grid and not vice versa (see Mertens on "Urban Planning in Magna Graecia" elsewhere in this volume). Despite their physical size, the buildings are therefore basically conceived not as stand-alone monuments but as landmarks emphasizing the urban system and the overall model of order this represents. This becomes even more evident where the temples show a correspondence over larger distances, as in the case of the temples at Syracuse (the Ionic *athenaion*, and the *apolloneion*) and Paestum (Temple of Neptune, the *athenaion*), or even when they lie outside the city walls, as at Selinus (town plan and the temples in the external sanctuary on the eastern hill).

Non-sacred public structures

It is obvious that structures of such breathtaking proportions can only be engendered by powerful political systems. We saw earlier how in the *agora* at Megara Hyblaea (seventh century B.C.) the desire to give form and a sense of place to the community entailed structuring public space with

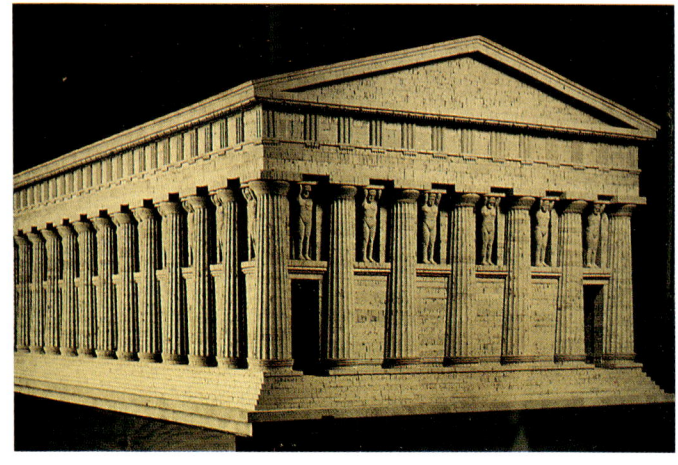

Plan and section of the *ekklesiasterion*
of Metapontum
monumental phase
of the 1st quarter 5th cent. B.C.
(Mertens drawing Schützenberger)

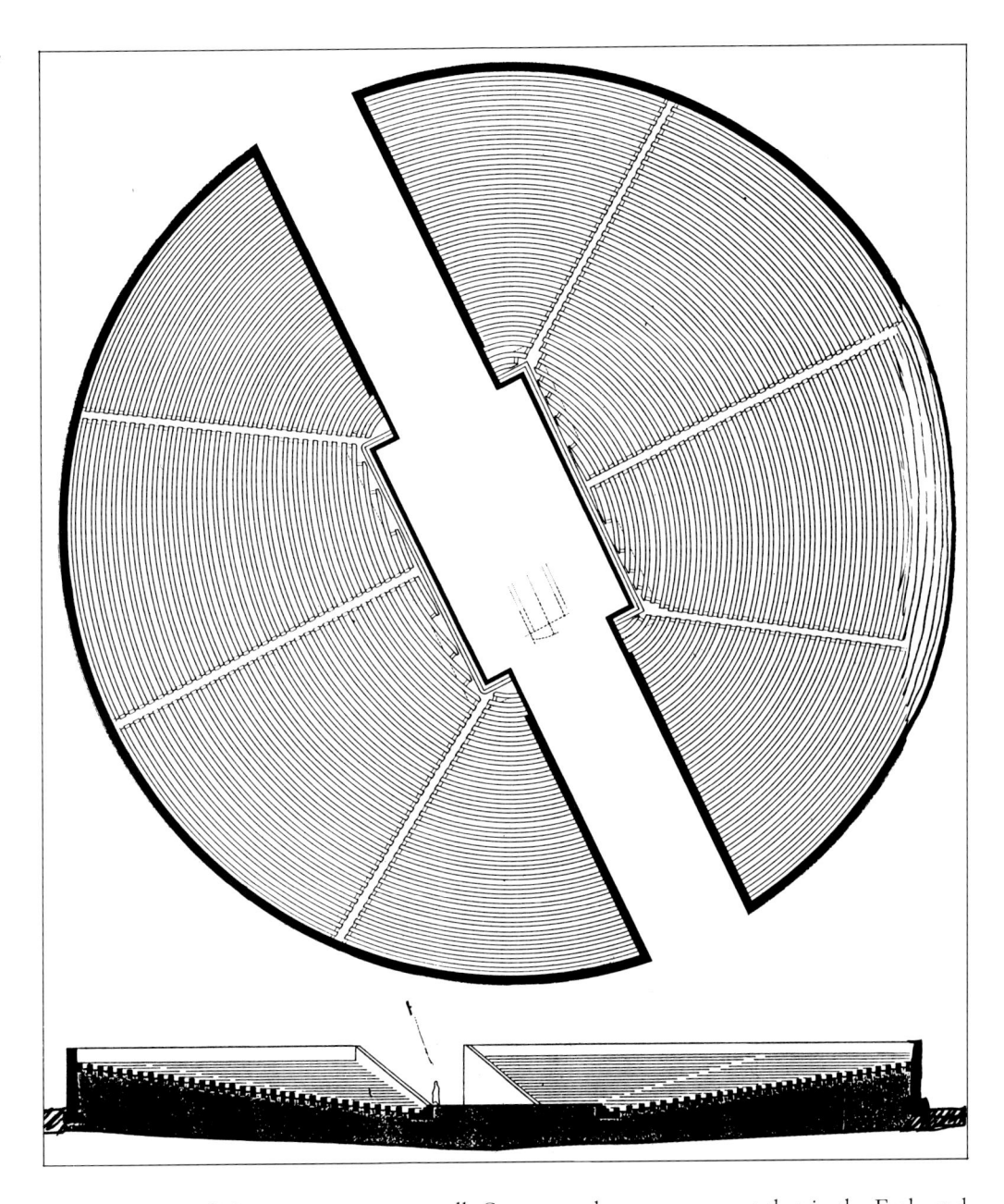

important non-religious monuments as well. Consequently, we can expect that in the Early and Late Archaic periods the prime importance accorded to the temples should have some correspondence in the other profane monuments. As things stand today, this idea is manifested most strikingly in the large roofless assembly structure in the *agora* at Metapontum, a building denominated *ekklesiasterion* for the time being. This was a place for public gatherings, and during its period of use in the mid-sixth century B.C., it had no equal in the entire Greek world. The *ekklesiasterion* is an excellent illustration of the social composition: the large circular structure (with all the symbolic and semantic pregnancy this form implies) could hold around 8,000 people gathered round a rectangular central space designed to accommodate a wide range of public events. Besides hosting events from the religious calendar (the *ekklesiasterion* was under the protection of the cult of Zeus Agoraios worshiped in the neighboring *temenos*), it is reckoned that the circular building also witnessed political rallies, which the entire eligible population attended from both city and surrounding *chora*.

It should be underlined that this building – which is chronologically parallel to the two main temples here at Metapontum – seems to be coeval with the original planned urban layout. The *ekklesiasterion* is a resounding confirmation of the colonists' capacity to address their functional needs by creating an independent and entirely novel type of building.

The Crisis of the Late Sixth and Early Fifth Centuries B.C.

Shortly before the close of the sixth century B.C. one begins to detect a growing lack of confidence in the once assured and self-reliant spirit of colonial architecture, a situation that gave rise to some radical internal contradictions. There are two basic reasons underlying this new indecisiveness: first, the architects began to realize the dead end to which certain popular choices were leading (I am thinking here in particular of the so-called Achaean style with its syncretic graft of the Doric and Ionic forms); second, the architects of Mainland Greece were meanwhile developing clear-cut and convincing canons for the architectural orders which, with the growing sense of the Greek *koine* or identity, would later assert themselves in crescendo.

In this phase of their history, which saw new floods of immigrants, the colonies betray a receptive attitude toward new ideas. This is particularly noticeable during the far-reaching political upheavals that shook Ionia, first at Samos and then in Asia Minor.

The outcome was an influential current of Ionic architecture that had nothing in common with previous Ionic tendencies, as we noticed in Archaic architecture of the Achaean colonies. The Ionic temple of Syracuse from the Late Archaic period, for example, built in pure Samian style, is undoubtedly conceived by craftsmen who immigrated from Samos, a large island in the Aegean. This workshop established the stylistic trend for a generation and more. A large temple erected at Catana (Catania, Sicily), and in particular the famous Ionic temple at Contrada Marasà near modern Locri, built in the second quarter of the fifth century, are the most significant testaments to the genius of these builders, who continued their activity through the fifth century, and whose works include the recently discovered Ionic temple at Caulonia, and the Ionic temple at Hipponium.

Another tendency under way in the Ionic style, probably influenced by original models from northern Ionia, can be detected in the singular Ionic temple at Metapontum. The monument in question can only be a model – not the product of a well-structured workshop. The basic forms themselves, namely the temple base, the capitals, moldings, and friezes, are inordinately abstract and stylized, and the manner of their execution suggests that the stonemasons and sculptors were not too familiar with true Ionic forms. As for the overall scheme of the temple, there is considerable freedom in the layout and originality in the composition of the structural elements of the Ionic order which is emblematic of the ease with which the colonial world managed to graft new experiences onto the traditional functional and structural requirements. The pseudo-dipteral temple plan in fact seems to foreshadow a characteristic typology that was not introduced to the Ionic architecture of Asia Minor until early Hellenism. The same applies to the remarkable composition of the entablature, in which a running frieze is combined with a dentelated cornice. In truth, both these qualities, the wide, spacious *peristaseis* and the importance of the running frieze on the entablature were already part of the peculiarities of the western Archaic temple, particularly in the Achaean colonies which – in their new stylistic formula – found their most congenial expression.

The Great Upturn of the Fifth Century B.C.

At any event, the Ionic phase was brief and insubstantial, and the temple at Metapontum, with its apparent anachronisms and forward-looking ideas, remains an isolated case.

The real advancement came with the Doric order, which began to show up in the major Siceliot cen-

Metapontum: capital of the Ionic temple

Reconstruction of the elements of the order of the Ionic temple at Metapontum
(Mertens drawing Schützenberger)

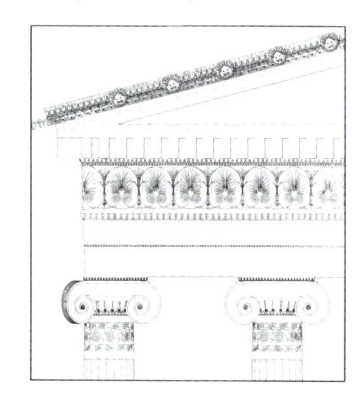

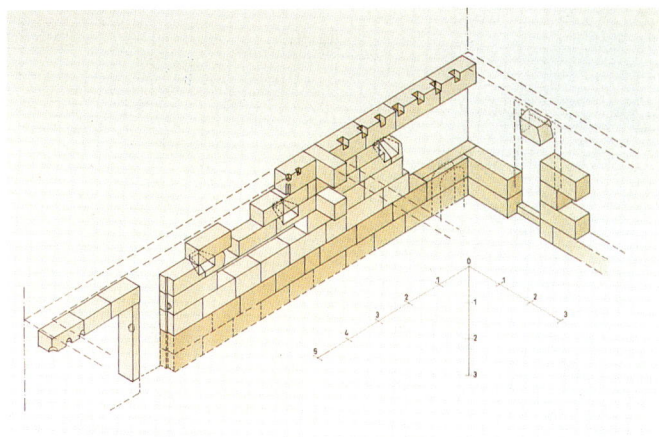

Selinus: wall of the monumental houses conserverd *in situ* first half 5th cent.

Selinus: reconstruction of the wall of the ground floor in the monumental houses first half 5th cent. B.C. (Mertens drawing Schützenberger)

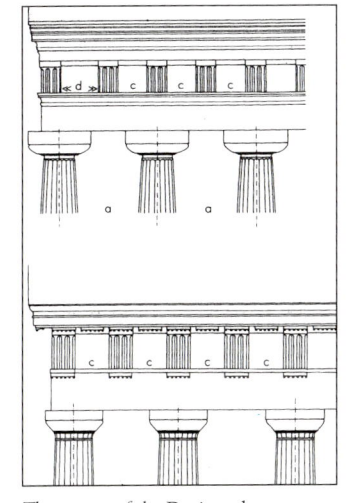

The corner of the Doric order
a) Archaic solution: equal intercolumniation widening of the first metope
b) Classical solution: regularly spaced frieze reduction of the first intercolumniation
(Mertens drawing Schützenberger)

ters. With their momentous transformations of a constitutional and social nature – accompanied by deep political turmoil – at all levels the Siceliot *poleis* led the way in the earlier fifth century B.C. The emergence of the great tyrannies at Acragas and Syracuse, with their dramatic social, economic, and cultural consequences, and the victory at Himera in 480 B.C. – a vital catalyst of forces – undoubtedly triggered the extraordinary renewal of interest in monumental architecture in general, and particularly in Doric temple architecture.

The phase of massive urban renewal, as exemplified by Syracuse with the installation of the Dionysian tyranny, and the arrival of huge quantities of new settlers, were an ulterior challenge to capacities the great technical and organizational prowess at work in the fields of urban planning, architecture, and engineering. Syracuse and Acragas, for example, were completely refitted with a complex system of water conduits. Besides the inscription on the stylobate of the *apolloneion* at Syracuse, this was the first instance in which the name of a person was directly equated with the operation, Phaeax, the inventor of the underground aqueducts of Acragas. It is known that Phaeax had to work with large forces of untrained workmen, including Carthaginian prisoners of war. These same hands were employed for building the *olympieion*, and the undertaking involved a substantial change of method. The utilization of an enormous quantity of stone blocks of almost standard shape and size for the foundations, the socles or base courses, and also for large parts of the walls, is undeniably linked to the availability of this workforce and betrays a very modern and rational outlook in dealing with such bold new technical objectives.

The profound restructuring and partial building *ex novo* of the residential areas engendered a new perception of the city: it became a constructed entity in itself. At this point the *insulae*, once they were seen as lots of land occupied by individual households often set apart from each other, were conceived and constructed as complete blocks, with all the consequences in terms of space, aesthetics, and hence also in terms of a new vision of the city as a built-up organism: a new reality that was in some cases accompanied by a new proportional arrangement of the *insulae* that affected the entire urban layout (e.g., Naxos and Neapolis; see the essay "Urban Planning in Magna Graecia" elsewhere in this volume).

In some cases this change in the quality of dwelling standards resulted in a considerable improvement of the standards of execution. The most conspicuous example is undoubtedly Selinus, where a large quota of the more central areas of the city in the first decades of the fifth century were constructed *ex novo* (albeit within lots defined a century earlier) with houses made of large squared blocks of stone whose quality and technique of execution were more customary for public buildings. For the time being the political and social reasons for this phenomenon are unclear. The houses, some of which had two floors, are built from large isodomic blocks; the units share their dividing walls, and seem to follow some common scheme. The lack of systematic archaeological excavations over a suitable area makes it impossible as yet to reach any conclusions about such observations, which are nonetheless highly illuminating on the question of the political, social, and economic configuration of the society that built such structures.

The new model: the temples in the Severe style
The new proficiency in organizational matters – aided by the availability considerable resources – kindled a surge of interest in monumental religious architecture. The joint victory of Acragas and Syra-

Temple of Hera Selinus viewed from the northwest (anastylosis)

Reconstruction of Temple E at Selinus the east facade (Mertens drawing Schützenberger)

cuse over the Carthaginians at Himera was promptly consecrated with the construction of two temples of great importance and impact: the so-called Temple of Victory erected upon the battle site, and the Temple of Athena in Syracuse itself. (The *olympieion* erected at Acragas is a case apart.) The two new temples – built with practically identical dimensions, ground plans, and orientation – provide a new model for temple design suitable to the environment and historical period, which is generally termed as the Severe style. Besides their shared stylistic and formal "austerity," which is typified by the capital with its rigid profile, the intention to set a standard by these two temples is evident in the extreme rationalism of the design, and particularly of the ground plan. The ratio of the number of columns (6 by 14) became a fixture hereafter for the larger temple monuments in the West (with the exception of the Temple of Hera at Selinus, having 6 by 15 columns). Other features include the perfect symmetry with which the *naos* (now with an *opisthodomos* or rear inner portico corresponding to the *pronaos* at the front) lies within the peristasis; the wide and spacious rooms of the *naoi*; the evenness in the interaxis and columns on each side. At this juncture a solution was sought for the awkwardness of the corner columns of the Doric order, a problem that was not ever considered in the Archaic-period temples. The conflict stems from the fact that, for evident structural reasons, the corner of the entablature must be occupied and marked by a triglyph, which therefore lies out of line with the axis of the column below. The solution to the problem lies either in widening the elements of the entablature, such as the corner metope, or by narrowing the gap between the columns toward the corner. To make the visual irregularities of this expedient negligible, the architects tried numerous ingenious ways of redistributing the columns or altering the entablature. In the case of the two temples in question, they chose to gradually contract the interaxis; for the *athenaion* in Syracuse, the distance between the entablature elements was almost imperceptibly increased. This so-called dual corner adjustment applied to both sides and front (1. interaxis from corner = 12 feet; 2. interaxis from corner 19 1/2 feet; normal interaxis = 12 3/4 feet) was subsequently taken up in the West. This new prototype of early Classicism in western Greece served the temple-builders of other important *poleis* – Selinus, Gela, Paestum, Croton – whose majestic monuments were completed within the first half of the fifth century B.C. Owing to their poor state of repair, the temples in Croton and Gela do not admit any precise affirmations about their background, whereas the *heraion* at Selinus and the Temple of Neptune at Paestum betray the two extremes of proportion and concept which that model embodied. The uncommon length, of the temple at Selinus reveals the difficulties of adapting the Archaic plan: the architects would not forgo the *adyton*, which had therefore to coexist with the new *opisthodomos*. Likewise, the frontage with its greatly slenderized columns and the consequent compensation made to the proportions with the entablature of equal height, betrays a lack of confidence in achieving the Classical balance. It cannot be ruled out, moreover, that these tendencies were prompted by new

Paestum: Temple of Neptune from the northwest

Reconstruction of the east facade of the Temple of Neptune at Paestum (Mertens drawing Schützenberger)

Greek models, particular those of Attica, including the supreme model of the first Parthenon, which preceded the Periclean temple in Athens today.
The other example, the Neptune Temple of Paestum with its decidedly more cumbrous and severe proportions, could be a reflection of coeval experiences under way in the Peloponnese, of which the Temple of Zeus at Olympia is a monumental example. In both cases, however, there is no prompt mediation with precise models, but rather with generic expressive and stylistic trends. Both the western temples are all too evidently tied and conditioned by formal and conceptual experiences of their own milieu, despite the marked breach with the linear Archaic tradition. As suggested above, the Temple of Hera attempted to merge the traditional religious conditioning with the new Classical form. Similarly, the Temple of Neptune, with its exceedingly bulky forms, and significant conceptual choices (such as the 6 to 14 column ratio, or the sophisticated exploration of the corner design problem) is too distinct and self-reliant to be an immediate response to any precise model, as in the case of the temple at Olympia. Perhaps we can imagine a more dialectical relationship between the features of the larger western temples of the Siceliot tyrannies with the great Greek sanctuary, which remained a crucial standard and link between Mainland Greece and the colonies. There is plenty of evidence to back up this idea, that the initiative for the construction of the Temple of Libon at Olympia may in some way have been stimulated by the phase of temple-building in the Severe style in the West.

New trends in the post-tyranny period: the golden age of Acragas
The glorious period of public monument construction – especially in Sicily – seems to come to a head in the first half of the fifth century B.C. One tends, naturally, to see this in connection with the general political and constitutional conditions established by the first of the tyrannies in Syracuse and Acragas. It should be sufficiently self-evident that to interpret monumental architecture as a direct expression of specific constitutional conditions is speculative and misleading. The creation of an important public gathering complex in the *agora* at Paestum, for instance, does not necessarily result from changes in the political setup, such as the institution of a pluralistic (not to say democratic) social matrix, and the contemporary, modernized reconstruction of a very similar *ekklesiasterion* of Archaic origin in the *agora* at Metapontum should make us cautious.
It is nonetheless astonishing to note that, in Acragas shortly before mid-century, the brief tradition of large-scale temple construction was interrupted, first on the so-called Temple of Heracles, then on the colossal *olympieion*. The construction of the latter seems to have been resumed in the last

Greek Architecture in the West

Paestum: axonometric reconstruction of the *ekklesiasterion - bouleuterion*

Acragas (Agrigento): the Temple of Juno Lacinia the east facade with indications of the fundamental proportions
(Mertens drawing Schützenberger)

quarter of the century; it was later abandoned definitively after the catastrophic fall of the city to the Carthaginians in 406 B.C.

This does not mean, however, that temples were not still being constructed. Actually, around 460 B.C. a veritable boom in temple-building began, establishing Acragas' fame among its contemporaries as the world's finest city, and "the eye of Sicily" (Pindar, *Pythian* XII.1; II. 9. 15). The famous temples, along the walls, which from then on would form an incomparable necklace around the *polis*, are all fairly contained in size; for Sicily they were the first temples on "human" scale, so to speak. At the same time, these temples have undeniable dignity and grandeur, each being peripteral and therefore a costly undertaking that aptly expresses the economic prowess of the city.

Furthermore, there seems to be significance behind the fact that the temples are of almost identical dimensions; their ground plans and detailing are also very closely related. They were commissioned according to equally similar criteria, and are undoubtedly designed by a coherent, well-organized, and highly active architectural school. Their design follows the principle of extreme rationality and transparency, based on the application of simple but cogent criteria of numeric proportion.

This allows us to follow closely, with concrete examples, the evolution from one temple to another, and explains how the architects of the Classical period developed the design of their monuments in a kind of dialectical discussion over the prototypes already erected: working from a precise knowledge of the metrological and, especially, of the proportional values of an archetype, that is, a monument already realized – and we know from Vitruvius that the architects of the Classical period were accustomed to making these criteria public – it was possible to design a new monument in similar terms, while simply adding the various adjustments that progress automatically dictated. This procedure in no way detracts from the monuments' artistic value, which depend solely on the wholesome proportions (which in turn depend on the experience and ability of the architect) but renders the complex process of the commission, design, and even execution, from the quarrying to the final touches on the finished monument, a sequence of actions that can be tightly controlled by the public administrators. The rationality and clarity of the outlook of the citizenry of these mature, affluent cities could hardly have had monuments of greater eloquence, nor indeed beauty.

The loss of singularity in the individual temple is at this point compensated by the synoptic vision of the overall urban plan, in which the temples combine and complement each other to perform a new role of immense importance. The specifics of site and position for each temple become a feature as vital as the temple itself. One can observe how, following their chronology, the temples came to fill all the major panoramic points of the city and surrounding *chora*, becoming landmarks for the entire city. An example of this can be experienced on the road to Gela or Caltanissetta, where one obtains a striking demonstration of the gradual ranking of the temples, first the Temple to Juno Lacinia, then the Concordia, and so on.

A new concept of "propaganda" afforded by planning and architecture had emerged, a more differentiated concept than the one underlying the large temple groupings of the Archaic period. The vision of the city styled upon panoramic criteria – a characteristic of the Late Hellenism – was being formulated.

Undoubtedly, it could hardly compete against Athens (but that applies to the entire Greek world),

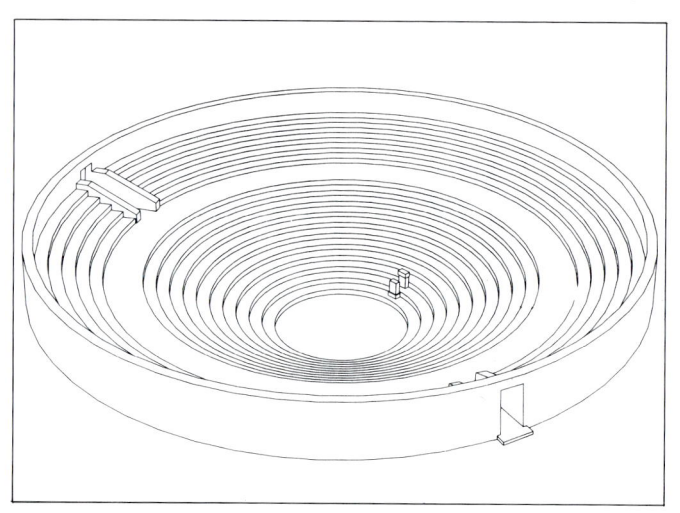

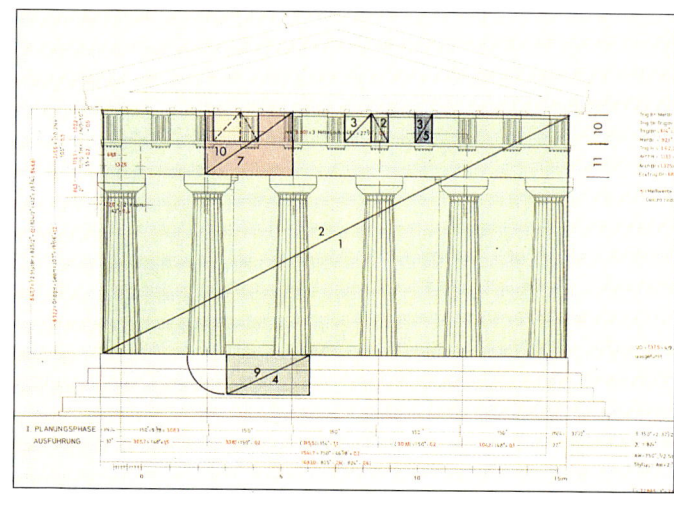

Acragas (Agrigento): the Temple
of Concord viewed from the northeast

Segesta: the great temple

with its unique, incomparable grouping of Classical monuments on the Acropolis. Once again, the most imposing public monuments in western Greece served to reinforce the colonists' image and sense of identity. At the same time they served to deepen the long and slow process of cultural assimilation of the old indigenous populations of the hinterland who, despite centuries of Hellenization, continued to maintain their innermost cultural spirit.

The spread of the Greek model in the non-Greek world
The aforesaid transition of the Greek temple from its function as a monument of Hellenic cultural supremacy to its new role as an archetype makes it "duplicable" (as in the case of Acragas). Furthermore, this change also made the application of the concept possible elsewhere. The case of Acragas showed that even the same building type and ground plan could be utilized indifferently for all the Greek forms of worship. It is therefore not surprising that the concept of the canonical Greek temple could be grafted onto non-Greek cultural environments.
The most conspicuous example is the much-discussed temple at Segesta, the Elymian town whose religious practices and deities are still largely unknown.
In the Mango quarter on the southern slopes of the town, building was undertaken as early as mid-fifth century, comprising a complete *temenos* with a midsize peripteral temple that excellently renders the Classical style found at Selinus; the temple was evidently designed and built by the busy workshops of that city. In an even more visually stunning situation is the large unfinished temple on the western hill. The building – erected on the ruins of a very early Elymian temple – seems to have been of particular political importance, a kind of propagandistic landmark, given that its construction was undertaken during the peak of Segesta's expansion, a period that had tragically implicated Athens in the affairs of the West. The temple and its design (which is also influenced by political changes) comprise features of exclusively Attic derivation, yet its overall pattern faithfully follows the evolution of the Siceliot temple. As the only example of building architecture of the later fifth century B.C., the building in fact draws on the monumental temples of the early tyrannies for its dimensions. It would

be hard to find a more proud expression of cultural identity. Of great significance is the fact that the temple is "unfinished," symbolizing the dashed hopes of Segesta: this great monument marks the interruption – through the chain of catastrophes and upheavals that affected most Greek and non-Greek cities toward the close of the fifth century – of the evolution of monumental sacred architecture in the Classical West. If we take a closer look at the various formal features, the tired profile of the capitals, the dry and rigid forms of the few moldings and triglyphs, we soon sense that the original force of expression was waning, despite the massive proportions. These are signs not only of a provincial milieu, but of the end of an era and the advent of a new set of values.

The crisis of the late fifth and early fourth centuries B.C.
The dramatic upheavals that overtook the Siceliot *poleis* at the end of the fifth century were matched in Magna Graecia by a more enduring though no less far-reaching crisis. In the field of architecture one notes that from the mid-fifth century the flow of major commissions all but dried up. Political motives – spurred by the increasingly aggressive sense of autonomy felt by the Italic peoples, but also linked to other environmental and economic problems, such as the great depression of Metapontum (Greek Metapontion) and other events – caused a conspicuous void that would last almost a century. In Sicily only Syracuse managed to escape the clutches of the Carthaginians and their dominance. Danger loomed perpetually on the horizon, however, and weighed decisively on future urban architecture and planning.

It is hardly surprising, therefore, that the manpower which had so far gone into building grandiose sacred and civil monuments were now put to work on creating massive defense works. The most impressive undertaking of this kind, which seems to epitomize the change of situation, are the Long Walls built by Dionysius I encircling the entire Epipolae Plateau, the fatal setting of the dramatic war against Athens. The awe-inspiring walls – longer than those Themistocles built around Athens – are all the more astonishing now that fieldwork has shown that Diodorus' reputedly hyperbolic description of them (XIV. 18. 2) is actually very accurate. Diodorus describes the undertaking in great detail, giving figures for the workforce and their equipment; the northern stretch of wall 30 *stadia* long (ca. 6 kilometers) was completed in a mere twenty days, under the watchful eye of Dionysius himself. A study of the quarries from which the wall-stone was extracted, together with the transport route, and the structure and techniques of the wall amply suggest that Diodorus was factual. One key item of information is the outstanding organizational abilities of Dionysius and his engineers, combined with a massive logistic apparatus, not to mention a vast workforce – the largest recorded for any undertaking in antiquity. We also know of new developments in the science of siege machinery, including the invention of the catapult, which was to have immediate repercussions on the design of defensive architecture. To complete the picture of the multiplicity of building activity all channeled toward the one objective of defense, Dionysius also undertook a complete restructuring of the ports at Syracuse, with the con-

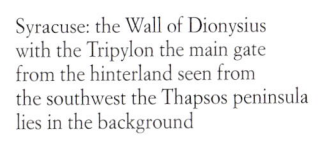

Syracuse: the Wall of Dionysius with the Tripylon the main gate from the hinterland seen from the southwest the Thapsos peninsula lies in the background

the construction of the arsenal, and not least the fortified palace on the island of Ortygia.

The massive Dionysian walling was not actually conceived exclusively as a form of defensive structure, making the barren plain of the Epipolae Plateau inaccessible to intruders, and hence a means of protecting the city. It undoubtedly had equal importance for the city's *chora*, to whose population the walls provided refuge; these were most likely the same people whom Dionysius put to work on this far-sighted scheme of security. In other words, with this scheme the city and its immediate territory were brought into a close, reciprocal relationship. It should be remembered the effect of seeing the huge band of white stone along the Epipolae hillside would have had on intruders. The wall created a new image of the city and of Dionysius' power.

The walls of Syracuse, however, are merely the most grandiose example of a wide variety of defense works that had become the principal building project under way in many *poleis* in this period. In Magna Graecia, meanwhile, the inhabitants of Locri (Lokroi Epizephyrioi) were also busy erecting a long defensive wall and the same thing was taking place in Locri's subcolony Hipponium (Hipponion). Such defensive works kept many towns busy throughout the fourth century.

The Major Recovery of the Later Fourth Century: the Start of Hellenism

It was not until the second half of the fourth century B.C. that the western colonial cities in both Sicily and Magna Graecia were once again stable enough to undertake urban renewal schemes and rebuilding. This generalization is not applicable everywhere, however, owing to the fairly complex political situation that prevailed. Paestum, for instance, ceded to Lucanian dominion, while the western half of Sicily was part of the Punic eparchy, with all the consequences of a slow and irreversible cultural about-turn. We will therefore limit our discussion to the more fortunate Greek *poleis* that managed to keep in the mainstream of the evolution of architecture and distinguish themselves once again with independent solutions that attest to an unbroken vigor in western Greek thinking.

Croton, Capo Colonna
katagoghion and *estiatorion*
the buildings for accommodating pilgrims in the great supra-regional sanctuary

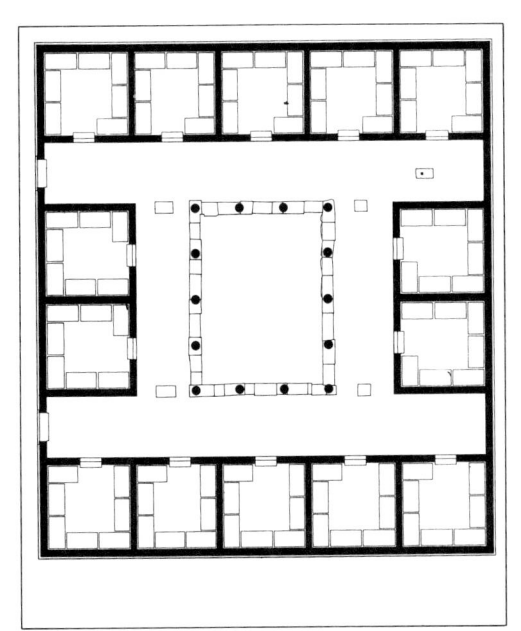

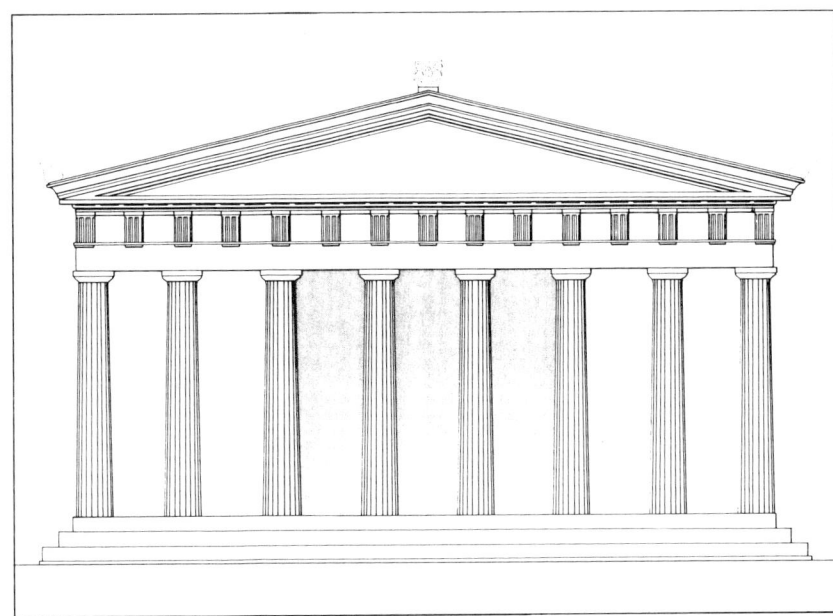

Croton: plan of the *estiatorion*
(Mertens drawing Schützenberger)

Crimisa (Cirò): reconstruction
of the Temple of Apollo Alaios Early
Hellenistic phase
(Mertens drawing Schützenberger)

In Magna Graecia, Metapontum is the *polis* that offers the most significant and complex examples. Coinciding significantly with the general upturn in the exploitation and management of the *chora*, large tracts of the city were rebuilt without changing the underlying urban layout (see essay "Urban Planning in Magna Graecia" elsewhere in this volume). One feature worth noting is the resourcefulness with which they resolved the main infrastructure problems, particularly as regards the main hydraulic plants. In the traditional fields of monumental architecture, sacred building became an almost marginal occupation. Once again Metapontum provides excellent indicators as to the changes under way. In the main urban sanctuary, only slight repair work was done on the great temples, which were actually not to last long anyway. Even more importantly, it seems that a divinatory cult made its home in the *agora* from early Archaic times, with an altar that was subsequently adorned with a grandiose architectural structure – a sure sign of the deep changes that were taking place in religious spheres. "Health" cults had begun to acquire increasing importance, as seen from the sanctuaries of Asclepius at Paestum and Acragas. In the second half of the fourth century B.C. the large extra-urban sanctuaries also seemed to draw more attention, to judge from the substantial architectural developments in some of the major sanctuaries, such as the *heraion* at Capo Colonna) and the ancient Sanctuary of Apollo Alaios at modern Cirò. Work on the former was carried out toward the close of the fourth century, with the construction of ample facilities to house pilgrims and wayfarers, built to designs that had evolved in Mainland Greece, such as the *estiatorion* and the *katagogion*; the latter sanctuary likewise hosted new structures of a similar nature. Of even greater importance was the reconstruction of the Temple of Apollo Alaios, where a magnificent stone peristyle of eight by nineteen columns was built, making this the only true peripteral temple of the post-Classical era in the entire West (apart from an as yet barely studied temple at Taormina), replacing the preceding Archaic structures in timber. In the face of this outstanding monument, with its anachronistic ground plan, we cannot but wonder whether the temple was perhaps intended as an evocation of the great Archaic past of the Greek colonies, which by this time had all but vanished.

A similar panorama can be seen in the Siceliot towns. At Megara Hyblaea, in the modest rebuilding scheme initiated by Timoleon, the most important monument had become a simple temple with twin columns *in antis*, carefully and precisely executed but of unassuming dimensions. Of a comparable size and plan was the coeval Temple of Empedocles (Temple B), the most significant Greek-style temple of Punic Selinus. In this little temple, which became famous in modern times for its yield of superb polychrome decorations, we can see a last attempt to implant Grecian architecture in a profoundly different cultural context. As for non-religious public building works, the onset of Hellenism saw a series of new definitions for the space known as the *agora*, or gathering place.

The *stoa*, which had already played a decisive role in the design of the western Greek prototype *agora* in Megara, assumed even greater prominence in this new context. A fixture in urban planning in the Late Classical and Hellenistic periods, the *stoa* in Mainland Greece had already shown its great versatility in creating and defining urban spaces, be they sacred or profane. Similarly, the *stoa* became

Greek Architecture in the West

an indispensable tool in the rehabilitation of the huge public areas of the colonial cities. At Metapontum, for instance, a large and well laid-out *stoa* on two stories closes the bottom end of the *agora* opposite the urban sanctuary. At Syracuse, which had meanwhile become the most important *polis* of the entire West, an amibitious system of *stoai* built on two levels crowned the theater, thereby forming a gigantic backdrop that dominated the whole of the Neapolis.

Western Hellenism

Syracuse: the fulcrum of Hellenistic architecture in the West
Syracuse was the focus and model of all the primary building projects in the West, culminating in the works undertaken by Hieron II, whose kingdom was the only one that could complete with the eastern Hellenistic realms.

Syracuse: Castle of Euryalus

Castle of Euryalus: axonometric reconstruction viewed from the west (H.J. Beste)

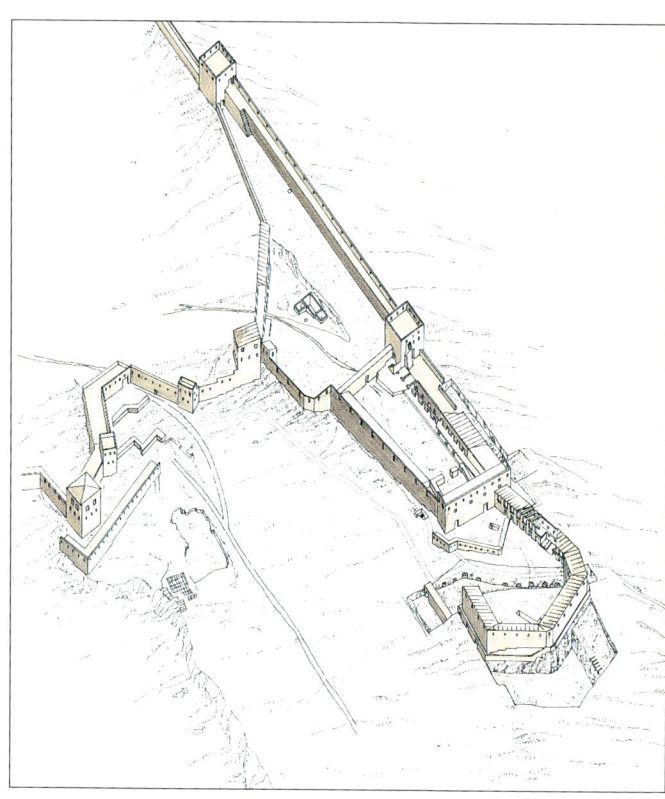

Greek Architecture in the West

Selinus: fortification of the acropolis viewed from the north

Selinus: model of the so-called North Gate on the acropolis viewed from the north (Mathieu-Fleig)

After the magnificent efforts of Dionysius the Elder, the main program of developments pivoted on the construction of siege works. It seems, moreover, that one of the greatest successors of Dionysius, Agathocles, created two of the fortifications of utmost significance and innovation: the new citadel of Euryalus at Syracuse, and a similar set of fortifications on the opposite end of Sicily, at Selinus. These two spectacular complexes embody the most advanced and radical ideas on "offensive defense," and are accompanied by an abundant share of Greek literature on the subject. The underlying concept of the defense works was to enable lightning sorties under perfect cover to waylay the enemy forces before they even got near the walls. The new tactics based on extreme mobility was a logical part of the new combat distances established by the invention of long-range weaponry, the catapult.

The north section of the bastions at Selinus are particularly cleverly devised. The structures comprise a large central gallery enabling forays protected by archers hidden in a three-story building, together with two large jutting towers on a semicircular plan, which housed the heavier artillery. The entire set-up was furthermore protected by a circuit of trenches and other minor works.

The siege works at Syracuse are comparable in design, though significantly more ambitious; the structure was amplified through to the third century B.C., particularly by Hieron II, until the fortress reached a size and complexity that remained unique throughout antiquity. The immense scheme, however, was never completed. Moreover, it seems as if it was never actually put into use: it remained a grandiose architectural enterprise of Hieron II, while exemplifying the engineering genius of its author. The enormous stone stronghold seems to emanate the spirit of that regal propaganda which informs the many megalomaniac works of Hieron II, such as the "altar" of over one *stadion* long built in the center of the Neapolis (Syracuse), complete with ample arcades; and not least the legendary

Syracuse: the theater

341

Syrakousiai, the largest sailing vessel ever built in antiquity. Nevertheless, Hieron's legacy of large-scale architecture is not limited to these clamorous achievements. The complete reworking of the Neapolis with the abovementioned system of *stoai*, but especially the construction (or perhaps the restincturing and enlargement) of the theater, were both undertakings of immense scope that allowed the unrivaled capital of the West to vie with the illustrious cities of Mainland Greece.

"International Hellenism" in the cities of the West
Like the *metropoleis* of the East, during the brief period of political continuity before the encounter with the Romans, so the western capital Syracuse stood as a model for all the smaller towns in its shadow: Helorus, Acrae, and particularly Morgantina, were endowed with *agorai* adorned with all the standard features of the period: theaters, meeting facilities, *stoai*, and large warehouses.
In certain areas the model that had been applied all over the Hellenistic world actually survived the Roman occupation, particularly in western Sicily, where throughout the second century B.C. favorable conditions endured to witness the evolution of a series of minor towns, including Tyndaris, Soluntum, Monte Iato, Segesta, to name only the better-known. Of particular distinction are their theaters, each with an elaborate two-story *skene*, which served as vital prototypes for the forthcoming development of the Roman theater. (In the same way, in Magna Graecia at the end of the fourth century the architects of Metapontum created the relative blueprint for the *cavea* or tiered theater seating.)
Syracuse also harbored another important Hellenistic type of building, namely the peristylar house. With their tall peristyles with two orders, Doric and Ionic, the splendid houses of Monte Iato and Soluntum offer the most characteristic examples. In Soluntum, the houses set into the steep hillside in the town are built on three stories (respectively for professional activities, residential, and domestic), and are therefore reminiscent of the fine examples of Hellenistic dwellings in Mainland Greece. These

Morgantina: the *agora* with the *ekklesiasterion* comprising three straight flights of steps and the theater

Segesta: reconstruction of the *skene* of the theater (Bulle-Wirsing)

Metapontum: reconstructed facade of the *kerkis* of the theater

homes are tangible evidence of the affluent and comfortable tenor of life enjoyed during this period, and they endorse the profound change of values that the society had undergone by this stage: there is no longer any distinction either in the elements or in the decoration of public and private monuments. These *poleis* of northwestern Sicily were in fact enjoying a season of unprecedented splendor. Despite being under Roman dominion – therefore protected and evidently favored by the new era of calm afforded by the *pax romana* – for some considerable time this sphere of the island seems to have been omitted from the profound cultural change under way in the rest of Sicily and Magna Graecia. Throughout the second century B.C. these towns saw not only the renovation of most of the private housing stock in compliance with the latest canons of Hellenism, but they also equipped themselves – in concord with the prevailing trend all across the Greek and Grecized world – with new monumental centers distinguished by imposing public facilities (theater, *bouleuterion*, *gymnasion*, etc.).

To obtain a picture of the prevailing standards elsewhere on Italian soil, it is enough to look at Paestum, which had altered profoundly since it passed to Lucanian dominion, and subsequently underwent radical restructuring immediately after it passed into Roman hands in 272 B.C. The renewal program was applied to both residential fabric and public areas, whereby the *agora* was summarily obliterated, together with its attendant facilities, and the Forum was rebuilt *ex novo* in accordance with Roman planning formulas, on the intersection between the two main streets. In this way a new complex monumental typology was carefully made to conform with the binding model afforded by the Roman capital.

Despite the restoration scheme, the Romans diligently conserved the ancient temples – not only at Paestum, but also in other towns and cities, apparently. It even looks as though (bar a few exceptions) the temples were not even adapted to the Roman forms of worship, but carefully protected as they were – restored, even – in full awareness of the incomparable cultural heritage that they represented. In some of the main monuments of new Paestum (i.e., the Dorico-Corinthian temple and the colonnades of the Forum) one notes an unmistakable recourse to much earlier architectural canons through the imitation of specific Archaic-Greek features, like some intentional form of "neoclassicism," an almost academic approach to the legacy of their Greek forebears, while at the same time signaling the definitive end to the world of Magna Graecia and the commencement of a new era.

Conclusions
To return to my opening remarks, it would be useful to summarize some of the characteristics that provide a common denominator in architecture, whose representative traits we have just followed in outline. Compared to Mainland Greece, which quickly sought to establish its main building typologies (above all the temple) through the institution of monumental building projects in durable materials (stone), and through the application of severe and logical formal apparatus (the orders), the colonies of the West unmistakably follow their own, quite distinct lines of development.

The monumentalization of each town's chief public buildings (and thence the private ones) seems to have been given critical precedence throughout the Greek colonial world. By thus demonstrating its cultural excellence or special fortune, each colony stressed its claim to the possession of the lands of

Soluntum: house with a peristyle
the so-called Gymnasium

the local populations, and its claim to the recognition and esteem of the entire Greek world, of which they never ceased to feel indissolubly a part.

The insistent theme of self-representation and self-assertion is always discernible in the magnificent temples of Syracuse, Selinus, and Acragas, and not least in the complex fortification measures and the "architectural utopias" of Hellenistic Syracuse. Likewise, in the temples built in the Severe style, the monumental tone is constantly perceivable, albeit tempered with respect to the Classical period. Even the individual architectural forms, with their noticeably bulkier and more overtly expressive forms compared to those of Mainland Greece, exude the spirit of grandeur.

The rapidity and autonomy with which the colonies in the earlier sixth century so swiftly managed to complete their first important monuments meant that they did not participate integrally or at the same speed in the lengthy, deep discussion taking place in Mainland Greece on the rules of architecture, that is, on the orders and the formal principles of proportion. In many colonies this inquiry was frequently interrupted or slowed down by the often dramatic upheavals in the social setup. The logic of strict and binding rules regarding form tended to give way to a general taste for abundant decoration. Nevertheless, as observed above regarding the Achaean colonies in Magna Graecia, there were attempts at consolidating a "colonial style" (loosely termed as "Dorico-Achaean," or the "Ionian Sea Style"), composed of the fundamental formal elements of the two main orders which, in Mainland Greece, crystallized into the distinct Doric and Ionic styles. The colonial world's ability to develop its own stylistic language through the merger of formal elements that have their roots in the different canonical orders was enduring, and manifested itself throughout the West; even during the fourth and third century B.C. this can be witnessed in the elaborate "Doric" cornices with their "Ionico-Siceliot" moldings in Sicily, together with the abundant formal apparatus of Tarentum's Hellenistic architecture. The flexibility and capacity to adapt expressed by this constant quest for identity through the development of a personal stylistic language was a rehearsal for the keen attention that the colonies were to pay to the functional aspects of architectural structure.

With their specific ground plans, the first temples in fact respond to a set of particular needs determined by the cult practices to be performed therein. For the gatherings of the townsfolk, the architects devised a building on a circular plan, thereby inventing a completely individual type of architecture, a very rare event in Greek architecture, which was based on a very limited range of basic building types. The major fortification complexes of early Hellenism were an immediate and unparalleled expression of the expanding sphere of siege science and the new war machinery. Here we have discussed the most notable cases only, but the same applies to all the other architectural types, and not least to the urban planning with its responses to the requirements imposed by the morphology of the terrain, to questions of traffic and mobility, and to all the complex rules that condition the design of infrastructure.

Another feature closely tied to the colonial architects' ability to elaborate new ideas are the organizational skills of the political-administrative bodies and those in charge of social operations in general. Their most conspicuous manifestation lies in two other phenomena that are specific to the construction of the colonies, namely a keen sense of experimentation (as noted at another level in their quest for a suitable formal expression), and an extraordinary range of floor plans and experiments in proportions and elevation design.

What is surprising is the receptiveness and promptitude with which the colonial architects managed to translate to such a large scale their highly diversified and heterogeneous ideas: projects so full of contradictions and unresolved conceptual problems such as those of the two contemporary Temples D and F at Selinus, which were large and costly monuments would be unthinkable in Mainland Greece. The architects were not short of funds in the colonies, and their optimistic outlook prompted them to explore their ideas on a full scale, whereas in Greece such schemes would have been discussed at length, and in the end shelved.

Closely related to this aspect of the liveliness of debate and the faculty of reaching swift decisions, is the sheer speed with which the colonists managed to put their architectural ideas into practice. Apart from the two colossal temples at Selinus and Acragas, which required more than one generation for their completion, most of the major monuments took a relatively short time to complete. This applies to all the temples in the Severe style. And if our hypothesis should be confirmed regarding the close ties between these monuments and the great tyrannies of the earlier fifth century, the time for realization and the completion of these colossal undertakings must have been briefer still. The technical structure of the *olympieion* in Acragas reveals clear signs of a premeditated rationalization of work procedures, a system that became a fixed postulate, especially in the case of the Classical temples of Acragas. Not only the technical and structural arrangement obeys this priority, but also the basic project itself. The most manifest example of this rationalizing spirit combined with the spectacular speed of execution, are the extraordinary fortifications built by Dionysius at Syracuse, an event whose details have been handed down from the early sources and confirmed by archaeological research.

The characteristics summarized here, to which one might add a great many less immediately conspicuous features of equal importance, belong to a cultural framework that is in part due to much more broader evolutive phenomena, which are valid for Mainland Greece as well. There can be no doubt, however, that certain of the most outstanding phenomena are deeply rooted in the specific conditions of the colonial world, and went toward defining that world. Consequently, it is not surprising to find them cropping up again – at least partially – here and there in today's colonial spheres. This seems particularly pertinent to the construction of North America, where the idea of an independent and self-reliant *apoikia* found fertile ground. The saying about the West being a kind of "America" for the Mainland Greeks is not as farfetched as it may at first seem.

Bibliography
General works: R. KOLDEWEY, O. PUCHSTEIN, 1899; J.J. COULTON, 1977; G. GRUBEN, 1980; A.W. LAWRENCE, 1983; R. MARTIN, 1961; A. GIULIANO, 1986-87, pp. 55 ff., pp. 132 ff., pp. 264 ff., pp. 554 ff., pp. 630 ff.; G. GULLINI, *Urbanistica...*, in *Megale Hellas*, 1983, pp. 205 ff.; G. GULLINI, *L'architettura*, in *Sikanie*, 1985, pp. 415 ff.; *Il tempio greco...*, CronAStorArt 16, 1985; D. MERTENS, *Per l'urbanistica...*, in *Megale Hellas..., Atti 21 ConcMGrecia*, 1981 (1982), pp. 97 ff.; E. GRECO, 1980 (with bibliography); F. PENSANDO, 1981; E. DE MIRO, Misc. Manni 2 (1980), pp. 707 ff.; W. HOEPFNER, E.L. SCHWANDNER, 1993; M. BIEBER, 1961; J.J. COULTON, 1976; F.E. WINTER, 1970; A.W. LAWRENCE, 1979; Y. GARLAN, 1974; J.P. ADAM, 1982.
On the origins: J.N. COLDSTREAM, 1977, pp. 317 ff.; H. DRERUP, 1969; W. MARTINI, *JdI* 101, 1986, pp. 23 ff.; A. MALLWITZ, *AA*, 1981, pp. 599 ff.; S. STUCCHI, *...tempio A di Prinias...*, in *Antichità Cretesi*, II, 1978, pp. 86 ff.; R.N. COOK, in *BSA*, 65, 1970, pp. 50 ff.; G. GULLINI, *Origini...*, in *ASAtene*, LIX, 1983, pp. 97-126; J.P. Descoeudres et al., *Greek Colonists...*, 1990; D. MERTENS, *Die Entstehung...*, in *Diskussionen zur archäologischen Bauforschung*, 6 (1995).
On the Archaic period: G. VALLET, F. VILLARD, P. AUBERSON, 1976; E. GABRICI, in *MonAnt*, XXXV, 1935, pp. 138 ff.; A. DE FRANCISCIS, 1979; P. ZANCANI MONTUORO, U. ZANOTTI-BIANCO, 1951-54; D. MERTENS, 1993; N. BONACASA et al., *Himera* I (1970); II (1976); R. MARTIN, in *ACSISMGr.*, X (1979), pp. 311-341; D. ADAMESTEANU-D. MERTENS, F. D'ANDRIA, *Metaponto I, NSc*, 1975 suppl. (1980); D. MERTENS, in *Neue Forschungen in griechischen Heiligtümern*, 1976, pp. 167 ff.; F. KRAUSS, 1959; R. OSTBY, *ActaAArtHist*, 6, 187, pp. 1 ff.; G.V. GENTILI, *Palladio*, 17, 1967, pp. 61 ff.; L. BERNABO BREA, 1986; D. MERTENS, *RM*, 86, 1979, pp. 103 ff.; N.A. WINTER (1993), pp. 273 ff.; I. ROMEI, *Xenia* 77, 1989, pp. 5 ff.; D. MERTENS, in *Scritti in onore di D. Adamesteanu*, 1980, pp. 37 ff.; D. MERTENS-A. DE SIENA, *BdA* NS. 16, 1983, pp. 1 ff.; S.K. THALMAN, 1980; B.A. BARLETTA, 1983; B.A. BARLETTA, in *AJA*, XCIV, 1990, pp. 45 ff.; D. THEODORESCU, 1974.
On the Classical period: D. MERTENS, 1984; G. GULLINI, 1980; D. MERTENS, *L'architettura*, in *Lo Stile Severo in Sicilia* (1990), pp. 75 ff.; H. LAUTER, *RM*, '83, 1976, pp. 233 ff.; L. POLACCO,-C. ANTI, *Il teatro antico di Siracusa* (1981).
On the post-Classical period: H. LAUTER, 1986; G. VALLET, F. VILLARD, 1966; W. VON SYDOW, *RM*, '91, 1984, pp. 239 ff.; *Odeon e altri "monumenti" archeologici* (1971); H.I. ISLER, *Quaderni ticinesi*, 10, 1981, pp. 131 ff.; H. LAUTER, *Die hellenistischen Theater...*, in *Hellenismus in Mittelitalien*, Kolloquium Göttingen 1976, pp. 413 ff.; K. MITENS, 1988; F. KRISCHEN, *Die Stadtmauern von Pompeji...*, in *Hellenistische Kunst in Pompeji* VII, 1941; K. DALCHER, 1994.

Henri Tréziny

Greek Military Architecture in the West

The Archaic urban defense systems
It is widely accepted nowadays that urban fortifications were built during the Archaic period of the Greek cities in the West, and, in particular, these were to be found in Campania (Elea, Cumae), Calabria (Locri, Caulonia), Lucania (Metapontum, Siris), and Sicily (Naxos, Leontini, Megara Hyblaea, Camarina, Monte Casale, Selinus, Himera).
Most of these fortifications date back to the sixth century and are easily linked (especially in Sicily) to the military activity of the contemporary tyrants. Others, however, have been ascribed earlier dates, such as the mid-sixth century (Camarina), or even the seventh century (Megara Hyblaea, Leontini, Monte Casale).
In establishing for the first time ever in the Greek world vast, homogeneous and well-planned urban settlements that rubbed shoulders with the sometimes hostile natives, the Greek cities of the West were probably also the first to build defensive walls. However, the remains of these defensive layouts, which were part and parcel of the founding of the city, reveal the superimposition of several other walls often at the expense of the earliest ones.
Although archeological data is scarce, there were almost certainly fortifications already in the seventh century on the military sites founded by Syracuse inland at Acrae in 664 and, especially Casmenae (Monte Casale) in 644 B.C. We know little about the great Greek cities along the coast, but we do know that there were tyrants in power already in the seventh century, and that there were wars between rival cities. For example, according to Polyaenus, Panaetius became the tyrant of Leontini toward the end of the seventh century, during a war between this city and Megara Hyblaea. It has been proposed to date back to the seventh century one of the phases of the fortifications of Leontini, but this is unlikely, in view of the numerous quarry marks which cannot be as old as this. The Archaic-period walls around Megara Hyblaea, including curving towers and a ditch in front which was cleared by F. S. Cavallari and P. Orsi at the end of the last century, were dated by the archeologists to the end of the sixth century. A recent examination of a ditch that was filled in the first half of the sixth century in the southern part of the city has provided indirect proof of the existence of an even older wall, from its few surviving blocks.
Sometimes the Archaic walls in the West were reinforced by towers (curved ones at Megara Hyblaea following the Bronze Age tradition, quadrangular ones on the Phoenician site at Motya) and by ditches. The aforementioned ditch at Megara Hyblaea must have been created by quarrying stone there for the walls of the city.

The upheavals of the fourth century
The war against Athens (413–412) made the Syracusans realize that the defense of the city could not be limited to the protection of the residential sectors (the island of Ortygia and the Achradina quarter), but that it had to be extended to control the Epipolae plateau, which dominates the city, and the

Fortifications of the Euryalus on the outskirts of Syracuse

overleaf
General view of the Euryalus at Syracuse from the south

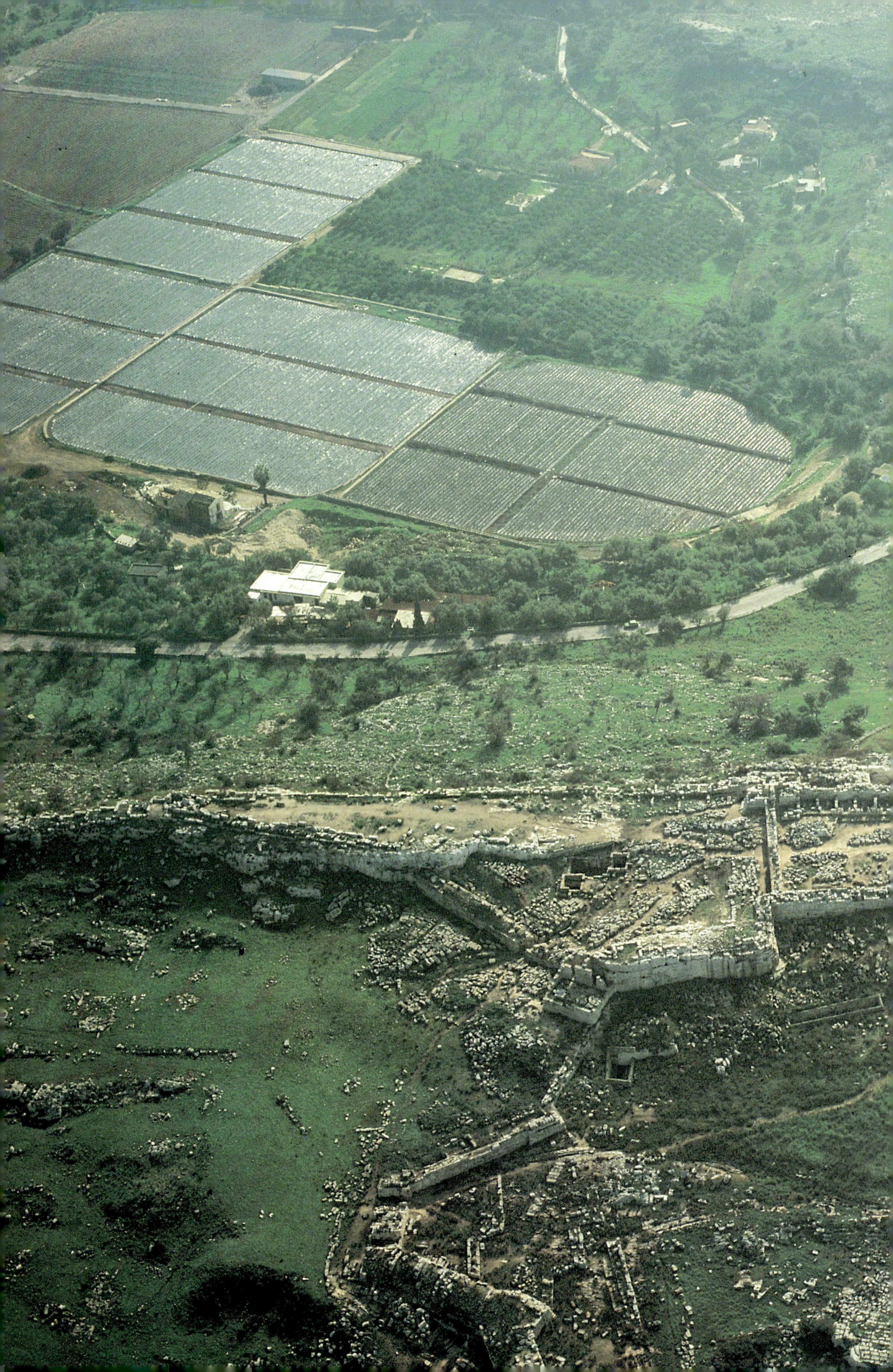

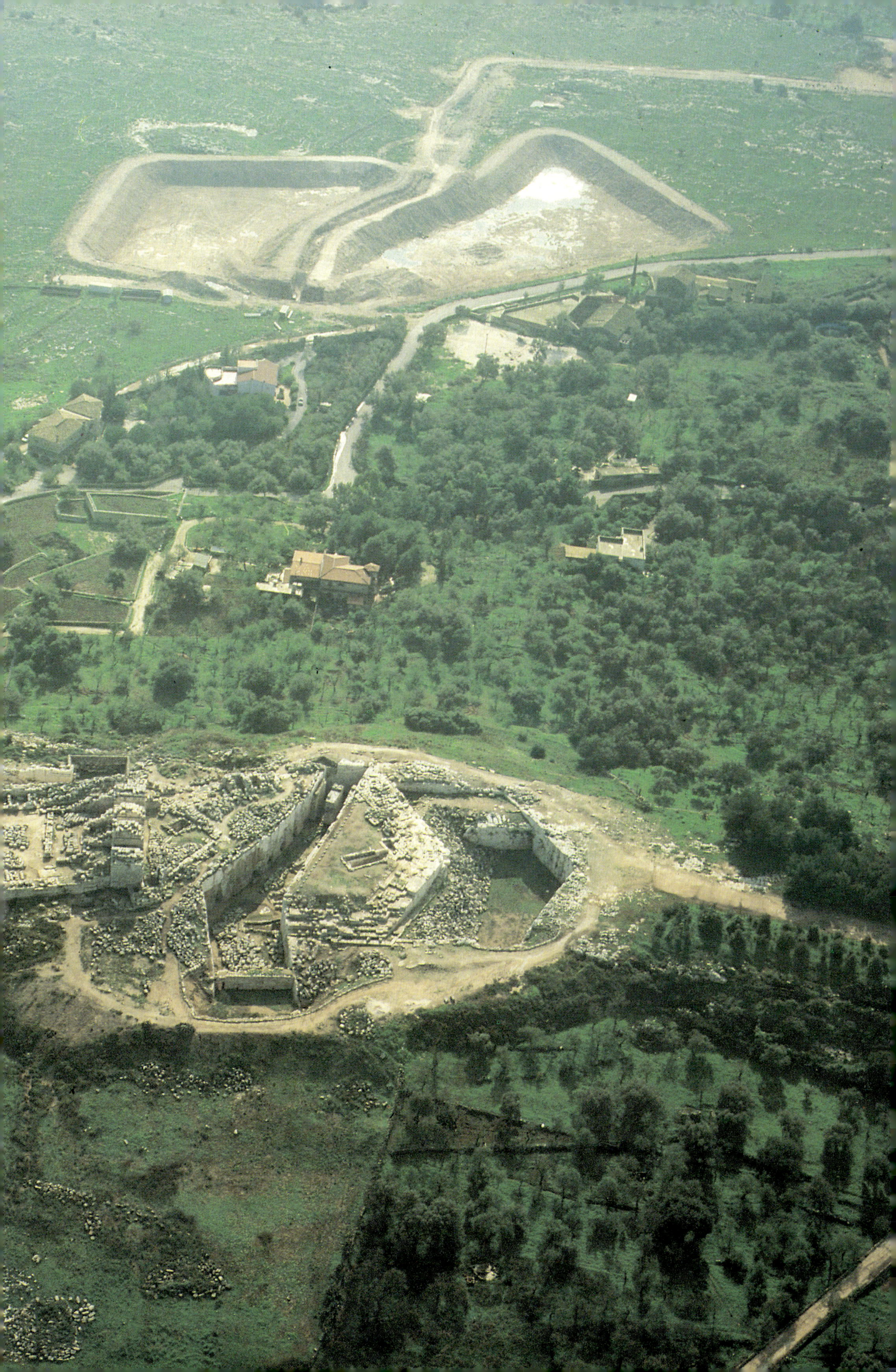

Greek Military Architecture in the West

The Euryalus
plan of the defensive system
end 5th - end 3rd cent. B.C.

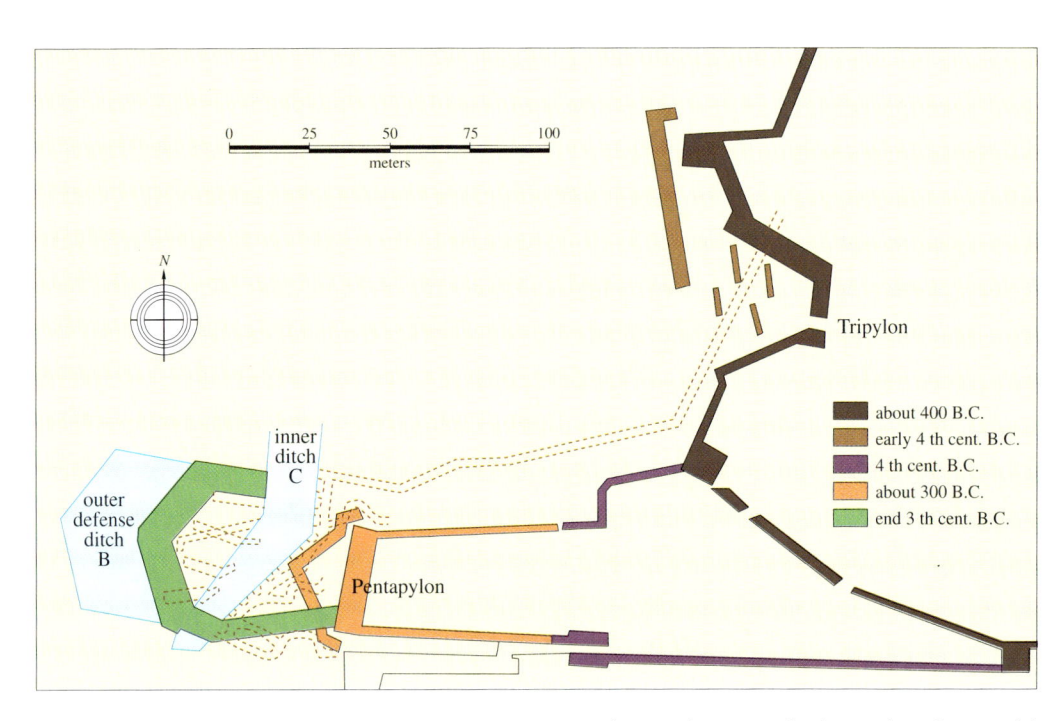

- about 400 B.C.
- early 4 th cent. B.C.
- 4 th cent. B.C.
- about 300 B.C.
- end 3 th cent. B.C.

Euryalus hill, which controls its access. Moreover, in 409 the Carthaginians had introduced powerful war machines and assault towers in their war against Selinus revealing just how vulnerable were the fortifications that nearly all dated back to the Archaic period.

In 402, Dionysius, the new tyrant of Syracuse, reinforced the defenses of Ortygia, which became his citadel, and built a large wall that surrounded the entire Epipolae plateau, an area at least eight times the size of the old city. Diodorus Siculus recounts that the new stone bulwarks were basically built against the rocky face and it appears they were reinforced by towers only at strategic points along it, such as near the main gates or posterns leading to the plateau. To the far west, the Euryalus, as the key to the defensive system, must have been protected by a small fort, about which little is known. From the middle to the end of the fourth century, during the reign of another tyrant, Agathocles, the main elements of the Euryalus defensive system were built. These included five imposing towers for the artillery batteries, the advance bastions, and the large ditches cut out of the rock which were to keep the enemy's war machines at a distance. The Euryalus was characterized by a complex network of galleries which connected the inside of the castle to the ditches. One of these passages, about two hundred meters long, led from the main ditch to the Tripylon, the great three-gated entrance for heavy traffic. The galleries were the means to quickly clearing away the material thrown in the ditches by the enemy as well as secretly moving troops from one spot to another along the defensive system. The basic part of this structure certainly dates back to the third century and was probably incomplete at the time of the Roman siege in 211. The first underground galleries may have been introduced in the fourth century in the Punic defensive system at Lilybaeum (Marsala), which would confirm the role played by the Carthaginians in the evolution of Siceliot defense techniques.

The destruction of the city of Selinus in 409 led to abandoning the old Archaic-period walls. The first walls of the citadel were built shortly afterward, perhaps during the tyranny of Dionysius. Here too, however, Agathocles is considered as responsible for the reinforcing of the fortress's defenses, by raising the first defense walls, introducing a huge semicircular battery, and vast ditches that could be reached from underground passages that were built rather than excavated, with a procedure similar to the one at the Euryalus. This was also abandoned at the time of the First Punic War, and the fortifications of Selinus never became as complex as those of Syracuse.

The important role played by the West in the evolution of defensive techniques has recently been much emphasized. We know that assault towers were used for the first time in the West by the Carthaginians during the conquest of Sicily at the end of the fifth century, but Dionysius of Syracuse was the first to utilize catapults while besieging Motya at the beginning of the fourth century.

The technique of building hollow walls in which the two facings of quarried stone are linked at regular intervals by smaller cross walls was generally attributed, after Scranton, to the engineers of the Alexandrian army. But L. Karlsson has noted that this technique had already appeared in Sicily at

Archaic wall
made of cyclopean masonry

Rampart built of unbaked bricks
over a cyclopean masonry socle
Gela
4th-3rd cent. B.C.

the end of the fifth century, at Selinus in fact, and preferred to attribute it to the engineers serving Dionysius of Syracuse. The new techniques developed by the tyrant's military engineers to resist the Carthaginian war machines later spread throughout Syracusan dominated Sicily and largely to the greater part of the Greek world.

Materials and bonds
Polygonal bonds, typical of the Ionian and island sites, can also be found in some sites in Sicily and Magna Graecia, depending on the origins of the settlers (Phocaeans at Elea), and in particular on the kind of materials utilized (lava from Naxos and the Aeolian Islands). A rectangular bond was the one most commonly chosen as from the sixth century. Examples can be found at Megara Hyblaea, Leontini, Locri, and Cumae, and quite certainly at Massalia as well. When good local stone could not be found, then the defenses were built with unbaked bricks, generally on a dry stone base or one made of river stones mixed with clay (Caulonia or Siris in the Archaic period), or on a wall made of cyclopean blocks of stone (Gela in the fourth century). Baked bricks were utilized for the same purposes in the Hellenistic age though more rarely (Elea, Rhegium).

The materials used on a site may change over the ages. The first wall surrounding Megara Hyblaea (seventh century) was characterized by a massive use of the poor local limestone quarried from the ditch in front, while the sixth-century wall was constructed with stone from the Melilli quarries, lying a few kilometers outside the city. White limestone from the nearby Saint-Victor quarries was used on the sites at Massalia until the fourth century, but in the second century there was a change to pink limestone shipped from the quarries at Cap Couronne, twenty kilometers away from the city but then part of its territory. The variety of materials used, just as at Elea or Pompeii, certainly depended on the organization of the building sites and very often on the extent of the territory and therefore on the relations with the neighboring natives.

The Greeks and the indigenous populations
Toward the end of the fourth century in Lucania there was a spread of fortification systems using large blocks of stone in the Greek style and with quarry marks written in the Greek alphabet. These were first considered to be Greek fortresses, traces of the passage of *condottieri* through Lucania. However, they were, in fact, built by the natives on the basis of the Greek originals, and perhaps were also erected by architects coming from the cities on the coast. In Provence too, the lovely walls of Saint-

Fortification with curving curtains of the type described by Philon of Byzantium at Pajares-Osuna, in Andalusia

Cyclopean masonry rampart built in the Greek style on the indigenous site Saint-Blaise, Provence 2nd cent. B.C.

Blaise were believed to be a Greek fortress, defending the territory of Massalia (modern Marseilles), but today they have been identified as an indigenous *oppidum* beyond the gates of the Greek city, perhaps the work of teams of craftsmen coming from Massalia. The spread of Greek technologies, examples of which can be found in all the regions surrounding the colonies, could also be due to native craftsmen becoming expert on the building sites of the Greek colonies along the coast, nor must we forget the role of mercenaries (from Campania, Gaul, and Iberia) who were on the payroll of the Greek and Punic armies as from the fifth century.

Greek fortifications and Rome
It is difficult to discuss Greek fortifications in the West without bringing up the subject of Roman ones as well. The Romans were in Naples from the end of the fourth century, at Tarentum (Greek Taras) from 271, and in Sicily from 241. Therefore, the Roman military engineers' adaptation of Greek construction technologies was a non-stop process that started long before Rome penetrated the Greek East. The Romans are also generally considered as being responsible for the spread of techniques already utilized in Greece, such as the construction of alternate layers of stone and brick, which G. Lugli defined as the "Roman style." It was, however, certainly much later on in the first century B.C. when Roman military engineers adopted designs straight out of Hellenist manuals. Such was the case of a text by Philon of Byzantium which recommended semicircular walls with the concave side toward the exterior, but no practical application of this project was known. The walls round Telesia, in Campania, built without doubt at the time of Sulla, provide a perfect example, and recent aerial photographic research has revealed that the site of Pajares-Osuna, in Andalusia, is probably of the same form. Another kind of structure (with the name of meander), only known through Philon's book, has perhaps found a concrete example in a wall of the first century recently discovered at Arles in Provence.
In spite of the distance that separated it from the Near East, birthplace of the oldest kinds of fortifications, and from the Hellenic kingdoms that were to develop defense systems of unrivaled complexity, Magna Graecia played a fundamental part in the history of fortifications. The colonial world at the dawn of the *polis* offered without doubt the oldest examples of walled cities. The confrontation with the western Phoenicians in Sicily contributed, as from the end of the fifth century, to considerably improving the techniques of besieging and defending from siege; nearer to Rome, it contributed to creating that same Roman defensive architecture that was to be its downfall.

Marcella Barra Bagnasco Housing and Workshop Construction in the City

Megara Hyblaea
reconstruction of Archaic houses

Pithekoussai
reconstruction of the plan
of Archaic houses
(from Ridgway 1984)

Foreword

The construction methods and styles used for building private homes, trade outlets, and workshops in the Greek colonies of the West are affected by several fundamental aspects: first, the way a given building relates to its urban context; second, the layout and role provided by the new spaces; third, the actual materials and building technology employed; and last, the evolution of architecture over the period spanning from the second half of the eighth century to the third century B.C.

For reasons of space, the discussion here will focus on a few select buildings in Sicily and Magna Graecia. The influence of Greek models on the building styles and techniques of the indigenous populations will not be analyzed, as this requires a separate discussion.

With the first wave of colonists to Italic soil during the Archaic period, several principal settlement features began to establish themselves: the detachment of the urban nucleus from the necropolis; a methodical street layout; the creation of designated public, civic, and religious areas. This is the stage at which the inclusion of specific private spaces was planned. Such spaces were comprised of strictly residential building stock, together with the relative infrastructure for everyday functions. These domestic units were grafted onto the urban fabric, whose street grid imposed conditions on the perimeter of the housing lots and *insulae*, even where a given area had not yet been fully developed.

Housing

The Archaic period (8th–6th cent. B.C.)
Surviving evidence of this particular period of Greek colonial development in Magna Graecia is scarce, whereas Sicily offers a fair range of extant fabric, particularly along the east coast.

On the whole, in comparison with the structures for general public use (either religious or civic), there are few examples of private construction from the Archaic period. This scarcity of archaeological evidence is due in part to the limited investigation of currently built-up areas, where excavations have rarely reached the deeper, Archaic levels, and in part to the fact that most common houses were built from perishable materials – wood, wattle and daub, and thatched roofs – which have not survived.

At Megara Hyblaea in Sicily, extensive studies made by the French enabled the identification of houses from the eighth century B.C., and others from the successive century in even greater number. Though scattered across the settlement area, the houses in question are nonetheless slotted into the street grid on which the subsequent township was based. Even the scant remains of houses excavated in Syracuse, contemporary to those of Megara Hyblaea, are already aligned with the street grid; similar alignment is also evident from the houses that have come to light at Sybaris in Magna Graecia. In both Megara and Syracuse the houses are very simple, single-cell, rectangular constructions measuring 12–16 square meters, probably roofed in thatch, in compliance with the prevailing custom of the time.

Similarly aligned on a main street of the Archaic period are two houses in Naxos, measuring 70 and 40 square meters respectively, which show a shift toward larger and more articulated dwellings from the mid-seventh to the sixth century B.C.

A different situation, however, had grown up in Magna Graecia, where the few surviving houses are free-standing buildings, whose precise relation with the urban layout has yet to be established. The

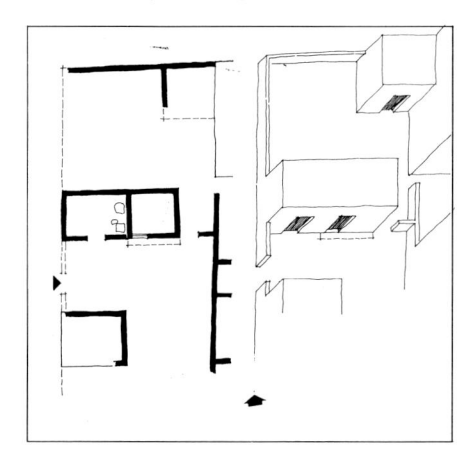

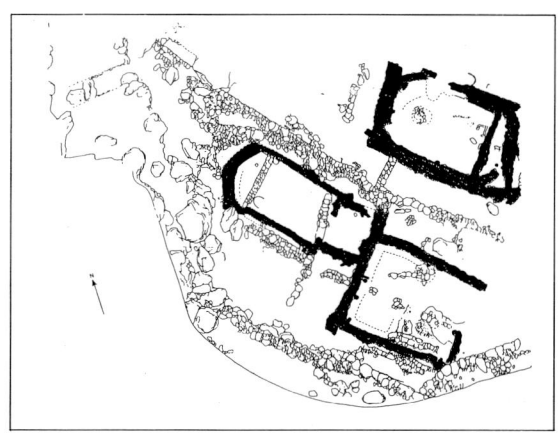

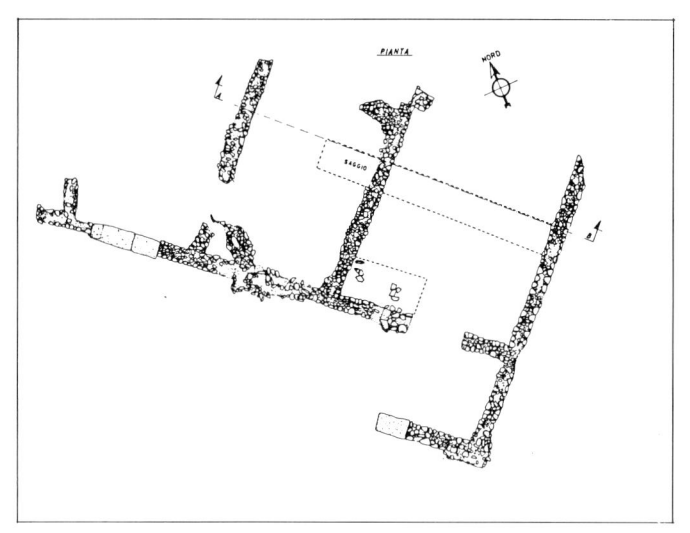

Policoro
survey of an Archaic house
Cospito-Caserta district
(from Tagliente 1986)

Elea
hypothetical reconstruction
of the Archaic house
of the acropolis
(drawing Barra Bagnasco)

finest examples of eighth-century housing (with the exception of certain isolated structures discovered in other *poleis*) are found in the Euboean colony of Pithekoussai on the island of Ischia. Here excavations have disclosed a craftsmen's quarter in which certain dwellings are combined with the workshops themselves). Of special interest is Building III, known as the "Ironsmith's Workshop." The building consists of a closed unit with a courtyard in front, whose floor was found to be littered with fragments of iron waste and other traces of metalworking activities. Room I alongside was evidently for dwelling purposes; it is divided into two parts: a rectangular room in front and a smaller interior unit with an apsidal wall, a feature common in Euboea, the homeland of the colonists of Pithekoussai.

An example of a more complex dwelling layout from the end of the seventh century B.C. has been found at Policoro, the site of the Greek colony Herakleia (Heraclea). Here, where archaeological remains relative to Siris on the Ionian coast have been found, stood a large abode of 115 square meters composed of three rooms facing south onto a forecourt that may have been arcaded.

This floor plan, which had already appeared in the West by the Archaic period, is generally defined as or likened to the *pastas* (vestibule) type, in which the *pastas* is a rectangular arcade that linking up the rooms at the north with the southern courtyard. Actually, the forecourt of the Policoro House – and likewise of most of those based on this scheme – represents a rather more limited arrangement, and forms part of the boundary wall of the house itself, erected to screen off the house from the outside.

Another, more complex, type of dwelling can be observed in the *megaron*, which is based on a rectangular scheme with a small front porch; the examples unearthed at Velia (Elea) date to 540–530 B.C. This type started on a fairly small plan of 22 square meters, but was gradually expanded until it covered an area of 60 square meters, to which the porch or forecourt was subsequently attached. One curious feature of the examples in question is that the owner – like that of the apsidal construction in Pithekoussai – was a potter. This seems to be evidence of the basic importance accorded to craftsmen in setting up the new colony, a class of worker that contributed significantly to the colony's survival.

The Classical period (5th–early 4th cent. B.C.)
Once again, the excavations in Sicily have yielded the most significant examples of dwellings for this period. A large quantity of finds have come to light at Himera on the south coast. Here, a general reworking of the town's layout in 476 B.C. entailed a systematic subdivision of the *insulae*, and the allocation of standard housing plots measuring 16 meters square. Despite this regular lot size, there does not seem to be any standard type of house of the kind that has turned up in similar contexts, such as at Olynthus in the Greek homeland. Practical needs and the specific requirements of the individual families may have dictated this random layout of the dwelling spaces. In some lots, however, there is widespread use of the covered three-room unit aligned with the street and looking inward to a large space, which was more likely a living room than an unroofed court.

Though fewer in number, the examples at Acragas (modern Agrigento) and Gela offer insights into the features of Classical housing, once again carefully slotted into a network of streets and *insulae*. The houses at Acragas, in the area of Porta V, between the sanctuary to the chthonic deities and the temple of Zeus, boast a floor space of 200 square meters, with a spacious L-shaped court. The houses at

Gela
survey of houses
5th cent. B.C.
(from De Miro 1979)

Megara Hyblaea
plan of House 49,19
with a peristyle
Hellenistic period

Morgantina
the Magistrate's House
Hellenistic period

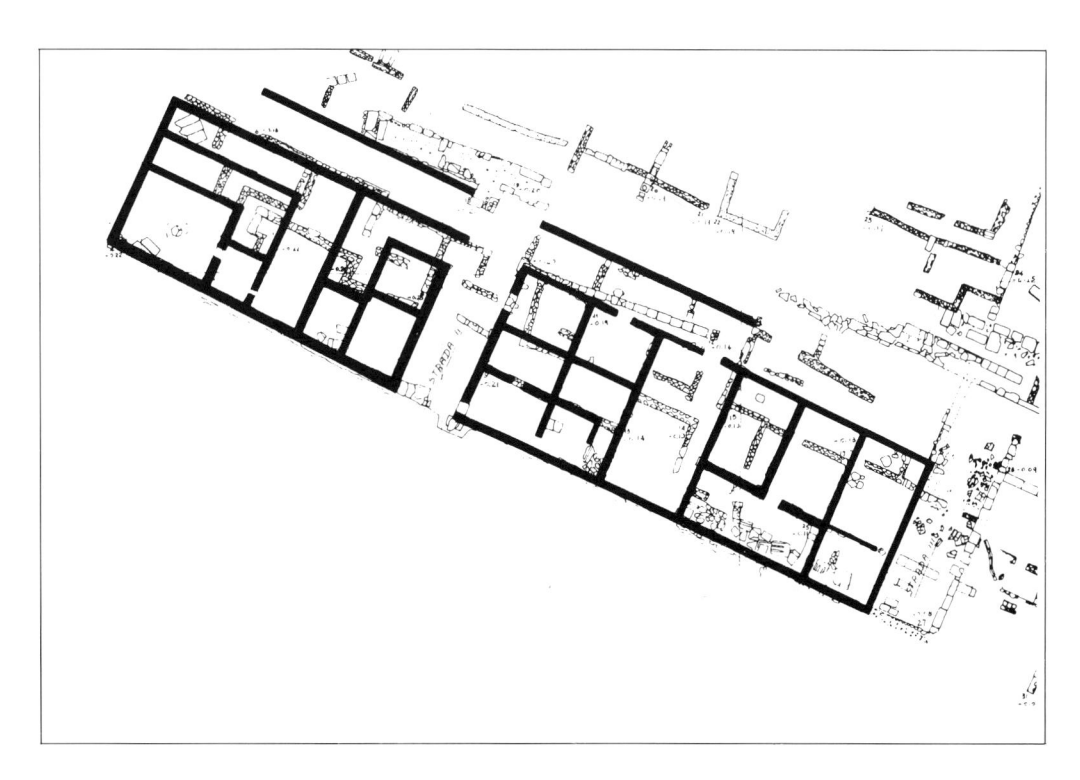

Gela are smaller, covering around 100 square meters, and are set with elongated rectangular spaces that have been identified as courtyards or enclosures for livestock.

The Hellenistic period (mid-4th cent. to 3rd cent. B.C.)
Compared to the Classical age, one of the typical features of this period is the greater care taken over private building. The home has become much larger, with more spacious rooms and the addition of two courtyards, demarcating the two specific zones of the house, one for receiving visitors, and one for private, family use.
Several houses in this group stand out from the rest, however, and again the finest examples are found in Sicily. The floor plan is more complex, and a peristyle has been added. A superb example – though not exactly representative of the living style of the colonists in question – is the "peristylar" house (House 49, 19) at Megara Hyblaea, with its pillared inner court. The building's perimeter is irregular, its longer sides measuring 25 meters and 41 meters respectively, and the house boasts around twenty rooms arranged around two courtyards, the first of which is arcaded. Three rooms have an entrance separate from the peristyle, which emphasizes the *andron* or banqueting room, which has a floor in crushed tiles and mortar.
Other examples of large Late Hellenistic dwellings have turned up at the site of the early Siculi set-

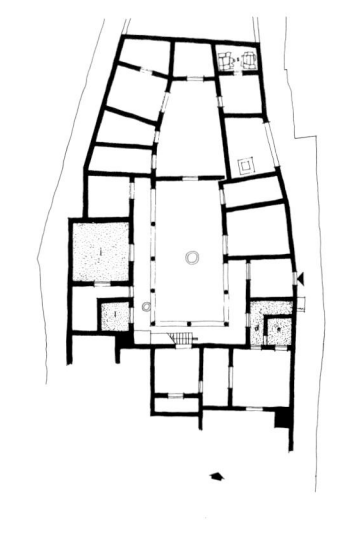

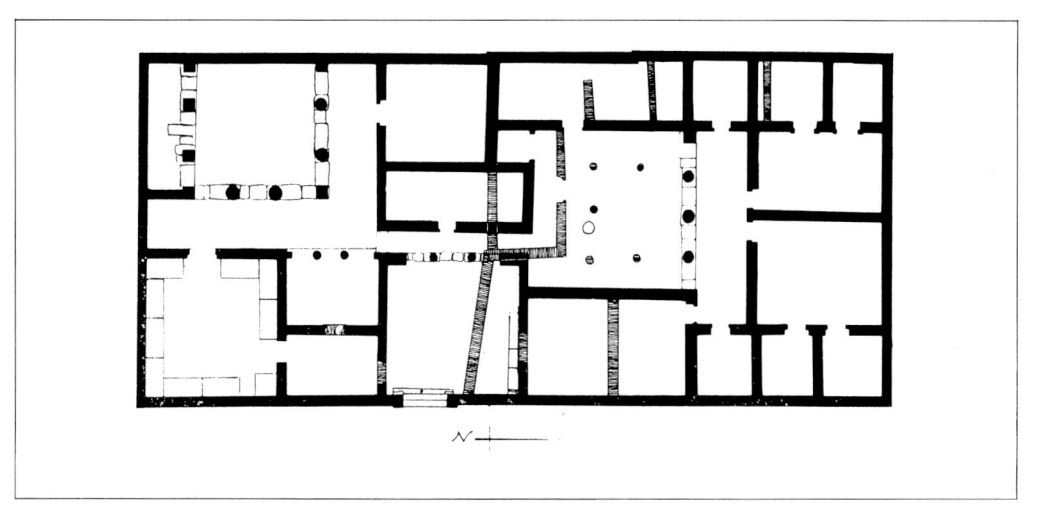

Monte Iato
house with a peristyle

tlement of Morgantina, later colonized by the Greeks (at Serra Orlando in the province of Enna): in particular, houses excavated in the various *insulae* west of the *agora*, such as the so-called House of the Arched Cistern, the Palmento House, and the Magistrate's House, which offer insights into the complex room arrangement that had developed by the advent of the Hellenistic period: spacious courtyards (often arcaded); halls for receiving visitors; numerous separate rooms in a variety of shapes, with elaborate wall and floor detailing. The Magistrate's House in particular is clearly divided into two parts: the *pastas*, or vestibule, with neighboring utility rooms, and the other for receiving visitors, with a sweeping peristyle and *andron*.

Two highly elaborate houses have recently been fully excavated, the first at Monte Iato, Sicily, about thirty kilometers south of Palermo, 800 meters above sea level; the other is in Magna Graecia, at Locri (the Greek colony Lokroi Epizephyrioi). The two dwellings exemplify two distinct types of layout in use in the second half of the fourth century through the third century B.C. The Monte Iato house, which has been excavated by a team of scholars from Zurich University, is a large construction of around 800 square meters with a considerable number of units serving a variety of functions, laid out on two stories around a peristylar court. The building's excellent state of conservation (favored by the extensive use of stone) has enabled excavators to identify all the architectural features, including the decorative detailing, including mosaic flooring and colored plasterwork ornamenting several rooms,

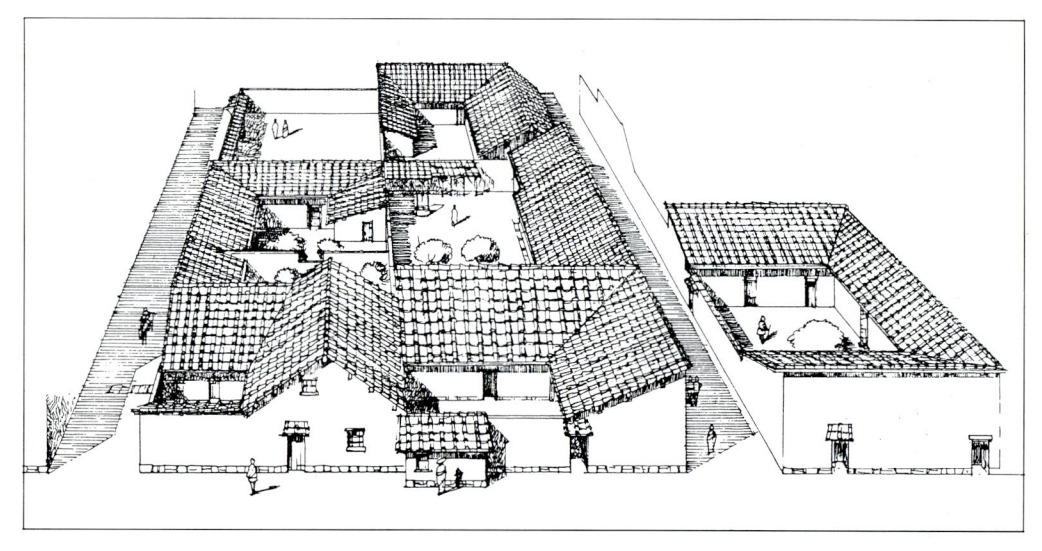

Locri, Centocamere district
reconstruction of houses
in blocks I2 and I3
(from Barra Bagnasco
drawing Boggio)

356

Locri
graphic reconstruction of the "Lions House" (from Barra Bagnasco drawing Boggio)

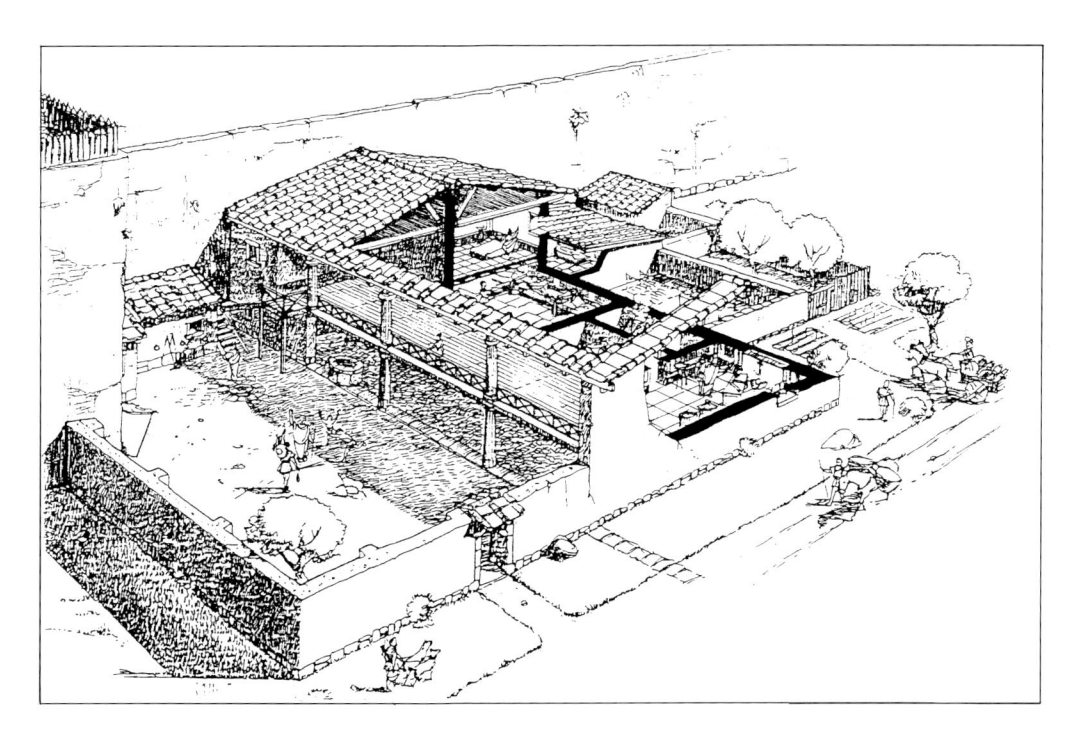

special reception rooms, including an *exedra* and two side *andrones*, together with a capacious bathroom with a lively color scheme and a rectangular tub filled from an elaborate spout in the form of a lion-head *protome*.

For the time being, the house unearthed at Locri is quite unique: it is called the "Lions House" for the reuse of limestone simas with lion-head water spouts. With a floor space of over 400 square meters, and probably a second story also, the Lions House stands out notably from the smaller or more modest units that have come to light in the street grid elsewhere on the site, in the Centocamere neighborhood. One of the principal explanations for the house's size is its particular location just outside the defensive wall, and hence free of physical building restrictions; however, upon closer examination, it appears that the complex was a gathering place for worship: it is probably an *adonion*. The Lions House in fact stands on the site of a former temple dedicated to Aphrodite, as testified by the remains of small votive deposits (*bothroi*) discovered in a chamber. Which reproposes the *pastas* scheme (the only extant example in Locri) common at Olynthus in the Greek homeland. The rooms at the north end of the building and the south court are linked by a long narrow arcade that gives onto the courtyard with two grooved plastered columns. The arcade is graced with colorful decorative work which has been reconstructed from the numerous extant fragments. It consisted of alternating bands of plasterwork in light blue, red, and speckled gray (to imitate marble). The functions so far identified for certain rooms include an *andron* (banqueting room) with a pavement laid with tiles and an unpaved surround of around one meter in width, where seven *klinai* (banqueting beds) once stood; a bathroom, with part of the tub in terra-cotta; and a latrine, slightly detached from the building, which is something of an anomaly in the Greek world and testifies to the considerable level of advancement of this particular house compared to those in town. Housing types of a reasonable size with a standard floor plan have been found within the street grid in the *polis* of Caulonia. Here, recent explorations in post-Dionysian layers dating to the second half of the fourth century B.C. have successfully identified the criteria for determining the lot proportions relative to the *insula* or street block, namely, two sets of six lots measuring 17.5 by 23 meters in two halves of the *insula* bisected by an *ambitus*. Investigations have also revealed traces of a repetition of the three-room type, in this case not the customary north-end type, but oriented to the west, divided from the courtyard via an arcaded corridor, which echoes the former *pastas* type.

Much simpler, and complying with repeat modules, are the houses unearthed in the Syracusan colony of Camarina on the south coast of Sicily. Excavations on the Timoleon level of the site (second half of the fourth century B.C.) have disclosed a strict grid of housing lots of standard dimensions. The ten lots lie either side of a central *ambitus* and cover an area of 17 by 12 meters, each with three (or four) rooms at the north end, and a courtyard at the south. This arrangement suggests the existence of a homogeneous class of the populace, perhaps small landowners.

Caulonia
reconstruction of the house types
Hellenistic period

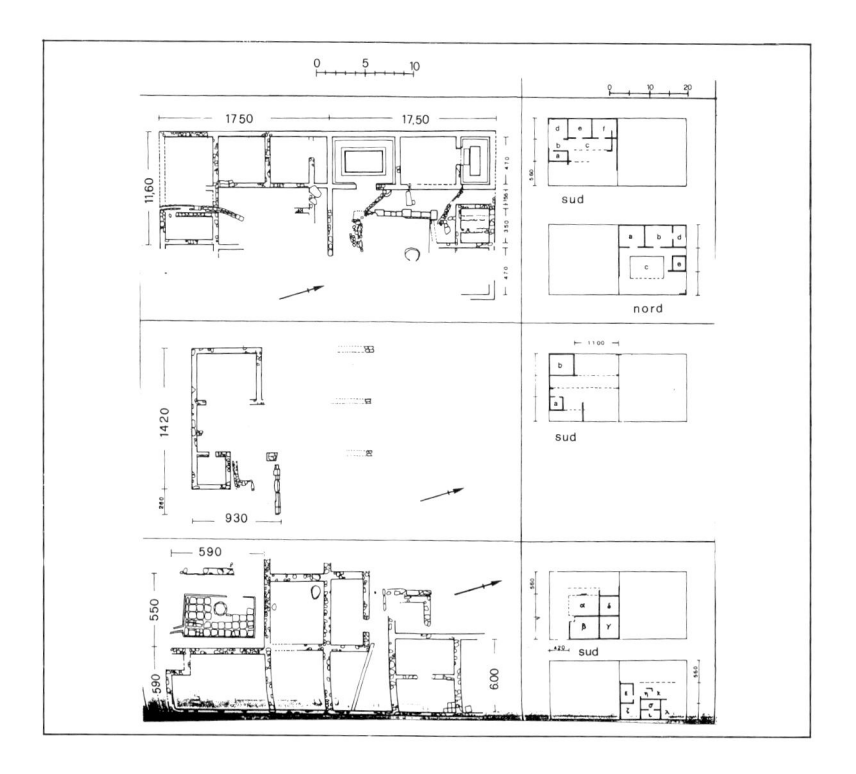

Shops and Craft Workshops

In order to obtain a clearer picture of everyday life in the Greek colony it is essential to know more about the various practices and activities pursued by the population. Although many manufacturing activities were actually practiced in the home – such as weaving (attested by the numerous loom-weights found exclusively in domestic settings) – in many cases there were fully-equipped laboratories and workshops. These are generally in the form of a small space accessed from the living area, with a separate entrance for clients. Numerous examples have come to light in the Greek *poleis*, starting with Athens and Olynthus. At Locri the shops conform to a cluster type (both inside and outside the city walls), with a large room on the street and two smaller rooms behind (probably storerooms).
As for the laboratories, the earliest examples have been found at the colonies of Pithekoussai and Elea. The most easily identifiable remnants are those pertaining to one of the oldest manufacturing activities of antiquity, namely the mass production of clay items that were used both for building and for votive or domestic consumption.
The most important material evidence is represented by the potters' kilns, often in reasonable state of conservation, which testify to the existence of entire neighborhoods (*kerameikos*) given over to the production of ceramic goods. The specifics of these neighborhoods are not always very clear, though they evidently included other infrastructure besides the kilns themselves: pits for purifying the clay ready for use, proper surfaces on which the craftsmen prepared their work, free areas for drying items and storing the finished products, and not least an abundant supply of water (usually drawn from a well).
Owing to the specifics of this particular kind of activity – which required ample working spaces, and produced unpleasant smoke and fumes – these neighborhoods required a certain degree of planning as regards their location and relationship with the rest of the urban fabric. Although the discovery of potter's kilns has largely been sporadic, making it impossible to tie them in precisely with the urban layout, the various examples that have come to light nonetheless indicate how the *kerameikos* might have been accommodated into the street grid. Small production plants are often linked to other specific functions of the city; many workshops, for instance, sprang up near shrines or places of worship, where there was a greater concentration of potential clients. A good example of this logic is found at Naxos, where two kiln workshops have come to light inside the sanctuary enclave, and likewise at the acropolis at Selinus (modern Selinunte). Generally speaking, the *kerameikos* quarter was in the heart of the *polis*, in order to cater for the constant demands for this type of product, and to facilitate the to-and-fro of materials.

Magna Graecia offers three important testimonies to three different ways in which the potters' quarter fitted in with the urban fabric, giving clues also perhaps as to the general importance accorded the artisan class as a whole.

In the ancient Greek colony of Metapontion (Metapontum), the pottery manufacturing quarter was active from the sixth to the fourth centuries B.C., and was set outside the city walls, though not far from the sanctuary enclave. In nearby Heraclea, the Hellenistic period saw the establishment of numerous small pottery workshops with kilns, where votive statuettes were the principal item of production; these workshops are dotted through the urban grid in the upper part of the city. The case of Locri is somewhat different. Here the potter's studio tended to be inserted within the perimeter of the *insulae*, inside the town walls but in a marginal position, near one of the main thoroughfares.

Most pottery kilns are round, though several examples of oval or square types have also come to light, always with the same basic design consisting of a combustion chamber below and a front channel for stoking and replenishing the fire; the dimensions also vary (diameter 1–3 meters), but the materials with which they are built are always tiles and bricks; often the kiln was located in a small room, in close contact (for ergonomic reasons) with the other spaces in which the clay items were worked. In Locri some kilns were built opposite each other, enabling the attendants to keep check on two production cycles at once.

Heraclea
Hellenistic kiln

Construction Techniques and Materials

The somewhat essential and straightforward construction techniques employed for house building evinces little or no evolution over time, nor distinctions from area to area. One of the determining factors of building was of course the availability of raw materials: where quarry stone was in good supply – as at Megara Hyblaea, Selinus, and Naxos – it was also employed for building homes. Elsewhere, and generally in the *poleis* of Magna Graecia, the lack of ready quarry stone led to rather less orderly building techniques, with foundations composed of an amalgam of river pebbles, recycled blocks of stone, kiln waste, broken tiles and brick. The walls were built up from this base compound in mudbrick and reinforced with wooden uprights. Over the seventh–sixth century B.C. the twin sloping roof was fully tiled, and fragments of tiles and coping are plentiful wherever excavations have been carried out.

Few of the houses from the Archaic and Classical periods bear signs of finery or elegance. The floors are never solid, and often the functions of rooms are not well defined. Notwithstanding this general lack of sophistication, traces of white plasterwork have turned up on both interior and exterior walls. During the Hellenistic period greater attention went into interior design and detail, and extensive evidence has survived in many different sites across Sicily, such as Morgantina and Monte Iato; Magna Graecia has yielded very few such cases (Caulonia and Locri). Interior details include delicate mold-

Locri, Centocamere district
Hellenistic kilns

Locri, Centocamere district
reconstruction of
the Hellenistic kilns in block I 2
(from Barra Bagnasco
drawing Boggio)

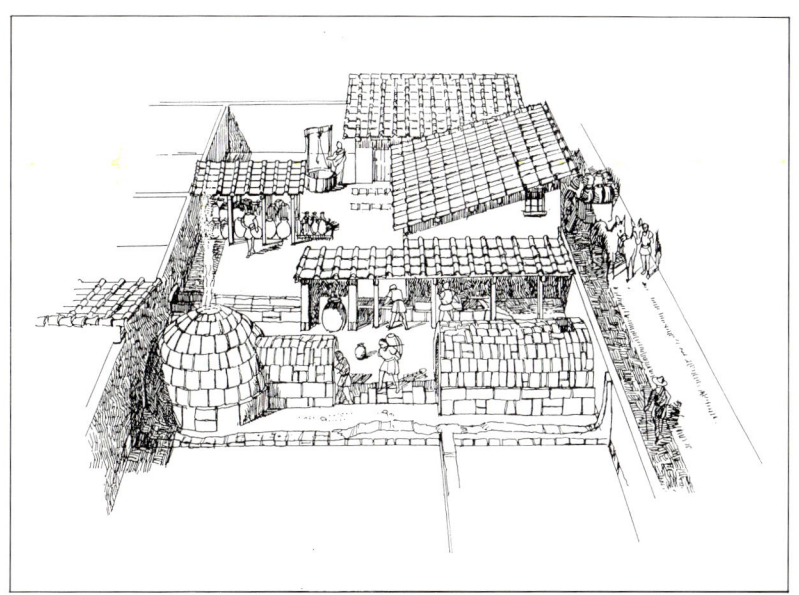

ings that decorated door and window surrounds or ran along the tops of walls; other decorative features included colored plasterwork in such key rooms as the *andron*, the typical symposium room in the Greek household. The houses at Morgantina exemplify the standard layout, by which the reception area (with or without a vestibule) was slightly set off from the living space, with an entrance of its own for reasons of privacy, and was usually the most elaborately decorated part of the house.

Conclusions

In their first two centuries on Italic soil, the Greek colonists devised a variety of different layouts for their homes, from the simple oblong house (Megara Hyblaea, Syracuse, Naxos), with the occasional apsidal variation (Pithekoussai), reaching more complex arrangements that went beyond the mere juxtaposition of different rooms, as testified by the splendid examples at the colony sites of Megara Hyblaea and Policoro.

In the ensuing period, the drift toward an ever more complex layout fostered greater variety in the floor plan. At this point, in fact, there is no longer a recurring house type from one *polis* to another, nor a regular way of laying out the rooms within the housing lot itself. While this may be due in part to an insufficient degree of information on our part, it is significant that, despite the extensive explorations carried out on the site at Himera (described above), it is still impossible to establish any standard floor plan in use throughout the various lots of the *polis*.

The most likely explanation for this apparently random design may be a disparity of income, or different types of activities practiced by the inhabitants of the colony.

A separate case is presented by the Hellenistic site of Caulonia, where the development of a new urban plan facilitated the creation of regularly shaped building lots, and the application of a standardized house layout within each one, focused on the *pastas*, or vestibule.

Despite these difficulties, several features have been successfully identified – features that were essential to the daily life of the family and therefore endured over time. First of all, a recurring feature is a fairly large outdoor area, which (even in the earliest constructions) could have been for livestock and crops, thereby fulfilling the role of *chora* within the housing lot. In the later, more complex layouts slotted into the street grid, this open space gradually evolved into a kind of "hub" around which the rooms were arranged, a system closed off from the street, conserving the privacy of family activities. This inward-looking scheme, with small doors and few or no windows onto the street, is a characteristic of the Greek house in antiquity, and was adopted throughout the West.

Another fairly frequent feature, also closely tied to the basic needs of daily life in the home, is the well (and, in the Siceliot colonies, water cisterns). These were in the courtyard, or the *pastas* (vestibule) in the larger homes. The design of the domestic water well is fairly standard throughout the Greek *poleis*; it measured 1–1.2 meters in diameter and was lined with purpose-made bricks, or with curved terracotta tiles fitted with footholds to facilitate maintenance.

For all the historical periods discussed here, it is not easy to reconstruct the furniture used by the average citizen, though the evidence suggests that homes were sparsely furnished with rudimentary, strictly functional items built largely in perishable materials that have not survived. One exception is the stone bench, which served as a seat during the day and a bed by night. To judge from vase paintings and *pinakes* (many of which have been found at Locri at the Mannella sanctuary), there were various types of chair, with or without backrest and arms, together with settles and chests, banqueting settees alongside which small tables may have been arranged to rest drinks upon.

Bibliography
M. BARRA BAGNASCO, in *Locri Epizefiri*, III..., 1989, pp. 5 ff.; idem, in *Magna Grecia*, IV, 1990; idem, in *Locri Epizefiri*, IV..., 1992, pp. 5 ff.; idem, in *SPABA*, XLV (1993), pp. 37 ff.; O. BELVEDERE, in *Himera*, II, 1976, pp. 577 ff.; C. BENCIVENGA, TRILLMICH, in *MEFRA* 95 (1983), pp. 417 ff.; F. D'ANDRIA, in *Metaponto*, I, NSc 1975 supplement, pp. 335 ff.; E. DE MIRO, in *Miscellanea in onore di E. Manni*, 1979, pp. 709 ff.; M.T. IANNELLI, S. RIZZI, in *RivStorCal*, n.s. VI (1985), pp. 281 ff.; H.P. ISLER, 1991; R. MARTIN, G. VALLET, in *Storia della Sicilia*, I, 1979, pp. 321 ff.; P. PELAGATTI, in *BArte*, 61, 1976, pp. 122 ff.; D. RIDGWAY, 1984; M. TAGLIENTE, in *Siris-Polieion*..., 1986, pp. 129 ff.; B. TSAKIRGIS, 1985; G. VALLET, F. VILLARD, P. AUBERSON, 1983.

Joseph C. Carter Agricultural Settlements

The chorai
The survival and success of the Greeks in the West was intimately bound up with their agricultural settlements, and their development was paralleled closely by that of the urban centers. A colony typically possessed a territory or *chora* immediately outside the urban center, a buffer area between Greek and indigenous populations, the *eschatia* – both protected by forts or *phrouria* along the routes linking their coastal plains with the interior. Here were produced the means of subsistence and later the surplus which brought prosperity. In most cases, however, only the city or *polis* is known in any detail. In Magna Graecia the fortunate exception is Metapontum, where both *polis* and *chora* (and the indigenous hinterland as well) have been the object of intensive archaeological investigation for more than a quarter-century. There has been limited investigation, too, of the *chorai* of Paestum (Poseidonia) and Croton.

In Sicily early discoveries of sanctuaries and necropolises outside Gela and other centers first revealed the existence of isolated farmhouses and the small agglomerations of a dispersed population in the territories of the colonies.

Now, intensive surveys at Himera, around Heraclea Minoa, Camarina and, most recently, Morgantina provide evidence for a pattern of life in the countryside that can now be said to have been habitual for the Greeks in the West.

The history of the agricultural settlements of the western colonies is the story of the transformation of indigenous territories into Greek ones. Although dispersed indigenous settlements (isolated farmhouses or small hamlets) are only rarely attested in the *chorai*, nowhere, almost certainly, did the

Plan of the *chora* of Metapontum
- farmhouses
- tombs
- lost settlements
- other
- research 1966-1971

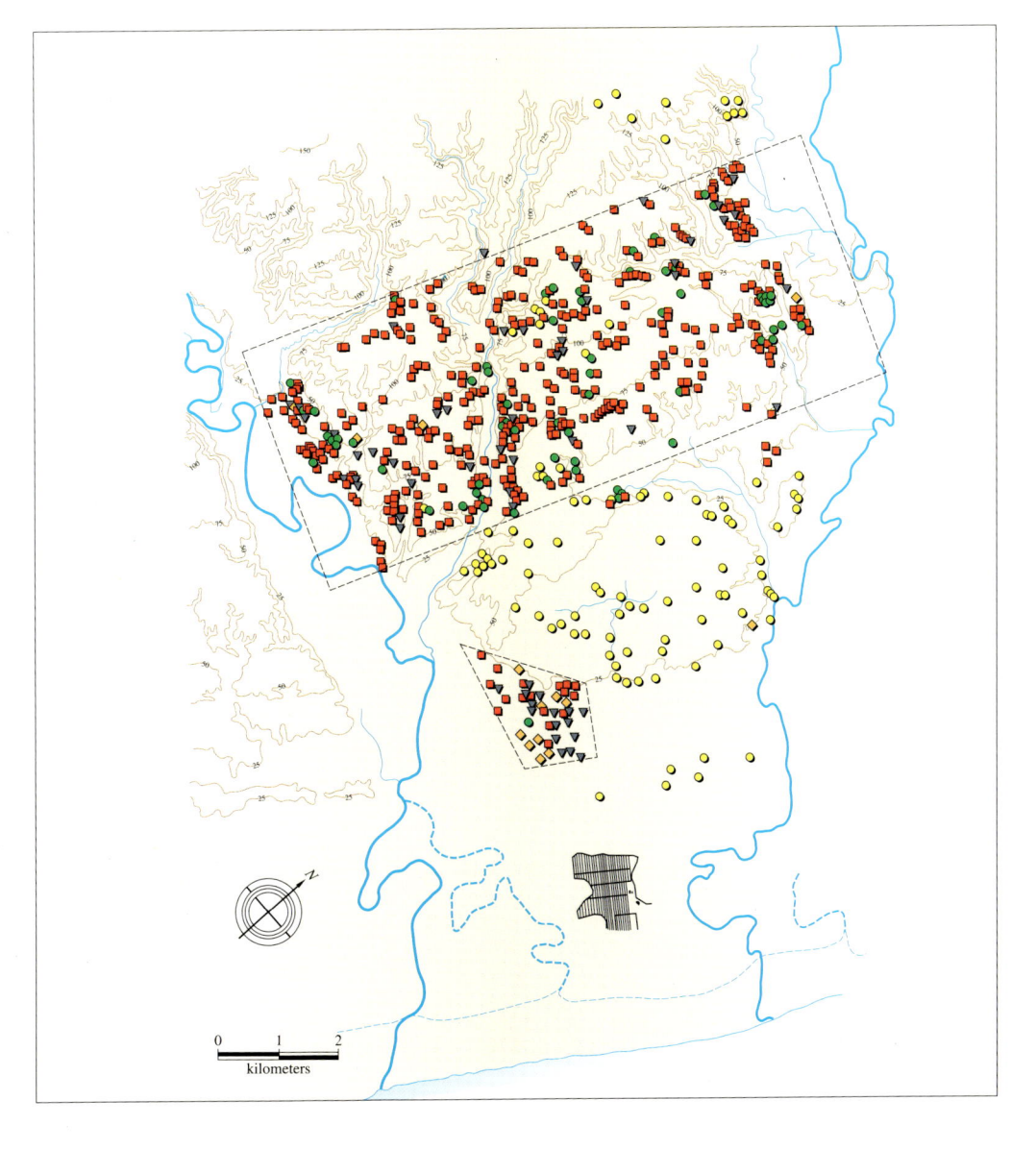

Agricultural Settlements

Reconstruction of the sanctuary
at Pantanello
in the earliest phase
ca. 580 B.C.

Survey of the farmhouses
in the area between the Basento
and Bradano Rivers
550-501 B.C.

Greeks find a virgin or a deserted territory. The most characteristic and visible expression of the new organization of the *chora* in the colonies was the uniform division of the land into strips and rectangular plots, reflecting the same mentality that is more widely evidenced in the preserved orthagonal grid plans of cities like Megara Hyblaea, Selinus, Metapontum, and Poseidonia (to cite only the most obvious examples).

It has been argued that this organization went back to the very founding of the colony, where it is presumed (on the basis of later documentary sources and the evidence of early colonial cities like Megara Hyblaea) that equality prevailed among the colonists, and that each colonist was assigned a uniform portion of the territory as well as a lot in the new city.

This may have been the case at some sites like Megara where unfortunately almost nothing is known of the *chora* but as the evidence accumulates at sites like Poseidonia and Metapontum, where the archaeological evidence for the *chora* is much fuller, it is more and more clear that the process of division may have taken place in stages. The geometrically shaped lots and the equality that they seemingly embodied may, indeed, be a relatively late phenomenon.

Rural sanctuaries

The earliest signs of life in colonial *chorai* were the sanctuaries. They lined major thoroughfares linking the urban center with neighboring colonies or indigenous centers. They were an integral part of the territory. Their location, often around springs, reflects primary concerns of the rural population with the fertility of the field and herds as well as with the health of the human population. They are in this respect, as well as in their physical appearance and arrangements, different from the cult places of the urban center. They were at first extremely simple, and often remained so. Some later rivaled those of the city in importance.

They could, like the extra-urban sanctuaries of Hera at Croton, Metapontum, and Poseidonia, have been frequented by all Greeks, colonist and foreigners, or they could, like the *thesmophorion* at Bitalemi outside Gela or the numerous cult places – marked by a small building or a votive deposit scattered at intervals throughout the *chora* – have served a more restricted group. The form and purpose of rural sanctuaries must have varied considerably depending on local circumstances even within the confines of a single colony.

The interpretation of extra-urban sanctuaries, both the larger and smaller ones as territorial markers, is often invoked to explain these places of worship beyond the walls and to provide a mechanism by which the expansion, or territorial aggrandizement of the new colony, could have been carried out. The theory assumed that the nascent and struggling *polis* was capable of farsighted and unified policy, and was confident of its corporate future.

It works best where the sanctuaries appear to be isolated, but intensive field survey has now shown that this was rarely if ever the case.

The first votives from the sanctuary of Artemis at San Biagio, six kilometers up the valley of the Basento are contemporaneous (late seventh century B.C.) with most primitive examples from the future urban settlement on the coast ("Sacellum C"). This is an example which fits the theory well. At this ear-

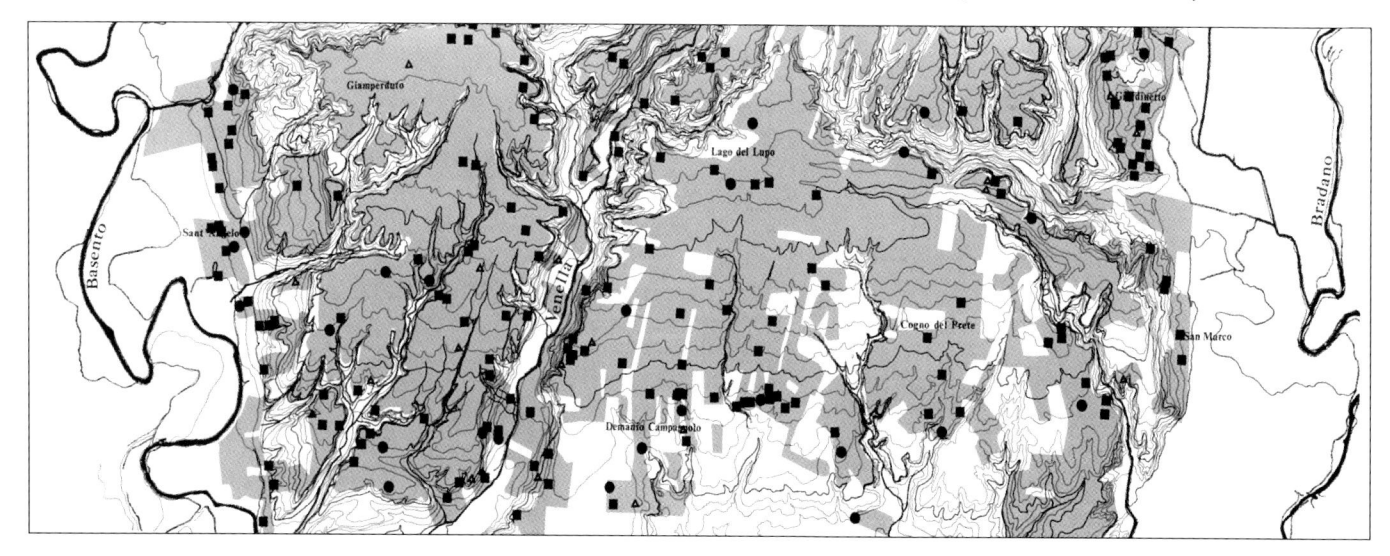

Plan of the *chora* of Metapontum
● sanctuaries
○ probable sanctuaries

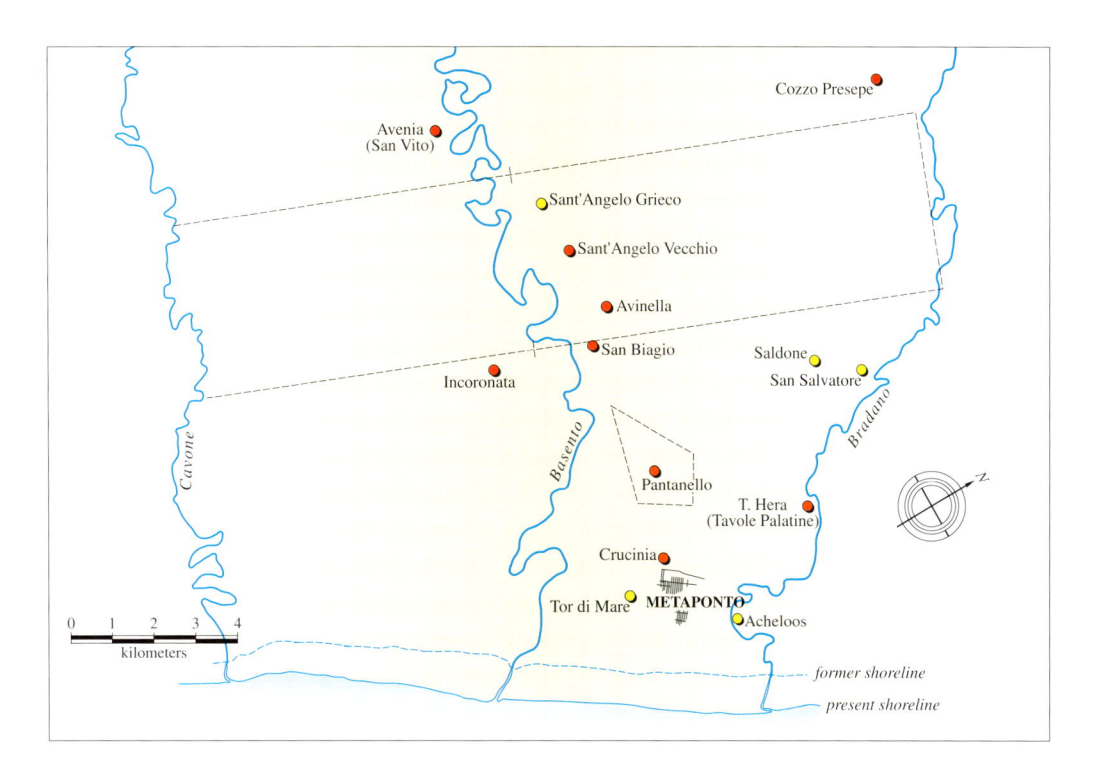

ly date, other evidence of life in the "city" as well as the colonial *chora* is scarce. What purpose could a sanctuary serve at this great distance and, apparently, without a resident rural population?

The territory of Metapontum, however, did not long remain deserted. By the mid-sixth century B.C., as intensive field survey has shown, it had begun to fill up with single-family farmhouses. Some of the earliest are the most distant from the city, and much further inland than San Biagio. At first they were limited to the valleys of the Basento and the Bradano. Then they spread up the valleys of the tributaries, and finally onto the high, gently rolling marine terraces between the valleys.

The sanctuaries like the first farmhouses were surely located on major roads into the interior. As the population grew so did the number of rural sanctuaries. Over a dozen are now known to date from the sixth and fifth centuries B.C., and they are distributed at regular intervals – on the average about three kilometers apart – along these major thoroughfares that follow the valleys. The interpretation as territorial markers, as evidence for an advancing frontier, cannot be justified for Metapontum. They may well, however, have served to define subdivisions by family group (or *genos*) within the territory. *Phylai* in the *chorai* of Metapontum and nearby Heraclea and family cults at Metapontum have been the subjects of recent studies. The similar scale of these rural cult places and the broadly similar characteristics of the cults to be inferred from the votives suggest an analogy with parish churches. In fact, some like San Biagio near modern Metaponto have continued (with interruptions) to be cult places down to the present.

The inhabitants of the *chorai* worshiped also at their hearths, as frequent finds of terra-cotta votive figures on farmsites show. To the gods venerated in local cult places should correspond in some way to those of individual local farmsites or *oikoi*. A striking illustration of this is the elaborate image of Artemis found in a modest farmhouse along the valley of the Venella about two kilometers from the Sanctuary of Artemis at San Biagio.

So far only one rural sanctuary site in the *chora* of Metapontum, Pantanello, has been completely excavated. It began to be used about 600 B.C., a generation after the earliest shrines in the city. Its importance greatly increased around 500 B.C. and at that time the worship of Dionysus was introduced. It continued to be frequented until the late fourth or early third century B.C. when it was completely reconstructed after a period of abandonment. With the decline of the *chora* in the third century, Pantanello, like all the sanctuaries of the *chora*, disappeared.

The "division roads"

The *chora* of Metapontum was traversed by "division lines," as aerial photography has shown. An excavated example in the Pantanello necropolis has shown that the "lines" were, in some cases at least,

Agricultural Settlements

roads. They were spaced about 210 meters apart, but there was much variation. It would be a mistake to assume automatically that the geometrization of the landscape was a unified system brought into being at one time at Metapontum, or anywhere else. Where the "division road" passes through the Pantanello necropolis, it is flanked by over eighty burials. None dates before about 480 B.C., which is roughly a century after the first colonial burials in this area and is a century and a half after the traditionally accepted "foundation" date of the colony (in the second half of the seventh century, B.C.).

A recent study employing satellite imagery has discovered a system of land division at Poseidonia, whose basic unit also seems to have been 210 meters. It, too, has been dated to the early fifth century B.C., when there are other signs of a general reorganization of life, both political and economic, in the colony (e.g., the appearance of the *ekklesiasterion*). The *ekklesiasterion* at Metapontum appeared in the mid-sixth century B.C. or earlier, but there are other signs that the geometrical system of "equal lots" was rather a redivision or subdivision of the land and wealth in a period of intensive economic and social change at the beginning of the fifth century B.C. There was a contemporaneous change in burial in the *chora*, which becomes much less exclusive. The introduction of the popular cult of Dionysus can also be dated to this period, and it was in just this period that the population of the *chora* reached its first, historical peak (with perhaps a thousand farmhouses between the Bradano and the Cavone). Similar phenomena can be observed elsewhere in the Greek world, for example in Attica where a recent study has shown that the division of the *deme* of Athene took place early in the fifth century B.C., after the democratic reforms of Cleisthenes.

By combining the evidence of the "division roads" at Metapontum with that of the spatial distribution of contemporaneously occupied farmhouses it is possible, at Metapontum – but in no other *chora* in the West, so far, to reconstruct the pattern of land plots. The average size of a plot occupied by a farmhouse for the *chora* as a whole was about 13 hectares, and this measure remains roughly constant for two centuries from the fifth through the fourth centuries B.C. In the wide plain of the marine terraces the average was 26 nectares.

The situation in the best preserved example of Greek land division, Chersonesus on the Black Sea, offers a close analogy, as the most recent research indicates – not only for the roads and size of plots, but also for the delay between establishing the colony and the geometrical division of the *chora*. The division by roads into rectangular lots of about 26 hectares on the Heraclean peninsula, and 17.5 hectares at Lighthouse Point (not 4.5 as previously thought) took place at the end of the fourth century B.C., a century after the "founding" and nearly two centuries after the arrival of the first Greeks in the area.

Survey of Metapontum
land division grid
Lago del Lupo district
500-450 B.C.

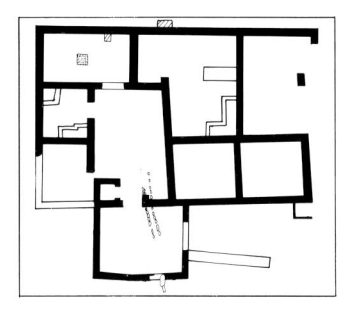

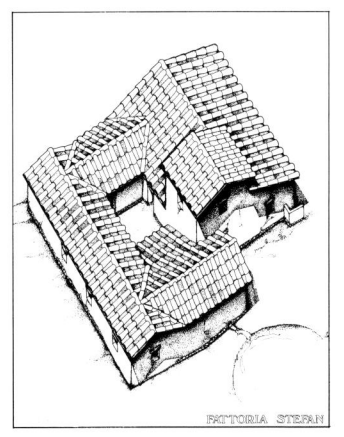

Plan and reconstruction of Fattoria Stefan

Plan of Fattoria Fabrizio

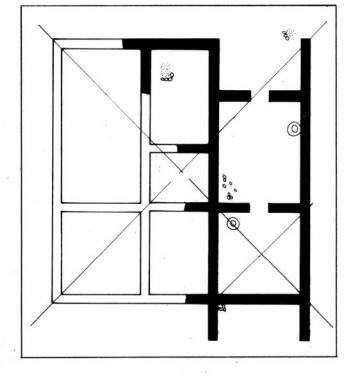

The farmhouses

The basic living unit of the *chora* was the farmhouse. Survey has shown that the *chorai* of Himera in Sicily, of Metapontum and Croton in Magna Graecia, were densely populated. There were on the average fifteen farmhouses per kilometer at Metapontum – of which about half would have been occupied in any given period – and a comparable number at Croton. Within a century from 550 to 450 B.C. or less, all of the available farm land in the *chora* was occupied by farmhouses. As noted earlier some of the earliest are among the farthest from the city.

This was the case at Himera, where the purpose like that claimed for the early sanctuaries, was to stake out the limits of the settlement. Farmhouses, as evidenced by the presence of burials, do not seem to have been numerous until the fourth century B.C. at Poseidonia (Paestum), and then were concentrated on the hills of the eastern edge of the *chora*. This pattern, it has been argued, was dictated by the type of "land use," by the olive cultivation (as opposed to cereal farming on the plains) and was influenced by the Lucanian takeover around 400 B.C.

The colonial Greek farmhouse, as we know from the relatively few excavated examples, was both a residence and a productive unit. The influence of the *pastas* plan that was broadly typical of Mainland Greece has been recognized.

The courtyard is seen as another essential and defining feature. Good examples of these generalizations are the two excavated farmhouses from the *chora* of Camarina, especially the Fattoria Capodicasa immediately outside the city walls and aligned with its street grid. The courtyard was on the north side of the square structure, and the kitchen in the southeast corner – an arrangement paralleled by some examples from southern Italy.

Few farmhouses of the early settlers of the colonial *chorai* are known in any detail. The exceptional cases, like the sixth-century establishment discovered in the hinterland of Siris, and that from Contrada Cugno del Pero in modern Metaponto show that they consisted of few rooms which served multiple functions.

Most sites that had a farm building in the fourth century B.C. had ceramic evidence of extensive occupation in the second half of the sixth or first half of the fifth century B.C., and traces of a structure which had clearly been cannibalized for its building materials. Their stone and tiles were reused in the walls of later farmhouses on the exact same sites. Despite the fact that there was extensive activity in rural necropolises in the second half of the fifth century B.C., no farmhouses of that period have yet been excavated at Metapontum.

A general reorganization of the *chora* took place late in the fourth century B.C., as the rural population surged again and building activity in the city resumed after a pause of over a century. This sudden revival has been thought to reflect new additions to the population drawn in all probability from Hellenized, indigenous centers. The renewal of the city and countryside at Metapontum and other sites in southern Italy in the late fourth century B.C. is paralleled in a more spectacular and sweeping way in Timoleonic Sicily.

Fattoria Stefan in the *chora* of Metapontum, in its final phase in the late fourth century B.C., had a central courtyard and the kitchen in Room 1 in the southeast. Tile in basins and benches in Rooms 2 and 4 and fragments of many *pithoi* in Rooms 1, 2, and 6 show that much of the ground story was given over to work. Loom weights were concentrated in Room 7, which because of its more substantial foundations has been reconstructed as a tower.

Here the women of the house were employed. This would have been normal farther east in the Greek world, for example in the *chora* of Chersonesus, but was a rarity in southern Italy (another exception is the fortified Lucanian farmhouse at Montegiordano).

Room 3 was probably a covered shed for animals. In contrast to the plans of the Camarina farms and several other from Metapontum (see below) this farmhouse probably grew by agglomeration rather than being planned by division within a square or rectangular outline. (Comparable are some recently explored farmhouses in Attica.) The walls were roughly parallel (compare Camarina above) with the "division road," the main road bisecting the *chora* between Bradano and the Basento. It ran close below its southeast wall.

The smaller one-story (?) farmhouse known as Fattoria Fabrizio was perhaps more typical of the *chora* of Metapontum in the fourth century B.C. Whereas Fattoria Stefan was located in the heart of the gently rolling terrace where the larger plots of ca. twenty-six hectares and, presumably, cereal cultivation predominated, Fattoria Fabrizio was on the slope of the Venella, along which the smaller plots were situated. The evidence of its location at a modest distance from cultivable land, and of its own-

Agricultural Settlements

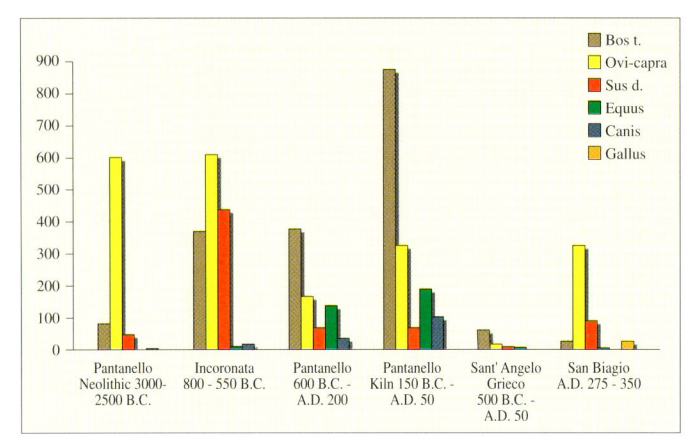

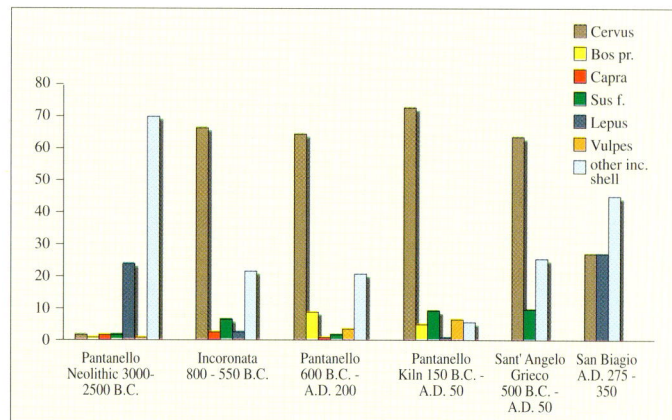

Domestic animal fossils
in the *chora* of Metapontum

Wild animal fossils
in the *chora* of Metapontum

ers' devotion to Artemis would indicate that at least part of their livelihood was gained by tending flocks. The votive plaque was found in Room 1.

Pithoi occupied Rooms 2 and 3, and a mortar was found in Room 4, together with a bronze strainer and a *lekane*, perhaps used in cheesemaking (a shed outside the square perimeter of the building). Ample evidence of a hearth in Room 5 indicates that it was the kitchen; Room 6 was virtually empty. The largest amounts of pottery and the highest ratios of fine to coarse ware were found in Rooms 2 and 3. Perhaps these were storerooms. The really unusual thing about the plan is the absence of a large accessible courtyard – but, as other excavated examples show, this may have been the rule rather than the exception in the *chora* of Metapontum.

Farmhouses in areas of Lucania under indigenous control, Tolve and Montegiordano, for example, show the pervasive influence of Greek architectural ideas – the courtyard, the tower, the *andron*, the bath – and, probably, of Greek systems for organizing agricultural production.

Crops and animals

The principal evidence for what the Greek farmers raised and the population ate are their organic remains, such as seeds, pollen, and bone. Unfortunately only at a few sites – such as at Camarina and Metapontum – has this material been systematically collected and studied. So the picture is necessarily incomplete. What is needed for Magna Graecia and the Sicilian colonies is the sort of wide-ranging paleobotanical project carried out at Chersonesus on the Black Sea – which has delineated the agricultural development of the colony, its relation to that of the pre-Greek indigenous population, and to its "subcolonies" in the western Crimea. Still, a great deal more is known of Greek agricolture in the West, now, than twenty years ago.

The study of pollen and seed remains from sites like Incoronata and Pantanello in the *chora* of Metapontum clearly show the dependence of the early colonists on cereals, especially barley; and the development by the mid-fourth century B.C. of an agriculture based broadly on cereals, grapes, and olives. Evidence for legumes and forage crops, including the earliest occurrence of alfalfa in the West, rounds out the picture.

Animal bones have usually been preserved and collected in significant quantities in a variety of sites in the *chora* of Metapontum, ranging in date from the Late Neolithic (ca. 3000 B.C.) to the Late Roman (ca. A.D. 340). This puts the Greek experience in a broad perspective. A primitive, prehistoric type of sheep, for example, was raised at pre-colonial Incoronata (eighth to seventh century B.C.). It completely disappeared from the *chora* with the arrival of a superior breed from the southeast (probably Greece) as the Achaean Greek colonists took possession of the *chora* in the sixth century B.C. That animal breeding was a major activity of Greek farmers here is amply indicated by the remains of superior breeds of horses and cattle. "Grazing indicators" (in the pollen evidence) show that grazing declined after 500 B.C.

The preponderance of cattle (the "tractors" of the ancient countryside) over other domesticated species on sites of the fifth and fourth century prove that the economy had shifted decisively to plow-based cultivation at the same time that the *chora* assumed it rigidly geometric appearance (cf. "Division Roads" above.).

Detailed study of the cattle from a deposit of the second century B.C. (under Roman domination) has revealed the startling fact that at Metapontum selective breeding of animals for size was still an im-

opposite
Bronze mirror
from the Pantanello necropolis
mid-5th cent. B.C.
Metaponto
Museo Archeologico Nazionale
Cat. 163

Agricultural Settlements

367

portant part of the economy when some historians had thought Magna Graecia was a wasteland. These were the largest cattle in the Roman world at the time.

The high percentage of elk (*Cervus elaphus*) bones at all sites in this period (and later) are silent testimony that large forests were not far off, and that the bounty of the *eschatia* included game, besides wood and pastureland.

Necropolises and health

Burials in small or larger necropolises in the *chora* are the securest proof that the population resident in the countryside was a permanent one, and that its social and economic level was generally on a par with (if not in some cases superior to) that of the urban center. From the tombs with fine Attic vases in the territory of Gela and Croton to the impressive stone cist tombs at San Biagio near Metapontum, the evidence of burials is eloquent.

A feature of these burials, which has only recently received the attention that it deserves, is the enormous amount of information about the population to be discovered from the study of the bones of the deceased themselves – information about mortality and population dynamics, nutrition, and physical appearance, and most of all about health status. Here the fullest information is again from the *chora* of Metapontum, from over 300 burials in the extensive area of tombs known as the Pantanello necropolis 3.5 kilometers from the city's walls.

The average life span of the Greek rural population was just over forty years for males, and just under that for females – a ripe age compared with what we know of other ancient populations. In stature they resembled pre-World War II peasants of Italy. In a colony renowned for its doctors, it is striking to find an apparently low level of health care (unset bones, rampant caries), but more striking is the evidence for disease.

The presence of thalassemia and therefore almost certainly of malaria has been diagnosed in a dozen cases – which illustrates the fatal consequences of an episode of catastrophic erosion of the river valleys (500–300 B.C.) – revealed by geomorphological investigations – and of the increasingly swampy conditions of the valleys documented by excavation.

The pain and premature death by disease, however, were even more widespread as the dramatic discovery of a form of trepomatosis, or syphilis, in endemic proportion has recently illustrated. Examination of teeth revealed a seventy percent rate of hypoplasia in the population, and this points to malnutrition or serious disease among most rural children. Recent studies of the urban necropolis of Crucinia confirm many of these findings, but also show an apparently better level of health care and fewer cases of severe illness. Clearly, the life that the Greeks succeeded in creating for themselves in the West was the result, too, of a silent triumph over most of the evils to which flesh is heir. It is only as we learn more about this aspect of their struggle that we can begin to appreciate fully their achievement.

Support for basin
with female figures
from the sanctuary area
at San Biagio
first half 4th cent. B.C.
Metaponto
Museo Archeologico Nazionale
Cat. 81/I

Bibliography

Agriculture in Ancient Greece (ed. B. WELLS) in *Acta Instituti Atheniensis*, Ser 4, 42, 1992; J.C. CARTER, "Agricoltura e pastorizia nella Magna Grecia" in G. PUGLIESE CARRATELLI (ed.), *Magna Grecia II*, 1987, pp. 173-212; "Metapontum – Land, Wealth and Population" in J.-P. DESCOURDRES (ed.), *Greek Colonists and Native Populations*, 1990, pp. 405-441; *Imera III: Prospezione archeologica nel territorio*, 1988; *Poseidonia Paestum: Atti del 27 Convegno di Studi sulla Magna Grecia*, 1987, (1988); C. PARIS PRESICCE, "La funzione delle aree sacre nell'organizzazione urbanistica primitiva delle colonie greche", in *Archeologia Classica*, 35, 1983, pp. 19-132; A. RUSSO TAGLIENTE, 1992; M. HENNEBERG, R. HENNEBERG, J.C. CARTER, "Health in Colonial Metaponto", *Research and Exploration*, National Geographic Society, 8, 4, 1992, pp. 446-459; A. SHCHEGLOV, 1992.

Claude Rolley   Sculpture in Magna Graecia

Krater from Vix
detail of the workmanship
on the neck with figures
of armed *kouroi*
end 6th cent. B.C.
Châtillon sur Seine
Musée Archélogique

The Problems

A new picture of Italiot sculpture, and of the other aspects of the civilization of Magna Graecia, has emerged from the series of finds that followed the land reform of 1950 and continue to be made. Although nearly all of them were presented within a short space of time, only rarely have they been studied in depth; and they have been given little attention by the historians of Greek sculpture. Despite the enormous quantity of material that has come to light, it has not been subjected to an overall assessment, as it ought to have been. This brief account will therefore begin with a number of general considerations, primarily of a theoretical character, that will permit the reader to have a better understanding of the works discussed.

Center and periphery: colonial or provincial?
The difficulties that are found when an attempt is made to obtain an overview of Italiot sculpture have various causes, some of which are common to Magna Graecia and Sicily. The works of the western Greeks are colonial products and their evident relationship with the sculpture of Mainland Greece is, to a certain degree, one of dependence. In particular, the studies of Greek sculpture focus on relations between mother cities and colonies, which – as may be noticed in a number of recent books – tend to reduce the sculpture in the West to a mere appendage to that of the Aegean world. In this regard, the equally apparent differences between the colonies and Mainland Greece have been explained from two different points of view. The first focuses on the contrast between *center* and *periphery*, a constant theme in art history. A long tradition – fostered particularly by German scholars – tends to label as "provincial" those works that, in the last analysis, would not have been produced if their makers had not been familiar with the output of Mainland Greece, or, to be more precise, of the areas that developed original styles: the Peloponnese and Attica, to which should be added, especially in the sixth century B.C., a number of the islands in the Cyclades. In this perspective, the sculpture of the western Greeks is considered to be more or less equivalent to that of Boeotia, which was also abundant in the sixth century, or the bronze statuettes of Arcadia. On the other hand, the "provincialism" of a work is regarded as evidence on which its attribution may be based. Thus, it has been affirmed that the famous krater of Vix was made in the Peloponnese, and not in Magna Graecia, because there is nothing provincial about it, while, on the contrary, the bronze *kouros* of Piraeus has been held to be Boeotian because its workmanship is mediocre. The origin of the krater is still open to debate, but it is necessary to find better arguments.

In this sense, the adjective "provincial" clearly implies a judgment regarding the object's quality. It is worth noting that in the same, essentially Germanic, tradition this expression is never used with refer-

opposite
Bronze *hydria* from the *heroon* at Paestum
540-530 B.C.
Paestum, Museum Archeologio Nazionale
Cat. 145/V

ence to Ionia, the area that included the major cities on the coast of Asia Minor and the nearby islands, although this had a large output of sculpture which was just as different from that of Athens or Corinth as was that of Poseidonia (Paestum) or Selinus. In this case, the scholars have been swayed by the prestige of Ionia, which, in the sixth century B.C., before the Persian conquest, was a land of scientists and philosophers, and the cradle of an original style of architecture. Or, just to give an example, if one of the great Athenian sculptors of the second half of the sixth century had seen the richly-dressed citizens of Samos in all their corpulence and self-importance, or the plump faces on the sculptured columns of Ephesus, he would have been as surprised as he would have been before the temples of Paestum and Selinus, and shown the same contempt as he would have done there.

From the book by U. Jantzen about the bronze statuettes of Magna Graecia and Sicily (1937), to the volume by E. Langlotz on the art of the western Greeks (1963), attempts were made in one or two cases to give historical substance to this contrast between the center and the periphery. This is particularly noticeable with regard to Tarentum. This was the only colony set up by the Spartans, and for a long period it enjoyed a special relationship with its metropolis. Now, as we shall see, numerous western works clearly imitate the forms of the artistic output of Laconia. As a result of this, the poorer Laconian products are described as Tarentine, so that, especially in Jantzen's book, everything that tends to be Laconian in style is attributed to the workshops of Tarentum. And the author does not seem to be at all puzzled by the fact that none of the objects clearly influenced by Laconian art was found in Tarentum.

The native populations
Before the excavations made after World War II up to the Land Reform, with the exception of Locri, Magna Graecia had yielded much less than Sicily, both as regards sculpture and all the rest. In particular, in the case of Sicily – influenced by an Italian tradition that reflected the ambition to restore the nation to its former greatness – the interpretation given was diametrically opposed to the previous one. The most outstanding names in this case are those of Pirro Marconi and Biagio Pace. In their terminology and historical interests there are, therefore, two corresponding orientations. The first lays emphasis on "anticlassicism," as in the case of Pace with regard to the sculpture at Selinus. What had been discovered up to then in Mainland Italy did not lend itself to this type of analysis, although evidently the "treasury" at the mouth of the River Sele, near Paestum, was later to yield a large quantity of material for this purpose. Other modern writers have highlighted the contribution, voluntary or otherwise, of the natives peoples with whom the Greek colonists came into contact. From the ancient sources, we know that these relations were not always hostile, and this has frequently been confirmed by the research of the last few decades, whether this be the study of the trade between the Greek and the natives – the clearest example of which has been provided by the excavation at Incoronata, near Metapontum – or an irrefutable fact: the founders of the colonies were almost exclusively men, and they married local women. In the Greek world, although women had no political rights, they often played an important religious role, and it should not be forgotten that they had almost all the responsibility for the raising of young children. Thus, through their beliefs and cults, they were able to influence sculpture.

But in this case, too, these considerations refer to Sicily, whether we are dealing with the Sanctuaries of Demeter and Persephone, or just of Persephone, or of such works as the female statue in the cemetery of Megara Hyblaea, which introduced an image of fertility and maternity to funerary art that was totally alien to what is to be found in the cemeteries of Mainland Greece. With regard to Magna Graecia, the hypotheses concerning the terra-cotta plaques from Locri, made for dedication in a sanctuary of Persephone, are oriented in another direction. There is, quite simply, an attempt to attribute in one statuette or another – as in the case of the *kore* of Rose (Cosenza), an Apollo from the sanctuary of Cirò, and the horseman from Grumentum – what a Greek would have considered to be mere clumsiness, to the failure on the part of the native bronze workers to fully understand Greek styles. These "clumsy" works have, in fact, been discovered outside the Greek cities – the small horse of Siris is an exception. But the Italiot products with which we are familiar do not lend themselves to the same analysis as the goddess suckling twins from the cemetery at Megara Hyblaea. The fact that even its modeling is not wholly "Greek" permits us to link the work's style and the religious belief it displays.

The multicentric nature of Greek art
However, this attempt to explain the difference between the sculpture of Magna Graecia and that of Mainland Greece is not sufficient. In fact, it could easily be extended to a large part of the Greek world. I have already referred to Archaic Ionian sculpture, which was so different from that of Athens or the

Little bronze horse from sacred ground at Siris
secondo half 7th cent. B.C.
Policoro
Museo Nazionale della Siritide

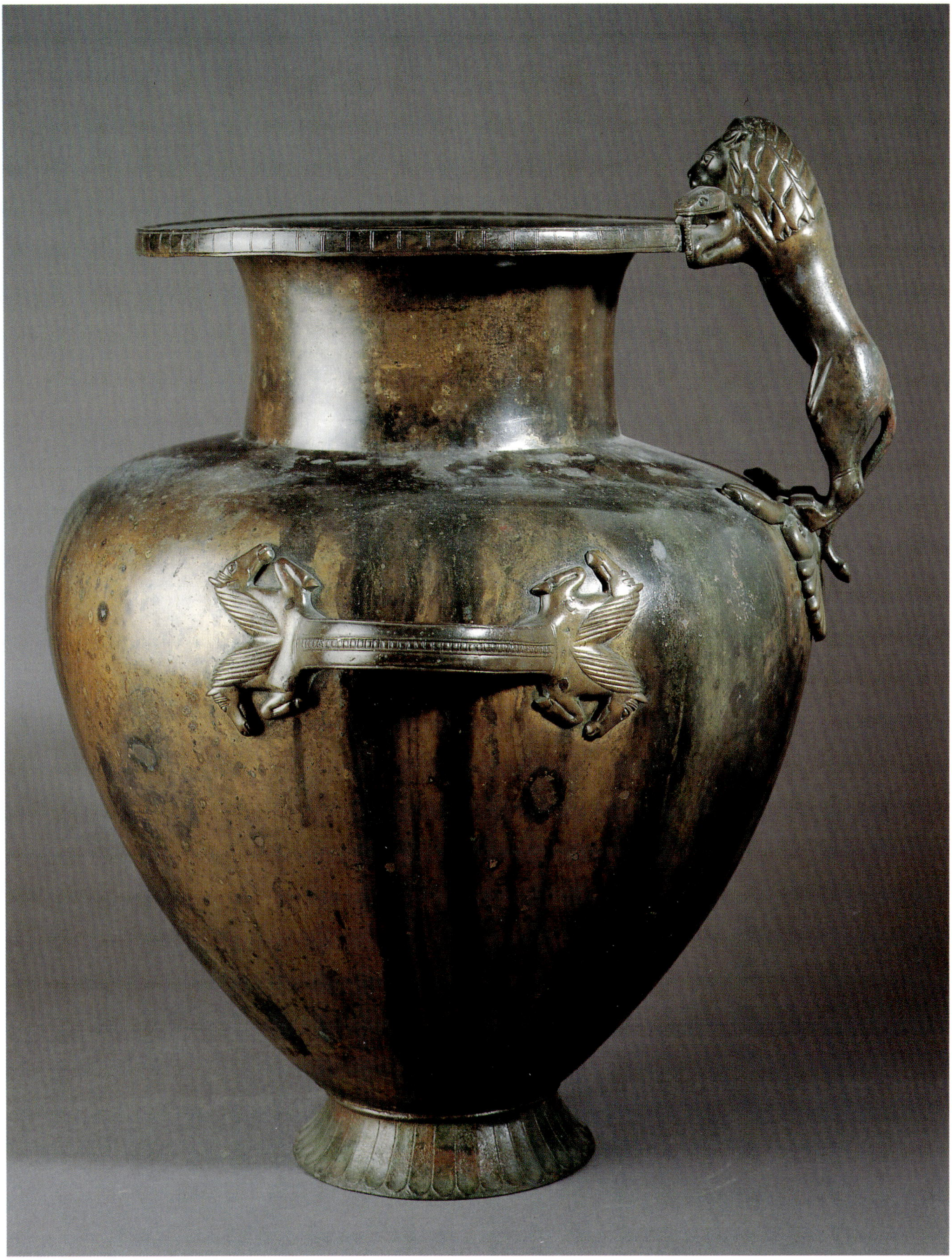

Peloponnese. But the Hellenistic world offers a comparable picture. Despite the characteristics that contemporary works generally share, there are the plastic arts of Hellenistic Egypt, with their two conflicting tendencies – the royal portraits and genre statuettes – that contrast with both the Pergamene styles (which aimed at dramatic expression) and the sobriety that was maintained by the Athenian workshops, imbued as they were with the Classical models that they had before their eyes. With regard to this period, too, there is an excessive tendency to relegate the West to a periphery that conceals its specific characteristics. It was only the Early Classical period – that of Phidias and Polyclitus – that merely had imitations, but not local or regional equivalents outside Mainland Greece.

The only way to fully comprehend Italiot sculpture is to see it in the wider context of Hellenism because, from the eighth to the second centuries B.C., Greek art was multicentric, just like that of northern and central Italy in the late Middle Ages and early Renaissance. In Greece a number of clearly defined styles developed, each of which corresponded to the output of one of the great *poleis* (city-states). These had their own cults, social structure, and culture, and were always in a state of unstable equilibrium in which there was a constant tendency to oscillate between the unity of the Greek world when it was confronted by the "barbarians" – that is, those who did not speak Greek – and diversity; and in a country perpetually at war, this often became hostility. Thus, as Langlotz demonstrated in 1927, we may distinguish different schools of art, in the strict sense of the term; their own clearly identifiable styles, were an expression of what would today be described as the cultural identity of their respective cities. The citizens and artists of each city who frequented the great Panhellenic sanctuaries during the games were able to see the works of the other cities. In the eyes of the sculptors, and also of some of the patrons, the rivalries were also of an artistic nature.

Consequently, certain cities provided social, economic, and cultural bases for artistic creation that were solid enough to favor the development of an original style that would then be handed down from master to pupil. From the beginning of the sixth century to the middle of the fifth, there were Argive, Corinthian, and Attic schools of sculpture, the birth of which was prefigured by the bronze statuettes of the eighth century. Elsewhere, distinctive styles only flourished for shorter periods: from the mid-seventh to the mid-sixth centuries on Naxos; for two or three generations at Sparta. The Persian conquest put an end to the development of the Ionian styles, although they continued to exist in the West. But the other regions of Mainland Greece did not evolve independent styles, and it is necessary to reflect on this in order to understand various aspects of artistic creation in the West. The bronze statuettes of shepherds from Arcadia tend to resemble each other, but regarding the details of the execution rather than the overall conception. As is clearly demonstrated by the splendid series of *kouroi* in the sanctuary of Ptoon, Boeotia, although it was rich, had recourse in turn to sculptors from Paros, Naxos, and Athens. Local artists with varying levels of ability imitated these models without ever evolving a Boeotian style. It is notable that the areas where a specific style was not developed were, broadly speaking, those that had never adopted – at least, not completely – the structure of the *polis*: they were the regions of the leagues and kingdoms, the model for which was, in the language of the ancients, that of the *ethnos*, the people.

Magna Graecia: influences and eclecticism
In view of what has been stated above, it is possible to attempt a definition of Italiot sculpture – the problems of which are not so exceptional as is often maintained – with reference to two or three issues. In the first place, that of the relations between the colonies and their mother cities should not be forgotten. Throughout the Greek world, the very fact that they were colonies influenced the birth of the workshops: we may observe – in the case of pottery, too, which was essential for everyday life – that there was a special form for the first generation that followed the foundation: at Thasos, Istria, and Massalia, to mention some examples that have been studied in depth. But, as we shall see, a careful comparison between the sculpture of the metropolis and that of its colonies brings to light, above all, specific parallels that are, however, of limited interest. A more complex problem arises from another observation. In the Archaic period, many different stylistic tendencies – more in the minor arts than in the large sculpture – were present in various cities, quite independently of the origin of their founders. The importation of objects, and the journeys of artists and craftsmen only partially explain this diffusion. Thus, a preliminary analysis identifies various stylistic currents: Laconian forms are found in bronzes and terra-cottas not only at Tarentum, but also elsewhere; the Ionian styles spread widely and their variations mixed together until, at the beginning of the fifth century, they were replaced by the marked influence of the art of Paros, for reasons and in ways that remain obscure. The Corinthian faces appear again not only in the terra-cottas of Metapontum and Sybaris, Achaean foundations where the presence of the forms

Bust of a woman
from Medma
first half 5th cent. B.C.
Reggio Calabria
Museo Nazionale
Cat. 169

Bust of a woman
from Medma
first half 5th cent. B.C.
Reggio Calabria
Museo Nazionale
Cat. 170

of the northern Peloponnese is understandable, but also at Siris, which was a colony of Colophon, an Ionian city. This complex and changeable picture is, therefore, very different from that of Mainland Greece, where the diffusion of styles was clearly delimited.

The creativity of the western artists allowed them to avoid producing mere copies, or derivatives, of the works of Mainland Greece. In Magna Graecia, through the combination of different borrowings, new forms were often elaborated, and these often resulted in genuinely original styles. Thus, the Zeus of Ugento mixes Laconian and Corinthian features, just as a century before the *perirrhanterion* of Incoronata had combined Ionian forms and Corinthian schemata. But what is merely a juxtaposition in the *perirrhanterion* results in a formally coherent work in the Zeus, at least if we forget the models that allow us to analyze its genesis. There is, as Fr. Croissant so aptly put it, an "inventive eclecticism," which, in its very origin, presupposes certain choices. This allows us to have a better understanding of the output of the bronze workers who made the *hydriae* from the *heraion* at Paestum and Sala Consilina, the cauldron from the tomb of Hochdorf in Baden-Württemberg, and the krater of Vix, attributed by some to Laconia and others to Corinth on the basis of various details. These comparisons are all appropriate: the synthesis could only occur in Magna Graecia.

From the workshops to the schools
Nonetheless, up to the fifth century, in the context of such a diverse and variable output, it is possible to identify areas that were more or less coherent. Thus, although Tarentum is another story, Metapontum, Sybaris, Croton, Siris, and Paestum have been described as an "Achaean area," with a number of features in common. These range from the diffusion of the objects known as "lamps of the Sele" to the imitation, in the figurines, of a type of face derived from Corinth, and – with the apparent exception of Paestum – the diffusion of types of simas in terra-cotta with relief decoration. Locri Epizephyrii, with its vast territory extending to the Tyrrhenian, was itself another area, while, despite the large number of finds, it is difficult to obtain a clear picture of the art of Rhegium.

In some cases we can go further. In the hundred-year period beginning with the mid-sixth century it is possible to distinguish various types of output, the originality and formal coherence of which are characteristic of styles associated with an individual city – and this prompts the question as to whether true schools existed, in the sense given to the term by Langlotz with regard to Mainland Greece. It was, in fact, P. Zancani Montuoro, in his publication of the metopes of the Sele *heraion*, who first proposed this type of analysis. The question is not, however, peculiar to Magna Graecia: it regards the birth of colonial schools that are independent of their metropolises, or of imports in general. With reference to an example outside Magna Graecia, it is clear that Cyrene, where large numbers of sculptures have been

Sculpture in Magna Graecia

discovered, had neither a style nor a school of its own; doubts remain regarding Thasos, a colony of Paros. The difficult and much debated problem of the coherence of the sculpture at Selinus, however, is beyond the scope of this essay. The clearest case is that of Locri, which was impervious to outside influences due to its aristocratic constitution. An output of luxury goods for the domestic market was developed here that may be paralleled with the bronze statuettes of Laconia in the sixth century; these were produced for dedication by the Spartans at the sanctuaries they frequented – that is, not only those in Laconia, but also at Olympia and Dodona. The close formal similarities that may be observed between the handles of the bronze mirrors from Locri and the terra-cottas from Medma reveal the same style, which is that of the city. Subsequently, the decoration of the temples, despite its quality, did not any longer have local roots. In Paestum, for two or three generations, the architectural sculpture was the result of the evolution of the same style, displaying strong Ionic influence, which, although it received contributions from outside, did not lose its continuity and coherence. Its appearance, with the decoration of the first temple (the so-called treasury) of the Sele *heraion*, marks Paestum's detachment from the "Achaean area." At

Clay *perirrhanterion*
with relief decoration
second half 7th cent. B.C.
Metaponto
Museo Archeologico Nazionale
Cat. 29

Sculpture in Magna Graecia

the same time, the architectural terra-cottas of Paestum are evidence of relations with Etruria that are difficult to interpret. For other areas, it is necessary to await the study of recent finds, especially at Metapontum, which has yielded a large group of statuary in stone and terra-cotta, and at Croton, where some recently discovered bronze statuettes are of excellent quality and, apparently, of the same style.

In the West, the Severe style is inseparable from Archaism, which it prolonged: the Battle of Himera did not mark a clean break, as did the Second Persian War in Greece. After 480 B.C., it is increasingly difficult to relate the western works and those of Mainland Greece, apart from the reliefs in Parian style, because of the situation in Greece. Athens only began to rebuild the temples of the Acropolis from 449–447 onward and, despite the sculptors mentioned by our sources, far fewer statues were made in Greece from 480 to 450 than during the previous thirty years. For this reason, too, the attributions – that is, the linking of names to works – for this period remains guesswork. The works that have, on various occasions, been associated with the name of Pythagoras of Rhegium are the best examples of these wholly arbitrary attributions, which tend to eclipse the much more interesting phenomenon of the partici-

Clay lamp with caryatids
580-570 B.C.
Paestum
Museo Archeologico Nazionale
Cat. 35

Sculpture in Magna Graecia

pation of western sculptors in the development of what we call the Severe style. This has been studied with regard to Sicily, but not for Magna Graecia, where the series of busts of Medma, for instance, would give us an invaluable insight into the transformations that took place contemporaneously throughout the Greek world.

Hellenistic sculpture
The early Classical period, that of Phidias and Polyclitus, made very little impression in the West: a male head from Metapontum shows continued links to the Severe style, while a splendid head of Athena from Tarentum, also in marble, is original, and it is more immediately expressive than the contemporary sculpture of Mainland Greece. This is a general phenomenon that may be observed from Lycia and Cyprus to Etruria. Thus, the carefully calculated equilibrium that the sculpture of the second half of the fifth century sought in Athens and Argos, and the rejection of expressivity that this implied, were not exportable: the Dioscuri of Locri, for instance, are cold and stiff.

But, just as the *Nereid Monument* of Xanthus displayed soon afterward the immediate impact abroad of the forms of the late fifth century, there was – at least in Tarentum – a sculpture of the fourth century that closely reflected what was happening in Mainland Greece. Above all, there are funeral *stelai*: from the fourth to the second centuries there was no equivalent of Syracusan sculpture in Magna Graecia. The most magnificent head from Tarentum of the first half of the fourth century is a life-size head of a woman in terra-cotta. The immediate cause of this was the political situation of the cities on the Ionian

Clay head of a woman
360-340 B.C.
Taranto, Museo Nazionale
Cat. 284

The Dioscuri
on horses supported
by tritons
marble statues
from the Ionic temple of Maracà
end 5th cent. B.C.
Reggio Calabria, Museo Nazionale
Cat. 195

Sea: the conflict with the natives did not, so it appears, permit the development of important workshops, despite the wealth of Tarentum. This prosperity, the reasons for which are still in debate, manifests itself more in the output of jewelry than in the statues, with the exception of the works commissioned from foreign artists. The most notable of these were two works by Lysippus: a pensive Heracles, and a Zeus. The latter, until the construction of the *Colossus of Rhodes*, was, with its height of 40 cubits (between 16 and 18 meters), the largest statue in the Greek world.

Thus, it is in the small-scale sculpture that we are obliged to seek the echoes of these statues, which must have made a profound impression when they were made, just as they impressed the Romans: but the splendid Dioscuro of Naples, which is, after all, only a bronze statuette, is not in itself the embodiment of a style. All this tends to contrast Tarentum with Syracuse; the wealth of the latter was at the service of the prestige politics of the tyrants, thus making it a major center for sculpture in the fourth and third centuries. The atlantes from Rossano di Vaglio, in Lucania, and a caryatid from Vasto, in the Iapygian area, which, around the beginning of the third century, revive motifs of the late fifth century, in a sense echo the series of Siceliot atlantes in stone: but none of the former were made by Greek hands. An atlas from Tarentum could be the link between the Sicilian models and the native imitations. A relief of a battle, from a hypogeum in Lecce, is, however, a perfect example of the standard Hellenistic output, and a similar work has been found at Tarentum itself. Probably it is necessary to distinguish here between the clients and the artists. Just as many of the fourth-century fortifications of native sites were clearly built by the Greeks, it is thanks to a kneeling satyr from Armento and some fragments, also half life-size, from various sanctuar-

Stone relief
with Orestes and Electra
in front of the tomb
of Agamemnon
350-330 B.C.
New York
The Metropolitan Museum of Art

ies (which were all wholly Greek), that we discover an output of bronze sculpture of the second half of the fourth century in the interior of Lucania. Evidently, before being summoned by the Lucani, these bronze workers had learned their trade in a Greek city.

Tarentum from the fourth to the second centuries
The very abundant series of terra-cotta figurines from Tarentum, as well as the lesser known one from Heraclea, is not particularly original, but there are distinctive details that allow these works to be identified. The preponderance of Aphrodite and the repertoire of theatrical subjects was general in the West as far as Lipari (Aeolian Islands). This distinguishes the whole of the western output from the tradition that extends from Tanagra to Myrina and then Alexandria, where, from the fourth to the second centuries, statuettes of elegantly attired women known as Tanagra figurines predominated.
On the other hand, the Tarentine predilection for funerary monuments in the form of small temples, known as *naiskoi*, often represented on large vases with the heroized figure of the deceased, led to the development of limestone reliefs that constituted the main output of the Tarentine sculpture in stone until the Roman conquest. The series begins with a splendid relief probably depicting Orestes and Electra before the tomb of Agamemnon, a theme that was entirely appropriate to the function of the work. This relief was made just after the middle of the fourth century, and nothing distinguishes its style from that of the works of Mainland Greece. Subsequently, battle scenes – including some in a mythological key – were predominant. These works are in fact adaptations, at times ambitious, of the prevailing repertoire, and are not easily datable. This is because this output – to tell the truth, more the work of craftsmen than of creative artists – continued without being influenced by the interruption of the large monumental friezes that occurred between the building of the Mausoleum around 350 B.C. and the Great Altar of Zeus at Pergamum in the first half of the second century.

Problems of boundaries
The Hellenistic sanctuaries of Campania, from Teanum to Capua, have yielded large terra-cotta heads similar to the terra-cottas discovered at Aricia, in Latium: the latter is certainly a sanctuary of Demeter, with Greek iconography. It has been possible to partially reconstruct a pediment decorated with large bas-relief figures, many seated statues, busts and other statues. The complex is in pure Hellenistic style, possibly of the third century; the material and style suggest that it is the work of Campanian artists.
This complex poses a question that may also be asked with regard to much older works: in southern and central Italy, where exactly is the border between what we may call "Greek" and what is Italic in nature? Much has been written in a somewhat fruitless attempt to establish, in relation to these two terms, the

Bronze statuette of Apollo
490-460 B.C.
Bari, Museo Archeologico
Cat. 160

style of a certain number of bronze statuettes of the sixth century. The answers are many and various, since both artists and works of art travel. It is highly probable that at Aricia the coroplasts spoke Greek to each other while they worked. On the other hand, it is very likely that the Archaic bronze horseman of Grumentum, for example, was made by a non-Greek bronze worker who deliberately imitated Greek art. In fact, he copied Greek forms, but the details of the surface and the lines are not Greek. The same occurred in the Hellenistic period with regard to the maker of the caryatids from Vasto or that of the telamones of Rossano di Vaglio, while the frieze with battle scenes from the Palmieri hypogeum in Lecce is similar to various funerary reliefs found in Tarentum.

In many other cases it is useless to try to come to a decision: it is simply of no importance. What really counts is the role played by Magna Graecia in the transmission of Greek styles to Italy. On the one hand, the fortifications built by the Greek architects for the Lucani in a period in which the latter threatened the Greek cities clearly demonstrate that artists and craftsmen traveled, regardless of the political situation. On the other hand, Campania had always been an area where cultures came into contact and mixed together, as testified by numerous cases. Examples of this interaction include the introduction of Greek funerary rites in a number of Orientalizing tombs at Pontecagnano; the presence of Etruscan features in the terra-cotta architectural decoration at Paestum; the early Hellenistic terra-cottas from Capua and Aricia. From the point of view of Greek culture as a whole, this alone would justify attributing a major role to the sculpture of Magna Graecia.

The originality of Italiot sculpture
May we, after all, describe the Italiot production of the plastic arts taken as a whole – quite apart from its currents and styles – as original? In this regard it is not possible to separate Magna Graecia from Sicily. If we compare the small bronze Apollo found near Bari with the athlete of Adranum, and also with the youth of Selinus, to give three almost contemporary examples, we have the impression that the western artists were seeking, first and foremost, to animate the figure, and that they gave more importance to the rendering of movement than formal balance. A number of mirror handles from Locri are decorated with figurines whose expressive postures seem to conflict with their function as a support. These examples, which date from the period of the Severe style – that is, the second quarter of the fifth century – are in contrast with the closed forms of the artists of Mainland Greece in the Archaic and Classical periods, who were always concerned with focusing the attention of the spectator on the interior of the figure. These western works are open forms, constructed according to schemata which in Mainland Greece were only developed in the second half of the fourth century with the *Apoxyomenos* of Lysippus or the bronze athlete of Antihythera.

The metopes of the first temple on the Sele River emphasize an aspect that is complementary to this. The accentuation of the significant elements tends to create an imbalance in the group of figures, and also in the profiles of a number of faces. This is strikingly evident in the metope with Heracles and the giant, and the same applies to the Leucippidae in flight. In the same sanctuary, the metopes of the second temple – the workmanship of which is much more refined – stress the decorative effects at the expense of the structure. Thus, unlike all the sculptors of Mainland Greece and, to a lesser extent, Ionia, the maker of the metope of the "dancers" was not particularly interested in the bodies covered with drapery forming folds on which the light so effectively plays: many of these young women have a bust in which there is no room for the second breast. A closer examination, however, reveals that, in the better preserved examples of these metopes, the sculptor has varied the schema by making only one of the two women smile: in order to make the dissimilarity between the facial expressions more evident, he has constructed two profiles according to two sharply contrasting schemata that appear to derive from models of different origin. It should not be forgotten that, in the same period, the painters of red-figure vases in Athens, using a pointed tool, sketched the outline of the naked body before drawing the clothed figure: in other words, they started out with the anatomical structure in order to reach a formal equilibrium.

This originality of the sculpture of Magna Graecia was most evident in the Archaic period – intended here in a broad sense, from the end of the seventh to the middle of the fifth centuries. Thus, in order to give it the credit it deserves, it is necessary to avoid the tendency that pervades classical studies of paying excessive attention to Athens. The balance, restraint, and sense of proportion that characterize some of the schools of Mainland Greece are only one of the many aspects of Greek art; Italiot sculpture manifests another. But it is not necessary to hypothesize native influences in order to explain the development of this art: it is just as Greek as that of Athens or Samos.

Clay votive statuette
last quarter 7th cent. B.C.
Cosenza
Museo Civico Archeologico
Cat. 32/I

Clay Daedalic statuette
mid-7th cent. B.C.
Naples
Museo Archeologico Nazionale
Cat. 31

Statuette of a woman
end 7th cent. B.C.
Metaponto
Museo Archeologico Nazionale
Cat. 33/II

The Works

The beginnings: the Daedalic style in the West
If we observe the chronology of sculpture in Magna Graecia, it will immediately be evident that the Italiot plastic arts made their first appearance at a late date, especially if they are compared with the figured pottery. The small bronze and clay sculpture of the second half of the eighth century, which flourished in Greece at the time of the first colonial foundations, had no equivalent in the West. Three small horses have been found at Syracuse, Tarentum, and Locri: in all three cases they were brought from their respective metropolises at the time of foundation, or shortly thereafter. A small horse from Siris, engaging but clumsy, is more recent and does not reflect a particular style. It was only around the mid-seventh century that the figurines of terra-cotta of the type we now describe as "Daedalic" (with reference to the legendary sculptor Daedalus) began to multiply. The overall coherence of this style does not prevent us from discerning variations on the main theme, which is exemplified in Greece by the large marble statue dedicated by the Naxian Nikandre at Delos: it consists of a standing woman, her arms hanging by her sides, wearing a foldless tunic with a belt round her waist and, more often than not, a cape over her shoulders. There are also a number of examples of a Cretan variant, in which the figure stands in front of a small plaque, and wears a *polos*, a cylindrical headdress having a ritual function. A more common variant, from Metapontum and Siris, resembles, with its face and the horizontal waves of the hair (what is incorrectly referred to as a "layered wig"), various Corinthian sculptures and figurines. It would appear that the same molds were used throughout the so-called Achaean area. In a splendid example, two fragments of which have survived (one is from Francavilla, near Sybaris), the tunic is embellished with a rich figured decoration in relief that reproduces the embroidery of the cloth.

Terra-cotta reliefs
It is in this context that the terra-cotta reliefs should be viewed; above all, they include the simas or gutters that adorned the edges of roofs. The earliest of these pieces, from Siris, includes a winged quadriga identical to those that appear on Cycladic vases of the mid-seventh century. A large terra-cotta basin for lustral water – the Greek name for which is *perirrhanterion* – found at Incoronata near Metapontum (until about 625 B.C., a trading post belonging to Siris), is embellished with a rich relief decoration stamped with molds on three different registers. The lower one juxtaposes scenes and isolated figures based on

mythological or epic themes, while the other two repeat the same designs all round the basin: two hoplites in combat over a dead body, a somewhat banal motif, and a divine couple on a chariot drawn by winged horses. Although the source of inspiration is nearly always Corinth, the winged horses are Cycladic rather than Ionian. This basin – the category of which is attested above all by examples with painted decoration – may be related to the enigmatic objects of which there is a complete example from the *heraion* at the mouth of the Sele, and fragments from Croton and Sybaris: it is more likely that they are incense burners rather than oil-lamps, as has previously been suggested. Around the central stem, the basin is supported by four figures of women holding their hands to their breasts in an ancient oriental gesture of fertility: but the oriental goddesses, which were imitated in Crete, are nude, while these figures wear the usual tunic, and the faces are in the late seventh-century style.

Tarentum
From the outset the workshops at Tarentum were different from the others. Here, too, terra-cotta predominated, with statuettes and antefixes – the ornaments used to conceal the ends of the imbrices

Clay Daedalic statuette
of a *kourotrophos*
end 7th cent. B.C.
Trieste
Civici Musei di Storia ed Arte
Cat. 37

Marble headless Kore
from Tarentum
525-500 B.C.
Berlin, Staatliche Museen
zu Berlin
Preussischer Kulturbesitz
Antikensammlung
Cat. 76

Sculpture in Magna Graecia

Bronze statue of Zeus
found at Ugento
ca. 500 B.C.
Taranto, Museo Nazionale
Cat. 77

(curved roof-tiles) – that, right from the start, had the semicircular form they maintained at Tarentum until the end. The motif of the antefixes is a frontal view of a woman's face; the first examples have a narrow, triangular form, which, in the Peloponnese, can be dated to the first quarter of the seventh century – although, in this case, they are certainly much more recent. Dating from shortly before the end of the seventh century, a number of heads of large statuettes are very precise copies of Laconian models; in them, the whole face is structured to emphasize the expression, with particular prominence being given to the eyes; it is quite possible that the molds were imported. But there are antefixes that are contemporary with these that have nothing Laconian about them: from the seventh century onward there exists, in fact, the vexed problem of the extent to which the mother city influenced the plastic arts in Tarentum.

The sixth century: the larger works of sculpture
To date, but one example of the marble *kouros* – that is, the most typical product of the Archaic sculpture of Mainland Greece – has come to light in Magna Graecia (at Metapontum), in marked contrast to Sicily. Also with regard to the second Archaic type, the *kore*, the only one in marble is the unfinished example found at Tarentum. The marble is Parian, and the work was certainly rough-hewn at Paros and then finished at Tarentum: this was standard practice in order to reduce the weight for transport and avoid the risk of damage to the finished work in transit. But was the sculptor Parian or western? The originality of the statue, the way the figure is dressed, and its similarity to a bronze statuette – originally a mirror handle – found at Satyrion, indicate that it may be the work of a Tarentine sculptor who went to Paros. However, the larger works of Archaic sculpture in the round in Magna Graecia that have so far been discovered are principally in bronze and, above all – as in Sicily – terra-cotta. The bronze Zeus found in a hiding place at Ugento, a Iapygian settlement, was placed on the top of a column, the limestone capital of which was also hidden on the same occasion. The abacus of the capital is adorned with rosettes that are more carefully executed on the main side: this decoration is Messapian, based on models of the Ionian Islands, demonstrating that it was made on the spot. But the statue is entirely Greek, as has been shown by a careful analysis that has revealed elements of Laconian origin, especially in the head, while the posture resembles that of Corinthian sculpture: it is an excellent example of the eclecticism of the Italiot works. That the sculptor is of Tarentine origin is suggested, in the first place, by the position of Ugento; but it has been proved without a shadow of doubt by a splendid terra-cotta head from Tarentum of approximately the same size, with a profile and structure that are identical. Now, the head from Tarentum lacks the representation of the hair, which is indeed strange. However, for this very reason, it has the appearance that the wax model of the bronze might have had before it was completed. Technically speaking, there is no difference between the modeling of clay and that of wax, and, in practice, the use of the two materials was often linked. With regard to terra-cotta, reference will be made first of all to a large fragment of a statue of a woman from Metapontum that has yet to be studied in detail. A clean break seems to suggest that it formed part of a group, possibly a pediment. It is in a poor state and the painted decoration has partially disappeared. It is, however, clear that it may be linked to the Archaic *korai* from the Athenian Acropolis: over the tunic, the folds of the *himation* descend in the characteristic wide flat zigzags; but the volumes are generally more massive. At Paestum many terra-cotta works are, as far as the style is concerned, different from both the series of metopes and different from each other. A standing male figure, wrapped in a cloak, unfortunately headless, displays features in common with statues in Samos, but it is distinguished from them by its slenderness. In this respect, a seated Zeus, possibly a cult statue, is surprising because its somewhat slender structure brings to mind Corinthian workmanship and its face either Corinthian or Athenians statues.

These observations, which take apart the works in an attempt to explain their genesis, should not cause us to forget their internal coherence. They indicate the variety of the solutions that were found: like the marble Siceliot *kouroi*, each of which is different from the other, the larger Italiot sculptures in the round appear today to be the result – often of excellent quality – of isolated commissions for which the sculptors, on each occasion, created a new, often original, balance between their own artistic skills and their temperaments. This impression is, perhaps, at least partially due to the limited number of works that have survived: the minor arts offer a more coherent picture.

The Laconian influence
Leaving aside pottery, which is very plentiful in Sicily, the clearest evidence of Laconian imports to the West is constituted by numerous bronze vases. Their diffusion is very striking, right from Gela to Atena Lucana, in the Vallo di Diano. But the heads of some terra-cottas and those that adorn the rims of some

Zeus enthroned
clay statue from
the urban sanctuary of Poseidonia
530-520 B.C.
Paestum
Museo Archeologico Nazionale
Cat. 65

Sculpture in Magna Graecia

Detail of the relief decoration
of a bronze *hydria*
6th cent. B.C.
Pesaro
Museo Archeologico Oliveriano

opposite
The *Grächwil Hydria*
ca. 570 B.C.
Berna
Bernisches Historisches Museum
Cat. 119

clay vases from Locri are casts taken from them. Thus, in Magna Graecia as a whole, there was more or less direct copying of Laconian forms. There are examples at Tarentum, with a bronze *peplophoros* and a number of terra-cottas, while a tripod embellished with cows and protomes of horses resembling Spartan bronzes has been found at Metapontum. A tripod discovered in a tomb at Trebeniste, in Illyria, was made by the same workshop as the one from Metapontum: at Trebeniste there are as many bronze vases from Magna Graecia as there are from the Peloponnese, and the two tripods are Italiot. The type of the horse protome, with the mane forming a crescent made up of parallel waves, narrow cheeks and a wide mouth, was copied by the sculptor of the horseman from Grumentum.

Two works have been attributed to Tarentum because they display Laconian influence. One is a bronze *hydria* found many years ago in a tomb at Grächwil, near Bern. The usual vertical handle has been replaced by a non-functional *ajouré* relief representing a goddess holding two hares and surrounded by other animals – four lions, two snakes, and an eagle. This "lady of the animals" resembles Laconian ivories and her face is Laconian in style; it was probably executed about the first quarter of the sixth century. A number of imitations – clearly not Greek – of these reliefs serving as handles are known; they have a similar design, but depict a hoplite between two horses, and were found in Picenum and the Bologna area, which indicates the route probably taken by the Grächwil *hydria*.

Another find in Laconian style with Picene associations was made in a Celtic tomb dating from the later part of the early Iron Age at Grafenbühl, a site near Ludwigsburg. It consists of two small sphinxes in a style similar to Daedalic, one in ivory and the other in bone, that were appliqués for furniture; the faces

Sculpture in Magna Graecia

Bronze tripod decorated
with heads and figures of animals
from Metapontum
mid-6th cent. B.C.
Berlin, Staatliche Museen
zu Berlin
Preussischer Kulturbesitz
Antikensammlung
Cat. 122

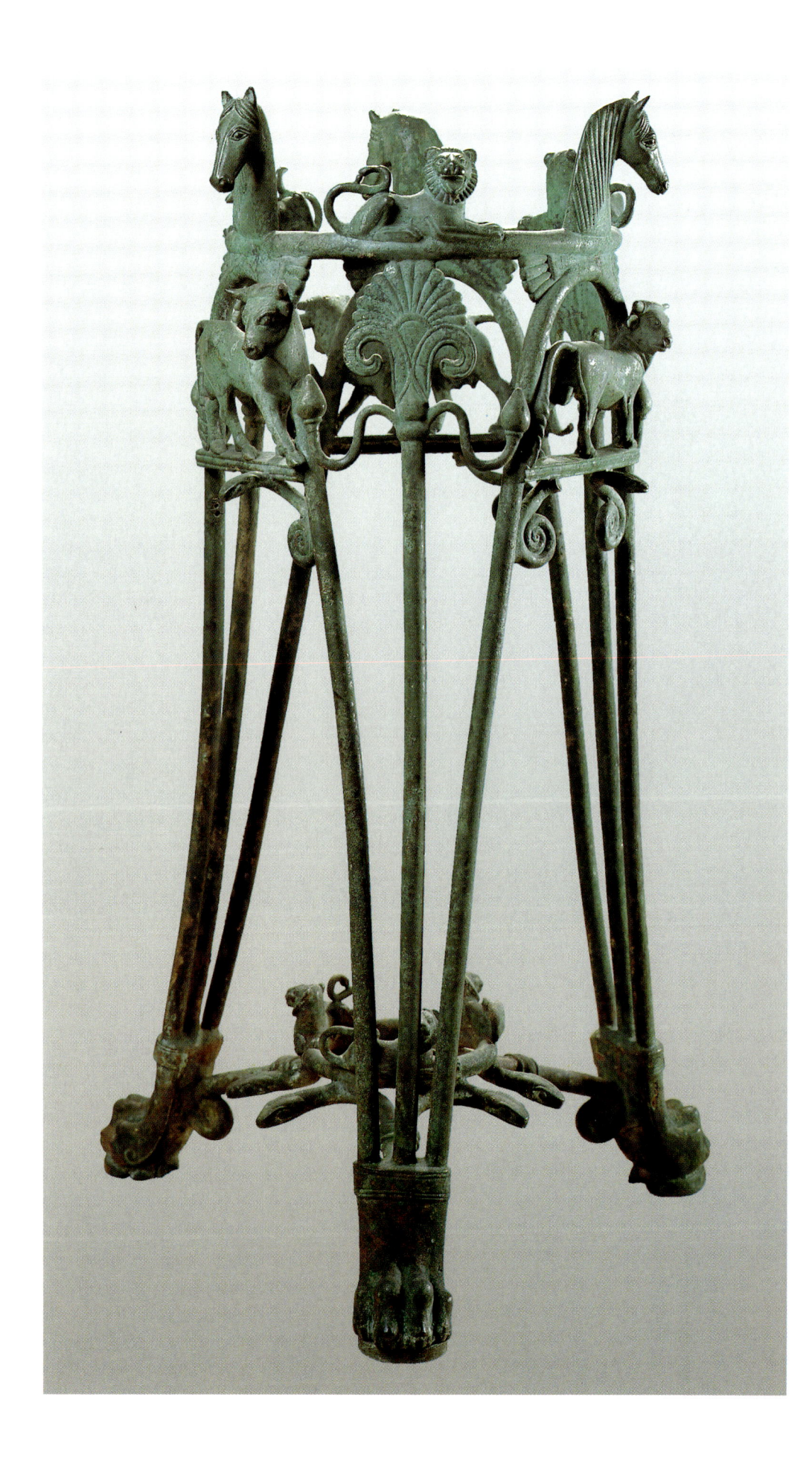

Bone sphinx
with amber face
from the princely tomb
di Grafenbühl
end 7th cent. B.C.
Stuttgart, Württembergisches
Landesmuseum

are made of amber. The only stylistic and technical parallel is provided by two ivory statuettes with amber faces found in a rich tomb at Belmonte Piceno, representing a winged goddess flanked by two acolytes. They are exactly the same size as the sphinxes (slightly less than 5 cm in height); they are not appliqués, but are very flat. Amber was often carved in southern Italy, but no figured amber has been found in any Greek site. In short, since the pseudo-handle of the Grächwil *hydra* is in marked contrast to the Greek types, it is probable that both the *hydria* and the sphinxes were made in Picenum. Nevertheless, they are in Laconian style, and it cannot be ruled out that their makers were Greeks, possibly Tarentines.

The Ionic influence
The influence of the Ionic forms is much stronger, more continuous, and more varied: the origin of many colonies must certainly have played an important role in this respect. But, in the early Archaic period, the most important factor was the activity of the seafarers of Rhodes and Samos, attested not only by the number of the imports, but also by the fact that the Ionic temple at Syracuse appears to have been built by Samians, who were also present at Gravisca, the harbor of Tarquinia. Numerous terra-cottas at Siris and Sybaris were made from molds of Samian terra-cottas. Historical research of the last few decades has focused on the activity of the Phocaeans in the Tyrrhenian Sea, both before and after the destruction of Phocaea by the Persians around 540 B.C. But a number of scholars have observed that, together with this evidence of a sizable Samian presence, there are no traces of Phocaean sculpture: it is doubtful, for instance, whether the foundation of Velia influenced the sculptors of the *heraion* at the mouth of the Sele, who, since before 540, had begun to work in a style deriving from East Greek models.
Ionian sculpture varied in Mainland Greece itself. At first, in Magna Graecia, there were forms that came from Ionia proper. The best examples are the metopes of the first temple of the Sele *heraion*; their coarseness should not be overemphasized because the very soft sandstone with which they are made has eroded considerably and many of the details, especially the drapery, have been effaced. There are close parallels for the profiles of the faces, which differ slightly from each other, in the pottery of East Greece, and the proportions of the stocky bodies are characteristic of the same region. This was the first great Italiot building project with architectural sculpture, and the artists – who were local – carved this stone that was so easy to work in a somewhat rough manner. This is clearly visible in the unfinished metopes in which the outlines and the various superimposed planes have already been sculpted: they were not seeking to represent the plump forms of their models in detail. We shall probably never know whether these works date to just before or just after 550 B.C. – that is, the fall of Siris, which was where this style probably originated. A little later Cycladic dress appears in the Italiot statuettes in bronze and terra-cotta; in the same period this was also represented on the Athenian Acropolis, with the *himation* draped across the tunic. The marble *kore* of Tarentum – especially if we accept the explanation for its incompletion given above – clearly indicates how the new styles may have arrived, accompanying, as it were,

Metope with figure riding a tortoise
from the *Heraion* at the mouth
of the Sele River
560-550 B.C.
Paestum
Museo Archeologico Nazionale

Metope with a *choros* of girls
from the *Heraion* at the mouth
of the Sele River
510-500 B.C.
Paestum
Museo Archeologico Nazionale
Cat. 69

the Parian marble. But, in this series of works, the western artists were more concerned with the decorative effects – which were often very refined – of the drapery than the structure of the body that it covers. A number of reliefs datable to the late sixth century were executed in this style: one, in terra-cotta, from Rhegium, and the metopes of the "dancers" from the second temple of the Sele *heraion*. And it is the same style that, in the second quarter of the fifth century, gave birth to the *Ludovisi Throne,* to which reference will be made later. Correct illumination of these works, which were made to be seen in sunlight, reveals the virtuosity of their very low relief. The conception of the relief, and the relationship between the figures and the background, are similar to those that may be observed in the reliefs of the "passage of the *theoroi*" in Thasos: as has so often been said, this style has an "international" aspect to it.

Terra-cottas in the Corinthian style
A series of terra-cotta figurines of the third quarter of the sixth century, found throughout the "Achaean" area, must be placed in a category of its own. It appears that the same molds were used in different sanctuaries, since only the added attributes give the offering a personal touch: the greatest numbers of jewels and animals were added to the figurines from San Biagio, in the territory of Metapontum. The narrower, clearly delineated faces and the characteristic arrangement of the hair, with vertical locks above the forehead, closely resemble Corinthian forms; these figures still wear the foldless *peplos*. With the exception of some aspects of the seated Zeus of Paestum, this style is not found elsewhere in Magna Graecia, although it is more widespread in Sicily.

Paestum and Locri: two contrasting situations
As P. Zancani Montuoro has pointed out, the only metope found in the city of Paestum – in reality, in the suburban sanctuary of Santa Venera – which represents Europa on the bull's back, constitutes the link between the two temples of the *heraion* by the Sele River, and is sufficient to demonstrate the continuity of the local workshops in a style that evolved in a coherent manner. It may also be related to a number of metopes of a later third series representing hoplites. There is another form of this Ionian sculpture in a corner of a roof in terra-cotta with a winged figure at the top: the same structure is also found at Didyma. But these cornices crowded with figures are found in Etruria as well, where the style of the sculpture is also Ionian. As regards the example from Paestum, the immediate origin of the type is uncertain. On the other hand, the last works in Ionian style, three marble heads of acroliths, at least one of which is well preserved, do not display any Etruscan influence, and are typical of the forms that the nascent Severe style was assuming in Magna Graecia. But the other works in Paestum are in a different style: a large terra-cotta statuette of a standing young man, wearing a cloak, recalls, as far as the type is concerned, the statues of Samos and Miletus, but its narrow torso is in contrast to the Samian bronzes, which widen out from the bottom upward. In a seated Zeus – also in terra-cotta – that may be a cult statue, there is the spare structure with strongly marked lines typical of Corinthian sculpture. Thus, at Paestum, as well as the makers of the metopes, there were sculptors whose origins and styles were extremely varied.
At Locri and in its territory – above all, at Medma – the coherence and continuity of the output are, in certain clearly defined series, much more evident: the terra-cotta votive reliefs from the sanctuary of Persephone at the foot of the Mannella hill, the terra-cotta busts from Medma, and some bronze stat-

uettes, nearly all of which are mirror handles. It is probably necessary to add here the *Ludovisi Throne*, which is the side of an altar, the only stylistic plastic parallels for which are the most attractive, and most Ionian, of the votive reliefs. In these three series – which have frequently been reproduced and commented on, but never seriously studied – it is possible to see how late Archaic evolved into the mature Severe style. With the exception of a number of pieces, they begin fairly late compared with the other Italiot output – shortly before the end of the sixth century – and they continue until the middle of the following century. The last series of objects offered in the sanctuaries of Locri, the mask protomes in terra-cotta, has been studied in detail. It is fairly difficult to link it to the other three series; it is, however, much further than, for instance, the protomes of Gela from those of Ionia, which are the most numerous in the whole Greek world; some of them display faces that are almost square, similar to those of the more recent Locrian bronzes.

Above all, it is for chronological reasons that the *peplophoros* type – that of the second quarter of the fifth century – is predominant at Locri in both the votive reliefs and the mirror handles; some, in the bronzes, are comparable to the most splendid examples from the north-eastern Peloponnese. In these statuettes, as in the more recent votive reliefs and the finest busts from Medma, the evolution of the style sometimes produces faces and drapery that are in marked contrast to the original Ionicism. The faces, in particular, are almost square and forcefully delineated. It has been observed that many bronzes from the Athenian Acropolis have faces that are similar to those in Locri, and it has been conjectured that they were Locrian offerings to Athens. Probably this hypothesis is totally unfounded: if there had been an influence, it would have been in the opposite direction, from Mainland Greece toward Locri, and the Severe style, with all its variants, was consistent in its character throughout the Greek world. On the other hand, the most advanced votive reliefs display the same predilection that the older ones had for rendering the drapery in a way that expands and, in a sense, flattens it. This makes these reliefs similar to the previous ones and – quite apart from the evolution of the forms – works such as the metopes of the second temple of the Sele *heraion*. The *Ludovisi Throne* is the result of the encounter of Ionicism of the mature Archaic period with a variant of the Severe style that appears to harmonize with it; one of Aphrodite's two maidservants on the principal face wears a tunic, the other a *peplos*. In the mirror handles with male figures, a peculiarity of Locri, the surface is always rendered in way that favors soft transitions, to the detriment of the representation of the musculature: in other words, the artist is interested in the play of light on the sur-

Pinax with the rape of Persephone
from the Sanctuary of Persephone
at Mannella
first half 5th cent. B.C.
Reggio Calabria, Museo Nazionale
Cat. 166/I

The *Ludovisi Throne*
front
ca. 460-450 B.C.
Roma,
Museo Nazionale Romano
Cat. 189

Sculpture in Magna Graecia

Bronze mirror with an ephebe
wearing a cloak for a handle
ca. mid-5th cent. B.C.
Reggio Calabria, Museo Nazionale
Cat. 161/II

Bronze mirror
with openwork handle
first half 4th cent. B.C.
Reggio Calabria, Museo Nazionale
Cat. 162

Marble head of a woman
from Tarentum
ca. 480 B.C.
Boston, Museum of Fine Arts

faces. Only in some of the busts from Medma is the construction nearly as solid as it is in the heads from the Peloponnese. In short, we are faced here with works of a unified school that lasted for three quarters of a century; as I have stated above, this is the only case in which this unity appears in the West.

Marbles in the Severe style
There is a tendency to date very disparate works to the second quarter of the fifth century: the importation of Greek marble was more frequent than in the preceding period, but it still regarded isolated works that should be examined individually, especially because the series of works which I have just discussed rarely offer sufficient opportunities. The famous seated goddess, which is now in Berlin, but certainly comes from Tarentum, must have been a cult statue, and this partially explains its rigidity. Faced with an unusual commission, the sculptor, either through timidity or in order to confer greater solemnity on the image, maintained Archaic forms in a number of details: the dress – the goddess wears a *himation* over a tunic – and also the locks of hair that descend to her breast, emphasizing its volumes. It is interesting to compare the diagonal folds of the drapery forming even zigzags with those of the last *korai* from the Athenian Acropolis, which were made thirty or forty years previously: this similarity is one reason why such works have been – and, unfortunately, often still are – described as the fruit of a *retardataire* provincial style. But, what in Athens shows the desire, not yet fully realized, to temper outmoded formulas, here manifests the deliberate will to maintain them, at least as far as the most obvious details are concerned: this is clearly shown by the choice of the dress, which is not, strictly speaking, a stylistic feature.

In other works, the Italiot sculptors produced variants of the Severe style – which was truly international – whether they were a woman's head from Metapontum, the present state of which allows us to appreciate, above all, the splendid hair raised above the neck, or three heads of acroliths, the first in the Ludovisi collection, the second in the Vatican Museums, and the third, made after the middle of the century, from the Temple of Apollo at Cirò. The first two are wholly frontal; as far as the head from Cirò is concerned, if it is photographed from the correct angle with good lighting, it is still possible to appreciate the solid, yet nuanced, structure, while the complex movements of the surfaces and the facial features show that it was turned and that the sculptor was careful to represent the foreshortening that resulted from this.

Enthroned goddess
statue from Tarentum
460 B.C.
Berlin, Staatliche Museen
zu Berlin Preussischer
Kulturbesitz Antikensammlung
Cat. 146

Head of Apollo
from the Temple of Apollo
at Cirò
440-430 B.C.
Reggio Calabria, Museo Nazionale
Cat. 191

Head of a woman
from Metapontum
470-460 B.C.
Metaponto
Museo Archeologico Nazionale
Cat. 149

450–350 B.C.: the Classical parenthesis
I have already mentioned that the forms of the early Classical period were not as successful in the West as those of the Severe style, although it is evident that sculpture was still being produced and terra-cottas offered. However, in Mainland Greece the output of bronze statuettes declined considerably up to the beginning of the Hellenistic period. The most recent marble work from Metapontum, the head of a young man, dates from the middle of the century. A slightly more recent head of Athena in Tarentum is remarkable for the vigorous modeling of the musculature and, above all, for its dreamy expression, which is due to the contrast between its small eyes and its large mouth with slightly drooping corners. The most ambitious works that have survived from the second half of the fifth century are *akroteria* from Locri representing the Dioscuri, who were reputed to have helped the Locrians in the battle of the Sagras. Two symmetrical groups in marble, which are more likely to be *akroteria* than the corners of a pediment, are supported by Tritons with raised arms: the Dioscuri, since they were seamen's gods, had marine associations. The two young men are shown as they are about to leap down from their horses. Viewed at eye level in the museum at Reggio Calabria, the instability of the postures, which have an almost photographic quality about them, is strikingly evident. But the groups were intended to be seen from below, and this explains why the sculptor chose the exact moment when the horsemen are about to touch the ground: the figures thus stood out much better. The hypothesis that the two groups were executed after the completion of the Parthenon is quite plausible. The rounded forms, which are not just the result of the wearing away of the surfaces, distinguish these works from what were probably their Attic models. A third group, in terra-cotta, in which a sphinx with an imposing bosom supports the hooves of a horse, is not nearly so well balanced: the horseman is heavy, while the horse's slender head and neck contrast

sharply with the rest of its body. All these works, although they are not easy to classify, are originals, and were probably made by western sculptors. By contrast, despite their skillful execution, many heads of women in marble from Tarentum, datable to the first half of the fourth century, are somewhat lifeless. They are examples of the models that must have been copied by the coroplasts who, from Tarentum to Paestum, including Heraclea (modern Policoro), produced vast quantities of terra-cotta busts.

It is difficult to understand why, for a long time, the finest bronze statuette, a squatting satyr from Armento, was considered to be Etruscan. It can be safely attributed to the second half of the fourth century on account of its complex posture, although the modeling of the musculature is still classical, as in the case of a woman's face from Rossano di Vaglio. But, as with the terra-cottas, it is difficult to identify specifically Italiot features. A small satyr from Metapontum, which is less ambitious than the one from Armento and was made shortly afterward, repeats the rotation of the torso; its head bears a slight resemblance to that of the bronze Marsyas from Paestum. The latter sculpture, which is particularly famous, has been variously dated on the basis of its supposed links with the Marsyas of the Roman Forum. Using very convincing arguments, a recent study proposed that it should be dated to the fourth century; it demonstrated that the proportions and the modeling of this statuette are intentionally unclassical because the figure portrayed was intended to be the personification of savagery. And, in fact, it displays a high degree of technical skill. But if the work really was, at that date, the work of a Greek sculptor, it would be quite unique, because, in the fourth century, it is only in the minor arts, such as terra-cottas and pottery, that these deformities are represented.

Toreutics

Although, as has already been mentioned, stone and bronze sculpture in the round was virtually non-existent in the Hellenistic period in Magna Graecia, the situation regarding toreutics was quite the contrary. While jewelry is outside the scope of this essay, decorative metalwork in relief, a branch of the plastic arts, is within it: it was produced in various series from the fourth century onward. Magna Graecia – chiefly Tarentum – played a major role in this output, although numerous questions have yet to be answered. A certain number of works of the fourth century, and sometimes of the third, are clearly Italiot, such as the shoulder straps from Siris, or the cheek-guards from Palestrina, which certainly came from Magna Graecia. The themes, the technique, and the style of these pieces were all indistinguishable from those of contemporary reliefs made in Mainland Greece, where, however, this technique was used principally for mirror-covers. A later disc of gilded silver depicting a nereid from Canosa, which decorated the cover of a *pyxis*, could have been a mirror-cover. It is an example of the silverware that, in the third century, was found in Tarentum and Alexandria; there was, in fact, trade between the two cities, the nature of which, despite recent studies, has not been fully clarified. A number of pointed helmets, in the form of a *pilos*, are decorated, especially at Tarentum, with repoussé reliefs in bronze; imitations made in terra-cotta also exist. Metal vessels with figured decoration raise more difficult problems, especially after recent excavations have unearthed the very rich contents of the Macedonian tombs of the mid-fourth century. The problem that existed before this discovery was that of distinguishing – with regard to the vessels of the Vesuvian cities – between those that were fourth-century Apulian or Campanian and those that were copies, since it is certain that in the half century, or century, before 79 A.D. the Campanian bronze workers had plenty of opportunities to see the fourth-century objects, of which they would often make faithful copies. A *situla* with repoussé decoration, purchased in Naples and now in Boston, is, however, one of the examples that may certainly be attributed to the fourth century. But a new problem has arisen with regard to the masterpiece of Macedonian toreutics: the large volute krater decorated with Dionysian themes that was discovered in a tomb at Derveni, near Salonica. The principal scene on this, depicting Dionysus and Ariadne surrounded by Maenads and Sileni, seems to be a more exuberant version of the frieze adorning the Boston *situla*. The form – overall and in the details – and the secondary elements of the decoration are the same that appear toward the middle of the fourth century in the large Apulian pottery kraters, which were made before the Derveni krater. The latter was found in a tomb of the late fourth century, and it appears that it cannot be attributed to a much earlier date. It will only be possible to date it more precisely when all the bronze vessels found at the site have been studied in detail. Numerous features of the decoration of the krater are, in fact, not Italiot, especially the types of the faces in the main scene, the forerunners of which were on mirror covers that are probably Corinthian. The form, however, is of Italiot origin: it clearly demonstrates that, among the artists and craftsmen with whom Philip II had surrounded himself in order to create an artistic milieu at court – which was destined to become specifically Macedonian – there were Apulians, and, probably, metal workers. And, for the moment, this is all that we know.

Marble head of Athena
first half 5th cent. B.C.
Taranto, Museo Nazionale
Cat. 192

Bronze statue of a satyr
from Armento
second half 4 th cent. B.C.
Munich, Staatlichen
Antikensammlungen
und Glyptothek München
Cat. 267

The reliefs from Tarentum
Aside from the terra-cotta reliefs, which seem to reflect the general development of Hellenistic art – until 209 B.C. at least – the most interesting series is the one comprising the limestone funerary reliefs from Tarentum. These are sufficiently numerous for us to be able to see their evolution, and many of them are associated with grave goods that allow them to be dated. They begin in the first half of the fourth century with friezes representing various subjects: battle scenes, a very commonplace theme; and at one time, so it seems, personages of the Underworld, which recall the subject-matter of pottery. Although it has been suggested that the most classical relief – of exceptional quality compared to what was generally a stereotyped output – represents Orestes and Electra before Agamemnon's tomb, because of the fragmentary state of the work, it is not possible to check this hypothesis. In fact, it is as close to the reliefs of Mainland Greece as are some funerary *stelai* of the same period: Orestes seems to have been sculpted by a faithful imitator of Scopas. On a frieze at Lecce, a horse rears like the one in the painting of Philip II's tomb, or in the mosaic of the battle of Issus found in the House of the Faun at Pompeii: the uniform character of the art of the fourth century and the fact that artists traveled extensively tended to eliminate regional differences.

In the third century, funerary monuments were generally embellished with a Doric frieze, so that the figured scenes were arranged in metopes. These often represent the deceased as a charging horseman who strikes his enemy to the ground with fervor and expressive power that is not found in the Aegean world

Limestone relief metope
2nd cent. B.C.
Taranto, Museo Nazionale
Cat. 333

before the friezes of the Great Altar of Zeus at Pergamum in the first half of the second century. Those who are surprised by this commit the same error that has already been made with regard to the fourth century: the West never knew the period – often described as the "sober style" – that, in third-century Greece, marked a reaction against the taste for movement, the use of space, and expressiveness that was typical of Lysippus and his pupils. One of these horsemen is so close to what is generally considered to be the equestrian statue of Alexander in the group Lysippus made after the battle of the Granicus that some believe it to portray Alexander. Although this is highly unlikely, the work shows that Lysippus' style continued to hold sway in Tarentum, while it had been forgotten in Athens, and did not have any followers either in Alexandria or, initially, in Pergamum in the groups of the Galatians. The rather odd composition of some of the metopes is due to the fact that only isolated examples have survived. Thus, frequently two superimposed figures run toward the exterior of the metope field, each of them to meet an adversary from whom they are separated by the triglyph; even stranger is the metope in which two young women flee in opposite directions from a danger that is not represented. Many figures are difficult to identify. In one case, it is more likely that they are Orientals with Persian crowns than Gauls, whose breeches they seem to be wearing; in Tarentum it is, therefore, a motif derived from works produced in the eastern half of the Mediterranean. But these unpretentious works are all marked by a taste for movement that is frequently unstable. Already perceptible in the friezes of the early fourth century, it becomes strikingly evident in those with the couples of figures fleeing toward the edges, because of the contrast between their diverging oblique lines. In conclusion, it is worth repeating what I have already observed with regard to the Archaic sculpture: there seems to be continuity between the Archaic works – in which the rendering of movement and action prevails over the concern for a balanced structure – and these reliefs. Apparently the work of skilled craftsmen rather than artists, in them the ardor of the warriors or fugitives results in curious, invariably centrifugal compositions.

Bibliography
As to the attitude of modern scholars toward the art of the Greek western world, the deepest analysis is by:
S. SETTIS, in *Atti del XXVIII Convegno di Taranto*, 1989, pp. 135-176.
As far as records are concerned, three major works illustrate the three stages of our knowledge of Italiot sculpture:
U. JANTZEN, 1937; E. LANGLOTZ, 1963; P. ORLANDINI, in *Megale Hellas*, 1983, pp. 3005-3554.
Besides, the whole series of Taranto's conferences *Atti*.

Giovanni Rizza

Siceliot Sculpture in the Archaic Period

By Greek tradition, the earliest sculptures known on the island of Sicily were the work of Daedalus: the *Chronicle of Lindos* (ca. 21–28) recalls a krater with embossed decoration which Phalaris of Acragas had dedicated at the sanctuary of Athena Lindia at Rhodes; the decorations featured representations of the Gigantomachy and of Kronos swallowing his children, and an inscription attested that Daedalus made it for King Cocalus. According to Pausanias (VIII. 46. 2) a statue crafted by Daedalus was kept at Gela; it had been brought by Antiphemus, the city's founder, after the occupation and sack of the Sican town of Omphake. Diodorus Siculus (IV. 78) recalls a golden honeycomb, strikingly lifelike, which Daedalus had made for the temple of Aphrodite at Eryx.

The convergence of memories of the south-central area of Sicily, which Greek tradition tells us was occupied by Sican tribes, has been regularly confirmed by archaeological finds, and seems to be a reflection of very early trading between Sicily and the Aegean world in a period long before the onset of colonization. The memory of King Cocalus, with whom Antiochus of Syracuse began his history of Sicily, and the tradition of a Cretan expedition to Sicily empowered by Minos, seem to concur in identifying the origin and area of the spread of these Aegean cultural influences, whose impact continued unabated throughout the Sican milieu through to recorded history, with formal tendencies that differed from those that were introduced in the course of Greek colonization drive in the eighth century B.C.

Two golden cups with embossed decoration and a series of incised oxen, together with two gold rings respectively representing a wolf and a cow suckling a calf, all disclosed at Sant'Angelo Muxaro (in today's Agrigento district), illustrate this artistic style which, even through to the seventh and sixth cen-

Gold embossed cup
with six lumbering oxen
from Sant'Angelo Muxaro
7th cent. B.C.
London, British Museum
Department of Greek
and Roman Antiquities

Siceliot Sculpture in the Archaic Period

turies B.C., continued to develop in peripheral areas, blending the Aegeo-Mycenaean tradition with forms and tendencies of a more local nature. The phenomenon is not limited to the figurative arts, but covers most of craft production and funeral architecture, which even through the seventh and sixth centuries continued to manifest itself in the Platani Valley in *tholos* tombs in true Mycenaean style.

While on Sican territory the somewhat meager heritage of Aegean tradition petered out, the influx of Greek colonists heralded a new chapter in the history of figurative arts by introducing, between later eighth and early seventh century B.C., the Late Geometric forms and style, and the incipient Orientalizing style. Two bronze figurines in the Museo Archeologico Regionale at Syracuse are the earliest evidence we have of sculptural art: they belong to the period shortly after the foundation of the colony, and have been dated to toward the end of the eighth century B.C. The first is a small horse in Late Geometric style from the Fusco necropolis; the second a standing male figure holding his phallus in his right hand, while the left hand is outstretched.

The little horse was either imported from Mainland Greece, or was fashioned by an immigrant craftsman; the other figure, which comes from the Plemmyrium, is instead a somewhat coarse imitation attributable to a local workshop.

These two pieces pose an insistent problem regarding early Greek sculpture in Sicily, namely, the relations on the one hand with the workshops in homeland Greece and the various speculations about the importation of finished work, of artists, or of material finished off on site; on the other hand we have the problem of relations with the indigenous populations, as regards the interpretation of Greek models, and from the point of view of the incidence of formal tendencies of the local tribes on the artistic output of the Siceliot towns and cities.

At any event, from the eighth century on, that is, from the foundation of the first colonies, the artistic production in Sicily developed along the lines of Greek aesthetics, which remain the framework by which Siceliot production is appraised.

Through to the end of the seventh century B.C., in most colonial towns in Sicily, relations with the workshops of the Greek homeland showed a marked bias toward the colonists' place of origin. At Gela, for instance, which was founded by emigrants from Rhodes and Crete, a group of clay statuettes testify to direct trade relations with Rhodes, Crete, and generally with the eastern Greek bloc: a fine head from the acropolis is thought to be from Rhodes; three female figures wearing the *polos* and layered hair from the sanctuary of the Sola *praedium* betray the forms of Cretan sculptural work. A complex lamp of human *protoma* and alternating rams, and a *pinax* bearing a decoration similar to that of the lamp, seem to be of Geloan manufacture, but reflect, with a provincial flair, forms of Cycladic and Rhodian sculptural work.

Bronze statuette of a horse
from the Fusco necropolis
second half 8th cent. B.C.
Syracuse
Museo Archeologico Regionale

Bronze male figurine
his right hand on his penis
his left hand forward
from Plemmyrium
second half 8th century
Syracuse
Museo Archeologico Regionale

Clay female figurines
from the sanctuary
at Predio Sola
end 7th cent. B.C.
Gela
Museo Archeologico Regionale
Cat. 42/II

Bone plaque with female figure
from Megara Hyblaea
650-640 B.C.
Syracuse
Museo Archeologico Regionale
Cat. 38

Clay oil lamp with human
and rams' heads
from the sanctuary at Predio Sola
630-620 B.C.
Gela
Museo Archeologico Regionale
Cat. 42/I

Special mention should be made of the Mormino collection, also presumed to be from Gela. This is a female figure constructed in accordance with the formulas of Daedalic style: a standing figure, her arms lying at her sides, braided hair, and *polos*. However, the details themselves seem to stray from the model, as in the zigzag veil, the decoration of the dress, the arrangement of the braids, and certain traits of the face – together, these details create a surface movement that helps dissolve the formal masses with a decorative verve that can be traced to Ionian spheres, but which may yet be linked to certain linear tendencies of indigenous Sicilian art. The Daedalic sculptures of Megara Hyblaea reveal direct links with the area of Corinth. A locally made clay head dating to Middle Daedalic, together with another head of Late Daedalic, evince the characteristics of Corinthian sculpture, as does the highly elaborate bone plaque from Middle Daedalic, which was probably imported from Corinth.

Corinthian influences were strong in Selinus, a colony of Megara Hyblaea, where the earliest examples of Daedalic sculpture date to the last quarter of the seventh century B.C. A female torso with chiton and cape, her arms fixed at her sides seems to echo the style of Middle Daedalic, but the slant of the plaits and the depth of the face place it at the end of the seventh century.

Only in the late seventh and early sixth century B.C. do we find in Sicily a rich production of stone sculptures in Daedalic and sub-Daedalic style. One marble group consists of votive lamps from the Malophoros sanctuary at Selinus; each differs from the others in style and quality of material. The best-known is a semicircular lamp decorated at the upper section with a human *protoma* in Daedalic style; the contained plasticity of the volumes, the smoothed over service of the marble, and the prevalence for Linear style, have led scholars to identify the pieces as having been made on the island, locally. The other samples, however, betray different treatment, ranging from the exasperated modeling of another *protoma* constructed by contrast of volumes, and the style of the *protoma* that decorate the remaining lamps in which the incision and volumes are combined in a hybrid type of modeling. A more precise knowledge of the quality of marble – which is considerably different from one piece to the next – might make it possible to attribute some of these pieces to local manufacture.

The use of locally quarried limestone for other pieces enables us to make a definite attribution to workshops in the *poleis* of the island. An unfinished *kouros* head is most certainly of local production. Local workshops were also responsible for the creation of two sitting figures from Acrae (Greek Akrai), datable to late seventh–early sixth century B.C. One represents a male figure lacking both the head and lower half of the body; the details of the figure's clothing were scored lightly into the surface, and perhaps completed with pigment. The second torso is female; her hair is arranged in plaits reaching her shoulders, and with her right hand she is holding to her chest an object that is no longer recognizable.

Marble votive lamp
with human head
from the Sanctuary of
Malophoros at Selinus
625-600 B.C.
Palermo, Museo Archeologico
Regionale "A. Salinas"
Cat. 43

Limestone female head
from Laganello
beginning 6th cent. B.C.
Syracuse
Museo Archeologico Regionale
Cat. 72

The production of southeast Sicily includes a sub-Daedalic head in the Museo Archeologico Regionale, Syracuse, originally from Laganello at the mouth of the Cyane River. In its overall monumental effect the handling seems to be composite: there are traces of Cretan style in the mouth and eyes, in the full lips, the shape of the nose and the arched eyebrows; on the other hand, one detects a Corinthian style in the cubic structure of the head, and the flattening of the mask-like face. Slightly over life size, the head has been attributed to a temple statue.

Also slightly oversize is another head in very fine *tufa* unearthed in the *naos* of Temple E at Selinus; in this piece the front parts, which are badly worn, and the facial traits are no longer discernible, but the structure (which is heavy and flattened at the front) and the position of the wig indicate likenesses with the one from Laganello; the softer surface treatment and stylization of the hair into a continuous undulating pattern suggest a provenance outside the Cretan or Peloponnese milieu (to which the Syracusan head belongs), and betray a dominant Ionian influence.

Of decidedly eastern Greek origin is the *kouros* head now at Agrigento. This piece is badly eroded and lacking the lower section, but the handling of the hair in large beads is reminiscent of Samian and Rhodian craftsmanship from the early sixth century B.C. That same sphere is also responsible for another *kouros* head, this time in marble, now at Agrigento.

Manifest Ionian influences can be found in two small bronze *kouroi* in the Museo Archaeologico at Palermo. The first, probably from Selinus, is standing with his arms at his sides; the construction of the body, with its narrow waist and small torso, is still close to the forms prevalent in Late Daedalic or Cretan, though perhaps mediated with Ionian influences (probably Samian). More evident divergence from the Samian workshops' output can be seen in the other *kouros*, from Selinus; the figure is more stocky overall, and stands with the left foot forward, while the arms are slightly bent, as if to follow the movement of the leg. The torso is broad and solid, the anatomical details scored hard into the surface. Both figures date to the beginning of the sixth century B.C.

Another piece dating to the early sixth century B.C. is the bronze statuette of Athena armed with spear and shield, found at Himera; the flattened cylindrical body and the helmet with its high crest can be traced to a type found in Crete – as noted by Palladius of Gortyn – which was also common in the Peloponnese. The structure of the head, heavy and square, has comparisons with work from the Peloponnese workshops, whose style also served as a model for the construction of the face. The clothing, with its slight flare toward the base, emphasized by the zigzag design along the hem, seems to suggest Ionian influences, and more specifically those of Samos.

Overall, in the Siceliot colonies the sculpture of the seventh century B.C. remains tied to the teaching of the workshops in the respective founding cities, interleaved with local interpretations and mixes that result in a composite style which, in the course of the late seventh and early sixth centuries B.C., assumed elements of the taste and style of eastern Greece.

Such elements are not limited to sculpture, but can be identified in the field of architecture also. As early as the beginning of the sixth century B.C. the Ionian elements begin to blend with the Dorian ones, creating composite forms that became specific to the western Greek sphere. At the Temple of Apollo in Syracuse, which has a Doric order, the *opisthodomos* was done away with in favor of a line of columns in the portico in front of the *pronaos*; this broke the balance of the Doric order established by the architects of Mainland Greece, emphasizing the front prospect of the building. It is significant

Siceliot Sculpture in the Archaic Period

Bronze statuette of Athena
from Himera
beginning 6th cent. B.C.,
Palermo, Museo Archeologico
Regionale "A. Salinas"
Cat. 45/II

that, in his inscription on the steps of the *pronaos*, the architect declares himself to be of Cnidian origin. The same floor plan dominates the *olympieion* built at Syracuse twenty years or so later, and likewise Temple C at Selinus. The temple complexes at Selinus built in the second half of the sixth century B.C. continue with this emphasis on the front prospect, as suggested by the Ionian architecture. Taking its cue from here, it further developed the floor plan in an independent and highly particular way. The nearness of the columns of Temple F and the disposition of the columns of Temple G mark a breach with the architecture of the Greek homeland, though they conserve the capitals and the arrangement of the entablature. In the last quarter of the century the construction at Syracuse of a full-fledged Ionic temple on the Samian model attests to the presence of Ionian stonemasons in the city, most probably from Samos itself.

The separate development, with local and colonial accents, which from as early as the beginning of the sixth century B.C. can be noted in the floor plans of the temple constructions, has a parallel in the importance accorded coroplastic decoration on temples, even when in Greece itself the clay superfetations were replaced first by limestone and then marble. The terra-cotta cladding, created originally to protect the wooden framework, began to take on a figurative role; such is the case with the terminal tiles (created to cover the central roof beam), which take on the form of horse and rider, serving as an *akroterion*. An example from Camerina, dating to the earlier sixth century B.C. shows how the horse and rider are perfectly adapted to the architectural form, giving rise to an unusual typology that is characteristic of temple decoration in Sicily.

Occupying the field of the main tympanum there must have been large Gorgon masks, like those found amid the ruins on Sicilian temple sites. A clay slab from the *temenos* of the Temple of Athena at

Terra-cotta face
of a sphinx from the area
of the Ionian temple
560-550 B.C.
Syracuse
Museo Archeologico Regionale
Cat. 57

Clay head
from Acragas
ca. 550-530 B.C.
Agrigento
Museo Archeologico Regionale
Cat. 62

Siceliot Sculpture in the Archaic Period

Clay plaque with a Gorgon
from the *temenos*
of the Athenaion of Syracuse
570-550 B.C.
Syracuse
Museo Archeologico Regionale
Cat. 56

Syracuse presents the full figure of the Gorgon in the conventional flying position, with Pegasus below the right arm and Chrysaor (now lost) under the left.

A marked use of polychromy – with a prevalence of red and black – can be noted on the examples mentioned above, together with some heads (perhaps sphinxes), which must have served as *akroteria*. Two of these are from Syracuse, respectively from the Ionic temple and the *temenos* of the Temple of Athena, and date to the first half of the sixth century B.C.; a third, from Acragas, seems to have been set in place in around 550 B.C., given its analogies with the *kouroi* of the Tenea group.

Numerous fragments of metope reliefs datable to between 560 and 550 B.C. have been unearthed at Himera near Temple B; they are mutilated and poorly legible, but the presence of such names as Heracles and Eurysthaeus on two of these suggest that they bore scenes of the Labors of Heracles.

As with the clay modeling, local workshops seem to have been responsible for a substantial quantity of reliefs at Selinus in limestone in the earlier sixth century B.C. The oldest group consists of six metopes, datable to the third decade of the century, originally from the defensive walls of the acropolis where they were reused as building material; three of them are decorated on the top with a Ionic style *kymation* with *ovuli*; the others are framed by simple moldings that serve as a frame. The average dimensions are seventy by eighty centimeters.

Limestone metope
with the Delphic triad
Apollo, Latona, Artemis
from Selinus
mid-6th cent. B.C.
Palermo, Museo Archeologico
Regionale "A. Salinas"

Limestone metope
with winged sphinx
from Selinus
mid-6th cent. B.C.
Palermo, Museo Archeologico
Regionale "A. Salinas"

Limestone metope
with Europa riding the bull
from Selinus
mid-6th cent. B.C.
Palermo, Museo Archeologico
Regionale "A. Salinas"
Cat. 73

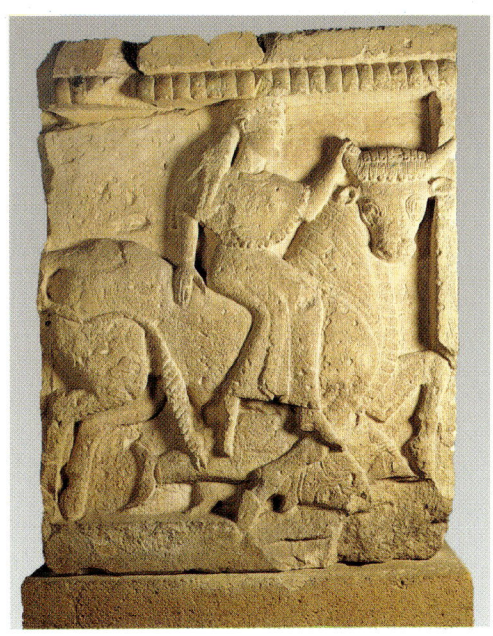

The three *kymation* metopes are reasonably similar to suggest that they belonged to the same architectural frieze. Respectively they represent the Delphic triad, a sphinx, and Europa astride the bull. The composition is characterized by a certain degree of cramming such that the figures barely fit in the field; Apollo, Europa, and the sphinx (with the tips of her wings) stretch from the very top edge of the metope, and almost spill out onto the border; in the Europa metope the horn, the left ear, and the lower right hoof of the bull break out of the field and cut into the frame. From the point of view of composition, all three metopes convey great motion, particularly as regards the Europa figure, but likewise discernible in the sphinx and triad metopes, whose composition seems to be spurred by the winged boots of Apollo and by the attributes of the three deities. The figures of the bull and the sphinx seem to suggest metal models; of special note is the emphasis on the outlines, which have been slightly endorsed to make the figures stand out from the ground; the gentle rounding of the margins of the figures gives the surface a softness reminiscent of Samian sculpture from the Archaic period.

The fourth metope, bearing the figure of Heracles(?) wrestling with a bull, was found in association with the others, but differs in the greater width of the setback and the lack of a frame round the other three sides; it has been noted that the tail of the bull resembles that in the Europa metope, though the figures themselves, almost entirely fashioned with the chisel, are too badly worn to allow a more critical reading.

The remaining two metopes come from a different section of the defensive wall of the acropolis. In the first, featuring Demeter, Kore, and Hecate, the position of the three standing figures has analogies with the metope of the three Delphic figures, but the difference can be seen in the greater isolation of the individual figures and of the group in the field of the metope; the upper offset is broadly chiseled, but there is nothing to suggest that it bore a *kymation* like the Delphic one, which therefore belongs to a different type. Considering the architectural elements, to yet another separate series belong the other metope, which is finished off at the base and top by two large offsets; it features a *biga* chariot seen from the front, with two riders and two rampant horses either side in heraldic pose. The relief seems to be a transposition of a drawing cut into the stone with clearly marked, angular outlines and the foreground smoothed over. Some incongruities suggest the piece was later tampered with to adapt it from an iconographic motif formerly composed of a "Potnia" figure on a *biga* with arms raised and hands resting on the heads of two rampant horses; to form the couple, the figure on the right was added, obscuring the original left arm of the central figure, while this same figure's hand remained visible alongside the horse's head, detached from the added figure, to whom it was supposed to belong. Other additions include the left arm of the central figure and the right hand of the side figure. The overall effect is pleasing, as with the other reliefs, testifying to a craftsman of lively and eclectic skills, and it has been commented that it conveys the expression of "a fully affirmed, evolved and identifiably Selinuntine style."

Limestone metope
with divine couple on a *biga*
and two rearing horses
at the sides
from Temple C at Selinus
575-550 B.C.
Palermo, Museo Archeologico
Regionale "A. Salinas"

Expressing another level of craftsmanship are the metopes from Temple C, also in limestone, datable to just before mid-sixth century B.C.; the three metopes represent Heracles and the Cercopes, Perseus and the Gorgon, and the *quadriga* of Apollo). The average dimensions are 115 by 147 centimeters.
The dynamic and decorative conception of the smaller metopes described above is overtaken here by sculptural approach dominated by a contained energy; the figures are represented as if frozen for a moment in mid-action, and are represented immobile, heads turned toward the observer. Thus we have Heracles bearing the two upside-down Cercopes, Perseus caught in the act of slicing through the Gorgon's neck, in the presence of Athena. The figures are conceived in the round, and stand out from the ground with an accentuated massing of form; the statuary nature is underscored by the frontality of the figures. In the *quadriga* metope, this tendency is carried to extreme consequences: the four horses, seen frontally, emerge from the ground if carved in the round; the *auriga* is fixed on a slightly more distant plane. The problem of rendering depth is not dealt with by using foreshortening, but by sculptural means by which the masses rest on a neutral background which accentuates the plastic values of the composition.
The formal handling of the metopes of Temple C betrays links with schools and art milieus in the homeland. The influences and suggestions from these spheres include optical correction that can be noted in the *quadriga* metope and in the one featuring Perseus and the Gorgon. The metope with the *quadriga* reveals accentuated asymmetry in the frontal view, most noticeable in the two lateral horses; the asymmetry is more emphatic if the piece is viewed from the right, while the view is considerably more balanced when viewed from the left. The same effects seem to have been sought in the Perseus

Limestone metope
with the *quadriga* of Apollo
from Temple C at Selinus
575-550 B.C.
Palermo, Museo Archeologico
Regionale "A. Salinas"

metope, in which the figure of Athena almost disappears when viewed from the left, hidden behind a protrusion of the frame, while she acquires a correct position when the piece is viewed from the right. With regard to the set of smaller metopes, those of Temple C are deeply innovative, not merely for the introduction of a plasticity that confers an in-the-round consistency to the figures, but also because the balanced optical corrections presuppose a specific viewing point for the entire series of metopes. The overall effect must have been completed and enlivened with color, traces of which can be seen here and there.

Influences and contacts with the workshops in the homeland, with a prevalence of Ionic features, can also be discerned in the sculpture in the round. A marble *kouros* from the necropolis of Megara Hyblaea, datable to around 550 B.C., bears an inscription on the right leg stating it belonged to the funeral monument of a physician, Sombrotidas son of Mandrocles. The absence of the *ethnos* indicates that the physician was from Megara Hyblaea itself, while the name of the father is typical of the eastern Ionian. The marble itself is Cycladic; its style has been compared with three *kouroi* (two from Delos and one from Actium) and attributed to the school of Naxos. There is some debate whether the Megara *kouros* was imported already finished, or if the marble was imported and the piece was actually worked locally. A section of unchiseled marble between the left arm and leg may have been deliberately left to facilitate transportation, hence giving viability to the first of the two hypotheses.
The use of the Megarian alphabet, however, suggests that the inscription was completed after its arrival in Sicily. Inscriptions on *kouroi* of this period have also been noted on Ionian production, but they

are usually votive in nature, and are inscribed on the forward leg. The funerary use and the unusual position of the inscription on the right leg would seem to be the fruit of adaptation to the Sicilian milieu. Decisive evidence of the local indigenous workmanship can be witnessed in the limestone statue portraying a seated *kourotrophos* figure suckling two babies in her arms; this piece was also found in the necropolis at Megara Hyblaea, and has been dated to around 550 in association with the grave goods of the tomb in which it was discovered. The statue has a single viewing angle, which is framed above by the ample cape, whose outline is repeated in the lower section by the border of the throne; the other three sides offer a single compact volume providing mass in support for the front surface. The style of expression used by the artist is that of eastern Greece, perhaps specifically Samian or Milesian; this is indicated by the turgidity of forms and the modeling of the folds of material; but while in the Samian groups the folds tend to be smoothed off at the borders with softer masses, here their lines are more endorsed and they tend to convey the underlying structure of the figure in the surface by means of a light overlay of relief on the supporting mass underneath.

The consistency and continuity of Ionian influence in the second half of the century are documented by a segment of an altar, dating to around ten years after the *kourotrophos* figure: it comes from the *temenos* of the Archaic Temple of Athena, Syracuse, and it is decorated with a palmette with two volutes painted red; the relief decoration adheres more closely to the eastern Greek style upon which the statues of Megara Hyblaea are based.
Of a slightly later date are two metopes from Temple F, Selinus. The bottom sections have survived, and they are datable to between the third and last quarter of the century; the representations feature episodes from the *Gigantomachy*. In one of these the figure of Dionysus slaying a giant has been identified; the group seems to repeat the scheme of the Perseus metope of Temple C, but the representation captures the dynamic moment of the action and is enhanced by a subtle interplay of folds on Dionysus' clothes, hinting at Late Archaic forms.
The second metope has been identified as representing Athena in the art of striking Enceladus lying on the ground. The powerfully drawn face of the giant, contracted with pain and framed by a thick beard of stylized curls, evinces the influence of the nearby Phoenician world, though it is not actually necessary to leave the Greek visual world to find similarities with the head of Antaeus in the krater by Euphronius. The metope from Temple F has links with the torso of a giant found at Temple G; it probably formed part of a tympanum; the dramatic expression of the mouth has parallels with the head of Enceladus. Another piece bearing the characteristics of Ionian sculpture is a votive relief from the *temenos* of the Malophoros. The piece features a couple moving across the visual field from left to right, with their torsos represented frontally and their legs from the side. The rhythmical movement of the legs and arms has sometimes led scholars to infer a dance of some kind, though the left hand of the male figure resting on the shoulder of his companion has led some to infer the representation of the myth of Hades and Persephone.
Sculptural works in clay play a significant role in art production in the later sixth century B.C. From the third quarter of the century comes a delightful female head found in the area of the Ionic temple at Syracuse. The delicately modeled features of the face are reminiscent of Ionian sculpture at the peak of the Archaic period; its chronology is inferred from comparisons with the group of sculptures around the *kore* of Lyons. Similar Ionic features can be seen in an antefix of a little later, found in the Fusco necropolis. Some scholars see a maenad in the somewhat wild nature of the narrowed eyes and heavy eyebrows. Attributable to the same artistic sphere is a fictile bust from Acragas, also datable to the last decades of the century.
Also belonging to the field of Ionic sculpture is a fine seated female statue from Grammichele; with the right hand she clutches to her breast an unidentified object, of which only the bottom section remains, while the left forearm is stretched out. The figure has been identified as a Demeter or Kore. The drapery with its dense runs of parallel folds, the stylized smile, the elaborate headdress, all show the influence of Ionic art. The lack of a more organic sensibility, making the figure rather heavy, has suggested provincial manufacture produced in a workshop in the region of Syracuse.
Of quite a different quality are two clay heads from Acragas, also datable to the end of the sixth century B.C. One of the heads, helmeted, perhaps portraying Athena, or a long-haired hero, is markedly asymmetrical when viewed frontally but these discrepancies disappear altogether when it is seen from the right; the shape of the eyes, the narrow lips, the modeling of the face, recall the sculptures of the tympanum of Aegina. The other head is also finely made, perhaps representing a female de-

opposite
Terra-cotta antefix
with female head
from the Fusco necropolis
last decades 6th cent. B.C.
Syracuse
Museo Archeologico Regionale
Cat. 60

Siceliot Sculpture in the Archaic Period

Siceliot Sculpture in the Archaic Period

Clay helmeted head
from Acragas
500 B.C.
Agrigento, Museo
Archeologico Regionale
Cat. 64

Clay female head
from Acragas
500-490 B.C.
Agrigento, Museo
Archeologico Regionale
Cat. 63

ity, carefully sculpted and finished off with a stylus. Here again, the asymmetry discernible in the shape of the cranium, eyes, and mass of hair falling on the shoulders, suggests it was designed to be viewed in three-quarter pose from the left. Both heads are thought to have originally belonged to a pediment decoration.

The sheer variety of components of sixth-century sculpture in Sicily reflects a certain flexing of the ties each colonial town had with its original city in the homeland. There was a manifest tendency to gather and combine cues from the different schools in the Greek world, while an overall local style began to emerge in which elements of taste and style originating in the eastern Greek world became more and more prevalent. The phenomenon was generalized and affected both sculpture and architecture; whether it be the Temple of Apollo, Syracuse, or Temple C, Selinus, the same Ionic component prevails, as manifested in the sculptural features. One of the more notable features of this phenomenon is undoubtedly the presence of immigrant craftsmen from the Ionian region, attested by such inscriptions as the one at the Temple of Apollo in Syracuse and the *kouros* of Megara Hyblaea; other evidence is the expedition of Pentathlon in around 580 B.C., who brought with him to Sicily a substantial group of Cnidians that subsequently settled in the Aeolian Islands.

At the end of the century the most notable expression of this tendency is the construction of the Ionic temple at Ortygia; its design, and the start of building work, presuppose the presence in Syracuse of settled Ionian craftsmen capable of taking on the responsibility for the endeavor. The interruption of work at the beginning of the fifth century, and the likely reutilization of the building material for the construction of the Temple of Athena in Doric style, would seem to imply substantial changes in the political and social climate in the city.

The explanation lies in the events that took place in Sicily at the start of the fifth century B.C.: Hippocrates' expedition to Gela, the establishment of the Dionysian tyranny in Syracuse, the destruction of such centers as Megara Hyblaea, Leontini, Catana, and Naxos, which for the entire sixth century had enjoyed considerable independence and sovereignty, altered the political balance throughout Greek Sicily, interrupting the course of self-reliant development of the individual towns and cities; as a result, the development of the figurative arts was affected, and from the beginnings of the Severe style we witness a new chapter in the history of Sicilian art.

Ernesto De Miro Greek Sculpture in Sicily in the Classical Period

The insular Ionic character of the Attic works at the end of the sixth century B.C., as in the case of the group of *Theseus and Antiope* from Eretria, was typical of a number of important sculptures. Datable to the beginning of the fifth century B.C., these have all been found in eastern Sicily. Here the coastal plain was covered with Chalcidian colonies whose ruling classes must have maintained solid ties with the Aegean world. This was before the first decade of the fifth century, when Hippocrates' expansionist expedition set off a train of dramatic events in which the tyrannical Geloan policy was interwoven with the obstinate desire of the Ionians to have settlements in the Chalcidian Siceliot world. At least, this is what is suggested by the vicissitudes of the Samians at Zancle (they were fleeing from the Persians). Two headless *kouroi*, probably for funerary use, in marble of the Greek islands – one from Leontini, the other from Grammichele, now in the Museo Archeologico Nazionale, Syracuse – already contain a harmonious vision of the body in their torsos. This led to a simplification of the anatomy, correlating the facial features and creating their expressivity with the softness of plastic forms; furrows sink into these, emphasizing the muscles and the bony crests. These effects are more severe in the first statue, with its elongated proportions, while they are better assimilated in the second, with its sense of balance and a more natural relationship between the planes.

Similar observations can be made with regard to the marble head of a *kouros*, probably from Leontini, now in the Museo Comunale, Catania. The perspectival distortion of this suggests that, with a three-quarters view from the left, it formed part of a group. In this work, the Ionic conventions of the bulging eyes and the protruding cheekbones are absorbed by the ample, solid structure of the face with its Attic flavor. Two draped torsos in Parian marble from Syracuse, one male and the other female, dating from the early fifth century, reveal the way the Attic style reacted to the decline of the Ionic influences with a mixture of elements. Thus, while in the male torso the hard lines of the drapery tend to be moderated by the compenetration with the soft, harmonious abundance of the planes of the body, in the torso of the acroterial Nike, with its more sober, solider planes, the drapery is less conditioned by them.

The Ionian and eastern Aegean presence in Sicily in the first quarter of the fifth century B.C. was now giving way to a web of cultural relationships with the Attic world. After the Persian Wars, this must have fully revealed the important role of Grecism to the western Greeks.

Although the importance of the relationship between artistic developments and commerce should not be exaggerated, it may be of some significance that in the late sixth-century Sicily the Euboic-Attic monetary system was adopted in the Dorian area and the areas surrounding it, especially Selinus, Acragas and Syracuse. This seemed to indicate that relations were being intensified. In fact, they appear to have been enriched in the Dorian area during the period of the tyrannies, in particular that of Theron at Acragas (488–472 B.C.) and Hieron at Syracuse (478–476 B.C.), by the revival of Peloponnesian cultural traditions, nurtured by the role of Sparta in the decisive antibarbarian event that was reflected in the recurrent Heracleidan myths of Pindar's Olympian and Pythian odes.

It is, however, certain that the major examples of sculptural art in the Severe style come from Acragas, in the period of the tyranny of the Emmenids. These include two sculptures in the round, one (inv. C18 53) from a well in the Rupe Atenea, the acropolis of the Greek city dominating the course of the Acragas River; the other (inv. A6.217) comes from the hill of the temples, or, more precisely from the area between the Temple of Heracles (a well) and the Temple of Zeus Olympius (the infill of the foundations). They are sculptures that, due to the perfection of their forms, are so close to works produced in Greece that they may reasonably be considered to have been imported or, at least, to have been made on the spot by Greek artists.

The first of the two sculptures is a *kouros*, known as the *Ephebe of Acragas*, a standing figure that can best be compared to the *Attic Ephebe* by Critius, which, however, it precedes slightly. The loosening of the Archaic rigidity is also evident in the way the right leg is put forward and the left leg is bent, and the way the arms are stretched out and the head is turned a little toward the side with the bent leg. But apart from these grammatical elements, the articulation of the structure has fewer anatomical effects in the torso, which in the corresponding parts appears almost equally rigid and compact.

The other sculpture is known as the *Warrior of Acragas*. It is the result of the piecing together of various parts – the head, the torso and right thigh – found in the area between the Temple of Heracles and the nearby Temple of Zeus, together with other marble fragments (a hand, drapery). There is no doubt that the sculpture, which represents a fallen warrior, formed part of a group. It has also been hypothesized that it belonged to the pedimental decoration of a temple (the Temple of Heracles), with the depiction of a scene from the *Twelve Labors of Heracles*, the fight between Heracles and Cycnus (this

Marble torso of flying Nike
ca. 480 B.C.
Syracuse
Museo Archeologico Regionale
Cat. 154

Greek Sculpture in Sicily in the Classical Period

Ephebos of Acragas
marble
ca. 480 B.C.
Agrigento
Museo Archeologico Regionale
Cat. 1

Ephebos of Acragas

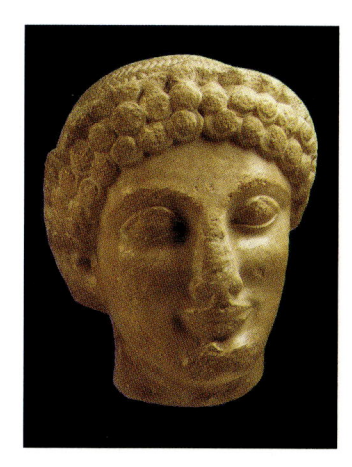

Archaic ephebic head
from Leontini
marble
beginning 5th cent. B.C.
Catania
Museo Civico "Castello Ursino"
Cat. 156

episode was frequently depicted by Attic vase-painters from the second half of the sixth century to the first quarter of the fifth century B.C.). It may also be supposed that in Acragas, during the tyranny of the Eumenids, it was worth insisting ideologically on the deities on which the civilization and welfare of mankind depend. While the relationship of Heracles with Demeter is well attested in the Greek world, and the figure of the civilizing hero found particular favor together with the Eleusinian deities in the period of the Pisistratid tyranny, it may reasonably be supposed that the same religious, cultural, and political operation may have been carried out in a period such as that of the great Siceliot tyrants of the earlier fifth century B.C.

While in the *Ephebe of Acragas*, under the luminous surface, all anatomical relief is toned down, in the torso of the *Warrior* – with the exception of the ample, harmonious surfaces of the pectoral muscles – the rich, yet controlled, anatomical details do not have a merely descriptive function, but contribute to the plastic force of the solid and compact structure of the body. With its ample, solid forms, the tension of the facial features, the sculpted details of the eyes, the lips, and the distinctive lines that descend obliquely from the mouth and nostrils, the head is closely related to that of the Amazon in the metope of Heracles and another lost metope of Temple E at Selinus. The scheme of the whole figure (the warrior, who has fallen on his left knee, with his right leg outstretched, attempts to defend his back with his shield) reflects a rhythmic and spatial concept that constitutes the main characteristic of the artist, so that the name of Pythagoras of Rhegium has been suggested. It is thought that this artist, an exile from Samos, was summoned to the hospitable court of Theron at Acragas, and that he may have worked with his circle in this splendid city, leaving his mark in other important cities of the island as well.

On the other hand, during the tyranny, Acragas appeared to be the site of a successful school of architectural sculpture in stone; the most magnificent manifestations of this were the lions' heads on the gutters of the Temple of Demeter on the slopes of the acropolis. At the end of the sixth century B.C. this school also produced the lion protomes of the gutter of the Temple of Heracles, the first that were made of limestone in Sicily.

Already, with the latter, the wholly local character of the workshop had been asserted: its works were notable for their convulsive plastic aggressiveness that carved into the compactness of the volumes, thus differentiating themselves from the contemporary Attic output in marble of the lion protomes of the Alcmaeonid Temple of Apollo at Delphi. This was characterized by softly modeled plastic compactness, which absorbed the sinuous wrinkles of the muzzle more satisfactorily.

It is probable that the subsequent output of the Acragantine workshop, responding to stimuli from Mainland Greece, reconstituted the plastic organicity into softer lines with the lion protomes of the Temple of Demeter. Thus, the tufts of the mane, although carefully carved, are arranged in thick uniformity, and there is a measured contrast between the pictorial vivacity of the mane and the dense, abundant plasticity of the face.

In the current stylistic evaluation, the capacity of this output to expand towards Gela in one direction (the protome of a gutter from Butera), and toward western Sicily in the other direction (Motya, Temple O at Selinus, the temple of Contrada Mango at Segesta), raises problems regarding its relationship with a similar, contemporary workshop at Himera, the most representative works of which are the lion protomes of the Temple of the Victory. Even if it did not have a common origin with the one at Acragas, the Himera workshop was influenced by it, and also had the benefit of Syracusan contributions. In this regard, it is worth noting that the temple at Himera, judging by what has been preserved, has its proportional equivalent in the Temple of Athena built by Dionysius at Syracuse, and the prototypes of the lions' heads on the latter appear to be those on the gutter of the south side of the temple at Himera. Concerning the lion protomes of the Temple of Victory at Himera, Marconi lucidly distinguished two sculptural types in the architectural decoration: these were, respectively, on the north and south sides of the building. This difference has recently been confirmed from a stylistic point of view by Mertens and Horn.

In the first type, the head of which is the artist's own model, the face has a square structure, the rounded ears are placed high up, the bulging eyes are almond-shaped, and the muzzle is broad with smooth corners. On this, the nose stands out; it is also wide and springs from a flat forehead that is only faintly marked by a light median line. The grooves on the muzzle and nose are only shallow ones and tend toward symmetrical geometrization; the two furrows parallel to the base of the nose have the effect of interrupting at a surface level the underlying structural unity. The hair of the mane, despite its flame-like conformation, appears to be flattened onto the neck and the tufts are in low relief.

In the second type (the one on the south side), the protome is oblong in shape, the ears are elongated,

Greek Sculpture in Sicily in the Classical Period

the forehead modeled and divided in the center by a deep furrow that, by continuing along the nose, contributes to the structural unity of the whole. For the mane, the new softer forms are preferred to the shaggy curls of earlier style, although there are still grooves creating deep shadows. While the transition from the surface of the muzzle to the cheekbones and the skull is a smooth one, the physical continuity between these parts and the wide nose is faulty due to the overemphasis of the eye sockets.

It is likely that the workshop of the protomes of the Temple of Victory functioned between 476 – when Theron consolidated his dominion over both Acragas and Himera with the introduction of large numbers of Dorians into the latter city – and 471 B.C., when the Himerans attempted to throw off the rule of Theron's son, Thrasydaeus, and defect to the Syracusan side. Around the mid-fifth century B.C. the importation into Acragas of a marble model, probably from the Cyclades (Museo Nazionale Archeologico, Agrigento, introduced a new factor to the stereotyped scheme of the gutter with lions' heads, which also influenced the subsequent sculptural output in the second half of the century.

The use of stone for decorative architectural features in the major sanctuaries of Sicily meant that there was less demand for the clay artifacts that had a long Archaic tradition. However, in the first half of the fifth century, outstanding examples of these were still being produced at Naxos and Gela.

In the latter city, there is a magnificent series of Silenic antefixes from Via Apollo, that are a far cry from the Ionic influences that persisted at Acragas. With their accentuated wrinkling and protuberances, the savage faces are an expression of compact, powerful plastic force in the decorative frame of hair and beard. At the same time, the tradition of the equestrian *akroteria* survives in an excellent horse's head, in which the Archaizing manner of the mane does not detract from the vibrant limpidity (which could almost be described as Phidian) of the protome.

In the first half of the fifth century, one of the best examples of the intensification and expansion of the production of terra-cotta sculptures was the female bust that was very common at Acragas and

Limestone lion-head downspout
from the Athenaion at Syracuse
480-470 B.C.
Syracuse
Museo Archeologico Regionale

Antefix with head of a bearded Silenus
from Gela
470-460 B.C.
Gela
Museo Archeologico Regionale
Cat. 184

Greek Sculpture in Sicily in the Classical Period

Marble head of a woman
from Temple E at Selinus
470-460 B.C.
Palermo, Museo Archeologico
Regionale "A. Salinas"
Cat. 153

Clay bust of a woman
from Grammichele
ca. 460-450 B.C.
Syracuse
Museo Archeologico Regionale
Cat. 179

Gela, and in their respective hinterlands. Its success can be ascribed to the cult of the chthonian deities, which was widespread under the tyrannies. But, while in the Acragas area, rather than participating in the new development in the early classical style, the type seems to adhere to the Late Archaic canons, the series from the Syracuse area, which are the model for the Grammichele busts, is quite different because of the plastic sensitivity of the volumes of the face. This counterbalances the very decorative effect of the mane, thus creating the sober monumentality typical of the period.
Also at Selinus, which was the last Greek outpost on the edge of the Punic eparchy, after it had overcome the isolation that preceded the Battle of Himera and abandoned its pro-Punic attitude, the new generation erected the imposing Temple E (the third in the history of the building) between 475 and 460 B.C. The sculptured metopes of this temple require a detailed explanation: they are in limestone, except for the parts representing female nudes, which are in marble from the Greek islands. These were found during the excavations carried out in 1831–1832 and 1865.
Three of the complete metopes (Heracles and Antiope, Artemis and Actaeon, Zeus and Hera) and the heads 50 and 53 of the Tusa catalogue belong to the east side, or *pronaos*, while the metopes of Athena and Enceladus, the so-called metope of Apollo and Daphne, and the heads 49, 51, 52, and 54 of the Tusa catalogue belong to the west side, or *opisthodomos*.
It is probable that the metopes of the west side are of earlier manufacture than those on the east side. The two surviving metopes on the west side and some of the heads of frieze of the *opisthodomos* have Late Archaic characteristics as far as their composition and style are concerned. By contrast, on the east side there is the emphasis on simplicity typical of the Severe style, with a quest for internal move-

Greek Sculpture in Sicily in the Classical Period

Ephebos di Mozia
marble
450-440 B.C.
Mozia
Museo Giuseppe Whitaker
Cat. 147

Warrior of Acragas
marble
480-470 B.C.
Agrigento
Museo Archeologico Regionale

ment and dynamic composition based on a relationship that is not only geometrical, but also psychological, and a plasticity that tends to assimilate motifs of linear style. With regard to this artist, who around 460 B.C. made conceptual and stylistic innovations, tackling problems similar to those that were coming to a head in the workshops of Mainland Greece in the same period, the name of Pythagoras has been suggested, as is the case with the *Warrior of Acragas*. Furthermore, it is possible to follow the development of his hypothetical artistic career with Magna Grecian and Siceliot works that began in Acragas (shortly after 480 B.C.), then proceeded to the metope of the *pronaos* of Temple E at Selinus, and finished with the Philoctetes of Syracuse.

The suggestion that the *Youth of Motya* in eastern Greek marble should be attributed to Pythagoras must certainly be taken seriously. The head is typical of the Early Severe style, with the rough skullcap framed in front and behind by rows of curls. The torso, which is covered with a very fine pleated chiton, has an animated rhythm, and this also seems to indicate that the statue should be dated to the second half of the fifth century B.C. In other words, it was conceived in a climate – that of Motya – that had already been enriched by the work of Phidias, and had cultural links with the rich, Hellenized cities of Phoenicia, or even with the peripheral environment of Cyprus. However, over and above any interpretations of the figure's posture (the right arm is raised, the left hand rests on the hip) and its dress (a long chiton with a wide strip of leather across the breast), it is probable that this masterpiece was made either in Acragas or Selinus (and was possibly taken to Motya after the Carthaginian sack

Greek Sculpture in Sicily in the Classical Period

of 409–406 B.C.). It probably represents a personage connected with the Panhellenic games (Theron himself, perhaps?). In my opinion, there is not such a striking contrast between the head and the clothed body, although the handling of the latter is stylistically linked to an output that includes the marble fragment from Selinus representing a horse's tail (inv. 1.14807 and 1.3894 in the Museo Nazionale Archeologico, Palermo).

Despite the beneficial effects of a recent restoration, the bronze *Ephebe of Selinus*, which lacks organic unity, proportion, and balance in comparison with the Hellenic model, is decidedly local in character. The influence of the sculptor Pythagoras is more evident in the small bronze from Adranum (inv. 31888, Museo Archeologico Nazionale, Syracuse). It represents a young athlete, probably in the act of offering a libation after his victory, if the right hand held a phial (this has not been found).

The distribution of the weight (with the trunk resting on the outstretched leg), the movement of the raised arm (with the right hand extended laterally and the palm turned toward the spectator), the energy expressed in the nude, and the way the athlete looks at his right hand all contribute to producing a deviation in the frontal view and a relationship between the volumes and space. Moreover, the latter is hardly affected by the flattening and elimination of the muscles of the forearm, and other clichéd devices of Archaic art.

In the later fifth century B.C. the Attic style became increasingly widespread in Sicily, as did the influence of Phidias' sculpture. Evidence of this is provided by the refined marble head in relief from Pachino (inv. 24837, Museo Archeologico Nazionale, Syracuse) and a larger-than-life marble head from the sanctuary of the chthonian deities at Acragas. The latter, considered to be of Demeter, because of its stylistic characteristics is thought to have been influenced by the sculpture in the manner of Agoracritus, in particular the veiled head (no. 203) of the Rhamnus *Nemesis*.

A number of large terra-cotta figures from the *akroterion* of Temple A of Himera, including two Nikes or Nereids, are notable for the distinctly naturalistic conception of the body and the chiaroscuro effects of the drapery. Clay female busts continued to be produced in the Gela, Acragas, and Syracuse areas, in which there is controversial evidence from the end of the fifth century B.C. The example recently found in a sacred well in Syracuse is particularly notable, especially because the bust, a part that

Marble head of Demeter
from Acragas
end 5th cent. B.C.
Agrigento
Museo Archeologico Regionale
Cat. 188

Marble head of a man
from Cape Pachynus
440 B.C.
Syracuse
Museo Archeologico Regionale
Cat. 187

Head of goddess
from Vassallaggi
beginning 5th cent. B.C.
Agrigento
Museo Archeologico Regionale
Cat. 178

is usually fairly lifeless, has been modeled by an extremely skilled coroplast.
At this point the problem of the most notable series of Acragas clay busts arises. These are usually considered to be a product of the flourishing post-Phidian period of the last decades of the fifth century B.C., and are collated with the work of the famous coin designers Cimon and Euainetus. Thus, both sculpture and intaglio may be linked to an Attic model of the late fifth century B.C. that has been mediated by a Siceliot artist. Recently, with a more careful consideration of the results of the excavations and a better knowledge of the classical output of the fourth century B.C. in Sicily, there is a tendency to link the Acragas busts, now in the archaeological museums at Syracuse, Agrigento, and Palermo, to the revival of the Classical style in the period of Timoleon, which, in a number of cases – terra-cottas, ceramics, and coinage – seems to be related to the output of the late fifth century B.C. Although this revival now appears to be simply a continuation of the Classical style from the period of Dionysius to that of Agathocles, it is certain that, together with the busts found by Rizzo in the caves of the rock sanctuaries at Acragas, there was pottery of the late fourth century B.C.
After the splendid period of the first half of the fifth century B.C., the Siceliot sculpture tended to bask in reflected glory, and its output was, at best, episodic. The resulting decline in vitality meant that, for the rest of the century, it is not possible to speak of an independent style with regard to this production.

Bibliography
G. Voza, in *La Sicilia antica II*, 1, 1980; E. Langlotz, M. Hirmer, 1968; V. Tusa, 1983; G. Rizza, E. De Miro, in *Sikanie*, 1985; *La statua marmorea di Mozia*, 1988; *Lo stile severo in Sicilia*, 1990; M. Mertens, Horn, 1988; Cl. Rolley, 1994, pp. 384 ff.; M. Barbanera, 1995; N. Bonacasa, 1995.

Nicola Bonacasa   Sculpture and Coroplastics in Sicily in the Hellenistic-Roman Age

By tradition, the Hellenistic period in Sicily does not close with the famous battle of Actium of 31 B.C., which marked the demise of the last Hellenistic kingdom, Egypt. From a strictly political standpoint, Hellenism ended in Sicily with the sack of Syrakousai (modern Syracuse) in 212 B.C. at the hands of M. Claudius Marcellus. But there can be no doubt that Greek cultural tradition continued to dominate the island, at least for the first one hundred and fifty years of the Republic. And in its turn, the Roman province of Sicily provided valuable feedback at artistic and cultural level to the metropolis, given that the sack of Syracuse and the removal to Rome of an infinite quantity of art works heralded the birth of a new phenomenon: the *initium mirandi Graecorum artium opera*, as noted by Livy (*Historiae* XXV. 40. 1–3). From the mid-fourth century B.C. two precise moments of artistic renascence on the island can be observed. Agathocles brought about sweeping political renewal to Sicily in 304 B.C. when he managed to establish a balance of power, heralding an unhoped-for openness toward the Hellenistic potentates of Epirus, Macedon, and Egypt (the king in fact married the Egyptian princess Theoxena). With the assumption of the title of *basileus*, and by fostering the birth of a federative and international state, Agathocles strove to instate a true Hellenistic monarchy of eastern stamp. However, his political outlook was not followed through by his successor. The second peak of artistic rebirth is attributable to the shift toward the more pragmatic internal economic policies of Hieron II (274–215 B.C.), regulated by the *Lex Hieronica* (Cicero, *Actio secunda in Verrem* III. 8. 19–20), and to the shrewd foreign policies of the tyrant king, who molded Syracuse on the other great capitals of the Hellenistic world and established solid and lasting ties with Alexandria, Rhodes, and not least Rome. As a result, Hieron's *basileia*, a token of farsighted independence, managed to mediate with dignity between the expansionistic pressures of the Lagids and the ongoing Romanization of the Mediterranean. The gigantic vessel especially designed for gala occasions, the *Syrakosia*, was built after 241 B.C. to designs by the naval architect Archias of Corinth, under the supervision of Archimedes (Plutarch, *Life of Marcellus* XIV). The ship – renowned for its sumptuous furnishings in mosaic, marble, and precious wood, diligently described by Moschion in Athenaeus' *Deipnosophistai* (V, 206d–209b) – was a gift from Hieron II to Ptolemy III and renamed the *Alexandris*, and undoubtedly marks the peak of the artistic exchange between Sicily and Egypt in the second half of the third century B.C. The second century B.C. and the first fifty years of the first witnessed the definitive collapse of Grecism in Sicily. It is not possible to identify a single official commission. Nonetheless, a strong feeling for Hellenistic culture can be noticed through the countless private commissions that continued almost to the end of the second century B.C. The written documentation confirms that Theocritus and Archimedes, both Syracusans, plus Sosiphanes, Rhinthon, Theodorus, and Nymphodorus, among a host of others, traveled from Sicily to Egypt, where they remained for some time. Similarly, among those who moved from Egypt to Sicily were Callimachus (who married a Syracusan woman), his nephew of the same name; Nicaeus of Miletus did likewise (and married the Syracusan girl Theogenis); lastly, it has been confirmed that Syracusan and Alexandrian merchants enjoyed uninhibited access to both the markets in question. This makes it easier to understand the emission of coinage in this period – issued by Agathocles and later by Hieron and his son Hieronymus – a fact that reflects the cosmopolitan tone and Syracuse's susceptibility to things Alexandrian. Furthermore, we can note that Hellenistic Sicily, with some considerable advance over Rome and southern Italy, was particularly sensible to Egyptian and Graeco-Egyptian cult worship, even before the reign of Agathocles. On the basis of this vast network of interest and exchange, it is hardly surprising that, with the mediation of Syracuse (the epicenter of Sicily's political and cultural life), the Hellenistic figurative arts – and Alexandrian in particular – spread through the island, especially during the third and second centuries B.C. The greatest number of artifacts have been yielded by excavations in Syracuse itself, Centuripe, and Morgantina for western Sicily; while evidence on the other side of the island has come to light at Soluntum, Ietae, and Lilybaeum.

The above observations regard the precise political and cultural choices of eastern Sicily. The Phoenician and Punic spheres of western Sicily had always had close ties with Egypt from the cultural and economic points of view. During Hellenism these ties with Alexandria became closer owing to the influx of Hellenized *emporia* along the Tripolitania seaboard. Unfortunately, the capture and sack of Syracuse in 212 B.C., the bloody civil unrest throughout Sicily in the second half of the century, and the serious backlash at political and economic level of this civil war, together with the disinterest of Rome for its province, Sicily, heralded the collapse of Sicilian artistic production. The late Sicilian-Alexandrian *koine* had not further issue, and the historian Strabo (*Geography* VI. 2. 2–8. 10) describes the state of abandon of the island through the first century B.C. The Mediterranean trading stations and artistic incentives had shifted their center of balance to Rome, mediated by Campania, Delos, and even Alexandria herself. Few specimens of sculpture are extant, and their quality is not consistent. The ship's ram in the Museo Archeologico, Paler-

Bronze statue of a ram
from Castello Maniace
Syracuse
beginning 3rd cent. B.C.
Palermo, Museo Archeologico
Regionale "A. Salinas"
Cat. 353

mo, is the only surviving example of Sicily's substantial bronze production; the sculptures in marble discussed below afford a meager idea of the craftsmanship of Hellenistic Sicily; and lastly, besides a few private portraits, there are no extant marble sculptures portraying the tyrants of Syracuse – works which were undoubtedly commissioned, given the existence of painted portraits (Cicero, *Actio secunda in Verrem* IV. 55. 123) and cast bronzes (Pausanias, *Periegesis* VI. 12. 2–4). The legacy of works in bronze that was steadily accumulating in Sicily (especially in Syracuse during the Hellenistic age) either through importation or as a result of the stimuli on local workshop production must have been considerable, such that they were reused on site or fell into the hands of the Romans, according to written accounts. Similarly, a great number of statues were erected by the city abroad. The Syracusan sculptor Micon, son of Nikeratos (Pausanias, *Periegesis* VI. 12. 2–4), the only craftsman whose name has reached us, is claimed to be the author of two bronze statues of Hieron II, on foot and one on horseback, consecrated at Olympia by the king's sons, probably after the peace of 241 B.C. Before continuing, it is worth asking ourselves if there was indeed a school of sculptors at work in the main cities of Greek-ruled Sicily. Some of the speculations against such a claim are often quite unjustified, at least as regards certain decorative and functional creations in marble, and various privately commissioned figurative works, undoubtedly executed in the country during the third century B.C. It seems reasonable to suppose that artists circulated from region to region, perhaps among certain major cities on the island, and worked the imported marble and initiated the casting of works in bronze. This notion is endorsed by a series of recent epigraphic discoveries at Segesta, which attest to a surprising number of foreign artists in other fields of artistic production, at least until the mid-second century B.C. The works found presuppose a cultivated and discerning class of patrons in Sicily in the period from the later fourth century through the end of the third and perhaps the early second. Generally speaking, in the second century the most representative sculptures were imported from abroad. We can begin our overview with a look at the extraordinary bronze ram in the Museo Archeologico Regionale, Palermo, the only survivor of a pair previously lodged in the Castello Maniace in Syracuse, and perhaps originally crafted to grace the tyrant's palace on Ortygia during the reign of Agathocles. This bronze masterpiece, produced in the first decades of the third century, has been ascribed to the circle of Lysippus, and presages that particular cultivated and intellectual vein that gave precedence to a bucolic expression and was represented above all by Theocritus in the field of literature, and in the Hellenistic figurative arts by the

Cuirass from the Scordia necropolis
last decades 4th cent. B.C.
Syracuse
Museo Archeologico Regionale
Cat. 385

Bronze head of Medusa
from Palazzolo Acreide
ca. 150 B.C.
Syracuse
Museo Archeologico Regionale
Cat. 371

category known as "country reliefs." The situation becomes more clouded when it comes to judging the small-scale bronze works, all of certain Sicilian provenance. The first piece (late third century B.C.) is an *ex-voto* executed with the solid cast method and boasts a splendid patina: an outstanding standing nude of Heracles wearing a large *leonte* on his head and carrying a bow in his left hand. The statuette came to light accidentally near a spring in the bed of the Irminio River near Cafeo (Modica). A decisive confirmation of the spread of Alexandrian themes and styles on the island can be seen in the small statue of Harpocrates, discovered at Soluntum in association with a stratum related to the first century A.D.; the piece is an example of a type mediated through an Alexandrian original of Praxiteles' school; according to the editors, the piece is linked to a statuette of Harpocrates found in the sea between the Camarina headland and the present-day village of Scoglitti. After the bronzes come the sculptural works in marble and malleable local stone. A small statue of Heracles found at Syracuse in 1909 in a man-made grotto dates to the start of the third century B.C.; the grotto seems to have served as both workshop and storeroom for the artist, and yielded lion-head water-spouts and other artifacts of minor importance. If this piece of carved marble was not assigned for use in some small house of worship, it is likely that it was a collectors' item. At any event, the sculpture is strongly reminiscent on a number of counts of the Agias portrait at Delphi, and demonstrates of how deep the influence of Lysippus' art had penetrated Magna Graecia and Sicily even for less important sculptural works. To date, few scholars have paid much attention to the quality and diffusion of limestone and malleable stone sculptures. In such works the local contribution is easy to identify, whether they be for private funerary monuments or for more public implementation. Throughout the third century B.C. we find striking expressions of architectural sculpture for insertion in theaters, a distinguishing feature of Sicilian Hellenism and denotes a marked specialization among craftsmen in the island. Most of these pieces are telamons and caryatids decorating the *proskenion* of the theaters at Ietae, Segesta, and Syracuse. The popularity of this kind of work peaked midway through the third century B.C., when the powerful naval shipyards at Syracuse first placed a set of three-meter-high atlas-figures on Hieron II's ceremonial vessel, a device introduced to support the ship's bridge. The starting date for the sculptural decorations in the theater at Ietae has been set at 300 B.C., together with the introduction of the stylistic device of coupled atlas-satyr and caryatid-maenad; the second couple were set in place approximately a quarter-century later. According to the wording over the *diazoma* in the theater at Syracuse, the large remnant of caryatid-maenad

Heracles small marble statue
found at Syracuse
Syracuse
Museo Archeologico Regionale
Cat. 358

Caryatid-maenad statue
from Monte Iato
320-300 B.C.
San Cipirello, Museo Civico
Cat. 376/I

Atlas-telamon statue
from Monte Iato
320-300 B.C.
San Cipirello, Museo Civico
Cat. 376/II

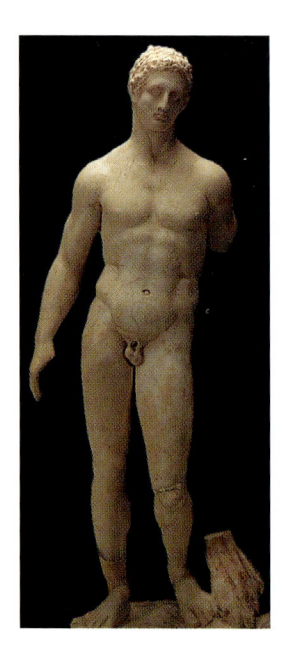

and the other fragments of telamon-satyr date to the age of Hieron II, to the period 238–214 B.C. This type of decoration, which entails bulky support figures integrated with the architecture, seems to be a western invention, recurring later outside Sicilian spheres. Private figurative sculpture began to assert itself over the third and second centuries B.C. with the growth of monuments for private buildings or tombs. Belonging to the height of the third century is an interesting male head, found in Syracuse in 1921 but regrettably in very poor state of repair. The piece denotes a post-Scopadaean stylistic influence, and seems to draw inspiration from the rhetoric of the iconography of the Hellenistic monarchies. Another piece, an idealized female portrait expressing pathos, has been dated to the close of the same century; the head once belonged to an iconic statue that was perhaps reutilized for the theater at Tauromenium (modern Taormina). The physiognomy of a wealthy middle-class woman with a personal and keenly dramatic expressiveness can be admired in a marble portrait found by chance at Syracuse in 1954. The rear of the piece was completed in gesso, while the face itself bears a strong resemblance to the well-known head of Arsinoë III from Boubastis, and other private works of Alexandrian manufacture (the Tell Timai group, for instance), dating to the early second century B.C. Such works were styled upon official Ptolemaic portraiture. Datable to the last years of the second century (or perhaps the early first) comes the superb head found in a cistern in Helorus, with its traces of polychrome detailing on the face. Stylistically, this piece belongs to the same category as the Tell Timai head at Cairo, and the technique of completion in gesso or stucco is typical of the Graeco-Roman workshops in Egypt. The sculptures executed for inclusion in public buildings or temples seems to have enjoyed an unchallenged predominance in Syracuse and Soluntum, with less importance in Centuripe and Tyndaris, throughout the second century. In this category are a handful of Hel-

Aphrodite Landolina
marble copy found at Syracuse
first half 2nd cent
Syracuse
Museo Archeologico Regionale

Marble head of a woman from Helorus
end 2nd-beginning 1st cent. B.C.
Noto, Museo Civico
Cat. 356

Female portrait marble
beginning 2nd cent. B.C.
Syracuse
Museo Archeologico Regionale
Cat. 355

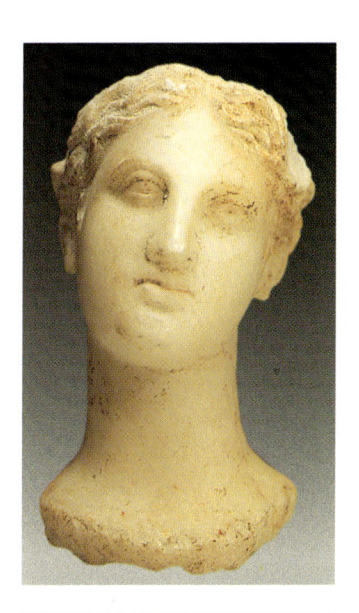

Zeus enthroned
limestone and marble statue
from Soluntum
ca. mid-2nd cent. B.C.
Palermo, Museo Archeologico
Regionale "A. Salinas"

Marble statue of a Muse
second half 2nd cent. B.C.
Syracuse
Museo Archeologico Regionale
Cat. 391

lenistic specimens (and their Roman copies) executed in or for Sicily; these are flanked by several Hellenistic sculptures of note in the island, of which copies were made in Roman times for Sicilian patrons. At this point, such works conformed with the stylistic currents of islands and centers in the Near East, and the Alexandrian theme material that prevailed in the public and private commissions simply disappears. One issue that remains to solve is the identification of the Aphrodite found in Syracuse by Saverio Landolina. If it is a copy (as seems likely) of the votive statue in the Aphrodite Sanctuary, after the outcome of the curious match between the sisters, according to the anecdotes bequeathed to us by the iambus-writers Cercidas and Archelaus (Athenaeus, *Deipnosophistai* XII. 554), then it is a superb one indeed fashioned directly on the original from Rhodes datable to the first half of the second century B.C., either imported or sculpted directly in Syracuse. Worth noting in the case of this sculpture (donated by Landolina) is the epigrammatic contrast of exquisitely Hellenistic cast, poised between the feigned coyness of the goddess and the boldness of her opulent nude forms of the utmost accomplishment. Another important figure, doubtless a temple statue, datable to the second half or close of the second century B.C., is the large-format enthroned Zeus from Soluntum, also identified with Hades-Pluto and Baal-Hammon. The media in this case are mixed: limestone for the body and throne, and marble for the head. Found originally in pieces, the sculpture has been carefully pieced together and restored by V. Villareale. This figure of Zeus is a notably refined work executed by a local master, an artist with a knowledge of contemporary developments in the Hellenistic world, but distinguishes his work by means of a provincial emphasis on the general traits and facial expression. Dating to the second century B.C. is another fine work, a statue representing Hygieia (assuming it is an original, as the present author does); this piece is a Late Hellenistic reworking of a prototype from the end of the fourth century. The classicizing tendencies of the time are discernible in the composure and frontality of the figure, together with the compositional virtuosity and decorative flair of the drapery. The renowned group of Muses from Syracuse comprises three small statues from the nymphaion built above the theater; the building seems to have served as the seat of the actors' guild. The figures in question have been endowed with a sinuous rhythm that is arrested by the obligatory frontal pose. From a technical and artistic standpoint, these marble figures would seem to be the creation of an island workshop (Rhodes perhaps?) active from the second half to late second century B.C. Now we pass on to two Muses sculpted from limestone, undoubtedly executed in Sicily by highly skilled local sculptors. The first is a life-size statue datable to the last twenty-five years of the third century B.C., lacking its head and arms (which were originally in marble and affixed to the body); the piece came to light in the digs at Morgantina. The second is a statuette conserved in the Palermo Museum, probably of Sicilian manufacture, and a superb early imperial-age replica of a harmonious Near East model from the beginning of the second cen-

Crouching Aphrodite marble
from Acragas
2nd-1st cent. B.C.
Agrigento
Museo Archeologico Regionale
Cat. 362

Hades and Cerberus
statue found at Syracuse
2nd cent. A.D.
Syracuse
Museo Archeologico Regionale

Hygieia small statue
found at Syracuse
last decades 2nd cent. B.C.
Syracuse
Museo Archeologico Regionale

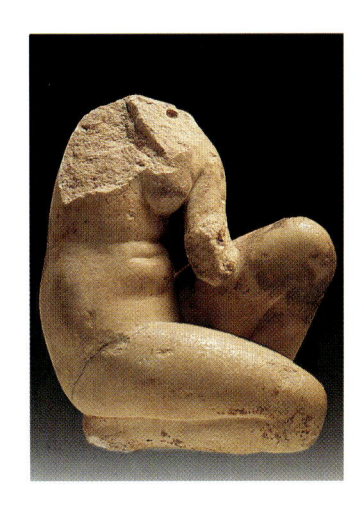

tury B.C. In Sicily this type of statue must have enjoyed considerable popularity, as they are associated with the production of the islands and of Asia Minor, and certainly designed to adorn public buildings of secondary importance, or even private dwellings. Among the sculptural works that were unquestionably destined for private use, are numerous small marble originals that must have been made to order. Two of these deserve a special mention: an elegant ephebic torso discovered at the site of Acragas (modern Agrigento) in the Hellenistic-Roman quarter; the figure dates to shortly after the mid-second century, and betrays a lingering urgency that is neatly attenuated by the frontal format; also from Acragas, attributable to an as-yet undefined Hellenistic milieu, is a crouching Aphrodite from the second or first century B.C., which could be considered a variation on the type sculpted by Doedalsas. Like the first, these two sculptures also subscribe to the Rhodian style. We now move on to the second set of sculptures that include Roman copies made in the imperial age derived from Hellenistic originals that were renowned in Sicily; such works were produced to order according to the style favored by imperial patrons. The group in question comprises five sculptures, each of which poses its own set of problems. Derived from a superb Hellenistic original from the late-third–early-second century B.C., the imposing statue of Hades-Pluto found in Syracuse in 1901 in association with the statuette of Hygieia belongs to the first group (and completely unrelated). The male figure is a variant, complete with cornucopia and three-headed Cerberus of the Hades-Pluto-Serapis kind commonly represented in standing format with headdress, scepter, and cornucopia. Irrespective of whether this statue was designed for the Syracusan *Serapeion* mentioned by Cicero (*Actio secunda in Verrem* II. 66. 160), the work is probably a Trajan reworking of a Hellenistic insular work; the technical and stylistic handling of the head, however, which betrays certain illusionistic traits, bears comparison with the Serapis from Alexandria. Another work that deserves attention is the marvelous Roman copy (not original) that has frequently been mistakenly tied to the altar of Hieron II, namely, the large bearded head (portraying Asclepius?) discovered in the amphitheater of Syracuse in 1834. Without a shadow of a doubt the ideal accents of the head fix the date to the second half of the third century B.C., and a close scrutiny of the stylistic clues pin the artifact to the early baroque period of Pergamum. According to a recent hypothesis proposed by archaeologists, the Syracusan head is a replica of the famous Asclepius from Pergamum by the sculptor Phyromachus. The headless statue of Asclepius in the Museo Archeologico, Palermo, most likely stems from a temple in the area of Acragas-Agrigento. It was found in one of the three cells of the Temple of Heracles. This excellent imperial copy derives from the outstanding Hellenistic original from the later second century B.C., which in turn emulated a fourth-century prototype. The grandiose standing figure of Zeus, formerly in Tyndaris and now in Palermo, was restored by V. Villareale and reconstrued (perhaps without justification) as an effigy of Zeus Ourios on the basis of iconographical

Sculpture and Coroplastics in Sicily in the Hellenistic-Roman Age

Headless statue of Asclepius
found at Acragas imperial copy
Hellenistic original dated
second half 2nd cent. B.C.
Palermo, Museo Archeologico
Regionale "A. Salinas"

Large statue of Zeus
from Tyndaris imperial copy
original dated 2nd cent. B.C.
Palermo, Museo Archeologico
Regionale "A. Salinas"

Old fisherman mutilated statue
imperial copy
original dated 3rd cent. B.C.
Syracuse
Museo Archeologico Regionale

material from Syracusan coinage issued during the later democratic period. The sculpture is of Roman manufacture, echoing a baroque tradition that was familiar in Syracuse, considering that the information from the coinage is endorsed by records of local worship of the deity in question (Cicero, *Actio secunda in Verrem* IV. 57. 128). To conclude the second group of sculptures taken into account here, mention should be made of an exceptionally fine statue depicting an old fisherman (Museo Archeologico Nazionale, Syracuse), regrettably mutilated and lacking its head. The conservative *ethos* of Hellenistic Sicily evident in all areas of the figurative arts unfortunately overlooked the crucial issue of the new Greek cultural vagaries. Not only are there no "genre" sculptural works in Sicily, but no collections have been made of the coroplastics or bronzes exemplifying that realistic and caricatural production that can be found everywhere in the Hellenistic centers of the *koine*. The statue in the Museum at Syracuse – a refined subject wholly Alexandrian in taste – only reached Sicily by dint of an informed Roman clientele. Together with numerous copies and replicas, this fisherman belongs to the type in the Vatican and Louvre Museums, and echoes an original that was created in Alexandria in the last twenty years of the third century B.C. The time has come to return to those island workshops that were accustomed to working malleable local stone, and whose activity was largely concentrated in Syracuse and neighboring towns. The workshops in question were fairly humble though in some cases not without artistic ambitions, as testified by the *proskenion* decorations at the theaters of Ietae and Syracuse mentioned earlier: while basically reiterating the models in circulation, in most cases they afford a simple translation of the wishes and tastes of the patrons. This is particularly true of works produced specifically for private use.

The craftsmen concentrated their efforts almost exclusively on producing works of a votive nature, or for funerary application: *pinakes* as *ex-voto* statues, funerary *stelai*, and *semata* for tomb decoration. Elsewhere, as in the large output of architectural elements inserted in public monuments and private buildings, the production of these workshops evince wholly original solutions. In the case of the sculpted water-spouts, one can easily note that those fashioned in the early fourth century B.C. evince a marked tendency for abstraction, clinging jealously to local styles, particularly as regards the output of the workshops of Gela (the Milingiana dripstone) and Acragas. The fine lion-head gutter made in Acragas falls into this local category. From the end of the fourth century and early decades of the third, one detects a shift toward an organic conception of sculptural form, but in the course of the third century B.C. this equilibrium is curtailed by a quest for baroque emphasis that is often violently expressive. The animal-head water-spouts of Gela, and even more so the lion-heads of the sanctuary of the Cyane fountainhead at Syracuse are so extreme that the very form seems to disintegrate.

On the question of locally produced sculptural works of a votive nature or for funeral chambers, the most Hellenistic one, and at the same time typical of Magna Graecia from the stylistic point of view, is undoubtedly the life-size male head in limestone from Megara Hyblaea. Like the metopes sculpted for the Tarentine funerary monuments, the relief work to which this head belongs was definitely funerary, and was executed in the first half of the third century by a cultivated Sicilian workshop that evinces considerable skill in enlivening the affecting expression of the head, achieved by an observant summary form of execution. In the hillside site of Acrae (Greek Akrai), on the southern flank of the ragged spur known as Colle Orbo, stand twelve large-format reliefs carved in niches cut into the rock face; these works are known as the "santoni" or saints, and are part of the rock sanctuary of Cybele, who was worshipped at Syrakousai, as testified by various monuments, including a *naiskos* in Pentelic marble that may have been imported from Greece. Also at Acrae, the second branch of the Intagliatella River running north–south, the so-called Via Sacra or sacred causeway, boasts the greatest number of insets for votive reliefs, together with the large relief cut into the rock, showing a sacrificial scene before an altar, being carried out by an armed warrior, with various onlookers standing about him. Having said this, we now pass on to a group of sculpted *pinakes*, authentic votive pictures equal to their painted counterparts; these were inserted into the votive alcoves in the caves in Syracuse, Acrae, and ancient Noto. One of the oldest of these, a relief found in place in the cave of Santa Venera at Acrae, represents the hero as a standing warrior accompanied by a shield-bearer. The typology and style are both traceable to around 300 B.C., and suggest links with the painted funeral *stelai* of northern Greece, Asia Minor, and Ptolemaic Egypt. Another item, a *pinax* from Syracuse, sculpted in soft local stone at the start of the third century, shows the hero in battle dress astride a galloping horse; this theme forms part of the iconographic schemes of the horseman hunting or doing battle. The disgregation that this theme underwent in time is evident from a mutilated relief from Morgantina (now in Syracuse), datable to the end of the third century B.C., again showing a horseman at the gallop, together with a serpent, in which the attributes and details have become more patently ornamental. Among the many fine articles of Syracusan production is an exceptional *pinax* in marble, sculpted undoubtedly in the

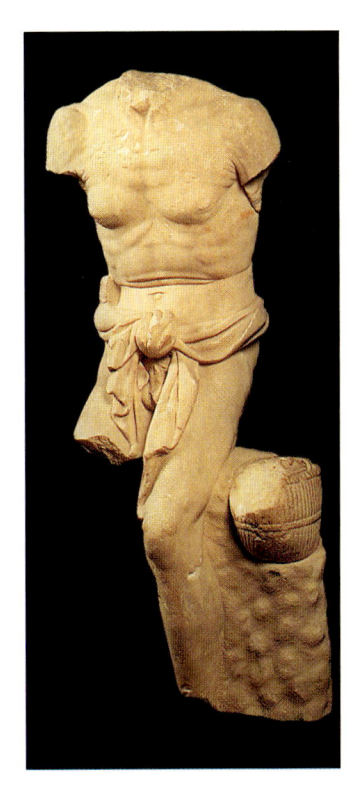

Downspout with head of an animal
beginning 3rd cent. B.C.
Gela
Museo Archeologico Regionale

Downspout
with head of a lion from the sanctuary
of the Ciane spring
first half 3rd cent. B.C.
Syracuse
Museo Archeologico Regionale

Relief with rearing horseman
and a serpent
beginning 3rd cent. B.C.
Syracuse
Museo Archeologico Regionale
Cat. 357

first decades of the third century by the same craftsmen who wrought the reliefs in the soft stone; the choice of a more costly material suggests a commission for a wealthy patron. The relief in question is a funeral piece, showing the deceased in a heroic situation: within the picture frame the scene contains a standing armed horseman with a cornucopia; in the middle ground stands the horse, in profile; at the left of the principal figure stands a shield-bearer with lance and shield; at the right a boy handing the hero his helmet. Further items of exceptional quality include two votive *pinakes* conserved in Syracuse. The first, from Acrae, represents the Delphi Apollo leaning on the *omphalos*, near the tripod, in the company of Artemis. The measured sense of composition, the rhythm dear to Praxiteles, the accomplished execution of the drapery, are all characteristics of high-quality sculpture from the first half of the third century B.C. The second relief comes from Camaro (Messina), and is dated to the third quarter of the third century; the piece represents draped female deities with *poloi*, all in perspective and in hieratic pose, probably representing Hecate or, more likely, Nymphs. The theme bears little relation with the cult of Demeter and Persephone. To close our discussion of sculpture, it should be pointed out that the monuments examined here all form part of a school of Hellenistic Sicilian sculpture that might be defined as provincial, and it would be a serious mistake to interpret it as belonging to an independent stylistic schema. What is in fact noticeable is an ongoing loss of inventive flair, a progressive dissolution of social incentive, a gradual retreat into the world of private commissions. By contrast, evidence of the considerable force maintained right through to the first century B.C. in the respective workshops of Cyrenaica and Alexandria – equal to the output of the Sicilian workshops using soft stone – comes in the form of an outstanding head of a crowned poet (Museo Archeologico, Syracuse), of African origin. While the examples of marble and bronze sculpture have been few and far between in Sicily, the evidence of terra-cotta production is widespread and of the highest quality. This category of medium convincingly testifies to the accomplishment of the craftsmanship of Hellenistic Sicily; the panorama that one gathers, particularly with regard to the relics brought to light in the necropolis and sanctuary deposits, is of a flourishing Sicily that is highly attentive to traditional fashions, without shunning international influences, between the second half of the fourth century and the last decades of the second, with significant echoes of a truly vast range of cultural areas. Excavations of the necropolis at the ancient colony of Lipàra on the Insulae Aeoliae (Lipari) yielded a vast hoard of terra-cot-

Sculpture and Coroplastics in Sicily in the Hellenistic-Roman Age

Statue of an actor
of the New Comedy
first half 3rd cent. B.C.
Lipari, Museo
Archeologico Regionale Eoliano
Cat. 240

Fat *silenus* with a flute satyric statuette
of the Middle Comedy
second half 4th cent. B.C.
Lipari, Museo
Archeologico Regionale Eoliano
Cat. 238/I

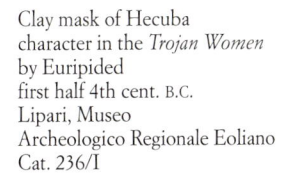

Clay mask of Hecuba
character in the *Trojan Women*
by Euripided
first half 4th cent. B.C.
Lipari, Museo
Archeologico Regionale Eoliano
Cat. 236/I

ta specimens on theatrical subjects. The complex was in use for over a century, from the first half of the fourth century to midway through the third B.C., and affords a treasury of goods of breathtaking range and quality, produced by Liparian craftsmen. This astonishing production began in workshops in Lipàra around 370 B.C. and was largely commissioned for funeral application, though it testifies to the links between theater, Dionysian rites, and the cult of the dead; there is evidence that production was brought to a drastic halt by the Romans in 252 B.C. In addition to tragic masks typical of the theater of Sophocles and Euripides, and to comic masks closer to the spirit of Aristophanes, the production of Liparian craftsmen has bequeathed us vital insights on important figures of the Greek theatrical universe, particularly as regards the kind of literary genre that the Alexandrian grammarians of the Hellenistic age called the Middle Comedy, of which no integral text has survived. More than three hundred items refer to the New Comedy of Menander and are datable to the first half of the third century, shortly before the death of Menander himself, and to the immediately ensuing decades. Through an in-depth study of the forty-four types identified, all from the third century B.C, made in close reference to the work of Julius Pollux (*Onomastikon* IV), a grammarian and sophist under the dynasty of the Antoninus, it has been possible to identify to the Menandrian masks, through which all the various characters of the New Comedy parade before us with startling freshness, due also to the bright polychrome decoration in lively colors obtained from the use of local kaolin. In the creation of the abundant faces of Menander's comedies, which are reflected in the Liparian masks, the artist has attempted to characterize the physiognomy of the characters through

431

Bust of a woman wearing a *polos*
from Morgantina
first half 3rd cent. B.C.
Aidone, Museo Archeologico
Cat. 382/I

outward hints at temperament, mixing them with casual traits and fleeting moods, bequeath us an extraordinary palimpsest of psychological insights which are all the more vivid the closer they attain to the literary prototypes of Menander. The large clay busts of the goddess became increasingly popular in Sicily from the Archaic period until the third century B.C., as testified by the busts from Grammichele and Acragas, Syracuse and Acrae, Morgantina and Centuripe, all centers in which the concentration of this type of bust is particularly high. There seems to be little doubt that at ancient Syrakousai – perhaps on the Neapolis promontory – Temples to Demeter and Kore were erected, built by Hieron to honor the city's triumph at Himera (Diodorus Siculus, XI. 26. 7), though it is not certain whether they were the ones witnessed by Cicero (*Actio secunda in Verrem* IV. 53. 119). To which of the two *thesmophoroi* goddesses (mother Demeter or young Kore-Persephone) the handsome set of terra-cotta busts should be attributed is unclear; despite the consistent composure in nearly all the specimens, they cannot claim the same level of nobility in the oval face, which is often framed by a thick head of hair and supports an imposing *kalathos*. These busts, executed with the mold method and with a minimum of manual interference, do not crop up frequently,

Bust of a woman from Morgantina
beginning 3rd cent. B.C.
Aidone, Museo Archeologico
Cat. 382/II

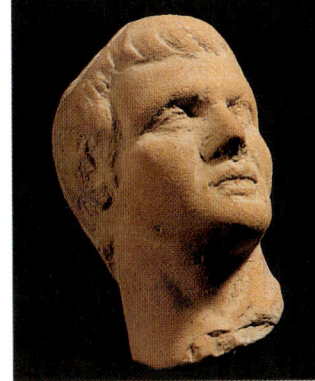

Clay head sait to be Agathocles
from Morgantina
first half 3rd cent. B.C.
Aidone, Museo Archeologico
Cat. 360

and rarely if ever do they appear in seriation, as the forms are varied and the faces have been endowed with personal traits. What is more important is that at different moments they evince contrasting esthetic directions: one pertaining to a jealous custody of the traditional, detached Greek style, the other more tenaciously Siceliot or western Greek, and hence more autonomous and explorative. In many such cases the smooth and anonymous bust (which is never bestowed with naturalistic features) one can perceive the vestiges of a pale painted band suggesting the opulence of the goddess's apparel. As is evident from the two most famous examples at Syracuse and Morgantina, the figured frieze is of particular interest not so much for the scene it represents as for the implementation of polychrome finish enhanced by a layer of overpainting that betrays stylistic links with that used for the ceramics of Lipàra and Centuripe. Before passing on to discuss the various types of coroplastics, which are more widespread and more reliably documented from the early third century B.C. on, it would be opportune to take a brief look at certain hypothetical "portraits," which afford tangible evidence of the efforts of the Siceliot artists to adapt their production. The two small third-century portraits, one supposedly of Agathocles, the other of a private fig-

Tanagra-style female figurines clay
from Centuripe
3rd cent. B.C.
Syracuse
Museo Archeologico Regionale
Cat. 366

ure, are both from Morgantina, and were certainly produced in the wake of the Syracusan workshops, which in turn repeated messages and signs from the official visual vocabulary of Agathocles and Hieron. This notion is sanctioned by the coinage of the period. Other items that deserve mention, though for different reasons, are two molds from the first half of the third century B.C.: the first, from Lipàra, bearing the portrait of Alexander the Great, half natural size, is probably a mechanical reproduction of an original that seems to echo the Alexander of the Museo Capitolino; the other mold shares the Hellenistic stamp of examples of this category of material found at Acragas, representing the head of Pan. Also from the start of the third century B.C. is the so-called Tanagrine mold, which began life at Athens itself but was later imitated and transformed in numerous centers (Tanagra, Olynthus, Alexandria, and in Asia Minor). These statuettes in very fine terra-cotta, made for tomb decoration, represent female figures in an extremely wide variety of poses, often wearing a blue *chiton* and white *himation* with red or gilded hair; some are portrayed in affected dance positions, others with masks and percussion instruments, attributes which suggest some orgiastic practice. The quality of execution is such that the entire category has often been classed as major sculptural production, rather than as traditional coroplastic repertoire. From the third to the second century B.C. there was a great demand for terra-cotta statuettes, which made their way to the necropolises and highly diverse places of worship across the island; many of these feature subjects from everyday life, rendered with the self-indulgent and gratified air typical of the intellectualizing and sophisticated culture that predominated midway through the Hellenistic era. Others portray deities in humanized attitudes (Aphrodite, Hades, and so forth), or even touch on themes from the middle world (satyrs, sileni, etc.) or personifications (amorini, etc.). The effigy of a young Hades from the large northern sanctuary at Morgantina belongs to the Praxiteles category that were most certainly standard production in the Syracusan workshops at the beginning of the third century B.C. The three standing, richly garbed female figures, respectively from the north and south sanctuaries of Morgantina, exemplify a rare elegance of pose and brilliant polychrome decoration; they are also chronologically antecedent and seem to take inspiration from the larger statuary types, which were often imported to Sicily from this period and circulated among the court of the Syracusan tyrant Hieron. The manifold cases of free interpretation among the Siceliot fictile workshops presented so far (Liparian masks; busts from Syracuse, Morgantina, and Centuripe; the medium- and small-format coroplastics) do not mean that Hellenistic Sicily was immured from developments in the rest of the Mediterranean – quite the opposite. Where the Siceliot craftsmen most excelled, in the production of pottery, that is, is exemplified by a superb satyr figure wielding his wineskin; the piece came to light in the Hellenistic necropolis and is datable on the basis of the chronology of the tombs unearthed in the final part of the third or early second century B.C. The satyr is a remarkable example of the coupling of Syracusan and Alexandrian sensibilities. The sheer vivacity of the subject, the sophistication of the execution and the excellent state of repair, the technical consistencies with other known examples, are strong indications that the five terra-cotta figures from Cairo, Alexandria, Kertsch, Phanagoria, and Syracuse (though this last is on a different scale) come from a single center of production. The panorama of coro-

Sculpture and Coroplastics in Sicily in the Hellenistic-Roman Age

Tanagra-style female figurine
from Soluntum
2nd-1st cent. B.C.
Palermo, Museo Archeologico
Regionale "A. Salinas"
Cat. 367

Dancing satyr
from Centuripe
2nd cent. B.C.
Syracuse, Museo
Archeologico Regionale
Cat. 365

Pan and a nymph clay group
from Centuripe
end 2nd cent. B.C.
Syracuse
Museo Archeologico Regionale
Cat. 363

Aphrodite fastening her sandal
from Centuripe
end 2nd cent. B.C.
Syracuse
Museo Archeologico Regionale
Cat. 364

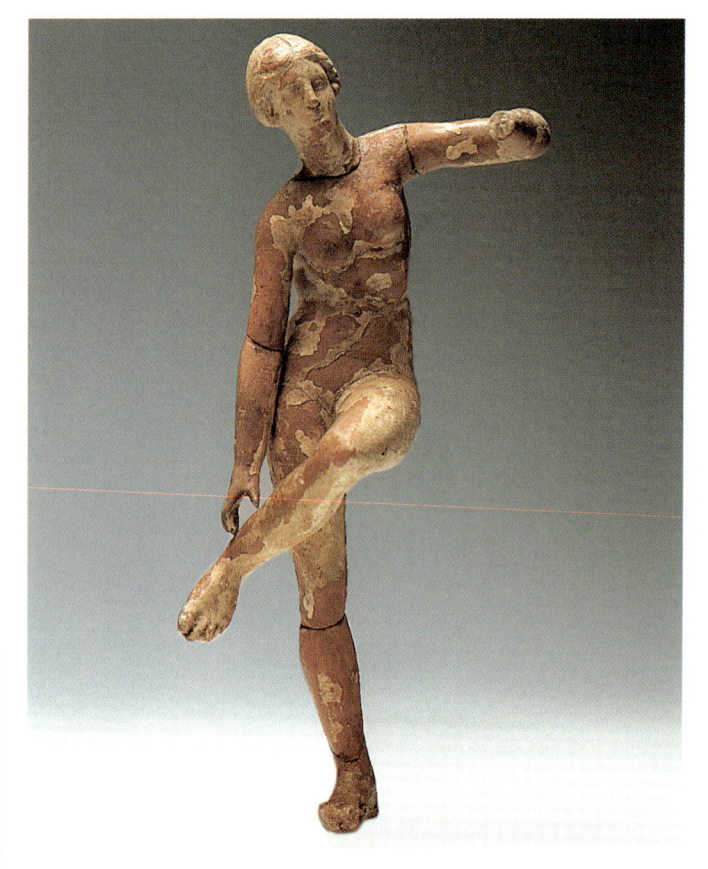

plastics production during the second century B.C. is virtually as varied as its counterpart, but it is less refined in terms of quality. Mention should be made first of the large statue of a dancing satyr, a delightful piece unearthed in the necropolis at Centuripe (in the Casino country), whose pose is reminiscent of the piece at the Taranto Museum, also from the second century; the latter is smaller and perhaps less striking in its rhythm, and is based on larger sculptural models. Next come two small statues from Centuripe, one featuring a female figure captured fastening or unfastening her sandal; it is striking for its complete nudity and the sheer elegance of the gesture. The second, a winged amorino, boasts singularly refined facial detail and a diligent study of the torso. Datable to the close of the second century, and perhaps as late as the first, comes another Centuripe group featuring Pan and a maiden, a somewhat tardy reworking of one of the many classical themes, fashioned with outstanding elegance by the Hellenistic *symplegmata*, whose statuary and relief works enjoyed resounding success throughout the third century. Another important category of work that should not be overlooked here, also from the first century B.C., is a group that is particularly well represented at the Museums of Agrigento, Morgantina, and Centuripe. In the first place is a statuette representing Aphrodite, kneeling in frontal pose, twisting her wet hair in imitation of the well-known pose of the Rhodian example. This particular theme is actually rare among coroplastic works, though examples from ancient Taras (Taranto) can be admired at the Museums of Agrigento, Morgantina, and Bari. Another piece, a rather poorly conceived Aphrodite Anadyomene (late first century), unearthed in the so-called Casa del Capitello Tuscanico at Morgantina, is a local and rather clumsy rendering of a well-known subject. Another piece with the same origins is a modest recumbent female figure on a high, elaborately embellished *kline*, wrapped in a thick *himation*; the piece is a "genre subject" that was a favorite among the workshops of Mirina. Our overview of the production of coroplastic in Sicily closes with a mention of such large-scale fictile works as sarcophagi (for example, the fine specimen found near Grammichele) and the round altars with applied relief ornamentation (examples of Gela, Soluntum, Lilybaeum). Also deserving mention are the four charming decorative figures, a pair of telamons and a pair of caryatids, which came to light in a Hellenistic house in the Calvario digs at Centuripe, a layer which has been dated to the first quarter of the first century B.C. These four specimens have evident links with the kind of telamon and caryatid figures that adorned the *proskenion* of the typical theater of this period, the same ones mentioned at the beginning of this essay when discussing local, Sicilian production of this complex type of decorative work that was already popular in the third century.

Luigi Beschi — Sculpture in Greek Cyrenaica

In memory of E. Paribeni and S. Stucchi

The colony of Cyrene was established on the tableland of the North African coast below Crete in 631 B.C. by settlers from the Dorian island of Thera who had fled for reasons of overpopulation and the urge to survive, taking in the intermediate ports of call, and directed to their goal by the oracle of Delphi, with the guide of Aristotle-Battus. As a colony, Cyrene's history is linked at numerous stages to that of the Greek *apoikiai* of the West. Owing to its geographical situation in the heart of what was known as the Pentapolis, a "five-city" group that included Barca, Ptolemais, Taucheira, and Euhesperides, the colony found itself engaged in a dense network of contacts, trade – and conflicts – with the indigenous populations of the region. The affinities between the types and practices of worship led to parallel forms of ritual and votive expression. In both cases, the Pentapolis' vantage point along crucial seafaring trade routes, together with the fertility of the land, gave rise to economic development and cultural exchanges of a similar nature. The political conditions were quite different, of course, and with them the historical backgrounds: particularly in the Archaic and Hellenistic periods, Cyrene was drawn into the sphere of influence of nearby Egypt, while Magna Graecia and Sicily formed part of the local history of the peninsula. The integration of new settlers from other islands in the Aegean in the early decades of the sixth century in the reign of Battus II, meant that Cyrene's tradition was inevitably comingled with those of the homelands of Sparta and Thera, and these in turn with the rest of Mainland Greece (and particularly the islands) to the point that it earned the title of "the largest, wealthiest, and southernmost of the Greek islands" (Chamoux). Cyrene stands like a spur on the southern Mediterranean thrusting out toward the West.

Like the western colonies, Cyrene was to assert its presence in the Panhellenic context of the sanctuaries of Olympia and Delphi with its frequent victories in the sports contests and with its *thesauroi*. As with Sicily and Magna Graecia, Cyrene's cultural calendar was attuned to events in the major centers of the homeland, as testified by commissions from abroad and a steady flow of imports, not to mention loans, which were often occasioned by the shortage of raw materials (such as marble for the production of statuary). Despite such links, Cyrene generated ideas and developments of striking originality and interest throughout the three principal periods of its history: the long monarchy through to the mid-fifth century, the democracy in the Classical period, and from the end of the fourth century its absorption in the Ptolemaic kingdom until the Roman dominion at the beginning of the first century B.C. Thus it was that the developments in the region's sculpture – abundantly produced in Cyrene and the rest of Cyrenaica, and often of the highest quality, with extraordinary cultural implications – can cast light on the colony's history, on its links overseas, and in particular on certain similarities with the western Greek world. But, as P. Lévêque recently observed, the sculpture produced by a given *polis* cannot be simply explained by the history of sculpture.

While Cyrene never gained fame for its sculpture, in other fields it boasted Callimachus for poetry, Aristippus and Carneades for philosophy, Theodorus for mathematics, and Eratosthenes for geography. Not even the later historiographers ratify the existence of a local school or a definable, independent style of production – nothing that can be said to stand out from a simpler tradition of taste, or from local craftsmanship catering to the modest demands of private commissions.

Production was in fact adapted to outside influences and configured to Hellenic or (to a lesser extent) indigenous-Libyan vernacular. The latter idiom made use prevalently of the limestone or sandstone in local supply, whereas the former turned to marble imported from island quarries (Paros) or from the Greek mainland (Pendelikon). Perhaps it was this very absence of marble that paved the way for a historical situation in which Cyrene was particularly fond of sculptural expression, and hence possessed a rich legacy of works of considerable appeal and mystery – far more than other cities of Greece. On the other hand, however, it was subordinated to "imports" or works otherwise generated outside the established "schools." As a result we find an Archaic period largely dominated by Cycladic and Laconian style, a Severe period punctuated with spurts of expression which (as in Sicily) seem to draw inspiration from Aegina or Paros, a Classical period that is closely linked with Athenian culture, and a more articulated Hellenistic phase, perhaps more closely tied to local forms of expression, but permeable to the *koine* of the period, and with nearby Alexandria in particular. Like some *basso continuo* in the background, artifacts of definite local production reflect the various shifts in taste and orientation among the official spheres. It is no coincidence, indeed, that the most signal Cyrenaic works recorded in literary sources were actually commissioned to "foreign" artists.

The sculptor Pythagoras of Rhegium (marking an early link between the North African colony and the western Greek world) completed two works for the sanctuary at Olympia: his statue of the athlete Mnaseas of Cyrene, called the Libyan, winner of the armed race of 456 B.C. (Pausanias, VI. 13. 7); and shortly afterward the *quadriga* or four-horse chariot of Cratisthenes, his son, who came in first in 448 B.C. (Pausanias VI. 18. 1).

Again Olympia celebrated its fourth-century athletes Eubotas (Pausanias, VI. 8. 3) and later Theocrestos (Pausanias, VI. 12. 7), winners of the chariot race. It is hardly surprising that at Cyrene itself, a city that specialized in horse-rearing and a frequent victor in Olympia and in the Nemean hippodrome (Pausanias, VI. 12. 7), the theme of the victorious *quadriga* crops up on numerous occasions in relief work on monuments. Similar presences can be found at Delphi: here in the fifth century another Cyrenaic *hoplitodromos*, Telesicrates (Pindar, *Pythian* IX) was commemorated; and in the fourth century B.C. mention is made of the two statues of Proros (Pausanias, X. 2. 3) and Polycles (Pausanias, X. 3. 1), who triumphed at the *stadiodromia* in 357 and 348 B.C. respectively; furthermore, two chariots, one symbolic and ideological, bearing the same figure of the Libyan Zeus Ammon (Pausanias, X. 13. 5), and the other, a more ambitious *anathema* on which run the verses of Pindar's account of the IV and V Pythian games: King Arcesilas IV, crowned by Libya on a chariot drawn by the nymph Cyrene. The author of the work was Amphion of Knossos.

The monumental relics themselves would seem to endorse this image, demonstrating that down through time the city was open to outside contributions and hence a melting pot for a variety of experiences bent to the tastes of the *polis*, catering to the ambitious commissions from both public and private spheres and orienting the work of local craftsmen. The public areas involved in this case were the major religious enclosures across the city, particularly the sanctuaries of Apollo (near the city's freshwater source), Zeus (on the east hill), Demeter (outside the walls), and the *agora* with its political and religious buildings. The private areas include the boundless necropolis, whose sheer variety of architectural structures and sculptural works is a reflection of the lively culture and religion of the colony.

The earliest relics, disclosed virtually by chance in 1966 in a quarry after the edge of the sanctuary of Zeus Lycaeus (perhaps a votive deposit made after the time of the Persian invasion of 515 B.C.), seem to stem from the around 560 B.C. or shortly thereafter. This was the reign of Arcesilas II, shortly before the Cyrenaeans imposed themselves over the Egyptians, and hence just prior to the first major urban planning and building projects. Together with the renowned Laconian cup (Bibliothèque Nationale, Paris) depicting a weighing scene before the sovereign, these vestiges demonstrate the ample scope of the colony's trade relations and cultural links. Two *korai* of superb formal and sculptural consistency were first thought to be linked to Samos, which at the time enjoyed special relations with Egypt, Cyrene and the West, and later with Chios. Now it seems more likely that they are linked to the central area of the Cyclades, given that the superb Kore from Myrrinous, signed by Aristion of Paros, began to attract works which have undeniable affinities with the earlier *korai* of Cyrene in terms of content and style. In the same hoard, furthermore, the torso of a *kouros*, bristling with inner tension and swathed in harmony, dated 550 B.C., together with a highly refined sphinx, formerly placed upon an Ionic votive column, suggest island manufacture. Belonging to the same period and place of origin are the precious fragments of a marble lamp with female *protome* (but lost during World War II) originating in the Apollo Sanctuary (around the altar of Artemis), which has been defined as the work of an island Sculptor. However, the privileged links with the renowned workshops of the central Aegean were interspersed with commissions and purchases in other prestigious centers of production of the Archaic period, whence the representations of the links with the homeland (though Thera itself tended to share the topics and solutions of the Cycladic artists) and with Laconian spheres. It was to this latter milieu that early researchers mistakenly attributed the series of *kouroi* dating from the first decades of the second half of the sixth century (at least some of which stem from the Apollo Sanctuary); now they are more convincingly attributed to island workshops, and hence in line with the evidence resulting from the casual finds of 1966. Nevertheless, it may be that, despite their fame for bronzework, the Spartan artists were also responsible for the exquisite repoussé plaques showing scenes of combat, and a *gorgoneion* found in a hoard at the sanctuaries of Zeus and of Apollo. Though dating to the very end of the century, a similar provenance has been attributed to the small Parian marble head, with its marked Ionian features; their delicacy, however, has close counterparts in the work of the Laconian sculptors (such as the small bronze Kore in Berlin). Few other works from the Archaic period (excepting those found at Athens itself) possess the intensity, subtle smile or distinction in the aristocratic arrangement of the hair. Other more explicit clues suggest direct links with the eastern Ionian area. A fragment of a Kore (provenance unknown), recently joined to the rest of its body from the American excavations carried out at the Demeter Sanctuary, offers outspoken affinities with Samian sculpture dating to the first half of the sixth century, a school whose specifics has been further confirmed by recent sensational discoveries. Samian artistry has also been discussed in connection to the possible existence of Ionian workshops in the African colony, perhaps manned by artist who arrived with the second wave of settlers in the time of Battus II. Together with the Therans and the Cretans, these newcomers may constitute the third tribe of Demonax's constitutional reform. Be that as it may, this is still insufficient as evidence for the formation and establishment of an authentic local production, given that E.

Silver tetradrachm
from Cyrene
London, British Museum
Department of Coins and Medals

Head of a woman
wearing a Severe-style diadem
ca. 480-470 B.C.
Cyrene, Museum

Funerary half figure
second half 5th cent. B.C.
Cyrene, Museum

Relief of a hoplite from the *agora*
5th-4th cent. B.C.
Cyrene, Museum

Paribeni, the most discerning of scholars studying Cyrenaic sculpture, claimed that throughout the entire sixth century the sculptures of Cyrenaica are either imported, or by "imported" sculptors. At the end of the century, two *korai*, facing twins (perhaps Artemis and Latona, composed in a triad with Apollo, and originating in his sanctuary), though sculpted in the international idiom of the Late Archaic *koine*, somehow echo the island schools in the placid structure of the bodies and the loose and musical rhythm of the drapery. Perhaps it is licit to claim some emergence of local manufacture at this time: not the birth of a school as such (which requires the initiating thrust of a great mind, together with the consistency of a specific, independent development), but the activity of local workshops working to guidelines suggested from elsewhere.

On the one hand, such an idea seems to be sanctioned by the decoration of the Temple of Apollo in its phase of around 500 B.C.; namely, the few fragments from the pediment, in local sandstone, seem to illustrate the mythical scene of the combat of the Nymph Cyrene with the lion, a subject that recurs on the *thesauros* at Olympia; stronger evidence still is afforded by the imposing *akroteria* in Parian marble. The latter in particular seem to offer a striking marriage of authentic Greek tradition and western colonial inspiration, according to an eclectic tendency that marked the end of a long period of permeability to outside influences, and the new impulse of incipient local production. This is particularly true of the huge *akroterion* emblazoned with a *gorgoneion* of Siceliot tradition, hemmed in by ample paired volutes and palmettes, denoting experimental, eclectic forays that had yet to coagulate into a discernible style.

On the other hand, this coincides with the advent of the monuments in the necropolis which, for their materials and religious implications, clearly represent a committed expression typical of the colony. Funerary *stelai*, occasionally fashioned from local limestone according to outside iconographic archetypes, are a rare occurrence. But from the start of the fifth century through to the Roman occupation (during which here too the use of popular, plebeian portraiture became current), the Cyrenaeans took up the widespread custom of endowing their tombs – whether male or female – with a female sculpture, first a bust and later a half-figure. Usually veiled, and often crowned with a *polos*, reflecting the iconography of the Eleusinian deities (as with the countless clay busts produced in Sicily and Magna Graecia), these figures thrusting from the ground (and hence chthonic) represent Persephone, the Goddess of the Dead. Direct references are eschewed; however, in one case alone her *polos* bears the inscription "Thea." Perhaps owing to this same religious reticence typical of the Eleusinians deities and which is here linked to the mystery of death, in many cases the austere, aggrieved face itself is omitted; in its place a plain, abstract colonnette. Between the inclusion and omission of the face lies an alternative, veiled face, in use during the Hellenistic period in particular, which caters to the same religious hesitancy while offering outlets for the virtuoso drapery carving in vogue at the time.

A long series of specimens which, though generally repetitive and rarely demonstrative of an original talent, nonetheless provide a more direct verification of the nature of local production in their range of types and styles and in harmony with the shift from Parian to Pentelic marble (and then back to Parian). In the first half of the fifth century these statues seem to pay heed to Cycladic influences. Later, throughout the Classical period, the focus shifts toward a more specifically Athenian model, before participating in the Hellenistic *koine*, with special adherence to the milieu of nearby Alexandria. In the transition from the Archaic to the Severe style, the initial wave of local production seems to have been oriented to an unelaborate strain of votive sculpture.

It was, however, precisely during the Severe period in the reign of Arcesilas IV, that a return was made to that particular mesh of outside stimuli characterizing the city's bonds with the main centers of production of the day. A few scattered fragments, all of outstanding originality and expressive force, testify to the ongoing influx of works from Ionian and island spheres, or of craftsmen from these areas. Despite its reduced size, the male torso with pronounced anatomical detailing echos the grandeur of the torsos of Miletus and Delos. The same applies to the double relief, whose subject matter is still unresolved (which, in the year A.D. 2, was infused with new life by a long inscription by the priest Pausanias); the piece has an innate authority which would seem to distance it from island monuments, such as those surveyed by Oxford relief, the Nisyros *stele*, or the Parian Icaria *stele*, thereby taking part in the as yet unsolved debate over the formation of the great master of the sculptures at Olympia, to which the Cyrenaic relief in question was at first accountably compared. And yet, at the same time, the Peloponnesian allusions cannot be ignored, as exemplified by the austere head of a boy, permeated with Aeginetan accents (perhaps due to the flight of some of the island's leading sculptors upon the invasion of the Athenians) which are discernible in a number of acrolithic faces and in a tautly modeled female head with diadem (perhaps a sphinx). This head in particular, defined by E. Paribeni as being "one of those faces that are easier to love than to describe," seems to herald a dialogue of sorts, at both technical and formal level, with some of the Severe-style works of western manufacture, through affinities with the fictile heads of Medma and the synthetic plasticity of the marble faces of

Bronze head of a man
ca. 340 B.C.
London, British Museum
Department of Greek
and Roman Antiquities

Selinus. It is through this and other artifacts that Cyrene, like Sicily, shows its openness to incoming stimuli, fostered by the political climate, respectively of the monarchy and the rule of tyrants.

Cyrene's subsoil has also yielded a significant series of figured bronzes of superlative accomplishment and interest. Dating to the end of the Archaic period and the dawn of the Severe style come two superb little bronzes whose miniaturistic features seem to embody the distant colony's interest in two subjects that were a popular feature of the major commissions for Panhellenic sanctuaries, namely, the standing *kouros* and the athlete in action. Both the bronzes in question (which disappeared during World War II) come from the Apollo Sanctuary. Despite its dimensions (barely 20 centimeters high) and the reduction of the torso and loss of facial detail, in one of these the vibrancy of the naked youth and the bold sense of large-scale statuary are reminiscent of the youth in the museum at Agrigento. The second bronze is based on the theme of the armed footrace and recalls the *hoplitodromos* of Tübingen, one of the best-known of all Greek bronzes. The Cyrenaic specimen is less stylized, more loose and daring in its movements, to the extent that it matches the spatiality of the "Leonidas" of Sparta, rather than Aeginetan rigor of that bronze. Both cases could have reiterated the athletic prowess of the colonies back in the homeland, as had in fact been asserted in the footraces (Telesicrates of Cyrene, victor at Delphi), and the chariot races (Arcesilas IV himself, victor at Delphi). It is certain that they document the shift in favor of a concerted commitment to figurative representation in tune with the inventions of the more advanced centers of production; all the more so, if these two examples unearthed during excavation work can be flanked by a third specimen, the "giant" *kouros* at the Metropolitan Museum, New York, which seems to have made its way from Cyrene through the market.

For the Classical period another bronze of considerable historical and artistic importance is once again a relic from the Apollo Sanctuary. This head, datable to the mid-fifth century B.C., must have briefly come to light at some stage, as it was found in a layer pertaining to before the fourth, in the southwest corner of the temple. And since the piece in question is a handsome effigy of a high-ranking noble, crowned by a royal headband fixed with a scarab brooch, it is thought to represent the last of the Cyrene kings, Arcesilas IV, whose athletic feats at Delphi are celebrated in two of Pindar's Epinician Odes (*Pythian* 4, 5). Fragment of a statuette that must have met its demise at the change of political regime; the statuette's technique and style reveal an auspicious fusion of Polyclitus' tradition with Attic culture, coeval with the metopes on the Parthenon. And lastly, perhaps the most renowned of all, the bronze portrait in the British Museum, once again from among the ruins of the Temple of Apollo, unearthed by the British archaeologists Smith and Porcher in 1860. The high cheekbones, sloping brow, short mustaches, and close curls all evince the aspect of a Libyan. Its realism, which is contained within the bounds of an elementary nobility and a controlled balance between inner structure and outward feeling and valor, would seem to justify its attribution to the second half of the fourth century B.C. and early Hellenism, in compliance with the portraiture of Lysippus.

As noted above, among the bronze masterpieces the portrait of Arcesilas IV betrays a certain Attic component. With the spread of democracy to the North African colony, and the growing hegemony of art under the Athenian statesman Pericles, Cyrenaic sculpture underwent a decisive change of style. Marked by the use of Pentelic marble, this change is noticeable in the new style of local funeral busts; yet it is even more evident in certain other relics, which testify to a direct dependence on Athenian cultural and sculptural models. For around a century thereafter the Attic influence took precedence, favored once again by imported wares (such as the massive influx of Attic wares, attested by no less than thirty-three pan-Athenaic *amphorae*) or the presence of artists from abroad. Alongside the local works, such as the relief of Niobids from the altar of Artemis, or the pair of sandstone funeral reliefs depicting Alcestis led by Heracles from Hades to Admetus and Pheres, a subject derived from the eminent Athenian relief of Orpheus and Euridice, a further striking testament to the spirit of Euripides' tragedy of 438 B.C., can be found in marble works of great plastic cogency, such as the hoplite relief from the *agora*, or the series of votive statuettes of Demeter and Kore. The former announces the onset of a Peloponnesian scheme to Dorian-influenced Cyrene, namely, the introduction of the *doryphoros* or spear-bearer figure dear to Polyclitus; the latter can be traced to the Eleusinian figurative tradition with examples that may well have been manufactured by some of the more noted Attic workshops of the late fifth and early fourth centuries B.C. Among the output of this particular phenomenon we find a series of noble, idealized heads, together with a group of decorative architectural pieces, including pediment sculptures and *akroteria*, with figures of Auras or Nikes, and the torso of Boreas, which recalls the airy apparition on the gable on the temple of the Athenians at Delos. Among the major public commissions was undoubtedly the decoration of the Temple of Apollo during the second half of the fourth century B.C., which coincided with Pratomedes' betyl or ritual column featuring Apollo Agyeus, set at the back of an exquisite exedra. In the course of his long term of studies on Cyrenaica, S. Stucchi made significant contributions to establishing the precise context of many sculptures, shedding light on their historical

Bust of a woman with a veil
from the necropolis
Cyrene
mid-4th cent. B.C.
Paris, Musée du Louvre
Département
des Antiquités Grecques
Etrusques et Romaines

Nike from the naval monument
in the *agora*
second half 3rd cent. B.C.
Cyrene, Museum

Head of Artemis
1st cent. B.C.
Cyrene, Museum

meaning; Stucchi brought together a group of fragments in Pentelic marble (some of breathtaking beauty, such as the Apollo seated on an altar), which purportedly composed the decorative spread of the main temple of Apollo near the fountainhead, according to a mosaic found at Neapolis: the arrival of the Greeks at Cyrene, guided by the Libyans. Reflecting the same local mythological tradition is one of the most unusual and problematic votive reliefs, namely, the painted sandstone *naiskos* (small shrine) dedicated to Lysanias, unearthed at the site of ancient Euhesperides, east of Benghazi. Besides the pending exegetic and chronological uncertainties with regard to this artifact, it seems certain that local deities are involved, as seen from the Eurypylus and the exotic pair of figures with breastplates over their long chitons, which also betray derivation from fourth-century Attic formulas.

The development of local manufacture paved the way for an interesting series of votive reliefs in Hellenistic style, which take their distance from the more refined tradition and are tinged with popular accents consonant with the culture of a mixed Greek and indigenous population; this fact is endorsed by the onomatology of numerous inscriptions and relics found in the necropolis.

This intermarriage of diverse traditions came increasingly to the fore in the early period of Hellenism, as the artistic dominance of Athens' role began to wane. In the necropolis a range of half-figure types and variants emerge, frequently based on models originating on the islands or Asiatic coast. The city, however, saw the rise of celebratory monuments that showed leanings toward the influence of the Lagids, who rose to power in 322 B.C. and held stable dominion (except for a brief spell of rule under King Magas), until the domain was annexed to Rome in 96 B.C. The public area of the typical Cyrenaic *agora* seems at this point to adopt an exhibitive (and hence celebratory) role, similar to that enjoyed predominantly by the sanctuaries in the Archaic and Classical periods.

Here were erected a number of monuments of remarkable originality and historical importance in the panorama of Hellenic art. One such masterpiece is the naval monument: first, a Nike set above the prow of a ship (foreshadowing the thrust of the Nike of Samothrace), perhaps to honor the victory of Ptolemy III over Seleucus II of Syria; second, near the round Temple of Demeter, the arrival point in the *agora* for the singing processions of Callimachus, the second half of the third century B.C. saw the erection of a vast relief depicting Aphrodite and Eros flanked by a pair of Thesmophoria deities. Recently, scholars have claimed that the relief contains precise allusions to Berenice II of Cyrene, and hence is likely to have been commissioned by Ptolemy. This is conceivable, given the fact that the same religious and topographical context has yielded a flank of an altar which, together with the figures of Aphrodite and Eros, features a Muse inspiring a poet, who can only be Callimachus, cantor of Berenice and one of the city of Cyrene's sons, a descendant by his father's line of the sovereign Battus, the *oikistes* or hero-founder of the colony, who was buried in that same *agora*.

In this same period and again in the *agora*, in the sanctuaries of Apollo and Demeter outside the city walls, one can begin to note the multiplication of iconic statues, a token of the Greek *eusebeia* and social ascendancy, whence the portrait with its expressions of signal authority and beauty. The faces of Ptolemy III, Berenice II, Ptolemy IV, and the two youths in the British Museum, London, comply with the progressive development of Alexandrian portraiture, leading to the heads of the early first century B.C., in which the traits are all but consumed by Late Hellenistic expressionism.

The continuous production of these iconic documents is offset by sculptural works of an idealized nature (votive statuettes mainly of infants, Eleusinian types with Isiac assimilations, and several superb heroic and divine heads) which conform with trends and stimuli from nearby Alexandria.

Subsequently, the Late Hellenistic period seems to witness the emergence of a "mannerist" master who, in his appeals to Classical archetypes with such works as an Alexander, a seated Demeter, and a small, delicate head of Artemis, seems to pave the way for Roman Classicism and thence to the trend for copying, which sees Cyrene once more intensely keen on the expressive and decorative opportunities offered by sculpture, such that the city became a focal point throughout the Greek world for its fund of superb works of this kind.

Bibliography
British Museum Coins, Cyrenaica, 1936. L. Naville, 1951; F. Chamoux, 1953; E. Paribeni, in *Atti e Memorie...*, N.S. 2, 1958, pp. 63-66; Idem, 1959; *Sculture... di Cirene*, 1959; G. Traversari, 1960; E. Rosenbaum, 1960; L. Beschi, in *Annuario...*, 47-48, 1969-70, pp. 133-341; J.G. Pedley, in *American Journal...*, 75, 1971, pp. 39-46; D. Withe, pp. 47-55; idem, in *Opuscula Romana*, 9, 1973, pp. 207-215; D. Withe, 1975-76, 2, pp. 14-32; A.L. Ermeti, 1981; E. Di Filippo Balestrazzi, L. Gasperini, M. Balestrazzi, in *Quaderni...*, 8, 1983; S. Stucchi, in *Studi A. Adriani*, III, 1984, pp. 851-857; L. Bacchielli, in *Quaderni...*, 10, 1985; S. Stucchi, 1987; E. Fabbricotti, in *Quaderni...*, 12, 1987; S. Stucchi, in *Quaderni...*,12, 1987, pp. 191-220; A. Laronde, 1987; S. Kane, 1992, pp. 72 ff.; J.C. Thorn, in *Libyan Studies*, 24, 1993, pp. 57-76.

Margot Schmidt

Southern Italian and Sicilian Vases

Among the precious legacies mankind has inherited from Magna Graecia are the painted vases of the Classical period. Some might consider this statement an exaggeration, or that – without exactly contradicting it – it should be circumscribed and limited inasmuch as other regions of the ancient world produced ceramics of equal quality, especially if we include the products made by the Athenian potters and vase-painters in the sixth and fifth centuries, when this kind of art was at its zenith, which were by far superior to other regional workshops. What was decisive for the development of vase-painting in Magna Graecia was that the artists steered their own course, introducing a repertoire of forms and images that distinguished them early on from the Attic models, whose influence was limited only to the start of their activity. The result is a treasury of artistic creations which must be considered utterly unique.

In the strict sense, by "Italiot" vase-making we mean the production of ceramics – in Apulia and Lucania as from ca. 440 B.C., and a little later, i.e., as from the fourth century B.C., in Campania and at Paestum – using the red-figure technique acquired from the mother country, instead of the earlier black-figure technique. Red-figure vases were also produced in Sicily from the late fifth century B.C. This kind of artistic production developed therefore in the cultural climate of the cities founded by the Greek colonists, in specific milieus that differed to a greater or lesser extent from those of Mainland Greece. Among the characteristics peculiar to the *poleis* was the highly profitable exchanges with the local populations living in the neighborhood of the Greek settlements. While on various occasions this proximity culminated in warfare, did however prevail peaceful coexistence and reciprocal influence for periods of varying length.

The spread and use of Italiot vases, even in remote settlements in the interior, together with their utilization in local necropolises together with other indigenous ceramics and products, are clear proof of the great influence of Italiot culture in Magna Graecia. Moreover, the role of these vases as carriers and interpreters of ideas and images should not be underrated. The way in which these images were assimilated by the local population provides us with significant information about the cultural level of the latter. It certainly cannot be said that the Greek cities in southern Italy were surrounded by "savages" without little or no civilization of their own. The shapes and decoration of several Italiot vases reflect the taste of their local customers. Traditional, non-Greek shapes (in particular, the *nestoris*, known as the "trozzella" in Italian) have been found decorated with the red-figure technique but illustrating people dressed in native costumes and bearing local weapons (for example, the Messapii in Apulia, the Oscans and Samnites in Campania).

Tarentum (Taras) and Paestum (Poseidonia) provide two opposites illustrating the relations between the descendants of the Greek settlers and the native peoples. On the one hand, we have the old colonial city of Spartan origin, in constant contact with the mother country, with rich traditions and a sophisticated Hellenic culture, and on the other, a city which was dominated, in the period we are examining, by the Lucani. The whole of the Paestan production of red-figure vases lies within this Lucanian period, excluding a brief interlude, from 336–332 B.C. If we consider Paestum as a "Lucanian

Messapic black-figure *nestoris* [two-handled storage jar]
500-475 B.C.
Copenhagen
Ny Carlsberg Glyptothek
Cat. 138

Messapic black-figure *nestoris*
end 6th cent. B.C.
Lecce, Museo Provinciale
Cat. 139

Black-figure *amphora*
from Campania
500-490 B.C.
Siena
Museo Archeologico Nazionale
Cat. 140

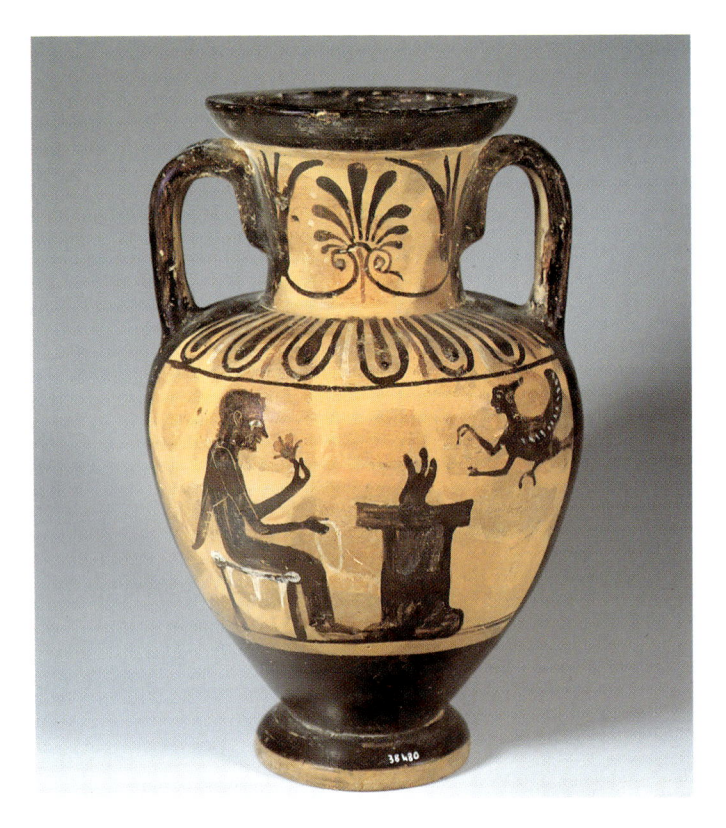

city," the classification of the subject matter becomes even more interesting, since the knowledge of the contents of the ancient tragedies has apparently remained unchanged. Evidence of this is provided by the vase-painting referring to Aeschylus or, more frequently, to Euripides. Highly amusing, extraordinary scenes from the comic theater are also present on Paestan vases. The only two Italiot vase-painters who signed their wares, Assteas and Python (no other signatures have survived from the other South Italian workshops) were active in "Lucanian" Paestum. These two leading vase-painters – who were probably potters as well – worked in one of the most important Paestan potteries. To return for a moment, to the beginnings of Italiot vases, in Athens the transition from black-figure to red-figure vase-painting took place as far back as the last quarter of the sixth century B.C. Why then did the production of red-figure vases only start in southern Italy several generations later, that is, toward 440 B.C.? The answer to this question is particularly complex and we must consider both external and internal causes. We will deal with the external causes first. After the long Peloponnesian War, toward the end of the fifth century B.C., the flow of imported wares from Athens declined drastically. Until then buyers in Magna Graecia had preferred to purchase original ceramic ware from Attic potteries instead of stimulating local workshops to adopt the Greek techniques (a fairly suitable comparison to this situation has sometimes been made with the modern phenomenon by which only authentic *haute couture* direct from Paris will satisfy certain tastes), now they had to try to satisfy their wishes by other means. At first the demand could be more or less met by the production of potters who had emigrated from Athens when the changed conditions of their own city forced them to seek their fortunes elsewhere. The fact that the first Italiot vases are hardly different from the Attic ones leads us to believe that they were indeed produced by these Athenian immigrants. One stimulus – though not the only one – was probably offered by the foundation of the Panhellenic colony of Thurii in the western area of the Gulf of Taranto in about 443 B.C. The new settlement grew up near the site of the once famous city of Sybaris, which had been destroyed. Athens played a major role in establishing the colony and therefore Athenian culture was able to spread in a more immediate way, without the time-consuming voyages across the sea. As early as 1893 Adolf Furtwängler upheld the view that it was the very foundation of the new colony that was decisive in starting the local production of red-figure vases. Furtwängler's theory need not be altogether discarded, although to the present day there have not been any discoveries (traces of kilns or suchlike) in the area of the ancient city to confirm it. However, in the area of the city of Metapontum, situated further east, excavations have brought to light material that proves the presence of an ancient workshop with fragments of vases that date from the time of the ear-

Red-figure *amphora*
from Nola
first half 5th cent. B.C.
Vatican City
Museo Gregoriano Etrusco
Cat. 141

Red-figure *amphora*
with the birth of Helen
from Paestum
ca. mid 4th cent. B.C.
Paestum
Museo Archeologico Nazionale
Cat. 216

ly-Lucanian Amykos Painter to the Dolon and *Creusa* Painters, of a slightly later date. In order to understand the internal causes of the delay in the spread of red-figure vase-painting, we should make a careful examination of the earlier production of pottery in southern Italy. Unlike the Greek motherland it seems that there was a lack of real interest in these areas in representing the human figure. The products of the ancient local potteries are all characterized by the preference for relatively abstract, ornamental, geometric designs. Even during the periods of closer contacts with Italiot vase-painting, the use of figurative subjects remained an exception (as for instance on very few Daunian and Messapic vases in Apulia). This characteristic appears to be applicable to the assimilation of the earlier black-figure technique as well. While, for example, in the late sixth century B.C. various workshops in Etruria produced some highly original black-figure vases, in southern Italy similar attempts were sporadic. Black-figure vases from Campania were influenced by Etruscan ware, while the rare local Apulian black-figure production proposed original but simplified silhouette figures, which differed from the attempts at characterization found in the ancient Attic models. It is interesting to note the survival of the black-figure technique in the production of one type of vase in particular, the small *Pagenstecher lekythoi*. These *lekythoi* seem to have been produced from the late 4th century B.C. at various places in Campania as well as in Sicily and the most successful examples prove that this style – only apparently obsolete – could nonetheless result in aesthetically satisfying results.

A particularly delightful example of probable local production but of a much earlier date, from the end of the 6th century, is the black-figure *amphora* of ca. 520 B.C. (Museo Nazionale, Taranto). The subject matter is a lively scene of a bird hunt with an owl as a decoy.

Early attempts at introducing the red-figure technique, dating to a previous period or, partly contemporary with the development of Italiot vases, are even rarer. One of the reasons for this could lie in the fact that this kind of technique was relatively difficult, and required the acquisition of certain skills. There is proof however that an isolated workshop in the province of Campania – the so-called "Owl-Pillar-Group" – was attempting to create red-figure vases before the mid-fifth century B.C. The rather clumsy application of this technique and the unusual style of the figures is appealing to modern eyes. Alongside the true red-figure vases, we should also mention the "imitations" with superimposed reddish slip, a few examples of which have been found in Apulia, while the majority came from Paestum and its surrounding area. The Paestan version of these imitation red-figure vases has been studied only recently, thanks to well-documented finds, and is now considered particularly significant in reconstructing the first period of Paestan pottery. These vases, with their rather opaque figures painted with diluted reddish clay, should not actually be considered as mere imitations of models whose craftsmanship was beyond their reach; instead they represent a particular form of decoration that probably corresponded more closely to the requirements and tastes of the craftsmen and their clients.

Southern Italian and Sicilian Vases

opposite
Apulian red-figure *krater*
with sculptor's workshop
attributed to Boston Group
first half 4th cent. B.C.
New York
The Metropolitan Museum of Art
Rogers Fund, 1950
Cat. 288

The fairly differentiated picture that we have today of the Italiot ceramic workshops is prevalently due to Arthur Dale Trendall, who spent nearly sixty years of his life (and after 1961, sometimes with the collaboration of Alexander Cambitoglou) examining and classifying the red-figure vases to date in Magna Graecia and Sicily. Future work in this field, that can draw on new findings and their contexts, will nevertheless remain indebted to the fundamental studies published by Trendall in several epoch-making volumes. Over the last few decades the present generation of scholars, particularly of Italians, has been able to make significant advances toward obtaining a proper focus of the native peoples. In this sense, the historical question of cultural receptiveness becomes a central issue: Italiot vases assume particular interest when seen in the context of reciprocal exchange, and their historical significance becomes more critical for our better understanding of the highly complex structure that is Magna Graecia, which owes much of its specific nature to its being rooted in the Italian peninsula.

We will now consider some of the characteristics of the various Italiot workshops. There were two distinct geographical groups: in the East, the areas on the Adriatic and the Ionian with their respective hinterlands, that is Apulia and Lucania (modern Basilicata); in the West, Sicily, Campania, and Paestum. The distinction (proposed by Trendall) between Apulian and Lucanian vases, while not being accepted today by all scholars as a rigid formula, is nevertheless a useful working model, since these regional groups developed along completely diverging lines until the end of the fourth century B.C.; however, in the later fifth century there still existed parallels and similarities between them. Thanks to the important discovery of the above-mentioned kilns at Metapontum, it has been possible to localize at least the initial stage of so-called Lucanian vase production. The concentration of the finds of Lucanian vases belonging to the period after ca. 380 B.C. – all brought to light in the interior and nearly always at a certain distance from the coast – suggests that the successors to this workshop were forced, apparently, to leave the Metapontine area. An examination of the vases and their more and more provincial style reveals that contacts with cosmopolitan Tarentum (Taras) had dwindled considerably, or had even ceased to exist. The most important city in the east of Magna Graecia, Tarentum must certainly have been one of the major centers of Italiot vase production; and yet no evidence to endorse this supposition – such as remains or materials used by workshops – has yet come to light. (With reference to the more recent discoveries of kilns that do not date back to the period in question, and for the presence of Tarentine clay, see also N. Cuomo di Caprio, "Les ateliers de potiers en Grande Grèce," *BCH*, suppl. 23, 1992, p. 69ff.). Given that the modern city of Taranto has been built directly over the ancient site, the possibility of carrying out excavations is extremely limited, and systematic research on a large scale is evidently to be excluded. On the basis of their characteristic differences, and depending on the statistics of their discovery, the Apulian vases of later production (mid-fourth century onward) can be attributed to various places of production. Throughout this period, in addition to Tarentum, where in all probability the Darius Painter and his colleague the Underworld Painter were active, there was another significant area with its own workshops, namely the Daunian territories north of Apulia (Canosa, Arpi). One of the vase-painters here was the highly productive Baltimore Painter (who it seems ran a flourishing, well-organized business), another was the highly original Arpi Painter.

In this rather brief survey, special attention should be paid to the Apulian vases which constitute about half (ca. ten thousand items) of the known production of South Italian red-figure ceramics. They have met with particular interest not only among specialists of ancient pottery. Leaving aside Attic vases, whose range of imagery is in fact quite different, no other kinds of vases have provided so varied and original evidence for the assimilation of Greek myths and their reproduction in ancient drama. Not are among Apulian vases are those decorated with a scene which is unique in its kind. There are, for example, mythological scenes that have no equivalents elsewhere and can sometimes (though not always) be linked to written texts which have survived in part or entirely. The favorite source of theme material in Apulia – and in the rest of Magna Graecia – appears to have been the tragedies of Euripides. The close connection with the contents of these works is already evident in the earlier Italiot vases, produced during the latter part of the author's lifetime or not long after his death. On this point, we should bear in mind the famous tomb discovered at the site of Heraclea (near Policoro), dating to about 400 B.C. The tomb contained, for example, a *hydria* with the oldest image known of the infanticide Medea fleeing on a chariot drawn by serpents. Considering the contents of the scene, the concept differs slightly from Euripides' version of the tragedy (staged in 431 B.C. in Athens): on the vase, Medea appears to be leaving her dead children behind her. Similar vase-pictures from the same source seem to be even more faithful to Euripides. For example, there is Dirce (from the myth of Antiope)

Red-figure *hydria*
with the infanticide Medea
fleeing on a chariot
drawn by serpents
end 5th cent. B.C.
Policoro
Museo Nazionale della Siritide

Red-figure *pelike*
with the torture of Dirce
tied to a wild bull
end 5th cent. B.C.
Policoro
Museo Nazionale della Siritide
Cat. 220/III

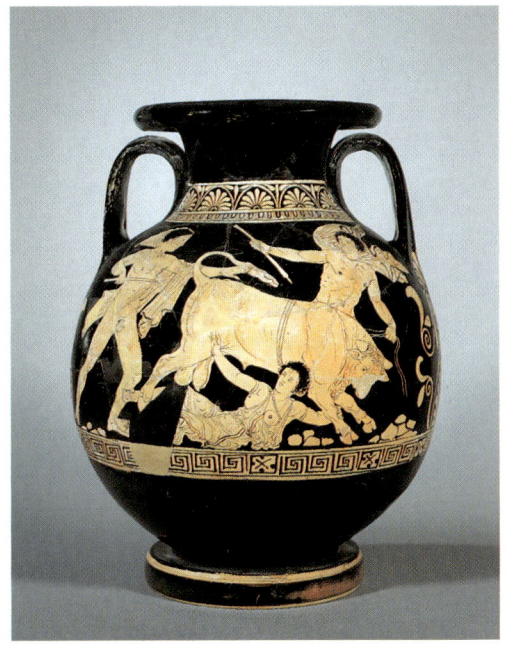

and, in particular, the scene with Heracles' children, the Heraclids, who, together with the aging Iolaus, are seeking refuge from their persecutor on an altar. This is a specifically Attic myth illustrating the noble role of protector assumed by the city of Athens. However, there is no trace of Euripides' tragedy of the Heraclids in the Athenian vase-painters' output, at least as far as we know today (the same is generally more or less the case of all the great Athenian theatrical works of the Classical period which seem to have left but indirect traces in the city's artistic production). Southern Italy, however, has revealed more than one representation of the Heraclids. Probably, the *pelike* bearing this subject, found in the above-mentioned tomb at Heraclea, had a special significance for the city, whose name clearly derives from Heracles. It must be noted, however, that the Labors of Heracles, one of the favorite subjects of Attic and other vases of Mainland Greece in the Archaic period, as well as the adventures of Theseus, were no longer popular with southern Italian painters and their customers.

The vase-paintings, to various degrees inspired by theatrical works, must be understood as evidence of a distinct artistic genre, and it would be a mistake to consider them merely as secondary sources for our reconstruction of literary texts, given that the material is transformed into an image, therefore involving the use of the specific medium of painting, and is expressed in a language that is very different from that of poetry.

Derivation from the stage, or rather the theatrical nature of the subject matter, may be grasped more directly, it seems, in the comical scenes. In this case, the actors are portrayed with their comic costumes and grotesque masks, and even the setting is included as a more or less improvised stage. These so-called *phlyax* vases were not produced only in Apulia. In addition to the considerable Paestan output, and the fine Sicilian examples of these farcical scenes, recent finds – in particular, the Würzburg bell-krater, belonging to the early Apulian period (about 370 B.C.), bearing a picture apparently drawn directly from Aristophanes' *Thesmophoriazusae*) support the thesis that the majority of the so-called *phlyax* vases did not represent rustic forms of local theater but rather were inspired by the Attic comedies. This supposition is even more convincing when we consider that – to our knowledge – *phlyax* plays were at their peak in southern Italy at the time of the poet Rhinton in about 300 B.C., when illustrations of comic situations on vases (perhaps wrongly defined as scenes from *phlyax* plays) had already ceased being produced about a generation earlier.

The problem of inspiration diacon either from the theater or from the broader realm of mythology, cannot be separated from the even more crucial question of the function of the vases. We should always remember that the majority of these vessels – and this is also true for the output of other workshops in southern Italy – were destined, from their conception, for tombs. The sepulchral character of the ceramic ware is reflected in some of the shapes which are impractical for daily use. For example, the tall *lutrophoroi*, a variety of the *amphorae* but with a much more complex structure, sometimes egg-shaped or cylindrical with handles shaped like spiralling tendrils, are typical funerary vases.

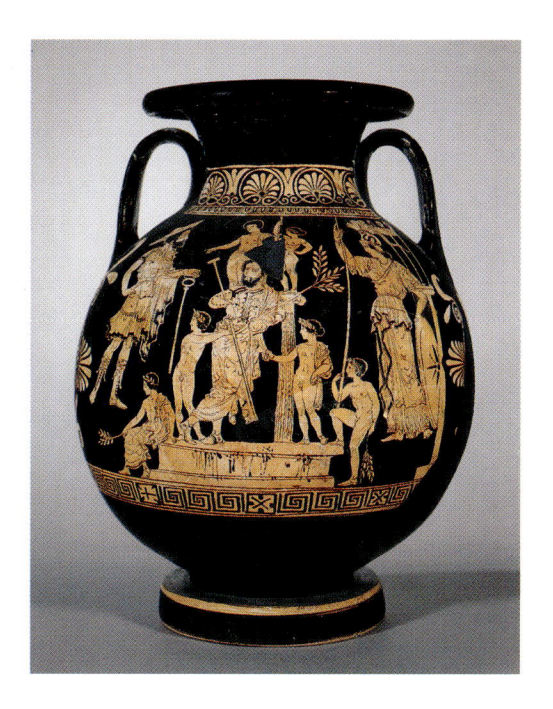

Red-figure *pelike*
with the legend of the Heraclides
end 5th cent. B.C.
Policoro
Museo Nazionale della Siritide

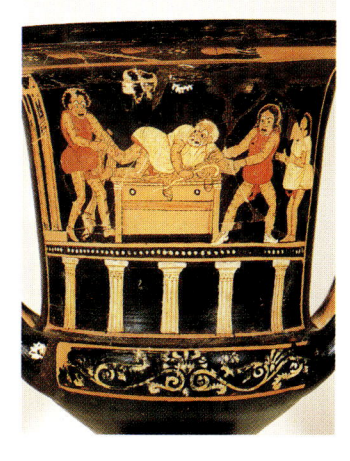

Kalyx krater from Paestum
with scene from a *phlyax* play
mid 4th cent. B.C.
Berlin, Staatliche Museen
zu Berlin Preussischer
Kulturbesitz, Antikensammlung
Cat. 227

The floral decoration which, in this case, involves the whole shape of the vase, evokes the wider context of funeral symbolism in Southern Italy. Painted decorations often include elaborate floral settings with polychrome buds and flowers. When these floral images become the central motif, represented inside the typical tomb 'naiskos' – as exemplified by some vases – the significance of their symbolic value becomes still more evident. They impart a consoling message that, even though we do not yet understand its nature, life exists beyond tomb.

Tomb scenes are the principal subject of many south vases, whereas such themes are all but lacking from Siceliote vase-painting. In Apulia, representations of shrines (*naiskoi*) increased considerably from the second quarter of the fourth century B.C. The tomb occupies the center of the scene, and is represented as an open building with columns, like a small temple. Inside it there are the dead, man or woman, sometimes accompanied by small groups of relations. The people within the *naiskos* are painted white; this may have two meanings. On the one hand, it refers to the whiteness of stone, making the human figures gravestone statues; on the other, the color white distinguishes and isolates the deceased from the other living human figures visible outside the shrine. The latter are in fact painted with red-figure technique, that is, with the color of life. The painters of the Apulian funerary vases developed a rich and highly significant system of symbols conveying an idea of life in transformation, and the omnipresence of memories as a source of vitality. The numerous gifts of the visitors to the tomb, such as flowery garlands, mirrors, fans, and various types of bowls, are primary components of this pictorial language.

All the symbols painted on the sepulchral vases of the late Apulian period – the large bunches of grapes and the ivy leaves, the tambourines and *thyrsi* held by the visitors – are clear references to the world of Dionysus, in his persona as god of the Dionysiac Mysteries. One noticeable feature is that, without exception, the bearers of offerings near the tomb are all young people, both male and female. They cannot, therefore, represent the families of the dead persons, as elderly people and children are absent. There are no signs of mourning or lamentation for the dead. They appear to carry out their pious rites quite serenely. Are these young men and women meant to be members of a mystic community, united by their confidence in a blissful life in the other world? The Dionysiac symbols referred to above indicate the kind of mystery that might have generated the religious significance of these burial scenes.

This brings us to a particularly important question concerning the study of Southern Italian vases. For a long time scholars have speculated as to whether the scenes they depict contain references to ancient mystery. The ties with Dionysus are self-evident; they can be discerned also on many other vases whose imagery does not refer explicitly to the tomb. Much evidence in Magna Graecia points to the fact that the Dionysiac, like the Eleusinian mysteries in the motherland, had widespread significance. In this respect, the words of the chorus in Sophocles' *Antigone* are frequently quoted

Southern Italian and Sicilian Vases

Red-figure *naiskos krater* attributed to the white Sakkos Painter ca. 320 B.C.
Matera, Museo Nazionale "D. Ridola" Cat. 336

(V. 1119) at the point in which Dionysus is named as the protector of Italy. This reading should not be discorded even though R.D. Dawe in his nex edition of the text from 1979 has proposed an emendation for the word "Italia".

By contrast, material evidence of the presence of the Orphic Mysteries in the images on Italiot vases is much harder to find. Obviously, one will have to look first at those representations that include the Thracian singer Orpheus himself, and particularly the underworld scenes painted on a specific group of Apulian monumental volute krateis – the so-called *Unterweltsvasen*, which are without real parallels in other areas of the ancient world. They convey a lively and complex image of the underworld, with the blessed and the damned or penitents, each one in his own place, ranged around the palace of the lords of the Underworld. Only a few mortals possess the privilege of returning to the world of the living, as a free choice, such as Heracles, who carried the dog Cerberus out of Hades, and Orpheus himself. The presence of Orpheus in the Underworld does not, however, seem to be motivated primarily by his mission, to save his wife Euridice. In fact, the heroine herself does not appear in any of these pictures except one. The aim therefore of the artists was perhaps to portray Orpheus, independently of his own personal myth, and to reveal him as the bearer of hope for all mankind, or, at least, for his own followers. It is very difficult to understand his role in these images especially because we are not sure how the story was thought to end in the period of the Apulian vases in the fourth century B.C. It appears that in an ancient variation on the myth of Hades, Orpheus did not fail, but really

Red-figure *naiskos krater*
attributed to the Copenhagen Painter
ca. 340 B.C.
Matera, Museo Nazionale "D. Ridola"
Cat. 339

succeeded in bringing Euridice back to life. Given this happy ending, he must have seemed much more suitable in the role of a sort of intermediary acting between mortals and the lords of the Underworld. But, if the Apulian pictures were in fact based on the idea of the disastrous attempt to reunite the mythical couple, there is still the fact that Orpheus, at one point, succeeded in moving the gods of the Underworld and in winning them over thanks to the charm of his music.

The presence of the three Judges of the dead (Minos, Rhadamanthys, and Aeacus\Triptolemus) in some of these depictions of the Underworld means that the place assigned to human beings here depends on their merits. Various motives lead us to believe that the task of these judges is not limited to the moment in which the dead enter Hades, but that throughout their sojourn in Hades they are continually judged for the good and evil they do. On the basis of their merits, the destiny of the dead might perhaps be improved or mitigated. Must the Danaids, who are often pictured in these images, really exhaust themselves eternally as they pour water and strive to fill the leaky *pithos*? On some of these Apulian vases, the representations of these "damned" women give the impression that they are not actually doomed to cruel and tremendous punishment, nor are they without any hope of reprieve – indeed, they appear to be serene. However, besides the Danaids, there are other condemned figures, chained and guarded by demons, and, lastly, there are the damned *par excellence*, Sisyphus and Tantalus, whose torments in the Underworld are eternal. There are then different levels of existence in the Underworld, ranging from the damned to the righteous (one of the

Southern Italian and Sicilian Vases

Red-figure *loutrophoros*
ca. 320 B.C.
Matera
Museo Nazionale "D. Ridola"
Cat. 328

latter being the seer Amphiaraos who is given a friendly welcome by Hades on several of the vases). We are led to infer that the judges continue to survey the conduct of men even after their death, and this might be connected to the famous cycle of reincarnations, the metempsychosis, forcing mortals to be reborne and to die again and again. There is sufficient evidence to suggest that these reincarnations were considered a sentence rather than a blessing. In some cases we can suppose, unfortunately without being absolutely certain, that echoes of the idea of the reincarnation cycle are also reflected in the pictures on Italiot vases.

We must keep in mind the destination of the vases as gifts for the dead, not only when trying to interpret the images that contain evident references to the tomb (*naiskoi* vases) or to the Underworld. The portrayal of a myth on a drinking cup for a *symposion* changes considerably when depicted on a funeral vase. Some myths are intrinsically linked to the theme of death, such as the story of Niobe mourning for the loss of all her children. In the Italiot representations of this myth, found both in Apulia and in Campania, there is hardly any reference to the cause of Niobe's unhappy destiny. She has been punished for the pride which led her, the mother of numerous children, to consider herself superior to the goddess Leto, who had only two children. The pictures on the sepulchral vases prefer, instead, to show the mother mourning inside the funerary monument, or over the tomb of her dead children. The bottom part of her figure, starting from the feet, is painted white to indicate the beginning of her turning into stone caused by her deep grief. It is hard to judge whether an image of this kind was meant to bring consolation and what the exact significance of the message was. Perhaps the message these mythological images had to convey was rather simple – to make men realize that even heroes have to bear trials and formidable destinies that are often much more cruel than those of mortals. Such a reflection might make the onlooker's own destiny appear easier to bear.

In the pictures showing Niobe at the crucial moment of her transformation into stone, the white pigment is not used as decoration, but is meant to give a precise message. This reminds us of the observation emphasized above, that the deceased inside the funerary monument depicted in the '*naiskos*' scenes were alsto painted white to characterize their new existence as separated from the living. The added colors, used frequently in the later Southern Italian vases, do not always have a deeper meaning; however, color was generally used to intensify the pictorial effect. It appears that the Italiot vase-painters closely followed developments in the realm of "great painting," and made an intelligent use of the new techniques. The use of colors and tones served to portray objects in an illusionistic manner, with, for example, the glint of the shining bronze shields of the warriors, or the superbly crafted precious vessels. The most knowledgeable use of color was achieved in painting the elaborate floral settings, florals which were sometimes even drawn in perspective. These florals decorated the necks of funerary kraters, and symbolized – as we said above – the vigor of life in continual renewal. In order to capture the qualities of an image as we perceive it with our senses, the painters tried to catch the play of light and shade, the bloom on a bunch of grapes, in which the side illuminated by the sun and the one in shadow were distinguished by different shades of color. The means used were still limited to those in the repertory of potters and vase-painters, but they were used with extraordinary ability. Naturally, the colors were achieved by nothing but different kinds of clay which, thanks to differing degrees of density achieved through dilution, provided a rich range of tones. Skillful employment of this type of coloring can be admired in the Gnathia pottery, which was produced from the second quarter of the fourth century B.C., most probably first in Tarentum and then in other workshops in Apulia and elsewhere. The Gnathia potters, whose vases were generally rather small, exploited the charm of the dark metallic painted surfaces, which contrasted markedly with the colored decoration, often consisting of miniaturistic vignettes recalling still lifes. The Gnathia pottery range, strongly tied to the Dionysiac tradition, included theater masks of outstanding realism. These masks corresponded to actual characters from the comic stage.

While this rather brief panorama of Italiot vase-painting has not been able to include a discussion of individual painters, we cannot ignore the most important Apulian vase painter, active in the second half of the fourth century, known as the Darius Painter. This name derives from one of his most important works, the monumental volute-krater in Naples, known as the "vaso dei Persiani" characterized by one of the very rare representations of a historical subject. The rather complex scene is an episode from the wars between the Greeks and the Persians. King Darius, identified by an inscription, is enthroned in the center. To understand the significance that this scene must have assumed in southern Italy in the third quarter of the fourth century, it is worth noting that, in that very period, the old rivalry between Greeks and Persians had suddenly flared up again: the peace im-

Apulian red-figure *amphora* with Orpheus and a dead person attributed to the Ganymede Painter
330-320 B.C.
Basle, Antikenmuseum Basel und Sammlung Ludwig
Cat. 214

Southern Italian and Sicilian Vases

Gnathia-style *lekythos*
ca. 340 B.C.
Taranto, Museo Nazionale
Cat. 327

Vase of the Persians
large volute *krater*
by the Darius Painter
detail
Darius enthroned holding
a council of war
second half 4th cent. B.C.
Naples
Museo Archeologico Nazionale

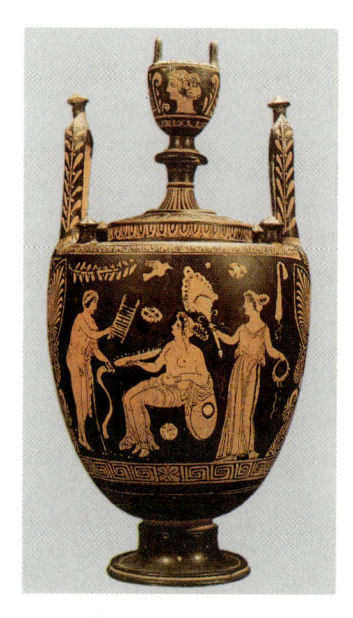

Nuptial *lebes*
combination vase
second half 4th cent. B.C.
Naples
Museo Archeologico Nazionale

posed by the Persians in 387–386 B.C. had led to the establishment of the Corinthian League in 338–337, as a reaction to that self-same "peace."

The works of this great master provide a perfect example of the pictorial achievements in Apulia mentioned above. One of his most remarkable qualities is the talent with which he characterized the human face and expressive features. His character studies give the impression that he was well acquainted with the new theories of physiognomy beginning to develop in his time.

The Darius Painter is one of the major representatives of late Apulian vase-painting, known as the ornate style, of which the elaborate and often very large volute-kraters are perfect examples. From the second quarter of the fourth century increasing numbers of these typical kraters were produced in Apulia, with Gorgon heads in relief attached to the end of the curving handles. This particular type was only been produced in Apulia. In fact, volute-kraters are rarely found west of southern Italy, even in their more simple, original form, inherited from Mainland Greece, and potters preferred to develop their own special shapes. There was a curious preference for "composite vases" in Campania, especially in Paestum. The basic shape, for example, could be a *lebes gamikos*, a container with a cover and curved high handles rising vertically; as the Greek name suggests, these were originally linked to the rites of marriage. They were fashioned in such a way that a second vessel – such as a small dish, a *lekane*, – could be placed on the flat knob of the lid. On top of this, there could be another much smaller and simpler *lebes gamikos* which, in turn, supported yet another vessel, this time a small *squat lethykos*. Many other kinds of combinations of basic shapes have been found, with a preference for the so-called "wedding container" and the *lekane*. Since the examples found were funerary vases, it is clear that these apparently hybrid shapes were not some kind of overblown ornamentation, but were probably expressing a message. We get the impression that the multiplication of certain shapes could be explained by the desire to underline the content of the message that each of these vases carries. Clearly the combination was worth more than the individual pieces, and this synergetic value had nothing to do with the exterior appearance; it was a question of transmitting this "something extra" to the dead. In more general terms, the composite vases concerned the reinforcing of single items involved in rites (which might not necessarily have been limited to the funerary sphere, but could have also referred to specific aspects of the world of the living).

We have already noted that the scenes depicting visits to the tomb typical of the majority of the Apulian *naiskoi* vases are totally unknown among Siceliot vases. In Campania, however, scenes around the tomb were very different in the early period. The center of the scene is occupied by a simple funerary *stele* rather than a monument. There is a lack of differentiation in the organization of space, and no distinction between the deceased and the living. Apulian influence is easily recognizable at the time when the vases produced in the western workshops begin to portray the characteristic group around the central *naiskos*. Relations between the various workshops are evident in these cases of Apulian influence. At Paestum, for example, in some works of the highly talented and original Aphrodite Painter one detects a transition in style from an Apulian (on rather an Apulianizing) to the Paestan phase. Potters and painters did not always remain in the same place (as can be seen in the Lucanian workshops). The Aphrodite Painter, who was active in Paestum, may provide an instinctive example of an individual craftsman who decided to travel to the West. Correspondences that can be observed between the early productions of Sicilian and Campanian workshops also reflect the mobility of these craftsmen. In spite of the specific stylistic features that developed over time in the main regions, Apulia, Lucania, and Campania, we ought not regard these various areas of production as distinctive self-contained units. Within these regions there were rather the individual cities and settlements with their local workshops to be considered. They were the ones responsible for establishing the productive structures, not the more abstract entities of the wider geographical regions as we know them today.

Pottery in Sicily developed along completely original lines. In the first half of the fourth century, the Greek or rather Siceliote area was limited to the east of the island, whereas the west was dominated by the Carthaginians. The period from the death of Dionysius I of Syracuse to the overthrow of tyranny in 342 B.C. upon the intervention of Timoleon was apparently little suited to the development of workshops of any quality. It is only partly true that the evolution of Siceliot vases can be examined with greater precision than the production of southern Italian workshops because we can rely on dated grave contexts. In fact, modern numismatists no longer agree about the dating on certain kinds of coins that had been confidently used to establish some of the dates in question. Among the more famous of the Siceliot vases are those rare specimens depicting scenes from the theater. They are particularly interesting because – in contrast with what we are used to from southern Italian vases reflecting scenes of tragedy – the Siceliot painters endeavored to represent at least part of the actual architectural structure of the stage.

There is no doubt that most of the imagery on Siceliot vases refers to the world of women, with numerous examples, and in a much more exclusive way compared to other Italiot vases, even though, in Apulia too, there are also frequent scenes that refer to the figure of Eros. The peak of this exclusiveness of female representations can be found on the typical vases produced on Lipari (Aeolian Islands). Here men do not appear at all. If there are no male figures, for whom, then, is Eros unveiling these solemn and lovely brides? Once again, the Lipari vessels are for funerary use. The women are presumably attending to a deity rather than a mortal: their destiny is another life altogether, in the Underworld. These scenes, which apparently refer to a wedding, are cogent proof of the close tie between marriage and death, a concept which seems to have been one of the principal beliefs of Magna Graecia.

The majority of the Lipari vases bear polychrome decoration. Numerous examples are colored with light blue, which was otherwise rarely used. The delicate use of colors continued in vases from Centuripe, a type that belongs to a later period of Siceliote production, already in the third century B.C. Through the finest vases produced at Centuripe, we can obtain a glimpse of the consummate skills of the great panel and wall-painters.

At the end of this survey let us again ask what this extraordinary world of images has to offer us. In fact, the vases of Magna Graecia require to be carefully deciphered. We must avoid misinterpreting their often bizarre forms as somewhat abstruse deviations of their creators. Everything about these vases is deliberate; everything was designed with a specific funerary significance. Even their shapes express hope in transformation rather than some form of annihilation. The mythical scenes decorating them, like some endless book of enchanting illustrations, convey a clear message: the destiny of heroes and heroines is not so different from that of humankind. The farcical scenes make us smile, as they did our forebears. And these are the scenes where we are still face to face with men as they really are: neither the rather unearthly Dionysiac initiates, nor the deceased who no longer belong to our world, nor the denizens of Hades.

Polychrome figured *pyxis*
by the Lipari Painter
first half 3rd cent. B.C.
Lipari, Museo Archeologico
Regionale Eoliano
Cat. 390

Angela Pontrandolfo   Wall-Painting in Magna Graecia

Figured globular *aryballos*
from the dwellings at Incoronata
mid 7th cent. B.C.
Metaponto
Museo Archeologico
Cat. 27

The ancient sources emphasize the importance of painting in the Greek cultural environment as an art of primary significance for poets and philosophers. By exploring the world of appearances and of perception, and in its capacity to analyze and reproduce the human passions, painting reveals numerous ties with the many fields of theoretical reflection. Simonides was thus to call painting "wordless poetry."

The written documentation that explicitly considered painting as a leading art compared to other figurative forms does not date back beyond the fourth century B.C. The accounts refer to artists whose active years can be placed between the fifth and the first half of the third century B.C., and they present an idea of painting of the Classical age re-elaborated and established as a model in the Roman epoch by Pliny the Elder in his *Natural History* (xxxv).

References to Magna Graecia are unfortunately few and far between, and do not allow us to reconstruct a history of names and artistic personalities. There is no evidence either of a deliberate desire to enhance the contribution made by western Grecism to the progress of pictorial art in the Italic world. The lack of written documentation is however made up for by the archaeological evidence. While being fragmentary and limited in number compared to other classes of materials due to its very fragility, this has in fact increased remarkably thanks to the discoveries made in the last fifty years in Italy and all round the Mediterranean. These recent additions have made it clear to historians that it is both impossible, misleading and perhaps useless to expect to retrace a straightforward history of painting, and that it might be better to try and reconstruct the specific nature of the various territorial environments into whose settings the pictorial documents merge as the outcome of complex systems of relations.

In the Archaic period when painting was an "outline of shadows" (as suggested by the Greek word *skiagraphia*, meaning "shadow painting"), the vast production of pottery in the Greek colonies of Magna Graecia and of Sicily as early as the seventh century B.C. shows that the Greek West was going through the same experiences as those on the continent and the islands. Figured vase-painting (given the lack of wall-paintings in this period) supplies the most direct evidence of the phases leading up to the invention of polychromy. The black outlines of the figures are filled with uniformly spread washes of color; the enriching details and features are drawn in relief. There are splendid examples from Megara Hyblaea, Syracuse, Gela, Naxos in eastern and southern Sicily, from Incoronata near ancient Siris on the Ionian coast, on the right bank of the Basento River, and from the *poleis* of Pithekoussai (Ischia) and Cumae in Campania.

The impact of these colonial productions on the neighboring non-Greek communities was certainly no less far-reaching than that of the imports from Greece itself. In particular, the structure of the aristocracies of southern Tyrrhenian Etruria made them potentially more receptive to and capable of developing actively the techniques and ideological models. The complex nature of these processes of acculturation comes to the fore indirectly in Pliny when the legendary figure of Demaratus, a noble exiled from Corinth and the father of Lucius Tarquinius Priscus, future king of Rome, is linked to the arrival of three craftsmen who were to create terra-cotta works and decorate them for temples and palaces. Their names are clearly etymological: Eucheir (to shape), Eugrammos (to paint), and Diopos (to install), and not surprisingly in another passage Pliny quotes a certain Eucheir as the "inventor of painting" and an artist by the same name is said to have been the teacher of Clearchos of Rhegium, the sculptor.

In yet another passage, however, Pliny supports the belief that painting in Italy had an autochthonous origin, as proved by the decorations on the temples of Caere, Lanuvium, and Ardea, and that, on the basis of information given by Varro, a Greek manner was introduced later on by two artists, Damophilus and Gorgasas, who were both able modelers and painters.

Given the contradictory character of the sources, modern research has rightly identified the crystallization and stratification of several traditions. On the basis of the archeological discoveries it has tried to focus on the influence exerted by the Greek cities of Sicily and Magna Graecia on the communities of Etruria and Latium, while an onomastic and stylistic analysis suggests that Damophilus and Gorgasas originate in the Chalcidian colonies of the Strait of Messina.

On the other hand, we should not ignore the fact that Epicharmus and Simonides mention a painter by the name of Scylax, a native of Rhegium, who painted a picture with a *kylix* inside an arcade at Phlius, in the Peloponnese.

The subject of this picture, situated according to Greek custom in a public place, is possibly echoed in the scenes of the so-called Tomba del Tuffatore or Diver's Tomb where a banquet is represented along the four side walls of the chamber.

Red-figure *krater* from Campania
detail of a scene of a *symposion*
340-330 B.C.
Naples
Museo Archeologico Nazionale
Cat. 351

The decoration of this tomb, discovered in Paestum (Poseidonia) in 1969, is the oldest documentation known to date of wall-painting in a Greek city, and the only one datable to the Classical period. Along the long walls the artists have painted the symposiasts lounging on beds with *kylikes* placed on low tables to the front. In one part of the short walls there is an ephebus holding an *oinochoe* used to serve wine who is walking away from a large garlanded krater (that contains the wine) sitting on a table, and in another part, a procession is taking place, led by a young naked youth with a blue drape on his shoulders, followed by a flautist and a bearded man leaning on a stick.

Some of the symposiasts are lying in pairs, lovemaking or amusing themselves with the *kottabos*, which consists in throwing the dregs of wine from their cups against a bronze instrument lying in the center of the room. Other figures are unaccompanied and are depicted playing the lyre or pipes; yet another is singing, with his hand to his forehead, a conventional gesture to indicate ecstasy.

The figured scenes on the four side walls undoubtedly form a common subject that is completed by another scene painted on the inner side of the ceiling block, which has given its name to the tomb: a young diver is flying through the air toward a pool, almost as if he flew over the blocks of square stones mounted one on top of another, which lie to the right-hand side of the greeny-blue background.

As soon as it was discovered in Paestum in 1969, the Diver's Tomb became famous for its uniqueness and was the subject of a heated debate between those (including its discoverer, Mario Napoli) who emphasized the great Greek painting characterizing the monument, and others, led by Ranuccio Bianchi Bandinelli, who tended to reduce its historical and artistic import, and consider it as the work of ordinary craftsmen and of a provincial nature, identifying the similarities with contemporary black-figure vase-painting produced in the nearby Campania under Etruscan influence. Moreover, another chamber tomb, now lost, decorated with painted scenes dating back to the first half of the fifth century, had been found in this area near Capua.

Today, twenty-five years after its discovery, the painting of the Diver's Tomb, which is datable to 480–470 B.C. given its style and that of the Attic *lekythos* found inside the tomb together with two alabaster unguent vases, can certainly be defined as a "hybrid." The way the figures have been represented and the composition of the scenes, especially that of the symposiasts lounging on their *klinai*, are perfectly "Greek" and just like the well-known and widespread pictures on the coeval red-

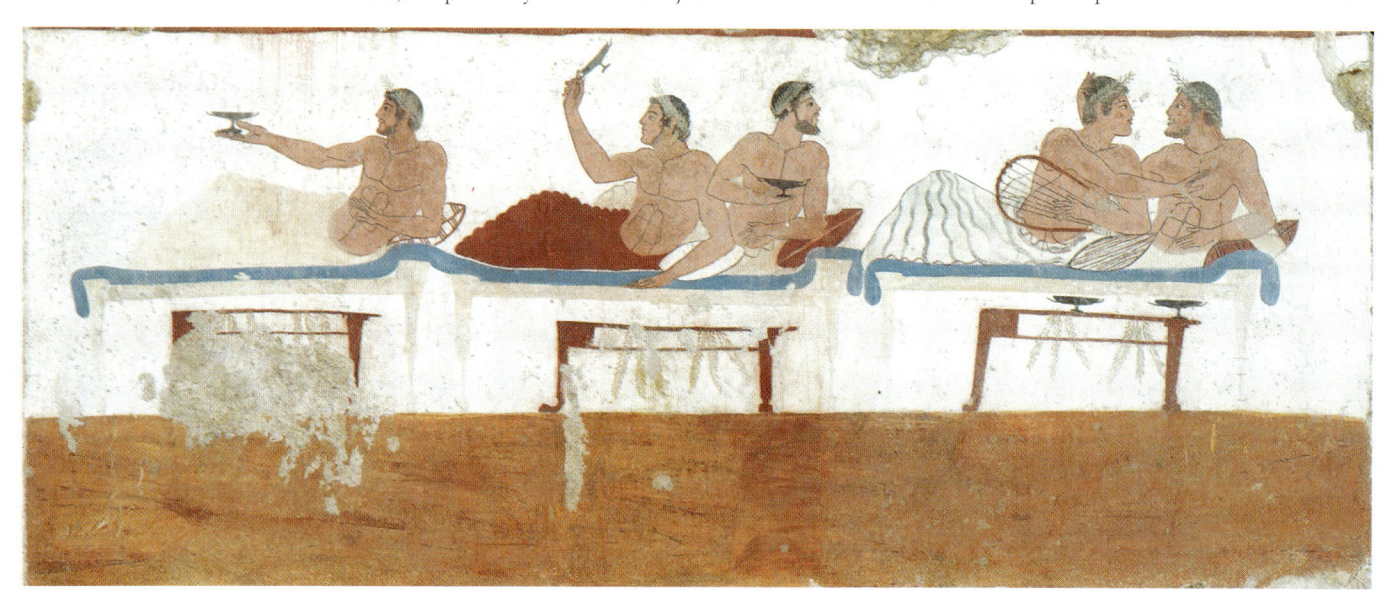

The Tomb of the Diver
long side slabs
480-470 B.C.
Paestum, Museo
Archeologico Nazionale

figure Attic pottery. Contrariwise, the mentality of decorating the inside of tombs with paintings is not at all Greek.

This custom was adopted at different times in some areas bordering on the Greek world, that had absorbed its cultural traits but whose societies had vertical structures. Examples are the frescoes of the sixth century B.C. discovered at Karaburun in Lycia and those in Macedon dating back to the dawn of Hellenism. Other examples can be found in Italy as from the seventh century in Etruria, at Veii, Caere, Clusium, and Tarquinii.

The "Greek" and the "Etrusco-Italic" aspects in the paintings of the Diver's Tomb cannot be isolated and are compounded in a harmonious unity which gives an idea of the complex nature of society in Paestum in the fifth century. On the one hand it irradiated political and cultural influence over the surrounding native communities, yet it was still a frontier city on the borders of the Etruscan territories in Campania to the north of the Sele, and tied to them intimately by osmosis.

The paintings of Paestum emanate their own undoubted fascination which lies more in the highly imaginative subject matter than in the techniques used to create them. The fresco was not very carefully painted and the use of color was hardly sophisticated; moreover, the execution was rapid and sketchy, leaving dripping trails of pigment. That more than one painter was certainly involved in painting the scenes on each wall is evident from the difference in brush strokes.

However, in examining these sketches, the couple of lovers, painted on one of the long walls, and the diving scene on the ceiling, have a unique and original appeal that stems from both the draftsmanship and the composition, which enriches the entire monument with a literary attribute to the point that the whole representation appears to become a story that stimulates the viewer to deep speculation that is neither easily nor immediately resolved.

The construction similar to a diving board from which the diver has leapt probably represents the *pulai* or pillars erected by Heracles at the end of the known world to mark the limit to what man may obtain knowledge of, and is therefore an extraordinary metaphor of death.

The dive transcends reality, and the diver symbolizes the passage from life to the ocean of death, which is a source of other forms of knowledge to which the noble man – the Greek citizen as exalted by Pindar in his *Odes* in the same years that these frescoes were painted – will obtain access, though not completely, through the experience of the *symposion* and of abandon caused by music, song, and eros.

The entire decorative program of the Diver's Tomb seems to try and celebrate, through its images, the conceptual links between the symposium that exalts the values that make a Greek citizen noble and the metaphorical representation of the passage to the afterworld. While full of Greek conceptual models, the paintings in the Diver's Tomb are in fact an exception, even as far as their contents are concerned, because they do not mirror the typical mental attitude of the Greeks who would normally never decorate the interior of a tomb with paintings, nor place the world of death together with that of the *symposion*, for the two worlds contradict each other.

It represents an exception to the rule which is also a sign of political integration, and it reveals a preference for an individual response to death which seems, through the very scene of the symposium, to exalt other forms of integration. The result is the feeling that this monument wants to emphasize the ideal union between the dead person, recognizable as a *mousikos aner* by the lyre placed beside him, and the guests at the symposium represented on the walls, almost as if certifying and sealing the identity and the membership of a group that launches beyond this life the pleasure of wine through the symbolism of the dive, and yet is conditioned as seen in the symposium by the rules that regulate it.

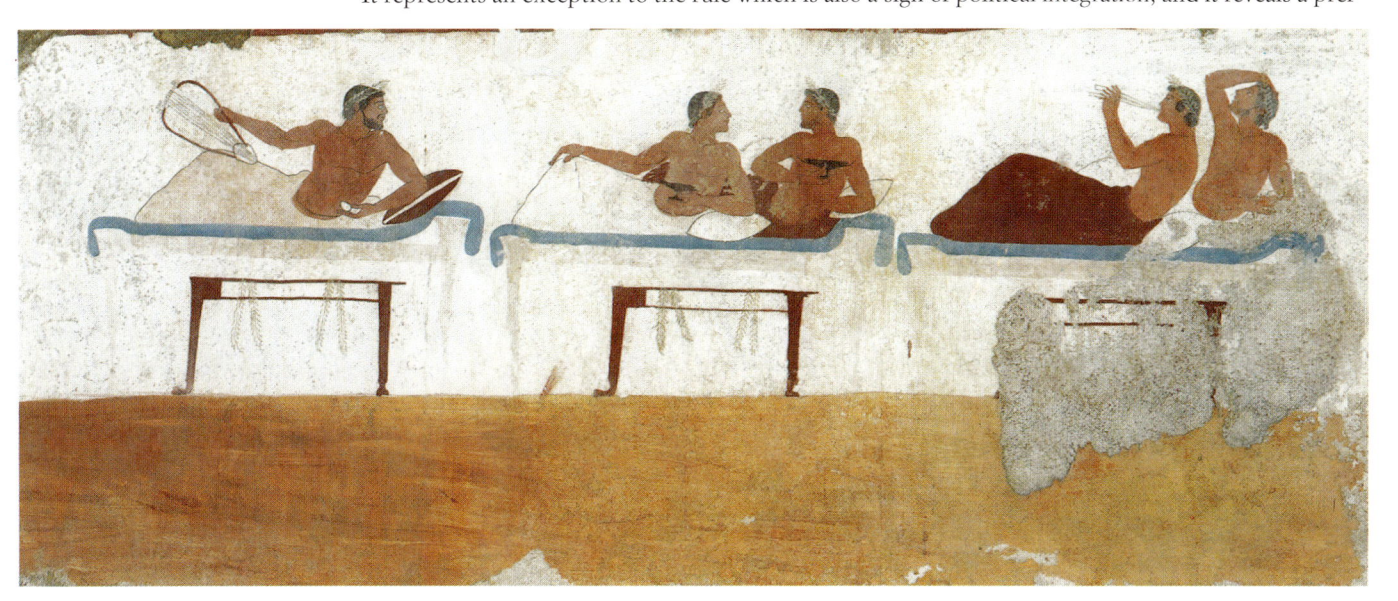

The narrative potential of the scenes and the intricate significance of the plot of this private monument make us realize how great the loss is of those pictorial heroic cycles that decorated public places or sanctuaries in Greek cities. An idea of what occurred in Magna Graecia, can be gleaned from a de-

The Tomb of the Driver
cover slab
480-470 B.C.
Paestum, Museo Archeologico Nazionale
Cat. 144

scription made by Pausanias (VI. 6. 4–11) of a painting that celebrated the liberation of the city of Temesa from a demon that was terrorizing it, thanks to the courage of Euthymus the boxer from Locri (three-times champion at Olympia in 484, 476, and 472 B.C.) who was so famous that he was even immortalized by the poet Callimachus in one of his *aetia*.

According to a recent convincing argument put forward by A. Rouveret, this painting was executed in the second half of the fifth century, perhaps because of a commission from the Panhellenic colony of Thurii founded at the same time on the site of what had been Sybaris in the Archaic age, before its destruction by Croton.

The subject was a series of personifications of places: the Sybaris River shown as a youth, the Calabros River, the Lyka spring as a nymph, Hera, the city of Temesa and, in the center of the whole composition, the demon chased away by the athletic hero. An inscription referred to the demon as Alybas. It was painted black and dressed in a wolf skin which rendered it even more terrifying but still very realistic.

Pausanias' description gives the impression that this painting, while being a typical subject of Magna Graecia, actually anticipated the types of composition to be adopted in Italiot pottery, in which the personifications of places act almost realistically to render the scene in which a mythical or mytho-

The Tomb of the Diver
short side slabs
480-470 B.C.
Paestum, Museo
Archeologico Nazionale

logical event is taking place, as if the intention is to communicate to the spectator that he too belonged to a geographical order that is also a cosmic order from the existential and philosophical point of view.

The figurative culture of the painter Zeuxis was influenced by speculative sophist philosophy. As Xenophon wrote, Zeuxis "found the way to calculate light and shade" and was one of those painters who, once having mastered their means of expression, became aware of the creative act in the artistic process. He was the subject of considerable controversy because of the extraordinary breakthrough made by his teaching, compared by Plato to that imparted by the Sophists. Zeuxis was to conclude the search for an idea of perfection expressed (like Polyclitus in sculpture) through a careful calculation of proportions, but at the same time, he achieved considerable success in understanding the deception of appearances.

Zeuxis was a western Greek by education, since he was born at Heraclea, probably Heraclea Minoa in Sicily, and had been taught by a certain Damophilus of Himera. During the first years of his career, before moving to Athens and then to Pella to the Macedonian court, he had received commissions from both Siceliot and Italiot patrons. He did in fact donate to the city of Acragas, then under the hegemony of Heraclea Minoa, one of his paintings, *Heracles as a child strangling the serpents*, and he made numerous paintings for the Temple of Hera Lacinia at Capo Colonna, near Croton (then the seat of the Italiot League), including one representing Helen, commissioned by the Acragantines, which was taken to Rome after the temple was sacked by Pyrrhus, and exhibited in the Porticus Philippi during Pliny's lifetime.

Zeuxis rose to fame thanks to this painting of Helen, which depicted the ideal perfection of beauty and was recorded in the proem of Cicero's rhetoric treatise *De Inventione*. In the same period, Gorgias, a sophist from Leontini who was famous for the seductive capacity of his oratory, composed a eulogy of Helen; and Euripides, in his tragedy of the same name, compares his heroine to a painting. An echo of Zeuxis' painting is recognizable in a small painting on marble from Herculaneum, now in the Museo Nazionale, Naples, which is a copy made at the end of the Hellenistic age. It illustrates five girls playing knucklebones and was executed using a monochrome technique on a white ground. Its structure and style are very close to the figures painted on pottery in the last decades of the fifth century B.C.

Procedures similar to those used by vase-painters were employed by the wall-painters who decorated the tombs found in some Hellenized settlements in southern Italy, datable to the late fifth century B.C. One of the particularly intense paintings illustrating a phase of the funerary rites is the semi-chamber tomb discovered at Ruvo, Apulia, in 1833, now on exhibition at the Museo Nazionale, Naples. A procession of women winds along the four walls, giving the impression of forming a circle round the dead man in the tomb. Their feet are moving in a fast dance, probably a *threnos*, to the beat of the notes played by the young lyre-players. The latter, dressed in white robes, set the rhythm of the whirling scene achieved through the expert use of the colors of the fluttering *peploi* and shawls which cover the heads and shoulders of the women. The lively reds, yellows, blues, white and black are spread over the figures in a rhythmic sequence that alternates them and doubles back on itself. The rhythm created by the color is in turn highlighted and brought out by the white borders on the dresses and shawls which seem to swing round the dancing figures, partly contrasting and partly accompanying the continual line of the arms painted in black outline on a white ground. The arms form a chain that gives visual expression to the unity of the scene because each dancer holds the hands, not of the two beside her, but of the one in front and the one behind her companions. The style of painting at Ruvo, with its ability to tell a story by fixing in the images a memorable scene of the rites, reveals the extraordinary cultural dynamism of western Grecism in its osmotic relationship with the Italic environment.

Apart from the figurative paintings, archeological documents also offer a considerable collection of decorative paintings, unmentioned by the written sources, which should not be ignored because they illustrate the long-term activity of highly specialized craftsmen taking part in the construction of the monumental buildings.

Part of this category are some painted tombs decorated with simple geometric and floral designs, dating back to the beginning of the fifth century B.C., and discovered both in some of the Greek cities in southern Italy and in the settlements of the natives in their spheres of influence: Gela and Vassallaggi in Sicily; Tarentum (Taras); Ugento and Cavallino in Messapia, and Gravina in the Peucetii area on the borders of Matera; Metapontum (Metapontion); and lastly, Paestum (Poseidonia) and some of the sites in northern Campania.

Some paintings have a tall red border at the base, whitewashed walls decorated halfway up and at the

Painted side slabs
from Tomb 87 at Spina-Caudo
4th cent. B.C.
Paestum
Museo Archeologico Nazionale
Cat. 262

top with regular red, blue, or black stripes. Others have a small floral frieze apart from the stripes, or, as in the case of a Tarentine sarcophagus, a series of lotus flowers with red berries and blue leaves. Botanical motifs cover the walls of another tomb in Tarentum and of a marble sarcophagus from Vassallaggi, while a Metapontine frieze in the center of the four walls comprises twigs of long green lanceolate leaves alternated with pairs of red flowers. Other tombs reveal rigorously geometric decorations designed along with the architectural structure of the monument and other decorative elements including even animated representations. At Ugento, one painting dating to the first years of the fifth century B.C., has a series of red ribbons hanging from the stripes drawn at the top of the walls and on the ceiling there are branches, birds, and objects suspended on cords. In a chamber tomb at Gravina there is a procession of horsemen and animals painted on a plain background [fondo risparmiato] in a limited area halfway up a wall between stripes above a high border at the base and a continuous black meander motif at the top.

Ornamental painting and scenes with figures unite in a decorative system along the walls of fourth-century tombs in Paestum. Here, the quantity of documents discovered has made it possible to analyze the special techniques and styles of the individual workshops, to distinguish the skills of the painters, to follow the evolution of painting from the production of good quality artistic craftwork to the achievement of high quality wall painting, and lastly, and most significantly, to glean the close relations between painters and clients.
The eighty frescoed tombs discovered at Paestum whose dates range within a period of just over one hundred years, although numerous, were in fact limited to select members of the Lucanian hegemonic groups that had taken over the Greek city at the end of the fifth century.
Right from the start of the series, two decorative systems are noticeable, which prove that wall-painting was already deep-rooted in the Greek city. One of the systems conceives the wall as an architectural space divided into several superimposing zones, indicated geometrically and with colored wash backgrounds – black or red in the lower part that becomes a border divided from the white upper zone by a series of alternate red, white and black stripes or by two branches working toward a rosette at the center. The second system considers the wall as a single space framed at the top by a branch frieze, and the whole surface is considered as if it was a fresh canvas, with a white ground called by the Greeks, a *pinax leukomenos*. It brings to mind the fifth-century Attic *lekythoi*, which were used exclusively in funerary rites.

The insertion of images in these two decorative systems highlights right from the start of the series the existence of two well-defined workshops with their own repertoires and figurative programs, even when they are depicting the same scenes.

One workshop, which evinces a more pictorial tradition compared to the other, created small figures set in a slightly larger field, surrounded on all four sides by a heavy, continuous black outline, whose white ground is brightened up by a few strokes of red, while brilliant splashes of green color the leaves of trees, the floral frieze and garlands which fill the whole short wall together with little animals and objects similar to the grave goods, something like a still life. The other workshop used a more structural, or architectural, decorative system, drawing monumental figures which occupied nearly the whole wall and which are emphasized by the high red border on which they stand. A discontinuous black outline, sometimes together with or substituted by a red one, serves to define the figures with their small heads, angular profiles and brush strokes that give a contour to the bodies.

There are therefore various well-defined figurative repertoires constantly corresponding to the different ways in which the artists have conceived the surface to be decorated. These decorative and figurative systems develop regularly not only in relation to each single wall but also to the whole composition of the four walls of the tomb that are interrelated by means of repetitive and traditional patterns, although there are occasional variations.

The frequency of the scenes represented in the tombs at Paestum has helped scholars analyze the sense of their composition. The paintings take on the role of a literary text and therefore give modern spectators the chance of making attempt at understanding the story told in pictures, which was obvious to the painters who had created them and to the public who were to enjoy them. These series of pictures, painted quickly on the spot with a technique similar to that of frescoes, and which were destined to be seen only for the brief period of the funeral rites, represent an ideal world as conceived by the Lucanian elites of Paestum.

All the tombs have scenes in common – chariot races, boxing, duels – which refer to the funerary games, a part of the rites, even though the figurative programs vary from workshop to workshop according to the requirements of clients with well-defined but not static ideals. They are homogeneous but not monolithic.

One kind of workshop seems to be more refined and more rigid in its adherence to sophisticated customs, the other is more dynamic in its capacity to bring together and mingle tradition with new symbolic compositions.

Ritual funeral dance
from Tomb 11 at Ruvo di Puglia
second half 5th cent. B.C.
Naples
Museo Archeologico Nazionale

Wall-Painting in Magna Graecia

The second type of workshop offered its clients a figurative program that became the fashion. The most successful image was that used in male burials, where the pictures celebrated the "homecoming of the warrior": the hero from the ideal point of view. The dead man is shown, weapons in hand, on his horse with the remains of his conquered enemy, while he rides toward a matron who offers him the instruments necessary for the rites of purification. This image idealizes military virtue and introduces the idea of etiquette giving it a public aspect, while bringing to mind, as a consequence, our loss as regards other non-serial and non-funerary paintings. Not surprisingly, this kind of iconography was adopted in the tombs of the Campanian aristocracies, especially at Capua and Nola, and it would not be mere conjecture to interpret it as the founding of an Italic figurative language, derived from the Greek tradition in its techniques and structures, but completely autonomous in its forms and content. All the paintings executed for the burial of women, both at Paestum and elsewhere in Campania, should be considered in this same light. The subjects are richly dressed women wearing local costumes or busy at their spinning, while in a painting at Cumae, a woman looks at herself in a mirror.

As from the mid-fourth century, new scenes appear in women's tombs at Paestum with images of the various phases of the funerary rites: the preparation of the body and the wake, weeping and wailing expressed through gestures, sacrifices and games. Tomb 47 at Andriuolo is extraordinary. The story goes as far as illustrating the dead woman's journey to the Afterworld. She is shown while about to step into Charon's boat. Charon, the ferryman, is painted with wings and a head like a Gorgon. This painting is typical of a new trend, keen on a natural representation of the scene and tending to overdo the expressiveness of the main components of the picture nearly always by means of color.

During the same period another type of decoration came to the fore that revealed greater technical expertise in attempts to express perspective and chiaroscuro. The artists have obviously learnt

Matron and handmaid
wearing funerary clothing
from a tomb at Cumae
4th cent. B.C.
Naples
Museo Archeologico Nazionale

The Black Horseman slab
from Tomb 58 at Andriuolo
340 B.C.
Paestum, Museo
Archeologico Nazionale
Cat. 261

from the figurative styles of both Tarentine and Macedonian early Hellenism. One example is Tomb 4/1971 at Andriuolo where the scene of a duel is elaborated according to a centripetal structure much like the one in the mosaic at Pella with the signature of the artist Gnosis.

These steps forward mark the end of the old decorative systems and the launching of new ones. Some monuments demonstrate the passage to the achievement of real paintings where each wall becomes a picture (but with considerable variations in the quality and execution) such as in the two short sides of Tomb 58 at Andriuolo. In particular, the picture showing a knight on a splendid black horse, could almost be called a "megalograph," created by expertly distributed overlapping colors.

Other paintings with a masterly use of more sophisticated techniques open up the way to expressive accomplishments exploring a new figurative language full of political and propagandistic significance in preference to the old. The chamber tombs discovered in the Spinazzo area of Paestum and some paintings at Capua are examples of this change. Here, the faces of the people, such as the old magistrate, have become realistic portraits.

These pictorial cycles all repeat the same program: a scene of farewell between two people on the central wall, and processions behind them on the side walls. They demonstrate the self-confidence of the artists in merging the ability to draw figures with strong outlines with both a knowledgeable use of color spread with brushes of different sizes and in a variety of tones, and a remarkable exploitation of shadow to highlight the objects as if they were really hanging on the walls.

These documents are the means to understanding the mediations and cultural climate in which the influence of the Italiot pictorial tradition of Tarentine origin gained ground in Rome where, at the end of the fourth century B.C., Fabius Pictor, a nobleman turned painter, decorated the temple of Salus with scenes representing historical events, highly praised for the benefit of posterity by Dionysius of Halicarnassus.

The very same period that saw the emergence of this historical and celebrative type of wall-painting, produced a second type, of excellent quality, that was exclusively ornamental. It played games

The Tomb of the Pomegranate
detail of the wall decoration
from Gnathia
end 4th cent. B.C.

with the structures that often led to scenographic architectural illusions. Examples of this type are the ceilings with fake beams, such as those in the so-called Pomegranate Tomb at Gnathia, or the vaulted ceiling of one of the Tarentine chamber tombs, which is decorated with tendrils and vine leaves that cover a pergola and is apparently a quotation of a ceiling painted by Pausias of Sicyon, who was the first to transform painting into an applied art.
Illusionistic perspective created both the painted columns on the walls of a tomb at Ruvo, forming a colonnade surrounding two birds perched on a bath, and the imitation windows of the Barbarossa and Lagrasta *hypogeia* near Canosa.

The area of Monte Sannace (Gioia del Colle) has yielded decorated walls with a tall blue lower border topped with check patterns filled with blue and yellow lines that appear to reproduce the pleats of a drape. These are bordered at the top by a frieze of *bucrania* and cups, and further up, by garlands and ribbons. The latter two elements comprise an elegant decoration in the *hypogeion* at Naples where pilasters, with female-headed capitals between volutes, and stuccoed cornices lend a rhythmic accent to the stretch of garlands and ribbons. The semicircular space that concludes the barrel vault of the central wall is filled with a splendid stuccoed and painted head of Medusa, exactly the same as the one on the pediment of the facade of a chamber tomb at Arpi (the so-called Medusa Tomb, whose interior is embellished with capitals with fine female heads and a painted floral frieze).
Right from the dawn of the Hellenistic age, Apulian society, like the Neapolitan one, displayed a preference for decorating the interiors of tombs like its houses. However, at the same time, adhering to Macedonian models, it produced monumental facades of an illusionistic nature, representing the gateway to the palace of Hades.
Part of this same tradition are the decorated doors, sometimes with people on the threshold, discovered at Tarentum and at Rudiae, and the figured frieze above the door – painted like a *naiskos* – of one of the chambers of the *hypogeion* of Cerberus at Canosa that represents the journey toward the underworld of a knight guided by Hermes.
The wall-paintings found in southern Italy testify, in spite of the gaps in the written tradition, to the quantity of knowledge and skills that developed in the Hellenic environment to which the cities of the West belonged in all respects. Above all, they teach us how the continual progress in techniques was accompanied by the consolidation of a common pictorial language, skillfully assimilated and re-elaborated in various ways according to regional traditions also by populations of non-Greek origin.
The figurative and decorative expressions of this pictorial language mark the stages of the process of elaborating a western culture whose specific character was the result of constant and uninterrupted exchanges between the native world and the Greek colonial cities.

Bibliography
Il Museo di Taranto..., 1988; G. ANDREASSI-A. COCCHIARO, 1987; A. CIANCIO *et al.*, 1986; E.H. CORRIGAN, 1979; S. DE CARO, in *RIASA* 1-3, VI-VII, 1983-84, pp. 71-74; M. MAZZEI, 1995; P. MORENO, 1987; M. NAPOLI, 1970; A. PONTRANDOLFO, in *Magna Grecia IV*, *Arte e artigianato* 1990, pp. 351-390; A. PONTRANDOLFO, A. ROUVERET, 1992; A. PONTRANDOLFO, G. VECCHIO, in *Napoli antica* 1985, pp. 283-293; *Principi imperatori vescovi*. 1992; A. ROUVERET, *BEFAR* 274, 1989.

The *hypogeion* of Cerberus
details of the wall decoration
at Canosa
4th cent. B.C.

Pier Giovanni Guzzo The Jewelry of the Western Greeks

Necklace of pendent disks
from Cumae
end 8th-beginning 7th cent. B.C.
Naples
Museo Archeologico Nazionale
Cat. 47/I

Dragon-shaped *fibula*
from Cumae
end 8th-beginning 7th cent. B.C.
Naples
Museo Archeologico Nazionale
Cat. 47/II

Apart from its intrinsic value, the jewelry of antiquity is usually appreciated as evidence of luxury and prestige. Nevertheless, it must necessarily be considered as archaeological material having historical interest, just like pottery or metal artifacts, or, for that matter, sculpture.

The fact that little importance has been attributed to antique jewelry in silver and gold has conditioned its study. Frequently, the jewelry of antiquity has been collected for its own sake, so that all knowledge of its provenance and its association with other finds has been lost. Thus, it is considerably more difficult to identify its links with specific cultures, and it is not always possible to provide absolute dating, or ascertain where it was made and used.

A field of study that has recently developed concerns the techniques used in the manufacture of jewelry, so that much more is now known about these. But, at the same time, it has been discovered that the goldsmith's techniques are both extremely conservative and widely diffused. Thus, from a historical point of view, even the most searching examinations of technique provide little useful information. The only exception to this is when, together with other criteria, they are used to identify modern articles made as imitations of antique ones.

The use of gold and silver for personal adornment was limited to the leading personages in the different cultural spheres of antiquity. Hence, a close study of this particular type of output allows us to have a greater insight into a socio-cultural stratum that, because it was dominant, is of notable importance for understanding that society as a whole. This is also because the extent of the diffusion of the ornaments made of precious materials is an important indicator of the standard of living, cultural development, the use of forms of self-aggrandizement, and so forth. When reliable excavation data are available, jewelry contributes to our understanding of ritual forms (whether funerary or votive), and archaeological differences between the sexes and age groups, and also provides "antiquarian" details regarding dress and the decoration of the person.

As far as the latter aspect is concerned, the finds representing jewelry are not as clear as archaeological excavations, nor do they cover all the cultures, which excavation investigates in a thorough manner. The same applies to the fairly limited number of epigraphic references to jewelry, which are generally confined to the sacred sphere.

The oldest gold jewelry from southern Italy known today comes from Calabria, Lucania, Apulia, and Campania. Important examples include: armlets in gold wire from Oppido Mamertina; spirals in gold wire from Torre Galli; circular *phalerae* with a central boss in sheet gold from Pisticci and Tursi; a bracelet in gold wire from Arpi; a circular *phalera* in sheet gold from Monte Saraceno; pendent discs in sheet gold from Cumae.

All of these finds repeat forms that had also been used for bronze jewelry. Hence it is clear that the metal used did not influence the output of these ornaments, which was already well-established in the Iron Age, even though gold was certainly introduced into the different cultures from outside the area, as there were no gold mines in southern Italy.

It is necessary, therefore, to try to identify the importers of the precious metal. Apart from Cumae and, in part, those situated in Lucania, the find-places do not always correspond exactly to the subsequent sites of Greek colonies. However, the same areas have yielded large numbers of other finds that can be dated to periods previous to the founding of the colonies, thus indicating that they were mainly frequented by Greek seafarers. It can, therefore, be postulated that unrefined gold was introduced into southern Italy by the Greeks in the course of their trade with the native communities. The metal would then be distributed to the other communities as part of the normal process of trade. And the finds, in which chance has played an important part (as in nearly all archaeological discoveries), have also been made on relatively remote sites, or ones that were not affected by colonial settlement, such as Arpi and Monte Saraceno.

With regard to the two latter sites, however, the importance of the pre-existing Adriatic amber trade should not be underestimated. In fact, old finds made at Noicattaro – they have not, however, been scientifically examined – comprise two gold discs, decorated with granulation, which were certainly made by a Greek workshop of the Geometric period.

The local origin of the oldest gold jewelry seems, therefore, to be attested both by the form of the finds, which is exclusively native, and by the mastery of metallurgical techniques displayed by these communities.

During the Archaic period, the founding and subsequent growth of the Greek colonies led to the setting up of a chain of trade relations, both with the exterior and with the remaining native communities in the interior.

The Greek colonies have not yielded many items of jewelry from this period. An exception is a series of statuettes, representing male and female figures, from Tarentum (Taras) and Metapontum (Metapontion). A recent find of the same type demonstrates that such figurines formed part of elaborate headdresses that were worn by women. They appear to portray the priestesses of local cults, chosen from members of the noble families.

The stylistic characteristics of the finds known to date seem to indicate that the goldsmiths' workshops producing such elaborate jewelry, evidently a symbol of social status, were located in Tarentum. In fact, other early jewelry has been found in Tarentum, including a silver diadem with a number of distinguishing features that are evidence of the independence of the Tarentine goldsmiths in this period. From Sybaris there is a breastplate in gilded silver sheet, with repoussé decoration consisting of palmette and lotus flower motifs. The reconstruction of the methods of burial indicates that it adorned a garment, probably a ritual one. The style of the decorative motifs does not permit identification of the workshop that made the breastplate, but it is likely to have been situated at Sybaris. This is also because other jewelry, mostly in silver, has been found on the nearby sites of Amendolara and Francavilla Marittima, indicating a close relationship between the Achaean colony and its satellite settlements.

While, in this case, it is possible to suggest an origin for the jewelry, this is not so with the elaborate silver necklaces, consisting of wires plaited in a herringbone pattern, found at Chiaromonte. In fact, there is an almost total lack of archaeological evidence regarding the jewelry output of Siris, which must have influenced the inland native area of Chiaromonte.

Similar necklaces, made with the same technique and the same material, have been found in the Archaic Greek necropolis at Cumae, which seems to suggest that the jewelry found at Chiaromonte was

Embossed gold pendent
from Noicattaro
6th cent. B.C.
Bari, Museo Archeologico
Cat. 103

Pectoral
embossed gold and silver
from Sybaris
599-575 B.C.
Sibari, Museo Nazionale
Archeologico della Sibaritide
Cat. 102

The Jewelry of the Western Greeks

Gold necklace with pendents
decorated with a woman's head
from Ruvo
end 6th-beginning 5th cent. B.C.
Taranto
Museo Archeologico Nazionale
Cat. 104

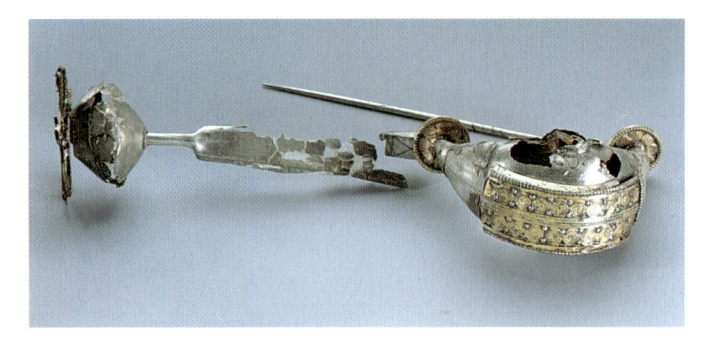

The Jewelry of the Western Greeks

Fibula with leech bow
from Pisciolo di Melfi
second half 5th cent. B.C.
Melfi
Museo Nazionale del Melfese
Cat. 109/I

Fibula with double bow
and duck's head catchplate
from Pisciolo di Melfi
second half 5th cent. B.C.
Melfi
Museo Nazionale del Melfese
Cat. 109/IV

imported from there. However, a pendant, also made of silver, was added to one of these necklaces, and there is no parallel for this in the Cumaean finds. Thus, it would appear to be prudent to await a more thorough investigation of the Archaic necropolises of Siris before coming to a conclusion.

In fact, it was during the Early Archaic period, at Cumae and, to a lesser extent, at Pithekoussai, that goldsmiths' workshops produced silver pendants on which Egyptian scarabs, or imitations of these, were mounted. The overall form of these pendants was derived from similar types used in the eastern Mediterranean, but the finds at Cumae and Pithekoussai are different in a number of details, for example their average dimensions. However, it is extremely likely that this jewelry produced in the Chalcidian colony was influenced by oriental models. In their turn, the Cumaean pendants inspired a limited number of pendants with closely related forms, although these used amber scaraboids rather than the Egyptian ones in *pâte de verre*.

In the sixth century B.C., precious ornaments must have also been widespread among the natives since, by the end of the fifth century, jewels were being produced – mostly in gilded silver – that were based on totally unhellenized formal and functional types, while the syntax of the decoration was mixed. Notable examples are the *fibulae* from the princely tombs of Melfi and the Daunian earrings.

What is not so obvious is whether the goldsmiths who made these objects were natives, or Italiots who worked exclusively for a native clientele. To judge by the much greater emphasis that is given to the form of these jewels, which is wholly Italic – unlike the decoration, which is added and, in a sense, irrelevant – it seems probable that the goldsmiths were Italic, even though they were well-informed about the contemporary Italiot production. As has been shown by ample archaeological evidence, the latter was commonly found in the native communities of the interior.

Parts of necklace in gold lamina
from Cumae
4th cent. B.C.
Naples
Museo Archeologico Nazionale
Cat. 247

The Jewelry of the Western Greeks

Pair of gold leech *fibulae*
from Cumae
4th cent. B.C.
Naples
Museo Archeologico Nazionale
Cat. 248/II

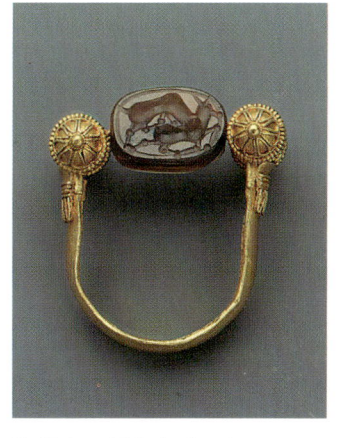

Gold ring with incised sardonyx
from Cumae
4th cent. B.C.
Naples
Museo Archeologico Nazionale
Cat. 249

Gold ring with a bezel
from Cumae
4th cent. B.C.
Naples
Museo Archeologico Nazionale
Cat. 248/I

Gold boat-like earring
from Tarentum
second half 4th cent. B.C.
Taranto, Museo Nazionale
Cat. 309

The Jewelry of the Western Greeks

Grave goods from Tomb 9
at Roccagloriosa
5th-4th cent. B.C.
Salerno
Soprintendenza Archeologica
Cat. 271

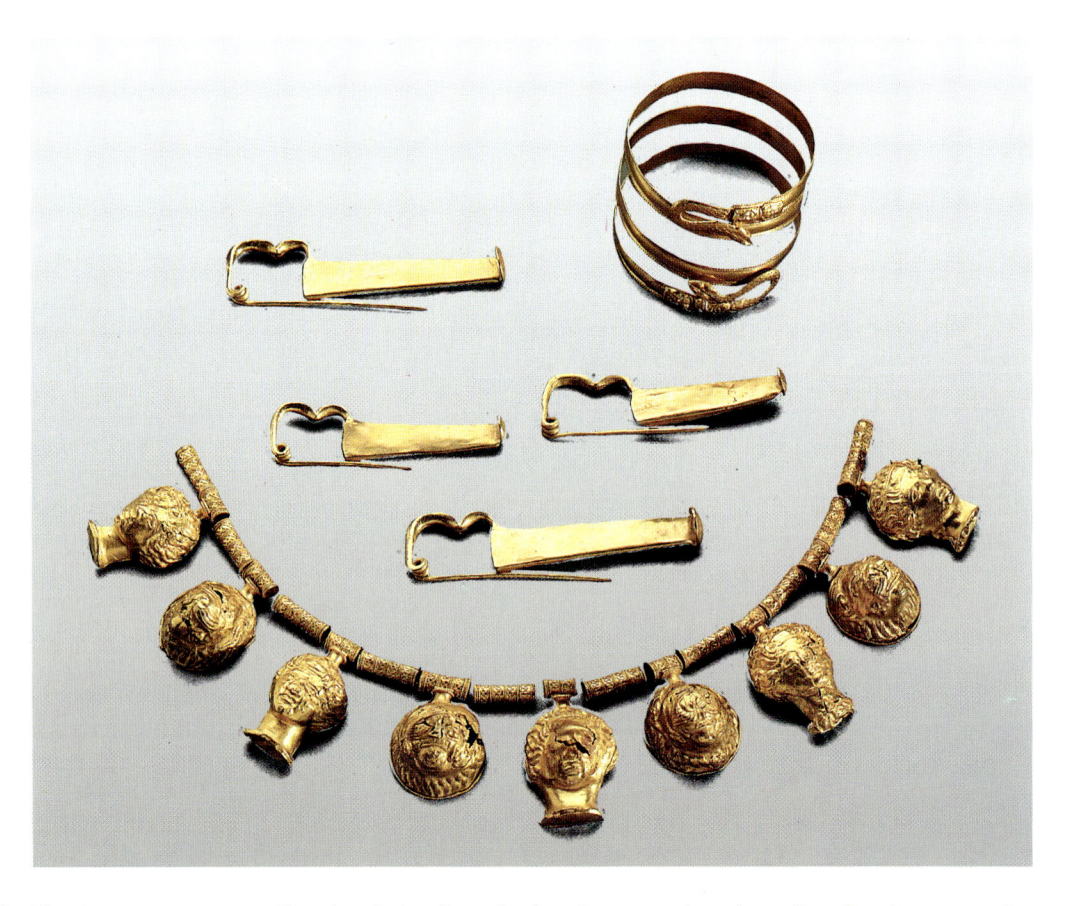

Gold necklace
from Pisticci
4th cent. B.C.
Naples
Museo Archeologico Nazionale
Cat. 283/I

Two important groups of jewelry, dating from the fourth century, have been found in the necropolises of Cumae and Tarentum. A similar group, from a slightly later date, has come to light in the necropolis of Teano dei Sidicini, while there are numerous Italic tombs (for instance, Roccagloriosa, Canosa, Armento, Sant'Eufemia) that have yielded single jewels or small groups of them.

In particular, archaeologists have sought to classify – and thus distinguish – the types produced in southern Italy and those from Mainland Greece. In fact, the fourth and third centuries were characterized by movements of peoples and expanding trade, while the establishment of magnificent centers of power, such as the capitals – some of them newly founded – of the kingdoms resulting from the exploits of Alexander the Great, led to the creation of styles suitable for a royal court, especially with regard to the production of jewelry. The latter was the consequence both of direct access to the sources of raw materials in the East, and of the institution of a powerful ruling class, comprised of dignitaries.

Thus, together with local products, which were, however, considerably influenced by types that were common in the whole of the Mediterranean area, it has been possible to identify some imports. Of these, the most important finds have come to light in Italic contexts. They include the treasure of Sant'Eufemia, the crown of Krithonios from Armento, and a diadem with polychrome enameling from Canosa. These types have only rarely – or, in some cases, never – been found in Magna Graecia, in either Italic or Italiot contexts. Moreover, these jewels are very similar to ones found in other areas around the Mediterranean. Finally, the general character of the funerary contexts where they were found indicates that they belonged to individuals having a high social status in their communities.

Although further finds may affect this opinion, it seems reasonable to conclude that these jewels are archaeological evidence of direct trade between Italic chiefs and Greek leaders in southern Italy, such as Alexander the Molossian and Pyrrhus, or else they are the booty acquired by Italic mercenaries in Greece.

On sites that were certainly Italiot, there is no jewelry of great value or showing particular technical skill. This seems to indicate that wealth was widely distributed in a fairly even manner: in fact, this corresponds to what may be gleaned from the relevant literary sources.

Imitations of jewelry in gilt terra-cotta were also fairly common. This is further evidence of the widespread desire to be considered "well-off."

The Jewelry of the Western Greeks

Pair of gold earrings
from Ginosa
end 4th-beginning 3rd cent. B.C.
Taranto, Museo Nazionale
Cat. 301/III

Gold diadem
from Ginosa
end 4th-beginning 3rd cent. B.C.
Taranto, Museo Nazionale
Cat. 301/I

Gold spiral finger ring
from Tarentum
end 4th-beginning 3rd cent. B.C.
Taranto, Museo Nazionale
Cat. 324

Pair of earrings
with double lion heads
from Tarentum
end 4th-beginning 3rd cent. B.C.
Taranto, Museo Nazionale
Cat. 313

The Jewelry of the Western Greeks

Gold bracelet
with antelope heads
from Mottola
first decades 3rd cent. B.C.
Taranto, Museo Nazionale
Cat. 302/I

Pair of earrings
with garnet head of African
from Tarentum
end 3rd-beginning 2nd cent. B.C.
Taranto, Museo Nazionale
Cat. 308

Gold diadem
with gold and enameled flowers
from Canosa
3rd cent. B.C.
Taranto, Museo Nazionale

opposite
Grave jewels found at Tarentum
comprising a gold
and garnet *sakkos*,
a pair of pendent earrings,
a gold, garnet and carnelian baldric,
a mesh necklace with pendents,
two spiral bracelets,
a gold and garnet
serpent-shaped ring
end 3rd-beginning
2nd cent. B.C.
Berlin, Staatliche Museen
zu Berlin Preussischer
Kulturbesitz Antikensammlung
Cat. 300

The Jewelry of the Western Greeks

The Jewelry of the Western Greeks

Amphora-shaped pendent
with chain
from Altamura
125-100 B.C.
Taranto, Museo Nazionale
Cat. 303/I

A special category of jewelry is that constituted by the small sheets of gold that were found in a tomb at Thurii; on these were written the formulas that ensured the deceased a safe and peaceful journey toward Hades.
With the conquest of Magna Graecia by the Romans, the use and production of jewelry decreased rapidly, a clear sign of the economic and political decline of the former Greek colonies. Only rarely is there evidence of an output of jewelry in the first century, for example in the case of two hoards excavated at modern Policoro. In these there are numerous jewels, which were made by eastern goldsmiths' workshops situated in Alexandria and, perhaps, Asia Minor. These hoards are archaeological evidence of the military activity – which allowed rich booty to be gained – that took place under the insignia of the Roman Republic in its progressive expansion. But the time had now come when Cicero was able to pronounce: "Magna Graecia deleta est" (Magna Graecia has been annihilated).

Gianfranco Maddoli   Cults and Religious Doctrines of the Western Greeks

God and man at the birth of a colony

According to Thucydides the historian, "Gela was founded by Antiphemus and Entymus who had led the colonists from Rhodes and Crete... and the city took its name from the river Gela, while the place where the acropolis was built, and which was the first to be surrounded by walls, was called Lindii..." (VI. 4.3). The foundation took place at the beginning of the seventh century B.C. The discovery of a fragment of a fifth–century Attic goblet dedicated to Antiphemus – a pious offering from an individual or a group for the annual holiday – is perhaps the clearest example of the colonists' veneration of the founder of their colony. The cult of the originator (*oikistes*) that spread after the death of a hero was the first to be "created" in the new colony and therefore symbolized the identity of the same. It constituted the basis of a local tradition and, as such, lasted over time. Its chief form of expression was the *enaghismos*, or the periodic ritual funeral commemorating the founder as the *archeghetes*, or primogenitor of the new city and of his own race which was multiplying there. The originator, who was destined to rise to the rank of the immortals, shared this title with Apollo, the deity that had authorized and guided his journey. An obvious example of this is the now famous inscription from Cyrene, a colony of Thera, that was also founded in the seventh century B.C., whose originator, the *basileus* Battus, was called *archegetes*, on a par with the god whose sovereign will he obeyed.

Of the many divinities comprising the Hellenic pantheon, Apollo had the task of defending the status quo, the harmony of the parts, the rigid observance of both the traditional and the positive norms, and was, first and foremost, the guardian of the law and of rites within the *polis*. He was also protector of the Muses, especially of that harmonic expression of their essence that is *mousike*, music (*mousike techne*), of health, the balanced harmony of the corporeal elements, and therefore of the art of medicine. Apollo was the father of Asclepius, another god of medicine, and of Hygieia, the goddess of health, whom we still invoke today when we use the word hygiene (from *hygieine* [*techne*] "the art that contributes to health"). With his knowledge of the mechanisms that regulate the order of nature and human society, Apollo was capable of foreseeing future situations and was therefore a prophetic god, who possessed and administrated the mantic art (from the Greek *manthanein*, "to learn, get to know"), or art of divination more than any other deity. Nobody was more capable than he of pinpointing the most suitable conditions and of offering the greatest guarantee of legitimacy for the founding of a colony, i.e., of a new settlement. Only by scrupulously following the suggestions, by respecting the rules and ritual obligations of the *archegetes* god could the colonists be certain that their difficult undertaking – it was usually a question of stealing land and landing places from the centuries-old settlements of the native inhabitants – would end in success.

Of the various sanctuaries dedicated to Apollo, the one which played a major role especially as regards the western colonial area, from the eighth century B.C. onward, was the *apollonion* at Delphi. The exceptionally favorable geographical position and the capacity of the sacerdotal class to cope with contrasting external pressures, made the *apollonion* the focal point of the *poleis* in both central Greece and the Peloponnese. A considerable number of oracles delivered by the Pythia, the priestess of Apollo at Delphi, have been handed down to posterity. They provided instructions, of varying ambiguity, concerning the places and methods to be used for founding a colony. The majority of these were certainly invented *ex eventu*, spreading a long time after the colony was founded so as to justify and legalize its existence. The late and fictitious formulation, however, is not enough to exclude the fact that originators about to lead a group of emigrants made constant visits to the sanctuary hoping for a positive sign.

Delphi was not the only, nor perhaps the oldest Apollonian sanctuary that was consulted. Apollo also resided on the island of Delos at the center of the Cyclades and at the crossroads of the sea routes to Crete and the eastern Mediterranean. The poet who wrote the *Homeric Hymn to Apollo* in the sixth century B.C. made the island speak with the following words: "Here, before anywhere else, [Apollo] will have a splendid temple built that will be the oracle for mankind" (*Hymn* 80–81). The Ionian *poleis* appealed to Apollo in the sanctuary at Delos, and, especially so, the Euboeans, who pioneered emigration toward the far-off shores of the Mediterranean, both eastward to Al Mina in Syria, where they established an *emporion* in the eighth century, and westward, creating the *emporion* at Pithekoussai and a colony at Cumae on the mainland opposite; the cities along the straits and the colonies on the eastern shores of Sicily as far as Leontini, including Naxos, the oldest and centrally sited colony whose name recalls the participation of emigrants from the Cycladic island near Delos.

Just outside the walls of Naxos there was an altar dedicated to Apollo *archegetes*, built by the early colonists and dedicated, as a highly symbolic gesture, to the god that had led them there. In time the altar became a ritual shrine because when the historian Thucydides was writing (end of the fifth century) the official envoys, the *theoroi*, invited to preside over the Panhellenic feasts in the mother country, made a

Sub-Geometric bichromic jug
with stylized figure (Zeus?)
over a sphere
surround by star motifs
with lightening in the center
5th cent. B.C.
Melfi, Museo Nazionale del Melfese
Cat. 137

Relief with the Delphic Apollo
and Artemis
first half 3rd cent. B.C.
Syracuse
Museo Archeologico Regionale
Cat. 370

sacrifice there before leaving Sicily (or certainly those from Naxos, and perhaps – as generally believed, but Thucydides is not clear about this – from all the other Greek cities in Sicily). In any case, while the link between the originator and Apollo, between the foundation of new colonies and the establishment of cults, is significantly and evidently confirmed here, it also points to the intimate interference existing between the human community organized into a political community and the divine world.

The fundamental characteristics of Greek religion
Greek religion was not a revealed religion with its origins in the figure and teachings of a founder; nor was it condensed into a sacred book, or elaborated in a sacerdotal literature. It was the result of a centuries-long experience in which the structures and articulations of the sacred peculiar to the Indo-Europeans absorbed, and were conditioned by the forms and religious convictions typical of the pre-Hellenic populations of the Aegean settlements, and of Asia Minor and Crete in particular. It was the product of a continuous evolution whose constants and variants formed a new equilibrium at different social and intellectual levels. Greek religion was expressed, therefore, in different forms in time and in space, while still within both common structures and the confines of continuity. Given this kind of evolution, an important and fundamental stage – following those of the inclusion of the Indo-European pantheon in pre-Hellenic Mediterranean piety (beginning of the second millennium B.C.), and of the order established during the peak of the Mycenaean civilization (sixteenth to thirteenth centuries B.C.) still strongly influenced by Minoan religion – comprised the centuries at the turn of the second millennium. The crisis following the fall of the Mycenaean kingdoms came to an end with the rise and alteration of new aristocracies, who ensured

their wealth (or land ownership) and rights through permanent warlike activity, based on an agonistic conception of existence. It was the epic poem – inspired by the heroic sources from the fallen but not forgotten Mycenaean world – that provided constant self-representation and the cultural medium for continual self-regeneration. The poet, who identified himself to varying extents with the bard that sang the epic poetry, reflects and, at the same time, transforms the society to which he belongs and which he represents. Homer, whose name sums up a centuries-old epic tradition in its final form of expression (it is thought that epic poems achieved their definitive form in the eighth century, at the time when the Greek world was coming to grips with the alphabet), is therefore the poet who describes, while portraying society in the Greek Dark Age (from about the eleventh to the ninth centuries), and reproposes – in canonical terms – the image that the reigning aristocracies had of the gods, whose anthropomorphous society was naturally modeled according to the values (and fears) of mankind. Shortly after, Hesiod, the seventh-century poet, was to register in his *Theogony*, the structure of the divine world which centuries of experience and epic celebration had elaborated. The historian Herodotus (second half of the fifth century) was at least partly right in affirming that "Hesiod and Homer ... are those who composed a theogony for the Greeks, giving names to the gods, sharing out the honors and the prerogatives, and describing what they looked like" (II. 53.2). He was only partly correct however, since Greek religion had had a clearly designed pantheon as early as the Mycenaean age (sixteenth to thirteenth centuries), even though this included a different membership and degrees of importance compared to the successive Homeric period. What neither Herodotus nor the poets of Archaic Greece could ever have known, we, men of the modern world, have learnt in the second half of the twentieth century, thanks to the deciphering of the clay tablets by Michael Ventris in 1952, which were written in the syllabic writing used in the Mycenaean world (Linear B script). These were destroyed by fires in the kings' palaces at the end of the thirteenth century and rediscovered during excavations as from the end of the last century. Zeus, Hera, Athena, Poseidon, Hermes, Ares, Artemis, and even Dionysus and perhaps Demeter, are clearly mentioned. Some deities who are well known to us (for example, Apollo) are absent or perhaps concealed behind other names. There are also the names of other gods who either disappeared or faded into the background of the following scene: sure proof that the history of the gods of the Greeks was one with the history of the men.

Olympian religiousness and chthonian religiousness
While writing from different standpoints, Homer and Hesiod, as we said above, reflected the society of the Archaic nobles where there was a hierarchical perception of the relationship between the gods and men which was completely geared to the social structure based on the net separation of the *aristoi* – in their own words, chosen by Zeus – and the common people who never could nor should rise to the social standing of the former. This distinction was extended to the man–god relationship. While the origins uniting them could not be denied (cf. the myth about Prometheus giving divine fire to mankind), the gods are placed on Mount Olympus. They are raised to a height that is inaccessible for ordinary human beings who will be guilty of *hubris*, that is to say, excessive pride and arrogance – a fault that demands inexorable punishment for just daring to go beyond the established limits. Apollo was the highest defender of Olympian piety which was expressed in the famous Delphic precepts: "Know thyself" (or recognize your own mortal nature, that you are only a man); "Nothing in excess" (given your human nature, do not aspire to what is not your due); "Be wise" (come to terms with the position you hold in the world and do not attempt to claim anything different).

Each of the Greek gods represents a specific field of the powers and forces that move and dominate Nature, and is a projection of the values and fears comprising the Greek cultural panorama. Every divinity expresses a particularly complex reality and interacts with the others operating in close fields or possessing similar qualities (the Greeks often express these connections in terms of filiation or kinship). Thus, for example, if Zeus is the god of light and of the sky which includes everything and therefore all the forces therein that surround and dominate nature ("Zeus is the heavens, Zeus is the earth, Zeus is the sky, Zeus is everything including that which is higher than this" is how Aeschylus put it), Hera is the goddess who superintends the fertility of women as brides and mothers, and in antiquity, she descended from the great female divinities of the Minoan age, and expresses even the maternity of nature in a wide sense, generating the fauna and flora. Aphrodite symbolizes and safeguards women in their love potential detached from marriage or not yet organized as such (Eros is her son). Athena is the goddess of practical intelligence, a projection of operative and intellectual vigor which inspires the arts, including the art of war. Ares, on the other hand, represents the force and cruelty of battles. As Jean Pierre Vernant wrote so clearly, "A pantheon, as an organized system which implies precise relations between the gods is, in a certain sense, a lan-

opposite
Apulian red-figure krater
with Athena seated and other gods
first half 4th cent. B.C.
New York
The Metropolitan Museum of Art
Rogers Fund, 1950
Cat. 288

Detail of the decoration
on the *François Vase*
showing the pantheon
570-560 B.C.
Florence
Museo Archeologico Nazionale

guage, or a particular form of apprehension and expression symbolizing reality." Such a projection depends on the complete humanization of the gods, who are conceived and presented with every human passion. They are sexually active; they form families with parents and children. They express the whole range of human feelings – benevolent and raging, adulterous and ambitious, envious and vindictive. The only thing that distinguishes them from mankind is their immortality. Homer provided a perfect, articulated and hierarchical definition of this polytheistic and anthropomorphic pantheon, which actually resulted in a new equilibrium inside the single aristocratic *poleis*, where one or another deity or a group of gods was worshipped locally depending on the more or less profound roots of the various native cults, or on the eventual deliberate "political" promotion of one god at the expense of the others.

Two considerably important deities occupied minor positions with respect to the gods on Olympus. They were Demeter, goddess of the earth, grain, and the agricultural world in general, and Dionysus, the god of wine and ecstasy. They represented the spontaneous and irresistible forces of nature which were the basis of the oldest form of Aegean piety, preceding the arrival of the Indo-Europeans, which flourished in Crete in particular. This religiousness was centered on the rhythms of birth, growth and death, and on the primary manifestations of male and female vitality. While being set and regimented to a certain extent in the ordered context of the Olympian deities, Demeter (with her daughter Persephone or Kore) and Dionysus (on the famous *François Vase* of Vulci, sixth century B.C., the procession of the gods shows Dionysus on foot, following the other gods riding in a carriage) continued to represent and to keep alive a deep religious feeling where man was a being totally submerged in the cosmic divine and played a role

in its destiny. If the myth about Prometheus – while not ignoring this sentiment – codified the distance between man and the gods, the myth of Dionysus (the son of Zeus and Persephone, raised in Crete in a cave, murdered, roasted and eaten by the Titans who were consequently struck by Zeus' thunderbolts, and from whose ashes, containing the divine child, man was molded; or, the son of Zeus and Semele who was then herself struck down by Zeus, and thus Dionysus was nurtured in his father's thigh to be born a second time) reproposed the deep-seated divine origins of man, and implied the course to be taken so as to be reborn and to reunite with the divine part of his heritage. This idea of death and rebirth – expressed in both the Dionysus and the Demeter myths (in the latter, Persephone, or Kore the young girl, is snatched from her mother, Demeter, by Hades, the god of the Underworld. Demeter, or mother earth, forces Hades to send Persephone back to her for a certain period of the year: spring and summer, the seasons of flowers and fruits) – forms the cornerstone of the chthonian type of religiousness, an expression linked to the vitality of the earth (*cthon*) which contrasts with the Olympian type. Here, the main forms of ritual and cultic expression are the initiation mysteries in honor of Demeter (the best-known and important ones are the Eleusinian mysteries) and of Dionysus. Many other very remote, cultic ceremonies can be linked to this idea, even though they involved important divinities, members of the Olympic pantheon. Locally, these forms of piety revealed their strongly Archaic origins and cultic characteristics that tended to contrast with the official religion of the *polis* developing towards the end of the Dark Age according to the requirements of the Homeric or post-Homeric aristocracies. The contrast between Olympian and chthonian piety constitutes a constant polarity in the Greek religion, which was represented, in accentuated terms

Cults and Religious Doctrines of the Western Greeks

485

Proto-Apulian red-figure krater
with the birth of Dionysus
out of Zeus's thigh
right, detail
end 5th-beginning 4th cent. B.C.
Taranto, Museo Nazionale
Cat. 197

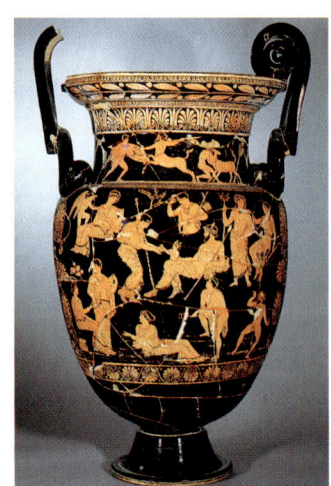

as from the fifth century, in the conflicting positions of two brothers, Apollo and Dionysus. The range of the cults and local emphases on various divine figures are particularly noticeable, not only in the rituals obviously (which did however always respect certain common characteristics) but also in the epithets which are attributed to the single deities. For example, among others, Zeus is Hypsistos (the Highest), Hieksios (Protector of suppliants), Horios (Protector of frontiers), Ourios (Favorably disposed toward navigation), Eleuthorios (Liberator, guarantor of the freedom won, for example, at the end of a tyranny), Kouros (Child, in Crete, where he was born according to a chthonian tradition). Moreover, very often the colonial cult of a divinity reproposed the same image, and therefore, the same epithet, of the god worshipped in the metropolis (for example, Zeus Atabyrios in Rhodes and in Acragas, the Rhodian colony in Sicily). Before returning to the specific subject of the Greek cults in the colonial areas in the West, we should not forget that, apart from the greater divinities (the Olympian pantheon assembles twelve of them – Zeus, Hera, Athena, Apollo, Artemis, Aphrodite, Ares, Poseidon, Hermes, Hephaestus, Demeter, and Dionysus – even though their names may vary within the group, such as Hestia for Dionysus) the Greeks worshipped many, many other "lesser" gods who could become considerably important on a local level, and even occasionally assimilate the character and functions of the closest "greater" god. Ample space in this realm was given over to the worship of heroes, human beings who had achieved divine immortality, a category which included a variety of figures, some deriving from Panhellenic sources (e.g. Heracles), others with exclusively local origins. Lastly, ever since the remotest times, the cult of the dead played a large part in the Hellenic religious sphere.

The gods and the polis: *from the metropolis to the colony*
The *polis*, the supreme form of the Greek state centered around a city, or community of people who recognize specific rights and duties (the term "city" used as a synonym here comes from the Latin *civ-*

itas, community of the *cives*, the *polis* is the community of the *politai*), was also, and perhaps, first and foremost, a community of a congregation. The community was dedicated to one or more cults that, in the first place, were official, promoted and celebrated by the local magistrates, that, secondly, were highlighted by the construction of temples which in turn became the cornerstone of the very economy of the *polis*, and lastly, that were organized according to a ritual calendar whose holidays punctuated the life of the community and whose ceremonies assigned a precise role to all its members, from the nobles to the lowest of the *politai*, both men and women, with special distinctions regarding age groups. In other words, religion, in the Greek cities, was the cement of social and political cohesion. There is nothing surprising or incomprehensible therefore about the fact that when a *polis* decided to set up a colony, it appealed to the local gods and made requests to Apollo for vigilant prognostications regarding the need to conserve the established order of the system and how to set up overseas a new balanced order based (certainly at first) on a similar cultic community.

Herodotus recalls (I. 164) that when the Phocaeans (citizens from Phocaea situated on the Ionian coast of Asia Minor in front of the island of Chios) decided to leave their mother country that risked invasion by Cyrus of Persia's army, they filled their boats, not only with their women and children, but also with "the statues of the gods from the temples and other votive objects." Moreover, once they had arrived at their destination, the island of Cirno (Corsica), they joined a nucleus of Phocaeans, who had already settled there, and founded the *apoikia* called Alalia "and built temples" (*hiera enhidrysanto*). This event took place in the mid-sixth century. At the end of the previous century, other Phocaeans had founded Massalia (Marseilles) at the mouth of the Rhone, and its citadel included the *ephesion*, the temple dedicated to Artemis of Ephesus, and the sanctuary of the Delphi Apollo, the god of the Ionian League in Asia Minor. Apollo certainly must have given his approval to the proposed new settlement suggested by Artemis through a dream sent to the aristocratic Aristarches, as narrated by Strabo (IV. 1.4) who refers to an old local tradition, perhaps already adopted by the historian Ephorus of Kyme (Cumae). Aristarches was ordered to take a model of the Ephesian temple with her so as to reconstruct a perfect copy in the new colony where she was the priestess. Artemis was worshipped above all the other deities

Relief of Dionysus and a satyr
beginning 2nd cent. B.C.
Policoro
Museo Nazionale della Siritide
Cat. 273

Aphrodite and Eros
mid-5th cent. B.C.
Reggio Calabria
Museo Nazionale
Cat. 176

in all the colonies founded by the Phocaeans, and it was the rule that "the image of the idol and the other rites observed in the metropolis were to remain unchanged." Diana Aventinensis had an identical symbolic representation in Rome, where she had been transferred by the Phocaeans who frequented the marketplace on the Tiber in the sixth century. The same situation was probably repeated at Elea (Greek Hyele), a colony founded on the Cilento promontory.

The example of Massalia illustrates indirectly how much the colonists were attached to the gods that were venerated in the mother country and in particular the importance ascribed to the patron divinities of their respective metropolises by the western colonies (but obviously not only those in the West). A few decades before Massalia was founded, Naucratis, the celebrated trading center, was set up in the Nile delta on the other side of the Mediterranean. Herodotus (II. 178) wrote that Amasis the pharaoh granted those who accepted his invitation to settle there, "spaces destined for raising altars and establishing sacred sites for the gods." A huge *hellenion* was built there as a common sanctuary for all the different ethnic groups of Greek extraction. Moreover, several *poleis* that were extraordinarily faithful to the cult of their respective patron deities, solemnly transported them overseas. At Naucratis consequently there was a *temenos* for Zeus built by the Aeginetans, a *heraion* constructed by the Samians, and an *apollonion* by the Milesians. An examination of the archeological stratigraphy in the oldest colonial settlements reveals clearly that, in the arrangement of the earliest buildings, the space for the *agora* of the gods, or for centralizing the official temple of the chief divinities of the local pantheon, was set out right from the start and respected in later transformations. This can be seen extraordinarily well at Megara Hyblaea in Sicily, at Metapontum and Paestum in Magna Graecia. The later town-planning schemes of the Classical age nearly always repeat the ancient layout of the sacred area, thus highlighting its different orientation. Himera is an eloquent example. The later model of Acragas, subcolony of Gela (580 B.C.), is significant and yet unusual. Its urban area was circled by a constellation of sanctuaries. The one for the most revered patron divinity, Athena, dominated the northwestern part of the acropolis, while a series of temples formed a chain along the southern side, according to a precisely defined layout. By contrast, Demeter's sanctuary stood in isolation at the walls' limits, in correspondence to the grotto that had been the most ancient place of worship, on the furthest point to the east of the northern side. At the tip of the southwestern side of the city, the largest temple ever built in Sicily, the *olympieion* dedicated to Zeus, was raised at the start of the fifth century in a place dedicated to sacred rites ever since Archaic times. It was the emblem of Theron the tyrant of Acragas.

The organization of sacred space together with the original layout of the seats of the divinities is just one of the elements that allows us to interpret the religious world of a *polis*, which is ever on the move like its historical and political events. The gods set up at the beginning, who generally reflected the status quo of the metropolitan pantheon, were later joined by other new ones, some of which acquired a greater significance compared to the others, due to a variety of reasons that cannot be pinpointed convincingly once and for all (for example, the development of certain social strata in the civic framework, protected by their own specific gods; political decisions leading to the promotion of some gods, or some cults, or certain aspects of the cults; wars, etc.). During the entire Archaic period and for the greater part of the Classical era, the image established by the cults at the time of founding the colony was certainly decisive. In many cases, the religious sphere of the colony reveals that of the metropolis where it has remained obscure, but generally it occurs the other way round. The original setup lasted a very long time; centuries later it is still possible to distinguish the gods of the colonies whose roots lay in their Minoan-Mycenaean heritage which, as we have already emphasized, can explain the cata-chthonian (subterranean) character of the religions of some colonial *poleis* whose founders came from the Aegean part of the world, where there were strong traditions of Cretan origin. Examples of this are Gela, Acragas, and Selinus; Cyrene, a colony of Thera, as well as Locri and Tarentum. Moreover, every colonial foundation constitutes a new start, anchored to its own identity, where the pioneer models undergo a slowing down of their natural evolution, putting a brake on development, adaptation, and change that instead follow a normal course inside the metropolitan area. The Greek religion of the western colonies can therefore be examined as a whole only to the extent that certain common characteristics can be isolated and if proven generalizations can be made. In reality, every local pantheon should be examined on its own, from the points of view of its relations with the metropolis and the cultural area of origin, and of the internal hierarchy of the divinities worshiped locally and their representation.

A few significant examples
While an analysis of the cults of all the western colonies is impossible here, we will describe a few significant cases and some of the divinities involved.

Epizephyrian Locri on the Ionian coast of modern Calabria offers a particularly interesting model of organization. A strong resemblance to the foundation of Tarentum (Greek Taras) by the *parthenoi*, the Spartan offspring of Spartan women of uncertain fatherhood, marks the establishment of Locri. The founders of the colony were tied to the metropolitan nobility of the Ozolian Locris through a matrilinear descendancy, reinforced by the story of Ajax, whose guilt in insulting Cassandra was expiated by the Ozolian Locrians who were forced to send two virgins to the Athena Ilias in Ilium (refounded Troy) every year. Athena, in fact, dominated Locri Epizephyrii in Italy from the heights of the acropolis at Mannella, where excavations have brought forth many statuettes of the goddess. As well as Athena, Zeus was venerated in the temple discovered at Casa Marafiori. The Archaic characteristics of the temple explain this coupling with Athena, who was probably an *Ilias* at Locri too, and the connected deep-rooted cult of the Dioscuri (the *dios kouroi* or sons of Zeus), the divine couple already present in the Mycenaean pantheon with the epithet of (*w*)*anakes*, "the sovereigns." The sanctuary dedicated to Zeus was the factor that established the Locrian *polis*. The recent discovery of a receptacle containing an archive of small bronze tablets proves that, with its economic reserves, the sanctuary functioned, in the Hellenistic age, as a real public bank. While being sited on the outskirts of the city, the Archaic cults of Aphrodite and Persephone were however central and decisive in the Locrians' religious sphere. One of the temples was near the seashore, in the Centocamere sanctuary, where the ancient practice of sacred prostitution was observed (it was also widespread at Cyprus and in Lydia, observed in Corinth and, in the West, in Sicily at the *aphrodision* at Eryx). The earnings went toward the upkeep of the temple. This was a typical phenomenon, during the Archaic period, occurring in the predominantly commercial centers. The sacerdotal organization including *hierodoulea*, the sacred offering to the goddess of love by the priestesses and other women consecrated in more or less stable terms, was a source of income for the city.

A very old graffito (seventh century B.C.) with the name of Kybala (Cybele) suggests that the cult was experienced in a very similar way to that of the eastern goddess who was identified by the Ionians in Asia Minor with Aphrodite. At the other end of the city, on the Mannella hillside, looking inland, stood the temple dedicated to Persephone, who seems to be more important at Locri than her mother Demeter. Evidence of this is provided by numerous decorated pottery items, and especially by the famous *pinakes*, small bas-relief terra-cotta squares depicting various scenes (about seventy different types have been catalogued), mostly manufactured in the first half of the fifth century. These continue to be a topic for considerable debate, even though it is fairly certain that most of the scenes depict a wedding, and more generally the theme concerns the passage of a girl to womanhood and marriage – represented in a ritual and mythical context full of symbolic implications – in the presence of deities and other figures that preside and confirm the sacred act. While apparently separated by their distinct geographical positions, the two cults of Persephone and of Aphrodite mirror the possible twofold destiny of women. In the former, they are considered and protected in their creative and reproductive role; in the latter, in their "sterile" role, subject to male eroticism. Both of these functions, however, constitute two differing sources of riches for the community.

The colonies designated as "Achaean" because their founding fathers came from Achaea in the Peloponnese (Sybaris, Croton, Metapontum, Caulonia on the Ionian Sea, and Poseidonia-Paestum on the Tyrrhenian Sea, whose history and origins are closely linked to those of Sybaris) all gave priority to the cult of Hera deriving from early antiquity. The hypothesis that the physiognomy of this great goddess was developed here, from precolonial sources active up to the time of the settlements, is possible, although, as yet, no documentary evidence has been found. She must, however, owe much to the Archaic models of Mycenaean extraction, imported by the colonists in the eighth century, which is the impression received from the great extramural sanctuaries at Capo Colonna (near Croton) and at the mouth of the Sele River (Paestum). This image can be integrated with the better-known ritual and mythical realities of the great *heraia* in the northern Peloponnese (Argos, Perachora, and so forth) and at Samos. Hera appears in southern Italy – as literary sources and archeological documentation show – as the queen of all nature (*panton genetla*), the patroness of animals and guardian of herds (*potnia theron*), the protectress of female cadences, of marriage, childbirth and maternity (*eileithyia* and *kourotrophos*), and lastly, as the lady of arms (*hoplosmia*).

In Croton the goddess is also Eleutheria, or "liberty," who set slaves free through a special procedure. This included the consecration to the goddess and therefore the transfer of one male or female slave or a whole group under her protection, who could then obtain from the goddess a liberating act recognized by the political community, after payment of a sum to the temple. The former slave then acquired, if not full rights as a citizen, a status of freedom that released him for ever from his previous subordinate state. Hera's power to do this is proved by the inscriptions found at the extramural sanctuary at Capo Colonna, which

Statue of Artemis
second half 2nd cent. B.C.
Potenza, Soprintendenza
Archeologica della Basilicata
Cat. 268/II

Pinax with figures of goddesses
in a cult scene
end 4th-beginning 3rd cent. B.C.
Lipari, Museo Archeologico
Regionale Eoliano
Cat. 350

Tablet with the epiphany
of the Dioscuri in a *naiskos*
second half 4th-first half 3rd cent. B.C.
Taranto, Museo Nazionale
Cat. 291/II

was one of the great Hellenic sanctuaries, universally accepted as an *asylia*, providing immunity and inviolability. This power is also ascribed to the city thanks to the results of recent excavations in the Vigna Nuova district, next to the walls, where not only votive offerings recalling the various different functions of the goddess (agricultural tools, axes, weapons, symbols of childbirth, etc.) have been found, but also chains and shackles, evidently offered in remembrance of a former state of slavery. A similar practice appears to be the case in Demeter's sanctuary at Heraclea in Lucania.

An excellent example of chthonian cults lasting into recent times is provided by Selinus, a sub-colony founded by the Megarians in 628 B.C. on the borders of the Punico-Phoenician sphere of influence, in the "Sicanian" zone of western Sicily that had certainly been frequented by the Greeks during the Mycenaean age. As far as a reconstruction based on archaeological documentation rather than on the written tradition is possible, the pantheon at Selinus was largely of Archaic and pre-Olympian origin, even though the "Olympian" gods obviously assumed important roles, as evidenced by the great temples in the city. The names of the gods that protected Selinus in the Classical period were written on the famous mid-fifth century inscription placed on the Temple of Zeus (Temple G), in the list of deities that had watched over the victory, the subject of this dedication. These were Zeus, Phobos, Heracles, Apollo, Poseidon, the Tyndarids (equivalent to the Dioscuri), with Athena, Malophoros, and Pasikrateia "and the other gods." A copy of their names was inscribed on a gold votive and placed in the temple dedicated to Apollo (perhaps Temple C), the *archegetes* god and maintainer of the status quo who is also the greatest guarantor of the alliances drawn up and inscribed on the votive offering.

Immediately next to the supreme Zeus are the personification of Terror (Phobos, the son of Ares, the god of war, in the *Iliad*) and Heracles, the heroic ancestor of the Dorian race. Heracles is the one who opens up the roads to civilization (a typically colonial emphasis of the hero's role). They are followed by the more important Olympian deities (with a combination of the Dioscuri with Athena, which we already saw at Locri). Lastly, two goddesses are remembered by a singular epithet: Pasikrateia, the "lady of all" (most probably Aphrodite or Hera, rather than Persephone) and the "bearer of fruits" (Malophoros), a goddess assimilated with Demeter and known also at Megara Nysa, the metropolis of Megara Hyblaea, which founded Selinus. An examination of the cult of the goddess Malophoros at Selinus, outside the city, has revealed its particularly Archaic savor, which has been considered incorrectly as the continuation of a native cult existing before the arrival of the Greek colonists. It has been said that the epithets used to invoke the goddess, "Potnia" and "Anassa," are typical of the Mycenaean vocabulary, and therefore a sign of the distant origins of the cult. These epithets have been combined with both that of a chthonian Zeus called Meilichius ("sweet as honey") to whom aniconic *stelai* were dedicated (without any human figures or with very simplified human features), and that of the cult of the infernal Hecate. Zeus Meilichius was invoked also as the giver of salvation (Soter) and his *stelai*, with the evolution from the simple stone to the sculpting of a human face (recalling the Punic *stelai* in nearby Motya), gave material expression to the encounter of the individual with "his" god that assured him the eternal sweetness of a future life: "I am Zeus Meilichius," "I am Meilichius." The goddess Malophoros, with her name so closely linked to the multiple fertility of nature, must certainly originate in the Minoan-Mycenaean religious world dominated by female deities personifying the inexhaustible and vital energies of the cosmos. We cannot exclude the possibility that her coupling with Zeus Meilichius represents the promotion of the couple, frequently invoked in the Aegean religion, and expressed by a goddess with a *paredros* next to her. The inclusion of Hecate confirms the image of a piety that is directed toward the Underworld, where half man's existence takes place, against the background of an intimate interrelationship between the cosmos and the divine that seems to lie far from the realm of Olympian and Apollonian religiousness. On the other hand, there are cults of the goddesses of the earth everywhere in Sicily, especially of Demeter and Persephone or Kore. The abduction of Persephone by Pluto took place, according to a widespread tradition, on a lake near Enna, according to others, at a Cyane spring near Syracuse, and the "holiest of goddesses" played major roles in all the colonists' rites as proved by the enormous amount of votive images referring to their cult. The Dionid tyrants were in particular the ancient holders of the priesthood dedicated to the goddesses from the days of the metropolitan cities at Triopium promontory on the Anatolian coast. It was the Dionids' task to promote the veneration of the goddesses, and it became an instrument of legitimization and prestige, and ultimately, of support of the tyrants' policies. Gelon, the tyrant of Syracuse, had huge temples built to the goddesses after winning the battle against the Carthaginians at Himera in 480 B.C., and encouraged the cult everywhere. Cicero was yet another witness to the omnipresent and ever-growing veneration of Demeter and Kore all over Sicily (which has always been referred to as the "granary" of the ancient world), a fact widely confirmed by the literary sources and archaeological excavations. In order to emphasize their universal importance, he invoked them last of all – *sanctissimae deae... cunctae Siciliae* – in his appeal to the gods that concludes the second oration against Verres (V. 72. 187–188).

Our survey of the divine and heroic figures represented in the religious world of the western Greeks could be extended much further. Athena has been mentioned briefly many times. Her cult has been confirmed nearly everywhere in the colonial settlements by temples, votive offerings, coins, and literary documents. The literary sources, together with some inscriptions, have very often proffered the epithets with which she was worshiped locally, and provide evidence of variants and cultic emphases either derived from the metropolitan areas or arising from the particular situation of the colonial sphere (Ilias, Myndia, Eilenia, Skyletria, Krathia, Polias, Longatis, Poliouchos, etc.).

We should also mention Artemis, *potnia theron*, the lady of life and death in the animal world and among the forms of existence not yet organized in political terms, who was very revered in some colonies, such

Pinax with Persephone and Hades receiving gifts
ca. 460 B.C.
Reggio Calabria, Museo Nazionale

Pinax with the rape of Persephone
ca. 460 B.C.
Reggio Calabria, Museo Nazionale

as Rhegium (where Artemis Phakelitis revealed traces of the Peloponnese due to the Messenians who took part in the foundation of the city) and Syracuse (Artemis Alpheioa and Potamia, linked to the myth of Alpheus and the Arethusa spring; Artemis Anghelos and Cydonia, from ties with the cults of Demeter, etc.). She was also known as the Ephesian Artemis in the aforementioned colonies of the Phocaeans. Then there were Dionysus, the various representations of Apollo and his son, Asclepius (a flourishing medical school grew up at Elea under their protection), Poseidon (who gave his own name to Poseidonia [Paestum] thanks to the primary role played by the god in Troezen, the mother country of these colonists), Hephaestus (linked to the primordial subterranean forces that were so alive and present in the geological reality of southern Italy and Sicily), Hermes, and so on. Much could be said also about the various cults worshiping fluvial deities, nymphs and local heroes. Some of these came from the epic world (Ajax, Diomedes, Philoctetes, Epeius, etc.), others from the sphere of divination (Calchas, Podaleirius, Machaon), and still more from isolated traditions linked to specific places, such as Dracon at Laus, Alibantes or Polites at Temesa, Eutimus at Locri. The latter was a real person, an athlete transformed into hero following his victories. Likewise, Philip the Butachides, was an Olympic athlete who died in Sicily at the end of the sixth century and who was venerated in a small temple near Segesta.

The extramural sanctuaries

A particularly interesting phenomenon, and the subject of much debate in recent years, is the presence of the large extramural sanctuaries. In truth, the question of their origin and functions is not limited exclusively to the West, as they have also been found in other areas of Hellenism. However, it was the examples in Magna Graecia that prompted scholars to investigate. These are the large sanctuaries (not the numerous small ones spread all over the territory of a colony) which lie a few kilometers away from the city, on promontories and certainly near the sea or at the mouth of important water courses and their relative ports. Sanctuaries with these characteristics were typical, in particular, of the three great Achaean colonies, Croton, Metapontum, and Paestum, where they were dedicated to Hera. Hera was also the tutelary deity, and, while enjoying a certain amount of independence and drawing together the different ethnic groups, she still lived in very close contact with the city. The three great *heraia* (at Capo Colonna, the *Tabulae Palatinae*, and at the mouth of the Sele) have been grouped together by analogy with the *apollonion* at Punta Alice, the *olympieion* at Syracuse, and the *athenaion* at Punta Campanella, Sorrento. The old hypothesis regarding their origins was that the sanctuaries were the continuation of previous places of indigenous cult worship (Ciaceri), but this has not been substantiated by archaeological findings. A second, different idea, based on the intimate knowledge of the ancestral tradition typical of the Greek colonists, was that the sanctuaries were a prosecution of ancient places of cult established by the Mycenaean voyagers who traveled up and down the coast of western Italy (Pugliese Carratelli). Other scholars (De Polignac) preferred the hypothesis of a deliberate establishment *ex novo* parallel to the foundation of the settlement as a means of integrating the native population and of controlling the surrounding territory. The debate is still in progress but, given the whole of our research to date, the origins of the interaction "external city – sanctuary" are more likely to be found in Mycenaean and proto-Archaic metropolitan Greece, which was certainly a source for the colonists when they considered introducing overseas a model that preceded the foundation of the colonies in more recent history (early examples were the *heraia* at Argos and Samos compared to their respective *poleis*, and the sanctuary at Perachora compared to Corinth), and that perhaps dated back to the Mycenaean age. The tablets in Linear B script unearthed at Pylos confirm a privileged relationship between Palace culture and a few important sanctuaries sited in various parts of the kingdom. It is still possible – and perhaps most likely – that in choosing the site of the extramural sanctuary the colonists of the eighth and seventh centuries were swayed by a sense of continuity, preferring certain places – headlands and fluvial ports – that had been formerly frequented by Mycenaean merchants. Sanctuaries set up as the continuation of native places of worship should instead be excluded. This hypothesis could be applied to nearly all the cases where scholars favored the idea of the Greek cult being the transformation and continuation of a local one, excepting, perhaps, the expressions of piety centered on natural phenomena such as rivers, springs, volcanoes and the like, which appeared, in the eyes of the ancients, whether they were Greek or non-Greek, intrinsically gravid with divine power. The Greeks, heirs and bearers of a much more organic and developed culture than that of the western native communities in the Iron Age, were much too consciously attached to their own well-structured religious traditions to consider changing those of the peoples they met and overpowered in the West. Loyalty to the original characters of the metropolitan pantheons was rather a factor of social cohesion, especially during the difficult phases of the settlement. Consequently, only after considerable time had passed, were there slight

Hera enthroned
marble statue from the *Heraion*
at the mouth of the River Sele
beginning 4th cent. B.C.
Paestum
Museo Archeologico Nazionale

and insignificant adaptations to native sentiments, deriving from the integration process and the need for political control. Models of earlier local religious cults never conditioned or upset in a decisive way the values and forms of expression of the Hellenes, who, at most, assimilated a few local accents, in particular, the cult of natural forces which both peoples felt were powers to be revered. The transfer of models and concepts occurs, in every course of colonization, from the more developed and civilized component to the subordinate one. The eventual countercurrent can only involve secondary and superficial aspects, which do not alter the identity of the culturally superior element.

From the cults to the religious doctrines
The wonder and fear provoked in every human group by the daily agitations of the forces that move nature and the universe bring about a variety of religious reactions. While acting within the same traditional framework, the humble peasant and the sailor, the citizen and the intellectual exaggerate or diminish, purify or reinterpret the contents and formulations of the belief they have inherited according to their own particular needs and susceptibility, and on the basis of collective knowledge.
New currents and digressions in religious philosophy developed over time alongside popular piety and

Zeus Meilichios from the Temple of Zeus Meilichios at Pompei
3rd-2nd cent. B.C.
Naples
Museo Archeologico Nazionale
Cat. 257

the accepted faith. These derived from more sophisticated interpretations of the Olympian and Dionysian cults, or expressed a religion of the intellect, deviating more and more from the old anthropomorphic polytheism. The doctrine of Pythagoras, the philosopher who emigrated to Croton from the island of Samos at the end of the sixth century, made its impact on southern Italian culture as a philosophical movement and also as a political and religious experience. Following in the oldest of traditions and formally respecting popular piety, but with a spirit and proposal of profound renaissance that would purify the theoretical and practical contents of the current religion, Pythagoras' religious message was centered on the immortality and the transmigration of the soul. The soul is a prisoner of the body because of its former sins. Either it succeeds in proving itself capable of leading a better life, during the period of reincarnation, or, after the death of the body, it must transmigrate through other bodies until it has acquired real knowledge, thanks to a rigorous existence, and with this, the right to withdraw forever from the corporeal prison. Knowledge is demonstrated in a rational course of progress that involves the whole of a man's existence. It is the *hodos tou biou* (the fabled Pythagorean "road of life") in which spiritual purification that can be verified in ethical attitudes and political behavior takes the place of ritual initiation in view of salvation. Not all men, however, (and not all to the same extent) have the strength to walk the straight and narrow with constant determination. Thus the disciples of the master are separated into two distinct groups: the mathematicians (from the verb *manthanein*, to learn), those who learn and absorb the teaching from start to finish and who are more closely bound up in the course; and the "acousmaticians" (from the verb *akouein*, to hear) or listeners, with their ears open but lacking in spirit. Leaving aside these two groups, there were then the masses who should be educated and whose pace on the road to maturity should be respected by introducing all kinds of pedagogic methods. This could include the traditional religion as well, which was accepted by Pythagoreans since the traditional pantheon provided a symbolic trace for interpreting the universe and for defining ethical behavior. It was the viewpoint of Apollonian theology which corresponded to the conception and the political interests of the ruling Pythagorean aristocracy, with Apollo, guarantor of the status quo and social harmony, as the core and cornerstone of a hierarchical society that should not be disturbed. Iamblichus, the neo-Platonic philosopher (fourth century A.D.), was the author of a *Vita Pythagorica* which drew together and conserved many old traditions linked with Pythagoreanism. He emphasized clearly the role assigned by the Pythagoreans to the *arche ton theon*, the government of the gods: it is particularly useful inasmuch as mankind needs the supervision of the gods as a brake on their behavior and as a threat, in order to impose order and moderation. Pythagoras himself was likened to Hyperborean Apollo, but it was not a case of deification. Rather, it was recognition of the authority of his teachings, in particular, in the religious sphere.

Xenophanes of Colophon, a sharp critic of anthropomorphic polytheism, came from the same Ionic environment in Asia Minor as Pythagoras did. He lived for years in Sicily and, according to Plato, was responsible for the founding of the Eleatic school that flourished at Elea (Greek Hyele) at the start of the fifth century B.C., and must have been the teacher of Parmenides. "Homer and Hesiod," argued Xenophanes indignantly, "attributed the gods all the qualities that mankind judges as disgraceful and reproachful: theft, adultery, reciprocal trickery." Moreover, "the mortals imagine that the gods are born, dress, speak, and look like them"; "If oxen, horses and lions had hands and could draw and act like men, then a horse would draw the gods like horses, the ox, like oxen, making their bodies exactly like their own." Leaving aside the debate regarding his relations with Parmenides, and the analysis of the fragments of his philosophy, it is obvious that, in living and working in Italy and Sicily, Xenophanes made a decisive contribution toward the philosophic and religious reflections of the western Greeks on themes such as the concept of the divine, of monotheism, of the relations between divinity and the world. He prepared the Greek world for the encounter with more advanced religious experiences than their own, such as Judaism, when he announced that "God is one, great among the gods and men, who differs from mortals both in body and spirit." A very deep religious experience is also at the heart of the philosophy of Parmenides of Elea, *aner pythagoreios* (Pythagorean man), as Strabo called him. Among the fragments of his writings there is a proem of a long lost poem in hexameters, a sort of epic tradition that proposed evoking Hesiod's *Theogony* (as Werner Jaeger noted). The latter had also been a divine revelation but Parmenides added a superior truth which went beyond it: the one and eternal Being. It was, once again, the allegory of a journey – in the wake of Pythagoras – toward the light, or toward the truth, along a *hiera hodos*, a "sacred path," which involved crossing the threshold of a gate guarded by Dike (Justice): the gate of knowledge. It was the mystic concept of the search for truth taken as both a religious and an intellectual experience, a rite of passage highlighted by the images of the gate and the *hodos*. It was the idea of a course to be followed that we have already seen in Pythagoreanism and which can also be found in the doctrine of Orphism. The doctrine of the philosophers at Elea could not be extricated from the coeval cultural milieu of the Achaean colonies. As Mondolfo said so clearly, the idea of salvation as the result of a journey to truth is a typical Pythagorean concept.

The subject of initiation continues, in conclusion, with a brief consideration of the profound religious experience of Orphism. While not being a phenomenon limited to the western Greeks, it was particularly widespread in Magna Graecia. In 1836 a small gold *lamina*, attached to the body by a chain, was found in a tomb in what had been Petelia (Strongoli, on the Ionian coast of modern Calabria). The characters on the *lamina* spoke of a journey in the nether world, of a spring to be avoided near a white cypress tree, and another one, gushing from the lake of Mnemosyne, to whose custodians the dead person was to announce: "I am a son of Gaea, the Earth, and of starry Uranus, my race is therefore heavenly… I am burning with thirst and dying. Hurry, give me the cool waters that rush from the lake of Mnemosyne." Once the guardians had recognized the origins of the dead person, they would give him water from the divine spring and the dead man would rise on high among the heroes.

The inscriptions on this and other *laminae* found later on have led to their cataloging as "orphic." The name of Orpheus, the legendary prophet and theologian of Thracian origin, embodied a series of myths

The marriage of Zeus and Hera on a metope from Temple E at Selinus
5th cent. B.C.
Palermo, Museo Archeologico Regionale "A. Salinas"

Cults and Religious Doctrines of the Western Greeks

Ritual axe with votive inscription
found at San Sosti
6th cent. B.C.
London, British Museum Department
of Greek and Roman Antiquities
Cat. 131

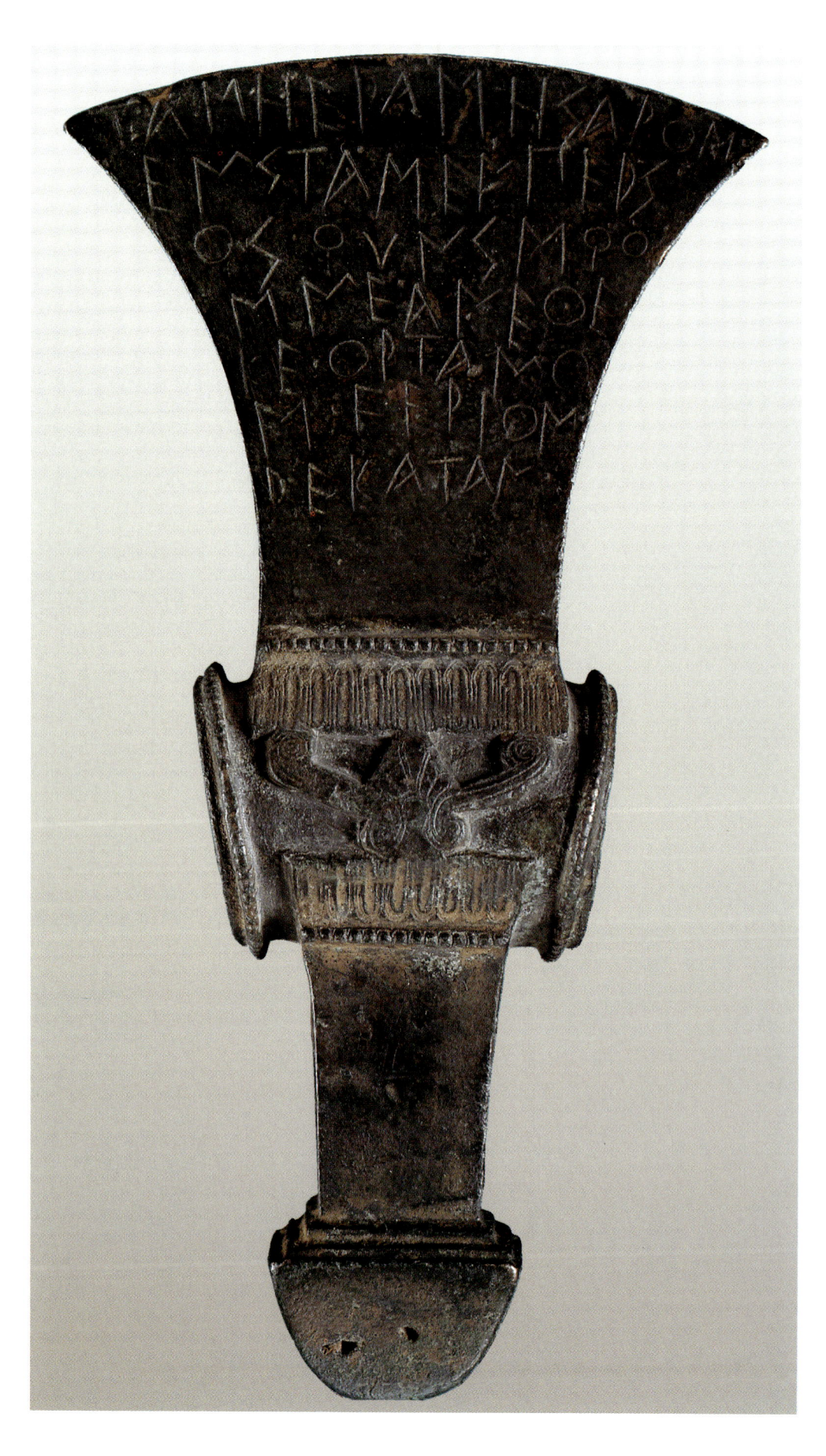

Cults and Religious Doctrines of the Western Greeks

Gold *lamina* with incised Orphic text found in a tomb at Petelia
London, British Museum Department of Greek and Roman Antiquities

and ideas centered on the destiny of man in the dramatic affairs of the universe. For the ancients, he was the bearer of a spark of divinity in a decadent and fragmented world (the myth of Dionysus murdered and devoured by the Titans, from whose ashes man was born). He may return, after a long journey leading to real knowledge, to reunite with the divine in a primeval union. It is up to man, the bearer of the divine seed of Dionysian origin, to choose, in the course of life, between the material and mortal element or the divine one. The rite of passage should help him understand, and therefore "remember" the truths necessary for recognizing which is the good spring for quenching his thirst, the source of reminiscence (Mnemosyne), in fact, of his own real origins. The knowledge of Orpheus (traditionally linked to another mythical poet, Musaeus), counters therefore the dominant influence of Homer, the inventor of an "Apollonian" concept which wanted the gulf between mankind and the gods to remain insurmountable. Its roots lie in the remote concepts of a Whole where men and gods originally shared the same nature and as such are destined to be reunited.

For a long time it was thought, quite wrongly, that the Orphic doctrine belonged to the lower and shunned strata of society. On the contrary, its theological and philosophical patrimony was very sophisticated. The remote concepts typical of the ancient chthonian religiousness were re-elaborated in the light of cosmologies and anthropologies that emerged from Ionian pre-Socratic thought, whose main but not only bridge with the West was Pythagoras. Being imparted strictly only to the *mystai* (those initiated in the mysteries), the doctrine was naturally prone to falsifications and limited interpretations, which perhaps explains a group of *laminae* full of distortions. Our knowledge of the authentic Orphic message, although incomplete, is entrusted to Plato, as far as the oldest testimonies are concerned – he came to Sicily and southern Italy in the years 388–387, and was in close contact with the Pythagorean of Tarentum (Greek Taras) – and to the text of the *laminae*. The real *bacchos*, the truly initiated man, according to the philosopher of the *Phaedo* (69c) is he who has philosophized correctly. The term *bacchos* belongs to the Dionysian vocabulary connected to the myth of the Cretan Dionysus, known with the epithet of *Zagreus*, and proves the contribution of a remote Cretan concept to the Orphic doctrine. However, the end of the journey through the Underworld, as far as the older and more faithful *laminae* are concerned, transformed the initiated not into a god but into a "hero." The hero returns to take part in the realm of divine immortality but he does not become a deity, thus respecting the distinction between men and gods that belonged to Apollonian theology. This detail, together with the fact that the doctrine of the *mneme* (the reminiscence) concerns more the intellectual sphere than that of the *psyche*, led to the conclusion of one of the greatest scholars of Orphism that the form in which this doctrine was expressed in southern Italy constitutes the mystic doctrine elaborated in a circle that looked to Pythagoras.

Recent excavations in a fifth-century tomb at Metapontum (Greek Metapontion), the town where Pythagoras was supposed to have died, yielded a simple set of grave goods. This included a small marble egg with a human figure emerging from the broken shell and a pendant with an androgynous figure, probably Phanes (the primogenitor in the doctrine of Orpheus, according to Proclus, the neo-Platonic philosopher), who was sometimes associated with Eros, who is the figure in the egg, the central object of Orphic cosmogonal symbolism. The finding is important because it also confirms the presence of women among the *mystai*. The coeval *lamina* found a few years ago at Hipponium, a subcolony of Locri Epizephyrii, was also part of the *viaticum* of a woman. It is one of the oldest, most complete and reliable examples of western Orphism, and deserves to be quoted entirely from the recent translation by Giovanni Pugliese Carratelli, as a conclusion to this rapid survey of the religious doctrine that expressed one of the highest concepts of the afterlife ever developed in antiquity:

> This (dictate) is sacred to Mnemosyne: (for the Mystes) on the point of death.
> You will go to the well-built houses of Hades,
> where, on the right, there lies a spring,
> and next to that a white cyprus tree stands.
> There the souls of the dead seek refreshment.
> Do not even approach this spring.
> Beyond you will find the cold water that runs
> from the lake of Mnemosyne, with its keepers to the fore,
> and they will ask you, with clear penetration,
> what you seek in the shades of murky Hades.
> Reply: "I am the son of the Earth and of starry Heaven;
> I burn with thirst and am fainting: quick, give me
> to drink the cold water that comes from the lake of Mnemosyne".
> They are merciful, as the king of the underworld wills,
> and will give you to drink from the lake of Mnemosyne;
> and when you have drunk you will travel the sacred path where
> the other *mystai* and *bacchoi* proceed in glory.

Bibliography

Among the great number of works on Greek religion see M.P. NILSSON, 1967³; 1961² and W. BURKERT, 1977. A simple and clear introduction to Greek religion is that by A. BRELICH, 1985; see also I. CHIRASSI COLOMBO, 1983. Quite useful are: K. KERÉNYI, 1963 (1951); W.C. GUTHRIE, 1987 (1950); J. FERGUSON, 1991 (1989).
On the role of religion in colonial foundations see I. MALKIN, 1987; oracles and foundations: G. PUGLIESE CARRATELLI, in *La Parola del Passato*, XLVII, 1992, pp. 401-410. Fundamental works for the western world are the studies conducted by E. CIACERI, 1911; G. GIANNELLI, 1963²; S. FERRI, 1929; G. ZUNTZ, 1971, and, lastly, by G. PUGLIESE CARRATELLI, 1990. A recent study on Greek religion in southern Italy is by G. MADDOLI-G. CAMASSA, in *Storia del Mezzogiorno*, I, 1, 1991, pp. 395-495. On Orphism: A. BOTTINI, 1992; G. PUGLIESE CARRATELLI, 1993. On the history on the studies see G. MADDOLI, in *Atti...* (1988), 1989, pp. 277-303.

Marcello Gigante   Literary Culture in Magna Graecia and Sicily

In this brief overview which, while avoiding a bland schematic approach, aims to provide a clear outline of the general and specific characteristics of the civilization of Magna Graecia, I will also deal with the more fundamental features of the culture. First of all, it is important to stress the unity of culture in Magna Graecia and Sicily against the background of the civilization of the Greek homeland. Just as Homeric poems contain subsets of unifying elements, so the vast sphere of culture unified by the Greek tongue contains the culture of Magna Graecia and Sicily, which was already perceived as such an entity by early historians and by the great poets of the era, Archilocus, Euripides, Callimachus, and their kind. In a fragment of Archilocus (fr. 22 West) we find a fertile plain irrigated by the Siris River, and likewise in a celebrate passage of *The Trojan Women* (verses 220–229), Euripides has the chorus extol the virtues of Sicily and Magna Graecia as the land of desire, of beauty, and the vigor of its inhabitants; such realms were ranked straight after Athens and the Peneo Valley. Such was the image of Magna Graecia in the mind of a fifth-century man of learning. In the *Origins* of Callimachus of Cyrene, a certain boxer from the colony of Locri Epizephyrii by the name of Euthymus, thrice winner at Olympia (in 484, 476, and 472 B.C.), by which he freed the city of Temesa from the obligation of paying the tribute of a virgin to the city's hero (fr. 635 Pfeiffer), and also Euthycles, winner of the pentathlon at Olympia (frs. 84–85). But most of all, Callimachus is noted for his praise of the colonial city of Locri (fr. 615) and the glory of the city of Croton, contained in his victory ode to the athlete Astylos (fr. 616). The strong bond between Mainland Greece and the colonies, however, in no way diminishes the autonomy and sheer originality of creative production in Magna Graecia – not just in the field of literature, but also in civil history, religious development, and the figurative arts. The starting point for the history of literature and writing in the Greek West is the Nestor *kotyle*, whose date has been unanimously fixed to between 730 and 725 B.C. The text of the epigraph in Chalcidian writing engraved in Pithekoussai on this Geometric-style cup runs: "I am the cup of Nestor, in which it is pleasant to drink. Whosoever drinks from this cup, alas, will be struck with desire for fair-crowned Aphrodite." There is evidence that in the eighth century B.C. Homer's epic poems were already popular in the West, not long after they were in fact composed. It is also striking that a iambic trimeter should be associated with a hexameter, in a system that might be called epodic: instead of slaking the drinker's thirst, the cup fuels his desire. The path of development of written culture in Magna Graecia and Sicily can be followed through several colonies which adopted the structure of the homelands, while achieving new contributions of their own. Locri was such a colony, and had already reached the status of *polis* by the seventh century, with a vast literary output that spread as far as Sparta. The Homeric poet Xenocrates wrote a form of paean that was conceived as a ballad consecrating heroic feats; in one such paean composed in honor of the god Apollo Xenocrates devised a new formula, the so-called "Locrian Harmony," which was entrusted to flutes rather

The extraordinary birth of Helen according to the literary tradition on an Apulian krater second quarter 4th cent. B.C.
Bari, Museo Archeologico
Cat. 217

Bronze tablet with inscription
concerning the management
of the Sanctuary of Zeus Olympus
at Locri Epizephyrii
350-250 B.C.
Reggio Calabria, Museo Nazionale

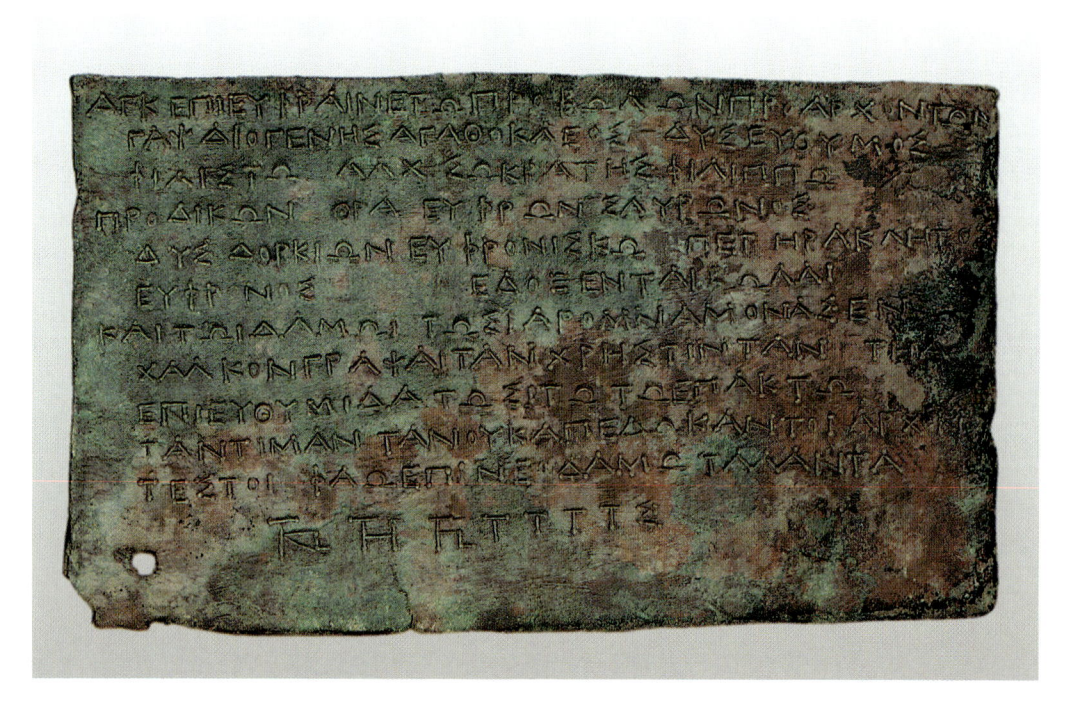

than lyres, a device that would later serve as a model for the great Theban poet Pindar. One of Pindar's Odes (*Pythian* II. 18–20) offers evidence that as early as the beginning of the fifth century there were already "virgins' cantos." One of these actually declares the underlying motive for its creation, namely that the virgins might sing the praises of the inhabitants of Locri for having spared the city from the threats of a tyrant. In the Hellenistic age all manner of love songs thrived – some rather hackneyed and crudely styled, whose subject matter revolved around acts of adultery. In one surviving example in ionic meter, an adulteress expresses her fears for the return of her husband at the first light of dawn, and begs her lover to make himself scarce. But Locri was also the home of the epigram. The great female poet Nossis is noted for several themes, mostly of an anathematic nature, but she was not above including autobiographical information, in imitation of the celebrated Sappho of Mytilene. Some of Nossis' works have reached posterity through the *Palatine Anthology* (in which Meleager identifies her with the iris flower), together with twelve epigrams that may have constituted her book of poems. Of this only the prelude and closing stanza have survived. The prelude is a kind of poetic manifesto (*Pal. Anth.* V. 170): "Nothing is more soave than love, yet all other delights come second: even the honey I spit from my mouth. Thus saith Nossis: she who is not favored by Cypris has no idea of what flower the rose is." The closing epigram (*Pal. Anth.* VII. 718), in which the poetess harks back to Sappho's model, runs thus: "O stranger, if you sail to Mytilene with hearty song to gather Sappho, that flower of the graces, tell her that I was friend of the Muses, that I was born at Locri and that my name is Nossis. Go!" Other epigrams are either anathematic (one is the dedication of the arms taken from the Bruttii by the Locrians; others to Locrian women portrayed with a keen realism), or convivial as in the epigram in which Nossis prays to me, all-powerful Hera, lady of Croton, to accept her gift (*Pal. Anth.* VI. 265). "Hera recovered who oft descending from heaven lookest on thy Lacinian shrine fragrant with frankincense, accept the linen garment which Theophilis, daughter of Cleocha, wove for thee with her noble daughter Nossis." But there are also certain epigrams of a historico-literary nature, in which the poet pays homage to Rhinthon of Syracuse, the creator of the *phlyakes* or buffoon actors who, as we shall see later, were a signal component of popular theater in the Hellenistic age. The aristocratic Nossis acknowledges Rhinthon's originality thus (*Pal. Anth.* VII. 414): "Laugh frankly as thou passest by, and speak a kind word over me. I am Rhinthon, one of the lesser nightingales of the Muses, but from my tragic burlesques I plucked for myself a wreath of ivy of my own devising." The archives of the Temple of Olympian Zeus, discovered by the scholar de Franciscis in 1972, have shed invaluable new light on the Dorian dialect in Magna Graecia, and has also provided clues as to the political and social history of Locri from the fourth [sixth] to the fifth century. The two bronze tablets found in the archives are similar in kind to those known as the *Tabulae Heracleenses* and are of the same importance in historiographical and literary terms. The various loan transactions documented in these tablets reveal the hand of a sort of Hellenistic accountant who, in order to relieve the boredom of his routine duties, used a literary style that epitomizes an "accounting

literature" of which very little is still known. One crucial item of news recorded in the tablets is the debt owed by the philosopher Plato to the city of Locri where, during his travels through Magna Graecia, he paid a call on Timaeus, one of the leading figures of the local Pythagorean school; another visit may have been paid to Philiston of Locri, a renowned physician. The workings of Timaeus' mind on the overwhelming questions of cosmology are contained in Plato's *Timaeus* dialogue (*Timaeus* 19e): "For our friend Timaeus is a native of a most well-governed State, Italian Locris, and inferior to none of its citizens in property or in rank; and not only has he occupied the highest offices and posts of honour in his State, but he has also attained, in my opinion the very summit of eminence in all branches of philosophy. (tr. R.G. Bury)" The nearby mainland colony of Rhegium (Greek Rhegion) was the birthplace of the sixth-century love-poet Ibycus, the greatest in all Magna Graecia. He spent part of his life in Sicily, and part on the island of Samos. Ibycus gave new direction to epic poetry, endowing it with lyricism; he was also responsible for a unique manner of acclaiming beauty that would serve as a model for a great many later poets. Rather than the heroic virtues extolled by Homer, Ibycus sang about love, and particularly the love of boys. One of the papyri found at the archaeological site of Oxyrhynchus on the Nile brought to light an important selection of Ibycus' work, notably the encomium for Polycrates, the young son of the Samian tyrant. The strophic handling betrays his debts to Stesichorus, though his own style differs in its unorthodox approach to epic poetry. Ibycus forsook the epic themes and motifs that were typical of his production while in the West, and instead began to adopt a rather fatuous style in tune with the palace circles he frequented, a style in which he celebrated the dazzling beauty of the youth in question, a beauty which in itself earned the boy his glory, rather than any military or athletic prowess. Here follows a section of this particular poem (*Oxyrhynchus Papyrus* 1790, published for the first time in 1922): "...destroyed the great, glorious, blessed city of Priam, son of Dardanus, setting off from Argos by the plans of great Zeus, enduring much-sung strife over the beauty of auburn Helen in tearful war; and ruin mounted long-suffering Pergamum thanks to the golden-haired Cyprian; but now it was not my heart's wish to sing of Paris, deceiver of his host, or of slim-ankled Cassandra and Priam's other children and the unmentionable day of the capture of high-gated Troy, nor shall I recount the proud valour of the heroes whom hollow, many-bolted ships brought to be an evil to Troy, fine heroes: they were commanded by lord Agamemnon, Pleisthenid king, leader of men, fine son born to Atreus. On these themes the skilled Muses of Helicon might embark in story, but no mortal man (untaught?) could tell each detail, the great number of ships that came from Aulis across the Aegean sea from Argos to horse-rearing Troy, with bronze-shielded warriors on board, sons of the Achaeans; among them foremost with the spear went swift-footed Achilles and great valiant Telamonian Ajax (who threw strong fire on Troy?); (with them also went) from Argos to Ilium Cyanippus, the most handsome man (descendant of Adrastus), (and Zeuxippus, whom the Naiad), golden-girdled Hyllis (conceived and) bore (to Phoebus); and to him Trojans and Greeks likened Troilus as gold already trhice-refined to orichalc, judging him very similar in loveliness of form. These have a share in beauty always: you too, Polycrates, will have undying fame as song and my fame can give it. (tr. D.A. Campbell)"
Love was not the only motor of the lyric poems of Ibycus, though it was undoubtedly preeminent. His bond with Sicily is further evidenced by a fragment (fr. 323 Page) in which he describes the mingling of the waters of Alpheus with those of Arethusa, and by a work traditionally attributed to him (or sometimes Stesichorus), *The Funeral-games of Pelias*. Together with the Cyclic poets, Homer was undoubtedly one of Ibycus' principal sources for subject matter. But likewise Archilocus left his mark on the Rhegian poet's output, which is also a reflection of the landscape of Magna Graecia. Despite his deference to the courtly predilection for the love of boys, Ibycus was by no means immune to feminine beauty. In a well-known piece (fr. 286) he exulted the universal puissance of Eros, who "bore down upon him like a strong northerly wind driven by Aphrodite, with such indomitable strength that the very roots of his heart were stirred." Ibycus is the first poet to draw analogies between the devastating deeds of Eros and the calm succession of the seasons in which Nature displays all its variety without toil or trouble. Ibycus' reverence for the beauty of boys, however, was not merely to indulge the tyrant of Samos: he used it as a pretext to compose a new type of poetry about beauty which shines like pure gold, and follows in the path of Homer when it affirms that "poetry bestows immortal glory." Indeed, in many respects Ibycus is a forerunner of Horace, and even of Shakespeare. Stesichorus was that sublime lyric cantor of epic themes and the inspirer of the figured metopes on the Temple of Hera at the source of the Sele River near Paestum. He is presumed to be from Himera in Sicily, though some sources indicate his birth in Mataurus in Magna Graecia. Stesichorus was doubtless deeply fond of the Italian heartland, though he was not the author of the songs praising the Locrian victory over the Crotonians. Many of the titles of Stesichorus' works have survived, which show an evident inspiration of the Trojan and the Heraclean Cycles: *The Sack of Ilium*, *Home-*

comings, *Geryoneis*; but he is particularly famed for his palinodes on Helen of Troy: in *Helen* he originally accused the woman of being the cause of all the misdeeds that befell the city, and was consequently deprived of his sight; subsequently, he withdrew the accusation and his sight was duly restored (fr. 192): "This story is not true: you did not embark on the fine-seated ships, nor did you reach the rock of Troy." Recent research has revealed that Stesichorus wrote about Jocasta exhorting her children not to persist in the fratricidal war. Little has survived of this Sicilian poet, but the extant fragments suggest a poet of immense stature. The city of Rhegium was actually the birthplace of Homer studies and of the first historians of the West. The first poet to cultivate the study of Homer was the rhapsodist Theagenes, who wrote a book on the art of poetry, on Homer's background and on his historical period, and inaugurated the linguistic inquiry into the works of the forefather of all Greek poetry, which he defended against the attacks of his contemporary, Xenophanes, a poet and philosopher. Theagenes defended the Homeric poets from the accusation of immorality, claiming that Homer expressed himself in allegorical form. He also compiled a critique of the written versions of Homer, comparing the vulgate lessons with the versions in his collection. Subsequently, between the fifth and fourth centuries B.C., the scholar Glaucus of Rhegium proceeded with the studies on Homer's work, but his most significant inquiry was into the development of musical form, in which he drew a distinction between the accompaniment of the *aulos* (a double-reed instrument) and that of the *kithara* (lyre), interpreting Orpheus, Terpander, Thaletas, and Olympus, whose chronology he tried to establish. His book bore the title *On the Ancient Poets and Musicians*. He is also reputed to have studied the Athenian tragic dramatist Aeschylus, claiming that he had taken Phrynicus' *Phoenissae* as a model for the *Persians*. One of the great pioneers of literary studies is Hippys, another native of Rhegium (fifth century B.C.), the first true historian of the Greek West. From the scant fragments that have survived, one can affirm that Hippys, the source for Hellanicus of Lesbos had a clear understanding of the historical unity of Magna Graecia and Sicily. Hippys may be considered a kind of bridge between history and the Roman legends. He was the author of a *History of Sicily* that earned the privilege of being epitomized, and a *Colonization of Italy*, that is, a history of the colonies of Magna Graecia. Similarly, in the works of the historian Lycus of Rhegium, who thrived in the late fourth and early third centuries, the history of Sicily is interwoven with that of Magna Graecia. Little is known of this scholar, but it is evident that his commentaries on Sicily were a source of material for the historian Timaeus of Tauromenium, as well as for Callimachus and the Chalcidian poet Lycophron. According to Lycus, Greek influence was considerable throughout the Adriatic, and in Corsica and Sardinia. The Panhellenic colony of Thurii in ancient Lucania, founded by the antagonist of Pericles' political legacy, Thucydides son of Melesias, was the birthplace of a major representative of Attic Middle Comedy, namely Alexis, who spent most of his life and work in Athens itself, though he never forgot his origins in Magna Graecia. His work is imitative of the Syracusan Epicharmus in its representations of Heracles and Odysseus. Alexis explored the fields of mythological and philosophical parody, and made fun of the Pythagoreans in particular, as we can see from the extant fragments of two comedies, *The Tarentines*, and *The Pythagorizer*. The links with the Italiot world are documented by such comedies as *The Bruttian Maiden*, a fragment of which has universal meaning (fr. 34): "Such is the life of men: just as a dice does not always fall the same way up, so life never maintains the same form, but is ever changing." Life seen as a banquet which, once over, one must leave, was represented by Alexis in several verses from *The Tarentines*, which were thus reworked by Giacomo Leopardi:

"Questa che chiaman vita sollazzevole,
oziosa, da spasso, o cosa simile,
son voci che si dicono per nascondere
la vera umana sorte. Ognun si accomodi
col suo parer; non voglio entrare in dispute;
ma per mia parte, io giudico che il vivere
sia tutto e in generale una scempiaggine.
Ciascun, da' regni morti e da le tenebre
venendo in questa luce, appunto capita,
non altrimenti che straniero ed ospite,
come dire a una festa: e chi da ridere,
mentre ch'ei vive e il può, trova più comodo,
più da ber, più da far l'opra di Venere,
e quattro cortesie, con miglior animo
da la festa al suo loco ha da tornarsene".

Gold *laminetta*
inscribed with texts inspired
by the Eleusinia
found at Thurii
4th cent. B.C.
Naples
Museo Archeologico Nazionale
Cat. 209

Commanding a key position in the history of the religious practices and literature in Magna Graecia are the so-called *Laminette Auree* or Golden Tablets, not only those of Thurii and Petelia, but also those of Hipponium (modern Vibo Valentia), origin of the oldest of all those found so far. The contents of these and others from Crete and Thessaly have been compiled in a volume by G. Pugliese Carratelli (*Le laminette d'oro "orfiche,"* Milan 1993). Endorsing previous research papers, this scholar has drawn a distinction between the *laminette* of Petelia and Hipponium from those found at Thurii: the former set has an underlying soteriological meaning related to the mystic cults (and hence to Orphism), and are characterized as *mnemosynai* and distinct from the formulas of recognition; the latter are of Eleusinian inspiration as the soul is not presented to the custodians of the fountain of salvation, but to the gods of the underworld, the most renowned of whom was Persephone. Other *laminette* belonging to the latter category include two plaques found very recently at Pelinna. The prime example of the former category is the one found in Hipponium, first published by G. Pugliese Carratelli in 1974:
Sacred to Mnemosyne was this [dictate for the *mystes*] when on the point of death.

You shall go forth among the well-built houses of Hades: on the right stands a fountain,
beside which rises a white cypress tree;
here descend the souls of the dead to seek relief.
Do not even come nigh unto this fountain;
but further ahead you will find the cool waters flowing
from Mnemosyne's lake: there attend the custodians,
who will ask you, with sure discernment,
what it is you seek amid the gloomy dusk of Hades.
Tell them: "I [am] son of the Depths and of the starry Heavens;
of thirst I am parched and weak: but give me forthwith

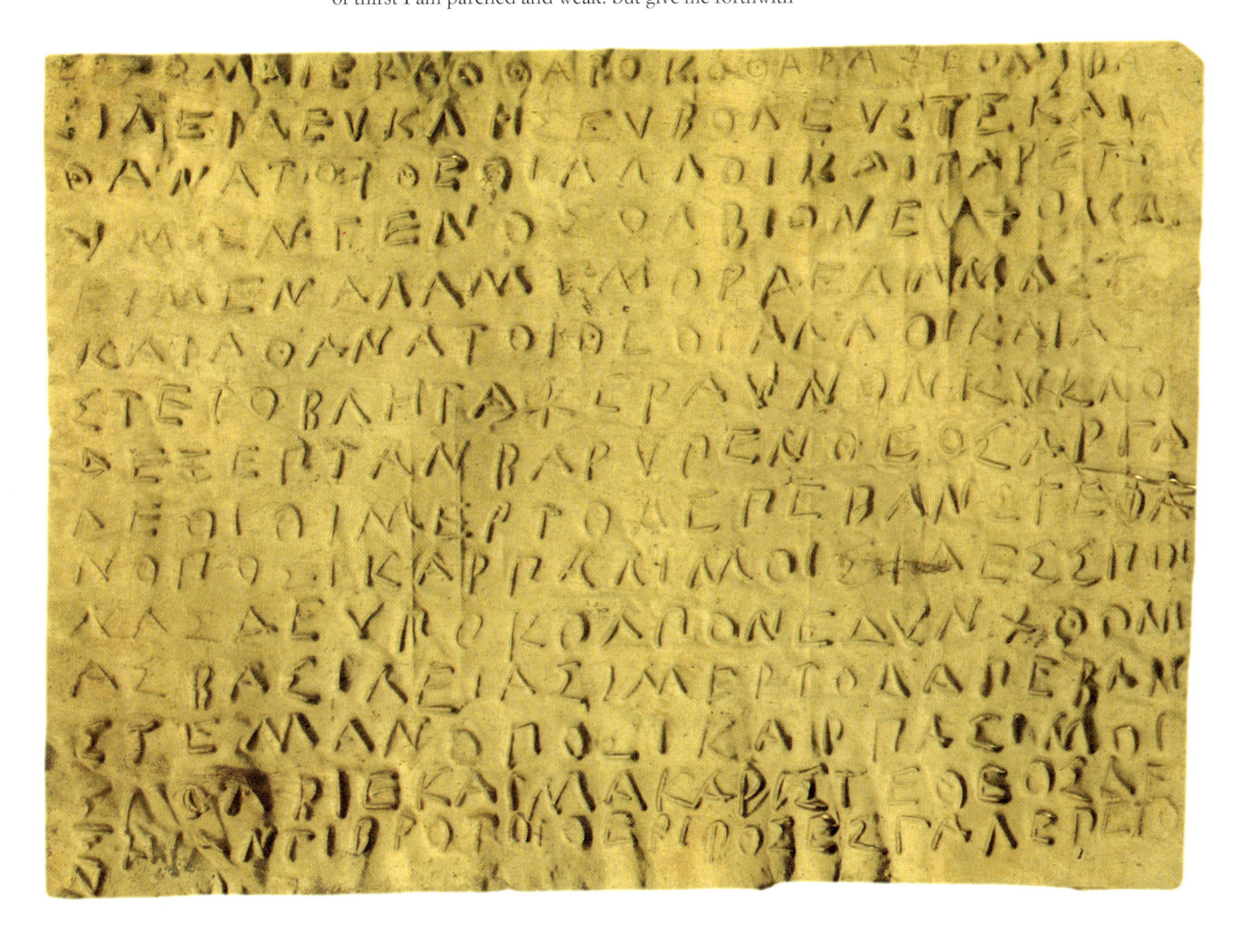

Small altar with a scene from
Sophocles' tragedy about
the myth of Tyro
end 5th-first half 4th cent. B.C.
Reggio Calabria, Museo Nazionale
Cat. 335

the cool waters of Mnemosyne's lake that I may drink."
And they will take pity for the wish of the sovereign of the Underworld,
and shall let you drink [the water] of Mnemosyne's lake;
and when you have drunk you will advance along the sacred way,
whither the other *mystai* and *bacchoi* proceed in glory.

An example of the latter category can be appreciated in this inscription from a *laminetta* unearthed at Thurii (II B, 1):

I come from among the pure ones, O pure queen of the Underworld,
Eukles and Eubuleus and other immortal *numina*:
that I declare I also belong to your blessed offspring.
But was subjugated by Destiny and the blinding dispenser of thunderbolts.
I fled from the dolorous cycle of grief,
and rose fleet of foot unto the pined-for corona;
I plunged into the womb of the Lady queen of the Underworld,
then descended fleet of foot from the desired corona.
"O happy and most blessed, *numen* will you become, immortal."
Like a kid goat I leaped toward the milk.

Leaving aside the differences of structure and style, and the stereotyped formulas that suggest an underlying Greek model, the two sets of Italiot plaques provide an outstanding testament to the sacred or mystic poetry of the period (composed in hexameters that do not always scan but whose idiom is freighted with meaning), a literary form that burgeoned in Magna Graecia, where Orphic rites paved the way for Pythagoreanism. The authors of these plaques betray a certain mysteriousness that accompanies the soul's approach to the afterlife. Without doubt, during the Hellenistic age the city of Tarentum (Greek Taras) enjoyed a period of extraordinary creativity prior to its capture by the Romans. Such philosophers as Archytas and Aristoxenus did much to further the civil and philosophical life of the Greek *polis*. The city seems to have been overshadowed by Pythagoreanism, but drama also flourished, with a mixture of autochthonous works and dramas imported from Athens (a fact documented in vase-paintings). Both the tragic and comic dramas of Athenian production were particularly popular in Tarentum, as in other *poleis* such as Medma and even in Locri itself. The Pythagorean philosopher Aristoxenus did not subscribe to the new form of theater that was invented by Rhinthon (or should we say, raised to the level of an authentic literary form); yet this type of drama is emblematic of the basic unity of Sicily and Magna Graecia. While originating in Syracuse, it became particularly popular in Tarentum. Rhinthon was an inspiration for *phlyax* vase-painters, particularly the Paestan painter Assteas, and he devised a kind of parody of the mythical repertoire of the great Athenian tragedians, especially of Euripides, whose work inspired many of the vase-painters of Magna Graecia. It has yet to be established whether the many vase-paintings and the extant historical and literary accounts necessarily indicate a revival of the performances of Attic tragedies whose text was established by Lycurgus in Athens in the year 386 B.C. At any event, the presence on certain vases of subjects taken from Attic dramas is highly significant as regards the popularity of these fundamental texts of ancient theater. This "revival" of subjects taken from dramatic works (principally from those of Euripides) sheds light on the growing trend for parody, a genre championed by Rhinthon of Tarentum, who can now be said with confidence to have chosen Aristophanes as his prime target. The new genre is generally described as "hilaro-tragedy," and came to be performed at all the Dionysiac festivals. The god Dionysus frequently crops up in phlyactic vase-painting (cf. the studies of the archaeologist Trendall). Among the known titles of Rhinthon's works are *Iphigenia in Aulis*, *Iphigenia in Tauris*, *Medea*, *Orestes*, *Telephus*, *Heracles* (of which these two iambic trimeters have survived: "In a tankard of wine you choked a large piece of genuine dry bread and some genuine loaves of wheat and barley"). The affinities with Euripides are self-evident; similarly we find Heracles portrayed as an eager drinker, in the wake of Epicharmus' portraits of the hero. Tarentum in fact boasts the greatest epigram poet of all Magna Graecia. A hundred or so epigrams of Leonidas have nearly all reached us through the fabled *Palatine Anthology*. Born toward the end of the fourth century B.C., Leonidas lived through the closing stages of the Greek *polis* Taras before its fall to the Romans in the year 72 B.C. It was in Epirus that the poet came to know King Pyrrhus, whom he held to be a descendant of Achilles. Leonidas composed epigrams for Pyrrhus and for Neoptolemus, who served as co-regent. Nothing else is known of Leonidas' life, except that he died far from his homeland, as he himself relates in a famous epigram (*Pal. Anth.* VII. 715), whose authenticity has paradoxically been questioned by some philologists: "Far from the Italian land I lie, far from my city Tarentum and this is more bitter to me than death itself; such is the life of wayfarers, though hardly a life; but the Muses loved me and in place of misfortune I have the sweetness of song. The name of

Orestes and Electra meet before Agamemnon's tomb
decoration on an Apulian krater from Tarentum
390-380 B.C.
Taranto, Museo Nazionale
Cat. 221

Literary Culture in Magna Graecia and Sicily

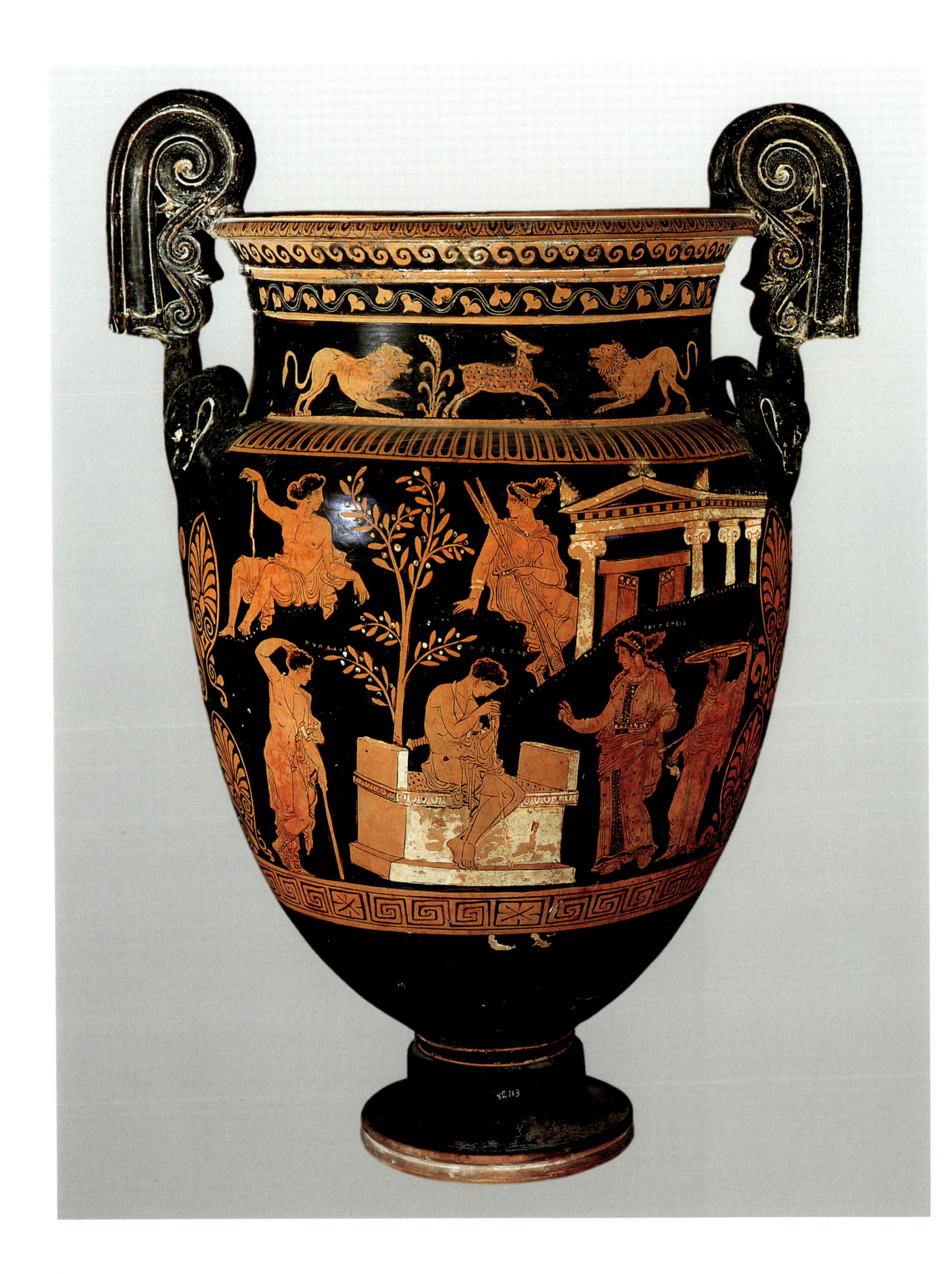

opposite
Orestes meets Iphigeneia
in the land of the Taurians
decoration on an Apulian krater
from Ruvo
350-325 B.C.
Naples
Museo Archeologico Nazionale
Cat. 225

Leonidas has not sunk into oblivion, no indeed – the gifts of the Muses proclaim it each day." The Muses in Leonidas' epigrams are of a varied nature: his were anathematic epigrams, extolling the virtues of the simple life, and hence linked to Sparta, the mother country of Tarentum; but he was also close to the Cynics and Pythagoreans. In one epigram, using a popular incantation-style formula, Leonidas expresses the superiority of his honest poverty (*Pal. Anth.* VI. 302): "Out, mice, clear out of my hut, the meal-tub of Leonidas has not the wherewithal to feed you too! This old man has barely enough crumbs of salt or bread buns for himself, yet I praise this life style, inherited from my forebears. So why, gluttonous mouse, do you sniff about in my hovel, seeing as you won't even get the leavings of my dinner? Be off! Go to someone else's house, where you'll certainly find better rations. What I possess is sheer simplicity." Among the various autobiographical epigrams exulting the poet's suffered inspiration and the loftiness of his self-confidence, the following two are cogently fashioned (*Pal. Anth.* VI. 300): "O Lathrian goddess, accept from poor Leonidas, the vagrant and penniless, these grateful figurines of olive-cake and this green fig which I plucked from the tree; take also five grapes which I pulled from the wine-giving bowers, O venerated goddess, and this libation from the dregs of my cup. As you spared me from sickness, so spare me this hateful penury, and I shall sacrifice a kid goat to you."

The other (*Pal. Anth.* VII. 736) runs: "O man, do not exhaust yourself in the life of a rambler, wandering from one land to the next. Do not deplete yourself: a simple shack is enough for a home, heated with a small fire. All you need is a plain bread-bun of unrefined meal, kneaded with your own hands in the hollow of a stone. All you need is a little mint and thyme, and a pinch of bitter salt which, when mixed with the rest, becomes so sweet." Leonidas was above all the common man's poet. He sang about humble craftsmen such as the carpenters Theris and Leonticus, the fisherman Diophantus, and the hunters Pigretes, Damides, and Clitor, together with the traveling musicians whose flute-playing accompanied the serenades of the young men carousing below the windows of their beloved. He was fascinated by novelties of all kinds, and praised the toys invented by Hermes in this fleet verse (*Pal. Anth.* VI. 309): "To Hermes, Philocles dedicated a solid ball, this boxwood rattle, the knucklebones he so loved and the spinning top – toys of his youth." While he sang his praise of Homer, Hipponax, and Erinna, he also composed about such figures as the "tippler" Maron and the old weaver Platthis, as in this epigram (*Pal. Anth.* VII. 726), which is a singular example of realism: "Many evenings and mornings old Platthis would forgo her sleep in order to keep destitution at bay. When she was already white-haired she sang a song of the spindle and distaff and that longtime working companion of hers; on her loom she toiled through to dawn and together with the Graces she ran the long stadium of Athena, or with her wrinkled hand on her wrinkled knee teased out enough thread for her weaving. Comely was she. But at eighty years Platthis saw the waters of Acheron: what fine things she had woven." Of all the *poleis* of ancient Sicily, the history of Sirakousai or Syracuse is undoubtedly the most fabulous, a city which in the age of the tyrants Dionysius the Elder and Younger was frequented by the likes of Aeschylus and Pindar. The city was the birthplace of Epicharmus, who wrote his special brand of comedy in Sicilian Doric, a style that flourished in the fifth century B.C. His rather short plays focused on the subjects of Homer and the Cyclic dramas. Little has survived of Epicharmus' *dramata*, which include *Odysseus Shipwrecked*, *Odysseus the Deserter*, *The Marriage of Hebe*, *Busiris*, *Hope or Riches*, *Land and Sea*. In the work *Busiris* Epicharmus assigned a servant the task of conveying the voracious appetite of Heracles when he was the guest of the king of Egypt: "If you saw him eat you'd die: his mouth gapes, his jaw cracks, his molars click, his canines gnash, his nostrils wheeze, and his ears wiggle." In *The Marriage of Hebe* the poet lists the various courses brought before Heracles, putting his words this time in the mouth of a deity: "He brings every possible kind of shellfish, limpets, whelks, cockles, oysters, razorshells, clams (hard to open but easy to swallow), mussels, and all other seashells, which are sweet on the palate and slither down the throat. ... Then comes the black shell ... and the other shellfish of such ignoble grittiness, which the humble man calls anthrophyte and we gods call white." Another delightful surviving passage of this comic poet's work is the monologue of the sullen social parasite: "I dine with whomever I please, when invited; as for those that don't want my company, I don't wait to be invited. At the table I am all good spirits, they split their sides laughing: whoever is paying gets lavish praise; and should anyone dare to contrary him, I lose my temper and give him what for. Then I go off, my belly full of food and wine; yet I have no servant-child to light my way! All on my own I stagger about, colliding and tripping, and find my own way home. And if I should have the ill-luck to run into the guards, Heavens! I usually get away with a couple of black-eyes, nothing more. When I get home in that state, there is no bed awaiting me! But it hardly matters, as the fumes of wine cloud the brain." The great Syracuse was also the home of Sophron, a mimographer much admired by Plato. Many discussions on the art of female and male mime have survived, and a Florentine papyrus (*PSI* 1214) offers

Pestan bell krater
with scene of satyric plays
ca. 330 B.C.
Naples
Museo Archeologico Nazionale
Cat. 228

a delightful glimpse of this art in a piece entitled *The Women Who Claim to Bring Down the Goddess*. Mention should also be made of Telestes of Selinus, whose work follows in the path of Timotheus of Miletus (the celebrated author of *Persae*), and who devised his own variation of the dithyramb.

Yet another important Syracusan author was Antiochus, logographer and author of a history of Sicily and Italy, and a likely source for the later work of Thucydides. Also in fifth-century Syracuse came the great Corax who, together with Tisias, founded the art of rhetoric and, to some extent, paved the way for the great sophist philosopher Gorgias of Leontini, the teacher of Polus of Agrigentum. The figure of Gorgias is well known. He theorized that things could be neither apprehended nor communicated, but he was also the author of several virtuoso pieces, including *The Encomium of Helen*, *The Defense of Palamedes*. Only one specimen of his prose writing has survived, a passage from *The Encomium of Helen*, giving a conception of the *logos* as a force to which mankind must submit his will: "The *logos* is a grand sovereign who, despite his tiny body and humble appearance, brings about the greatest works of mankind: he can curtail fear, remove anguish, spread pleasure, and fuel pity." One of the historians who covered the reign of the tyrant Dionysius of Syracuse was Philistus, a glimpse of whose work is afforded by a recently discovered papyrus. In his wake, Sicily witnessed the rise of the great Timaeus of Tauromenium, who had an extraordinary influence on the historians that followed him. It was Timaeus that another important historian, Polybius, accused of having a too bookish concept of history.

Of the work of Theocritus (who served as a model for Virgil) – inventor of the bucolic idyll but also author of epigrams – a worthy example of his most celebrated idylls are the *Thalysia*, and *The Spell*. Of the works of this poet, Idylls IV and V are particularly relevant here, as they are set in Magna Graecia. Idyll IV (*The Herdsmen*), here is the song of Battus and Corydon against the background of Croton and the Lacinium Promontorium (Capo Colonna), sacred to Hera (*The Herdsmen*, 15–37):

BA. Certainly there's nothing left of that calf yonder
  but the bones. She doesn't live on dewdrops,
  does she–like the cicada?
CO. Faith, no. Sometimes I pasture her by the Aesarus
  and give her a nice truss of soft hay,
  and sometimes it's on shady Latymnum that she frisks.
BA. The bull's thin too–the ruddy one.
  I shope Lampriadas's folk may get such another
  when the demesmen sacrifice to Hera:
  they're [rascals] in that deme.
CO. And yet the bull is driven to the saltings,
  and to Physcus's, and to the Neaethus,
  where all good things grow–restharrow, fleabane and fragrant balm.
BA. Wretched Aegon,
  your cows too will come by their deaths
  because you, like others, have fallen in love with a cursed victory.
  And the pipe that once you made yourself is getting flecked with mildew.
CO. Nay, by the Nymphs it is not,
  for as he going off to Pisa he left it me for a present.
  I am something of a player myself,
  and can strike up Glauca's tunes, or Pyrrhus's, well enough.
  I sing the praise of Croton: "A bonny town Zacynthus is"
  and of the Lacinian shrine that fronts the dawn–
  where boxer Aegon devoured eighty loaves all by himself.
  There it was, too, he seized the bull by the hoof
  and brought it down from the hill and gave it to Amaryllis.
  The women shrieked loudly, and the herdsman laughed. (tr. A.S.F. Gow)

From the fifth Idyll (*The Goatherd and the Shepherd*) comes a picture of Sybaris and the plains around the Athenian colony of Thurii, with its network of live-giving streams (1–2, 14–16, 70–73, 120–127, 145ff.); the arbitrator of the singing competition between the goatherd Comatas and the shepherd Lacon is the woodcutter Morson:

CO. Keep away from Lacon,
  the shepherd from Sybaris, my little kids;
  yesterday he stole my fur.
LA. No, by the Pan of the river banks himself!
  It was not Lacon, son of Calerides
  who stripped the fur off your back!
  Let me throw myself down from this crag
  into the Crathis, like a madman.
CO. Sure, for the nymphs, my dear Morson,
  you need not show any propension for Comatas
  nor have any preference for him.
  These sheep are the property of Sibirtha of Thurii,
  but the nannies, my dear, belong to Eumara the Sybarite.
CO. Morson, somebody is already
  swallowing a bitter pill
  haven't you realized? Quick, run and grab
  the onions from the tomb of an old hag.
LA. I'll pinch someone too, Morson,
  and you'll see him. Now he's going to Alentum
  to uproot cyclamins.

The tunnyfish seller krater
with characters from the comedy
380-370 B.C.
Cefalù
Museo della Fondazione Culturale
Mandralisca
Cat. 233

Phylax scene
with Heracles, Iolaus
and Eurystheus
decoration on an Apulian
red-figure *oinochoe*
second quarter 4th cent. B.C.
Taranto, Museo Nazionale
Cat. 224

Co. Milk is flowing over Himera, not water,
    You, Crathis, take the wine down
    and fruit will grow on the cannella herb.
La. Honey is flowing from Sybaris
    and the girl at dawn with the jug
    can gather honeycomb instead of water.
Co. Cheer up, my little horned ladies
    I'll bath you all
    in the pond at Sybaris tomorrow.

The next in succession is Moschus, author of *The Runaway Love* and *Europa*, who was much appreciated (and translated) by Leopardi, who defined Moschus as the "Greek Virgil."

At the height of the Hellenistic age, Syracuse witnessed the emergence of the epigrams of Theodoridas, who continued the diverse poetic production of his precursors Leonidas and Nossis through the second half of the third century B.C. His epigrams, which have reached posterity through the *Palatine Anthology*, were gathered by Meleager, who chose wild thyme as his emblem: the nineteen extant epigrams reveal that the poet was more preoccupied with death than with love. Theodoridas is also important for his descriptions of the countryside of Sicily and Magna Graecia, and to some extent was the inventor of spring poetry. The epigrams on Euphorion and Mnasalces have provided scholars with the poetic "manifesto" of Theodoridas; while other epigrams show the poet a master of anathematic verse. In conclusion, Theodoridas as a poet was immersed in the history of Sicilian Doric poetry, and in the history of the Hellenistic epigram; closely following the example of Callimachus, he has distinct personality, and goes hand-in-hand with his more famous contemporary Theocritus.

Bibliography
For further information on the synthesis above, see my essays in *Enciclopedia dello Spettacolo*, IV, 1957, series 1513-1518; 1967; 1971; in *La Parola del Passato*, CLIV-CLV, 1974, pp. 22-39; in *Storia e cultura del Mezzogiorno...*, 1979, pp. 3-7; in *Letterature comparate...*, 1981, pp. 243-245; in *Taras*, VIII, 1988, pp. 7-33.
I have contributed to this theme with other writings published in *Atti dei Convegni tarantini di Studi sulla Magna Grecia* starting from 1965. *Megale Hellas...*, 1983, pp. 585-640; 1987, pp. 527-563; *Magna Grecia*, III, 1988, pp. 259-284, contain other outlines of mine on the literary civilization of Magna Graecia.

Valeria Lanzara Gigante The Literary History of Cyrenaica

When the first group of Dorians set foot on the shores of Libya, following their leader, Battus, to found a settlement among the hills and dales of Azili, the water of the Cyra spring was just an uncontaminated promise of civilization. The inescapable response of the oracle had driven them there from Thera on the other side of the Mediterranean.

The city of Cyrene, whose birth was veiled by legend like every adventurous expedition of the ancient colonists, was founded in the name of Apollo. Its history, as narrated by Herodotus, emerges from the flashes of Pindaric images. Cyrene is a nymph loved by the god among the twin peaks of Myrtussa (the Hill of Myrtles). Apollo, in the form of a crow, on Battus' right, leads the expedition to the site of the city. Once on Libyan soil, Battus regains the power of speech at the amazing sight of lions. Apollo, the most beloved of all the gods, is venerated in a great temple on the acropolis. He is omnipresent, with all the names linked to his cult, in the epigraphs of Cyrene. In his honor, belted warriors dance with the yellow-haired Libyan women at the Carnean feasts that celebrate him as the ancestral divinity of the founding fathers. This is the *Hymn* dedicated to the beloved god by Callimachus, outstanding son of a land destined to become the cradle of versatile genius.

Literature was already produced in Cyrene in the two centuries filled with wars and silences following its foundation, if it really was the Cyrenaic Eugammon who wrote the *Telegony*, the closing poem of that epic cycle that Callimachus was to criticize so heavily three centuries later. The story of Telegonus, the son of Odysseus and Circe, and later husband of Penelope, seems to be the most suited, among the various subplots of the cycle, for satisfying uncultured curiosity about the developments of the mythical affairs, and no less important is the announcement in it, that apart from Telemachus, Eustathius meets another son of Odysseus and Penelope called Arcesilas, who was the legendary ancestor of the kings of Cyrene.

However it was primarily in the Hellenistic age that literature and science both flourished in Cyrene. Encyclopedic learning that characterized the culture of the Hellenistic world is the training ground for Cyrene's intellectuals, for mathematicians such as Theodorus, a disciple of Protagoras and master of the Platonic Theaetetus, Nicoteles, emulator of Conon of Samos in studies on the theories of the cone, and geographers, such as Amometos, author of a *Navigation from Memphis*, and of a monograph on the Attacori, a far-off people similar to the Hyperboreans, living in a region with sunny hills.

Generous mother of fine intellects, Cyrenaica was, however, to remain only the land of origin for many of its sons attracted by other centers of culture, in particular by Alexandria, the capital of the Ptolemaic kingdom, set up, with the blessing of its enlightened rulers, to become the goal of intellectuals from all the known world.

Aristippus, founder of the Cyrenaic school which identified pleasure with the purpose of life, calm movement in contrast with the wild movement of pain, emigrated to Athens, attracted by the fame of Socrates. Early in life, Callimachus left Cyrene to become first a schoolmaster at Eleusis, a suburb of Alexandria, and then leader of the men of letters drawn to the library and museum of Ptolemy II Philadelphus. A variety of interests stimulated Callimachus to undertake research in a wide range of fields, but principally, apart from literary and philological studies, he produced works on geography, toponymy and folklore. His writings, more than eight hundred according to the *Suda*, included works in verses and prose, and among the latter there was a gigantic *catalogue raisonné*, with the title *Pinakes*, of all the literary works belonging to the library, divided into sectors and arranged in alphabetical order. His familiarity with the precious papyri provided him with the erudition at the base of his poetry. It is easy to pick out in his verses the echoes of his innumerable studies, some traces of which can be found in a few titles, *About Nymphs, Birds, Winds, Rivers*, etc.

Originality and elegance made Callimachus a magnetic and inevitable reference for Greek and Roman authors, and even though he never became the director of the library, he was certainly the master of young poets such as Apollonius of Naucratis, known as Apollonius Rhodius, the author of *Argonautica*, and Eratosthenes, another native of Cyrene, an all-round genius, who tended toward philosophical and scientific studies, but was not averse to experimenting poetry. Callimachus, like all genial minds, was not without followers and critics. He turns vehemently on the latter, whom he considers instigated by envy, in the prologue of *Aetia* (*Origins*), the work in elegiac distichs on a series of myths linked together by the tenuous thread of the *aetion*, the search for their origins. The critics contested his choice of an essential and delicate style, a new form of art that, in eliminating the superfluous, abandoned the overwhelming power of the canto for a more subtle form of seduction. The new style upset the parameters of artistic creation.

Relief with the nymph Cyrene
London, British Museum
Department of Greek
and Roman Antiquities

Emphasis gave way to moderation. The unity of the work broke up into a multitude of suggestions. Resonance faded to a whisper.

Callimachus asserted firmly the principles of his poetry: brevity, originality and lightness. He retorted contemptuously to his malign disparagers, using the fairy-tale image of the metalworking genies, the Telchines. To the accusation of exaggerated conciseness he called up the examples of Mimnermus and Philetas, whose little pieces were worth more than the great tall one, and he invoked for poetry the yardstick of art and not the Persian rod. The secret of the new art, the voice of a cricket countering the braying of the ass, the narrow path never trod by carts, was revealed to the poet, as he first started to write verse, by Apollo the god who protects poetry (*Aetia*, fr. 1, 23f. Pf):

"…poet, feed the victim to be as fat as possible
but, my friend, keep the Muse slender."

It is again Apollo who guarantees Callimachus' poetry in the last lines of *Hymn II*. To Envy who whispers in his ear,

"I admire not the poet who singeth not
things for number as the sea…"

the god replies praising the trickling stream that springs from an undefiled fountain and beats the current of the Euphrates.

The aristocratic concept of art, an irreversible process that leads to isolation, emerges from the provocative lines of the twenty-eighth epigram (trans. A.W. Mair, London 1969):

"I hate the cyclic poem, nor do I take pleasure
in the road which carries many to and fro.
I abhor, too, the roaming lover,
and I drink not from every well;
I loathe all common things."

and from the sense of the eighth epigram:

"but mine, O Lord, the monosyllable!"

The literary controversy finds its natural place in the *Iambi*, thirteen compositions in which the metric variety corresponds to the richness of the themes. The collection opens with the name of Hipponax (Ἀκούσαθ' Ἱππώνακτος, "Listen to Hipponax") the inventor of the *choliambus* and the starting point for the evolution of this genre. In *Iambus IV* the dialogue between the laurel and the olive conceals the points of the dispute with one of the poet's rivals (expressed in the *Diegesis*, or exposition) in the relaxed tone of a fable. In the six hymns which have survived together with the epigrams, the distinctive characteristic is, as in the rest of his work, innovation in the wake of tradition. The narrative patrimony of the Homeric hymns opens up to a multitude of subjects. The myth is suggested, narrated, sometimes limited to a swift allusion. The divine image is placed at the center of a cluster of stories that mingle the contrasting dimensions of reality, the grotesque, and the surreal. The delicate style entrusts to the rhythm of the hexameter the anomalies of a deliberately new language. The talent of the poet is to draw out from an elaborate weave of neologisms and glosses exquisitely designed scenes, iridescent reflections of the Μοῦσα λεπταλέη: the gushing of rivers in waterless Arcadia at the birth of Zeus, the herd of deer with horns of gold captured in the Parrhasian foothills by Artemis of the deadly arrows, the dance of the Cyclades round Asteria, the divine island of Apollo, fragment of a star heaven-fled into the deep, consecrated with the name of Delos. But the poet can also change his tune. As a narrator, his talent does not forget the pathetic, it condescends to the affected, and looks at the funny side of things. The ancient tale blooms intact and new in the brilliant sequence of the single episodes.

Callimachus is everywhere an admirable creator of images, studied in their tone and chiaroscuro. The use of pathos promises perpetual substance to the shadow of the knife reflected in water as it plunges to the hearts of the oxen on the eve of the wedding of Acontius and Cydippe, and to the

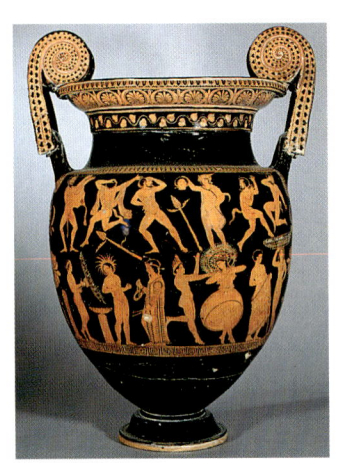

Red-figure krater with a ritual dance from the Carnea festival attributed to the Carnea Painter end 5th cent. B.C. Taranto, Museo Nazionale Cat. 198

pained amazement of Tiresias blinded in the meridian peace of Mount Cithaeron. The knowledge of the art permits the clear picture of the hut in the fragments of *Hecale*. The distant glow of Arsinoe's pyre, spied from the snowy peak of Mount Athos, in the poem *Ektheosis Arsinoes* (for the deification of Arsinoe) introduces a slight shudder in the regal tale of immortality.

The poet was tied by devotion and gratitude to the monarchs of Alexandria. He offered tributes to the divine person of the king that were tempered with reserve. The king's direct dependence from Zeus allowed him, following Hesiod's example, to exalt his greatness without going beyond the limits of rationality. The unhappy destiny of Cyrenaica under the rule of Magas created a tension which the poet must have disliked, and it ended only with the marriage of Ptolemy III Euergetes with Berenice, the daughter of Magas, and the annexing of Cyrenaica. The poet's trust was expressed in the *Hymn to Apollo* (67f.):

> "… and swear that he would vouchsafe a walled city to our kings.
> And the oath of Apollo is ever sure."

The perhaps now elderly poet composed for his new queen and countrywoman the *Coma Berenices* (or *The Lock of Berenice*), in 1.IV of the *Aetia*, that sang of the rise of the regal plait among the stars, a new constellation between Aquarius and Orion.

Two Cyrenaic scholars were members of Callimachus' circle: Ister, his pupil and friend, and Philostephanus, a bibliographer and bibliophile, whose work is reduced to a fragment in distichs. It describes the extraordinary and evil nature of a small lake in Sicily which casts back on its shores anyone who dares to swim there.

Six funerary epigrams are all that remain of the work of Theaetetus, the epigrammist, mentioned by Callimachus in his seventh epigram as one who traveled a "splendid path." These return to the traditional themes of Hellenistic epigrams: the dialogue between a buried corpse and a passer-by, the subjects of death *ante diem* and of shipwreck. The second epigram is an epitaph for Crantor, the philosopher, and helps to put Theaetetus' poetical activity into chronological order. In the fourth epigram the poet weeps for the whole house of Antagoras that has been burnt to the ground. That Hades' eye will distinguish each one of the dead in the horrid promiscuity of the ashes is the only flash of brilliance that redeems Theaetetus' faded Muse.

Eratosthenes also came from Cyrene, but the epitaph written for him by Dionysius of Cyzicus (*Palatine Anthology* VII. 78) reveals that he was not buried in his family tomb there. His all-round brilliance was expressed not only in philosophical and historical writings, and studies in mathematics, astronomy, and chorography as listed in the *Suda*, but Eratosthenes was also a poet. The instrument he invented for the duplication of the cube and the measurement of proportional averages is described in an epigram of doubtful attribution which includes his name in the last line. In the astronomical field he was fascinated most by the legends linked to the celestial bodies, and in literature by the research into theater, and in particular, ancient comedy. He became director of the library in Alexandria and was known by the nickname of "Beta," or "Second Best," perhaps because of the envy of his rivals, or more likely because he lacked that special extra that distinguishes erudition from genius. There are only fragments of his poetic works, but these prove his adherence to the Callimachean school and his taste for the *aetion*. In the legends about the god in *Hermes*, a short poem in hexameters, or epyllion in the current literary style, there is a revived interest in astronomy in mythological terms, recalling the *Katasterismoi* where he had collected the myths concerning forty-four stars.

High up in the heavens, Hermes can observe the movement of the celestial spheres in harmony with the music of the lyre he had built from the shell of a tortoise. He recognizes the Milky Way and, below, the five zones into which the earth is divided (fr. 16):

> "… two are darker than the deep blue, one is rough and red through fire,
> its core, exposed to the heat, is totally scorched:
> Sirius is upon it, inflamed by the ever consuming rays.
> The opposite ends, the poles, are icy,
> and flooded continually with water that is not water but ice that fell from heaven
> and enveloped the earth and it is very cold there.
> The other two zones, between the heat and the ice, on opposite sides, are both mild,

Fragment of a papyrus scroll with lines from a Sapphic ode (fr. 98 Voigt)
1st cent. B.C.
Milan, Università degli Studi
Istituto di Papirologia
P. Mil. Vogl. inv. 1243

and give life to grain, the germ of Eleusinian Demeter,
and men are in the antipodes in these zones…"

In *Erigone*, the poet wrote in couplets the story of Icarius, the peasant entrusted by Dionysus with the gift of the vine. Details such as the sacrifice of the goat and the jump onto the bag made from its skin, hypothesized by Hyginus (*De Astronomia* II. 4), which probably go back to the legends about the origin of the tragedy, reveal the erudite and etiologic character of Eratosthenes' poetry. The few fragments indicate the choice of an allusive style along Callimachean lines. An example of this is fr. 25: καὶ βαθὺν ἀκρήτῳ πνεύμονα τεγγόμενος, "wetting the lung thoroughly with pure wine," which brings back a flash of Alcaeus (fr. 347: τέγγε πλεύμονας οἴνωι, "wets the lungs with wine").

Eratosthenes is also attributed, but not definitively, with the epigram of a poet from Cyrene (Athenaeus II. 36 E) in which the Sapphic suggestion of the tempest of love (fr. 47), transferred to the dangerous power of wine, is confirmed in the revival (ἐτίναξεν) of the last line:

"Wine is as powerful as fire,
when it overtakes man: it upsets him
as Boreas and Notus do the Libyan sea,
revealing what is hidden in the depths,
and ravaging the whole of his mind."

The expulsion of the scholars from the museum in 127 B.C. by Ptolemy II Euergetes (known as "Big Belly"), who had been king of Cyrene for a period, brought Alexandria's sparkling intellectual life to an end. The last glow from Cyrenaica, which likewise faded into decline, was the work of Menecles of Barca, the historiographer of Libya and the foundation of Cyrene, following in the footsteps of Callimachus' antiquarian interests, and also severe critic of the intrigues of the royal dynasty. The new Euergetes was vindictive and criminal. He preferred to get rid of the kingdom of Cyrene with a will that excluded it from the possible possessions of the Ptolemaic crown and ceded it to Rome, the new power blazing upward. For Cyrenaica, the illustrious mother of great minds, offered like Pergamum as a legacy to Rome, the *stele* of Ptolemy Neoteros was notice of the end.

Bibliography
For an overview of Cyrenaic civilization see: F. CHAMOUX, 1953; G. PUGLIESE CARRATELLI, *Maia*, 16, 1964, pp. 99-111; P.M. FRASER, 1972; A. LARONDE, 1987; *Cirene…*, 1990.
On Challimachus' relations with Cyrene: M. VALGIMIGLI, C. ANTI, in *Africa italiana*, 2, 1929, pp. 211-230; G. COPPOLA, 1935; idem, in *Aegyptus*, 42, 1962, pp. 27-97; idem, in *Aegyptus*, 43, 1963, pp. 141-191; 356-383; F. WILLIAMS, 1978; C. MEILLIER, 1979; G. PASQUALI, in *Scritti filologici*, I, 1986, pp. 154-301; P. BING, 1988, pp. 91-146.
For Alcaeus' and Sappho's fragments refer to the edition by E.M. VOIGT, 1971; for Callimachus' work refer to R. PFEIFFER, 1949-53; for Teeten's epigrams refer to A.S.F. GOW, D.L. PAGE, 1965; for Eratosthenes fragments refer to J.U. POWELL, 1925; for Philostephanu's fragment refer to H. LLOYD-JONES, P. PARSONS, 1983.

In a well-known passage in Plato's *Gorgias* (493a) the author refers to the Orphic doctrine of the human body as a "tomb" of the soul, an immortal soul anxious to return through recurrent purified reincarnations to the divine sphere from which it has suffered exile due to past transgressions. In this context he introduces a vivid portrait of the fate awaiting in Hades those who were incapable of curbing their desires: condemned to "pour water with a sieve" into a vessel which, like their insatiable souls, is riddled with holes. This idea is attributed to a "shrewd fellow, of Sicilian or perhaps Italic stock, who dissertated on the myths." It has been guessed that Plato was alluding to Empedocles ("the Sicilian"), or to the Pythagorean philosopher Philolaos ("the Italic"); both attributions are legitimate in their own right (though the second perhaps more tenable, as a little later on at 493d another parable-image is introduced, borrowed from "the same school," thereby hinting at Pythagoreanism). Plato's vagueness about whether it was a Sicilian or an Italic is deliberate, as if he intended to freight it with further allusion: from the Athenian house where he portrays Socrates and Callicles discussing justice, temperance, and happiness, the author points to a land – Magna Graecia and Sicily – where discussions on the human soul abound amid religious and philosophical speculation.

Other focal points of the western Greek world, such as Cyrene, spawned quite different brands of philosophy. Here taught Aristippus (ca. 435–366 B.C.), originally a disciple of Socrates in Athens and later an itinerant teacher in numerous Greek cities, including Syracuse (Greek Syrakousai); there are plenty of anecdotes about his sly mixture of adulation and impertinence toward his tyrant lord Dionysius; and when he returned to his homeland in the last years of his life Aristippus is purported to have founded a school of his own. The fundamental precepts of the Cyrenaic school are the identification of physical and momentary pleasure as the highest good (with regard to which the sage maintains his intellectual superiority, careful to control the circumstances rather than be overwhelmed), which is closely linked to hedonism, the key role of subjective impressions on the gnoseological plane. The kernel of Aristippus' ideas was later developed by Aristippus the Younger (nicknamed *Metrodidaktos*, meaning "taught by the mother," Arete), and then developed further in multiple directions by Hegesias, the pessimistic advocate of suicide as a solution to the ills of life; by Anniceris and Theodorus, nicknamed the "atheist" for his rationalistic outlook on religion. When Theodorus left Cyrene for political reasons he went to Athens where he stayed until the fall of Demetrius of Phalerum; on his way back to Cyrene he enjoyed a brief spell in the court of Ptolemy. Not long afterward, midway through the third century B.C., the school's cycle seems to have come to an end. It may be argued, however, whether it was a real school at all. At any event, from what the written sources disclose, the Cyrenaics were drawn to problems that were central to the ongoing debate in Athens, the unchallenged capital of intellectual activity (another philosopher who left Cyrene for Athens was Carneades, head of the Athenian Academy midway through the second century B.C.), or to the relation with their political protector of the moment.

By contrast, the doctrines of Pythagoras or Empedocles or Parmenides seem to be more "physiologically" tied to that peculiar *humus* of Magna Graecia and Sicily over the sixth and fifth centuries B.C. Actually, they disclose more or less close relations with the Orphic cults, whose rapid diffusion locally is attested by the inscribed golden plates discovered in tombs at Thurii, Hipponium, and Petelia (datable to late fifth–early third century B.C.), which served to accompany the soul of the deceased initiate to the afterlife, a kind of "pass" to receive the acknowledgment of the gods, and ensure the purification that finally liberated the soul from the dire cycle of earthly incarnations.

Actually, the entire system of Orphic eschatology is still very much open to debate, given its deep links with all the other mystery religions of the period, and above all given the difficulties involved in extrapolating from the texts and archaeological finds of later date the particulars of the beliefs and practices which most directly refer to the so-called Orphic writings: hexametric poems attributed to the mythical Orpheus, circulating in the sixth and fifth centuries B.C. Orphism apparently did not include a dogmatic system, established by some written authority or institutional control (the only proper Orphic sect so far confirmed is the one based in ancient Olbia, on the Black Sea). There certainly existed an Orphic movement, however, that allowed a vast range of individual speculation and religious feeling. Its influence can be detected (to an extent that varies from case to case) wherever elements crop up, such as soul-body dualism, belief in metempsychosis, the practice of purification through initiation rites, an ascetic lifestyle in which vegetarianism was essential, as it was believed souls entered all living beings (Burkert, 1982; Zhmud, 1992). These elements are in fact recognizable to varying degrees and in a variety of combinations in several manifestations of philosophers in Magna Graecia. The character of these manifestations is interesting, and, despite strong internal divergences, can be described as a complex pattern of Orphic-related loci.

Gold *lamina*
with Orphic inscription
from Hipponion
end 5th cent. B.C.
Vibo Valentia, Museo Archeologico
Statale "Vito Capialbi"
Cat. 213

The Pythagorean movement was particularly absorbed in religious issues, which earlier observers perceived in terms of its intertwining with Orphism (Herodotus, II. 81; Ion of Chios in Diogenes Laertius, VIII. 8). Pythagoras, born in Samos ca. 570 B.C., left his homeland in his old age (perhaps owing to his hostility toward the tyrant Polycrates) and settled ca. 520 in the Greek *polis* of Croton, Italy. Here he gathered around him a community of followers which in some ways foreshadows the later philosophical schools (such as Plato's Academy at Athens), and seems to have been organized like a sect which abode by an alternative lifestyle, held regular meetings, respected different levels of initiation to the master's teaching, and observed secrecy regarding his innermost tenets. The group attempted to influence Croton's political development, aiming to steer it toward an aristocratic program of the conservation of ethical and religious values. At an early stage, Pythagoras became personally – and successfully – involved in the clash between Croton and Sybaris (ca. 510 B.C.). Later, however, the community incurred popular disapproval, and its leader was eventually forced to flee to Metapontum, where the master probably ended his days early in the fifth century. A later and more far-reaching public outcry against the "sect" led to the burning of its meeting places, which had meanwhile spread throughout Magna Graecia; at which point the Pythagoreans dispersed (including Philolaos, mentioned in Plato's *Phaedo* as being the teacher at Thebes of Simmias and Cebes). The exodus was probably complete by the first decades of the fourth century B.C. The only one to remain in the Italian peninsula seems to have been Archytas of Tarentum, a friend of Plato and more or less of the same age, mathematician and musicologist, and a politician of considerable status in the city. At any event, the major questions dealt with by the Pythagoreans were being taken up by the work of Plato.

The doctrinal core that grew up around the idea of the immortality of the soul (with transmigration and its relative taboos, particularly as regards food, and severe living rules in order to ensure a wise identification with the divine) seems to be more plausibly attributable to Pythagoras himself (usually, as we know, it is extremely difficult to distinguish his contribution from those that accumulated more or less anonymously in the school's long existence; so much the more for the fact that a large quota of tradition such as the Neoplatonic tradition of Iamblichus and Porphyry, Pythagoreanism extends historically straight into Platonism). It is not impossible that Pythagoras came into contact with the religious cultures of other countries (tradition has it that he traveled to Egypt, Mesopotamia, and Phoenicia), working on some of his ideas before settling in Magna Graecia. Here they found fertile soil and bore fruit in a relationship of action and reaction with the host milieu. Xenophanes of Colophon, who also migrated around the same period from his homeland in Ionia, to Elea on the Tyrrhenian coast of Magna Graecia, draws an ironic picture of Pythagoras running to defend a dog that was being beaten, in whose barking he recognized the voice of his friend (fr. 7). Pythagoras may also be the "wise man" who so thrilled Empedocles (fr. 129) for his extraordinary ability to reach out with his mind and seize the time covered by ten or even twenty human lives. Here we can already glimpse the role assigned to memory (which later sources focus on with insistence) as the fundamental principle of cognitive experience, the faculty that permits the individual to accumulate experience in self-awareness and recall, through past lives, his original belonging to divinity. It is appealing to think that this motif was borrowed from earlier mystery cults, coloring the Orphism of Magna Graecia with a characteristic philosophical hue: in fact the texts on certain gold plates – such as those of Hipponium and Petelia, but also (thereby complicating the hypothesis) on one found at Pharsalus in Thessaly – invoke the goddess Mnemosyne rather than Persephone or other gods, appealing on behalf of the initiate for a gift of those purifying "fresh waters" that liberate the human from the burden of earthly existence (Pugliese Carratelli, 1993).

The Pythagoreans were also responsible for major contributions to the fields of mathematics (including the discovery of the incommensurability of the diagonal of a square with its side), astronomy (the cosmology of Philolaos), music (the formalization of the musical intervals in terms of numerical relations,

Coin from Samos
with the effigy of Pythagoras
250 A.D.
London, British Museum
Department
of Coins and Medals

Pythagoras
clypeate image
5th cent. A.D.
Aphrodisias, Museum

Head of Parmenides
first half 1st cent. A.D.
Ascea Marina
Depositi della Soprintendenza
Cat. 397

perhaps the work of Pythagoras himself, is behind an important series of inquiries and experiments conducted by Hippasus and Archytas). Details of the group's scientific acquisitions are discussed elsewhere in this volume, but it is worth noting here that the Pythagoreans' interest in exact sciences went hand-in-hand with their religious trend, which allowed for accentuation in either direction, and, moreover, as regards their scientific research, allowed for a wide variety of directions according to the personal bent of the sect member, who was left free to operate without institutional regulations. The most widely accepted presupposition was probably the theory of the reducibility of all reality to numbers (deriving perhaps from the idea that all things can be represented by a figured combination of points); this offered food for thought for both Plato and Aristotle: while on the one hand it favored a symbolic and at times mystic interpretation of numbers (with sacred inferences, or moral equations such as virtue or justice), on the other it fostered an interest in a formal and quantitative level of reality.

According to Timaeus, one of Pythagoras' pupils was Empedocles (Diogenes Laertius, VIII, 54). This statement, clashing with the accepted dates for the philosopher (490–430 B.C.), is due to the habit of ancient biographical tradition of translating intellectual affinities into school relationships. As it happens, the philosophy of Empedocles overlaps in many areas with that of the Pythagoreans (irrespective of whether Pythagoras was the subject of the fragment no. 129 cited above). One thing is certain: as attested by the hundred-odd extant verses of the *Purifications*, Empedocles subscribed to the concept of the immortality of a soul migrating through several cycle of lives on earth (*ergo* his rejection of animal sacrifice), achieving final liberation and rejoining its divine source. There is evidence, moreover, that his native milieu was open to Orphic influences, as testified by archaeological evidence (Bottini, 1992, p. 114) and by the famous verses of Pindar's *Olympic* (61ff.) dedicated to the tyrant of Acragas, Theron, winner in the *quadriga* in which the poet lauds the happy condition awaiting the worthy in the next life, "honored among the gods" (compare frs. 146f. of Empedocles), and finally, for those who manage to distance themselves from wrongdoing through a long cycle of reincarnations, "near to the tower of Kronos."

Empedocles also wrote a poem entitled *On Nature*, in which, in reply to Parmenides' negation of becoming (see below), he put forward a highly influential explanation of phenomena change, through a combination of four "roots" – earth, air, fire, and water – in themselves unchangeable and eternal: two cosmic principles – Love and Hate – respectively foster the union and separation of the elements. Here also the process of knowledge (both sensory and intellectual) is explained by the material interaction between the bodily organs and the effluence of particles emanated by objects. The reduction of principles of consciousness to the physiological mechanisms of a mortal body is deemed to contrast with the notion of an immortal soul, the divine principle that had alighted temporarily on man, and the focus of the *Purifications*. Modern interpreters tried several times, in several different ways, to reconcile those two different principles; but, even if a conclusive solution to this problem is hardly possible, the two principles could well coexist in Empedocles' intellectual world.

It has been guessed that Empedocles wrote the *Purifications* in his youth, before passing onto more sober and critical inquiries into nature; alternatively, it has been speculated that the *Purifications* in fact predates the profession of materialistic faith contained in *On Nature*, after which he is supposed to have undergone religious conversion, withdrawing his earlier statements. We do not need this kind of speculation. The poem on physical matters is veined throughout with a religious discourse, as shown in the identification of the initial stage of the cosmic cycle as a state in which Love is absolute, such that the elements merge in absolute unity, without distinction. This is the Sphere, motionless and perfectly round in its isolation, whose description reflects the influence both of Xenophanes' attack upon anthropomorphic theology of gods, and of Parmenides' image (also affected by Xenophanes) of Being in its spherical wholeness (compare frs. 27–29, and 134 of Empedocles with Xenophanes frs. 14, 15, 23–25; Parmenides, fr. 8, vv. 29ff., and 49). Here is evidence of the intention to see the traditional idea of divinity within the new coordinates of the inquiry into nature, a line of inquiry that Empedocles shared with other exponents of philosophy in Magna Graecia (and not just here, witness Heraclitus). Other outlooks linked to a rational approach to theology include Pythagoras' theology of numbers; the progressive moralization of the ancient myths advanced by Xenophanes' on the unity and singleness of divinity; more indirectly, the inclusion of this theme from Xenophanes in Parmenides' discourse on the characteristics of Being; the list of arguments on the eternity of the gods should include fr. 1 of the writer of comedy Epicharmus, native of Megara Hyblaea (Sicily), who lived between the sixth and fifth century B.C., and whose work borrowed from the work of the Pythagorean and Eleatic schools, and from Heraclitus.

This brings us to Parmenides of Elea, who has been left out so far though he lived from ca. 520 to 440 B.C. and hence before Empedocles, whose system presupposes that of the latter, as mentioned above. In this overview of the points of contact with the Orphic movement, the philosophy of Parmenides is undoubtedly out of line (except for the religious references in the proem, see below). His ontological analysis is a strenuous exercise of variation on the theme "being is, non-being is not," and presupposes a notion of logical truth (I would say "secularized") inasmuch as it draws purely on the powers of reason to demonstrate that Being, the only "thinkable" thing, is unique (duplicity would imply the reality of non-being), complete in itself, and unchangeable (if it were to change, it would become something other than itself, and hence non-being), and therefore it is also eternal.

On epistemological questions, Parmenides establishes a clear-cut opposition between two paths and methods of research: the first, the path of truth followed by the philosopher, is the only one that grasps Being in its exclusive existence; the second, the way of opinion mostly followed by mortals, corresponds to the illusory belief in the perceivable world. Nonetheless, the second part of Parmenides' poem is taken up with a cosmological theory, perhaps proposed as the best possible approximation to the principles of the system (scholars, noting that the Pythagorean Amynias in Diogenes Laertius, XI. 21, is said to have been a disciple of Pythagoras, have attempted, albeit rather unsuccessfully, to identify traces of Pythagoreanism in this part of the poem).

Taking a completely anti-empirical outlook is Parmenides' pupil Zeno, with his elaborate and well-known paradoxes denouncing plurality and movement (the paradoxes of the "dichotomy," the "stadium," the race between "Achilles and the tortoise," and the "arrow"), which earned him the title of "father of dialectics" (Aristotle, in Diogenes Laertius, VIII. 57, and IX. 25; the word "dialectic" here is meant as a cognitive process that focuses exclusively on the formal aspect of reasoning, of which Parmenides is undoubtedly the founder). In Melissus of Samos, who spiced the debate launched by Parmenides with the idea of the infinity of being, the removal of the empirical world was complete (Leszl, 1988). But the distance from Parmenides does not lie in this feature alone. The fact that both Zeno and Melissus wrote in prose, while Parmenides (and later Empedocles also) expounded his ideas in hexameters – the standard epic verse – is evidence of Parmenides' wish to submit himself to the aegis of poetic tradition, thereby conferring an aura of authority to the exposition of his thought. The famous proem contains the description of a journey made by the philosopher in a carriage drawn by winged horses, leaving the beaten track for a threshold beyond which a nameless goddess reveals to him the existence of the two paths of inquiry and explains their contents to him (occupying the rest of the poem). Recently, the goddess has been identified as Mnemosyne, mother of the Muses, who, according to the text of several gold plates, offers the final purification to those who in life have successfully attained initiation into the truths of the afterlife (Pugliese Carratelli, 1988); the same image of the two paths seems also to allude to that crossroads (cited in the plates, in Pindar, and in several well-known Platonic myths on the afterlife) where the souls of the uninitiated go in one direction returning to earth reincarnation, while the initiates proceed definitively to the realm of otherworldly beatitude (Sassi, 1988). Irrespective of the various hypotheses, the fact remains that the proem is freighted with overtones of initiation rites, by which Parmenides aims to endow his thought with an aura of divine origin. It is true that his discourse is based not on visionary ideas but on strict axiomatic reasoning. One can therefore suppose that, in order to introduce his philosophy to a milieu that was particularly sensitive to questions of the soul's fate, he borrowed religious notions in order to confer some kind of ratification to his exposition, a process that has parallels in the way the Pythagoreans capitalized on the legend that burgeoned around their founder, or the way in which Empedocles invoked the protection of the Muse (fr. 3ff.; 23, v. 11; 131) and propagandized to his disciple Pausanias and the citizenry of Acragas his extraordinary magical powers, worthy of a god (fr. 111f.). In comparison with Empedocles' attitude, Parmenides' evocation of religious ideas is more outward and formal, and one cannot doubt the structural importance of the philosopher's self-representation to his public.

All in all, the interplay of affinities and differences that can be detected in philosophical thought in Magna Graecia gives the impression of a tight mesh of internal relationships – an impression that is endorsed if we include medicine. A proper school may never actually have existed on Italic soil, at least not in the sense intended by the Greek physician Galen when he spoke of "Philistion, Empedocles, Pausanias, and their fellow doctors of medicine in Italy" after "those of Cos and Cnidos" (*De Methodo Medendi*, <H>I<H>, 1; as a matter of fact, also the existence of schools on Cos – the birthplace of Hippocrates – and Cnidos is still unproven). Galen's attention in this respect is fully justified, however, by the legacy of medical research that had been performed in the western Greek world.

Even Parmenides, not entirely crushed by the ontological reduction of the intelligible world, seems to have been working in the field of human physiology and medicine. The circulation of doxographical manuals of his opinions in these matters may lie behind his presence in lists of founders of medical schools circulating among medieval Arab milieus, which probably conserve traces of earlier Hellenistic historiographical research. Likewise, this must be the reason for the inscription of his name on a herm found at the Italiot colony of Elea together with two other herms and a statue dedicated (first century B.C.) to members of a local medical college, with sacral undertones (Pugliese Carratelli, 1990; in my opinion, the distinction between *physikos* for Parmenides and *iatroi* for the others listed in the dedication has an Aristotelian slant, as a philosopher who may have influenced the physicians indirectly, through his own research into nature or *physis*).

At all events, the Pythagoreans' interest in medicine is overall more significant (anyway, the milieu was propitious: witness the illustrious itinerant physician Democedes of Croton, son of an Asclepian priest, whose fame predates possible contacts with Pythagoras). The Pythagorean theory of the universe as a "harmony" of opposites – an effective notion on both micro- and macrocosmic levels – is equatable with the idea of a close bond between bodily well-being and wisdom. This idea prompted research (perhaps already in earlier Pythagoreanism) into ways of maintaining a balance of the former (with an accent on dietetics that was aided by an ascetic lifestyle) with the latter (with an emphasis on the cathartic effects, physical and spiritual, of music, which was seen to be an earthly reflection of the

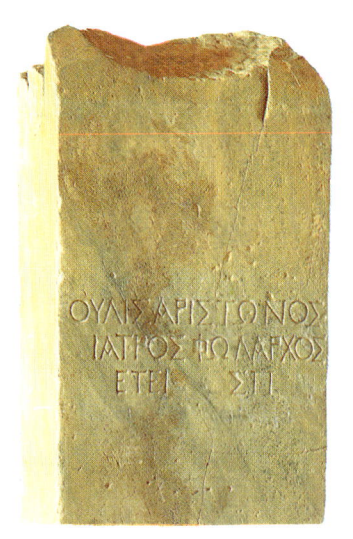

Herm of Oulis, son of Ariston
found at Elea
1st cent. A.D.
Velia, Acropoli, Cappella Palatina
Cat. 398

Herm of Oulis, son of Ieronumos
found at Elea
1st cent. A.D.
Velia, Acropoli, Cappella Palatina
Cat. 399

harmony governing the world). The notion of harmony lies behind the famous definition of Alcmaeon of Croton, a younger contemporary of Pythagoras, but also an independent researcher into the mechanisms of perceptive and intellectual knowledge, who stated that health is the product of a physical balance among the various opposing forces (wet or dry, hot or cold, sweet or bitter), and that sickness results from a bias of one of these forces, caused by outside factors (fr. 4).

Similarly, Empedocles entertained an interesting relationship with medicine, and claimed to have magical powers, offering to cure the sick by means of his "healing voice." It should be remembered that the philosopher-physician was highly skilled in rhetoric, such that Aristotle himself attributed him with having indeed invented the art (as Zeno was attributed with inventing dialectics in the passages from Diogenes Laertius quoted above). Moreover, the same source (VIII. 58) quotes Empedocles as having among his disciples the rhetor and sophist Gorgias of Leontini; in Plato's work of the same name (456b), he is supposed to have helped his brother by "persuading" the sick to accept the therapy. Seen overall, these accounts offer an intriguing vision of the interplay between medicine and rhetoric (as a technique of persuasion) that may have been characteristic of this particular phase of Sicily's cultural development, which also witness the figures of Corax of Syracuse and his pupil Tisias, who are traditionally credited with the first treatises on the art of rhetoric. But the magic performances of Empedocles must have comprised those incantations and ceremonies of purification that were oth-

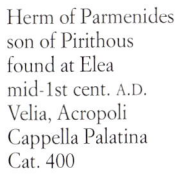

Herm of Parmenides
son of Pirithous
found at Elea
mid-1st cent. A.D.
Velia, Acropoli
Cappella Palatina
Cat. 400

erwise scorned as charlatanism (in the Hippocratic treatise *The Sacred Disease*, chapter 18). These gifts existed with no apparent discomfort alongside biological doctrines that pivoted on the four-element idea and influenced a great deal of "field work," negatively, as argued by the author the Hippocratic work *On Ancient Medicine* (chapter 20), in which Empedocles is accused of focusing on the elementary principles rather than on the empirical study of action and reaction of the body. The scheme of the four qualities hot, cold, dry, wet (linked to fire, air, earth, and water) is central to the etiology of Philistion of Locri, active in the first half of the fourth century B.C. (and whose attention to the question of breath and breathing brings him close to Philolaos, who realized that proper breathing was necessary for maintaining body warmth).

In closing, it is interesting to note that in those inquiring into health and sickness, two different theories of the soul seem to cohabit, as for instance in Empedocles (as noted above): in one the soul is basically seen as a vital principle tied to bodily faculties; in the other it is immortal and separate from the body. But Alcmaeon likewise merged his research in physiological phenomena and health with the idea of an immortal soul in eternal motion, and hence sharing the divinity of the heavenly bodies (Aristotle, *De Anima*, I. 2. 405a. 29): mortality stems from man's inability to create a full circle, joining the beginning with the end. Elsewhere, cohabiting in Pythagorean thought, perhaps even in the same author (though the attribution is still debated), are a definition of the soul as "harmony" of bodily opposites and sharing in its destiny (cf. Aristotle, *De Anima* 407b. 27; Plato, *Phaedo* 5e and ff.), and a dualistic theory as exemplified in the passage from *Gorgias* cited at the start of this essay, which underlines the soul's imprisonment in the body (thereby suggesting its final liberation therefrom). The cohabitation of these two points of view posed some problems at conceptual level. Later, Platonic psychology went some way to solving the issue, ascribing an "appetitive" soul with a lower order of functions and links with the body, and the "intellectual" soul with proximity to the divine. But it was nevertheless cohabitation, and confirms the crucial importance of eschatology in the philosophical and scientific thought of Magna Graecia.

In fourth-century Athens several authors of Middle Comedy satirized the local imitators of the Pythagorean way of life, and were consequently dubbed "Pythagorists" or "Pythagorizers" (which nonetheless implied some continuity with the ancient Pythagoreans). The heavy-handedness of satire, highlighting the ascetics' indifference to outward, material things to the point of neglecting cleanliness, or the oddity of vegetarianism (ironically made to symbolize destitution by Aristophon, fr. 9 Kock; presumably often disregarded, according to Alexis, fr. 220 Kock) are explained by the predilection of the comic dramatists (which started with Aristophanes' satirical portrait of Socrates in *The Clouds*, and evidently tickled the Athenian theater-goers) for the figure of the muddleheaded philosopher quite heedless of the practical matters of everyday life. The ascetic zeal of the Pythagorean sect must have seemed particularly odd, with its obsession for moral uprightness and the afterlife (in Aristophon's portrayal, fr. 12 Kock, the Pythagoreans are the only ones to be admitted to Pluto's dining table, owing to their piety). The "Pythagorizers" were also labeled "Tarentines" in the titles of two comedies (by Alexis of Thurii, and Cratinus the Younger) thereby stressing their eccentricity with respect to the Athenian cultural milieu, underlining their geographical distance in a moment when the migration of the Pythagoreans from the West must have been complete. For the same reason, perhaps, to label them as out-of-date, Aristophon lumps the Pythagoreans together with "those of former days" (fr. 9 Kock).

But Plato, too, became a target of the comic satire for his frugal lifestyle, and for his conception of the dualism between body and soul (cf. Aristophon, fr. 8 Kock; Alexis, fr. 158; Cratinus the Younger, fr. 10). Reflecting on "those of former days," Plato in fact penetrated the depth of the question of the soul (and the intrinsically linked questions of *virtue* and *salvation*). He introduced this question to Athens (together with the dialectics of the Eleatic thinkers), thereby ensuring the lasting attention of theoretical philosophy, though not the conciliation with the needs of practice and politics.

Bibliography

Quotations, supposedly literal, follow, as usual for pre-Socratic philosophers, H. Diels's numeration, 1903, VI, edited by W. Kranz, 1951; reference to the sources has been made in relation to indirect records. Specific reference has been made to the following texts: A. Bottini, 1992; W. Burkert, in *Jewish and Christian Self-Definition*, III, 1982, pp. 1-22; W. Leszl, in *Magna Grecia*, III, 1988, pp. 197-226; G. Pugliese Carratelli, in *La Parola del Passato*, XLIII, 1988, pp. 337-346; idem, 1990, pp. 421-430; idem, pp. 269-280 (merging various essays published in a number of issues of *La Parola del Passato*); G. Pugliese Carratelli, 1993; M.M. Sassi, in *La Parola del Passato*, XLIII, 1988, pp. 383-396; L. Zhmud, in *Hermes*, CXX, 1992, pp. 159-168.

Vincenzo La Rosa   The Impact of the Greek Colonists on the non-Hellenic Inhabitants of Sicily

In the stratified and polycentric labyrinth of the island's history, the Sicans, Sicels, and Elymi are little more than names. The record of these populations, which were without any literary tradition, is entrusted entirely to material culture, and hence all other information is left to the Greek historians and commentators to provide. Such information is given as episodic, by-the-way comments that are never really prompted by an interest in the populations in question, and have capriciously survived the disappearance of so many works of the authors of antiquity. The history of these populations is a virtually anonymous one, largely devoid of any real events. The Late Iron Age (Finocchito *facies*, ca. 750/730–650 B.C.) saw the beginnings of interaction with Greek culture in the eastern part of the island, a process that provided the only relief in the island's development, through to the end. In the westerly regions of the island and the Caltanissetta and Agrigento areas unaffected by the process of Italicization that had previously characterized Sicel territory, the Greek influence was added to the Mycenaeanizing aspect of Sican culture.

The abandonment of Pantalica (whose identification with the Hybla centre has recently been questioned) toward the mid-eighth century basically coincides with the arrival of the Greeks. The necropolis near Villasmundo in the Marcellino Valley has yielded several imported Greek vases dating to the second half of the eighth century B.C. Anterior even to the foundation of the colonies are two cups from the Finocchito necropolis, in association with Cycladic shapes characteristic of the end of Middle Geometric. At Finocchito the impact with the local Syracusan culture (and the armed parties of the region) is exemplary. After the phase known as South Pantalica (represented by few tombs), the population and economic growth testified by the grave offerings of phases IIA and IIB (corresponding to the colonial generation of 735/730–700 B.C., and the first half of the seventh century through 665 B.C.?) has been quite justifiably related to the ongoing process of territorial aggregation triggered by the threatening presence of Greek colonists. The scissor penetration effected by the Syracusans along the coastal route to Helorus and the mountain path to Acrae, determined the violent end of the "kingdom" of Finocchito, and the razing of the defense works encircling the settlement. At the necropolis of Butera, the introduction of cremation rites and the earliest traces of imported Greek wares (first and second quarter of the seventh century B.C.) suggest a wholly different impact between the natives and the colonial milieu of Gela. The Cretan style of certain funeral enclosures, a fact given new emphasis of late, seems to imply that a garrison of people of Cretan origin (Rizza) may have been stationed at Butera (perhaps identifiable with the Omphake centre cited as the first stage in the Geloan penetration effort).

In the sphere of this clash-encounter between prevailing and subordinate cultures, there are certain lingering, shared features worth noting. One is the "pacific" approach of the Chalcidians as opposed to the "violent" approach of the Dorians. Another is the inestimable cultural weight and sheer number of the native women in the early colonial communities. In truth there was little room for peaceful coexistence, what with the need to overrun and seize control of the land, to recruit workpeople, and to ensure that colonial products continued to spread ever further inland. The reorganization of the territory – with the likely retreat of the more exposed communities further into the interior – may have sparked, in the first phase of the process, a certain degree of aggregation and synechism between tribal circles. But the ensuing movements were the direct outcome of armed campaigns pursued by the Greeks in answer to their growing needs. For their part, there is strong evidence of native interest in all things Greek. The path of development of the young Sicel *ethnos* – which enjoyed relative affluence and was probably ruled by a warrior aristocracy – underwent a series of traumatic events as they were severely outmatched by the Greek newcomers. The ancient writers mockingly announce this dramatic change of historical course began when the warrior-king Hyblon accorded a group of land-hungry colonists the right to settle in the coast of the Syracusan territory: the foundation was named Megara Hyblaea.

The *apoikia* of Selinus in the central west of the island cannot date to before the mid-seventh century. With respect to the eastern end of the island, this discriminating factor is coupled with the lack of involvement in the process of Ausonio-Italic penetration during the Final Bronze Age, and with the upshot of a different outlook with the Aegean peoples. In the necropolis of Sant'Angelo Muxaro (generally identified with the Camicus of kings Cocalus and Minos), dozens of *tholos* tombs document the weight of the Mycenaean tradition, while the precious goldsmith's workshops of the seventh century attest to an enduring affluence. One native settlement (dating from mid-eighth to early seventh century B.C.) has been located on the Manuzza hilltop at Selinunte (ancient Selinus); a "mixed" excavation level (containing local and Greek material, together with remnants of hut bases) bear witness to a phase in which there was some degree of cohabitation between locals and people of Greek stock, a phase that preceded the foundation of the colony proper. In the case of the foundation of Acragas (modern Agrigento), the native peoples had perhaps already withdrawn to the immediate vicinity, gathering into small communities around "long-established cult sites" (De Miro).

Another process that is particularly hard to pin down, more so than the late impact with the Greek world, is

Two gold rings
with a cow feeding her calf
and a wolf
from Sant'Angelo Muxaro
7th cent. B.C.
Syracuse
Museo Archeologico Regionale

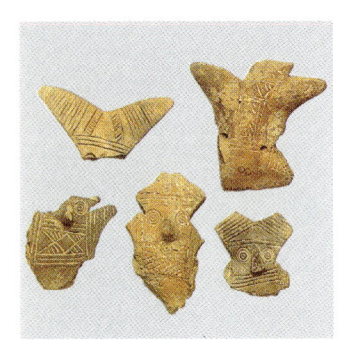

Fragments of handles
of jars or vases
incised decorations
with human faces
from Segesta
7th cent. B.C.
Palermo, Museo Archeologico
Regionale "A. Salinas"

Vase handle with an appendix
in the form of a human face
and sides like raised arms
from the Vanella cave at Segesta
7th cent. B.C.
Palermo, Museo Archeologico
Regionale "A. Salinas"

the formation of the Elymian culture in the Sican framework, despite the recent identification of a proto-Elymian phase (S. Tusa). Among the rather scant archaeological evidence, typical items of this particular cultural milieu include handles from cups or open vases decorated with schematic human faces of a type that denotes parallels with vessels of Iapygian manufacture (S. Tusa). The most natural comparisons, however, are those with the forked handles characteristic of the Thapsos *facies*, a type that has so far been found as far as the Platani Valley. A slightly different case is offered by the geometric painted ware, whose affinities with Sican production may be the result of shared influence from the Greek workshops. For certain fragments, however, the decorative syntax or the representation of animal figures have no comparisons among Sicilian production, and evince a vague Cycladic or even Cypriot vein; alternatively, the influence might be from the easternmost shores of the Mediterranean basin, permeated through Greek culture. While the material evidence is hard to pin down, the linguistic data are also somewhat unclear. In the Segesta waste tips on Monte Barbaro, which ceased to be used in 420–410 B.C., the inscriptions scored into the pottery in Greek characters have triggered diverging opinions, though there is a fairly general conviction that the idiom is of Indo-European origin. Such differences of opinion reflect the dichotomy of the literary tradition with regard to the origins of the Elymi (i.e., whether they are Italic or Trojan-Anatolian).

The few clues that can be interpreted with greater confidence suggest a typically Sican context in which perhaps only in the second half of the seventh century B.C. emerge features of a material culture hitherto unmatched in this area. To judge from our current knowledge, one might even exclude the existence of a specific Elymian territory, and consider instead the possibility of the allocation of ethnic minorities in individual settlements within a cultural framework that had already been consolidated, and this at a relatively late stage. The faint eastern Greek or Cypriot traits could therefore be evidence of contacts with the Hellenic world before the arrival of these ethnic minorities on Sicilian soil, thereby justifying the rapid and peaceful emergence of the two settler towns of Segesta and Eryx (modern Erice), where the imposing defense works are an outspoken statement of the inhabitants' keen concern over the consolidation of the Carthaginians at the isle of Motya. With their stronger cultural background, affluence, and greater adaptability, not to mention their commercial flair, the Punic newcomers soon strengthened their position within their respective host communities, shepherding them toward a more typically urban conformation. In a subsequent phase these townships may have constituted economic and cultural datum-points for a territorial network, encouraging the idea among ancient writers of an authentic people. The ambitions of the Greeks at Selinus on the one hand, and those of the Punic communities on the other, made the Elymian towns a kind of third force in the region, and conditioned the entire political development, with marked repercussions on the history of the island as a whole.

Finocchito's violent destruction in the east of the island, and the *apoikia* of Selinus in the west have traditionally marked the end of the cultural and political independence of the native peoples. The foundation of secondary colonies at Camarina and Acragas at the start of the sixth century signaled the completion of the systematic zoning of the territory in question, which only at its westernmost limb experienced an unsuccessful bid by Pentathlon (580 B.C.) and Dorieus (510 B.C.) to regain control. From the outset, the individual colonies opted for more natural methods of penetration into the interior, with the multiple intention of swelling their *chora* (territory) and markets, of garnering more work hands, and of containing the expansion of other Greek neighbors. On the other hand, the spheres of influence also fostered the emergence and consolidation of indigenous cultural "provinces" that became deeply engaged in the bitter struggles during the period of the tyrannies. Some colonies, such as Camarina, tried to construct their fortunes on a policy of receptiveness toward the local population. In the early phases in particular the latter adopted an ambivalent stance: owing to their fear of sieges and inbred warrior mentality, they tended to safeguard their identity and yet were irresistibly drawn to the ideology and culture of the hegemony around them. This type of ambivalence, which prevailed through to the times of Ducetius' military campaigns, slackened in the second half of the fifth century B.C., when the process of acculturation was basically complete. Theutus (a Sican from Ouessa, the first chief recorded after Hyblon) and Ducetius respectively represent the chronological extremes of this process. Archaeological finds have confirmed the progressive expansion, both in time and space, of the Greek colonial radius, and shed light on the impact this had on the local cultural situation, revealing a series of variants: indigenous settlements that assimilated Greek culture or which played host to small nuclei of Greek-speaking people in their midst; on the other hand we find Greek settlements that make ample use of local manpower. As for the generalized "invasion" of Greek products – pottery in particular – this was fueled in some cases by the establishment of military garrisons, or by the setting up of specifically Greek urban nuclei (Sabucina, Morgantina). Regarding other centers, such as Monte San Mauro (Caltagirone) or Monte Saraceno (Ravanusa), the new settlements were superimposed directly on the existing indigenous village. This process shows some peculiarities in the western part of the island, where Greek activity found itself up against Punic interests; such contention

Small globular *amphora* with incised geometric motifs and stylized head of a bull on the shoulder from the Entella necropolis
7th cent. B.C.
Palermo, Museo Archeologico Regionale "A. Salinas"

Clay fragment with bull decoration from the Vanella cave at Segesta
second half 7th cent. B.C.
Palermo, Museo Archeologico Regionale "A. Salinas"

over land did not actually escalate in military terms until the fifth century B.C., and until then the Elymian town of Segesta managed to play off the opposing forces to its own advantage.

In Camarina's inland region, excavations at Castiglione show that the centre was razed at the end of the sixth century, perhaps in the course of Hippocrates' military endeavors. One striking datum is the contemporary presence in the necropolis of two distinct types of tomb: native burials in rock-cut chambers and individual grave inhumations probably reminiscent of the Greek practice. The overall uniformity and repetitiveness of the grave offerings, the presence of Greek artifacts (not usually of any great value), the somewhat crude local imitation of colonial products, are recurring features in all the cemeteries for this period. The coexistence of funeral rites of varying traditions (circular burials of the *tholos* chamber-tomb variety, individual sarcophagus inhumations, simple grave burials, *cappuccina* types, and even burial in *pithoi* (so-called *enchytrismoi*) are all found at Monte Bubbonia in the Mazzarino district, where the assimilation of Greek culture became total around the close of the sixth century B.C. In the heart of the Mendolito district on the bed of the Simeto River, an urban center has been identified which was probably abandoned with the foundation of Adranon (Roman Adranum), toward the end of the fifth century. A stretch of the defense walls in lava stone shows a double rampart construction, one of which near the city gate itself was enhanced with one long public inscription written in Greek characters, but in a language that shows affinities with the Oscan dialects.

The allusion on the inscription to types of organized civil structures coincides in the Mendolito district with a fairly widespread literacy. From the nearby Centuripe comes a plain *guttus* of a shape that denotes fifth-century manufacture, bearing the celebrated inscription in the Sicel tongue; scholars have detected certain linguistic divergences in this inscription from the epigraphs found in the Mendolito area.

The growing ability to read and write and the "warrior" component re-emerge at Montagna di Marzo, which may be identifiable with Erbessus. The numerous and brief epigraphs on pottery – mostly of indigenous manufacture – have recently been enhanced by an amphora of a very crude type that was evidently in wide use, datable to the late sixth–early fifth century; the painted inscription, on two registers, contains references to the usage of the *symposion*. Chamber-tomb 31 of the east necropolis (first half fifth century B.C.) contained two sarcophagi of warriors with typically Greek weaponry and a sumptuous grave offerings (besides a hundred or more clay vessels of Greek and local manufacture, and a dozen in bronze). The twelve incised (graffiti inscriptions on Attic *kylikes* and *skyphoi*), all in the Sicel tongue, have provided a few important personal names such as *italo* and *mares*, recorded by Aelianus as *archegeta* of the Ausoni tribes. As far as the necropolis typology is concerned, up to now there is no confrontation to the hoard of skulls unearthed at Rossomanno di Valguarnera (all carefully set in line, some placed inside *paterae* of local manufacture). The only precedents for this kind of generalized acephaly are those in the second archaeological level at the Butera necropolis.

Alongside the burial items, the religious sphere provided a preferential meeting-point with the Hellenic culture. As in Magna Graecia, the emergence of cult ritual in the indigenous settlements is directly linked to the advance of urbanization, but also to the growing self-imposition of the local aristocracies. The problem in such cases is how to assess the acceptance of certain artifact types (architectural or otherwise); it is also difficult to pinpoint forms of religious syncretism: as for the Greeks exchanges of this kind are highly improbable. Several years ago G. Pugliese Carratelli put forward a fascinating hypothesis, by which both Greek and indigenous worship derived from the Minoan-Mycenaean cult of the Great Mother of Crete. The presence of votive offerings of both Greek and local manufacture in the same cult-places (i.e., in the Greek colonies and in native townships), raises the issue of grave offerings, and should therefore be seen in light of the same basic self-affirmation in cultural and ideological terms (and, in the case of the elites, in political terms, too).

From an archaeological point of view, nothing is known about the most important Sicel cults, which are all situated in areas of high geoseismic activity. The temple of the god Adranus, traditionally defended by a hundred dogs, probably stood on the eastern slopes of the volcano, not far from the town that took his name. The Paternò district, where numerous springs of ferro-sulfurous water can still be found in the Salinelle area, was the site of a sanctuary dedicated to the goddess Hybla, whose acolytes were renowned fortune-tellers and interpreters of dreams. In the Catania plain, near the lake of Naftia (now dried up) stood the sanctuary of the Palici (the progeny of gods Adranus and Aetna, according to a certain written tradition).

It is still impossible to estimate the outcome of this commingling and differences in the two votive deposits that were discovered in the Grammichele area distinguished by two large statues of female deities, whose manufacture has been respectively attributed to a Sicel workshop (in the *contrada* of Poggio dell'Aquila) and Siceliot (in the *thesauros* of Terravecchia). The presence of these works indicates that the involvement of the local craftsmen was not limited to laying out and decorating the buildings themselves, but attained the iconographycal attributes of the cult itself. The rare examples of statuary, which were all created without using molds, includes a clay bust unearthed not far from the mouth of the Simeto River (datable perhaps to the first half of the fifth century B.C.) which does not seem to be modeled after the Greek prototypes. The detailing of the overflowing breasts of this "Simeto Goddess" can only really be attributed to the general line of fecundity sphere.

However, other useful clues are afforded by a group of Sicel bronze figurines which, despite their formal inadequacies, evince a progressive adaptation to the Greek prototypes. The earliest bronze of the group is the figurine from the Plemmyrium, based on the Geometric model, of a man in the act of masturbating. Whereas the Italic influences can be discerned in the couple-type, characterized in some cases as gift-bearers. A good example is the Vizzini bronze in which one of the figures, both with an owl-looking face, holds out a large bowl in the left hand. Other Greek-based types such as the *auriga* type, appear only in the Archaic period. Yet others, such as the warrior type, crop up with a range of significant variants: the statuettes (with or without weapons), grip the lance in the left hand; with the right hand (when the shield was omitted) the figures were portrayed in a simple gesture of offering or supplication.

Regrettably, the written testimonies are even less complete than the picture offered by the extant material evidence, except for notes on the figure of Ducetius. There must have been a certain receptivity toward the Sicels, to judge from the *hypothesis*, the tragedy of the *Women of Aetna* commissioned by Hieron from Aeschylus to celebrate the capture of Catana (modern Catania) and the foundation of the new colony, Aetna. Much detail can be found in Diodorus Siculus' accounts of the deeds of Ducetius, who was active around the mid-fifth century, the only authentic military and political leader, whose name (like that of the Celtic chief Brennus) would seem to stem directly from his role as commander (*dux*). Born in a hamlet bordering the Palici sanctuary, Ducetius was a member of an aristocracy that was completely Hellenized but which frequented the nearby *heroon* at Caratabia. Ducetius tried to imbue the local indigenous context with customs and a political fabric that echoed the Greek tyrannies, exploiting the never extinguished nationalist-warrior *ethos*. His is a good example of "counter-acculturation," that is, the native attempt to stave off a complete cultural takeover is evident, and in which the subjugated party adopts the same devices as its opponents to safeguard its identity. Ducetius brought his policies into play after the expulsion of the Deinomenids, following in the wake of the budding pro-Sicel democracy of Syracuse, who had decided to combat the *xenoi*, to whom the tyrants had accorded citizenship. Things came to a head in 453 B.C. with the constitution of the *synteleia* (a kind of military federation), to which "all towns of the same ethnic group adhered, excepting Hybla." That this move got under way in the Palici area is suggested by the transferal of Menaenum down to the plain, and the consequent foundation of a new center, Paliké, near the celebrated Palici sanctuary site. After the defeat

Painted antefix
from a votive deposit
at Terravecchia di Grammichele
6th cent. B.C.
Syracuse
Museo Archeologico Regionale

Enthroned goddess
from Poggio dell'Aquila
at Terravecchia di Grammichele
second half 6th cent. B.C.
Syracuse
Museo Archeologico Regionale

Clay bust of a goddess
from the Plain of Catania
first half 5th cent. B.C.
Adrano, Museo Civico

in 450 B.C. at Nomai, Ducetius was taken prisoner by the Syracusans, and pleaded for his life to the *ekklesia*, who sent him on a comfortable exile to Corinth. This decision sparked new conflicts among the two most powerful Greek colonies on the island, Syracuse and Acragas (Agrigento), who wrestled for control over the northern coastlands. In this very area, Ducetius, who had meanwhile returned from Corinth, took a garrison of Greek natives of the Peloponnese together with indigenous men under Arconidas of Erbita and founded Cale Acte (448–447 B.C.). The leader's death in 440 B.C. foreshadowed the definitive crushing of the Sicels at Trinakrie, one of the centres around the Palici sanctuary territory. From the political point of view, the most significant legacy of Ducetius is the *synteleia*. There is no sure evidence for some form of Sicel "league" (as a sort of self-contribution, and therefore as a unified administration) anticipating the *synteleia*, although the sheer rapidity with which this political entity emerged and took root is remarkable. The notion, however, that the ethnic links themselves were sufficient basis for political aggregation may not be far off the mark – such developments are typified by the Osco-Sabellian social patterns.

At Sabucina, which rose on Sican territory, the first phase of town planning dates to the seventh century B.C., and was superimposed on the circular huts of the period known as North Pantalica. The presence of proto-Corinthian material and the borrowing of motifs from Rhodian and Cretan wares from the very outset suggest a certain receptiveness to Geloan influence. In the course of the sixth century the township was given a ring of defense works, probably in view of the installation of a Greek garrison (from Acragas rather than Gela?): a similar presence can be seen in finds from the western necropolis, in use from the late sixth to later fifth century B.C. (yields include an interesting locally made animal-figures krater, imitating Attico-Corinthian prototypes, in this case employed as a cinerary urn). A town's destruction level (mid-fifth century) may concide, ac-

Bronze figurine of a man
with right hand on his penis
from the Plemmyrium
near Syracuse
second half 8th cent. B.C.
Syracuse
Museo Archeologico Regionale

Couple making offerings
on a truncated conical base
bronze
end 8th-first half 7th cent. B.C.
Syracuse
Museo Archeologico Regionale

cording to some scholars, with the deeds of Ducetius. The town was rebuilt in the second half of the century, orientated to a new direction, and the new *enceinte* was provided with square towers. The reuse of previous tombs bears witness to a phase of economic recession that endured through the later fifth century and eventually saw the temporary abandonment of the site, probably in connection with the Carthaginian advance. Evidence shows a general return of well-being here as elsewhere, during the period of Timoleon. The unusual layout of the settlement was probably the fruit of a combination of different experiences (which E. De Miro has even referred to Mycenaean tradition, or to the Italic customs of the Sissizi), as may be inferred at Sabucina from the siting and consistency of the religious enclave just outside the walls. The earliest phase (seventh century) is represented by the remains of a rectangular *sacellum* complete with a ritual bench and two votive furrows. Later that century (toward the end?) the building was abandoned; it was overbuilt by one of the three circular, coeval constructions that symbolize the sanctuary's heyday; the layout basically reproduces the local prehistoric hut arrangement. The votive offerings, arranged perhaps in natural pits used as rudimentary *bothroi*, were prevalently of indigenous manufacture, though Greek specimens are not unknown. Hut *Sacellum* A has yielded a deep beaker on a disc base (which has been likened to Minoan stone chalices), a bronze belt, an Attic *lekythos* of the last quarter of the sixth century, and the famous model of a prostyle temple on a pedestal (second half of the sixth century) which is a plastic decoration imitating Greek pototypes. Hut Sacellum B has yielded a tiny, schematic model of a tent-type building, evidently based on an indigenous construction, and decorated with horse *protomai* (seventh century?), together with several fictile statuettes of seated female figures similar to those found in Gela-Acragas sanctuaries, dedicated to chthonic deities. On top of the third circular construction, abandoned in the mid-sixth century B.C., a rectangular building was raised (of the type known in the Gela-Acragas sanctuaries), which was the only one of the entire enclave left in use. A round altar, votive deposits, and offerings, testify, by this time, to the Greek stamp of the cult in question, which resembles the *thesmophoria* cult. As for the *sacella* huts, it is important to note that there exist quite a few and that they display marked similarities of chronology, concentration, and layout. This cultural homogeneity, the important location in the town's layout, the cult-business needs presuppose the existence of a full-fledged priesthood, as a distinct class of the society. An attractive though unproven hypothesis is that a tribal organization (with its own dominant groups) was reflected in this multiplicity of the religious buildings.

In the sacred enclave at Polizzello, protected by a ring of *aggere* walls, new excavations indicate a situation parallel to that of Sabucina, with three hut *sacella* on a circular plan, plus a fourth exedra-shaped building, which has been interpreted as a sort of *theatron* for ceremonial practices. The two levels of occupation at the sanctuary (which E. De Miro has hypothetically dubbed "pan-Sican") span the seventh and sixth centuries; the strikingly rich yield of votive offerings includes pendants and jewelry fashioned from bone and amber, *fibulae* in silver or set with bone, together with artifacts in iron. Among the articles from the previous excavations are vases of local production bearing human and animal figures both painted and incised. Among the bronzes, a male gift-bearer is of a rather stockier type than its contemporary counterparts found elsewhere on Sicel territory; another piece has a curious trident form, in which links with the Mycenaean coroplastic can be detected. At Sabucina as at Polizzello the evidence testifies to purely indigenous religious practices which even before the arrival of the Greek colonists had achieved a certain articulation, which evolved sanctuary-type complex structures. The strongest clues of Aegean cultural influence can be found at Polizzello, the far-

Bronze warrior
making offerings
second half 6th cent. B.C.
Syracuse, Museo
Archeologico Regionale

Bronze warrior
with cuirass and wide belt
making offerings
from Mendolito di Adrano
first half 5th cent. B.C.
Syracuse, Museo
Archeologico Regionale

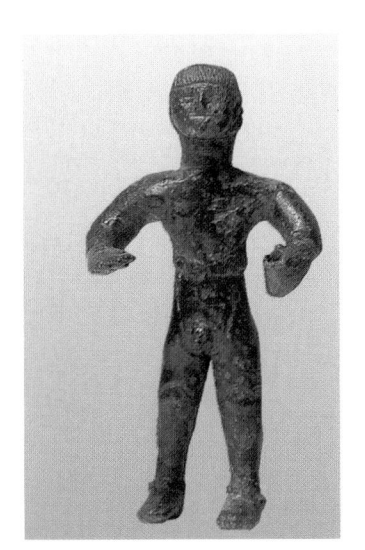

thest from the Sicel heartland, whereas Sabucina boasts a clearer evidence of Hellenic presence, identifiable in the sheer continuity of indigenous ritual practices as those of Greek type.

Another characteristic of the Sican area is the widespread presence of fictile models. This type of theophanic evocation – which in Sicel area manifests itself in cult statuary of the kind found at Grammichele or the Plain of Catania – is in nearly all cases based on the representation of cult buildings, some of which are discernibly of Greek derivation. It is not possible to establish whether the *tholos* type (which in historical Greece verges on a full-fledged *heroon*) is actually alien to this phenomenon. There is something to be said, however, for the suggestion that votive miniatures of sacred buildings in the Caltanissetta-Agrigento region is indicative of the resounding importance which architecture had in the Minoan-Mycenaean world. As for the nature itself of the cults represented, it is less clear here than in the eastern areas discussed above. Possible reminders of the tomb-temple of Minos, dedicated to Aphrodite, or to the Cretan cult of the *meteres* at Enghion, are nowhere to be seen. If we rule out the kind of links with the chthonic sphere observed at Sabucina, and De Miro's suggestion of a possible *telesterion* or building for initiation rites at Polizzello, the only viable indication seems to be the frequent discovery of stylized bull *protomai* of Late Minoan derivation, created in relief on various little amphorae with incised or painted decoration.

Likewise, very little literary information has emerged for the Sican area, too. At the necropolis of Sant'Angelo Muxaro, the definitive abandonment of the *tholos* tombs (in the first decades of the fifth century B.C.) can probably be linked – assuming the identification of the center with ancient Camicus – to a precise historical event. As the place became a hotbed of resistance for Hippocrates and Capis, fellow kinsmen of the Acragantine tyrant Theron, the centre fell under the yoke of the tyrant of the Emmenidai family who, on the discovery of the tomb of King Minos, gave back his remains to the Cretans (Diodorus Siculus, IV. 79. 4); these Cretans were most likely not of Aegean stock, and at the time wielded no political consequence in this specifically Hellenic world, but nonetheless clung to a precise cultural identity of their own from within the Acragantine territory. It is possible that these events were taken up in part by Sophocles in his *Kamikoi* (and linked perhaps to the *Daidalos*), and parodied by Aristophanes in his *Kokalos*. The Athenian public's interest in the western area of Sicily, and hence in a saga in which it saw this same territory represented, is connected to a phase that followed the death of the tyrant Theron: the instrumental pro-Elymian political line assumed by Athens (including the dual treatise with Segesta, the earliest of which dates to 458–457 B.C., and the second just prior to the Sicilian expedition) affected an area of the island traditionally of Sican culture, in which "national" sagas had already surfaced before the emergence of the various Elymian nuclei. These territory, furthermore, offered ample opportunity for links with the figure of Daedalus who, in the hands of the Attic historiographers, had become an Athenian hero of sorts.

In conclusion, the west-central area of the island has different basic characteristics with respect to the eastern side. One of its most signal features is the association of impressed and incised ware with painted ware, and with a far more elaborate decorative syntax than appears in Sicel territory. In many cases, moreover, the influence of the Greek Orientalizing style is very evident: the incomprehension or inorganic interpretation of the Greek models, with a marked sense of *horror vacui*, engendered some very typical compositions whose preoccupation with human and animal figures may well be traced to Minoan-Mycenaean tradition.

From the second half of the fifth century B.C. the material evidence that can be referred to the specifically

Column krater
with four-legged animals
from the Sabucina necropolis
second half 6th cent. B.C.
Caltanissetta, Museo Civico

Conical cup with disk foot
from the Sabucina sanctuary
second half 7th cent. B.C.
Caltanissetta, Museo Civico

native milieu becomes virtually negligible in both Sican and Sicel territories, before petering out almost completely. By contrast, information in the written sources increases for the period, albeit sporadically, and offers few actual cases in which one is able to extrapolate an identifiable trend. The wholesale assimilation of Greek culture on the part of the native inhabitants succeeded in smoothing over the ethnic and cultural distinctions between the two most substantial nuclei; this is compounded by the arrival of growing streams of mercenaries from Campania as well as by the increasing pressure of the Carthaginians, and the ongoing political and military concentration of force being implemented during the Agathocles period. The sustained state of conflict and the subsequent bouts of destruction and internal struggles, the abandonment of settlements and their repopulation, together with the massive migrations of people (sometimes over very brief periods), mark serious upheavals in the fabric of the communities under study, which, in shedding their cultural substance, combined with the Greek, Punic, Elymian, and Campanian input to make way for the emerging reality of Roman Sicily.

From the archaeological standpoint, for many centers of the mid-fifth century only a few sets of grave offerings include the latest types of locally manufactured artifacts. One of the most significant features – and not just with regard to indigenous spheres – was the so-called renaissance during the Timoleon period, which ran out between the death of Agathocles and the retreat of Pyrrhus. The few years that mark the heyday of the career of this Corinthian *strategos* Timoleon, (from 344 to 337 B.C.) who saw the deposition of the tyrant Dionysius and the defeat of the Carthaginians on the Crimisus River, represents an epoch of intense fervor, boosted presumably by a sharp rise in the population, and characterized by new political allegiances and groupings, through the concession of citizenship to substantial quotas of the native population and immigrant mercenaries. The numerous Sicel, Sican, and Elymian villages and towns that underwent civil and urban reorganization in this period (Ietae, Segesta, Punic Soluntum, and the Syracuse-dependant Morgantina, to name but a few), are little different from those of Greek foundation.

The social and political structures. The indigenous populations in the history of Greek Sicily
The warrior *ethos* remains one of the enduring constants in the history of Sicel social makeup, as was inevitable in a country marked by a high rate of armed conflict throughout the Greek age, not to mention the spillover of events in the Syracusan on State. It seems likely that a dominant class with initial warrior characteristics evolved from a situation of enduring or permanent forms of activity, assuming the connotations of a mercenary class, fueled by the influx of disinherited migrants and people of lowly standing. Such a development was further abetted by the numerous Greek garrisons stationed in the indigenous settlements, garrisons whose ranks were inevitably swelled with members of the local population.

Nevertheless, the documented agricultural use of the land would seem to indicate that most of the local inhabitants were assigned to farming or were local landlords of some kind, who more or less saw to the regular supply of produce to the Greek towns. There is much to suggest, indeed, that personal status within the community was essentially tied to land ownership. Large groups of local-born people would have tilled the land in what were known as the *campi leontini* (Leontine fields) or the various *chorai* around the other Greek *poleis*. There is even a chance that among the ranks of the serfs *Kyllirioi* (the slaves) combating the Syracusan *Gamoroi* (the landowners) were many soldiers of Sicel stock. A certain woman *Sikanà*, mentioned in the *defixio* of Selinus (in which there is also mention of a *Tyrrana*) may not have been a slave exactly; similarly, a *Sikelos* and a *Sikanos* (of immigrants-*metoikoi* or slaves?) are recorded as active among the potters in the *Kerameikos* quarter in Athens (where one of the hillocks south of the city bore the place-name *Sikelia*). At the time of the Athenian expedition to Sicily, a *Sikanos* with fifteen ships was dispatched by the Syracusans at Acragas (Agrigento) to intervene in the cross-fighting and break the neutrality (Thucydides, VII. 46 and 50). In Rome, moreover, a certain Q. Claelius Siculus (whose relationship with the island cannot be better defined) served as consul in 498 B.C. Lastly, it may be that the merchant figure referred to as *Hyblesios* in the inscription on an Attic cup of the second half of the sixth century (found at Gravisca in Etruria) was effectively of island stock.

Clay model of a small temple in antis on a pedestal from the circle *Sacellum* A in the Sabucina sanctuary second half 6th cent. B.C. Caltanissetta, Museo Civico

Clay model of a tent-shaped building with horse heads from the circle *Sacellum* B in the Sabucina sanctuary 7th cent. B.C. Caltanissetta, Museo Civico

Trilobate *oinochoe*
with painted decoration
from Montagna di Polizzello
7th cent. B.C.
Syracuse, Museo
Archeologico Regionale

Small *amphora*
with stylized
relief bulls' heads
and incised decoration
from Montagna di Polizzello
7th cent. B.C.
Palermo, Museo Archeologico
Regionale "A. Salinas"

At least from the seventh century onward, there is strong evidence for the emergence of an elite connected to religious functions. The political and social status of those who attended to cult business has been proven, as in the case of the Palici sanctuary, attested by the right to *asylia* and by the ordeals linked to the boiling craters, from which water, carbonic anhydrite and other vapours came out. The acolytes of the goddess Hybla, who were known for their skilled interpretation of dreams (*enipnion exegetai*), enjoyed the greatest respect of the mother of Dionysius; and according to written sources, those of the *meteres* in Enghion were in charge of no less than 3,000 heads of livestock. Mention should also be made of the priesthood at the western end of the island, at the Aphrodite sanctuary on Mount Eryx, who were entrusted with presiding the sacred prostitution.

As for the local chieftains of earlier, pre-Greek times, an aside by Diodorus (V. 9. 1) notes that "the Sicels entrusted their most valorous men with the command, whereas the Sicans were unable to agree over who should take power and so fought among themselves for several years". Of the names that have been passed down to posterity, the mythical figures of Cocalus and Xouthos, and likewise Hyblon and Arconidas are all connected to the monarchy. The status as king, for individual villages, was mentioned by Diodorus even for the earliest periods of the Sican history (Diodorus, V. 6. 2). Theutus, meanwhile, is cited as "lord" of Ouessa, while the term tyrant (on the Greek model) is applied to a certain Agyris of the eponymous town of Agyrion; a *hegoumenos* is said to have ruled over Inessa in the times of Ducetius. The latter alone, who began his career as a simple chieftain of his birthplace, assumes the connotations of an ethnarch, a political and military commander. The power setup does not always seem to pivot on the individual villages and towns, however. The information we have regarding Arconidas, the relations between Herbita and the settlements in the district (after Ducetius' attempts!) would seem to suggest forms of territorial networking. Given the tradition of absolute power rather than democracy, there is something out of place about the public epigraph from the Mendolito area, dated to the second half of the sixth century: the terms *touto* and *verega*, notably of Osco-Umbrian origin, presuppose some form of civil organization – perhaps on a military basis – that is more compatible with the exercise of power within sets of "juridical-political units" of a relatively spread-out nature. The hypothesis that the original tribal setup, trough the emergence and the consolidation of certain elites, may have evolved over time toward more differentiated social patterns, is therefore quite tenable. By the same standard, it is logical to infer that the prevailing Greek influence fostered the gradual development away from village aggregations toward para-urban patterns; in which the existence of defense works or public religious buildings is an indirect token of the new "political" connotations.

Both Sicans and Sicels were attracted yet overwhelmed by the stimuli to amalgamate, yet without forgoing their inherent desire to be different and cling to a physiognomy of their own in comparison with the Greeks; in such a physiognomy the unifying aspects vie with specific elements of remote ascendancy. To this "minor" Sicily, being neither Greek nor Punic, belongs the original effective division of the island into two areas – a division which, despite the many centuries in which Sicily was a province of Rome, continues to linger to this day. The Sicel–Sican dichotomy may merely represent the start of a chain of phenomena that lead toward the same way: the western region of the island saw the tenacious survival of the Aegean tradition, the Phoenician-Carthaginian presence, as well as a more incisive Arab one; while the eastern region witnessed a stronger Italic influence, a greater number and variety of Greek colonies, and the long Byzantine "renaissance." And yet it is in the heart of the indigenous world that we should look for the embryo of the rural model of economy (still weak, as were the elites) which would later make Sicily the great supplier of grain to the Mediterranean. In fact, the dramatic contrasts between indigenous villages and colonies, between coastland and interior, between rural and town economy, between dominant and submissive cultures, have somehow permeated the island's history, even in recent times.

Bibliography
General treatise (from which this contribution has been taken): V. La Rosa, in *Italia omnium terrarum parens*, 1989, pp. 3-110. I have again dealt with some specific topics of the same themes in *L'ospitalità...*, in *Siculorum Gymnasium*, XLV, 1992, pp. 103-106; *Influenze di tipo egeo...*, in *Kokalos*, XXXIX-XL, 1993-94, I, 1, pp. 9-47. In recent bibliography the following works are of specific relevance: *Gli Elimi e l'area elima*, 1990; *Atti Giornate internazionali...*, 1992; D. Pancucci, M.C. Naro, 1992; E. Procelli, R.M. Albanese, in *Not. Scavi*, 1988-89, I supplement, 1992; *Kokalos*, XXXIV-XXXV, 1988-89 (but 1992-93); *Storia e archeologia...*, 1993 (especially regarding the new data about Sabucina put forward by R. Mollo Mezzena); R.M. Albanese, E. Procelli, 1993; G. Di Stefano, 1995. Useful references can also be found in the recent *Ancient Sicily* (*Acta Hyperborea*, 6, 1995), edited by T. Fischer-Hansen.

The Impact of the Greek Colonies on the Indigenous Peoples of Campania

At the beginning of the Iron Age today's region of Campania was inhabited by peoples having a variety of different ethnic origin and culture. To the extent of present knowledge, the earliest settlements are those of Capua, Pontecagnano south of Salerno, and Sala Consilina in the Vallo di Diano (bordering Basilicata). These centers were created at the beginning of the ninth century B.C. by colonists from the coastlands of southern Etruria, and are contemporary with the major settlements in that area: Tarquinii, Veii, and Vulci. The creation of the first proto-urban settlements went hand-in-hand with colonial expansion of the Etruscans, demarcating the transition from the Bronze Age to the Iron Age.

As with other cases of proto-historic evidence, these centers are known particularly for their necropolises. As in Etruria, the burial grounds are characterized by cremation, a practice that continued side-by-side with inhumation in Campania. The cremated bones of the dead were conserved together with the personal effects (*fibulae*, jewelry, weapons for men, and weaving tools for women) in an urn capped with a bowl for a lid; in some of the male tombs, the lid is a pottery imitation of a bronze helmet. These features are all typical of the Villanovan culture that dominated Etruria during the Early Iron Age.

The adoption of imported funeral rituals is accompanied by other peculiarities in the physical organization of the land: the large tract of land designated for residential building is clearly marked off at the outset from the burial area. This is densely set with tombs that tend to spread out in concentric waves; soon after, however, the development model changed, and special "clan" areas began to take form. While in the first half of the ninth century B.C. the society offers evident signs of equality, by mid-century patent clues of emerging class stratification begin to show: the more eminent male tombs contain weapons, and those of the women bronze spindles; in same graves, burial goods become more abundant and costly.

Imported objects begin to appear, some originating in regions considerably distant from the Tyrrhenian, such as the "curtain" vases in Basilicata; certain types of sword in Calabria; pots with "feathered" decoration from Sicily, and several bronze items of Sardinian manufacture. This does not necessarily mean that these items betoken commercial activity as such: depending on the objects in question, they may be ceremonial or even marriage gifts. But the liveliness of the contacts reveals an otherwise unsuspected mobility among the indigenous populations. The length of the journeys they took presupposes aims of some importance. It is likely that the basic stimulus was the quest for metals or other elementary goods; equally likely is the occasional involvement of mediators, such as the Phoenicians. But this does not mean that economic and political developments were any less vibrant: at the end of the ninth century B.C., at the dawn of the Greek "rediscovery" of the West, Pontecagnano was experiencing a burst of growth.

Like Pontecagnano, Capua lies at the center of a fertile river valley, not far from the estuary. The site's position facilitated its role as a way station for trade by sea, while fostering good links with the populations of the interior. Through the system of rivers comprising the Volturno, Liri, Sacco, and Tiber, Capua was in constant exchange with Latium (Lazio) and the Etrurian interior higher up the Tiber, a region dominated by the cities of Clusium (Chiusi) and Volsinii (Orvieto). Both Capua and Pontecagnano are somewhat extraneous to the cultural situation in the rest of Campania, as the local *facies* observed a different burial rite, from which derives the name "grave culture" owing to the exclusive observance of inhumation. So far, evidence exists from the mid-ninth century B.C. of a people denominated as Opici by the early historians, who gradually assumed both name and physiognomy of the Campanians. In the typical tomb of this culture, often lined and roofed in shingle, the body is inhumed supine, together with personal effects; the vases are usually set next to the feet or legs, and on rare occasions near the head. The vases tend to vary in style from those of Pontecagnano and Capua; the decoration is in relief, comprising a series of grooves and protrusions, whereas in the Villanovan culture the vase patterns were usually incised or impressed on the surface.

Even greater differences can be seen at socioeconomic level. Evidence shows that the settlements, which lived from farming, reached the size and configuration of small villages, a fact endorsed by other sources. In the Sarno Valley, these nuclei are fairly close to one another. In each case the area assigned for the burial ground is large in comparison; the graves themselves, often of vast dimensions, were set in the middle of a large circular area, probably covered with a kind of hut reserved for the dead. The huts thus created lay along narrow parallel lanes, creating an imitation village.

Clay helmet with figured apex
beginning 9th-mid-8th cent. B.C.
Pontecagnano, Museo
Archeologico dell'Agro Picentino
Cat. 15

The only exception from this layout is the settlement at Cumae, before it became the acropolis of the Greek colony. The settlement, which must have included a port and controlled the whole of the Campanian coast toward Lazio, seems to have been chosen as a site not only for agricultural reasons, but as a strategic political and trading way station. In two tombs from the pre-Hellenic necropolis appear the first tangible signs of the Greeks' arrival: three bowls of purified clay with painted decoration; these date to the late ninth–early eighth century B.C.

This was the moment in which, after a long period of stasis that followed the collapse of the Mycenaean reigns, the Greeks resumed their seafaring activity. Most ships set sail from Euboea, the large island off the Attic coast which, unlike other regions of Greece, had survived the Greek Dark Age unharmed. In the wake of the Phoenician ships, the Euboean vessels dropped anchor at the Sicilian coast and also strayed further into the Tyrrhenian waters. Their cargo included the typical vessels for wine consumption: drinking cups, frequently with a decorative band with rows of chevrons between the handles. These vessels, intended for exchange with the more affluent members of the indigenous populations, have turned up in modest quantities in Veii, Capua, Cumae, and Pontecagnano; some isolated examples have also turned up elsewhere in the Tyrrhenian region. The fact that they were included in the indigenous grave goods – particularly those of eminent members of the society – is evidence that the local milieu acknowledged and accepted these sophisticated tokens of production (pottery) and consumption (wine), demonstrating a certain openness toward the Greek world. At least in the so-called Villanovan communities, contact and exchange was greatly aided by the liveliness of trade in the local milieu.

The Impact of the Greek Colonies on the Indigenous Peoples of Campania

Euboic-style krater
made in Pithekoussai
730-700 B.C.
Sarno, Museo

Imported Greek cup
with chevron decoration
from Tomb 3 at Cumae
first half 8th cent. B.C.
Naples
Museo Archeologico Nazionale

Cup decorated with birds
from Tomb 248 at Capua
second quarter 8th cent. B.C.
Naples
Museo Archeologico Nazionale

It has yet to be ascertained what instigated these adventurous merchants to embark on perilous journeys, apparently unliable to economic return. Perhaps theirs was a quest for metals, their goal being the mineral resources of the Monti della Tolfa between Tarquinii and Caere, or the metal-bearing hills opposite Elba. This seems the most likely motive, though their eventual scope was perhaps more ample, and comprised all those opportunities – big and small – that characterize the ancient practices of seafaring peoples.

One of the key phases of these early contacts between newcomers and indigenous folks was the establishment of a stable *emporion* at Pithekoussai on the Isle of Ischia. This venture, the first signs of which date to the middle of the eighth century, heralds the end of haphazard trade patterns and the start of more enduring, continuous relationships: Pithekoussai was settled by craftsmen and merchants who thereby established themselves at the western tip, so to speak, of a navigation route that led back to Al Mina on the coast of northern Syria, at the mouth of the Orontes River. The *emporion* of Pithekoussai on Ischia served as the destination of luxury goods brought from the east, such as semi-precious stone seals of Cilicia. Here, skilled Euboean metalworkers fashioned raw materials from mainland Etruria, and sold them back to the indigenous tribes as finished goods. Furthermore, local craftsmen took their important skills on the road and went to work in Etruria itself, making coveted Greek-style vases together with prized items wrought from gold.

The food supply of the Euboean *emporion* came from the surrounding countryside of the island; but as the yield was insufficient, the islanders purchased what they lacked from the mainland tribes. This made for lively contacts with the indigenous villages in the Sarno Valley, where the

The Impact of the Greek Colonies on the Indigenous Peoples of Campania

Silver *oinochoe*
from Tomb 928 at Pontecagnano
7th cent. B.C.
Pontecagnano, Museo
Archeologico dell'Agro Picentino

Protection for a horse's head
embossed bronze *lamina*
from Tomb 4461 at Pontecagnano
end 8th cent. B.C.
Pontecagnano, Museo
Archeologico dell'Agro Picentino

tribal elites were evidently attracted to Greek culture, and tried to emulate it. Their efforts were curtailed, however, when Euboean settlements became self-sustaining.

A major change came with the creation of the first full-fledged colony, Cumae, which was established in 740 B.C. on the mainland. This new enterprise was promoted by the same Euboeans who had rediscovered the West. But the foundation of a city is quite different from setting up an emporium: it presupposes the political control of an extensive territory, and entails reproducing the hierarchical organization of homeland society. Consequently, such a venture causes upheavals in the overall equilibrium of the host area, a change to which the region of Campania was particularly suited owing to its ethnic and political complexity.

The Euboeans' first move was a violent one: they razed the indigenous town (on the current site of the acropolis). Those, among the natives, who were not slayed, and chose to remain, were obliged to live on the surrounding land and work as menials. This all took place with the tacit acceptance of Pontecagnano and Capua, and indeed the aristocratic class of Cumae entertained enduring political relations with the latter.

The Opici withdrew further inland and established themselves on the Apennines, in contact with the Caudini, the most advanced of the Samnite tribes. The native towns, such as Calatia, Suessula, Caudium, and Abella, including those that predated this stage of development, seem to have flourished after the foundation of Cumae; in certain native tombs from the second half of the eighth century B.C., the grave goods include Greek cups.

The colony of Cumae stood as a model and a partner for its neighbors Pontecagnano and Capua, and its presence helped catalyze the important changes already under way in these indigenous centers. At the end of the eighth and beginning of the seventh century B.C. a process came into play by which the members of the local aristocracies up and down the coast began to adopt sim-

Silver *kotyle*
from Tomb 928 at Pontecagnano
7th cent. B.C.
Pontecagnano, Museo
Archeologico dell'Agro Picentino

Bronze cauldron
with bulls' heads
from Cumae
7th cent. B.C.
Copenhagen, Nationalmuseet

ilar behavior and customs, coalescing into a homogeneous group, irrespective of ethnic differences. This process is demonstrated by similarities in funeral rites and goods. The tombs of the *principes* at Pontecagnano contain silver or bronze vases and *fibulae*, the same types that can be observed in the "princely" tombs elsewhere in Lazio and Etruria, and not least in the most sumptuous tomb in Cumae itself: Tomb 104 of the Fondo Artiaco. The tombs in question evince funeral rites of the heroic, Homeric type; by mid-eighth century cremation had given way to inhumation, and yet the *principes* continued to observe cremation rites, in Homeric style, and their cremated bones were put in bronze vases or silver urns. The source of this custom is undoubtedly Euboea, as exemplified by the tombs in the *heroon* at the western gate of Eretria; the channel by which the custom spread across the West, was undoubtedly Cumae. However, Cumae gradually blended into its Tyrrhenian context and began to endow the tombs of its *aristoi* with grave goods of Etruscan production. This explains why for many years the most sumptuous of the cremation burials in Cumae was mistaken for an Etruscan tomb.

As in Etruscan and Latin spheres, Tyrrhenian society assumes a gentilicial structure, with large groups of parentage, which also absorbed the so-called *clientes*. The basic running of the society was in the hands of the *gentes*, who had skills in all areas of activity, fostering and conducting relations with *gentes* of other towns and cities; this same class of people bore the burden of war or the costs of founding new settlements.

The growing Etruscan hegemony in Campania in the late eighth and early seventh centuries B.C. was the fruit of the joint venture of gentilicial groups or, in some cases, the result of the enterprise of a particular *gens* rather than a question of political pressure or domination. The pervasive nature of the Etruscan "supremacy" is epitomized by the spread of the Etruscan language. Though showing traces of local influence, Etruscan became the spoken and written language common to all the non-Greek areas of the region, as testified by the highly numerous vase inscriptions. This said, however, the openness of certain townships to outside cultural influence can be seen in the occasional inscription in Achaean, which was spoken in the nearby town of Poseidonia (Paestum). Two important vase inscriptions from Fratte and Pontecagnano testify, in this frontier country, the custom of the *symposion* (drinking party), a social ritual that saw the aggregation of people of different ethnic extraction. Here and there we also encounter traces of attempts at written transcriptions of the local spoken language.

The Etruscan ascendancy in the region had repercussions on the balances within the Opic world, galvanizing processes of political reorganization and growth. The outcome of these processes can be seen in the re-foundation of such earlier centers as Caudium; other towns, such as Nola, Nuceria (Nocera), Pompeii, and Fratte were built from scratch. Other towns, like Marcina, were the fruit of the efforts of the nobility, as its name suggests. The new towns grew up as focal gathering points at the center of vast tracts of farmland, which had until this stage been dotted with villages. Such is the case of the Sarno Valley, where the scattered populations converged to form the township of Pompeii.

The local craftsmanship also betrays the predominance of Etruscan tastes and culture through the standardization of pottery production in the famous *bucchero* wares typical of Etruria. The typical *bucchero* piece is made of clay that is dark both on the surface and inside. The wares were finished to give the piece a characteristic metallic sheen, which explains why they were so popular. While in the seventh century B.C. lightweight *bucchero* vases with their gleaming surfaces were imported, by the end of the century many towns across Campania had set up production workshops. Through gradual standardization, these workshops adopted the thicker, less refined type in use in Etruria, and did not hesitate to introduce shapes and decorative motifs of local invention. Such was the appeal of this form of pottery that in the sixth century B.C. the most common wares in Etruscan towns in Campania seem to have been *bucchero*. Only the particularly advanced towns, such as Pontecagnano, saw the emergence of figured pottery, produced by Etr-

Bucchero kantharos
with Greek inscription:
ΑΠΟΛ (APOL)
second half 6th
to beginning 5th cent. B.C.
Pontecagnano, Museo
Archeologico dell'Agro Picentino

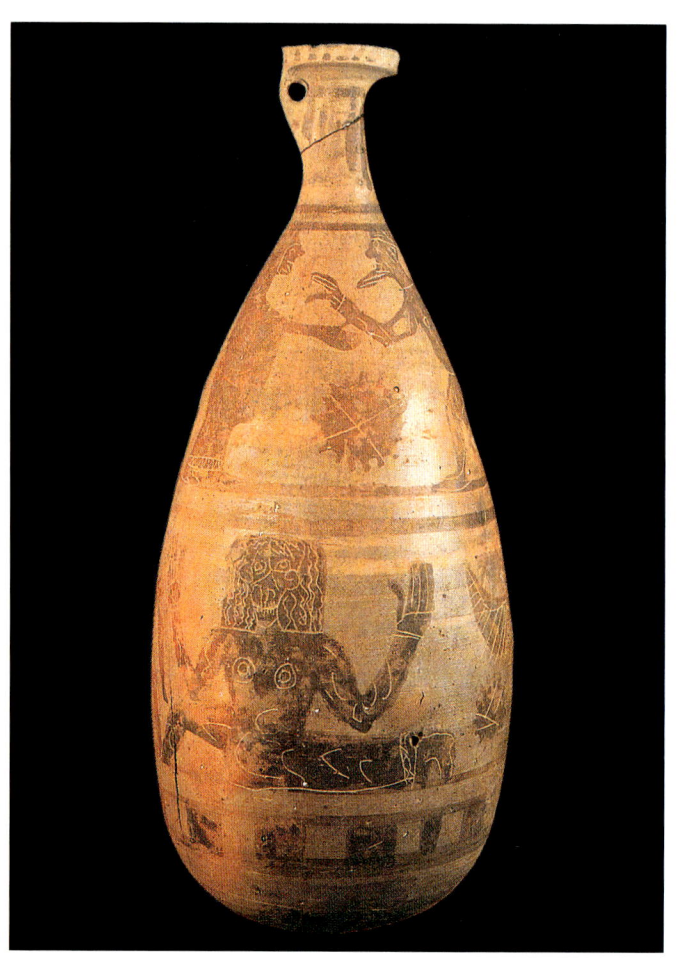

Alabastron with running *gorgoneion*
local production
beginning 6th cent. B.C.
Pontecagnano, Museo
Archeologico dell'Agro Picentino

Antefix with head of woman
inserted in a lotus flower
end 6th cent. B.C.
Capua
Museo Provinciale Campano

uscan craftsmen imitating the renowned pottery of Corinth. This kind of production became particularly diffuse in Pontecagnano and Capua.

After a period in which some vases by the Gorgon Painter group made their appearance, Attic vases became more frequent only after mid-century. Evidence of production by masters of red-figure vases has turned up in Nola in particular, with fewer examples in Fratte, whereas there is widespread evidence of Ionian cups and other wares of Ionian tradition.

In the course of the sixth century B.C. Pontecagnano's status altered in favor of the rising Greek *polis* of Poseidonia on the one side, and on the other of the new Etruscan town of Fratte, near modern Salerno. The dominating township in Campania at this point had become Capua.

From the end of the seventh century, the funerary goods in local tombs are rich in Corinthian pottery and bronze vessels, testifying to an affluent, cultured nobility. By this stage Capua had become an important trading center for luxury goods arriving from a wide variety of places in the Greek and Italic worlds. The discovery outside Campania of warrior tombs containing Corinthian helmets and other pieces of armory, together with bronze pitchers and bowls similar to those found in Capua, are outspoken evidence of the city's key role in spreading Etruscan cultural features through Basilicata and the Ofanto River area.

In the first half of the sixth century B.C. Capua saw a conspicuous increase in monumental architecture. This surge of building is testified by the huge amount of architectural terra-cottas and figured antefixes. The sheer variety of forms produced and the vivacity of the outside cultural influences – first Corinthian and then Ionian – are evident from the wealth of material that has come to light in the suburban sanctuary of the Fondo Patturelli. After mid-century, Capua found itself vying with Cumae and Pithekoussai in the production of a particular system of architectural revetment, which went into widespread application in Campania, from the Marica Sanctuary to the mouth of the Garigliano, to the Archaic temple to Apollo in the forum, Pompeii, to the shrine on the acropolis of Fratte near Salerno, to the building that may have been a *thesauros* for a Campanian city in the Achaean colony of Poseidonia. These temples, with their typical Capuan stamp, were the outward expression of Capua's political and cultural dominion – a supremacy which it enjoyed by dint of the lasting covenants between the Capuan and Cumaean nobility.

Until the first decades of the fifth century B.C. the production of Capua's craftsmen was notably varied and prolific. Besides the architectural terra-cottas mentioned above, the city boasted its particular brand of black-figure pottery, and especially the production of coveted bronzework and an extraordinary type of *lebes* whose lid was decorated with miniature figures sculpted in the round. And yet it was the very surge of development of Capua that determined the city's eventual demise: the constant expansion of building activity and craft production drew ever-increasing numbers of agricultural workers into the city to man the workshops and builders' yards.

The political balance along the coast had meanwhile undergone internal changes. The new Greek colonial city, Neapolis, founded toward the year 470 B.C., cast a shadow over Cumae. With considerable foresight, the governors of Neapolis allowed an increasing number of Campanians a say in the city's management. As a result, the stark contrast between the equality practiced in Neapolis, and the continued submission practiced in Cumae and Capua inevitably began to take its toll. At length, the Campanians toppled their overlords, first at Capua (423 B.C.) and subsequently at Cumae (421 B.C.); the way in which these decisive changes took place is graphically described by Livy, who explains how the seizure of power in Capua came from within, after a sustained period of cohabitation between Etruscans and Campanians in the city.

With the fall of Capua and Cumae, events swung further in favor of Neapolis which, owing to its political acumen in social questions, benefited from excellent relations with the Campanians. After expeditions into Sicily, and the reduction of the expansionist and political ambitions of Athens, Neapolis became one of Greece's principal frontier cities in the West. Corn from the Campanian countryside flowed to the port, to be acquired by the Athenian ship, bringing – among other goods – the figured vases, now reserved for a colonial market. In the course of the fourth century Neapolis became a vital turbine for a vast region of inland farming territory, which itself gradually came to be populated with villages and towns: the city became a magnet for people of Campanian and Samnite descent, who amassed around the site of the early Greek settlement, Palaepolis.

The new setup was subsequently compromised by the emergence of a new pole in the fertile coastal plain: in 343 B.C. the Samnites, a hill people that had so far remained relatively excluded from Greek and Etruscan relations, attacked the Sidicini, who turned to the Campanians for help. Rome saw the occasion for a new frontier in the south, and ran to its new ally's aid, marking the onset of the wars with the Samnites. These wars would end with the definitive assertion of Rome as the major power in Campania.

Notwithstanding the persistent skirmishes between Romans and Samnites, the second half of the fourth century B.C. was not a bleak period. Among the many important developments were the growing sanctuaries of Capua, Cales, and Teanum; the emergence of a flourishing red-figure vase production at Capua and Cumae. With regard to these vases, their immense popularity throughout Campania and Samnium is indicative of the relative affluence of the peoples of these regions. The Caudine tribe was the more advanced amongst Samnite tribes. In long years of contact with the Greeks and Etruscans, it became part of a cultural Campanian *koine*. Legends arose to the effect that the Samnites were in fact from Sparta. The written sources claim that Pontius Herennius, the father of the victorious leader at the Caudine Forks, had met and conversed with Archytas of Tarentum, and also Plato.

The final collapse of the Italiot world followed on the heels of the third Samnite War, upon which the Romanization of the entire southern region of the peninsula was complete.

Bibliography
On Campania in the Iron Age: B. D'AGOSTINO, in *Popoli e Civiltà dell'Italia Antica*, 2, 1974, pp. 11 ff.; P. GASTALDI, in *Annali I.U.O. ArchStAnt*, I, 1979, pp. 13-58; W. JOHANNOWSKY, 1983; B. D'AGOSTINO, in *Magna Grecia - Prolegomeni*, 1985, pp. 209-244; idem, in *Annali I.U.O. ArchStAnt*, IX, 1987, pp. 23-29; B. D'AGOSTINO, P. GASTALDI, 1988; G. COLONNA, in *Storia e civiltà della Campania - L'Evo antico*, 1991, pp. 25-68; S. DE NATALE, 1992; W. JOHANNOWSKY, in *Annali I.U.O. ArchStAnt*, n.s. 3, 1996, forthcoming.
On Campania in historical times: E. LEPORE, in *Storia di Napoli*, I, 1967; B. D'AGOSTINO, in *Popoli e Civiltà dell'Italia Antica*, 2, 1974, pp. 179 ff.; M. FREDERIKSEN, 1984; S. DE CARO, 1986; L. CERCHIAI, in *Annali I.U.O. ArchStAnt*, IX, 1987, pp. 41-54; A. MELE, 1987, pp. 155-178; B. D'AGOSTINO, in *Italia omnium terrarum alumna*, 1988, pp. 531 ff.; L. CERCHIAI, 1990; G. GRECO, A. PONTRANDOLFO, 1990. The whole subjert has been reconsidered in a brilliant work by L. CERCHIAI, *I Campani*, 1995.

The Impact of the Greek Colonies on the Indigenous Peoples of Lucania

It is by now common knowledge that the term "colonization," when used in reference to the movements of Hellenic peoples to the area in the West that came to be Magna Graecia, has a very different meaning than the usual one for modern and contemporary history; indeed, its sole function is to conjure up a very variegated set of personalities, events, and situations.

This consideration is all the more true when examining the relations that these "colonizers" established with the peoples they called *barbaroi*. It is important to note that the colonizers had various origins and different military might and aspirations, and that they acted in the absence of a prior theoretical framework, given how very early on this was all starting to happen, and even when it was at its most intense. The *barbaroi* – whom archaeologists lump together under the name of the Italic people – in their turn were even more varied in terms of ethnic origin, language, demographic importance, and culture. The research sector has shed a great deal of light on individual *de facto* situations, offering minutely detailed information. Nevertheless, today it seems possible to mark out the broad lines that will permit us to step back and gain a perspective on the phenomenon, without, however, lapsing back into the all-embracing and equally generic idea of "Hellenization" which traditionally goes hand in hand with that of "colonization."

Colonization may take one of two forms (even if, obviously, the ultimate aims are substantially the same): either the total elimination by military force of any autochthonous presence (an attitude that seems to be peculiar to the Achaeans), or complete assimilation (perhaps sought by the eastern Greeks). In the case of Lucania, it seems that we can make a geographical distinction, as both approaches were taken only in the farmland (*chora*) that is the natural and vital extension of the city-state outside of the urban limits (this means that in the evolution of things, the *chora* must have emerged very early on). Outside of this district, defined both visually and psychologically by the line of foothills of the hinterland, the Greeks never showed any intention of expanding the territory of their exclusive competence.

This general attitude did not escape the notice of Sybaris, which, after the rout of Siris, acquired the control of most of the Oenotrian territory, which stretches between Calabria, Basilicata, and Campania; what is often described as an "empire" in anticipation of successive stable territorial dominions of the monocratic type seems instead to have taken shape as a political and economic domination over a vast heap of different entities, both Greek and indigenous (the four *ethne* and twenty-five *poleis* mentioned by Strabo, VI. 1. 13).

Proof of this lack of structural homogeneity, compensated in any case by these Italic satellite entities' complete dependence on the *polis*, may be found at the critical time of the war of 510 B.C., when the former did not seem to be involved at all, and the destruction of Sybaris by the people of Croton triggered the collapse of the entire system and the destabilization of a vast territory; within a generation's span, many settlements shrank to the size they had at their beginning, around the first half of the previous century, to then disappear completely.

Beyond the *chorai*, therefore, stretched the lands of the *barbaroi* or the Oenotrians, usually mountainous and not very fertile. Further inland were the peoples conventionally known as the "North Lucani," as distinct from the historically defined Lucani and instead kindred to the Apulians who had settled along the northeastern strip of modern Basilicata (further north were the Daunii and then the Peucetii).

Relations with all these peoples were long dominated by what is summed up in the term "acculturation process." The absence of an expansionistic thrust beyond the limits described above is, in fact, compensated by other valid reasons for interest in the hinterland: the very deployment of the colonies along the coast of the peninsula implies the need to guarantee safe transit if not to the men then at least to the goods, along the river valleys (of, respectively, the Sinni and the Agri, whose navigability is mentioned by Strabo [VI. 1. 4] and then of the Basento and the Bradano) that ran between the Ionian and Tyrrhenian shores, significantly enhancing trade relations that arose in view of the complementarity of the respective territories.

On the other hand, on a more patently political level, the establishment of friendly relations with non-Greek neighbors very probably took place very quickly in response to a primary need of the various *poleis*, which were afflicted by perennial instability in both external and domestic relations. In any case, there is little doubt that both the inhabitants of Siris and the Achaeans (Sybarites and Metapontians) implemented the open-relations strategy, and this quickly fell into a fairly constant pattern as far as exchange of material goods and especially of customs, giving rise to genuine "behavior models."

The first of such models is linked to most of the region and has to do with the rapport established with the type of community most common in the Archaic period, that is, one in which differences of social rank and wealth were contained within unitary structures of an aristocratic type, each one the holder of

The Impact of the Greek Colonies on the Indigenous Peoples of Lucania

Sitting deity statue
from Garaguso
470 B.C.
Potenza, Museo
Archeologico Provinciale
Cat. 151

a residential nucleus in villages that were not necessarily subject to the rule of a common authority; in the case of the Oenotrian center of Chiaromonte, the placement of a small sacred area at the center of several nuclei seems highly significant, as it may have served as an element of community cohesion. Judging from the architectural evidence, the predominant dimension was the ceremonial one, where the material and spiritual were more readily reconciled.

Economic transactions, alliances, and perhaps even forms of exchange introduced by intermarriage came to be established in the context of ritual practices in which religious values certainly must have played a decisive role, as suggested by the function of such non-Greek sanctuaries as that at Garaguso, in the Metapontian hinterland. Here, toward the beginning of the fifth century, a precious votive, clearly the work of a city-dwelling craftsman, was presented: a small marble statue of the goddess enclosed within a limestone model of a temple.

It may not be a coincidence that the same site has also yielded a funeral assemblage dating from the late fifth century that is so similar to the standard Greek ritual as to suggest that the occupant of the grave was a native of Metapontum. The most evidence is provided by the funerary assemblages, which are primarily made up of everyday objects, in particular "kitchen sets" (for cooking meat) and dinner sets, an unmistakable sign of the adoption of the practice of banqueting, where wine played an important role as a social catalyst. Such a circumstance provided a major outlet for imported Greek and Etruscan wares.

Of course, it is highly likely that what the graves yield represents only the funeral feast; however, there is no reason to believe that this departed to any great extent from the banquets presumably held in what we might call the earliest example of a palace (*anaktoron*), that is, the building in Serra di Vaglio decorated with the so-called horseman's frieze in clay, the work of a Metapontian craftsman. This palace is one of the clearest examples of acculturation and stands in contrast with the huts devoid of any proportional harmony, which were widely used during the same period.

The male members of such elite classes lost no time in adopting Greek arms and armor, which were more effective and showier than the traditional proto-historic ones; many were given the attributes of horsemen, which, moreover, confirms how ideologically pregnant was the acquisition of such bronzes as the *Horseman of Grumentum* and its less famous companion in Boston, an item that was certainly presented as an offering to some Italic sanctuary. For the entire Archaic phase at least, the adoption of Greek weaponry did not constitute any real risk for the Greeks, since these "loans" retained an episodic and individual character within the context of a system that remained pre-political; they did not lead to the acquisition of the hoplite-type tactics – whether mounted or on foot – that were the true secret of the Greeks' military superiority. As for the female members – notably in the Oenotrian area – the most obvious sign of privilege is represented by the opulence of the large jewelry parures and the exaggerated complexity of the headdresses and attire, which were encrusted with metals, bone, and amber. Here the ostentation of riches assumes a particular form (and probably indicated the personal part of the dowry) that must have to do with the local early Iron Age traditions, but it also reflects customs of an eastern and Greek matrix, signs of that particular fondness for luxury items (*tryphe*, *habrosyne*) for which Ionian Greeks as well as Etruscans have been criticized. Recent discoveries at the urban cemetery of Metapontum show this predilection at work in an Archaic nucleus, marked as much by ritual complexity as by a clear intention of ostentation, in sharp contrast with the extreme sobriety and regularity that usually mark Greek funerary customs.

The most striking instance of this phenomenon of cultural (and probably political) interaction can be seen from a series of large tombs that came to light at Braida di Serra di Vaglio, mentioned above in connection with the possible *anaktoron*.

In the male tombs, the panoply is enhanced by unique pieces, such as the "Argive" hoplite-type shields with embossed decoration, together with several items of a parade-horse's bridle set.

The fact that this bridle was made for a pair of horses (given that the artifact recurs in other Italic contexts, as yet insufficiently investigated) tends to suggest that the warriors in question had a two-horse chariot at their disposal (evidence of which has turned up in the Melfi district, where the Etruscan influence is manifest); alternatively it may imply a second mount in the care of a shield-bearer, exactly as seen in a frieze unearthed a few meters away.

At any event, the find is cogent evidence of the ongoing endorsement of a model that was patently aristocratic; in one case, the point of reference was the Tyrrhenian aristocracy, in another, the *hippeis* of the nearby colonial elites.

The corresponding female tombs exhibit a parallel fund of jewelry, in one instance with further *unica*

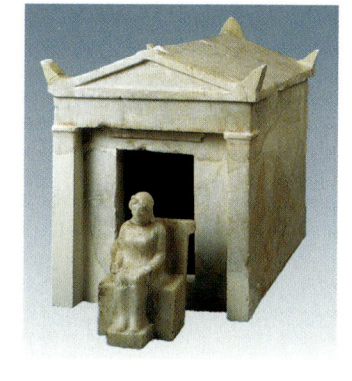

Model of a temple
with sitting deity
from Garaguso
470 B.C.
Potenza, Museo
Archeologico Provinciale
Cat. 151

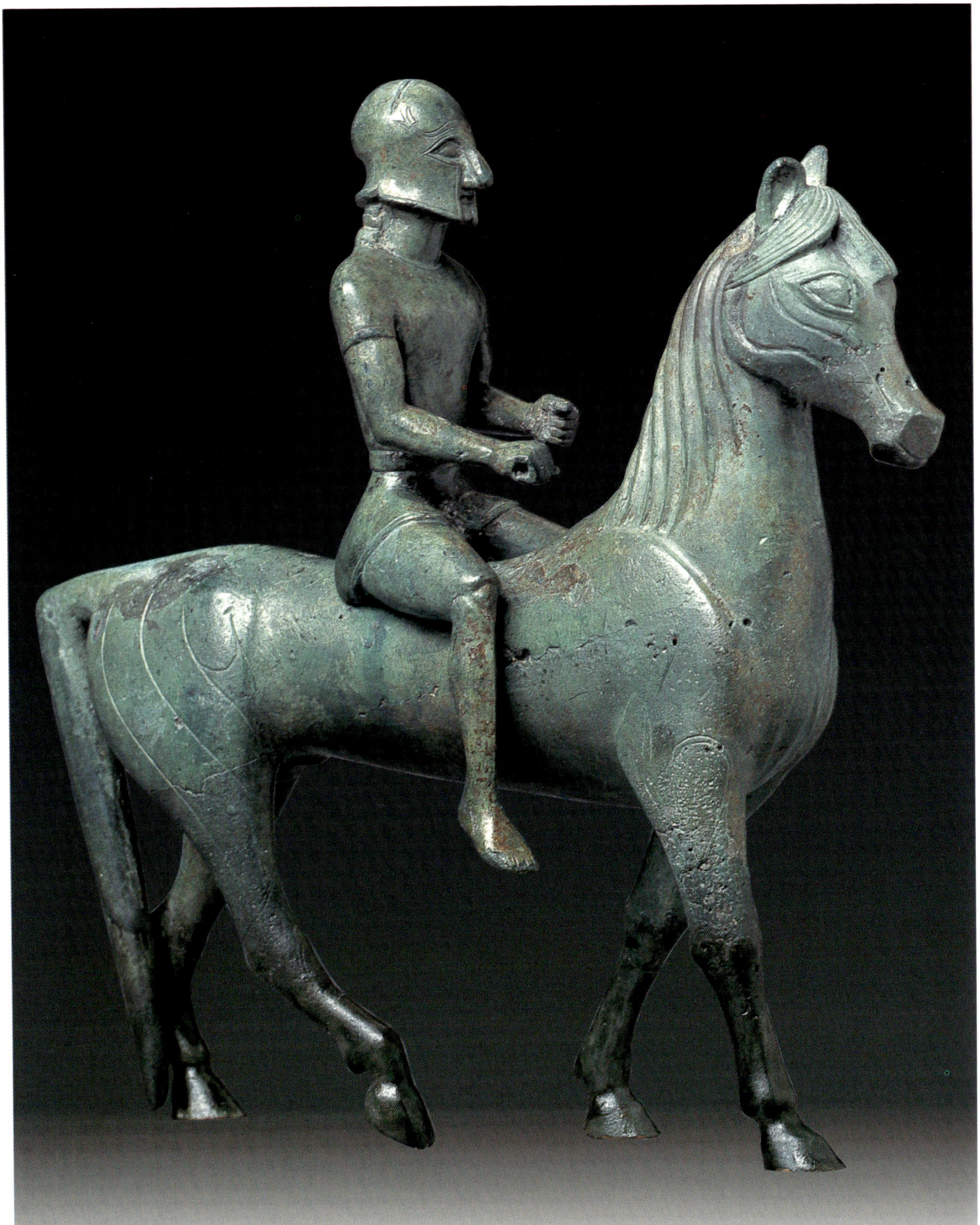

opposite
The Horseman of Grumentum
560-550 B.C.
London, British Museum
Department of Greek
and Roman Antiquities
Cat. 113

Fragment of a plaque
with a mounted groom
from the clay frieze
of the building at
Braida, Serra di Vaglio
second quarter 6th cent. B.C.
Potenza, Museo
Archeologico Provinciale
Cat. 150

Corinthian type bronze helmet
from Chiaromonte, Tomb 170
6th cent. B.C.
Policoro, Museo
Nazionale della Siritide
Cat. 115

in gold. Overall, therefore, the tomb involves a set of personalities of such high rank that one might even bracket them as "kingly", though in the rather limited sense that such a term can have in the context of these somewhat diminutive and relatively sparsely peopled Italic communities. In any case, the deceased were in a position to engage Greek craftsmen, performing the role of patrons rather than clients or beneficiaries of gifts of luxury products, albeit made in series.

The transitional phase from Late Archaic to Classical was also a period that marks a veritable leap in the acculturation process in terms of ideology and religion; how closely the two phenomena are related is conveyed by the *Life of Pythagoras* by Porphyry, knowledgeably discussed by Alfonso Mele, who points out the inclusion of *basileis* and *dynastai*, native kings and lords, among the scholar's many followers.

There is ample evidence relative to this and similar transformations in practices and attitudes, particularly in the tombs of the "emerging" classes in the northeast area of the region.

They stand out for their exterior structure (with solutions ranging from the large wooden "chambers" of Ruvo del Monte to the structures of Pisciolo di Melfi, where a stone coffin for the corpse and a single ritual urn were found alongside a ditch-repository, and the deep pits of Lavello) as well as the makeup and ritual aspects of their assemblages, just as varied, but in any case always aimed at giving the deceased an aura of great distinction. With the males, apart from the interest of the symposiac practices, evolutive with respect to the Archaic banquet, the abandonment of the military theme is common to both Ruvo del Monte and Pisciolo di Melfi. In the latter, the male occupant is provided with a two-wheeled chariot, perhaps more closely linked to a ceremonial procedure than to a method of combat, and above all a spectacular series of jewels, nearly identical to those of his companion.

Such changes are not found at Lavello, probably because of the specific circumstances in that part of the native world. Here, even though the emphasis remains on the warrior status (now expressed through a post-hoplitic panoply), objects related to the *paideia* (flute, strigil) were added, as well as, and especially, a full-blown sacrificial set (in bronze and silver), with a spoon (probably for honey) and *phialai* clearly of eastern Greek origin, possibly descended from some Archaic jewelry of Chiaromonte.

As yet another burial suggests, this kind of privilege was extended to some female members of the local society, who were provided with all that was needed for slaughtering, roasting and boiling meat and serving wine. In all probability, such gear should be seen in relation to the role of *mater familias* built up around the sphere of the *hestia*, the domestic hearth, at the center of the family nucleus (*oikos*) where

Figured amber
with satyr and maenad
500-480 B.C.
London, British Museum
Department of Greek
and Roman Antiquities
Cat. 107

Grave jewels from Tomb 102
at Braida di Vaglio
ca. end 6th cent. B.C.
Potenza, Soprintendenza
Archeologica della Basilicata
Cat. 106

women were viewed as competent and independent members of society, an outlook that is unusual in Magna Graecia.

On the other hand, this same assemblage shows such a striking resemblance to the sequence of the Etruscan pictorial cycle in the Golini I hypogeum at Volsinii (Orvieto) illustrating the preparation and celebration of a banquet in the next world before the infernal royal couple Hades-Persephone as to suggest that the custom of banqueting had also taken on symbolic and allusive values within the context of eschatological concerns, perhaps, as mentioned, accepted by this elite in the perspective of a direct link between social privilege and "hope of salvation."

A very similar attitude turns up again at Ruvo, where the myth of Eos (Aurora), who stole away a young lover, carrying him off to an otherworldly dimension, is depicted on the krater of the male burial and on the bronze candelabrum of the female one. Likewise, at Serra di Vaglio the burial goods included a krater with the same subject alongside a reproduction of the panther sacred to Dionysus and a doll with jointed limbs, one of the toys which, according to the Orphic doctrine, the Titans used to beguile and capture the infant god. The probable purpose of the latter to indicate the infant condition does not in fact cancel its religious value conferred through a "talking" symbology in the climate generally favorable to the worship of Dionysus that existed throughout Magna Graecia (bear in mind the chorus of Sophocles' *Antigone* [1118 s.] that invokes the "protector of illustrious Italy").

The specific link between Dionysus and the infant condition is moreover testified to in a grave at nearby Bantia (Banzi). This burial demonstrates the adoption of the specific funerary custom linked to the celebration of the festivals of the *Anthesteria*, documented by the adoption of the small sacred *chous* of Attic manufacture.

In terms of settlement structures, decisive clues are once again quite scarce. It is possible that there existed a harmony of an isonomic kind among the elite groups, foreshadowing a more political form of organization, in which the exercising of power is entrusted to "republican" magistracies that appropriately express the structure. By isonomic we mean a form of supremacy of one or more among the various aristocratic nuclei. Our deduction hinges upon the evidence provided at Serra di Vaglio (where the Late Archaic residential area seems to be at least in part made up of a series of houses fitted out with Greek architectonic terra-cottas and organized around a more important structure) and at Lavello (where there are two examples of the same kind of "palace").

All the above-mentioned examples belong to the transition period between the fifth and fourth centuries B.C. Thus, they foreshadow the deep innovation in most of southern Italy that came with the migration of the Samnite peoples from the highlands of the central Apennines toward the coastal stretches opposite, within the context of ethnogenic processes that came to involve some of the already-resident Italic peoples and led to the formation of the Lucanian alliance.

The Impact of the Greek Colonies on the Indigenous Peoples of Lucania

Pair of gold braid fasteners
from Tomb 43
at Pisciolo di Melfi
5th cent. B.C.
Melfi
Museo Nazionale del Melfese
Cat. 110

Gold necklace
from Tomb 955 at Lavello
end 5th cent. B.C.
Matera
Museo Nazionale "D. Ridola"
Cat. 108

Pair of Daunian-style
Attic red-figure jugs
450-440 B.C.
Malibu, Collection
of the J. Paul Getty Museum
Gift of Malcolm Wiener
Cat. 143/I

On a "civic" level, this phenomenon had very important consequences, all colored by a radical modernization, the widespread adoption of Greek technology, practices, and behavior.
The final "model," therefore, is one of ethnic and political self-awareness, and shows how the peoples of Lucania took advantage of Greek culture. The Lucani were very far, for example, from the Celts who, having invaded the Po Valley part of Etruria, destroyed its urban structures; they kept alive Poseidonia (Paestum), conquered in about 420 B.C., and set up Laus according to an urban plan that was perfectly Greek; they adopted a monetary economy and introduced the official use of the language written in an alphabet derived from the Greek one of the Tarentine-Ionian type.
In the hinterland, where cities continued to be absent, although most of the population lived on simple farms (these, too, modeled on Greek schemes), a few settlements instead sprang up that were endowed with massive wall enclosures similar to those erected to protect a network of highland centers functioning as refuges and military strongholds. Such settlements were perfectly abreast of the Greek military technology of the time.
Thanks precisely to the use of written language, documented by the phrase ἐπὶ τῆς Νυμμέλου ἀρχῆς, *epi tes Nymmelou arches* (under the legitimate authority of *Nymmelos*), carved in a block of the wall of "new" Serra di Vaglio, as well as the epigraph found at the back of the fortress of Raia San Basile near Muro Lucano ("*maio arrio in hi meddikio*"), we can see how the construction or successive maintenance of these structures were the fruit of the activity of a magistrate (called in the second case by the typical Oscan name *meddix*), within the context of what must be defined a genuine union of states. In confirmation of this, Strabo (VI. 1. 3) recalls how the *basileus*, supreme chief of the entire Lucanian *nomen* in war, was chosen from among those who practiced *archai* (even if in all likelihood they still also belonged to that branch of *familiae illustres* from which Livy (VIII. 24. 4) informs us Alexander took 300 Messapian, Bruttian, and Lucanian hostages in 333 B.C. It is clear that we are now in the presence of entities furnished with *nomoi* and *politeiai*, laws and stable political and legal orders; in a complete reversal of the perspective, they now became the object of an ideological and philosophical consideration by the Greek *poleis* that was anything but disinterested, and came along with a new awareness – especially after the violent end of the war of 390–389 B.C. (Diodorus Siculus, XIV. 100–102) – of the mortal danger that these *barbaroi* could represent, the same *barbaroi* that archaeologists can point out as the protagonists of a perfectly successful process of Hellenization.

Bibliography
E. GRECO, *Archeologia della Magna Grecia*, 1992, with complete previous bibliography; the reference to the study by A. Mele regards "Il pitagorismo e le popolazioni anelleniche d'Italia", in *Annali del seminario di studi del mondo classico. Archeologia e storia antica* (= *AION ArchStAnt*), III, 1981, pp. 61 ff.

Ettore M. de Juliis   The Impact of the Greek Colonies on the Indigenous Peoples of Apulia

The impact of the Greek colonies on the indigenous peoples of Apulia cannot be described as having taken place in a single, precise episode, not even during the initial phase. It occurred over different periods and in different ways, in relation to the ethnic group affected. Nor should the phase of "precolonial" contacts be overlooked, even if we limit it to the historical phase of Greek colonization. In any case, before discussing this more recent phase, it should be mentioned at least in passing that when the Mycenaean ships started plying the coasts of southern Italy in the last centuries of the second millennium B.C., they must have brought the first cultural stimuli of a Hellenic type to the peoples of the Italic peninsula. This may be seen both in certain aspects of crafts techniques (refined pottery with painted decorations) and in the religious sphere, where the main Greek gods became known and associated with the indigenous ones. The memory of such contacts, which found its way into Hellenic legend – where the West is the setting for many of the exploits of demigods and heroes – must have made the Italic barbarians less strange in the eyes of the historic-age Greeks, thus easing somewhat the renewal of relations after the crisis of the Hellenic "Middle Ages". Concrete proof of these resumed contacts is offered by fragments of Greek pottery in some sites of the Salentine Peninsula, especially along the coast, which was the first landing point on the westward trade route. The fragments dating from between the end of the ninth and the first half of the eighth century B.C. are rare and they belong to the Corinthian and, to a lesser degree, Euboean and Cycladic pottery styles (*oinochoai, skyphoi, protokotylai*, to which may be added the large containers for shipping, such as large *amphorae, hydriai*, and *pithoi*). These have been found in the Iapygian settlements of Otranto and Porto Cesareo. This initial phase, which preceded the foundation of all the Greek colonies in Italy and Sicily, was followed by a much better documented one in the second half of the eighth century, contemporary to the earliest colonies, which culminated in the foundation of Taras (Tarentum) in the Iapygian territory at the close of the same century. This second phase is marked by fine pottery tableware from Corinth (*Aetos 666*-type *kotylai*, Thapsos-type *skyphoi* with panel and early proto-Corinthian vessels), as well as shipping vessels, especially in the coastal sites of Otranto and Satyrion (Porto Saturo), but also in such inland sites and Vaste, Cavallino, Muro Leccese, Valesio, and Monte Sannace. The Hellenic influences discussed thus far were a distinctly local phenomenon, where they represented the exotic or prestigious element for the dominant group in the respective native communities. The natives of Apulia were the Iapygi, divided into the three tribal groups, proceeding from south to north, of the Messapii (or Calabrians and Salentinians), the Peucetii (or Pediculi) and the Daunii. For a better understanding of the scope and forms that Greek colonization assumed in Apulia it is necessary at this point to describe the main features of the Early Iron-Age Iapygian culture which the Greeks encountered and later became part of when they founded Taras.

The Iapygian settlements of this period vary according to whether they are located on the coast, in the plains, or in the hills of the interior. The former are compact, converging around naturally defended sites, that is, on points of land that stretch into the sea or lacunar areas. The plains settlements, instead, occupy large areas with scattered groups of huts and tombs that are linked to a gathering point easier to defend in the face of danger. In the absence of such a possibility, the defense of the settlement or part of it was probably entrusted to simple palisades and ditches. The dwellings themselves were oval-plan or round huts with walls and roofs made of branches or reeds supported by posts and waterproofed by layers of clay. In south-central Apulia this kind of hut has a low dry stone wall around the perimeter of the base. Closely linked to the nuclei of huts and therefore inside the settlement are the cemeteries, which throughout the region are of the inhumation type with the corpse laid on its side and arms and legs bent. By far the most common type of grave is the ditch kind; next comes the tumulus type, especially in central Apulia. For infants, burial was in urns (*enchytrismos*). The grave goods consisted of metal objects and clay vessels. *Fibulae* have been found in abundance, including the kinds commonly unearthed in southern Italic cemeteries (the serpentine bow, the so-called Sicilian and the two-piece types), as well as others typical of the Adriatic area, such as the double-spiral kind (the so-called eye-glass *fibulae*) in a number of variations. The small figured bronze pieces, both in plate and cast, have similar origins and were found primarily in the northern area; these are in no way inferior either in terms of technique or style to contemporary Hellenic specimens. The same may be said of the small terra-cotta figures and the painted pottery. The latter dates from the final phase of the Bronze Age and is characterized by globe or biconical shapes modeled without the help of the wheel and decorated with mat brown-black geometric motifs against the pale ground of the vase in a style known as "Iapygian Geometric." Starting in the eighth century, the shape and decorations of the pottery made in the north took on a distinct form known as "Proto-Daunian Geometric." In the second half of the same century, both styles show the influence of Late Geometric Corinthian pottery – which had in the meantime become fairly common in the Iapygian territory – from which they adopted many geometric motifs. Proto-Daunian pottery became common well outside the area of its production, in Campania and along the Adriatic (Picenum, Dalmatia, and Istria), reaching as far as Slovenia.

Biconical Iapygian pot
with geometric decoration
from Cavallino
first half 7th cent. B.C.
Lecce, Museo Provinciale
"Sigismondo Castromediano"

Small imitation Corinthian
Iapygian pot
with geometric decoration
from Cavallino
first half 7th cent. B.C.
Lecce, Museo Provinciale
"Sigismondo Castromediano"

Moving on to observations of a more general nature, it is certain that the most widespread and substantial source of wealth for the Iapygian peoples was agriculture, supplemented by animal husbandry. Crafts, too, were fairly well developed and must have satisfied the needs of the internal market, permitting a remarkable and lasting autonomy. This, however, did not stand in the way of relations and forms of exchange with other peoples, already long before the arrival of the Greek colonists in the region, for example, Daunian contacts with the peoples of Campania and the Adriatic area or those of the Messapii with the Epirus region and Greece itself. In this period the Iapygian peoples do not appear to have been broken down into social classes; the archaeological documentation instead seems to show socially undifferentiated groups, led by chieftains. Therefore, the community's economic surplus was used by the chieftain and his family to purchase prestige goods that exalted his position of importance within his sphere of belonging. The picture of the Iapygian culture that results from the description thus far helps to answer a longstanding question, that is, why Greek colonies were absent in Apulia except for Taras (Tarentum), founded in a not earlier phase and on the fringe of that territory. It is true, but only in part, that the quest for metals would have driven the first Greek navigators to the Tyrrhenian shores of the peninsula, rather than to the Adriatic. But this argument does not hold water for the colonies interested in populating and exploiting the agricultural resources of new territories. In fact, the proximity of Apulia to the areas of origin and the fertility of its plains should have in any case attracted the interest of the first Greek colonists. If this did not occur, there must have been other reasons: the dense and widespread population in the Iapygian territory, the links that the indigenous populations maintained among themselves and with other groups and the control of the seas by Illyrian as well as, presumably, Iapygian "pirates." Finally, the high level of civilization attained by the indigenous peoples of Apulia must have contributed in a determining way to discouraging Greek colonization in this region.

This cultural setting provided the backdrop for an event rich in consequences: the occupation of the Tarentine area by Spartan colonists. This was undertaken on the advice of the Delphic oracle, which is said to have answered the *oikistes* or Greek colonial expedition chief Phalanthus thus: "I will give you Satyrion and I will even let you inhabit the rich town of Taras and become the scourge of the Iapygi" (Strabo, VI. 3. 2). The arrival of the Spartans is traditionally dated 706 B.C., when life in the two thriving Iapygian villages – one on the Tarentine peninsula and the other, Satyrion, a few kilometers south of Taras, on the coast – was interrupted and destroyed. After occupying the most important harbor in the gulf, the Spartans must have immediately moved to conquer the surrounding territory, indispensable for the survival of the new city, seizing it, just as the oracle had foreseen, from the Iapygi who were forced to retreat to the interior. Archaeological proof of the immediate occupation of the hinterland by the Tarentines to the detriment of the Iapygi is offered by the recent discovery at L'Amastuola (near Crispiano) of a Greek-type settlement from the first half of the seventh century, which lies immediately over a Iapygian village of huts. A possible, further westward expansion by the Tarentines was checked during the second half of the seventh century by the founding of Metapontum, promoted for this purpose by Sybaris.

The founding of Taras (Tarentum) marks the start of the encounter and clash between the Hellenic and Iapygian cultures. The latter, however, lost its compactness and began to separate into its three main regions: Messapia, Peucetia, and Daunia. Both the independent development of the three ethnic groups and the intensity of their relations with the Greek world – highest in the Salentine area and lowest in faraway Daunia – must have contributed to this phenomenon. In fact, for the entire Archaic period, notwithstanding continual military clashes, various aspects of the Greek civilization penetrated the entire Messapio-Peucetian world. This came to a halt in 473 B.C., the year traditionally assigned to the harsh defeat suffered by Tarentum and Rhegium at the hands of the allied forces of the Messapii and Peucetii. From that moment, relations between Tarentum and the non-Hellenic populations of Apulia entered into a deep crisis that lasted about fifty years before a new and definitive wave of Hellenic colonization. During the Archaic period, however, a few fundamental traits of Greek civilization were passed on once and for all to the indigenous peoples and in many cases completely replaced the original ones. Here, we can only mention them in passing, while pointing out how difficult it is to find archaeological confirmation of changes in the spiritual sphere. One thing that the Iapygi clearly adopted from the Greek world may be seen in the private buildings, with the abandonment of the wattle-and-daub huts and the introduction of houses with a regular floor plan, composed of a drystone base and mudbrick walls, and roofed in clay tiles. Even the well-established native pottery craft yielded to the Greek influence, at first only at a technical level, with the introduction of the wheel, and later at a stylistic level, with the production of pottery decorated with bands, a commonly used motif, and in a rather unsuccessful attempt, brown-figure vases. Such innovations appeared early on in Messapia and, through contacts with Metapontum across the Bradano Valley, in Peucetia; they came rather late to Daunia and were restricted to the Ofanto River area.

Bronze statue of Zeus
from Ugento
ca. 500 B.C.
Taranto, Museo Nazionale
Cat. 77

Proto-Lucanian red-figure *hydria*
by the Amykos Painter
430-400 B.C.
Naples
Museo Archeologico Nazionale

The urban plan adopted early on in Cavallino still seems to be an isolated case and has been subject to various reconstructions. It evolved between the mid-sixth and the first twenty-five years of the fifth century and was interrupted when the crisis broke out between the Iapygi and Tarentines. In other sites, as at Monte Sannace, Greek-type buildings have been found, but their distribution lacks any principle of urban planning. As early as the Archaic phase, but especially in the period that followed, the Greek model was adopted for the construction of urban fortifications, often made of regular courses of hewn stones. Moving on to the sphere of religion and cults of worship, it is certain that the identities of the native deities and the Greek ones soon merged, as shown by the existence of such mixed sanctuaries as Monte Papalucio, near Oria. There are also examples of figures of deities with Greek features worshipped in native sites, such as the famous bronze statue of Zeus found in the Messapian community of Ugento and almost certainly made in Tarentum. Worthy of particular attention is the diffusion, especially in the Salento area, of inscriptions in the Messapian language, thanks to the adoption of an Archaic-period Laconio-Tarentine alphabet starting in the second half of the sixth century. And although initially limited to the aristocracy, the Greek practice of the *symposion* enjoyed great favor, as evidenced by the pottery and metal utensils found in the richest funerary assemblages. Similarly, a typical custom of the Hellenic *paidea* – that is, the practice of attending the *gymnasion* – is documented early on in a rich painted grave at Ugento from the end of the sixth century.

During the fifty years' crisis between Tarentum and the non-Hellenic populations of Apulia, the latter intensified their relations with other Greeks, that is, those who had settled at Metapontum on the Bradano and the Athenians along the Adriatic coast. This situation began to change in a decisive way during the last

Proto-Apulian red-figure krater
end 5th-early decades 4th cent. B.C.
Taranto, Museo Nazionale
Cat. 197

thirty years of the fifth century, after the war between Thurii and Tarentum, which ended in favor of the latter, and after the foundation of Heraclea in 433–32 B.C., which closed off Metapontum on the western shore. In fact, Metapontum's firmly held leading role in relations with the native centers of Peucetia and southern Daunia during the middle decades of the fifth century was gradually taken over by its old rival, Tarentum. By the second quarter of the fourth century B.C., this process was complete as confirmed by an examination of the red-figure pottery produced in the two centers and imported into the Daunio-Peucetian territory. A similar phenomenon may be noted along the Adriatic coast, where toward the close of the fifth century products from Athens had already became scarce as an obvious consequence of the disastrous end of the Peloponnesian War. The political and military importance of Tarentum during the fourth century, when it was also the chief city of the Italiot League, makes this city the true protagonist of the deep and definitive Hellenization of the Apulian territory. This phenomenon embraces all of the fourth century and the first decades of the following one, until the defeat the Tarentines suffered in the war with the Romans, that is, until the start of the later process of Romanization. The most obvious feature of this new phase of Hellenization consists in the northward expansion of some of the Hellenic cultural influences that had already been absorbed in the Archaic phase by the native centers of central-southern Apulia. This may be seen in certain technological innovations, such as the introduction of the pottery wheel, as well as in the acquisition, at less and less exclusively elitist levels, of a Greek ideology, as reflected, for example, by the practice of the *symposion* and the *gymnasion*. An identical transformation may be seen in the sphere of religious beliefs and funeral rites, not always easy to interpret. And in a different, though no less important sphere, that of the

Manduria
remains of the Messapic walls

Limestone *stele*
with Messapic inscription
from Cavallino
second half 6th cent. B.C.
Taranto, Museo Nazionale

martial arts, the Hellenic example, tested countless times in combat, must have been powerful and determinant for the native populations, which, with the acquisition of hoplite weaponry and with the strategic use of the cavalry, could compete on equal terms with the armies of the Italiot cities. Similarly, there was a marked improvement in urban fortification, which intensified during this era of political instability; perhaps thanks to the direct involvement of Greek architects, the most advanced construction techniques and devices of Hellenic siege machinery were adopted. The diffusion of powerful urban fortifications makes up the cause and effect of the definitive acquisition by the non-Hellenic populations of the Greek urban settlement model and the general abandonment of the vicano-village mode of occupying the territory, which had been typical of the Iapygian peoples from the very outset. Finally, a veritable *koine* took shape in crafts production, where there was a shift from a stage in which the native elite demanded of the Italiot and Greek craftsmen refined workmanship in metals, stone, gold, and pottery to one in which the same objects were made directly by the various indigenous centers after Italiot craftsmen had established local workshops. This phenomenon has been clearly identified in the area of Apulian figured pottery, where the more recent products – characteristic among which are the vessels of monumental size – have been attributed to such centers of northern Apulia as Canosa and Arpi. But at some earlier stage the vast diffusion of figured vessels must have been a powerful vehicle for Greek culture, as it carried with it, in addition to the objects as such, and the use for which they were made, infinite representations of gods, demigods and heroes of Greek religion and mythology. Thanks to these contacts, the non-Hellenic peoples became familiar with the rites, customs and theatrical representations – including the *phlyakes*, or burlesques, which were brought to literary respectability by Rhinthon right in Tarentum during the city's final phase of independence and found new vitality in Rome with the evolution of the *Atellanae fabulae* and the Plautine comedy.

Bibliography
D. YNTEMA, in *Studi di Antichità 3*, 1982, pp. 83-131; F. D'ANDRIA, in *Forme di contatto...*, *Atti del convegno di Cortona (24-30 May 1981)*, 1983, pp. 287-295; E.M. DE JULIIS, *I popoli della Puglia...*, in *Magna Grecia-Prolegomeni*, vol. I, 1985, pp. 145-188; idem, *Gli Iapigi...*, 1988; idem, *L'origine...*, in *Italia omnium terrarum alumna*, 1988, pp. 591-650; F. D'ANDRIA, ibidem, pp. 651-715.

Pier Giovanni Guzzo

The Greeks in the Po Valley

The Adige River forms a dividing line – and a link – between two aspects of material culture during the Bronze Age: in fact, Mycenaean ceramics have been found along this line.

The northern Bronze Age culture, which was notable for its vitality, was part of a central European network. The "Mycenaean" finds in the Po Valley have been ascribed to "diffuse trade" (that is, they formed part of a series of exchanges between partners who were different on each occasion), not to the actual presence of Mycenaean seafarers. This model seems to correspond closely to what we know of this ancient world, both because of the analogy with what Herodotus (IV. 31–33) states with regard to the offerings that the Hyperboreans made to the Apollo of Delos, and to the fact that, in the find-places, there does not appear to be any significant variation in the tendencies that have already been noted that can be related to an external stimulus. Moreover, as further confirmation of this, the end of the hypothetical Mycenaean presence did not cause any changes: the links with the European cultures continued without traumas after the Palace culture had collapsed.

The suggested lack of direct links between the Po Valley and the Mycenaean world, on the one hand, and the lack of interest on the part of the inhabitants of the Po Valley in having direct relations with the Mycenaeans, on the other, would justify the mythical aura surrounding the origin of amber as related in the oldest Greek sources and the variety of sites that are mentioned. The notable similarities between the comb found at Frattesina Polesine and the one from Enkomi (Cyprus) do not seem to be sufficient to modify the working hypothesis: the link was formed in the opposite direction to that followed by the raw material, as in the case of the mold of a finned ax from the "Oil Merchant's" House at Mycenae, without the producers having direct relations. Furthermore, the pottery from Lefkandi and Khaniá seems to form part of the normal European commerce between the Po Valley and the Greek Peninsula.

The fact that the Etruscans controlled the territory north of the Apennines is demonstrated by the erection and inscription of the *cippi* found at Rubiera, probably before the end of the seventh century B.C. Although they are unique, these *cippi* attest to the precise toponyms, the magistratures, and the settling of families. The origin of the people who settled the northern regions is still in debate, as are the routes they took across the Apennines and the nature of the relations between the Etruscans and the Umbrians on the Adriatic side. The latter are particularly important because they were one of the links in the "Adriatic chain." Nonetheless, whichever hypothesis may be preferred, there is no doubt that the Etruscans controlled the territory north of the Apennines. In fact, the problems of interpreting the production ascribed to the Orientalizing period of the Felsina (Bologna) area should all be seen in relation to those linked to the similar stage in the Orientalizing period known to have occurred in Etruria. The same applies to the less distinct sphere of the Venetic Orientalizing period, to the prolonged production of *situlae*, and the figure-painted transalpine artifacts. These were all derivations, which progressively became more distant, of Etrurian influences and models: this is demonstrated by, for instance, the tripod from Vetulonia found in Tomb 49 in the Pelà necropolis at Este, which, as far as is known, did not have any equivalent of oriental origin. The organization of the territory north of the Apennines also required the control of the oldest routes across the Po Valley and the Alps; these led to the mouth of the Po, where trade with the Adriatic took place.

The development of navigation in the river mouths, including those on the Adriatic (see Herodotus, I. 163), and the foundation of Massalia (Marseilles), with its rapid development, appear to be the main reasons, essentially external in nature, that induced the northern Etruscans to set up the trading settlement (*emporion*) of Spina. Although it is clear that the sea obtained its name from Adria and not Spina, there is a lack of archaeological evidence associated with the chronological layer providing confirmation of the origin of the name. It appears, therefore, to be more appropriate here to employ the abstract model of the trading settlement, applying it to the whole of the Po Delta, and omitting a detailed analysis of what we know – much or little as the case may be – with regard to individual sites.

Through the trading settlement of the delta, the northern Etruscans (during the Archaic period they controlled the whole of it) now came into direct contact with the Greek seafarers. But independent enterprises, such as those of the Aeginetans, were no longer tolerated. For the Greeks who reached the well-regulated trading settlement, it was the threshold to a new world, and this was rationalized according to the models of the epic and the myth. That the trading settlement acted as a filter with regard to undesired independent activity on the part of the Greeks is demonstrated by the continuous flow of Etruscan goods that crossed the Alps in the direction of the German "princes." Moreover, this contention is not modified by the fact that there were Greek goods as well: the older northern alphabets derived from the Etruscan one, not the Greek one. The *symposion*, and its furnishings, are no longer uniquely Greek, as they had been assimilated long before by the Etruscans, whether in Etruria or in the Po Valley. On a belt-hook from Carceri, Este, there is the representation of an Atestine at a *symposion* while a woman offers him a *kylix*. It

Bronze tripod
made in Vetulonia
from Tomb 49
at Pelà di Este
7th cent, B.C.
Este, Museo Atestino

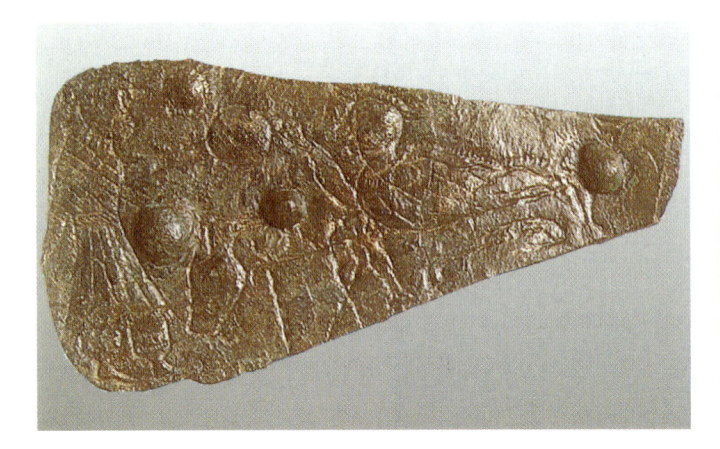

Bronze clasp of a belt
with scene of a symposium
from the Carceri d'Este
necropolis
first half 5th cent B.C.
Este, Museo Atestino

Incised bronze cup
with the earliest inscription
in the Venetic language
first half 6th cent. B.C.
Este, Museo Atestino

was the Etruscans, in fact, who allowed women to take part in the entertaining, while the man's clothes and cap are typically northern. In any case, he is not wearing a wreath. Further evidence of Etruscan predominance in the acculturation of the Po Valley is provided by what is believed to be the oldest Venetic votive inscription found so far, because of the derivation of the alphabet used, as well as the shape of the vessel on which it is engraved. The exchange of goods between the Greeks and Etruscans included a wide variety of objects, but the filter of the delta trading settlement divided the carriers into two groups. As far as the delta there were many of them: Greeks and Apulians, for instance. But they were not allowed to go beyond. Similarly, in a later period, Strabo recorded that the Illyrians put wine into wooden barrels after it had been unloaded at Aquileia, which was, once again, described as an *emporion* (V. 1. 8).

In the delta, Spina seems to have played a dominant role, as is shown by the building of a treasury (*thesauros*) at Delphi (Strabo, V. 1. 7). From its title, which contains a specific mention of the inhabitants of Spina (Strabo, IX. 3. 8), it has been deduced that the trading settlement was independent of Felsina. The latter is called *princeps Etruriae*, and even though too little is known about the organization of political power in northern Etruria, it is likely that it had responsibilities outside its own territory, so that, for instance, it may have controlled Spina on behalf of all the twelve city-states. And if the proposed model corresponds with reality, the *emporion* must have comprised all the ports of the delta, as is demonstrated by the archaeological finds in the area (this is now divided between the regions of Emilia-Romagna and Veneto). On the other hand, the independence of the title to the treasury tends to stress what the Greeks were already aware of, probably more than in the case of other equally efficient ports, without there being any mention of the control over Spina by other political entities. This was evidently an unnecessary element in its trade relations with areas outside its territory and was of no interest to travelers. In fact, that the independence indicated by the title of the treasury was only apparent may be inferred not only from comparisons with Gravisca, but also from Strabo (IX. 3. 8), where the annotation *ton peri ton Adrian* (i.e., on the coast of the Adriatic Sea) has been added to the ethnic. As far as we know, there was only one Spina in antiquity: the geographical information seems, therefore, to indicate that the whole of the upper Adriatic, and not just Spina, had participated (or wanted to participate) in the construction of the treasury.

The modern area of Romagna can be considered to form part of the Po Valley, both from a geographical point of view and also because it is a vital link in the chain of trade relations in the Adriatic area. It has been ascertained that it was culturally influenced by the Umbrians in the Archaic period. And on a Middle-Corinthian krater there is a figure defined with this ethnic, confirming that they were on familiar terms. This archaeological evidence precedes the attempt made by the Etruscans living on the Adriatic, together with the Umbrians, Daunii, and others, to seize Cumae (Dionysius of Halicarnassus, VII. 3). While the Corinthian inscription is evidence of direct knowledge, the expedition against the Cumaeans shows that this direct knowledge was no longer generally accepted. And, given the chronological layer of the expedition, its concurrence with the presumed initial stage of the building of the delta trading settlement is not at all surprising.

One might well ask why the Etruscans decided to attack Cumae. In fact, a reasonable explanation has recently been offered – namely that Cumae vied for trade with the Etruscan cities on the Tyrrhenian, with whom the Etruscans on the Adriatic were allied – and it hardly seems necessary to add anything to this, apart from the observation that the Etruscans living in the Po Valley gave a show of solidarity on this occasion (this was, of course, in their own interest) with the Etruscans living in Etruria. And the latter included the inhabitants of Caere and Vulci, whose products were distributed toward the north. Once the trading settlement had been set up on the Po Delta, the ports along the coast controlled by the Umbrians must have ceased to have their previous function for the seafarers, who would have been obliged to head directly for the Po Delta by the aggressive Etruscan privateers, ably commanded by important personages. Nonetheless, in the course of time there has been a steady rise in the number of Greek finds in Romagna, in parallel with the increase that has occurred in the whole of the Adriatic area. The operative range of the Etruscan privateers is probably demonstrated by the archaeological finds from the Archaic and Classical periods on the Picene coast. Here, judging by the finds, the seafarers were free to come ashore and trade, and, in this respect, they were favored by the lack of a political structure in the Picene villages.

The particular interest of the role played by Spina in the relations between Greeks and Etruscans lies in the evidence of Hellenic cultural traits in this trading settlement, rather than in the abundance of the imports. Although the huge bowl by the Penthesilea Painter, from Tomb 18 C VT, still represents "barbarian" ostentation of the function of intermediary that the owner performed, there are sporadic examples of white-ground *lekythoi*, a type of funerary vase, and, in the course of time, figure-decorated *choai*. With regard to the latter, mention should be made of those of Italiot manufacture; their presence was not fortuitous, but evidently, in order to meet demand, imitations were required when it was not possible to obtain them from the original source.

It has already been pointed out that the rapid fall in the output of figure-decorated pottery in Athens in the last quarter of the fifth century had only a minimal affect on the volume of imports arriving at Spina. Even when Dionysius the Elder began to control the Adriatic there was not a sudden upheaval in this area, to judge by the archaeological finds. It is my opinion that these more recent events demonstrate the validity of the interpretative model that has been employed previously. So long as there was a need for trade with areas outside the Po Valley, whoever the carriers might be, the trading settlement on the delta continued to perform this function, to its own benefit.

Another confirmation of the validity of this model, and the fact that the trading settlement cannot be limited to a single site, is constituted by the colonization of Adria by the Syracusan tyrant Dionysius. His aim was evidently that of participating in the trade in the delta, and, judging from the availability of mules, this had excellent results. But, if we proceed from the economic implications to the political ones, the colonization by Dionysius, seen together with other events, assumes an aspect that is explicitly anti-Etruscan and, probably, anti-Athenian. Within the same area, Dionysius in fact encouraged competition between the ports of Adria and Spina. However, his attempt does not appear to have been wholly successful, despite the favorable accounts disseminated in the fields of hydraulics and mythology. Besides the relative brevity of Dionysius' political endeavors – these were not continued by his son, who withdrew to Apulia – the cause of this defeat lies in the importance that Spina had now assumed in its hinterland, which was, generally speaking, still controlled by the northern Etruscans.

Red-figure cup
with the rape of Ganymede
attributed to
the Pentesilea Painter
from Spina
5th cent. B.C.
Ferrara, Museo Nazionale

Detail of red-figure vase
attributed to the Master
of the Berlin amphora
from Spina
ca. 490 B.C.
Ferrara, Museo Nazionale

Red-figure *oinochoe*
from Spina
ca. 430 B.C.
Ferrara, Museo Nazionale

The Etruscan dominion was, however, now coming to an end: this was due to the expansion of the Celts in the north and the attacks of the Romans in the south. The production of pottery in the upper Adriatic tended to display the mark of southern Etruscan influences rather than direct Italiot ones. Thus, a single "banqueter," which shows possible Tarentine influences, even though it is made of local clay, is countered by the more recent terra-cottas of Spina, which are difficult to relate to specific cultural areas. The imports of vessels overpainted in white have been considered to be of Italiot origin, but this does not necessarily mean that the tin and silver *paterae* with the apotheosis of Heracles are Italiot, given their similarity to the output of Volterra and Cales. The resumption of north Etruscan piracy in the Adriatic in the last quarter of the fourth century seems to have signaled the beginning of the end of the commercial role of the delta. The Gauls of Picenum were in contact with the Greeks, as is demonstrated by a number of finds of jewelry in their respective necropolises. On the other hand, the relatively few jewels found at Spina continued to reflect the Etruscan tradition, although they had independent characteristics, and did not indulge in direct acquisition. As a result of the progressive decline of the peaceful trading settlement, the Etruscans turned to piracy in a desperate attempt to maintain the standard of living that they had previously reached.

If the above hypothesis corresponds to reality, after the decline of the delta ports Greek products were no longer distributed directly to the interior. However, the only commodity that it is possible to follow over an extended period is wine, which was transported in Greco-Italic containers.

Nonetheless, the upheavals in the overall political balance of ancient Italy that took place in the third century do not appear to have left any archaeological evidence that will substantiate this contention. At the end of the century, a hoard of coins at Castelfranco Emilia was sealed up; this consisted mainly of Syracusan issues in the period from 345 to 210 B.C., together with Carthaginian and Campanian coins. In my opinion, the find is not so much a sign of the "Adriatic expansionism of the Syracusan tyrants" as the rich booty of a participant in this campaign who had survived the war – or might this soldier even have taken part in the capture of Syracuse under Marcellus?

Should this not have been the case, an explanation would have to be found both for this long-lasting fidelity to Syracusan commercial outlets (as we have seen, these were not so enduring in the northern Adriatic) and also for the overall composition of the hoard. With regard to the latter, while the presence of Carthaginian coins may be ascribed to Hannibal's invasion, it is more difficult to account for coins from either Acragas or Suessa Aurunca at Castelfranco Emilia.

However, it was not before the time of Julius Caesar that there was a significant Greek presence in northern Italy. In fact, he included five hundred Greeks among the five thousand new settlers that he transferred to Comum (Como) in order to reinforce the old colony there. "He also granted citizenship to them and he enrolled them in the list of citizens, and not only did they settle there, but they also gave the colony its name, because all the inhabitants were called Neocometi, which translated into Latin means Novum Comum" (Strabo V. 1. 6). And Catullus of Comum was the best-known example of a *neoteros* poet.

Pier Giovanni Guzzo   The Encounter with the Bruttii

The Greeks were certainly not new to encounters with barbarians in the West. These included, for example: the fraudulent oath with the Sicels surrounding what was to be Locri; the genuine agreement with King Hyblon of the future city of Megara Hyblaea; the forays against the natives living on the heights overlooking the Strait of Messina; the dealings, whether there was a pecuniary element or not, with the Oenotrians in order to obtain the foundation of Elea (Greek Hyele).

The encounter with the Bruttii (or Bruttii) followed the ones that have just been mentioned, which, for the Greeks, were their first contacts and their first settlements; the chronological diversity also led to a diversity of the nature of the relationship. The dynamic thrust that characterized the earliest period of the settlers in the west – at times theirs was the desperation of the disinherited, inducing them to become the "torment of the Iapygi," for instance – was now countered by a peaceful reaction that neither the weak, unstable alliances within the Italiot League, nor the short-lived charisma of Architas of Tarentum were able to withstand.

In the fourth century B.C. the Italiots were well-established, with a solidly structured society: the "reaction" was also a gradual decline, based on production and culture, which was, however, very different from that of the Italics. But the changed balance of power in the Mediterranean meant that there was an inversion in the relationship of the forces in comparison with the pre-existing situation. The various Italic tribes, who originated from Samnite stock, spread along the Apennines, bearing down on the Campanian plain, then on Cumae and Neapolis. In the unceasing search for new pastures and better opportunities, first Paestum (Poseidonia) then Laus came under Italic domination, while the remnants of the archaic tribes of the Oenotrians, the Chones, and the western Daunii were infiltrated, subjected, or even, so it appears, annihilated.

The Bruttii were subjected to the southern Samnite branch of the Lucani. Their name, possibly derived from an Illyrian root, seems to be linked to a Iapygian and Messapic word meaning "deer", which was their totem. This derivation, which has parallels in both antiquity and the field of anthropology, appears to be more acceptable than an etymology based on cultural similarities.

The Bruttii were well known to the Greek writers by the end of the fifth century. Probably it was not by chance that one of the first to mention them was Aristophanes, in a passage so isolated that it has given rise to a number of attempts to seek a different interpretation of the meaning. The comic dramatist was very well informed about the events connected with the Panhellenic foundation of Thurii (this was, in fact, almost exclusively ascribable to Pericles). It was here that the boundary was fixed between the Lucani and the Bruttii on the Ionian coast. Paolo Poccetti, the scholar who has most recently analyzed (in a very coherent manner, I should add) the isolated account, has made a number of reflections on the oratorical technique and the cultural area to which the passage seems to allude – although this might well be that of the Italiots rather than of the Bruttii.

And, while the testimony has been confirmed, with the certainty that the adjective used by Aristophanes referred to the Bruttii, it needs to be stressed that – in Athens at the time of the dramatist – it was clearly the Italiots to whom the adjective referred, in a comic context, even if it related to one of the less well-known Italic tribes.

Bruttian inscription
from the Sanctuary of Apollo Alaios
at Crimisa (Cirò Marina)
first half 3rd cent. B.C.
Reggio Calabria, Museo Nazionale

This was also because Aristophanes' raillery was contemporary with the progressive conquest of political independence from the Lucani by the Bruttii. Diodorus Siculus and Strabo are particularly brutal in this regard: "slaves", "fugitives", "bastards", and "shepherds" are the terms they use to describe this people.

In the recent close analytical study of a passage from Plato by Mario Lombardo, there is no explicit mention of the Bruttii. But the socio-economic situation outlined by the philosopher is no different, in qualitative terms, from that described by more recent authors, both in a general sense, and with explicit reference to their political independence.

By contrast, the term that Aristophanes uses to describe the Italiots with regard to their oratorical ability is surprising – unless, that is, there is a parallel (a very cryptic one, however) with the account handed down by Justin of the pedagogic capacity of the Bruttii that was recognized by their Lucanian masters. Thus, once again there is a general synchronism in the evidence relating to the period preceding the fateful date of 356 B.C. (when the Bruttii obtained their independence from the Lucani).

In fact, as Justin relates, it was customary for the young Lucanian nobles to spend a period of time among the Bruttii; this was devoted to their education before entering public life, especially with regard to military skills. The Bruttian pedagogues, according to the detailed account, toughened them up so they could face the difficulties of life far from the luxury offered by towns. But since we know that, when military difficulties arose, the Lucani (and Bruttii) chose a king for the whole people from

The Encounter with the Bruttii

Embossed bronze lamina cuirass
from a tomb at Laus
4th cent. B.C.
Reggio Calabria, Museo Nazionale
Cat. 266/II

Phrygian type helmet
made of embossed bronze lamina
from a tomb at Laus
4th cent. B.C.
Reggio Calabria, Museo Nazionale
Cat. 226/I

among the ordinary magistrates, this special institutional figure must be credited with both military and political skills. An excellent example is wise old Herennius. In fact, during their education, the young Lucani were not only strengthened physically, but they were also initiated into the subtleties of dialectics, under the guidance of the Bruttian "shepherds."

The final obtaining by the Bruttii of their independence from the Lucani, recorded by the Greek sources, can, therefore, be interpreted in two different ways. On the one hand it may be considered to crown a long struggle that finally resulted in the recognition of the cultural, political, and military importance of the Bruttian sages, while, on the other, it can be seen as the exclusively military succession of a rabble lacking any distinguishing features, apart from that of being able to defeat their former rulers.

Certainly, the political and diplomatic exigencies of Dionysius' expansionism at the expense of the Italiot cities were among the reasons for the recognition of their independence and the fact that it was recorded in the ancient sources. Indeed, Timoleon, when he went to Syracuse to restore it after the turbulent period of the two tyrants, took Thurii (once again!) into his care, so as to allow its inhabitants to keep the Bruttian bands at a safe distance; up to then, these had continually endangered its security. This was on land: on the sea, however, it was only thanks to the divine intervention of Boreas (the north wind) that the raids of the Syracusan ships had been warded off.

The Encounter with the Bruttii

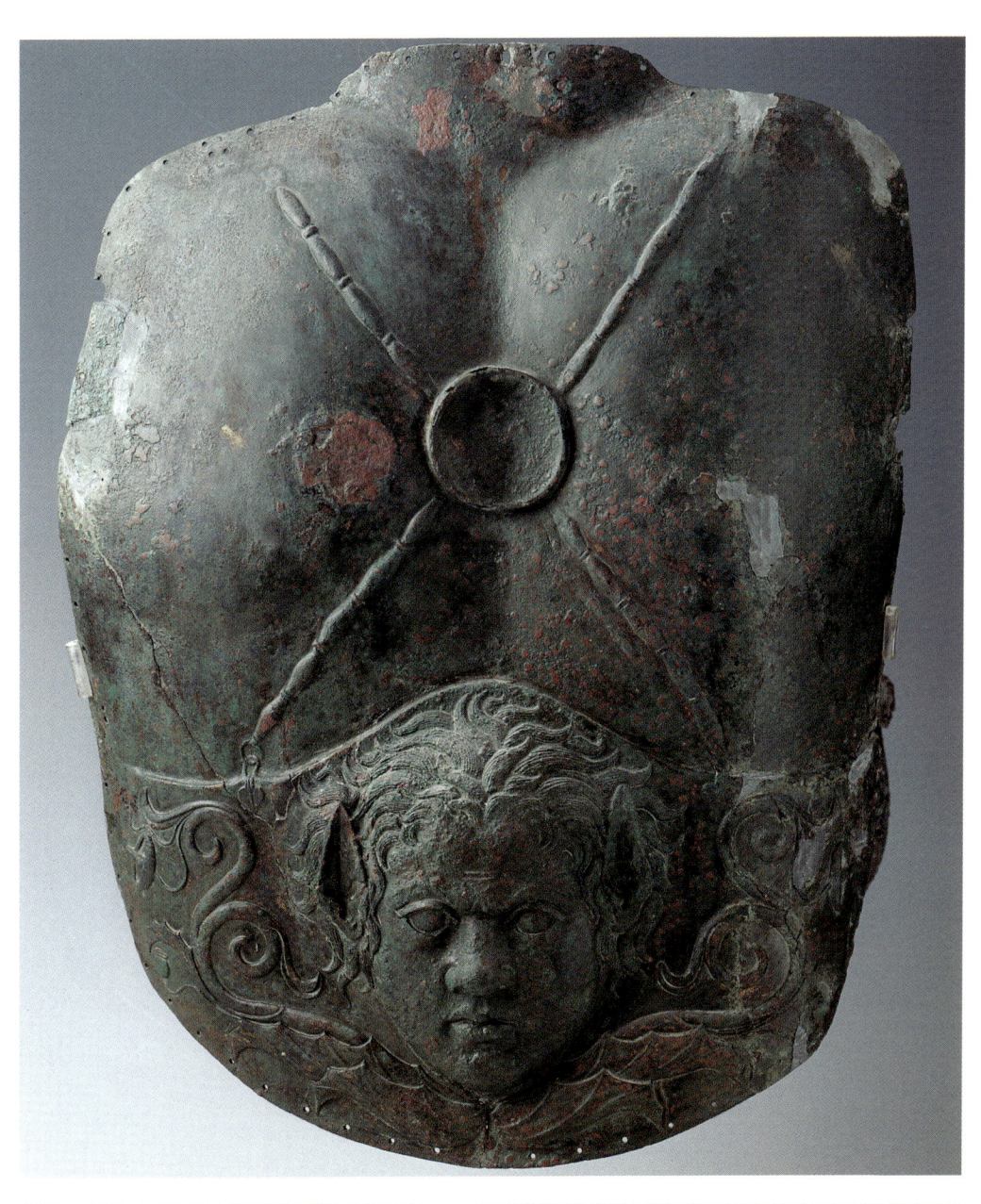

Bronze lamina belt
with silver lamina inserts
from a tomb at Laus
mid 4th cent. B.C.
Reggio Calabria, Museo Nazionale
Cat. 266/V

Silver coin
of the Bruttian confederation
with Greek inscription:
ΒΡΕΤΤΙΩΝ
3rd cent. B.C.
Syracuse, Museo
Archeologico Regionale
Gagliardi Collection

In contrast with the variegated, complex picture given by the literary sources with regard to the encounter between the Italiots and Bruttii, archaeology has contributed relatively little. The literary description of Petelia as the metropolis *ton Leukanon* (of the Lucani) seems to confirm that the chronological level of this stronghold, situated between the end of the Sila, the mouth of the Neto and the Ionian coast, was precedent to 356 B.C., despite the fact that even in Alexander the Molossian's day, almost a generation later, the literary distinction between Lucani and Bruttii was not entirely clear. However, in the area surrounding modern Strongoli, there have been no archaeological finds attesting to the Italic settlements that can be definitely dated to before 356 B.C. And the half-dozen or so sites (Rossano, Crichi, Santa Sofia d'Epiro, Lamezia-Moscatello) that can be archaeologically dated to the period at the turn of the fifth century have yielded finds that are extremely difficult to interpret. In fact, their absolute dating does not appear to justify their exclusive attribution to the Bruttii, who were still subservient to the Lucani in this period.

Even so, the topographical distribution of the archaeological evidence now at our disposal, together with the coeval hoards of coins that have been found outside the Italiot territory, are factors that merit closer examination. These are, in fact, finds made south of the line that divided the Lucani from the Bruttii from the end of the fifth century, although this distinction was not politically significant. Once again, they are finds relating to grave goods. Although originally these were probably very simple, later on, Greek and Italiot products, as well as coins, were also acquired, as they constituted the material sign of the coveted goal of Italic expansion. They are, in fact, finds made on the edges of the territories of Italiot cities. This testifies to their control of the area, as if they were waiting for the right moment to swoop down onto the plain in order to take possession of it. Indeed, this was a process that was already under way at Cumae, Neapolis, Paestum, and Laus.

Today there is a lack of archaeological evidence of settlements and of everyday objects at this chronological level. But this is not only the result of the random nature of the excavations: it should also be remembered that, in the period being considered here, the Bruttii were a nomadic people dependent on a predominantly pastoral economy.

It is tempting to link the small Archaic bronze figures brought to light at Tiriolo and Cosenza with the early Bruttii, for whom the archaeological evidence is indeed slight, when they encountered the Italiots living on the coast. Both these sites, in fact, played an important role in later events, and Cosenza was recognized as the *metropolis ton Brettion* (main town of the Bruttii) until the tragic events involving Hannibal. This was probably to counterbalance, from a political point of view, the previous *metropolis*, Petelia, which wavered between the Italic roots of its people and the alliance with Rome that had been forged by its nobility. These bronzes were linked to the distinctive votive rituals of the Italics in general; in this case, because of the sites where they were found, they may be attributed to the Bruttii. But, without being adequately informed about the general context of the individual finds, we cannot say whether they testify to the functioning of a culture contemporary with the arrival of the Bruttian vanguard in the various areas being considered, or if they were placed in the votive deposits after 356 B.C.

And this was when the phase of the first encounter had given way to that of confrontation and conflict, only to be followed by reciprocal acceptance. It was also the time when the Bruttian tribes settled in their impressively fortified villages, and when their leaders, and their women, were buried in chamber tombs with the material signs of their military and economic power, and the more subtle – but still visible – ones of their unremitting desire to become part of the Italiot cultural world, and thus permit the encounter to most fully bear fruit.

Carlo Tronchetti   The Greeks in Sardinia

After a period in which the Mycenaeans entertained relations with the islanders of Sardinia, evidence for which has been found in various areas of the Greek world, there followed a gap of several centuries in which there are no signs that the inhabitants of the island had any dealings with the Greek world.

The period extending from the end of the second millennium B.C. until the eighth century B.C. was an extremely complex one during which Cypriots and Phoenicians – in a broad sense – appeared in the western Mediterranean, with contacts and trade relations from which the Greeks themselves seemed to be excluded.

However, the situation changed during the eighth century. In fact, as is well known, this was a period in which there were many new developments. One of the most important, at least from our point of view, was the beginning of the colonization of the West by both the Greeks and the Phoenicians. Although – in its initial stages, at least – the phenomenon did not lead to fierce competition or hostility (we shall see the evidence for this later on), there seemed to be a demarcation line separating the areas colonized by the Greeks from those settled by the Phoenicians. The latter were situated in the southwestern part of the Mediterranean: the coast of North Africa with Malta, the coast of Sicily opposite it, southern Sardinia, the Balearics and the southern part of the Iberian Peninsula.

The Phoenicians began to establish colonies in Sardinia around 750 B.C., after they had traded there for decades. As far as we can tell today, the oldest colony was Sulcis, present-day Sant'Antioco, a small island off the southwest coast of Sardinia. More or less contemporary with this were Tharros, situated at the entrance to the Gulf of Oristano, Bithia and Nora further east, and probably also Cagliari. There were also smaller settlements, such as Cuccureddus near Villasimius, at the eastern extremity of the coast of southern Sardinia.

Although the main scope of this essay is to throw light on the presence of the Greeks in Sardinia, this long preamble on the Phoenicians is necessary, first, to enable the reader to fully comprehend the island's historical background, and, secondly, because the Greek material regarding this period (from the eighth century to the first half of the seventh century B.C.) has mostly turned up in the Phoenician colonies, or, when found in native settlements, is evidently the result of trade between the Sardinians and the Phoenicians.

It is only fairly recently that Greek objects have been found at this chronological level in Sardinia. In contrast with the ample finds of Late Geometric material at Carthage and in Spain, until a few years ago, Sardinia had yielded very little. Thus, only one vase had been found at Sulcis, the provenance of which was a matter of debate until, thanks to the finding of fragments of the lid, it was possible to attribute it to a Pithekoussan workshop and date it to between 720 and 690 B.C.

This attribution, which was confirmed by the excavations on the island of Ischia, was particularly important for the historical reconstruction. In fact, the excavation of Pithekoussai, the earliest Greek colony in the West, has revealed the presence of groups of Semitic peoples in the Greek community. The discovery of a Pithekoussan vase at Sant'Antioco filled a gap in the archeological evidence regarding the route leading to the mines of the Iberian Peninsula, which has been elucidated by B. B. Shefton in an exemplary manner.

The fortunate discovery of the first settlement of the Phoenician colony of Sulcis in 1983, the excavation of which is still taking place, has revealed a wealth of new archaeological evidence. In fact, the excavations of the dwellings have unearthed, together with Phoenician material, a large quantity of shards of Greek Geometric pottery of Proto-Corinthian, Euboean, and Pithekoussan origin. To date, the cups of the Aetos 666 type are the oldest finds; the material may be dated to a period spanning from the second half of the eighth to the early seventh centuries.

The integration of the Greek and Phoenician cultural elements is manifest in a number of important pieces. The one in which this is most evident is the fragment of the shoulder of an *amphora* with a typically Phoenician shape decorated with a bird that is thoroughly Greek both iconographically and stylistically. Then there is a series of shards of locally produced cups with a type of decoration that derives its syntax from similar Greek pieces; this phenomenon has also been noted at Al Mina, where the two peoples were present together.

At the current stage of studies, it is perhaps premature to assert that there was a Greek presence in the Phoenician colony of Sulcis, because, as S. Moscati has rightly pointed out, the data we have available are insufficient. However, this supposition can be regarded as a working hypothesis, especially on the basis of the first vase mentioned above, the Pithekoussan urn. In fact, this was found in the *tophet*, a necropolis and Sanctuary that had an important religious function in the Phoenician cities

Pithekoussan urn
with fragments of the lid
from Sant'Antioco
8th-7th cent. B.C.
Cagliari, Soprintendenza Archeologica

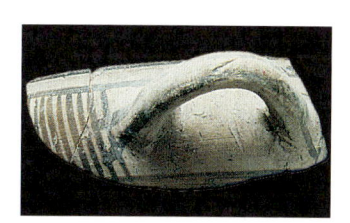

Fragment of the Aetos 666 cup
from Sant'Antioco
second half 8th-beginning 7th cent. B.C.
Cagliari, Soprintendenza Archeologica

The Greeks in Sardinia

Fragments of a Phoenician *amphora*
with Greek decoration
and of a Phoenician cup
with a Greek-style decoration
from Sant'Antioco
end 7th-mid 6th cent. B.C.
Cagliari, Soprintendenza Archeologica

Eastern Greek cup
from Tharros
end 7th-first half 6th cent. B.C.
Cagliari, Soprintendenza Archeologica

Balsam pot in the shape
of Nile River god
from Tharros
7th-6th cent. B.C.
Cagliari, Soprintendenza Archeologica

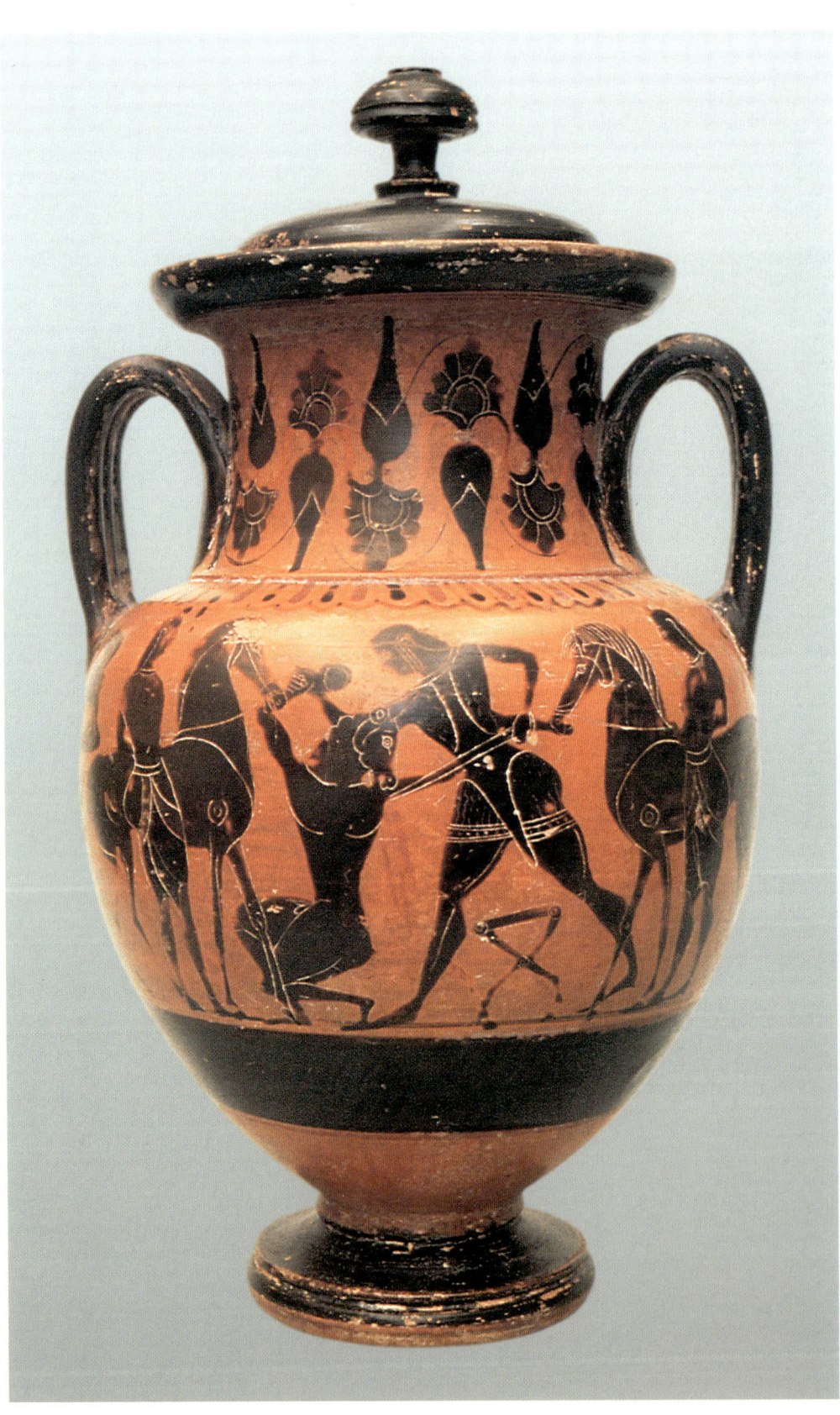

Attic red-figure *amphora*
of the Hyblaea Group
from Tharros
end 6th-5th cent. B.C.
Cagliari, Soprintendenza Archeologica

Gold necklace
from Tomb 87
at Monte Luna, Sernobì
4th cent. B.C.
Cagliari, Soprintendenza Archeologica
Cat. 314

Gold ring
with incused female face
from Sernobì
4th cent. B.C.
Cagliari, Soprintendenza Archeologica

in Sardinia. Stillborn babies, or those who died shortly after birth, were deposited in them, and sacrifices also took place there.
The discovery of an imported urn used in a religious context of such significance may be a sign of the presence of "foreigners" (in this case Greeks) who had become part of the community and participated in its rites, but used the objects from their own cultural tradition. Another possible explanation is that at least one of the couple was Greek (in this case, I believe it was probably the woman). In the *tophet* at Sulcis, this phenomenon is found in only a few other cases at the same chronological level. These do not involve Greek vases, but ones with shapes deriving directly from native types, thus lending credibility to the theory that there were mixed couples. Moreover, a Greek presence, albeit a small one, in the Phoenician colonies would not be surprising, especially in the light of the splendid interpretation of the sources describing the mythical colonization of Sardinia undertaken by Pulci Doria. From these, it may be deduced that there was a core of relations with the Euboean world in a generally Phoenicianizing context.
But, even if there really was a Greek presence in the Phoenician colonies in Sardinia, this must have been extremely limited, both as regards the numbers of individuals involved and its duration, as it only regarded the early stages of colonization. After this period, however, it is unlikely that Greek groups were physically present on the island, despite the fact that a large number of objects produced in Greece have been found there.
In the Archaic period, from the late seventh century to the mid-sixth century B.C., the major Phoenician cities in Sardinia imported a large quantity of material, most of which was Etruscan, but including a much smaller quantity of Greek material. From the coastal settlements, these objects were distributed to the indigenous communities in the interior. Apart from a few Corinthian pieces, mostly dating from the late seventh century, the first half of the sixth century was characterized by pottery from Mainland Greece, especially the B2-type "Ionian" cups.
The constant repetition of the association of Etruscan material with that of Greek origin – the latter, as has already been mentioned, forming a much smaller proportion of the total than the former – makes the conjecture that the Greek products were also distributed in Sardinia through trade with Etruria extremely convincing. This hypothesis has been generally accepted, especially now that many shards decorated with bands, formerly ascribed to eastern Greek workshops, have been attributed to

Phoenician workshops, and the possibility that the *Serdaioi* (allies of the Sybarites), mentioned in a famous Delphic inscription, were, in reality, the inhabitants of Sardinia has been ruled out. In effect, a number of passages from Herodotus seem to indicate an "Ionian" interest in Sardinia, with proposals for sailing to the island and setting up colonies there. This has been used as an argument in favor of a direct presence, or at least a trading one, of the Greeks on the island. In reality, an analysis of the passages reveals that the plans to go to Sardinia were abandoned, and alternatives were found. Furthermore, these events took place in a period in which Sardinia was already under Carthaginian domination – that is, after the first treaty between Rome and Carthage, in which the island was considered to be part of the metropolitan territory of the North African city – so that they were subsequent to the arrival of Greek material from the East.

In conclusion, there are absolutely no traces of Greek settlements in Sardinia, and such written evidence as we have available states that Greek material reached the island through Etruria.

In the late sixth, fifth and, above all, fourth centuries B.C., an ever-increasing quantity of Attic pottery was imported into Sardinia: firstly black-figure, then red-figure and black-paint vessels. In fact, it was the latter that, between the last decades of the fifth century and the end of the fourth century, constituted alone the fine table service, and was very widely distributed. It also gave rise to a whole series of local imitations that were in widespread use during the third century. It is impossible to say exactly how this material reached the island, whether with the Carthaginians serving as middlemen or by direct contact with Athenian merchants. Generally speaking, as various sources attest, relations between Athens and Carthage were excellent. Moreover, two passages from Aristophanes, one in *Knights* (vv. 173 ff.) and one in *Wasps* (vv. 699 ff.), describe Sardinia as being the most westerly outpost of the Athenian commercial empire.

The contiguity of the territory dominated by Carthage to that inhabited by the peoples of Greek origin in Sicily led to the progressive Hellenization of the Punic customs. This took place through the introduction of deities such as Demeter and Kore, whose cult was extensively diffused in Sardinia, and the adoption of styles and iconographies that have been found at Sant'Antioco in a group of *stelai* in the *tophet*, in which the image of the deity is inserted in a small temple having typically Greek shapes and decoration.

Finally, a number of gold jewels, which can easily be distinguished from the contemporary Punic output on the island, came from Magna Graecia, in all probability from Tarentum. Rings with incuse faces, a necklace (or bracelet?) consisting of a gold chain with pendants in the form of small *amphorae* and a clasp in the form of a rosette with two whorls of petals, and small gold sheets with the Gorgon's head found at Senorbì, a small village inland from Cagliari, are all evidence of the penetration of these foreign luxury objects of Greek origin into the Punic culture.

Bibliography
C. Tronchetti, *RivStFen*, 1979, pp. 201-205; M. Gras, in *Il commercio greco...*, 1981, pp. 83-95; F. Nicosia, in *Ichnussa*, 1981, pp. 421-476; C. Tronchetti, *I Greci e la Sardegna, Dialoghi di Archeologia*, 1985, pp. 17-34; P. Bernardini, C. Tronchetti, in *Sardegna preistorica...*, 1985, pp. 285-307; M. Gras, 1985; S. Moscati, *RANL*, 1985, pp. 265-271; C. Tronchetti, *EVO*, 1986, pp. 117-124; P. Bernardini, *RivStFen*, 1988, pp. 75-89; C. Tronchetti, 1988; C. Tronchetti, in *Sardinia in the Mediterranean...*, 1992, pp. 364-377.

Mario Torelli

The Encounter with the Etruscans

"Ephorus states that these two cities (Naxos and Megara Hyblaea) were the first Greek colonies to be founded in Sicily, in the tenth generation after the Trojan War: previously, in fact, there was a great fear of the piracy of the Etruscans and of the primitive character of the barbarians of this area, so that no one wanted to sail there, not even for trade." This very well-known passage that Strabo (VI. 267) quotes from the work of Ephorus, the authoritative historian of Aeolian Cyme (in fact, he was himself interested in Italy, especially Cumae, which was founded by a Chalcidian and a Cumaean from Aeolis), gives an accurate picture of the economic, political, and cultural contexts in which the Greeks first sailed to Sicily and the Italian peninsula and came into contact with the Etruscan world.

There is no doubt that the Etruscan piracy (Giuffrida Ientile, 1983; Gras, 1985) conditioned the oldest Greek settlements in the West in various ways. It was not by chance that, from 770 B.C. onward, security reasons prompted the Greeks to set up – on the model of the Phoenician trading posts so vividly described by Thucydides (VI. 2. 6) – the first stable presence in this part of the Mediterranean, the Euboean settlement of Pithekoussai, on an island (Ridgway, 1984; Buchner and Ridgway, 1993). Despite the threatening presence of the volcano Mount Epomeo, this was hospital and sheltered, being well-provided with harbors, and it allowed rapid access to the Etruscan mainland, both in Campania, which was already occupied by large settlements between the Gulf of Salerno and Capua, and in Etruria proper. Certainly preceded by pre-colonial seafarers who were largely of Euboean origin, as is demonstrated by Middle Geometric Cycladic and Corinthian pottery of the late ninth and eighth centuries B.C. found in Etruria, Campania and Sicily (Descoeudres and Kearsley, 1983; D'Agostino, 1989), the settlement of Pithekoussai, where Chalcidians and Eretrians lived together in prosperity (Strabo, V. 247), was immediately opened to other immigrants who served the purposes of a settlement that was an intermediary between East and West. In fact, it organized the trade in luxury goods of oriental or Greek manufacture (D'Agostino, 1977A; D'Agostino, 1977B) that were very much in demand by the nascent aristocracy of the continent, with the iron from the rich Etruscan sources of supply (Zifferero, 1991), together with other equally important commodities from the rest of the Italic area, such as slaves, copper, alum, hides, and grain. From this point of view, besides the evidence of individuals of Phoenician culture settling in the island, the numerous ritual vases from southern Etruria (the so-called spiral *amphorae*) found in women's tombs at Pithekoussai confirmation of the presence of Etruscan women who had married the Greek inhabitants of the island. These are certainly the most concrete signs of the intensive trade between Euboean merchants who had settled in the *emporion* (trading settlement) at Pithekoussai and the Etruscan heartland, which comprised the area between the mouth of the Tiber and that of the Arrone. In accordance with an Archaic tradition, this trade included the matrimonial sphere; in fact, it existed as early as the ninth century B.C. between Sardinia and Etruria (Torelli, 1981A).

From the outset, the attraction for the Etruscans of the Greek colonial settlements in Italy and Sicily was in proportion to the role attributed by the Etruscan "princely" class to specific Greek models in the construction of their ideology that served the ends of a political hegemony destined to last for centuries. In the Archaic period, before the assertion of Syracusan power and the appearance of Athens in the West, the Greek colonial cities, as Pithekoussai had already done, certainly accepted individuals of Etruscan origin, in the same way that Italiots and Siceliots settled in the Etruscan *poleis*. However, after the Pithekoussan period there is only occasional evidence of the presence of Etruscans in the Greek colonial cities. Thus, for example, it is debatable whether the very rich individual buried in Tomb 104 of the Fondo Artiaco in the Cumae necropolis (Tocco Sciarelli, 1985) is a Euboean aristocrat linked to funeral ceremonies of a Homeric cast used in Mainland Greece or rather an Etruscan nobleman who had been admitted to colonial society in accordance with the precepts of hospitality and *philia* (friendship). Traditionally, relationships of this type were frequently mentioned with reference to the vicissitudes of the tyrant of Cumae, Aristodemus: on the one hand, the Cumaean aristocrats whom he had exiled found refuge in the Etruscan city of Capua (Dionysius of Halicarnassus, VII. 10. 3), on the other, the tyrant harbored the Tarquins after their expulsion from Rome (Livy, II. 14 and 21; Dionysius of Halicarnassus, VI. 21) and formed his bodyguard from the Etruscans taken prisoners in the battle of Aricia, "among whom were his close friends" (Dionysius of Halicarnassus, VII. 7. 4). The analogies with the situation in the Siceliot area are very evident; here Telines, grandfather of Gelon, the tyrant of Gela, defeated during a *stasis* (uprising) in his homeland, found refuge in the Sicel city of Maktorion (Herodotus, VII. 153). In other words, the Italiot and Etruscan aristocrats, who continued to maintain close relations with their peers outside their own territories during conflicts and social disputes (these were very frequent in the Archaic period), could count on the solidarity of their friends in the cities of the other nation. Important evidence of these alliances, roughly contemporary with the vicissitudes of Aristodemus, is provided by a Paestan symposiac inscrip-

The Sostrato *stele*
with inscription dedicated to
the Aeginetan Apollo
from Gravisca
end 6th cent. B.C.
Tarquinia, Museo Nazionale
Cat. 7

tion under the foot of an Attic cup of the late sixth century B.C. found in a tomb in the Etruscan city of Pontecagnano; this testifies to the solidarity between members of the Etruscan aristocracy of this town with the nobility of Paestum (Poseidonia), which was situated nearby, even if they did not necessarily belong to the same *hetairiai* (Torelli, 1984): the famous painted Tomb of the Diver at Paestum could be the corresponding proof, shortly afterward, of the presence of Etruscan aristocrats in the same Achaean colony (Greco, 1982).

Besides this, there is a considerable corpus of epigraphic texts. These include Etruscan inscriptions attesting to the integration of individuals of Greek origin into Etruscan society, and, in the case of the Greek warehouse of the port of Tarquinii, Gravisca, Greek epigraphic texts (Torelli, 1982), in which the presence of Greeks in Etruscan cities is well documented. This is the result of the considerable social mobility – with subsequent integration – at all levels of the wealthier Archaic societies of the Italian peninsula (Ampolo, 1981; Torelli, 1988). None of these epigraphic texts, whether Etruscan or Greek, can be related with certainty to the western Greeks. On the other hand, it is well known that in the Greek trade of the Archaic period (Mele, 1979), the aristocracy – apart from the well-known case of Demaratus, the Euboean element appears to be dominant in this, and inserted in the higher social levels – was substituted in the late seventh century B.C. by mercantile activity that was still largely controlled by the leading aristocratic families of Greece, especially Ionia in Asia Minor, but materially carried out by individuals whose social level was modest and confined to the *emporia*. These were, in fact, wholly dominated by the eastern Greek carriers and agents, often slaves, from Ionia in Asia Minor. Finally – should we wish to draw a parallel in this sense – the available evidence provides only rare instances, such as the Etruscan character mentioned in a *defixio* (enchantment) at Selinus (Arena, 1989, p. 61), of the presence Etruscans of a lower social level in the Greek colonial cities.

For a long time, however, until the establishment of Roman hegemony, mercantile objectives dominated the relationship between the western Greeks and Etruscans: they were epitomized by the *emporia* and piracy, which, in the Archaic period, were two sides of the same coin (Mele, 1979, pp. 59 ff.). Regarding the archeological remains, these objectives are attested by Greek material in Etruscan contexts and, more rarely, by Etruscan material in Greek colonial contexts (Gras, 1985); in literary sources they are illustrated by the characterization of the maritime vocation of both Greeks and Etruscans as an essentially piratical one. Etruscan piracy, a problem that the western Greeks had had to face from the outset, and, in a more general sense, the strong presence of the Etruscans on the seas (Cristofani, 1983), continued to put considerable pressure on the whole Greek colonial area. Around the middle of the seventh century B.C., Aristonothos, a vase-painter with an eclectic background (Schweitzer, 1955), but having a substantially Euboean and Cycladic matrix, worked for the Etruscan aristocrats of Caere. On the famous krater in the Museo del Palazzo dei Conservatori, Rome, he vividly expresses the Etruscan aspiration to thalassocracy, representing it in both direct and symbolic forms: on one side there is the engagement between an Etruscan ship and a Greek one, and, on the other, the blinding of Polyphemus, a metaphor for the victorious battle of the Etruscan client in the guise of Odysseus against a Cyclops that alluded to the Greeks of Sicily (Torelli, 1987, 20–23). Naturally, the Greek literary sources insisted on the negative connotations of this Etruscan piracy. By recounting myths and legends relating to the Etruscan pirates, beginning with the abduction of Dionysus (Homer, *Hymn to Dionysus*), which some considered to have occurred in the sea off the coast of Sicily (Euripides, *Cyclops*; Nonnus of Panopolis, *Dionysiaca*), the sources insisted on the cruelty of the Etruscans and the unpleasant aspects of their predatory activities. These included their custom of binding prisoners face to face with dead bodies (Aristotle, *Protrepticus*, fr. 60 Rose; Virgil, *Aeneid*, VIII. 478–488), which even became proverbial (Hesychius of Alexandria, s.v. Τυρρηνοί δεσμοί, [*Tyrrhenian Bonds*]), as well as the incredible reputation for practising cannibalism that the Etruscan pirates had at times earned (Hyginus, *Fabulae*, 274. 20).

Evidently, the piracy of the Etruscans was matched by that of the Greeks; evidence for this was the initial Chalcidian settlement of Zancle (Messina), and then the Cnidian-Rhodian colony of Lipara, although obviously, when referring to the Greeks, our sources do not mention the savage cruelty that was attributed to the Etruscan pirates. In a famous passage, which was confirmed in the literature of antiquity (Pausanias, IV. 23. 7), Thucydides (VI. 4. 5–6) states that the first inhabitants of Zancle were pirates who allowed the Greeks to control the straits; this was a thorn in the side of the Etruscans, who aspired to control the seas. However, the Etruscan threat to the straits must have continued for a long time from the Greek point of view, because the rationalist mythographer Palaephatus (Περί ἀπιστῶν [*De incredibilibus*] XX) asserted that the monster Scylla was none other than the ever-present danger of the destruction by Etruscan vessels of ships passing through the straits. In this respect, the occupation of Lipara in 580 B.C. by Cnidian-Rhodian colonists led by Pentathlus was equally important. In the prehistoric era, Lipara and the Aeolian

Krater made by Aristonothos
with the blinding of Polyphemus
from Caere
mid 7th cent. B.C.
Rome, Musei Capitolini
Cat. 6

The Encounter with the Etruscans

Islands played a fundamental role in the control of the lower Tyrrhenian. From the Neolithic to the early Iron Age, evidence of this is provided by an almost continuous series of exports of Aeolian material to distant destinations, and, in particular, of imports to the island of material of varied provenance (Bernabò Brea, 1958), among which Mycenaean pottery was conspicuous right from its first appearance on the coasts of the central western Mediterranean (Vagnetti, 1983). As is well known (Diodorus Siculus, V. 9. 4), the distinctive economic and political organization instituted in the island by the Cnidian-Rhodian colonists required the labor force to be divided into two parts: one was assigned to working the land, the other to "defense from the pirates" – that is, naval operations and privateering, in this case presented in a defensive light. Thus, longstanding, intense rivalry led to conflict between the Etruscans and the Liparaeans, as the sources repeated on various occasions (Diodorus Siculus, V. 9. 4–5; Strabo, VI. 275; Pausanias, X. 11. 3–4, and X. 16. 7). During this struggle, the Etruscans besieged and possibly conquered the island: this was when the tragic episode recounted in Callimachus' *Aetia* (fr. 93 Pfeiffer) may have taken place. Involving the sacrifice of a Greek from Lipara by the Etruscans (Colonna, 1984), a rite that was frequently practiced by the Etruscans using prisoners of war (Torelli, 1981B), this may have been the occasion on which the Etruscans dedicated a tripod at Delphi (Colonna, 1989), an event which may be associated with the Etruscan offensive on the straits referred to by Strabo (VI. 257) in connection with the tyrant Anaxilas of Rhegium around 490 B.C. (Ampolo, 1987). The revenge of the Liparaeans, narrated in a heroic tone by the sources (Pausanias, X. 11. 3), followed shortly afterward, and resulted in a much larger votive offering at Delphi, datable to the years between 480 and 450 B.C. (Vatin, 1993).

The events relating to the Straits of Messina and Lipara that have just been discussed should be seen in the context of a notable deterioration of the conflict between the Etruscans and the western Greeks. This may be linked to the increasingly complex sociopolitical organization of the *poleis* of Etruria and Magna Graecia, which was now capable of involving land armies in Campania and Latium, from the clashes under the walls of Cumae to the Battle of Aricia; all of these episodes were dominated by the Cumaean tyrant Aristodemus. In this phase, from the late sixth century B.C. onward, the alliance between the Etruscans and Carthaginians was consolidated in the Tyrrhenian Sea area (Pallottino, 1963; Ferron, 1966). The following are the most important stages in this alliance, which was to develop into a form of isopoly between Etr-

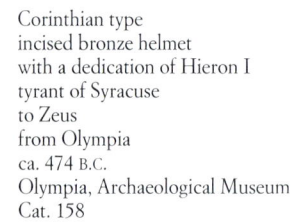

Corinthian type
incised bronze helmet
with a dedication of Hieron I
tyrant of Syracuse
to Zeus
from Olympia
ca. 474 B.C.
Olympia, Archaeological Museum
Cat. 158

Gold lamina with inscriptions in Phoenician and Etruscan found at Santa Severa beginning 5th cent. B.C.
Rome
Museo Nazionale di Villa Giulia

uscans and Carthaginians that was mentioned by Aristotle (*Politics* III. 9. 1280a): the battle of the Sardinian Sea, in which the Carthaginians and Etruscans fought the Phocaeans during the fourth decade of the sixth century B.C. (this was the matrix of the Greek colonization of Elea and the Etruscan settlement of Aleria [Gras, 1972]); the treaty of 509 B.C. between the Romans and Carthaginians (Bengtson, 1975, II. 16–20); the battle off Cumae in 474 B.C. between the Etruscan fleet and that of Hieron of Syracuse. There is striking archeological evidence of the latter event in the form of two Etruscan helmets found at Olympia, one of the Corinthian type and the other of the Negau-Vetulonia type (Egg, 1988, p. 248), bearing dedicatory inscriptions by Hieron of Syracuse (Tod, 1946, 22). The Etrusco-Punic alliance had a profound influence on the relationships between Etruria and the Greek colonial world, especially those with Sicily (Pallottino, 1973–74). The dominant Greek city in this context appears to be Syracuse: as a result of the previously mentioned deterioration of the conflict, it now began to be directly involved in the Tyrrhenian area, which had previously been dominated by the fleets of the colonies of Magna Graecia. Immediately after their victory at Cumae in 474 B.C., the Syracusans stationed a garrison at Pithekoussai. Then, in 453 B.C., Syracuse launched a direct attack on the heart of Etruscan wealth, Elba, which it first sacked with a squadron commanded by Phayllus, and then went so far as to occupy, albeit temporarily, with a fleet of sixty triremes commanded by Apelles. The same line of conduct was followed two generations later with the famous sack of Pyrgi (Colonna, 1985); ordered in 384 B.C. by the tyrant Dionysius of Syracuse, this is an event that once again formed part of the endemic conflict with Carthage and its faithful allies, the Etruscans. It is small wonder, therefore, that right from the outset of the westward expansion of the nascent Athenian imperialism – with Diotimus' expedition to Neapolis and the treaties with Segesta, Rhegium, and Leontini – Athens was the most important ally for both Carthage and the Etruscans (with whom the propagandistic argument of the distant Attico-Pelasgian συγγένεια [origin] was used); this was put to the test by the Etruscan participation in the Athenian expedition against Syracuse (Torelli, 1975).

Thus the relationship between Etruria and the Greek colonies, with the political organization of the Etruscan cities along the lines of the Greek city-state that took place in the Archaic period, tended to assume the typical forms of the relations of the Greeks with the barbarian peoples, especially the Etruscans. Although the Greek ethnographers (Sassi, 1988) attributed a barbarian status to the latter, they considered

Eulogy of the Spurinas
inscription from Tarquinia
1st cent. A.D.
Tarquinia, Museo Nazionale

Etruscan silver coin
from Populonia
4th cent. B.C.
Florence
Museo Archeologico Nazionale

that they were in a sense close to themselves, in particular because the Etruscans were identified with the Pelasgians (Briquel, 1984), while, in the Etruscan aristocratic families, the practice of searching for Greek origins and genealogies – which had, in fact, being going on for some time – became increasingly common. Thus, as we have already seen in the case of the krater by Aristonothos, the Etruscan aristocrats tended to use the myth of Odysseus as a vehicle for promoting their public image: his western wanderings constituted a metaphor that was used in a polysemic sense. While, on the *pyxis* of Pania, the representation of Odysseus being threatened by Scylla as he sails past her and the rescue of his companions from Polyphemus' cave serve as an allegory for the *metis* (astuteness) of the Etruscan aristocrats before the perils of the great journey toward the underworld, in the tomb of Orcus II at Tarquinii the scene of the blinding of the Cyclops takes on additional triumphal meanings with regard to the Syracusan arch-enemy (Torelli, 1983). This was the pride of the Tarquinian patrician family of the Spurinas, who were protagonists of the Etruscan expedition with Athens against Syracuse in 414 or 413 B.C. (Torelli, 1975).

The Etruscan ships engaging in piracy and organized trade continued to sail both in the seas around Sicily and in the whole of the Tyrrhenian, leaving just a few archeological remains in the form of wrecks, such as those off Elba, Montecristo, and Torre della Meloria (Commercio etrusco, 1985). It is not, therefore, by chance that the epigraphic evidence of commercial correspondence on small lead plates, which has brought to light Greek letters connected with the colonies of Pontus, Massalia, and Emporion, has recently been enriched by an Etruscan text of the fifth century B.C. found in the south of France at Pech Maho (Lejeune, Pouilloux, Solier, 1988). In this respect, between the late sixth and the third centuries, the Etruscan "base" of Aleria in Corsica played a vital role in the control of the middle and upper Tyrrhenian on the west coast; on the east coast, this role was played by Populonia, the only Etruscan city that issued silver coins from the Archaic period onward. This is believed to be linked to the Euboean weight standards (Hackens, 1976); among the fourth-century material found in the necropolis at Aleria (Jehasse, 1982) there is no lack of pottery from Magna Graecia, witness to the degree to which this Etruscan settlement was at the center of trade that also involved the Greek colonies. A parallel case on the Adriatic coast in the same period was the archeological evidence of Spina (Berti, Guzzo, 1993), where pottery from Magna Graecia has been found; but, together with this, in the tombs at Spina there are numerous Italiot coroplastic products. This is very important from an ideological point of view, since this modest material, having little economic significance, was clearly intended to transmit and assert religious and eschatological beliefs; further attention will be given to this question below.

On the Etruscan coast, the presence of Greek *emporia* of Euboean and Greek colonial origin in the nascent cities of southern Etruria gradually extended during the eighth century B.C. from the oldest ports on the Tiber and its mouth to the coastal towns of Caere, Tarquinii, and Vulci, which, for the whole of the Archaic period, disseminated Greek culture to the rest of the country. The process continued in the seventh century B.C., and eventually involved the rest of maritime Etruria, with the substitution of the trade partners in the last quarter of the century, so that the Euboeans were replaced by the Greeks from Ionia. From the outset, however, the trade in merchandise was accompanied by the diffusion of culture, lifestyles, and, above all, technology of Greek origin (Torelli, 1982B), leading to the rapid Hellenization of the Etruscan ruling classes. Thus, in the Archaic period, Magna Graecia certainly made an immense contribution to the technological and cultural development of Etruria.

Buchner (1975) has rightly stressed the role played by Pithekoussai and Cumae in the manufacture of Orientalizing jewelry that was so popular with the rich Etruscan "princely" class, just as the Euboean matrix was of decisive importance for the development of the contemporary Etruscan Geometric and Late Geometric pottery (Canciani, 1974–75). However, it should be noted that the study of Greek loanwords in Etruscan (De Simone, 1968–70) has revealed that hardly any of these came from the Euboean or Ionian area. This seems to suggest that a central role was played in this trade by Tarentum, the Achaean colonies, and, above all, Syracuse; the importance of the latter was emphasized by Hencken (1958) on the basis of the evidence provided by the material culture. In any case, the Etruscans owed a great deal to the Euboeans: although the origins of the Etruscan olive cultivation are controversial (Gras, 1985, pp. 212 ff.), the perfection of the Etruscan techniques of viticulture (Gras, 1985, pp. 266 ff.) may probably be attributed to the Euboean colonies, since the definition of "aminaean" given by the Latin sources to the Etruscan custom of cultivating vines in festoons seems to have originated in the area around Neapolis, which was close to Euboean Cumae. But the most significant cultural element deriving from contact with the Euboean colonies was the adoption at the end of the eighth century B.C. by the Etruscans – and also by the Latins – of an alphabet of Chalcidian origin (Cristofani, 1978; Pandolfini, Prosdocimi, 1990), a choice that may be attributed to the prestige and importance of the colony of Cumae.

Krater made by Eurythios
in the Corinthian style
found at Cerveteri
ca. 600 B.C.
Paris, Musée du Louvre
Département
des Antiquités Grecques
Etrusques et Romaines

Oenotrian Geometric style jug
with tentlike decoration
found at Vulci
first half 8th cent. B.C.
Rome
Museo Nazionale di Villa Giulia

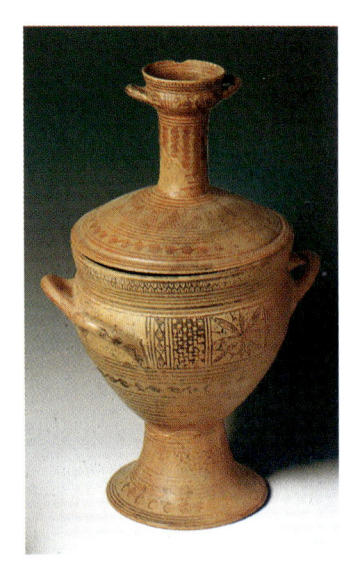

Euboic Late Geometric *krater*
found at Pescia Romana
730-710 B.C.
Grosseto, Museo Archeologico
e d'Arte della Maremma

In the seventh century B.C., in addition to the Euboean colonies and Syracuse, the other colonies in Italy – Tarentum and the Achaean cities – began to play an increasingly important role in the transmission of culture to Etruria. A major contribution of the western Greek area was the introduction of the practice of using heavy materials for roofing (Wikander, 1993); in the second half of the seventh century B.C., this spread from southern Etruria to the rest of the area. Various parts of the Greek world were responsible for the creation of the Etruscan cultural models, although the Greek colonial element prevailed (above all, the Achaeo-Tarentine one), which mediated the contemporary experiences from both the mainland Greece, on the axis Sicyon, Aetolia, and Corcyra, and the Ionian area. These innovations, which took place right through the sixth century B.C., were due to craftsmen from Magna Graecia – originally they may have been itinerant – who worked in teams on the construction of houses and their roofs, including the painted decoration, in accordance with the paradigmatic model of the three semi-mythical *plastae* (clay-molders), Eucheir, Eugrammos, and Diopos (Torelli, 1979). It is significant that a craftsman called Diopos worked at Camarina in the sixth century B.C. and "signed" a painted antefix (Pelagatti, 1977). The so-called second phase of Etruscan architectural decoration must have also been heavily influenced by the experience of the Siceliots. At the end of the sixth century B.C. (Colonna, 1986, pp. 468 ff.), perhaps at the same time as the transformation of the Etruscan *poleis* into republican states (Torelli, 1992), this decoration radically changed the appearance of the revetments of the Etruscan temples. In fact, according to tradition, the decoration of the temple of Ceres, Liber and Libera in Rome, dedicated in 493 B.C. (Dionysius of Halicarnassus, VI. 17. 2–4), was the work of two Greek artists, Damophilus and Gorgasus (Pliny *Natural History*, XXXV. 154), who are likely to have been of Siceliot origin, especially if Damophilus was the grandfather of the homonymous painter of Himera, who taught Zeuxis (Torelli, 1985).

In the Classical period, the contribution of the western Greeks to the culture and art of the Etruscans became more difficult to identify, because the only evidence available is circumstantial. Although there were national traits in some of its artistic traditions, Etruria – which was now wholly open to the ideas and aesthetic innovations that originated in the great centers of Hellenic culture – could be considered to be a province of the vast outer Greek world, in which the receptive and transmissive function of the Greek colonies was of major importance. In this sense, the role of Magna Graecia and Sicily appears to be that of an intermediary, although, unlike the situation in the Archaic period, this is difficult to define. And, on occasion, functions and stimuli that it did not possess have wrongly been ascribed to Magna Graecia. For

Vase made by Bocchoris
in the Orientalizing style
from Tarquinia
end 8th cent. B.C.
Tarquinia, Museo Nazionale

example, it has been suggested that it was the unique, direct matrix of the architectural, pictorial, and sculptural forms of Middle and Late Hellenistic Etruria, whereas, in fact, they were often common – and possibly independent – derivatives of the artistic creations of the great cultural centers of Mainland Greece, especially those commissioned by the aristocrats of the Macedonian world. In the West, these derivatives appeared to be influenced by the analogous ideological requirements of the small ruling classes, whether Etruscan or from Magna Graecia.

Nonetheless, this intermediary role of Magna Graecia existed, and continued to be extremely important, as certain distinctive features of Etruscan religious beliefs seem to indicate. There is, in fact, no doubt that, in the fifth and fourth centuries B.C., the religion and ritual of Etruria were notably influenced by the Italiot and Siceliot areas. The presence of votive statuettes in tombs at Spina of this period has been alluded to above; this phenomenon occurred especially where the contact between the western Greeks and the Etruscans was very close and long-lasting. The same applies to the Paestan statuettes of Argive Hera found in many tombs of the fifth and fourth centuries B.C. at Pontecagnano, the evidence of a strong western Greek imprint given in the same period to the cult of the *emporion* of Gravisca, where there was even a specimen of a *pinax* of the Locrian type, possibly from Medma (Torelli, 1977), or the links with Magna

Polychrome terra-cotta antefixes
with a silenus head and a maenad head
ca. 500 B.C.
Rome
Museo Nazionale di Villa Giulia

Graecia of the cults of Demeter, Ceres, and Vei in Rome (Coarelli, 1988) and at Veii (Comella, Stefani, 1990). It is likely, however, that – apart from this vigorous underlying fabric of mystery-religion and redemption that was so intensely experienced by the people – much more complex messages, nourished by the same soteriological vein and known to have existed in Magna Graecia in the late fifth and fourth centuries B.C. (Bottini, 1991), reached even the highest levels of Etruscan society. In effect, the many derivatives of the doctrine of Orphic and Pythagorean origin cannot be ignored. Very complex from a conceptual point of view, and certainly originating from Magna Graecia, they were widespread in the eschatology of the aristocratic classes in the Classical and Hellenistic periods (Torelli, 1986), once again confirming the centrality of the contribution of the western Greeks to the formation of the ideology of the ruling classes of Etruria.

Bibliography
C. AMPOLO, in *Gli Etruschi e Roma...*, 1981, pp. 45-70; C. AMPOLO, in *Atti XXVI...*, 1987, pp. 45-71; R. ARENA, 1989; H. BENGTSON, 1975²; L. BERNABÒ BREA, 1958; F. BERTI, P.G. GUZZO, 1993; A. BOTTINI, 1991; D. BRIQUEL, 1984; G. BUCHNER, in *Contribution à l'étude...*, 1975, pp. 59-86; G. BUCHNER, D. RIDGWAY, in *Mon-Al*, monographic essay IV, 1993; F. CANCIANI, in *DArch*, VIII, 1974-75, pp. 79-85; F. COARELLI, 1988; G. COLONNA, in *MEFRA*, XCVI, 1984, pp. 557-578; G. COLONNA, in *Santuari d'Etruria*, 1985, pp. 127-141; G. COLONNA, in *Rasenna*, 1986, pp. 369-530; G. COLONNA, in *Atti II Congresso Internazionale Etrusco*, I, 1989, pp. 361-374; A. COMELLA, G. STEFANI, 1990; *Il commercio etrusco arcaico*, 1985; M. CRISTOFANI, 1983; M. CRISTOFANI, in *Lingue e dialetti...*, 1978, pp. 403-468; B. D'AGOSTINO, in *MonAL*, XLIX, 1977A; B. D'AGOSTINO, in *Annales ESC*, XXII, 1977B, pp. 207-226; B. D'AGOSTINO, in *Atti II Congresso Internazionale Etrusco*, I, 1989, pp. 63-78; J.-P. DESCOEUDRES, R. KEARSLEY, in *BSA*, LXXVIII 1983, pp. 9-53; C. DE SIMONE, Wiesbaden-1968-70; M. EGG, in *Antike Helme...*, 1988, pp. 222-270; J. FERRON, in *Latomus*, XXV, 1966, pp. 689-709; M. GIUFFRIDA IENTILE, 1983; M. GRAS, in *Latomus*, XXXI, 1972, pp. 698-716; M. GRAS, Roma 1985; E. GRECO, in *AION*, IV, 1982, pp. 51-56; T. HACKENS, in *Contributi introduttivi...*, 1976, pp. 221-270; H. HENCKEN, in *AJA*, LXII, 1958, pp. 259-272; J.-L. JEHASSE, one 1982²; M. LEJEUNE, J. POUILLOUX, Y. SOLIER, in *RAN*, XXI, 1988, pp. 19 ff.; A. MELE, 1979; M. PALLOTTINO, in *CahTun*, XI, 1963, pp. 22-28; M. PALLOTTINO, in *Kokalos*, XVIII-XIX, 1972-73, pp. 48-70; M. PANDOLFINI, A.L. PROSDOCIMI, 1990; P. PELAGATTI, *Cron Catania*, XVI, 1977, pp. 43-65; D. RIDGWAY, 1984; M.M. SASSI, 1988; B. SCHWEITZER, in *MDAI(R)*, LXII, 1955, pp. 78-106; G. TOCCO SCIARELLI, in *Napoli antica*, 1985, pp. 90-99; M.N. TOD, 1946²; M. TORELLI, 1975; M. TORELLI, in *PP*, 1977, pp. 398-458; M. TORELLI, *N.H.*, XXXV, pp. 151-152, 1979, pp. 307-312; M. TORELLI, 1981A; M. TORELLI, in *Le délit religieux...*, 1981B, pp. 1-7; M. TORELLI, in *PP* 202, 1982A, pp. 304-325; M. TORELLI, in *Il commercio greco nel Tirreno...*, 1982B, pp. 67-82; M. TORELLI, in *DArch*, III, I, 1983, 1, pp. 7-17; M. TORELLI, in *AION...*, VI, 1984, pp. 277-280; M. TORELLI, in *Magna Grecia...*, 1985, pp. 379-398; M. TORELLI, in *Rasenna*, 1986, pp. 159-237; M. TORELLI, 1987; M. TORELLI, in *Storia di Roma*, I, 1988, pp. 241-261; M. TORELLI, in *Ostraka*, I, 1992, pp. 249-274; L. VAGNETTI, in *Modes de contacts et processus...*, 1983, pp. 165-185; C. VATIN, in *Ostraka*, II, 1993, pp. 145-167; Ö. WIKANDER, 1993; A. ZIFFERERO, in *SE*, LVII, 1991, pp. 201-241.

The Rhythm of the Greek "Emporion"

From the Phocaeans to the Massaliots (ca. 600–540 B.C.)

The oldest Greek objects found in southern Gaul date from the third quarter of the seventh century B.C. (goblets and *oinochoai* of the authentic or imitation sub-Geometric Proto-Corinthian type from Agde and Mailhac). There has sometimes been the temptation to connect these isolated relics with the movements of Rhodian sailors mentioned by the authors of antiquity and whose presence in the area is commemorated in the name of the Rhône (Rhodanos). Yet the only Mediterranean imports that have subsequently been verified in the lower Rhône Valley and along the eastern coast of the Languedoc during the course of the last quarter of the century are of Etruscan manufacture (*amphorae*, and black *bucchero* ware). Apart from two Greek cups (with Ionic filleting), among the valuable objects from the "chieftain" tumuli discovered in the hinterland of lower Provence, estimated to date to the late seventh and middle sixth centuries (Pourrieres, Vauvenargues, Pertuis, and Cadarache), were Etruscan bronze vases (*oinochoai* and bead-rimmed bowls). In the *polis* of Massalia (modern-day Marseilles), which was founded around 600 B.C., twenty-five percent of the fine pottery and ninety percent of the *amphorae* for the entire first half of the sixth century were still of Etruscan origin.

Therefore, in their travels in the West the Phocaeans, discoverers "of Tyrrhenian, Iberia, and Tartessus" (Herodotus, I. 163), probably found an existing Etruscan distribution network which they themselves became part of for many decades. Traveling in the opposite direction to the Etruscan traders, the Etrurian *amphorae* probably either represented the return cargo of ships carrying Gallic products, or cargo that had been loaded in various ports of call by sailors, who thus guaranteed a link with the eastern basin of the Mediterranean, as could have been the case with the (Phocaean?) navigator whose existence was revealed by the Giglio shipwreck.

There is another viable hypothesis, however, which would attribute a more dynamic role to the Phocaeans. It is possible that the Etruscan phase that most likely preceded the foundation of Massalia did not last as long as is generally thought; in fact it could be placed around the year 600 B.C., which would embrace both the period of Phocaean exploration and the period of the first settlement. This was the era in which the Phocaeans, landing at *Ostia Tiberis*, forged bonds of friendship with Tarquinius Priscus and in which, according to M. Torelli, they secured "the establishment of the Gravisca *emporion*." This traffic, in which Etruria was such an essential force, was what induced the Phocaeans to settle in southern Gaul, irrespective of whether they were its promoters, or its beneficiaries. Their settlement at Alalia on the eastern coast of Corsica could also belong to the same scenario, in approximately 560 B.C., even though Herodotus (I. 165) is somewhat laconic on the matter ("following an oracle they founded a city which they called Alalia"), and Corsican archaeology is for the moment silent.

Would archaeological evidence endorse the supposition of a "commercial" reason for Phocaean colonization, as various texts seem to suggest? According to Aristotle, who is quoted by Athenaeus (XIII. 576a), "the Phocaeans from Ionia who were involved in *emporia* [trading] founded Marseilles"; whereas Plutarch (*Solon* II.7) recounts that a certain aristocrat, Protis, who thought highly of sea trade, "founded Marseilles after having won over the Celts who lived near the Rhône." F. Villard was probably right in observing that the founding of Marseilles followed all the stages of a classic *apoikia* or colony, a process that the information supplied by Aristotle, Strabo, and Pompeius Trogus allows us to reconstruct with some precision.

During this period the pottery imported to and used in Marseilles, where Etruscan imports occupied a notable place (particularly as regards *amphorae*), was essentially of Greek stamp. The majority of this was made up of Massaliot products of gray clay and, above all, light-colored clay, which attested to the presence of all the varieties of finer tableware. The importation of Corinthian or Spartan vessels was rare in comparison to ware from eastern Greece (e.g., Rhodian bowls, wine tumblers from Chios, and the famous B2 Ionic cups), and Attica (cups, *lekanoi*, and *amphorae*).

It seems that the Phocaeans (and the Massaliots, since it is difficult to distinguish them) chose the route toward the extreme West – and the renowned opulence of Tartessus, where they cultivated the friendship of its king, Arganthonius – along which they established the settlements of Agatha (Agde), Emporiae (Ampurias), Hemeroscopium (Cape Nao), and Maenaca. In Gaul the diffusion of commercial *amphorae* and pottery imported to (or made in) Marseilles, was limited to a select few localities that were either near Phocaean colonies (Saint-Blaise, the Baou de Saint-Marcel, and Tamaris) or the Agde hinterland (Bessan). Elsewhere, some coastal or inland sites have yielded a small number of objects that probably arrived there as a result of sporadic commerce or indirect trade.

Proto-Corinthian style sub-Geometric cups from Tomb 83 (above) and Tomb 115 (below) of the Peyron necropolis at Agde third quarter 7th cent. B.C.

Marseilles and the expansion toward Gaul (ca. 540–400 B.C.)

The period around 540 B.C. saw a turning point from both archaeological and historical points of view. The principal event was the emergence of Massaliot-produced wine, which was celebrated by a new form of *amphora* initially made of feldspathic clay and then, after 525, out of micaceous clay, employing a technique that was used through to the second century B.C. This fact probably marked the access of the Phocaeans of Massalia to territories worthy of its name, and the new clay *amphorae* spread the mature city's name far and wide. Also in these last decades of the sixth century Marseilles soon minted its first silver coins, the "Auriol type."

Was it merely a coincidence? These signs of economic independence follow in the wake of two events whose consequences are as evident as they are difficult to evaluate. Around 545 B.C. the conquest of native Phocaea by the Persians resulted in an exodus of the population, who arrived "in Corsica [i.e., Alalia] and Marseilles" (Antiochus of Syracuse, quoted by Strabo, VI. 1. 1). The activities of the new arrivals on Alalia led five years later to an Etrusco-Carthaginian coalition which, following a sea battle in Alalian waters, once again forced the Phocaeans into exile and resulted in the founding of Elea (Greek Hyele). This Alalian battle has been assessed in various ways, since Herodotus (I. 167) wrote that the Greeks attained a "Cadmeian" victory, meaning that the victors emerged from the conflict as bedraggled as the vanquished. However, the immediate result, to judge from the necropolis tombs dating from the late sixth to mid-third centuries, was probably the establishment of an Etruscan colony at Alalia. It is worth noting that the Massaliots seem to have kept out of that conflict and to have continued frequenting the Gravisca *emporion*.

We can offer the following as proof of the importance of Marseilles in the second half of the sixth century: a) the large increase in Attic imports into Marseilles itself and the indigenous sites of southern Gaul, a phenomenon which is magnificently illustrated by the Lequin wreck 1A (Porquerolles Island); b) the diffusion of Massaliot pottery products in southern Gaul and of wine *amphorae* that found their way to Etruria, Magna Graecia, Sicily, Sardinia, and Spain. Can it be assumed that the small number of Massaliot *amphorae* unearthed in Burgundy and Switzerland, and the discovery at the Mount Lassois *oppidum* of Attic vessels in association with the *Vix Krater*, the largest Greek bronze krater so far found, demonstrates the onset of commercial trade with the tin mines of Britannia from 530–520 B.C.? Must Marseilles be inserted in an economic world system centered on Etruria? As far as relations between the Celts and the Mediterranean were concerned, were the routes that began in the Etruscan settlements in the Po Valley and crossed the Alps more important than the Rhône-Saône corridor? Was there not a need in this area to favor a form of non-commercial distribution connected to the existence of hierarchical societies and to the special social significance of alcohol consumption, and which could be contrasted to the non-stratified societies of southern Gaul, where all of the settlements have yielded large

Massaliot *amphorae* used as building rubble from Place de Gaulle at Marseilles 4th cent. B.C.

The Greeks in Gaul and Corsica

Large bronze krater
probably made in Magna Graecia
from the princely tomb at Vix
(Côte d'Or)
end 6th cent. B.C.
Châtillon-sur-Seine, Musée Archéologique

quantities of *amphorae*?; c) and finally the era in which Marseilles constructed its votive treasury at the sanctuary of Delphi.

In the first half of the fifth century the importation of Attic pottery into Massalia undoubtedly suffered a downturn, but it soon recovered to reach its highest level (forty percent of fine tableware) around the year 400 B.C. In the indigenous sites the percentage of vessels and Massaliot *amphorae* continued to increase. Massaliot *amphorae* together with Attic red-figure ware were found in three inland sites in Gaul, thus testifying to a likely establishment of new relations. The three sites were at Lyon-Vaise, at Bourges on the Loire, and at Bragny at the confluence of the Saône and the Doubs; this last site is notable for its enormous quantities of ironwork from the last decade of the century.

Retreat or reconversion (ca. 400–125 B.C.)
From the mid-fifth century Massaliot *amphorae* had already ceased to be found beyond the Ligurian Sea and the Gulf of Lyons. From the end of the century it seems that in this area the Massaliots began to carry out a policy of colonization that was designed to guarantee them both a proper monopoly and above all, according to Strabo (IV.1.5), dominion over the sea, even at the risk of leaving the continent to the barbarians. From these colonies, or *epiteichismata* (fortresses), as Strabo termed them, we can follow the geographic and chronological positioning, from east to west: Nicaea (Nice) which was possibly founded in the second half of the third century; Antipolis (Antibes) whose date is uncertain; Olbia (Hyères) which dates back to around 330 B.C.; Tauroeis (Six-Fours) which probably dates back to the third century; Rhodanoussia on the Rhône, and Agatha (Agde), which was refounded around 400 B.C. It is difficult to understand the functions of these colonies but, apart from Agde, they do not seem to have been used as commercial *entrepôts*. On the Provençal coast it appears that they were mainly military outposts established to counter the Ligurian pirates operating along the Italian route, and in fact it was in this era that Massaliot *amphorae* became popular in Genoa and a series of imitations of the heavy Massaliot drachma, which the Phocaean colony minted in imitation of the Syracusan tetradrachm and the Elean drachma, began to appear in the upper reaches of the Po. Furthermore, two events took place in southern Gaul at the beginning of the fourth century: the diffusion of Massaliot *amphorae* (as well as pottery made out of light-colored clay) either continued to spread or at least remained stable in the indigenous coastal centers, while their popularity began to decline in inland settlements and they were not replaced by other products. It was only at the start of the Second Punic War and the Roman conquest of Spain that Greco-Italic and later Italic *amphorae* began to progressively substitute Massaliot *amphorae*. In the beginning this happened in the city of Massalia and the western coastal sites (Pech Maho, Lattes), where the phenomenon was noticeable from the end of the third century up to approximately 175 B.C., but it gradually spread to the inland regions and eastern Languedoc.

This double process can be seen as a consequence of the reinforcement of the role of the local coastal ports as gateway communities and consumer areas and, at the same time, as a reinforcement of a linear hierarchical system of distribution on the part of the local people themselves, in whose spheres eastern

Greek goods from the Warrior's tomb, no. 163 at Ensérune (Hérault) beginning 3rd cent. B.C.
below: black-painted pottery from Rhode (Rosas, Catalonia) the Massaliot colony
right: pale clay Massaliot and black-painted Rhodian pottery
Nissan-lez-Ensérune, Musée d'Ensérune

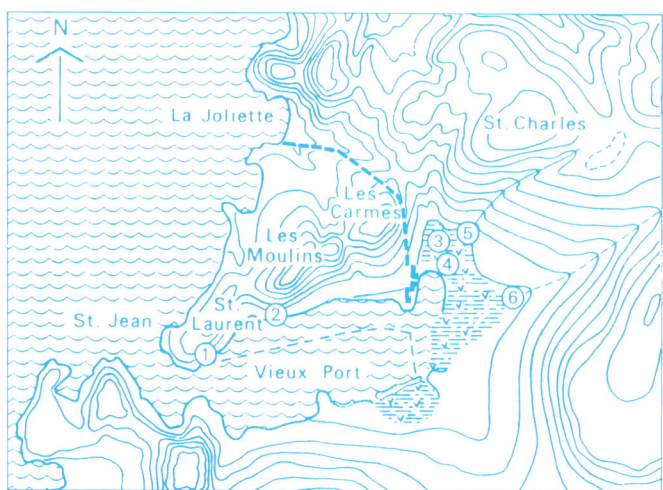

Marseilles, general view
of the ancient site
with the Old Port in the foreground

Map of the ancient site
of Marseilles
1 bight
2 Greek shore
3 marsh
4 sea bottom
5 mouth of the River Frache
6 mouth of the Lacydon springs
--- Hellenistic fortifications

Water pipes at Les Moulins
Marseilles
6th cent. B.C.

Languedoc represented something of an exception owing to the establishment of special ties with Massalia (*philia* or *xenia* relations, or even tax obligations).

Marseilles in the Roman province
The Roman army had already intervened in 154 B.C. against the Deciates and Oxybii from Liguria who attacked the Massaliot colonies of Antipolis and Nicaea. However, in 125–123 B.C. Marseilles itself was threatened by Salluvii, and the Roman intervention was a result of the creation of the Province of Transalpine. For its part, Massalia obtained the right for the entire Provençal coastal strip to come under its authority, but from that moment on Roman legions maintained order, as was clear on the occasion of the Salluvii rebellion in 90 and the campaigns of Gaius Valerius Flaccus in 83 and of Pompey and then Fonteius in 77 B.C. In 102, on the occasion of the intervention against the Ambrones and Teutones on the Aix-en-Provence plain, a canal was built from Fos to Arles on the orders of the consul Marius, and subsequently the Massaliots collected a toll from the ships that used the canal. The Phocaean city probably benefited from a condition of *civitas foederata*, and its inhabitants even managed to conserve this after they had found themselves on the losing side in the conflict between Pompey and Caesar and had been conquered by Caesar's troops. Caesar's victory forced Massalia to hand over arms, ships, and treasure; it also lost control of Antipolis and its territory was reduced to the immediate vicinity of the city, together with Nicaea, Olbia, and the islands of Stoechades (the Hyères Islands). In the third century A.D. Nicaea was still governed by the *duumvir Massiliae, agonothetos et episcopos Nicaeensium*, who was probably a magistrate from Massalia charged with administrating justice and supervising the application of decisions that came from the metropolis in the homeland. Greek culture also flourished in Massalia, and in fact the city has yielded more Greek inscriptions from the Roman period than for the entire period of its independence. Despite the benevolent behavior of the Romans, at least up to the year 49 B.C., and the numerous benefits that the city derived from this, after the creation of the Province, Massalia had to deal more and more with the presence of Roman settlers and merchants in Gaul. As Cicero noted around about the year 70, "not one piece of silver changed hands in Gaul without its being registered in the accounting books of the Roman citizens" (*Pro Fonteio* XI). By the last quarter of the second century Massaliot *amphorae* had ceased to circulate in Gaul. Massaliot wine production was reserved for the city itself, although no locally produced *amphorae* have so far turned up in digs. However, it is also probable that Massaliot merchants – thanks to their traditions and a sound knowledge of the country – continued to participate in trade between Gaul and Italy, symbolized by Italic *amphorae* or black-painted Campanian vessels. The trade in Massaliot wine only recovered in the later first century B.C., with a type of flat-bottomed *amphora* that has been discovered in particular in the Carmes hills.

Marseilles and Its Colonies

Topography, urban planning, architecture
Caesar and Strabo have provided us with sundry information on the general appearance of the city of Massalia in the first century B.C. "Marseilles is surrounded by the sea on almost three sides; the re-

Aerial view
of Olbia in Provence (Hyères, Var)
Massaliot colony

Olbia in Provence
Letter on an *ostrakon*
made of Campanian
pottery
"Hail, I will send you
a letter about the slaves"
2nd cent. B.C.

Archaic Ionic capital
from Massalia
ca. 510 B.C.

maining part, the fourth side, is the only part that is accessible by land. Even here, the part that extends toward the acropolis, is defended by the nature of the land and by a rather deep gorge" (Caesar, *De Bello Civili* II.1). Strabo specifies that the *Ephesion* and the sanctuary of the Delphi Apollo rose up on the acropolis. A reconstruction of the ancient coastal shoreline clearly shows that the site of the city, composed of the three hills of Saint-Laurent, Moulins, and Carmes, stretched out like a peninsula into the open sea and the Bay of Lacydon (modern Vieux-Port), and encompassed a marshy area as it moved inland.

The twenty years of research carried out in this area during the time of the great town planning project has made it possible to accurately map the evolution of the city. It appears that in ancient times the city was initially confined to the Saint-Laurent hills and that it excluded the present Bourse area and did not reach its maximum extension until the end of the sixth century. It was not until the late fifth century that the Lacydon marshes were slowly filled in and drained to the north and south of the "horn" of the port, thus making it possible to construct the great access road in the east of the city. The houses were built in terrace-form on the slopes of the hills and in regular blocks in the lower areas, using stone, wood, and unbaked brick for their construction. The oldest section of the town walls (in ruins) were made of white limestone and they apparently date to the fourth century. We know that during this period there were three principal necropolises, in the north (valley of Joliette), the east (the Sainte-Barbe necropolis had simple inhumations and cremations; cremation enclosures in the Bourse area; and sarcophagus inhumations in Rue Tapis-Vert), and on the southern bank of the Lacydon in front of the old city. The best-conserved monuments date from the Late Hellenistic period and they include various hydraulic constructions (*dromos* wells, large quadrangular block fountains, and a monumental reservoir) and above all the pink limestone walls. The remains of the Porte d'Italie which formed part of these walls can today be seen in the Bourse gardens.

Among the colonies of Marseilles only Olbia "the Blessed" has been definitely localized and excavated (at the point where the western sand-dunes of the Île de Giens meet dry land). It was a 165-meter square-shaped settlement surrounded by a defensive wall made of large uncut boulders (replaced in the second century B.C. with squared blocks), with just the one gate in the east, in the part of the old port (now silted up). Inside this square the houses were built in a geometric pattern, with two large orthogonal axes (*plateiai*) that defined four areas, each one of which was in theory divided into ten rectangular blocks of 11 by 34.5 meters by a set of narrower streets (*stenopoi*). The buildings had stone foundations and walls of unbaked brick.

Society and religion
In Massalia the splendor of the mercantile aristocracy is cogently expressed by the stability of its institutions, which are described by Aristotle in a text that has since been lost as being like a balanced oligarchy in which the power, following an evolutionary process proposed by Aristotle himself (*Politics*

Light drachma
obverse: head of Artemis
reverse: lion and legend
Massalieton
2nd cent. B.C.

v. 6), was concentrated in an ascending hierarchy. This consisted of a political body that was open only to noble families, an assembly of Six Hundred *timouchoi*, and a Council of Fifteen, which was "a permanent commission for dealing with current business, three of which enjoy precedence" (Strabo, IV. 1.5). The result, as Cicero, a convinced conservative, noted, was that "the population enjoyed a status that was little more than servitude."

The law imposed customs in which fidelity to the old traditions, austerity, and discipline dominated, and these included a limit on pomp at funerals and on women's dowries, a ban on the consumption of wine by women, the obligation for strangers entering the city to surrender their arms, the exclusion from the city of mendicant clergymen, a ban on indecent entertainment, and a limit on the freeing of slaves, to name but a few.

The cults and religious festivals celebrated in Massalia and its colonies were strictly tied to the Ionian origins of the city. Unfortunately, archaeological finds relating to these practices have been rather rare. The principal cult was that of Artemis of Ephesus, which had a temple on the Massaliot acropolis and in the Rhône delta. Her cult statue was famed for its resemblance to that of the Aventine Diana, and her likeness appeared on the reverse of the drachma minted by the city. The other most important cult was that of Delphi Apollo. The Ionic capital monument that dates from approximately 510 and which was found isolated at the foot of the Massaliot acropolis, was probably linked to a temple dedicated to one or other of these cults. In Massalia itself the people also worshipped Athena, Dionysus, Apollo Thargelios, Leucothea, Zeus Patroos and maybe Demeter Thesmophoria. Finally, some fifty or so *naiskos stelai* made of local limestone in the shape of miniature temples with the image of the seated goddess testify to the existence of an urban *heraion* to Cybele. The cult of Aphrodite is attested to at Antipolis and Olbia; that of Heros (Heracles?) at Olbia and Tauroeis; that of the Dioscuri at Agde, and that of Mother Goddesses at Olbia. A rocky sanctuary on the Île de Giens has yielded more than three hundred examples of dedications inscribed on pottery, bearing the names of Greek and local dedicatees.

The Impact of the Greek Presence on Local Culture

It is true that Greek Massalia was the originator of many different activities in southern Gaul, such as the production of wine and oil, the use of the potter's wheel, the construction of mudbrick buildings, the introduction of coins, the progressive establishment of a market economy, sculptures in stone, and the use of the alphabet. However, not all these influences had the same impact, since they were often either restricted to small quotas of the population, or they appeared later. They did, nonetheless, prepare the ground for the subsequent acculturation under the Romans.

Naiskos stele of Cybele
Rue Négrel, Marseilles
end 6th cent. B.C.

Naiskos stele of Attis
Rue Négrel, Marseilles
end 6th cent. B.C.

Head of two-face deity
from the sanctuary
at Roquepertuse
(Bouches-du-Rhône)
3rd cent. B.C.
Marseilles, Musée de la Vieille Charité

Terra-cotta cup
with Gallo-Greek graffito inscription
from the *oppidum* at La Cloche
Pennes-Mirabeau
(Bouches-du-Rhône)
end 2nd-first half 1st cent. B.C.
Marignane, Mairie-dépôt des fouilles
de La Cloche

Let us look at two emblematic examples, the southern Gaul school of sculpture and the adoption of the Greek alphabet for writing Gallic. We are lucky in being able to follow the development of stone sculpture under the influence of Mediterranean styles over the course of three generations. The first phase of the third century is represented in Roquepertuse by two squatting statues, in hieratic pose, and by the two inclined heads similar to the double-faced *hermae* of Greek production. Here the use of the flat chisel and of polishing reminds us once again of the Celtic method of working wood. In the artifacts unearthed at Entremont, which date from approximately the middle of the second century, the style is still rather rigid but the craftsmanship, which sometimes involves a drill and a chisel, is smoother and the subject range is wider, such that female portraits, standing figures, an equestrian statue, and animals appear beside the squatting warriors. Finally, at the beginning of the first century, in a column capital composed of human heads, found in Glanum, we find a form of art that has become mixed. "Even if the capitals are Mediterranean in type (vegetable *calykes* in the form of clumps of acanthus leaves in the Corinthian order), the figures, with their simple style of large ears, big eyes framed by heavy eyelids, and clumsy mouths, recall the traditions of Entremont, and the elements of Italo-Grecian religious and mythical iconography (Dionysus/Bacchus, Apollo, Hermes/Mercury, Pan, the Cyclops, Africa) are mixed in with people wearing Gallic torcs that come directly from the Celtic world" (Fr. Salviat).

Caesar and Strabo both confirm that the Gauls wrote using the Greek alphabet. In fact archaeology has revealed the existence (from the second century B.C. to the first century of the present age, of a Gallo-Grecian form of epigraphy in which the Ionic alphabet of Massalia was radically adapted to fit the Gallic pronunciation. The earliest examples consist of ownership markings scratched on common tableware; other examples are of inscriptions found on votive and funeral tablets. It would appear that the use of the written word developed on two fronts: first, among the aristocratic classes, resulting in a form of lapidary epigraphy that seems to have been practiced to a greater degree by the inland communities; and second, among ordinary people, albeit limitedly, as can be seen in the pottery scratchings and the fact that the coastal settlements were apparently more receptive to writing.

Bibliography
M. Bats, G. Bertucchi, G. Congès, H. Tréziny, in *Etudes Massaliètes*, 3, 1992; L. Jehasse, J. Jehasse, in *Gallia*, XXV, 1973.

The Greek and Celtic Worlds: a Meeting of Two Cultures

It is thanks to the Greeks that, toward the end of the sixth century B.C., the Celts emerged from the anonymity of a population without history. The fact that their name appeared in the works of the scholars of Asia Minor, who at the time were laying the foundations of history and ethnography, in all probability was not due to the discovery of their existence among the peoples who at the time were generally referred to as Hyperboreans. It was more likely due to the desire to classify the existing information about the known world in a different way from the traditional mythical framework, which by then was inadequate for the needs of the urban Mediterranean communities developing at the time. The numerous contacts linked to the expansion of commercial trade required that the new peoples be identified, since it was important to distinguish and localize them approximately, at least.

The identification of the Celts, therefore, was linked to the intensification of relations with both the immediate and the more distant neighbors of the western Mediterranean colonies, even if this probably did not signal the beginning of relations between the Hellenic world and the Celtic world, which up to that time had been marginal although certainly not unknown to the Greeks. The legendary stories that tell of exchanges with the distant western and northern peoples appear to be memories of ancient contacts that have been handed down over the years, we are left today with, but a few objects, scattered without apparent logic over time and space, as evidence of these contacts. According to a passage by Diodorus Siculus, inspired by a lost work on the Hyperboreans by Hecataeus, an island as big as Sicily rose in the ocean facing the northern part of the Celtic lands. This island had fertile soil and a temperate climate, and its inhabitants practiced a particular cult with a circular temple dedicated to Apollo, which was apparently visited by Greeks from Athens and Delos for the purpose of worship. This description could easily be applied to the island of Britain with its circular shrines linked to the cult of the sun, well-represented by the impressive megalithic monument at Stonehenge. There are also frequent references to the recurrence of nineteen-year periods in relation to the God, which allows us to reconcile the lunar year with the solar year. This cycle, in fact, corresponds exactly to the ideas about the calendar and astronomy which those monuments revealed. It is therefore possible that the passage in Hecataeus, like other texts concerned with the mythical age of the heroes, is an echo of ancient contacts with western peoples that preceded by many years the colonization of the western Mediterranean.

It does, however, seem certain that the development of relations between the Greek world and the Celtic world, which according to archaeological studies definitely took place in the sixth century B.C., was a consequence of the activities of the Greek colonies and trading posts founded at the beginning of the century on the northern coast of the western Mediterranean and on the Adriatic coast. The decisive role of Massalia (Marseilles) has long been recognized, since its excellent position at the mouth of the Rhone made it easy to arrive at the heart of the transalpine territory inhabited by the Celts. It is only recently, however, that the true value of the role played by the Greco-Etruscan trading posts in the Po River delta and the cities of Adria and Spina has been recognized. These posts quickly became the departure points for the transalpine traffic that crossed Veneto, as well as strategic points for commerce between Greece and Etruria. The settlements in the Mantua area and the agglomerations on the southern coasts of the great lakes (Como–Prestino to the north of Milan, and Golasecca–Sesto Calende–Castelletto Ticino further west), which had then already urban characteristics, also played a very important role.

Thanks to certain inscriptions, the oldest of which date back to the second quarter of the sixth century B.C., we have known for a decade or so that this area – now called Lombardy – was inhabited from the beginning of the last millennium B.C. by a Celtic-speaking people who were therefore related to the transalpine Celts, a fact that must have had a certain amount of influence on the increase in commercial traffic.

It is not always easy to establish the route by which a given product or influence of Greek origin traveled, whether it was the Rhone route or the Alpine one, althought the fact that they were both used has been clearly demonstrated. For example, the Châtillon-sur-Glane fortress on the Swiss plateau has provided us with fragments of a type of pottery classed as Phocaean, which is characteristic of the Massalia (Marseilles) area, together with shards of pottery manufactured in northern Italy. Since at least some of the objects of Greek origin discovered north of the Alps definitely followed the same commercial route utilized at the time by the Etruscans from the Po Valley, the discovery of a Greek object at a central European site is not necessarily evidence of direct contact. Likewise, the area where Attic black-figure vases have been found (an area spread out over the Alps) cannot be considered as proof of the irradiation of Greek culture in the Celtic world. The most northern example of such an object found so far – a fragment of a goblet with palmette – was discovered in the small, rural village of Kadan, in western Bohemia. It dates back to the beginning of the fifth century B.C., and is one of numerous examples that indis-

Bronze cauldron
made in Greece
from the princely tomb
at Hochdorf
second half 6th cent. B.C.
Stuttgart
Württembergisches Landesmuseum

putably come from the Po area of Etruria. It probably arrived in Bohemia as a result of the frequent contacts the area had with the Etruscan world. This demonstrates how difficult it is to establish the precise origins of the Mediterranean influences that were undoubtedly present in the so-called princely spheres of the transalpine Celts in the sixth and fifth centuries B.C. Even the more valuable objects, the great bronze vases like the Grachwill *hydria*, the Vix *krater*, or the Hochdorf cauldron, which are generally attributed to the Tarentine workshops – could have followed either one of the routes, and have arrived having had no further direct contact with their place of origin. It is highly likely (albeit almost impossible to prove) that Greek merchants or adventurer-explorers penetrated the Celtic world.

One exception is represented by the conception and technical construction of one of the successive walls of the Heuneburg hillfort on the upper reaches of the Danube, which was built toward the middle of the sixth century B.C. with quadrangular bastions of mud-brick laid on a stone base. This type of construction, very different from walls built according to the local tradition, which were made of wood and stone, has many similarities with ramparts found in Magna Graecia, and it represents an unrepeated attempt to establish locally a prestigious example of military architecture based on the Greek model. It has been suggested that the scheme might have been imported by some local inhabitant who had formerly lived in that part of the Mediterranean, but it seems more likely that it was the result of the intervention of a Greek who was well-versed in the subject. The Heuneburg bastion is emblematic of the transient impact of Greek influence on the Celtic world, and was apparently an isolated at-

Decoration on a gold torc
from Waldalgesheim (Rhineland)
second half 4th cent. B.C.
Bonn, Rheinisches Landesmuseum

Decoration on a gold torc
unknown provenance
second third 4th cent. B.C.
London, British Museum
Department of Greek
and Roman Antiquities

tempt at grafting construction techniques; in fact it was later replaced with a traditional type of wall. The funeral statues of individuals represented in "heroic nudity" that appeared among the transalpine Celts in the sixth century B.C. were also a result of Greek influence, although in this case they came from across the Adriatic. It is in fact along the coasts of central Italy and Istria that we find the best comparisons to the warrior adorning a tumulus in Hirschlanden, a burial ground close to the Hohenasperg fortress near Stuttgart, Germany. The figure is nude with a conical headgear, a large torc and a short dagger attached to his belt that denote his rank. Other statues of similar but decidedly more primitive manufacture testify to a temporary vogue in the area for this type of monument.

There are other examples, but the final balance seems a clear indication that the Celtic world was not very receptive to influences of Greek origin, which are almost imperceptible from the end of the sixth century B.C. The La Tène culture of the historical Celts developed in the following century, due almost exclusively to the influence of the Etruscans, whose became the Celts' principal and possibly only intermediaries with the Mediterranean world. A period in which the Greeks attempted – though with little lasting success – to establish direct contact with the transalpine peoples was apparently followed by a withdrawal phase, a return to a more Mediterranean orientation.

It was only at the beginning of the fourth century B.C. that some transalpine Celts migrated down into the Italian peninsula and established direct contact with the cities of Magna Graecia. Celtic mercenaries, who were probably Senones recruited from Syracuse's trading port at Ancona, were part of the expeditionary force sent in 369–368 B.C. to Greece by the tyrant Dionysius of Syracuse, while other Celtic mercenary troops also in Dionysius' pay fought in the south of the peninsula. This type of activity, more frequent and widespread than attested by written sources is probably the best explanation for the rapid Hellenization of the Senones whose burial grounds have yielded a large number of luxury goods, such as jewels and vases of Italiot origin, and have also revealed evidence of methods of body-care typical to the Greek world, such as the use of strigils and other utensils. The proximity of the Ancona *emporion* evidently facilitated sea contacts, particularly with Taras (Tarentum), but the Senones' territory also afforded a means for crossing to the Tyrrhenian coast and, in particular, to Campania, which was the principal source of supply for coral, a material that was highly sought-after by the Celts from the beginning of the sixth century B.C.

For these reasons, it is nowadays believed that the revival of Celtic art, undoubtedly characterized by the assimilation of Greek and in particular Italiot models, began among the Senones of the Adriatic. This new tendency is known as either the "Continuous Vegetal Style," because of the prevalence of vegetable subjects such as garlands of palmettes and tendrils, or the "Waldalgesheim Style," whose name is taken from a grave in the Rhine Valley still considered to belong to the beginning of this development. This new style quickly spread among the transalpine Celts, bringing the art of the La Tène period to its apogee and introducing it to refined forms of dynamic composition. The acculturation of the Senones appears to have been very rapid, and their participation in the birth of the new vegetal style is testified to by a few rare artifacts dating from before the middle of the fourth century: the Filottrano torc and scabbard, the Moscano di Fabriano (Ancona) scabbard and fibula. The links that they have with analogous transalpine pieces clearly demonstrate that they were the first of the series, and still very close to the Italiot models. The objects that have reached us give us a very incomplete idea of the intensity and breadth of the influence of Magna Graecia. However, we can appreciate its extent by looking at the influence exerted, even as far as Bohemia, by the refined decoration of the Campanian *fibule*, and above all by the vogue for the so-called Herculean knot, which was common for a short time among the transalpine peoples but is attested to by the numerous examples found in the vast area that extends from Ireland to the Carpathian Basin. It is therefore possible that the influence exerted by the Italiot populations on the Celts was not limited to formal borrowings, and it is highly likely that the interest shown by the Celts from the early second quarter of the fourth century B.C. for the transitory forms of the "plastic metamorphosis" (well-illustrated in the first instance by the Filottrano scabbard) was inspired by the Pythagorean and Orphic doctrines, which some early writers associated with the doctrine of the Druids. The Danubian expansion and the "Great Expedition" of 280 B.C. created new areas of contact between the Celtic and the Hellenistic worlds. The spread of the Galatians into Asia Minor led to the rather rapid, almost complete Hellenization of the Celts, who were therefore sometimes referred to as Gallo-Greeks (*Hellenogalatai*). The only things that remained of the Celtic civilization at this stage were a few surnames, slight traces of the language that was still spoken up to the end of the fourth century, and some *fibulae* deriving from the La Tène period and datable to the third and second centuries B.C. The weaponry probably also conformed to the local manufacturing style, if we can believe the stone reliefs at Perga-

The Greek and Celtic Worlds: a Meeting of Two Cultures

Gold torc with Herculean knot
from Clonmacnoise, Ireland
beginning 3rd cent. B.C.
Dublin, National Museum of Ireland

Ornate bronze bracelet
with Celtic version
of the Herculean knot
second half 4th cent. B.C.
Saint-Germain-en-Laye
Musée des Antiquités Nationales

The Greek and Celtic Worlds: a Meeting of Two Cultures

Kantharos from Tomb G3/993
at Pećine
3rd cent. B.C.
Požarevac, Narodni Muzej

Bronze handle of a drinking horn
from Tomb 17
at Jászberény-Cseröhalom
end 3rd-beginning 2nd cent. B.C.
Szolnok, Damjanich János Múzeum

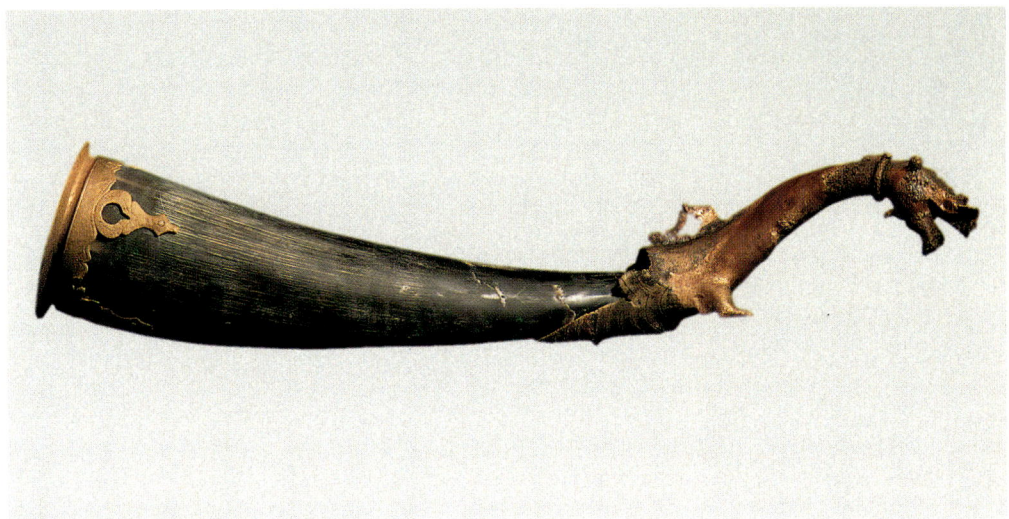

mum, on which the La Tène-type elongated shield (called *carnyx*) and the war trumpet are to be seen beside Greek weapons. The record left behind of the sacking of the Delphi sanctuary by Brennus' marauding army is indisputably one of the most successful incidences of propaganda in antiquity. It conceals in fact a much more complex reality, in which the actual clashes were probably no more numerous than the instances of collaboration and pacific exchange. There is evidence dating from the earlier third century B.C. testifying to such contacts, not only with the Italian or Balkan Celts but also with those from other geographical regions, particularly from those areas in which mercenaries and contingents for the military expeditions were regularly recruited. In the West, these areas were represented by the territory along the banks of the Rhone and the Languedoc; in the east by the territories along the middle Danube, an area that was freshly populated or perhaps had been settled in much earlier times. The Hellenistic influence was more evident in the Danube basin, which served as the starting point for the said "Great Expedition." Apart from Greek-made bronze vases, which could have been either the fruits of barter or plunder, we find a considerable number of terra-cotta vases that were undoubtedly inspired by metal or ceramic Hellenistic *kantharoi*. It is also evident that the Celtic artists adopted new iconographic subjects, no longer chosen at random but carefully selected according to their requirements, which demonstrated a good knowledge of the Hellenistic master-craftsmen's repertoire of bronze artifacts and jewelry. This was the case, for example, of the *ketos*, a sea dragon in notched clay, which in some central European works of art replaced the traditional griffin-headed snake monster.

A Hellenistic model could possibly explain the precise disposition that is hidden behind the appearance of disorder and spontaneity of the golden torc of Lasgraïsses. The floral cluster separated by the volute of an obliquely inclined band could have been inspired by garlands similar to the luxurious examples found in the necropolis at Canosa in Apulia.

The extraordinary ability of the Celtic artists in the third century B.C. to assimilate stylistic models and render them almost unrecognizable makes it virtually impossible to distinguish the copies from the originals, and only a few evident cases can be safely attributed to them. However, these examples are proof of a much more widespread phenomenon fostered by a sound knowledge of Hellenistic culture on the part of groups or individuals who, after acquiring this knowledge during their service in the military campaigns, returned to their country of origin.

The adoption of coins by the Celts, which were primarily used as a reliable form of retribution for mercenary engagements, gives an idea of the extent of influence the Hellenistic world had on the Celts. The most common models were Macedonian coins, such as the gold stater and the silver tetradrachm of Philip II and Alexander the Great; but the Ambiani of northern Gaul also imitated a coin of Tarentine mintage, and the so-called Roman-Campanian coins were imitated in the area that is now Bavaria. The exact chronology of the initial phase of the coinage of Celtic money is still under discussion, but it appears that knowledge of money was widespread among the Celts toward the end of the third century B.C., when the appearance of coins of smaller denomination than the stater, and the parallel use of gold and silver testify to the elaboration of a system used for barter.

The first Celtic *oppida* appeared in the first decades of the second century B.C., and were the result of a socioeconomic transformation whose most evident symptom was the adoption of coinage. It is clear that the contribution of the Hellenistic world must have played a decisive role in this apprenticeship to urban life. It was certainly no mere chance that the central European Celts still used the Greek alphabet at the beginning of the first century B.C. Caesar spoke of its use among the Helvetii, and the alphabetic sequence inscribed on some shards found at the *oppidum* site at Manching (Bavaria) strongly confirms this.

In adopting an urban model the Celts could not do better than follow the Hellenistic model, which had become the urban model *par excellence*. However, if in the sixth century B.C. the direct transplant of formal and unsuitable simple elements led to their rejection (a good example of which was the Heuneburg hillfort bastions), the birth of the *oppida* was, on the contrary, the result of two centuries of assimilation and adaptation to urban life and a socioeconomic system that was followed by a part of the Celtic people. This part was definitely a minority, but it was particularly influential and active and had the capacity and the time to adapt the Mediterranean model to the necessities and the possibilities of the Celtic world, thus beginning a fundamental chapter in the history of the settlement of Celtic (Europe). The Hellenic contribution to Celtic culture was, therefore, not so much due to the diffusion of Greek culture, but rather to how much the Celts understood and borrowed from it, so that when they came into direct contact with the Hellenistic world they were able to use this knowledge to their advantage.

Gold stater
from the Armorica area
3rd-2nd cent. B.C.
Paris, Bibliothèque Nationale
Cabinet des Médailles

Gold stater
of the Sequani
3rd-2nd cent. B.C.
Paris, Bibliothèque Nationale
Cabinet des Médailles

From the Early Colonies to the Fifth Century B.C.

"*Nam re etsi a Numa concepta est curiositas superstitiosa, nondum tamen aut simulacris aut templis res divina apud Romanos constabat. Frugi religio et pauperes ritus et nulla Capitolia certantia ad caelum, sed temeraria de caespite altaria, et vasa adhuc Samia, et nidor ex illis et deus ipse nusquam.*"
Tertullian, *Apologeticus* XXV. 12f.

Sicily and southern Italy
Arts and crafts in Sicily and southern Italy from around the mid-eighth century B.C. to the beginning of the fifth lack uniformity. The Greek colonists attempted to transmit the artistic motifs of the homeland throughout their new lands on the Italian peninsula. As early as the end of the eighth century B.C., however, figurative characteristics of a wholly local nature began to emerge both in colonial production and in that of the local, indigenous workshops. Among the Greek citizens participating in the process of colonization were countless artisans, whose primary task it was to produce bronzes, ceramics, terra-cottas. Doubtless, these craftsmen not only imbued their work with the traditional stylistic features of their hometowns, but began to bend their repertoire in order to cater to a local clientele of different tastes and background, thereby creating a "colonial style," which was characterized by an immediacy otherwise unencountered in the art of the Greek homeland. The constant flux of new migrant craftsmen from Greece provided considerable mobility in the assumption of styles and modes of expression which, while lacking the elegance of their Greek counterparts, vaunted an engaging naturalness and immediacy. For their part, the local craftsmen absorbed much of the incoming colonial ideas. While often misinterpreted and never fully grasped in an organic sense, the ideas thus assimilated gave birth to new inventions of mixed indigenous and colonial character that had repercussion on the culture within the colonies themselves. These opening remarks will help the reader understand why it would be misleading to consider the art of Sicily or Magna Graecia – or for that matter, of Apulia, Campania, or the Apennine and Adriatic regions – as something specific and unitary. Similarly, the labels "indigenous" and "colonial" are only indicators to help us identify phenomena that actually require investigating individually, according to area, as a means to defining a multiplicity of arts and crafts. It is not possible to speak in terms of artistic continuity or cultural independence, only of input and influences – often purely casual – which tended to slip into a local vernacular where the influence of authentic Greek formal culture was not constantly present.

From the end of the sixth century B.C. the influence of the colonial culture of the *poleis* on the artistic trends in the host lands shows signs of diminishing. The Greeks' attention turned from Sicily and Magna Graecia in order to deal with the demands of the Persian Wars and with the increasing pressures from the Punic peoples of Carthage and the native Etruscans. At the end of the seventh century, society in Sicily and Magna Graecia underwent deep changes, with a drift toward class stratification, compared with the previous aristocracy, in a sort of belated emulation of the social fabric of the original Greek oligarchies. Mass culture as such began to wane, and in its place emerged authentic dynasties, which cultivated the more sophisticated ideas typical of the Greek *poleis* (though these motifs were largely exclusive to rarefied social classes and therefore not in vogue throughout the population). The dismemberment of the lower-middle class that formed a common denominator among the Greek colonies (and the disparity that began to articulate itself in the needs of the different classes) favored the decadence of that "common" culture which had predominated in the early colonies of the West, albeit a somewhat rough culture susceptible to multiple influences. From their very foundation, the built-up areas of colonial cities were subdivided on an orthogonal pattern. The sanctuary buildings were largely Doric in style (due to the prevalence of Dorian immigrants). But this transposed style was quite different, and expressed an utterly novel monumentality and potency unprecedented in the Greek homeland. In time, this style began to undergo Ionic influences, betraying the desire to assimilate the monumental architectural forms of the eastern Greek world, resulting in totally hybrid forms of architecture.

Sculptural form, in the antique Daedalic tradition, broke away from its sources, particularly as regards buildings for worship. Myths were given a more local slant, with sagas in a mode more accessible to the colonial populations, based on the grandiose subjects of the poet Stesichorus. The sobriety of homeland sculpture was remolded with a new narrative delight, sometimes even anecdotal, and with great attention to detail. Staid Classicism gave way to more sturdy forms, spiced with gestural emphasis and deliberate hierarchies. The delayed preferences and unexpected adaptations of style, and the interference of heterogeneous styles, all betray the indiscriminate way in which formal motifs were borrowed simply as pointers for new and quite independent inventions. The few extant examples of local sculpture evince a certain heaviness, an earthy adherence to the material from which they are fashioned. Such local characteristics are most evident in the terra-cotta figures from the sanctuary hoards. As for vase decoration, the Classical topics tend to be impoverished by their compliance with local styles and tastes, with a somewhat bloated, coarse appearance. Alongside this colonial production, the native workshops developed types and styles of their own, particularly as regards pottery. Here the once handsome Greek vase shapes become stunted, clumsy, decorated with uneven and haphazardly arranged figures (sometimes merely to create a pattern). Among the examples of bronzework, a series of animal figures hark back to a distinctly "pagan" and earthy style. The terra-cottas and sculptures are predominantly seated, female figures depicting fertility, gazing fixedly ahead. The underlying preference for expression through symbolism is exemplified by the awkward placement of the bulbous eyes, and the limited number of features portrayed in the full figures, with their emphasis on the bust and head.

The craft production in regions that were, apparently, less affected by Greek colonial influence – such as Apulia, Picenum, and part of Campania – is more typical, the fruit of more independent branches of local culture, discernible in the shapes adopted and in the customary devotional items found in the sanctuary deposits. Most of these are weapons, utensils, funerary *stelai*, jewelry, and votive terra-cotta figures. The Greek influence shows in the pattern only, which is sometimes employed to lend formal syntax, but nonetheless remains ornamental. Classical myths or otherwise religious subjects are often introduced purely for playing out local styles, and represent customs that are virtually incomprehensible to the modern observer, including funeral rites and battles that fail to establish independent iconographical categories. The scenes thus illustrated are merely episodic, often obscure, owing to their fortuitous inclusion; many are executed in bold lines that recall more robust types of composition, but remain infantile and are lost in narrative minutiae, replete with detail and juxtapositions. This is the product of a basic mentality that is patently different from the categorical order typical of the Greek world. Some works, despite their often narrative immediacy and appeal, lack consistency in both quantity and quality; their presence is haphazard, and they have left no mark on the figurative culture of ancient Italy.

Sicily
The settlement along the coastlands of colonists with such a precise political organization inevitably caused upheavals in the life-styles of the native populations with which they came into contact. It may be that the bronze found on the coast was actually brought by the Greeks to be traded with the inland tribes for local iron. The Mendolito hoard also includes several masks (with others from the Acragas-Agrigento district) datable to the second half of the eighth century B.C.; these masks are in the form of stylized human-featured *protomai*, and are among the earliest extant examples of native art. As for pottery production, soon after the arrival of the first colonists, certain local potters began turning out vases in imitation of the Greek varieties.

The singular nature of colonial art in Sicily becomes more manifest in the seventh century B.C. The archaeological evidence indicates that even before the mid-seventh century there were vase-painters' workshops active at Syracuse and Megara. Similar evidence has been found for Gela. Local pottery soon began to assimilate a Greek style whose specific production site has yet to be pinpointed. An *oinochoe* from Polizello attests to traces of Greek forms, in the surface decoration in particular, with its inchoate Geometric accents and exuberant decorativism based ostensibly on the human form.

An even more consolidated native style is evident in the small bronze figures of animals. The most important of these, datable to around the end of the seventh century B.C., come from a votive deposit found in Castronuovo, the contents of which is largely composed of votive gifts from local shepherds. The spontaneity and immediacy of these animal representations testify to a direct and alert hand; the skill with which the animals' features are captured is particularly evident in a krater from Sabucina. Effectively, the vase takes its form from sixth-century Corinthian production, and yet the decoration is quite native in character: a wolf is portrayed in a ferocious stance, its forequarters greatly upscaled and its head viewed frontally.

Local production also shows certain distinct traits of its own as regards architectural models. One found at Sabucina derives from those that were frequently offered to the sanctuaries. However, the building rests unnaturally on a base; the antefixes and spectral *akroteria* at the crown of the building are particularly crudely fashioned, suggesting that the Greek model served merely for ideas for the native craftsman; while the heavy decoration is aimed at demonstrating the building's grandeur.

The typical characteristics of indigenous art in Sicily are found mainly in sculpture. Excavations at Megara have yielded a limestone figure of a woman suckling two babies. The theme itself originated in Mainland Greece in the sixth century. But the once clear forms of the Ionian subject have been altered: in this case the solemn, immobile figure of the woman proffers the hefty, heavily swaddled babies with powerful hands. She seems to be bearing her progeny like trophies symbolizing her affluence. The lower part of her clothing is rather unnaturally arranged, and the decoration suggests a taste for exhibition (even in the rendering of the toes). The same concept can be inferred from a seated figure found at Grammichele. Here the craftsman has employed terracotta, a more humble material, but also a more malleable one and seems to have reveled in it. While the surfaces are fluid, the figure is heavy and earthbound, like the clay from which it is fashioned. In this case too, the prototype can be found among the seated figures of sixth-century eastern Greece; here, however, the artist has put the emphasis on the earthly immanence of the figure (perhaps a female deity), by making the body stout and adopting a constrained frontal pose. The huge hands, the head slightly tilted up, the bulbous eyes, the faintly marked mouth, the heaviness of the clothing, show that the artist was more interested in the emblematic features of the divine presence, an emphasis that has detracted from the overall organic feel of the figure. The entire piece is projected toward the observer, and designed to be viewed head-on only.

Locally made bronzes tend to manifest the sculpting abilities of the native populations. One particular piece, from Mendolito, features a gift-bearer who, protected by his shield (perhaps once holding a spear in his left hand), is wearing full parade gear. The brash freshness of the figure, whose face is merely sketched, with his clergyman's haircut and bulky, flabby legs, is exemplary of the artistic limits of the local workshop production in the first half of the fifth century B.C.

Apulia

The region of Apulia developed under quite different auspices from Sicily. It appears that contacts with the Greek homeland were continuous (at least as far as regards the settlements in the Gulf of Taranto) from Mycenaean through the start of Geometric. However, a new wave of culture came to the region with the foundation of Taras (Roman Tarentum). The native inhabitants – the Daunii in the north, the Peucetii in the central region, and the Messapii in the south – had already formed a culture of their own, consisting of full-fledged urban settlements with certain common characteristics. Even before the arrival of the Greek colonists to Tarentum, these indigenous peoples had established contact with the opposite coast of the Adriatic. The Greek newcomers, therefore, were not dealing with subaltern populations – at least not culturally speaking – but with peoples possessing an established civilization of their own. Consequently, the Greeks found themselves forced to negotiate, rather than impose themselves, in order to make their own culture prevail. This may explain why local Apulian production was richer and more varied than that of Sicily, at least as far as artistic quality is concerned; it also means that Apulian crafts were the most strongly characterized of indigenous art throughout Magna Graecia.

Until a few decades ago the definition of Apulia's artistic culture was based almost entirely on the study of ceramic production. The discovery of hundreds of fragments of engraved and painted *stelai* in Daunia raised again the issue of the region's civilization in the historical age. For the most part, the *stelai* originate from the various necropolises of ancient Sipontum (though similar specimens have turned up in other Daunian sites). The *stelai* are fashioned from slabs of local limestone, and present schematic portraits of the deceased, standing upright, the head only hinted at, the body clad in embroidered cloth and adorned with necklaces, *fibulae*, other body ornaments and weaponry (in the case of male *stelai*). These ornaments make it possible to ascribe a chronology to each monument, at least from the seventh century B.C. Several scenes bear witness to the complexity of the iconography that had developed, together with a compositional talent that was unknown among other indigenous peoples. Regrettably, the *stelai* have not always been found in direct association with the tombs they originally adorned. Consequently, we have yet to supply a more detailed definition of the dating of these pieces, a reliable reconstruction of their chronological order in order to fathom the dynamics of such a complex class of items. The exegesis of certain funerary scenes depicting offertory processions (probably in honor of the deceased) and hunting scenes remains unclear. The sheer fixity of the figures (accentuated by the rigid or sketchy facial features), together with the opulence of the decoration (traced with a straightedge and compass), the barbarian abundance, and the studied arrangement of certain scenes (which acquire the status of true representations) raise these Daunian *stelai* above the other artifacts, and testify to a crafts production that may denote an authentic school of sorts. In fact, these *stelai* assimilate Greek models. When a more thorough study has been completed, revelatory comparisons will be made with the early type of Greek funerary *stelai* (of which very few examples have survived, perhaps because most were inscribed on wooden boards, no longer extant; some links, however, can be discerned in the stone pieces in the cemeteries of Athens, Paros, and Crete). Although the underlying stylistic traits are doubtless Greek (though as yet not pinpointed to a particular milieu), the scenes have been transformed to represent a purely local use: rather than attest to some simplistic assimilation of outside iconography, such subject matter could be transformed by the evolved Daunian culture to represent episodes of local tradition. The production of these *stelai* must have continued over a long period; it is furthermore feasible that they provided cues for other forms of sculpture (such as the head – perhaps for funerary purposes – found at Gnathia, datable to the sixth century B.C.).

Active relations between Apulia and Greece are confirmed by the importation of weaponry. In the seventh century B.C. a Cretan helmet seems to have reached the Italian peninsula, and the following century the shield grips discovered at Noicattaro. The indigenous art of Apulia is particularly well represented by indigenous ceramic works. Apulian vases subscribe to a set of characteristic shapes that are quite distinct from their Greek counterparts, and seem to draw inspiration from earlier works of local origin (thereby displaying an extraordinary consistency through prehistory and history). The vases in question are large-format items with an ample body; many were made for water storage, which was fundamental in such a dry region as Apulia. Their polychrome decoration is highly vivacious; in many cases they are further enhanced by relief work which, while not interfering with the vase walls or structure, flow uninhibitedly over it. The earliest specimens (ninth century B.C.) were discovered in Apulia (though examples were exported to Picenum and to the opposite coast of the Adriatic, testifying to Apulia's busy trade links abroad). The peak period of vase production in the region runs from the seventh to the fifth century B.C. The ceramics of Daunia have a characteristically dark and almost forbidding use of color, with sharp, resonant patterns. Some are given an additional relief motif, as in the type with a monster-animal, its paws resting on the rim (and the handle representing a misshapen head); other vases are decorated with small, hastily sketched figures. Peucetian production follows a more fragmentary style, its patterns less geometric though more rhythmic in the decorative motifs. In Messapian production, the decoration is more minute, its colors dimmer but the decorative patterns on the whole more organic. Daunian influence can be detected in a funerary bell (?) unearthed in the necropolis of Sala Consilina, datable to the sixth century B.C. The piece documents the assimilation of complex scenes of Greek Geometric (probably Attic), though reworked to represent more specifically local motifs. Two centuries later, after Geometric had been superseded in Mainland Greece it continued to flourish throughout Apulia. It is very unlikely that the Geometric style developed autonomously in Daunia; more probably (given the unmistakable links between features of local Geometric and that of Greece), craftsmen with firsthand knowledge of the Geometric style migrated to Apulia in the eighth century, leaving behind them certain fossilized ideas of the style with the indigenous population. Several antefixes of Daunian origin offer further evidence of the assimilation of the Geometric style; others betray a certain Daedalic influence, but are linguistically inferior (and were perhaps passed on from Etruria, through Campania). A series of small bronzes from Lucera, perhaps dating to the beginning of the seventh century B.C., demonstrates the presence of bronzeworkers with sufficient skill and self-assurance to reproduce those anecdotal features to which the Etruscan forgers were so partial in the eighth and seventh centuries B.C. (which derive from decorative bronze pieces from Greece, and from the Peloponnese in particular, perhaps mediated through Cumae and Campania).

Campania and southern Italy
At Ischia and Cumae on the mainland the colonists turned out vases that rivaled their Greek counterparts in quality. One krater illustrating a dramatic shipwreck incident (datable to the end of the eighth century) shows the craftsman's profound appreciation of the large-scale scenes borne by Attic funeral kraters. In this case, however, their assimilation is not simply a banal evocation of borrowed subject matter. The capsized ship, the struggling oarsmen assailed by huge fish (one of which is devouring the head of a sailor), the barbarians' acute sense of the destiny which, to their mind, haunted the colonists (in a more earthy, less epic vein than the scenes found on funeral vases of Athenian production) qualify the unknown Ischian vase-painter as the first illustrator of Greek life in the West. The grasp of certain mainland motifs (especially the highly singular ideas of Athenian origin) is formidable in the workshops in the Greek colony of Metapontum (second quarter of the seventh century B.C.). Besides executing special one-off commissions, the colonial workshops mass-produced pottery which, though derived from prototypes imported from Mainland Greece or brought down from Etruria, achieve an independent style utterly of their own; the buyers of such vessels were from Cumae and the coastland area of modern Salerno (and perhaps even Etruria itself). Similar phenomena characterize Etruscan production, particularly from Cerveteri, Vulci, and Veii, where the bird decoration (perhaps of Euboean tradition) is enlarged and transferred to the surface of pottery and wall-painting (witness the tomb at Veii) as early as the eighth century B.C. The motif predates the arrival of craftsmen from the Greek homelands – who quickly absorbed the Etruscan cultural climate – which went on for the whole of the seventh century B.C.

Ceramic art in Campania developed largely on the same lines as that of Sicily, in the sense the indigenous peoples very soon began to absorb the influences of the Greek culture with which it came into contact. The outcome, however, was different: the process of filtering Greek influences was very rapid indeed. Inland Campania possessed a varied culture of its own (witness the necropolis at Capua). The indigenous culture of Campania was diversified and well-developed (fostered by the sheer abundance of agricultural produce), and had established precise relations with the peoples of central Italy and Daunia; in fact it enjoyed a certain hegemony throughout Campania, but also around Salerno and in the valley populations in the interior. The arrival of the Greek colonists spurred the native peoples to generate an artistic *koine* that, when seen alongside that of the colonists, betrays a marked independence (and a certain degree of formal autonomy also). Of likely Greek influence are the bronze figurines that characterize the very early phases of Campanian production. With their engaging natural treatment, the figurines are charged with considerable expressive potential. The production of small bronzes was not limited to Campania alone, but through this region the stimulus reached peoples in the interior and as far down as Lucania. The incoming Greek types gave new impetus to local styles, such as the one Tertullian attributed to the Romans during the reign of King Numa (see Latin quote at the start of this essay). The establishment of cult worship by the colonists prompted the native populations to better define their own. Indigenous sanctuaries were created and developed, such as those at Capua, Montecassino, at the mouth of the Garigliano River, and at Cales. In these sanctuaries the local peoples practiced their own forms of worship, and made votive offerings to their deities. These innumerable votive items were in clay, and were mostly fashioned on-site in the sanctuaries themselves, ready to be sold to the pilgrims who visited during the ritual feast days. It is not yet clear whether the craftsmen were exclusive, or if the votives were produced under commission by artisans of renowned ability: great is their affinity with the artistic creations of the bread-bakers and sweet-makers. Generally speaking, the extant examples lack stylistic skill, and while on occasion they can be traced to the Greek monuments of which the craftsman may have had some knowledge (monuments that are invariably reworked with countrified boldness, without much concern), in most cases it would be pointless to attempt an identification of cultural origin. The figures presented are lanky, unsteady, their arms and legs elongated, their meager bodies surmounted by sketchy, improbable heads. In some instances, the craftsman seems to have felt a rush of creative enthusiasm, and the clay appears to take the upper hand, resulting in an abundance of curls, and the incisions become exuberant and betray a paucity of restraint that is untypical of the Classical world. Similar phenomena, at formal level, are perceivable in the production of certain cinerary urns, such as those of Pontecagnano. The encounter with the colonists prompted the native populations, moreover, to build temples with broad, low eaves. To decorate these buildings they devised Gorgon antefixes (either whole or simply with a gruesome head), with women capturing birds (perhaps in imitation of Artemis), or with women in flight: an entire range whose meaning is barely comprehensible. The human features seem to travel haphazardly over the surface of the clay, the faces emphasized to make them apparently more visible to the observer; the various parts of the body do not coalesce into an organic idea, but often provide a figurative schema that is utterly divorced from the organic forms from which they derive. When, in the second half of the sixth century, Campania was incorporated into the cultural sphere of the Etruscans, the local motifs received further impulse from a more well-defined iconographic repertoire, at which point the antefixes gained a nimbus, the figures became more articulated, despite a singular paucity of formal values. From Capua this repertoire spread through the whole of central and southern Italy. Local pottery workshops assimilated the subject matter of the Etrusco-Corinthian ones, perhaps at Pontecagnano. During the sixth century, and for part of the fifth, Capua seems to have experienced a surge of importance. This period saw the first so-called "mother" figures, dedicated in a sanctuary near the town. The figures featured a seated female figure sculpted from local tuff, holding one or more infants. A similar figure had emerged in Sicily, as exemplified by the specimen found at Megara. In this case, however, the rendering is cruder, more approximated. The earliest sculptures of this category are hewn from blocks of tuff, according to size; the figures tend to be schematic, their features merely hinted at. In time, however, the execution became more complex, the number of babies proudly borne in their arms steadily multiplied in boastful proclamation of fecund motherhood. The statues were offered by the women of Capua to the goddess that had assisted them through childbirth. This ritual, and the strong earthbound sense of assessing a life by the amount of progeny, are further evidence of a farming culture, ever tied to the land whence it sprang. The Capua neighborhood, probably a sanctuary near a freshwater spring, is the origin of a terra-cotta head of local stamp, perhaps dating to the fifth century B.C. In this unusual piece, the last vestiges of Classicism have completely disappeared. The artist seems to revel in the exploitation of the material alone; the mass of hair consists of overlaid pieces of clay, the beard from clumps of compressed clay; the eyelids and brows are scored in with a stylus. Despite his efforts, however, the artisan's work is formally inchoate. Recent finds in Lucania (Serra di Vaglio, Lavello, Melfi) and especially the plentiful grave goods in princely tombs testify to how the customs of the Lucanian population attuned themselves to cultural conventions dictated by their aristocracy in the seventh century (which had assimilated the characteristics of the previous eighth-century aristocracy). A chief feature of this situation is the vast use of amber, perhaps imported from a Hellenized center in Picenum; of *fibulae* in silver; of bronzework, still adhering to the Archaic iconography; of goldwork, perhaps ordered directly and imported from Greece itself, like the weapons.

The Atestine or Situla culture
At the town of Este near Padua, the culture known as Atestine or Situla has been more precisely defined and grouped into four phases (spanning the eighth century B.C. through Roman times). This subdivision is of a

Greek Influence on Italic Art

The *Capestrano Warrior*
funerary statue from the Picene area
6th cent. B.C.
Chieti, Museo Nazionale

scholastic and generic nature, and does not actually correspond to precise cultural epochs. While the material evidence found at Este has been considerable – to the extent that the culture has been assigned separate phases – the characteristics of the so-called Atestine culture are highly complex if we limit our study to the sphere of this city alone, which was more receptive than creative as regards artistic forms that cover a broader geographical area and hence comprise a wider range of artistic expression.

The Atestine culture is the byproduct of a merger of several different cultural currents. The Hallstatt culture further north had shown a traditional skill in metallurgy (with a whole repertoire of characteristic decorative motifs of distant Celtic culture) and a highly active trade network typical of the Baltic Sea for the diffusion of artifacts through busy trading that covered the regions on either side of the Alps. Through the Etruscan city of Felsina (Bologna), the Atestine culture was in direct contact with the Etruscans, and provided a crucial bridge for many technical and visual devices of their Italic neighbors, including the Etruscan forms for certain objects and perhaps the more organic sense of narrative arrangement of the features of a more Orientalizing culture (features in which the Atestine culture abounds). Today, however, it is difficult to ascertain exactly how these Orientalizing elements actually spread and became an intrinsic part of this culture's essential heritage. The question of the Etruscan contribution to the early phases of Atestine culture remains still unsolved, notwithstanding the recent finds. The lack of information regarding how these motifs were actually assimilated – whether they were transmitted via traveling craftsmen, or by sea – (and above all the impossibility of establishing the periods and phases of this assimilation) means that, for the time being at least, the phenomena involved cannot be more precisely defined. Undoubtedly, the assimilation of Orientalizing motifs did not take place too early; the first evidence in fact dates back to the seventh century B.C. Among the common products of Atestine culture are items for domestic use, such as the characteristic *situlae*; the *fibulae*, with their striking plasticity; and not least weaponry, including heavy belts, helmets, daggers, and the like. Generally speaking, techniques of metalworking were widespread, such as embossing and engraving on copper and bronze. The sheer naturalness of certain scenes represented in this way is astonishing: soldiers on the march, cultural pageants, and athletic contests. While many such processions of figures – at times of monstrous animals – betray a certain narrative backwardness, the composition itself is thorough and carefully calibrated. Some of these scenes are among the scant few of early Italy to possess a convincing and quite characteristic grasp of narrative. But the entire issue of Celtic influence needs to be reassessed in light of the discovery of several princely tombs at Verucchio near Rimini, on the Adriatic. The superb wooden items of the grave goods (e.g., the decorated intaglio throne) and other artifacts in bronze, gold, amber, ivory (perhaps from a hippopotamus), attest to the existence of two trends of craftwork as early as the seventh century. A Celtic current is particularly noticeable in the woodwork and goldwork; the other (in a Greek vein) was composed of craftsmen with outstanding talents in the production of items in ivory, and particularly in amber, imported from the Baltic.

Picenum

The artistic culture of the Picenum region has yet to be given greater definition. While new discoveries on the one hand have brought greater firsthand knowledge of the material evidence of the region, on the other they have so far failed to enable any concrete judgments on the basic attributes of the so-called Piceni peoples. Thus said, our knowledge has been much advanced by the discovery of such necropolises as those at Campovalano, Novilara, and Numana on the coast; and Fabriano, Capestrano, and in part also Alfedena further inland. The overall impression is distinctly unitary, and fits in with the picture offered by certain sporadic finds (at Pitino, Ripatransone, Rapino, Belmonte, Bellante, Loreto Aprutino, and Guardiagrele, for instance). From the ninth century B.C. these territories were under external influence: on the one hand, they experienced the penetration of the so-called Villanova culture; on the other, the influence of Apulia or, more precisely, of the Daunii. During the eighth and seventh centuries B.C. – and to a greater degree in the sixth – the Picene settlements were under fairly precise cultural influences: the Atestine to the north, the Etruscan to the west (through the Apennine passes), Daunian culture from Apulia in the south; and, lastly, Greek culture itself, which arrived by sea. The Picene culture took some time to form, and drew on from a variety of disparate sources, not acquiring any real individuality perhaps until toward the close of the sixth century B.C. But it would be a serious mistake of methodology to infer that Etruscan culture prevailed over the formation of Picene culture: the Etruscan contribution seems to have declined steadily, while it seems viable to affirm that the Celtic influence – and particularly the Greek and Daunian ascendancy – were more important.

Certain artifacts that have been unearthed in the burial grounds testify moreover to the diversity of provenance. The plentiful objects made of amber may well have come from the Baltic; the ivories are undoubtedly of eastern origin (perhaps from Laconia). Phoenician imports are also attested. The vast quantities of imported bronze items suggest an accumulation of material that had gone out of use, in a region that possessed a considerable amount of exchange goods (testified by the traditional custom of accumulating less sought-after materials that were nonetheless very popular among the community, which possessed its own foundries and finishing workshops). From midway through the sixth century Greek influence steadily increased, as affirmed by the diffuse importation of Attic black-figure vases. By the end of the fifth century, Greek influence had become predominant. And yet one can detect a certain reluctance among local craftsmen and workshops in the stubborn division between the Greek *emporion* and their own markets, which were often no more than a few hundred yards from each other. Among the characteristics of these people was their continued interest in other outside cultures, their inherent independence and attachment to their own rites and routines, and not without reason: they were accustomed to a comfortable, affluent life-style.

Among the more characteristic forms of archaeological evidence are the *stelai* marking several tombs in the necropolis of Novilara. These can be better understood when compared with those of Daunia (in some cases the similarities are striking, though the specimens in question evidently belong to a far broader cultural sphere, given the analogies with funerary sculptures of Nesazio in Istria, where there is evidence of imported Apulian pottery). The *stelai* are carved with lively hunting scenes, and battles on land or sea. In one case, the reverse of the *stele* carries a long, continuous spiral decoration of Celtic tradition. The chronology of these slabs is still under discussion, but where the *stelai* are still in place, the evidence suggests a date of mid-seventh century B.C. Unlike the Daunian *stelai*, with their somewhat static though well-crafted anthropomorphic designs, the Novilara *stelai* are noticeably more spontaneous. The carvings offer scenes of combat conducted by the Novilara tribes both on land and at sea. Such battles might be linked to sagas that were typical of the narrative heritage of all peoples of the Classical world. The wealthy townsfolk appear to have transposed their own deeds into mythical stories: the figures doing battle become legion, and the beasts in the hunt assume fearful proportions. Even animals not native to the peninsula, such as lions, make their appearance, together with winged demons, monsters, and symbols, all depicted in a farfetched mortal fray. The narration of sagas and the inclusion of personal biographical detail are done with a fresh, albeit ingenuous, immediacy (in the characterization of the feats portrayed and in the assimilation of the iconographical repertoire). The figures are never more than sketched; the composition is created by haphazard layering on different planes; the scenes reflect a basic desire to fill rather than construct a sense of space, which as a result remains vacant. Owing to the craftsmen's technical shortcomings in working the stone, the designs are frequently overrun with somewhat exuberant spiral patterns.

In the Warrior's Tomb at Fabriano, datable to the mid-seventh century, the *situlae* embossed with monstrous animals forms, and the shields engraved with corteges of horsemen, hoplite soldiers, and animals, are evidence of a fairly definite contact with the Orientalizing milieus of Este and the Alpine region. Our appraisal of Picene culture can only become definitive with the long-awaited publication of material from the tombs of Pitino and Numana. A princely tomb (of a woman) datable to approximately mid-sixth century B.C. entails a set of grave goods with abundant imported pottery, bronzes, silverwork, and ivories; the deceased's tumulus included two entire chariots. Upon close analysis, the grave goods suggest that craftsmen of Greek origin in the Picene area worked pieces of amber imported from the Baltic. The representation of the human figure, which already by the seventh century B.C. manifested that fresh sketchiness of certain small bronzes (probably portraying gift-bearers, in which relief and *stelai* figures are copied in the round), continued in the approximation of figurines surmounting or hanging from bronze pendants, and found an outlet in monumental applications toward the end of the sixth century. The site at Numara has yielded a colossal head in a crested helmet, presumably once crowning a funeral statue. While the execution of the head is markedly disorganic, almost as if it were inflated from inside, with small eyes and the features barely hinted at, the monumental effect of the whole is undeniable. The sculpture poses the problem of determining just how the craftsmen managed to achieve such imposing representations for these immense tomb statues, which rear up in defense of the dead.

Excavations carried out in the necropolis of Campovalano have yielded a considerable quantity of material, most of which seems datable to the sixth century B.C., and allows for a more in-depth assessment of the Picene civilization. Another find, a large *olla* with applied decoration on the lid and figures carved into the body (animals and combatants) could date to the sixth century in relation to Falisco-Etruscan material, but also seems to borrow from the engraved *stele* repertoire (the presence of a glass spindle whose place of origin is not definable testifies to the importance of women in the spheres of the Picene aristocracy). Despite the highly reduced dimensions of the figures represented, the numerous human-figure *protomai* betray a basic monumentality that strongly distinguishes them from the small bronzes. A *stele* from Belmonte demonstrates the quality obtained by isolating figures on a given plane, lifting them out of the narrative context.

Picene art offered a basis from which the warrior peoples inhabiting the interior made their explorations into form and design. The decoration of the earliest weaponry found in the necropolis at Alfedena (sixth century B.C.) illustrates the extent of this tribe's assimilation of the standard designs of Picene processional arms. Picene craftsmanship also shows through in what is perhaps the most significant sculpture yet discovered in central Italy, namely, the *Capestrano Warrior* (Museo Archeologico Nazionale, Chieti). This towering statue, sculpted from limestone and enhanced with some painted details, guarded the tomb of one of the leading chieftains buried in the necropolis. Supported on either side by pillars carved laterally with representations of two spears, the warrior's head is crowned with a striking, wide-brimmed parade headpiece and his face is obscured by a mask. His folded arms are adorned with armbands and he wears a stiff necklace. In his right hand he seems to be clutching a commander's banner; the sword with its embossed hilt hangs from his chest harness, and likewise a dagger. His heart is protected by two armored pectoral disks, his abdomen by a heavy, belted piece of armor, his legs by shin-plates; he is shod in sandals. An inscription presumably once bore the deceased's name. But this magnificent warrior is not an isolated case in Picene production. In addition to the Numana head, an inscribed *stele* has been found at Guardiagrele (which closely matches the first) and a female bust from the same necropolis at Capestrano. The sculptures affirm that statues for the deceased were a fairly regular occurrence in the burial grounds, providing a form of signpost. Some scholars consider the sculptures to be basically upscaled transpositions of the motifs used in a great deal of small statuary and sculptural reliefs, or of the figures carved into the *stelai*; others, however, have drawn attention to the *kouroi* figures that adorn some tombs in Mainland Greece. Such comparisons nonetheless fail to account for the religious purpose and iconographic basis to the *Capestrano Warrior*. Without doubt, the statue was originally part of a funerary structure. It may well have been a portrait of the deceased, armed for his last battle parade, defending his name as a warrior and his family's estate against death, alone, on the plain of the cemetery. In this theatrical and essentially earthly defense of his pride and estate, the warrior is a worthy precursor of those Romans of high lineage recorded by Polybius (*Histories* VI. 53), whose effigies were placed on display beneath the rostrum in the forum, before the public, and were adorned by family members with masks of their illustrious ancestors. The *Capestrano Warrior* is also an effigy of a deceased person, propped up by posts under his arms, his face hidden by a mask, disguising his inability to command. His arms are still, and his right hand vainly grips a banner. But the "awfulness" of this personage is supposed to reach out beyond the living, by dint of the memory of his ancestry, and the inscription may be the equivalent of the *cursus honorum*, a biography of the warrior, as it were. The stunted head, the slender flanks, the body with its almost female listlessness, the minutiae of the personal ornaments (an outspoken sign of affluence), while detracting from the organic sense of the whole, by no means diminish the sheer fixity of the deceased's pose.

The sculpture has an innate monumentality alien to the Italic world (and starkly contrasting with the patently human features of the great *kouroi* figures): such monumentality stems from the ability to play out features that identify and underline the moral, warrior nature of the deceased in question. The ideology that can be discerned in the Capestrano figure is not a chance episode but the upshot of an iconographic and stylistic codification. For this reason it is not alone, and the others associated with it are the manifestation of a civilization with an inherent cohesiveness, a society that found a bastion against the ravages of time in the military ranks and juridical classes of the upcoming civilization of republican Rome, after centuries of uncertainty. The *Capestrano Warrior* represents the pinnacle of the Picene craftsmen's skills in monumental artistry (a feature assimilable with Rome itself).

Liguria

The discovery of a large necropolis at Chiavari, in one of the rare cultivable valleys of the Ligurian coast, has raised new issues regarding the history of the region's artistic production. The necropolis has yielded a great number of tombs (datable to the seventh century B.C.), which, on the one hand, betray similarities with the Etruscan and Faliscan cultures; on the other, they also show a certain independence at formal level, in the shapes and decorative designs, which tend to have elements of a still generic nature when compared with other manifestations of eastern-influenced culture on the peninsula.

Campania and Southern Italy from the Fifth Century to the Invasion of Hannibal

> *"Nec enim temere ullus pulchrior in urbem aut speciosor triumphus intravit. Ante hunc diem nihil praeter pecora Vulscorum, greges Sabinorum, carpenta Gallorum, fracta Samnitium arma vidisses: tum si captivos aspiceres, Molossi, Thessali, Macedones, Bruttius, Apulus atque Lucanus; si pompam, aurum, purpura, signa, tabulae Tarentinaeque deliciae."*
> Florus, *Epitome de Gestis Romanorum* I. XIII. 26f.

Central and southern Italy
The situation in these regions changes between the early fifth century B.C. and Hannibal's invasion of the peninsula. Once again, it is impossible to provide an articulate picture of the various manifestations of artistic expression. Here we will only point out how, in various separate geographical zones, certain trends emerged denoting several different cultural backgrounds. The written sources are not helpful in this issue. Actually, some of them, such as the epigraphs, tend to label the period preceding the fifth century as being subaltern, a supposition that is simply not corroborated by the archaeological evidence, which instead emphasizes the splendor of the fifth and of the fourth centuries B.C.

First, however, we must comprehend the state of the native world in the fifth and early fourth centuries B.C.: it was no longer simply a culture posing a sort of "counterreaction" to that of the colonial spheres, but a culture which, in order to survive intact, was obliged to raise its standards to a more civilized, dignified level. This inclination is most conspicuous in the constitutional, juridical, and military codes, which at this point in time assume an overriding importance and paved the way for a separate articulation of public law. The road to independence must have been long and fraught with difficulties, undermined from within by dissidence, and never far from complete disruption. It was in such circumstances that Rome rose against its rival cities on the peninsula, assimilating certain aspects of the native cultures, and gradually emerging as the cultural hub of central Italy. The tribes inhabiting the mountainous areas of the country continued to fine-tune their organization, particularly their armies, while the aristocracies collapsed completely. Meanwhile in Apulia, and to some extent in Campania, the towns tended to upkeep a tone of civil life of their own kind: it was these cities in particular that proved to have assimilated the features of the colonization of Thurii. During this period, which saw some of the grimmest years in the history of the peninsula (including invasions perpetrated by the forces of Carthage in the south, and by the Gauls in the north), the first signs of a common trajectory began to manifest themselves, signs that would lead to a gradual unification, investing the native tradition with broader civil values. The panorama changes from the mid-fourth century.

The populations of Apulia and to some extent those of Campania attempted to assimilate as far as possible the characteristics of the incoming civilization, which had its origins largely in Macedonia. It was no longer a question of evoking the outdated idiom of Atticism (which had been proposed through the foundation of Thurii), but of interpreting the classical themes through the revision of the Macedonian state and then in the Hellenistic courts. The Hellenistic culture found particularly fertile ground at Taras (Roman Tarentum), and from here it spread through the rest of the peninsula, with resounding consequences in Etruria. In Sicily, the city that most readily assimilated the Hellenistic idiom was Syracuse, though to a lesser degree. Despite this diffusion, the influence of Hellenistic culture was limited to the constitutional and civil structures of the cities in southern Italy and Sicily. This limit was handed down from colonial culture, whose aim was to form isolated and self-defining mores, impervious to things exotic. In the case in question, this entrenched restriction was even more accentuated: the new culture being welcomed was a class culture, based on features of the courtly spheres of northern Greece, Egypt, and the Orient, a culture whose style and schema were to be reiterated. It was not formative for the intermediate social classes or those below, and for this reason Rome was its most crude exponent, crude but self-assured and outspoken.

In the third century B.C. mainland Italy was characterized by a fashion or tendency toward Hellenism rather than by an authentic Hellenistic culture as such. This fashion was restricted to specific spheres of the society, and not always tolerated among the middle classes. At the end of the third century B.C. the peninsula faced its most difficult test: for fifteen long years the Carthaginian troops under Hannibal raided the peninsula. An endless struggle emerged between the Punic and the Roman civilizations, a struggle which saw the latter finally victorious, albeit at a terrible price. The Roman juridical codes showed their mettle and abilities, but at the end of the Second Punic War the country was on its knees: the artisan livelihood of the smallholder farmers was destroyed, and with it the economy of the intermediate and subaltern classes, which had in part modeled themselves on Hellenistic society. As regards the intermediate and subordinate culture, the start of the second century saw the disappearance of Hellenistic subject matter (or at most, it tends to remain fossilized on bygone themes). The native culture, meanwhile, is shapeless and inexpressive in formal terms. From the above outline, it is clear that it is practically impossible to split up the artistic production of the fifth to second centuries B.C. into precise areas. Instead we are forced to trace somewhat broad outlines to describe cultural spheres that share affinities of some kind, or even generic features.

In contrast with this affirmation, certain noble families of Rome assimilated the typical features of Hellenistic luxury, as attested by the portraits of Scipio Africanus (on a ring) and Flamininus (a gold coin). These were the canons to which the Roman *nobilitas* aspired from the early decades of the first century B.C.

Apulia and most of southern Italy (especially Campania) are a case in point. At the time of the foundation of Thurii there must have been a great many vase-painters among the colonists residing in these regions. These craftsmen were responsible for the introduction of Athenian motifs to local vase production. Soon, however, especially in Tarentum, new trends began to emerge in local pottery, as the very shapes of the vases themselves became exaggerated, far larger than their Attic prototypes, and were embellished with eccentric relief decorations (of local stamp), with a tendency toward "rural" monumentality; in other cases, the shapes became more elaborate, often typical of the funerary type. Vase decoration, which in Attic examples as early as the second quarter of the fifth century had begun to attest to the shortcomings of two-color (black and red) surface decoration for representing the conventions of Greek painting, attempted to expand the possibilities with the addition of coloring that departed markedly from the prerogatives of linear decoration on pottery (white, purple, yellow, gold). A first phase in a Hellenizing style was followed by vases infused with native motifs. The warriors represented in the *sacella* (corresponding to those carved into the monumental *stelai* of Athens in the fourth century B.C.) fill the belly of the vases of this period.

The Classical essentialness gives way to an imaginative description of weaponry, ornament, and local custom. On some examples, the plant motifs become preeminent and overscaled, filling the neck and the backs of the vases. Overall, the production is substantially disorganic, corresponded by the immediacy of some of the mythical scenes, overdramatized, exotic, or patently comical (in a truculent assimilation or parody of the saga repertory being developed by the highly evolved society of Athens). Alongside this natural, carefree rendering of the smaller figures was an evident taste for narrative simplification, such as in the erotic or banquet scenes. By the middle of the fourth century the ceramics begin to carry hints of a shift toward a more complex and refined art of the type that prevailed in the Macedonian court. Highlighting appears on certain vases, testifying to the attempt to emulate the major themes of painting in the Greek homeland, using a wide palette of colors; other vases strive to reproduce toreutic patterns in terra-cotta. The so-called Gnathian ware, which declined at the beginning of the third century B.C., denotes the assimilation of the more advanced cultural milieu that prevailed in both Athens and Egypt. Other artifacts produced in Tarentum include coroplastic production, a category that affords a vast quantity of heads in the round, statuettes, *pinakes* (some of which show an outstanding level of workmanship), all testifying to the existence of workshops with a considerable output. The numerous funerary monuments of this Greek colony often comprise relief decorations sculpted into the limestone (friezes and metopes) that suggest an interest in some of the more complex visual challenges being tackled by the artistic community in Greece itself. Some of these monuments comprise fictile antefixes of considerable quality, whose subject matter is evidently Hellenistic.

Tarentum was the source of the diffusion of certain iconographical and formal ideas in painting that soon spread throughout Apulia (and were transmitted as far as Etruria); similarly, Tarentum hosted a great many gold- and silversmiths, whose work found a wide public and was widely imitated. Indeed, the Macedonian lesson had been well learned. A similar panorama, albeit less intense, is documented in Sicily. Here coroplasts and vase-painters thrived, and some turned out specimens with notably fine polychrome decoration. Vase factories sprang up at Paestum (Greek Poseidonia) and elsewhere in Campania, but this production is clearly nothing more than a local, colonial, representation of the art that was evolving in the Greek homeland.

The gold workshops and the engravers of Alexandrian tradition had a marked effect on the more elaborate artistic production of Sicily. It is worth examining indigenous production which, though ostensibly drawing from Hellenistic models, achieved a set of formal values of its own; indeed, alongside the Hellenizing vases, the local workshops continued to turn out vessels modeled on their own designs. Among the more characteristic types are the large-format *askoi*, which on occasion (as in the case of the *askos* from Lavello) offer an unsophisticated if intense narrative of a funeral rite. The figures are barely sketched in and are wholly local in style and taste. Other examples are adorned with female heads seen frontally, as if to match the *protomai* featured on the larger figure-painted vessels. Still others are enhanced by an elaborate but somewhat cumbersome decoration of figures or sculpted *protomai* that seem to herald the transfer of toreutics to the realm of pottery art. The vase-painters who worked on these items were most likely also engaged to decorate the interiors of the tombs of some of the more wealthy patrons. In Apulia (at Ruvo and Canosa), in Lucania (in the superb series at Paestum), in Campania (at Capua and Cumae), these painters were called in to decorate the sarcophagi and mortuary chambers (with dancing girls, devotees, warriors, battle scenes, funeral rites, scenes of the afterlife). These paintings are executed with a vivid palette, with figures crowding the field, more through simple juxtaposition than through an organic idea of distribution.

The authors of these representations reveal the limitations of their craft, however. While they achieve considerable skill in the decoration of vase surfaces, when required to illustrate the walls of sarcophagi or tombs – spaces of much larger dimensions – they seem to balk, and their compositions are laborious and rather basic. (This is a repeat of a phenomenon common in Etruria in the later sixth century, by which the "pontic" potter, on their arrival from the East, found themselves painting the large surfaces of the tomb walls.) In the vast majority of cases, the artists prove incapable of enlarging their vase-painting without destroying the iconographic and stylistic substance of the figures. These reappear in overabundant and approximate scenes, demonstrating the technical shortcomings of craftsmen unable to transfer their skills to works of different dimensions (that require a different kind of ability). Where in other conditions perhaps the passage from vase-painting to painting wall compositions for funerary chambers and sarcophagi might have spawned a "school," in southern Italy the level of craftsmanship was too limited to supersede such elementary difficulties.

Craftwork in Campania seems to have enjoyed a greater measure of independence, perhaps because the region was further from the principal centers of colonial art. Not enough is known of the production of the Hellenized towns along the coast, whose craftsmen undoubtedly produced works of greater scope than those of the inland towns. The most significant hoards are those of Capua. Here the production of statues in tuff, given up as votive offerings on the part of mothers, was continuous. However, the original, Classical stamp of the early specimens of such votive statues gives way to exclusively local forms. The seated mother-figures display their progeny in accordion fashion, their pride lying in the sheer number of children borne, in some case exceeding the dozen, a pride that somehow seems to supplant a more intimate feeling for their offspring. The rather overblown gesture and the stockiness of these rural figures are insufficient justification for the basic shortcomings and uncouthness of their execution.

The production of terra-cotta figures seems to have provided the Campanian artists with a more congenial outlet for their skills. Besides the common terra-cotta figurines, the workshops turned out certain large-format types, either life-size or even larger. And yet this upscaled type of statue was no more than an enlargement of the figurines, and the poor results are similar to those obtained by the vase-painters with their murals and sarcophagus paintings (the scale makes the subjects dull and ungainly, their details overdone, with a basic lack of consistency). The resulting art is close on pastiche. In vain the craftsman has tried to conceal his rawness with gimmicks of the kind we find among the coroplasts, who resorted to using bits of clay to supplant the creation of real sculptural details, with little balls or cubes of more "liquid" material. The basic sketchiness verges on caricature, and these figures of youths like "stuffed shirts" with no real framework and futile gesturing, these heavy, earthbound women, suggest a society that preferred to parody rather than emulate the subject matter of the refined Greek originators.

There is, however, one notable area of Campanian production that stands out above the rest, and that is the group of votive busts found in the sanctuaries. In this case, given the rank of their clients, the craftsmen paid scant attention to stylistic canons and produced artifacts of an entirely freer, more sincere type. Some of these are strikingly immediate, though crudely rendered, with a deliberate overstatement of features. The faces gaze at the observer, and the artists have dilated the material unnaturally, showing skill not so much in establishing a sense of organic form to the figures, as in endowing the individual anatomical details with plasticity (sometimes outrageously mis-scaled). Such figures are an eloquent testimony to this culture's conviction that clay was the craftsman's premier medium.

To this period belongs one of Campania's most singular pieces, a metope unearthed in association with the triangular forum at Pompeii, perhaps datable to the third century B.C. The main, uncommonly broad field is set with three figures in relief: Athena, perhaps Daedalus pinning his son Icarus to a wheel (or possibly Hephaestus pinning down Ixion). The stocky figures stare out at the observer, gesticulating in some pageant. They seem to communicate among themselves only for the consent of those attending the scene. The implacable weapons of Athena have been forsaken for the tools of the carpenter, those same tools that the Campanian craftsmen used habitually in their daily work, and whose prominence here seems to overlay the myth with the ingenuity of a class of workers proud of their craftsmanship.

Owing to its inherent characteristics in even earlier times, Campania is the region which, ever verging on formal breakthrough, was able to mediate the tendencies of Hellenistic art for the southern part of the peninsula and the Apennine region. On either side of the Apennines, in central and southern Italy – and particularly in the territories that correspond to today's Abruzzo, Molise, Campania, Apulia, Lucania, part of Calabria, and by induction part of Lazio, the Marches, and Umbria – the land was covered with woods that nonetheless permitted grazing for livestock, except in a few rare places where the forest was too thick. Until more recent times these were the best areas for raising livestock such as sheep and swine.

The region's chief characteristics were the structure of the flocks and herds, the regular seasonal transfer of animals from one area to another, the market economy, characterized by the return to the valley grazing grounds in early autumn after passing spring and summer in the foothills. The people were nomadic, despite having sturdily fortified towns, and hence were particularly suitable go-betweens for cultural characteristics picked up during their travels, and particularly at the market fairs. This way of life facilitated a kind of ongoing cultural osmosis, particularly in the case of Apulia and Campania, along those sheep-tracks in the countryside over which the drovers traveled with their folds, one of the primary sources of livelihood for the mountain populations of ancient Italy. This pastoral civilization was governed by strict laws of conduct tied to age-long customs; yet it was permeable to outside influences, adapting foreign practices to its own mode of life. The interchange that took place between the farmer cultures of Campania and Apulia and the trader communities of the Greek colonies in no way interrupted the seasoned habits and ways of life of the native populations. The herdsmen must have been well-armed, a necessary precaution against marauders and predators, and their capital was presumably composed of easy-to-carry items. Their forms of worship were inevitably tied to the changing grazing periods; the temples or sanctuaries were sited along the transhumance routes, which were dictated by the presence of springs and brooks, by choice pastures, and by key intersections with other drover routes. The votive offerings given up at the sanctuaries consisted largely of cast bronze coins minted in towns all over central and southern Italy. Other gifts include statuettes depicting herdsmen and soldiers, Heracles and Mars, or of women; small vases; terra-cotta animal figures; statues portraying the gift-bearers, and any number of heads (male and female) fashioned in the likeness of the dedicator, or models of parts of the body testifying to a cure granted by the deity.

The sanctuary at Carsoli in Abruzzo gives an idea of what these sacred shrines were like, with their clustered, mobile pavilions in which the craftsmen sold bronze pieces or made articles in terra-cotta on-site, adapting their work to suit the tastes of the clientele, and taking casts from old molds and then touching up the facial features; such pieces may have been fired *in situ*. There are numerous documented cases in which a single mold was used to cast prototype heads, that were later given details to make them male or female, or they were made to look older or younger, or given beards, and so on. Those with less ready cash had the option to buy a half-head in profile to hang on the sanctuary wall. Rarely did the craftsmen create completely original, one-off works. They basically offered buyers a series of prefabricated, vaguely Hellenistic models with little or no individual detailing; sometimes they were merely symbolic, as in the case of the heads, the most common type of sanctuary offering; these mementos shed light on the human condition of some suffering person. The small bronzes represent Heracles, the footloose but mature Heracles dressed in the pelt of the Nemean Lion, his club raised seemingly in defiance of the difficulties that nature lay in the way of the farming community, a Heracles only remotely reminiscent of Lysippus' exquisite portraits now in Taranto, which the craftsmen had probably heard tell of. Others represent Mars, ready to defend the herdsmen from would-be aggressors. Sometimes the bronzes depict Jupiter or Minerva; in others the gift-bearers themselves, clothed in heavy woolen garments, pictured as they offer up sacrifices to the chosen deity. These deities, as one can infer from the dedications on a number of small vases, were indigenous personifications of ever-present nature, defense against illness, gods of war, spirits of good fortune or love; deities of menial domestic life or the most humble work: Asclepius, Vulcan, Juno, Salus, Bellona, Minerva, Fortuna, Vesta, Venus, and Saturn.

The first manifestations of this agrarian culture show up in the sixth and fifth centuries B.C., but it was not until the fifth century that the inner articulations began to emerge, a development testified by the advent of important material evidence in the sanctuary hoards. These hoards became steadily more numerous and spread across the Apennine area, across central and southern Italy, affirming the predominance of Italic cults and their assimilation up and down the peninsula. Attributable perhaps to the fourth and third centuries is the statuette of a Samnite warrior (now in Paris) which, despite evidence of a generic Campanian style, belongs to the same milieu as the *Capestrano Warrior*. Other statuettes, such as those of Pietrabbondante (mid-third century B.C.), though somewhat coarse and elementary, evince a certain flair for design, an immediacy that exonerates them from the accusation of incompetence: the heads are too small or too large, certain features (such as hair) painstakingly detailed, the ingenuously ardent pose of the gift-bearers, all reaching out toward the observer, in parade dress. All these aspects are indicative of an artistic mode that enjoyed wide popularity among the Italic populations, despite its formal insufficiency.

On occasion, as in the case of certain highly rare terra-cotta heads – and some in bronze (such as one from Abruzzo, now in Paris) – the artifact is evidently the handiwork of a common craftsman, perhaps of urban, Italiot extraction (e.g., from Taras-Tarentum), possessing some skill in portraying the physiognomy of the client bringing his offering to the sanctuary; the results are sometimes unusually well calibrated for works of Italic production. Despite their rarity, these works did not become a trend owing to the fortuitous nature of the offerings and of those who commissioned them. The production of central Italy lacked figurative continuity, making it impossible to create schools of art as such, which would have stimulated the craftsman to give the piece true characterization; a proper maturity of the milieu is missing and the works that do emerge are more often than not the chance product of a particularly inspired craftsman or client.

It would be simplistic to suggest that the panorama in question was a shared, coherent one. Actually, the contents of certain votive hoards – and the Lavinio hoard in particular (near Rome), together with those at Cerveteri and Tarquinia – demonstrate an extraordinary complexity of visual ideas that still need more in-depth appraisal. Alongside items in clay no more than modestly fashioned, some ingenuously following Classical ideas (e.g., the figure of Athena), is an imposing series of votive heads of unusual freshness and successful characterization, some of which reach the heights of masterpieces (anticipating the canons of Roman portraiture of the first century B.C. The trend in the cities for commissioning portraiture is particularly noticeable among the finds from the fourth and third centuries. The distinctly Hellenized bronze armor unearthed in Lazio and the bronzes and ivories found at Palestrina attest to the fact that the dominant classes of Rome at least were in possession of a formal culture satisfied by experienced craftsmen who were at times capable of turning out true works of art.

From the Invasion of Hannibal to the Battle of Actium

> *"Infesta, mihi credite, signa ab Syracusis illata sunt huic urbi. Iam nimis multos audio Corinthi et Athenarum ornamenta laudantes mirantesque, et antefixa fictilia deorum Romanorum ridentes."* Livy, XXXIV. IV. 4; from a speech by Cato, 195 B.C.

Peninsular Italy
The period that spans the invasion of Hannibal and the battle of Actium is undoubtedly one of the hardest to place among the periods of art history in the Italian peninsula, which is largely identified with Rome.
The literary sources are all outspoken about the large quantities of art works which, particularly in the second century B.C., were imported to Italy from the eastern Mediterranean in the form of booty. Equal emphasis is placed on the vast accumulation of capital, as if Rome and the peninsula had soaked up most of the wealth amassed in the Mediterranean. On the other hand, the archaeological evidence that can be traced to Italic workshops – and to those of Rome itself – afford undeniable proof of the dismal decline in the standards of workmanship. This deterioration is unmistakable in the coins, being the most "official" token of the Republic. The wars with Hannibal, waged with equal fierceness by either side, were seen as a battle for survival, conducted for over fifteen years up and down the peninsula, and had debilitated the economy of the entire country, or most of it. The more servile classes of the population were utterly downtrodden, and even the middle classes saw the utter collapse of the family-based economy that had fostered the Hellenizing figurative culture so characteristic of the third century B.C.
Despite all this, under the guiding dominance of Rome the peninsula experienced a binding force that lent unity at political, juridical, and administrative levels. Few regions of the land escaped the ravages of the invasion. Campania, to some extent, emerged intact, and the coastal areas of the region in particular managed to cling to a certain crafts tradition of Hellenistic cast. But the rest of southern Italy was unable to struggle to its feet after the fearful beatings. The diffusion of the *latifundium* (estate) and the spread of malaria caused the steady impoverishment and eventual abandonment of the land, with the consequent plunder of some of the oldest sanctuaries of the country, of which the ransacking of those in Sicily by the men of the notorious Gaius Verres in the first century B.C. is a terrible example. This poverty is belied by the wealth and complete adhesion to Hellenistic fashion by the leading families in Rome. The public buildings commissioned by noblemen (crammed, moreover, with treasures plundered from the East) were all built in Hellenistic style. The residences and the ornamentation of the more powerful figures were made to rival those of the great sovereigns of the Hellenistic world. This process became exclusive in the earlier first century B.C.
This helps us understand why, through the rejection of Hellenistic culture (or that part of it on which Roman society in the third century was based) and the exhibition of presumed Roman cultural traditions (actually non-existent, unless we include the traditional violation of the juridical codes by the very figures who were supposed to uphold them), the figurative art of the peninsula underwent an abysmal decline, and only a few buildings (public works such as the sanctuaries in Latium-Lazio) and a few other artifacts, imported directly to Rome from the East, offer any evidence of artistic quality (in some cases of the highest order, it must be said). However, the portraits of the ancestors and *nobiles* show considerable formal accomplishment at times. In these conditions, the cultural idiom of the native populations is patently elementary and destitute. The superb examples of craftsmanship that span the third century diminish dramatically in both quality and number (at least as regards the middle and lower classes).
This decline is particularly noticeable for those classes of artifacts that were produced consistently over time, from the third century to the first: in the votive hoards, the material attributed to the second century B.C., and

particularly the terra-cotta heads, confirm this debasement of formal handling. A series of female busts serving as signposts for the tombs of the Palestrina necropolis evince a progressive decline in stylistic quality (almost parallel to the steady degeneration of the images of Rome on coin issues): the examples dated to the second century are notably crude; the facial treatment coarse and haphazardly rendered, the hands tense, and the clothing sketchily represented with a few careless details. The burial grounds of Beneventum and Tarentum have yielded a series of crudely made busts, some of which may date from the second century B.C.
Campania seems to be alone in maintaining an acceptable standard in its artistic production. The funerary monuments, statues, and *stelai* of Pompeii, Capua, and Teanum (probably datable to this same period) show evidence of an attempt to transfer coroplastic tradition to the carving of stone. The bodies are almost unnaturally elongated, the folds in the clothing are without pattern, the figures flattened on the surface, the heads set too large on meager torsos with stooping shoulders. Though magniloquent in a fashion, the figures are vacuous. Some improvement is discernible from the beginning of the first century B.C. It is not, however, a revival of some earlier tradition, but a mere provincial assimilation of a specifically urban, Roman art, which in the early first century began to assume an organic pattern. In this respect, there are a fair number of funerary *stelai* that echo the motifs of this urban repertoire.

On a *stele* from Capua two leisurely posed male figures are inscribed on a broad upper band, while the smaller band below presents a slave-selling scene. Far from repudiating his origins, the new citizen steadfastly wishes them to be recorded and represented on his tomb. Certain other funeral pieces are adorned with lion figures. It has not yet been established exactly when this animal came to be used in Italic funerary sculptures: their diffusion is well documented in Aquileia, Emilia, Samnium, Sabina, Picenum, Campania, Apulia, and in Rome itself. With their bulky bodies and huge heads, the lion figures stand as fearsome guardians of the dead, and though menacing, they are more like dogs than felines.

Some *stelai* in Umbria and Picenum denote a striking revival of traditionalistic features; other *stelai* show both acute naiveté and fundamental artistic insufficiency, with a stubborn frontal pose; the more significant features (including the mere accessory details) are brought out on the surface; neither the parts nor the decoration have been composed into a whole. The heads of the deceased are crammed into superimposed registers; at this juncture, the municipal device conveys no more than provincial vanity.

The monuments which can more appropriately be defined as "Italic art" and attest to a revival of features of an earlier period are those found in Samnium. A funerary monument unearthed at Amiterno was found to bear at least two reliefs: one with a funeral scene, the other showing gladiators in combat (also with a funerary function). The reliefs, dated around mid-first century B.C., tend to contradict each other: the procession is full of precise details, gestures, and exuberance in the figures, to the detriment of the overall coherence; the distribution on two registers shows a sincere and fresh narrative flair. In the gladiator relief, however, the ungainly figures seem to emerge from a woolly, inert material, and reveal a tendency to cram the picture field.

Another relief, conserved at Sulmona, and without doubt a funerary piece, offers a portrayal of the practice of transhumance, showing a flock accompanied by herdsmen pushing their personal assets in a cart. The figures stand out sharply against the uniform and undefined field of the plain stone background; their execution is inadequate and sketchy, inartistic in every sense, even anecdotal (without the accompanying inscription it would be difficult indeed to determine the period to which the work belongs). But the scene, at the start of the great drovers' way that led southward from the Pian di Cinque Miglia, is an atemporal representation of a custom which for long centuries formed an economic and social framework for the whole of central Italy. This picture of human labor was turned into a proverb (which, as with all proverbs, is merely a fossil of tradition): "Do not distrust yourself," runs the epigraph, like a caption almost. At the end of the drovers' way, at Lucera, we find another relief work picturing a herdsman in a cloak, strongly traced against the wood in the background of the relief. But by the first century B.C., the drovers were no longer a cultural category. They were neither warriors nor spreaders of culture, only a class of men serving the *latifundium*, meek subjects without prospects, living under the yoke of time.

Bibliography

General works:
O. Montelius, 1895-1910; T.J. Dunbabin, 1948; G.V. Kaschnitz-Weinberg, in *Handbuch....*, 1950, pp. 311 ff.; G. Pugliese Carratelli, D. Adamesteanu, L. Forti, A. Frajese, M. Gigante, G. Gullini, P. Orlandini, C. Rolley, A. Stazio, A. Szabò, L. Vagnetti, *Megale Hellas...*, 1983; D. Ridgway, 1984; G. Pugliese Carratelli, N. Bonacasa, E. De Miro, A. Di Vita, S. Garraffo, F. Giudice, G. Gullini, E. Joly, G. Monaco, G. Rizza, A. Stazio, A. Szabò, V. Tusa, G. Voza, *Sikanie...*, 1985; G. Pugliese Carratelli, A.M. Chicco Bianchi, G. Colonna, B. D'Agostino, F.

D'Andria, E.M. De Juliis, R. De Marinis, V. Kruta, M. Landolfi, F. Roncalli, *Italia...*, 1988; G. Pugliese Carratelli, C. Ampolo, D. Briquel, P. Cassola Guida, B. D'Agostino, C. De Simone, A. La Regina, V. La Rosa, M. Lejeune, M. Lombardo, N. Negroni Catacchio, N.F. Parise, R. Peroni, A.L. Prosdocimi, *Italia...*, 1989; *La grande Roma dei Tarquini*, 1990; *Antiche genti d'Italia*, 1994.

On the themes of Italic art (so far hardly defined on a critical level) see R. Peroni, G. Colonna, in *Enciclopedia...*, IV, 1961, pp. 251 ff.; G.V. Kaschnitz-Weinberg, 1965; R. Bianchi-Bandinelli, A. Giuliano, 1973; A. Giuliano, in *Xenia*, 3, 1982, pp. 3 ff.

Some studies only are mentioned either for the records they illustrate or for the critical evaluation they put forward. Sicily and southern Italy (from Greek colonization up to the fifth century B.C.).

On Sicily:

B. Pace, 1935-1949 (second ed. 1 vol., 1958); P. Orlandini, in *Kokalos*, X-XI, 1964-1965, pp. 539 ff.; G. Vallet, F. Villard, 1964; G. Rizza, in *Cronache...*, 4, 1965, pp. 7 ff.; C.A. Di Stefano, in *Archeologia Classica*, XVIII, 1966, pp. 175 ff.; V. La Rosa, in *Cronache...*, 7, 1968, pp. 7 ff.; F. Villard, in *Ann. Atene*, LIX, 1981, pp. 133 ff.; M. Frasca, in *Bollettino d'Arte*, 76 (year LXXVII), 1992, pp. 19 ff.

On Apulia:

B.M. Scarfì, in *Monumenti...*, XLV, 1960, cc. 145 ff.; B.M. Scarfì, in *Notizie Scavi*, 1962, pp. 1 ff.; B. Neutsch, in *Apollo*, 1, 1961, pp. 53 ff.; S. Ferri, in *Bollettino d'Arte*, 1962 e ff.; F. Johansen, in *Archeologia Classica*, XXIV, 1972, pp. 256 ff.; P.G. Guzzo, in *Bollettino d'Arte*, 69, 1976, pp. 60 ff.; E.M. De Juliis, 1977; M.L. Nava, 1980; E.M. De Juliis, 1988; *Archeologia dei Messapii...*, 1990.

On Campania and southern Italy:

H. Koch, 1912; P. Mingazzini, in *Monumenti...*, XXXVII, 1938, cc. 693 ff.; A. Adriani, 1939; P.C. Sestieri, in *Notizie Scavi*, 1952, pp. 86 ff.; G.Z. Giglioli, in *Studi Etruschi*, XXIII, 1954, pp. 405 ff.; G. Buchner, in *Römische Mitteilungen*, 60-61, 1953-1954, pp. 37 ff.; M. Napoli, in *La Parola del Passato*, XI, 1956, pp. 386 ff.; S. de la Genière, in *MEFRA*, LXXII, 1961, pp. 7 ff.; E. Hill-Richardson, in *Memoirs...*, XXVII, 1962, pp. 153 ff.; W. Johannowsky, in *Bollettino d'Arte*, 1963, pp. 131 ff.; D. d'Agostino, in *La Parola del Passato*, LXXXVIII, 1963, pp. 67 ff.; F. Parise Badoni, 1968; A.D. Trendall, 1967; J.N. Coldstream, in *University...*, 15, 1968, pp. 86 ff.; M. Napoli, 1970; D. Adamesteanu, 1971; A. Pontrandolfo, 1982; P.G. Guzzo, 1989; L. Cerchiai, 1995; *Fratte....*, 1990; E. Laforgia, in *AION*, XIV, 1992, pp. 69 ff.; A. Bottini, 1992

On Metapontum's workshops of terra-cottas, lastly:

P. Orlandini, in *Bollettino d'Arte*, 73, 1988, pp. 1 ff.

On the Atestine culture:

P. Jacobsthal, 1969; O.H. Frey, 1969; G. Fogolari, A. Prosdocimi, 1988; L. Capuis, 1993; *Il dono delle Eliadi...*, 1994.

On the Celtic culture:

M.T. Grassi, 1991.

On Picenum:

P. Marconi, in *Monumenti...*, XXXV, 1935, cc. 274 ss; A.V. Salis, in *Sitzungsberichte...*, 1936-1939, 1; G. Moretti, in *Bullettino...*, n.s., 1936-1937, pp. 94 ff.; A. Boëthius, in *La Critica d'Arte*, IV, 1939, pp. 49 ff.; A. Boëthius, in *Eranos*, LIV, 1956, pp. 202 ff.; H. Jucker, in *Antike Kunst*, 7, 1964, pp. 3 ff.; V. Cianfarani, in *Bollettino d'Arte*, 1966, pp. 1 ff.; V. Cianfarani, in *Rivista...*, XV, 1968, pp. 5 ff.; K.W. Beinhauer, 1985; F. Parise Badoni, M. Ruggeri Giove, 1980; R. Papi, 1990; *La civiltà picena nelle Marche*: Studies in honor of Giovanni Annibaldi, 1992 (among them the study by G. Colonna, *Apporti etruschi all'orientalizzante "piceno": il caso della statuaria*, pp. 92 ff.: which has to be cautiously examined); J.J. Basile, in *Revue des archéologues...*, XXVI, 1993, pp. 9 ff.

On Ligurian art:

N. Lamboglia, in *Rivista di Studi Liguri*, XXVI, 1960, pp. 91 ff.; XXX, 1964, pp. 31 ff.; XXXII, 1966, pp. 251 ff.; XXXVIII, 1972, pp. 103 ff.

From the fifth century to the invasion of Hannibal:

S. Ferri, in *Opuscula*, 1962, pp. 317 ff.; L. Breglia, in *La Critica d'Arte*, VII, 1942, pp. 29 ff.; R. Bianchi Bandinelli, in *La Critica d'Arte*, VII, 1942, pp. 18 ff.; A. Cederna, in *Notizie Scavi*, 1951, pp. 169 ff. On Lavinio votive deposit see the exhibition catalogue: *Enea nel Lazio*, 1981; M. Torelli, 1984; G.Q. Giglioli, in *Archeologia Classica*, IV, 1952, pp. 174 ff.; A. Cederna, in *Archeologia Classica*, V, 1953, pp. 187 ff.; A. Mainri, in *La Parola del Passato*, X, 1955, pp. 50 ff.; G.O. Onorato, 1960; F. Tiné Bertocchi, 1964; G. Colonna, 1970; M.L. Vollenweider, 1972-1974.

See the exhibition catalogue: *Roma medio repubblicana. Aspetti culturali di Roma e del Lazio nei secoli IV e III a.C.*, 1973; *Hellenismus in Mittelitalien*, in *Abhandlungen...* 97, 1976; V. Cianfarani, L. Franchi Dell'Orto, A. La Regina, 1978; I. Rainini, 1986; M.J. Strazzulla, 1987; C. Perassi, *Correnti artistiche...*, in *Athenaeum*, n.s. LXVI, 1988, pp. 345 ff.; P. Cassola Guida, *Bronzetti friulani...*, 1989; A. Pontrandolfo, A. Rouveret, 1992; *Corpus delle stipi votive in Italia* (edited by M. Torelli and A. Comella).

From the invasion of Hannibal to the battle of Actium:

M. Rostovzev, in *Antike Plastik....*, 1928, pp. 213 (see also: *Storia economia e sociale dell'impero romano*, 1933, plate III, 5, XII, 2); G. Rodenwaldt, in *Jahrbuch*, LV, 1940, pp. 12 ff.; L. Forti, in *Memorie...*, 6, 1942, pp. 43 ff.; H. Fuhrmann, in *Mitteilungen...*, II, 1949, pp. 45 ff.; A. Giuliano, in *Römische Mitteilungen*, 60-61, 1953-1954, pp. 172 ff.; T. Dohrn, in *Römische Mitteilungen*, 67, 1960, pp. 98 ff.; R. Bianchi Bandinelli, in *Dialoghi di Archeologia*, I, 1967, pp. 7 ff.; R. Bianchi Bandinelli, L. Franchi, A. Giuliano, A. La Regina, M. Torelli, F. Coarelli, in *Studi Miscellanei*, 10, 1967; M. Torelli, in *Dialoghi di Archeologia*, II, 1968, pp. 32 ff.; P. Pensabene, in *Römische Mitteilungen*, 82, 1975, pp. 263 ff.; B.M. Felletti, 1977; S. Diebner, 1979; G. Zimmer, 1982; O.S. Brendel, 1982 (on p. 197 some valuable writings by F. Coarelli are mentioned); S. Diebner, 1986; L. Todisco, 1994, *passim*.

Eugenio La Rocca

Greek Artists in Republican Rome: A Short History of Sculpture

"Infesta, mihi credite, signa ab Syracusis illata sunt huic urbi, iam nimis multos audio Corinthi et Athenarum ornamenta laudantes mirantesque et antefixa fictilia deorum Romanorum ridentes" (Believe me, alien works of art have been brought to this city from Syracuse; already I have heard too many people who extol and admire ornamentation from Corinth and Athens, and deride the terra-cotta antefixes of the Roman gods. Livy, XXXIV. 4. 4).

When, in 195 B.C., Cato thus protested against the proliferation in Rome of ornamentation from Corinth and Athens, Greek culture had already thoroughly permeated the life of the city, while the age of the sobriety typical of the ancient Latin traditions now seemed remote. In the evident contrast between the concepts of *austeritas* (severity) and *paupertas* (poverty) and those of *luxuria* (luxury) and *avaritia* (avarice), it is interesting that the latter, seen as synonyms of corruption and decadence, were – according to the most intransigent of the conservatives – a consequence of Greek influence. It was, therefore, inevitable that this negative judgment also involved the domain of art, which had been stigmatized by Cato.

But a more thorough analysis, from a historical point of view, reveals a strange contradiction between this opinion and the apparently incompatible consciousness of the cultural superiority of the Greek world. This very consciousness helps to explain both the search for closer links and common origins, and also the creation, dating probably from the fourth century B.C., of the myth of Rome as a Greek *polis*, founded by the descendants of the Trojan refugees in Italy. Equally significant is the request, addressed to the Attalids in the second century B.C., for the *acus*, a conical black stone, probably a meteorite, which, according to the testimony of Varro (I. 1. 6. 15), was venerated as a representation of Cybele and kept in a temple dedicated to her in Pergamum. Moreover, its supposed provenience from Mount Ida, which had important Trojan associations (rather than from Pessinus), was used by Rome to strengthen the myth of a common Greek origin.

With regard to art and architecture, the forms and modes of the Greek heritage must have been introduced to Rome in ancient times, since Pliny relates that as early as the fifth century B.C., for the decoration of the *cella* of the Temple of Ceres, Liber, and Libera on the slopes of the Aventine, two Siceliot artists, Damophilus and Gorgasus, referred to as *plastae* (modelers in clay) were employed (*Natural History*, XXXV. 154). The quality of their work must have been excellent, since in 31 B.C., when the building burnt down, the paintings and the *crustae* (probably terra-cotta reliefs) were carefully salvaged and then installed in the new building dedicated to Tiberius in 17 A.D.

But aside from purely artistic considerations, it is significant that this temple – although it was a product of the Etrusco-Italic tradition, insofar as it employed the Tuscan order – represented a culturally and politically innovative choice for Rome since it involved the acquisition of forms and models that were typically Greek. This is clear not only because artists who had been trained in the Greek tradition were commissioned to decorate the *cella*, but also because of the type of cult chosen: that of a triad resembling the Greek group of Demeter, Dionysus, and Kore, gods that were venerated in southern Italy and Sicily. These are choices that have specifically political implications if they are seen in the context of one of the thorniest problems in Rome in the middle Republic, that of the strained relations between patricians and plebeians. Vowed in 496 B.C. by the dictator Lucius Postumius, the temple was dedicated in 494 by a philodemocratic consul, Spurius Cassius, and housed the popular assemblies. Thus, from a political point of view, the building became the symbol of the new balance of power that had been created in Rome, as well as being the religious center of the Aventine area, which was becoming increasing "plebeian" in character. The choice of foreign models and the triadic cult of Ceres, Liber, and Libera may, therefore, be interpreted both as intentional detachment from the conservative tradition of the senatorial order, and a polemical response to the Capitoline patrician triad. Aside from the possible political implications, the fact remains, however, that Rome now formed an integral part of the vast network of relations and trade in the Mediterranean that had allowed the diffusion of the basic elements of Greek culture, often through southern Italy and Sicily (the priestesses of the cult of Ceres, Liber, and Libera, for instance, must have been selected in the cities of Magna Graecia).

At the end of the fifth century, another Greek cult was introduced to Rome: that of Apollo Medicus, whose temple, dedicated in 431 B.C., was in the Prata Flaminia (Flaminian meadows) – that is, in the southern Campus Martius near the Tiber, which was an area outside the *pomerium*. Because of this, the temple was used for the meetings of the senate whenever it had to receive foreign delegations or magistrates holding *imperium*, who could not enter the *pomerium* of Rome.

Despite the introduction of individual cults and artistic models, it does not appear that, at this stage of Roman history, religious buildings had already been influenced by the canonical types of Greek architecture. In fact, the Tuscan model was dominant: this was characterized by a high podium and by fairly wide intercolumniation, at times even araeostyle – that is, with exaggeratedly wide spaces between the columns – as in the case of the Temple of Ceres, Liber, and Libera. This structure was made possible by the use of wood for the roof and often for the columns as well; the tympanum was still open, with three load-bearing beams (*columina*) that jutted out into the cavity of the pediment and were covered with large terra-cotta ornaments. The overall appearance of these buildings must have been a far cry from the harmonious proportions that Greek architecture had developed at the same time and despite the fact that, as far as architectural ornamentation was concerned, the presence of craftsmen from Mainland Greece, or at least from the Greek world, was becoming increasingly common – possibly to a greater extent than has been ascertained hitherto.

In this regard, the discovery of a splendid fragment of a terra-cotta statue representing a wounded warrior in the Esquiline area is interesting; because of its superb use of form and magnificent polychromy it has been attributed to Damophilus and Gorgasus, or, at any rate, Greek artists, to whom, if this is correct, credit should go for the high level of coroplastics in Rome. Although the provenience of the piece is uncertain, it is likely that it formed part of the revetment of a temple, possibly that of Ceres, Liber, and Libera, the rubble of which, after the fire of 31 B.C., may have been used to fill the area of the Esquiline cemetery. There may, on the other hand, have been a sanctuary near the Esquiline Gate, where the traces of a votive deposit have been found.

The increasingly widespread penetration of Greek culture in Rome is attested by a certain heterogeneity of the finds, as in the case of the urn in Parian marble from a shaft grave in the Esquiline cemetery. Elegantly embellished with a pictorial decoration and added *akroteria* (possibly bronze), the urn – probably also of Parian production – bears witness to the diffusion of high quality Greek artifacts. Furthermore, it confirms that Rome was now a participant in the broad network of trade in the Mediterranean, especially in view of the fact that similar urns have been found in the cemeteries of Spina and Cerveteri. Not far from Rome, at Lanuvio (Lanuvium), another tomb, known as the Tomb of the Warrior, which was certainly that of a man of high rank, has yielded a type of burial strongly influenced by Greek traditions, due to the presence of a panoply of armor as well as a number of objects indicating the deceased's athletic and heroic ideals (discus and bronze strigils, alabaster, bag containing sand).

Contacts, firstly with the numerous *poleis* of southern Italy and then, following the military conquests, with the major cultural centers of Greece and Asia Minor, favored the progressive assimilation of the

Fragment of a clay statue
of a wounded warrior
from the Esquiline Hill
Rome, Antiquarium Comunale

Marble funerary urn
from the Esquiline Hill necropolis
Rome, Antiquarium Comunale

motifs of Greek art that, from the fourth century B.C. onward, began to influence the styles of Roman art. The phenomenon is well attested, and in a continuous manner, by the widespread diffusion of terra-cotta works, which were mostly made in molds and were sometimes finished off with a pallet, and which, thanks to the transmission of models from Rome, now the dominant power, reached the peripheral areas of central Italy. Especially in the early centuries of the Republic, this penetration must have proceeded hand in hand with military occupation and the subsequent foundation of colonies.

Even in the most ancient examples, the rendering of Greek Hellenistic models is so precise that it is clear that if Greek craftsmen were not already working in Rome, models were being transmitted through copies from Greece to Italy at an early date – presumably in the form of molds or plaster casts. This may be deduced from the close analogies with the contemporary Greek output of the fourth and third centuries, as has already been observed with regard to the celebrated *Mars of Todi*; this is a bronze statue of the late fifth century B.C., presumably of Volsinian production, that is believed to have been made in an eclectic style using molds taken from Greek bronzes.

Thus, the larger works of Greek sculpture, especially those made by the circle of Polyclitus, became aesthetic models, which often arrived after elaboration by the artists of Magna Graecia. At first, such models were reproduced schematically, to such a degree that they became stereotypes, remote from the function and significance of the archetype. It was only after a couple of centuries that they were fully assimilated by Roman art.

Unfortunately, with regard to terra-cottas, the state of preservation of the sculptures only rarely permits a detailed analysis of the forms. This is the fortunate case of the terra-cottas that decorated the ends of the beams of the open tympanum of the Temple of the Scasato at Falerii Veteres, as well as the pedimental group of the Temple of Juno Curitis at Tivoli. In particular, the modeling of the body and the wholly Alexandrian expressivity of the face framed by a thick wavy hair of the so-called Apollo of the Scasato, as well as the fashioning of the female figures with rich and elegant drapery on the Tivoli pediment, can only have been made by a workshop with considerable experience in the field of red-figure pottery (possibly established by a Greek craftsman) that was able to produce skillful, precise copies of Greek statues, perhaps with the use of casts. For example, in the nude statue of a man with a *chlamys* over his shoulders, from Tivoli, it is possible to discern the influence of the Argive models of around the middle of the fourth century, such as the *Athlete of Koblanos* or the *Hermes* of the Andros type, while, in the statues of women, the severity of the forms and the balance between body and dress suggest Greek archetypes dating from the fourth century B.C. Hence, the terra-cottas from Tivoli may be dated to the mid-third century, or even the late fourth and early third centuries.

This information is of vital importance for the light it throws on the artistic currents and the diffusion of knowledge in central Italy; it may, therefore, also be related to Rome itself, where, unfortunately, only a few recent finds bear witness to the development of a refined coroplastic output.

The architectural terra-cottas found in the area of the Temple of the Magna Mater on the Palatine Hill, which may have belonged to the nearby Temple of Victoria, can be dated to the end of the fourth or the beginning of the third centuries. They consist of two faces, unfortunately very fragmentary; their close similarity to those of the Scasato appears to confirm the existence of itinerant craftsmen in the Etrusco-Latian area, according to a tradition that had already been affirmed from the end of the fifth century for the decoration of public buildings. From this point of view, it is not necessary, therefore, to ascribe the terra-cottas from the Palatine to the possible removal of Faliscan craftsmen to Rome following the conquest of their city in 241 B.C.

With regard to the adoption of Greek models, that of the types relating to the portraits of Alexander the Great – which was very precise – needs to be considered separately. Already at the end of the fourth century, in fact, these models had a strong influence over the physiognomy of the Roman portrait, and were extremely popular in central-Italic coroplastics. A number of typical elements, such as the hairstyle and the "pathetic" contraction of the eye with the eyebrows exaggeratedly arched, are found as distinctive signs that could be rendered in a very simple manner – for instance, in votive figures or funerary portraits – or with skillful and precise modeling, as in the case, mentioned above, of the *Apollo of the Scasato*. Even more persuasive is the *Fortnum* head, now in Oxford: its model, expressed accurately, has been identified as the so-called *Rondanini Alexander*, now in Munich, and, like the latter, portrays a youth with thick wavy hair and melancholy upturned gaze. The face is modeled with smooth surfaces, while only the details are characterized by a strong taste for the picturesque. The position of the hand, partly closed and touching the cheek, together with the "pathetic" expression, link this head to the Alexander of the Erbach type, and suggest that it belonged to the statue of

Terra-cotta male head from the Esquiline Hill known as the *Fortnum Head*
Oxford, Ashmolean Museum

Colossal statue of Minerva
from Lavinio
Pratica di Mare
Depositi Soprintendenza Archeologica
Cat. 402

Greek Artists in Republican Rome: A Short History of Sculpture

Terra-cotta statue of a woman
identified as Kore
from Ariccia
Rome, Museo Nazionale Romano
Cat. 405

a seated mourner with his head resting on his hand. The hypothesis that this is a funerary statue is reinforced by the fact that this fragment was found on the Esquiline Hill, which was used as a cemetery until the second century B.C. It cannot, however, be ruled out that it formed part of a pedimental relief similar to those found at Tivoli or Falerii, and that it represented a young hero leaning on a column in a thoughtful attitude.

With all its peculiarities, the Greek archetypes continued to be adopted right through the Republic until the Augustan age. And the different levels at which forms and styles were assimilated are strikingly evident in the abundant output of terra-cotta works. Of fundamental importance in this regard are the series of sculptures in terra-cotta found in the votive deposit of the Sanctuary of Minerva at Lavinio; they may be dated to a period extending from the fifth to the second centuries B.C. (and possibly even later, due to the presence of terra-cotta revetments datable to the late first century). In this case, the progressive adoption of the Greek models, in a manner that was increasingly mature and conscious, is illustrated by the comparison between the still schematic rendering of a statuette of Minerva dating from the fifth century, with the flattened structure of the body, the regular folds of the *chiton*, and the stylized face with almond-shaped eyes, and that of another statuette of the goddess, attributed to the second century, the modeling of which displays total adherence to the Greek Hellenistic styles, especially those of the contemporary terra-cottas of Myrina.

Some finds near Rome have revealed another interesting aspect of the Roman coroplastic output: the existence of a Central-Italic *koine* influenced by models from Magna Graecia, possibly Tarentine ones. Of particular importance is the material found in the votive deposit of a sanctuary at Ariccia that was perhaps dedicated to the cult of Ceres, Liber and Libera: here two typological series – the first consisting of large busts cut off at the height of the breast, the second of enthroned goddesses – are of high formal quality and display a dramatic use of light effects obtained with a skillful use of the pallet. The large busts are certainly reminiscent of those that were offered to the chthonic gods in Sicily, but the style of the heads of Ariccia seems rather to have been influenced by Tarentine models, especially if the latter were derived from the capitals decorated with heads of gods from Canosa, or the splendid head in limestone from Bolsena, now in the Museo Barracco, Rome.

Two other terra-cottas that certainly had an architectural function are contemporary with, and typologically similar to, those of Ariccia: one is a head of a boy from Monte Antenne, near Rome, the other is a fragment of a female figure from the votive deposit of San Salvatore at Lucera, in Apulia. Seminude and portrayed as she is lifting a veil, the figurine appears to be part of a group representing an abduction scene, possibly Aeolus raising Aura, as in the *akroteriai* in Athens and Delos.

In Rome, too, in a chamber tomb in Via Santo Stefano Rotondo, among the grave goods of a young man, unfortunately now largely stolen, there were – aside from a strigil and pieces of pottery that date the context to the first decades of the third century B.C. – a number of interesting fragments of terra-cottas imported from Magna Graecia. Of particular interest are corner elements with winged *genii*, female heads emerging from acanthus leaves, and the *quadrigae* driven by Nike over the waves of the sea represented by tritons.

On the reverse of a *denarius* struck in 113 or 112 B.C. by the minter L. Marcius Philippus there is an equestrian statue on a plinth: the horse is shown galloping with its front legs raised, with a support disguised as a tree trunk clearly visible under its belly, while the rider holds a laurel branch in his right hand as a sign of victory. It has been suggested that he is Q. Marcius Tremulus, who defeated the Hernici in 306 B.C., and was the only victor in his family before 113 B.C. The interest of this coin lies in the iconography of the equestrian statue, which resembles one of the most famous Greek archetypes, that of the group representing Alexander and horsemen that Lysippus made after the battle of the Granicus, and it is likely that a monument of this type was erected in Rome toward the end of the fourth century B.C.

In fact, in this period, an ever-increasing number of honorific statues must have invaded the public areas of the city, following the dictates of the most fervent political propaganda. Pliny (XXXIV. 15) provides evidence of the presence in Rome of artists from Magna Graecia between 285 and 282 B.C., when the first public statue was erected in Rome at the expense of foreign citizens. The citizens of Thurii, in fact, donated a statue and a golden crown to the tribune of the people, Gaius Elius, responsible for a law against the Lucanian Stennius Stallius, who had plundered their city twice. On another occasion, when a siege of Thurii was raised thanks to Gaius Fabricius, the citizens dedicated a honorific statue to him. It is, however, difficult to ascertain whether artists were sent to Rome from Thurii in order to make these honorific statues, or whether they were made in Thurii itself.

Naturally, the diffusion of honorific statues gave an important impetus to the development of portraiture during the Republic. One of the works that is most pertinent to the comprehension of this complex phenomenon and the evaluation of the contribution of early Greek Hellenism is still the bronze head known as the *Capitoline Brutus*. It must have formed part of a full-length statue, as is indicated by a slight twisting of the head that is perceptible in the musculature of the neck, but it is not possible to ascertain whether it was, for example, an equestrian statue. The work may be attributed to the late fourth century or the first half of the third century B.C. because of the similarities to a number of paintings from Etruscan tombs, especially the one with a portrait of Velthur Velcha in the Tomb of the Shields at Tarquinii, which has been dated to the third quarter of the fourth century B.C. The influence of the iconography of contemporary Greek portraits, such as the statue of Demosthenes by Polyeuctus, dated about 280 and known from numerous copies, is very evident, but there are also affinities with other, older works, such as the bronze, attributed to Democritus and dated to the second half of the fourth century, that is known from a copy in the Villa of the Papyri at Herculaneum. Aside from the possible models, contemporary or earlier, the *Capitoline Brutus* – a true precursor of Roman portraiture that has been variously dated from the fourth to the first centuries B.C. – allows a number of interesting considerations to be made with regard to the extent to which Greek culture was adopted, and, above all, the degree of formal variation that the Italic artists and craftsmen managed to achieve. The complex facial structure of the *Demosthenes*, divided into planes with notable effects

Terra-cotta bust of Ceres
from Ariccia
Rome, Museo Nazionale Romano
Cat. 404

Fragment of a clay statue of a woman (Aura?) found among the offerings in the votive deposit at San Salvatore
Lucera, Museo Civico "G. Fiorelli"
Cat. 290

of light and shade, is, in the *Brutus*, simplified and made more regular; nonetheless, it still manages to express the moral rectitude and severity of its subject. It is no coincidence, in fact, that its iconography seems to have been derived from Greek prototypes intended to commemorate men with outstanding civic and political virtues, statesmen, or else orators and philosophers, for whom it was felt that reference to higher moral qualities should take precedence over the creation of a faithful portrait. That the Greek Hellenistic portrait had reached a perfect balance between expressiveness, physiognomy, and integrity is demonstrated by such works as the celebrated portrait of Menander executed by Praxiteles' sons, Cephisodotus and Timarchus. In view of this, it is clear that, in the *Capitoline Brutus*, the Greek figurative repertoire has been assimilated and adapted, through the use of synthesis, to serve specific purposes. In fact, the *Brutus*, although its formal qualities are exceptional, is not an isolated phenomenon, and other portraits, with different merits, may be seen in relation to it, so that the widespread diffusion of the Greek artistic repertoire may be postulated. This diffusion is, however, associated with patrons of high social standing – that is, members of the Roman and Latian aristocracy who were embarked on political careers.

The late third century B.C. marks the beginning of what Veyne (*Diogene*, CVI, 1975, p. 14ff.) has described as the "second Hellenization" of Rome, when mere adoption of Greek models became real assimilation, with the concerted selection of iconographic forms, often with formal variations that are indicative of the skill – at times notable – of the Italic artists and craftsmen. This is the period of the conquest of Syracuse (in 212 B.C.), followed by that of Tarentum (in 209). They were sacked, respectively, by the plebeian M. Claudius Marcellus and the patrician Fabius Maximus, both of whom embodied the Roman attitude to Hellenization.

According to the sources, Marcellus was the first to introduce the truly Greek notion of *charis* (grace) to Rome (Plutarchus, *Parallel Lives*, Marcellus XXI. 2. 4), whereas, in reality, as we have already seen, relations with the Greek world dated back to long before this period. Thus, valuable works of art were not brought to Rome merely to be paraded as spoils of war: both Claudius Marcellus and Fabius Maximus expressed a desire to claim the merit for their introduction into Rome, which favored the diffusion of Hellenic culture. Marcellus himself, in fact, believed he was a connoisseur, but, in this attitude of his, there may also be an attempt to turn the tables, politically speaking, on the senatorial order that tended to confuse ideologically the forms of public and private Hellenization with the corruption of the traditions of their ancestors.

Despite this, the patrician Fabius Maximus, although he was not seeking political revenge and apparently indifferent to things artistic, also brought a rich booty of art treasures back to Rome: these included the colossal bronze of *Heracles* made by Lysippus, which he dedicated on the Capitoline Hill together with an equestrian statue of himself, the evident aim of which was the promotion of his public image (Plutarchus, Fabius Maximus XXII. 8). Although their ideologies and political aims were different, these two leaders helped to overcome the prejudices of a large part of the Roman ruling class with regard to Hellenistic culture. Indeed, Cato believed the Romans had such a great capacity for corruption that he predicted the empire would be lost when they were totally imbued with it (Plutarchus, Cato XXIII. 2).

But, during the second century B.C., the controversy was gradually set aside, while the Hellenization of Rome gathered momentum. The conquests in Greece and Asia Minor had permitted direct acquaintance with the great capitals of the Hellenistic kingdoms: the triumphant Roman magistrates, to whom the modesty of their cities compared to the splendor of the Greek ones must have been evident, were accompanied by a heterogeneous retinue of artists, scientists, and men of culture. The Roman sources, which give great importance to this new departure in the history of Rome, establish the beginning of what is described as "*luxuria*" or "*luxuria asiatica*" at the victory of Scipio Asiaticus over Antiochus III at Magnesia in 189 B.C. and of Gnaeus Manlius Vulso over the Galatians of Asia in 186 B.C.

Livy (XXXIX. 22. 9) mentions that Scipio Asiaticus took artists from all over Asia to Italy; again in 186 B.C., Marcus Fulvius Nobilior, in order to celebrate his victory over the Aetolians, brought other artists from Greece. The echo of these events, which were destined to change the course of art history in Rome, may be found in Pliny (XXXIV. 34): "*Mirumque mihi videtur, cum statuarum origo tam vetus Italiae sit, lignea potius aut fictilia deorum simulacra in delubris dicata usque ad devictam Asiam, unde luxuria.*" (And it is incomprehensible to me that, since the origin of the statues is so ancient in Italy, wooden or earthen statues of deities were dedicated in the temples until the conquest of Asia, from where luxury was derived.)

While the spoils of war continued to arrive in Rome in ever-increasing quantities, with large numbers of works of art – such as those stripped from Corinth by Lucius Mummius Achaicus or those brought from Macedon by Quintus Caecilius Metellus – in the city there were now not only important Greek artists, who were given the task of creating the most important works, but also an increasing number of minor artists and craftsmen. They were responsible for figurative works (the large number of cult statues, for instance) and the decoration of public and private buildings. Thus, a heterogeneous and extremely vital circle of artists was being formed around the Roman patrons; most of the latter were victors, and, within a short space of time, they had imposed the use of the Greek modes in all their various forms.

But, in second-century Rome, in parallel with the introduction – in a somewhat unsystematic manner – of the contemporary Hellenistic artistic currents, it was evident that another extremely interesting phenomenon was coming to the fore. In marked contrast with past attitudes, in fact, the Greek language and the immensely rich culture that was associated with it were now considered to have made a major contribution to the literature and philosophy of Rome, and to be an essential part of a high-ranking person's education. As early as 212 B.C., *Ludi Scaenici* (theatrical shows) with the Latin version of a number of Greek texts were held at the Apollinare in the Prata Flaminia, and, also in the third century B.C., Livius Andronicus had been the first to adapt a Greek tragedy for a Roman audience. Now, however, the diffusion of Greek culture was assuming different dimensions, because numerous aristocratic families began to adopt an increasingly open-minded position that permitted them

Bronze bust
the so-called *Capitoline Brutus*
Rome, Musei Capitolini

Colossal head of a goddess
(formerly in the Albani Collection)
Rome, Musei Capitolini

Colossal marble statue
of *Athena Parthenos*
Rome, Musei Capitolini

to reconcile Roman tradition with philhellenism, despite the fact that their knowledge of the Greek language and culture was still somewhat superficial. The case of Lucius Aemilius Paullus is significant: after the victory over Perseus in 168 B.C., he asked for, and obtained, a tutor and a painter "*ad triumphum excolendum*" (in order to perfect the victory) from Athens (Pliny, XXXV. 135), and the choice fell on the Athenian Metrodorus, a pupil of Carneades who was both philosopher and painter. It was in this period, in fact, that, for the first time, Athens began to be perceived as a center of culture and learning based on a glorious past. And this was, perhaps, one of the reasons why, generally speaking, Greece was always treated with particular respect, aside from such exceptional cases as the destruction of Corinth in 146 B.C.

In the second and first centuries B.C., from the end of the Second Punic War until just before the principate, a general renewal took place in Rome. In effect, this period, in which there were notable ideological and political innovations together with new cultural ferment, paved the way for the formation of the Empire. Aside from the military operations, thanks to which, with incredible rapidity, Rome became the mistress of the Mediterranean, it was a change in the social order that had a decisive effect on art and architecture. In fact, the situation was now much more complex than it was during the middle Republic, when political power was firmly in the hands of a few *gentes* (groups of families). The new political developments allowed members of socially inferior families to emerge, members of the equestrian rank, often of provincial origin, who had become rich in a short space of time and were anxious to become part of the ruling class. The modification of the original political equilibrium, due to the arrival of these *novi homines*, caused the aggravation of the struggle for power, especially during the first century B.C. and after the reform of Gaius Marius in 107 B.C. Subsequently, the army – now professional and, hence, linked to its general – became a decisive instrument of political coercion.

All this explains how, with the exacerbation of the political contest, the systems of electoral propaganda and self-promotion must have been boosted. The prestige deriving from public works gave a strong impetus to building activities and the production of sculpture in Rome. Munificence, which was one of the aspects of the political struggle between the *optimates*, led to the construction of buildings that were more and more imposing due to both the complexity of their structures and the use of increasingly precious materials, thanks to the enormous wealth deriving from the spoils of war.

Even though at this stage it is not possible to speak of a building program comparable to the one promoted by Pericles, with all the political implications that were linked to it, it is undeniable that, in Rome, this was a period of major developments in architecture and urban planning, and the contribution of models and concepts from the Greek Hellenistic world was, once again, of fundamental importance. Unfortunately, the general appearance of the cities in this period can only be reconstructed very approximately; although it may seem reductive, it is, in fact, very useful to make a comparison with the layout of the most important colonies. It has been possible, for example, to demonstrate that, as regards the religious architecture, the Greek model, although it continued to develop and spread, did not replace the Tuscan one; until the first century B.C., this was used with all its variants, and was often combined with decorations of the Italic type.

One of the first temples in Rome to be built on a Greek plan seems to have been that of the Magna Mater on the Palatine Hill; this was vowed in 204 B.C. and dedicated in 191. It is no coincidence that it was intended to contain the baetyl of the goddess Cybele obtained from the Attalids: this was the period of the progressive expansion of Rome in the eastern Mediterranean, and the gradual adaptation to Greek Hellenistic architectural models is, perhaps, the first sign of the presence of Greek craftsmen in the city. But it was only in 146 B.C. that there was concrete evidence of a Greek architect working in Rome: this was Hermodorus of Salamis (presumably the city in Cyprus), who, in his long career – it appears that he was still active in 102 B.C. – built the Navalia, the naval dockyards of the Campus Martius, and two important temples, also in the area of the Campus Martius. They mark the introduction into the religious architecture of Rome of a model that was purely Greek, both as regards type and material: both temples were, in fact, peripteral, and were built on a low *crepidoma* in Pentelic marble.

Nothing has survived of the Temple of Jupiter Stator; known only from Vitruvius' description, it was erected by Metellus Macedonicus on the northern side of the Circus Flaminius as part of the Porticus Metellus, after his victory in 146 B.C. It appears, however, that the remains now under the church of San Salvatore in Campo belonged to another temple attributed to Hermodorus, that of Mars in the Circus, built for the consul Iunius Brutus Callaicus, who vowed it in 138 B.C. during the war against the Lusitani (Priscian, *Institutio* VIII. 4. 17). In the latter case, re-examination of the remains has per-

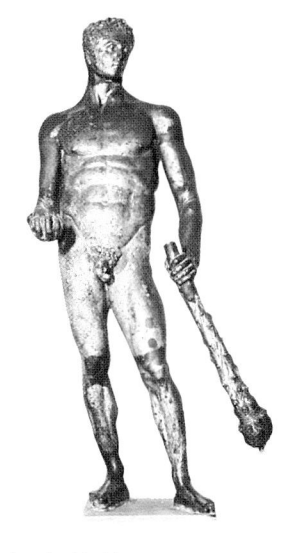

Colossal gilded bronze statue
of Heracles
Rome, Musei Capitolini

mitted the temple to be seen as part of the Ionic tradition, as is revealed by the fragments of the architrave and the coffering of the peristasis, as well as the unusual form of the bases of the six columns that are still visible; these are of a type in the Ionic tradition (the so-called *Lesbian Wulstbasen* [bulging bases]) for which there are no precedents in Rome.

But, going back to the edifices built by Metellus Macedonicus, they are undoubtedly the most revealing evidence of the progressive adaptation of the Roman outlook to the Greek one. Quite aside from the specific contribution of Greek architects and artists, they caused the Italic architectural structures and decorative motifs to be transformed in accordance with the Hellenistic models, which had, in fact, already entered the sphere of Roman politics. In this sense, the layout of the Porticus Metellus, which was innovatory for Rome, is exemplary: having four sides closed by porticos, it resembled that of a *temenos*. In the porticoed square, the disposition of the sculptured groups was reminiscent of that of the *anathemata* for the victory over the Galatians in the Sanctuary of Athena *Nikephoros* (bringer of victory) at Pergamum. Part of Metellus' spoils of war consisted of the superb group by Lysippus of thirty-four bronze equestrian statues representing Alexander the Great with his officers who had fallen in the battle of the Granicus. Taken from the Macedonian city of Dion and brought to Rome, the group must have acquired a strong symbolic value, linked as it was to an image of power and conquest. At the same time, there is no doubt that Metellus wished to identify himself with Alexander, and even surpass him, given that he had defeated his heirs.

Later on, also in the Campus Martius – almost as if he wished to take a prudent attitude with regard to self-promotion toward the Senate – Pompey built a huge complex. The structure of this, which was divided into public and private sectors, was very similar to that of the Ptolemaic palaces of Alexandria. The hub of the complex was a theater in brick (the first in Rome) with a temple dedicated to Venus Victrix on the top of the *cavea*, while behind the *scenae frons* was attached a large quadriporticus adorned with tapestries and sculptures representing the personifications of the conquered provinces. The celebratory function of the complex was stressed by the presence, on the side of the quadriporticus furthest from the theater, of a curia-nymphaeum used for extraordinary meetings of the Senate; this was dominated by a statue of Pompey portrayed triumphant as Neptune. Since Pompey had held the office of *curator annonae*, from a propaganda point of view, the position of the curia between the quadriporticus and the porticus Minucia, where the free distribution of grain to Roman citizens took place, was not fortuitous. Lastly, since Pompey's urban villa was probably situated close by, the planning of the complex clearly resembled that of the large palaces of the Greek Hellenistic dynasties, from which Pompey must certainly have drawn inspiration. Only Julius Caesar went further: rather than merely adapting it, he completely revised a structure of the Greek type to meet new ideological requirements. With the creation of his new forum, the porticos of which enclosed the Temple of Venus Genetrix, he had transformed the religious model of the temple surrounded by a *temenos* into a highly symbolic monumental complex. In keeping with this new approach was the equestrian group in which Caesar was represented as Alexander on the back of his favorite horse, Bucephalus. This use of architectural space, closed to city traffic and meant as a public meeting place in the presence of the rich *manubiae* (proceeds from booty) of the benefactor, appears to be the logical end result of the germinal idea present in the Porticus Metellus.

In reality, therefore, the Greek models that were introduced to Rome made a major contribution to conveying specific messages. Thus, in order to serve propagandistic and self-promotional ends, they assumed a role that went far beyond that of the Greek precedents by drawing inspiration from the dynastic forms of the Hellenistic East. But, eventually, these were also surpassed and transformed into a creation that – thanks to the coherence of its architectural and ideological principles – became typically Roman, as was the case with the Imperial Fora.

The high level attained by architecture in the second and first centuries B.C. was matched by similar excellence in figurative art. The analysis of its constituent parts allows us to build up, for the whole of the late Republic, an extremely eclectic picture involving the fusing of other vigorous currents from the Greek world and the underlying Classical style. There were, therefore, the ideal conditions for them to influence each other, and create models that were a harmonious and skillful synthesis of artistic styles. Rome, which was rich and powerful politically, but lacked its own school of art, favored the development of a hegemonic ideology that bore its most interesting fruit in these two centuries.

It was inevitable that the different artists who came to Rome brought with them their own heritage of artistic languages. Despite the general diffusion of ideas throughout the eastern Mediterranean, the dominant style in this period was still heavily influenced by a number of schools, each with its own idiom: the Attic school, strongly imbued with its Classical past; the Pergamene school, which grew up around the artists who had created the groups dedicated by the Attalids after their victories over the Galatians and the Great Altar of Pergamum; the Rhodian school, which appeared to favor the so-called *sfumato* style in the Praxitelean tradition; and the Alexandrian school, the exact nature of which is still uncertain, although it seemed to be mainly interested in realism and the representation of landscape. To these may be added the contemporary output of Asia Minor and the islands, especially Paros, although this is still difficult to define in stylistic terms.

Of the workshops active in Rome, one of the most important seems to have been an Attic one that was famous for two sculptors from the *deme* of Thoricus: Polykles and Timarchides. Their activity has been reconstructed in a very reliable manner from the end of the third century to the beginning of the first century B.C. The evidence examined by Kirchner and then Halbicht, together with the remains of a number of their works, have permitted the reconstruction of their lineage, which began with Polykles, a *proxenus* of the Aetolians in 210 or 209 B.C., then his two sons, Polycles II and Timarchides I, who were followed by the two sons of each of them, Timocles and Timarchides II, as well as Polycles II and Dionysius, active between 185 and 147.

Their works formed part of the great Athenian tradition, with the revival of motifs and formal elements of the sculpture of the fifth and fourth centuries B.C., which were, however, often influenced by the contemporary baroque style. These were not, therefore, merely accurate copies, but rather the reelaboration of classical prototypes in order to produce works that were expressions of a new sensibility and style. Thus, the models of the Classical tradition, especially the Phidian one, helped to stimulate the elaboration by individual artists of the most famous subjects. It is significant that, while the family of these artists was active in Rome, it also produced cult statues for the new sanctuaries in Greece (at Elatea and in Athens itself), as well as honorific statues for the rich Italic merchant class at Delos. One of the most outstanding works executed for the Romans must have been the *Apollo* holding a *cithara* described by Pliny (XXXIV. 35) and attributed to Timarchides. It may have been the colossal cult statue executed when the Temple of Apollo Medicus was rebuilt, possibly in 179 B.C., during the censorship of Marcus Aemilius Lepidus and Marcus Fulvius Nobilior. A huge hand, found during the excavation of the Temple, may have belonged to this cult statue. From an iconographic point of view, the type has been linked to a variant of Praxiteles' *Apollo Lyceus*, but with more abundant drapery that hangs down the statue's legs, and a more accentuated twisting of the body, resembling that of the *Venus of Milo*. It may, therefore, have been an eclectic work, in which the substantial classical element was influenced by the Hellenistic baroque. This type also rapidly became popular in Asia Minor (a Hellenistic variant has been found at Tralles).

A colossal head, possibly a beardless Hercules, found on the slopes of the Capitoline Hill, has, however, been attributed to Polycles; he was mentioned by Pliny as one the sculptors who had, around 150 B.C., revitalized the techniques of bronze working. This hypothesis is based on the testimony of Cicero, who remembered (*Ad Atticum* VI. 1. 17) a *Hercules* by Polycles on the Capitoline Hill, near the Temple of Ops. In the head, in fact, the pathetic traits are skillfully combined with the typical schemata of the Praxitelean tradition, such as the shape of the eyes and the small, full mouth. The attribution to Polycles has, on the basis of a stylistic comparison, brought to light a resemblance between the *Hercules* and the head of an acrolith representing a goddess, formerly in the Albani collection and now in the Museo Capitolino; it is thought to have belonged to the Juno Regina in the homonymous temple that was rebuilt by Metellus. According to Pliny (XXXVI. 35), in the Temple of the Juno Regina, beside other works, there were two statues of the goddess, one by Timarchides, and the other by Polycles and Dionysius. The sculptor of the first statue must have been, therefore, Timarchides I, who made the *Apollo Medicus*; in the decade 180–170 B.C., his output may be linked to the construction of the Temple of Juno and the restoration of the Temple of Apollo, which took place during the censorship of Marcus Aemilius Lepidus. On the other hand, the second statue was probably the work of his sons, Polycles and Dionysius, who also made the cult statue in the neighboring Temple of Jupiter Stator, one of the buildings erected by Metellus; the architect was Hermodorus and it is, therefore, datable to the period between 148 and 131 B.C. However, it is not possible to give a more precise chronology for these works.

The Classical tradition, which, in the works of these Attic artists became an original synthesis reflecting the current taste, is found in a large part of the sculptural output of the period, especially in that related to cults. In accordance with a tradition that was becoming codified in the Roman world, the Phidian style was considered to be the most suitable for the representation of the gods. Thus, the mag-

Marble statue of a woman
the so-called *Cesi Juno*
Rome, Musei Capitolini

nificent colossal statue of Minerva, now in the entrance-hall of the Museo Capitolino, conforms to the rigorously Greek type of the Athena Promachos: in a sense, the Roman Minerva has assimilated the Greek Athena. The contribution made by the Greek artists to the creation of works of this level must have been of fundamental importance. In addition to the marble works, there were those in bronze, such as the colossal statue in gilded bronze of Hercules (now in the Museo Capitolino), from the round Temple of Hercules in the Forum Boarium, possibly dedicated by Aemilius Paullus after his victory over the Macedonians in 168 B.C. In addition, there were numerous cult statues made according to the technique of the acrolith, which was also widespread in the Greek world and harked back to the great chryselephantine sculptures of the Classical age.

In the Temple of Mars in the Circus, the cult group consisted of two statues, a colossal seated statue of Mars – perhaps of the so-called Ludovisi type – and a nude Venus. The latter, which, in Pliny's opinion (XXXVI. 26), was more beautiful than the Praxitelean ones, was sculpted by Scopas, perhaps Scopas Minor, who was known in Rome because he also executed a statue of Hercules Olivarius. The temple of this deity was identified with the one in Pentelic marble in the Forum Boarium before A. Ziolkowski demonstrated that it was the Temple of Hercules Victor, dedicated by Lucius Mummius after the conquest of Greece in 146 B.C.

The acrolith that dominated the *cella* of the temple B in Largo Argentina, in Rome, must also have been the work of a Greek sculptor with Classical tendencies; it has been identified as the one vowed in 101 B.C. by Quintus Lutatius Catulus to Fortuna Huiusce Diei, a goddess whose cult was linked to astrology, so that she was, to some extent, comparable to the Greek Kairos. A similar classicistic imprint, derived from Greek models of the fifth and fourth centuries B.C., and rendered with great precision, is found in other heads belonging to acrolithic statues, and also in the fragment of a cult statue from the Via Appia (perhaps the *Tempestas* of the homonymous temple dedicated by the various Cornelius Scipio at their tomb). This consists of a foot wearing a sandal finely decorated with tritons and nereids, and it resembles the sandals embellished with the battle of Lapiths and Centaurs worn by Phidias' cult statue of *Athena Parthenos*.

In the same period, it is certain that works in the Hellenistic baroque style were also to be found in Rome, for example the so-called *Cesi Juno* in the Museo Capitolino, an original statue believed to have been made in Pergamum, although it cannot be excluded that it was the work of one or more artists who arrived in Rome with a victor. Also of interest is a series of works in *peperino*, which, with their dramatic expressiveness – still strikingly evident despite the original stucco finish – are almost certainly derived from Greek Hellenistic models: an example is the splendid head of a woman in the Museo Capitolino. The most outstanding work in this current was the *Aphrodite* by Doedalsas; according to Pliny (XXXVI. 35), this was displayed in the Porticus Octaviae, the rebuilt version of the Porticus Metellus.

The marble group of the *Dioscuri*, found in fragments at the Spring of Juturna (close by the Temple of Castor), where it had been erected after Aemilius Paullus' victory at Pydna in 168 B.C., clearly demonstrates that another style also existed in Rome. Probably the work of Greek sculptors, it displays a noticeable use of Archaic stylistic schemata in the rigid frontality of the horsemen standing beside their horses, which are also rendered in an intentionally schematic manner. This emulation of the Archaic style may be explained as an interesting case of religious conservatism, probably reflecting the desire to imitate the most ancient statues, which were the object of particular veneration.

Once again the Temple of Apollo Medicus offers an opportunity for expanding on what has already been stated with regard to the variety of artistic currents present in Rome from the second century B.C. onward. According to Pliny (XXXVI. 34), in fact, a large number of works by a famous artist of the Rhodian school, Philiscus, were displayed in the temple. They included nine Muses, Apollo, Apollo nude, Artemis and Leto: in all probability a woman's head, found near the *cella* of the Temple, belonged to one of the Muses. Pliny (XXXVI. 35) also states that in the Temple of Juno Regina, together with the statues made by Timarchides and his sons Polycles and Dionysius, there was a *Venus* by Philiscus. The works by the latter, dating from the second quarter of the second century B.C., together with those of the Attic sculptors who, as we have seen, were active for a longer period, throw light on the ways in which models were diffused. Thus, Rome may be compared to the Hellenistic cities: in other words, it received, produced, and exported artistic models in much the same way as Pergamum, Alexandria, or Antioch did. And it is quite possible that M. Aemilius Lepidus commissioned the group of the Muses directly from Philiscus. But the latter's workshop, like the other Rhodian ones, must have had to meet a considerable demand for mass-produced works, since various groups of Muses have also been

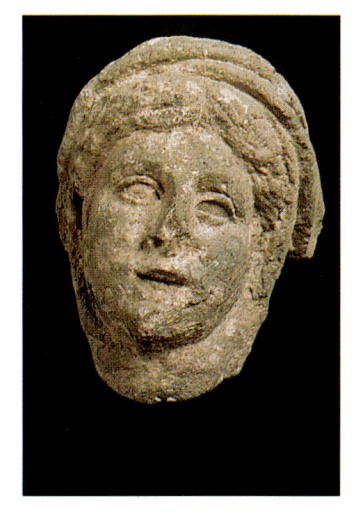

Head of a woman in *peperino*
funerary monument
found in Via di San Lorenzo
Rome, Musei Capitolini

Slab from the so-called
Altar of Domitius Ahenobarbus
detail of the procession
of Poseidon and Amphitrite
Munich, Staatlichen Antikensammlung
und Glyptothek München

found both in Asia Minor and Alexandria. From Rome, where all these currents came together, the codified models were then transmitted to the provincial centers, which – although their output was a humble one in terra-cotta – were, in fact, heavily dependent on the urban models. A typical example is the colony of Luni, founded in 177 B.C. by M. Aemilius Lepidus, who had been censor of Rome in 179 B.C.: in the Temple of Luna, the group of the Muses with Apollo and Luna reproduces, on a smaller scale, the types ascribable to the Muses by Philiscus and the *Apollo* by Timarchides, dedicated in the Temple of Apollo Medicus in Rome.

This is perhaps an appropriate point to attempt a brief reappraisal of the coroplastic production in this period: the long-standing Roman and central-Italic tradition does not appear to have declined in the least, despite the arrival *en masse* of Greek artists who were experts in the working of more precious materials. Terra-cotta works datable to the second century B.C., such as the splendid fragments of the so-called Domus Tiberiana on the Palatine Hill, or the seated statue of a woman from a private *sacellum* at Ostia, display an extraordinarily high level of workmanship; this is particularly evident in the great care taken over the details and the handling of the drapery. Even more significant are the two pedimental groups found in Rome at the church of San Gregorio al Celio and near the second milestone of the Via Appia Nuova. The first pedimental group, representing a sacrifice to a divinity, displays a marked Classicism that does not, however, lack the typical devices of the most advanced Hellenistic style. On the other hand, in the second pediment, unfortunately badly damaged, the influence of the Attic sculpture of the second half of the fifth century B.C. is very evident. Both these pedimental groups may be dated to around the middle of the second century B.C., although the second one may date from the end of the century because of its Classicistic forms in the Neo-Attic style.

Clearly influenced by works available on the Roman market, the coroplastic output continued, therefore, to be in great demand, and it may well be that the marked conservatism that was so typical of the Roman ruling class, especially with regard to cultic matters, was favorable to it. Right through the second century, in fact, cult statues influenced by the Archaic type were made in wood, terra-cotta, or stuccoed stone. In the Temple of Juno Regina, on the Aventine Hill, the statue had been brought from Veii, and was, therefore, Archaic, but also the other statues dedicated subsequently were, as the sources relate, in cypress. Together with the new cult statues, often colossal and acrolithic, the majority of the statues of Roman divinities were in terra-cotta, and, in any case, until the late Republic, the most ancient statues – some of which were small *xoana* – continued to be venerated.

It is not surprising, therefore, that, in the second half of the first century B.C., Arcesilaus, an artist from southern Italy, possibly Tarentum, was commissioned to make two important statues in terra-cotta, one for the Temple of Venus Genetrix, in the Forum Iulium, and the other for the Temple of Felicitas. These temples were among the most outstanding architectural achievements in pre-Augustan Rome. Thus, the fact that, once again, coroplastics was chosen as the medium for the cult statues indicates that the tradition of the "*antefixa fictilia deorum Romanorum*" (terra-cotta antefixes of the Roman gods) to which Cato referred had certainly not been abandoned; rather it had taken an evolutionary course that was heavily influenced by the contemporary marble output, which itself displayed the mark of Hellenistic influence, as the previously mentioned examples of Luni and Rome reveal.

Greek Artists in Republican Rome: A Short History of Sculpture

In the field of architecture excessive importance should not, however, be ascribed to the use of marble as a building material, although it was becoming increasingly widespread. In reality, with the exception of Athens, which had marble quarries close by, no Greek city was built of marble. In the vast majority of cases, the buildings were constructed in freestone that was covered with plaster or stucco, and only a few monuments were in marble: this applied to Alexandria and Antioch, and pre-imperial Miletus and Ephesus. It is only to be expected, therefore, that few marble remains from the Hellenistic age have survived in such important cities as Alexandria, where the use of stucco predominated.

Rome followed this tradition, which only began to change from the Augustan era onward, when, thanks to the exploitation of the quarries near Luni, marble replaced more humble materials in public buildings. In view of this, it is hardly surprising that, in the period when the great marble edifices of Hermodorus were being constructed, or the rebuilding, completed in 69 B.C., of the Capitoline Temple of Jupiter with a number of columns brought from the *Olympieion* in Athens, was underway, other buildings, such as the quadriporticus of Metellus and various important temples, continued to be constructed in stone faced with stucco. Thus, the Temple of Honos et Virtus, designed by the architect Gaius Mucius for Gaius Marius, and entirely built in *peperino*, was, for instance, among the most highly-praised in republican Rome and, according to Vitruvius, worthy of the tradition of the Greek temples.

Supported by the critical theories of the philosophical school of the Middle Stoa, principally of Posidonius of Apamea, who was responsible for the first concrete application of analogies between artistic forms and rhetoric, the mounting wave of Classicism – which, in the great cult statues, reached its highest, most rigorous manifestation – became an integral part of Roman art. The case of the so-called Altar of Domitius Ahenobarbus, probably the base of a Roman triumphal monument, is exemplary in this regard. Four sculptured slabs from this were found among the ruins of the Temple of Mars (un-

Marble statue of a seated woman
from the area
of the Theater of Pompey
Rome, Musei Capitolini

Marble statue of Apollo as a citharist
Rome, Musei Capitolini

der the church of San Salvatore in Campo). Three of them represent the marriage of Poseidon and Amphitrite who, in the Hellenistic iconography, symbolize rule of the seas, while the fourth one depicts a census in the presence of Mars near an altar (Ara Martis in Campo). In fact, the most interesting of the four reliefs is the last: while the first friezes, now in Munich, are clearly influenced by the Hellenistic style of the second century B.C., and probably formed part of a Greek naval monument that was dismantled and brought to Rome, the one with the census scene (now in Paris) draws on – despite the poor syntax of the figures on the neutral ground – models of the fourth century B.C., which are, however, also imbued with the Hellenistic style. The relief is datable to the early first century B.C., after the Marian reform of 107 B.C. (the soldiers are wearing heavy armor), but it is interesting that it was juxtaposed with the other reliefs, without any concern for the clash of styles. Evidently, it met functional and propagandistic requirements (perhaps of a personage who, after a naval victory, had become censor). Echoes of the Hellenistic style in the now familiar Classical schema, rendered at times with the uninspired repetitiousness of the Roman craftsmen, are also found in the figures of the episodes of the most ancient story of Rome sculpted in the marble reliefs of the Caesarean period that adorned the Basilica Paulli (the so-called Basilica Aemilia) in the Forum Romanorum.

The decoration of the huge Pompeian complex in the Campus Martius must have been very typical of the artistic taste of the period. Pliny informs us (XXXVI. 41) that the fourteen statues representing the nations conquered by Pompey were by Coponius. They may have been displayed in the quadriporticus, perhaps in niches on the sides of the Curia-nymphaeum where the statue of the victor stood, almost as if they were paying homage to him. Unfortunately, however, nothing can be said with regard to the artistic accomplishments of Coponius because no remains that can be ascribed with certainty to his cycle of the *Nationes* have been found. Only a headless statue of a seated woman and a group of colossal statues, now in Rome (Palazzo Borghese), Naples, and Paris, representing Apollo and the Muses, have been attributed to the Pompeian complex. Another two statues in a similar style, now in the Museo Capitolino, an *Apollo* with the tunic and cloak of the citharist and a priestess (possibly Hygieia), help to identify the salient features of the sculpture of this period. This is characterized by rough carving without final polishing, thus revealing a stylistic procedure in the Hellenistic tradition applied to a rigorously Classical schema.

But, although, in the vast output of the last centuries of the Republic, the degree to which the Classical repertoire was assimilated varied, as did the results in artistic terms, the high quality of some products is indicative of what was now a profound acquisition, from both the rational and critical points of view, of the Greek artistic heritage. Thus, innovatory processes were started that led to increasingly important developments.

When Quintilian (*Institutio Oratoria* XII. 10. 8) stated that Polyclitus had represented the human body with "*decor supra verum*" (elegance rather than realism), he was evidently referring to a schematization that, as had already happened with regard to the Phidian divinities, considered the style of Polyclitus to be the highest expression of the virtue of heroes and superhuman beings. This is demonstrated by the solid structure of the so-called *Terme Prince*; this does not, however, lack allusions to works by Lysippus – his Alexander with a spear, for instance – especially in the dramatic handling of the face. This bronze original in the Museo delle Terme, probably datable to the second quarter of the second century B.C., may have represented a Hellenistic sovereign (perhaps Attalus II before his accession to the throne), or a Roman in a heroic pose after the Hellenistic mode, but, in any case, it constitutes an excellent synthesis of a wide variety of Classical canons. It also is interesting to see how, in the first century B.C., another nude – the marble statue of a youth at the Museo di Villa Albani – is an example of a different procedure. With a distortion typical of the Polyclitean canon – noticeable in the much more delicate forms – it appears to be the expression of a conscious reaction against the Classical model: oriented toward the creation of a new one, it prefigures the currents that inspired, in the later Empire, the celebrated groups of Orestes and Electra in Naples, and Orestes and Pylades at the Schloss Fasanerie. The maker of this work, Stephanos, proudly signed that he was a pupil of Pasiteles: because of the innovatory message it contains, it is believed to be the copy of an original by the great Greek sculptor, who, together with Arcesilaus, was one of the most outstanding artists working in Rome in the mid-first century B.C.

The ferment that must have enlivened the artistic activity at this stage produced such splendid works as the youth in the Museo Albani; and although it sought to abandon the Classical canons, it was derived from the profound knowledge of them. It was no coincidence that Pasiteles, who may have originally come from southern Italy, was mentioned by Pliny (XXXVI. 39) as the author of a treatise on the

Colossal marble statue of a woman (Hygieia?) Rome, Musei Capitolini

nobilia opera – that is, the Greek works worthy of being remembered and copied. He must have been endowed with an encyclopedic culture and a profound knowledge of a wide variety of the most outstanding works of the past. The distinctive characteristic of this artist – and of his colleagues, too – must have been an erudite eclecticism, which resulted in the refined elegance of the so-called Campana reliefs. To this aspect should be added an interest in the most extreme naturalism resulting from philosophical studies relating to *mimesis*, in the sense of an excellent imitation of nature. According to Posidonius of Apamea, it was possible to proceed from this level to a higher concept only through the imagination. This was able to express, in an original manner, what went beyond the visible world – beyond, in other words, what was subject to imitation.

The anecdote about Pasiteles, who, so it appears, risked his life in order to draw a wild animal in a cage, is particularly significant. Nonetheless, the fact remains that these artists tended to favor coroplastics. This medium required a malleable material that permitted the subjects to be represented in a more fascinating manner thanks to the light and shade effects obtained with the pallet, which were more attractive than those that could be created in bronze or marble. Due to the lack of originals, it is difficult for us to know to what extent the output of these artists had cast off the formal schemata of the Greek heritage in order to interpret it with a different sensibility. We do know, however, that Arcesilaus modeled the *Venus Genetrix* in the Forum Iulium, and contracted to make the cult statue of the Temple of Felicitas for a million sesterces. He was also noted for his *proplasmata*: these are usually interpreted as being models, but they could also be finished sculptures in terra-cotta that were intended to be copied. However, according to Pliny (XXXV. 155), connoisseurs were willing to offer sky-high prices for them. An idea of the quality of these works may be obtained from the splendid statue of a seated woman from Ostia and the pedimental sculpture from the Via Appia Nuova, where the clay is fashioned with a skill that even permits the creation of effects of transparency, as in the *chiton* of the female figure. The basic concept is formally Classical, but, in the general eclecticism of the works, there is also an erudite revival of the stylistic features of the Severe style that, in accordance with the taste of the period, led to borrowings such as the *Nikai* on the monumental base in basalt found near the Temple of Fides on the Capitol (possibly a monument dedicated to Sulla), right up to the Augustan age, when this archaizing cultural current began to symbolize forms of outmoded morality. It was, therefore, this style, which was only in part Classicistic, that pervaded the pre-Augustan artistic currents with regard to both sculpture and architecture. Thus, the eclecticism of the forms and the superimposition of the models are explained by the fact that the Corinthian order, now well-established in the Greek world, took longer to secure acceptance than the Doric and Ionic orders, as in the so-called Temple of Portunus in the Forum Boarium, or in the temples of the Forum Holitorium. This also explains the refined Archaism in the temple dedicated by Pompey to Hercules at the Ara Maxima in the Forum Boarium, which not only used an original work by Myron as a cult statue, but must also have been araeostyle after the Etruscan models (Vitruvius, *De Architectura* III. 3. 4).

Thus, the artists, famous or otherwise, of Greek origin, or with Greek training – some of them prob-

Base of an honorary monument possibly dedicated to Sulla
Rome, Musei Capitolini

ably had their workshops in Rome – and the indeterminate, but substantial, number of artists whose workshops developed in this milieu, must have produced works that were an expression of eclectic Classicism. At the same time, the works of art collected by the celebrated orator Asinius Pollio offer further confirmation of the peculiarity of the taste of this period. The prevailing eclecticism must have conditioned the constitution of one of the most important art collections in the ancient world, which was a splendid example of the taste of cultured Romans in the Caesarean period. Pliny (XXXVI. 33–34) provides a list of the *monumenta Pollionis*, an impressive series of sculptures, some of them colossal, by past and contemporary artists, some of whom were active in other areas of the Mediterranean, especially Rhodes. They were displayed to the public in Pollio's gardens, in grottoes and *nymphaea*, or else in the center of water-filled grottoes, rather like what was to happen later with the Rhodian groups at Sperlonga. The location of the collection is uncertain: it may have been situated in the Horti Asiniani, which, it appears, were on the site where the Baths of Caracalla were later built (in them, in fact, the most important works mentioned by Pliny were to be found) rather than in the Atrium Libertatis, Pollio's library at the foot of the Capitoline Hill. Pliny's list includes works by Stephanus, Arcesilaus, Cleomenes, Eniochus, Papylus (a pupil of Praxiteles), Eutychides, and, naturally, Apollonius and Tauriscus of Tralles, sculptors of the famous group (now in Naples) representing Dirce being bound to a bull by Amphion and Zethus, which had been brought to Rome from Rhodes. It appears this was a splendid original that it would, in fact, have been difficult to copy. According to Pliny, the artists considered themselves to be pupils of Menecrates, who was believed to have been one of the sculptors of the Great Altar of Pergamum; it is, possible, therefore, that the so-called *Farnese Bull* was executed around the middle of the first century B.C., and was almost contemporary with the *monumenta*. This explains the particular characteristics of the execution, which, overall, was very plastic, yet, at the same time represented the details in a meticulous and analytical manner. But, aside from these exceptional examples of artistic prowess and the splendid monumental buildings that were rapidly changing the face of the city, the lesser works were the ones that reflected the extent to which Greek culture now influenced the Roman world. This assimilation began to affect forms that, traditionally, had been considered to be Roman, such as portraits and honorific statues. From the second century B.C. onward, these became extremely popular, and were adapted to the growth of the ruling class, the members of which were increasingly interested in individualistic portraits for propaganda purposes. Other rich personages who did not, however, have political ambitions, aspired to leave their mark; on occasion, they commissioned major works, as in the case of the Sanctuary of Fortuna Primigenia at Praeneste. They may have been merchants from provincial towns, especially in Latium and Campania, with profitable business interests all over the Mediterranean. Decimus Cossutius, the Roman architect whom Antiochus IV employed for works in Athens (the Olympieion) and in Syria, belonged to a wealthy family, possibly of Sabine origin, that had links with the quarrying of marble in the East. It was, therefore, inevitable that the influence of Hellenic models on these personages was enormous; above all, it could be used for self-promotional ends with greater freedom from political restraints,

Base of an honorary monument possibly dedicated to Sulla
Rome, Musei Capitolini

Marble group representing
the punishment of Dirce
the so-called *Farnese Bull*
Naples
Museo Archeologico Nazionale

because they lived in the provinces and, in any case, in a milieu outside the control of the senatorial censorship. This accounts for the two important statues from Delos portraying private citizens according to the *schemata* of heroic nudity that, in this period, were the types in greatest demand, perhaps because they alluded in generic terms to the virtues and inherent qualities of the subject. The works in question are the *Pseudoathlete* (now in Athens) and the celebrated *Ofellius Ferus*, a merchant of Campanian origin whose wealth was probably derived from the slave trade, since his statue was displayed in a niche of the so-called Agora of the Italians, which was devoted to this activity. As may be inferred from the inscription, in the free port of Delos this personage must have been a respected member of the Italic community. In any case, his colossal statue was certainly executed by the famous Attic sculptors, Dionysius and Timarchides, who, as we have seen, worked both in Rome and Greece on important commissions. The discovery in Rome of the so-called *Terme Prince* reveals that the type had spread, presumably from the middle of the second century B.C. onward, to the city as well, although it was probably intended for private edifices, such as dwellings or buildings constructed *ex manubiis* (with the money obtained from the sale of booty). Unlike the *Prince*, which fully respects the Classical canons, in the *Pseudoathlete* the contrast between the Classical forms of the body and the marked individuality of the face is strikingly evident. This is a Roman version of the portrait of the Greek heroic type that was later to be found in such works as the so-called *General* of Tivoli, and evolved into the Actium type of the portraits of Augustus. In the types of public portraiture, the canonical one in *toga* or cuirass must have been extremely popular, especially because it was the only type displayed in official buildings, in accordance with a tradition that was precursed by the Greek statues – as is evident if the Roman republican statues are compared with the honorific ones of Rhodes and Cos. Unfortunately, few examples have survived. Of particular importance are the two sculptures known as the *Togate Statue* of Bergamo and the *Orator* of Florence, who is portrayed in the pose that is typical of a leader addressing the crowd. This personage, Aulus Metellus,

Bronze statue of Aulus Metellus
the so-called *Orator*
Florence
Museo Archeologico Nazionale

may have been a Roman citizen holding a high public office, who wished to celebrate thus his new status. The high stylistic quality of the two sculptures, one marble, the other bronze, resembles that of the output of the Greek workshops of the first century B.C.; in fact, the large number of togate figures from Delos representing Italic merchants were probably Athenian. On the other hand, the majority of the statues and portrait busts must have been produced by Roman workshops. The salient characteristics of these works – the marked verism of the facial features with an exaggerated emphasis on detail – have given rise to the hypothesis that there was a typically Roman matrix for this type, which is specifically linked to the middle class and its aspiration to distinguish itself by creating a new style. In reality, even in the oldest portraiture, the influence of the Greek models was of decisive importance, above all due to the contribution of the numerous currents associated with them. This was especially true in the Hellenistic age, when the desire to create a realistic portrait and the need to represent the higher moral virtues were perfectly balanced. The portraits of Pompey, which are, fortunately, known to us thanks to a series of copies of the imperial age, are splendid illustrations of the way in which – depending on the particular requirements of the moment – artistic currents and techniques were developed that were already present in Hellenistic portraiture. Particularly in the dynastic portrait, this had already developed a remarkable capacity to adapt to the function of the statue and the message it was intended to convey. The first portraits of Pompey (the Venice type) display the influence of the basic model that can be traced back to the statue of Menander executed by Praxiteles' sons. Subsequently, the need to portray a mature man and cautious politician meant that the traits of maturity were accentuated – as in the *Pompey* of the Copenhagen type – reflecting the style that was also present in the portraits of Crassus. Only in a few cases, linked to particular merits with regard to the state and the city, did the Senate authorize the creation of larger sculptural works. Although it was not the first of its kind, the equestrian statue of Sulla, erected in the Forum on the *rostra*, must have acquired particular importance from a propaganda point of view if the same honor was bestowed on Pompey and Caesar. Although it is significant that they were the product of a provincial milieu, the honorific monuments dedicated on Delos to the most important figures of the day must have been more imposing. These include the one dedicated to Gaius Marius, perhaps on the occasion of his mission to Asia in 99 B.C.; erected in the Agora of the Italians, it was executed by an Ephesian sculptor, Agasias, who was active in the late second and early first centuries B.C. Judging by the few extant fragments (now in Athens), which include a splendid kneeling warrior with disheveled hair and a suffering face, it must have been an equestrian statue after the Hellenistic type of the combat between a horseman and a barbarian. From a political point of view, the group must have had an important propagandistic function, and, for this reason, the type was repeated on coins, such as the *denarius* of A. Licinius Nerva of 47 B.C., but not even Octavian dared to impose this type in the area of the Forum when, in 43 B.C., the Senate honored him with an equestrian statue on the *rostra* that was intended to resemble the Sullan one.

Bibliography

T. Holscher, 1967; F. Coarelli, in DArch, II, 1968, pp. 302 ff.; P. Gross, in REL, LVII, 1970, pp. 85 ff.; Kl. Fittschen, in MDAI(R), LXXVII, 1970, pp. 177 ff.; F. Coarelli, in DArch, IV-V, 1970-71, pp. 241 ff.; J.D. Breckenridge, in ANRW, I, 4, 1973, pp. 173 ff.; L. Castiglione, in MAIU, IV, 1973, pp. 28 ff.; U.V. Hiesinger, in ANRW, I, 4, 1973, pp. 159 ff.; *Roma Medio-Repubblicana...*, 1973; P. Gros, in *L'Italie préromaine et la Rome républicaine...*, 1976, pp. 387 ff.; P. Zanker, 1976; F. Coarelli, in PBSR, XLV, 1977, pp. 1 ff.; F. Coarelli, in "Prospettiva", Suppl. I, 1977, pp. 35 ff.; H. Flashar, 1978; T. Holscher, in MDAI(R), LXXV, 1978, pp. 315 ff.; T. Holscher, in Tainia, 1978, pp. 351 ff.; A. Stewart, 1979; Kl. Tuchelt, 1979; T. Holscher, in JDAI, XCV, 1980, pp. 265 ff.; M. Torelli, in MAAR, XXXVI, 1980, pp. 313 ff.; F. Coarelli, in *L'art décoratif à Rome...*, 1981, pp. 229 ff.; H. von Hesberg, in *L'art décoratif à Rome...*, 1981, pp. 19 ff.; F. Coarelli, "Opuscula Instituti Romani Finlandiae", II, 1982, pp. 119 ff.; Chr. Habicht, in MDAI(A), XCVII, 1982, pp. 171 ff.; P. Zanker, in WZBerlin, XXXI, 1982, pp. 307 ff.; F. Coarelli, in *Architecture et societé...*, 1983, pp. 191 ff.; T. Holscher, 1984; M. Kreeb, in BCH, CVIII, 1984, pp. 317 ff.; E. La Rocca, in *Alessandria e il mondo ellenistico-romano...*, III, 1984, pp. 629 ff.; M.R. Hofter, 1985; G. Lahnsen, in MDAI(R), XCII, 1985, pp. 261 ff.; L. Giuliani, 1986; G. Hübner, in *Altertümer von Pergamon*, XV, 1986, pp. 127 ff.; M. Cristofani, 1987, pp. 95 ff.; H.G. Martin, 1987; L. Pietilä, Castrén, 1987; E. Simon, in JDAI, CII, 1987, pp. 291 ff.; E. La Rocca, in BCAR, XCII, 1987-88, pp. 265 ff.; R.R.R. Smith, in *Ritratto ufficiale e ritratto privato*, 1988, pp. 493 ff.; A. Ziolkowski, in "Phoenix", XLII, 1988, pp. 309 ff.; J.P. Morél, in *Cambridge Ancient History* (2ª ed.), XIII, 1989, pp. 477 ff.; H.R. Goette, 1990; M.D. Fullerton, 1990; L. Anselmino, L. Ferrea, M.J. Strazzulla, RendPontAc, 63, 1990-91, pp. 193-262; V.C. Goodlett, Aja, 95, 1991, pp. 669-681; F. Oueyrel, BCH, 115, 1991, pp. 389-464; M. Forte, P. Desantis, S. Sani, 1992, pp. 185-223; G. Hafner, 1992, pp. 17-32; M.J. Strazzulla, 1992, pp. 161-183; M.A. Tomei, RM, 99, 1992, pp. 171-228; G. Zimmer, 1992, pp. 301-313; W. Fuchs, 1993; F.H. Pairault-Massa, 1993, pp. 243-268; M.J. Strazzulla, 1993, pp. 317-349; P. Moreno, 1994.

Raffaella Farioli Campanati

The Legacy of the Western Greeks
in the Art of Late Antiquity and the Middle Ages

Throughout Late Antiquity and the Middle Ages, in the complex and tormented history of the West one notes – with varying intensity depending on the epoch or political and social context – the importance of Greek artistic culture, in its new and broader meaning as "Byzantine." This culture emerged in that part of the Roman Empire that was heir to the civilization of the great Hellenistic cities of the Near East and Mediterranean which, together with the growing input from Eastern and Sassanid cultures, maintained vital links under the protective aegis of Constantinople, the "New Rome."

In artistic spheres, even within the evolution of a more organic grasp of form and its relationship with physical or conceptual space, the legacy of the Hellenistic tradition furnished a constant fulcrum for the evolving art transmitted from Constantine's capital. Providing a bridge between Europe and Asia, Constantinople was destined to become the absolute metropolis under Justinian, completely supplanting the earlier capital, Rome, in all its functions. It was therefore to Constantinople that the successive rulers in the West turned their attention, thereby endorsing as it were the legitimacy of the capital's *imperium*: from the sovereigns of Ravenna in the Valentinian-Theodosius line of Constantinople to Theodoric, from the exarchs (provincial deputies), and later the Carolingian and Ottonian rulers to the Normans. This explains the Hellenizing slant to the art works commissioned by the sovereigns and members of the more privileged classes, and likewise the cultural leanings of the various courts, whose ceremonies, banners, and sumptuary arts strove to emulate the splendors of the imperial liturgy of Constantinople. While it is undeniable that Byzantine artistic culture constitutes a vital component in the formation of Carolingian and Ottonian art – and similarly of Norman art in Palermo – in some regions of Italy where contacts with the metropolis and further East were more direct and enduring, Byzantine culture bore greater weight as it was the local expression of immigrant Greek and eastern craftsmen, as in the case of Rome and particularly Sicily and Lower Italy. Given that the brevity of the present essay affords insufficient space to delve with any depth into the complexities of the issues of Byzantine culture from the end of Late Antiquity through the advent of Norman domination, we are obliged to make a careful selection from among surviving material evidence, focusing on those works that were patently commissioned by a Hellenized clientele; this narrows down the field of study to Sicily and Lower Italy, but includes Rome. As regards these regions – all heirs to ancient Greece and directly dependent on Constantinople as of the sixth century, as Sicily was until the Arab occupation (A.D. 878), together with Calabria, Lucania, and Longobardia after the dominion of the Longobards in the tenth century as Byzantine *themi* (administrative districts) and later united under the Byzantine Catapanato in the mid-tenth century – artistic expression was one of the aspects of a deeply rooted and enduring Hellenization, on a par with the various forms of ecclesiastic literature (hymnography, hagiography, and theology) characteristic of the cults of the Hellenized populations. While Hellenization was undoubtedly more incisive at a linguistic and literary level, and particularly so in Sicily and southern Calabria, it should be noted that the documentation of artistic production is rather scarce and discontinuous. In fact, material evidence only becomes more abundant after the Norman conquest (A.D. 1067) and the consequent transition of the diocese from the patriarchy of Constantinople to the hands of the Church of Rome. The greater quantity of Byzantine art works produced under the Normans – to some extent because the survival of works and monuments was more facilitated than in previous periods – might seem contradictory, when in fact it endorses the authenticity of the Hellenization process, which did not take the form of importation (as was the case of the commissions of Desiderius, the abbot of Monte Cassino Abbey, or the mosaics of Norman Palermo), nor of the bookish cult of the Norman kings in the great monastic foundations), but rather the outcome of a gradual evolution over the course of the centuries, fueled by lingering Greek liturgical practices and monastic institutions, and perhaps also on the basis of a deeply ingrained linguistic substrate. Things evolved diversely in other Byzantine sites and regions, such as at Ravenna, which, from the time of the conquest of Justinian (A.D. 540) upheld its status as capital, first as the chief seat of the prefecture, then of the Exarchate, through to the Longobard conquest (A.D. 751), or at Bari, a Byzantine capital for almost 200 years; these two cities were "never Hellenized, either linguistically or in religious matters" (Falkenhausen). Hence, as regards the situation affecting the southernmost regions of the ancient realm of Magna Graecia, there is evidence not so much of self-induced Hellenization – an orientation that was quite alien to the policies of Constantinople – as of a natural process of absorption closely tied to the monastic activity, which remained "one of the principal vectors of Hellenization" (Bulgarella).

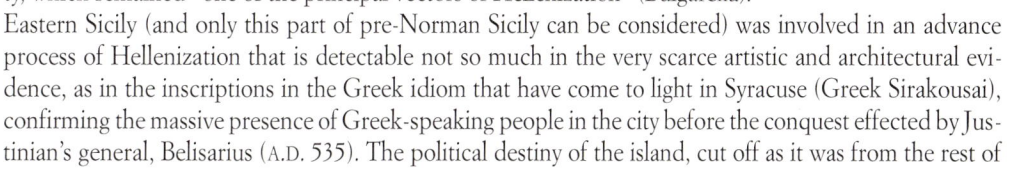

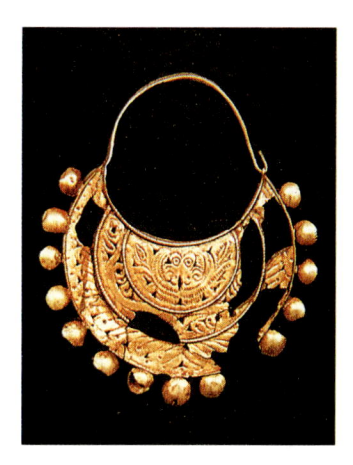

Eastern Sicily (and only this part of pre-Norman Sicily can be considered) was involved in an advance process of Hellenization that is detectable not so much in the very scarce artistic and architectural evidence, as in the inscriptions in the Greek idiom that have come to light in Syracuse (Greek Sirakousai), confirming the massive presence of Greek-speaking people in the city before the conquest effected by Justinian's general, Belisarius (A.D. 535). The political destiny of the island, cut off as it was from the rest of

Half-moon earring
from Racineci
8th-9th cent. A.D.
Syracuse
Museo Archeologico Regionale

Pluteus with a griffin
and winged horse
10th-11th cent. A.D.
Cagliari
Museo Archeologico Nazionale

Fragmentary *pluteus*
from San Marciano
10th cent. A.D.
Syracuse
Museo Archeologico Regionale

the Italian Exarchate and the spreading Longobard conquest of Lower Italy, brought it immediately into the sphere of government of Constantinople. Two signal events – first, the sojourn (albeit briefly from A.D. 663 to 668) in Syracuse of the Byzantine Emperor, Constans II Pogonatus, but also Sicily's becoming a *thema* in the seventh century, together with the territories of the Bruttii (today's Calabria); subsequently Otranto and Naples were snatched from the jurisdiction of the Exarchate. The second significant event came in the eighth century when Sicily and Calabria broke away from the Church of Rome, and passed under the wing of the Patriarchy of Constantinople. These two events basically ratified the Hellenization already under way at linguistic and liturgical levels, and undoubtedly influenced the development of art throughout the regions concerned. In this context, a further contribution to the process came in the form of the colonies of Greek monks, whose activities are documented from the first half of the seventh century, as attested by the letter Maximus the Confessor sent to the *hegumenoi* in the Sicilian monasteries. These monks were most likely originally from the eastern reaches of the Byzantine Empire, laid waste and overrun by the Persian and Arab hordes. In the period that followed Justinian's conquest, compared with the territories of Lower Italy in which Byzantine culture did not assert itself until after the Longobard conquest (ninth century) and the constitution of the *thema* of Longobardia, Sicily was already Hellenized from both linguistic and religious points of view. Despite the scarcity of extant material, or the rare and sporadic yields of archaeological digs, the overall architectural substrate betrays a prevalent adhesion to North African typologies, with contingent features to those of Constantinople and the Near East at Nesima, Zituni, and in the basilica of San Giovanni in Syracuse itself; these tendencies are also discernible in the floor plan of certain rock-cut chapels (e.g., San Micidiario at Pantalica, Sant'Alania at Leontini). Among the sculptural works found, Syracuse has yielded *plutei* from San Marciano, carved on-site, whose layout of incised geometric and vegetal patterns evince Sassanid decorative tendencies. A larger number of extant sculptures cover the seventh century, when the sumptuary arts in Sicily were dominated by certain types of jewelry that became popular throughout the Aegean. The production of sculpture, of which the few surviving examples betray a noticeable Byzantine imprint, continues through the period of Arab domination, as can be inferred from certain indicative fragments of sculpted plaques datable to the tenth century. Lastly, in the area of pictorial works, an important fresco predating the Arab dominion in the ninth century graces the vault of part of the hypogeum of Santa Lucia in Syracuse; the painting's layout is accommodated in a large cross subdividing the four quadrants, an arrangement that was completely novel for the period but came to be repeated in later medieval churches in Cappadocia and in the Balkans. In Syracuse the great gem-studded cross echoing certain sumptuary pieces – with its central medallion bearing the figure of Christ set between two others featuring the archangels and a *clipeus* with the Virgin in prayer at the foot of the main upright – associates the theme of the *parousia* to that of the *deesis*, in compliance with the Byzantine standards of the East (Velmans). The quadrants of the cross are densely filled with the *Forty Martyrs of Sebaste*, pictured in a Syrian version; a caption-inscription in Greek (yet to be deciphered) may shed further light on the missing elements that completed the composition. In pre-Justinian Campania too one notes a certain prevalence of the effects in both architecture and painting (burial-niche mosaics of bishop figures in the San Gennaro catacombs) of the highly fertile exchanges with traders in North Africa: in San Giorgio Maggiore (fifth century A.D.) in Naples the

Chancel of the Oratory
of Sant'Aspreno
10th cent. A.D.
Naples, Oratorio di Sant'Aspreno

insertion of dosserets between the capitals and spandrels above is indicative of early relations with Aegean Greek spheres; furthermore, the plan of San Lorenzo Maggiore (mid-sixth century) with its apse locked into the side wall and flanked by *pastophoriai* evokes the standard morphology of types common in Syria and Asia Minor. In this church in particular, and in Santa Maria Capua Vetere, the floor mosaics make direct reference to Syrian models, which in turn borrowed from their specific Palestinian forerunners, whose use was inaugurated by Paolinus at Cimitile (Naples) and Fondi (Latina) with the introduction of theophanies, respectively of the Trinity and Judgment, expressed in symbolic form which, in the abstract conception of the large cross inside the *clipeus* or shield device, seem to presage the later mosaics of Giovanni II (A.D. 535–555) in the apse of the basilica of Stefania in Naples, featuring a *Transfiguration* in parallel with the apse mosaics of Sant'Apollinare in Classe, Ravenna (A.D. 549).

Another identifiable contribution of "Greek" origin can be seen in the eighth century in the saint cults of Constantinople, which had a marked influence on such cults elsewhere, recorded in the list of local liturgical festivals (the so-called *Calendario marmoreo*), and integrated with the contents of a Greek *synaxarion* (documenting a saint's life), which is probably datable to the period in which the Duchy was part of the Byzantine *thema* of Sicily. The gradual "Byzantinization" of the Duchy of Naples – which was effectively linked to the historical and geographical patterns that crystallized in Lower Italy after the Byzantine reconquest and institution of the *thema* of Longobardia (in the year A.D. 891–892) – became more accentuated in the tenth and eleventh centuries as more and more people of Italo-Grecian stock migrated from Calabria and Sicily (the *bioi* of the monk-saints Nilus of Rossano, Sabas of Collesano, and Macarius), and was endorsed by the foundation of Greek monasteries. Relations with Constantinople, which were without doubt fostered by the busy trade activity of the cities along the coast, and with Amalfi in first place, are evident in a spreading Hellenization – as testified by the use of Greek characters in the notary registers, as part of the lively interest in Greek culture on the part of the local aristocracy of the Duchy (and especially by the *doux* Sergius and other members of his family) and of the Neapolitan clergy; such circles accommodated most of the translators of the Neapolitan school: lives of the Byzantine saints and the famous translation of the *Romance of Alexander*, which was overseen by Archdeacon Leo and commissioned by Duke Giovanni III.

In the sphere of visual arts, besides the few albeit significant extant examples of churches – San Costanzo in Capri (with its inscribed cross floor-plan), and San Giovanni a Mare in Gaeta – the area of greatest interest from the eighth and ninth centuries is sculpture and statuary, as these show remarkable comparisons with works in Mainland Greece and the East and for the unitary development that links such arts with the somewhat scant documents in Naples, Cimitile (Santi Martiri), Sorrento, and Capua, to which examples from Sardinia (at Assemini and Dolianova) can be linked. Among the most distinguished artifacts in this category are the marble gates of the Sant'Aspreno Oratory, Naples, founded in late eighth–early ninth century by Cabulus and Constantina, mentioned in the inscription carved into the upper listel of the *plutei*, fixed to small pillars that evince remarkable parallels with similar Sardinian pieces (e.g., at Assemini). The *plutei* are enhanced by a two-dimensional rhomboid relief bordered by a twine molding with bipeds either side a central *kantharos* and a mixture of four-footed animals and imaginary creatures, all in flight. The

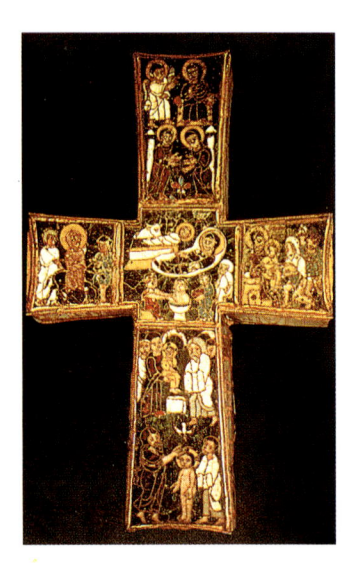

Enameled cross of Pope Pasquale I
817-824
Vatican City, Museo Sacro
della Biblioteca Apostolica

Illuminated page
from the *Homilies
of St. Gregory of Nazianzus*
9th cent. A.D.
Milan, Biblioteca Ambrosiana
Ambrosiano E 49-50 inf. p. 119

composition and subject matter are decidedly oriental, and were copied from imported decorated fabrics; the designs are of Sassanid origin, and turn up in Sorrento in other later works adopting a similar relief technique, such as the panel designed with fantastic or heraldic animals within a *clipeus* (probably dating to the construction of the cathedral); other related works include the large panels designed with animals around a Tree of Life (Sorrento, Cimitile, Capua, and San Macario in Sardinia). A comparison with other material confirms the cultural exchanges that took place between Campania and Sardinia, and the prevalence of the Byzantine and eastern artistic imprint. One item that harks back to Byzantine marble icons is the local version of the archangel of Capua, which has successfully conserved the dignity of the prototype. The progressive Hellenization of the Duchy of Rome is reasonably well documented, particularly as regards the institution of Greek monasteries – encouraged over the seventh and eighth centuries – by the "Greek" popes (i.e., Syrian, Greek-speaking Sicilian, and Greek proper) that developed with the constant stream of immigrants, originally of people fleeing the Persian and Arab invaders (seventh century) and subsequently during the Iconoclasm, of persecuted Melchites and Byzantine iconodule or icon-worshipping refugees. This influx of people of Greek and oriental stock comprised members of religious orders as well as Greek-speaking lay citizens, who must have made up a considerable quota of the population of Rome, although, as for Ravenna, the spoken idiom remained Latin. The Greek-spoken religious material, revived from the seventh century by major figures such as Sophronius of Damascus, John Moschus, and Saint Maximus the Confessor (who distinguished himself for his considerable contribution to doctrine during the Monothelite crisis), the monk Theodore (Bishop of Tarsus and later Archbishop of Canterbury), and the renowned translator Cardinal Anastasius Bibliothecarius (ninth century), had a constant and lasting effect on the life of the Church of Rome (liturgical psalmodies, the introduction of new cults for eastern saints) in the delicate diplomatic relationships with Constantinople as regards the theological and dogma conflicts under way and for political reasons. These lofty cultural figures were responsible for the circulation of many Greek texts and the commission of superb illuminated manuscripts, the focus of scriptorial arts in the Greek monasteries in Rome. The manuscript *Vat. Gr.* 1666, dated to the year A.D. 800, containing the translation of the *Dialogues* of Saint Gregory the Great, curated by Pope Zacharius himself, followed by other codices replete with illuminations, such as the *Manuscript of Patmos* 171, and then in the ninth century the *Ambrosiano* E 49–50 inf. (*Homilies of Saint Gregory of Nazianzus*) whose style is close to that of the *Cod. Gr.* 923 (*Sacra Parallela*) in the Bibliothèque Nationale, Paris, manuscript that Weitzmann now considers to be of Palestinian origin. The first two are unquestionably the work of Roman *scriptoria*. A precedent from the seventh century, constituted by the splendid illuminated manuscript of a profane subject, the *Dioscuride Gr.* 1 in the Biblioteca Nazionale, Naples, whose model was the famous codex commissioned at Constantinople around 512 by Anicia Giuliana, documents the activity of the monastic *scriptoria* in Rome and the high level of culture of the client, perhaps in this case a member of the Roman aristocracy with a classical background living between Rome and Constantinople. In monuments, from midway through the sixth century A.D. certain eastern elements begin to show through in the church mosaics (e.g., San Lorenzo fuori le Mura, Sant'Agnese, the chapel of San Venenzio, Santo Stefano Rotondo), and in certain other cases – most notably in Ravenna – equipped with liturgical devices that are alien to Roman tradition; other novel features include the use of *opus sectile* floors, typical of the eastern reaches of the Byzantine Empire in churches tied to "Greek" church figures, such as the lower oratory of the Palestinian monastery of Saint Sabas (now called Mar Saba) and Santa Maria Antiqua, linked to the palazzo on the Palatine Hill, where the deputy of the Exarchate performed his functions. The church contains works that document a phase starting A.D. 567–568 (the possible date of the remnants of superb wall-paintings featuring an *Annunciation* scene), which saw non-Roman painting with captions written in the Greek tongue. The papacy of Saint Martin I (A.D. 649–653) saw the creation of the panel bearing the noble and ethereal panels of Saint Solomon and the Maccabean sons, portrayed in a wide range of soft and luminous hues, and on a pillar nearby the figure of the angel of the "first" Annunciation, one of the finest testaments of the fresh Hellenistic vein in the art of Constantinople. This Hellenistic style is likewise evident in the rest of the church's decoration, and is the basis of the grandiose pictorial program furthered by John VII, "*graecus natione... vir eruditissimus*," one of the "Greek" popes who collectively held the papal throne almost uninterruptedly from A.D. 606 to 752, the date marking the fall of the Exarchate (A.D. 751). Pope John VII, son of the Byzantine deputy Platon, the *curator palatii*, was doubtless in close contact with metropolitan spheres, and during his brief term as pope (A.D. 705–707) did much to sponsor the arts, as testified by the many surviving works. To push his ambitious programs he seems to have made use of craftsmen summoned from Constantinople (Nordhagen). He completely restored the church of Santa Maria Antiqua, which subsequently became the chapel to the neighboring papal residence on the Palatine (which John hoped to turn into a *patriarchia*). Thus the church acquired a *bema* or sanctu-

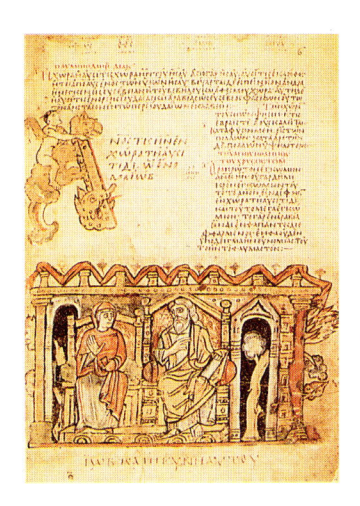

Illuminated page
from the *Libro di Giobbe*
first half 9th cent. A.D.
Vatican City
Biblioteca Apostolica Vaticana
Vat. Gr. 749, f. 6r

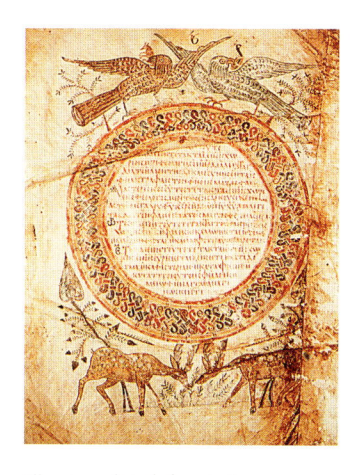

Illuminated sixth frontispice
from the manuscripit
of the *Homilies*
of St. Gregory of Nazianzus
941
Patmos
Saint John's Monastery
Patmos 4 Gr. 33, p. 6

ary, an *ambo* or raised pulpit with relative frescoes, plus other frescoes throughout the presbytery and apse: above the figure of Mary in the apse niche, two orders separated by a broad band of dark red ground (bearing the inscription in white letters reminiscent of manuscript lettering) depicted a sweeping *Adoration* scene with rows of angels and God's children. Regrettably, very little remains of this work, which was executed in confident, broad brush-strokes, a style which recurs in the presbytery Christology cycle, and has prompted precise comparisons with illumination works from Constantinople, and with the mosaics commissioned by the pope for the atrium of St. Peter's, of which only slight traces remain. Among the other paintings of Santa Maria Antiqua attributed to Pope John VII are those on the apse niche walls, portraying the figures of the Church Fathers (*palimpsestos*), and in the presbytery again, over the velarium, with the striking portraits of the Apostles set off against the gilded *clipeus* device. Such works evince a grasp of greater structural solidity. It is here in this place of worship belonging to the Byzantine jurisdiction (and later tied to John VII's program), and, to some degree, in certain decorative phases of the church at the monastery of San Saba, with its important monastic *scriptoria*, that we can follow the developing expression of non-Roman art, a courtly art pertaining to a Greek cultural elite. The fresco works executed from the mid-eighth century are informed with outside subject matter, in this case from Palestine (e.g., the *Crucifixion* in the Capella di Teodoto), and one detects a certain linear emphasis and simplification, and the figures are more rigid even in the more lively scenes; the inferior workmanship (evident also in wall-paintings in other buildings in Rome) may be attributable to local craftsmen trained in foreign workshops, probably in Rome itself, or to iconodule painters the fled the Iconoclasm. In this case, however, the authors would mainly be refugees from Constantinople and the regions affected by the sweeping repression of icon worship.

The influx of iconodule artists, which in the eighth century included Melchites in flight from Persia, played a considerable role in the foundation of Greek monastic institutions, often on the initiative of the papacy. The new monasteries joined the three documented institutions of the seventh century, composed of Cilicians (Aquae Salviae), Armenians (on the Esquiline), and for the most part Palestinians (San Saba).

The tide of religious refugees from Constantinople, a phenomenon that repeated itself with the crisis provoked by Photius (the city's patriarch), was swelled further by the influx of Italo-Grecian monks fleeing from Sicily and Lower Italy with the incursion of the Arab forces. As a result, new monasteries sprang up everywhere. Nevertheless, it appears that the foundation of the monasteries of San Silvestro (A.D. 761) and Santa Maria in Campo Marzio (before A.D. 807), San Passede (first third of the ninth century), and Santi Stefano e Cassiano (mid-ninth century) are all directly related to the influx of iconodule monks (Sansterre). Among the artistic contributions of the "Greek" monks, such as the wall-paintings and other separate works (i.e., icons, whose presence in Rome during the Iconoclasm is considerable) – which in the past were perhaps overrated and are now reassessed by more recent studies (Weitzmann, Mango) – one can detect the effects of the Greek monastic *scriptoria* and by the diffusion via codex illuminations of contemporary eastern Greek artistic tendencies. A likely product of this derivation from monastic illumination is the monumental fresco work in San Saba, of which we can still admire the splendid representation of the *Healing of the Lame Man*, datable to the seventh–eighth century (Gandolfo), together with the aforementioned panels in the presbytery of Santa Maria Antiqua; the latter derive from a prototype used in the later manuscript (A.D. 880–886) *Gr.* 510 in Paris (Kitzinger). This inflow of artistic models can be observed particularly well in the ninth-century codices cited above. In the eclectic *Book of Job* (*Vat. Gr.* 749), while the illuminations of the first group evince stylistic references (Belting) with some of the wall-paintings of San Saba, the second group is informed with a completely different idiom, a "new style" definable as post-Iconoclastic, so to speak, with figures against a gold ground that indicate parallels with the art of the metropolis. This new style was by no means an isolated phenomenon, but echoed the widespread trend in Cappadocia and Salonica (Belting); fifty years later similar traces can be seen, albeit in a reduced form, in the crypt paintings in the church of Santa Marina at Carpignano (near Otranto), part of the Greek colonial district of the Salentine Peninsula. The said group includes an *Enthroned Christ* and an *Annunciation*, which were commissioned in A.D. 959 by the priest Leo from a painter of modest stature, Theophylactos. This style is later discernible in two other fresco works in the Byzantine church of San Pietro, Otranto, namely the *Last Supper* and a *Christ Washing the Disciples' Feet*, both datable to the tenth century; similar influences can be found in the successive decoration (A.D. 1020) of the crypt at Carpignano, the handiwork of the Greek painter Eustatius, who seems to have based his efforts on his predecessor's work, albeit in a debased version.

From these testaments and from other paintings in some of the small rock-cut churches (with particularly successful results in the crypt dedicated to Santo Stefano in the village of Vaste (ancient Bastae), the noble figure of Saint Andrew and the later portraits of Christ amid angels, and the slender, ascetic images of the Saints), besides the more numerous and better qualified documentation of the period ensuing the Byzan-

Saint Solomon and the Maccabees
649-653
Rome, Santa Maria Antiqua

The Apostle Andrew
detail of the frescoes
in the presbytery
8th cent. A.D.
Rome, Santa Maria Antiqua

tine domination (particularly in the thirteenth century in Apulia in the abbey church of Santa Maria delle Cerrate, and in San Mauro at Gallipoli, in the Salentine Peninsula), in which one can read how the artistic culture of Byzantine Apulia was close in style and subject matter to the oriental provinces, and particularly to the Greek mainland, with which links are well documented from the ninth through the eleventh century. However, with respect to the strictly Byzantine production, the painted works of Apulia and Basilicata boast a peculiarity of their own, namely the prevalence of iconic and devotional images of both saints and bishops, inserted in more complex narrative programs, which may stem from the greater immediacy of religious expression typical of a "minor" patron, whose cultural pretensions were notably less complex.

Relations and exchanges with the Greek homeland are also discernible in sculpture – notably in Bari (the capital of the *thema* of Longobardia, and subsequently of the Byzantine Catapanato) and in Trani (archdiocese in A.D. 987); such works qualify Apulia as an authentic Byzantine province: *plutei* bearing fantastic creatures (Bari, Trani) or decorated with geometric figures in sequential patterns according to the Middle Byzantine schemes that occur in San Nicola, together with other geometrizing decorations executed with incision, witness the architrave over the portal of Bari Cathedral (probably produced in the site workshop set up in 1034 by Bishop Bisantius), together with door surrounds, and fragments of iconostasis epistyles at Bari and Trani. To the sepulchral sculpture category belong two sarcophagi of Siponto (Greek Sipontion) and Troia, fragmentary slabs, and a fine tomb slab at Bari, a masonry tomb front (maybe imported and used for the sepulcher of the Byzantine commander and logothete Basilius in 1075). Of certain local manufacture is the icon at Trani representing the *Hodighitria Virgin*, whose surround bears an inscription in Greek regarding the patron, the turmarch Delterius, whose name is recorded in a document dated 1039.

In "Greek" Calabria, which belonged to the *thema* of Sicily from the seventh century until the Arab conquests, the swift Hellenization that preceded the later ninth-century Grecizing phenomenon in Apulia, was repeatedly fueled by monks and other religious members haling from the Orient, and from Greece in particular (especially the Peloponnese) in a mutual exchange, as documented by the many writings on the lives of the monastic saints (the so-called *bioi*). Here the cross-references with the Greek territories are evident everywhere: the gypsum plaques from Santa Maria di Terreti (now in the Museo Nazionale, Reggio Calabria) are, in fact, decorated with numerous marble reliefs of a kind that was frequent in Greek lands in the Near East (cf. close comparisons at Episcopi near Volos, Greece), with a surround bearing an inscription in pseudo-Kufic, and with a running composition of *orbicula* with pairs of winged animals or quadruped either side of the Tree of Life, inspired by the precious fabrics woven in eastern Byzantine lands.

Similar references can be found in the celebrated surviving examples of architecture based on the five-

Saint Mark's church at Rossano
11th cent. A.D.

domed Greek cross plan, such as the church known as the Cattolica (Stilo) and San Marco (Rossano), both similar in concept to churches in Crete. As for painting activity in Calabria – evidence of which is scarce and always fragmentary – the second and more legible decorative phase (eleventh century) of the church of Scalea, with its saint figures (including San Fantino Iuniore, a hegumen from the famous Mercourion monastery nearby), shows affinities of style and subject matter with the cycles in Corfu and in the Peloponnese (Falla). Whereas the image of the *Hodighitria Virgin*, which was worshipped from the tenth century on as the *acheropita* in the ancient cathedral of Rossano (home of the superb *bios* of Saint Nilus of Rossano), is thought to be identifiable in the fresco work in the present church (Falla), its contents could be a reflection of an earlier metropolitan version, and has been linked to similar figures on seals found in Calabria, one of which is attributed to a tenth-century patriarch of Constantinople.

Stylistic parallels have also been suggested with certain illuminations contained in the celebrated codex *Homilies of St. Gregory Nazianzus (Patm. Gr. 33)* executed in Reggio Calabria in October 941 by the monk Nicola and his son Daniele. This codex is among the richest and most elaborately decorated manuscripts of Byzantine production. The fact that the codex was in Patmos in 1201 is a sure indication of the cultural exchanges that took place between the Greek world and Lower Italy, further endorsed by paintings in Calabria, Apulia, and the Salentine Peninsula throughout the thirteenth century, and not least by the hegumen Nectarius (1220–35) of the famous abbey of Casole, recommending to the *metropolita* of Corfu a young Greek painter, Bardanes, who had worked in Apulia.

Bibliography

G. JACOPI, in *Clara Rhodos*, VI-VII, (1932-33), pp. 580 ff., ill. 1-27, plates, I-IV; K. WEITZMANN, 1935, pp. 37 ff.; R. DEVRESSE, 1955; S. BORSARI, 1963; A. PERTUSI, in *CISAM* (ninth week), 1962, 1964, pp. 75-133; idem., in *L'eremistismo...*, 1965, pp. 383-417; P.J. NORDHAGEN, in *Acta ad archeologiam...*, 3, 1968, pp. 110; A. GRABAR, 1972; C. MANGO, in *CISAM* (twentieth week), 1973, pp. 683-721; H. BELTING, in *DOP*, XXVIII, 1974, pp. 3-29; E. FOLLIERI, in *Calabria bizantina*, 1974, pp. 71-94; A. PERTUSI, in *Calabria bizantina*, 1974, pp. 17-46; A. GUILLOU, 1976; A. GRABAR, in *Il passaggio dal dominio bizantino...*, 1977, pp. 231-247; C. BERTELLI, in *Atti del XVII Convegno...*, 1978, pp. 117-130; V.v. FALKENHAUSEN, in *Atti del XVII Convegno di studi...*, pp. 61-90; G. MANGO, in *Habitat...*, 1978, pp. 45-62; G. SCHIRÒ, in *Atti XVII Convegno...*, 1978, pp. 11-58; K. WEITZMANN, 1979; F. BULGARELLA, in *Atti...*, 1980, pp. 89-129; idem, in *Il Mezzogiorno dai Bizantini...*, III, pp. 129-249; C.D. FONSECA, in *La Puglia fra Bisanzio e l'Occidente*, 1980, pp. 37-44; A. GUILLOU, in *La Puglia fra Bisanzio e l'Occidente*, 1980, pp. 5-36; idem, in *Storia d'Italia*, III, pp. 7-128; V. PACE, in *La Puglia...*, 1980, pp. 317-400; G. CAVALLO, in *I Bizantini in Italia*, 1982, pp. 427-612; V.v. FALKENHAUSEN, in *I Bizantini in Italia*, 1982, pp. 3-136; R. FARIOLI CAMPANATI, in *I Bizantini in Italia*, 1982, pp. 139-426; R. FARIOLI CAMPANATI, in *Rivista di studi bizantini e slavi*, II, 1982, pp. 283-296; M. GIGANTE, in *I Bizantini in Italia*, 1982, pp. 615-651; V. PACE, in *I Bizantini in Italia*, 1982, pp. 497-612; J. M. SANSTERRE, 1983; M. FALLA CASTELFRANCHI, in *Rivista storica calabrese*, VI, 1-4 (1985), pp. 389-413; V.v. FALKENHAUSEN, in *Atti del Congresso int. di Studi Amalfitani* (1981), 1986, pp. 9-31; idem, in *Atti VI Convegno Int. di storia...*, 1986, pp. 134-173; R. KRAUTHEIMER, 1986; idem, *Roma, Profilo di una città, 312-1308*; T. VELMANS, in *Atti del VI Convegno...*, 1986, pp. 341-354; G. MATTHIAE, 1987-88; L. BERNABÒ BREA, 1988; R. FARIOLI CAMPANATI, in *CISAM* (thirty-fourth week), (1986), 1988, I, pp. 99-118; P.J. NORDHAGEN, in *Bisanzio, Roma...*, 1988, pp. 593-619; M. FALLA CASTELFRANCHI, in *Italian Church Decoration...*, 1989, pp. 81-100; F. GANDOLFO, in *Fragmenta picta*, 1989, pp. 183-187; M. FALLA CASTELFRANCHI, 1991; F. BOLOGNA, in *Storia e Civiltà della Campania...*, 1992, pp. 171-259; G. CAVALLO, in *Storia e Civiltà della Campania*, 1992, pp. 277-290; V.v. FALKENHAUSEN, in *Storia e Civiltà della Campania*, 1992, pp. 7-35; G. FIACCADORI, in *Storia e Civiltà della Campania*, 1992, pp. 145-170; idem, in *Storia della Calabria antica*, 1994, pp. 707-762.

Second Part

Catalogue of Works on Exhibit
Bibliography
Index of Names

Recent Discoveries

2
Two prow-shaped consoles

150–100 B.C.
Vita/Salemi limestone
h 36 cm; l 80 and 92 cm
w 39 and 40 cm
Segesta, Magazzini di Casa Barbaro
inv. 2671, 2673

The consoles were discovered in 1993, together with a third one similar to those on exhibit, in the great hall of the *tablinum* in a wealthy Hellenistic house, known as the "Casa del Navarca." It was the presence of these special prow-shaped architectural elements that led to the identification of the probable owner of this lordly residence: "Heracleus, navarchus segestanus," who died between 73 and 71 B.C., the victor of a naval battle, who captained a ship supplied by Segesta, (Cic., *Verr.* II, 5, 43, 45, 48, 86, 111, 120).
The items from Segesta represent a kind of boat that was widely used in the Greek world. It was characterized by the trifid ram placed on the horizontal extension of the lower strake, along the waterline.[1]
We can compare these particular examples with a series of Hellenistic monuments dating to the second and first centuries B.C., that belong to the famous representation of a ship that is the base of the *Nike of Samothrace*.[2] The consoles from Segesta have the following characteristics in common with these monuments: a) the particular shape of the oars case which, seen from the front, gives the impression of a pair of wings; b) the curve of the lower face of the oars case typical of the "Rhodian type" and the downward slant of the upper face; c) the particular junction of one of the upper strakes with the base of the oars case.
The consoles from the Casa del Navarca prove that there were local craftsmen at Segesta who knew the great works that characterized artistic production in the Greek islands during the Hellenistic period. Once again they draw us to the culture and civilization of Asia Minor which, according to the data acquired during research in recent years, have strongly influenced the history of the architecture of the ancient city after the Roman conquest in 225 B.C.
The lower part of the consoles represents the prow of a ship whose structural details appear in a schematic way in bas-relief.
All the same, we can recognize on the side of the ship: a) the lower strake, situated along the waterline, whose horizontal extension is formed by the trifid ram (*embolon*); b) the two upper strakes which confine the jutting and somewhat squashed oars case; the edge of the parapet of the bridge. On the slightly convex bridge there is a more or less square base (with a side of ca. 17 cm) whose unfinished horizontal surface reveals two holes in correspondence to the lower corners and, on one of the consoles, a line incised down the middle.
The prows of the ships were doubtlessly decorated with other elements – prepared separately and probably utilizing different materials (bronze?) – which could be inserted by means of the small holes visible on the consoles. We can reasonably believe that there were two *proembola* and the *stolos* on the parts corresponding to the two upper strakes and the straight stem (on one of the consoles there are all three holes).
It is less easy to formulate a hypothesis about the object which must have lain on the square-shaped base on the bridge of the boat: it was linked either to the functioning of the room (bracket lamp or oil lamp); or to the celebrative nature inherent in the representation of the ships (a statue of a god, or a heroic image of the owner himself). In other words, the holes must have formed a setting for the other structural elements of the ship fabricated separately: perhaps the "bow beam" that supported the *apostis*.[3]
The surface of the back of the pieces (ca. l 41 cm) has only been rough-hewn in order to aid the insertion of the elements in the wall.

R. Camerata Scovazzo

[1] This element appears for the first time on the Attic *stele* of Democleides (National Museum, Athens), and it occurs frequently in the Classical and Hellenistic periods, cf. BASCH, 1987, pp. 299–301.
[2] Such as the altar in Rhodes museum; the monument of the terrace of the Temple of Athena at Lindos; the Asclepian galley found at Isola Tiberina, cf. BASCH 1987, pp. 354 ff.
[3] BASCH 1987, p. 362, fig. 774.

8
The Gela wreck

The following objects were found together with the wreck of a Greek ship that had sunk at the beginning of the fifth century B.C. off the shores of Gela, just 800 meters from the present coastline.[1]
The archaeological research was begun after two local scuba divers made the discovery in 1988. Since then five excavations have been carried out which succeeded in exploring the whole of the ship that lies at a depth of between four and five meters, and in retrieving the articles of trade and the ship's furnishings. The area where the ship lay was covered, at the time of the discovery, by a thick layer of stones comprising the ballast that had been loaded in various ports during the voyage, to replace the merchandise sold, and to keep the ship stable. The ballast must have been stored originally within wooden dividers which smashed at the time of the wreck.
The Gela wreck is one of the few ships dating to the Archaic period that have been found in the Mediterranean Sea, and certainly one of the most complete. It is 17.40 m long and 6.40 m wide. The maximum height is 1.30 m in the areas of the stern and prow. It can be classified as belonging to the class of those built using the "shell" method. The load-bearing structure of the ship is, in fact, the planking, comprising pinewood planks of various lengths, which constitute the shell inside which lay 17 oak floor timbers and the keelson.
The construction technique of the ship is rather particular. The planking, four lengths of which have survived whole, was bound together with vegetable cords passing through holes bored obliquely along the seams of the same planks and held by small wooden treenails.
It was therefore a ship that was sewn together, built using a common method in the ancient world, and already in use in the third millennium. The oldest known example of this method is the Cheop's ship, but Greek boats of a similar kind were involved in the Trojan War according to Homer.
Sewn ships, dating chronologically from the sixth century B.C. to the Middle Ages, have been found in other areas of the Mediterranean. The most ancient examples include the Bon Porté boat, the two ships buried under Place Jules Verne in Marseilles, and the Etruscan boat found off the Isola del Giglio (Baia Campese), dating back to the Archaic period.
Later examples are the sewn ships of Israel (Ma'agan Michael; fifth century B.C.) and of Kerenya (fourth century B.C.), the Valle Ponti wreck, near Comacchio, which is a river boat from the Augustan period, the Cervia wreck (of Byzantine origin) and the Nin wreck on the eastern coast of the Adriatic Sea, dating to the Middle Ages.
The sewn planks system is combined on the Gela ship with the use of tenons and mortises, and this particular technique provides a further clue to its dating, as it became the custom in shipyards after the early decades of the fifth century B.C.
The most obvious find that has survived is the step of the mast, 52 cm wide, flanked by two large and solid wooden pieces that are rounded and shaped at their ends.
The step has many rectangular cavities designed, apart from receiving the foot of the main mast, to block the guide planks serving to maneuver the mast and for the necessary counter-thrust when the ship was at sea. The whole wooden structure of the ship was reinforced and kept together by the oak keelson which extended from the first floor timber to the poop, fitted by joints over the floor timbers.
Inside, the hull had been lined with tar to improve its impermeability, and it was probably covered with lead plating on the outside, parts of which have been discovered during the excavations.
In many points, from the prow to the stern, vegetable fiber matting has been found, which must have originally been laid as a covering, as in the case of the two Marseilles ships.
The boat was carrying a load of various goods including not just *amphorae*, but precious items, imported from Greece, as well as material for use on board and fiber baskets made from gramineous plants. The latter, whose borders were finished with a strip of fig wood, were covered with a layer of tar and probably served to contain foodstuffs, for the crew, or for selling in the markets of the cities where the ship came to anchor.
Many of the *amphorae* found are Chian and must have held the famous and excellent wine from Chios. But there are also *amphorae* from Lesbos, Samos, and eastern Greece, as well as Attic and many Massaliot types. There are only a few Corinthian *amphorae* of the A and B types, and of the Punic type, used for transporting olive oil.
The variety of types of *amphorae* recov-

ered leads us to believe that the ship had stopped in ports, along its journey, that were emporiums, containing warehouses of various goods, ready to be loaded on board passenger ships and to be sold in markets along the ports of call.

However, there were also precious goods, an extra load, which included four little clay altars, described below, several black painted Attic vases, bowls, cups, oil lamps, Ionic cups of the B2 type, *skyphoi* and Ionic *amphorae* of the striped kind, a trilobate black-figure Attic *oinochoe* with a scene of a *Gigantomachy* (Athena throwing the giant Enceladus), and a black-figure *lekanis*, unfortunately in pieces, which portrays a man wrapped in a cloak and looking over his shoulder. There are also five Attic *askoi*, two of which are painted black and three are red-figure vases, the latter with scenes painted on the upper part, that can be attributed to the school of Epictetus, and which are therefore datable to the decade around 490 B.C. The first *askos* shows two young reclining banqueters, the second portrays two naked and drunken sileni, and the third, depicts a silenus and a maenad lying naked on cushions, drinking.

Probably some of the objects recovered, such as the little clay altars, the clay wild piglet and the arm of small wooden statue, comprising the figure of a god, might have been used on board for religious rites during the voyage, with the purpose of appealing for divine protection with prayers and sacrificial offerings. But it is also possible that these objects might have been sold once the ship reached its destination.

Other finds during the excavation, utilized by the crew, which included saucepans, bowls, achromatic jugs, the bronze handle of a strainer whose tip is a duck's head, a clay flute exactly like the ones found in the Giglio wreck, and the bronze studs decorating the wooden furniture on board, give us a clear picture of the self-sufficient manner characterizing the sailors' life on board during their long voyages.

Given its special and varied cargo and its good state of conservation, the Gela wreck may be considered as exceptional compared to the other discoveries made in the Mediterranean Sea.

I
Attic red-figure "askos"

500–490 B.C.
orange clay
h 4 cm; diam 10 cm
whole
Gela, Museo Archeologico Regionale inv. 36349

The item belongs to the "deep *askoi*" class. The body has a central opening and a rod-like handle between the small spout and the outer side of the upper and rising wall; the vertical spout widens at the lip; ring foot.
On the upper horizontal surface there are symmetric designs on either side of the central hole, showing two reclining banqueters, in profile, with naked torsos and the lower part of their bodies wrapped in flowing *himatia*. Both are lying on a cushion and one is raising a *kylix* in his right hand, while the left is bent and raised; the other banqueter has a *kylix* in each hand.
Two inscriptions from left to right have been painted above the two figures and read: ΕΠΟΙΕΣΕΝ ΚΑΛΟ.[1]
The *askos* is attributed to a master of the Epictetus school and is dated to the decade between 500–490 B.C.

II
Attic red-figure "askos"[1]

500–490 B.C.
orange clay
h 4.5 cm; diam 8.3 cm
Gela, Museo Archeologico Regionale inv. 36350

It belongs to the "deep *askoi*" class. Body with central opening and a rod-like handle attached horizontally between the spout and the outside edge of the upper wall; vertical spout with flanged lip; ring foot.
Two naked, drunk sileni, painted on the upper surface, are arranged symmetrically on each side of the central opening. One of the sileni has his left arm raised, the hand bent toward his head: the other, retrorse, is holding a phial in his right hand, and a drinking horn in his left.
There is a painted inscription in the space above the second silenus, which reads, from right to left: ΕΠΟΙΕΙΝ.
The *askos* is attributed to a master close to the Epictetus school, and is dated to the decade between 500–490 B.C.

III-IV
Two clay small altars

fine, nut-brown, compact, fine clay with mica inclusions; carefully rubbed down and polished white slip
h 8 cm; w 9 cm; l 36 cm; h 9 cm
w 8 cm; l 34.3 cm
Gela, Museo Archeologico Regionale inv. 30245, 30246

The altars are rectangular with a flat top and back surface. The sides have a jutting cornice and are concave in the center.
The brown and reddish painted decoration is spread over three areas. The border around the base bears a double wave pattern. On the concave surface there is a design of seven leaf palmettes alternated with lotus flowers; along the crown there is a double contrasting frieze of black- or red-painted leaves, with traces of white paint.
The shape of these objects is rather unusual and it is hard to find corresponding items in the Greek, Magna Grecian, and Siceliot environments. The type of clay and the decoration make them comparable to items from the Peloponnesian area.
They probably had a cultual function on board.

V
Tripod

bronze
h 6.4 cm; diam 27 cm
recomposed
Gela, Museo Archeologico, inv. 36243

Bronze tripod comprising a ring supported by three low lion's claw feet, lead soldering.

M.R. Panvini

[1] For the first information about the Gela wreck, see Panvini 1989, pp. 193–200; Fiorentini 1992, pp. 25–37; Panvini 1993.

10
Bearded male head

bronze; lost wax cast
h 34.3 cm; max w 19 cm
Reggio Calabria, Museo Archeologico Nazionale
probably from the Porticello wreck (Villa San Giovanni)[1]

The piece represents a bearded head of dense curling locks bearing a *taenia*, or headband, with a central slot; the head formerly belonged to a full-length statue. From the front, the fracture at the root of the nose makes it difficult to establish whether the person represented is a deity or a sovereign. The forehead and temples are framed by tight coils of hair, which curl round the cheeks and the back of the head; the handling of the curls is highly accomplished: above the headband they are more loosely arranged, but get thicker toward the forehead; the mustaches are formed of threads around the man's lips, and are incised into an insert of bronze that was cast separately. Down over the chin the beard hair is longer and softer-looking. Behind the left ear is a cavity in the headband, perhaps for an insert of curls, cast separately. The bone of the brows is fairly pronounced, creating deep oval cavities around the eyes; the lips are full. Seen from the side, despite the damage from a blow, the nose gives the man an austere and commanding appearance. The eyebrows are incised with delicate lines. Undoubtedly, the eyes and lips would have conferred a coloristic slant to the figure, a different demeanor; the portrait is enhanced by the contrast between the face, hair, and beard. Owing to the state of the patina, the style of handling of the face itself cannot be categorized, though the transition between surface planes denotes a certain flatness.

Generic analogies enabled the new head from Porticello to be ascribed to that of a class of herm of the "Athens-Venice-Sorrento type", well-known from the numerous Roman copies[2] (which Curtius has labeled Group D), the archetype of which is attributed to Agoracritus' early period.[3] However, the Porticello head differs from the examples cited by its shorter hair and beard.

The handling of the uncommonly full beard, the rendering of the mustaches, and the elegant incisions of the hair held in the headband, give this new piece affinities with the *Münchener*

König (Glyptothek, Munich);[4] the Roman copyist has accentuated the vein of expressive coolness of the archetype. Similar in aspect, though more lively than the Porticello head is the famous head belonging to the *Borghese Anacreon* (replica in Copenhagen; heads of same type in Berlin and at Palazzo Altemps, Rome), whose archetype Furtwängler attributed to the young Phidias. The Copenhagen exemplar is thought to be a copy of the statue of the poet seen by Pausanias on the Athenian Acropolis, together with that of Xanthippus, father of Pericles. Belonging to the same artistic milieu is the so-called Capaneo, the neo-Attic relief in Villa Albani, derived from scenes of the *Amazonomachy* of the shield of the Parthenos.

Until we have a more in-depth study of the piece – which is currently being restored – particularly when a bivalve impression has been made (cf. Appendix, below), the most likely attribution for the time being is fifth century, probably in a non-Attic milieu, with traces of the Late Severe style. The banded head is less likely to be a deity than some personage of royal standing, as yet unidentified.

E. Lattanzi

Appendix
Technical observations

The conservative restoration of this piece was entrusted to the I.C.R. laboratory.[5] During its period abroad, the head seems to have been tampered with on numerous occasions: the outer surface was subjected to a reactive chemical treatment to remove the incrustations, involving the application of tampons on the crown of the skull, and elsewhere, particularly on the lips, evidently to determine the presence of different material; this has entailed the loss of almost all the patina, such that at first sight the mouth could be mistaken for a copper insert.

There are also signs of a cast having been made, which has left traces of siliconic rubber and wax in the grooves and notches.

The effect of this operation, which has incurred dire conservation problems, combined with the crude method adopted for cleaning it, has had a devastating effect on our chances of interpreting the work in full, since most of the original patina has been lost.

Furthermore, the specimen must have been subjected to radiation, as the readings from thermoluminescence tests carried out on residues of the casting operation were questionable, and have therefore hampered dating the piece, which in this casis highly problematic.

The earth used for the casting must have been removed at an early date, as the seawater incrustations covered the thin layer of residue earth clinging to the skull and the internal surface of the bronze. In the course of cleaning the earth (discussed below) was removed in small blocks that could be perfectly recomposed; once this was done, the laboratory proceeded by taking samples for analysis and studying the various surfaces.

The metal was revealed to be a binary alloy with very slight traces of other elements, chiefly lead.

The head is the fruit of a single cast, and terminates in an oblique line half-way down the neck; the head was joined to body (not extant) by welding, of which conspicuous traces have survived.

The mold used for the cast was created with a bivalve impression, with the join running from the center of the face to the center of the nape, dividing the head precisely down the middle.[6]

In correspondence with the two parts one can see a flat bronze furrow, applied by hand and cast with the rest of the head; its purpose was clearly to strengthen the piece where it was weakest, along the join of the cast.

This procedure is a rarity for the execution of head casts, among the finds that have reached us, and may be explained by the fact that the piece has very few notches: the very compactness of the volumes of the hair and beard, in addition to the hardness of the rendering, suggest that the cast may have been executed from a sculpted prototype created expressly by the craftsman for this specific work from an existing sculpture, perhaps in marble (a hypothesis to be confirmed with caution).

Traces of a brace of some kind can also be detected in the center of the neck, below the weld.

Given the technical specifications outlined above, it seems possible to affirm that the head was cast using the indirect technique.

The lips (which tests have proved to be also in bronze) are currently being analyzed to establish the execution technique involved, i.e., whether they were cast together with the head, or by a block of precast bronze inserted into the wax, as suggested by the slight change in level that emphasizes their outline.

Visible behind the left ear, high up, at the end of a curl, is a deep slot for an insert that would have started from the headband.

It is unclear as to whether or how this element was indeed applied, as there are no traces whatever of welding nearby; nevertheless, along the neck, slightly toward the base, a small, square-shaped pit is visible, a missing metal link perhaps, since lost, which may have been detached by damage, as suggested by the state of the top of the left ear.

It seems unlikely that the shallow slot midway along the headband was a setting for a gem; there is not the slightest trace of such an insert, either on the original pieces or on the repairs; furthermore, the slot is blocked by a few curls of hair.

Inside the head, the small, square distancing pins are made of iron, except for one, which is round and of bronze. The two pins at the crown of the head pass through the metal; the others are respectively situated in line with the headband (3) and the beard (3), and are only visible on the inner surface; consequently, for the outer sections of the head one can infer that the casting-on method was used, at least in part.

As for the headband, the repair work done above the right ear is visible, where an iron pin has been fixed; other repairs are detectable from the anomalies of the forward section, which is broader, protruding and with evident flaws where it joins with the rest.

On the other hand, the beard shows no indication of repairs or irregularities in the handling of the locks.

The head is the result of an imperfect cast, as testified by the unevenness of the metal and the numerous repair pins; the harsh knocks it has received – apparently deliberately inflicted to detach the head from the body – damage of which numerous traces remain, have caused a large crack to appear at the root of the nose, which corresponds to the most defective part of the piece, and therefore the most fragile; the fracture, moreover, spreads out either side; other clues include the deformation of the nose, the forehead, and several of the curls of the beard.

The residue casting earth, which has clung inside the crown and the chin, is comprised of three layers a few millimeters thick, and composed of an argillaceous matrix to which a superfine dose of quartzose was added; the resulting compound was mixed with fine hairs, which lie parallel, suggesting a manual application.

These data do not conflict with the observations made regarding the indirect method for casting of the head, as borne out by the layers of finishing in question.

The statue has proved to come from the sea, as testified by the incrustations and the analysis of the patina.

At the time, the investigations made indicated the provenance as an ancient ship that sank off Porticello;[7] there is no direct proof, however, among the evidence now available, of this head's belonging to the famous shipwreck.

On the contrary, although the composition of the metal alloy of this head in many ways matches that of the fragment of a nude figure from Porticello (the only ones that could be inferred to belong to the same statue), there are notable technical differences, such as in the quality of casting, in the way the pieces are welded, and in the welding pins used.

The question therefore remains open, and the lack of certainty on the issue has numerous implications. If we are to believe that the pieces all come from the same shipwreck, the date for this head falls between mid-fifth century (as suggested by the casting hypothesis, noted above, regarding the original from which it derives) and the end of the fifth–early fourth century B.C., considered to be the date when the ship sank.[8] If we question this hypothesis, we are left without a *terminus ante quem* or a working hypothesis for the original of the piece: the bronzes of the wreck off the coast of Porticello, are thought to be part of a cargo bound for Sicily, as recently put forward by Maurizio Paoletti.[9]

As for an absolute chronology, the main clues lie in the composition of the alloy,[10] and the fact that it contains no lead whatsoever undoubtedly places the piece in or near the orbit of the Porticello bronzes; the heavy lips and the diagonal cut of the neck speak in favor of an early date.[11]

As for the *terminus post quem* afforded by the original, further in-depth investigations need to be made before we can safely identify a date for it, as, given the deformations undergone by this piece and the parts probably fitted after casting, the original may have been considerably different from the piece under study.

G. Prisco

[1] For the head's history, see E. LATTANZI, "Un'altra testa dal relitto di Porticello'" in *VIII Rassegna di archeologica subacquea*, Giardini Naxos, 1993 (forthcoming). The piece was given back to Italy by the Antikenmuseum, Basel, in 1993.
[2] See list in PARIBENI 1953, p. 41, no. 6; cf. also TRAVERSARI 1973, N6, cat. 14.
[3] CURTIUS 1931, p. 62, no. 3; cf. also POULSEN, pp. 1 ff., figs. 1 ff.
[4] SCHLOERB, VIERNEISEL 1979, pp. 117 ff.
[5] For a broader study of the head from the viewpoint of conservation and execution techniques, see G. PRISCO, P. FIORENTINO, contribution to the conference entitled "I Bronzi di Riace vent'anni dopo," Rome, November 1995.
[6] The only examples of plaster casts made from a bivalve system that have come to my attention are the face masks from Sabratha (cf. Barone 1994, esp. the head of Satyrus, no. 94, pp. 55 ff., pl. XXII, which has been established as deriving from a marble original).
[7] For the technical specifications of the Porticello bronzes, cf. FRAZZOLI, VLAD BORRELLI, FIORENTINO 1976; P. FIORENTINO, M. MARABELLI, M. MICHELI, "Indagini ed interventi di conservazione sui reperti bronzei di Porticello," in *BdA* 24, 1984, pp. 15 ff.
[8] For the chronology of the Porticello wreck and an analysis of the material found, see JONES EISEMAN, SISMONDO RIDGWAY 1987.
[9] For different views [on the route] followed by the Porticello ship, see PAOLETTI 1995.
[10] For the use of metal compounds as chronological indicators, see P.T. CRADDOCK, "The Composition of the Copper Alloy used by the Greek, Etruscan and Roman Civilizations. 2. The Archaic, Classical and Hellenistic Greeks," in *Journal of Archaeological Science*, 4, 1977, pp. 103 ff.
[11] For more on lip-casting techniques as a chronological indicator, see BOL 1985, pp. 90 ff.; for the slanting line of the neck in Late Archaic and Classical statuary, see MATTUSCH 1988.

55
Fragment of wall-facing with painted figures

ca. 570–560 B.C.
intense orange-pink, solid, compact clay, with fine lithic inclusions and a thick clay wash on the surface; black, purple paint and occasional traces of white paint
h 22.5 cm; w 76.5 cm; t 3.1 cm
recomposed from four fragments comprising only the upper part; right side missing; slightly abraded
Naxos, Museo Archeologico, inv. 2352
probably from Naxos; Scalia-Maloprovvido suburban sanctuary (p.lla 66 f. 5, rectangle 11, excavations 1991)

This presumably once square piece of wall-facing is decorated with a group of three painted figures. Three surviving holes prove that it was attached to the walls of a building, which could be identified with some caution as Sacellum H. A large part of the upper side as well as a part of the left is conserved. This makes it possible to calculate the original length of about 83 cm, taking into account the certain equidistance between the holes and the presumed central position of the scene. This size is more or less equivalent to the facing of the metope of Thermos. As regards the height, the volume of the heads of the figures suggests between 88 and 90 cm, very similar to the height of the aforementioned metope.[1] The scene, painted on a light, perhaps pale yellow, ground, is framed at the top by a frieze of alternate black and purple tongues. A thin, black line ends it on the side, unlike the Thermos and Calydon metopes, that are characterized by large painted frames.[2] This last detail would have made it easier to attach some more panels alongside this one, with other painted scenes, suggesting the possibility that the whole composed a continuous frieze. The hypothesis is confirmed by the failure to find any triglyphs, while the exact positioning on the wall is still uncertain and problematic. This facing is one of the rare vestiges of Archaic monumental painting and is, in fact, unique among Siceliot architectural remains of the early decades of the sixth century B.C. Serving as a wall decoration for a building, it was discovered inside the vast extramural sanctuary to the west of Santa Venera. Together with other fragments of similar facings, that bore different subjects, this one was found in the area in front of the west prospect of the *Sacellum* H. This was a long rectangular *in antis* building (15 m x 7 m), whose ceramic materials permitted its being dated to the start of the sixth century B.C. The first nucleus of this sanctuary, built beside the city gates, almost as if it guarded them, was identified in 1977. Further and more recent excavations have ascertained its considerable expansion, over 10,000 sq.m, and its somewhat enigmatic organization, almost certainly the result of the aggregation of neighboring *temene*.[3] Evidence of a cultual nature is a limited presence concerning two female deities: the terrible though rare, Enyò, and Athena.[4] The mend to the piece, and the total absence of distinctive signs in the figures, make it difficult to fathom the subject matter and the identity of the characters protrayed. Of the figures only three incomplete heads have survived. Their arrangement (two facing left, the other right, at descending levels from left to right) enables us to envisage a scene in which two standing figures face a third, seated (the lower one on the left). All three heads appear to be male, owing to the remains of a long pointed beard (figure on right), and the apparent absence of white pigment, which was reserved for depicting women.[5] Stylistically, the sharp outlines of the figures put them in the same category as the fragments from Gordium,[6] or those of the narrow plates of Boccanera.[7] Yet they are particularly close to the figures featured on the metopes of Thermos.[8] The pictorial technique is the same, and despite the extent of decay, the style used is polychrome, in which colored linear drawing is associated with black-figure painting technique.[9] Strong resemblances can also be noted in the handling of the black hair encircled by purple headbands, Internal grooves cut in a decisive hand describe the curls of hair, which fall on the forehead in round spiraling locks. As for what can be determined from the remains of the figure on the right, the outline of the large frontal eye, with its well-distanced arching brow is the same.[10]

M.C. Lentini

[1] DINSMOOR 1975, p. 75
[2] CHARBONNEAUX, MARTIN, VILLARD 1978, figs. 3, 33–34; MERTENS, HORN 1978, pp. 31 ff., fig. 1; DYGGVE 1948, pls. XVIII-XX.
[3] PELAGATTI 1980, pp. 702 ff.; idem 1993, p. 282; LENTINI 1993.
[4] GUARDUCCI 1985, pp. 9 ff.; PUGLIESE CARRATELLI 1985, p. 39; LENTINI 1993.
[5] PAYNE 1925, p. 124.
[6] BIANCHI-BANDINELLI, PARIBENI 1992, no. 65.
[7] RONCALLI 1965, pp. 28-55, nos 16-20, pls. XII, XIII, XV.
[8] KOCH 1914, pp. 244 ff., pls. XIII-XIV.
[9] VILLARD 1989, pp. 134 ff.
[10] KOCH 1914, pls. XIII-XV.

59
Antefix with silenian mask

530–510 B.C.
bright pink clay with thick and dense lithic inclusions; on the surface remains of the cream colored slip, black and purple paint; from a new mold
h 18 cm; w 11.5 cm; t 2.5 cm
a large part of the beard is missing, and the nose is chipped; slightly abraded
Naxos, Museo Archeologico, inv. 2351
probably from Naxos; extra-urban votive depository West of Santa Venera Prop. Coop. Sole Nascente (p.lla 101 f. 5, saggi 9–11, excavations 1992)

The face, obtained from a rectangular slab, is thin. The forehead is low and prominent, and framed by large black painted curls, indicated by the deep incisions, that slip out from under a white band decorated with little purple vertical crosses. The rest of the hair, which projects beyond the roof tile joint, is expressed by less deep and wider spread incisions. A brown and flowing beard, marked by a sinuous, sculptured line, invades the hollow cheeks, and highlights the high and sharp cheekbones. The eyes are narrow oblique slits, lined in black, with a round, black pupil in the center. The sharply defined eyebrows are painted the same color. The nose is large and snub. This feature and the long horsey ears in particular, portrayed from the front, with a great disk earring in the lobe[1], identify the person as Silenus, and reveal the ambiguous and disturbing nature of the daemon who was Dionysus' inseparable companion.[2] Little of the satyr's fierce and wild character transpires from the almost hieratic composure of this mask.[3] The "thoughtful" expression on his face suits the prophesying, often associated with wine, with which the Sileni were gifted, and which is expressed in the reply full of pained knowledge given by one of them to King Midas: not to be born is the best thing for man, but once born, he must desire to return as soon as possible to the kingdom of night and Hades.[4] Such an attitude is doubtlessly accentuated by the fleshy mouth. The corners turning down, follow the line of the thick drooping whiskers.
The mask constitutes the plastic completion of the front end of the roof tile. Designed to decorate the eaves of a roof, the mask, together with a few bowls and three *oinochinai*, was left in a

small irregular-shaped earthy trench (2.50 m x 1.20 m). The little votive deposit, perhaps a true *thysia*, dating to the last decades of the sixth century B.C., stands in an area outside the ancient city, to the west of Santa Venera. The site, very near the modern 114 highway, should be positioned along the ancient route connecting Naxos and Catana, that was later replaced by the Roman Via Pompeia.[5]
The antefix belongs to Type A, the most archaic type according to Pelagatti's classification, which now totals about forty items, mostly found in the sacred areas of the city.[6] The composition of the face like the appearance of the mouth, which characterize the type, have much in common with the lovely Silenian mask in the British Museum.[7] Another comparison can be made with a group of masks from Syracuse and from Megara Hyblaea. In both cases, the important role of eastern-Greek models in creating the type comes out clearly.[8] There can be no doubts now about ascribing the antefix of this type to the coroplast workshops of Naxos, whose products have been found as far as Syracuse and Lentini.[9]

M.C. Lentini

[1] PELAGATTI 1977, p. 51, pl. 1:4.
[2] CARPENTER 1986, pp. 76 ff.
[3] PELAGATTI 1965, p. 86.
[4] ROHDE 1970, p. 531.
[5] PELAGATTI 1980–1981, p. 702; idem. 1993, p. 285.
[6] PELAGATTI 1965, pp. 81 ff.
[7] HIGGINS 1954, p. 142, n. 523.
[8] PELAGATTI 1965, p. 88, pl. XXXIII: 1–3.
[9] PELAGATTI 1977, p. 52.

61
Painted antefix

550–540 B.C.
orange-pink hard clay with fine sandy inclusions; remains of the whitish slip on the surface; brown and purple paint; from a mold
h 14.5 cm; w 12.8 cm; t 2 cm
diam roof tile 18 cm
almost complete, except for the lower left edge; decoration abraded
Naxos, Museo Archeologico, inv. 1225
probably from Naxos; suburban area west of Santa Venera. Prop. Soc. immobiliare Sedis (p.lla 73 f. 5 Pelagatti excavations 1973)

An unusual seated figure of Silenus himself, naked, in black relief dominates the light ground. The full silhouette is painted in brown wash, and highlighted against the ground by a confident incised line, painted simply along the outline of the shins and the right hand. Numerous incisions indicate the anatomic parts distinguishing the dark mass of the body which contrasts with the lively polychrome head, discernible in the occasional traces of purple and white and in particular by the gaps left where the two colors are missing.
This is one of the few painted antefixes discovered in excavations at Naxos. It is also one of the few examples of the complete figure of Silenus, the others being the one from Gela showing the daemon as he bears a wineskin on his shoulders, and the two relief sileni from Medma.[1]
This antefix belongs to the flat slab type which ends the semicircle of the roof tile.[2] It was discovered, together with fragments of similar items, in an area outside the ancient city, west of Santa Venera.[3] It certainly must have decorated the edge of the roof of a small building. Given the lack of remains of buildings, the sacred nature of the place should be confirmed by the finding of some fragments of architectural ceramics, and by the context of the very excavation whose composition identifies it as a votive environment, datable to the years around the mid-sixth century B.C. This presentation of Silenus is different and rare, of eastern-Greek origin. It is quite obviously a contrast to silenian masks usually produced on numerous antefixes at Naxos which prefer to show the benevolent nature of the daemon. The obscene and grotesque figure alludes rather to the playful and wild cult of Dionysus, a primary and essential aspect little known so far at Naxos.
The identity of the figure is confirmed by his usual characteristics: the long tail, just distinguishable flattened under his buttocks, and the pointed horse-like ears. It shows the left side of Silenus, with his legs bent under his chin, while the chest is held erect and turned slightly in the opposite direction. An enormous ardent phallus erupts from between his thin legs. Its red painted tip almost touches his nose. The open right hand is stretched out; the other one is leaning on the ground to maintain his unstable equilibrium. The feet have been chipped away but they were probably relatively large and not hoofed.[4]
The oversize phallus is an essential and constant characteristic of the so often ithyphallic sileni, without excluding the fact that the phallus plays a leading part in the Dionysian religion, whose cult includes numerous obscene and playful elements.[5]
The representation of the legs recalls a more archaic practice, that of the slight and tiny body compared to the head. Its rhythm and posture is similar to the Alcyoneus on the Caeretan *hydria* from Vulci.[6] The twisted bust, leaning backward from the cumbersome protruding phallus, and the position of the arms contribute movement and a comical cast to the figure.
The comic effect increases with the head that certainly represents the most peculiar part of the figure. A comparison with the above-mentioned Alcyoneus is again highly fitting. In both cases, the excessive features are dominated by an enormous nose.
The savage nature of the famous Silenus on the tetradrachms from Naxos is revealed in quite a different way: the violence and madness that pervade the features do not exceed the categories of human expression.[7] Those of this Silenus are nightmarish, as frightening as those of a nocturnal apparition. *Nyctipoloi*, nocturnal mice, is the term Heraclitus used for Dionysus' adepts.[8] The glare, the horrendous deformity of the face evoke the artificiality of the mask. Aristotle (*Pr.* XXXI, 7; *Poet.* 5, 14) defined the comic one as "ugly and deformed, but without any expression of pain." And mask-like, the head conserves the union of hair, beard and face. The former are one flat cap, a wig rather than real hair. They can be compared, like the horsey forehead, to those of the figures on an Ionic vase from Karnak in the Ashmolean Museum, Oxford. The latter are recognizable as the men, disguised as satyrs, who carried Dionysus' boat during the Anthesteria.[9] In spite of the farcical tone and the immediate comicality of the picture, there is absolutely no reference to cultual events. It would therefore be hard to deny the subject the identity of Silenus in order to attribute him with that of an adept of the god, masked as Silenus.

M.C. Lentini

[1] ADAMESTEANU 1953, pp. 1 ff., pl. 1; VAN BUREN 1973, p. 147, pl. XVI, fig. 64; PELAGATTI 1984–1985, p. 294.
[2] PELAGATTI 1977, pp. 64 ff., figs. 24–25; WINTER 1993, p. 279.
[3] PELAGATTI 1993, p. 277.
[4] CARPENTER 1986, pp. 76 ff.
[5] BERARD, BRON 1986, p. 119; KEUIS 1985, pp. 75 ff.
[6] EAA, II, p. 515, fig. 709.
[7] CAHN 1944, p. 114, pl. XII, R45.
[8] JEANMAIRE 1991, pp. 271 ff.
[9] BOARDMAN 1958, pp. 3 ff., figs. 2, 5.

Recent Discoveries

82
Statuette of an enthroned goddess

ca. 550 B.C.
clay
h 40 cm; w 12.2 cm
Paestum, Museo Archeologico
Nazionale, inv. 48428
Paestum, southern urban sanctuary

The statuette is of a goddess sitting on a throne with her hands extended that must have once held her attributes, now lost. The oblique almond-shaped eyes, the pronounced chin and triangular forehead characterize the long, oval face. The back of the throne is decorated with two sphinxes placed symmetrically on each side of the goddess. Her arms lie on the arms of the throne, while the lower part of the terra-cotta is built like a lectern. The surface reveals traces of a whitish slip and a reddish painted decoration.[1]

F. Longo

[1] The statuette is mentioned by P. ORLANDINI in *Paestum*, p. 169, fig. 13.

83
**Votive deposit at Scrimbia
Vibo Valentia**

A large votive deposit was explored from 1979 to 1981 in the Scrimbia quarter of Vibo Valentia, the central part of the urban area of ancient Hipponium. The considerably important material discovered is now being studied, and a part is on exhibit in the Museo Archeologico. The area around the excavations had previously been disturbed by building sites so the reconstruction of the sanctuary to which the votive deposit belonged, the definition of the nature and extension of the sacred place, and the eventual identification of monumental buildings have been rendered impossible.

The objects of the large votive deposit range from the first half of the sixth to the beginning of the fifth century B.C., while a smaller one nearby contains items belonging to the whole of the fifth century B.C. The Scrimbia ceramic objects (only partly restored and analyzed) include numerous black-figure and Attic fragments, some examples of Chalcidian and Laconian pottery, as well as numerous miniaturist and achromatic examples of local production.

There are a very large quantity of coroplastic artworks at Scrimbia, and they provide a panorama of great interest regarding the artistic scene at Hipponium in the Archaic period, which maintained very close ties with Locri Epizephyrii, the mother country, and the other Locrian subcolony, Medma, but the artworks also include types and shapes that do not coincide with those ascribed to the Locrian milieu.

There are both standing female figures at Scrimbia as well as enthroned ones and some of them are relatively large. Then there are some plastic vases imitating the western-Greek styles (and a few imported ones), numerous heads especially small ones, occasional figures of a reclining banqueter, and some fragments of Locrian pinakes in the later deposit. On the whole, these offerings are related to the cult of a female divinity, with evident similarities to the votive deposits of Mannella at Locri and of Calderazzo at Medma.

I
Votive figure of a standing goddess

540-500 B.C.
terra-cotta, hand modeled
h 47 cm 
Vibo Valentia, Museo Archeologico inv. 20848.

The goddess is enthroned, and while her body has been shaped by hand, other highly stylized parts have been assembled in a clumsy way. On the upper part of the torso the short *apoptygma* of the *peplos* has been portrayed as a square developing horizontally (the breasts shown in slight relief are unnaturally distant) which derives from the smooth horizontal plate, known as the "lectern" type, a famous Locrian product.[1]

Beneath the *apoptygma*, the trunk is very large, and the lower part of the body is only slightly indicated, appearing almost one with the rather schematic low-backed throne. The rather fat arms of the goddess are relaxed with her hands resting on her knees.

On her head, the goddess is wearing a polos that is slightly flared at the top. Her hairstyle comprises a mass of almost undifferentiated hair above the forehead, with deep rod-like horizontal incisions, and two long, thick plaits reaching her bosom, also represented by similar incisions.

The head is relatively small, slightly long, but with a robust structure, marked cheekbones and a large chin. The eyes are only partly sunk in their orbits. The nose is short; the mouth, large with thin and contoured lips. Large disk earrings are attached to the broad ears.

Only the head has been made in a mold with a slight defect in the area of the eyes. It is completely different from the heads of the Locrian "lectern statues" (which is the source of the body of this figure), and reveals compact masses and simplified surfaces very unlike the stylistic language of the eastern Greek tradition of the Locrian prototype.

II
Votive figure of a standing goddess

end 6th to beginning 5th cent. B.C.
terra-cotta
h 56 cm
Vibo Valentia, Museo Archeologico inv. 20881

The body has been modeled by hand into a roughly stylized shape. The reduction at the waist is heavily accented, and the lower part of the body is large and smooth. The toes of the goddess peep out from under the hem of her slightly flaring *peplos*. The ample area of the *apoptygma* of the *peplos* on the upper part of the body (where the breasts and the slight rise of the neckline are emphasized plastically) are not separated from the arms and the mass of hair falling on to her shoulders that forms a fluid contour. The joined arms are unnaturally short: the right one is bent, because the hand is clasping against the bosom a rather indecipherable attribute, that was perhaps once colored (a flower?). The left arm is extended along the body.

The head, the only part produced with a mold, is large in comparison. The hairstyle is composed of long locks. The large ears are decorated with disk earrings. The forehead is broad; the eyes, with their distinct lids, are wide set and only slightly sunk beneath the arching brows which form an angle with the long nose. The cheeks spread amply to the sides; the lips are full and contoured at the corners and the chin is prominent.

This type of rather large face, with its oval shape thinner at the base, regular features and rather unaccented structure, is very common in the ambit of Locri and the subcolonies, and reflects the Locrian Ionicizing tradition with its Atticizing inflections typical of late Archaism.

The body repeats, without any innovation, the shapes already defined in about the mid-sixth century B.C., and the evident disproportions. Limited interest in the modeling of bodies and in the systematic coordination of the image is also noticeable in other examples of the Archaic coroplastic works of art from Scrimbia.

The votive deposit at Scrimbia is characterized by an exceptional quantity of bronze offerings of various kinds: there are some mirrors, many umbilicate *paterae*, several cauldrons (the majority with beaded edges), a trilobate *olpe* decorated with a lion's head, a sieve with a duck's head handle, a statuette of a fragmentary and very damaged draped female figure.

The defensive weapons are particularly important. There were at least 12 helmets, 6 greaves and 9 shields, some of which were richly decorated. The arms' offerings at Scrimbia are the largest group known so far in a sanctuary of Magna Graecia, and are the evident expression of the upper classes, presumably aristocrats, whom we imagine to be the same at Hipponium and in the mother city, Locri Epizephyrii, where

Recent Discoveries

the aristocratic class derived its origins from the legislative code drawn up by Zaleucus. Such conspicuous offerings of weapons strongly characterize this aristocracy as it celebrates its own position in relation to both the community of the *polis* and to the gods. In the cult practiced at Scrimbia there seem to be tutelary values as well as references to a probably chthonic female divinity, such as that represented by the terra-cotta statuettes and the offerings of clay fruit. Before being able to achieve deeper knowledge of the Scrimbia cults, which may have involved several divinities, it is obviously necessary to make a systematic examination of all the votive objects, a task still to be completed.

Of all the weapons found in the votive deposit at Scrimbia, the shields have the greatest problems of conservation, because the *laminae* of the bronze facings are very thin and have only survived as fragments which makes their recomposition extremely difficult. At present, attempts are being made to achieve the reconstruction of parts of the shields.

The edges of the shields, decorated with multiple braiding, have 6, 7, or 8 rows of scrolls, with other slight variations in design that have proved the presence of at least nine shields, as well as other examples decorated with incised bronze *lamina* emblem centerpieces (one of them is a *gorgoneion*), and attached to leather or wood backings. The fragmentary conditions of the shields make it impossible to ascertain to which shields the remains of the varying kinds of *Schildband* belonged. For the moment, only limited parts of single palmette and trapezoidal side plate harnesses have been recomposed, while the figured *Schildband* described here has almost been completed.

III
Schildband with figured scene from shield

ca. 570 B.C.
bronze *lamina* with incised decoration
l 73 cm
recomposed
Vibo Valentia, Museo Archeologico
inv. 89540

The curved *lamina* (*porpax*), designed to block the left forearm, is fixed with small globular studs on the inside of the shield and continues toward the top and bottom with two fillets that have simple braiding on the borders, decorated with four-figured scenes one on top of the other and separated by a tongue molding. The two fillets end at the top and bottom with large palmettes arising out of volutes.

The upper fillet contains the following figures, from top to bottom: Zeus, to the left, attacks a winged Typhon bearing two thin, twined snakes on his chest and the lower half of his body portrayed as a serpent; a young genius, with huge extended wings, wings on his feet and a smooth disk placed in the center of his body, is represented with the "running kneeling" convention; to the right, Heracles, identified by his club and quiver hanging on his left, is strangling the Nemean Lion; two heraldic lions sitting facing each other but with their heads turned outward and one foreleg raised. The lower fillet has the following scenes, from top to bottom: two hoplites, with crested Corinthian helmets, swords in the sheaths by their sides, and shields shown in profile, are facing each other with their lances ready; two winged horses facing in a heraldic manner, with one foreleg raised and the other placed on a low central piece with volutes; the battle between Zeus and Typhon; the winged genius running to the right.

These last two scenes are identical to the first two of the upper fillet, and are placed in the same sequence, suggesting that a matrix comprising the two scenes was used to prepare both fillets.

The lower fillet compares exactly to Type XXXI of the *Schildband* of Olympia, whose scenes are identical to those of the ones from Hipponium, which would confirm, therefore, its Peloponnesian fabrication. The upper fillet has not been found at Olympia.

IV
Chalcidian-type helmet

second half 6th cent. B.C.
bronze *lamina* with incised decoration
h 27 cm
Vibo Valentia, Museo Archeologico
inv. 89537

All the helmets found in the votive deposit at Scrimbia belong to types that have already been found at Olympia. Only one of the helmets is a Corinthian type, the rest are Chalcidian helmets. Most of them have a round-ended falcate chin guard, two have ram-headed chin guards and two have angular-ended chin guards.

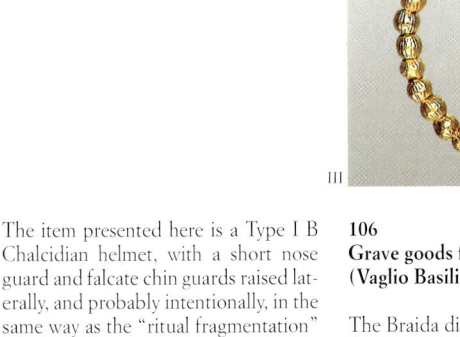

The item presented here is a Type I B Chalcidian helmet, with a short nose guard and falcate chin guards raised laterally, and probably intentionally, in the same way as the "ritual fragmentation" of other helmets was practiced as a further form of consecration at the time of interment in the votive deposit.[1]

The eyebrows, above the eye openings, are represented allusively by a contoured rise, united at the center and extended laterally toward the ears. Just above them, a thick series of embossed parallel locks of hair, descend from the curved hull-shape that separates the cap from the lower part of the helmet.

A figured decoration is incised above the curved part which is almost completely reconstructable in spite of the damage to the surface. A vertical palmette rises from volutes in the center, above the forehead. Simple braiding, reduced to a few remains, runs above the curved part and ends with two palmettes lying horizontally next to the spaces for the ears.

On either side of the cap, there are two symmetrical figures of bearded tritons, facing the front part of the helmet. The lower part of the body is a fish with three sinuous curves, and it is divided lengthwise, with traces of scales engraved along the back. The upper part of the body is human, and is shown from the front. There are traces of the pectoral muscles, ribs, of the epigastric arc with the abdominal partitions. The arms are bent, and the hands extended: one on high, in front of the face, the other down, behind, toward the tail of the fish. The bent arms stance seems to suggest the rapid strokes of swimmers. The head is drawn in profile. The triton has a pointed beard and long hair which descends straight down at the back. Very few traces have remained of the features of the face and the top of the head which have been incised where there is a slight swelling of the cap that has been hammered on the inside of the helmet.

The remarkably precise, lively figured decoration, with its sense of design, has little in common with the Olympian helmets, and brings up again the possibility of western fabrication.

C. Sabbione

[1] For weapons from Scrimbia, cf. *Atti Taranto* 1991, pp. 241–217 (C. SABBIONE); for the Olympian shields, see KUNZE 1950, pp. 32-33, pl. 58; BOL 1989, pp. 147-148, pl. 58.

106
Grave goods from Tomb 102 at Braida (Vaglio Basilicata, Potenza)

The Braida district is a large flat area at the foot of the north-eastern slopes of mount Serra San Bernardo whose summit (1,090 m) bears one of the most important and complex Italic centers in what was to become Lucania.[1]

The tomb, like all the others discovered so far, is a shaft grave with a wood coffin that was probably covered by a tumulus of large stones.

According to the studies of M. and R. J. Henneberg, the coffin contained the body of a six- to seven-year-old girl, who lay in a fetal position, according to the typical custom of this area. The associated grave goods include a quantity of bronze bowls (two *lebetes* on iron legs, two bowls with a beaded border and a *stamnos*) associated with a grater, *andirons*, skewers and tripods in iron. The pottery items comprise both miniaturist shapes of probable colonial production such as the red-painted *oinochoi*, and normal sized vases. The majority of the latter belong to a local sub-Geometric class, especially the *kantharoi*, dippers, and the small jugs, as well as a large column krater identical to the one in Tomb 101, and some little biconical pots and *pyxides* on tall feet with designs of running animals (horses?) of Corinthian inspiration. Attic production is represented by a Kassel-type *kylix*.

The rich and complex jewelry is of particular note, especially the following gold items: a diadem placed on the forehead, a pair of ring elements lying at the sides of the head, level with the ears, a series of beads near the nape of the neck, probably belonging to a necklace or a sort of "chain" used in the hairstyle, another bead separate from the others, two finger rings found near the breast, a large set of amber beads of varying size and shape, level with the breast, and lastly, a series of various kinds of silver *fibulae*, mixed with the previous beads.

I
Diadem

gold
l 32.4 cm; max w 3.6 cm
recomposed, lacunar
Potenza, Soprintendenza Archeologica della Basilicata, inv. 95207

Sub-rectangular cut and embossed *lamina*, with traces of the silver fastener.

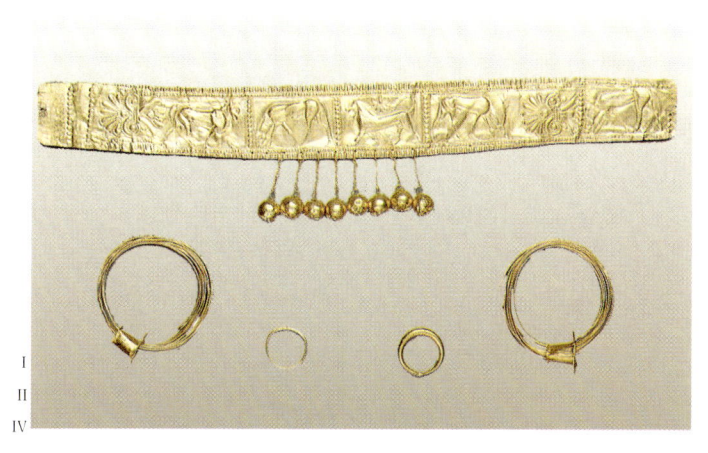

The present state of the impressed decoration (obtained with a technique somewhat similar to that of the golden laminae of Delphi) seems to be the result of extensive reworking. It is composed in the following manner: to the far left, there is a smooth area (except for two parallel rows of beading), followed by a horizontal palmette of the same kind as those on the *Schildbänder*, with a beaded border on the top and bottom, and then by a strip of tongues (at the base only, due to the slipping of the mold).
The base of the palmette (with scrolls and faint traces of a figured element) lies over the first of four metopes – all framed by beading – which contain, a bull passant facing right, a horse *paissant* facing left, a lion passant facing left and a stag *paissant* facing right. After the last metope there is a second palmette unexpectedly bent to the left. A double vertical row of beading isolates the last part of the *lamina*. It contains a fifth metope with a horse paissant facing left. The head of the animal lies beyond the beading. To the fore there are evident traces of an earlier stamp, whose subject was a four-legged animal, perhaps the same.
The long sides of the band are decorated with tongues. On the lower side, however, they have been partly eliminated by an oblique incision made along the sides of the metopes (2 to 4). Underneath these, holes have been made to attach the chains bearing the globule whose base has been decorated with a rosette shaped cutter.
From its general appearance, the diadem cannot be compared to the products of western goldsmiths[2]; it evokes instead the impressed items discovered in eastern Greece.[3] This ambiance is confirmed also by the globule pendant, typical of Rhodian workshops and, more generally, by the decorative syntax based on the sequence of metopes each one containing just one animal.[4]
The reference to Corinthian production seems, however, to be the prevailing influence on the iconography, starting from the bull and the stag *paissant*.[5] The image of the horse is clearly modeled on the prototype of the latter: the only differences being the neck and head of the two animals.[6]
As far as the lion is concerned, as well as being comparable to Corinthian ceramic designs, there is a similarity with the "Argive" *Schildbänder*,[7] without excluding that the wide open jaws with the tongue clearly shown, are a characteristic feature of the Ionian area, as demonstrated by both the coinage and the pottery ware.[8]

II
Pair of braid fasteners or ornaments for the ears

gold
diam. 6 cm
complete
Potenza, Soprintendenza Archeologica della Basilicata, inv. 95208 and 95209

Wire bent in half and then wound in several spirals[9] which run along a small *lamina* truncated cone, delimited at the wider end by a circular crown, decorated at the edges with beading.
The chief element can be compared to the "rings" made of silver that were relatively common in the Ripacandida necropolis quite close by. In this case, it was clear that they were to be used as braid fasteners, since there is evidence of single ones found lying in correspondence to the occiput.
The minor one can be distinguished instead, for its reduced size and for what could be called its "indirect" function, from a series of precious metal objects, already known as "balsam holders," used by the native population in the Apulian-Lucanian area between the sixth and fourth centuries. Recently it has been suggested that these are in fact ornamental objects for earlobes.[10]

III
55 beads

gold
spacers h 0.2 cm
small beads: h 0.5 cm; max diam. 0.5
large beads: h 1.3 cm; diam. 1.5 cm
largest bead: h and max diam. 3 cm
complete
Potenza, Soprintendenza Archeologica della Basilicata, inv. 95210

Rounded *lamina*; the series includes: 11 tubular items, probably used as spacers; 44 spheroid or bi-conical pod-like items: 21 small, 22 large, 1 larger than the rest. Both of the holes of the larger beads are characterized by a thin spiraled strip trimming.[11]

IV
2 finger rings

gold
diam. 2 cm
complete
Potenza, Soprintendenza Archeologica della Basilicata, inv. 95211 and 95212

Solid band with a shallow small lozenge-shaped setting.[12]

V
281 beads

amber
Potenza, Soprintendenza Archeologica della Basilicata, inv. 95181–95206

The group includes 22 types of different shapes and sizes. The smallest beads are disks either, cylindrical, or reel-shaped. The other non-figured beads (excepting a few completely undefinable ones) are globular or lenticular, ribbed, ovoid, spherical-capped, lozenge, cylinder, drop and ribbed-fusiform,[13] and disk shapes. The figurative ones represent shell valves,[14] small *amphorae*, ram heads of various sizes, boars, crouching four-legged animals,[15] and human heads – unfortunately abraded.
The largest bead is a crouching winged sphinx whose features chiefly recall the class "of the satyr and maenad," without excluding, however, possibilities of contacts with the small but qualitatively significant group "of Armento".[16]

VI
37 fibulae

silver
recomposed
Potenza, Soprintendenza Archeologica della Basilicata, inv. 96620-96656

The group can be divided into four kinds of *fibulae*: 25 (including one miniature) simple arc types (sometimes with an elbow at the top) with an elongated catchplate ending in a spherical knob;[17] 8 of a similar type but with a double arc and a band of gold with a herringbone pattern attached at the junction of the two arcs; 3 with a double curving arc, a long catchplate with a pentangular profile ending in a tang for the application of an apophysis; 1 simple leaf arc.[18]
In a few cases amber beads are strung along the tongues.
A hypothesis of "colonial" fabrication can certainly be put forward for the diadem, an exceptionally important discovery, worthy of its definition as a specially commissioned piece. As far as the other items of jewelry are concerned, native craftsmanship can in no way be excluded, but they were probably part of a palace-based activity, the work of traveling craftsmen with various cultural origins.

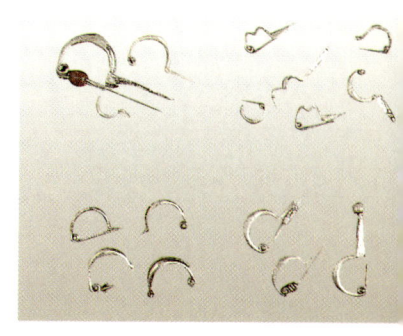

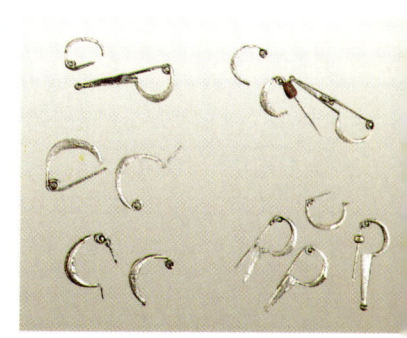

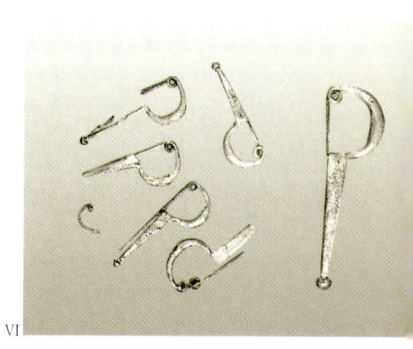

E. Setari

---

[1] For the site, see GRECO 1991; for the necropolis, see BOTTINI, SETARI 1995; BOTTINI, SETARI 1995 a.

[2] Cf., however, two pieces, in metope spaces, in *Oro*, p. 257, nn. 106 ff.

3. MARSHALL 1911, p. 69, n. 905 ff.; also DE RIDDER 1924, p. 9, nn. 93 ff., pl. II (from Attica).

[4] Rhodian productions: MARSHALL 1911, nn. 1103 ff.; in general, cf. some relief *pithoi* from Phaestus: SCHAEFER 1957, pp. 20 ff., nn. 48 ff.

[5] Bull: PERACHORA II, pl. 48, 1125 a (proto-Cor.); compares well also with the Attic one: CVA Louvre III He, p. 161, 1–2. Grazing stag: PAYNE 1931, pls. 10, 5; 11bis, 1; late proto-Cor. and transitional.

[6] This fairly unusual type, is, in fact, particularly ancient: cf. some proto-Attic krateres: CVA Berlin Antiquarium I, A32, A35, pls. 20 ff., 25 ff.; and an *oinochoe* probably from Cycladic Cumae: DUGAS 1925, pl. XIII b; ORLANDINI 1991, p. 3.

[7] Respectively: PAYNE 1931, pl. 16, Transitional; BOL 1989, pl. 34.

[8] Respectively: CVA London British Museum II Dm, pl. 5 f.; BODENSTEDT 1976, pl. 9.

[9] For the goldwork see GUZZO 1993, p. 243.

[10] Ibid., pp. 259 ff.: cylindrical earrings with an expanding plane; GUZZO 1991.

[11] GUZZO 1993, p. 192.

[12] Ibid., pp. 175 ff., group VIII.

[13] STRONG 1966, nn. 94 and 100, from Armento.

117
Grave goods from Tomb 101 at Braida (Vaglio Basilicata, Potenza)

The tomb had a structure similar to Tomb 102 (see cat. 106). The lower part of the coffin was given over to the vases, of both pottery and metal ware. The coffin contained a large pseudo-column krater, a few "Ionian" cups, various vases with bichrome sub-Geometric and striped decorations. The bronze items comprised a lebes with iron feet, four bowls with braiding on the lip, a *podanipter*, a strainer and a grater. There were also iron goods: a tripod, a bundle of skewers, tongs and a pair of andirons. In the same space between the interred body (a male of 60 or more, according to the determinations by M. and R. J. Henneberg) and the southeast side of the coffin, there were two iron lanceheads and a bent shield. The half lying on the ground and the space beside it contained two *prometopidia*, two *prosternopidia*, two belts and two lance heads crossed in such a way that the respective hilts were opposite each other. The south corner of the coffin revealed a pair of bronze greaves with an incised decoration. Above them there was a large black-figure Attic band-cup, and, nearer the dead man, two iron swords and a black-painted kylix of the "Bloesch C" type. An "unbuckled" belt was lying at waist height.

I
Circular shield

bronze
max diam. 90 cm
Schildbänder: ww 7.5 and 7 cm, ll 22.5 and 19 cm
Potenza, Soprintendenza Archeologica della Basilicata, inv. 95144

A large part of the slightly convex, outer facing made of soldered *lamina* has survived. The *lamina* has a wide border (bent to allow it to be attached to the wood or leather backing) with braiding comprising five concentric circles.[1]
The following *lamina* elements were attached on the inner side: five engraved rosettes serving to attach the straps for carrying the shield on the back; two small, flaring rhomboidal plates with a loop (eye), perhaps designed to fix the grip (that has not survived), and lastly, the harness whose extremities extend into two fragmentary, embossed fillets (*Schildbänder*).
Between the end of the harness and the beginning of the above fillets there are a couple of slightly wider rectangular plates, worked in the same manner: a double dotted frame on the outside, surrounding the figure of a lion passant, facing right, with its jaws wide open. Both the *Schildbänder* end with a large engraved palmette (Type A, Kunze classification, Kunze 1950). The inner space, which is framed by a dotted border, is subdivided into metopes, one set over the other (two in the upper part, three in the lower), separated by panels with a similar frame. In two cases these surround a simple braid, in the third, a meander. The three lower metopes contain a Gorgon, a horseman and a centaur, all facing right. The first and second subjects are repeated in the two upper metopes. The pairs of images have been cast from dies obtained from the same matrixes.
From the typological point of view, this *Schildband* belongs to the "Argive"[2] hoplite class of shields, known, in particular, from the discoveries at Olympia. This is one of the rarest classes in Magna Graccia. Between complete and fragmented examples, these total less than ten, and are the examples of Melfi, Chiuchiari,[3] Banzi (found in 1995), of the Metapontine tomb whose burial goods are divided between Metaponto and St. Louis (on exhibit), of the Tomb IV of Noicattaro (on exhibit), the *Schildbänder* of Mottola,[4] and of the votive deposit of Hipponium at Scrimbia (on exhibit).
While displaying an apparent similarity to their Olympian counterparts, the *Schildbänder* are, in fact, clearly independent from the iconographical and stylistic points of view. This becomes all the more evident when we begin to analyze the single parts, starting from the lion passant which has never been discovered among the "Argive" fillets. Moreover, the pattern adopted here corresponds to one already utilized in proto-Corinthian, Rhodian, and Attic black-figure ceramics.[5] The centaur (whose body to the fore is completely human), with the branch raised above its back, is likewise unknown at Olympia, but it has been found in proto-Corinthian ceramics.[6]
The Gorgon, shown in profile in the "running kneeling" stance, is, however, a common presence, except for her legs being in a different position, which usually corresponds instead to a Gorgon with her head facing front.[7]
This kind of horseman with his right arm stretched back to bear the kentron does not appear either to belong to the "Argive" types, but it was found in proto-Corinthian and proto-Attic ceramics,[8] and also became a part of the repertory of the architectural clay slabs with relief decorations in the Achaean colonial milieu.[9]
The schema of the Braida *Schildband* seems to be closest to that used in Attic black-figure vase-painting in the mid-sixth century[10] which also appears on bronze *lamina* in the Corinthian sphere.[11] The general similarity to the horsemen of the *Schildbänder* found at Olympia[12] is further mitigated by the walking pace of the horse: the raising of one foreleg and of one hind leg evokes the formal language of the late sixth century,[13] subsequent even to that on a gold lamina of Delphi.[14]

II
Pair of prometopidia

bronze
h 44 cm; max w 17.5 cm; diam. disk 13.5 cm
Potenza, Soprintendenza Archeologica della Basilicata, inv. 95145, 95146

Both the examples, which are fragmentary and recomposed, are formed of bronze soldered *lamina* cut to the shape of a horse's head (a close-knit series of tiny holes indicates the presence of leather padding). A concave disk with a flat border (with similar perimetral holes) apparently to protect the poll of the horse, is attached to the top by means of a complex tang inserted in the posterior part. The remains of various hook elements serving to attach it to the harness can be seen on the inside.
A bas-relief fills the ground whose subject is a *potnia theron*[15] holding a pair of large waterfowl with talons.[16] Like the feet and head of the goddess, these are plastic and stand out against the flatness of the body. In one of them, the breast is covered with a large *gorgoneion* inserted in a pattern of decorative elements comprising rows of stripes with rosettes, a chain of palmettes and a chain of lotus flowers,[17] and tongues at the base. A decoration of various rows of meanders on a spotted ground, ending with a tongue pattern and other minor motifs,[18] inserted in a tiny and condensed[19] sequence appears along the lower part of the robe, beneath the pair of birds. •
The other example has a series of

[14] Ibid., n. 94; cf. some examples in rock crystal from Piraeus: SEGALL 1938, pl. 26, n. 94.
[15] Ibid., nn. 84 ff. (rams), 76 ff. (wild boars), 63 ff. (four-legged animals).
[16] NEGRONI CATACCHIO 1989, BOTTINI 1990, MASTROCINQUE 1991.
[17] GUZZO 1993, p. 144, group IV.
[18] Ibid., pp. 148 ff., group VI; p. 157, group IX.

stripes comprising running lotus flowers (with more complex ones in the center), large rosettes, opposing triangles, curving meanders, wave, and braid patterns.[20]

At the moment none of these characteristics correspond to those of the numerous similar items found elsewhere.[21]

The rendering of the goddess by means of more than one technique recalls to a certain extent that of an older Attic clay plate with the Lady of the Serpents.[22] The face, framed by thick, vertical, and still labyrinthine plaits, can instead be coupled, from the stylistic point of view, with an embossed female head contained in a bronze disk, that perhaps came from Olympia.[23]

The *gorgoneion*, crowned by pairs of entwined snakes, while not being dissimilar to the Archaic antefixes produced in the Tarentine and Metapontine areas, generally recalls her counterparts in Attic black-figure ceramic ware,[24] but differs from them, however, in the chain of rings forming the tresses, which can be found in a well-known ivory from Samos[25] and in a Spartan *akroterion*.[26] The perforated eyes, like those of the potnia, serving for inserts in another material, bring to mind the *gorgoneion* on a greave from Ruvo (London).[27]

III
Pair of prosternopidia

bronze
56 x 29 cm ca.
recomposed
Potenza, Soprintendenza Archeologica della Basilicata, inv. 95147, 95148

Ample, roughly rectangular plate (corresponding to the chest of the horse) which was attached by two long straps to the sides of the neck. A series of closely spaced little holes along the edges prove the original existence of padding. The central part is shaped in relief in a pseudo-anatomical manner. A palmette is embossed at the base of each of the side fillets.

This was a relatively rare kind of horse harness. Other similar items are known, coming from Ruvo, Ginosa, and from a group at the Getty Museum,[28] but they are completely different. There are also various examples in the former Maler Collection.[29]

On the whole, it does seem possible to attribute the fabrication of both the shield and the harnesses to colonial workshops, capable of enlarging the classical repertory and of producing some significant stylistic improvements while still remaining substantially faithful to tradition.[30]

A. Bottini

[1] BOL 1989, pl. 9.
[2] FORENTUM II, p. 102.
[3] BOTTINI 1989, p. 171.
[4] DELL'AGLIO, LIPPOLIS II, 1, p. 180.
[5] For the proto-Corinthian, see PAYNE 1931, pls. 1–3; *Perachora* II, pl. 16, 272 d; stylistically very close, especially for the rendering of the open jaws; for the Rhodian production, see SCHIERING 1957, pp. 53 ff; for the Attic, *CVA*, Louvre, III He, pls. 120 ff.
[6] PERACHORA II, pl. 48, 114 b; but cf. the embossed silver sheath of the iron sword from the Bernardini Tomb at Praeneste, in CANCIANI, VON HASE 1979, n. 40.
[7] BOL 1989, pls. 70 and 60 respectively.
[8] Respectively: PAYNE 1931, pl. 1,7; PERACHORA II, pls. 15, 254 a; 32, 736 a; 47, 980; CVA, Berlin, Antiquarium, I, pls. 32, 33.
[9] Cf. Braida: LO PORTO, RANALDI 1990, pl. III, 6; Francavilla Marittima: *Megale Hellas*, fig. 323.
[10] *CVA*, Louvre, III Ha, pl. 10, 3; Louvre III He, pls. 193, 4; 194, 1–2.
[11] *Perachora* I, p. 147, pl. 48, 10; 11; pl. 49, 5.
[12] BOL 1989, pl. 47 H 10 e–f; pl. 49, H 15 a–d; pl. 55 H 29 βδ; pl. 61 H 36 βδ; pl. 81, H 80, H 81.
[13] Cf., for example, the southern side of the frieze of the Siphnian Treasury at Delphi: DAUX, HANSEN 1987, II, pls. 106, 108, section III block CL.
[14] AMANDRY 1962.
[15] Cf. *the potnia* on disks for harnesses from Salamis in Cyprus of the 7th cent.: KARAGEORGHIS 1974, pl. 89; 10. *Olympiabericht*, 1981, pp. 102 ff. in part. A *potnios* is depicted on a very particular pair of p., probably of Etruscan origin, of the first half of the 7th cent.: BERGER 1982, pp. 264 ff.; CAHN 1989, p. 76, W32 a–b; the corresponding female figure appears on an Etruscan bronze relief (Copenhagen): JOHANSEN 1979, fig. 3.
[16] SCHAEFER 1957, pp. 67 ff., pl. X,2; BLOESCH 1943, also on the possible Corinthian origin of the type.
[17] cf. KLEEMAN 1958, fig. 10: Siphnian Treasure, Delphi.
[18] Cf. the winged *potnia* on a gold plate from Kameiros: MARSHALL 1911, n. 1128, pl. XI.
[19] This recalls the rendering on Cretan *laminae*: KUNZE 1931, e.g., pls. 36 and 40.
[20] On the whole there are possibilities of comparing these to bronzes with incised decoration of Rhodian production: VILLARD 1965.
[21] BOTTINI, SETARI 1995, p. 22.
[22] STEWART 1990, fig. 41.
[23] HEILMEYER 1988, pp. 68 ff., 1.
[24] *LIMC* IV, ad v., pp. 285 ff., nn. 36 ff.
[25] Ibid., n. 291: STEWART 1990, fig. 23.
[26] Ibid., n. 29: *Rivista dell'Istituto nazionale di Archeologia e Storia dell'Arte* 9, 1960, p. 157, fig. 64.
[27] *LIMC* IV, cit., n. 253.
[28] For Ruvo, see *JdI* 24, 1909, p. 143, fig. 17: in the center there is an embossed but flat *gorgoneion*; for Ginosa: DELL'AGLIO, LIPPOLIS II, 1, pp. 76 ff., n. 40, 9–10; p. 180; for the American museum, see: *GettyMusJ* 12, 1984, p. 239; *quadriga* and pair of embossed Nike *stephanephorai*.
[29] SCHUMACHER 1890, pp. 150 ff., n. 786: with relief *gorgoneion*; n. 787: a sphinx in the center and chains of lotus flowers at the sides; the body is in bas-relief, the head is three-dimensional.
[30] Cf. the coinciding considerations about Sicily in CALDERONE 1991.

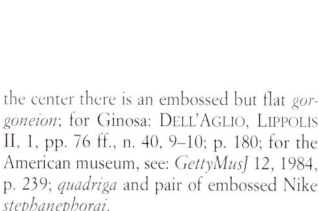

135
Black-figure kalathos

depurated clay, polished and painted with very diluted black paint
h 19.5 cm; diam. 27.2 cm
recomposed
Metapontum, tomb 260
Metaponto, Museo Archeologico Nazionale, inv. 319209

The *kalathos* is part of the grave goods found in Tomb 260, discovered in the western necropolis at Metaponto, in the Crucinia district,[1] inside a rather substantial group of graves dating between the last decades of the sixth century and the first century B.C. It lies alongside an extra-urban route probably connecting the city and the *heraion* of the so-called Tavole Palatine.[2]

The inside of the necropolis is interesting for the elements of affinity and continuity expressed in the repetition of specific architectural shapes and in the strong concentration of space. The most frequent types of tomb are the tile covered cist, the limestone slabs, and the monolithic sarcophagus.

Tomb 260 is in fact a sarcophagus, made from a block of yellowish, fine limestone, cut out from the inside, with a slab of the same stone to cover it. It lies north-west-south-east, with the head to the north and the body is supine.

The upper half of the *kalathos* was found outside the sarcophagus, in the north-east corner, as if it was intentionally separated from the other part which was recovered from inside the tomb together with other grave goods. The vase has a small hole going through the center of the base. Outside the sarcophagus, the upper half was found together with a small black-painted *amphora*, recognizable as a part of the service used in the specific rites of the funeral. There can be no doubt about the conditions of the find: while numerous lesions and fractures are present on the cover, it did in fact protect all the objects on the inside.

The remainder of the grave goods is composed of a black-painted *lekythos* with a palmette design on the shoulder and a red-figure *lekythos* with a winged female, two bronze mirrors (one with a plastic handle and suspension ring), a twin pyxis and an *alabastron*, both made of alabaster.

The *kalathos* has a truncated conical shape that is bell-shaped at the top. There is triple ribbing along the lip and along the base line that defines the flat bottom. A couple of horizontal relief stripes interrupts the profile of the body almost at the center. The inside has been treated irregularly with diluted black paint, that has resulted in a bluish iridescent rather metallic sheen. On the lower part of the outside, there is a double fret pattern alternating with a checkered design. On a groundless stripe in the upper part there is a continuous frieze of ten black-painted male figures, in the act of dancing round a monumental *kantharos*. The single figures, wrapped in long stylized ivy shoots, have additional touches of purple to highlight bands, hairstyles and footwear, as well as the handles of the *kantharos*. The anatomical details, muscles, special features and contour lines are incised. The central frieze is bordered at the top by a sequence of dotted diamonds, painted with almost wavy brush-strokes, and at the base by stylized lotus buds. The scene is a symposiac *komos* arranged around the large wine jar.[3]

The attitudes are typical of well-known iconographic schemata, such as wrestling and athletic activities, with the spatial dimension highlighted by the twisting of the symposiasts, by their rhythmic movement and the evolution of the rotating arms. The whole composition recalls the frieze with the game of ball on the base of a statue in the Athens museum. The single figures are shown in profile or in a three-quarters position, and are always well drawn. However the limits of the craftsman are evident when, for choreographic reasons, he has to portray a retrorse glance accompanied by a gesture of the arms. This item is of decidedly Metapontine origin, embracing different kinds of artistic experiences and styles. There is an exaggerated Archaicizing in the way certain characters are presented, such as in their bulging muscles and the way the features of the face are shaped that was typical of artists working in the last decades of the sixth century B.C. By contrast, there are some noteworthy solutions, such as those adopted for the figures to the left of the kantharos which seem to be better defined and executed. In this sense, they recall the black-figure techniques still in use in the fifth century in the production of Panathenaic *amphorae* (the Berlin Painter and his disciples, the Robinson Group).[4] Doubts about dating the vase toward the end of the sixth century are further enhanced by an examination of the other objects composing the grave goods. The date of the red-figure *lekythos*, which is also ascribable to Metapontine production given the quality of the clay and the characteristics of the paint[5], could be settled, thanks to the scene it bears and to certain details typical of the manner of the Bowdoin, Providence, and Pan Painters, at between the first and the second quarter of the fifth century B.C. The *kalathos* is not a usual object to be found in the necropolises of the Greek colonies, but it seems to have been widely used in the non-Greek environment (Pisticci, Alianello, Oppido Lucano, and Melfi Pisciolo). It often appears in paintings on *lekythoi* in the urban necropolis of Metapontum, together with a female figure, and in fifth-century contexts.

A. De Siena

[1] Lo Porto 1966.
[2] De Siena 1992.
[3] Greifenhagen 1929; Bérard, Bron 1986.
[4] Beazley 1944.
[5] San Pietro 1991; D'Andria 1980.
[6] Beazley 1963; Boardman 1974.

183
Antefix with a silenian mask

450 B.C. ca.
pale orange clay with thick and rare lithic inclusions, clay wash of the same color on the surface, black and purple paint, from a new mold
h 20.5 cm; l 15 cm
whole, with lesions and a gap near the right cheekbone, roof tile recomposed
Naxos, Museo Archeologico, inv. 2350
probably from Naxos, eastern quarter
Prop. Rosai (Sample 11 Pelagatti excavations 1981)

The head is in full relief. The features are serene and perfectly humanized. The only element which betrays the wild nature of this figure are the horse-like ears. These little, pointed ears lie horizontally, against the flat and compact mass of hair. The latter provides a geometrical frame to the balding temples characterized by two deep parallel furrows. The nose is regular, only the nostrils are dilated sensuously. The shape of the face with its slanting eyes, sunk between the eyebrows and sharp high cheekbones, acquires plasticity from the play of light and shadow over the colored surfaces: the black of the hair against the red of the circular band attached to the roof tile, and of the interior of the ears, as well as the brown of the short roundish beard and drooping whiskers contrasting with the scarlet mouth. Like in theatrical masks, the mouth is sufficiently open so as to reveal the teeth. That this is an expedient to indicate the mystic ecstasy or more realistically the ritual excitement, is a point that finds a precise correspondence in certain Attic red-figure drinking bowls of the late sixth century B.C.[1] The savagely gaping mouth of the Silenus of a well-known antefix from Thermos could represent a distant antecedent.[2] While both the receding hairline and the position of the ears always bring us back to the Attic type of representation of the satyr, as he appears in particular in the vase-painting from the early decades of the fifth century.[3] The same can be said of the humanizing process that pervades the features of the face. The mask from Naxos provides therefore a reassuring, playful, and one could add, civilized image of Silenus.[4]
The mask constitutes the plastic conclusion to the front end of the roof tile. Like roof tile no. 81, it decorated the eaves of the roof of a building. It was actually discovered near the urban sacellum F dating to the Classical period.[5] This is the only complete roof tile whose original coloring is also well-conserved. It belongs to the Type C class, the latest according to Pelegatti's classification. While having considerable stylistic affinities with a variation of the preceding Type B, that can be dated to the mid-fifth century, only very few examples of this kind have been found. It should, however, like the more archaic Type A, be considered as a creation of a workshop from Naxos, from where it must have been exported beyond the Straits, as the very close similarity with the lovely Limbadi mask, in Medma territory proves.[6]
Lastly, it is worth mentioning that Naxos has accounted for more silenian images than any other western colony. Different kinds were produced in local workshops for more than a century and utilized in covering sacred buildings, private residences as well as the heads of some lidded tombs. These are a sign of the importance and spread of the Dionysus cult in the city, and an indirect document of the controversial origin of this city from the large island of the same name, beloved by the god, in the Aegean Sea.

M.C. Lentini

[1] See, for example, Boardman 1975, figs. 85:1, 106.
[2] Winter 1993, p. 131, fig. 55.
[3] See, for example, Boardman 1975, figs. 252, 299.
[4] Bérard, Bron 1986, pp. 128 ff.
[5] Pelagatti 1977, p. 48, n. 20; Idem, 1984–1985, pp. 680 ff.
[6] Pelagatti 1977, pp. 53 ff., pl. II.

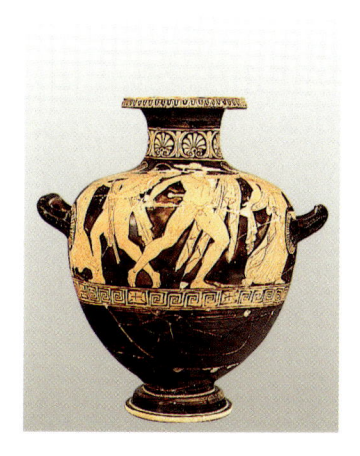

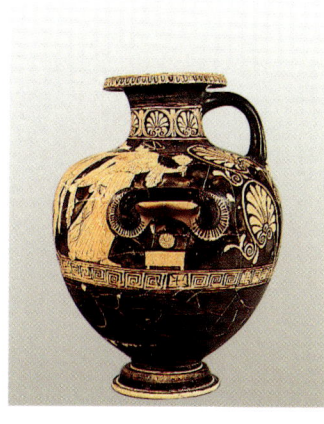

218
Proto-Lucanian red-figure hydria

425–400 B.C.
light brown clay, shiny black paint with brown blotches
h 46.8 cm; max diam. 35 cm; diam. foot 15.5 cm
recomposed
The Amykos Painter
Metaponto, Museo Archeologico Nazionale, inv. 297066

The *hydria* is part of the grave goods of Tomb 11 at Metaponto (Pizzica-Pantanello district), which is made of slabs of *carparo*. It lies north-south and contained the skeleton of a twenty year-old woman. Apart from the *hydria*, there were a black-painted *skyphos*, three one handled cups decorated with black painted stripes, an iron blade, bronze tweezers, six iron *fibulae* with bone facings, a bronze mirror with a suspension ring and dove-shaped attachment, six tablets of a whitish, chalky substance for make-up.
Flanged mouth with curving lip, short neck, rather wide at the shoulder; horizontal loop handles curving upward, straight upright handle, molded foot.
On the body, in the space between the two horizontal handles, there are two consecutive scenes. To the left: the first female figure looking to the right wears a long pleated *chiton*, drawn in at the waist by a girdle. Her hair is styled with a *krobylos*. She extends her arms toward a naked male figure in profile, with a *himation* falling over his arms and a *petasos* on his shoulders. In his left hand he holds two long lances.
Then there is another naked male figure, with a *himation* falling on his left extended arm, and a *petasos* on his head, shown as he is about to strike a retrorse female figure with his short sword. The woman is wearing a long pleated *chiton* with an *apotygma*, drawn in at the waist by a belt. Her hair is collected in a *krobylos* held in place by narrow ribbons. Her right hand is staying the *himation* over her left arm. She has a mirror in her left hand.
The first and fourth figures are partly covered by the base of the handles.
There is a decoration of ova alternated with dots on the outer edge of the mouth, and a series of palmettes on the neck. Under the figured scene there is a stripe with inscribed meander squares alternating with inscribed crosses. Beneath the upright handles, there are two palmettes, one over the other, bordered with others between scrollwork. The bases of the horizontal handles are decorated with black-painted tongues. Beneath the left one, there is a single leaf scroll, beneath the right one, a rectangle and painted disk with black paint decorations.
Unlike other cases in which the extremely general scenes represented cannot be identified with any precise myth, here the vase appears to be illustrating the meeting of Electra and her brother Orestes, and his successive murder of Clytemnestra.
An examination of the people in the scene reveals many characteristics that are typical "signature-motifs" of the Amykos Painter's work. These include the very rich style of the draping, the highlighted borders of the fabrics, falling in sinuous folds,[1] their unciform finish on the front of the clothing,[2] the rendering of the profiles[3] and the hair, depicted as a single mass surrounded by curls.[4]
A very similar compositive scheme can also be found on another hydria and on a nestoris illustrated by the same vase-painter.[5]

G. Scarano Indice

[1] TRENDALL 1967, pl. 17, nn. 1, 3, 4: cloak of the male figure to the left, central female figures to the right; pl. 18, n. 1: cloak of male figure.
[2] Ibid., pl. 10, n. 2: female figure to the right; pl. 11, nn. 1, 2: central female figure; pl. 20, n. 3: female figure to the left.
[3] Ibid., pl. 18, n. 4: male figure with *petasos*, pl. 20, n. 3: male and female figures; pls. 20, 21, nn. 3, 5, 6: for the mouths drawn with a brief downward stroke.
[4] Ibid., pls. 20, 21, nn. 3, 5.
[5] Ibid., pl. 18, n. 4; pl. 17, n. 1.

260
Figurine of Eros sleeping

4th cent. B.C.
clay
h 4.5 cm
recomposed
Paestum, Museo Archeologico Nazionale, inv. 133152
Heraion of the Sele River

The tiny terra-cotta figurine is of a winged little boy, lying inside a cradle with only the lowest part of his body covered. His head rests on both his arms lying behind his head. The image of Eros lying asleep on a flower, a rock or some other support, spread from the Hellenistic period onward. In an example of this type coming from Ruvo, (British Museum, London), and on another fragment of a terra-cotta mold coming from Taranto (Copenhagen), Eros is shown lying in a cradle with his cheek resting on the palm of his left hand and with his right arm lying behind his head.[1]

F. Longo

[1] For the iconography of Eros sleeping, see LIMC, III, pp. 916 ff., n. 783 in particular; cf. PALUMBO 1986, p. 65, n. 235; SIEVEKING 1916, pp. 42 ff., pl. 103, 2.

262
Two painted stone slabs from Tomb 87 in the Spina-Gaudo necropolis Paestum

limestone
plastered part: h 136 cm; w 200 cm
Paestum, Museo Archeologico Nazionale, inv. 133459

I
Slab with a scene of a funeral procession

Southern horizontal slab from a gable-roofed cist tomb.
In the central part of the slab there is a white ground picture (74.5-76 cm), framed at the base by a red border (39-45 cm) and at the top by a branch turning leftward with an undulated stem and long leaves inside two red stripes. The picture is of a funeral procession showing three women walking to the left, at a certain distance, one from the other. The subdivision of the space and the decorative system used conform to Type III,1, of the Pontrandolfo-Rouveret classification, which appears in other painted tombs dating between the second and the third quarters of the fourth century B.C. The same association of this decorative system and the funeral procession scene can be found in the painted stone slabs in Tombs 27 (east and west), 56 (west and north) and 8 (south and north) of the necropolis at Andriuolo, and in the Barlotti Tomb of the necropolis at Spina-Gaudo, found in 1977.
The first woman, to the left of the scene, is barefooted and is wearing a red, sleeveless gown. A red-bordered veil trails from her tall diadem. On her head she is carrying a tray of offerings, including black-painted jugs, eggs and pomegranates. Behind her, there is another woman, dressed in the same way, but with her hair loose, and cut to the height of her cheeks. She is painted as she crosses her arms on her breast in the typical manner of weeping mourners. The third woman is wearing a white gown with brown vertical stripes. It has a red border at the front and is decorated with a running wave scroll pattern. The veil on her head is decorated with brown stripes and hangs from a tall diadem. The secondary decoration is composed of a narrow red drape in the center and two festoons at the side formed from an M-shaped branch. The branches of the festoons are the same as the one painted on the upper part of the slab, with a red stem and diluted red painted leaves. The drape and festoons are suspended from the lower red stripe above the figured scene. The latter ends at both sides with a palmettes and scroll design and a pomegranate.
The procession of women carrying offerings and making gestures of lament is fairly common in the painted tombs at Paestum. This particular picture is linked to the figured scenes on the other stone slabs within the same context, and in the specific case of Tomb 87 at Spina-Gaudo, it is linked to the slab placed on the opposite side that represents the scene of a prothesis.

II
Stone slab with a scene of a prothesis

Northern horizontal slab.
The subdivision of the space and the decorative system is identical to that of the southern slab with the funeral procession, belonging to the same tomb (see no. 15). The painted scene has a white ground and measures 76-80 cm, while the red border at the base is 39-45 cm.
The scene portrayed is a *prothesis* with two women shown as they are preparing the dead woman for her lying out. The funeral bed, in the center of the scene, is covered with a white fabric that has an embroidered border, painted in red and yellow, comprising straight horizontal stripes, zigzags, running wave, and spots.
The dead woman is lying on the bed with her feet to the left, in a slightly oblique position. She is wrapped in a white shroud that has a red ribbon on it. The head is held up by two white cushions with red borders, and it is decorated with a tall diadem bearing a veil with brown stripes. The dead women's feet, wearing yellow bootees, are resting on another white and red bordered pillow. Two women stand, one at the head and the other at the foot of the bed. They are wearing red, sleeveless gowns and are busy preparing the dead women who clasps an *alabastron* in both hands. The woman, to the left, has no veil and her loose hair has been cut to the height of her cheeks. She is holding out a red ribbon. The woman, on the right, wears a high diadem with a vertically striped veil, and a red necklace. She appears to be giving instructions.
The secondary decoration is composed of a festoon in the center with an M-shaped branch and two narrow red drapes on either side. The branch of the festoon, like the decoration on the upper part of the slab, comprises a red stem and leaves painted with diluted red paint. The drapes and the festoon are suspended from the lower red stripe above the figured scene. The sides of the picture both end with a red palmette and scroll design and a pomegranate. A yellow bird cage and an upturned *kalathos*, painted with a black and yellow decoration, hang from nails on the wall.
The scene of the *prothesis*, which is one of the most common subjects of the painted tombs in Paestum, as from the mid-fourth century B.C., seems, in the majority of cases, to capture the moment of private pain, involving exclusively female figures and children. In their recent work on the painted tombs at Paestum, Pontrandolfo and Rouveret have examined the scenes illustrating the *prothesis*, distinguishing four groups deriving from the positioning of the mourners, their gestures and the type of funeral couch. The slab described here belongs to the "d" group together with the painted slabs from Tombs 57 (south) and 8 (west) in the Andriuolo necropolis and from the Barlotti Tomb (east) in the Spina-Gaudo necropolis, which adopted the same decorative system: III,1, of the Pontrandolfo-Rouveret classification.

F. Longo

264
Helmet and cuirass from Tomb 40 of the Santa Croce necropolis, Eboli

The tomb lies in the necropolis at Eboli, in the heart of the Sele Valley, which was inhabited by the Eburini, whom Pliny mentioned (*Nat. Hist.* III. 11. 98) when writing about the Lucani, placing them between the Bantini and the Grumentini. The tomb is situated in the largest burial ground, within a group of nine graves, datable to the second half of the fourth century B.C. which most likely comprise a family plot. The burial goods of the male members are characterized not only by rich metal and ceramic objects but also by offensive and defensive weaponry. In this particular tomb, whose burial goods can be dated to between 340-330 B.C., the armor was not worn by the dead man: the cuirass and helmet were leaning against one of the short sides of the shaft grave, behind and above the stone couch respectively, according to the custom of accumulating arms taken as trophies, which occurs frequently in tombs of the same period in the Paestan necropolis, at Gaudi,[1] the "real equivalent" of the arms decorated on the walls of some coeval Lucanian tombs.[2]

I
Helmet of the southern-Italic Chalcidian type

bronze
h 25.7 cm; 22.1 cm without chin guards; w 14.4 cm
recomposed, deformed
Paestum, Museo Archeologico Nazionale, inv. 133157

The cap, comprising the incomplete and smooth upper part and the top part of the occiput, is only just distinguishable from the smooth high neck guard protecting the nape of the neck, and from the frontal part. Ribbing on the latter with a cuspidate design develops into two spirals or volutes at the temples. On the sides, the fairly ample depressions follow the curve of the ears. The lower parts of the mobile and rather long chin guards are triangular-shaped whereas the upper parts are lobate. They are joined to the cap by means of an iron pivot inserted in a beaten laminar hinge, incised with a wave scroll motif and reinforced with bronze tacks. The chin guards are each decorated with a ram's head in relief.

The eye, mouth and wool of the animal have been finished with a burin.⁵
The helmet belongs to the B/I group of the Bottini classification: helmets with long neck guards and relief spirals on the temples.⁴ The ram's head decoration on the chin guard has been found on other helmets and not just on the "southern-Italic Chalcidian" types, but the style is quite different.⁵ A satisfactory comparison of the heads of rams on the chin guards can be made between this helmet and another one found in Tomb 164 of the necropolis at Gaudo, Paestum, even though the rams of the latter are fabricated in greater relief and with more precise details. The Gaudo helmet has two little tubes on the cap for bearing plumes (whereas originally there must have been three). The absence of a third tube on this helmet could be due to the hole in the upper part of the cap.

II
Short anatomical cuirass

bronze, hammered *lamina*
breastplate: h 37 cm; w 27.6 cm
back-plate: h 29.5 cm; w 29.5 cm
connecting plates: hh 8.6 and 8.9 cm
ww 11.6 and 12.6 cm; t 0.15 cm
recomposed
Paestum, Museo Archeologico Nazionale, inv. 133158

Breastplate: the edge (which is only slightly distinguishable at the lower extremity by an incised line) has a series of little holes, 3-6 mm apart, that serve to attach it to the leather padding. At shoulder level and on the sides of the chest there are traces of the body of palmette-shaped iron hooks (2 x 1 cm) attached to the *lamina* by means of beaten bronze tacks. These were necessary to anchor the breastplate and backplate in their places together with the rectangular plates on the shoulders and along the sides, but only the lateral ones have survived. The latter, with a similar row of small holes along their edges, were fixed to the back-plate by means of a bronze pivot inserted in a hinge.
Back-plate: the edges also have small holes for the padding while, at shoulder level, there are traces of the body of one of the two iron hooks, attached to a laminar reinforcing piece, incised with a running wave motif, serving to join it to the shoulder plates. The hinges of the side plates were made by hammering the end part of the *lamina* incised with a running wave design which is repeated along the hinges attached to the sides of the back-plate.
The anatomical, stylized shape was embossed. The collar bones are emphasized on the upper part of the breastplate, while the lower part includes pectoral muscles and the epigastric arc designed with ribbing at the center of the abdomen that forms a sort of cuspidate rectangle. The ribs are only faintly emphasized by the relief (three on each side). The umbilicus, the lines of the groin, and the partitions of the abdomen are marked by slightly depressed lines, while signs of soldering reveal that the nipples were made of inserts. The backbone is shown on the back-plate by means of two long vertical ribs meeting at the top where the shoulder blades are indicated by a light relief.⁶
This kind of anatomical cuirass, comprising a breastplate and a back-plate of the short type, leaves not only the sides but also the lower part of the belly uncovered. The latter, however, was usually protected by a wide belt in the tradition of Italic defensive armor. Anatomical cuirasses of the short type have been found at Eboli, Ruvo, Scordia, and Campobasso. The most satisfactory comparison, however, can be made firstly with a similar cuirass found in Tomb 37 in the same necropolis at Eboli, where the one described here comes from, and secondly, with one conserved in the British Museum (London), which is indicated as coming from southern Italy.⁷

M. Cipriani, F. Longo

¹ Rouveret in *Atti Taranto* 1987, p. 398.
² Pontrandolfo, Rouveret 1992, p. 433.
³ Cipriani, "Eboli preromana. I dati archeologici: analisi e proposte di lettura," in *Italici*, p. 135, fig. 40.
⁴ Bottini in *Forentum*, II, p. 97.
⁵ For this class of helmets, see Stary 1981a, Stary 1981b, Stary 1982, Dintsis 1986, Pflug, in *Antike Helme*, pp. 145 ff, Cahn 1989.
⁶ Cipriani, in *Italici*, p. 135, fig. 40; Armi, p. 161.
⁷ For the British Museum (London) cuirass, see Connolly 1982, p. 17, fig. 2. The cuirass from Tomb 37 of the Eboli necropolis is mentioned by Cipriani in *Italici*, p. 135, fig. 11.

275
Graves goods from Tomb 191 at Heraclea

The tomb, which was excavated in 1982, is sited in the crowded necropolis just beyond the point where the great east-west *plateia* leaves the urban area of Heraclea, in the Madonnelle quarter. It is a shaft grave tomb measuring 120 x 60 cm, lying on an east-west orientation, just sixty cm below ground level. This is a child's tomb with rich grave goods formed by twelve female figurines. Most of these are upright and similar to the Tanagra figurines, and one is a dancer. These were placed, together with the other grave goods, a long-stemmed drinking bowl, a small drinking cup and a *guttus*, around the buried child.

I
Female figurine

beige clay
h 19 cm
slightly chipped
Policoro, Museo Nazionale della Siritide, inv. 200758

Figurine of a naked sitting woman with her breasts clearly shown. The arms are extended along her thighs. The head is slightly bent forward. Her hair is styled in a high chignon with a sausage curl decorated with impressed dots. There is a suggestion of undefinable earrings. Considerable traces of white wash.

II
Female figurine

beige clay
h 14.5 cm
recomposed, chipped
Policoro, Museo Nazionale della Siritide, inv. 200757

Figurine of a woman sitting on a shaped stool, with a circular air hole on the back. She is wearing a *chiton* and a *himation* wrapped around her waist and legs. The arms are extended to the front. Considerable traces of white wash. Square base. Roughly shaped body. The hair is centrally parted in front and gathered in a chignon at the back of the head.

III
Female figurine

beige clay
h 14.5 cm
recomposed
Policoro, Museo Nazionale della Siritide, inv. 200756

Figurine of a woman dressed in a chiton, sitting on a shaped stool with a footrest. Circular air hole on the back. She is leaning forward with her arms extended. A serpent is wound around her left arm. A cylindrical *cista* lies at her feet. Her locks of hair are parted centrally and gathered in a sausage curl and then in a bun at the top of her head. She is wearing a long *chiton*. Considerable traces of white wash and of a reddish color on the hair. It has been shaped in a perfunctory manner.

IV
Female figurine

beige clay
h 12.5 cm
recomposed
Policoro. Museo Nazionale della Siritide, inv. 200754

Figurine of a woman dressed in a chiton, sitting on a shaped stool with a footrest. Circular air hole on the back. She is leaning forward with her arms extended. A serpent is wound round her left arm, another one is on her right shoulder. A cylindrical *cista* lies at her feet. Her locks of hair are parted centrally and gathered from a sausage curl in a chignon on the nape of her neck. Disk-shaped earrings. Considerable traces of white wash and a reddish color on the hair.

V
Female figurine

pink-beige clay
h 18.1 cm
chipped
Policoro, Museo Nazionale della Siritide, inv. 200769

Dancing girl wearing a chiton and a himation. She is standing on her left foot. Her right leg is raised with the foot turning to the left. One arm is extended to the side while the left one lies against the twisting body with its evident breasts. Traces of white wash. Rectangular air hole on the back.

VI
Female figurine

beige clay
h 16 cm
chipped
Policoro, Museo Nazionale della Siritide, inv. 200759

Figurine of a woman standing on her right leg while the left one is flexed. Her left arm is bent, with her hand resting on her hip. She is wearing a chiton, drawn in at the waist, with its lower edge painted brown. Considerable traces of white wash. Disk-like base with a concave profile.

VII
Female figurine

beige clay
h 21.5 cm
chipped
Policoro, Museo Nazionale della Siritide, inv. 200761

Figurine of a standing woman dressed in a *chiton* and a *himation*. Her weight lies on her left leg to the front, while her right leg remains behind her. Her right arm is raised across her breast under the *himation*, and the left one is bent on her hip. Her hair is parted centrally in front. Undefinable earrings. Considerable traces of white wash. Disk-like base with a slightly concave profile.

VIII
Female figurine

beige clay
h 21.5 cm
slightly chipped
Policoro, Museo Nazionale della Siritide, inv. 200753

Figurine of a standing woman wearing a *chiton* and a *himation*. Her weight lies on her right leg while the left one lies slightly behind. The right arm is bent on her breast under the *himation* and the left is bent at her side. Her hair is parted centrally. Undefinable earrings. Considerable traces of white wash. Disk-like base with a slightly concave profile.

IX
Female figurine

beige clay
h 21.5 cm
slightly chipped
Policoro, Museo Nazionale della Siritide, inv. 200753

Figurine of a standing woman wearing a *chiton* and a *himation*. Her weight he's on her right leg while the left one is slightly behind. The right arm is bent on her hip and the left one hangs by her side. Both are underneath the *himation*. Her hair is parted centrally at the front and gathered in a chignon at the nape of her neck. She is wearing a crown of ivy leaves with a ring-like element in the center. Considerable traces of white wash, of a blue color on the *himation*, and of red on the hair. Truncated pyramidal base. Circular air hole on the back.

X
Female figurine

beige clay
h 23.1 cm
chipped
Policoro, Museo Nazionale della Siritide, inv. 200752

Figurine of a standing woman dressed in a *chiton* and a *himation*. Her weight is on her left leg, while the right one is behind her. The right arm is bent beneath her breast, under the *himation*, like the left one at her side, bearing a drum. Locks of hair are held back by the crown of circular elements and gathered in a bun on the top of her head. Disk earrings. The *himation* is colored pink and brown at the top and along the lower border. Traces of white wash. Disk-like base with a concave profile. Circular air hole on the back.

XI
Female figurine

beige clay
h 21.1 cm
chipped
Policoro, Museo Nazionale della Siritide, inv. 200755

Figurine of a standing woman with a *himation* over her left arm and *chiton* drawn in at the waist. Large locks of hair are held in place by a crown and by a dotted sausage curl. They are gathered at the top in a complex bun. Undefinable earrings. Traces of white wash. It has been shaped in a perfunctory manner. Disk-like base with a concave profile. Oblong air hole on the back.

XII
Female figurine

beige clay
h 14.5 cm
chipped
Policoro, Museo Nazionale della Siritide, inv. 200762

Figurine of a standing naked woman with the right leg crossed over the left one. Her right arm is leaning against a pillar, while the left one is bent on her hip. The *himation* lies over the left arm and back. Traces of white wash. Square air hole on the back. Roughly shaped.

XIII
Female figurine

beige clay
h 17.5 cm
chipped and abraded
Policoro, Museo Nazionale della Siritide, inv. 200764

Figurine of a woman standing on her right leg with the left one bent forward. She is leaning on a little pillar. The *chiton* is folded over at the waist below the naked torso. Her right arm hangs at her side. The hair is centrally parted and gathered in a large chignon at the nape of her neck. Square base. Circular air hole on the back. Roughly shaped.

XIV
Tall footed drinking bowl

beige clay
h 17 cm; max diam. 19.2 cm
Policoro, Museo Nazionale della Siritide, inv. 200761

Cup on a tall trumpet-shaped foot with molding near the top. Cap-shaped bowl with flat-rimmed mouth. Decoration with white wash ground and a flower with alternating brown and pink petals painted in the center of the bowl.

XV
Drinking cup

beige clay
h 8 cm; diam mouth 4.3 cm
Policoro, Museo Nazionale della Siritide, inv. 200767

Drinking cup with tall cylindrical neck and flanged mouth; truncated conical foot.

XVI
Guttus

beige clay
h 7.5 cm; max diam. 8.3 cm
Policoro, Museo Nazionale della Siritide, inv. 200760

Black-painted, double conical *guttus*. Groundless truncated conical foot. Double knotted cord handle attached below the start of the neck. Oblique cylindrical beak. Inscription on the shoulder: ὑγιεῖα. The presence of this, not infrequent, inscription on vases, provides a key to the recognition of the divinity in question, already indicated by two of the figurines among the grave goods, with their arms extended and the *cista* at their feet. It is possible that the serpent round the left arm of the female figurine C, came out of this basket, and likewise the second serpent on the divinity's shoulder (figurine D). The iconographical reference is clearly Hygieia, goddess or personification of health who appears to belong, in the Greek pantheon, to the group of health-giving divinities such as Asclepius, but she can also be associated with others, not linked to healing, such as Demeter and Athena. Demeter does, however, appear to have been considered at Eleusis as a health-giving goddess. In fact, a coin has been found at Metaponto combining the head of Demeter and the inscription of Hygieia. According to tradition, this divinity is particularly tied to Asclepius (and is usually considered his daughter), so much so that she bears his most important attribute: the serpent. The images frequently show the serpent winding round the body of the goddess, sometimes up to her shoulders. Occasionally she is shown sitting, but always in the act of nurturing the serpent. In fact, Hygieia is normally represented as the nourisher of serpents, as in figurines C and D. The epigraphic and iconographic evidence of Hygieia found in Tomb 191 are correlative to other archaeological data recently acquired concerning the colony of Heraclea. The discovery of a damaged, life-size, marble head has been particularly important. This was found as construction rubble in the central insula of the acropolis (A zone). The features of this high grade head seem to recall the iconographic qualities of the aforementioned goddess. Moreover, the weighty ideological and religious significance of this work of art at Heraclea, where marble *agalmata* are decidedly rare, should also be emphasized. Furthermore, a black-painted fragment from an *eschara* found in the so-called Sanctuary of Dionysus, in the area near the altar consecrated to the divinity, bears a dedication to Asclepius.[2]
In conclusion, evidence has been found, in two different areas, relating to the presence of a cult easily identifiable in the grave goods of Tomb 191. The health-giving character of the divinity is probably associated, in the grave, with a "salvational" significance expressed in surrounding the dead child with the figurines. It also appears to suggest the title of "mother" or divine protectress suitably applied to Hygieia as a religious figure. The discovery of fragments of eggshells on the deposition level might offer symbolic proof of the chthonian-regenerating quality known to exist in spheres permeated by particular religious tendencies.

S. Bianco

[1] DAREMBERG, SAGLIO, a.v.
[2] PIANO 1991, p. 203.

280
Burial goods from Tomb 1/83 of the Pizzica necropolis at Metaponto

The grave was discovered in 1983 at Pantanello, a few kilometers to the west of Metaponto. It is part of a group of tombs lying along the "Basento Roads," one the main routes leading from the Greek city to the interior of the region, that were systematically examined by the University of Texas from 1982 to 1986.[1]
The "barrel" type tomb, with its roof made of huge semicylindrical tiles, contained the few remains of a young girl's skeleton.

I
Figurine

clay; lower part produced from a mold; the back, with the large circular air hole in the center, was handmade, and the drum attached
h 12 cm; w base 7.9 cm
recomposed
Metaponto, Museo Archeologico Nazionale, inv. 284021

Figurine of a woman sitting on a rock. The head faces front, while the body is in a three-quarters position. The right arm lies on the left leg; the left arm is extended to hold the drum. The legs are crossed with the right one slightly to the fore.
The woman is wearing a long *chiton* with a *himation* draped over it. The latter covers her head and the whole of her whole body, except the front of her breast. She is wearing earrings and has a melon-shaped hairstyle.
The position of the figure recalls the early Tanagra figurines whose production began at the end of the fourth century B.C. and reached a peak during the following century.[2] This figurine, made of local clay, is closely linked to types frequently found at Taranto.[3]

II
Bracelet

bronze and gold, cast and hammered
diam. 5 cm; t 0.8 cm
gold plate only partly conserved
Metaponto, Museo Archeologico Nazionale, inv. 284022

Flattened bronze band plated with a thin gold *lamina* terminating, at both ends, in a lion's head made from a die with anatomical details engraved very carefully (orbits perforated probably for inserts made of another material). Truncated conical connecting piece edged at both ends with one knurled wire and two smooth ones, and decorated with a series of lanceolate leaflets on the lower junction.[4]
The bracelet can be attributed to Tarentine goldwork of the early decades of the third century B.C.[5]

III
Necklace

gold and pâte-de-verre
cast and hammered
l 26.5 cm
part of clasp missing
Metaponto, Museo Archeologico Nazionale, inv. 284023

Double chain comprising small rings of thin wire, flattened at the center and doubled back, connected by a wire wound round the clasp. The latter was originally composed of two facing lion heads (only one has survived), made from a die and with incised anatomical details, including a tiny ring for the hook at one end. The junction of the two parts is a truncated conical element of blue pâte-de-verre inserted between two little gold cylinders decorated with a knurled wire.
The necklace belongs to Type II A of the Tarentine production,[6] especially common from the beginning of the third century B.C. onward.[7] The production techniques and the nature of the anatomical details of the lion's head are so similar to those of the bracelet described above, that we can presume they came from the same workshop.

IV
Coin

300–275 B.C.
bronze
weight 2.4 gr; diam. 0.10 mm
Metaponto, Museo Archeologico Nazionale, inv. 284024

Metapontum mint
obv.: indistinct wreathed right profile of a head
rev.: two upright ears of barley

The most interesting items of the grave goods are the gold chain and the gold-plated bronze bracelet which clearly prove the dead person to be a female, probably a child. The presence of personal ornaments is generally evident at the end of the fourth century and for the whole of the third century B.C. in children's graves, not only in the area of Metaponto, but also along the whole of the Ionian coast, especially at Heraclea. Confirmation that the tomb is that of a little girl comes from the clay figurine that should be considered not so much a "real object" to be used as a toy, but rather a "symbolic object" linked ideally to the world of play.
It is interesting to note how there is a probable relation between the clay figures and the sex of the dead person. Female figurines are never found in boys' tombs. The latter contain either male figures (boys, satyrs or phallic figures) or animals (piglets).[8]
Moreover, it appears that the coin, which was usually placed in the mouth of the dead person, is nearly always only found in children's graves, and has, in all likelihood, a precise eschatological meaning.
Considerations about the style of the precious objects made in the Tarentine tradition and about the utilization of gold-plated bronze allow us to establish the date of the grave goods as the early decades of the third century B.C. The figurine would also lead us to this period, while decisive confirmation arrives from the bronze coin with the double ear of barley, minted at Metapontum in the first quarter of the third century B.C.[9]

A.L. Tempesta

[1] CARTER 1990, pp. 8 ff.
[2] KLEINER 1942, pp. 15 ff.
[3] HIGGINS 1970, p. 275, pl. 46,2.
[4] *Ori Taranto* 1984, pp. 254 ff., n. 169, even though it is a closed ring type.
[5] GUZZO 1994, p. 33, n. 54.
[6] *Ori Taranto* 1984, p. 215, n. 148.
[7] GUZZO 1994, p. 32, fig. 16, which draws it into the Tarentine sphere.
[8] This appears to be deducible from the typological study of the necropolises of Heraclea: PIANU 1990, p. 231 ff.
[9] JOHNSTONE 1989, pp. 121–136, with the previous bibliography.

281
Headstone of tomb

clay
h 35 cm; w 70.5 cm; t 2.3 cm
complete
Metaponto, Museo Archeologico Nazionale, inv. 319201

Headstone: the semicircular slab was produced from a matrix with cylinder impressed decorations; the semi-elliptic relief slab was also produced from a matrix and then applied with a bond made of refined clay (the same used for the slip). The letter K on the back was incised with a round-pointed instrument after the slab was baked.
The headstone belongs to Tomb 117 of Metapontum's urban necropolis (property of Giacovelli, Crucinia district), immediately to the north of highway no. 175 leading to Matera.[1]
It was found under a shallow mound which was the reason for the partial removal of the cover. The grave was lying on a ne–sw axis and comprised a cover of large semicircular "barrel" roof tiles (w 90 cm, av. l 60 cm)[2] closed on the short side, in correspondence to the head, by a semi-elliptic slab with a relief decoration. On the inside, the skeleton was lying supine with the skull to the ne, and the few burial goods – a black-painted patera, a skyphos and a few broken tiny amber beads – were placed at the height of the hips. The grave goods can be dated to the last decades of the fourth century B.C.
By far the most interesting discovery among the terra-cotta tiles was the headstone with a bas-relief achieved by attaching a pseudo-antefix. A choice that constituted a clear sign of conferring distinction on this particular grave, even though it was inserted quite regularly with respect to the layout of the group of neighboring tombs and did not differ from other contemporary tombs as regards the composition and typology of the grave goods.
The semicircular slab has a border at the base[3] with a rightward meander pattern alternating with a lotus bud inside a rectangle and a broken rectangle design composed of two L-shaped elements. The relief is fairly fresh and clear-cut in spite of a some imprecisions in the impression and defects on the cylinder.[4]
Two oblique borders[5] comprising bas-relief decorations utilizing the cylinder technique, with an olive twig motif, connect the meander border at the base

to the relief slab attached at the top.⁶ The latter is the shape of a rather irregular ogive. The relief is fresh, and the details accurate, even though there are some anomalies in the rendering of the features of the face and hair between the two halves of the slab, mostly likely due to the coroplast's utilization of two different matrixes. The image is full-faced, with a large nose, and slightly open generous mouth. The person is wearing a Phrygian cap. The face is surrounded by soft wavy curls which part, in the lower part, to reveal the side facings of the cap.

The first observation that springs to mind is the remarkable craftsmanship of the coroplast expressed in the utilization of shapes and techniques of the Greek artistic language elaborated together with formal and iconographic solutions of his own creation. The combination of the cylinder technique with its very low, decorative relief contrasts very effectively with, and highlights, the plasticity of the face obtained by reutilizing two matrixes of antefixes and then attaching it to the cover slab by means of a pure clay bond. The flowing of the hair which fills the background with stylized locks, the invention of the two facings of the Phrygian cap, and the "cut" carried out immediately above the same cap, allow us to pinpoint the coroplast's own decisions, independent of the faithful reproduction of current models and an established repertory.

It is hard to provide an explanation of the figure. Judging by the features⁷, it is probably female, but there are no specific attributes except for the leather cap. This can be interpreted in several ways, since it was often worn in antiquity by both mortals and the gods. There are numerous representations of youthful figures with Phrygian caps in the coroplastic art, the ceramics and in the toreutics of Magna Graecia in the fourth century B.C., and, in particular, in the latter half of the century.⁸ The closest comparison that can be made is with a group of antefixes dating to the last thirty years of the fourth century B.C., discovered in the area of the sanctuary and theater at Metaponto.⁹ These have a female head with a Phrygian cap and have been interpreted in various ways: as Athena, as a highly improbable Medusa, after the passage of the cap, as Perseus¹⁰, as Artemis Bendis¹¹, or, in a more convincing way, as an amazon.¹²

An examination of the ample bibliography on the subject reveals the tendency to recognize more or less direct allusions to the catachthonian world and to place an accent on the funerary symbolism of the amazons – whether represented as figures or as isolated heads – especially in Italiot art.¹³ In this context, the presence of the head of an amazon in the decoration of the covering of a lidded tomb is highly significant.¹⁴

On the other hand, it should not be forgotten that, sometimes, in the Magna Grecian sphere, the choice of images is dictated by purely decorative requirements, as is the case of many other subjects frequently utilized in the Italiot figurative repertory of the fourth century B.C.

A.L. Tempesta

¹ For the first presentation, see DE SIENA.
² Two have survived, but originally there must have been three tiles for the cover, making the overall length of the tomb ca. 1.80 m. The southwestern part of the tomb was completely removed by a power-driven machine.
³ h 5.3 cm, l ca. 69.5 cm.
⁴ A fracture of the cylinder is visible on the upper part of the frieze, while an evident error can be seen in the L-shaped element connecting the lower frame and the meander, "added" later by the engraver.
⁵ Left border, h 3.8 cm, l 29.5 cm; right border, h 3.8 cm, l 27 cm.
⁶ The latter was attached before the cylinder decoration was made because the olive twig motif is present on the outer edge of the pseudo-antefix.
⁷ For the question of the ambiguity of the physical aspect of the orientals, see Moret 1975, pp. 149 ff.
⁸ Particularly close to this one, are, for example, the female heads in relief that decorate the volutes of the krater (Louvre K74) attributed to the homonymous artist and dated to the mid-century. Cf. *RVA I*, p. 374, n. 120, pl. 125, 1–2; or the head with a Phrygian cap emerging from a corolla on the neck of a volute *krater* of the Underworld Painter (330–310 b.c.): *RVA II*, p. 534, n. 289, pl. 198.
⁹ TEMPESTA 1995.
¹⁰ HERDEJURGEN 1973, p. 54ff.; see also MERTENS, HORN, in *EAA*, Suppl. 1994, s.v. "Antefix".
¹¹ SCHAUENBURG 1974, pp. 176 ff.
¹² For the iconography of the amazons, see VON BOTHMER 1957; lastly, DEVAMBEZ, in *LIMC I*, s.v. "Amazones", pp. 586–653.
¹³ MORET 1978, pp. 85 ff., DEVAMBEZ, art. cit., p. 648.
¹⁴ On the basis of the discoveries made so far, antefixes and pseudo-antefixes at Metaponto decorated sacred and public buildings and, later on and to a lesser extent, private buildings as well (see TEMPESTA 1995) while there is no evidence to their being used in funerary settings, unlike what occurred at Taranto (LAVIOSA 1954, p. 220f.) and in numerous other centers of Magna Graecia and Sicily (MERTENS, HORN in *EAA*, suppl. 1994, with bibliography for the single centers).

330 I
Phrygian type helmet

second half 4th cent. B.C.
bronze *lamina* with embossed decoration, probable retouches with burin especially on the front and chin guards
overall h 34 cm; l from neck guard to brow 24 cm; t 0.3-0.6 cm
almost complete with occasional fractures and frequent splintering; many small integrations; "lumpy" corrosion and fragmentation problems at the edges
Florence, Collezione Ceccanti (notifica ministeriale 27033), inv. CC451
probable Italiot fabrication of the second half of the 4th century B.C.
from southern Italy

The hemispherical cap, which is deformed and squashed lengthwise, ends at the top with a forward curving apex, like a Phrygian cap. On this, there is a double lamina, with its top edges cut to a running wave design and decorated with rays united by little arcs at the base, that has been attached by a series of rivets, but only the lower ones have survived. The laminae begin from a single piece that has been cut and decorated with an upside down palmette, volutes and rosettes, and applied earlier to the base of the curving apex. This palmette constitutes the ideal ending of the rich floral composition that decorates the front of the cap, comprising an acanthus plant from which a six-petaled palmette with a shield-shape in the center is sprouting, volutes ending with rosettes, scrolls terminating in a palmette and leaf.

The front piece has a sinuous outline, a slightly flared base and its horizontal edge is bent outward. It is decorated with a series of heavily incised, distinct, curling locks.

The depressed neck guard is decidedly flared at the base, has lateral extended lobes and its edges bend outward. It is decorated at the center with the same basic pattern as the front of the cap. Scroll designs on the lobes grow out of two narrow acanthus leaves ending in leaflets and bell-shaped flowers.

The mobile chin guards have curved edges and a hinge. They are decorated with a griffin, in profile, standing on a rocky relief. The triangular head of the griffin with a beard and pointed ears is nearly full-faced. The foreleg is raised (the right one on the left chin guard, the left one on the right chin guard). It has a wide, curving wing and its tail ends in scrolls and leaflets. Judging by the rendering of the details, the griffin on the left chin guard could have been produced by a blunt punch.

On the right side of the cap, over the chin guard, there is the hammered "eye" base of a little rod fixed with a nail, which must have held one of the minor *lophoi*. These supports must have been hidden by the laminae with straight-edged bases and curving outlines (curving in the opposite sense to those of the chin guards) nailed to the sides of the cap and decorated with a male head shown in profile with a Phrygian style helmet complete with a crest and fixed half-moon chin guard. (The punch utilized to create the decoration of the two laminae seems to be the same one, used back to front.)

By its shape and decoration, this helmet can be assigned to Type IIB, a classification recently established by P.G. Guzzo¹, and it is the most complete example, since it conserves the embossed decorations not only on the cap and the neck guard, but also on the chin guards and side *laminae*.

The rich, floral motifs decorating the cap and the neck guard are not so different from similar motifs, sometimes completely re-arranged and laid-out, to be found on the "Phrygian" helmets in Paris and Perugia², on the *prometopidia* from San Giorgio Lucano and Canosa³, and on the Marcellina-Laus cuirass.⁴

The type and the rendering of the locks on the front piece are very similar to those on the rounded cap helmets from Catanzaro and Rome.⁵ In spite of certain fractures and formal contradictions, the design of the griffins is particularly unusual.⁶ The large wing and naturalistic, lean body have been represented in great detail, whereas the head is more rigid and roughly drawn, and the tail ends in an elegant scroll, not without a certain emphasis from the decorative point of view. The style of the male heads with the "Phrygian" helmets is decidedly refined and perceptive. These can be compared in general to the relief heads that decorate the handles of an Apulian *nestoris*⁷ and to the lid of a *pyxis* in the Jatta Collection.⁸ The delicate profile of the warrior is looking to the curved side of the *lamina* almost as if it was pictured standing out against a shield. The plastic rendering, with the great, wide eye, the slight mention of the lid, the incised pupil, regular nose and full lips, is fluid and not overindulged. Three soft locks lie over the temple. The airy crest fixed directly on the cap, the enlarged front, highlighted at the base by a small relief border which continues along the lower part of the cap as it reaches the long, considerably bent neck guard, make this helmet quite unusual. From the typological point of view, the helmet worn by these heads, without any decoration or any cutout for the ears, with the crest directly attached to the cap, seems to be very similar to Type I of the Guzzo classification,[9] numerous examples of which have been found in Bulgaria and in Macedonia, but which does, however, have a visor on the front. We cannot exclude the possibility that the craftsman chose to represent a kind of helmet that has not yet been discovered, and which could be considered as a variation of Guzzo's Type I or as a passage between Type I and Type II. As far as the function, the significance and the numerous, rather interesting iconographical references are concerned, there is a certain affinity between these heads and the (stylistically more harsh and sharp) ones incised on the back of the cuirass (Thetis Foundation) more recently identified with the Dioscuri.[10] This identification, considered to be the only one that coincides with the Italiot culture of the period (the same period to which this helmet can be ascribed) could be valid in this case too, if the perfect duplication of the head and, above all, the presence of the griffins (placed in a subordinate position with respect to the heads) did not evoke the question (the historic and cultural aspects of which should certainly be studied) of an identification with the Arimaspeans. In this case the mythical monsters with only one eye, belonging to the legendary world of the Hyperboreans and sometimes confused with the latter[11], could be attributed with a apotropaic significance perhaps combined with protective qualities. The Arimaspeans[12] were a particularly favorite subject at Taranto in the second half of the fourth century B.C., where they were represented on the golden terra-cotta tombs[13] and on the carved stone *akroteria* of funerary monuments.[14] The Arimaspeans-Hyperboreans fighting the griffins on these monuments, seem to imply protective qualities rather than ideological ones, that should be linked probably to the legend of Aristeas of Proconnesus, author of the *Arimaspea*, which was well-known in the Pythagorean circles at Tarentum connected with the Academy.[15]

L. Lepore

330 II
Anatomical cuirass comprising breastplate and back-plate

hammered and embossed bronze *lamina*; h 44 cm, chest 38 cm, diam neck 14.6 cm, t 0.5 cm, on both plates frequent splintering and large hole at the base of the breastplate considerable fractures recomposed with integrations; "lumpy" corrosion and fragmentation problems at the edges
Florence, Collezione Ceccanti (notifica ministeriale 27033), inv. CC 485, 486
southern Italy

The anatomical rendering is precise but only slightly emphasized except for the pectoral muscles, the back bone and the line of the ilium. The umbilicus is depressed and raised. The "button" nipples were perhaps made of a different material (copper?) and then inserted. The plates have a low neck whose edge is bent markedly outward, likewise, the edges of the armpits and the bottom of the plates.
The breastplate still has two rings on the shoulder, attached by means of staples, bent back and flattened on the inside (one of these is decorated with four ribs). There are two rings on the left side; one ring and the remains of another two on the right side.
The back-plate has two rings on the shoulder with their relative staples and two holes (perhaps for another two rings) near the ends of the neck. There is one ring (upper) and the remains of another (medium) on the right side; an upper ring and the hole for a lower ring on the left side.
Judging by the surviving rings, the remains of the staples and the holes, originally the cuirass must have had a total of six rings (three on each plate) on the right side; four rings (two on each plate) on the left side; six rings on the shoulders (four on the back-plate, two on the breastplate).
On both edges of the sides of each plate, large rivets fix four bronze fillets that have been hammered simply (h. 24 cm, w 5 cm, t 0.3 cm). The joints have been masked by thin bronze laminae (max h 3 cm) embossed with a chain of contrasting and extended, stylized palmettes (with a crown of beading on the central element). The little *laminae* have been fixed with a series of smaller rivets. They have beading on the edges and the ends are bent under and fixed with another two slightly larger rivets.

The remains of two hinges can be seen on the right side of the back-plate, beneath the decorated *lamina*. There are traces of probable hinges on the left side.
On the right side of the breastplate, where there are a few fragments of the decorated *lamina*, two groups of three holes can be seen (perhaps serving for the hinges) and an uneven edge that was probably cut and filed in antiquity.
The latter observations bring us to the conclusion that this cuirass, which was originally a type with hinges on both sides and rings on the sides and shoulders, must have been both enlarged and its system of attachment (superimposition of the side pieces) completely modified.
The cuirass can certainly be considered as an "Apulian" variant of the class of long anatomical cuirasses, cataloged by Zimmerman.[1] It does not seem to enter into the categories recently established by Bottino.[2] The hook system extending down both sides and the number of rings presumably present on the shoulders and on the plates are characteristics only found on this cuirass.
As regards the shape (the narrow shoulders, the wide neck, the characteristic curve of the armpits, the not very accentuated curve of the lower part) and the type of anatomic modeling (in particular the rendering of the pectoral muscles), it is very close to the cuirass (Naples) coming from the Monterisi Rossignoli hypogeum at Canosa.[3] The decorative use of small embossed laminae, as well as the functional adoption of additional *laminae*, are evident in the cuirass of Tomb 669 II at Lavello,[4] which is a much more developed type and came from a context dated as the last quarter of the fourth century B.C.
As far as the modifications of the cuirass are concerned, the doubt remains as to whether they were carried out simply to widen an originally narrower cuirass, or whether they were a recomposition of the parts of two separate cuirasses of a similar size and shape.

L. Lepore

[1] GUZZO 1992, p. 23.
[2] ADAM 1982, nn. 1–2, pls. I,II a, III.
[3] BOTTINI 1989, pp. 706 ff. It is interesting to compare these with Greek products from Scythian territory.
[4] GUZZO 1992, pp. 25 ff., pl. III, 1–2.
[5] ADAM 1982, nn. 6–7, pl. VI.
[6] Convincing comparisons of these have not yet been found; see, however, the retrorse sphinxes of the chin guards of the "Phrygian" helmet in the Louvre, in DINTSIS 1986, p. 218, n. 56, pl. 19,6.
[7] SCHAUENBURG 1974, p. 137ff., figs. 1–4. In this case the head wears a Phrygian cap and is interpreted as Bendis.
[8] SICHTERMANN 1866, n. K 107, p. 61, pl. 155. Another head interpreted as a female head with a "Phrygian" helmet of the same kind as the real one examined here.
[9] GUZZO 1992, p. 22f.
[10] ZIMMERMANN 1989, pp. 11 ff.; GUZZO 1990, p. 141; GUZZO 1994, p. 31, n. 48.
[11] BOLTON 1962, p. 20ff.
[12] Occurs frequently in Kertsch ceramic ware and in also in the Italiot production, particularly the Apulian ware, and is depicted on the so-called golden *kalathos* from the Bliznitsa tumulus on the Taman peninsula: Artamonov 1969, p. 74, pls. 291–294.
[13] LULLIES 1977, p. 235ff.
[14] LIPPOLIS 1994, p. 127, table 3.
[15] BOLTON 1962, pp. 142 ff.
[16] ZIMMERMANN 1982, p. 138.
[17] BOTTINI 1991, p. 100, with preceding bibliography.
[18] MAZZEI 1992, pp. 172 ff., n. 6, p. 175.
[19] BOTTINI 1991, p. 101.

373
Gold grave goods from Tomb 20 at Abacaenum (the Cardusa necropolis at Tripi)

The remains of a Greco-Roman settlement with its relative necropolises, situated in an area known today as Tripi, on the Tyrrhenian coast of Messina, has been identified with Abakainon, an indigenous town of very remote origin that was later Grecized, and after became a Roman "municipium" with the name of Abacaenum. It is known through literary texts and coins minted there in the fifth and fourth centuries B.C.
After limited projects in 1952 and 1961, the Soprintendenza of Messina and the Tripi town council began a systematic excavation of a vast sector of the Greek necropolis in the Cardusa district.
The 52 tombs discovered so far, which can mostly be dated to the end of the fourth and the third centuries b.c., have particularly complex structures, and in some cases, markedly monumental qualities. The majority are crowned with an *epitymbion* comprising a small pyramidal monument with one or more large parallelepipedic steps made of local sandstone. A *stele* which was sometimes inscribed with the name of the dead person, was mounted on a dado on top of the pyramid. This type also appears, in Sicily, in the late Classical and Hellenistic necropolises at Leontini, Tyndaris and Messana. There are also cist tombs with large sandstone slabs as well as more modest ones with clay slab covers or lids. This sector containing the necropolises is fairly homogeneous, on the whole, and corresponds to a wealthy class. It therefore provides important contributions to the knowledge not only of the customs and funeral rites but also of the socioeconomic situation of this little known center, and of the various expressions of its material culture and craftsmanship.[1]

Tomb 20

The tomb is an *epitymbion* comprising a sandstone dado measuring 50 x 50 x 30 cm with a hollow for a quadrangular *stele*, that has not been found. The dado was attached to two slabs (80 x 32 cm and 74 x 30 cm) by means of two large lead coated iron pivots. Beneath there was a quadrangular pit (measuring 155 x 95 cm) roughly 55 cm deep, that contained the remains of the cremation. The gold objects, including the fragments of the crown were discovered in different places and at different levels of the pit, while the clay goods were found grouped together on the north-east side. These included six very damaged vases that can only be partly recomposed, a tapering *unguentarium*, Forti Type III, two pyriform *unguentaria*, Forti Type IV–V,[2] a small black painted lekane, a heavily damaged tiny black-painted bottle, a small squat spherical vase with no foot, of the ink-pot type.

I
Ring

gold
diam. setting ca. 2.5 cm
Patti Marina, Antiquarium della Villa Romana, inv. 7061

Plain gold lamina with roundish setting. Flattened.

II
Ring

gold, milky chalcedony
max h 2.7 cm
Patti Marina, Antiquarium della Villa Romana, inv. 7062

The scarab-shaped mobile setting has a four-legged animal engraved on the back. The ring is formed of two twisted wires united to a flat wire with lion's head clips at the sides. The scarab is held in place by a twisted wire that runs underneath the clips and by a band with a minute decoration of an egg motif and braiding. It is slightly deformed.
Examples of lion's head clips dating to the fourth century B.C. have been found at Taranto, while a similar twisted ring type (also found in southern Russia and dating to the fifth and fourth centuries B.C.) belongs to a later period. The Tripi ring differs from the Tarentine ones for the band around the scarab.[3]

III
Ring

gold, garnet
diam. 1.8 cm
Patti Marina, Antiquarium della Villa Romana, inv. 7063

The ring has a flat band and a faintly relief oval setting containing a smooth convex garnet.[4]

IV
Crown

gold, bronze
diam. ca. 17.5 cm; long leaves 2.5–2.7 cm; band 0.5 cm ca.
Patti Marina, Antiquarium della Villa Romana, inv. 7064

The crown is composed of forty-nine gold *lamina* lanceolate myrtle leaves with a hammered midrib, attached by gold wires to a gold-plated bronze band. It has been recomposed from some fragments.

V
Ribbon diadem (?)

gold
l 32 cm; w 0.6 cm
Patti Marina, Antiquarium della Villa Romana, inv. 7065

This is a gold *lamina* band with two holes at its bent ends.

VI
Ribbon diadem (?)

gold
total l ca. 33 cm; w 0.6 cm
Patti Marina, Antiquarium della Villa Romana, inv. 7066

The band, comprising four fragments, is similar to the one described above.

VII
Three elements of a chain

gold
w 1.3 cm
Patti Marina, Antiquarium della Villa Romana, inv. 7057

These are minute gold wire links, united in pairs and soldered at the center to a tiny ivy leaf. One is damaged.

VIII
Five rosette-shaped bracts

gold
diam. ca. 4 cm
Patti Marina, Antiquarium della Villa Romana, inv. 7068

These are gold *lamina* rosettes with five petals, a central hole and ribs separating the petals. They are damaged.

IX
Fourteen tubular beads

gold
l ca. 0.4 cm
Patti Marina, Antiquarium della Villa Romana, inv. 7069

These are tiny tubular beads made of smooth gold lamina. Together with the chain elements (inv. 7067) they were perhaps part of the same miniaturist style necklace.
Gold *lamina* jewelry is a typical item of funeral goods and these examples can be compared to others, dating to the Hellenistic and Republican period in Sicily, found in sites such as Lipari, Tyndaris, Naxos, etc. The two rings (inv. 7062 and 7063) were certainly the personal property of the dead person, and can be compared to similar Tarentine items of the fourth and, especially, of the third centuries B.C. The pottery articles in the grave, in particular, the two *unguentaria*, would appear to date the deposition as not before the end of the third century B.C., if not the beginning of the following century, while the rings could date back one or two generations.
G. Maria Bacci Spigo

[1] VILLARD 1954, pp. 45–50; CAVALIER 1966, p. 89; BERNABÒ, BREA 1975, pp. 9-11.
[2] FORTI 1962.
[3] *Ori di Taranto*, n. 189, p. 282; for rings with a scarab, see pp. 251 ff; GRIEFENHAGEN 1970, vol. I, p. 48, nos. 1020 ff., pl. 25.
[4] *Ori di Taranto*, p. 297, no. 229, p. 262.

387
Grave goods from Tomb 2 in the indigenous necropolis at Valle Oscura (Marianopoli)

The grave goods described below, normally on exhibit in the Museo Archeologico, Marianopoli, totaled seventy-two items including vases, jewels and a clay statue.
The sides of the tomb were constructed with plastered stone slabs. It measured 3.90 x 2.40 m. This tomb is part of a Greek necropolis dating to the Hellenistic age, lying on the N and N-E slopes of Monte Castellazzo, a mountain on the outskirts of Palermo, close to the Madonie range, near the modern town of Marianopoli.
Monte Castellazzo has been the subject of systematic research. It is well-known in archeological literature because it has been identified with Mytistraton, the site mentioned by the ancient sources in describing the First Punic War.
Both Tomb 2 and the other three coeval ones excavated near it, were probably destined to be used by the same family group, and they had chosen a sector of the prehistoric necropolis.

I
Red-figure hydria

clay
h 34 cm; diam 21.2 cm
Marianopoli, Museo Archeologico
inv. AG 20056

Globular body with horizontal shoulder decorated with an ivy-leaf pattern. The principal side has a scene of a gynaeceum where women are preparing for a marriage. In the center, there is a naked woman wearing slippers, with jewels on her arms and ankles. She is leaning over the basin of a louterion to pour in a liquid from a *lekythos* in the palm of her left hand. A dove is flying behind her. A little handmaid, holding a mirror and with a himation draped over her left shoulder, stands, ready to serve, in front of the central figure. Behind the handmaid there is another woman, dressed in a draped chiton and adorned with jewelry, who is holding a casket from which an embroidered ribbon hangs. Behind her, we get a glimpse of a *kline* and cushion. On the left side there is a woman, wearing jewelry and a tightly pleated robe, who is carrying a round object in the left hand. A xylophone is hanging to the top left.

The ground on the secondary side is decorated with a palmette and flowery volutes to the side, while two female heads, with their hair gathered in a sakkos and diadem, are painted in profile under the handles. The jewels and the additional touches to the details are painted white yellow and gold.

II
Black-figure hydria

clay
h 27 cm; diam. 17 cm
Marianopoli, Museo Archeologico
inv. AG 20050

Globular body with a horizontal shoulder decorated with an ivy-leaf pattern. On the principal side, there is a picture of a religious scene, with female figures to the sides of a small column that bears a little temple. To the right, a woman, veiled by a corner of her *himation*, seems to be removing it and revealing her bust, decorated with a long necklace. She is holding a string instrument lying on a *louterion* in her left hand. To the left of the column, another female figure is sitting with a *kithera* in her left hand, while her right hand rests on the kline. She is wrapped in a *himation* that leaves her bust uncovered. There is a dove behind the woman, and, to the top left, there is a lyre. On the secondary side, there is a palmette with flowery volutes. Underneath the handles, there are two heads of women with their hair gathered in a *sakkos*. The colors of their diadems and earrings have been added later. The jewels and details of the scene have been painted afterward in white, yellow and gold. Siceliot production, attributed to the "Lentini-Hydriai Group."

III
Red-figure stamnos-shaped pyxis

clay
h 24.1 cm; diam. 15.3 cm
Marianopoli, Museo Archeologico
inv. AG 20012

Ovoid body with vertical handles rising from the shoulders, and a cylindrical mouth to the lid. Two left profiles of female heads have been painted on the body. They are wearing diadems and jewels on their necks and ears, while their hair is gathered in a *sakkos*. There are palmettes and scrolls under the handles. Siceliot production.

IV
Black painted globular lekythos

clay
h 26.5 cm; max diam. 20 cm
Marianopoli, Museo Archeologico
inv. AG 20042

V
Gnathian-style lekane

clay
h 13 cm; max diam. 16 cm
Marianopoli, Museo Archeologico
inv. AG 20082

Lekane decorated in the Gnathian style, with white and yellow vine leaves and shoots on the lid and a white palmette on the knob.

VI
Gnathian-style lekane

clay
h 13.8 cm; max diam. 16.5 cm
Marianopoli, Museo Archeologico
inv. AG 20083

Lekane decorated in the Gnathian style, with white and yellow vine leaves, shoots and grapes on the lid and a white four-petaled rosette on the knob.

VII
Gnathian-style lekane

clay
h 17.4 cm; max diam. 11.4 cm
Marianopoli, Museo Archeologico
inv. AG 20079

Lekane decorated with white and yellow vine leaves on the lid and a white daisy on the knob.

VIII
Gnathian-style lekane

clay
h 8 cm
Marianopoli, Museo Archeologico
inv. AG 20068

Lekane decorated with white and yellow vine leaves on the lid and a palmette on the knob.

IX
Gnathian-style lekane

clay
h 8.4 cm
Marianopoli, Museo Archeologico
inv. AG 20069

Lekane decorated with white and yellow vine leaves on the lid and a black-painted palmette on the knob.

X
Gnathian-style lekane

clay
h 14.6 cm; max diam. 16 cm
Marianopoli, Museo Archeologico
inv. AG 20081

Lekane decorated with white and yellow vine leaves on the lid and a black-painted palmette on the knob.

Recent Discoveries

XI
Gnathian-style lekane

clay
h 9 cm; max diam. 12.7 cm
Marianopoli, Museo Archeologico
inv. AG 20046

Small *lekane* decorated with white and yellow ivy leaves on the lid and a black-painted palmette on the knob.

XII
Gnathian-style lekane

clay
h 10 cm; max diam. 12.4 cm
Marianopoli, Museo Archeologico
inv. AG 20078

Small *lekane* with white rosettes and scrolls on the lid.

XIII
Red-painted skyphos-shaped pyxis

clay
h 20 cm; max diam. 15.8 cm
Marianopoli, Museo Archeologico
inv. AG 20013

Red-painted *skyphos*-shaped *pyxis* decorated with additional white-painted floral motifs along the border beneath the lip and the lid.

XIV
Red-painted skyphos-shaped pyxis

clay
h 16.3 cm; max diam. 11.5 cm
Marianopoli, Museo Archeologico
inv. AG 20088

Red-painted *skyphos*-shaped *pyxis* decorated with additional white-painted floral motifs along the border between the handles and the lid.

XV
Skyphos-shaped pyxis

clay
h 17.3 cm; max diam. 12.8 cm
Marianopoli, Museo Archeologico
inv. AG 20044

Black-painted *skyphos*-shaped *pyxis* decorated with additional white- and yellow-painted floral motifs on the body and lid.

XVI
Gnathian style skyphos-shaped pyxis

clay
h 16.3 cm; max diam. 13.4 cm
Marianopoli, Museo Archeologico
inv. AG 20047

Black-painted *skyphos*-shaped *pyxis* decorated with additional white-painted convolvuluses.

XVII
Pyxis with lid

clay
h 12.8 cm; diam. 8.4 cm
Marianopoli, Museo Archeologico
inv. AG 20097

Pyxis with a cover, and knob in the shape of an *aryballos*-style *lekythos*. Running wave pattern between the two handles; swastika beneath the handle.

XVIII
Gnathian style skyphos-shaped pyxis

clay
h 11.2 cm
Marianopoli, Museo Archeologico
inv. AG 20086

Skyphos-shaped *pyxis* decorated with additional white- and yellow-painted vine shoots and grapes and ivy leaves.

IX
Black-painted stamnos-shaped pyxis

red clay
h 18.2 cm; max diam. 8 cm
restored
Marianopoli, Museo Archeologico
inv. AG 20015

XX
Black-painted stamnos-shaped pyxis

reddish clay
h 7.7 cm; max diam. 10.7 cm
Marianopoli, Museo Archeologico
inv. AG 20049

Black-painted *stamnos*-shaped *pyxis* with metallic gloss, with additional white decoration on the shoulder.

XXI
Black-painted stamnos-shaped pyxis

nut-colored clay
h 8,7 cm; diam 8.8 cm
recomposed
Marianopoli, Museo Archeologico
inv. AG 20074

Black-painted *stamnos*-shaped *pyxis*, decorated with a groundless running wave motif in the border between the handles.

XXII
Black-painted guttus

clay
h 4 cm; max diam. 11.3 cm
Marianopoli, Museo Archeologico
inv. AG 20064

Lenticular and leguminous-shaped body.

XXIII
Gnathian-style skyphos

nut-colored clay
h 12.9 cm; diam. 9.7 cm
recomposed
Marianopoli, Museo Archeologico
inv. AG 20084

Skyphos in the Gnathian style. Black-painted ovoid body, with thin sides, decorated with additional white- and yellow-painted floral motifs.

XXIV
Red-figure bombylios

orange clay
h 4.7 cm; max diam. 8.3 cm
Marianopoli, Museo Archeologico
inv. AG 20043

On the body, female head in profile, looking right, with diadem and hair gathered in a *sakkos*. Palmettes at the sides.

XXV
Red-figure bombylios

orange clay
h 19 cm
Marianopoli, Museo Archeologico
inv. AG 20059

On the body, naked male offerer (ephebus) with a long necklace on his chest. He holds a *patera* in the right hand and a lantern in the left. Palmettes at the sides.

XXVI
Red-figure Pagenstecher lekythos

nut-colored clay
h 19.4 cm; diam. 6.9 cm
Marianopoli, Museo Archeologico
inv. AG 20090

In the center, standing woman with naked bust and body wrapped in a *himation*. She holds a plate in the left hand, and a rod in the right. Palmette underneath the handles. Additional white paint to render the bust of the woman, the rod, the plate, and the folds of the mantle.

XXVII
Black-figure lekythos

nut-colored clay
h 17.7 cm; max diam. 7.7 cm

Marianopoli, Museo Archeologico inv. AG 20051

In the center, sitting woman with naked bust and body wrapped in a *himation*. Her right hand is leaning on a swan. Palmette under the handle. Additional white paint to render the bust; of the woman, the folds of the mantle and the wings of the swan.

XXVIII
Black-figure lekythos

nut-colored clay
h 17.2 cm; max diam. 6.5 cm
Marianopoli, Museo Archeologico
inv. AG 20052

In the center, woman sitting on a stool, with naked bust and the legs covered by a *himation*. There is a swan behind her. Palmette under the handle. Additional white paint to render the bust of the woman and the folds of the *himation*.

XXIX
Red-figure bombylios

nut-colored clay
h 12.5 cm; max diam. 7.3 cm
Marianopoli, Museo Archeologico
inv. AG 20058

XXX
Black-figure bombylios

nut-colored clay
h 12.5 cm; max diam. 7.3 cm
Marianopoli, Museo Archeologico
inv. AG 20057

Bombylios decorated with black-painted palmettes and a wide black stripe in the center of the body.

XXXI
Black-figure lekythos

nut-colored clay
h 15.7 cm; max diam. 6.5 cm
Marianopoli, Museo Archeologico
inv. AG 20053

Black-figure fusiform *lekythos*. On the front, sitting offerer, in right profile. The lower part of the body is wrapped in a draped *himation*, and the naked bust is rendered by additional white paint. Palmette between scrolls under the handle.

XXXII
Black-figure lekythos

nut-colored clay
h 15.5 cm; max diam. 5.6 cm
Marianopoli, Museo Archeologico
inv. AG 20085

Black-figure fusiform *lekythos*. On the front, sitting offerer, in right profile. The lower part of the body is wrapped in the *himation* and the naked bust is rendered with additional white paint. Palmette under the handle.

XXXIII
Black-figure bombylios

nut-colored clay
h 8.7 cm; max diam. 5.8 cm
Marianopoli, Museo Archeologico
inv. AG 20048

Small *bombylios* decorated with palmettes and a central black-painted stripe.

XXXIV
Pagenstecher lekythos

nut-colored clay
h 10.8 cm; max diam. 4 cm
Marianopoli, Museo Archeologico
inv. AG 20077

Left view of a swan (additional white paint on the wings and neck). Palmette with scrolls underneath the handle.

XXXV
Pagenstecher lekythos

nut-colored clay
h 10.3 cm; max diam. 4 cm
Marianopoli, Museo Archeologico
inv. AG 20099

Left view of a swan (additional white paint on the wings and neck). Palmette with scrolls underneath the handle.

XXXVI
Pagenstecher lekythos

nut-colored clay
h 11.7 cm; max diam. 4.4 cm
Marianopoli, Museo Archeologico
inv. AG 20062

Left view of a swan with wings spread (additional white paint on the wings and neck). Palmette with scrolls underneath the handle.

XXXVII
Pagenstecher lekythos

nut-colored clay
h 11.7 cm; max diam. 4.4 cm
Marianopoli, Museo Archeologico
inv. AG 20098

Left view of a swan (additional white paint on the wings and neck). Palmette between scrolls underneath the handle.

XXXVIII
Pagenstecher lekythos

nut-colored clay
h 12.2 cm; max diam. 4.4 cm
Marianopoli, Museo Archeologico
inv. AG 20100

Left view of a swan (additional white paint on the wings and neck). Palmette with scrolls underneath the handle.

XXXIX
Pagenstecher lekythos

nut-colored clay
h 12.5 cm; max diam. 4.3 cm
Marianopoli, Museo Archeologico
inv. AG 20095

Left view of a swan (additional white paint on the wings and neck). Palmette between scrolls underneath the handle.

XL
Pagenstecher lekythos

nut-colored clay
h 10.2 cm; max diam. 3.9 cm
Marianopoli, Museo Archeologico
inv. AG 20061

Left view of a swan (additional white paint on the wings and neck). Palmette between scrolls underneath the handle.

XLI
Gem

pâte-de-verre
max diam. 3 cm
Marianopoli, Museo Archeologico
inv. AG 20104

Oval pâte-de-verre gem engraved with monkey.

XLII
Statuette of a flautist

terra-cotta
h 10 cm
Marianopoli, Museo Archeologico
inv. AG 20060

XLIII
Alabastron

alabaster
h 21 cm
Marianopoli, Museo Archeologico
inv. AG 20016

XLIV
Mirror

bronze
h 12 cm
Marianopoli, Museo Archeologico
inv. AG 20054

The grave goods can be dated to 330–310 B.C., also because a bronze coin of the helmeted "Athena/Pegasus type", belonging to the time of Timoleon, was found in the same tomb.

M.R. Panvini

[1] First information in FIORENTINI 1980-81, pp. 583-592.

Works on Exhibit

Authors of the Files

A.A	Arcangelo Alessio		L.L.	Lucia Lepore
G.A.C.	Gaetana Abruzzese Calabrese		Mar.L.	Marinella Lista
I.A.	Irène Aghiou		F.L.	Fausto Longo
B.A.	Beatrice Amendolagine		S.L.	Silvana Luppino
G.M.B.S.	Giovanna Maria Bacci Spigo		A.M.	A. Marongiu
Ad.B.	Adele Bellino		G.A.M.	Grazia Angela Maruggi
L.B.B.	Luigi Bernabò Brea		L.M.	Laura Masiello
R.B.P.	Roberta Belli Pasqua		M.A.M.	Maria Amalia Mastelloni
S.B.	Salvatore Bianco		G.M.	Giovanni Mastronuzzi
F.B.	Francesca Boitani		M.M.	Marina Mazzei
A.M.B.	Anna Maria Bombaci		M.M.H.	M. Mertens Horn
M.B.	Mariarosa Borriello		M.M.-D.	Myriame Morel-Deledalle
A.B.	Angelo Bottini		G.N.	Giuseppe Nicolosi
G.B.	Grazia Bravar		R.P.	Rosalba Panvini
R.C.S.	Rosalia Camerata Scovazzo		A.P.	Annamaria Patrone
V.C.	Vanna Canalis		E.P.	Elvira Pica
M.G.C.	Maria Giuseppina Canosa		C.A.P.	Carlos A. Picón
G.C.	G. Castellana		E.C.P.	Elisa Chiara Portale
M.C.	Marina Cipriani		G.P.	Gabriella Prisco
R.C.	Rosalba Ciriello		P.R.	Paul Roberts
A.C.	Assunta Cocchiaro		M.R.	Matilde Romito
A.D'A.	Amelia D'Amicis		M.Rub.	Marina Rubinich
A.Dell'A.	Antonietta Dell'Aglio		P.I.R.	Pamela I. Russel
A.D.S.	Antonio De Siena		G.R.	Gemma Russo
C.A.F.	C. A. Fiammenghi		C.S.	Claudio Sabbione
M.T.G.	Maria Teresa Giannotta		V.S.	Vincenzo Santoni
M.G.	Massimina Gigante		A.S.	Assunta Sardella
T.G.	Teresa Giove		G.S.I.	Giovanna Scarano Iudice
M. Gorg.	Mariantonietta Gorgoglione		T.S.	Teresa Schojer
C.G.	Costanza Gualanella		E.S.	Elisabetta Setari
L.G.	Lorenzo Guzzardi		R.S.	Roberto Spadea
J.J.H.	J.J. Hermann		U.S.	Umberto Spigo
M.T.I.	Maria Teresa Iannelli		A.L.T.	Anna Lucia Tempesta
M.I.	Mario Iozzo		G.T.	Gabriella Tigano
H.P.I.	Hans Peter Isler		L.T.	Laura Trombetta
M.L.	Mimma Labellarte		A.T.	Amedeo Tullio
A.L.	Adele Lagi		A.V.	Agata Villa
G.L'A.	Gilda L'Arab		M.L.V.	Maria Luisa Viola
G.F.L.T.	Gioacchino Francesco La Torre		K.Z.	Karl Zimmermann
E.Latt.	Elena Lattanzi		V.Z.	Vincenzo Zumbini
M.C.L.	M.C. Lentini			

1	**Statue of an ephebe** ca. 480 B.C. marble h 102 cm (about 2/3 of its true h) reconstructed; some parts missing Agrigento, Museo Archeologico Regionale, inv. C 1853 Agrigento, from a cistern near San Biagio	The stance, with the right leg slightly forward and the outstretched arm which perhaps held a phial; the generalized treatment of the nude body; and the type of head, full oval, with a low forehead, heavy eyelids, a sensuous mouth, and short threadlike locks of hair that encircle and frame the face all indicate the influence of the Severe style in its early stage (cf. the ephebe of *Kritios*). The polish of the surface and the treatment of this figure suggest a certain mannerism.	RIZZA, DE MIRO 1991, p. 224, fig. 238; *Stile severi*, pp. 115-116, 158-161, and more bibliography; ROLLEY 1994, pp. 300-301. E.C.P.	

2 *see Recent Discoveries*

3 I	**Small earthenware model of a boat** about mid-third century B.C. clay h 8.5 cm; max l 43 cm; w 9 cm Milan, Archaeological Deposit inv. ME 0046 Milazzo, necropolis (building site Via Ciantro FMC 6, part. cat. nos. 309-783), tomb 5, internal furnishing	Realised in a mould, it shows a long, slim hull with pointed keel. Part of a short raised and decorated bow is conserved in the bows, probably of a horn or short volute type; to the stern an incomplete, volute *aphlaston*. The keel is well modelled. The two rowlocks stick out on each side of the boat between two beams of the gunwhale. Two triangular platforms at the bow and stern could indicate the forecastle and poop deck.	TIGANO 1991, pp. 52 ff., pl. I, figgs. 3-4; BASILE 1993, p. 84; TIGANO 1994, p. 34, fig. 6. G.T.	

3 II-V	**Group of four rowers** ca. mid-third century B.C. Milazzo, Archaeological Deposit inv. ME 0047, 0048, 0049, 0050 Milazzo, necropolis (building site in via Ciantro, FMC 6, part- cat. nos. 309-783) tomb 5, external furnishing	**II** refined clay, modelled by hand, stuffed and overpainted in white 4.5x3.5 cm; complete It has been made with two clay rods placed side by side to form the lower limbs, the torso and arms stretched forward. The head, modelled separately, shows well defined features. **III** refined clay, modelled by hand 4x4 cm It shows legs together, torso leaning slightly backwards and arms stretching forwards. The head is characterised by summary indication of features such as the hooked nose, pointed beard and big ears. On top of the head is a typical pointed hat.	**IV** refined clay, modelled by hand 4x3.5 cm It shows outstretched legs, the trunk bent backwards and arms stretched forwards. The head shows summary indication of features (hooked nose, pointed beard, big ears) and is covered with a characteristic pointed hat. **V** refined clay, modelled by hand 3.8x3 cm fragmentary It shows legs outstretched and togehter, trunk lightly leaning backwards and arms stretched forwards. TIGANO 1991, pp. 58 ff., fig. 7; BASILE 1993, p. 84, fig. 6. G.T.	

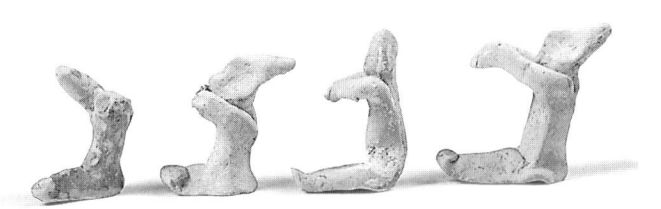

4	**Fragment of small votive model of a war ship (pentekonteros?)** end sixth-beginning fifth century B.C. clay, well conserved polychrome h 5.2 cm; w 6.8 cm Lipari, Museo Eoliano, room X inv. 15990 Lipari, acropolis, 1950 digs	Part of beaked prow on which the great apotropaic eye is painted; below this are two *zosteres* (strakes of gunwhale) in high relief, ending in the projecting *proembolion* (the upper beak). Below a successive large portion of hull painted in white is a small part of another *zoster* (decorated with two big white spots on a reddish background); to the end of which the *embolon* (the real beak) was to be inserted.	JOHNSTON 1985, pp. 78-79; SPIGO 1991, pp. 71-73. U.S.	

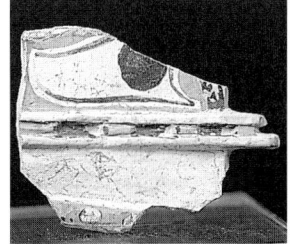

Works on Exhibit

5

Late Geometric krater

725-700 B.C.
clay, brown glaze, thrown on a wheel
h 17 cm; diam. brim 20 cm
partially reassembled
Pithecusa, Museo Archeologico
(being refitted), inv. 168813
Lacco Ameno, necropolis of Pithecusa
sporadic

Groups of seven dashes on the brim and, among horizontal lines, a row of recurring S's and dots on the lip. On the body, a figurative frieze painted with a shipwreck scene; in the centre a big overturned ship stands out and on the other side of the vase an enormous fish devours a shipwrecked person.

BUCHNER, RIDGWAY 1993, p. 696, pls. CCIV-CCV. C.G.

6

Krater of Aristonothos

ca. mid-seventh century B.C.
refined clay, slip, glaze
h 36 cm; diam. rim 33.5 cm
reassembled and integrated
Rome, Capitoline Museum, formerly Castellani Collection, inv. 172
Caere

Groups of vertical dashes on the lip. A figurative scene unfold on the upper half of the body; below is a chequered band and sunburst of cusps alternating with buds. A crab is between the handle attachments.
Side A: the blinding of Polyphemus (*Odyssey* IX, 382 ss) with Aristonothos's signature painted behind the figure of the cyclops; *side B*: naval battle.

MARTELLI 1987, pp. 263-265. G.L'A.

7

Anchor with dedication from Sostratos to Apollo

end sixth century B.C.
medium grained marble and brilliant crystals
h 115 cm; w 37 cm; t 18 cm
Tarquinia, Museo Nazionale
inv. II 4094
Gravisca, Greek sanctuary: "alpha" building

It is half of an anchor stock which would have measured nearly 2.50 metres in length. It bears an incised dedication in Dorian and the Aegina alphabet "I am of Apollo of Aegina, Sostratos made (to make), the (son of)...". It is about Sostratos, son of Laodamas, remembered by Herodotus (IV. 152), for the incredible riches accumulated by him in commerce.

TORELLI 1971, pp. 44 ff.; *Civiltà degli Etruschi*, 1985, p. 185, 7.1.9. F.B.

8 *see Recent Discoveries*

9

Head of an old man with long beard the so-called philosopher of Porticello

fifth century B.C. (460-440 B.C.)
bronze - cire perdue casting
h 42 cm; l 30 cm
Museo Nazionale di Reggio Calabria
inv. 17096
From the wreck discovered in the deeps in front of Porticello (Villa S. Giovanni, Reggio Calabria), 1969

Head belonging to a statue, of which fragments remain, of a person dressed in *chlamys*. The aquiline nose, mouth hidden by thick moustaches, emaciated cheeks, small, deep-sunken eyes are strongly distinctive (the right one conserves the iris in vitreous paste; the eyelashes are of bronze plate; the forehead is bony and wrinkled). The beard is particularly long, with locks worked separately and soldered on. A thin fillet, today lost, encircled the head. It is probably a portrait; perhaps the oldest Greek portrait yet known.

G. FOTI 1969, pp. 137 ff.; E. PARIBENI 1984, pp. 1 ff.; ROLLEY 1994, I, pp. 394 ff.; PAOLETTI 1994 pp. 119 ff. E. L.

10 *see Recent Discoveries*

11

Corinthian aryballos with black figures

575-550 B.C.
refined clay, glaze, thrown on the wheel
h 10.2 cm; diam. 9.5 cm
Boston, Museum of Fine Arts
inv. 01.8100
Boeotia

Among the first images of Ulysses and the Sirens in Greek art, the *aryballos* shows the hero tied to the mast of his boat; the Sirens sing from a rock and two great birds fly over the scene. A person behind the Sirens might be Circe.

SCHEFOLD 1992, pp. 298-300, 319-320; *LIMC*, VI, 1, p. 962, no. 151. P.J.R.

12

Chalcidian amphora with black figures

ca. 540 B.C.
clay, glaze, thrown on the wheel
h 41 cm; diam. 85 cm
Paris, Bibliotèque Nationale
Cabinet des Médailles, n. 202
Vulci

Palmettes and lotus flowers on the neck. A frieze of horsemen on the shoulder. The battle between Heracles and Geryon in front of Athens is depicted on the body; all the figures are indicated with inscribed names. Attributed to the Painter of Inscriptions.

CVA Paris, Bibliothèque Nationale, 1 (7), pp. 19 ff., pls. 25-26. I.A.

Works on Exhibit

13 **Attic kylix type A with black figures**

550-540 B.C.
clay, slip, glaze, thrown on the wheel, graffito, overpainting
h 10.4 cm; diam. rim 19.3 cm
Taranto, Museo Archeologico Nazionale, inv. 52155
Taranto, 10.III.1949, via F. Di Palma tomb III

Side A: Heracles saves Hesione by getting into the sea monster's mouth in order to cut off its tongue. Between the handle attachments are a cloaked person and dolphins.
Side B: Horseman between groups of male characters.
Inside: ring with point of glaze.
Can be placed in the vase painting production of Lydos.

BOARDMANN 1990, p. 113, fig. 179.
L.M.

14 **Attic cup with red figures**

ca. 480 B.C.
refined clay, glaze, thrown on the wheel
h 5.5 cm (without foot); diam. 29.4 cm
reassembled
Vatican City, Museo Gregoriano Etrusco, inv. 16563
Vulci

Attic cup decorated on the inside with Heracles in the cauldron; on the outside of the bowl are scenes of the battle between Achilles and Hector. Attributed to the circle of Douris.

ARV, I, p. 449.
G.L'A.

15 **Earthenware helmet with figured peak**

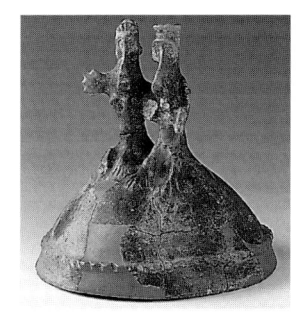

beginning ninth-mid-eighth century B.C.
polished mixture
max h 26 cm; diam. 25.6 cm
reassembled and integrated
Pontecagnano, Museo Nazionale dell'Agro Picentino, inv. 13769
Pontecagnano

The smooth cap is decorated, a little above the edge, with a toothed ropey finish with notches impressed by a small wheel. The top of the cap is decorated with a sculptured group of figures who, because of the position of their lower limbs, seem to be sitting. On the left, a female figure encircles the shoulders of the other figure shown as male by his anatomy and *polos* or helmet with hole for inserting a *lophos* which he has on his head.

Pontecagnano II, p. 162, fig. 32.2.
A.L.

16 **Mycenaean ae type female statuette**

1375-1300 B.C.
terra-cotta, painting
Taranto, Museo Archeologico Nazionale, inv. 7212
Taranto, Scoglio del Tonno, 1899

Female idol with red-brown reticulated decoration on the front and on the back in the upper part of the body; with decoration of vertical bands down to the base and a big central band behind indicate the skirt; traces of decoration on the head.

TAYLOUR 1958, p. 115, tav. 13; VAGNETTI 1985, p. 133, fig. 180.
M.G.

17 **Ingot of ox skin**

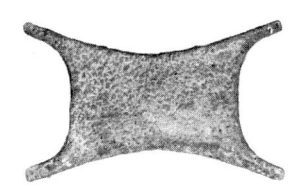

Middle Bronze Age
copper, fused
w 65 cm; max h 40.5 cm; t 3.5 cm
27.360 kilos weight
Ozieri, Civico Museo Archeologico inv. OZ 8302
Ozieri, Bisarcio area

Copper ingot made like animal skin. It shows considerable bubbles and cracks deriving from imperfect fusing. On one of the surfaces the letter *tau* of the Mycenaean Linear A and B is impressed.

VAGNETTI, LO SCHIAVO 1987, p. 224, fig. 28.3a.
A.M.

18 **Mycenaean painted alabastron**

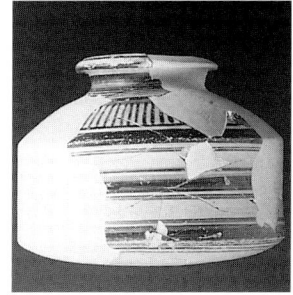

1400 B.C.
clay
14x10.5 cm
Sassari, Museo Nazionale "G.R. Sanna"
Orroli (Nu), Nuraghe Arrubiu

The oldest Mycenaean product discovered in Sardinia, it is the element of certainty in dating the setting up of the nuragic complex and in the comparative dating of finds of material culture associated to it in that it was found in fragments under the oldest beaten flooring.
V.C

19 I-XXII

Furnishing of tomb D at Thapsos

fourteenth-thirteenth cent. B.C.
Syracuse, Museo Archeologico
Regionale "P. Orsi"

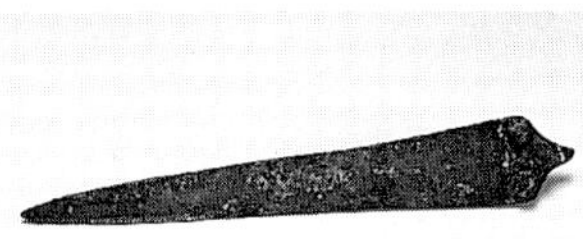

Besides the objects on exhibit, the furnishing included other Mycenaean vases and amber beads.

I
Small three-handled Mycenaean vase

clay, wheel, complete
h 14 cm; diam. 9.2 cm
inv. 69343

II
Mycenaean sack-like alabastron

clay, wheel, reassembled
faded decoration
h 7.6 cm; diam. 5.7 cm
inv. 69341

III
Two-handled Mycenaean angular alabastron

clay, wheel, missing a handle and part of the neck
h 7.7 cm; diam. 5.7 cm
inv. 69341

IV
Two-handled Mycenaean angular alabastron. Decoration of groups of lines and bows

clay, wheel, complete
h 8.7 cm; diam. 7.2 cm; inv. 69339

V
Low single-handled cup with fish bone and concentric circle decoration

clay, wheel, complete
h 4 cm; diam. 12 cm; inv. 69342

VI
Mycenaean deep cup with decoration of bands of lines and waves

clay, wheel, complete, small hole in the bowl
h 11.8 cm; diam. 18.5 cm; inv. 69346

VII
Small pitcher with decoration impressed and enlivened with white grey mixture. Three fragments reasssembled on the handle

Thapsos culture
grey mixture, three handle fragments recomposed
h 12 cm; diam. 5.6 cm; inv. 69332

VIII
Small flask with tall surmounting handle and cylindrical spout, with impressed decoration

Thapsos culture
greyish mixture, handle with small lacuna, damaged
h 14.3 cm; diam. 4 cm; inv. 69333

IX
Small jug with red glaze

Borg in Nadur culture
clay, complete, glaze cracked
h 9.5 cm; diam. 7 cm; inv. 69334

X
Small dagger with triangular blade and median ribbing

oxidized bronze, complete
l 17 cm; inv. 69360

XI
Cypriot pitcher type WSW

clay, handle reassembled from three fragments
h 19.5 cm; diam. rim 4x3 cm
inv. 69335

XII
Small Cypriot pitcher type BRW

clay, reassembled from three fragments
h 14.4 cm; diam. 3.1 cm
inv. 69337

XIII
Small Cypriot pitcher type BRW with traces of white bands of decoration

clay, complete
h 13.3 cm; diam. rim 2.7 cm
inv. 69336

XIV
Three hundred small annular elements from a necklace

bone
diam. 0.4 cm; inv. 69335

XV
48 biconical elements

vitreous paste
diam. 0.7 cm; inv. 69364

XVI
12 elements from a necklace of annular form

semi-precious stone, dark red colour
diam. 0.3 cm; inv. 69368

XVII
30 beads from a necklace in annular form

vitreous paste
diam. 0.3 cm; inv. 69367

XVIII
50 beads from a necklace in annular form of brown colour

vitreous paste
diam. 0.3 cm; inv. 69366

XIX
Heartshaped pendant with cylindrical perforated appendix

gold, complete
h 1.9 cm; inv. 69362

XX
Small annular necklace clip

end fifteenth-fourteenth century B.C.
gold, complete, crushed
diam. 0.4 cm; inv. 69363

XXI
7 discoidal and annular beads

end fifteenth-fourteenth century B.C.
amber in good state of preservation; one piece reduced to half
diam. min 0.8 cm, max 2 cm; inv. 69371

XXII
3 biconic-shaped elements from a necklace

end fifteenth-fourteenth century B.C.
gold leaf, one slightly damaged
l 2.1, 1.5, 1.4 cm; inv. 69361

*Archeologia Siciliana
Sud-Orientale*, pp. 35-40   E.C.P.

20 I-XXVIII

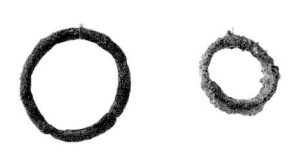

Furnishing from tomb 4 at Villasmundo

second half eighth century B.C.
Syracuse, Museo Archeologico
Regionale "P. Orsi"

I
Amphora with painted geometric decoration

clay, neck restored
h 22.5 cm; diam. rim 15.7 cm
inv. 69877

II
Small amphora with painted horizontal bands of faded decoration

eighth century B.C.
clay, wheel, one handle reattached, decoration, superficial cracking
h 11.7 cm; diam. rim 8 cm
inv. 69896

III
Small amphora with decoration painted with hatched angles

second half eighth century B.C.
clay, wheel, small lacuna on lip
h 28.8 cm; diam. 16.3 cm
inv. 69888

IV
Trilobed oinochoe with painted geometric decoration

second half eighth century B.C.
clay, wheel, no handle and chipped lip
h 14.2 cm; diam. 8x7.1 cm
inv. 69886

V
Trilobed oinochoe with painted geometric decoration

clay, wheel, complete
h 13.4 cm; diam. rim 7x6,5 cm
inv. 69897

VI
Capenduncola with surmounting handle

grey mixture, recomposed and reintegrated
h 7.4 cm; diam. 8 cm
inv. 69897

VII
Kotyle type Aetos 666

mid-eighth century B.C.
clay, wheel, reassembled, with abrasions and chipping on the lip
h 10 cm; diam. 15.2 cm
inv. 69878

VIII
Kyathos of Cycladic production with geometric decoration

mid-eighth century B.C.
clay, wheel, reassembled with small lacunas on the bottom
h 7.4 cm; diam 9.2 cm
inv. 69875

IX
Kyathos of Cycladic production with geometric decoration

mid-eighth century B.C.
clay, wheel, reassembled
h 6.8 cm; diam. 9.6 cm
inv. 69876

X
Capenduncola with surmounting handle

grey mixture, restored and reintegrated
h 7.2 cm; diam. 8 cm
inv. 69898

XI
Capenduncola with surmounting handle and globular body, with impressions on the shoulder

dark beige mixture, reassembled and restored
h 9.7 cm; diam. 6.2 cm
inv. 69899

XII
Amphora with painted decoration

clay, wheel, reassembled with small reintegration on body and lip
h 25.3 cm; diam. 15 cm
inv. 69874

XIII
Amphora with decoration painted in bands and wavy lines

clay, wheel, complete, with reintegration on the lip
h 25.7 cm; diam. 16 cm
inv. 69879

XIV
Small trilobed achrome oinochoe

clay, wheel, complete
h 9.3 cm; diam. mouth 6x5.2 cm
inv. 69881

XV
Small trilobed oinochoe with painted geometric decoration (faded)

clay, wheel, nearly all the lip is missing
h 9.8 cm; diam. 4.9x4.3 cm
inv. 69883

XVI
Large one-handled bowl with conical appendix, painted geometric decoration

clay, wheel, complete, with damage
h 9.5 cm; diam. 22 cm
inv. 69892

XVII
Large one-handled bowl with painted geometric decoration

clay, wheel, handle incomplete and damaged
h 13 cm; diam. 20 cm
inv. 69890

XVIII
Large one-handled bowl with painted geometric decoration

clay, complete, with chipping on the lip and damage
h 13.5 cm; diam. 21 cm
inv. 69889

20 XIX
Large one-handled bowl with traces of reddish colour

clay, reassembled from several fragments, encrusted and chipped on the lip
h 10.3 cm; diam. 25 cm; inv. 69894

XX
Achrome bowl with handle and hole passing through

clay, complete, with chipping on lip heat blister inside and damaged
h 7 cm; diam. 16.5 cm; inv. 69894

XXI
Large one-handled bowl with painted decoration in bands

clay, reassembled and reintegrated
h 9.5 cm; diam. 19 cm
inv. 69885

XXII
Large bowl with handle and decoration painted in bands and impressed furrows

clay, complete, damaged
h 12.6 cm; diam. 18.5 cm
inv. 69893

XXIII
Spear tip

iron, three fragments reassembled incomplete at the tip and tang oxidized and encrusted
l 16 cm; max w 3.5 cm
inv. 69907

XXIV
Spear tip with tang

iron, reassembled from two fragments oxidized
l 26.5 cm; inv. 69908

XXV
Spear tip

iron, incomplete in three fragments reassembled, corrosion, oxidized encrusted
l 16.5 cm; max w 3 cm
inv. 69909

XXVI
Spear tip

iron, broken at the base, oxidized
l 17.2 cm
inv. 69910

XXVII
Finger ring in gold with superimposed ends

iron, complete, oxidized and covered with encrustation
diam. 2.3 cm
inv. 69922

XXVIII
Ring in oval section

bronze, oxidized, with a break
diam. 3 cm
inv. 69924

Archeologia Siciliana Sud-Orientale, pp. 57-63; KEARSLEY 1983, pp. 41, 4811.

E.C.P.

Works on Exhibit

21

Late Geometric kotyle from Rhodes, the so-called Nestor Cup

725-700 B.C.
clay, glaze, thrown on the wheel
h 10.3 cm; diam. 15.1 cm
partially reassembled
Pithecusa, Museo Archeologico
(being refitted), inv. 166788
Lacco Ameno, necropolis of Pithecusa
tomb 168

Under the lip, a large panel divided into two superimposed parts: the upper one shows a division into sections decorated with lozenges, meanders and "Rhodian trees"; the lower one, inside lines and horizontal zig zags, has a reverse inscription in the Euboic alphabet – "Nestor's... the good cup to drink from. But whoever drinks from this cup will be straightaway consumed by desire and love for Aphrodite of the beautiful crown."

BUCHNER, RIDGWAY 1993, p. 219, pls. CXXVI-CXXVIII.
C.G.

22

Fragment of Late Geometric krater

725-700 B.C.
clay, glaze, thrown on the wheel
max h 9 cm
Pithecusa, Museo Archeologico
(being refitted)
Lacco Ameno, Mezzavia hill
area Mazzola

On the lip, groups of four vertical dashes surmount a band with wavy vertical lines. On the shoulder there is a panel, defined by four vertical lines, with the head and part of the body of a winged creature; above the panel a reverse inscription with the potter's signature: "...inos m'epoiese[e]...".

BUCHNER 1972, p. 371, pl. XCIII, 2.
C.G.

24

Stamnos

second half of the seventh century B.C.
clay; slick
h 13.5 cm; max diam. 18 cm
Gela, Museo Archeologico Regionale "Paolo Orsi"
Gela, perhaps from the ancient necropolis

A *stamnos* produced locally, with decoration in brown paint: a crown with rays painted around its space, *fasces* of parallel lines, and a broken curve frame each side of a metope containing two heraldic griffins (side A) and two winged creatures (a crow and a crane?) face to face (side B). Iconographic-stylistic dependence on orientalized Cretan ceramic art is evident, together with Corinthian touches (the rays).

ADAMESTEANU 1953, pp. 245-246, pl. CIX, 2; RIZZA, DE MIRO 1985, p. 154, pl. 136.
E.C.P.

25

Figured dinos

end seventh century B.C.
pink terra-cotta, slip
h 17.7 cm; diam. 32.5 cm
Agrigento, Museo Archeologico Regionale, inv. AG 4328
Montechiaro, Castellaccio di Palma
found in 1957

Dinos portraying the *triskeles*: three legs in movement with a face in front at their intersection. This vase is one of the earliest witnesses of the *triskeles*, which will become the symbol, with its three legs, of the three-pointed island, Trinacria.

G. CAPUTO, pp. 3 ff.
G.C.

26

Figured dinos with Bellerophon

mid-seventh century B.C.
refined clay, thrown on the wheel
h 22 cm; diam. 40 cm
Metaponto (MT), Museo Archeologico Nazionale, inv. 298978
Incoronata di Pisticci (MT), sample S

Body with very flattened profile, apodal, distinct curved lips, false sculpted handle with ring and reel. On the main side, Bellerophon riding Pegasus, battling with the Chimaera and brandishing a spear with his right hand is depicted, while on the other side a deer in the act of being caught by a couple of opposing lions is portrayed.

ORLANDINI 1988, pp. 6-16, pl. II.
A.D.S.

27

Figurative globular aryballos

mid-seventh century B.C.
refined clay, thrown on the wheel
h 27.7 cm; max diam. 25.5 cm
Metaponto (Mt), Museo Archeologico Nazionale, inv. 298980
Incoronata di Pisticci (MT), sample S

Globular body with distinct low foot and wide outward-turning lip. On the mouth a chequered motif is painted; on the body there is a double figured scene within metope-like frames. In the main one a pair of opposing griffons in front of a palmette are depicted with two backward-looking lions on the sides; the other side is entirely filled with a rich phytomorph motif.

ORLANDINI 1988, pp. 1-6, pl. I.
A.D.S.

28		**Dinos** 650 B.C. refined clay h 24.7 cm; max diam. 45 cm Policoro, Museo Nazionale della Siritide, inv. 41147 Acropolis of Herakleia	*Dinos* with an oblique edge, flattened spherical body and false ring handles. Decoration inside a panel. *Side A*: battling horses with central tripod. *Side B*: battling horses with central *louterion*. Applied decoration of groups of cruciform rosettes.	ADAMESTEANU 1980, pp. 32-33. S.B.
29		**Earthenware perirrhanterion** second half seventh century B.C. refined clay, moulded, parts missing h 78 cm; diam. bowl 78 cm Metaponto (MT), Museo Archeologico Nazionale, inv. 125064 Incoronata di Pisticci (MT), sample G	Wide bowl with cylindrical support, on which three figurative bands in relief are superimposed. In the first, in succession, are depicted a pair of heraldic lions, Heracles killing the centaur, Ulysses with the sorcerer Circe (?), and a pair of Gorgons. In the second a battle scene is portrayed six times, and in the third the motif of the divine couple in a chariot pulled by winged horses is repeated. The outside of the bowl is decorated with a sculpted bean motif	while a lion and panther facing each other with a palmette and lotus flower in the middle follow each other around the lip. ORLANDINI 1980, pp. 175-238, pls. I-XXIII. A.D.S.
30		**Relief statuette in Daedalic style** mid-seventh century B.C. clay, matrix h 17 cm; w 10.6 cm; t 1-1.8 cm fragmentary in the upper part Naples, Museo Archeologico Nazionale, inv. CS 106 Santangelo Collection	Female figure, portrayed frontally in very low relief. The lower part, with the skirt decorated with three orders of figurative scenes, remains: Ajax carrying the body of Achilles, a dance of young girls and one of young men.	ORLANDINI 1983, p. 336, fig. 303. M.B.
31		**Daedalic statue** mid-seventh century B.C. terra-cotta, matrix h 5 cm; w 3.4 cm; max t 1.6 cm Naples, Museo Archeologico Nazionale, inv. 20672 Cuma	The bust, arms and shoulders covered with *epiblema* of the female figure remain. The face, characterised by great bulbous eyes, is framed by the hair, which is flattened on the top of the head and arranged in thick, compact horizontal bands ending in three fine ringlets.	SCATOZZA, HOERICHT 1987, p. 45, pl. V. M.B.
32 I-II		**Votive statuette** 625-600 B.C. clay, matrix h 18.4 cm; w 3.4 cm Cosenza, Museo Civico, inv. 2591 Corigliano Calabro (CS), Cozzo Michelicchio area Standing female figure with *polos* and *himation*; hair in curls over the forehead descending in three pearl-studded ringlets each side; big eyes with thick curved eye-	brows; small high ears; outlined bust; waist distinguished by narrow *peplos* decorated with latticework; smooth dress; outlined feet. The back is smooth and flat. GUZZO 1987, pp. 166-168. V.Z. **Votive statuette** end seventh-beginning sixth century B.C. clay, matrix h 11.8 cm; w 3 cm Cosenza, Museo Civico, inv. 2594	Corigliano Calabro (CS), Cozzo Michelicchio area Standing female figure with *polos* and *himation*; round, protruding eyes; thin smiling lips; long, rounded chin; hair divided into two plaits on each side with fish-bone incisions; smooth tubular dress; long arms attached to the body; feet barely sketched in. The back is smooth and convex. GUZZO 1987, pp. 166-168. V.Z.
33 I-II		**Small plaque with female figure** 652-600 B.C. clay, matrix h 6.2 cm; w 3.6 cm lower part missing Metaponto, Museo Archeologico Nazionale, deposit no. 38, inv. 128748 Metaponto, (MT), Sanctuary of Apollo Lycian Bust of female deity of the Late Daedalic type, standing, with arms stretched along	her sides; Dorian *peplos* with *apoptygma* and hair like *etagenparruke*. OLBRICH 1979, p. 100, pl. I, type A1, p. 194, pl. XLVII, type C1. A.L.T. **Female statuette** end seventh century B.C. clay, matrix, by hand, added details h 8.6 cm; w 4.2 cm fragmentary Metaponto, Museo Archeologico	Nazionale, inv. 147146 Metaponto, (MT), Santuario di Apollo Licio, to the north of temple B Female bust of Daedalic derivation, standing, with arms folded and hands clasped on chest; narrow Dorian *peplos* held at the waist by a thin belt and hair like *etagenparruke*. OLBRICH 1979, pp. 120 ff., pl. IX, type A 39. A.L.T.

Works on Exhibit

| 34 | **Small plaque with hierogamia**

end seventh century B.C.
clay, matrix
h 10.7 cm; w 7.3 cm
fragmentary
Metaponto, Museo Archeologico Nazionale, inv. 30054
Metaponto (MT), Sanctuary of Apollo Lycian (1964?) | Small plaque in high relief representing the sacred marriage of Zeus and Hera. Zeus, on the left, is dressed in a short *chiton* and crowned; Hera, on the right, is wearing a Dorian *peplos* narrow in the waist and a low *polos* on her head. | OLBRICH 1979, p. 102, pl. I, type A5.
A.L.T. |

| 35 | **Earthenware lamp on caryatids**

580-570 B.C.
terra-cotta
h 17 cm; caryatids h 10.5 cm
diam. 17.5 cm
reassembled and integrated
Paestum, Museo Archeologico Nazionale, inv. 48496
Paestum, *Heraion* of Foce Sele | The vessel is on a high foot, supported by a flared cylindrical shaft, hollow inside, with raised rim on which three female figures are positioned, with the function of caryatids, with plaited hair obtained by incision and hands clasped to their chests; female heads, similar to those of the caryatids, are applied to the lip. | ZANCANI MONTUORO 1960, pp. 69-77, pls. XVI-XVIII, fig. 1; ORLANDINI 1983, p. 354, fig. 327.
F.L. |

| 36 | **Female head in Daedalic style**

mid-seventh century B.C.
clay, matrix, by hand
4.6x4 cm
Taranto, Museo Nazionale, inv. 9395
Taranto, with no further data of the discovery | On the hair, curled over the forehead and falling down the shoulders in two rigidly waving masses, is a *polos*. The face is triangular, with rounded chin and slight cheekbones; curved eyebrows, protruding eyes, straight nose, thick lips. | BORDA 1979, pp. 25, 29-30, fig. 1.
G.A.C. |

| 37 | **Kourotrophos in Daedalic style**

end seventh century B.C.
clay, matrix, by hand, on the wheel
h 20 cm
incision and painting
Trieste, Museo Civico di Storia ed Arte, inv. 2393 (T229)
Taranto | Standing female figure holding a child in her arms; the woman wears a rigid tubular *chiton* and a short *epiblema*; her hair in big plaits down the sides of her face and curls over her forehead is covered by a band. | BORDA 1982, I, pp. 85-89, III, pls. 13-15.
G.B. |

| 38 | **Bone plaque with a female figure**

650–625 B.C.
bone, with a metal bar on the reverse side
h 8.2 cm; w 2.2 cm
Syracuse, Museo Archeologico Regionale "Paolo Orsi", inv. 84818
Megara Hyblaea | Perhaps part of a buckle. It depicts a female figure in full frontal stance, the arms hanging down on each flank, the body clothed in a long dress with fine decoration engraved on it (scales on the breast, curves on the belt, tongue shapes and a network pattern on the skirt). The iconography and the type of head – a *polos* (with tongue-shapes decoration), braided hair, and a "U"-shaped face – place it in the Daedalus canon. | RIZZA, DE MIRO 1985, p. 168, fig. 151; *Sicilia greca*, p. 93, n. 24; ROLLEY 1994, pp. 151-152, fig. 135.
E.C.P. |

| 39 | **Female clay statuette**

early sixth century B.C.
clay
h 22 cm
well-preserved polychrome
Syracuse, Museo Archeologico Regionale "Paolo Orsi", inv. 64490
Syracuse, Spanish Garden necropolis tomb 4 | Standing female figure, with the forearms outstretched in a gesture of offering, a round object in the right hand. The body is clothed in a long, tubular dress, high-waisted with the waist indicated by a narrow pattern, two necklaces on the breast, a low *polos* and a hair band, the hair detailed (in braids that lie flat) only in front. | *Archeologia Siciliana Sud-Orientale*, pp. 92-93, n. 317, pl. XXIX; *Sicilia greca*, p. 97, n. 39.
E.C.P. |

Works on Exhibit

40

Ivory plaque with the figure of Potnia Theron

ca. 630 B.C.
ivory, an iron bar on the reverse side
h 9.2 cm; w 5 cm; t 2-3 cm
Syracuse, Museo Archeologico Regionale "Paolo Orsi", inv. 13540
Syracuse, Fusco necropolis, tomb 139 (1893)

The plaque, part of a buckle, depicts Artemis as Potnia Theron, an iconography dating to very ancient times. The goddess, winged, dressed in a long gown with decoration engraved on it, is accompanied by a goat figure in profile at her shoulders, and has placed her hands on it in a protective gesture.

JUCKER 1961, p. 195, fig. 120; *LIMC* II (1984), p. 628, n. 56, pl. 447. E.C.P.

41 I

Small head of a woman

572-550 B.C.
clay; executed with a mold *polos* (missing) applied
h max 6.6 cm
incomplete
Syracuse, Museo Archeologico Regionale "Paolo Orsi", inv. 21429
Gela, *Thesmophorion* of Bitalemi

A small head belonging to a statuette of a woman. The representation of the face is particularly detailed, as is that of the hair with spiral curls on the forehead and its main bulk, animated with ample horizontal waves, at the sides on the face.

MEOLA 1971, pp. 69, 77, plate V a (see pl. V b). E.C.P.

41 II

Statuette of a woman

575-550 B.C.
clay; executed with a mold; *polos* (missing) and hair applied; finished with a pallet
h max 17.4 cm
incomplete
Syracuse, Museo Archeologico Regionale "Paolo Orsi", inv. 21294
Gela, *Thesmophorion* of Bitalemi

The figure of a woman wearing a *chiton* with a belt round her waist and a mantle covering her back and both arms, falling symmetrically in front. The head was originally surmounted by a *polos*; the hair consists of braids flowing over the shoulders; the face lacks distinguishing traits, and is triangular in accordance with the schemata of the Ionic coroplastic output.

MEOLA 1971, pp. 69-70, 76, pl. XX b. E.C.P.

41 III-IV

Statuette of a woman

late seventh century B.C.
clay, handmade, incomplete
Syracuse, Museo Archeologico Regionale "Paolo Orsi"
Gela, *Thesmophorion* of Bitalemi

A torso representing a woman wearing a smooth dress with her arms touching her body. The head, surmounted by a low *polos*, is characterized by a U-shaped face, animated by large bulging eyes and a prominent nose; the mouth is tightly closed; the hair forms a fringe on the forehead and braids, lacking in detail, at the sides of the neck.

MEOLA 1971, pp. 50, 76, pl. I b; DE MIRO 1983, p. 100, fig. 110, p. 101. E.C.P.

Statuette of a woman

late seventh century B.C.
clay, handmade; applied *polos* (missing) and hair, h 17.3 cm

Syracuse, Museo Archeologico Regionale "Paolo Orsi", inv. 21296
Gela, *Thesmophorion* of Bitalemi

Standing figure of a woman wearing a smooth *chiton* with a short mantle over her shoulders. The head, executed perfunctorily, comprises a wig lacking in detail and a trapezoidal face animated by wide-open eyes.

MEOLA 1971, p. 68, pl. XX a. E.C.P.

41 V

Clay votive offering from the sanctuary of Bitalemi at Gela

ca. 550 B.C.
clay
incomplete
Syracuse, Museo Archeologico Regionale "Paolo Orsi", inv. 21428
Gela, *Thesmophorion* of Bitalemi

MEOLA 1971, pp. 66-67, 77, pl. XVII c (cf. pl. IV b). E.C.P.

42 I

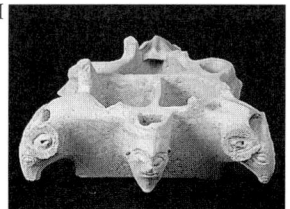

Earthenware oil-lamp with alternating human and ram heads

630-620 B.C.
clay
h 11 cm; max diam. 26 cm
Gela, Museo Archeologico, inv. 7711
Gela, out-of-town Sanctuary of Predio Sola

Oil-lamp of triangular form, with six reservoirs superimposed on two separate levels. The three upper ones are connected to the rams' heads which protrude at the angles; the lower ones are connected to the human heads placed in the middle of each side. The three cone sides are decorated with a rhombic grid in black glaze; the details of the human heads are shown in graffito and thin lines of red colour. Produced locally, it recalls the marble examples of Greek-insular provenance.

ORLANDINI 1963, cc. 33-41, n. 1, figg. 14-16, pls. VIII a-c, IX a-b. R.P.

Works on Exhibit

42 II

Three earthenware female statuettes

end seventh century B.C.
clay
max h 75. cm; 7.5 cm; 7.3 cm
fragmentary in the lower part
Gela, Museo Archeologico, inv. 7497 7498, 7499
Gela, out-of-town Sanctuary of Predio Sola

They are all identical; they are wearing a narrow-waisted dress down to the feet and have their arms along their sides. There is a tall *polos* on the head; the face is structured on converging planes; the hair is arranged in horizontal planes, on the shoulders. Produced in the Gela workshops, they reflect the late Daedalic and Cretan sculptured forms.

ORLANDINI 1963, 43, nos. 3-5, pl. X, b-c-d.
R.P.

43

Oil-lamp with human head

625-600 B.C.
marble
h 7.4 cm; max w 21.5 cm
Palermo, Museo Archeologico "A. Salinas", inv. 3892
Selinunte, Malaphoros Sanctuary

Of a semi-circular form, it has three protrusions with holes for being hung up. On the straight side a head of Daedalic type is sculpted; with a long face, nearly rectangular, big eyes with incised irises, a big nose, thin mouth. The hair is held on the forehead by a diadem decorated with volutes and gathered into heavy plaits at the sides.

GABRICI 1927, 162-163, fig. 95 (159), pl. XXIII, 1-1a; TUSA 1983, p. 133, no. 42, fig. 45.
A.V

44

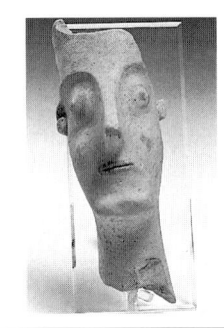

Small earthenware head

end seventh- beginning sixth century B.C.
terra-cotta of yellow-orange colour slip, applied brown colour
h 15 cm
Agrigento, Museo Archeologico Regionale, inv. AG 19896
Agrigento, 1972-76 excavations, west sector, hill of the temples

Figure of female deity with tall *polos*. The statuette, which is to be taken back to a first phase of use for worship of the place from which the piece comes, shows the confluence of geometric-proto-Daedalic features and precedents of a sub-Minoan Cretan sphere.

DE MIRO 1994, pp. 59 ff., fig. 5.
G.C.

45 I

Statuette of an offerer

end seventh century B.C.
bronze, solid casting
h 8.7 cm; base w 3.2 cm
Palermo, Museo Archeologico "A. Salinas", inv. 2604
Himera, temple A

Represented in the act of offering two objects with the tubular arms outstretched. A low *polos* is on the large head; the hair falls onto the shoulders in two masses; the big eyes are almond-shaped and the nose and chin are quite pronounced. The body, of cylindrical form, is covered by a long *peplos* with *apoptygma*.

BONACASA 1970, p. 91, pl. XXXII, 1; DI STEFANO 1975, p. 61, n. 101, pl. XXV.
A.V.

Statuette of Athena

beginning sixth century B.C.
bronze, solid casting
h 18.6 cm; base w 3 cm
Palermo, Museo Archeologico "A. Salinas", inv. 2606
Himera, temple A

It is a very archaic representations, of Xoanon type, of Athena Promacos. The goddess is depicted in the act of hurling the spear; her left arm held a shield. A helmet with tall *lophos* is on her head. The features of the face are squarish and rigid with bulbous eyes; the hair falls on the shoulders in a mass, decorated by incised lines.

BONACASA 1970, pp. 89, 91, pl. XXXI; DI STEFANO 1975, p. 8, no. 8, pl. III.
A.V.

46 I-II-III

Statuette of a hoplite

ca. 530 B.C.
bronze, cast
12.5x4 cm
Sibari (CS), Museo Nazionale Archeologico della Sibaritide
inv. 65148
Francavilla Marittima (CS), Sanctuary of Athena on the Timpone Motta, area of building I

The figure, presenting a slight twist, wears a helmet with tall *lophos* and a breastplate decorated with incised spirals. The right hand which held the spear is near the chest; the left which raised the shield is at waist height. The hair falls down his back in a long, thick mass of triangular shape with incised curls.

CROISSANT 1993, p. 558, pl. XLVII.
S.L.

Female statuette

575-550 B.C.
bronze, cast; 9.7x3.2 cm
Sibari (CS), Museo Nazionale Archeologico della Sibaritide
inv. 65144
Francavilla Marittima (CS), Sanctuary of Athena on the Timpone Motta area of building I

Standing female figure (Athena Hippia?), with forearms oustretched and hands closed into fists which have a hole passing through vertically. On the sides of the heavy face two bands of hair fall with horizontally incised curls. She wears a *peplos* and belt, with a cloak and enlarged hem.

STOOP 1970-71, pp. 45-48, pl. XVII.
S.L.

Tablet with Archaic inscription

beginning sixth century B.C.
bronze, incision; 24x12x0.3 cm
Sibari (CS), Museo Nazionale Archeologico della Sibaritide
inv. 64676
Francavilla Marittima (CS), Sanctuary of Athena on the Timpone Motta area of building II

The tablet carries an inscription incised in Achaean reverse alphabet in six lines. A tenth of the prize offered to the goddess is probably obtained from the series of considerable prizes with which the cities of origin used to integrate the simple crown of olives reserved for the Olympic winners.
"Kleombrotos, son of Dexilaos dedicated, having won at Olympia (the race) of equals in height and stature, after having promised in a vow to Athena a tenth of the prizes."

STOOP, PUGLIESE CARRATELLI 1965-66, pp. 14-21, 209-214, pl. IV; GUARDUCCI 1967, I, pp. 110-111.
S.L.

Works on Exhibit

| 47 I | **Necklace**

end eighth-beginning seventh century B.C.
electrum, lacking most of the amber beads, modern string
l 31.5 cm; 20.72 gr
Naples, Museo Archeologico Nazionale, inv. 126418
Cuma, bottom Maiorano (from a ditch-tomb); Stevens Collection | The necklace is made up of thirty small electrum discs alternating with groups of gold pearls with a central pendant in gold leaf of an elongated spheroidal form. The discs, of diminishing dimensions from the centre to the ends, are decorated with granulation and have a central setting containing an amber bead. | GUZZO 1993, p. 187, C.I A 1.   T.G. |

| 47 II | **Fibula**

end eighth-beginning seventh century B.C.
electrum, complete
l 6 cm; 9.32 gr
Naples, Museo Archeologico Nazionale, inv. 126419
Cuma, bottom Maiorano (from a ditch-tomb); Stevens Collection | Electrum *fibula* like a dragon with filigree and granulated decoration which finely ornament the body of the *fibula*, the small circular disc soldered to the elbow of the bow, and also the minute gold sphere thread on the needle. | GUZZO 1993, p. 143, F.I L 1.   T.G. |

| 48 | **Slab of a frieze with departure scene**

650-625 B.C.
clay, moulded
h 20.7 cm; l 36 cm
reassembled
Metaponto, Museo Archeologico Nazionale, inv. 128746
San Biagio della Venella (Bernalda, MT) sanctuary area | Slab bordered by two edges above and below; a departure scene has been realized in relief with an armed warrior screened by the big round shield, in the act of getting onto a chariot pulled by winged horses; in front of the chariot driven by a charioteer the figure of another armed soldier who reproposed the same scene in the long frieze, is barely visible. | MERTENS, HORN 1992, p. 105, fig. 13, pl. I.   M.L.V. |

| 49 | **Slab of a frieze with a procession of worship scene**

575-550 B.C.
clay, matrix
h 4.5 cm; max l 45 cm
fragmentary
Metaponto, Museo Archeologico Nazionale, inv. 134482
Metaponto, Urban Sanctuary *sacellum* C | A scene of a procession of worship develops on a base plinth in relief towards the right with a two-wheeled chariot and pair of horses driven by a backward-looking male figure; two female figures are seated in the chariot and one of them seems to hold a flower in her right hand. | MERTENS, HORN 1992, p. 114, fig. 28, pl. 9.   M.L.V. |

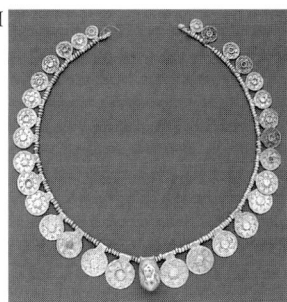

50 — Earthenware relief frieze

575-550 B.C.
terra-cotta
Potenza, Museo Archeologico Provinciale
Serra di Vaglio, Braida district

Seven fragments pertaining to a continuous frieze representing a duelling scene between dismounted hoplites.

slab inv. 1/3387
Fragment of upper right corner part pertaining to the left slab, reassembled from two fragments
h 10.6 cm; w 23 cm; t 2.6 cm

Incomplete figure of hoplite with Corinthian helmet and spear with leaf tip and median ribbing. With his left arm, by means of the *porpax* and *antilabe*, he holds the inside of the shield.

slab inv. 32/3418
Fragment of central part pertaining to the left slab
h 23 cm; w 9.9 cm; t 2.2 cm

Incomplete figure of mounted palfrenier. In his right hand he grips the *kentron* which curves to meet the horse's rump.

slab inv. 7/3393
Fragment of lower right corner part pertaining to the left slab
h 16 cm; w 19.5 cm; t 2.2 cm

Incomplete figure of advancing hoplite with circular shield, defined at the bottom by a double band in relief.

slab inv. 43/3428
Fragment of upper left corner part pertaining to the right slab
h 8 cm; w 18.2 cm; t 2.5 cm

Incomplete figure of hoplite. Relief of the head with Corinthian helmet and its tall *lophos*, of the shoulders, the left arm bent to hold a spear and a circular shield in the right (only the upper edge is visible). At the top on the left Greek alphabet sign.

slab inv. 51/3436
Fragment of central left part pertaining to the right slab
h 13.5 cm; w 13 cm; t 2 cm

Incomplete figure of hoplite whose left leg and circular shield are visible.

slab. inv. 46/3431
Fragment of central part pertaining to right slab
h 8.5 cm; w 11.7 cm; t 2.8 cm

On the left the hoplite's arm, with marked emphasis of the biceps, raised to hold the spear. On the right a double horse's head with marked anatomical details.

slab inv. 57/3442
Fragment of lower right corner pertaining to the right slab
h 22.8 cm; w 24.2 cm; t 2.5 cm

Incomplete figure of mounted palfrenier who holds two horses with very elongated bodies and stylized tails, manes and musculature. The palfrenier wears a *chiton* and holds a whip. The figured scene is defined, at the bottom, by a double band in relief. Hole for fixing.

LO PORTO, RANALDI 1990, pp. 291-315; GRECO 1991, pp. 30-31.   Ad.B.

Works on Exhibit

51		**Female protome akroterion** 600-590 B.C. clay, matrix h 49.2 cm; w 52 cm partially reassembled Metaponto, Museo Archeologico Nazionale, inv. 147155 Metaponto, Sanctuary of Apollo Lycian	Fragment of *akroterion* with female (?) *protome* of the Argive school in *mezzotondo*; the face, of sub-Daedalic features, is framed by snail-like curls over the forehead and long "beaded" plaits; the strong and robust neck is "cut" at the base. M.L.V.	
52		**Protoarchaic antefix with female protome** 620-600 B.C. clay h 19 cm; w 25.5 cm Trieste, Museo Civico di Storia ed Arte, inv. 3782 (T14) Taranto	A female face has been applied to the crescent-shaped field of the antefix with sharp outlines and of triangular form. The wide arch of the eyebrows continues down the nose, prominent and pointed. The hair is in pearl-studded plaits, on the sides of the face with the uncovered ears, and in small curls over the forehead.	BORDA 1979, pp. 73 ff., fig. 23. G.B.
53 I		**Antefix with gorgoneion** end sixth century B.C. clay, matrix, finished by hand and spatula 18x24 cm Taranto, Museo Archeologico Nazionale, inv. 17580 Taranto, Vecchio Museo	Semi-elliptical slab. Wide face; oblique eyes with prominent pupils; small ears placed on the temples; dilated nose; large mouth with tongue hanging between long fangs; distinct and prominent chin; beard with pointed locks; hair with stylized fringe and beaded plaits.	LAVIOSA 1954, p. 232, no. 4, pl. LXVII, 4; ORLANDINI 1983, p. 402, fig. 420. L.T.
53 II		**Antefix with gorgoneion** end sixth century B.C. clay, slip, traces of colour, matrix finished by hand and spatula 18.5x20 cm Taranto, Museo Archeologico Nazionale, inv. 17584-50784 Taranto, 10.6.1934, via Dante corner via Leonida	Circular slab. Full face surrounded by a crown of small snakes; oblique eyes; dilated and deformed nose; snarling mouth with tongue hanging between short fangs; hair executed on the forehead with a double row of snail-like curls.	ORLANDINI 1983, p. 402, fig. 421. L.T.
53 III		**Antefix with head of Silenus** end sixth century B.C. clay, slip, traces of colour, matrix retouching by hand and spatula 19x14 cm Taranto, Museo Archeologico Nazionale, inv. 17573 Taranto, Vecchio Museo	Semi-elliptical slab. Face of Silenus with oblique eyes; snub nose; long lips together; thin moustaches; long, cat-like ears; hair of short, segmented locks ending in curls over the forehead and beaded plaits at the sides of the face; graffito beard with fish-bone motifs.	ORLANDINI 1983, p. 403, fig. 425. L.T.
54		**Slab with dancers called Griso-Laboccetta** 525-500 B.C. terra-cotta, by hand, painting h 69.5 cm; w 96 cm; t 17 cm Reggio Calabria, Museo Nazionale Reggio Calabria, sacred area between the streets Tripepi, Torrione 2 Settembre and Palamolla	The slab represents two female figures (Nereids?) in rapid movement towards the right. They are wearing *chitones* articulated by horizontal pleats; hems of a dark brown colour edge the cloak which is over the dress. A small cloak, it too edged in dark brown, covers only part of the shoulders. Of the two girls' faces the long plaits of yellow ochre colour remain, furrowed by wide horizontal dashes.	LATTANZI 1987, p. 83. R.S.

55 *see Recent Discoveries*

Works on Exhibit

56	**Tablet with figure of Gorgon** ca. 575 B.C. clay h 56 cm; w 50 cm well-preserved polychrome, reconstructed, some parts missing Syracuse, Museo Archeologico Regionale "Paolo Orsi" Syracuse, Athenaion	Clay tablet from an architectural facade, frontal or metope (4 holes indicate that it was nailed to a wooden beam). It depicts the theme of the monstrous birth from the Gorgon slain by Perseus – on the right side of the scene Pegasus is preserved, and perhaps Chrysaor was also represented.	Rizza, De Miro 1985, pp. 187-188, fig. 179; Schefold 1992, p. 86, fig. 66 (at p. 84). E.C.P.
57	**Face of a sphinx** 560–550 B.C. clay, slick, traces of polychrome, stick retouching h 12 cm parts missing Syracuse, Museo Archeologico Regionale "Paolo Orsi" Syracuse, the Ionic Temple area	Unfortunately only the face remains. This work is distinguished by high-quality workmanship and by the expressiveness of the large eyes accentuated by colour. It represented a sphinx, perhaps on an *akroterion*.	*Archeologia Siciliana Sud-Orientale*, p. 75, no. 273, pl. XX; Rizza, De Miro 1985, p. 188, fig. 180. E.C.P.
58 I	**Antefix with leonine protome** 550-525 B.C. ca. 490-480 B.C. (Kenfield) clay, slip, well preserved polychrome h 21.5 cm; w 24.6 cm Aidone, Museo Archeologico inv. 67-174 Morgantina, Cittadella district	Antefix of leonine protome contained within the mane and paws.	Allen 1970, p. 377, pl. 95, fig. 26; Kenfield 1990, pp. 270-272, pl. 45 f. A.M.B.
58 II	**Antefix with a maenad's head antefix** mid-sixth century B.C. clay, slip, well conserved polychrome h 22.5 cm; w 20.5 cm Aidone, Museo Archeologico inv. 58-1950 Morgantina, Cittadella district	On the white slip covering all the head, the reddish-brown and black of the hair, features of the face and especially the wide open eyes and long lashes stand out.	Mertens, Horn 1991, pp. 11-12, fig. 3; Kenfield 1993, pp. 25-26, fig. 11. A.M.B.

59 *see Recent Discoveries*

60	**Antefix with a female protome** late sixth century B.C. clay h 20.2 cm Syracuse, Museo Archeologico Regionale "Paolo Orsi", inv. 1414 Syracuse, Fusco district (1843)	Depicting a maenad, in view of the vaguely feral character of the face, or else a nymph, this antefix, together with a second similar one, was part of a chapel or of a grave monument. The head, in Ionian style, is characterized by *stephane*, the hair densely wavy on top and with braids down to the neck at each side, large almond-shaped eyes accentuated by the plastic value of the eyelids and eyebrows, sensuous lips, and a pointed chin.	Mertens, Horn 1991, pp. 12-13, figg. 4-5, e pl. III b for an identical sample; Rizza, De Miro 1985, p. 194, fig. 209). E.C.P.

61 *see Recent Discoveries*

62	**Head of kouros or sphinx** 550-530 B.C. pinkish coloured terra-cotta, slip h 23 cm Agrigento, Museo Archeologico Regionale, inv. AG 1316 Agrigento, 1951, from a well to the north of the Temple of Heracles	The head, conserved practically to the shoulder line, presents long hair gathered in plaits (in curls over the forehead, in knots on the back). Current identification gives it as a *kouros*; identification as a sphinx is preferable.	De Miro 1994, pl. 27, p. 65. G.C.

Works on Exhibit

63

Earthenware female head

500-490 B.C.
brown coloured terra-cotta
h 19.6 cm
Agrigento, Museo Archeologico Regionale, inv. AG 20508 (formerly PA 3450)
Agrigento

Head belonging to a cult statue of a female figure in the round, generally identified as a deity (Kore-Persephone?). The head has long hair divided into wavy bands, parted in the centre over the forehead, and falling onto the shoulders closely following the neck.

L'arte della Magna Grecia, 1968, pl. VI-II, and 44, pp. 251-252.

G.C.

64

Helmeted head

500 B.C.
orange coloured terra-cotta, slip with traces of red colour
h 20 cm
Agrigento, Museo Archeologico Regionale, inv. AG 1275
Agrigento, 1953-54 excavations from the area between the Temple of Zeus and the Sanctuary of the Chthonic Deities

Head protected by a Chalcidian type helmet with long hair gathered into plaits which come out from under the helmet at the nape. It can be attributed to a cult statue in the round, perhaps of helmeted Athena, which could have belonged to a frontal group.

DE MIRO, 1998, fig. 66, p. 65.

G.C.

65

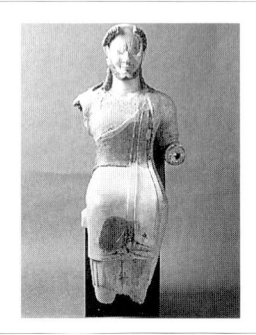

Earthenware statue of an enthroned deity

530-520 B.C.
painted terra-cotta
h 90 cm
reassembled, fragmentary
Paestum, Museo Archeologico Nazionale, inv. 133149
Paestum, southern urban sanctuary

Male figure sitting on a throne without a back. He is wearing a clinging *chiton* which lets the forms of the body be seen while the *himation* leaves the right part of the bust uncovered. Long plaits fall to his chest, his shoulders and down his back. Most probably it is a cult statue of Zeus.

ORLANDINI 1983, pp. 379-380, figg. 392-393.

F.L.

66

Head of male statue

end sixth century B.C.
clay, colour, matrix
24x15 cm
Taranto, Museo Nazionale, inv. 4008
Taranto, no further information of the find

Hair gathered on top of the head and placed in rigid, flat locks over the forehead ending in spiralling curls. The head is enclosed by a *lemniskos* with the ends falling either side of the wide neck. Oval face with pronounced cheekbones; elongated eyes with convex eyeballs; prominent nose; thick lips.

LIPPOLIS 1995, p. 44, pl. 2, I, 8, pl. XV, 5.

G.A.C.

67

Part of a metope

510-500 B.C.
stone
l 67 cm; h 38 cm; t 14 cm
the lower left part is missing, chipping
Naples, Museo Archeologico Nazionale
Posidonia, near the stream Capodifiume, not far from the walls

On the fragment the bust of a female figure facing frontwards remains. She is dressed in a *chiton*; the position of the hips indicates that she was seated, with the legs in profile, possibly on the back of an animal, traces of which remain. It is probably an image of Europa on the bull. Two rosettes are on the sides of the head which reach the limits of the slab.

Napoli 1969, pp. 381-382

M.B.

68

Metope with Heracles and Halcyone

560-550 B.C.
sandstone
max h 83 cm; w 152 cm; max t 31.2 cm
reassembled
Paestum, Museo Archeologico Nazionale, inv. 133155
Paestum, *Heraion* of Foce Sele

Slab complete with metope and triglyph. In the metope area the figured relief presents a bearded male person with a *chiton* who seizes a larger, kneeling nude figure by the hair from behind and sticks his sword into the other's kidneys.

ZANCANI, MONTUORO 1964, pp. 76-83, pls. XVIII, b-d, XIX-XX; VAN KEUREN 1989, pp. 72-77, pls. VII.b, VIII-IX, XIXa.

F.L.

Works on Exhibit

| 69 | **Metope with chorus of young girls**

510-500 B.C.
sandstone
max h 85 cm; max w 71.6 cm
max t 22.5 cm
Paestum, Museo Archeologico Nazionale, inv. 133156
Paestum, *Heraion* of Foce Sele | The metope represents two young girls who flee or dance towards the right with the right arm stretched forwards and the left holding up the hem of the *chiton*. | Zancani Montuoro, Zanotti Bianco 1951, pp. 141-146, pls. XLI, XLIV, fig. 40; Orlandini 1983, p. 366, fig. 358.
F.L. |

| 70 | **Male head**

ca. 530 B.C.
limestone, traces of colour
14x6x10.3 cm
Sibari (CS), Museo Nazionale Archeologico della Sibaritide, inv. 7529
Sibari, Parco del Cavallo | Surviving part of a high relief with features of the face, perhaps originally bearded, executed partially in the round. The head is slightly bent forwards, with hair encircled by a smooth fillet (or visor of an Attic helmet?) and curled snail-like. Archaic profile with pointed nose, bulbous eyes, thin lips (although marked). | Zancani Montuoro 1972-73, pp. 62-66, fig. 4, pl. XXX.
S.L. |

| 71 | **Inscription from Olympia**

550-525 B.C.
bronze
h 8.9 cm; l 15.2 cm; t 0.5 cm
Olympia, Archaeological Museum inv. B4750
Olympia, Thesauros of the Sybarites | Bronze slab with holes for fixing it. It shows, incised in the Achaean alphabet, the stipulation of a treaty of "friendship" between the Sybarites and their allies the Serdaioi, in the eyes of Zeus, Apollo and the other gods and the city of Poseidonia. | Kunze 1961, pp. 207 ff.; *SEG*, XXII 1967, no. 336; E. Greco 1990, pp. 39 ff.
G.L'A. |

| 72 | **Female head**

ca. 590–580 B.C.
limestone
h 55.8 cm
broken at the base of the neck; chips and abrasions on the surface
Syracuse, Museo Archeologico Regionale "Paolo Orsi"
Syracuse, from Langanello, at the mouth of the Ciane River | Large female head, probably depicting a goddess, with a *polos*, hair in spiral curls down to the forehead and thick pearly plaits flowing down on the neck, a face elongated but massive. | Rizza, De Miro 1985, p. 171, fig. 162; Rolley 1994, p. 307, fig. 316. E.C.P. |

| 73 | **Metope with Europa on the bull**

mid-sixth century B.C.
tufa
h 84.2 cm; w inf. 67.5 cm; t 31.5 cm
Palermo, Museo Archeologico "A. Salinas", inv. 3915
Selinunte, Acropolis | The bull is depicted in profile, but with its head facing to the front, as it traverses the sea, symbolised by two dolphins. Europa, on the back of the animal, seizes a horn with one hand. Some of the details are treated with special decorative care, as for example the curly hair, the bull's neck and eyes and the nymph's cloak and pleated dress. | Giuliani 1979, pp. 43 ff., pl. 10; Tusa 1983, p. 113, no. 5, figs. 24-26. A.V. |

| 74 | **Head of a youth**

c. 530 B.C.
tufa
h 19.5 cm
fragmentary in the posterior part
Palermo, Museo Archeologico "A. Salinas", inv. 3900
Selinunte, temple C | The high forehead is topped by hair divided in the middle into two bands. The eyebrow arch is barely hinted at; big, curving eyes; inconsistent rectilinear lips; robust and prominent chin. | Giuliani 1979, pp. 32, 61, pl. 7,3; Tusa 1983, p. 134, no. 47. A.V. |

75	**Kouros of Sombrotidas** ca. 550 B.C. marble h 119 cm the head, right arm, and lower part of the legs are missing Syracuse, Museo Archeologico Regionale "Paolo Orsi", inv. 49401 Megara Hyblaea, southern necropolis (1940)

The statue, intended for the monument at a grave, has an inscription in the Megara alphabet written on the right leg:
Σομβροτίδα·τō hιατρō·τō Μανδροκλέος.
This inscription designates the person honored, a person of Ionian origin, perhaps from Samos – as indicated by the naming and by the practice of putting the inscription on the leg of the figure – who nevertheless had become a citizen of Megara Hyblaea (evidence of origin missing), perhaps thanks to his being a physician.

RIZZA, DE MIRO 1985, pp. 173-174, figs. 173-175; ROLLEY 1994, pp. 299-300, fig. 14.
E.C.P.

76	**Headless kore** 525-500 B.C. marble h 35.5 cm; w 12 cm Berlin, Staatliche Museen, inv. SK 578 Taranto

The *kore*, headless, without hands or forearms, not a finished work, presents the left leg forward and the arms stretched out. It wears a *chiton* with oblique *paryphe*, and a short *himation* draped on the right shoulder. There is no trace of hair on the back.

BLUMEL 1963, p. 28, pls. 52-54.
G. L'A.

77	**Statue of Zeus** about 500 B.C. bronze, cast base 32.5x8.8 cm; h 74 cm Taranto, Museo Nazionale inv. 121.327 Ugento

Bronze sculpture surmounting a Doric capital with abacus decorated with a series of rosettes. The male figure, with legs apart, represents the deity in the act of hurling lightening, while it holds an eagle in its left hand.

DEGRASSI 1981; LIPPOLIS 1985, pp. 31 ff.
E.L.

78	**Fragment of female head** ca. 480 B.C. marble h 14.8 cm; w 15.5 cm Boston, Museum of Fine Arts inv. 00.307 Taranto (?)

Head of Athena; the upper part has been predisposed to take a helmet. Eyes, lips and hair have been executed in an exaggerated way. The back is of coarser workmanship.

COMSTOCK, VERMEULE 1976, no. 26; ORLANDINI 1983, p. 369, fig. 363.
J.J.H.

79	**Head of acrolyte in marble** 500 B.C. large grained marble h 17 cm; w 10.5 cm Paestum, Museo Archeologico Nazionale, inv. 133150 Paestum, to the north of the IV votive offerings of the southern urban sanctuary

Above the forehead, the head presents a band and a horse-shoe shaped groove in which a veil was to be positioned, executed probably in stucco. In the rear part the piece has been longitudinally cut.

ORLANDINI 1983, p. 369, fig. 365; ROLLEY 1995, pp. 107 ff., pls. XXII, XXV, 1.
F.L.

80	**Head of acrolyte in marble** beginning fifth century B.C. small-grained and shining marble h 15.5 cm; max w 7.2 cm fragmentary Paestum, Museo Archeologico Nazionale, inv. 133151 (old inv. 4851) Paestum, southern urban sanctuary

A narrow projecting band (1 cm) at the base of the neck and another prominent band (2 cm) on the forehead. The back part of the face, only rough-hewn, leads one to suppose the presence of part of a helmet realised most probably in stucco. The rear part of the head presents a clean longitudinal cut.

ORLANDINI 1983, p. 369; ROLLEY 1995, pp. 107 ff., pls. XXIII, 3-6 and XXV, 2.
F.L.

81 I-VIII

I
Support for a basin

first half fourth century B.C.
clay, matrix, with hand retouches
h 22.6 cm; diam. 15.5 cm
partially reassembled
Metaponto, Museo Archeologico Nazionale, inv. 292623
San Biagio alla Venella (Bernalda, MT)
sanctuary area

It is made up of four identical standing female figures, with arms along their sides, dresses held in at the waist, *epiblema* barely visible on the shoulders. The face is surrounded by small tongues of hair on the low forehead and groups of small plaits falling onto the shoulders with quadrangular pearls. Small connecting slabs between one figure and the other have been applied later.

PARIBENI 1973, p. 145.   M.L.V

II
Female statuette

550-525 B.C.
clay, matrix, by hand
h 22.3 cm; w 14.3 cm
partially reassembled
Metaponto, Museo Archeologico Nazionale, inv. 29892
San Biagio alla Venella (Bernalda, MT)
out-of-town sanctuary, votive offering no. 1 (1973)

Bust of female deity of Ionian type, with tall flared *polos*, crowned by elements of pine cone; small discoidal *fibulae* and a serpent's protome on the shoulders; right arm raised to hold a spear (now lost).

OLBRICH 1979, p. 158, pl. XXX, type A 124.   A.L.T.

III
Female statuette

525-500 B.C.
clay, matrix, by hand
h 30 cm; w 14.5 cm
partially recomposed
Metaponto, Museo Archeologico Nazionale, inv. 29893
San Biagio alla Venella (Bernalda, MT)
out-of-town sanctuary, votive offering no. 1

Bust of female deity of Ionian type with tall, conical head covering curving forwards; large wheels applied to the shoulders (one is conserved); sickle-shaped haloes and arms stretched out.

OLBRICH 1979, p. 156, pl. 28, type A 121.   A.L.T.

IV
Female statuette

525-500 B.C.
clay, matrix, by hand
h 30.5 cm; w 23.5 cm
partially reassembled
Metaponto, Museo Archeologico Nazionale, inv. 29894
San Biagio alla Venella (Bernalda, MT)
out-of-town sanctuary, votive offering no. 1 (1973)

Bust of female deity of Ionian type with flared *polos* adorned by lance-shaped leaves; wheels applied to the shoulders; sickle-shaped haloes and arms stretched out not conserved.

OLBRICH 1979, p. 151, pl. 24, type A 106.   A.L.T

V
Female statuette

525-500 B.C.
clay, matrix, by hand
h 27.2 cm; w 27.5 cm
partially reassembled
Metaponto, Museo Archeologico Nazionale, inv. 29902
San Biagio alla Venella (Bernalda, MT)
out-of-town sanctuary, votive offering no. 1 (1973)

Bust of female deity of Ionian type with tall flared *polos* crowned by elements of pine cones; big wheels applied to the shoulders; sickle-shaped haloes and a deer held in the arms.

OLBRICH 1979, p. 157, pl. 29, type A 122; ORLANDINI 1983, p. 398, fig. 406.
    A.L.T.

VI
Female statuette

525-500 B.C.
clay, matrix
h 58.1 cm; w 26.7 cm
reassembled and integrated
Metaponto, Museo Archeologico Nazionale, inv. 29907
San Biagio alla Venella (Bernalda, MT) out-of-town sanctuary, votive offering no. 1 (1973)

Female deity of Ionian type with tall flared *polos*, sculpted wheels applied to the shoulders; sickle-shaped haloes; arms stretched out to hold an animal not conserved; lower part in simple and smooth tubular support.

ORLANDINI 1983, p. 398, fig. 408.
    A.L.T.

VII
Female statuette

525-500 B.C.
clay, matrix, by hand, remains of colour
h 44.8 cm; w 10 cm
reassembled
Metaponto, Museo Archeologico Nazionale, inv. 29911
San Biagio alla Venella (Bernalda, MT)
out-of-town sanctuary, votive offering no. 1 (1973)

Female deity of Ionian type, standing, with cylindrical *polos* adorned by three applied wheels; hair rendered in "tongues" on the forehead and *parotides* on the shoulders where four wheels have been applied (two on each part); arms stretched out with small holes at the ends; lower part of quadrangular section, hollow back, with widened supporting base.

OLBRICH 1979, pp. 146 ss., tav. 21, tipo A 99.   A.L.T.

VIII
Statuette of Zeus Aglaos

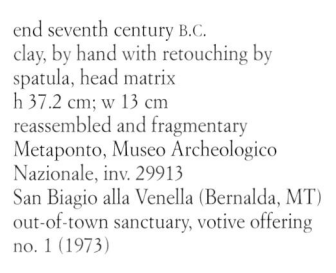

end seventh century B.C.
clay, by hand with retouching by spatula, head matrix
h 37.2 cm; w 13 cm
reassembled and fragmentary
Metaponto, Museo Archeologico Nazionale, inv. 29913
San Biagio alla Venella (Bernalda, MT)
out-of-town sanctuary, votive offering no. 1 (1973)

Zeus, standing, of Daedalid type, with low *polos* decorated by incisions; snail-like curls over the forehead; arms stretched out with small circular hole in the left hand closed in a fist; Dorian peplos narrow at the waist from which the tips of the feet peep out.

PARIBENI 1973, pp. 458 ss., tav. C1; MERTENS-HORN 1992, pp. 91-94, tavv. 24-25.   A.L.T.

82 I

Earthenware bust from a statuette of an armed female deity

second half sixth century B.C.
terra-cotta
h 15.5 cm; max depth 2.9 cm
Paestum, Museo Archeologico Nazionale, inv. 1884
Paestum, southern urban sanctuary

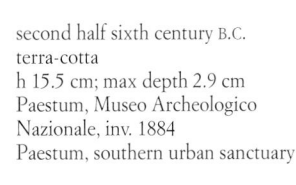

Hollow torso in the rear part. The head surmounted by a low *polos* is conserved; long plaits fall from the nape to the shoulders and chest leaving the breast free. The left arm is stretched forwards while the right one is raised to wave a spear, now lost, probably of metal. The figure is interpreted diversely as Athena *Promachos* or Hera *Hoplosmia*.

SESTIERI, BERTARELLI 1989, p. 32, fig. 17.
    F.L.

82 II see Recent Discoveries

Works on Exhibit

82 III

Earthenware statuette of an enthroned female deity with small horse

mid-sixth century B.C.
painted terra-cotta, matrix
h 37 cm
reassembled and integrated
Paestum, Museo Archeologico Nazionale, inv. 1937
Paestum, from the I votive offering of the southern urban sanctuary

The figure, wearing a *polos* decorated with leaves, clasps a small horse to her chest. The details of the goddess's face, her dress, the throne and the horse are rendered with the colour still clearly visible on the lozenges of her dress. The goddess represents Hera Hippia.

ZANCANI MONTUORO 1961, p. 35, pl. XII, 1; G. GRECO 1992, p. 255, pl. LIV, 4.
F.L.

83 I and II see Recent Discoveries

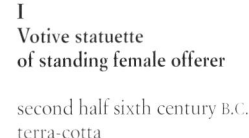

84 I-VIII

I
Votive statuette of standing female offerer

second half sixth century B.C.
terra-cotta
h 17.5 cm
Reggio Calabria, Museo Nazionale inv. 5591
Locri Epizefiri, Sanctuary of Persephone in Mannella district

The figure presents a *peplos* flaring towards the bottom, with unusual small cloak of curved contours on the chest. The arms have been applied separately: the right one is stretched along her side with a small jug in her hand; the left one is bent upwards to hold a vase on her head, of which a stump remains.

SABBIONE 1970, p. 109, fig. 12.
C.S.

II
Votive figure of standing female deity

ca. mid-sixth century B.C.
terra-cotta, by hand, matrix
h 61.5 cm
Reggio Calabria, Museo Nazionale inv. 5804
Locri Epizefiri, Sanctuary of Persephone in Mannella district

The figure, in *peplos* with low *polos* and arms rigidly bent forwards, presents the lower part as elongated and practically cylindrical with a flat, squarish thorax, called "leggio".

ARIAS 1976, pp. 483-487.
C.S.

III
Votive statuette of enthroned goddess

ca. mid-sixth century B.C.
terra-cotta
h 24 cm
Reggio Calabria, Museo Nazionale inv. 5587
Locri Epizefiri, Sanctuary of Persephone in Mannella district

The lower part of the figure and the throne, decorated with applied discs, have been realised very schematically with a plaque worked by hand and bent backwards; the torso with *peplos* and the head with hair divided horizontally on the sides of the face, stylistically deriving from Corinthian models, have been produced with a matrix.

SABBIONE 1970, p. 149, fig. 22.
C.S.

IV
Votive figure of an enthroned goddess

second half sixth century B.C.
terra-cotta
h 59 cm
integrated
Reggio Calabria, Museo Nazionale inv. 5775
Locri Epizefiri, Sanctuary of Persephone in Mannella district

The goddess, seated rigidly with arms along her body on a very schematized throne, is wearing the *peplos* and a cloak with smooth hem which falls right to the ground. On the head is a low *polos* with an applied central disc; hair in long locks over her forehead and long plaits. Strong-structured, ovoidal face.

SABBIONE 1987, pp. 54-55.
C.S.

V
Large votive protome of female deity

second half sixth century B.C.
terra-cotta
h 26.5 cm
Reggio Calabria, Museo Nazionale inv. 5764
Locri Epizefiri, Sanctuary of Persephone in Mannella district

Hair covered with a band, *stephane* and veil which fall laterally behind the ears adorned with big applied earrings. Big face with rounded forms and sculpturally marked features.

BARRA BAGNASCO 1986, pp. 26-27, pl. II (type A I).
C.S.

VI
Large votive protome of female deity

second half sixth century B.C.
terra-cotta
h 28 cm
Reggio Calabria, Museo Nazionale inv. 7569
Locri Epizefiri, Sanctuary of Persephone in Mannella district

Hairstyle with tall *stephane* and applied discs at the top; veil which falls behind the ears adorned by big applied earrings. Wide, rounded spaces in the face; gradual passages above all around the eyes, from the curved arch of the eyebrows and the mouth.

BARRA BAGNASCO 1986, pp. 30-31, pl. IV (type A III).
C.S.

VII
Large votive protome of female deity

second half sixth century B.C.
terra-cotta
h 29.5 cm
Reggio Calabria, Museo Nazionale inv. 5901
Locri Epizefiri, Sanctuary of Persephone in Mannella district

Hairstyle with *stephane* and veil which fall behind the ears, leaving long locks of hair placed around the forehead uncovered. Elongated, ovoidal face, quite heavy.

BARRA BAGNASCO 1986, pp. 56-57, pl. XIV (type B IX).
C.S.

VIII
Large votive protome of female deity

second half sixth century B.C.
terra-cotta
h 23 cm
Reggio Calabria, Museo Nazionale inv. 5570
Locri Epizefiri, Sanctuary of Persephone in Mannella district

Low *polos*; hairstyle of long locks with the three central ones shorter; hair indicated by dense striation; ears with accurately modelled lobes; elongated face of squarish structure developed in depth; high cheekbones; long nose; relatively thin lips.

BARRA BAGNASCO 1986, p. 83, pl. XXXIII (type C XVI).
C.S.

Works on Exhibit

85 I — **Relief of a recumbent person with phiale**

end sixth century B.C.
clay, colour, matrix, the spherical elements of the diadem by hand
31x44.5 cm
Taranto, Museo Archeologico Nazionale, inv. 50367
Taranto, 30.4.1934, Cortivecchie district, Oberdan street corner Minniti (votive offering)

Oval face with hair encircled by a *stephane*. Nude bust, right hand lying on the same knee; the left is holding a *phiale* at chest height. A *himation* is wound around the left forearm and encompasses, as it falls in thick rigid pleats, the lower part of the body lying on a *kline*, of which the depositional plane remains.

LIPPOLIS 1995, p. 112, D.3, g.9.
G.A.C.

---

85 II — **Statuette of a recumbent person on a kline**

fourth century B.C.
clay, slip, colour, matrix, by hand
25x20x7 cm
Taranto, Museo Archeologico Nazionale, inv. 20048
Taranto, 15.7.1919, Cortivecchie district, western side of Regina Elena street, owner D. Acclavio (votive offering)

Lying on a *kline* with a high back and pair of cushions. Curly, disorderly hair tied with a *lemniskos* falling to the left of the head. Oval face, thick curly beard. Nude bust, sides covered by a *himation*.

DE JULIIS 1983, p. 68, fig. 141; LIPPOLIS 1995, pp. 110-111, D.3, g.3.
G.A.C.

---

86 — **Relief with banqueting figure**

end sixth century B.C.
yellow-orange coloured terra-cotta with white slip, details in red colour
h 19.8 cm; w 16.5 cm; t 2.8 cm
Agrigento, Museo Archeologico Regionale, inv. AG 20516 (formerly PA 3467)
Agrigento, from the sanctuary near San Biagio

The relief represents a male figure lying on a *kline*. His left elbow is on a cushion, the corresponding hand holds a cup. Wearing a *himation* which leaves the thorax uncovered and only half of the lower body covered, the banqueter has his head turned to the front; the hair bound by a band rendered with colour which falls onto his shoulders.

GRIFFO 1942, p. 121.
G.C.

---

87 I — **Female protome**

clay
max h 12.5 cm
some parts missing
Syracuse, Museo Archeologico Regionale "Paolo Orsi", inv. 84257
Francavilla in Sicily, votive offering

Female *protome* with veil and diadem, hair parted in the middle and arranged in delicate waves down to the forehead. The face – a narrow oval with a slight smile and almond-shaped eyes greatly elongated and heightened by prominent eyelids – and the precise, uniform rendering of the hairstyle suggest a certain mannerism. Belongs to a stylistically homogeneous group of *protomai* that may be assigned to Naxos.

SPIGO 1987, p. 285 (*Pprot* 18), pl. XXII, 1, complete piece of the same type; UHLENBROCK 1989, pp. 18 ff., figs. 15-20.
E.C.P.

---

87 II — **Female protome**

520–500 B.C.
clay
max h 26 cm; max w 22 cm
parts missing
Syracuse, Museo Archeologico Regionale "Paolo Orsi", inv. 84479
Francavilla in Sicily, votive offering

Female *protome* with veil and diadem, hair arranged in delicate wavy locks and parted in the middle. The very narrow oval face, enlivened by delicate modulation of the areas around the eyes, nose, and lips, is reminiscent of great Athenian sculpture (cf. *kore* no. 674 on the Acropolis).

SPIGO 1987, pp. 287-288 (*PProt*, 20), pl. XXIV, 1, for another piece of the same type.
G.C.

---

87 III — **Female protome**

520–500 B.C.
clay
h 30 cm; max w 21 cm
reconstructed
Syracuse, Museo Archeologico Regionale "Paolo Orsi", inv. 85476
Francavilla in Sicily, votive materials

Female *protome* with veil and diadem. Hair in long curls arranged in locks on the forehead. The sensitive modelling of the face, the proportions and rendering of the physiognomy reflect Attic sculpture of the late sixth century B.C.

SPIGO 1987, p. 288 (*PProt*, 21), n. 61, pl. XXIV, 2; *Sicilia greca*, p. 110, no. 82.
E.C.P.

Works on Exhibit

88

Fragmentary clay kore

510–500 B.C.
clay
parts missing
Syracuse, Museo Archeologico
Regionale "Paolo Orsi", inv. 44158
Agrigento

Female figure dressed in a *chiton* with delicate folds and a transverse *himation*, with a roll of folds along the slanting upper border and a swallow-tail motif around the waist, at the line of fracture. The type of head and folds of the drapery suggest the iconographic-stylistic influence of the Attic *korai* of the late sixth century B.C.

MARCONI 1929b, p. 179, fig. 108 (p. 177).
E.C.P.

89

Bust of female deity

490-480 B.C.
pinkish terra-cotta, white slip
h 23.5 cm; w 19.5 cm; t 10 cm
Agrigento, Museo Archeologico
Regionale, inv. AG 21020
(formerly PA 3445)
Agrigento, 1925 excavations, from the rocky sanctuary near S. Biagio

Bust of Persephone with youthful features and long hair arranged like a ribbon over the forehead and like strings of pearls at the sides of the neck. The goddess was decorated with a diadem, as well as with a necklace: a hole in the centre and two at the sides (that on the left conserved) served to apply, on this last, a *lamina* in precious metal.

MARCONI 1929, p. 182, fig. 115.
G.C.

90

Female clay statuette

mid-sixth century B.C.
clay
h 31 cm
Syracuse, Museo Archeologico
Regionale "Paolo Orsi", inv. 78087
Monte San Mauro in Caltagirone

The body of the figure is a simple plaque: apart from the slight projection of the breast and brief indication of feet, only the head and arms (with forearms outstretched) are sculpted; the dress is completely smooth; a necklace on the breast.

SCHÜRMANN 1989, p. 30, no. 42, with ref.; SZABÓ 1994, pp. 95, 106, 111 ff.
E.C.P.

91

Female statuette

early fifth century B.C.
clay
h 38.5 cm
including the reconstructed base
Syracuse, Museo Archeologico
Regionale "Paolo Orsi", inv. 14314
Grammichele

A female figure with diadem, dressed, like the *korai*, in a cape and *chiton*, with a medium *paryphe* incongruously duplicated (the hem held in the left hand). With the weight on the left leg and the right leg slightly forward, the left arm outstretched, the right hand on the breast and holding a lotus flower.

HIGGINS 1954, pp. 298-299, no. 1089 (pl. 149).
E.C.P.

92 I-III

I
Female protome

ca. 510 B.C.
clay
h 22.4 cm; max w 18.1 cm
two holes for hanging
reconstructed, traces of polychrome
Syracuse, Museo Archeologico
Regionale "Paolo Orsi", inv. 21301
Gela, *Thesmophorion* of Bitalemi

This *protome*, one of the finest examples of the production at Archaic Gela, belongs to the so-called "Meander Polos type" identified by Uhlenbrock, defined thus because of the characteristic decoration of the *polos*. The shape of the face – large and triangular, with almond-shaped, almost horizontal, eyes, a flat-bridged short nose, and delicately modelled lips – is a physiognomy seen in the Attic and Ionian *korai* of the late sixth century B.C.

UHLENBROCK 1988, pp. 44-45, 68, no. 19, pl. 2 a-b.
E.C.P.

II
Female protome

ca. 500 B.C.
clay
h 10.5 cm
one hole for hanging
Syracuse, Museo Archeologico
Regionale "Paolo Orsi", inv. 21319
Gela, *Thesmophorion* of Bitalemi

This *protome* belongs to the "Puffy Hair type" as named by Uhlenbrock, consisting of models in a reduced form, characterized by voluminous hair, simplification of the sculpting of the face and of the eyes, with flattened eyeballs.

UHLENBROCK 1988, p. 81, no. 28 a (cf. pp. 86-87, pl. 40 c-d).
E.C.P.

III
Female protome

mid-fifth century B.C.
clay
reconstructed
Syracuse, Museo Archeologico
Regionale "Paolo Orsi", inv. 21431
Gela, *Thesmophorion* of Bitalemi

Female figure standing with a baby in her arms, completely enveloped, along with the child, in a cloak, in a style first seen in Sicily (Syracuse, Selinus, and Gela) in the fifth century B.C. The theme of the *kourotrophos* recurs in numerous examples of diverse types, among the votive materials of the sanctuary at Bitalemi, probably through a connection with the chthonic cult practiced there.

ORSI 1906, 703 ff., fig. 529, HADZISTE-LIOU, PRICE 1978, p. 54, ill. 588
E.C.P.

93		**Female votive mask** sixth century B.C. clay h 50 cm; w at the base 46 cm Gela, Museo Archeologico, inv. 7369 Gela, out-of-town sanctuary of Predio Sola	Large female mask, with diademmed head, covered by the veil which falls at the sides of the ears to the shoulders. The hair is arranged over the forehead in thick waves and the chest is adorned by two rows of pendants (five taurine *protomai* in the first row and five spherical drop pendants in the second). It is the largest and most complete votive mask of Sicily, typologically comparable to examples from Agrigento and Gela itself.	ORLANDINI 1963, 19-21, no. 31, figg. 11-13. R.P.
94		**Large earthenware protome** 500-475 B.C. clay mixed with lava debris h max 29 cm; l 41 cm Gela, Museo Archeologico Gela, acropolis, from the bottom of a cistern	Horse head pertaining to an equestrian statue, probably supported by a sphinx. The head, characterized by the plasticism of the muzzle and accentuated realism, is a masterpiece of Siceliot coroplastic. The dating is confirmed by comparisons with the horses that appear on Geloan didrachms.	ORLANDINI 1958, pp. 123 ff., pl. III. R.P.
95 I		**Inscribed lithic herm** mid-fifth century B.C. tufa h 62 cm; max w 41 cm very corroded head Palermo, Museo Archeologico "A. Salinas", inv. 5675 Selinunte, Malophoros Sanctuary	Herm of the god Meilichios. On the main face it presents the inscription in Greek characters: *ho* Μιλίχιος τᾶ- ς πατριᾶς τᾶν h(ε)ϱ- μιō παιδōν καὶ τᾶν Εὐκλέα παί- δ(ō)ν. It is about a votive offering of the noble group of the daughters of Hermias and the daughters of Eukles.	MANNI PIRAINO 1973, pp. 98-100, no. 68, pl. XLI; MOSCATI-DI STEFANO 1991, p. 43, fig. 35. A.V.
95 II		**Female protome** 550-525 B.C. clay, executed with fresh matrix hole for hanging it h 8.5 cm Palermo, Museo Archeologico "A. Salinas", inv. 111 Selinunte, Malophoros Sanctuary	Hair arranged in two symmetrical and compact bands, finely incised. Elongated almond-shaped eyes with well drawn eyelids; ears executed decoratively; thick, well modelled lips.	GABRICI 1927, 217, pl. XXXIX, 6; *Sicilia greca*, p. 113, no. 96. A.V.
95 III	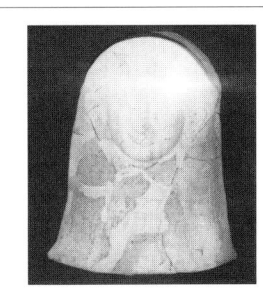	**Female protome** 530-520 B.C. clay, slight traces of colour h 25.5 cm Palermo, Museo Archeologico "A. Salinas", inv. 130 Selinunte, Malophoros Sanctuary	Oval face with prominent chin; long almond-shaped eyes with thin, well modelled eyelids; fleshy mouth. The head is surmounted by a tall *stephane* and a long veil which leaves the ears uncovered; these are rendered decoratively and adorned with discoidal formed earrings. Two small holes on the left ear.	Unpublished. A.V.
95 IV		**Female protome** 525-500 B.C. clay, internally hollow h 19.5 cm Palermo, Museo Archeologico "A. Salinas", inv. 116 Selinunte, Malophoros Sanctuary	Head surmounted by *polos* and long veil falling onto the chest. Hair of dense waves and with small arc motifs over the forehead. Big ears decorated with disc earrings. Irregular face due to a defect in the matrix, with elongated almond-shaped eyes, prominent nose and lips of a rectilinear cut.	*Sicilia greca*, p. 113, no. 98. A.V

95 V		**Standing female figure** end sixth century B.C. clay, executed with double matrix and smoothed by spatula h 12.2 cm fragmentary Palermo, Museo Archeologico "A. Salinas", inv. 225 Selinunte, Malophoros Sanctuary	The head is surmounted by a *polos* and diadem; the hair is arranged in rows of pearly curls over the forehead and falls in long plaits onto the chest and in a compact mass, marked by horizontal furrowing, onto the shoulders. Protruding bulbous eyes; widely curving eyebrows; pronounced nose; slightly curving lips. She wears a pleated *chiton* and a *himation*.	Unpublished.	A.V.
95 VI		**Standing female figure** 525-500 B.C. clay, executed with single matrix (worn out) and smoothed by spatula vent on the back h 25 cm Palermo, Museo Archeologico "A. Salinas", inv. 229 Selinunte, Malophoros Sanctuary	The hair, arranged in a compact mass on the forehead and tied by a *stephane*, falls to the shoulders in long plaits. Oval face with almond-shaped eyes; pronounced nose; twisted mouth due to a defect in the matrix. She is wearing *chiton* and *himation*, The right arm is bent onto the chest and the hand is holding an object; the left one is close to the body and the hand is lifting a piece of the dress.	GABRICI 1927, 262, pl. LXVII, 6.	A.V.
95 VII		**Standing female figure** end sixth century clay h 22.5 cm Palermo, Museo Archeologico "A. Salinas", inv. 21920/1 Selinunte, Malophoros Sanctuary	The figure is encompassed by a long *himation* which covers the blue coloured *chiton*. the right arm is clasped to the chest, while the left, stretched out, is holding the dress. Robust neck and face.	TUSA 1971, pp. 213-214, pl. XVa; *Sicilia greca*, p. 164, no. 325.	A.V.
95 VIII		**Goddess enthroned with a panther** second half sixth century B.C. clay, executed by matrix, finished by spatula, internally hollow, vent in the base; traces of colour (white on the *himation*, red *chiton* with black bands) h 20 cm Palermo, Museo Archeologico "A. Salinas", inv. 10302 Selinunte, Malophoros Sanctuary	Compact hairstyle in a smooth band over the forehead, tied by a tall *polos* with a long veil. Oval, rather full face; well marked eyebrow arcs; very elongated eyes; prominent chin and nose; small fleshy mouth. The forms of the breast are barely hinted at. A small panther is crouching in her lap, rendered plastically. The feet of the figure, whose triangular tips can be seen, are on a low stool.	Unpublished.	A.V.
95 IX		**Enthroned female statuette** 500-490 B.C. clay h 26 cm Palermo, Museo Archeologico "A. Salinas", inv. 2 Selinunte, Malophoros Sanctuary	The figure has a tall *polos* on her head. The hair is divided into two symmetrical bands over the forehead, held by a *stephane*. Very elongated oval face with protruding eyes and robust chin. The hands lie on the knees. The chest is adorned by three necklaces with pendants in the form of acorns and medallions with *gorgoneion*; the ends of the necklaces are fixed onto the shoulders by disc clasps. The throne is also adorned with four *gorgoneion* medallions.	GABRICI 1927, 272, pl. LIX, 7.	A.V.
95 X		**Enthroned female statuette** end sixth century clay h 24.5 cm Palermo, Museo Archeologico "A. Salinas", inv. 9 Selinunte, Malophoros Sanctuary	A tall *polos* is on the head of the figure. The hair is divided into two symmetrical bands over the forehead, falling in a compact mass on the sides of the neck. Elongated face; oblique eyes, pointed nose and chin; mouth stretched according to the archaic scheme. Flattened body, dressed in a *chiton* and rigid overdress, adorned by a necklace with three pendants. Two disc *fibulae* are on the shoulders. The arms are not expressed; the feet rest on a stool.	GABRICI 1927, cc. 293-295.	A.V.

95 XI

Enthroned female statuette

500-490 B.C.
clay
h 21.5 cm
Palermo, Museo Archeologico
"A. Salinas", inv. 152
Selinunte, Malophoros Sanctuary

The head is encircled by a *stephane*. The hair, divided into two symmetrical bands over the forehead, is rendered by parallel furrows and falls to the shoulders in two compact masses. Oval, rather irregular face; mouth stretched according to the Archaic scheme. She is wearing a pleated *chiton* and a smooth overdress.
The chest is adorned by three necklaces with pendants in the form of acorns, fixed at the shoulders by double palmette clasps. The wrists are adorned by three armillas.

GABRICI 1927, 272, pl. LIX, 4; *Sicilia greca*, p. 113, no. 99. A.V.

95 XII

Enthroned female statuette

end sixth-beginning fifth century B.C.
clay
h 33 cm
Palermo, Museo Archeologico
"A. Salinas", inv. 266
Selinunte, Malophoros Sanctuary

Lacking forearms which were applied. The head is covered with a veil. The hair, arranged over the forehead in a band of narrow locks, falls in a compact and wavy mass down the sides of the neck. Oval face, almond-shaped eyes, robust nose, strongly curved mouth and prominent chin.
She is wearing a pleated *chiton* and smooth overdress; two necklaces with pendants in the form of acorns and discs and a central hanging crescent-shape, are fixed to the humerus by discoidal *fibulae*.

GABRICI 1927, 269, pl. LVI, 2. A.V.

95 XIII

Female head from bust

mid-sixth century B.C.
clay, internally hollow
h 12.5 cm
Palermo, Museo Archeologico
"A. Salinas", inv. 37352
Selinunte, Malophoros Sanctuary

Low *polos* on the head; hair divided into two compact bands over the forehead and gathered into long, narrow, latticework plaits falling onto the chest. Elongated oval face. The eyebrow curves are well marked; large protruding eyes with curved upper and straight lower; corroded nose; fleshy lips drawn with the typical Archaic curve; prominent chin.

Unpublished. A.V.

95 XIV

Shaped balsam-container

550-525 B.C.
clay, executed with double matrix and retouched with spatula
h 25.4 cm
Palermo, Museo Archeologico
"A. Salinas", inv. 128
Selinunte, Malophoros Sanctuary

Standing female figure. The head is encircled by a *stephane* which supports the edge of the balsam-container, in the form of a *kalathos*. The hair falls to the shoulders in long, knotted plaits. The elongated face is characterised by slender eyes and big ears. She is wearing a *chiton poderes* and *himation* with dense pleats. A dove is in her left hand.

GABRICI 1927, 211, pl. XXXVIII, 1; *Sicilia greca*, p. 113, no. 97. A.V.

95 XV

Shaped balsam-container

end sixth century B.C.
clay, executed with double matrix and smoothed by spatula
h 22.3 cm
Palermo, Museo Archeologico
"A. Salinas", inv. 131
Selinunte, Malophoros Sanctuary

Standing female figure. The rim is shaped like a *kalathos* on the head. The hair forms two swollen bands over the forehead and falls in long, smooth plaits onto the bust in a compact mass, in horizontal bands down the back. She is wearing a *chiton poderes* and *himation* with dense pleats. Arms stretched out and hands closed.

GABRICI 1927, 213, pl. XXXVIII, 10. A.V.

95 XVI

Shaped balsam-container

end sixth century B.C.
clay, executed with double matrix and refinished by spatula, traces of polychrome
h 25.6 cm
Palermo, Museo Archeologico
"A. Salinas", inv. 134
Selinunte, Malophoros Sanctuary

Standing female figure. The head is encircled by a *stephane*. The hair is styled in long, knotted plaits. Oval face with almond-shaped eyes and well modelled eyebrows. She is wearing a *chiton poderes* and *himation*. A dove is in her left hand.

GABRICI 1927, 211, pl. XXXVIII, 4. A.V.

Works on Exhibit

95 XVII

Female head

500-475 B.C.
clay
h 12.5 cm
Palermo, Museo Archeologico
"A. Salinas", inv. 439
Selinunte, Malophoros Sanctuary

Oval face with well defined features: prominent chin, robust neck. The hairstyle, especially elaborate, is arranged in rows of snail-like curls; the diadem, fragmentary, was decorated with discoidal elements. Pearl-like earrings.

GABRICI 1927, c. 288, pl. LXX, 2-2a; *Stile severo*, p. 285, no. 118. A.V

96

Statuette of enthroned female deity

510-500 B.C.
orange coloured terra-cotta with sandy coloured slip
h 29.5 cm
Agrigento, Museo Archeologico Regionale, inv. AG 1145
Agrigento, 1953-55 excavations, sector to the south west of the Sanctuary of the Chthonic Deities

The statuette, which can be attributed to the iconographic, so-called Athena Lindia type, has a *polos* on the head, shoes on the feet and is wearing a *chiton* with false sleeves held at the shoulders by big *fibulae* and at the sides by the deity's hands. The dress is decorated by three superimposed rows of pendants (heads of bulls, rams, drums, heads of Silenus).

DE MIRO 1994, fig. 61 and p. 55. G.C.

97

Little altar with scene of a zoomachy

late sixth century B.C.
clay, sculpted by hand
h 21 cm; max l 51.2 cm
depth 8.8 cm
reconstructed, with some parts missing
Syracuse, Museo Archeologico Regionale "Paolo Orsi", inv. 18670
Centuripe, from the necropolis area

This representation, in high relief, consists of a smooth base and an upper border outlined by an astragal. The theme, auguring good fortune in Archaic imagery, is of a fight between a lion and a bull, with the bull falling onto its forelegs and succumbing to the attack of the lion, which is sinking its teeth into the bull's neck.

VAN DER MEIJDEN 1993, pp. 42-44, 54 ff., 257, Tk 44, with preceding bibl., and p. 373 for more documents. E.C.P.

98 I

Little clay altar

550–540 B.C.
clay
h 34.8 cm; w 52.2 cm
depth 24.5 cm
well-preserved polychrome
Paris, Louvre Museum, inv. CA 5956
Sicily

At the top and at the bottom: curves, ovals, tongue shapes. On the short sides the following scenes are painted: *side A*) Circe, nude, standing (in the pose of a *kouros*), stirs a potion in front of one of the companions of Ulysses (who has a human body and a pig's head); *side B*) Heracles battling a centaur; *front*) fight between Heracles and Triton, who is characterized by fish that he holds in his hand and by a multiform body (human torso, serpentine lower limbs, and fish tail). In relief, with details painted, figures placed paratactically.

VAN DER MEIJDEN 1993, pp. 81, 83-87, 115, 302-302, *MY 24* with preceding bibl. E.C.P.

98 II

Shaped earthenware support

sixth century B.C.
clay
h 15 cm; w 24 cm; depth 13 cm
Gela, Museo Archeologico
Gela, sacred area of the ex-railway station

Low, cubic support. On the front is the figure of a crouching demon or *telamon* with upraised arms. The face is of the mask type.

DE MIRO 1986, p. 395, pl. VIII, 1. R.P.

98 III

Little altar

550-530 B.C.
clay, female figure executed separately and fixed to the wall
h 56 cm; l 37 cm
fragmentary
Gela, Museo Archeologico
Gela, sacred area of the ex-railway station

Large fragment of earthenware *arula* with figured scene squared off by projecting frame. On the left a female figure with open wings, in the design of the "race on one's knees", is wearing a *chiton* with *paryphe*, which leaves the left breast uncovered. With the left arm she is hugging to her chest a young man depicted in 3/4, with his face facing to the front and short *polos* on his head. They are possibly Gorgon and Chrysaor, or Eos and Kephalos.

DE MIRO 1986, pp. 393-394, pl. VI. R.P.

99	**Little altar with the struggle of Heracles and Acheleo** fifth century B.C. terra-cotta h 27 cm Reggio Calabria, Museo Nazionale inv. 5115 Locri Epizefiri, necropolis in Lucifero district, 1956 excavations	The relief scene on the front side is framed within two Ionic columns. Heracles, characterised by the club, bow and quiver hanging on the tree to the left, beats Acheloüs, represented as a bull with a human head. The *arula* was reused in the structure of a fourth-century B.C. tomb.	Novaco Lofaro 1966, pp. 131-140.	C.S.
100	**Small earthenware pillar with Greek epigraph** sixth century B.C. terra-cotta, fragmented h 38.5 cm; max w 13 cm; max t 6.5 cm Naples, Museo Archeologico Nazionale, inv. 112880 San Mauro Forte	The small pillar is pyramidal in shape and rests on a small base with mouldings. The inscription, in late Archaic Achaean alphabet, arranged from the top to the bottom on the four faces, carries a dedication in verse to Heracles. The author of the object and dedication is the potter Nikomachus who asks to have great fame among men in exchange for the god.	Guarducci 1967, III, p. 556.	T.G.
101 I	**Matrix of small female statue** second half sixth century B.C. brown coloured terra-cotta h 11.4 cm; w 7.3 cm Agrigento, Museo Archeologico Regionale, inv. S3 Agrigento, 1927 excavations, to the west of the Sanctuary of the Chthonic Deities, outside the walls	Female deity with *polos* on her head and wearing a peplos belted at the waist and with an *apoptygma*. The body and head of the goddess, who has long hair in wavy locks falling behind her shoulders, are depicted totally frontally; the arms are glued to her sides.	Marconi 1929c, pp. 580 ff.	G.C.
101 II	**Matrix of a mask of a female deity** third quarter sixth century B.C. yellow-orange coloured terra-cotta h 38 cm; w 28 cm; t 14.3 cm Agrigento, Museo Archeologico Regionale, inv. C239 Provenance unknown, from the collections of the ex Museo Civico of Agrigento	Earthenware matrix of mask of a female deity executed in a mould, of large dimensions. The goddess was veiled with her forehead adorned with a *stephane* and earrings.	De Miro 1994, p. 65, fig. 62.	G.C.
102	**Breastplate** 599-575 B.C. silver and gold, *repoussé* 7.3x27.5x0.3 cm Sibari (CS), Museo Nazionale Archeologico della Sibaritide inv. St. 44241 Sibari, Stombi	Crescent-shaped *lamina* with small, smooth tongue of triangular form at the left end and formed of three superimposed layers: two in silver and the third, external, in gold. Borders are edged by a series of embossed tongues with concave surfaces; central band decorated by eight alternating couples of a chain of palmettes with seven petals and opposing open lotus flowers. The pairs are linked by volute ribbons and united by a rounded central element.	Guzzo 1973, pp. 65-74.	S.L.
103	**Pendant** sixth century B.C. gold, *repoussé* 8.3x6.2 cm Bari, Museo Archeologico, inv. 1659 Noicattaro (BA)	Of trapezoid form, a hare running on a row of five rosettes is represented in the central part defined on three sides with a guilloche motif; on the border, at the top, three ribbed tongues have been fixed for hooking it to the upper part, not conserved, destined to be hung up. On the lower edge three hanging lotus flowers are fixed, decorated naturalistically.	De Juliis 1983, p. 139, pl. XXXI; Guzzo 1993, type VIII A1, pp. 75, 233.	M.L.

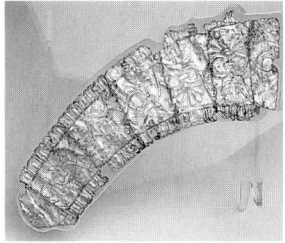

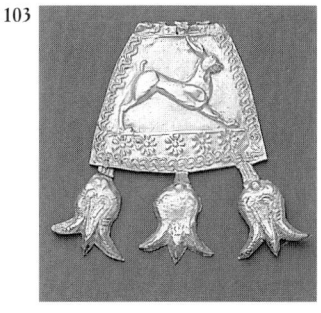

Works on Exhibit

104

Gold necklace with female protome pendants

end sixth-beginning fifth century B.C.
gold, lamination, bean motif, *repoussé*
h heads 2 cm
Taranto, Museo Archeologico Nazionale, inv. 6429
Ruvo (BA), "Caldarola acquisition"

Forty-three biconical beads, decorated with bean motif; six female *protome* pendants with a horizontal cylindrical passage in the upper part. Front facing heads with tongued hair, marked by short horizontal dashes.

Guzzo 1993, pp. 52, 191, C II A 1 (necklace), pp. 71-73, 228, P V A 1 (pendants).
M.G.

105

Female protomes (eight)

end sixth-first quarter fifth century B.C.
sillver, gold, lamination, *repoussé* gilding
h from 3.4 to 4 cm
Taranto, Museo Archeologico Nazionale, inv. 12024-12031
Taranto, from a tomb, no further information

Fully front-facing heads; hair in steps over the forehead with plaits to the sides of the head: *stephane* with widened arch; full oval; frontal ears drawn in detail; slightly oblique almond-shaped eyes; short, straight nose; lips raised at the edges. A small female figure, leonine *protome* and two acorns belong to the same group of findings, worked in the same techniques and with the same materials.

Guzzo 1993, L IV A 1, pp. 106-108, 266, 332.
M.G.

106 *see Recent Discoveries*

107

Figured amber

amber, engraved
h 18 cm; w 9.5 cm; max t 4.5 cm
London, British Museum
inv. 18.651.3.46
Armento?

Kneeling on the right is a bearded satyr; on the left a maenad covered with an ample *himation* is caught in an apparently vigorous movement with her right leg lifted and the left depicted in the act of jumping. A deer is between them.

Strong 1966, pp. 61 ff.; Negroni Catacchio 1989, pp. 659 ff.
G.L'A.

108

Necklace

end fifth century B.C.
gold
l 13 cm
Matera, Museo Ridola, inv. 338225
Lavello, tomb 955

Four bunches of grapes in double *lamina* and decorated surfaces, with eyelets for hanging. Seven ornaments in the form of acorns with surfaces partially decorated with granulation and eyelet for hanging. Two biconical ornaments decorated with horizontal incised bean motif. Eight cylindrical ornaments with embossed decoration.

Donne, p. 127, no. 170, p. 154, fig. 170.
R.C.

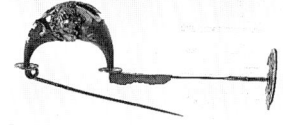

109 I-IV

I. Fibula with leech bow and rectangular laminated decoration

second half fifth century B.C.
silver and gold, lamination, *repoussé*
h 4.6 cm; l 14.9 cm
nearly entirely reassembled
Melfi, Museo Archeologico Nazionale inv. 52840
Pisciolo (Melfi), tomb 43

Double valve bow decorated with a gilded rectangular *lamina* in double spirals on dual register, inside boundary knurling. On the lateral bands, a braided drop motif inside bean motif. Two small discs with knurled edge and spirals are hooked to the ends. Long rectangular pin with incised hour-glass motifs; terminal biconical element decorated with a rosette.

Tocco 1971, p. 120, pl. XLIX; Guzzo 1994, p. 31, fig. 6.
M.L.V.

II Fibula with leech bow and rectangular laminated decoration

second half fifth century B.C.
silver and gold, lamination, *repoussé* fragmentary
h 4.7 cm; reconstructed l 14 cm
Melfi, Museo Archeologico Nazionale inv. 52838
Pisciolo (Melfi), tomb 43

Same type and decoration as *fibula*.

Tocco 1971, p. 120.
M.L.V.

III Fibula with leech bow and rectangular laminated decoration

second half fifth century B.C.
silver and gold, lamination, *repoussé*
h 4.5 cm; reconstructed l 15 cm
partially reassembled
Melfi, Museo Archeologico Nazionale inv. 52830
Pisciolo (Melfi), tomb 48

Same type and decoration as *fibula*.

Tocco 1971, p. 126.
M.L.V

IV Fibula with double bow and pin ending in duck protome

second half fifth century B.C.
silver, cast
h 3.2 cm; reconstructed l 14.7 cm
recomposed, fragmentary pin
Melfi, Museo Archeologico Nazionale inv. 51448, 51473
Pisciolo (Melfi), tomb 48

Double broken bow with central thread of *godron* and small globes with the edge knurled and the two bows soldered. Long rectangular pin decorated with incised hour-glass motifs ending in duck *protome* with incised rhomboid motifs and eyes like small globes. Double winding spring.

Tocco 1971, p. 125, pl. LIII; Guzzo 1994, p. 31, fig. 8.
M.L.V.

Works on Exhibit

110

Pair of plait holders

fifth century B.C.
gold
h 2.5 cm; diam. 6.6 cm
Melfi, Museo Archeologico Nazionale
inv. 52841-2
Pisciolo (Melfi), tomb 43

Tubular *lamina* with bent end decorated in filigree and on the upper border by two bands with ribbon meanders bordered by concentric lines.

Tocco in *Popoli anellenici*, p. 121.
R.C.

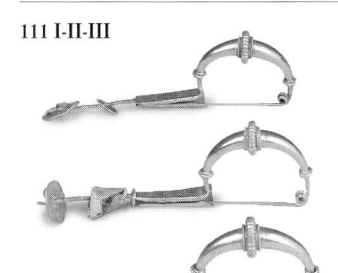

111 I-II-III

I
Fibula

within first half fifth century B.C.
gold, lamination
h 3.5 cm; l 11.2 cm; l bow 4.2 cm
Potenza, Museo Archeologico Provinciale, inv. 176/3604
Banzi, ditch tomb (1963 excavations)

Fibula with simple enlarged bow, smooth, tripartite by a knurled row between two discs. Rectilinear, filiform tongue connected to the bow by a double spiral spring. Long pin with *apophysis*, bounded by mobile discs with braided edges, of different diameters. The pin is decorated on the upper face by two series of broken lines converging on the centre divided by triangular motifs.

II
Fibula

within first half fifth century B.C.
gold, lamination
h 3.2 cm; l 11 cm; l bow 4.3 cm
Potenza, Museo Archeologico Provinciale, inv. 177/3605
Banzi, ditch tomb (1963 excavations)

Same type and decoration as *fibula* inv. 176/3604.

III
Fibula

within first half fifth century B.C.
gold, lamination
h 3 cm; l 11 cm; l bow 4.3 cm
h cm 3; l cm 11
Potenza, Museo Archeologico Provinciale, inv. 178/3606
Banzi, ditch tomb (1963 excavations)

Same type and decoration as *fibula* inv. 176/3604: the pin's mobile discs enclose a small bone cylinder.

Guzzo 1993, pp. 22-23, p. 156, figs. 1-2.
A.B.

112

Mesonfalica phiale

end fifth century B.C.
silver
h 3-3.5 cm; diam. 17.3 cm
Melfi, Museo Archeologico Nazionale
inv. 331981
Lavello, tomb 599

Body with crushed cup, rounded walls at the bottom, short edge bent inwards. A second *lamina* with *repoussé* decoration in the perimeter band with a circle of palmettes and nine alternating leaves and lotus flowers, included between two rows of points in relief, is above the *omphalos*.

Forentum, II, 1991, p. 37, pl. XIV, figs. 53-54.
R.C.

113

Bronze horseman

560-550 B.C.
bronze
h 25.5 cm; l 27 cm
London, British Museum
inv. GRA 1904.7-3.1
Grumento

Horseman with Corinthian helmet and short tunic, horse walking, incised anatomical details.

Jantzen 1937, pp. 26 ff., p. 46; Walters 1951, pl. I.
G.L'A.

114 *see Recent Discoveries*

115

Helmet

sixth century B.C.
laminated bronze
max h 27 cm; w 19.7 cm; depth 29 cm
Policoro, Museo Nazionale della Siritide, inv. ?
Chiaromonte (Pz), Sotto la Croce district, tomb 170

Helmet of Corinthian type. Eyebrow arch executed in relief and lengthened with a curve to the sides; the borders were defined by a band of incised dashes then cut separately. It presents a pair of large curved *alae* in *lamina* cut out and soldered to the cup. It was originally equipped with a central *lophos*.

Bottini in *Armi*, pp. 71 ff.
S.B.

687

116		**Helmet** fifth century B.C. bronze, lamination h 43 cm; diam. 21 cm Karlsruhe, Badisches Landesmuseum inv. F432 Canosa	Holed eyes, cut out nose protector, joined cheek pieces. Incised decoration of a lion on the left and a bull on the right.	A. BOTTINI in *Antike Helme*, p. 135, no. 4, type C. G.L'A.

117 *see Recent Discoveries*

118 I		**Shield** 599-575 B.C. bronze, *lamina*, hammering, *repoussé* diam. 86 cm; t 0.1-0.9 cm Bari, Museo Archeologico, inv. 5554 Noicattaro (Ba), Calcara district, tomb IV discovered 16.5.1905	Formed of a smooth spherical segment fixed by nails to a leather support; the border is decorated by a multiple guilloche motif with intervening dots. The arm harness of anatomical form, with a row of scarabs on the joints, *lamina* bands for fastening decorated with mythological subjects within metope-like squares, has also been conserved.	NISTA 1978, pp. 15-16; DE JULIIS 1983, p. 117, pl. 72:1; CAHN 1989, p. 16. M.L.
118 II		**Large belt** 599-575 B.C. bronze, *lamina*, *repoussé* 102x12.5 cm; t 0.2 cm Bari, Museo Archeologico, inv. 5559 Noicattaro (Ba), Calcara district, tomb IV discovered 18.5.1905	Decorated with a continuous frieze of *quadrigae* galloping, driven by a charioteer with short loin-cloth and stretched to spur on the horses with the *kentron*. In the empty spaces between the horses hooves, dogs chasing wild boar have been depicted. The frieze is bound by a Doric *kyma*; along the upper edge a row of small holes indicate the fastening of the *lamina* to the leather support. A rectangular plaque reinforces the belt from the in-	side, having been broken in ancient times. NISTA 1978, pp. 26-29, pl. XIX; ROLLEY 1990, pp. 187-188. M.L.
119		**Hydria of Graechwill** 570 B.C. bronze, cast h 57.2 cm; diam. rim 28.3 cm reassembled and integrated Berne, Musée d'Histoire, inv. 11620 Magna Graecia	Trumpet foot, swollen ovoidal body; neck of concave profile; out-turned lip. The lateral small stick handles figure lions and sphinxes at the joints, while the vertical handle is made of a *Potnia Theron* surrounded by lions, dogs and birds, realised in the round.	ZIMMERMANN 1987, pp. 244-246. K.Z.
120	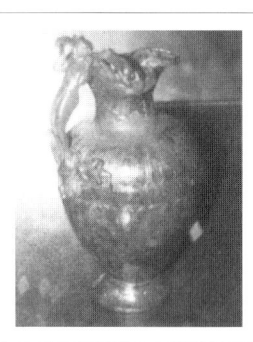	**Bronze oinochoe** end sixth-beginning fifth century B.C. bronze, cast, relief bead work and incised phytomorphic motifs, handle cast separately h 18.5 cm; w 9.5 cm Taranto, Museo Nazionale, inv. 134913 Ugento (LE), 13-7-1970 Salentina road no. 52, tomb 2	Trilobed rim with squared lip; ovoid body with bead work on two registers separated by a band with incised guilloche motif; conical trunk foot decorated with petals and lotus flowers incised between rows of pearls; the handle in the form of a *kouros* with feet resting on a *gorgoneion*, between two rams, and the arms raised high to keep back two lions.	LO PORTO 1970-1971, pp. 116-119, pl. XLVII, A-B; ROLLEY 1991, pp. 194-195. G.M.
121		**Hydria** 580–570 B.C. bronze, border, handles and feet cast separately and welded on h 42 cm; max diam. 34 cm entire diam. border 17 cm the shoulder reconstructed incorrectly Syracuse, Museo Archeologico Regionale "Paolo Orsi" Gela, necropolis district, Spinasanta tomb V (1931)	Horizontal handles with spiral decoration of birds' heads; vertical handle with two serpents at the top, linear decoration, and a lower spiral decoration attachment ornamented by a fine female *protome* of sub-Daedalic conception. It belongs to the so-called Telesstas group.	ROLLEY 1982, pp. 32 ff., no. 3, figs. 127-130; GAUER 1991, pp. 99-100, and more bibl. E.C.P.

122

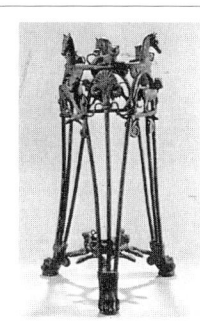

Bronze tripod

mid-sixth century B.C.
bronze, cast
h 75.4 cm
Berlin, Staatliche Museen
zu Berlin Preussischer Kulturbesitz
Antikensammlung, inv. F768
Metaponto

Tripod decorated with *protomai* and figures of animals, palmettes and lotus flowers.

JANTZEN 1991, p. 27, no. 14.   G.L'A.

123

Bronze lebes

mid-sixth century B.C.
bronze
fused *protomai* with engraved retouching
h 21.5 cm; max diam. 53.7 cm; border ext. diam. 41.5 cm; int. diam. 35.4 cm
reconstructed
Berlin, Staatliche Museen
zu Berlin Preussischer Kulturbesitz
Antikensammlung, inv. 8600
Lentini, necropolis (1883–1884)

Probably used as an urn for ashes, it has an echinoform shape. Four rams' heads are welded onto the border; they are alike, but with variations in detail, most notably in the fourth, perhaps made by a different sculptor, though from the same workshop. The adoption of a ram's *protome* instead of the more common one of lions or griffins, and the special style of drawing, lead one to suppose that this *lebes* was produced locally.

JANTZEN 1937, pp. 54, 57-58, no. 5; DE MIRO 1976, p. 68, figs. 3, 5   E.C.P.

124

Mesomphalos phiale

beginning sixth century B.C.
bronze, cast
h 6.7 cm; diam. 25 cm
Palermo, Museo Archeologico
"A. Salinas", inv. 12081/3
Castellazzo di Poggioreale (Trapani)

The external surface is incised with guilloche motif and impressed dots on the edge; three galloping horses, finely decorated, are on the bowl. On the bottom are various floreal fillers. A ring of bead work frames the very prominent *omphalos*.

DI STEFANO 1972b, p. 244c, fig. 8; *Sicilia greca*, p. 25, no. 322.   A.V.

125

Cast-out phiale with surface in rilief

seventh century B.C.
bronze, *repoussé* decoration
h 2.6 cm; diam. 14.5 cm
Syracuse, Museo Archeologico
Regionale "Paolo Orso", inv. 23306
Gela, La Paglia necropolis (1903)

Great central rosette of six petals, with a raised central *omphalos* rendered by a triple strand, bordered by a band of small tablets. The main decoration consists of four pairs of animals (a bull and a horse) faced by a lone bull.

VAGNETTI 1972, pp. 198-199, pl. II, 2.   E.C.P.

126

Outlined applique with figures

ca. 530 B.C.
bronze, hollow behind, tube with a circular attachment behind the head
h 32.5 cm
Syracuse, Museo Archeologico
Regionale "Paolo Orsi"
Camarina, necropolis

Applique for a piece of furniture or a vase in the form of a female figure, with the arms raised in the act of holding up a palm in relief on a moulded plate. The figure wears a *chiton*, with a central *paryphe* and heavy folds along the legs, and a cloak whose two borders fall along the sides of the body.

RIZZA, DE MIRO 1985, p. 209, fig. 219.   E.C.P.

127

Patera with shaped handle

fifth century B.C.
bronze
h 5 cm; diam. 30 cm; l of the grip 18 cm
Melfi, Museo Archeologico Nazionale
inv. 50392
Melfi, Chiuchiari, tomb F

Thin, slightly outward turning border distinguished by notching; body with convex profile, wide bottom. The handle in the form of Archaic *kouros* with raised arm, presents, higher up, an attachment shaped like a volute capital with palmettes coming off like a fan; lower down, an attachment shaped like a palmette.

TOCCO in *Popoli anellenici*, p. 104.   R.C.

Works on Exhibit

128		**Handle of patera** 530-500 B.C. bronze, cast, fragmentary l 25.8 cm; w 10.9 cm Metaponto, Museo Archeologico Nazionale, inv. 123226 San Biagio alla Venella (Bernalda, MT) out-of town sanctuary	Handle in the form of a *kouros* covered by a loin-cloth and with arms raised to hold a couple of small crouching rams; head of ram on the base; palmette coming from the volute of the juncture with the bowl.	ORLANDINI 1983, p. 377, fig. 386. A.L.T.
129		**Bronze patera with shaped handle** 500-490 B.C. bronze l 50.2 cm Agrigento, Museo Archeologico Regionale, inv. AG 11406 Monte Adranone, tomb 3 of the southern necropolis	Bronze patera of hemispherical bowl with hanging ring and handle shaped in the form of a *kouros*. The juncture of the handle and *patera* presents two palmettes placed symmetrically at the sides of a double volute; a double volute surmounted by a palmette decorates the opposite end. The *kouros* of the handle is nude and has long hair; his arms are raised and his hands, with the palms opened frontally, correspond to the palmettes of the juncture.	PUGLIESE CARRATELLI, FIORENTINI, p. 123, figs. 137a-b. G.C.
130		**Applique of siren protome** 570-550 B.C. bronze h 12 cm; w 10.5 cm London, British Museum, inv. BR 495 Blacas Collection	*Applique* pertaining to the juncture of the handle of a big basin; it represents a winged goddess in the act of running. Probably of Taranto production.	WALTERS 1899, no. 495; BURN 1991, pp. 104-105. P.R.
131	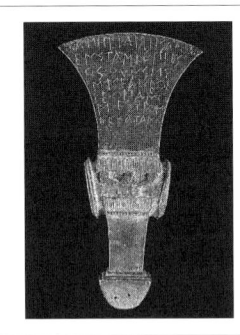	**Axe from San Sosti** sixth century B.C. bronze max l 16.7 cm London, British Museum inv. GR 1884.6-14.31 (Bronze 252) S. Sosti (CS)	Axe-hammer with hole for the insertion of a wooden handle. On one face of the wider end the following epigraph can be read: "I am sacred to the goddess Hera who has her sanctuary on the plain. Kyniskos, the sacrificial slaughterer, dedicated me, as a tenth (of the reward) of his services".	GUARDUCCI 1967, III, pp. 43 ff.; PUGLIESE-CARRATELLI 1983, p. 38. G.L'A.
132	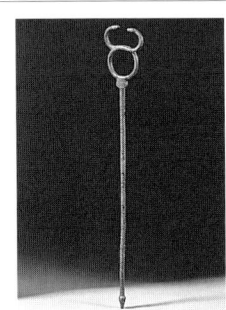	**Caduceus with inscription** 450-420 B.C. bronze h 46 cm London, British Museum inv. GR 1875.8-10.3 (Bronze) Sicily?	The inscription in Ionian dialect on the stick can be translated like this: "I am the public property of the Longanesi". It is probably the caduceus of the herald of the city of Longane in north eastern Sicily.	WALTERS 1899, no. 319. P.R.
133		**Perirrhanterion with black figures** 599-575 B.C. clay, thrown on the wheel, with sculpted applications h 28.8 cm; diam. bowl 18.8 cm nearly completely reassembled Metaponto, Museo Archeologico Nazionale, inv. 29961 San Biagio alla Venella (Bernalda, MT) sanctuary area votive offerings no. 1 (1973)	Moulded bell-shaped support with distinct trumpet foot; careened bowl with flat, out-turned rim and four sculpted rosettes applied. On the support, painted decoration on two registers: zoomorphic friezes with pairs of facing animals; lionesses and cervids low down; sphinxes and swans high up; rosette fillings. On the external careened rim of the bowl, two lionesses and more pairs of facing swans; on the inside bottom, a	frieze of differing lotus flowers, alternating by twos. ORLANDINI 1983, p. 354, fig. 330. LM.V.

134 I	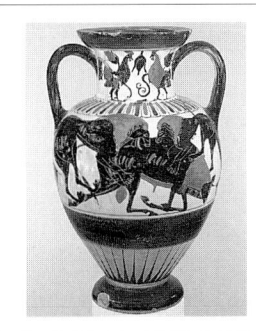	**Chalcidian amphora with black figures** end sixth century B.C. clay, glaze, thrown on the wheel h 37.5 cm New York, Metropolitan Museum of Art, Rogers Fund 1946, inv. 46.11.5	On both sides of the neck are two facing cocks. *Side A*: two lions attack a bull and pull it to its knees. *Side B*: two lions attack a wild boar.	Iozzo 1993, pp. 108-109, 112-113, fig. 20, pls. CI-CVI. C.A.P.
134 II		**Chalcidian amphora with black figures** ca. 540 B.C. clay, glaze, thrown on the wheel h 26.4 cm; diam. 10,9 cm New York, Metropolitan Museum of Art, Fletcher Fund 1956 inv. 56.171.1	*Side A*: Hephaistos, with a drinking horn, is depicted on the back of a donkey pulled by a satyr; Dionysus follows him, also with a drinking horn. *Side B*: two banqueters; below the klinai is a young waiter and dog. Attributed to the Painter of Orvieto.	Von Bothmer 1957b, pp. 165 ff.; *LIMC*, IV, p. 639, no. 134; Iozzo 1993, pp. 50, 54-55, fig. 9, pls. XXXVIII-XXXIX. C.A.P
134 III		**Chalcidian psykter with black figures** 560-550 B.C. refined clay, glaze, retouching in white and red h 42 cm; max diam. 32 cm Museo Nazionale di Villa Giulia inv. 50410 Cerveteri, Castellani Collection	The vase, equipped with double wall and hole on the bottom, served to keep the drinks fresh. *Side A*: within panels, a satyr ambushes a maenad near a big palm with leaves falling in a fan-shape. *Side B*: a male figure moving towards the right followed by three female figures wrapped in a single cloak. "Group of the Amphorae inscribed".	Mingazzini 1930, p. 181, pls. XXXVII, 1, 2; Vallet 1958, pp. 211 ff. F.B.
134 IV		**Chalcidian kylix with black figures** ca. 520 B.C. clay, slip, glaze, overpainting and graffitti h 5.2 cm; diam. rim 23.4 cm reassembled and partially reintegrated Florence, Museo Archeologico Nazionale, inv. 115087 Cerveteri, G. Campana Collection probably from an Etruscan necropolis	The *kylix* with hemispherical bowl and surmounting handles is decorated on both sides with a pair of big male eyes placed to the sides of a rapacious nose surmounted by a bud. The eyes are bounded by sinuously curved eyebrows and the nasal-lip folds, as well as by the silenus-like ears which are flanked by multipetal palmettes which come together at the handles in slender volutes. Circle of the Painter of Phineus.	Iozzo 1993, pp. 74, 87, 183, pl. XCIV (AG 67). M.I.
134 V		**Chalcidian hydria with black figures** 530-520 B.C. clay, slip, glaze, thrown on the wheel graffito, overpainting h 16.9 cm; diam. rim 10.2 cm Taranto, Museo Archeologico Nazionale, inv. 20145 Taranto, 8.X.1925, F. Di Palma road 72 tomb 1	Tongues on the shoulder. *Side A*: facing sphinxes; in the background filling of rosettes. *Side B*: backward-looking lions to the sides of an upside down palmette placed below the handle. Sunburst in the lower part of the body.	Keck 1988, pp. 272-273, S-G 8; Iozzo 1994, p. 220, TA 10, pl. XLVII.1. L.M.
134 VI		**Chalcidian skyphos with black figures** ca. 540 B.C. refined clay h 20.9 cm; diam. 30 cm Naples, Museo Archeologico Nazionale Santangelo Collection	*Side A*: abduction of the Delphic tripod. Hercules, helped in the context by Hermes, disputes the tripod with Apollo who, in his turn, is helped by a winged Artemis. An Erinys is behind the tripod. Rosettes in the background. *Side B*: context between two hoplites in the presence of two women.	Rumpf 1927, p. 100, pls. CLXXI-CLXXIV. Mar.L.

Works on Exhibit

134 VII

Chalcidian amphora with black figures

530-500 B.C.
clay
h 27.7 cm
Reggio Calabria, Museo Nazionale
inv. 21053
Matauros (modern Gioia Tauro)
tomb 116 Musumeci

Decoration of lotus buds on the neck and of panels on the body. *Side A*: young horseman with horse which goes off at a gallop and, reinforcing the dynamics of the scene, a dog which bounds off at a run. *Side B*: horseman and horse walking. Attributed to the Group of Phineus.

SABBIONE 1987, pp. 112-113; IOZZO 1993, pp. 69 and 87.
C.S.

135 *see Recent Discoveries*

136

Etruscan-Corinthian kotyle by the Painter of the Bad Wolf

beginning sixth century B.C.
clay, polychrome
h 17.1 cm; diam. 19.7 cm
Pontecagnano, Museo Nazionale dell'Agro Picentino, inv. 35272
Pontecagnano, tomb 856

Figures emerge from the background among which that of the Gorgon, characterised by the gesture of the raised arms with hands open to the sides of the head. The wolf with its enormous, wide-open mouth, shows a considerable lengthening of the muzzle and polychrome execution of the body within incised lines.

CERCHIAI 1990, pp. 106-109, figs. 51-53 and 91.
A.L.

137

Sub-geometric bichrome jug

fifth century B.C.
refined clay, glaze
h 16.5 cm; diam. 7.9 cm
Melfi, Museo Archeologico Nazionale
inv. 118259
Ripacandida, tomb 14

Outward turning rim; handle with ribbing; extra decoration made up of lines and lattice-work in black and brown glaze. An icon is depicted on the two faces which show a stylised human figure above a sphere within which there is a flash of lightning; all around a series of star motifs.

A. BOTTINI in *Popoli e civiltà*, vol. VIII, 1988, p. 243, pl. 80; BOTTINI-TAGLIENTE c.s.
R.C.

138

Messapian amphora with black figures

500-475 B.C.
clay, glaze, thrown on the wheel
h 33.3 cm; diam. 24 cm
Copenhagen, Ny Carlsberg Glyptotek
inv. 509.9

Decoration of palmettes, lozenges and lotus flowers on the neck. Figured frieze on the shoulder. *Side A*: scene of a duel between Aphrodite, on the right (indicated by the inscription) and Athena, on the left. On the fallen warrior's shield is the inscription AINIAS. *Side B*: three warriors, one of whom fallen and identifiable by the inscription KAPAN, in the presence of Zeus.

FISCHER, HANSEN 1992, n. 119.
G.L'A.

139

Messapian amphora with black figures

end sixth century B.C.
clay, glaze, thrown on the wheel
26.6x2 cm
Lecce, Museo Archeologico Provinciale, inv. 425
Taranto (?)

A horizontal branch with long leaves is on the neck; bead work on the shoulder; rays on the rim and base of the body; opposing palmettes on the handles; rosettes. On the body, *side A*: small, nude male figure with *chlamys* passed behind his shoulders is turned to the left in the act of picking fruit from a tree with his right hand, while with his left he brandishes a club. On the sides, in symmetrical positions, two birds are turned towards the scene, while on the right a third is turned outwards. *Side B*: palmettes joined by plant volutes.

CVA Lecce I, p. 10, pls. IX, V-VI, X, V; D'ANDRIA 1988, p. 663.
M.T.G.

140

Bell-shaped amphora with black figures

500-490 B.C.
clay, slip, glaze, overpainting
h 24 cm; diam. rim 11.2 cm
reassembled
Siena, Museo Archeologico Nazionale
inv. 38480
Chigi-Zondadari Collection

Amphora with distinct neck, overturned *echinus* foot and handles with double sticks. *Side A*: female figure seated on a *diphros okladias*, dressed in a *chiton* and with a pomegranate in her right hand in the act of sacrificing before a double *aulos* player. *Side B*: female figure seated on a *diphros*, with a flower in her left hand and a crown in her right, and a flying Siren. Attributed to the Group of Diphros.

MANGANI in CYGIELMAN, MANGANI 1991, pp. 67-68, no. 44, pl. XXX.
M.I.

141

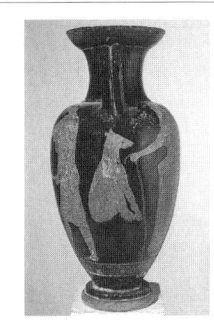

Nolan amphora with red figures

first half fifth century B.C.
clay, glaze, thrown on the wheel
overpainting
h 36.5 cm; diam. 57 cm
The Vatican, Museo Gregoriano Etrusco, inv. 18001
Nola

The figured decoration, bounded at the bottom by a band of meanders, moves around the vase evolving in three scenes. A young woman, with chiton and *hydria* on her head goes towards a big *pithos* positioned under one of the handles; next an old man with chiton and *himation* who looks at a big dog lying on a rocky elevation; then two young men, one with chiton and short sword, the other wrapped in the *himation*. Attributed to the Group of the Pilaster of the Civetta.

TRENDALL 1953, I, p. 43.   G.L'A.

142

Grave goods from grave 21 in the native cemetery of Valle Oscura (Marianopoli)

end sixth century B.C.
Marianopoli, Museo Archeologico

The collective grave 21 forms part of a vast cemetery located on the southern slopes of the Montagna di Balate, between Caltanissetta and Marianopoli, in a wide valley known as the Valle Oscura. The numerous finds were situated along the south-west wall, in the center of the grave, or at the bottom of it.

I
Attic black-figure column-krater

orange clay
h 23 cm; diam. rim 15 cm
reassembled
inv. 927

Side A: Dionysus, bearded and cloaked, is depicted lying down. On his right there is a recumbent maenad wearing a sleeved chiton with folds. In the background there is a leafy tree bearing white fruit and, at the sides of the scene, two cloaked figures.
Side B: scene of an attack with helmeted warriors armed with spears and bearing shields with central *episema*.
Two apotropaic eyes are depicted under the handles.
Attributed to the Mikra Karaburum Group.

II
Attic black-figure column-krater

orange clay
h 21 cm; diam. 14 cm
reassembled
inv. 928

Side A: three helmeted warriors, with spears and shields.
Side B: Dionysiac *komos* with dancing maenads and, in the center, two satyrs.
Two apotropaic eyes are depicted under the handles.

Attributed to the Mikra Karaburum Group.

III
Attic black-figure kylix

orange clay
h 14.5 cm; diam. 13 cm
reassembled
inv. 921

Between the handles, a continuous series of black lines.

IV
Ionic cup, type B2

orange clay
h 10 cm; diam. 17.5 cm
reassembled
inv. 920

V
Attic kylix, Kassel type

orange clay
h 9 cm; diam. rim 13 cm
reassembled
inv. 923

With a frieze consisting of purple and black ornamentation under the rim.

VI
Attic kylix, Band cup type

orange clay
h 6.5 cm; diam. 13 cm
reassembled
inv. 922

VII
Ionic kylix, type B2

orange clay
h 8.5 cm; diam. 12 cm
reassembled
inv. 924

VIII
Attic kylix

orange clay
h 7.5 cm; diam. 13.2 cm
reassembled
inv. 925

Frieze of *guttae* in black paint between the two handles.

IX
Trilobate oinochoe, locally made

buff clay
h 18 cm; diam. 14 cm
reassembled
inv. 937

Ovoid body, partly painted.

X
Trilobate oinochoe, locally made

light brown clay
h 21 cm; diam. 16 cm
reassembled
inv. 936

Ovoid body, partly painted.

XI
Trilobate oinochoe, locally made

light brown clay
h 21 cm; diam. 14 cm
reassembled
inv. 935

Ovoid body, partly painted.

XII
Trilobate oinochoe, locally made

reddish clay
h 19 cm; diam. 16.5 cm
reassembled
inv. 948

Flattened globular body. The brown decoration consists of three circular bands on the body; on the shoulder there is a frieze of birds; on the neck a waving line between circular bands; on the bottom, a radial decoration.

XIII
Trilobate oinochoe, locally made

light brown clay
h 22 cm; diam. 19 cm
reassembled
inv. 945

Globular body. Decoration painted in brown, consisting of a series of waving lines on the neck and the body; on the shoulder, a band.

XIV
Trilobate oinochoe, locally made

buff clay
h 19 cm; diam. 15.5 cm
reassembled
inv. 947

Globular body. On the shoulder a frieze depicting four birds, painted in brown with purple touchings on the winds. On the neck, a band of purple colour, defined by brown lines; on the body brown and purple circular bands. On the bottom, a radial decoration.

XV
Trilobate oinochoe, locally made

light brown clay, buff slip

h 19 cm; diam. 16.5 cm
incomplete; inv. 950

Geometric type decoration, painted in brown, consisting of vertical bands on the body. On the neck, concentric circular lines.

XVI
Trilobate oinochoe, locally made

orange clay, buff slip
h 15.5 cm; diam. 15.5 cm
incomplete, reassembled
inv. 949

Globular body, with linear decoration painted in brown.

XVII
Trilobate oinochoe, locally made

grayish clay
h 16 cm; diam. 14 cm
reassembled
inv. 946

Globular body with geometric decoration painted in brown, consisting of a continuous sequence waving lines on the shoulder and the bottom.

XVIII
Small trilobate oinochoe, locally made

reddish clay
h 15 cm; diam. 11 cm
inv. 944

Linear decoration painted in light and dark brown. On the body, in the center, a horizontal bough; other two boughs are painted on the neck.

XIX
Trilobate oinochoe, locally made

grayish clay
h 15.5 cm; diam. 13 cm
reassembled
inv. 942

Globular body and linear decoration painted in dark brown. On the shoulder, stylized boughs.

XX
Trilobate oinochoe, locally made

light brown clay
h 17 cm; diam. 18 cm
reassembled
inv. 941

Linear decoration painted in brown. On the body, horizontal band and on the shoulder a continuous sequence of waving vertical lines.

XXI
Trilobate oinochoe, locally made

reddish clay
h 22 cm; diam. 14.5 cm
reassembled
inv. 940

Linear decoration painted in brown, partly faded. On the body, concentric circular bands.

XXII
Trilobate oinochoe, locally made

reddish clay
h 18 cm; diam. 14.5 cm
reassembled
inv. 941bis

Globular body with linear decoration painted in brown, mostly faded. It consists of a sequence of concentric circular lines.

XXIII
Trilobate oinochoe, locally made

reddish clay
h 17 cm; diam. 14 cm
reassembled
inv. 964bis

Globular body. Linear decoration painted in dark and light brown. On the neck, a band is defined by concentric line and framed by a continuous waving line; on the body, circular band defined by concentric lines, and on the shoulder three rosettes with dotted petals.

XXIV
Column-krater, locally made

reddish clay
h 21 cm; diam. 18 cm
reassembled
inv. 951

On the shoulder a band is framed by a sequence of waving vertical motifs painted in brown. On the body, circular brown band. The neck, the rim and the foot are brown.

XXV
Krateriskos, locally made with geometric decoration

red clay
h 9 cm; diam. 9 cm
reassembled
inv. 957

On the shoulder radial band; on the body and foot concentric circular bands.

XXVI
Small column-krater, locally made

reddish clay, buff slip
h 16 cm; diam. 15 cm
reassembled
inv. 952

Linear decoration painted in brown and red. On the neck, a band is the fined by concentric lines and a continuous zig-zag motif.

XXVII
Small trilobate oinochoe, locally made

red clay
h 14 cm; diam. 7 cm
reassembled
inv. 939

Ovoidal body; brown glaze, faded.

XXVIII
Column-krater, locally made

reddish clay
h 17 cm; diam. 17 cm
reassembled
inv. 954

Linear decoration painted in brown. On the shoulder, two opposing birds. On the body, circular band and lines. Rim and neck covered with brown colour.

XXIX
Column-krater, locally made

reddish clay; abraded surface
h 15 cm; diam. 14.5 cm
reassembled
inv. 953

Floral decoration in brown and red. On the neck, waving line.

XXX
Black-glazed krateriskos of Laconian type

orange clay
h 12.5 cm; diam. 12.5 cm
reassembled
inv. 929

XXXI
Column-krater with geometric decoration, locally made

redish clay
h 18 cm; diam. 18 cm
reassembled
inv. 956

On the shoulder, band defined by concentric lines and framed by lozenges; On the body concentric band and lines.

XXXII
Black-figure column-krater locally made

redish clay
h 16 cm; diam. 18 cm
reassembled
inv. 955
On the shoulder a sequence of birds and stylised rosetta. On the body circular concentric lines.

XXXIII
Column-krater with linear decoration locally produced

light brown clay
h 15.9 cm; diam. 17 cm
reassembled
inv. 958

XXXIV
Achrome bowl

light brown clay
h 67 cm; diam. 14.5 cm
inv. 961

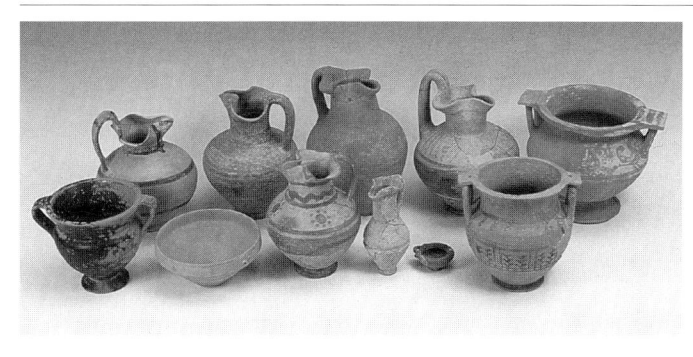

Conic body and vertical rim.

XXXV
Bowl, locally produced

lith brown clay
h 75 cm; diam. max 16.5 cm
inv. 962

Vertical rim and conic body with linear decoration painted in brown. It contained 700 beads of amber necklace and animal bones.

XXXVI
Bowl with linear decoration locally produced

reddish clay
h 11 cm; diam. 27 cm
inv. 960

XXXVII
Bowl with linear decoration locally produced

reddish clay
h 15 cm; diam. 27 cm
inv. 959

It contained the beads of an amber necklace.

XXXVIII
Kothon decorated with bands

light brown clay
h 2.5 cm; diam. 5 cm
reassembled
inv. 938

Vertical rim and conic body.

Restaured.

XXXIX
Oil-lamp

reddish clay
h 2.5 cm; diam. 4.5 cm
inv. 931

Flat rim painted in red glaze.

XL
Oil-lamp

reddish clay
h 2 cm; diam. 3.7 cm
inv. 930

Flat rim painted in red glaze.

XLI
Oil-lamp

reddish clay
h 2.3 cm; diam. 5.3 cm
inv. 934

Flat rim; traces of black glaze.

XLII
Oil-lamp

reddish clay
h 2.5 cm; diam. 5.5 cm
inv. 932

Flat rim; traces of black glaze.

XLIII
Oil-lamp

light brown clay
h 2.4 cm; diam. 5.7 cm
inv. 933

Flat rim; traces of red glaze.

XLIV
Necklace

amber
inv. 963

84 amber beads and aries-shaped pendant.

XLV
Dagger

iron
l 31 cm
inv. 1053

XLVI
3 rings

bronze
inv. 1058-1060

XLVII
Ring (elikes)

bronze
inv. 1057

143 I-II

I
Attic jug in Daunian form with red figures

450-440 B.C.
clay, glaze, thrown on the wheel
h 35 cm; diam. 34.5 cm
reassembled, fragmentary
Malibu, The Paul Getty Museum
Gift of Malcolm Weiner
inv. 81.AE.183.1

Vase in subgeometric, Daunian form with horn-shaped handles, red figure painting technique. The figured scene is disposed on a double register separated by a band of ovoli. Upper register, *side A*: in the centre a winged male figure (Boreas?) between two pairs of draped women who flee, alarmed; *side B*: winged female figure (Eos?) pursuing four young men with short chlamys (among whom is Cephalus). Genre scenes in the lower register. Scene of pursuit also on the lip. Attributed to the circle of Polygnotos.

JENTOFT NILSEN 1990, pp. 243 ff., pl. 25.   G.L'A.

II
Attic jug in Daunian form with red figures

450-440 B.C.
clay, glaze, thrown on the wheel
h 41 cm; diam. 36 cm
reassembled, fragmentary
Malibu, The Paul Getty Museum
Gift of Malcom Weiner
inv. 81.AE.183.2

Vase in sub-geometric, Daunian form with horn-shaped handles, red figure painting technique. The figured scene is disposed on a double register separated by a band of ovoli. Upper register, *side A*: Menelaus on the left follows Aphrodite who hands him a small Erote, and Helen moves rapidly towards the right; behind Menelaus are two, badly conserved figures. Side B: a bearded man (Priam?), richly dressed and seated on an altar with sceptre in his right hand and the left raised in a gesture of despair; two male characters follow, one on foot (Achilles?), the other fleeing on horseback (Troilus?), and a female figure (Polyxena?). In the lower register genre scenes. Attributed to the circle of Polygnotus.

JENTOFT NILSEN 1990, p. 247, pl. 26.   G.L'A.

144

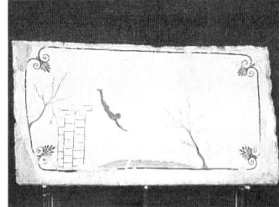

Covering slab from the tomb called the Diver's

480-470 B.C.
limestone
194x98 cm
Paestum, Museo Archeologico Nazionale, inv. 23103
Paestum, Tempa del Prete

Covering slab from a box tomb plastered and painted in the fresco technique. A line of black cornice with volutes and palmettes in the four corners bounds the main scene of a young man in the act of diving into a mirror of water. The scene is framed by two trees which grow from the edge of the cornice itself and, on the right side, by a structure composed of three pilasters, each one built with seven squared blocks. The scene has been given a symbolic value: it is to represent the passage from life to death which happened after crossing through the gates of Hades (the pilasters) and the river Oceanus (the mirror of water).

NAPOLI 1970, in particolare pp. 149 ff.; PONTRANDOLFO 1990, pp. 351-352, fig. 529.   F.L.

145 I-VII

I
Bronze hydria

530-520 B.C.
bronze, cast, hammering, *repoussé*
h 41.7 cm; diam. 32.5 cm
Paestum, Museo Archeologico Nazionale, inv. 49803
Paestum, from the *heroon* of the *agora*

Annular foot, ovoidal body, rounded and oblique shoulders, cylindrical neck with slightly concave profile. The vertical handle, decorated by a row of talus and pearls, is like a ribbon. The upper juncture is made up of a pair of lions lying down who seize the rim of the vase; the lower one by two rams who flank a female head emerging from a palmette. The horizontal handles present a median line in the centre with talus and pearls and, laterally, little rounds, with two palmettes incised on their external surface. The junctures are instead made up of palmettes in relief with palmiped protomes developing from them.

STIBBE 1992, pp. 16 ff., fig. 24, p. 55 - F2.   F.L.

II
Bronze hydria

530-520 B.C.
bronze, cast, hammering, *repoussé*
h 42.8 cm; diam. 34.5 cm
reassembled
Paestum, Museo Archeologico Nazionale, inv. 49804
Paestum, from the *heroon* of the *agora*

Shape as the *hydria* inv. 49803.

STIBBE 1992, pp. 16 ff., fig. 25, p. 55 - F2.   F.L.

III
Bronze hydria

530-520 B.C.
bronze, cast, hammering, *repoussé*
h 41.7 cm; diam. 32.5 cm
Paestum, Museo Archeologico Nazionale, inv. 49800
Paestum, from the *heroon* of the *agora*

Shape as the *hydria* inv. 49803.

STIBBE 1992, pp. 16 ff., fig. 26, p. 55 - F3.   F.L.

IV
Bronze hydria

540-530 B.C.
bronze, cast, hammering, *repoussé*
h 41.4 cm; diam. 30 cm
Paestum, Museo Archeologico Nazionale, inv. 49802
Paestum, from the *heroon* of the *agora*

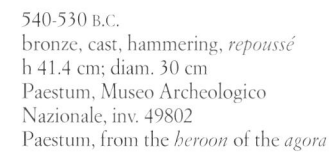

Trumpet foot with profile *kyma* reversa and bead work decoration; expanded body; shoulders decorated with incised bead work and joined to the body by a soft, continuous line.
The vertical handle, decorated by a row of pearls, ends at the top with a lion's head turned towards the inside of the vase. High up it presents a reel juncture, the lateral rounds of this are decorated on the outside with an upside-down palmette flanked by two sphinxes. The horizontal handles, like a ribbon with raised edges, are decorated with a row of talus and pearls and have junctures made up of double leonine protomes in relief.

STIBBE 1992, pp. 9-10, fig. 13, p. 53 - B6.   F.L.

V
Bronze hydria

540-530 B.C.
bronze, cast, hammering, *repoussé*
h 43.5 cm; diam. 35 cm
Paestum, Museo Archeologico Nazionale, inv. 49801
Paestum, from the *heroon* of the *agora*

Similar in shape to the *hydria* inv. 49803. The vertical handle is made up of a lion in the round which, high on its back legs above a palmette with rounded leaves and volutes from which develope snakes's heads, appears at the rim of the vase framed by other heads of serpents. The horizontal handles like ribbons are decorated by a row of pearls while the junctures are made up of double equine protomes in relief with bent fore legs.

STIBBE 1992, fig. 9, p. 56 - G11.   F.L.

VI
Bronze amphora

540-530 B.C.
bronze, cast, *repoussé*

h 37.8 cm; diam. 27 cm
Paestum, Museo Archeologico Nazionale, inv. 49807
Paestum, from the *heroon* of the *agora*

High foot with concave profile decorated with bead work; cylindrical neck; rounded shoulders; body tapering towards the bottom. The ribbon handles of median ribbing and slightly raised edges present a palmette with rounded leaves and incised volutes on a flat surface at the lower juncture. The upper juncture is made up of two appendixes which lengthen upwards assuming the shape of closed fists into which a mobile handle was fixed.

STIBBE 1992, p. 49, fig. 63, p. 61 - Nn.
F.L.

VII
Attic amphora of black figures with the apotheosis of Heracles

510 B.C.
clay
h 58 cm
foot reassembled
Paestum, Museo Archeologico Nazionale, inv. 133153
Paestum, from the *heroon* of the *agora*

Side A: the apotheosis of Heracles who enters Olympia guided by Athena, distinguished by a helmet with tall *lophos*; Hermes and Apollo, who plays the lyre, accompany him while Artemis, beside the horses, seems to be welcoming the hero. *Side B*: in the centre of the scene, between two couples of maenads and satyrs, Dionysus, crowned with grape leaves and with a drinking horn and two branches of ivy and grape leaves in his hands, appears with a ram and Hermes, who, as on the main side, is wearing the *petasos* and has the *caduceus* in his hands. Attributed to the Painter of Chiusi.

BEAZLEY 1971, p. 170, n. 6.   F.L.

---

146 **Enthroned female deity**

ca. 460 B.C.
marble
h 151 cm
Berlin, Staatliche Museen Zu Berlin Preussischer Kulturbesitz Antikensammlung, inv. SK1761
Taranto, Pizzone district (?)

The goddess is sitting on a throne with high back and resting her feet on a stool; her arms are stretched to hold the attributes. She is wearing a *chiton* with an overdress and a cloak. Her face is animated by a slight smile; her hair is arranged in a triple crown over her forehead while it is gathered in a *sakkos* on the nape. Above the hair a support for a diadem can be noticed.

BLUMEL 1940, n. A17, pp. 16 ff.; ORLANDINI 1983, p. 439.   G.L'A.

---

147 **Ephebe from Mozia**

450-440 B.C.
Statue in white, large-grained red marble probably of insular provenance
h 1.81 m
Mozia, Museo Giuseppe Whitaker inv. I.G.4310
Mozia, Zona K (1979)

The statue from Mozia represents a young man with vigorous, athletic body whose forms are hinted at rather than covered by a long, close-fitting tunic of thin material arranged in very fine, dense pleats.
A large band, which would have been decorated with a bronze element applied to the two holes visible in the middle, holds the dress at chest level. The statue has no feet or arms; only part of the left hand with fingers embedded in his side remains.

Atti Marsala 1988.   R.C.S.

---

148 **Headless torso of a warrior (?)**

first decades fifth century B.C.
limestone, missing part of the lower limbs, the left arm and the entire right half of the body
h 41.2 cm
Metaponto, Museo Archeologico Nazionale, inv. 135653
Metaponto, urban sanctuary

Male (?) torso armed with cuirass on short, thickly pleated, wavy *chiton*, also visible in the short sleeve coming out from under the waistcoat. The curved bust appears taut in the effort of probably holding a bow. The sight practically in profile, and the non-worked back lead to a hypotheseis of a frontal use for the statue.

ORLANDINI 1983, p. 404, fig. 440.
M.L.V.

---

149 **Female head**

470-460 B.C.
marble, bronze, fragmentary
h 18.5 cm; diam. 49 cm
Metaponto, Museo Archeologico Nazionale, inv. 135652
Metaponto, Sanctuary of Apollo Lycian near temple C (1973)

Head of female deity (Io?) with long hair swept into waves over the temples and nape. There are bronze insertions along the contours of the narrow, elongated eyes, on the ears (for earrings, not conserved) and on the forehead (probably for inserting two small taurine horns).

ORLANDINI 1983, p. 438, figs. 433-434.
A.L.T.

Works on Exhibit

150

Athlete's head

about mid-fifth century B.C.
marble
h 22.6 cm
Metaponto, Museo Archeologico Nazionale, inv. 30357
Metaponto, urban sanctuary

Young, beardless face of full. Slightly frowning forehead for the effort sustained; the hair arranged in disordered curls or intentionally flattened onto the skull; the right, slightly swollen ear conserved might indicate the representation of a young athlete after a competition, possibly boxing. The hole currently present on the top of the well worked head, is perhaps attributable to the support for a *meniskos*.

ORLANDINI 1983, p. 438, fig. 443.
M.L.V.

151

Small temple

470 B.C.
marble, traces of colour
h 42 cm; l 51 cm; w 36 cm
Potenza, Museo Archeologico Provinciale - Garaguso

Rectangular plan *in antis*, double sloping roof, rectangular opening at the front framed by two small pilasters crowned with small capitals on which the smooth trabeation rests. The rear side is completely smooth.

Statue of seated female deity

470 B.C.
marble, traces of colour
h statuette 21 cm; h throne 16 cm
w throne 12.5 cm
Potenza, Museo Archeologico Provinciale - Garaguso

Seated female figure with *chiton* and cloak; the hair is arranged in locks under a diadem. The holes in both hands and in the lap indicate that the goddess is in the act of holding a child (*kourotrophos*) or small animal in her stretched out arms. The throne is worked in a single block with the statuette and has a parallelepiped shape.

SESTIERI, BERTARELLI 1958, pp. 67-78.
Ad. B.

152

Head of ephebe

ca. 470 B.C.
limestone
h 15.2 cm
broken at the base of the neck; nose chipped
Palermo, Museo Archeologico "A. Salinas", inv. 14804
Selinunte

The hair is gathered into a typicle style *krobylos*. The oval face is well modelled with elongated eyes and thin, horizontally cut lips.

BISI 1969, pp. 34 ff., pl. XI; TUSA 1983, p. 138, no. 57; *Stile severo*, p. 223, no. 69.
A.V.

153

Female head

470-460 B.C.
insular marble
h 19.3 cm
reassembled from four fragments
Palermo, Museo Archeologico "A. Salinas", inv. 3926 (3984)
Selinunte, temple E

The head was part of a metope today lost; it presents a slight twist towards the left. The face is oval, eyebrows prominent, lips fleshy, neck robust. The modelling is soft and rich in *chiaroscuro*. The upper part, of backfill, is missing.

Stile severo, p. 200, no. 31; MARCONI 1994, pp. 155-156, pls. 88-89.
A.V.

154

Torso of Nike in flight

ca. 480 B.C.
marble
max h 76 cm; max w 46 cm
max t 29 cm
the torso, headless, with the upper part of the legs
Syracuse, Museo Archeologico Regionale "Paolo Orsi"
Syracuse, temple of Athena

Perhaps intended as an *akroterion*, this statue depicts a Nike running towards the right, with the legs in profile, the breast forward, the left hand on the flank, the right arm outstretched. The locks of hair on the breast, the baring of the right breast, and the *ductus* of folds give the impression of impetuous movement.

RIZZA, DE MIRO 1985, p. 228, fig. 244; ROLLEY 1994, p. 301.
E.C.P.

155

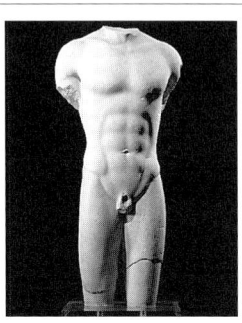

Headless kouros

early fifth century B.C.
marble
max h 103 cm; max w 53 cm
parts missing
Syracuse, Museo Archeologico Regionale "Paolo Orsi", inv. 26624
Lentini, discovered outside the area of the ancient city

Probably intended for funeral purposes, it perhaps goes with the head in the Museo di Castello Ursino (cat. 156). The rendering of the abdominal partitions, the sculpting enlivened by *chiaroscuro*, and the graceful proportions of the figure show affinity with Attic works influenced by the sculpture of the Cyclades.

RIZZA, DE MIRO 1985, pp. 210, 223, fig. 229, with bibl.; ROLLEY 1994, p. 300.
E.C.P.

Works on Exhibit

| 156 | Archaic ephebic head, Kouros of Lentini

beginning fifth century B.C.
max h 25 cm
Catania, Museo Civico di Castello Ursino
Lentini | Big, natural head. Flat, low and disappearing forehead; arched eyebrows; very protruding eyes; small and finely contracted mouth in the corners; robust chin. Hair made of a sphere striated by undulations radiating from the top, of a crown of curls, and at the rear of a sort of pad divided into small masses. | LIBERTINI 1930, pp. 3-4, no. 1, pls. I-II; LANGLOTZ 1968, p. 273, pls. 48-49.
G.N. |

| 157 | Helmet

ca. 474 B.C.
bronze
h 20 cm; w 24 cm
London, British Museum
inv. GR 1928.6-10.1
Olympia, Sanctuary, bank of the Alpheus | Helmet of Negau type; on the cap an inscription in Greek-Doric and Syracusan alphabet with dedication from Hieron of Syracuse to Zeus, similar to the inscription on helmet no. 158. | LAZZARINI 1976, p. 317, no. 964; EGG 1986, p. 198, no. 185.
G.L'A. |

| 158 | Helmet

ca. 474 B.C.
bronze, engraving
h 19.2 cm; w 18 cm
Olympia, Archeological Museum
inv. M9
Olympia, bank of Alpheus | Helmet of Corinthian type decorated with a palmette on the sides of the eye-piece. On one side a dedication from Heiron, tyrant of Syracuse, to Zeus as an ex-voto for the victory won at Cuma in 474 B.C.: "Hiaron the Dinomenide and the Syracusans (offer) to Zeus, (booty) of the Etruscans at Cuma". | LAZZARINI 1976, pp. 47 ff., no. 964b; M. CRISTOFANI in *Civiltà degli Etruschi*, p. 256, no. 9.21.2.
G.L'A. |

| 159 | Bronze kriophoros

end sixth-beginning fifth century B.C.
bronze
h 10.7 cm
Metaponto, Museo Archeologico Nazionale, inv. 31142
Metaponto, urban sanctuary | Nude male figure with hands stretched forwards; the left probably held a stick. The feet hint at movement and the left one is forward. The body results quite massive with few calligraphic details, only on the abdomen. The bearded head has short hair close to the skull emphasised by deep, parallell incisions. The ram is held over the shoulders with its hooves crossed on the front. | ROLLEY 1989, pp. 5-117, figs. 1-3.
A.D.S. |

| 160 | Statuette portraying Apollo

490-460 B.C.
bronze, solid casting, engraving cold
h 25 cm
Bari, Museo Archeologico, inv. 4396
Ceglie del Campo (BA), south east railway station | Depicted in the act of advancing with bow grasped in the left outstretched hand, while the right, closed in a fist to hold the arrows or branch of laurel, is along the side of the body. The right leg is pushed forwards with the foot solidly on the ground. The head is covered by smooth hair articulated in a double order of curls over the forehead, whereas behind the nape it folds into a single band. | CASSANO 1988, pp. 353-354.
M.L. |

| 161 I | Mirror with handle in the shape of an offering athlete

ca. 480-450 B.C.
bronze
h 33 cm
Reggio Calabria, Museo Nazionale
inv. 4779
Locri Epizefiri, necropolis of the Lucifero district, tomb 865 | The figure of a young, nude athlete who held a *patera*, now lost, in his right hand in a gesture of libation, is placed on a small, quadrangular-shaped base, and it is linked by a small volute element with the disc, adorned by engraved tongues. | CARUSO 1981, pp. 48-49.
C.S. |

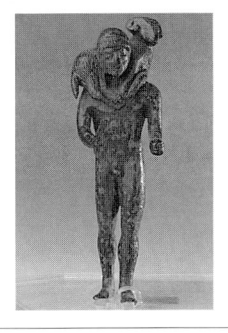

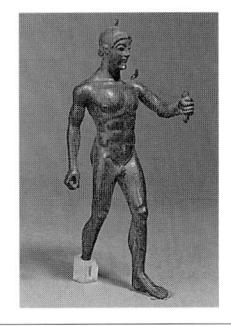

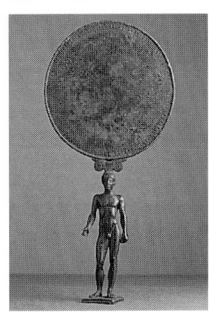

Works on Exhibit

161 II		**Mirror with handle in the shape of a cloaked ephebe** ca. mid-fifth century B.C. bronze h 34.5 cm Reggio Calabria, Museo Nazionale inv. 4490 Locri Epizefiri, necropolis of the Lucifero district, tomb 622	The figure of the ephebe in the round and with a complex hairstyle held by a diadem is completely wrapped in a cloak which leaves the weight of the body to be seen, placed on a circular moulded base and joined to the disc by an element similar to an Ionic capital.	CARUSO 1981, pp. 30-31.	C.S.
161 III		**Handle of a mirror in the shape of a young girl in a peplos** ca. mid-fifth century B.C. bronze h 17.2 cm Reggio Calabria, Museo Nazionale inv. 6736 Locri Epizefiri, Sanctuary of Persephone in the Mannella district	The figure, with left leg forward, is wearing a *peplos* of dense vertical pleats. The gesture of loosening a lock of hair and holding out a ball in the left hand probably indicates an offering to the deity of young people's games and hairstyles from a young girl preparing for her wedding.	ARIAS 1976, pp. 548-550.	C.S.
161 IV		**Mirror with handle in the shape of a siren** second half fifth century B.C. bronze h 33 cm Reggio Calabria, Museo Nazionale inv. 4496 Locri Epizefiri, necropolis of the Lucifero district, tomb 632	From the flat handle originally covered in another material, a complex motif of lotus flowers and volutes rises, onto which a siren is placed in a frontal position. It has feline paws, a bird's body with wide folded wings and a female head with hair in wavy locks; a curved element decorated with ovuli and palmettes functions as the link to the moulded disc.	CARUSO 1981, p. 13.	C.S.
161 V		**Mirror with relief decorated handle with Electra** ca. 400 B.C. bronze h 35.6 cm Reggio Calabria, Museo Nazionale inv. 4837 Locri Epizefiri, necropolis of the Lucifero district, tomb 975	The flat handle is joined to the moulded disc by a pierced plaque with Electra in a *peplos*, seated on the tomb of her father Agamemnon (characterised by the arms of the deceased) as she sadly embraces the vase which she believes contains the ashes of her brother Orestes.	COSTABILE, CARUSO 1982, pp. 371 ff., pl. 95.	C.S.
162		**Mirror** first half fourth century B.C. bronze h 29 cm; diam. of the disc 23 cm fragmentary handle Reggio Calabria, Museo Nazionale inv. 5762 Medma (Rosarno), from a tomb in the Grizzoso district	The disc decorated with two concentric circles has been cast separately compared to the handle which was soldered by means of a small plaque decorated with impressed ovuli. The handle, of pierced work, represents a satyr with an animal skin on its shoulders caught in the act of caressing a youth who is sleeping. The scene is framed in a natural environment rendered with rocks and stylised trees on the same plane as the figures.	IACOPI 1950, pp. 193-200; SABBIONE 1987, pp. 123-124.	M.T.I.
163	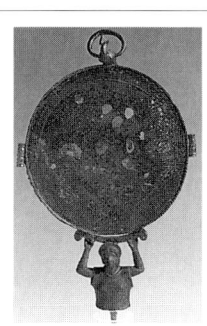	**Bronze mirror** mid-fifth century B.C. bronze diam. 16.1 cm Metaponto, Museo Archeologico Nazionale, inv. 305283 Metaponto, Pantanello necropolis tomb 350	Disc in bronze *lamina* with suspension ring in the form of a duck; lateral rochets and grip as a female figure with arms raised to join the stylised volutes of an Ionic capital. On one side is depicted the myth of Actaeon who, kneeling and in profile, with a deer skin over his shoulders, is devoured by dogs. The female figure most probably had a wooden hand grip.	CARTER 1990, pp. 95-98.	A.D.S.

164		**Mirror** mid-fifth century B.C. bronze, cast of unattached pieces engraving h 36.2 cm; diam. 15.5 cm partially reassembled, missing an Erote Metaponto, Museo Archeologico Nazionale, inv. 9998 Pisticci (Mt), necropolis, Casinello-San Teodoro district, tomb 08/04/53	Disc mirror adorned by engraved *gouillon* and beaded fillet; support of subtriangular form with ends finishing in half palmettes and volutes which support an erotes in flight. The handle is made up of a standing female figure holding a small rabbit in her outstretched right hand, while with the left she raises a part of her Doric peplos. The figure rests on a moulded conical-trunk base ending in three leonine paws.	LO PORTO 1968, p. 117, pls. 48-49. A.L.T.
165		**Little altar with winged Nike** mid-fifth century B.C. terra-cotta h 27.7 cm Locri, Antiquarium, inv. 79119	The relief scene on the front is framed by three pilasters with Ionic capitals. The personification of victory, in a *peplos* with great folded wings, holds a band, probably to honour a victorious athlete.	V. ORIGLIA, in *Locri Epizefiri III*, pp. 170-171, pls. XXXIII, XXXVI. C.S.
166 I		**Locrian pinax with abduction of Kore-Persephone** first half fifth century B.C. terra-cotta h 22.5 cm Reggio Calabria, Museo Nazionale inv. 28270 Locri Epizefiri, Sanctuary of Persephone in the Mannella district	The scene represents the rape of Kore-Persephone, dressed in a *peplos* and with a cock, attribute of fertility, by a young man with a *chlamys* on his shoulders (variously identified as one of the Dioscuri or as an envoy from the god of the Underworld) who jumps onto a charriot pulled by two winged horses.	PRUCKNER 1968, pp. 70 ff., pl. 14,4. C.S.
166 II		**Locrian pinax with procession scene** first half fifth century B.C. terra-cotta h 25 cm Reggio Calabria, Museo Nazionale inv. 57482 Locri Epizefiri, Sanctuary of Persephone in the Mannella district	On the right the priestess in a *chiton* and with veiled head holds a cup and slender sceptre and is preceded by a young girl who is carrying folded material (the marriage *peplos?*) on her head and by a child who is holding a stem with pine cone, attribute of fertility like the cock represented on the ground.	ZANCANI MONTUORO 1960, p. 41, pl. III. C.S.
166 III		**Locrian pinax with a ball being offered to Persephone** first half fifth century B.C. terra-cotta h 28 cm Reggio Calabria, Museo Nazionale inv. 28272 Locri Epizefiri, Sanctuary of Persephone in the Mannela district	On the left, a young girl in a *peplos* offers a cock and ball to Persephone on a throne, the goddess, dressed in a *chiton* and with veiled head, who is holding a cup. In the centre, is a piece of furniture on which folded material (perhaps the marriage *peplos?*) has been laid; below, a palmiped with unfolded wings. At the top, a *hydria* and two *paterae* are imagined hanging on the wall.	PRUCKNER 1968, pp. 48-49, pl. 7, 6. C.S.
166 IV		**Locrian pinax with Persephone and Dionysus** first half fifth century B.C. terra-cotta h 27 cm Reggio Calabria, Museo Nazionale inv. 58729 Locri Epizefiri, Sanctuary of Persephone in the Mannella district	Bearded Dionysus, wrapped in a *himation*, is holding behind his shoulders a long vine-shoot with large bunches of grapes and offers a *kantharos* as a sign of homage to Persephone, in a throne with a *chiton* and veiled head, who is holding a cock and ears of wheat, symbols of the fertility of animals and plants.	ORSI 1909, p. 424, fig. 7. C.S.

166 V	**Locrian pinax with Persephone and Hades on a throne** first half fifth century B.C. terra-cotta h 28 cm Reggio Calabria, Museo Nazionale inv. 21016 Locri Epizefiri, Sanctuary of Persephone in the Mannella district	Persephones and Hades are represented on a richly decorated throne; they bear several typical symbols of fertility; the cock, ears of corn, a branch with flowers and a libation cup. Under the throne is another cock and on the right a long stem supports a pine cone, another attribute of fertility.	ORSI 1909, p. 424, fig. 8.	C.S.
166 VI	**Locrian pinax with goddess and boy inside a basket** first half fifth century B.C. terra-cotta h 26 cm Reggio Calabria, Museo Nazionale inv. 61046 Locri Epizefiri, Sanctuary of Persephone in the Mannella district	An enthroned goddess, possibly Persephone, with a *chiton*, *himation* and diadem, raises the cover of a basket inside which there is a half-lying child, variously identified as Ploutos, or Brimos, or even Dionysus, to whom the *kantharos*, depicted under the piece of furniture supporting the basket, would allude. At the top, a mirror is suspended.	ORSI 1909, p. 469, fig. 40.	C.S.
167	**Pinax** 470–460 B.C. clay max h 22 cm; max w 21 cm reconstructed, some parts missing Syracuse, Museo Archeologico Regionale "Paolo Orsi", inv. 85649 Francavilla in Sicily, votive offering	The scene, present in the Locrian pinakes and known in Francavilla in three different variants, depicts the opening of the mystical basket, held by Persephone (on the right) in her lap, in the presence of a standing female figure (Ilithia?) who crowns the divine boy that issues from Persephone (Dionysus, Iacchus, or Pluto).	SPIGO 1987, pp. 307-308 (PPin 12), pl. XXX,2.	E.C.P.
168	**Female head** 500-480 B.C. clay h 26 cm; w 13 cm Reggio Calabria, Museo Nazionale inv. 2893 Medma (Rosarno), votive offerings of the Calderazzo district	The head, identified as that of the goddess Athena, is characterised by the classic, Archaic smile, by the swollen ocular globes, and the locks of "snail-like" hair which characterise the terracotta of the first decades of the fifth century B.C.	ORSI 1913, p. 79, fig. 87; MILLER 1983, p. 391, no. 924.	M.T.I.
169	**Female bust** first half fifth century B.C. clay h 38 cm; w 31 cm Reggio Calabria, Museo Nazionale inv. 2887 Medma (Rosarno), votive offerings of the Calderazzo district	The bust is very squarish with slight hinting of the breast. The very sculptured face has hair divided into two swollen bands which cover the ears, to which two globular earrings have been applied.	ORSI 1913, pp. 76-77, fig. 84; MILLER 1983, p. 380, no. 925.	M.T.I.
170	**Female bust** first half fifth century B.C. clay h 37 cm; w 25.5 cm Reggio Calabria, Museo Nazionale inv. 2891 Medma (Rosarno), votive offerings of the Calderazzo district	Squarish bust with slight hinting of the breast. The hair is arranged in three braids of "snail-like" curls.	ORSI 1913, pp. 78-79, fig. 88; MILLER 1983, p. 325, no. 223, pl. 21.	M.T.I.

171		**Standing female statuette** first half fifth century B.C. clay h 44 cm; w 16 cm Reggio Calabria, Museo Nazionale inv. 1123 Medma (Rosarno), votive offerings of the Calderazzo district	The figure of an offerer, covered by a *himation* and *chiton* treated with ample pleats, is holding a piece of the dress with her left hand and the right holds perhaps a lost *patera*. On her face, double bands of hair which lengthen into flat locks, falling onto the shoulders.	ORSI 1913, pp. 83-90, fig. 98; MILLER 1983, p. 312, no. 99, pl. IX.	M.T.I.
172		**Female statuette seated on a throne** first half fifth century B.C. clay h 41 cm; w 23 cm Reggio Calabria, Museo Nazionale inv. 1127 Medma (Rosarno), votive offerings of the Calderazzo district	The deity is dressed in a *chiton* and *himation* of dense pleats. In her hand she has a casket or small piece of furniture and is seated on a throne with a back decorated with projecting palmettes and supports of leonine paws.	ORSI 1913, pp. 91-95, fig. 103; MILLER 1983, p. 306, no. 23.	M.T.I.
173		**Female statuette seated on a throne** first half fifth century B.C. clay h 45.7 cm; w 23 cm Reggio Calabria, Museo Nazionale inv. 1128 Medma (Rosarno), votive offerings of the Calderazzo district	Female figure with covered head, seated rigidly on a throne, her hands holding a dove with spread wings.	ORSI 1913, pp. 91-95, fig. 105; MILLER 1983, p. 307, no. 34.	M.T.I.
174		**Female head** first half fifth century B.C. clay h 18.5 cm; w 13 cm Reggio Calabria, Museo Nazionale inv. 1071 Medma (Rosarno), votive offerings of the Calderazzo district	Hair divided into two sculpted bands which fall onto the neck in big, flat plaits. The features of her face are spread in the so-called "Archaic smile".	ORSI 1913, pp. 107-113; MILLER 1983, p. 342, no. 474.	M.T.I.
175		**Kriophoros** first half fifth century B.C. clay h 38 cm; w 13 cm Reggio Calabria, Museo Nazionale inv. 3487 Medma (Rosarno), votive offerings of the Calderazzo district	The statuette represents a bearded man, covered in a long cloak, who is carrying a ram on his shoulder as an offering to the deity.	ORSI 1913, pp. 119-124; MILLER 1983, p. 318, no. 157, pl. 12.	M.T.I.
176		**Group of Aphrodite with Eros** mid-fifth century B.C. clay h 33.5 cm; w 18 cm Reggio Calabria, Museo Nazionale inv. 607 C Medma (Rosarno)	The terra-cotta group represents the upper part of a veiled female figure dressed in a *chiton* and *himation* which falls in soft folds; on her left shoulder she is carrying a winged erotes which rests on her bent arm.	ORSI 1913, pp. 127-129; SABBIONE 1987, p. 126.	M.T.I.

Works on Exhibit

177

Female bust

beginning fifth century B.C.
clay, internally hollow, executed with fresh matrix
h 34.2 cm
Palermo, Museo Archeologico "A. Salinas", inv. 309
Selinunte, Malophoros Sanctuary

The treatment of the hair is particulary accurate as it is arranged over the forehead in a raised band of dense waves and gathered in big, smooth plaits which fall to the breast. The face presents protruding almond-shaped eyes with slightly raised eyebrows and a rectilinear cut to the mouth. Holes in the ears for earrings.

Bovio, Marconi 1969, p. 29, 258, pl. LXV; *Sicilia greca*, p. 114, no. 103. A.V.

178

Protome of female deity

beginning fifth century B.C.
yellow-orange terra-cotta, slip
h 29 cm; w 26 cm; t 8.5 cm
Agrigento, Museo Archeologico Regionale, inv. AG 2614
Vassallaggi (Caltanissetta) sanctuary (1961)

Protome of female deity, including part of the bust, equipped with a double hole for suspension above the forehead.

De Miro 1962, p. 144, pl. LIX, fig. 2. G.C.

179

Clay female bust

460–450 B.C.
clay, stick retouchings
h 42 cm; w 34.5 cm
reconstructed and reassembled
Syracuse, Museo Archeologico Regionale "Paolo Orsi", inv. 20403
Grammichele, votive materials in Pojo Aquja (1901)

A smooth bust, originally painted, and adorned with a necklace. On the head there is a high *polos* with a round pad at its base; long hair parted in the middle above the forehead and in regular waves delineated by a stick.

Rizza, De Miro 1985, p. 239, fig. 278; *Stile severo*, p. 267, no. 102, and further bibl. (fig. at p. 268). E.C.P.

180

Ephebe

480-460 B.C.
bronze, head and arms cast separately
bits of metal added to the body
eyes filled with vitreous paste
h 84.7 cm
Palermo, Museo Archeologico "A. Salinas", (temporary deposit)
Selinunte

Standing on the left leg with the right one bent; right hand stretched out, probably to hold a *phiale*; the left also probably held an object, lost. The hair is characterised by a series of locks disposed radially around the head.

Rizza, De Miro 1985, pp. 224-225, figs. 233-234; *Stile severo*, pp. 239-241, no. 82. A.V.

182

Athlete

end fifth-beginning sixth century B.C.
bronze, solid cast
h 28 cm
dark green patina
Gela, Museo Archeologico, inv. 35721
Gela hinterland

Standing figure of an athlete, perhaps a discus-thrower, with his left leg forwards and slightly bent, arm raised and turned forwards, the other arm lowered and turned backwards. The structure of his body is solid, the anatomy and muscular masses are at times distinguished in an exaggerated way. The face is framed by hair and moustaches, and the hair, gathered over the forehead in a pad with a big central knot, is rendered by irregular locks.

De Miro 1976, pp. 59, 82. R.P.

183 *see Recent Discoveries*

184

Antefix with the head of Silenus

470–460 B.C.
clay
h 23 cm; max w 11.5 cm
partially reconstructed jar
Gela, Museo Archeologico Regionale inv. 8294
Gela, via Apollo (Molino Di Pietro)

Part of the decoration of the roof of a sacred building, this antefix is characterized by a mask-like, ornamental rendering of facial features, accentuated by the harsh molding of the surface: parallel creases on the forehead, sculpted eyebrows, wrinkles around the eyes, equine ears, snub nose, thick lips, mustache, and little plaits of hair and beard in the form of a mane.

Orlandini 1954, pp. 259-266, pls. LXXXV,2, LXXXVI,2; *Stile severo*, p. 256, no. 93, and bibl. E.C.P.

Works on Exhibit

| 185 | **Antefix with the head of Heracles**

460–450 B.C.
clay
max h 21 cm; max w 17.6 cm; t 2.7 cm
polychrome traces, parts missing
Syracuse, Museo Archeologico Regionale "Paolo Orsi", inv. 49544
Syracuse, via Carso | Belonging perhaps to a grave monument. The figure, depicted in left profile, is recognizable as Heracles thanks to the *leonte*, a feature of which appears on the nape of the figure's neck. The crown of laurel alludes to the hero's rise to Mount Olympus, a theme appropriate to a funeral setting. | PARIBENI 1967, pp. 282 ff., fig. 3; *Stile severo*, pp. 260-261, no. 96.   E.C.P. |

| 186 | **Antefix with head of Acheloüs**

end fifth century B.C.
yellow-orange terra-cotta, slip
h 21.4 cm; w 18.2 cm
Agrigento, Museo Archeologico Regionale, inv. 6079
Agrigento, from a well to the north of the Temple of Heracles | Antefix shaped as the face of Acheloüs, fluvial god, depicted here with antropomorphic features, not taurine, but with a definite silenic look. | PUGLIESE CARRATELLI, FIORENTINI 1992, p. 86, fig. 87.   G.C. |

| 187 | **Male head from a funerary stele**

450–440 B.C.
marble
max h 25 cm; max w 28 cm
max t 5 cm
hole for a hinge (traces of lead within it); broken at the base of the neck
Syracuse, Museo Archeologico Regionale "Paolo Orsi", inv. 24837
Pachino, Burgio district | It depicts a person of mature age, bearded, in left profile. The rendering of the hair and beard, the former in curls calligraphically engraved in curved peaks, the latter in long, fine, wavy locks, reflects motifs of the Severe style, but there are also more advanced traits such as the treatment of the eyes, with eyelids distinct from the eyeball and narrow, shadowed eye sockets. | ROSS HOLLOWAY 1975, pp. 37-42; *Stile severo*, pp. 168-169, no. 6.   E.C.P. |

| 188 | **Head of female deity**

end fifth century B.C.
white marble
h 35 cm
Agrigento, Museo Archeologico Regionale, inv. AG 9245
Agrigento, 1954 excavation, from a cistern between the Sanctuary of the Chthonic Deities and the Temple of Zeus | The head belonged to a female statue of considerable dimensions, more than 2 metres. The inclined, veiled head probably belonged to a cult statue: identification with Demeter has been proposed. | GRIFFO 1987 pp. 142 ff. fig. 131.   G.C. |

| 189 | **Ludovisi Throne**

460-450 B.C.
marble | h 104.1 cm; l 1.44 cm; depth 72 cm
fragmentary
Rome, Museo Nazionale Romano inv. 8570
Rome, Villa Ludovisi 1887 ("Horti Sallustiani")

On the front, in the centre, a female figure visible from the waist up; the lower part of her body is hidden by a veil – she is wearing a light *chiton*. Two female figures, one with a *chiton*, the other with a *peplos*, headless, resting on rocky ground, carry it. On the short side on the left is a nude, young flautist, seated; on the short side on the right is a woman with a *chiton* and *himation*, seated, holding a box from which she takes a grain of incense to throw in the *thymiaterion* in front of her.

D. CANDILIO in *Museo Nazionale Romano*, pp. 54 ff.; ORLANDINI 1983, p. 440.   G.L'A. | |

| 190 | **Boston Throne**

marble | h 96 cm; l slabs 161 cm, 55 cm, 73 cm
Boston, Museum of Fine Arts, inv. ???
Provenienza ???

Main relief: two cloaked women to the sides of a winged Eros who is holding a balance with two male figures. *Lateral reliefs*: an ephebe who is playing the lyre on one; a bent old man on the other. The ends of the slabs are filled with volutes and palmettes. | COMPTOCK-VERMEULE 1976, pp. 20 ff. ORLANDINI 1983, p. 441.   G.L'A. |

191		**Large head of Apollo** 440-430 B.C. marble of Grecian type, bronze max h 41.3 cm; w (referred to the neck) 20.5 cm a large fragment of the left hand and another three fragments of fingers have been preserved Reggio Calabria, Museo Nazionale Cirò Marina (*Krimisa*) inside the cella of the Temple of Apollo Alaios	The whole belongs to a large acrolyte. A bronze wig would have been attached to the bare cranium; the holes for fixing it are evident. The orbital cavities would have been filled with bone and vitreous paste. Most probably, the idol represented Apollo standing with his head bent towards the ground and possibly carrying a bow and *patera*.	Orsi 1932, pp. 135-170; Orlandini 1983, p. 437. M.H.
192		**Head of Athena** first half fifth century B.C. white marble of Aegean provenance addition of metal elements h 29 cm Taranto, Museo Archeologico Nazionale, inv. 3899 Taranto	The statue is attributable with all likelihood to local production, as several stylistic features show (oval with emphasising of the jaw, inflated surfaces of the cheeks, fleshy lips), which are found in other sculptures of the Magna Graecia area.	Belli Pasqua 1991, pp. 34-38, II. 1 (and prec. bibl.). R.B.P.
193		**Female statue draped as a votive offering from Sorrento** third century B.C. h max 83 cm; w 50 cm; depth 23 cm Sorrento, Museo Correale di Terranova Sorrento, via dell'Accademia, 1911	Female figure sitting on a doe. She wears a *chiton* and cloak. Also the back of the statue has been sculpted. The figure leans on a tree trunk. The following inscription runs along the base: ΑΔΑΣΑΝΘΗΚ (ἁδας ἀνέθηκ[ε)	Levi 1924, p. 375 no. pl. XIX; Staehler 1985, pp. 326 ff.
194		**Draped female statue next to a quadruped as a votive offering from Sorrento** third century B.C. white marble (Penthelic?) from Greece h max 39 cm; w 48 cm; depth 27 cm Sorrento, Museo Correale di Terranova Sorrento, via dell'Accademia, 1911	Female figure lying on a saddle on a quadruped facing leftwards. The *chiton* that the female figure wears reveals part of her body, while her cloak covers the saddle and falls on the animal's back.	Levi 1924, pp. 375-384, pl. XXX; Staehler 1985, pp. 326 ff.
195		**Group with Dioscuro from the temple of Marasà** end fifth century B.C. marble from the island of Paros h 126 cm (140 cm with the base) Reggio Calabria, Museo Nazionale inv. 89538 Locri Epizefiri, Ionic temple of Marasà	One of the Dioscuri gets off a horse sustained by a triton with human bust and fish body. Together with an analogous, specular group it decorated the western front of the temple, celebrating the Dioscuri's miraculous help (they came from the sea on horseback, which the triton alludes to) to the Locrian army in the victorious battle of the Sagra River.	De Franciscis 1960, pp. 1 ff.; Costabie 1995, pp. 5 ff. C.S.
196		**Proto-Lucanian hydria with red figures** 430-440 B.C. refined clay, glaze, thrown on the wheel h 48 cm; diam. rim 17.3 cm Naples, Palazzo Reale, inv. 81949 Ruvo (?)	The vase shows two figured scenes separated by a band decorated with ovuli and palmettes. On the shoulder are three people, one of whom (Heracles?) is seated on a rock, opposed by a group of four Amazons. On the stomach a Dionysian procession is depicted. Attributed to the Painter of Amykos.	*RFVA*, I, p. 36, no. 137, pl. 12, 3-4. Mar.L.

197		**Proto-Apulian volute krater with red figures** end fifth-beginning sixth century B.C. clay, glaze, thrown on the wheel overpainting h 87.5 cm; diam. 51.6 cm Taranto, Museo Archeologico Nazionale, inv. 8264 Ceglie del Campo (BA), 1898 via G. Martini, *hypogeum*	*Side A*: on the neck, a *centauromachia*; on the front, birth of Dionysus from Zeus' thigh in front of other deities of Mount Olympus, arranged on two staggered planes. *Side B*: on the neck, three satyrs lay a table for Heracles; on the front, on two registers, battle scene between Greeks and Amazons. The krater is attributed to the Painter of the Birth of Dionysus.	RFVA, I, pp. 33-37; LABELLARTE 1988, pp. 315-317; D'AMICIS 1991, pp. 138-145.	A.D'A.
198		**Proto-Lucanian volute krater with red figures** end fifth century clay, glaze, thrown on the wheel applications *à la barbotine* overpainting h 82.8 cm; diam. 47 cm Taranto, Museo Archeologico Nazionale, inv. 8263 Ceglie del Campo (BA), 1898 via G. Martini, *hypogeum*	*Side A*: Dionysus seated on a rocky elevation between Artemis and a satyr on the right, a flautist and orgiastic maenad on the left. *Side B*: on the upper register, sileni fleeing in front of Perseus who is raising the cut-off head of Medusa; on the lower register, scenes of a ritual dance, linkable to the cult of the god.	LABELLARTE 1988, pp. 312-315; D'AMICIS 1991, pp. 132-137.	A.D'A.
199		**Lucanian nestoris with red figures** ca. 380 B.C. clay, glaze, thrown on the wheel h 67.5 cm; diam. 48 cm London, British Museum, inv. F179	*Nestoris* with rosettes applied to the handles. The neck is decorated with a meander and branch of laurel on the main side, with a trace of ivy and branch of laurel on the other. *Side A*: Dionysus and a satyr under a pergola, among satyrs, maenads and a papposilenus. *Side B*: Dionysian *thiasos* with five characters. Attributed to the Painter of Brooklyn-Budapest.	LCS, I, p. 113, no. 482	G.L'A.
200		**Krater from Paestum with red figures** mid-fourth century B.C. clay, glaze, thrown on the wheel h 39 cm, diam. 43 cm Paris, Musée du Louvre, inv. K240 Paestum	Bell-shaped krater. *Side A*: Dionysus, with a crown and thyrsus, on the back of a panther, between a papposilenus and a maenad flautist, who proceed towards the right preceded by a child satyr. *Side B*: standing female figure with *phiale*, Eros with horn and *phiale*; between them a duck; on the left a stele. Attributed to the Painter of the Louvre K240.	TRENDALL 1987, p. 45.	G.L'A.
201		**Siceliot situla with red figures** second half fourth century B.C. clay h 18.7 cm Reggio Calabria, Museo Nazionale inv. 4795 Locri Epizefiri, necropolis in the Lucifero district, tomb 844	Pouring spout and bridge handle above the mouth. On the neck, procession of three nereids transported by a dolphin and two mythical marine animals. On the body an old, nude silenus, seated, is surrounded by maenads and young satyrs, some of whom are dancing. Attributed to the circle of the Painter of Maron.	SPIGO 1987, p. 4, no. 37.	C.S.
202		**Sculpted vase in the form of a maenad** mid-fourth century century B.C. clay h 18.5 cm fragmentary Reggio Calabria, Museo Nazionale inv. 4823 Locri Epizefiri, necropolis in the Lucifero district, tomb 934	The dancing maenad, with crown of leaves on her complex hairstyle, is wearing a *chiton* which leaves her right breast uncovered and a panther skin on her left arm, with a drum hanging from it.	ARIAS 1984, pp. 677-679.	C.S.

203		**Krater in the Gnathia style** 330-320 B.C. clay, thrown on the wheel, glaze, slip overpainting h 31 cm; diam. 38.3 cm Lecce, Museo Provinciale, inv. 1010 Rudiae	Bell-shaped krater. *Side A*: under the rim, vine-shoot, knotty, zig-zag branch with bunches of grapes, leaves and tendrils. In the centre, a dancing maenad dressed in a long *chiton* and cloak, is holding a drum in her right hand and a torch in her left; a double file of dots make up the ground line. *Side B*: under the rim, near the handles, dry graffito branch with small painted leaves arranged in the corner. Close to the Painter of the Bottle of the Louvre.	*CVA*, Lecce, I, IV, pl. IV, 2-4; Forti 1965, pp. 60, 61, pl. XVIIc; Green 1968, p. 37. M.T.G.
204		**Relief with figure of banqueter** end fifth century B.C. yellow-orange coloured terra-cotta no slip h 28.5 cm; w 17.5 cm Agrigento, Museo Archeologico Regionale, inv. C 287 Provenance unknown, from the collections of the ex Museo Civico of Agrigento	The relief represents a young banqueter lying on a *kline*. Dressed in a *himation* which, having fallen from his shoulders, leaves his thorax exposed, he has a diadem formed by two bands with two adorned rows between them, covering his head. He is holding a *kantharos* in his left hand.	Marconi 1929, p. 188, fig. 122. G.C.
205		**Pinax with recumbent figure** first half fourth century B.C. clay, executed in matrix with retouchings by spatula reassembled h 42.5 cm; w 33.1 cm Metaponto, Museo Archeologico Nazionale, inv. 135679 Metaponto, Theatre, votive offering sector E1 (1979)	Relief on high base, representing male bearded figure (Dionysus), adorned with *taenia* and *stephane*, and with a *kantharos* in his right hand, half-lying on a *kline*; to the left is a veiled, female figure dressed in a *chiton* and *himation* with a nude young man at her feet. At the top, in the background is an equine *protome* in profile towards the left. Unpublished.	F. G. Lo Porto 1966, pp. 165 ff., figs. 28-32, pls. VII-VIII; *Metaponto* I, pp. 419 ff., figs. 61-62; Letta 1971, pp. 61 ff.
206		**Pinax with maenad and satyr** clay, executed in matrix with retouchings by spatula reassembled and fragmentary h 36.2 cm; w 26.1 cm Metaponto, Museo Archeologico Nazionale, inv. 134555 Metaponto, Apollo Licio sanctuary, votive offerings, sacellum E (1977)	Relief with dancing maenad and satyr. The maenad is holding a big cornucopia with her left arm and is wearing a light, fluttering chiton; to her right the bearded satyr, with his head adorned by a *taenia* and completely nude apart from tall footwear, is holding a large krater with small columns in his right arm. Unpublished.	Lo Porto 1988, p. 22 ff.
207		**Block of tufa with Greek inscription** fifth century B.C. h 113 cm; w 86 cm; t 27.5 cm tufa, fragmented Naples, Museo Archeologico Nazionale, inv. 129874 Cuma, (Correale)	The inscription, engraved on the internal face of a tufa slab, broken in two pieces, which served to cover a large sepulchre, warns: "It is not right to be entombed here, unless one has been initiated to the Bacchic cults". The epigraph evidently belongs to an initiate of mysteries, a follower of the cult of Dionysus.	Jeffery 1990, pp. 239-240, no. 12. T.G.
208 **209** **210**		**Golden Orphic tablets** fourth century B.C. gold, complete h 2.8 cm; w 4.7 cm	h 2.5 cm; w 4.6 cm h 3.6 cm; w 5.1 cm Naples, Museo Archeologico Nazionale, inv. 111623-111625; 111463-111464 Thurii The tablets, conventionally called "Orphic", come from two funerary tumuli, the so-called Timponi, situated in the land of Thurii. They had the function of *vademecum* to guide the deceased to the next world so that he could reach,	thanks to his condition of initiate, a privileged situation of beatitude, avoiding the painful cycles of reincarnation. Guarducci 1974, pp. 7 ff.; Pugliese Carratelli 1983, p. 41, fig. 9. T.G.

Works on Exhibit

211
212 Golden Orphic tablets

fourth century B.C.
gold, complete
h 5.4 cm; w 2.9 cm
h 2.3 cm; w 8.1 cm
Naples, Museo Archeologico
Nazionale, inv. 111623-111625;
111463-111464
Thurii

The tablets, conventionally called "Orphic", come from two funerary tumuli, the so-called Timponi, situated in the land of Thurii. They had the function of *vademecum* to guide the deceased to the next world so that he could reach, thanks to his condition of initiate, a privileged situation of beatitude, avoiding the painful cycles of reincarnation.

GUARDUCCI 1974, pp. 7 ff.; PUGLIESE CARRATELLI 1983, p. 41, fig. 9.
T.G.

213 Lamina in inscribed gold

end fifth century B.C.
gold, engraved
h 3.2 cm; w 6 cm
Vibo Valentia, Museo Archeologico
Statale "Vito Capialbi", inv. 1671
Hipponion, (Vibo Valentia), western
necropolis (INAM), tomb 19

Extremely thin *lamina* in gold, folded back four times on itself and placed on the high part of the deceased's sternum. It presents a Greek inscription engraved in sixteen lines, which provides the deceased with all the instructions necessary to guide his spirit, initiated into the Orphic doctrine, on his other-world journey. The folding was perhaps a ritual act, destined to preserve the sacred text from profane eyes.

FOTI-PUGLIESE CARRATELLI 1974, pp. 91-126; PUGLIESE CARRATELLI 1993.
M.T.I.

214 Apulian amphora with red figures

330-320 B.C.
clay, glaze, overpainting, thrown
on the wheel
h 86.5 cm
Basle, Antikenmuseum, inv. 540

Side A: inside a *naiskos*, from the roof of which a helmet, a shield and two wheels are hanging, is Orpheus with his lyre and a seated dead person with a roll of papyrus in his left hand. Four people are arranged around them, two male and two female, with offerings. Side B: two female and two male figures with offerings are seated all around a stele. Attributed to the Painter of Ganymede.

SCHMIDT-TRENDALL-CAMBITOGLOU 1976, p. 11, pl. VII c-d.
G.L'A.

215 I Alabastron

last quarter of fifth centruy B.C.
alabaster
h 29.5 cm; diam. rim 7.5 cm
Potenza, Soprintendenza Archeologico
della Basilicata, deposits, inv. 318636
Metaponto (Mt), funerary furnishings,
Torretta district

Large bottle for perfume of tapering shape with distinct neck and very wide upper disc. Two small lateral grips are on the upper part of the body.

BOTTINI 1988, pp. 1-18; IDEM, 1992, pp. 64-85.
E.P.

215 II Pendant

last quarter fifth century B.C.
bone
h 5.8 cm; w 1.8 cm
Potenza, Soprintendenza Archeologico
della Basilicata, deposits, inv. 318637
Metaponto (Mt), funerary furnishings
Torretta district

Engraved, anthropomorphic pendant represents, on one side, a nude male figure with arms along his sides and, on the other side, a draped female figure. In place of the breasts, two large cavities with traces of bronze indicate the presence of applications. Extremely summary treatment of both faces.

A. BOTTINI 1988, pp. 1-18; IDEM 1992, pp. 64-85.
E.P.

215 III Small sculpture portraying Helen

last quarter fifth century B.C.
whitish limestone
h 5.8 cm; max w 4.2 cm
Potenza, Soprintendenza Archeologico
della Basilicata, deposits, inv. 318638
Metaponto (Mt), funerary furnishings
Torretta district

Small sculpture in the form of an egg with irregular opening on the front side which frames a child-like figure, crouching inside with its hands resting on the edge. Rounded head with smooth, thick hair, features rendered by engraving, Traces of red paint.

A. BOTTINI 1988, pp. 1 ff.; IDEM 1992, pp. 64-85.
E.P.

215 IV

Cylindrical pyx

last quarter fifth century B.C.
white marble
h 6.1 cm (total); h body 5.4 cm
diam. base and cover 15.2 cm
Potenza, Soprintendenza Archeologica della Basilicata, deposits, inv. 318639
Metaponto (MT), funerary furnishings, Torretta district

Cylindrical *pyx* in profile, slightly flared, large base disc with three list feet. Supporting tooth for the cover which presents a nearly flat pommel grip, emphasised by a red band. On the walls of the body a standing, draped male figure with profile to the left and stretching out a vase is barely visible.

A. BOTTINI 1988, pp. 1 ff.; Idem, 1992, pp. 64-85.
E.P.

216

Bell-shaped neck-amphor with red figures showing the birth of Helen

mid-fourth century B.C.
clay
h 62.7 cm; reassembled
Paestum, Museo Archeologico Nazionale, inv. 21370
Paestum, Adriuolo, tomb 24

Depicted on the main side, in the centre of the composition, is Helen coming out of a big egg on an altar on which the signature of the painter is painted: *Pithon egrapsen*. The newborn stretches her arms towards her mother, Leda, who rushes up from the left while, on the opposite side, old Tyndareus assists at the miraculous birth. In the upper part of the vase are the half-busts of Hermes, Aphrodite, the maenad Phoiba and the papposileno Tybron. On the opposite side, Dionysus, with his legs wrapped in a *himation*, is sitting between a silenus and a maenad.

TRENDALL 1987, pp. 139-140, no. 240 and pp. 142-143, pl. 89; PONTRANDOLFO-ROUVERET 1992, p. 323, fig. of p. 322.
F.L.

217

Apulian krater of the phylakes with red figures

375-350 B.C.
clay, overpainting, thrown on the wheel
h 34 cm; diam. 26.6 cm
Bari, Museo Archeologico, inv. 3899
Bari, corso Vittorio Emanuele, bought in 1900

In the centre of the stage two actors are acting: on the right, a male character makes a sign to stop the old man, who is in front of him, armed with a two-edged axe and meaning to hit the egg, which is miraculously opening to let out Helen, the only character not in *phylakes* costume.
A female figure identifiable as Leda, wife of the king of Sparta, to whom the egg had been entrusted and who is therefore Helen's adoptive mother, assists at the event from a half-open door. Attributed to the Painter of Dijon.

RFVA, I, p. 148; *LIMC*, IV, 1, no. 5, p. 503.
M.L.

218 *see Recent Discoveries*

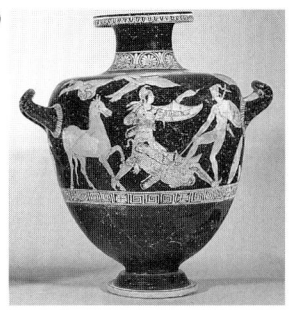

219

Lucanian hydria with red figures

second half fifth centruy B.C.
refined clay, thrown on the wheel
h 31 cm
Metaponto, Museo Archeologico Nazionale, inv. 128551
Metaponto, Saldone necropolis

In the centre of the scene of the main side a male figure clearly detaches himself; in profile, bearded, laureate and with the attributes of Zeus. On both sides two fleeing female figures going in opposite directions. It is probable that it is the amorous pursuit of the nymph Aegina on the part of the god. Work attributable to the Painter of Pisticci.

CARTER 1976, pp. 846-847; pl. CXXXIV.
A.D.S.

220 I

Pelike with red figures with Athena and Poseidon

end fifth century B.C.
clay
h 45 cm; max diam. 33.5 cm
Policoro, Museo Nazionale della Siritide, inv. 35304
Herakleia, western necropolis

Side A: warrior on horseback with Doric inscription which identifies him as Poseidon. He is armed with trident and defensive panoply. To his right is a young horseman, possibly Hermes.

Side B: Athena on a *triga* next to another female figure. She is wearing a shield with radial *episema* and a two-pointed stick to incite the horses to gallop. The scene seems to refer to the contest between Poseidon and Athena for the conquest of Attica.

DEGRASSI 1965, pp. 12 ff.
S.B.

220 II

Hydria with red figures

data
clay
h 44.5 cm; max diam. 32.2 cm
Policoro, Museo Nazionale della Siritide, inv. 35214
Herakleia, western necropolis

Accessory decoration of band of ovuli around the rim with frieze alternating with palmettes, lotus buds and meanders. *Side A*: scene with the death of Sarpedon, whose name comes to us through the work of Patroclus. On the upper part is the transportation of Prince Lycian in flight by *Thanatos and Hypnos*. *Side B*: ample decoration with palmettes.

DEGRASSI 1965, pp. 12 ff.
S.B.

Works on Exhibit

220 III — Pelike with red figures

end fifth century B.C.
clay
h 40.6 cm; max diam. 30.5 cm
Policoro, Museo Nazionale della Siritide, inv. 35297
Herakleia, western necropolis

Accessory decoration with frieze of palmettes and meanders. *Side A*: scene of the punishment of Dirce tied to a bull with the possible figures of Anfione and Zeto at the sides. *Side B*: four young men conversing in pairs.

DEGRASSI 1965, pp. 12 ff.   S.B.

221 — Apulian bell-shaped krater with red figures

390-380 B.C.
clay, thrown on the wheel, overpainting
h 45 cm; diam. 51 cm
Taranto, Museo Archeologico Nazionale, inv. 4605
Taranto, perhaps from excavations in the Arsenale Militare, 1913

Meeting between Orestes and Electra near Agamemnon's tomb: a funerary monument, with dado relief portraying battle scenes and surmounted by a column and the standing statue of the deceased with his offensive and defensive weapons, stands out.
On the tomb are bands and ritual vases in bronze; around it are offering figures. Attributed to the Painter of Sarpedonte.

RFVA, I, p. 164.   E.L.

222 — Apulian volute krater with red figures and Orestes at Delphi

390-380 B.C.
refined clay, glaze, thrown on the wheel, overpainting
h 76.5 cm
complete
Naples, Museo Archeologico Nazionale, inv. 82270
Ruvo

Side A: on the cover, female figure, perhaps a muse, is holding a lyre and plethron. On the body, the nude hero with ruffled hair seeks refuge in the Delphic temple, where he embraces the *omphalos*. To his left Erynis can just be seen, holding a snake. Apollo, in the centre, opposes him, with bow and arrows and holds his right hand out towards the priestess Pythia who flees in alarm. On the extreme right of the scene Artemis is visible flanked by two dogs. Inside the temple two tripods are visible. *Side B*: on the cover, papposilenus with the *narthex*. *On the body*: Dionysian scene. Attributed to the Black Fury Painter.

RFVA, I, p. 167, 13.   Mar.L.

223 — Apulian krater with red figures

380-370 B.C.
clay, glaze, thrown on the wheel, overpainting
h 48.5 cm
Paris, Musée du Louvre, inv. K710
Armento

Under the lip a band of laurel and ovuli motif; underneath the figured scene a band of meanders and crosses; palmettes and plant volutes under the handles. *Side A*: the purification of Orestes at Delphi. *Side B*: two young-men and a woman. Attributed to the Painter of the Eumenides.

RFVA, I, p. 97, no. 229.   G.L'A.

224 — Apulian oinochoe with red figures

375-350 B.C.
refined clay, glaze, thrown on the wheel, overpainting
h 21.8 cm; diam. 12.5 cm
Taranto, Museo Archeologico Nazionale, inv. 56048
Taranto, 17.6.1952, the Carmine district, Piazzale Sardegna, tomb 62

On the body, between a metopal square bounded, at the top, by ovuli and a row of ivy leaves, at the bottom, by a band of meanders and laterally, by an arrow motif, is a *phylakes* scene: In the centre, is Heracles in the act of making love spells with the *iynx*, after having put down the bow and club. On the right, hoary Jolas, leaning on a stick, admonishes the hero, while to the left, King Eurysteus, with *polos* crown and short cloak, advances leaning on crutches.

TRENDALL 1967, pp. 18, 64, no. 122, tav. VIII a; DE JULIIS, LOIACONO 1985, pp. 266-267, no. 307.   G.A.M.

225 — Apulian volute krater with red figures

350-325 B.C.
well refined clay
h 62.6 cm; diam. 32 cm
Naples, Museo Archeologico Nazionale, inv. 82113
Ruvo (found May 1836)

Side A: scene of the meeting of Orestes with Iphigenia, now priestess of Artemis in Tauris. On the bottom, Pylades, Orestes seated on the altar with bowed head, Iphigenia and temple servant. At the top, Apollo and Artemis, with double spear, divided by a laurel shrub. To their left, Ionic temple with open doors, partially covered by high ground. *Side B*: two opposing couples, on the right the woman has a veiled head, on the left, the young people have entwined hands. Circle of the Painter of Ilioupersis.

RFVA, I, p. 193, no. 3.   Mar.L.

Works on Exhibit

227		**Krater from Paestum with phylakes scenes** mid fourth century B.C. clay, glaze, thrown on the wheel h 37 cm; diam. 36 cm Berlin, Staatliche Museum zu Berlin Preussischer Kulturbesitz inv. F3044 S. Agata dei Goti	Calyx krater. Side A: scene of a robbed miser, with four people indentifiable by inscribed names. In the background two hanging female masks. Side B: Dionysus with *phiale* and thyrsus, followed by a satyr carrying a torch and egg. Signed by Asteas.	TRENDALL 1987, p. 84.	G.L'A.
228		**Bell krater from Paestum with red figures** ca. 330 B.C. refined clay, glaze, thrown on the wheel h 35 cm; diam. 32 cm Naples, Museo Archeologico Nazionale, inv. 81417 S. Agata	Bell krater. *Side A*: Papposilenus with *thyrsus*, holds up a bird in front of a Siren roosting on a rock, in front of which is a snake. *Side B*: two draped youths, leaning on sticks. Attributed to Python.	TRENDALL 1987, p. 160, no. 288, p. 154.	G.L'A.
229		**Bell krater from Paestum with red figures** 350-330 B.C. clay, glaze, thrown on the wheel h 56.5 cm; diam. 53 cm London, British Museum inv. 1917.12-10.1 Paestum	Bell krater by Python. *Side A*: Orestes on an *omphalos* between Athena, on the left, and Apollo and a fury, on the right. Above the scene female busts and those of a Fury and a young man (Pylades?) have been arranged. *Side B*: Dionysus between a maenad and a silenus; above are busts of a silenus and a maenad.	TRENDALL 1987, p. 145, pl. 91.	G.L'A.
230		**Chalice krater with red figures** early fourth century B.C. clay h 42.5 cm Syracuse, Museo Archeologico Regionale "Paolo Orsi," inv. 36334 Syracuse, Fusco necropolis	*Side A*: the principal scene, inspired by Aeschylus' Choephoroe, depicts the reunion of Electra, seated on the tomb of Agamemnon (in the center), and Orestes (on the right), in the presence of Pylades (on the extreme left) and a *canephora*. *Side B*: a satyr and a maenad. Attributed to the Painter of Dirce.	TRENDALL 1967, p. 203, no. 26; TRENDALL 1989, p. 29, fig. 60.	E.C.P.
231		**Siceliot calyx krater with red figures (circle of the Painter from Syracuse 47099)** 360-340 B.C. clay h 34 cm; diam. 33 cm Lipari, Museo Eoliano, room XXII inv. 9405 Lipari, necropolis of the Diana district tomb 730 (used as a cinerary)	*Side A*: three moments from the tragedy of Euripides, *Alcmena*. On the right, Hermes, who was probably entrusted with the prologue; in the centre, Alcmene about to be burnt on the pyre erected by her consort Amphitryon, to punish her for her unknowing adultery with Zeus, the *deus ex macchina* who will come to Alcmene's help in the epilogue. *Side B*: the scene, possibly attributable to the lost tragedy *Le donne di Colchide* (P. Ghiron Bistagne), represents the fatal falling in love of Medea - an erotes, in the centre, is hurling a spear at her - and Jason. TRENDALL, WEBSTER 1971, p. 76, III, 3, 7; TRENDALL 1983, p. 272, no. 29 d; SPIGO 1987, p. 34. U.S.		
232		**Fragment of a chalice krater with red figures** ca. 330–320 B.C. clay max h 24 cm; diam. ca. 30 cm Syracuse, Museo Archeologico Regionale "Paolo Orsi," inv. 66557 Syracuse, Fusco necropolis, tomb 34	Side A: the scene, in an artificial setting of columns, is from Oedipus Rex by Sophocles: Tiresias, the white-haired old man on the left is speaking to Oedipus about the death of Laius while Oedipus, in the center, between the two girls, Antigone and Ismene, listens thoughtfully; Jocasta, covers her face in dismay, like the woman on the right. *Side B*: three standing figures in flowing gowns.	F. GIUDICE in *Sikaria*, p. 259, fig. 299; TRENDALL 1989, p. 236, fig. 429.	E.C.P.

233	**Bell krater of the tunny fish seller** 380-370 B.C. clay, traces of slip h 38 cm Cefalù, Museo Fondazione Culturale Mandralisca, inv. 2 Lipari, necrolpolis of the Diana district, excavations of Barone Enrico Pirajno di Mandralisca (1864)	*Side A*: to the left, an old fishmonger cuts a portion of tunny fish; on the right, the client, a small man with thin legs, hol out the money to pay. *Side B*: two young lovers talking. Attributed to the "Painter of the tunny fish seller".	TRENDALL 1967a, p. 208, no. 54; TRENDALL 1967b, pp. 83-84, no. 191; GIUDICE 1985, p. 256, fig. 285; TULLIO 1991, p. 68, fig. 55. A.T.	
234	**Theatrical backdrop** third century B.C. painted terra-cotta h 32.2 cm; w 28 cm; t base 8cm Naples, Museo Archeologico Nazionale, inv. C.S.362 Santangelo Collection	The terra-cotta reproduces a scenic backdrop in the form of a door; four columns with Ionic capitals frame, low down, three doors; a second order of columns holds up a tympanum pediment, with a female bust in the centre and a disc *akroterion* at the corners. The architectural prospect is inserted between two high towers.	FORTI, STAZIO 1983, p. 672, fig. 700. M.B.	
235	**Arula** end fifth-first half fourth century B.C. clay, matrix h 52 cm; l 73 cm; depth 32.5 cm Reggio Calabria, Museo Nazionale inv. 2871 Medma (Rosarno), from tomb 19 of the necropolis found in the Nolio district, in the winter of 1914	The front side of the arula is decorated with a scene, from the Sophoclean tragedy relative to the myth of Tyre; her two sons, Pelia and Neleo, are depicted in a gesture of supplication, seated above an altar, as they surround their mother, for whose liberation they have killed cruel Siderus, who lies on the ground. The old father, Salmoneus, is present in the scene, depicted on the right, fleeing in desperation. PAOLETTI 1982, pp. 372-375, pl. 95,1-2.	M.T.I.	
236 I-II	**Pair of masks from the same tragedy** first half fourth century B.C. clay h 7.9 and 8.7 cm Lipari, Museo Eoliano, room XXIII inv. 18401 b-c Lipari, necropolis, trench XLV 1993 (owner Mirto), tomb 2486	Small earthenware models of masks of Hecuba and Taltibio, characters from the tragedy *Le Troiane* by Euripides. Hecuba's expression of profound pain and Taltibio's contrasting sentiment allude to the moment when the small Astianatte was killed and given to the grandmother in order to be buried, while Andromache is taken away as a slave and the flames rise over Troy.	BERNABÒ BREA 1995, pp. 3-9; CAVALIER 1995. L.B.B.	
236 III-IV	**Pair of masks from the same tragedy** 350-330 B.C. clay h 7.2 and 6.6 cm Lipari, Museo Eoliano, room XXIII inv. 15420 h-g Lipari, necropolis, trench XXIII 1985 tomb 2184	Earthenware models of masks of Pelops and the child Chrysippus, characters from the lost tragedy *Chrysippus* by Euripides. The convivial crown which encircles their heads alludes to the fact that the rape of Chrysippus by Laius happened during a banquet.	BERNABÒ BREA-CAVALIER 1991, pp. 161 ff., pls. CXXXVII-CXXXVIII. L.B.B.	
237	**Four masks belonging to the same comedy** ca. 350 B.C.	clay h 7.7, 7.7, 8.3 and 8.7 cm Lipari, Museo Eoliano, room XXIII inv. 14593, 14590, 14592, 14591 Lipari, necropolis, trench XXXIX 1982, tomb 1987 Four comic masks evidently from the same comedy, not identifiable. Male, beardless mask, perhaps a young god, who might have intervened in the prologue to explain the facts prior to the	comedy. Another bearded male mask with convivial crown (from the same matrix of the Blepiro of the *Ecclesiazuse*). Two female masks, one with a sinciput chignon and the other with a convivial crown (from the same matrix of the Prassagora of the *Ecclesiazuse*, modified by the addition of a crown). BERNABÒ BREA-CAVALIER 1991, pp. 45 ff., 58 ff., pl. XXIX. L.B.B.	

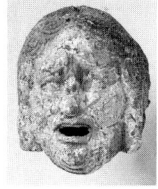

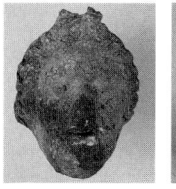

Works on Exhibit

238 I		**Satiric statuette of the age of the middle comedy** second half fourth century B.C. clay h 7.2 cm Lipari, Museo Eoliano, room XXII inv. 15156, Lipari, necropolis, trench XXXVI 1984, (property Zagami) votive ditch M	Papposilenus plays the double flute swaying on his legs. He is nude with a cloak falling behind his shoulders.	Unpublished. Cfr. BERNABÒ BREA 1981, p. 65, D 8, fig. 62. L.B.B.
238 II		**Satiric statuette of the age of the middle comedy** second half fourth century B.C. clay h 8 cm Lipari, Museo Eoliano, room XXIII inv. 11331 Lipari, necropolis, trench XXXIII 1972	Papposilenus as a philoshopher, standing, leaning against a small pilaster, with a *himation* around the lower part of his body.	BERNABÒ BREA 1981, p. 67, D 13 a, fig. 66. L.B.B.
238 III		**Satiric statuette of the age of the middle comedy** second half fourth century B.C. clay, white slip h 9.8 cm Lipari, Museo Eoliano, room XXIII inv. 10581 Lipari, necropolis, trench XXXI 1971	Indecent, nude satyr with great wine-skin on his shoulders.	Umpublished. Cf. BERNABÒ BREA 1981, pp. 63-64, D 1 b, fig. 59. L.B.B.
239 I		**Statuette related to the middle comedy** second half fourth century B.C. clay, white slip h 12 cm Lipari, Museo Eoliano, room XXIII inv. 15128 g Lipari, necropolis, trench XXXVI 1984, tomb 2123	An old bawd with convivial crown.	BERNABÒ BREA-CAVALIER 1995, p. 94, pl. LVIII, 5. Cfr. BERNABÒ BREA 1981, p. 90, E 54, fig. 125. L.B.B.
239 II		**Statuette related to the middle comedy** second half fourth century B.C. clay, traces of white slip h 13.1 cm Lipari, Museo Eoliano, room XXIII inv. 3463 Lipari, necropolis, trench XV 1953 sporadic	Callipygean flute-player who, holding a double flute in her right hand, repeats the gesture of the young Syracusan girls which Athens tells us of; they invited a passer-by to be the judge of their beauty contest.	BERNABÒ BREA 1981, p. 110, F 1 b, fig. 181. L.B.B.
239 III		**Statuette related to the middle comedy** ¹ half fourth century B.C clay, white slip h 10 cm Lipari, Museo Eoliano, room XXIII inv. 6955 Lipari, discharge in front of the urban walls of the fourth century B.C., 1971	The ashamed one: Phrygian flute-player (as the cap indicates) in very thin, dancer's dress who, crouching down, hides herself by crossing her arms in front of her chest and clasping the double flute.	BERNABÒ BREA 1981, p. 110, F 3 d, fig. 182. L.B.B.

239 IV		**Statuette related to the middle comedy** second half fourth century B.C. clay, white slip h 10.4 cm Lipari, Museo Eoliano, room XXIII inv. 3161 Lipari, around the altar of the sanctuary of the Maggiore ground, Trench XXIII 1955	Standing, comic actor with convivial crown in the typical phallic costume of the "middle comedy". Head bowed towards the left.	Bernabò Brea-Cavalier 1965, p. 303, B 115 b, pl. CLXI, 3; Bernabò Brea 1981, pp. 81-82, E 29 b, fig. 97. L.B.B.
239 V		**Statuette related to the middle comedy** second half fourth century B.C. clay, white slip h 10.9 cm Lipari, Museo Eoliano, room XXIII inv. 10783 Lipari, necropolis, Trench XXXI 1971	Comic actor in phallic costume and with convivial crown, perhaps in the part of a slave taking refuge on a quadrangular-shaped altar; motif which frequently recurs in the depictions of the "middle comedy".	Bernabò Brea 1981, p. 81, E 28 g; cfr. fig. 96 ibidem. L.B.B.
239 VI		**Statuette related to the middle comedy** second half fourth century B.C. clay h 11.5 cm Lipari, Museo Eoliano, room XXIII inv. 10661 Lipari, necropolis, Trench XXX 1971	The rejoicer: standing, comic actor in phallic costume who crosses his arms over his chest.	Bernabò Brea 1981, p. 85, E 41g; cfr. fig. 110 ibidem. L.B.B.
239 VII		**Statuette related to the middle comedy** second half fourth century B.C. clay h 6.9 cm Lipari, Museo Eoliano, room XXIII inv. 3150 Lipari, necropolis, Trench XVII 1953 sporadic	Standing, clownish statuette of Heracles in phallic costume with a sulky look. He has a leontea on his head and is resting his right hand on the club on the ground.	Bernabò Brea-Cavalier 1965, p. 302, B 111 a, pl. CLXV, 7; Bernabò Brea 1981, p. 74, E 2 a, fig. 72. L.B.B.
240		**Statuette of actor of the middle comedy** first half third century B.C. clay, white slip and traces of added colour h 10.5 cm Lipari, Museo Eoliano, room XXIII inv. 13474 f Lipari, necropolis, Trench XXXVI 1979, (property Zagami), tomb 1817	Statuette of comic actor in the part of *Hegemon Presbytes* of the "new comedy" (no. 3 in the Polluce catalogue). It is a mask with a double expression, with one normal eyebrow and the other raised, so that the character could show himself to be good-natured or angry according to which side he showed to the public.	Bernabò Brea-Cavalier 1995, p. 58, tav. LXVI, 1. Cfr. per il tipo: Bernabò Brea 1981, p. 150, nos. 11-12, fig. 238. L.B.B.
241 I	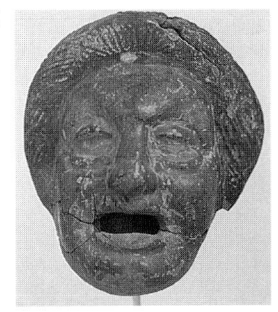	**Mask related to the new comedy** first half third century B.C. clay, well preserved polychrome h front 7.3 cm Lipari, Museo Eoliano, room XXIII, inv. 10778 Lipari, necropolis, Trench XXXI 1971	Mask of *Kolax* (the adulterer), one of the parasites (Polluce's mask 17), which smiles nastily and has a smooth forehead like that of the dog which licks its owner.	Bernabò Brea 1981, p. 189, fig. 306. L.B.B.

Works on Exhibit

241 II	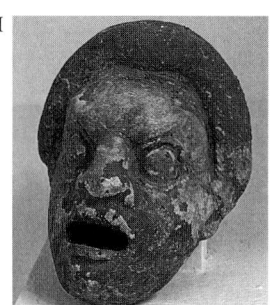	**Mask related to the new comedy** first half third century B.C. clay, well preserved polychrome h 8 cm Lipari, Museo Eoliano, room XXIII inv. 11289 Lipari, necropolis, Trench XXII 1972	Mask of *Parasitos* (Polluce's mask 18), florid and aquiline nose (*epigrypos*).	BERNABÒ BREA 1981, p. 192, fig. 314. L.B.B.
241 III	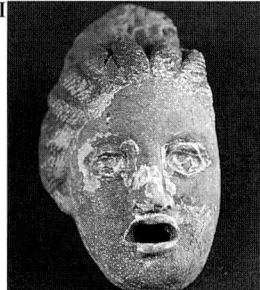	**Mask related to the new comedy** first half third century B.C. clay h 8.6 cm Lipari, Museo Eoliano, room XXIII inv. 9771 (9721) Lipari, necropolis, Trench XI 1971 sporadic	Small earthenware model of female mask identifiable as the *Pallaké* of the "new comedy" (cf. Polluce's mask 37). It is the mask of *Chrysis* in Menander's *Samia*.	BERNABÒ BREA 1981, p. 224, fig. 380. L.B.B.
241		**Mask related to the new comedy** first half third century B.C. clay, well preserved polychrome h 12.5 cm Lipari, Museo Eoliano, room XXIV inv. 12980 Lipari, necroplois, Trench XXVII 1983, votive ditch	Earthenware model of the courtesan mask classified by Polluce (mask 38) as *Teleion Etairikon* (the *etericita perfetta* symbol of the category), with locks of hair pulled back above the ears.	BERNABÒ BREA 1981, p. 228, fig. 389, pl. XL. L.B.B.
241 V		**Mask related to the new comedy** first half third century B.C. clay, well preserved polychrome h 19 cm Lipari, Museo Eoliano, room XXIV inv. 12965 (12695) Lipari, necropolis, Trench XXXVII 1978, votive ditch	Big model of mask of the *Oulos Neaniskos* (Polluce's mask 12), the brazen youth with eyes too open and only one line on his forehead. Convivial crown detached and applicable.	BERNABÒ BREA 1981, p. 171, fig. 266, pl. XXVIII. L.B.B.
242	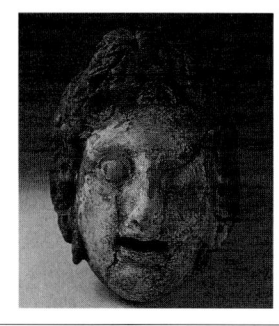	**Mask of Ule (the curly headed)** first half third century B.C. refined clay, whitish slip, well preserved polychrome h 16.5 cm Cefalù, Museo Fondazione Culturale Mandralisca, inv. 121 Lipari (?), excavations carried out in 1864 by Enrico Pirajno di Mandralisca (?)	Big mask representing an honest woman, no longer very young (a woman or mother), who has been recognised as a character in Menandrean comedy. The face, quite full, is characterised by big, protruding eyes and thick, curly hair of a red colour. The elaborate hairstyle differentiates the example in the Cefalù Museum from the others known.	TULLIO 1979, p. 29, pl. VII, 1; BERNABÒ BREA 1981, pp. 214-216, fig. 359; BONACASA 1985, p. 312, fig. 371; TULLIO 1991, p. 83, fig. 86. A.T.
243		**Theatrical comic mask** third century B.C. terra-cotta, moulded, back realised by hand, applied crown, traces of colour h 11.5 cm; w 10 cm Taranto, Museo Archeologico Nazionale, inv. 4069 Taranto, 15.VI.1888, the S. Lucia district, found lying on the ground	Thin, elongated face; eyes half-closed with upper eyelids smooth and slightly lowered; straight nose; open mouth; hair hidden by a convivial crown with flowers and leaves with traces of pink colour. It is possible to recognise in the example under consideration the *deuteros episeistos* (the second which makes the hair wave).	BERNABÒ BREA 1981, p. 186, fig. 304. G.A.M.

244

Comic actor with child in his arms

first half third century B.C.
clay, slip, remains of colour
h 15.4 cm; base 4.8x3.8x1.7 cm
body obtained from two matrixes
head applied, circular vent in rear
Taranto, Museo Archeologico
Nazionale, inv. Patroni 4258
Taranto, 30.5.1896, Regio Arsenale
near Villa Pepe, sepulchre XIII

Standing on a rectangular base with right leg slightly forwards, right arm bent onto his chest and the left raised to clasp a baby in swaddling clothes, he has a bearded face with open mouth and protruding eyes; he wears a short cloak which leaves his right shoulder and arm uncovered. The actor with child in his arms is to be identified with *Hegemon Therapon* (main servant).

MARUGGI 1988, pp. 195-198, cat. 17.7b, pl. XXXIX.
G.A.M.

245

Theatrical comic mask

second-first century B.C.
terra-cotta, remains of colour, moulded
h 26.5 cm; w 17.7 cm
Taranto, Museo Archeologico
Nazionale, inv. 20068
Taranto, 10.2.1932, via Regina Elena
house of the Mutilated, cemetery and cremation

Bald skull; big, staring eyes with contracted, asymmetrical eyebrows; large, twisted aquiline nose; open mouth; sticking-out ears. The mask under consideration is identifiable as a type of "parasite" of Menandrean comedy.

BIEBER 1961, p. 100, fig. 377; ALESSIO 1989, p. 106, no. 77.
G.A.M.

246

Statuette of a dioscuro

300 B.C.
bronze
h 45 cm
lacunae on the left hand
Naples, Museo Archeologico
Nazionale, inv. 5022

The young, male figure, characterised by the tall conical headcovering which covers practically all his hair of short, barely moving locks, probably carried a spear in his right hand.

ORLANDINI 1983, p. 501, figs. 539-540.
M.B.

247

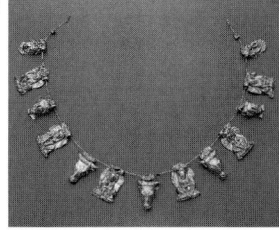

Elements from a necklace

fourth century B.C.
gold
max h 3.7 cm; weight 24.50 gr
Naples, Museo Archeologico
Nazionale, inv. 126431
Cuma, tomb furnishings, already
Stevens Collection

Thirteen elements of a necklace in gold lamina. The pendants are made up of two small heads of Hercules depicted as young and beardless with his head covered by the *leontè* knotted under his chin; two young, bearded heads of Achelos characterised by two small, pointed horns and pointed, sticking out ears; three buchranes and six front-facing, winged sphinxes.
Each pendant has an identical suspension cylinder decorated in front with a flower with six or eight petals worked in filigree.

GUZZO 1993, p. 200, P. IV C2.
T.G.

248 I

Ring

fourth century B.C.
gold
diam. 2.5 cm; weight 21.92 gr
deformed setting
Naples, Museo Archeologico
Nazionale, inv. 126408
Cuma, tomb furnishings, already
Stevens Collection

Ring made up of a cylindrical row of stones and setting formed by two discs in golden lamina separated by a dense network of gnurled thread. Corresponding to the soldering of the stones to the setting are two Caryatids in the round. The lower disc is decorated with an olive branch; the upper one with a *Gorgoneion*.

GUZZO 1993, p. 168, A.IV 1.
T.G.

248 II

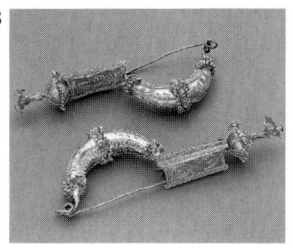

Pair of fibulae

fourth century B.C.
gold
l 8.5, 9.2 cm; weight 10.14 gr
Naples, Museo Archeologico
Nazionale, inv. 126406-407
Cuma, tomb furnishings, already
Stevens Collection

Pair of gold fibulae of the "leech" type with a long pin of triangular section decorated in filigree and ending with a biconical capsule which lens to form a flower with thirteen petals from which two pistils rise. The thickened bow is decorated with palmettes and has an ornamental motif of a spiral enclosed by two vertically folded wave laminae in the centre and at the ends.

GUZZO 1993, p. 153, F. VII D 1-2.
T.G.

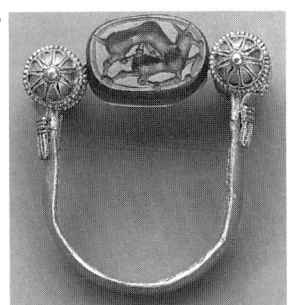

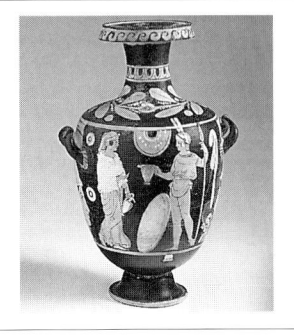

249	**Ring** fourth century B.C. gold and sardonyx diam. 20 cm; weight 7.97 gr Naples, Museo Archeologico Nazionale, inv. 126458 Cuma, tomb furnishings already Stevens Collection	Ring with ribbon row of stones finishing in two cylinders decorated with filigree and enclosed by hemispheres reproducing the corolla of a flower. The small cylinders hold a hinge around which a scarab in engraved sardonyx rotates and, on the flat face, a lion devours a deer.	BREGLIA 1941, p. 41, no. 100. T.G.
250 **I-II**	**Pair of fibulae** fourth century B.C. gold l 8.5, 8.9 cm; weight 13.76, 13.94 gr Naples, Museo Archeologico Nazionale, inv. 131634-131712 Teano, tomb 79	Pair of golden fibulae of "leech" type with bow richly decorated with dense vegetable motif in filigree and rosettes. In the central part of the bow, two small cornices in relief are divided by five rosettes with central buttons. The big rod also presents complex decoration in filigree like the biconical sphere placed at the end and terminanting in a flower.	GUZZO 1993, p. 154, F. VII D 5-6. T.G.
251	**Lucanian lekythos with red figures** 360-350 B.C. refined clay, wheel, overpainting h 27 cm; diam. 6.5 cm Naples, Museo Archeologico Nazionale, inv. 81855 Paestum	On the neck, decorated motifs in rays; under the handle, palmettes and half-palmettes. Scene with, in the centre, a richly dressed goddess seated on a rich throne adorned with palmettes and statuettes. To the sides of the goddess, on the left, laureate Eros; on the right, standing female figure holding a patera. Rosettes and shrubs in the background; next to the female figure, incense burner of *Thymiaterion*. Attributed to the Painter of the Primato.	RFVA I, p. 166, no. 925, pl. 72, 5-7. Mar.L.
252 **I-II-** **III-IV**	**Painted tomb slabs** 330-320 Bc tufa, painted plaster short side slabs: 112x94x10 cm long side slabs: 112x97x16 cm Naples, Museo Archeologico Nazionale, inv. 224929 Nola, via Crocefisso	The two short slabs portray, respectively, an armed horseman with head covered with a helmet with curved horns, and a youth wrapped in the himation. On the long slabs: a young horseman with shield and a procession of women.	DE CARO 1983-84, pp. 71 ff.; *Meisterwerke* 1995, pp. 82-85. M.B.
253	**Hydria with red figures** 350 B.C. clay, glaze h 38.3 cm; diam. 12.4 cm lacking vertical handle about 350 B.C. - Group of the Libation (AV II), Painter Astarita and ...., bell production Naples, Museo Archeologico Nazionale, inv. 182721 S. Agata dei Goti, Gargiulo Collection	On the mouth and neck motif of ovuli; on the shoulder crown of laurel from right to left; under the vertical handle, palmettes in a fan among plant volutes. Departure scene; warrior with Oscan armour holding out a *skyphos* to his lady. She is draped and holding an oinochoe for the libation rite in her hand. Under the handles: male heads with *pilos*. Decorative motifs in the background; balls, fillets and festoons. Attributed to the circle of the Painter Astarita.	LCS, I, pp. 400, 273, pl. 156, no. 4. M.L.

| 254 | **Earthenware group with two women playing dice**

340-330 B.C.
terra-cotta, remains of colour
h 21 cm; w 11.5 cm: lenght 23 cm
London, British Museum, inv. D 161
Capua | The two women, dressed in soft chitons, are leaning forwards for the game of Astragalus. The ancient authors, like Herodotus and Aeschines, describe the variants of this game; perhaps the two women depicted are playing it by throwing the die into the air then to catch them again on the back of their hands. | HIGGINS 1967, p. 129, pl. LXI A. R.R. |

| 255 | **Akroterial disc with the depiction of Heracles and the lion Nemean**

second half fourth century B.C.
clay
internal diam. disc 62-64 cm
external diam. 78-81 cm
l tile 82 cm; h tile 25-26.5 cm
Fratte di Salerno, Scigliato district (1955) | The disc represents Heracles struggling with the lion Nemean, both depicted with arched backs, on the inside of the circular space. This earthenware akroterion possibly belongs to a cult building where the figure of the hero was a subject for particular veneration, as moreover was widespread in that period among the Italic populations. | G. GRECO, in *Fratte* 1990, p. 68, fig. 78, p. 81, figg. 118 and 119. M.R. |

| 256 | **Four fragments of a figured frieze**

beginng third century B.C.
terra-cotta, by hand
A: max l 22 cm; max h 28 cm
B: max l 27 cm; max h 28 cm
C: max l 37 cm; max h 16 cm
D: max l 36 cm; max h 28 cm
Naples, Museo Archeologico Nazionale, inv. 21487 (A) 21488+21491 (B), 21496 (C) 21497+20707 (D) | Pompei, area to the west of the Triangular Forum

Fragment A represents a horseman holding a shield on his left arm on a horse galloping towards the right. Fragment B shows a horseman, shield on the left, on a horse rearing to the left. Fragment C, a horseman leaning far forwards on a horse galloping to the right. Fragment D, a horseman with his bust twisted to the left on a horse galloping to the right. Such fragments, together with a further twelve, were part of a frieze certainly destined to decorate a public building, identifiable, possibly, as the *Palestra Sannitica* in Pompei. | D'AGOSTINO 1982, pp. 63-93. M.B. |

| 257 | **Statue of the so-called Zeus Meilichios**

third-second century B.C.
terra-cotta, face executed in matrix body executed in detached parts and juxtaposed
h 189 cm; base 46x62 cm
Naples, Museo Archeologico Nazionale, inv. 22574
Pompei, from the so-called Tempietto of Zeus Meilichios | The bearded male figure is crowned and covered with a large cloak which leaves the bust uncovered and which is arranged over the front to form ample, triangular drapery. This was identified in the nineteenth century as that of Zeus Meilichios, on the basis of an Oscan inscription (found near Porta di Stabia), which cited a cult place dedicated to this god. | RUSSO 1991, pp. 110 ff. M.B. |

| 258 | **Earthenware statuette of Aphrodite or Hera kneeling**

first half fourth century B.C.
terra-cotta
h 17 cm
Paestum, Museo Archeologico Nazionale, inv. 56649
Paestum, Heraion di Foce Sele | Kneeling, nude female figure wrapped in a cloak holds a dove in her right hand. The goddess is assisted by two small erotes or demons, one of which has its hand on the chest of the goddess while the other helps her to remove her cloak. | ZANCANI MONTUORO-ZANOTTI BIANCO 1951, p. 14, pl. VI; ORLANDINI 1990, p. 187, fig. 62. F.L. |

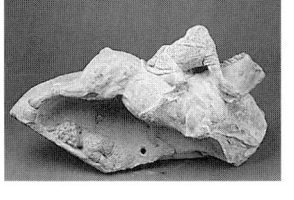

Works on Exhibit

259 I-III

I
Thymiaterion

fourth century B.C.
terra-cotta
h 22.3 cm
Paestum, Museo Archeologico
Nazionale, inv. 56652
Paestum, Heraion di Foce Sele

Small bust of female figure with uncovered breast which emerges from a crown of leaves; on her head, covered by a cloak, she bears a lily with eight rounded petals. Eight ornaments from a necklace can be made out on the neck.

ORLANDINI 1983, p. 503, fig. 578.
F.L.

II
Thymiaterion

fourth century B.C.
terra-cotta
h 18 cm
Paestum, Museo Archeologico
Nazionale, inv. 48569
Paestum, Heraion di Foce Sele

Small bust of female figure cut below the breast. The young girl with bared breast wears a sash or necklace around her neck decorated with wolf teeth; on her veiled head, covered with a cloak, she bears a lily with five pointed petals, one of which is fragmentary.

STOOP 1960, p. 8, pl. III, 3.
F.L.

III
Thymiaterion

fourth century B.C.
terra-cotta
h 14.6 cm
Paestum, Museo Archeologico
Nazionale, inv. 48570
Paestum, Heraion di Foce Sele

Small bust of female figure cut off at breast height. The young girl, wearing a low-cut dress, has a lily with eight rounded petals on her head. Inside the lily burnt traces can be noted.

TOCCO SCIARELLI, DE LA GENIÈRE, GRECO 1992, p. 396, pl. LX (first figure on the right).
F.L.

260 *see Recent Discoveries*

261

Painted slab, the so-called black horseman

340 B.C.
limestone
max h 146 cm; max w 98 cm
Paestum Museo Archeologico
Nazionale, inv. 21599
Paestum, Andriuolo, tomb 58

Western slab of a woman's box tomb with double sloping roof. The scene, which represents a man on horseback, occupies the entire wall. The rider is depicted in parade dress with red chiton, baldric, belt, shin-guards, helmet with red and black feathers and shield in the left hand, and is on a black horse with white hooves and muzzle.
The horse proceeds towards the right where a krater decorated with palmettes and surmounted by an enormous yellow bouquet tied to a red sash is depicted.

PONTRANDOLFO, ROUVERET 1992, pp. 45-46, fig. 37, p. 153, figg. 4-5, pp. 336-337.
F.L.

262 *see Recent Discoveries*

263

Lucanian nestoris with red figures

fourth century B.C.
clay, glaze, thrown on the wheel
h 85 cm; diam 43 cm
Karlsruhe, Badisches Landesmuseum
inv. W372
Castelluccio

Handles with two roundels decorated with rosettes; superimposed ornamental bands on the neck, palmettes under the handles. The figured scenes are bounded at the top by a wave motif and, at the bottom, by a band of crosses and meanders.
Side A: Ares hands over arms to Aphrodite; an Erote with crown and jug flies about above them and a band is in the background.
p: Aphrodite seated, surrounded by three Erotes. Attributed to the Painter of the Primato.

CVA Deutschland, Karlsruhe 2 (8), pp. 40-41, pl. 78; LCS, I, p. 170, no. 258.
G.L'A.

264 *see Recent Discoveries*

265

Two bronze shoulder protectors

390-340 B.C.
bronze, embossed
h 17cm; l 11.5-10.8 cm
London, British Museum, inv. W285
Siris?

Plaques to cover the shoulder straps of a double valve cuirass. They are decorated in high relief with scenes of Amazzomachia. On the best preserved piece one can observe the very fine rendering of both the Amazon, with his rich drapery, and the Greek of vibrant musculature.

WALTERS 1899, no. 250; ROLLEY 1986, pp. 170, 172.
P.R.

266 I

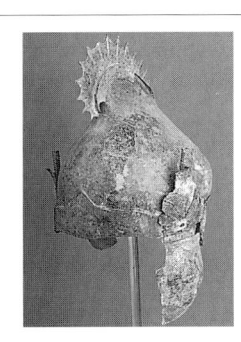

Phrygian type helmet

fourth century B.C.
bronze *lamina* with embossed decoration
max h 36.5 cm
Reggio Calabria, Museo Nazionale inv. 11805
Laos (Marcellina - CS), room tomb

Hemispherical helmet with upper rise of the "Phrygian cap"; movable shoulder protectors fixed with eyelet fastener; cavity for the ears and neck protector turned towards the outside. Above the cheek-piece, a *lamina* with leaf veining hides a small cylinder for inserting plumes. On top of the helmet, double *lamina* in crested profile decorated in rays.

Guzzo in *Laos* II, 1992, pp. 22-25.
G.F.L.T.

266 II

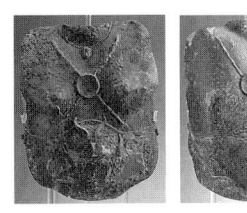

Bivalve cuirass

fourth century B.C.
bronze *lamina* with embossed decoration; damascening in silver
front valve h 34 cm; w 27 cm
back valve h 37.5 cm; w 29 cm
Reggio Calabria, Museo Nazionale inv. 11803-11804
Laos (Marcellina - CS), room tomb

Short cuirass of anatomical type. The two valves are joined by four rings; the front shows a *torque* around the neck with mask pendant (Medusa?). On the chest and back two rows of alternating oblong and lenticular elements entwine, with discoidal *phalera* in the centre, ending in eyelets which hold up a richly decorated belt. Between plant volutes and floral motifs, in the centre of the front side, a *protome* of Pan; on the back, head of a satyr. The absence of reinforcements in iron or lead suggests an exclusive use only for parades.

Guzzo in *Laos* II 1992, pp. 25-30.
G.F.L.T.

266 III

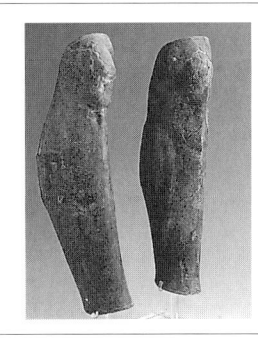

Pair of shin-guards

fourth century B.C.
bronze *lamina* with embossed decoration
h 39.1 cm
Reggio Calabria, Museo Nazionale inv. 11806-11807
Laos (Marcellina - CS), room tomb

The articulation and musculature of the embossed calves is evident; the edge of the whole *lamina* is marked by a raised border decorated with thin fillets.

Guzzo in *Laos* II 1992, pp. 30-31.
G.F.L.T.

266 IV

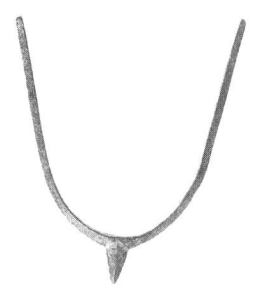

Spur

fourth century B.C.
cast bronze
l 7.3 cm; opening 6.3 cm
Reggio Calabria, Museo Nazionale inv. 19153
Laos (Marcellina - CS), room tomb

Spur of curved shape in rhomboidal section with triangular point.

Guzzo in *Laos* II 1992, pp. 30-31.
G.F.L.T.

266 V

Belt

mid fourth century B.C.
bronze lamina with *appliques* in silver *lamina*
fragment a: max l 17.5 cm with hooks 13 without; h 10.4 cm; t 0.1 cm
fragment b: max l 26.7 cm; h 10.4 cm t 0.08-0.1 cm
Reggio Calabria, Museo Nazionale inv. 11808a-b
Laos (Marcellina - CS), room tomb

The two ends are preserved: *a*, with three hooks of a "wolf's head" type, fixed, with rivets, to the back of the lamina; *b*, with two rows of three holes for fastening, framed by palmette appliques of silver. Preserved on *a* is a frieze of plant volutes and palmettes along the border with hooks, fixed by two bronze lists; three figures of Scylla in profile in the act of freeing a winged creature; an archer in front of the first Scylla; a fragmentary figure, ascribable to a triton, behind the archer, On *b*, apart from the six palmettes, a shield and an Amazon with axe and bow are preserved.

Guzzo in *Laos* II 1992, pp. 35-53.
G.F.L.T.

267

Statuette of a satyr

second half fourth century B.C.
bronze
h 41 cm; w 34 cm
Munich, Staatlichen Antikensammlungen und Glypthek München, inv. 720y
Armento

Bearded satyr, kneeling in 3/4, with right arm raised and left parallel to the body; fragments of something remain in his hands.

Furtwangler 1900, n. 441; Hus 1975, tav. 48.
G. L'A.

Opere in mostra

268 I		**Draped female statuette** end second-first century B.C. greyish-white marble h 33 cm; w 16 cm; depth 7.5 cm Potenza, Soprintendenza Archeologica della Basilicata, Deposits, inv. 70753 Rossano di Vaglio	Headless female statuette with *chiton* and *himation* standing on her left leg, the right bent slightly forwards. Her missing right forearm was bent forwards and held an attribute, the left falls down her side.	DENTI 1992, pp. 67-72.	E.P.
268 II		**Statuette of Artemis** second half second century B.C. Greek marble h 56 cm; w 25 cm; depth 15 cm Potenza, Soprintendenza Archeologica della Basilicata, Deposits, inv. 70754 Rossano di Vaglio	Headless statuette representing Artemis with *chiton* and *himation* running to the left; left supporting leg is forward, the right one is back and flexed. Right arm is stretched down, the left bent forwards. Lacking hands, quiver on the back and the front part of the feet.	DENTI 1992, pp. 47-53.	E.P.
268 III		**Statuette of Artemis** second half second century B.C. Greek marble (?) h 48.5 cm; w 19 cm; depth 21 cm Potenza, Soprintendenza Archeologica della Basilicata, Deposits, inv. 70755 Rossano di Vaglio	Headless statuette of representing Artemis in a *peplos* with right supporting leg forwards and the left back. The *apotygma* is fixed by a thin belt which holds the quiver on the back. Lacking right arm and left forearm.	DENTI 1992, pp. 54-61.	E.P.
269	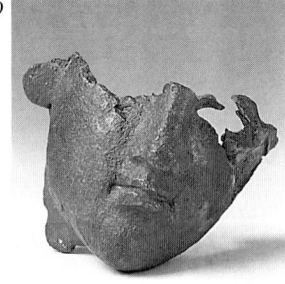	**Fragment of a woman's head in bronze** end fourth-beginning third century B.C. bronze, cast max h 7.7 cm; w 10 cm Potenza, Soprintendenza Archeologica della Basilicata, Deposits, inv. 54296 Rossano di Vaglio	Lower part of female face of which the orbital cavities, straight nose, small mouth with lateral dimples and full, elongated chin are visible. Disc earring on the preserved ear.	ADAMESTEANU, DILTHEY 1992, pp. 31, 74, 76.	E.P.
270	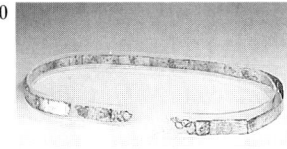	**Belt** third century B.C. silver and gold h 2 cm; max l 94 cm Potenza, Soprintendenza Archeologica della Basilicata, Deposits, inv. 75347 Rossano di Vaglio	Belt in silver *lamina* of embossed decoration with *protome* of radial Helios repeated twelve times; palmette on flower volutes and acanthus on the better conserved end. A small *lamina* in gilded silver with the same *protome* of Helios is soldered to this. Terminals of snake heads with coiled bodies.	GUZZO in *Leukania*, pp. 82, 83, 85, 86.	E.P.
271 I-II-III-IV	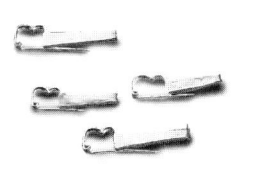	**Fibulae** fifth-fourth century B.C. gold, bow cast, stirrup in beaten lamina inv. 48112 l 7.6 cm; max h 2.4 cm inv. 48113 l 7.7 cm; max h 2.4 cm inv. 48114 l 7.4 cm; max h 2.4 cm inv. 48115 l 9 cm; max h 2.5 cm Salerno, Depositi Soprintendenza inv. 48112, 48113, 48114, 48115 Roccagloriosa (SA), La Scala district tomb 9	Bow broken into two small bows widened at the centre. Long stirrup of channel-form ending in a button, in lamina rolled with a hammer. The buckle tongue connects to the bow by a double spiral spring.	GUALTIERI, FRACCHIA 1990, pp. 207-212.	C.A.F.

Works on Exhibit

271 V

Necklace

first half fourth century B.C.
gold
female head pendants h 3.5 cm
lion head pendants diam. 3 cm
cylindrical links l 1.1 cm; diam. 0.6 cm
Salerno, Depositi Soprintendenza
inv. 48122
Roccagloriosa (SA), La Scala district
tomb 9

The necklace is made up of 5 female head pendants of thin embossed *lamina*, 4 lion head pendants also embossed and 10 cylindrical linking elements, each consisting of a small cylindrical cannon in golden *lamina* with beaded borders, decorated with filigree.

GUALTIERI, FRACCHIA 1990, pp. 207-212.
C.A.F.

271 VI

Bracelet

first half fourth century B.C.
gold lamina
diam. 6.5 cm
Salerno, Depositi Soprintendenza
inv. 48123
Roccagloriosa (SA), La Scala district
tomb 9

Bracelet with triple spiral and central convexity beaded along the borders. Both the ends of the spiral finish in a snake's body coiled into a bow. The two ends of the laminated band end with a small motif of opposing human faces joined to each other at the tops of their heads, from where the snake's body departs.

GUALTIERI, FRACCHIA 1990, pp. 207-212.
C.A.F.

272

Tablets of Heraclea

end fourth-beginning third century B.C.
bronze
h 124.3 cm; w 37.5 cm; t 1 cm
h 184.5 cm; w 38.5 cm; t 1 cm
Naples, Museo Archeologico Nazionale, inv. 2480-2481
Policoro

Two bronze tablets, containing the reports of the *oristai*, special magistrates having the task of recuperating some lands belonging to the Sanctuaries of Dionysus and Athena Polias in the territory of Herakleia. The land, usurped by private people, would then be divided into lots to be rented out.

PUGLIESE CARRATELLI 1983, pp. 44-45, fig. 16.
T.G.

273

Relief with Dionysus and a satyr

beginning second century B.C.
pentelic marble
max h 36.5 cm; w 38.5 cm
max depth 8 cm
Policoro, Museo Nazionale della Siritide, inv. 45275
Herakleia, Acropolis (Zone C)

A silenic character at the side of a rocky cave with a *himation*, in the design of the banqueter lying on a a *kline* covered with a wild beast's skin, holds a *phiale mesomphalos* in his right hand, a cornucopia in his left. In front is a satyr in the act of pouring from an *oinochoe*. The design and attributes recall the sphere of Dionysus-Hades.

H. DE LACHENAL, in *Leukonia*, pp. 148-151.
S.B.

274

Part of funerary furnishings of the so-called Goldsmith's Tomb

second century B.C.
iron, bronze, bone, ceramics, vitreous paste, rock crystal, chalcedony
Policoro, Museo Nazionale della Siritide
Herakleia, southern necropolis
tomb 68

Collection of metal instruments for working *lamina* in precious metals. Three scalpels, a hammer, an anvil, a file, a needle, pincers, pushers, nine awls, small bar, clasps and bronze rings can be noted. As well, there are seven weights, five small bases and fifty figured moulds, besides clasps and settings of vitreous paste and material like rock crystal, chalcedony and pumice stone. A thin-walled glass and a rolling mill are among the ceramic objects.

L. GIARDINO, in *Leukania*, pp. 152 ss.
S.B.

275 *see Recent Discoveries*

Works on Exhibit

276		**Spiral ring** farth-third century B.C. gold l 3.6 cm; strip w 0.4 cm Policoro, Museo Nazionale della Siritide, inv. 49462 Herakleia, southern necropolis tomb 22	Ring wound in a spiral in convex *lamina* decorated with dots on the borders. Moulded laminate elements of palmettes with an opposing rosette ending in a double snake *protome* are applied to the ends.	BIANCO 1992.	S.B.
277		**Mirror** fourth century B.C. bronze h 44 cm; diam. 23.1 cm Policoro, Museo Nazionale della Siritide, inv. 46844 Herakleia, southern necropolis tomb 58	Disc with raised border and handle with quadrangular outline with figured, *à jour* scenes. In the picture, bounded by two small Ionic columns and at the top by a decorated ovuli cornice, is a female figure. On the two sides are winged spirits and at the bottom on the right, an *amphora*.	PIANU 1990, p. 69.	S.B.
278		**Disc with Aphrodite** fourth century B.C. terra-cotta diam. 23.5 cm; t 0.4 cm Policoro, Museo Nazionale della Siritide, inv. 45078 Acropolis of Herakleia	Irregular disc with head of Aphrodite with hair in wavy locks divided on the forehead and held by a diadem. On the two sides is an *erotes* with large wing turned frontwards and kneeling in profile on one leg. At the top are two suspension holes.	Museo Siritide, tav. 31.	S.B.
279 I		**Matrix of a tanagrine** end fourth-beginning third century B.C. terra-cotta h 21 cm; w 10.5 cm Policoro, Museo Nazionale della Siritide, inv. 35932 Acropolis of Herakleia	Matrix of a standing "tanagrine" leaning on her left leg with flexed right leg. She is wearing a *himation* and *chiton*. Hair and locks divided over the forehead. Left arm bent behind her waist and right arm on her chest visible under the folds of the *himation*.	Museo Siritide, fig. 46.	S.B.
279 II		**Matrix of Artemis-Bendis** fourth centruy B.C. terra-cotta h 28 cm; w 17.4 cm Policoro, Museo Nazionale della Siritide, inv. 35338 Acropolis of Herakleia	Matrix of Artemis-Bendis with lion skin on her head and paws falling onto the shoulders. Has a Phrygian type of head-covering and hair in locks divided over the forehead. It is dressed in a cloak and short *chiton*. It is fragmentary laterally and in the lower part.	Museo Siritide, fig. 45.	S.B.
279 III		**Matrix of pinax** fourth century B.C. terra-cotta h 31.5 cm; w 28 cm fragmentary Policoro, Museo Nazionale della Siritide, inv. 35945 Acropolis of Herakleia	Slack matrix of *pinax* with standing female figure. Hair in wavy locks divided over the forehead. Right arm bent at the waist and the left holding a basket of eggs. She is wearing a *chiton* and long veil. She is in front of a person, fragmentary from the thorax up and dressed in flowing robes on the lower part, lying on a *kline*.		

280-281 *see Recent Discoveries*

Works on Exhibit

282	**Crown of gilded bronze** second half fourth century B.C. bronze and clay with gold leaf diam. 32 cm Metaponto, Museo Archeologico Nazionale, inv. 128739	Circular bronze bar into which stems of ivy leaves, berries, bunches of grapes, grasshoppers and locusts are inserted. The bodies of the insects, berries and grapes have been realised in clay while all the rest is in bronze. All the elements which make up the crown have a thin covering of gold leaf.	GAIS 1982, pp. 54-56; *Ori Taranto*, p. 90, n. 18. A.D.S.
283 I	**Elements from a necklace** fourth century B.C. gold l 5.9 cm; weight 15.9 gr fragmentary, modern thread Naples, Museo Archeologico Nazionale inv. 120301 Pisticci, tomb in the Cinque Carra district (1886)	The necklace is made up of two conical, beadworked clasps, a small terminal cylinder decorated in filigree, thirty-six beads of flattened rosettes and a central cylindrical pendant of filigree decorated *lamina*. From this, another pendant, formed of six plaits of thread of different ls with rosettes and small globes in beadworked *lamina*, hangs.	GUZZO 1993, p. 195, C. III A 1. T.G.
283 II	**Pair of earrings** fourth century B.C. gold h 3 cm; weight 6.48 gr fragmentary Naples, Museo Archeologico Nazionale, inv. 120303 Pisticci, tomb in the Cinque Carra district (1886)	The earrings, of the particular shape deriving from spiral types, have a tubular body in gold lamina which is decorated with vegetal filigree motifs in the central area and terminate with two female heads. The heads, with hair gathered onto the nape, also have the same type of *helikes* earrings, reproduced in miniature.	GUZZO 1993, p. 248, O. III B 1. T.G.
283 III	**Ring** fourth-third century B.C. gold and cornelian diam. 2.4 cm; weight 14.7 gr Naples, Museo Archeologico Nazionale, inv. 120302 Pisticci, tomb in the Cinque Carra district (1886)	Gold ring of thin bar with big oval setting formed by a finely decorated gold band of minute incisions into which a cornelian has been inserted. On the stone a butting bull turned towards the right, which recalls the types on Thurii coins, has been engraved.	GUZZO 1993, p. 165, A. III A 1. T.G.
284	**Female earthenware head** 360-340 B.C. clay, matrix h 36 cm Taranto, Museo Archeologico Nazionale, inv. 4006 Taranto, provenance unknown	Pertaining to a life-size statue, it can be attributed to an icon-like, standing female type, balanced on the left supporting leg with the right flexed, according to a scheme of ponderation which concludes with the head, bowed and turned in the direction of the relaxed leg. On the hair, divided into two bands swept neatly backwards in a soft way, a gold diadem with vegetal decoration and mounted on a support of perishable material is portrayed.	E. LIPPOLIS, in *Ori Taranto*, p. 119, n. 48. E.L.
285	**Veiled female head** second century B.C. sculpture, white marble from the Aegean h 40 cm Taranto, Museo Archeologico Nazionale, inv. 3905 Taranto	The head probably belongs to a funerary statue. Distinctive stylistic features of the very bowed oval, bounded by two areas of shade formed by the veil falling onto the neck, of the half-open lips and of the shading of the eyes which give it a moving feel.	BELLI PASQUA 1991, pp. 91-93, IV 16. R.B.P.

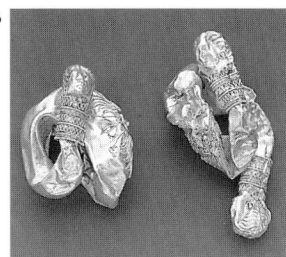

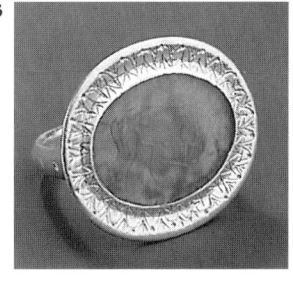

286 Veiled female head

mid-fourth century B.C.
marble
max h 35 cm; w 25 cm
breaks and chipping
Kansas City, the Nelson-Atkins
Museum of Art
(Purchase: Nelson Trust)
inv. 33-3/4
Taranto

Female head cut off just below the neck, of 3/4, slightly bowed. It is covered by a veil which leaves the locks of hair over the forehead free to frame the fully oval face. On the auricular lobes are holes for inserting earrings.

LANGLOTZ, HIRMER 1968, p. 68, tav. 135.
G.L'A.

287 Female head

first century B.C.
parian marble; sculpture, added element worked separately
h 28 cm
Taranto, Museo Archeologico Nazionale, inv. 3897
Taranto

To include in the ambit of the Coptic tradition of the late Hellenistic period, as the manieristic taste shows, evident in the contrast between the rendering of the polished fresh complexion and the heaviness of the hairstyle, rendered roughly moreover in the locks divided by sharp, deep furrows.

BELLI PASQUA 1991, pp. 110-113, V 2.
R.B.P.

288 Apulian column krater with red figures

first half fourth century B.C.
refined clay, glaze, thrown on the wheel
h 51.5 cm
New York, Metropolitan Museum of Art, Rogers Fund, 1950, inv. 50.11.4

Column *krater* decorated with plant shoots on its neck; the figured scenes are framed by a double band decorated with dots. *Side A*: sculptor realising a statue of Heracles in the presence of Zeus, a Nike and the same Heracles. *Side B*: Athena and a Dioscuro, with Pan and Hermes at the top on the left; lower down Eros pursues a bird. Attributed to the Boston Group.

RFVA, I, p. 266, tav. 89,1.
G.L'A.

289 I-II

I
Female bust

third century B.C.
refined clay, traces of colour
h 16.5 cm; w face 15 cm
base max 21.5 cm
Melfi, Museo Archeologico Nazionale
inv. 337263
Lavello, Gravetta Sanctuary

Thick neck; full face; ears barely hinted at on whose lobes are holes to which earrings would have been fixed. Hair differentiated in the centre, with waves parallel to the forehead and three plaits applied to the sides of the neck. Over the forehead, cushion diadem with bundle of intertwined cavetti in the middle of a Herculean knot, tied by four small bands.

A. BOTTINI in *Leukania*, pp. 17-18.
R.C.

II
Male bust

third century B.C.
refined clay, traces of colour
h 16.5 cm; w face 15 cm
l base 21.55 cm
Melfi, Museo Archeologico Nazionale
inv. 337164
Lavello, Gravetta Sanctuary

On the left shoulder a raised "rope" forms the border of the drapery. Thick neck, full face. The hair is rendered in parallel bands of overlapping, semi-circular locks, gradually more irregular and summary towards the top of the head, where they cease completely.

A. BOTTINI, in *Leukania*, pp. 17-18.
R.C.

290 Nude female earthenware bust

mid-second century B.C.
clay, matrix, traces of colour, hair modelled by hand
h 43 cm
Lucera, Museo Civico, inv. 389
Lucera, votive offerings of San Salvatore

The bust depicts a nude female deity, Aphrodite or Persephone. The arms were originally raised; the left one held a piece of the veil resting on a shoulder. On the left flank is the hand of a male figure which encircled her back.

D'ERCOLE 1990, pp. 258-259, p. 261, n. 2, tav. 92b, 93, 94a.
M.M.

291 I		**Tablet with the epiphany of the Dioscuri inside a naiskos** second half fourth-first half third century B.C. clay, matrix; 43x30.5 cm Taranto, Museo Archeologico Nazionale, inv. 4109 Taranto, 25.2.1914, the Solito quarter Fabrizio district	*Naiskos* with triangular pediment with architrave resting on two amphorae, which in turn insist on a pilaster. The nude Dioscuri with chlamys on their shoulders, standing, each hold a *mesomphalos* and a palm branch. They have cushioned headcoverings on their heads and high footwear on their feet knotted above the calf.	LIPPOLIS 1995, p. 55, pp. 117-118, D.3, g.25. G.A.C.
291 II		**Tablet with the epiphany of the Dioscuri inside a naiskos** second half fourth-first half third century B.C. clay, slip, matrix; 44x40 cm Taranto, Museo Archeologico Nazionale, inv. 4123 Taranto, 25.2.1914, the Solito quarter Fabrizio district	*Naiskos* with triangular pediment with architrave resting on two amphorae, which in turn insist on a pilaster. The Dioscuri, with shoulders and the lower parts of their bodies wrapped in a *himation*, are both on horseback on a high trapezoidal base and each hold a *mesomphalos* and palm branch.	LIPPOLIS 1995, tav. XV, 1, pp. 55 ss. G.A.C.
292 I II		**I** **Antefix with female head** beginning fourth century B.C. clay, matrix, retouching by hand and spatula 19.8x20.5 cm Taranto, Museo Archeologico Nazionale, inv. 17554 Taranto, Vecchio Museo	Semi-elliptical slab. Face bowed to the left; eyes with incised pupils and irises; small mouth with fleshy lips; short curly hair separated by a middle, slightly raised, parting; traces of a *himation* on the shoulders; small cross-shaped earings sustaining an inverted pyramid and pearl necklace with crescent. ORLANDINI 1983, p. 505, fig. 560. L.T.	held by a diadem, are visible at the sides of the temples. ORLANDINI 1983, p. 505, fig. 573. L.T.
		II **Antefix with veiled female head** third century B.C. clay, matrix, retouching by hand and spatula, remains of colour Taranto, Museo Archeologico Nazionale, inv. 17594 Taranto, Vecchio Museo Circular slab with raised border. Female head covered with veil gathered at the height of the neck by the left hand shown in close-up. Some locks of hair,		
293 I		**Arula** first half fourth century B.C. clay, matrix h 22.5 cm lower base l 27.5 cm; w 18.5 cm upper base l 27.8 cm, w 19 cm t slab 2 cm Taranto, Museo Archeologico Nazionale, inv. 208343 Taranto, 27.4.1914, Masseria Vaccarella, sporadic find	Parallelepiped. On the front, between two moulded cornices, scenes of initiation to marriage: on the right, a female figure, probably Aphrodite or Kore-Persephone, with *chiton* and *himation*, pushes an erote depicted in the act of holding out the taenia to the figure on the left; the bride: She is seated on a *kline* and is taking off her veil. A handmaid is at her feet. Next to the *kline* is the nuptial casket on a *hydria*. On the lateral faces are elaborate phytomorphic motifs.	LIPPOLIS 1995, tav. XXII, 1. G.R.
293 II		**Arula** second half fourth century B.C. clay, matrix h 22.5 cm lower base l 26.5 cm; w 20 cm upper base l 28.3 cm, w 19.7 cm t slab 1.8 cm Taranto, Museo Archeologico Nazionale, inv. 208386 Taranto, 1912, Regio Arsenale sporadic find	Parallelepiped. On the front, between two fluted columns surmounted by Doric capitals, a female figure in profile is depicted on the right, probably Aphrodite, dressed in a *chiton* and *himation* about to get into a *chariot*; on the left, two winged figures, one female the other male, push the chariot along the surface of the sea suggested by wave motifs. On the lateral faces elaborate phytomorphic decorations.	LIPPOLIS 1995, tav. XXII, 2. G.R.

294		**Earthenware arula** ca. 510-490 B.C. terra-cotta, matrix h 18 cm, w 35 cm Cambridge, Harvard University, Fogg Art Museum Bequest of Frederick M. Watkins inv. 1972.48 southern Italy	Rectangular arula with hollowed out sides and profiles projecting to the upper and lower borders. On the front a Dionisian scene is depicted: under a pergola, a silenus with a *kantharos* in his right hand advances, followed by a maenad on horseback and a boy satyr.	HANFMANN, WALDBAUM 1973, p. 33, n. 11. G.L'A.
295 I		**Female bust** fourth century B.C. terra-cotta h 52 cm; w 31.5 cm reassembled Matera, Museo Nazionale "D. Ridola" inv. 5918 Timmari, votive offerings	On her head the *polos* is adorned with studs with a ropey finish at the bottom. The hair is combed into long, smooth locks. The *chiton*, with stylised drapery in radial pleats is held up on the shoulders by big buttons. Soft, oval face, wide forehead, big eyes, straight thin nose, fleshy mouth with raised corners. The neck is adorned with a necklace of discoidal and lanceolate elements.	LO PORTO 1991, p. 107, n. 70, tav. XLV. A.P.
295 II		**Female bust** fourth century B.C. terra-cotta h 22 cm; w 20cm reassembled Matera, Museo Nazionale "D. Ridola" inv. 5958 Timmari, votive offerings	The chiton, in a low V, is decorated in the middle with a big disc button and by four other smaller ones on the shoulders. The face is oval and softly modelled, the chin strong and round; the expression of the eyes moving because of the depth of the orbital arches; the nose is straight and the mouth fleshy. The hair raised up on the head is knotted into a *krobylos* and is encircled with a crown of ivy leaves and berries.	LO PORTO 1991, p. 102, n. 58, tav. XXIX. A.P.
295 III		**Disc antefix** fourth century B.C. terra-cotta h 18 cm; w 26 cm reassembled Matera, Museo Nazionale "D. Ridola" inv. 6212 Timmari, votive offerings	Lacking the lower part, it has two holes for suspension at the top. In the middle, an oval female face of soft modelling, distinct eyelids, regular nose, fleshy mouth, low front from which the curls, divided in the middle and held by a diadem, irradiate.	A. BOTTINI 1988, p. 78, fig. 103. A.P.
295 IV		**Female bust (Persephone)** fourth century B.C. terra-cotta, moulded and shaped by a spatula h 33 cm; w 20 cm reassembled Matera, Museo Nazionale "D. Ridola", inv. 5960 Timmari, votive offerings	The arms are folded on the chest and the left hand holds a small box. It has a *stephane* with small leaves and *polos* on its head, disc earrings with pendats at her ears and a necklace with lanceolate elements around her neck. Light drapery can be perceived at the sides of her neck down to her chest.	LO PORTO 1991, p. 93, n. 33, tav. XXXI. B.A.
295 V		**Male torso** fourth century B.C. terra-cotta, moulded h 16 cm; w 6 cm Matera, Museo Nazionale "D. Ridola" inv. 5825 Timmari, votive offerings	Part of a male statue, lacking the head, arms and lower half of the legs. The figure rests on the left leg, the torso is slightly turned to the left. The modelling is soft and mellow.	BOTTINI 1988, fig. 110, p. 82. A.P.

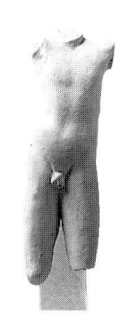

295 VI		**Female bust** fourth century B.C. terra-cotta, moulded h 21 cm; w 15.5 cm Matera, Museo Nazionale "D. Ridola" inv. 5952 Timmari, votive offerings	The bust, with V-shaped *chiton* and *himation* on the shoulders has arms folded onto the chest with the right hand holding a pomegranate, and the left a bowl of fruit. The head is placed on the long neck, the oval face is slightly asymmetric; a diadem, in part restored, is on the hair, combed like a "melon". Reassembled and restored.	Lo Porto 1991, p. 100, no. 53, pl. XXXVII. A.P.
295 VII		**Base of thymiaterion** fourth century B.C. terra-cotta, moulded h 28 cm; w 15 cm reassembled Matera, Museo Nazionale "D. Ridola" inv. 5118 Timmari, votive offerings	A sculpted ropey finish of ovuli runs along the corners and a chain of small double spirals is impressed on the base. On three analagous sections an identical female figure in profile to the right with hair of entwined locks, a short-sleeved *chiton*, and holding a pomegranate in her right hand and a lotus flower in her left, emerges in basrelief.	Lo Porto 1991, pp. 76-77, no. 6, pl. XXIII. B.A.
295 VIII		**Female head** fourth century B.C. marble h 8.5 cm; w 6.5 cm; depth 8 cm Matera, Museo Nazionale "D. Ridola" inv. 5137 Timmari, votive offerings	The face, with a slight asymmetrical structure, reveals delicate and dry modelling. It has thick eyelids, a straight nose in line with the spacious forehead, half open lips and rounded chin. Over the forehead a mass of hair divided into two, of wavy locks combed backwards and gathered at the nape.	Lo Porto 1991, p. 155, no. 212, pl. LXXI. B.A.
295 IX		**Female head with diadem** third century B.C. terra-cotta h 27 cm; w 17 cm; depth 18 cm reassembled Matera, Museo Nazionale "D. Ridola" inv. 5956 Timmari, votive offerings	Hair in waves, divided over the forehead and treated in locks finished with a spatula. It bears a diadem bordered with sculptured rosettes and two showy disc earrings with an internal disc and pendants in the form of pyramidal buckets.	Lo Porto 1991, pp. 105-106, n. 66, tav. XLIII. B.A.
295 X		**Female head** fourth century B.C. terra-cotta, moulded h 8 cm; w 8.2 cm; depth 5 cm Matera, Museo Nazionale "D. Ridola" inv. 6058 Timmari, votive offerings	The head with a low *polos* has hair divided in two over the forehead. The wavy locks are gathered at the temples in two bands which leave two disc earrings visible. The face of a large, square structure gets smaller at the chin, marked with a dimple. The eyes have upper eyelids in relief; the nose is straight and the lips closed and of a slightly sinuous cut.	Lo Porto 1991, p. 87, no 26, pl. XXVI-II. B.A.

296 I-XXV

Furnishings from a tomb at Egnathia

Discovered in July 1939 in the area of ancient Egnathia (Fassano, BR); the composition of the furnishings indicates a female connotation to the tomb.

I Hydria in Gnathian style

clay, glaze, wheel, overpainting
h 24.8 cm: diam 6.7 cm
Taranto, Museo
Nazionale, inv. 54351

Out-turned rim, ovoid body, disc foot, knotted vertical handle. On the neck a series of inverted "S", rosette, necklace with pendants; on the shoulder palmettes, series of dots, pairs of lines; on the body, wave motif, lines and tremolo segments.

II Bottle in Gnathian style

clay, glaze, wheel, overpainting
h 12.7 cm; diam 4.1 cm
Taranto, Museo
Nazionale, inv. 54351

Out-turned rim, globular body on low stem, ring foot. On the neck lines and sticks; on the shoulder lines and bands; on the body, network among lines.

III Polychrome hydria

clay, slip, wheel, impressions
h 33.5 cm; diam 10.8 cm
Taranto, Museo Nazionale
inv. 54349

Out-turned rim, ovoid body, bell-shaped foot, vertical ribbon handle; lines marked on the shoulder and body.

IV Patera mesomphalos

clay, slip, matrix, by hand
h 3.5 cm: diam 17.3 cm
Taranto, Museo Nazionale
inv. 54352

Out-turned rim articulated by twelve protuberances; on the inside twelve hollow ovoids and *omphalos*, two holes for suspension.

V Patera mesomphalos

clay, slip, matrix, by hand
h 3.5 cm: diam 17.3 cm
Taranto, Museo Nazionale
inv. 54353

Out-turned rim articulated by twelve protuberances; on the inside twelve hollow ovoids and *omphalos*, two holes for suspension.

VI Patera mesomphalos

clay, slip, matrix, by hand
h 4.3 cm; diam 19.5 cm
Taranto, Museo Nazionale
inv. 54354

Out-turned rim articulated by twelve heads with *pileus*; on the inside twelve hollow ovoids and *omphalos* emphasised by an impressed line.

VII Patera mesomphalos

clay, slip, matrix, hand moulded
h 4 cm; diam 19.5 cm
Taranto, Museo Nazionale
inv. 54355

Out-turned rim articulated by twelve heads with *pileus*; on the inside twelve hollow ovoids and *omphalos*.

VIII Miniature situla

clay, wheel
h 5.6 cm; diam 3.8 cm
Taranto, Museo Nazionale
inv. 54359

Distinct rim, concave on the inside; body of convex profile; high cylindrical foot; ribbon handles.

IX Earthenware figurine

clay, slip, matrix, traces of colour
h. 28.2 cm
Taranto, Museo Nazionale
inv. 54372

Standing female figure wearing a *chiton* and cloak; naked hands raised to the head; flat rectangular base.

GRAEPLER 1989, p. 27, pl. VIII, 2.

X Earthenware figure

clay, slip, matrix, by hand, traces of colour
h 28.1 cm
Taranto, Museo Nazionale
inv. 54360

Standing female figure, dressed in *chiton* and *himation* which drops to knee level; head covered by cloak.

GRAEPLER 1989, p. 27, pl. VIII, 2.

XI Earthenware figure

clay, slip, matrix, by hand, traces of colour
h 22.7 cm
Taranto, Museo Nazionale
inv. 54369

Standing female figure, leaning on a pilaster with the right hand, holding a fruit possibly. The upper part of her body is nude; the lower part covered by a cloak; on her left shoulder a dove. Flat, rectangular base.

GRAEPLER 1989, p. 27, pl. VIII, 2.

XII Earthenware figure

clay, slip, matrix, by hand, traces of colour
h 22.8 cm
Taranto, Museo Nazionale
inv. 54370

Standing female figure, leaning on a pilaster with the right hand, holding a theatrical mask. The upper part of her body is nude; the lower part covered by a cloak.

GRAEPLER 1989, p. 27, pl. VIII, 2.

XIII Earthenware figure

clay, slip, matrix, hand moulded, traces of colour
h 22.8 cm
Taranto, Museo Nazionale
inv. 54370

Standing female figure, leaning on a pilaster with the right hand, holding a theatrical mask. The upper part of her body is nude; the lower part covered by a cloak.

GRAEPLER 1989, p. 27, pl. VIII, 2.

XIV Earthenware figure

clay, slip, matrix, hand moulded
traces of colour
h 11.1 cm
Taranto, Museo Nazionale
inv. 54367

Standing female figure, dressed in *chiton* with high belt, band of cloth on her hsoulders and arms.

GRAEPLER 1989, p. 27, pl. VIIII, 2.

XV Earthenware figure

clay, slip, matrix, hand moulded
traces of colour
h 19.5 cm
Taranto, Museo Nazionale
inv. 54368

Standing female figure, dressed in large *chiton* with *apoptygma* which arrives under her knees and in a cloak wrapped around the head.

GRAEPLER 1989, p. 27, pl. VIII, 2.

XVI Earthenware figure

clay, slip, double matrix
traces of colour
h 24 cm
Taranto, Museo Nazionale
inv. 54361

Nude seated female figure, with legs together, arms folded, hair in the "melon" style.

GRAEPLER 1989, p. 27, pl. VIII, 2.

XVII Earthenware bust

clay, slip, matrix, traces of colour
h. cm 12
Taranto, Museo Nazionale
inv. 54363

Female bust wearing a *chiton* veil on the head and shoulders, crown of ivy leaves on the forehead, earrings.

GRAEPLER 1989, p. 27, pl. VIII, 2.

XVIII Earthenware bust

clay, slip, matrix, traces of colour
h 13.1 cm
Taranto, Museo Nazionale
inv. 54364

Female bust emerging from a calyx of leaves, dressed in a *chiton* without sleeves; hair in the "melon" style with padded crown of ivy leaves and earrings.

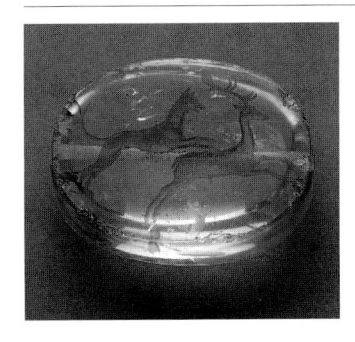

GRAEPLER 1989, p. 27, pl. VIII, 2.

XIX Group of Eros and Psyche

clay, slip, matrix, hand moulded
traces of colour
h 16 cm
Taranto, Museo Nazionale
inv. 54362

Standing, embraced: Eros of an infantile type on the right, with a cloak on his shoulders and fan in his right hand; Psyche on the left, dressed in a *chiton* and *himation* with hair in the "melon" style and pad.

GRAEPLER 1989, p. 27, pl. VIII, 2.

XX Pair on a kline

clay, slip, matrix, by hand, traces of colour
h 10.3 cm; l 11.6 cm
Taranto, Museo Nazionale
inv. 54350

Recumbent male figure, holding a lyre in his left hand; his right hand is lying on the nape of a female figure.

GRAEPLER 1989, p. 27, pl. VIII, 2.

XXI Bearded old man

clay, slip, matrix, hand moulded
traces of colour; h. cm 11.7
Taranto, Museo Nazionale
inv. 54365

Standing figure wearing a *chiton* and short cloak. Prominent belly.

GRAEPLER 1989, p. 27, pl. VIII, 2.

XXII Papposilenus

clay, slip, double matrix, traces of colour; h 12.2 cm
Taranto, Museo Nazionale
inv. 54366

Dressed in a *chiton* and short cloak, right hand on his long beard, prominent stomach, face with silenic features, holes on the edge of the *chiton* for suspension of mobile legs.

GRAEPLER 1989, p. 27, pl. VIII, 2.

XXIII Dove

clay, slip, matrix, hand moulded
h 9.5 cm; l 9.2 cm
Taranto, Museo Nazionale
inv. 54357

Closed wings, anatomical details barely hinted at, feet in relief on the conical-trunk base.

GRAEPLER 1989, p. 27, pl. VIII, 2.

XXIV Goose or duck

clay, slip, matrix, by hand
h 7.1 cm; l 6.9 cm
Taranto, Museo Nazionale
inv. 54358

Globular body, feathers divided into upper and lower parts, anatomical details barely hinted at, holes for insertion of feet in another material.

GRAEPLER 1989, p. 27, pl. VIII, 2.

XXV Seal

rock crystal
h 2.5 cm; l 5.8 cm
w 4.5 cm
Taranto, Museo Nazionale
inv. 54373

Scarab-shaped seal with a hole through its length. On one side a dear hunted by a dog caught in the act of jumping.

Ori Taranto, p. 316, cat. 273.

A. DELL'AGLIO-D. GRAEPLER in *Ori Taranto*, pp. 428-434.   A.dell'A.

---

297 I-XIII

Furnishings of a tomb at Taranto

Discovered in December 1909 in via Duca degli Abruzzi, in the garden of the S. Francesco di Paola church. In the course of recent re-arrangement of the Deposits of the Museo Nazionale di Taranto, all the elements of the furnishings which confirm the dating proposed in the first edition of the context have been recuperated.

I Dancer

clay, slip, double matrix, traces of colour
h 36.5 cm
Taranto, Museo Nazionale
inv. 4092

In a dancing movement, with legs crossed, feet on point, dressed in a transparent fluttering *chiton*, left breast bare, hair held by a *stephane*. Two vertical holes at the back.

II Dancer

clay, slip, double matrix, traces of colour
h 35.2 cm
Taranto, Museo Nazionale
inv. 4096

Body and head, without *stephane*, obtained from the same matrix as figure inv. 4092. Different, though, the position of the arms. Two vertical holes on the back.

III Dancer

clay, slip, double matrix, traces of colour
h 23.6 cm
Taranto, Museo Nazionale,
inv. 4106

Caught in a twisting movement, she wears a *chiton* and a cloak. *Stephane* on her forehead.

IV Dancer

clay, slip, double matrix, traces of colour
h 20.5 cm
Taranto, Museo Nazionale
inv. 4098

The dancer is wearing a long *chiton*; her hair is gathered.

V Dancer

clay, slip, double matrix, traces of colour
h 23.9 cm; base 3.4 cm
diam 9.1 cm
Taranto, Museo Nazionale
inv. 4102

Nude, right leg forward, left back on its point, ferine ears. Small hole on the back and under the left arm. Circular base.

VI Satyr

clay, slip, double matrix, traces of colour
h 30 cm
Taranto, Museo Nazionale
inv. 4103

Nude, represented running; muscular body, left arm wrapped in a wild beast's skin with the paws knotted on his chest and which also covers the shoulders; beardless face, ferine ears, frowning forehead.

VII Satyr

clay, slip, double matrix, traces of colour
h 29.6 cm
Taranto, Museo Nazionale
inv. 4095

Nude, represented running; muscular body, left arm wrapped in a wild beast's skin with the paws knotted on his chest and which also covers the shoulders; berdless face, ferine ears, frowning forehead.

VIII. Satyr

clay, slip, double matrix, traces of colour
h cm 19.3; base cm 3.5; diam. cm 9.7
Taranto, Museo Nazionale, inv. 4199

Standing satyr, with a young beadless face, ferine ears, circular base.

IX Satyr

clay, slip, double matrix, traces of colour
h cm 18.7; base cm 3.9; diam cm 11.6
Taranto, Museo Nazionale, inv. 4097

Naked, running satyr, beardless face, ferine ears, two small horns on his forehead, circular base.

X Sleeping maenad

clay, slip, double matrix, traces of colour
h 9.6 cm; l 30 cm;
Taranto, Museo Nazionale
inv. 4104

Lying prone on a rocky base covered with a wild beast skin, lower part of the body covered by a cloak, *strophion* around her breast, profiled head, arms raised and bent.

XI Artemis

clay, slip, double matrix, traces of colour
h 21 cm; base 3.5 cm; diam. 9.5 cm
Taranto, Museo Nazionale
inv. 4100

Standing, dressed in a short *chiton* with apotyma and high belt, very small bust, footwear. Circular base.

XII Female bust

clay, slip, double matrix, traces of colour
h 19.8 cm; w 16.1 cm
Taranto, Museo Nazionale
inv. 4101

Dressed in a *chiton* belted under the breast and buttoned on the shoulders; hair held by a pad, earrings

XIII Tropaion

clay, slip, double matrix, traces of colour
h 16.1 cm
Taranto, Museo Nazionale
inv. 4105

Elmo a berretto frigio con visiera, corazza anatomica sopra al vestito, schinieri, scudo di tipo "celtico".

A. Dell'Aglio D. Graepler, in *Ori Taranto* 1984, pp. 476-481, CXXXVI; Graepler 1994, pp. 295 ff.

A.Dell'A.

298

Earthenware applications

second half fourth century B.C.
clay, slip, matrix, gilded lamina, colour
Taranto, Museo Nazionale
inv. 12339-12356; 14715
Taranto, tomb 1, the Tesoro district
28.7.1909

Numerous applications in gilded terracotta testify to the deposition of a decorated wooden coffin. The single applications were arranged to create friezes which used generic subjects, like rosettes or *gorgoneia*, or more narrative ones, as in the frequent animal theories, often animated by assaults of griffins or felines, or in the Dionysian scenes. In the case under examination, the specific funerary value is denoted by two rare plaques with portrayals of Scylla in a male and female version.

D. Graepler, in *Ori Taranto*, pp. 393-396.

E.L.

299

Bottle

325-300 B.C.
silver, gilded lamina, hammering, engraving
h 10.5 cm
Taranto, Museo Nazionale
inv. 119169
Taranto, via G. Maturi corner via Vaccarella, tomb 18, 19.5.1961

The bottle, of an unusual shape, is decorated with a necklace of rosettes, opposing buds and *lonchiai*. The short cylindrical neck lacking a distinct lip, might indicate the presence of a cover.

E. Lippolis, in *Ori Taranto*, no. 4, p. 54.

E.L.

Works on Exhibit

300 I-III

Jewellery from Taranto

end third-beginning second
century B.C.
Berlin, Staatliche Museen zu
Berlin Preussischer Kulturbesitz,
Antikensammlung, inv. 1980.17-22

Possibly coming from a tomb context, the jewels exhibited here were discovered in Taranto at the beginning of the last century.

I Sakkos

gold, garnets, knurling
diam 9 cm
reassembled

It is made up of a lamina strip at the base, a gridwork cup with garnets in the points of intersection and a central medallion with a head of Medusa. The strip is adorned with floral motifs and, on one side, presents a Herculean knot worked à jour.

II Earrings

gold
h 5.5 cm

Pair of pendant earrings with winged female figures; the joint with the pendant is marked by a rosette.

III Bandolier

gold, garnets, cornelians
l 10.8 cm

Double knit realised with two golden stitches alternating with a precious stone; in the centre is a Herculean knot partly in garnets, movable and connected to the necklace with hinges and linking cones; they too partly of garnets.

301 I

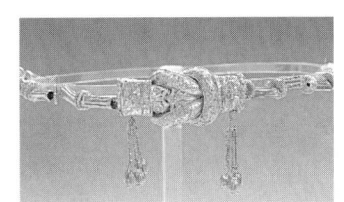

Diadem

end fourth-beginning third
century B.C.
gold, filigree, chains
max l 32.2 cm
Taranto, Museo Nazionale
inv. 22406
Ginosa, the Chiaradonna district,
Girifalco tomb, 1927

The diadem, preserved among the objects of a tomb's furnishings together with the earrings (cat. nos. 563-564), presents an innovative formal solution, re-elaborating the traditional phytomorphic elements of the local ornamental lexicon to enrich the surface of the central Herculean knot, an element of apotropaic value.

E. Lippolis, in *Ori Taranto*, no. 52, pp. 121-122; Guzzo 1993, p. 214.
E.L.

301 II

Pair of disc earrings with conical pendant

end fourth-beginning third century
B.C.
gold, mould, filigree, knurling
h 6.7 cm
Taranto, Museo Nazionale
inv. 22407 A-B
Ginosa, the Chiaradonna district
Girifalco tomb, 1927

Lamina disc decorated with an elaborate phytomorphic composition in filigree. Conical pendant, in smooth lamina, with Lesbian Kyma around the base and threads wound spirally around the body. Hook made of a hollow cylinder in lamina soldered onto the back part of the disc.

T. Schojer, in *Ori Taranto*, pp. 173-174, no. 91, p. 424; P. Guzzo 1993, p. 253, fig. 54.
T.S.

302 I

Bracelet

first decades of third century B.C.
gold, fusion (gold ingot), double
mould (protome), filigree, knurling
h 28 cm; diam. 7.7 cm
Taranto, Museo Archeologico
Nazionale, inv. 54.118
Mottola (Ta), bought 21.12.1936

Open circle, twisted band, helicoidal, with deep furrowing, ends in antelope protomes with very precise anatomical details, hollow eyes for inserting stones, filigree decoration on elements in lamina.

A. Dell'Aglio, in *Ori Taranto*, no. 167, pp. 243-245, XCI, pp. 434-435; Guzzo 1993, III, A1, pp. 78-79, 314-315.
A.Dell'A.

302 II

**II
Ring with engraved bezel**

280 a.C. circa
gold, engraving
diam. band cm 2.3
bezel cm 2.9x2.4
Taranto, Museo Nazionale, inv. 54117
Mottola, 21.XII.1936, (purchased)

The bezel shows the profile of an elderly woman characterized by marked facial traits, "melon" hairstyle, and jewellery (disk earings with erotes-shaped pendant). The band is attached to an unusually large circular bezel

A. Alessio, in *Ori Taranto*, pp. 260, 289 ff., cat. 210; Guzzo 1993, p. 165, no. 3.
A.A.

Works on Exhibit

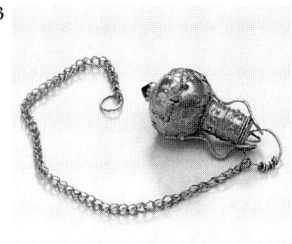

303 I

Amphoriskos pendant with chain

125-100 B.C.
gold, garnet, enamel, mould, knurling filigree, enamel applications, engraving
chain l 15.3 cm
pendant h 3.7 cm; diam. 1 cm
Taranto, Museo Nazionale
inv. 40.107
Altamura (BA), 4.6.1975, via Genova

Chain of large "double" knit. *Amphoriskos* of globular body, with decorative geometric and phytomorphic motifs in filigree. Ferrule in faceted garnet, set among lanceolate lamina leaves.

A. DELL'AGLIO, in *Ori Taranto*, n. 163, pp. 232-233, CXL, pp. 495-496; GUZZO 1993, V, F1, pp. 73-74, 231, 301.
A.Dell'A.

---

303 II-III

II
Ring set with garnet

end second century B.C.
gold, red garnet, polished
diam. band cm 1.3; bezel cm 1.1x0.6
Taranto, Museo Nazionale, inv. 40109
Altamura, 4.VI.1975, from a tomb of via Genova

A translucent garnet with a convex surfaced is set in the bezel. .

A. ALESSIO, in *Ori Taranto*, pp. 265, 300 ss., cat. 242.
A.A.

II
Ring set with garnet

end second century B.C.
gold, red garnet, polished
diam. band cm 2; bezel cm 1.6x1.1

Taranto, Museo Nazionale, inv. 40108 Altamura, 4.6.1975, from a tomb of via Genova

The bezel is enriched by an oval translucent garnet bead with convex surface. the band consists of a bent lamina..

A. ALESSIO, in *Ori Taranto*, pp. 265, 300, cat. 241.
A.A.

---

304 I

Sceptre

end third-beginning second century B.C.
gold, ivory, engraving, cutting
l 51 cm; h 3.6 cm
Taranto, Museo Archeologico Nazionale, inv. 22439
Canosa, Tomb of the Gold

The shaft, in perishable material, possibly wood, was covered with a pierced golden lamina. It seems to be of local production, realised also by assembling elements of diverse provenance, like the terminal element in bone or the two *Nikai* summararily applied to it.

E. LIPPOLIS, in *Ori Taranto*, pp. 320-326; P. GUZZO in *Principi*, p. 530 E.L.

---

304 II

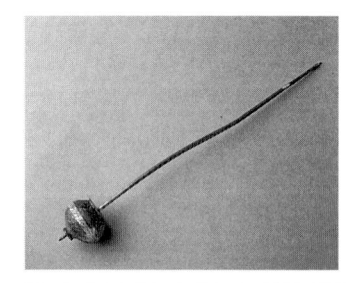

Hairpin

end third-beginning second century B.C.
silver, gold leaf, fusion, hot gilding engraving
l 18.5 cm
Taranto, Museo Nazionale,
inv. 22431
Canosa di Puglia (BA), 14.5.1928
tomb of the Gold

Long, tapering, cylindrical shaft; spheroidal head decorated by a gilded median band with engraved wave motifs and partly dotted in the background; on the base a gilded vegetal garland.

E. LIPPOLIS, in *Ori Taranto*, pp. 358-359, no. 326; GUZZO 1992, p. 531, no. 18.
L.M.

305

Crown

fourth century B.C.
silver
max h 5.2 cm; l 31 cm
Melfi, Museo Nazionale
inv. 53134
Melfi, Cappuccini, tomb C

Lamina in repoussé silver; in the middle a rosette with eight petals and dotted ribbing. To the sides two shoots of oak leaves with rosettes under the shaft.

G. TOCCO 1971, in *Popoli anellenici*, p. 113.
R.C.

306

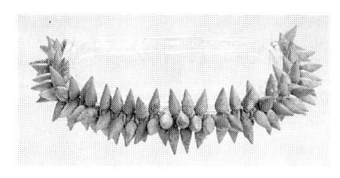

Funerary crown

second half fourth century B.C.
clay, mould, slip, red colour
l 25 cm
Taranto, Museo Nazionale
inv. 12037
Taranto, 3.V.1909, Arsenale Militare tomb 356

It is composed of one hundred conical elements with lower end like a ring to pass a thread through uniting them in a double opposing series and in a central row where they are arranged in a horizontal or oblique sense.

Ori Taranto, pp. 418-419, appendix LXII.1.
L.M.

Works on Exhibit

307

Seal with golden tie

fifth century B.C.
gold, engraving, chalcedony
l 23 cm; seal h 2.7 cm
Taranto, Museo Nazionale
inv. 12.023
Monteiasi (TA), the Amoroso district
(bought 30.6.1912)

Golden tie with tubular, fish-bone knit; cylindrical seal in chalcedony, on whose surface a deer attacked by a lion is depicted; passing hole in the long sense, into which a thin gold bar with eyelet terminals is inserted.

Ori Taranto, pp. 310-311, 314, no. 7; Guzzo 1993, pp. 56-57, 207, fig. 34.
A.D'A.

308

Pair of circular earrings

end third-beginning second century B.C.
gold, garnets, mould, filigree
engraving, incision
h 1.8-1.4 cm
Taranto, Museo Nazionale
inv. 22634, 22635
Taranto, 27.3.1922, the Vaccarella district, tomb 3

Circle of threads intertwined and wound spirally. On one end, modelled garnet of a head, set in a lamina capsule covered with raised spirals of thread to render the thick, curly hair. On the other end, smooth pin for the hood. In the second earring, the garnet represents a black woman, with the addition of a chignon on her nape.

T. Schojer in *Ori Taranto*, pp. 190-191, n. 130, p. 453, CXXIII; Guzzo 1993, p. 259, fig. 53.
T.S.

309

Earring in the shape of a boat with filigree decoration

second half fourth century B.C.
gold, mould, filigree, granulation, knurling, engraving
9.9x5.8 cm
Taranto, Museo Nazionale
inv. 110090
Taranto, 22.2.1958, via Umbria, room tomb 23

Boat in lamina, entirely decorated by an elaborate vegetal composition. Surmounted by a palmette, it presents laterally two seated *Nikai*, two rosettes and two doves. From the lower part small chains of double knit hang to which are suspended a palmette and seven small stylised *amphorae*.

T. Schojer, in *Ori Taranto*, pp. 154-157, cat. 68, pp. 414-415, appendix LIII; Guzzo 1993, pp. 250-251, fig. 43.
T.S.

310

Pair of disc earrings with inverted cone pendant

second century B.C.
gold, garnet, pearl, green vitreous paste, mould, filigree, granulation knurling, engraving
h 4.7-5 cm
Bari, Museo Archeologico
inv. 1662 bis
Ceglie del Campo (Bari)

Lamina disc with granulated triangular borders and bezelled garnet, surmounted by a "crown of Isis". Central biconical pendant. At the sides, two small chains in double knit with small terminal *amphorae*, and two in simple knit with clasps in gold, pearl and vitreous paste and bell-shaped terminals.

T. Schojer, in *Ori Taranto*, pp. 165-166, cat. 80; Guzzo 1993, p. 254, fig. 45.
T.S.

311 I

Pair of disc earrings and triple pendant with flying creature

end second-beginning first century B.C.
gold, white and brown vitreous paste
green enamel, mould, filigree
granulation
h 3.1-3.3 cm
Taranto, Museo Nazionale
inv. 50635 A-B
Taranto, 15-5-1934, via Gorizia, room tomb

Lamina disc with granulated and filigree rosette and long hook. Central pendant in vitreous pasta representing a swan with neck bent low, its feet on an abacus in golden lamina and an acorn necklace around its chest. Lateral pendants of double knit chain with knots and bell terminals.

T. Schojer, in *Ori Taranto*, pp. 168-169, cat. 84, pp. 504-505, appendix CL; Guzzo 1993, p. 251, fig. 56.
T.S.

311 II

Pair of disc earrings and triple pendant with flying creature

second century B.C.
gold, brown vitreous pasta, mould
filigree, granulation, knurling
h 3.5-3.7 cm
Taranto, Museo Archeologico Nazionale, inv. 6430 A-B
Taranto, 9.5.1911, piazza d'Armi tomb 4

Lamina disc with border of filigree petals and rosettes in two layers of petals: long hook. Central pendant made of a dove in vitreous paste with its head turned to the side and a necklace around its chest. Lateral pendants in double knit chain with knots and bell terminals.

T. Schojer, in *Ori Taranto*, pp. 169-170, cat. 85, pp. 501-502, appendix CXLIII; Guzzo 1993, p. 251, fig. 57.
T.S.

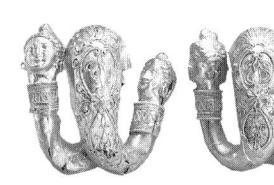

Works on Exhibit

Pair of helix earrings

second half fourth century B.C.
gold, mould, filigree, knurling
h 2.5
Taranto, Museo Archeologico
Nazionale, inv. 54.733 A-B
Taranto, 3.7.1954, via Cagliari n. 13
tomb 5

Body in empty tubular lamina, spiral twisted, with central thickening where an elaborate floral weave in filigree developes. Ends thinned with female *protomai*. The two heads, with minute *helix* and *sakkos* earrings, are inserted into a collar soldered to the body and decorated with a wavy thread of filigree.

Ori Taranto, pp. 178-179, cat. 103, p. 379; Guzzo 1993, p. 103, n. 55, p. 248, n. 1.   A.D'A.

312 II Helix earring

end fourth-beginning third century B.C.
gold, mould, filigree, knurling
h 2.2
Taranto, Museo Nazionale,
inv. 12.036
Taranto, 20.4.1905, via Principe Amedeo, sporadic find

Body in empty tubular lamina, smooth, spiral twisted, with central thickening. Ends thinned with female two-fronted protomes, with Phrygian cap and minute *helix* earrings, inserted into a collar soldered to the body and decorated with a wavy thread of filigree.

Ori Taranto, p. 180, cat. 105, p. 423; Guzzo 1993, p. 248 no. 3.   A.D'A.

313 Pair of earings with double leonine protome

end fourth-beginning third century B.C.
gold and brown enamel, mould
filigree, knurling
h 2-1.9
Taranto, Museo Nazionale
inv. 40156 A-B
Taranto, 1.6.1974, via Cugini, tomb 2

Arch of intertwined threads wound in a spiral. At one end a leonine protome in moulded lamina, with mane divided into wavy locks, hollow eyes for the insertion of vitreous paste or a stone and accurately modelled muzzle with engraving around the mouth, on the ribbon and the facial sketches. On the other end, a protome of smaller dimensions and less accurate modelling.

T. Schojer, in *Ori Taranto*, pp. 183-184, cat. III, p. 424, appendix LXXXII; Guzzo 1993, p. 257.   T.S.

314 Necklace

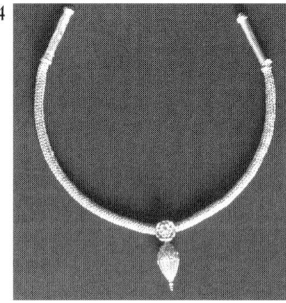

fourth century B.C.
gold, filigree, knurling, granulation
lamination
l 24.8 cm
Cagliari, Soprintendenza Archeologica
Monte Luna (Senorbi, CA), tomb 87

Necklace of thin threads of gold entwined to form a double fish-bone motif. At the ends of the chain are two cylinders in which the fasteners were placed. Pendant in the shape of an acorn. The join between the pendant and the necklace is hidden by a rosette.

Pisano 1988, p. 383.   V.S.

315 Ring with scarab

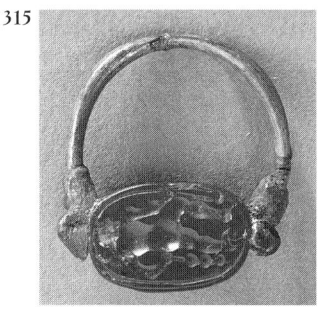

end fourth century B.C.
silver, honey-coloured chalcedony
engraving
diam. circle 1.5 cm
scarab 1.4x0.8 cm
Taranto, Museo Nazionale
inv. 40100
Taranto, 4.3.1975, from tomb 32 in via Alto Adige

Scarab decorated on the flat face with standing Heracles leaning on a club and holding in his left hand a branch or something similar. In origin the chalcedony turned on a filament passing through the ends of the bar shaped like a cone on which the spiral was then wound.

A. Alessio, in *Ori Taranto*, pp. 276 ss., cat. 176; Guzzo 1993, p. 172, no. 9.   A.A.

316 Ring with engraved bezel

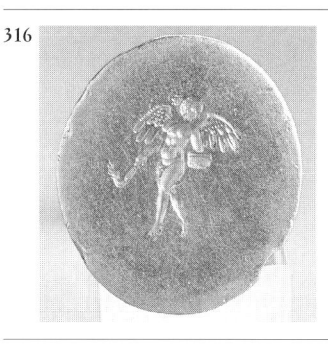

beginning third century B.C.
gold, engraving
diam. circle 1.7 cm
bezel 2.6x2.4 cm
Taranto, Museo Nazionale
inv. 40163
Saturo (Leporano, TA), 17-18.VI.1977
from a store-room

The subject is composed by an exquisite *erotes* portrayed in flight with wings unfolded and head turned backwards, intent on holding a container and a torch.

A. Alessio, in *Ori Taranto*, pp. 259, 289, cat. 208; Guzzo 1993, p. 165, no. 10.   A.A.

317		**Ring with scarab** 350-325 B.C. gold, engraved with burin, *repoussé* relief diam. circle 2 cm scarab 1.6x1.1 cm Taranto, Museo Nazionale inv. 4526 Taranto, 25.IX.1909, from tomb 442 found in the area of the Arsenale	On the base of the scarab is depicted seated Electra, with bowed head, intent on removing the cloak covering her head. The daughter of Agamemnon, is indicated by name in relief with two groups of distinct letters on part of the *himation* (HAE-KP). The end of the bar is shaped like a leonine *protome*.	A. ALESSIO, in *Ori Taranto*, pp. 254, 281 ff., cat. 188; GUZZO 1993, p. 171, no. C1. A.A.
318		**Ring with scarab** ca. 340-330 B.C. silver, darkish honey-coloured chalcedony, engraving, round pointed drill diam. circle 2.2 cm scarab 1.9x1.4 cm Taranto, Museo Nazionale inv. 4666 Taranto, 18.6.1915, from tomb 5 in the Vaccarella district	Anatomical rendering on the back of the scarab by engraving. On the base, a pair of horsemen galloping towards the left, armed with javelins. Ring ends shaped as small cupolas.	A. ALESSIO, in *Ori Taranto*, p. 276, cat. 174; GUZZO 1993, p. 172, n. 7. A.A.
319	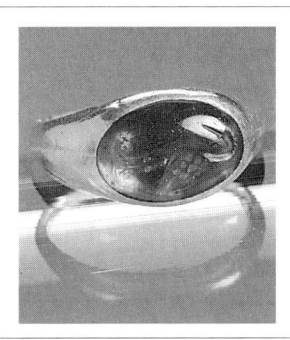	**Ring with mounted stone** end second-beginning first century B.C. gold, brick-red coloured garnet, round pointed drill diam. circle 1.4 cm setting 0.9x0.6 cm Taranto, Museo Nazionale inv. 50637 Taranto, 15 5.1934, from a room tomb in via Gorizia	Ring in heavy gold which mounts an oval stone on whose convex surface a standing *heron* is depicted, seen in profile to the left, on a base line.	A. ALESSIO, in *Ori Taranto*, p. 301, cat. 243. A.A.
320	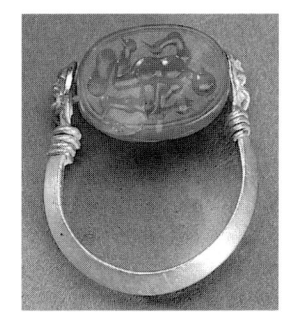	**Ring with scarab** 325-300 B.C. gold, honey-coloured chalcedony engraving, round pointed drill diam. circle 2.8 cm scarab 1.5x1 cm Taranto, Museo Nazionale inv. 54752 Taranto, 5.12.1934, from a tomb in via Iapigia	On the base of the scarab, warrior in bent position with right knee on an elongated element with rounded end, probably a rocky relief; seen in profile, he appears armed with a dagger and a sort of club. He is nude apart from a headcovering. The chalcedony is held by a golden thread wound as a spiral around the end of the bar shaped as a leonine *protome*.	A. ALESSIO, in *Ori Taranto*, p. 280, cat. 185; GUZZO 1993, p. 174, no. E1. A.A.
321		**Ring with mounted stone** second half second century B.C. gold, emerald, engraving diam. circle 1.5 cm setting 0.9x0.7 cm Taranto, Museo Archeologico Nazionale, inv. 22442 Taranto, 23.III.1933, from a room tomb in via Gorizia	On the stone, of a slightly convex surface, the figure of a filiform insect, recognisable today only from the cast, was engraved.	A. ALESSIO, in *Ori Taranto*, p. 300, cat. 240. A.A.
322		**Ring with scarab** 325-300 B.C. silver, pale violet-coloured chalcedony engraving, drill diam. ring 1.8 cm scarab 1.6x1.2 cm Taranto, Museo Archeologico Nazionale, inv. 106516 Taranto, 15.XI.1956, from tomb 2 in via Bellini	The scarab, always with detailed back, has the image of a palimped on its flat face, possibly a duck, depicted in profile towards the left within a cornice of dashes. The gold bar is of the commonest type, with ends of cupolas.	A. ALESSIO, in *Ori Taranto*, p. 276, cat. 175; GUZZO 1993, p. 172, n. 8. A.A.

323

Ring with revolving stone

end third-beginning second century B.C.
gold, whitish pink agate, engraving
diam. ring 1.6 cm; stone 1.0.6 cm
Taranto, Museo Nazionale
inv. 11769
Taranto, 25.10.1960, from tomb 1 in via Sardegna

Gold bar made up of an entwined thread linked to a smooth one with ends of phytomorphic, conical trunks, crossed by the filament which holds up the agate, shaped like an astragalus.

A. ALESSIO, in *Ori Taranto*, pp. 254, 282, cat. 189; GUZZO 1993, p. 175, no. Ea1. A.A.

324

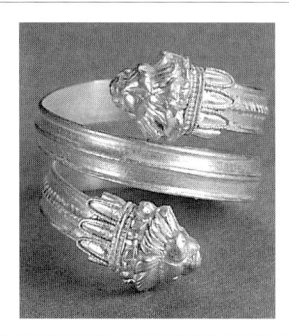

Spiral ring

end fourth-beginning third century B.C.
gold, mould, filigree, engraving
diam. circle 1.9 cm
Taranto, Museo Nazionale
inv. 12632
Taranto, 11.3.1966, from a tomb in via Molise

Spiral with external ribbing and enlarged borders, finishing at the two ends with lion protomes; hollow in that they are obtained by lamina worked separately and then soldered. The grafting onto the ring is masked by a smooth thread between two knurls and by a small collar of petals with filigree borders.

A. ALESSIO, in *Ori Taranto*, pp. 261, 292, cat. 217; GUZZO 1993, p. 244, n. III A1. A.A.

325

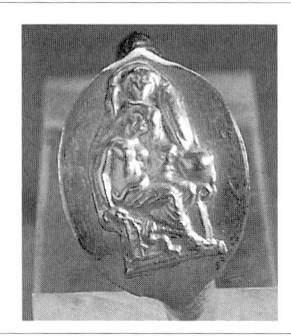

Ring with relief setting

second quarter fourth century B.C.
gold, *repoussé* in the mounting
diam. ring 1.8 cm; setting 2.2x1.9 cm
Taranto, Museo Nazionale
inv. 22417
Taranto, 11.10.1932, from a tomb in via Crispi

The scene, which occupies the setting, shows two female figures of mournful aspect; they are recognisable as Electra, with head covered by a *himation*, seated on an altar, and behind her, her faithful nurse standing. The group is probably represented near Agamemnon's tomb, to which the attributes present on the right (shield and sphere) might allude.

A. ALESSIO, in *Ori Taranto*, pp. 256 ff., 283, cat. 192; GUZZO 1993, p. 168, no. B1. A.A.

326

Ring with engraved setting

end fourth century B.C.
gold, engraving
diam. circle 1.9 cm
bezel 2.2x1.8 cm
Taranto, Museo Nazionale
inv. 22626
Taranto, 22.1.1923,
(bought B. Ricciardi)

On the mount, an elegant female figure adorned with earrings and bracelets, with her hair gathered into a *sakkos*, leans on a pilaster holding a crown in her left hand.

A. ALESSIO, in *Ori Taranto*, pp. 259, 288 ff., cat. 207; GUZZO 1993, p. 164, no. 6. A.A.

327

Lekythos in style Gnathian

340 ca B.C. circa
clay, glaze, wheel, overprinting
h cm 16.8; diam. rim cm 4; diam. foot cm 6.8
Taranto, Museo Nazionale, inv. 54745
Taranto, 30.12.1942, district Lupoli tomb 1

The boy shows two vertical blossoms, a female figure seated on a *disphros*. She is holding a mirror; her hair is gathered on her head and tied with a ribbon; her legs are wrapped in a *himotion* Her breast is uncovered.

WEBSTER 1968, p. 5, no. 4; FORTI-STAZIO 1983, p. 659, no. 666. G.A.M.

328

Apulian loutrophorus with red figures

ca. 320 B.C.
clay, overpainting
h cm 110; diam. 38 cm
Museo Nazionale "D. Ridola" Matera
inv. 164531
formerly in the Rizzon Collection

Side A: inside a *naiskos* a woman, with diadem, sits between two maids, one holding an umbrella, the other a box. Four offerers at the sides. At the bottom, a row of objects of the female *oikos*; basket with fruit, box, lyre, stool with crown. On the neck, winged female figure with diadem and bust coming out of acanthus plant volutes.
Side B: funerary stele surmounted by a beaded *Kylis*. Attributed to the Passano Group.

TRENDALL, CAMBITOGLOU 1992. M.G.C.

| 329 | **Fragment of basin in Gnathian style**

mid-fourth century B.C.
clay, glaze, wheel, overpainting graffito
h 21.5 cm; w 26 cm
Taranto, Museo Nazionale
inv. 4638
Taranto, 1909, Arsenale della Marina Militare, found lying on the ground | Body with convex profile, moulded lip. Decoration: nude *hetaera* with an abundant and flaccid body and a torch in her right hand dances towards a half-closed door. At the top, on the right, ivy shoots and, corresponding to the figure, the graffito name KONNAKIS, ascribable to the person herself. | WEBSTER 1968, p. 5, no. 3. G.A.M. |

330 see Recent Discoveries

| 331 | **Cuirass**

end fourth century B.C.
bronze, *lamina*, hammering
h 53 cm; diam 35.5 cm
Bari, Museo Archeologico, inv. 6075
Canosa, Ipogeo Varrese, discovered February 1912 | The cuirass is formed by two valves modelled plastically according to the anatomical features of a male torso. The two *gyala* are articulated among themselves by three pairs of fasteners placed on the shoulders and along the flanks, each flanked by heart-shaped plates with fixing rings. | ZIMMERMANN 1979, p. 178, no. 19; E. RICCHETTI, in *Principi*, p. 328, no. 2. M.L. |

| 332 | **Funerary stele**

350-325 B.C.
insular white marble
h 91 cm; w 53 cm
Taranto, Museo Nazionale
inv. 3920
Taranto, via F. Cavallotti | Narrow, elongated *stele* with architetural framing preserved only in the two corner pilaster strips and lacking the original tympanum crowning. The deceased is represented together with elements indicative of the funerary environment (apple offered to the serpent) and of his social *status* (weapons); the figure is standing, in heroic nudity, and with his *chlamys* rolled on his left arm. | LIPPOLIS 1994, p. 113, fig. 79. E.L. |

| 333 | **Metope of Doric frieze**

second century B.C.
soft stone, sculpture with noticeable traces of chiselling
max h 46.8 cm; max w 39.5 cm
Taranto, Museo Nazionale
inv. 6185, 6186, 6187
Taranto, piazza d'Armi, property Augenti-Ramellini, 15.7.1991 | Three sculptured metopes probably pertaining to the frieze of the trabeation of a funerary *naiskos* or to the crowning of its podium. Following each other from the left, two figures in oriental costumes, two Greek warriors and two female figures, possibly to represent a scene of rape or outrage. The figures are elongated and the drapery linear. | LIPPOLIS 1994, p. 124, fig. 98. E.L. |

| 334 | **Earthenware group with banqueters**

third-second century B.C.
clay, hand moulded, slip, traces of colour
base 17.5x14 cm; max h 14 cm
Egnazia, Museo Nazionale, inv. 9398 EGN
Egnazia, (Savelletri di Fasano) tomb 78/3 or "of the Banquet". | Rectangular base with two *klinai* in a corner on which four figures are placed; one sitting and three lying. Parallel to a *kline* a rectangular table with four feet, food and a bowl. At the end of the same *kline*, a round table with three feet with food and a basin. Between the two tables a small servant.
One figure closes the group, turned towards the banqueters, in movement and originally supported. | ANDREASSI, COCCHIARO 1987, pp. 48-49, pl. X. A.C. |

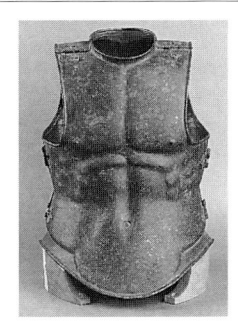

335

Apulian krater with red figures

340-330 B.C.
refined clay, glaze, wheel, overpainting
h 142 cm
fragmentary in part and integrated
Naples, Museo Nazionale
inv.81394
Ruvo, tomb discovered in 1834

Side A: on the neck, a siren among floral clusters; below, the race between Enomaus and Mirtilus, on one side, and between Pelops and Hippodamia, on the other. On the body: celebration of the funeral of Archemorus in front of the gods and heroes, around a building with Ionic columns; all the characters are indicated by the inscriptions.
Side B: on the neck, under a series of rosettes, Dionysian scene. On the body, Heracles in the garden of the Hesperides with the portrayal of Atlas holding the celestial vault. Attributed to the Painter of Dario.

RFVA, II, p. 496, n. 42; AELLEN 1992, p. 86. M.L.

336

Apulian mascheron krater with red figures

ca. 320 B.C.
clay, overpainting
h 123 cm; diam. rim 56 cm
Matera, Museo Nazionale "D. Ridola", inv. 164510
ex Collection Rizzon

Side A: in the centre, in *naiskos* Hades and Persephone on a *kline*. To the left, Megara and the Heraclids and Hekate with a torch. On the right, Hermes with *caduceus* and Orpheus in oriental clothes with a lyre. At the bottom, the offerers. On the neck, quadriga driven by Nike and, at the top, female head among plant volutes of acanthus. On the handles overpainted heads of Io and women bearing *thymiatrion* and a torch. *Side B*: in the centre in *naiskos*, seated woman. Four offerers at the sides. On the neck, in the middle, a seated woman with crown and box among offering women. On the handles masks of Io. Attributed to the Painter of the white *sakkos*.

TRENDALL, CAMBITOGLOU 1992. M.G.C.

337

Apulian hydria with red figures

mid-fourth century B.C.
refined clay, glaze, wheel
h 40.8 cm; diam. 16.8 cm
New York, Metropolitan Museum of Art, inv. 56.171.65

Scene of offers at the tomb: three female figures are arranged around a funerary *stele* which rests on a base with pomegranates and two hanging *kylikes*. The women bear crowns, bands and *paterae*. At the bottom on the right, a basket of eggs. Attributed to the circle of the Painter of the Ilioupersis.

RFVA, I, p. 205, tav. 65,2 G.L'A.

338

Apulian mascheron krater with red figures

340-330 B.C.
clay, overpainting
h 61 cm; diam. rim 50 cm
Matera, Museo Nazionale "D. Ridola"
inv. 164563
formerly in the Rizzon Collection

Side A: in the centre *naiskos* with young dancing girl with diadem. At the side, on the left, sorrowing pedagogue with lyre; on the right, crying woman. On the neck female head among plant volutes, foliage and flowers. *Side B*: woman with drum and crown and youth with *thyrsus* and bunch of grapes. In the middle stele. Mascherons: *on side A*, overpainted heads of Io; *on side B*, heads of Io. Attributed to the Copenhagen Group 4223

TRENDALL, CAMBITOGLOU 1992. M.G.C.

339

Apulian mascheron krater with red figures

ca. 340 B.C.
clay, overpainting
h 80 cm; diam. rim 44 cm
Matera, Museo Nazionale "D. Ridola"
inv. 164509
formerly in the Rizzon Collection

Side A: in the centre *naiskos* with a bearded man sitting among two standing youths. The youth on the left wears a helmet. To the sides another two youths alternate with two offering women. On the neck, Gannymede abducted by the swan among the pedagogue, who runs up with a stick and ball, and a youth with a circle. At the top on the right, a small fountain building. *Side B*: two youths and two offering women around a funerary stele. Mascherons: overpainted heads of Io in white and yellow on Side A. Attributed to the Painter of Copenhagen 4223.

RFVA, II, p. 468, tav. 167,5. M.G.C.

340 I-III

I Earthenware statuette of Apis

third century B.C.
refined clay; h 12.7 cm
Melfi, Museo Archeologico Nazionale
inv. 336745
Lavello, tomb 601

Lying-down statue of Toro Api - recognisable for the lunar gradient between its horns - symbol of Osiris and his birth.

A. BOTTINI, in *Museo Venosa*, p.76. R.C.

II Earthenware statuette of Dionysus as a child on a ram

third century B.C.
refined clay, traces of colour; h 12 cm
Melfi, Museo Archeologico Nazionale
inv. 336678; Lavello, tomb 605

Figure of the child Dionysus, seated astride a ram; barely hinted facial features, curly hair. On the upper part of the legs is a hint of drapery covering.

BOTTINI 1991, pp. 157 ss. R.C.

III Earthenware statuette of a child on a cock

third century B.C.
refined clay, traces of colour; h 10.9 cm
Melfi, Museo Archeologico Nazionale
inv. 335664
Lavello, tomb 906

Three-quarter view of child seated on a cock with an arm resting on its wing.

BOTTINI 1991, pp. 157 ss. R.C.

341		**Oinochoe with red figures and polychrome** end fourth century B.C. refined clay, glaze, overpainting h 63 cm; diam. foot 15.6 cm Melfi, Museo Archeologico Nazionale inv. 334896 Lavello, tomb 669	Main decoration: at the top, *quadriga* driven by an erotes. Above the horses, three doves with garlands. At the bottom, three-quarter female figure, seated and looking behind with a mirror, basket and bunch of grapes. On the left erotes with *thymiaterion* and *situla*. On the right, youth seated in three-quarters looking behind with a basket, ball and bunch of grapes. On the neck motifs of plant volutes with female heads in the middle; on the shoulder, bands of	rosettes alternating with female heads. Rear side: complex series of palmettes among plant volutes. M.P. FRESA, in *Forentum II*, p. 55. R.C.
342		**Polychrome Lebes gamikos with sculpted decoration** first decades second century B.C. clay, traces of colour, wheel, moulded applications Taranto, Museo Nazionale inv. 22796 Taranto, via Leonida, 14.5.1926	Conical-trunk cover with Erote applied to the pommel. The *lebès* presents an elongated ovoidal body divided into two zones: the lower one is beaded on the main side; the upper is decorated with female figures and an applied Nike. On the neck, a necklace with pendants. Ribbon handles with *telamones* on the front junctures and erotes applied to the top.	L. MASIELLO, in *Ori Taranto*, p. 457, no. 17, CXXVI. E.L.
343		**Askos with polychrome and sculpted decoration** end fourth- third century B.C. clay, plaster, colour, hand moulded h of vase 47.3 cm h of statue 24 cm Bari, Museo Archeologico, inv. 6006 Canosa (BA), Ipogeo Varrese, discovered February 1912	The *askos*, of globular body, presents complex pictorial and sculptural decoration: this last is made up of two *gorgoneia* applied to the front of the vase and to the rear handle attachment; to the sides of the mouth, two rearing horse protomes; on the shoulder and top of the handle, three worshippers. Polychrome floral motifs are painted on the sides of the gorgonian protomes; on the flanks of the vase, two winged seahorses.	F. VAN DER WIELEN, in *Principi*, no. 4, pp. 311, 314. M.L.
344		**Pyx with polychrome sculpted decoration** beginning third century B.C. clay, plaster, traces of colour, moulded medallion h 17 cm; diam 31.5 cm Leyden, Rijksmuseum van Oudheden inv. K 1980/5.1 Canosa	Cylindrical *pyx* with inner-turning rim for the cover; this last, in slightly convex profile with central medallion in relief, presents concentric grooving and an external frieze. The medallion represents an erotic scene with three figures.	F. VAN DER WIELEN, in *Principi*, pp. 520 ff.; BASTET 1982, 11 pp. 155 ff. G.L'A.
345		**Flask** third century B.C. terra-cotta, matrix, traces of colour h 29.3 cm; diam. 26 cm; t 4 cm Naples, Museo Archeologico Nazionale, inv. 16270 Canosa	The flask, whose body is composed of two joined discs, rests on two quadrangular feet and has two handles on the sides of the neck. Decorated on both faces with the sea monster Scylla with female bust, two dog heads at the sides and fish tale endings of the dragon body, which winds in two symmetrical coils at the sides of the monster.	S. DE CARO, in *Museo Napoli*, p. 84. M.B.
346 I		**Locrian inscribed tablet no. 12** 350-250 B.C. bronze h 11 cm Reggio Calabria, Museo Nazionale inv. 40545 Locri Epizefiri, archives container from the sanctuary of Zeus Olympus	A loan conceded by the Locrian Sanctuary of Zeus Olympus to the Locrian *polis* in the year of the eponymous Timodamus, is registered here. The work of several magistrates whose names and positions (*hieromnamones* for the treasury, *proboloi proarchontes*, *prodikoi*) are indicated. The sum of 1785 talents, 5 sesterces, 18 1/2 litres, was destined to the reinforcing of the town walls; the graphic scheme at the bottom alludes to the planimetry of a tower.	COSTABILE 1992, p. 253. C.S.

346 II III	**II Locrian inscribed tablet no. 13**	**III Locrian inscribed tablet no. 20**	Costabile 1992, p. 253.	C.S.
	350-250 BC bronze h 12.3 cm Reggio Calabria, Museo Nazionale inv. 40546 Locri Epizephyrii, archives container from the sanctuary of Zeus Olympus	350-250 B.C. bronze h 22.5 cm Reggio Calabria, Museo Nazionale inv. 40553 Locri Epizefiri, reliquary of the archive of the sanctuary of Zeus the Olympian		
	The text, which follow an analogous scheme to tablet 12, registers a loan from the treasury of Zeus to the Locrian *polis* for a "contribution (split over the three months of Boukatios, Agreios, Hippodromios) to the *basileus*". Costabile 1992, p. 255. C.S.	The text records the repayment by the city of loans from the treasury of Zeus: it gives the names of the eponymous magistrate Onasimos, of the magistrates who made the repayment on behalf of the city (proboloi, prodikoi, polemarchoi, phatarchos) and of those who receive the sum of 300 silver talents on behalf of the sanctuary (hieromnamones).		

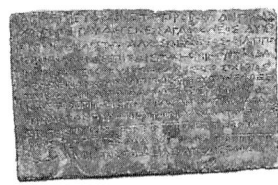

347	**Antefix in the form of a female head**	Locri Epizephyrii, sanctuary of Persephone in the Mannella district	Foti 1976, p. 354, pl. XXXI.	C.S.
	ca. mid fourth century B.C. terra-cotta h 22 cm Reggio Calabria, Museo Nazionale inv. 6215	Bipartite coiffure of long wavy locks, fastened on the top of the head by a three-banded diadem; rosette earrings, necklace with ovoid pendant in relief. Large ovoid face, sunken eyes with thick eyebrows and engraved iris and pupil, narrow mouth with fleshy lips.		

348	**Female figure holding a statuette of Artemis**	The standing female figure, perhaps a priestess, dressed in a peplos and with a bipartite coiffure on her forehead, raises her hands to hold above her head a small statue of Artemis; the goddess has her bow in her left hand and a fawn in her right; the priestess's attitude may be making a ritual display or participating in a procession.	Barra Bagnasco 1984, p. 47, fig. 13.	C.S.
	late fifth-early fourth century B.C. h 23.5 cm Locri, Antiquarium, inv. 96630 Locri Epizephyrii, excavation of the residential area of Centocamere district			

349 I	**Small model of cave**	Type without tank. Tall narrow mouth flanked by two applied lion's heads with large halo-like manes; cavity divided by wings into several areas; the lion masks of the front are repeated on the second diaphragm; on the walls stalactites, concretions and irregularities of the rock are represented in relief.	Arias 1946, p. 157, fig. 23; F. Martorano, in *Costabile* 1991, pp. 73 ff., figg. 126-130.	M.R.
	third-second century B.C. terra-cotta, hand-made with moulded elements applied separately h 45.6 cm; l 35.2 cm reassembled and integrated Reggio Calabria, Museo Nazionale inv. 357 Locri Epizephyrii, Grotta Caruso			

349 II	**Herma with three nymphs and Pan in the cave**	Plaquette surmounted by three female heads with low headdresses; at the sides two stylized thyrsi. In the lower half: Pan, with goat's hooves and horns, sits on a stool inside a cave with his left hand resting on his syrinx.	Foti 1972, p. 72, no. 25; Costabile 1991, p. 99, fig. 176.	M.R.
	late fourth-early third century B.C. terra-cotta, moulded h 17.7 cm; l 7.5 cm Reggio Calabria, Museo Archeologico Nazionale, inv. 101 Locri Epizephyrii, Grotta Caruso			

Works on Exhibit

349 III — **Herma with three nymphs and Pan in the cave**

late fourth-early third century B.C.
terra-cotta, moulded
h 16.5 cm; l 9.5 cm
reassembled
Reggio Calabria, Museo Archeologico Nazionale, inv. 108
Locri Epizephyrii, Grotta Caruso

Plaquette surmounted by three female heads; at the sides two thyrsi. In the lower half: Pan standing inside a cave playing the syrinx.

ARIAS 1946, p. 146, fig. 9; COSTABILE 1991, pp. 156 ff., fig. 254. M.R.

349 IV — **Herma with three nymphs and bull with human face**

fourth century B.C.
terra-cotta, moulded
h 16.3 cm; l 8.7 cm
Reggio Calabria, Museo Archeologico Nazionale, inv. 117
Locri Epizephyrii, Grotta Caruso

Plaquette surmounted by three female heads. At the bottom, in a doorway with a fluted frame, appears the forepart of a bull with a bearded male head viewed frontally, representing a river-god (Acheloüs?).

COSTABILE 1991, p. 221, fig. 343 M.R.

349 V — **Herma with three nymphs and bull with human face**

fourth-third century B.C.
terra-cotta, moulded
h 18 cm; l 9.9 cm
Reggio Calabria, Museo Archeologico Nazionale, inv. 110
Locri Epizephyrii, Grotta Caruso

Plaquette surmounted by three female heads with low headdress; at the sides two thyrsi. In the lower half: a bull with beardless male face stands erects, in profile looking left, on a rectangular base, on which is written: Euthymou [hi] e [ra] / E[u]thymou (sacred to Euthymos); opposite the animal is a small "altar" for libations, with a small basin on top seen in perspective.

ARIAS 1987, pp. 5 ff.; COSTABILE 1991, p. 200, fig. 321. M.R.

349 VI — **Nude seated female statuette**

late third-early second century B.C.
terra-cotta, moulded, with retouching by stick
h 19.8 cm; l 8.9 cm
lacunose
Reggio Calabria, Museo Archeologico Nazionale, inv. 286
Locri Epizephyrii, Grotta Caruso

Hair gathered in a bun behind the head and adorned with a low headdress (polos); chubby face; folds of the neck indicated; arms lying along the body, interrupted at the elbows, where the holes for the insertion of the forearms are visible; swollen abdomen, back slightly curving forwards. Hollow inside.

R. LEONE, in *Costabile* 1991, p. 118, fig. 194. M.R.

350 — **Votive pinax**

late fourth-early third century B.C.
clay, white slip, traces of colours
h 13.6 cm; l 13 cm
Lipari, Museo Eoliano, Depositi inv. 1950
Lipari, Diana district, trench XXIII/II/1955, votive ditch around the altar of the sanctuary of the Maggiore land

Pinax with representation of two goddesses at either side of an altar, behind which a priestess plays the double flute. The right figure is perhaps Kore with the pomegranate; the left one, which has a lanceolate fan, may be Ilitia.

Cf. BERNABÒ BREA 1958 b, p. 127, pl. 47, fig. 2; BERNABÒ BREA-CAVALIER 1977, fig. 151. A.S.

351 — **Campanian red-figure crater**

Purified clay, varnish, turned on lathe overpainted
h 52 cm; diameter 26 cm
Naples, Museo Archeologico Nazionale, inv. 85873
provenance unknown

Bell krater. Side A: symposium scene with three banqueters, one of whom embraces a girl; on the left a flute-player, on the right a boy with a water-bucket. The scene is framed by columns and adorned with tendrils, masks, hanging objects and doves. Side B: female figure sitting between three standing women, offering. Attributed to the C.A. Painter.

LCS, I, p. 460, no. 70, pl. 178,1. M.L.

352
I-IV

Treasure of silver from Paternò

375-3265 B.C.
Berlino, Staatliche Museen zu Berlin
Preussischer Kulturbesitz
Antikensammlung
Paternò (CT), 1909

I Kylix

diam. 13.5 cm

This cup, a duplicate of two other cups which are part of this same treasure, is of a type which larcks feet and has raised, curved handles; the inside of the cup is engraved with delicate floral decoration.

II Olpe

height 7.6 cm

An *olpe* with an outward-curving brim, a short concave neck, and a rounded swelling body engraved with delicate vegetable decoration (a design of bean pods). This type of *olpe*, well-known among black-figure ceramics in 5th-century B.C. Greece, persisted in southern Italy until the middle of the 4th century.

PFROMMER 1987, p. 21, nota 92, p. 180, con bibl. prec.

III Pyxis

A jewelry case, with ring and fastener, shaped like a seashell in accordance with a motif developed by the engravers at Tarentum. An octopus is engraved on the outside.

PFROMMER 1987, pp. 20, 180, and prec. bibl.

IV Mesomphalos phial

diam. 24.3 cm

A gold-plated silver phial. An oval cavity inside, just below the rim, has an engraving of vines and palmettos, and female heads with conical hats in high relief. The *omphalos* is encircled by a small band with a *kymation* from Lesbos on it, and a delicate design of leaves anbd palmettos. This type of phial was common in Apulia, in clay versions too

PFROMMER 1987, pp. 20, nota 90, 180, con bibl. prec.   E.C.P

353

Ram

early third century B.C.
bronze, cast by cire perdue
h 79 cm; l 138 cm
Palermo, Museo Archeologico
"A Salinas", inv. 8365
Syracuse, Castello Maniace

The sole survivor of a pair which in the Middle Ages adorned Castello Maniace in Syracuse. The animal is resting on its haunches, with large staring eyes, open mouth, ears sticking up above its spiral horns. The fleece is finely modelled in long wavy tufts. A fine example of Sicilian craftsmanship, strongly influenced by the Lisippean school.

COARELLI 1980, p. 164, figg. 90-91;
GRECO 1995, pp. 418-421.   A.V.

354

Colossal head of a divinity

1st-century B.C. (?) replica
of an original dated ca. 180 B.C.
marble
height 53 cm
chipped at the base of the neck
Syracuse, Museo Archeologico
Regionale "Paolo Orsi", inv. 693
Syracuse, Amphitheatre (1834)

Probably part of a cult statue, this is the head of a bearded male god. Is was once erroneously presumed to be connected with the Altar of Hieron II of Syracuse, but experts tend now to identify this head as that of the god Asclepius. It is done in the style of works produced at Pergamum, and this evident fact has recently led B. Andreae to consider it a replica made in the Augustan era (whereas R. Wilson places it in the late Hellenistic age). Both regard it a replica of the celebrated Asclepius of *Phyromakos*.

BONACASA 1985, p. 298, fig. 332, and prec. bibl.; ANDREAE 1993, pp. 84-91, 96-106, pls. 12,1-3; 14,1; 15,1-2.
E.C.P.

355

Portrayal of a female

late 3rd-early 2nd century B.C.
marble, the back side an unfinished surface
diadem made separately, and missing
height 29.8 cm
chips and surface abrasions
Syracuse, Museo Archeologico
Regionale "Paolo Orsi"
Syracuse (1954)

This portrayal of a female conveys pathos: she is looking up and to the right, her eyes gazing into the distance, her lips slightly parted. The type of physiognomy – long oval face, low forehead, regular mouth – and the simple hair style, with the hair parted in the middle at the front and gathered in a *toupet* at the nape, show the influence of Ptolemaic portraiture, specifically in the effigies of Arsinoes III, for example the head of *serapeion* in Alexandria.

BONACASA 1985, p. 295, fig. 334, and prec. bibl.   E.C.P.

356

Small female portrait from Helorus

second century B.C.
female head from Helorus
white marble, 9 x 9 cm
Museo Civico of Noto, Deposits
inv. SR 7001
From a cistern opposite the Stoa, Voza excavations

Young woman with wavy hair bound back, with curls in front of the clearly-depicted ears. Head inclined, sad expression, long neck. Traces of brown on the pupils and the eyebrows, pink on the lips, coppery red on the hair. Chipped on the top left. At the back the marble has been cut, perhaps in order to put the piece in place; it is broken in places, and there are traces of stucco.

BONACASA 1985, p. 295, fig. 324.   L.G.

Works on Exhibit

357

Pinax with the figure of a galopping horseman

early 3rd century B.C.
limestone
height 27.3 cm
chipped at the edges
Syracuse, Museo Archeologico Regionale "Paolo Orsi", inv. 839
Syracuse

This depicts an armed horseman galloping towards the left, his right hand stretched out towards the horse' head. The clamide he wears is flying about, in the background, and the horse's forelegs are off the ground; these details suggest the vehemence of the ride. The same details are a recurring motif in Hellenistic *imagerie*, and influence military iconography: one thinks, for example, of the battle of Alexander, or more specifically, of the *pugna equestris* of Agathocles displayed in the *Athenaion* in Syracuse.

BONACASA 1985, p. 309, fig. 359, and prec. bibl. E.C.P.

358

Statuette of Heracles

early 3rd century B.C.
marble
height 50 cm; height of the head 6.8 cm
traces of red coloring (a *leonté*), some small parts missing, base restored in antiquity
Syracuse, Museo Archeologico Regionale "Paolo Orsi", inv. 30575
Syracuse, Achradina district, from a man-made cavern used as a workshop and depositary by a sculptor

Recognizable as Heracles because of the *leonté* (partly preserved) which hangs from his left arm. He holds his club in his left hand and the golden apple of the Hesperides in his right. Nude, standing, his weight on his right leg, the left slightly extended and drawn back as if in a swinging motion. The pose, the physical anatomy, and the type of head – relatively small, with deepset eyes that are gazing into the distance – are clearly imitative of the work of Lysippus.

BONACASA 1985, p. 294, fig. 318. E.C.P.

360

Small male head

first half of the third century B.C.
clay, traces of polychrome
h 4.2 cm
Aidone, Museo Archeologico
inv. 55-2634
Morgantina

Male head with portrait-like features, perhaps representing Agathocles. He is turned to the left, with thick tufts of hair over his forehead, sunken eyes with pronounced superciliary arch, aquiline nose, deep furrows at the sides of the mouth, powerful neck.

BELL 1981, p. 210, n. 714, pl. 114. A.M.B.

361

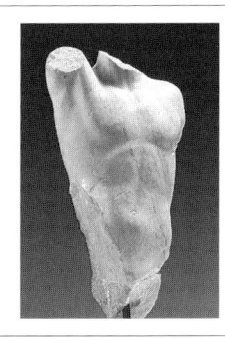

Male torso

third-second century B.C.
white marble
h 34.5 cm; w 17 cm; thickness 12.5 cm
Agrigento, Museo Archeologico Regionale, inv. C 1855
Provenance unknown, from the collections of the former Museo Civico of Agrigento

Torso of male figure which the anatomy suggests was fairly young. The standing figure may have been represented in the act of pouring a liquid from a pitcher held in his hand, on the model of Praxiteles' Pouring Satyr.

PUGLIESE CARRATELLI-FIORENTINI, p. 105, fig. 105. G.C.

362

Statuette of crouching Aphrodite

second-first century B.C.
white marble
h 22.5 cm; w 18.5 cm
thickness 10.5 cm
Agrigento, Museo Archeologico Regionale, inv. C 1854
Provenance unknown, from the collections of the former Museo Civico of Agrigento

Small statuette representing Aphrodite crouching at her bath, in the act of wringing her hair with her hands. The type to which the piece belongs is a late Hellenistic reworking of Aphrodite at the bath of Doidalsas, attributed to Rhodian sculptors.

DE MIRO 1994, pp. 57 ff, pl. 30. G.C.

363

Group in clay: Pan and a maiden

late 3nd century B.C.
clay
height 19.6 cm
Syracuse, Museo Archeologico Regionale "Paolo Orsi", inv. 43263
Centuripe, necropolis in the Cannatelli district

A maiden, nude and kneeling, perhaps a nymph, intent on bathing (you see the border of her gown, folded, behind her left leg), is taken by surprise by Pan, who is attempting to raise her from behind, holding her by the arms. This is a type of scene originating in the first half of the 2nd century; the sculptor here reproduces the scene, "correcting" it, in the classicist sense withthe two figures faring each other.

BELL 1981, pp. 173-174 (no. 352); BONACASA 1985, pp. 331-332, fig. 383. E.C.P.

364

Statuette of Afrodite

150-125 B.C.
clay
h cm 27.2
reconstructed
Siracuse, Museo Archeologico Regionale "Paolo Orsi"
inv. 35957
Centuripe, the Mammana collection

The goddess is depicted nude, balancing on her right foot, in the act of removing, with her right hand, the sandal (originally painted on) of the raised left foot.

LIMC II (1984), *s.v. Aphrodite*, p. 58, no. 469, pl. 45; BONACASA 1985, p. 331, fig. 381. E.C.P.

365

Statuette of satyr

late 3rd - earky 2nd century B.C.
clay, moulded by hand and with a stick, well detailed on both front and rear
h cm 34; h of head cm 5.5; traces of polychrome, some parts missing
Siracusa, Museo Archeologico Regionale "Paolo Orsi", inv. 49960
Centuripe, necropolis in the Casino district, tomb 18 (1942)

In the act of dancing, smiling, his satir's appearance made evident cy the goat hair on his flanks and by certain details of the head (small equine ears, little horns on the forehead, a wild head of hair, and a Dionysiac crown of vine leaves).

BONACASA 1985, p. 331, fig. 334; *Sicilia greca*, p. 202, no. 356. E.C.P.

366 I-IV

I. Statuette of a muse

late 3rd - earky 2nd century B.C.
clay; h cm 33
slick, traces of polychrome
Muses' attribute missing
Siracusa, Museo Archeologico Regionale "Paolo Orsi", inv. 46824
Centuripe, necropolis in the Casino district, tomb 18 (1932)

Fully clothed female figure, seated on a rock projecting laterally, the head and bust turned to the left at 3/4 angle. On her left she is holding, to judge from the positions of the arm, a musical instrumlent, a Lyre.

Sicilia greca, p. 173, no. 370, fig. (p. 242). E.C.P.

II. Statuette of Aphrodite

late 3rd - earky 2nd century B.C.
clay; h. cm 26
traces of polychrome, part missing (the left arm) and parts reconstructed (the left foot)
Siracusa, Museo Archeologico Regionale "Paolo Orsi", inv. 46827
Centuripe, necropolis in Casino district, tomb 18 (1932)

Semi-nude, standing on the right leg, wrapped in a mantel that covers the back and the left shoulder, hanging down behind,; right arm raised.

Sicilia greca, p. 173, n. 371; cfr. LIMC II (1984), *s.v. Aphrodite*, pp. 79 ff., ns. 707-711, pl. 71 (part. n. 708). E.C.P.

III. Statuetta of a dancer

late 3rd - earky 2nd century B.C.
clay; h. cm 15.5
parts reconstructed; traces of polychrome

Siracusa, Museo Archeologico Regionale "Paolo Orsi", inv. 46829
Centuripe, necropolis in Casino district, tomb 18 (1932)

Sicilia greca, n. 368, p. 173. E.C.P.

IV. Statuetta di danzatrice

late 3rd - earky 2nd century B.C.
clay, h cm 21
reassembled fragmentary unsculpted back; traces of polychrome

Siracusa, Museo Archeologico Regionale "Paolo Orsi", inv. 46828
Centuripe, necropolis in Casino district, tomb 18 (1932)

Sicilia greca, n. 369, p. 173 E.C.P.

367

Female Tanagra statuette

second-first century B.C.
clay
h 42 cm
Palermo, Museo Archeologico "A. Salinas", inv. 1032
Soluntum

Figure of a young woman, finely draped in a dress and cloak with many folds. The right arm is bent back, with the hand resting on the shoulder; the left arm, slightly bent, holds the cloak. The neck is long and sinuous, the features of the face are well modelled, the typical "melon" hairstyle is elegant. It belongs to the class of the so-called Tanagra statuettes, which were widespread in the artistic koiné of the Hellenistic period.

VILLA 1993, p. 364, tav. LXVI, 5. A.V.

368

Statuette of Harpocrates

early first century A.D.
bronze, full cast, details added by engraving
h 10 cm
Palermo, Museo Archeologico "A. Salinas", inv. 7762
Soluntum

The god is represented as a naked, standing child, leaning against a gnarled trunk from which hangs one edge of the cloak that covers his shoulders. The bowed head is encircled with a crown of leaves and surmounted by the crown of High and Low Egypt. The left hand holds the horn of plenty; the index finger of the right hand touches the lips. This iconographical type was common in the Hellenistic period; it originated from Praxiteles.

TUSA 1972-73, p. 402; DI STEFANO 1975, pp. 4-5, no. 3, pl. I. A.V.

Works on Exhibit

| 369 I | **Panel with painted wall decoration**

first century B.C.
stucco painted encaustically
max size 155 x 83.5 cm
Palermo, Museo Archeologico "A. Salinas", inv. 2299
Soluntum | Decoration in the "second Pompeiian style": on a base of violet orthostats, which are separated by a yellow rectangle, is a violet square decorated with a garland of fruit, ears of corn and leaves, from which long embroidered bands hang down. Under the garland is depicted, as if suspended in mid air, a female mask of a reddish colour, with brown hair bound by a ribbon. | WILSON 1990, pp. 30-31, fig. 24.   A.V. |

| 369 II | **Panel with painted wall decoration**

first century B.C.
stucco painted encaustically
max size 153 x 119 cm
Palermo, Museo Archeologico "A. Salinas", inv. 2300
Soluntum | Decorative pattern similar to the preceding one (inv. 2299). In this panel, however, is depicted a bearded male mask of a brown and yellowish colour, with the hair rendered in thick untidy tufts adorned by a crown of berries and leaves. The panel also includes part of an adjacent square, of which one can see the beginning of a garland with a band, adorned with three pine-cones. | BEYEN 1938, pp. 44-46, fig. 6 a-c.   A.V. |

| 370 | **Relief with the figure of Delphic Apollo**

late 3rd century B.C.
limestone
Siracusa, Museo Archeologico Regionale "Paolo Orsi", Palazzolo Acreide | This relief presents, almost fully rounded, a semi-nude androgynous figure leaning lightly on an *omphalos* placed on a quadrangular base, and also a female figure standing, richly clothed, holding a large tripod in her right hand. In View of these two attributes, an Apollonian identification seems probable; although a different identification (Aphrodite with Persephone) has recently been suggested. | *LIMC*, II (1984), *s.v. Apollon*, p. 267, no. 675, pl. 238, prec. bibl.: BONACASA 1985, p. 310, fig. 354; POLACCO 1992, pp. 173-202, pls. 1-10.   E.C.P. |

| 371 | **Applique**

3rd century B.C.
bronze, lead attachment, domaged on the right, green patina
h cm 16.5; w cm 12
Siracusa, Museo Archeologico Regionale "Paolo Orsi", inv. 94750 | Full face, with elongated eyes; fleshy lips. The hair, parted on the forehead, falls on the shoulder. | N. BONACASA, in *Sikanie*, p. 293 n. 342.   C.C. |

| 372 I | **Jewelry from Avola**

The pieces presented here are part of a smal treasure found in 1914 near Avola, inside a clay vase; the treasure also included a gold earring and three hundred coins from the 4th century B.C., from Syracuse and Persia, now dispersed.. | I
Pair of bracelets

330-300 B.C.
gold
max. diam.cm 5.5;
w of the band cm 1.3
London, British Museum
GRA 1923.4-21.1 and 2

Bracelets terminating in a serpent's head (identical in the two examples) | and worked with decoration of acanthus leaves, spirals, and ovals.

WILLIAMS 1988, p. 79, a, pl. 32, 1.4. |

| 372 II |  | II
Ring

340-300 B.C.
gold, filigree, high relief
max. diam.cm 2; max.diam. cm 2.4
London, British Museum
GRA 1923.4-21.3 | Ring with a setting for a stone, raised, elliptical, and depicting a figure, in high relief, of a maenad dancing. This ring belongs to a well-known collection of jewelry from Tarentum and its vicinity, probably created in the same workshop, whiwh was probably i nTarentum. | WILLIAMS 1988, pp. 79-80, b, pl. 34,1-2. |

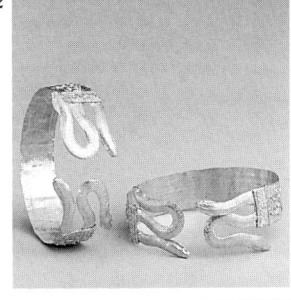

373 see Recent Discoveries

Works on Exhibit

374 | **Funerary shrine**
first century B.C.-first century AD
tufa
h 108 cm; w 58 cm; t 54.8 cm
Palermo, Museo Archeologico
"A. Salinas", inv. 1069
Lilybaeum

Shrine in the form of a *naiskos*, on a rectangular plinth decorated with festoons. The columns, which are of the Tuscan type, are painted with the sign of Tanit and the caduceus. On the background is depicted the scene of a funeral banquet. At the bottom traces of the inscription; at the sides figures of a boy and a maidservant.

Manni Piraino 1973, pp. 44-45, n. 19, tav. XIII; Di Stefano 1984, pp. 165-166.
A.V.

375 | **Head of a male**
later half of thr 3rd century B.C.
limestone
h cm 28.3
broken at the base of the neck
Siracuse, Museo Archeologico
Regionale "Paolo Orsi"
Megara *Hyblaea*

Originally part of a relief, the head has about it an air of pathos and drama thanks to the upward-turned gaze, the structure of thedeepset eyes, and the flowing movement af the "leonine" hair. These characteristics, of Alexandrine derivation, recur in black stone reliefs at Tarentum and Etruscan-Italic clay heads from the mid-Hellenistic periods..

Langlotz 1968, pp. 310-311, n.o 155; Bonacasa 1985, p. 309, fig. 346.
E.C.P.

376 I | **Statue of a maenad**
320-300 B.C.
from Monte Iato (Soprintendenza Beni Culturali di Palermo)
local limestone
h 1, 99 m
Museo Civico, San Capirello (PA)
inv. S 11
From the stage building of the theatre of Iaitas (Monte Iato)

A caryatid made of three blocks, originally inserted in the corner of a wall. It represents a follower of Dionysus, god of the theatre. She wears a peplos and a crown of ivy. With her upraised hands she supported a section of architectural entablature.

Isler 1991, pp. 49-52, 76-77, figs. 11-12.
H.P.J.

376 II | **Statue of satyr**
320-300 B.C.
local limestone
h 2.04 m
Museo Civico, San Capirello (PA)
inv. S 13
From the stage building of the theatre of Iaitas (Monte Iato)

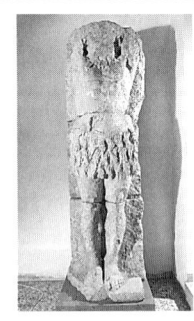

A telamon made of three blocks, originally inserted in the corner of a wall. It represents a follower of Dionysus, god of the theatre. A garland encircles his chest and he wears a fur skirt, the costume of actors. With his upraised hands he supported a section of architectural entablature.

Isler 1991, pp. 49-52 e pp. 76-77, figs. 11-12.
H.P.J.

377 | **Statuette of Artemis the huntress**
late fourth-early third century B.C.
terra-cotta
h 37.5 cm; l 28 cm
Agrigento, Museo Archeologico Regionale, inv. AG 1314
Agrigento, 1951, from a well north of the Temple of Heracles

Statuette representing the goddess Artemis as huntress, viewed frontally, running towards the right, preceded by a small feline. She is dressed in typical hunting garb: boots, short peplos over short chiton with false sleeves, leather corslet with a belt round the waist.

Griffo 1987, p. 142, fig. 129.
G.C.

378 | **Statuettes of the group from piazza Vittoria in Syracuse**
late 5th-early 4th century B.C.
clay
Syracuse, Museo Archeologico Regionale "Paolo Orsi"

I
Statuette of a female

clay
h 36.3 cm; w at thez base 13.2
reconstructed, inv. 84847

Dressed in a chiton tucked up below the knee and a himation arranged in a "U" and revealing her breast; with a lrage polos decorated with a double row of a 5 rosettes and with a veil. Her right leg bears her weight, and i ncorrespondence, the right arm holds up a large torch, while in her left she holds a piglet, her hand under its belly.

I
Statuette of a female

clay
h 36.5 cm; w at the base 13.6
reconstructed, inv. 84849

Very similar to the preceding statuette, but the head is different, characterized by a smooth, relatively low *polos* and an abundance of hair, massed especially at the temples. The figures is slightly inclined to the right. Other differentiae: the position of the piglet, held close to her waist, and the design of the base of the statuette.

III
Statuette of a female

clay
h 33 cm; w at the base 8.5 cm
reconstructed, inv. 84852

Standing with the weight on the left leg, the figure wears a light chiton with an oval neckline, and a mantle thrown over the left shoulder and around the lower part of the body. In her right hand she hodls a piglet by the hind legs, and in her left hand a small torch. A high *polos*, smooth and bell-shaped, with a tubular diadem at the base; hair parted in the middle and arranged on the sides of the face, which is oval; splendid earrings;

Sicilia greca, p. 115, no. 110.

IV
Statuette of a female

clay
h 32.3 cm; w at the base 10.4 cm
reconstructed, inv. 84854

Ihe chiton – up below the knees and partially covered by a *himation* arranged in a "U" – is tied at the waist, creating a pleasing ensemble of folds; the *polos* is decorated with rosettes in relief and framed by a veil. In her righr hand the figure holds a piglet, head down, and in the left a large torch, holding it near her body on the side of her non-weight-bearing leg.

Sicilia greca, pp. 115-116, n. 111; cfr. BONACASA 1992, pp. "'-24, tav. 13, I.

V
Fragmentary statuette of a female

clay
h 25.2 cm; reconstructed, some parts missing, inv. 84858

Perhape this figure had both foreams outstretched, in a gesture of offering. It is characterized by a hairstyle that combines archaic elements (little globular ringlets arranged in three rows around the face) and fashionable (the top-knot).

Sicilia greca, p. 116, n. 112.

VI
Statuette of Artemis

clay
h 26 cm; w at the base 10.7 cm
inv. 84859

The goddess wears a chiton with many folds, a mantle, and half-boots, which latter characterize her as a huntress; she carries a spear in her left hand, and with her right caresses a stag standing by her side. Hair in a top-knot.

Sicilia greca, p. 116, n. 113.

VII
Statuette of a female

clay
reassembled and reconstructed

This figure, presents another variant on the theme of offering. It is distinguished by the vessel full of gifst carried on the left arm. this element is also represented in the iconography by the "offering of the piglet".

VIII
Statuette of a female

clay
reconstructed

The figures holds a vessel full of gifts on her left arm, rather than a piglet; in her right and she holds up a large torch.

BIGNASCA 1992, pp. 26-28, tav.23.3.

IX
Statuette of a female

clay
reconstructed, some parts missing

The tendency to grandiosity and the accumulation of attributes is even more evident in this type, a variant of the preceding one: here, the higher position of the right hand on the torch emphasized the torch-holding gesture, making the figure seem more grand, and the addition of a little animal (a piglet?), standing on the vessel and burdering it even more, increases the opulence of the offering.

VOZA 1976-77, p. 556 ss., tav. XCVIII, f.

X
Statuette of a female

clay
reconstructed

This statuette presents a different image, returning to the traditional elements of the typt: the ductus of the clothing is different, even though the base of the chiton is tucked up as usual; she holds the piglet close to her breast with her left hand, while the right holds perhaps another offering (fruit?); the head is clearly inclined to the left, altering the customary solemn frontality of the type.

Sicilia greca, pp. 115-116; BIGNASCA 1992, pp. 20 ss.   E.C.P.

379

Relief with recumbent figures

3rd century B.C.
limestone
max h 25 cm; max l 35 cm
some parts missing, ample traces of polychrome
Syracuse, Museo Archeologico Regionale "Paolo Orsi", inv. 66954
Syracuse, piazza della Vittoria, from the "well of Artemis"

This relief depicts a pair of banqueters stretched out on a *kline*, with the bust facing out while the lower part of the body is in profile; the male figure holds a patera in the right hand; his female companion is taking a bunch of grapes from the *trapeza* with food the foreground; on the left is a little server. Perhaps of funerary significance, like a series of analogous portrayals honoring the dead; and given the setting of its discovery, a votive purpose is also possible.

VOZA 1968-69, pp. 362-364, *Archeologia Sicilia Sud-Orientale*, pp. 103-104, n. 359. Cfr. DENTZER 1982, *passim*.
    E.C.P.

Works on Exhibit

380		**Statuette of Aphrodite** second-first century B.C. orange-coloured terra-cotta h 11.5 cm Agrigento, Museo Archeologico Regionale, inv. AG 1280 Agrigento, 1953-54 excavations, area of Sanctuary of Chthonic Deities	Statuette represente Aphrodite crouching at her bath, in the act of wringing her hair with both hands, typologically traceable to a late Hellenistic variant of the Aphrodite at the Bath by Doidalsas.	GRIFFO 1987, p. 113, fig. 96. G.C.
381		**Female bust** later half of the 3rd century B.C. clay h 46 cm traces of polychrome Syracuse, Museo Archeologico Regionale "Paolo Orsi", inv. 40772 Centuripe, "cave near the Chiesa Madre"	The traditional portait bust is here altered, in the direction of an attempt to obtain a solemn, hieratic image; one notes the increased size, the importance of the *polos*, the symmetri and descriptiveness of the *chiome*, the enlargement of the eyes and the fullness of the face, especially around the mouth.	LIBERTINI 1926, pp. 95-96, pl. XX, 1; BONACASA 1985, p. 313, fig. 393. E.C.P.
382 I		**Female bust with polos** first half of the third century B.C. clay, with slip, well-preserved polychrome h 48 cm; w 35.6 cm Aidone, Museo Archeologico inv. 58-2147 Morgantina, Serra Orlando district	Oval face framed by thick hair parted on the forehead and bound back in parallel waves. Prominent nose and small fleshy mouth showing a slight smile. Bust not modelled. Particularly striking is the colour of the eyes, of the red lips and of the pink panel on the bust.	BELL 1981, p. 142, n. 113 b, pl. 32. A.M.B.
382 II		**Female bust** early third century B.C. clay, with slip, traces of polychrome (red-brown, pink) h 44 cm; w 36.9 cm nose integrated Aidone, Museo Archeologico inv. 57-2050 Morgantina, Serra Orlando district	Oval face with large almond-shaped eyes and protruding eyelids, dimple on the chin. "Melon" hairstyle gathered in a large bun behind the head. Chiton gathered under the bosom by a girdle, naked arms on which are visible traces of spiral bracelets.	BELL 1981, pp. 146-147, n. 145, tavv. 40-41. A.M.B.
382 III		**Female bust** second half of the third century B.C. clay, with slip, well-preserved polychrome h 30.4 cm reassembled and integrated Aidone, Museo Archeologico inv. 58-2139 Morgantina, Serra Orlando district	Oval face with large eyes, slight smile and dimple on the chin. "Melon" hairstyle gathered in a bun behind the head. Adorned with diadem, necklace, spiral bracelets, and a pendant on the chest; holes for ear-rings in the lobes. Chiton gathered under the bosom with a pink ribbon. Particularly striking are the pink of the lips and the yellow of the jewels.	BELL 1981, p. 147, n. 149, pl. 42. A.M.B.
383		**Female statuette on kline** third century B.C. clay, traces of polychrome h 13.3 cm; w 14 cm Aidone, Museo Archeologico inv. 59-1997 Morgantina, Serra Orlando district	Cloaked figure, reclining on a kline and with the left arm resting on two cushions. On the hair is a polos from which a veil hangs down. Head turned to the right; phiale in the right hand. Pink complexion, turquoise phiale, magenta upper part of the kline.	BELL 1981, pp. 137-138, n. 89, tav. 21. A.M.B.

Works on Exhibit

384

Female statuette

late fourth century B.C.
clay
h 62 cm
Aidone, Museo Archeologico
inv. 57-806
Morgantina, Serra Orlando district

Cloaked figure with polos, standing on the right leg, with the right arm stretched forward and the left one (missing) near the body. Oval face framed by hair parted on the forehead and drawn back in thick waves which fall in two tresses on the shoulders. Adorned with drop-earrings and a diadem in front of the polos. Draped in a chiton and in the thick folds of a himation which leaves the right arm free.

BELL 1981, p. 132, n. 56, tavv. 13-14.
A.M.B.

385

Bi-valve breastplate

late 4th century b.c.
bronze
max h 32.5; max w 30 and 33 cm
Syracuse, Museo Archeologico Regionale "Paolo Orsi",
inv. 4285842859
Scordia (Catania), from a collection of funeral objects

A bi-valve breastplate, anatomically molded, of very accurate workmanship. It farmed part of the armor buried with the dead warrio, together with his sword-belt, a dagger, and two lances.

BONACASA 1985, p. 293, fig. 344, con bibl. prec.
E.C.P.

386

Funerary emblem in the from of a trophy

kate 4th-early 3rd century B.C.
limestone
h 82 cm; max diam 43 cm
chips, abrasions, and parts missing
Syracuse, Museo Archeologico Regionale "Paolo Orsi", inv. 24291
Syracuse, Fusco necropolis

Trophy used as a funerary *sema*. Belonging to a well-known Hellenistic type, as evident in the shape of the breastplate, ridig, indications of shoulder plates and *pteryges*, and a large "pathetic" *gorgoneion* figured in relief.

BONACASA 1985, p. 308, fig. 345, con bibl. prec.
E.C.P.

387 *see Recent Discoveries*

388

Pisside with the scene of a nuptual offering

later half of the 3rd century B.C.
clay. Tempera; gilding; applied plastic ornamentation
h 56 cm
reconstructed; lacking feet; well-preserved polychrome
Catania, Institute of Archeology of the University
Centuripe

Below the border, "architectonic" moulding in relief: leonine protomai, patere, a kymation in the style of the court of Hieron; at the base, a circlet of acanthus leaves. The scene depicts the offering of gift to the bride, seated in the center on a kline, between two maidens. The nuptual theme, in virtue of its funerary-eschatalogical implications, recurs very often in the repertoire of art objects from Centuripe. The scene painted on the cover may have a funerary significance.

JOLY 1985, p. 353, fig. 436.

389

Equipment of tomb 2287 of the necropolis of the Diana district (Lipari)

ca. 340 B.C.
Burial in a coffin made of sun-dried bricks, with internal equipment (1987 excavations)

I
Campanian red-figure Lebes Gamikos (Mad-Man Painter)

clay
h ?? cm
Lipari, Museo Eoliano, Room XXII
inv. 16364e

Side A: woman sitting on a rock, looking back to the left. Draped in a thin chiton - unlaced so as to reveal the bosom - and a himation which covers the legs; she holds a mirror in her left hand. On the right in the main field an infula. Side B: a woman standing in profile facing left, almost entirely draped in the himation, holds a mirror in her right hand. Under each handle is a large palmette.

Sicilia greca, p. 169, n. 350, fig. a p. 239; U. SPIGO 1993, p. 42, tav. 34.

II
Red-figure Lekane (workshop of the NYN Painter)

clay
h 13 cm; max diameter 18 cm
Lipari, Museo Eoliano, Room XXII, inv. 16364f

On the lid, which did not originally belong to the vessel but was adapted, are represented two female heads in profile facing right, with their hair bound in the sakkos; diadems

Sicilia greca, p. 169, n. 351, fig. a p. 239; SPIGO 1993, p. 43, tav. 35,1.

III
Red-figure Lekane (workshop of the NYN Painter)

clay
h 11.7 cm; max diameter 21.3 cm
Lipari, Museo Eoliano, Room XXII
inv. 16364g

On the lid, which did not originally belong to the vessel but was adapted, are represented two female heads in profile facing right, with their heads bound in the sakkos; diadems encircling the head, earrings and necklaces overpainted in white. The heads alternate with two fan-like palmettes, edged with white, and flanked by squat leaf-whorls.

Sicilia greca, p. 169, n. 351, fig. a p. 239; SPIGO 1993, p. 43, tav. 35,2.

IV
Ovoid black-figure Pagenstecher lekythos

clay
h 14.7 cm
Lipari, Museo Eoliano, Room XXII, inv. 16364a

It represents a woman dressed in a chiton sitting on a rock looking at herself in a mirror held in her right hand; her left hand rests on a rock behind her. On the reverse side a large stylized palmette between leaf-whorls with semipalmettes and lozenge-shaped flowers or large buds. Probably of Sicilian manufacture.

Sicilia greca, pp. 169-170, n. 352, fig. a p. 240; SPIGO 1993, p. 43, tav. 35,4.

V
Siceliot Lekane with lid decorated in the Gnathian style

clay
h 19.5 cm; max diameter 21 cm
Lipari, Museo Eoliano, Room XXII

Sicilia greca, p. 170, n. 353, fig. a p. 240; SPIGO 1993, p. 43, tav. 35,3.

VI
Lekythos in the shape of a female head

clay
h 12.2 cm
Lipari, Museo Eoliano, Room XXII, inv. 16364l

Hair parted on the forehead in two thick masses of dense spiral curls, gathered at the back in a sort of sakkos. White colour on the face, brown on the hair, red on the lips. Mouth in black paint, deformed. Probably of Sicilian manufacture.

Sicilia greca, p. 170, n. 354, fig. a p. 240; SPIGO 1993, p. 43, tav. 35,4.

VII
Little globular bottle with decoration in black paint

clay
h 9.7 cm
Lipari, Museo Eoliano, Room XXII inv. 16364i

The decoration consists of two bands separated by a third one in black paint. In the upper band, on the belly: a series of ovules alternating with little lozenge-shaped garlands. In the lower band, at the level of the bottom of the vessel: pattern of stylized astragals between pairs of vertical strokes. Shoulder and mouth in black paint.

Sicilia greca, p. 170, n. 355, fig. a p. 240; SPIGO 1993, p. 43, tav. 35,4.   U.S.

390

Equipment of tomb 144 from the necropolis of the Diana district (Lipari)

300-275 B.C.

Burial in a box made of stone slabs; equipment external, to the south-east, in a a container of unbaked clay

I Polychrome figured pyxis (Lipari Painter)

clay
h 25.8 cm; max diameter 6.8 cm
Lipari, Museo Eoliano, Room XXIV, inv. 2761

Side A: due women draped (red-brown and light-blue himatia) sitting on one large rectangular "block" covered with two cloths (one light blue, the other with red stripes). *Side B*: large female head in profile facing right, with the hair gathered in a sakkos. Lid: large motif of "cushion" between olive-branches, in light blue and white. Recurrent in the Aeolian production of the first half of the third century B.C., of which the "Lipari Painter" is the founder, are the richness of the colours added which contribute to the construction of the figures, and the subject-matter, which centres on the mundus muliebris and the wedding, in connection with the cultual sphere of Aphrodite and with aspects of funerary Dionysianism.

A.D. TRENDALL in BERNABÒ BREA-CAVALIER 1965, p. 281; BERNABÒ BREA-CAVALIER 1986, p. 5, figs; 46, 58, 103-104.

II Siceliot olpe with Gnathian decoration

clay
h 18.5; max diam. 7 cm
Lipari, Museo Eoliano, room XXIV, inv. 276a

BERNABÒ BREA-CAVALIER 1965, p. 49, pl. CXXX, 2 c.

III Siceliot skyphos in black paint

clay
h 9.2 cm; diameter 8.5 cm
Lipari, Museo Eoliano, Room XXIV inv. 276a

Disc-shaped moulded foot, deep vessel with ovoid profile, thin stick-handles set obliquely and bent back upwards.

BERNABÒ BREA-CAVALIER 1965, p. 49, pl. CXXX, 2 d.

IV Two little plates in black paint of Siceliot manufacture

clay
h 18.5 cm; max diameter 7 cm
Lipari, Museo Eoliano, Room XXIV inv. 276c, e

Low flared foot, narrow convex and jutting-out rim.

BERNABÒ BREA-CAVALIER 1965, p. 49, pl. CXXX, 2 a, b.

V Black-painted lamp of Siceliot manufacture

clay
l 10.3 cm
Lipari, Museo Eoliano, Room XXIV inv. 276e

Hollow internal pillar; long beak with rounded end.

BERNABÒ BREA-CAVALIER 1965, p. 49, pl. CXXX, 2 e.   U.S

Works on Exhibit

391		**Statuette of a muse** later half of the 2nd century B.C. marble h. 83cm. lacking the head, feet, and the left side of the base, which was sculpted separately Syracuse, Museo Archeologico Regionale "Paolo Orsi", inv. 14533 Syracuse, from the "nymph's grotto" above the theatre.	Standing, in a flexible pose, on the rightleg, holdingthe borderof her mantle in her right hand, the figure is dressed in a light chiton, high-waisted, and a *himation* wrappeg around the legs and over the left arm. The draperyhas been rendered with great virtuosity, accentuating the effects of tra sparency, in accordance with late-Hellenistic taste.	LANGLOTZ 1968, p. 312, pl. 161; BONACASA 1985, p. 296, fig. 321. E.C.P.
392		**Askos shaped in the form of a satyr** late 3rd century B.C. clay h. 16 cm. ; l. 17,9 cm. reconctructed from fragments Syracuse, Museo Archeologico Regionale "Paolo Orsi", inv. 55081 Syracuse, necropolis in the Grotticellidistrict	A vase in the form of a satyr, crowned with ivy and with a *pardalide* on its back, set on a distended leather bottle. Other *askos* of this type - from Alexandria (which has the most examples), Phanagoria, Pantikapaion, and Amisos and iconographic study of the Alexandrine documentationsuggests that this type originated in the Ptolemaic capital: it would have been a decorative sculpture, perhaps a statue ornament in a garden, from the late 3rd century B.C.	*Archeologia Sicilia Sud-Orientale*, pp. 113-114, no. 377, pl. XXV; BONACASA 1985, p. 331, fig. 385. E.C.P.
393 I		**Female statuette** second half of the third century B.C. clay, with slip, traces of polychrome h 21.5 cm Aidone, Museo Archeologico inv. 57-2054 Morgantina, Serra Orlando district	Cloaked figure, velato capite, standing on her right leg with head and body turned towards the left. Left hand at her side, right hand on her breast. Pink himation. Expressive face with furrows at the sides of the nose and mouth and a dimple on the chin.	BELL 1981, p. 178, n. 383, tav. 81. A.M.B.
393 II		**Female statuette** third century B.C. clay h 34 cm Aidone, Museo Archeologico inv. 57-1872 Morgantina, Serra Orlando district	Cloaked figure, standing on her right leg, with head and body turned towards the left. Left hand on her side, right arm along her body. Full, oval face with prominent chin, hair partedon the forehead, drawn back and tied in a bun. A furrow on the hair shows the presence of a diadem.	BELL 1981, pp. 174-175, n. 359 a, tav. 74. A.M.B.
394		**Male statuette** early third century B.C. clay, traces of polychrome (pink purple) h 35.5 cm Aidone, Museo Archeologico inv. 57-719 Morgantina, Serra Orlando district	Cloaked male figure, perhaps Hades, standing on his left leg; body turned towards the right, right arm stretched forward and left arm bent to support the himation which slips down from the left shoulder to leave the thorax uncovered. Oval face, hair parted on the forehead and tied behind the head in a plait which falls over the right shoulder. A furrow on the hair shows the existence of a garland or a crown.	BELL 1981, p. 167, n. 295 a, tav. 66. A.M.B.
395		**Shaped vase** mid third-second century B.C. clay, thin walls h 15.2 cm - without handle 11.7 cm w 15.8 cm; front thickness 5.3 cm back thickness 6 cm; plinth 2.4 cm Messina, Museo Interdisciplinare Regionale, inv. 3652 Messina, necropoli "Orti della Maddalena", Caserma di Artiglieria recupero 1936-37 (out of context)	Represents a sculptural group - the she-wolf and the twins - of great significance. This is the first depiction of it in the form of a shaped vase, and the only example so far found in "Magenta Ware", a class characterized by modelled vases in the shape of small animals. The iconography, which was of great importance in the Roman world, here has one of its earliest testimonies, perhaps the earliest of all in a funerary context. This suggests a link between ce-	ramic production and coin typologies which has yet to be explored. The group shows a taste for realism of a Hellenistic type. SGUAITAMATTI 1991, pp. 117 ss.; MASTELLONI 1993, pp. 39-40. M.A.M.

Works on Exhibit

397	**Portrait-head supposedly of Parmenides** first half of the first century AD fine-grained white marble, yellowish patina h 37 cm; w at the temples: 13.8 cm Ascea Marina, Depositi Soprintendenza, inv. 43511 Velia, Southern Quarter, so-called Insula II	This head seems similar to a herma bearing the inscription Parmenides (inv. 17421). It is therefore of great importance, for it is the earliest portrait which attempts a posthumous reconstruction of the features of the great Eleatic philosopher. There is a notable similarity between this portrait of Parmenides and the iconographical type of the Hellenistic period now definitely attributed to Metrodorus.	FABBRI-TROTTA 1989, pp. 102-104, tavv. LVII-LVIII. C.A.F.
398	**Herma of Oulis (son of) Ariston** first century AD white marble with grey veins h 129.5 cm recto; 134.5 cm verso Velia, so-called Cappella Palatina inv. 17422 Velia, Southern Quarter, so-called Insula II	About 21 cm from the top is engraved the following inscription, on three lines:	FABBRI-TROTTA 1989, pp. 69-73, tav. XXVII, 1. C.A.F.
399	**Herma of Oulis (son of) Ieronumos** first century AD white marble with grey veins slightly tapering h 124.5 cm Velia, so-called Cappella Palatina, N.I. Velia, Southern Quarter, so-called Insula II	On the right side are two circular holes. The lower part has been restored. About 28 cm from the top is engraved the following inscription on three lines:	FABBRI-TROTTA 1989, pp. 73-74, tav. XXVIII, 2. C.A.F.
400	**Herma of Parmenides (son of) Pireto** mid first century AD white marble with grey veins upper w 30 cm; lower w 28 cm upper thickness 17.2 cm; lower thickness 15 cm Velia, so-called Cappella Palatina inv. 17421 Velia, Southern Quarter, so-called Insula II	About 20 cm from the top is engraved the following inscription on two lines: This herma is dedicated to the famous Eleatic philosopher who lived in the fifth century B.C..	FABBRI-TROTTA 1989, pp. 74-75, tav. XVIII,1; PUGLIESE CARRATELLI 1991, pp. 269-280. C.A.F.
401	**Senatus Consultum de Bacchanalibus** date unknown bronze 27 x 28 cm Vienna, Kunsthistorisches Museum inv. III 168 Tiriolo (Cz)	Consular decree of 186 B.C. which forbade Roman citizens, those who had Latin rights and allies to celebrate rites connected with the cult of Bacchus. Livy (XXXIX, 8, 19) mentions the popular disorders which often broke out in various parts of the peninsula during the Bacchanalia.	I.L.L.R.P., n. 511; PAILLER 1988; DESY 1993. G.L'A.
402	**Clay statue of Minerva** fifth century B.C. terra-cotta, traces of colour h 196 cm reassembled, lacunose Pratica di Mare (Lavinio), inv. ??? Depositi Soprintendenza Archeologica Lavinio	This statue represents the goddess standing with her helmet, the aegis with the Gorgoneion and a costume with a waistcoat of scales and a snake belt. She has a sword in her right hand, while in her left she holds the shield, decorated with snakes round the edge, and in the centre quadrupeds facing one another, birds, and crescent moons; the shield rests on the head of a triton next to the goddess.	CASTAGNOLI 1979; G. PUGLIESE CARRATELLI, in *Scritti Adamesteanu*, pp. 577-578. G.L'A.

403	**Bronze tablet with dedication to the Dioscuri** mid to late sixth century B.C. bronze max l 29.1 cm; h 5 - 5.3 cm; thickness 0.1 - 0.15 cm Pratica di Mare (Lavinio), Depositi inv. ??? Lavinio, Sanctuary of the Thirteen Altars	Thin plate with four holes at the corners and one near the centre to fix it with nails. The inscription, which reads from right to left and is in an archaic Latin alphabet, attests the presence of a Greek cult at Lavinium: "Castorei Podlouqueique / qurois".	CASTAGNOLI 1975, pp. 441-442. G.L'A.
404	**Clay female bust** ca. 300 B.C. terra-cotta h 72 cm; w 50 cm; depth 37 cm Rome, Museo Nazionale Romano inv. 112375 Ariccia, loc. Castelletto, 1927	Frontal bust with head slightly raised. Full, oval face, eyes looking upwards; the hair, which has a central parting, is divided into two bands bound by a ribbon knotted on the head, and falls softly on the shoulders, back and bosom. The goddess wears a diadem of corn-ears, earrings with a rosette and a pyramidal pendant, and a necklace which ends in two snake-heads. The chiton is fastened on the right shoulder by three round buttons; on the left shoulder it is	covered by a mantle. Interpreted as Demeter/Ceres. A. ZEVI GALLINA, in *Roma medio-repubblicana*, pp. 321-322; ORLANDINI 1983, p. 502. G.L'A.
405	**Clay female statue** ca. 300 B.C. terra-cotta h 115 cm; max w 51 cm; depth 82 cm reassembled and integrated Rome, Museo Nazionale Romano, inv. 112377	Seated figure of young female, identified as Kore. She wears a long chiton with a high girdle and short sleeves, a himation, and sandals; on her head a diadem with floral applied elements holds her wavy hair, which swells on the temples and is gathered behind the head, after which it falls in thin wavy strands; she has button earrings with pyramidal pendants. She sits on a backless throne which has a footrest with a moulded outline; in her left hand she holds a little votive pig.	A. ZEVI GALLINA, in *Roma medio-repubblicana*, p. 327; ORLANDINI 1983, p. 502. G.L'A.
406	**Ercules'head with Leonte** 2nd century B.C. terracotta, matrix cm 37x34,15 Sassari, Museo Archeologico G.A. Sanna Golfo di Olbia	The life-size statue shows Hercules wearing the skin of the Nemican lion. It was found amoung ear ther ware artifacts produced at Olbia.	
407	**veoled female head** 3rd-2nd century B.C. cm 8x4,5x4,8 Padria (SS), Museo Civico Santuario district S. Giuseppe	The head, probably part of a statuette, is wrapped in a veil.	
408	**Child head** 3rd-2nd century B.C. terra-cotta cm 10,5x7,4x4,5 Padria (SS), Museo Civico Santuario district S. Giuseppe	The small head, damaged on its left side, has curls near the ears and parted hair. The neck has a hinge which served to attach the child's head to the body.	

Works on Exhibit

409	**Female face** 3rd-2nd century B.C. terra-cotta cm 9,4x8x3,8 Padria (SS), Museo Civico Santuario country S. Giuseppe	Female headwiht a particular style hair, recostructed from fragments.	
410	**Stone steles of Cybele** sixth century B.C. limestone, traces of colour 1) h 48 cm; l 30 cm; thickness 23 cm 2) h 50 cm; l 31.5 cm; thickness 25 cm Marseilles, Musée d'Histoire inv. 8375, 83710 Marseilles, 1863	These form part of a group of 47 steles found together, which all represented a female deity sitting inside a naiskos; in the two examples on show the goddess, identified as the Great Mother Cybele honoured by the Phocaeans, holds a lion on her knees.	SALVIAT 1992, pp. 141-150. M.M.-D.
411	**Centaur** bronze alt. cm 11,2; lungh. cm 10,8 Madrid, Museo Arqueólogico Naciónal, inv. 28835	Bald-headed and bearded centaur.	HOMENAJE ALMAGRO, II, pp. 377-383. G.L'A.
412	**Female statuette** fifth-third century B.C. bronze, cast h 11.6 cm; thickness 1 cm Madrid, Museo Archeologico Nacional, inv. 28835 Jaen	Figurine of a praying woman, standing, dressed in a tight-fitting chiton which reaches down to her feet, with a V-neck and short sleeves; over the chiton she wears a mantle with a dotted edge, fastened on the right shoulder. Hair in long tresses, ears visible.	ALVAREZ OSSORIO 1941, p. 83, no. 457. G.L'A.
413	**Headless Kore** ca. 510 AD island marble h 120 cm Cyrene, Museum of Sculpture inv. 14009 Cyrene, Sanctuary	Broad, square shoulders; the peplos is arranged obliquely with wide, sinuous folds. Three long tresses fall on the breast, while on the back the hair descends in predominantly vertical lines. This figure probably formed a group together with another headless kore from the same sanctuary.	PARIBENI 1959, pp. 11-12, pl. 13. G.L'A.
414	**Faceless bust** late sixth-early fifth century B.C. white marble of medium grain h 41.2 cm; w 34.5 cm Cyrene, Museum of Sculpture inv. 11136 Cyrene, eastern necropolis	Faceless cylinder crowned by a low polos in the form of a truncated cone; on the forehead is a band of wavy hair, above which there are long tresses that fall on the shoulders, while from the polos a veil falls over the back. The cylinder fits on to a slightly rounded bust, with a wide-necked chiton.	BESCHI 1969-70, pp. 210-221, fig. 61. G.L'A.

416	**BVeiled female bust** mid fourth century B.C. island marble, traces of working with a drill h 72 cm; w 48 cm; chipped Paris, Musée du Louvre, inv. MA 1777 Cyrene	Bust of a woman draped in a cloak which falls from her head and covers her right hand, while the left hand, which has a spiral bracelet around the wrist, holds it on the shoulder. The head is turned towards the left, the hair is parted in tufts on the forehead. The back is flat, and shows folds opening out like a fan.	BESCHI 1969-70, pp. 281-282, no. 105a. G.L'A.
417	**Veiled female head** third-second century B.C. island marble max h 30.5 cm; max lower w 12 cm fragmentary, chipped Cyrene, Museum of Sculpture inv. 11029 Cyrene	Female head with elongated face, covered on the right side by a veil; hair in narrow tresses; on the left ear-lobe is a hole for the insertion of an earring. The back too has been worked.	BESCHI 1969-70, p. 312, no. 159. G.L'A.
418	**Sacred relief**	fourth century B.C. Pentelic marble 92x2.30 cm Cyrene, Museum of Sculpture inv. 15004 Cyrene, agorà	Two slabs with a deep jutting ridge on the outer sides; the figures stand on a small base. In the centre Aphrodite, in a light chiton, and a young winged Eros seem to diverge from the axis of the composition; the two lateral figures, which are badly preserved, have been identified as Demeter and Kore; they are dressed in robes with heavy folds.
419	**Stele of the founders** fourth century B.C. marble h 153 cm; w 56-63 cm thickness 27-31 cm; broken in the lower part; deeply engraved letters filled with red paste Cyrene, Museum of Sculpture	This tapering stele has a rectangular hollow chiselled in its upper part. The stele carries the decree containing the constitutional principles which had governed the growth of the colony founded by Theraean immigrants led by Battus; the inscription expressly mentions the placing of the stele in the sanctuary of Pythian Apollo at Cyrene.	PUGLIESE CARRATELLI G. IX, I, no. 3; 1987, pp. 25 ff. G.L'A.
420	**Metope** first century B.C. marble 55.5x62.5x3 cm Vatican City, Biblioteca Apostolica Vaticana	Derived from a Greek original of the fourth century, it shaws a horseman.	MAGI 1964. G.L'A.
421	**Corinthian Helmet** bronze, lamination, engraving 34x20x23 cm Venezia, Collezione Centro Studi Ricerche Ligabue	Corinthian helmet with bone plaques. G.L'A.	

Works on Exhibit

422

Corinthian Helmet

bronze, lamination, engraving
30x21x27.5 cm
Venezia, Collezione Centro Studi Ricerche Ligabue

Courinthian-type helmet decorated with figures of animals.   G.L'A.

423

Poseidon

terra-cotta
33x21 cm
Venezia, Collezione Centro Studi Ricerche Ligabue

Bearded male figure on a *Vline*.
      G.L'A.

Bibliography

Bibliography

AA.VV. (a cura di ANTI C.), *Sculture greche e romane di Cirene*, Padova 1959.

AA.VV., *Agriculture in Ancient Greece* (ed. by WELLS B.), Stockholm 1992.

AA.VV., *Apoikia*, "Studi in onore di G.Buchner" ("AION ArchStAnt", N.S. 1, 1994).

AA.VV., *Bibliografia topografica della colonizzazione greca in Italia e nelle isole tirreniche*, Pisa-Roma, I, 1977 - XI, 1992.

AA.VV., *Bronze Age Trade in the Mediterranean* (ed. by GALE N.H.), Goteborg 1991.

AA.VV., *Cirene. Storia, Mito, Letteratura*, Urbino 1990.

AA.VV., *Da Cocalo a Ducezio. Incontri fra genti nella Sicilia antica*, Atti VII Congresso Internazionale Studi Sicilia Antica (Palermo 1988), in "Kokalos", XXXIV-XXXV, 1988-89 (ma 1992-93).

AA.VV., *Dal sillabario minoico all'alfabeto greco*, in "La Parola del Passato" 31, 1976.

AA.VV., *Eikon. Aegean Bronze Age Iconography: Shaping a Methodology* (ed. by LAFFINEUR R.- CROWLEY J.L.) "Aegaeum", 8, 1992.

AA.VV., *Fenici e Arabi nel Mediterraneo*, Convegno in Roma (ottobre 1982), Roma 1983.

AA.VV., *Il commercio etrusco arcaico*, Atti Incontro di studio (Roma 1983), Roma 1985.

AA.VV., *Il Museo di Taranto: cento anni di archeologia*, Taranto 1988.

AA.VV., *Il tempio greco in Sicilia, architettura e culti* (a cura di G. RIZZA), "CronAStorArt", 16, Catania 1985.

AA.VV., in DESCOEUDRES J.P. (ed.), *Greek Colonists and Native Populations*, Oxford 1990.

AA.VV., in *La statua marmorea di Mozia*, Roma 1988.

AA.VV., in *Lo stile severo in Sicilia*, Palermo 1990.

AA.VV., *L'habitat égéen préhistorique* (par DARQUE P. et TREUIL R.), Paris 1990.

AA.VV., *La cité antique? À partir de l'œuvre de M.I.Finley*, in "Opus" VI-VIII, 1987-89.

AA.VV., *La civiltà micenea. Guida storica e critica* (a cura di MADDOLI G.), Roma-Bari 19922.

AA.VV., *La Crète mycénienne* (Actes de la Table Ronde, Athènes, Mars 1991, par FARNOUX A. e DRIESSEN J.), in corso di stampa.

AA.VV., *La Magna Grecia e il mare. Studi di storia marittima*, a cura di PRONTERA F., Taranto 1996.

AA.VV., *La Sicilia antica* (a cura di GABBA E.-VALLET G.).

AA.VV., *La transizione dal miceneo all'alto arcaismo. Dal palazzo alla città* (C.N.R.), Roma 1991.

AA.VV., *Le dessin d'architecture dans les sociétés antiques*, Actes du Coll. de Strasbourg (26-28 Janv.1984), Strasbourg 1985.

AA.VV., *Lo stile severo in Sicilia. Dall'apogeo della tirannide alla prima democrazia*, Palermo 1990.

AA.VV., *Lo Stretto crocevia di culture*, Atti del XXVI Convegno di Studi sulla Magna Grecia, Napoli 1993.

AA.VV., *Magna Grecia*, I-IV, Milano 1985-1988.

AA.VV., *Magna Grecia*, Milano 1990.

AA.VV., *Momenti precoloniali nel Mediterraneo antico*, Convegno in Roma (marzo 1985), Roma 1988.

AA.VV., *Naxos.Gli scavi extraurbani oltre il Santa Venere (1973-75)*, in "Not. Sc." 1984-85 (1988), pp.253-497.

AA.VV., *Odeon e altri "monumenti" archeologici* (1971).

AA.VV., *Phönizier im Westen* (Symposium in Köln, April 1979), Mainz 1982 (= Madrider Beiträge, 8).

AA.VV., *Princìpi e forme della città*, Milano 1993.

AA.VV., RASMUSSEN T. and SPIVEY N.(eds.), *Looking at Greek Vases*, Cambridge 1991.

AA.VV., *Storia e archeologia della media e bassa valle dell'Imera*, Atti IIIgiornata di Studi sull'Archeologia licatese (Licata-Caltanissetta, 1987), Palermo 1993 (soprattutto per i nuovi dati di Sabucina proposti da MOLLO MEZZENA R.).

AA.VV., *The Role or the Ruler in the prehistoric Aegean* (ed. by REHAK P.), "Aegaeum", 11, 1995.

AA.VV., *Transition. Le monde égéen du Bronze moyen au Bronze récent*, "Aegaeum", 3, 1989.

AA.VV.., *Les civilisations égéennes*, Paris 1989.

ACCAME S., *La lega ateniese del secolo IV a.C.*, Roma 1941.

ACQUARO E.-AUBET M.E.- FANTAR M.H., *Insediamenti fenici e punici nel Mediterraneo occidentale*, Roma 1933.

ADAM J.P., *L'architecture militaire grecque*, Paris 1982.

ADAMESTEANU D., *Dios agora*, in "ParPass" 1979, pp. 296-312.

ADAMESTEANU D., *Popoli anellenici in Basilicata*, Napoli 1971.

ADAMESTEANU D., SEG XXIX 1979, 955.

ADAMESTEANU D.-MERTENS D.-D'ANDRIA F., *Metaponto I*, "NSc" 1975 Suppl. (1980).

ADAMESTEANU D.-VATIN C., *L'arrière-pays de Metaponte*, in "CRAI" 1976, pp. 110ss.

ADRIANI A., *Cataloghi illustrati del Museo Campano. I - Sculture in tufo*, Alessandria d'Egitto 1939.

ADRIANI A., *La nécropole de Moustafa Pacha*, in "Annuaire du Musée Gréco-Romain", 1933/34-1934/35, Alessandria 1936.

AGNELLO S.in "Archivio Storico Siracusano", 1972-73, pp.91 ss.

ALBANESE PROCELLI R.M., *Ripostigli di bronzi della Sicilia nel Museo Archeologico di Siracusa*, Palermo 1993.

ALLEGRO N.-VASSALLO S., *Himera.Nuove ricerche nella città bassa (1989-92)*, in "Kokalos", XXXVIII, 1992, pp.79-150.

AMPOLO C., *I gruppi etnici in Roma arcaica: posizione del problema e fonti*, in *Gli Etruschi e Roma. Studi in onore di M.Pallottino*, Roma 1981, pp. 45-70.

AMPOLO C., *Il nuovo contratto di Camarina: aspetti giuridici ed economici*, in "La Parola del Passato", 224, 1985, pp.331-336.

AMPOLO C., *La città antica, guida storica e critica*, Roma 1980.

AMPOLO C., *La funzione dello Stretto nella vicenda politica fino al termine della guerra del Peloponneso*, in Atti XXVIConvegno di studi sulla Magna Grecia (Taranto 1986), Taranto 1987, pp. 45-71.

AMPOLO C., *Organizzazione politica, sociale ed economica delle "poleis" italiote*, in PUGLIESE CARRATELLI G. (a cura di), *Magna Grecia. Lo sviluppo politico, sociale ed economico*, Milano 1987.

ANDREASSI G.-COCCHIARO A., *Necropoli d'Egnazia*, Fasano 1987.

ANDRONIKOS M., *Vergina II. The "Tomb of Persephone"*, Athens 1994.

ANDRONIKOS M., *Vergina. The Royal Tombs and the Ancient City*, Athens 1987.

ARENA R., *Iscrizioni greche arcaiche di Sicilia e Magna Grecia, I. Iscrizioni di Megara Iblea e Selinunte*, Milano 1989.

ARNOLD C.-BIUCCHI-BEER L.-TOBEY-WAGGONER N.M., *AGreek Archaic Silver Hoard from Selinus*, in "American Numismatic Society, Muscum Notes", 33, 1988, pp.1-35.

ARNOLD-BIUCCHI C., *The Randazzo Hoard 1980 and Sicilian Chronology in the early Fifth Century B.C.*, The American Numismatic Society, New York 1990.

ASHERI D., *La popolazione di Imera nel Vsecolo a.C.*, in "Rivista di Filol. e istr. class." 1973, 4, pp. 457 ss.

Atti dei Convegni di studi sulla Magna Grecia, Taranto 1961 e ss.

Atti del II Congresso Internazionale di Micenologia (Roma-Napoli, ottobre 1991), in corso di stampa.

Atti Giornate internazionali di Studi sull'area elima (Gibellina 1991), Pisa-Gibellina 1992.

BACCHIELLI L., *Due statuette di Cirene: testimonianze della produzione arcaica locale*, in "Quaderni di Archeologia della Libia", 10, 1985.

BACCHIELLI L., *I"luoghi" della celebrazione politica e religiosa a Cirene nella poesia di Pindaro e Callimaco*, in *Cirene. Storia, Mito, Letteratura*, Atti del Convegno della S.I.S.A.C. (Urbino, 3 luglio 1988), Urbino 1990, pp. 5-33.

BACCHIELLI L., *Le pitture dalla "Tomba dell'altalena" di Cirene nel Museo del Louvre*, in "Quaderni di Archeologia della Libia", 8, 1976, pp. 355-383.

BAFICO S., *Greci e Fenici ad Alghero*, in "Archeo", 74 (aprile) 1991, p. 18.

BALDASSARRE I., *Osservazioni sull'urbanistica di Neapolis in età romana*, in *Neapolis*, Atti Taranto XXV (1985), Napoli 1986, pp. 221-231.

BALDASSARRE I.-ROUVERET A., *Une histoire plurielle de la peinture grecque*, in *Céramique et peinture grecques: modes d'emploi*, Actes du Colloque, Paris 26-28 Avril 1995 (in corso di stampa).

BALMUTH M. (ed.), *Studies in Sardinian Archaeology III*, Atti del Convegno *Nuragic Sardinia and the Myceneaean World* (Roma 1986), "British Archaeological Reports" 387, Oxford 1987.

BARBANERA M., *Il guerriero di Agrigento*, Roma 1995.

BARLETTA B.A., *An "Ionian Sea" Style in Archaic Doric Architecture*, in "AJA" XCIV, 1990, pp. 45ss.

BARLETTA B.A., *Ionic Influence in Archaic Sicily. The Monumental Art*, Gothenburg 1983.

BARRA BAGNASCO M., *Aspetti di vita quotidiana*, in BARRA BAGNASCO M. (a cura di), *Locri Epizefiri*, III. *Cultura materiale e vita quotidiana*, Firenze 1989, pp. 5 ss.

BARRA BAGNASCO M., *Edilizia privata in Magna Grecia: Modelli abitativi dall'età arcaica all'ellenismo*, in *Magna Grecia*, IV, Milano 1990.

BARRA BAGNASCO M., *Le strutture e la vita dell'area*, in BARRA BAGNAsco M. (a cura di), *Locri Epizefiri, IV. Lo scavo di Marasà Sud.Il sacello tardo arcaico e la "casa dei leoni"*, Firenze 1992, pp. 5 ss.

BARRA BAGNASCO M., *Scavi in Magna Grecia dell'Università di Torino*, in "SPABA", XLV (1993), pp.37 ss.

BASCH L., *Le Musée imaginaire de la marine antique*, Athènes 1987.

BASILE J.J., *The Capestrano Warrior and related Monuments of Seventh to Fifth Centuries B.C.*, in "Revue des archéologues et historiens d'Art de Louvain", XXVI, 1993, pp. 9 ss.

BATS M.-BERTUCCHI G.-CONGÈS G.-TRÉZINY H. (a cura di), *Marseille grecque et la Gaule*. Actes du colloque international d'histoire e d'archéologie et du V Congrès archéologique de Gaule méridionale (Marseille 1990), "Etudes Massaliètes", 3, Lattes/Aix-en-Provence 1992.

BATS M.-BERTUCCHI G.-CONGÈS G.-TRÉZINY H. (a cura di), *Marseille grecque et la Gaule*, Actes du Colloque international d'Histoire et d'Archéologie et du Ve Congrès archéologique de Gaule méridionale - Marseille, 18-23 novembre 1990="Études massaliètes", 3, Paris 1992.

BEAZLEY J.D., *The Development of Attic Black-Figure*, Berkeley, California, 1951 (1986).

BECHTEL F., *Die griechischen Dialekte*, Berlin 1921-1924.

BEINHAUER K.W., *Untersuchungen zu den eisenzeitlichen Bestattungsplätten von Novilara (Provinz Pesaro und Urbino)*, Frankfurt a.M. 1985.

BELL M.III, *Observations on Western Greek Stoas*, in *Eius Virtutis Studiosi: Classical and Postclassical Studies in Memory of F.E. Brown* (edd. SCATE R.T.-REYNOLDS SCOTT A.), Hanover-London 1993, pp. 327-341.

BELTING H., *Byzantine art in southern Italy*, in "DOP", XXVIII, 1974, pp. 3-29.

BELVEDERE O. (a cura di), *Himera III*, Roma 1988.

BELVEDERE O., *Himera, Naxos, Camarina, tre casi di urbanistica coloniale*, in "Xenia", 14, 1987, pp. 11 ss.

BELVEDERE O., *Tipologia e sviluppo delle abitazioni*, in *Himera*, II, Roma 1976, pp. 577 ss.

BENCIVENGA C.-TRILLMICH, *Resti di casa greca di età arcaica sull'acropoli di Elea*, in "MEFRA", 95 (1983), pp. 417 ss.

BENGTSON H., *Die Staatsverträge des Altertums*, I-II, München 19752.

BÉRARD J., *La colonisation grecque de l'Italie méridionale et de la Sicile dans l'antiquité*, Paris 1957.

BÉRARD V., *Les navigations d'Ulysse*, 4 voll., Paris.

BERNABÒ BREA L., *Il tempio di Afrodite di Akrai*, Napoli 1986.

BERNABÒ BREA L., *La Sicilia prima dei Greci*, Milano 1958.

BERNABÒ BREA L., *Le isole Eolie dal Tardoantico ai Normanni* (Biblioteca di "Felix Ravenna", 5), Ravenna 1988.

BERNABÒ BREA L.-CAVALIER M.-BELLI P., *La tholos termale di San Calogero nell'isola di Lipari*, in "Studi Micenei ed Egeo-Anatolici", XXVIII, 1990, pp.7-78.

BERNARDINI P., *S. Antioco: area del Cronicario. L'insediamento fenicio*, "RivStFen", 1988, pp.75-89.

BERNARDINI P.-TRONCHETTI C., *La Sardegna, gli Etruschi e i Greci*, in AA.Vv., *Sardegna preistorica.Nuraghi a Milano*, Milano 1985, pp. 285-307.

BERTELLI C., *Impulsi classici e loro trasmissione nell'ambiente artistico della Magna Graecia*, in Atti del XVII Convegno di studi sulla Magna Graecia (Taranto 1977), Napoli 1978, pp.117-130.

BERTI F.-GUZZO P.G., *Spina. Storia di una città tra Greci ed Etruschi* (Catalogo della mostra), Ferrara 1993.

BESCHI L., *Divinità funerarie cirenaiche*, in "Annuario Scuola Archeologica Italiana di Atene", 47-48 (N.S. 31-32), 1969-70, pp. 133-341.

BIANCHI BANDINELLI R., *Arte plebea*, in "Dialoghi di Archeologia", I, 1967, pp. 7 ss.

BIANCHI BANDINELLI R., *La pittura antica*, Roma 1980.

BIANCHI BANDINELLI R., *Palinodia*, in "La Critica d'Arte", VII, 1942, pp. 18 ss.

BIANCHI BANDINELLI R.-FRANCHI L.-GIULIANO A.-LA REGINA A.-TORELLI M.-COARELLI F., *Sculture municipali dell'area sabellica tra l'età di Cesare e quella di Nerone*, in "Studi Miscellanei", 10, 1967.

BIANCHI R.-BANDINELLI-GIULIANO A., *Les Etrusques et l'Italie avant Rome*, Paris 1973.

BIANCOFIORE F., *Civiltà micenea nell'Italia meridionale*, Roma 1967.

BIEBER M., *The History of the Greek and Roman Theater*, Princeton 1961.

BING P., *"Callimachus Hymn to De-los". The Well-Read Muse. Present and Past in Callimachus and the Hellenistic Poets*, Göttingen 1988, pp. 91-146.

BOARDMAN J. (ed.), *The Oxford History of Classical Art*, Oxford 1933.

BOARDMAN J., *Athenian Black Figure Vases*, London 1974.

BOARDMAN J., *Athenian Red Figure Vases: The Archaic Period*, London 1975.

BOARDMAN J., *Athenian Red Figure Vases: The Classical Period*, London 1989.

BOARDMAN J., *Greek Sculpture. The Archaic Period, a handbook*, London 1978.

BOËTHIUS A., *Il guerriero di Capestrano: due ipotesi*, in "La Critica d'Arte", IV, 1939, pp. 49 ss.

BOËTHIUS A., *Livy 8, 10.12 and the Warrior Image from Capestrano*, in "Eranos", LIV, 1956, pp. 202 ss.

BOLOGNA F., *Momenti della cultura figurativa nella Campania medievale*, in *Storia e Civiltà della Campania. Il Medioevo* (a cura di PUGLIESE CARRATELLI G.), Napoli 1992, pp. 171-259.

BONACASA N. et al., *Himera* I (1970); II (1976).

BONACASA N., *Lo stile severo in Grecia e in Occidente*, Roma 1991.

BONNET C.-JOURDAN-ANNEQUIN C., *Héraclès - D'une rive à l'autre de la Méditerranée - Bilan et perspectives*, Actes Table Ronde Rome 1989, Bruxelles-Roma 1992.

BORGNA E., *L'arco e le frecce nel mondo miceneo*, Roma 1992.

BORSARI S., *Il monachesimo bizantino nella Sicilia e nell'Italia meridionale prenormanna* (Istituto Italiano per gli studi storici, 14), Napoli 1963.

BOTTINI A., *Archeologia della salvezza*, Milano 1991.

BOTTINI A., *Archeologia della salvezza*, Milano 1992.

BOTTINI A., *Archeologia della salvezza*, Milano 1992.

BOTTINI A., *Archeologia della salvezza.L'escatologia greca nelle testimonianze archeologiche*, Milano 1992.

BREGLIA L., *Posizione della Campania nell'arte italica*, in "La Critica d'Arte", VII, 1942, pp. 29ss.

BRELICH A., *I Greci e gli dei*, Napoli 1985.

BRENDEL O.S., *Introduzione all'arte romana*, a cura di SETTIS S., Torino 1982.

BRENOT C., *Catalogue du Fond Général*, in *De Phocée à Massalia*, Marseille 1981, pp. 17-54.

BRIQUEL D., *Les Pélasges en Italie. Recherches sur l'histoire de la légende*, Roma 1984.

British Museum Coins, Cyrenaica, London 1936.

BRUNO V.J., *Form and Colour in Greek Painting*, New York 1977.

BUCHNER G., *Figürlich bemalte spätgeometrische Vasen aus Pithekussai und Kyme*, in "Römische Mitteilungen", 60-61, 1953-1954, pp. 37 ss.

BUCHNER G., *Nuovi aspetti e problemi posti dagli scavi di Pithecusa con particolari considerazioni sulle oreficerie di stile orientalizzante antico*, in *Contribution à l'étude de la société et de la colonisation eubéennes* (Cahiers du Centre Jean Bérard, 2), Napoli 1975, pp. 59-86.

BUCHNER G.-RIDGWAY D., *Pithekoussai I*, Roma 1993.

BUCHNER G.-RIDGWAY D., *PithekoussaiI*, in "MonAL", s. monografica IV, 1993.

BUCK C.D., *The Greek Dialects*, Chicago-London 1955.

BULGARELLA F., *Bisanzio in Sicilia e nell'Italia meridionale: i riflessi politici*, in *Il Mezzogiorno dai Bizantini a Federico II* (*Storia d'Italia*, diretta da GALASSO G.), III, Torino 1983, pp. 129-249.

BULGARELLA F., *Testimonianze cristiane antiche e altomedievali nella Sibaritide*, in Atti del Convegno Nazionale a Corigliano-Rossano, 1978 (Vetera Christianorum, Scavi e ricerche, 3), Bari 1980, pp.89-129.

BULTRIGHINI A., rec. a *Polydispion Argos* ("Bulletin de Correspondance Héllénique", Suppl.XXII, 1992), in "Rivista di Filologia e Istruzione classica" 121, 1993, pp.67-71.

BURKERT W., *Craft versus Sect: The Problem of Orphics and Pythagoreans*, in *Jewish and Christian Self-Definition*, ed. by MEYER B.E.-SANDERS E.P., III, London 1982, pp. 1-22.

BURKERT W., *Griechische Religion der archaischen und klassischen Epoche*, Stuttgart 1977 (trad. it.*IGreci*, Milano 1980).

BUSOLT G.(-SWOBODA H.), *Griechische Staatskunde*, München, I, 1920.

CACCAMO CALTABIANO M., *La monetazione di Messana*, Antike Münzen und Geschnittene Steine Bd. XIII, Berlin 1993.

CAMASSA G., *La codificazione delle leggi e le istituzioni politiche delle città greche della Calabria in età arcaica e classica*, in CINGARI G.(direttore), S*toria della Calabria*, Roma-Reggio Calabria, I, a cura di SETTIS S., 1988, pp. 630-649 (bibliografia pp. 655-656).

CAMASSA G., *Le istituzioni politiche greche*, in *Storia delle idee politiche, economiche e sociali*, I (a cura di FIRPO L.), Torino 1982, pp. 3-1265.

CANCIANI F., *Un biconico dipinto da Vulci*, in "DArch", VIII, 1974-75, pp. 79-85.

CAPOVILLA G., *Callimachea et Lybica*, in "Aegyptus", 42, 1962, pp. 27-97.

CAPOVILLA G., *Callimaco e Cirene storica e mitica*, in "Aegyptus", 43, 1963, pp. 141-191, 356-383.

CAPUIS L., *I Veneti*, Milano 1993.

CARBÈ A., *Note sulla monetazione di Selinunte.Contributo della numismatica alla storia e al patrimonio religioso della città*, "Rivista Italiana di Numismatica", 1986, pp.3-20.

CARLIER P., *La royauté en Grèce avant Alexandre*, Strasbourg 1984.

CARTER J.C., *The Pantanello Necropolis 1982-1989. An interim Report*, Austin 1990.

CASSANO R. (a cura di), *Principi imperatori vescovi. Duemila anni di storia a Canosa*, Venezia 1992.

CASSOLA GUIDA P., *Bronzetti friulani a figura umana tra protostoria ed età della romanizzazione*, Roma 1989.

CASSOLA GUIDA P.-ZUCCONI GALLI FONSECA M., *Nuovi studi sulle armi dei Micenei*, Roma 1992.

CASSON L., *Ships and Seamanship in the Ancient World*, Princeton 1971.

CASSON L., *Ships and Seamanship in theAncient World*, Princeton N.J. 19862.

CASSON L., *The Ancient Mariners*, Princeton 1991.

CASTAGNOLI F. (a cura di), *Enea nel Lazio* (Catalogo della mostra), Roma 1981.

CAVALLARI F.S.-HOLM A.-CAVALLARI L., *Topografia archeologica di Siracusa*, Palermo 1883 (con Appendice edita nel 1891).

CAVALLO G., *La cultura greca. Itinerari e segni*, in *Storia e Civiltà della Campania*, Napoli 1992, pp. 277-290.

CAVALLO G., *La cultura italo-greca nella produzione libraria*, in *I Bizantini in Italia* (Collana "Antica Madre", diretta da PUGLIESE CARRATELLI G.), Milano 1982, pp. 427-612.

CECCARELLI I., CICERCHIA E., COARELLI F., LA ROCCA E., MANGANI E., MONACO E., PICOZZI M.G., PISANI SARTORIO G., RICCIOTTI D., SANTORO P., SOMMELLA MURA A., STRAZZULLA M.J. (a cura di), *Roma medio repubblicana. Aspetti culturali di Roma e del Lazio nei secoli IV e III a.C.* (Catalogo della mostra), Roma 1973.

CEDERNA A., *Carsoli. Scoperta di un deposito votivo del III secolo a.C. (prima campagna di scavo)*, in "Notizie Scavi", 1951, pp.169 ss.

CEDERNA A., *Teste votive di Carsoli*, in "Archeologia Classica", V, 1953, pp. 187 ss.

CERCHIAI L., *I Campani*, Milano 1995.

CERCHIAI L., *I Campani*, Milano 1995.

CERCHIAI L., *Il processo di strutturazione del politico - I Campani*, in "Annali I.U.O. ArchStAnt", IX, 1987, pp. 41-54.

CERCHIAI L., *Le officine etrusco-corinzie di Pontecagnano*, Napoli 1990.

CHAMOUX F., *Cyrène sous la monarchie des Battiades*, Paris 1953, pp.104-114, 138-142.

CHAMOUX F., *Cyrène sous la monarchie des Battiades*, Paris 1953.

CHAMOUX F., *Cyrène sous la monarchie des Battiades*, Paris 1953.

CHIRASSI COLOMBO I., *La religione in Grecia*, Bari 1983.

CIACERI E., *Miti e culti nella storia dell'antica Sicilia*, Catania 1911.

CIANCIO A. ET AL., *Tombe a semicamera sull'Acropoli di Monte Sannace*, Fasano 1986.

CIANFARANI V., *Osservazioni sul restauro del guerriero di Capestrano*, in "Rivista Istituto Nazionale di Archeologia e Storia dell'Arte", n.s., XV, 1968, pp. 5 ss.

CIANFARANI V., *Stele d'arte medioadriatica da Guardiagrele*, in "Bollettino d'Arte", 1966, pp. 1 ss.

CIANFARANI V.-FRANCHI DELL'ORTO L.-LA REGINA A., *Culture adriatiche di Abruzzo e di Molise*, Roma 1978.

CIASCA A., *Fenici*, in "Kokalos", 34-35 (1988-89) [1992], pp. 75-88.

CLAVEL-LÉVÊQUE M., *Marseille grecque.La dynamique d'un impérialisme marchand*, Marseille 1977, pp.79-84, 115-124.

CLERC M., *Massalia, Histoire de Marseille dans l'Antiquité des origines à la fin de l'Empire romain d'Occident (476 ap. J.-C.)*, Marseille, I, 1927, pp.424-434.

COARELLI F., *Il Foro Boario*, Roma 1988.

COARELLI F., in *Siritide e Metapontino, Storia di due territori coloniali*, Atti del Convegno (Policoro, 31 ottobre-2 novembre 1991), 1996.

COARELLI F., *La "pugna equestris" di Agatocle nell'Athenaion di Siracusa*, in *Nuove ricerche e studi sulla Magna Grecia e la Sicilia in onore di P. Arias*, Pisa 1983, pp. 547-557.

COARELLI F.-TORELLI M., *Sicilia*, Bari 1984.

COLDSTREAM J.N., *A figured Geometric Oinochoe from Italy*, in "University of London Institute of Classical Studies, Bulletin", 15, 1968, pp. 86 ss.

COLDSTREAM J.N., *Geometric Greece*, London 1977, pp. 317 ss.

COLDSTREAM J.N., *Geometric Greece*, London 1977.

COLONNA G., *Apollon, les Etrusques et Lipara*, in "MEFRA", XCVI, 1984, pp.557-578.

COLONNA G., *Apporti etruschi all'orientalizzante "piceno": il caso della statuaria*, in *La civiltà picena nelle Marche*, Studi in onore di Giovanni Annibaldi, Ripatransone 1992, pp. 92 ss.

COLONNA G., *Bronzetti votivi umbro-sabellici a figura umana, I: periodo "arcaico"*, Firenze 1970.

COLONNA G., *Il santuario di Leucotea-Ilizia a Pyrgi*, in G. COLONNA (a cura di), *Santuari d'Etruria* (Catalogo della mostra, Arezzo 1985), Milano 1985, pp. 127-141.

COLONNA G., *Le civiltà anelleniche*, in PUGLIESE CARRATELLI G. (a cura di), *Storia e civiltà della Campania - L'Evo antico*, Napoli 1991, pp. 25-68.

COLONNA G., *Nuove prospettive sulla storia etrusca tra Alalia e Cuma*, in Atti IICongresso Internazionale Etrusco (Firenze 1985), I, Roma 1989, pp. 361-374.

COLONNA G., *Urbanistica e architettura*, in PUGLIESE CARRATELLI G. (a cura di), *Rasenna*, Milano 1986, pp. 369-530.

COMELLA A.-STEFANI G., *Materiali votivi del santuario di Campetti a Veio*, Roma 1990.

CONSOLO LANGHER S., *La Sicilia dalla scomparsa di Timoleonte alla morte di Agatocle.L'introduzione della "Basileia"*, in GABBA E.-VALLET G.(a cura di), *La Sicilia antica* (vol.II della *Storia della Sicilia*), Napoli 1980, pp. 289-342.

CONSOLO LANGHER S., *Problemi di storia costituzionale siceliota*, in "Helikon", 9-10, 1969-70, pp. 107-143.

COOK R.M., *Greek Painted Pottery*, London 19722.

COOK R.N., *The Archetypal Doric Temple*, in "BSA", 65, 1970, pp. 50ss.

COPPOLA G., *Cirene e il nuovo Callimaco*, Bologna 1935.

CORDANO F., *Antiche fondazioni greche*, Palermo 1986.

CORDANO F., *Antiche fondazioni greche.Sicilia e Italia meridionale*, Palermo 1986, pp.124-137.

CORDANO F., *La città di Camarina e le corde della lira*, in "La Parola del Passato", 49, 1994, pp. 418-426.

CORDANO F., *Le tessere pubbliche dal tempio di Atena a Camarina*, Roma 1992.

CORDANO F., *Le tessere pubbliche dal tempio di Atena a Camarina*, Roma 1992.

Corpus Inscriptionum Graecarum I-IV, Berlin 1828-1877.

CORRIGAN E.H., *Lucanian Tomb Paintings Excavated at Paestum 1969-1972: A Iconographic Study*, Columbia University 1979.

COSTABILE F., *Finanze pubbliche. L'amministrazione finanziaria templare*, in PUGLIESE CARRATELLI G. (a cura di), *Magna Grecia.Lo sviluppo politico, sociale ed economico*, Milano 1987.

COULTON J.J., *Greek Architects at Work*, London 1977.

COULTON J.J., *The Architectural Development of the Greek Stoa*, Oxford 1976.

CRISTOFANI M. (a cura di), *La grande Roma dei Tarquini*, Roma 1990.

CRISTOFANI M., *Gli Etruschi del mare*, Milano 1983.

CRISTOFANI M., *L'alfabeto etrusco*, in PROSDOCIMI A.L. (a cura di), *Lingue e dialetti dell'Italia antica*, Roma-Padova 1978, pp. 403-468.

CULTRERA in "Not. Sc." 1943, pp. 33-42, 124-126 (Giardino Spagna).

CUSUMANO N., *Una terra splendida e facile da possedere.IGreci e la Sicilia*, Roma 1994.

D'A. DESBOROUGH V.R., *The Greek Dark Ages*, London 1972.

D'AGOSTINO B., *Grecs et "indigènes" sur la côte tyrrhénienne au VIIe siècle. La transmission des idéologies entre élites sociales*, in "Annales ESC", XXII, 1977B, pp. 207-226.

D'AGOSTINO B., *I paesi greci di provenienza dei coloni e le loro relazioni con il Mediterraneo Occidentale*, in PUGLIESE CARRATELLI G. (a cura di), *Magna Grecia - Prolegomeni*, Milano 1985, pp. 209-244.

D'AGOSTINO B., *Il coperchio di cinerario da Pontecagnano*, in "La Parola del Passato", LXXXVIII, 1963, pp. 67 ss.

D'AGOSTINO B., *Il mondo periferico della Magna Grecia*, in *Popoli e Civiltà dell'Italia Antica*, 2, Roma 1974, pp. 179 ss.

D'AGOSTINO B., *Il processo di strutturazione del politico nel mondo osco-lucano. La protostoria*, in "Annali I.U.O. ArchStAnt", IX, 1987, pp. 23-29.

D'AGOSTINO B., *La civiltà del Ferro nell'Italia meridionale e nella Sicilia*, in *Popoli e Civiltà dell'Italia Antica*, 2, Roma 1974, pp. 11ss.

D'AGOSTINO B., *Le genti della Campania antica*, in PUGLIESE CARRATELLI G. (a cura di), *Italia omnium terrarum alumna*, Milano 1988, pp. 531ss.

D'AGOSTINO B., *Rapporti tra l'Italia Meridionale e l'Egeo nell'VIIIsec. a.C.*, in Atti II Congresso Internazionale Etrusco (Firenze 1985), I, Roma 1989, pp. 63-78.

D'AGOSTINO B., *Tombe "principesche" dell'orientalizzante antico da Pontecagnano*, in "MonAL", XLIX, 1977A.

D'AGOSTINO B.-GASTALDI P. (a cura di), *Pontecagnano II. La necropoli del Picentino 1. - Le tombe della I Età del Ferro*, Napoli 1988.

D'ANDRIA F. (a cura di), *Archeologia dei Messapii*, Lecce 1990.

D'ANDRIA F., *Greci e Indigeni in Iapigia*, in *Forme di contatto e processi di trasformazione nelle società antiche*, Atti del Convegno di Cortona (24-30 maggio 1981), Pisa-Roma 1983, pp. 287-295.

D'ANDRIA F., *Messapi e Peuceti*, in *Italia omnium terrarum alumna*, a cura di PUGLIESE CARRATELLI G., Milano 1988, pp. 651-715.

D'ANDRIA F., *Scavi nella zona del Kerameikos (1973)*, in AA.VV., *Metaponto*, I, "NSc", 1975 Supplemento, pp. 335 ss.

DALCHER K., *Das Peristylhaus 1 von Iaitas: Architektur und Baugeschichte*, Zürich 1994.

DE CARO S., *Saggi nell'area del tempio di Apollo a Pompei*, Napoli 1986.

DE CARO S., *Una nuova tomba dipinta da Nola*, in "RIASA" 1-3, VI-VII, 1983-84, pp. 71-74.

DE FRANCISCIS A., *Il santuario di Marasà in Locri Epizefiri, 1. Il tempio arcaico*, Napoli 1979.

DE JULIIS E.M, *Gli Iapigi, Storia e Civiltà della Puglia preromana*, Milano 1988.

DE JULIIS E.M, *L'origine delle genti iapigie e la civiltà dei Dauni*, in *Italia omnium terrarum alumna*, a cura di PUGLIESE CARRATELLI G., Milano 1988, pp. 591-650.

DE JULIIS E.M., *Gli Iapigi. Storia e civiltà della Puglia preromana*, Milano 1988.

DE JULIIS E.M., *I popoli della Puglia prima dei Greci*, in *Magna Grecia-Prolegomeni*, a cura di PUGLIESE CARRATELLI G., vol. I, Milano 1985, pp. 145-188.

DE JULIIS E.M., *La ceramica geometrica della Daunia*, Firenze 1977.

DE LA GENIÈRE J.-ROUGETET J., *Recherches sur la topographie de Sélinonte, campagne 1985*, in "Rendiconti Lincei", XL, 1986, pp.289-297.

DE LA GENIÈRE S., *La Céramique géometrique de Sala Consilina*, in "MEFRA", LXXII, 1961, pp. 7 ss.

DE MIRO E., *Architettura civile in Agrigento ellenistico-romana e rapporti con l'Anatolia*, in "Quaderni dell'Istituto di Archeologia", Università di Messina, 3, 1988, pp. 63-72.

DE MIRO E., *La casa greca in Sicilia*, Misc. Manni 2 (1980), pp. 707 ss.

DE MIRO E., *La casa greca in Sicilia. Testimonianze nella Sicilia centrale dal VIal III secolo a.C.*, in *Miscellanea in onore di E.Manni*, Roma 1979, pp. 709 ss.

DE MIRO E., *La valle dei templi*, Palermo 1994, pp.21-49.

DE MIRO E., *Topografia archeologica*, in AA.VV., *Sikanie* (a cura di G. PUGLIESE CARRATELLI), Milano 1985, pp. 563 ss.

DE NATALE S., *Pontecagnano II. La necropoli di S. Antonio: Propr. Eci 2. Tombe della Prima Età del Ferro*, Napoli 1992.

DE POLIGNAC F., *La naissance de la cité grecque*, Paris 1984.

DE POLIGNAC Fr., *La naissance de la cité grecque*, Paris 1984.

DE SENSI SESTITO G., *Considerazioni sulle strategie di Archita*, in "Miscellanea di studi storici", 8, 1990-91, pp. 25-34.

DE SENSI SESTITO G., *La Calabria in età arcaica e classica.Storia, economia, società*, in CINGARI G.(direttore), *Storia della Calabria*, I, a cura di SETTIS S., Roma-Reggio Calabria 1988, pp. 230-232 (bibliografia pp. 293-294).

DE SENSI SESTITO G., *La Sicilia dal 289 al 210 a.C.*, in GABBA E.-VALLET G.(a cura di), *La Sicilia antica* (vol.II della *Storia della Sicilia*), Napoli 1980, pp.343-370.

DE SIMONE C., *Die griechischen Entlehnungen im Etruskischen*, Wiesbaden 1968-70.

DESCOEUDRES J.-P.-KEARSLEY R., *Greek Pottery at Veii: Another Look*, in "BSA", LXXVIII, 1983, pp. 9-53.

DESCOEUDRES J.P. (ed.), *Greek Colonists and native Populations*, Canberra-Oxford 1990.

DEVRESSE R., *Les manuscrits grecs de l'Italie méridionale. Histoire, classement, paléographie* (Studi e Testi, 183), Città del Vaticano 1955.

DI FILIPPO BALESTRAZZI E.-GASPERINI L.-BALESTRAZZI M., *L'emiciclo di Pratomedes a Cirene*, in "Quaderni di Archeologia della Libia", 8, 1983.

DI STEFANO C.A., *Nuove ipotesi sui bronzetti di Castronovo*, in "Archeologia Classica", XVIII, 1966, pp. 175ss.

DI STEFANO G., *Camarina.Guida alla città antica*, Ragusa 1993.

DI STEFANO G., *Indigeni e greci nell'entroterra di Camarina*, Ragusa 1995.

DI STEFANO G., *Litri e decalitri da Camarina*, in "Archeologia viva", XIII, 45, maggio-giugno 1994, pp. 46-49.

DI VITA A., *L'urbanistica*, in *Sikanie. Storia e civiltà della Sicilia greca* (coll. *Antica madre*, VIII), Milano 1985.

DI VITA A., *La penetrazione siracusana nella Sicilia sudorientale*, in "Kokalos", II, 1956, pp. 177 ss.

DI VITA A., *Le fortificazioni di Selinunte classica*, in "Annuario Atene", LXII, 1984 (1988), pp. 69-79.

DI VITA A., *Selinunte fra il 650 ed il 409: un modello di città coloniale*, in "Annuario Atene", LXII, 1984 (1988), pp.7-62.

DI VITA A., *Town Planning in the Greek Colonies of Sicily from the time of their Foundations to the Punic Wars*, in *Greek Colonists a.Native Populations*, Canberra-Oxford 1990, pp. 343-363.

DI VITA A., *Tucidide VI, 5 e l'epicrazia siracusana*, in "Kokalos", XXXIII, 1987, pp. 77 ss.

DICKINSON O., *The Aegean Bronze Age*, Cambridge 1994.

DICKINSON O., *The Aegean Bronze Age*, Cambridge 1994.

DIEBNER S., *Aesernia - Venafrum*, Roma 1979.

DIEBNER S., *Reperti funerari in Umbria a sinistra del Tevere. I sec. a.C. - I sec. d.C.*, Roma 1986.

DIELS H., *Die Fragmente der Vorsokratiker*, Berlin 1903 (Berlin 1951[6], hrsg. KRANZ W.).

DIELS H.-KRANZ W., *Die Fragmente der Vorsokratiker*, I-II-III, Berlin 1956[8].

DOHRN T., *Ein Frauenbildnis in Teramo*, in "Römische Mitteilungen", 67, 1960, pp.98 ss.

DOUMAS CHR., *The Wall-Paintings of Thera*, Athens 1992.

DRERUP H., *Griechische Architektur in homerischer Zeit*, Göttingen 1969.

DRÖGENMÜLLER H.P., *Syrakus*, Heidelberg 1969.

DUNBABIN T.J., *The Western Greeks*, Oxford 1948.

DUŠANIĆ S., *The ὅρκιον τῶν οἰκιστήρων and Fourth-century Cyrene*, in "Chiron", 8, 1978, pp. 55-76.

EFFENTERRE H.VAN, *La cité grecque des origines à la défaite de Marathon*, Paris 1985.

EGG M., *Italische Helme mit Krempe*, in AA.VV., *Antike Helme. Sammlung Lipperheide und andere Bestände des Antikenmuseums Berlin*, Mainz 1988, pp. 222-270.

EHRENBERG V., *Die Stadt der Griechen*, Zürich 1965[2] (trad. it.Firenze 1967).

ERMETI A.L., *L'agorà di Cirene*, III, 1. Il Monumento navale, Roma 1981.

FABBRICOTTI E., *Divinità greche e divinità libie in rilievi di età ellenistica*, in "Quaderni di Archeologia della Libia", 12, 1987.

FALKENHAUSEN V. v., *I Bizantini in Italia*, in *I Bizantini in Italia*, Milano 1982, pp. 3-136.

FALKENHAUSEN V. v., *Il ducato di Amalfi e gli Amalfitani fra Bizantini e Normanni*, in Atti del Congresso int. di Studi Amalfitani (1981), Amalfi 1986, pp.9-31.

FALKENHAUSEN V. v., *Il monachesimo greco in Sicilia*, in Atti VI Convegno Int. di storia sulla civiltà rupestre medievale del Mezzogiorno d'Italia – La Sicilia rupestre nel contesto della civiltà mediterranea (Catania-Pantalica-Ispica, 1981), Galatina 1986, pp. 134-173.

FALKENHAUSEN V. v., *La Campania fra Goti e Bizantini*, in *Storia e Civiltà della Campania*, Napoli 1992, pp. 7-35.

FALKENHAUSEN V. v., *La dominazione bizantina in Italia meridionale*, Bari 1978 (1ª ed. it.).

FALKENHAUSEN V. v., *Magna Graecia bizantina e tradizione classica*, in Atti del XVIIConvegno di studi sulla Magna Grecia (Taranto 1977), Napoli 1978, pp. 61-90.

FALLA CASTELFRANCHI M., *Disiecta membra. La pittura bizantina in Calabria (secc. IX-XIII)*, in *Italian Church Decoration of the Middle Ages and Early Renaissance* (ed. by TRONZO W.), Bologna 1989, pp. 81-100.

FALLA CASTELFRANCHI M., *Per la storia della pittura bizantina in Calabria*, in "Rivista storica calabrese", VI, 1-4 (1985), pp. 389-413.

FALLA CASTELFRANCHI M., *Pittura monumentale bizantina in Puglia*,

Milano 1991.
FARIOLI CAMPANATI R., *La cultura artistica in età giustinianea in Italia*, in XXXIV Settimana CISAM (1986), Spoleto 1988, I, pp. 99-118.
FARIOLI CAMPANATI R., *La cultura artistica nelle regioni bizantine d'Italia dal VI all'XI secolo*, in *I Bizantini in Italia*, Milano 1982, pp. 139-426.
FARIOLI CAMPANATI R., *Quattro sarcofagi mediobizantini in Italia*, in "Rivista di studi bizantini e slavi" (Miscellanea Agostino Pertusi), II, 1982, pp. 283-296.
FELLETTI B.M.-MAJ, *La tradizione italica nell'arte romana*, I, Roma 1977.
FERGUSON J., *Among the Gods*, London-New York 1989 (trad. it. *Fra gli dei dell'Olimpo*, Bari 1991).
FERRI S., *Divinità ignote*, Firenze 1929.
FERRI S., *La "prothesis" apula di Lavello* (1929), in *Opuscula*, Firenze 1962, pp. 317 ss.
FERRI S., *Stele "Daunie"*, in "Bollettino d'Arte", 1962 ss.
FERRON J., *Les relations de Carthage avec l'Étrurie*, in "Latomus", XXV, 1966, pp. 689-709.
FIACCADORI G., *Calabria Tardoantica*, in *Storia della Calabria antica*, Roma-Reggio Calabria 1994, pp. 707-762.
FIACCADORI G., *Il Cristianesimo*, in *Storia e Civiltà della Campania*, Napoli 1992, pp. 145-170.
FIORENTINI G., *Gela, la città antica e il suo territorio*, Palermo 1985.
FISCHER-HANSEN T. (ed.), *Ancient Sicily*, in "Acta Hyperborea", 6, 1995.
FOGOLARI G.-PROSDOCIMI A., *I Veneti antichi. Lingua e cultura*, Padova 1988.
FOLLIERI E., *I santi della Calabria bizantina*, in *Calabria bizantina*, Atti del I e II incontro di Studi Bizantini, Reggio Calabria 1974, pp. 71-94.
FONSECA C.D., *La civiltà rupestre in Puglia*, in *La Puglia fra Bisanzio e l'Occidente* (a cura di FONSECA C.D.), Milano 1980, pp. 37-44.
FORTI L., *Un gruppo di stele del Museo Campano*, in "Memorie dell'Accademia di Archeologia, Lettere e Belle Arti della Società di Napoli", 6, 1942, pp. 43 ss.
FRAJESE A. (a cura di), *Opere di Archimede*, Torino 1974.
FRASCA M., *Tra Magna Grecia e Sicilia: origine e sopravvivenza della coppia amuleto a figura umana*, in "Bollettino d'Arte", 76 (anno LXXVII), 1992, pp. 19 ss.

FRASER P.M., *Ptolemaic Alexandria*, Oxford 1972.
FREDERIKSEN M., *Campania*, Roma 1984.
FREY O.H., *Die Entstehung der Situlenkunst - Studien zur figürlich verzierten Toreutik von Este*, Berlin 1969.
FUDA R.-VAN COMPERNOLLE R.-COSTABILE F., *La costituzione locrese nel IV-IIIsec. a.C.*, in COSTABILE F. (a cura di), *Polis ed Olympieion a Locri Epizefiri.Costituzione, economia e finanze di una città della Magna Grecia.Editio altera e traduzione delle tabelle locresi,* Soveria Mannelli 1992, pp.203-228.
FUHRMANN H., *Zwei Reliefbilder aus der Geschichte Roms, II. Der Imperator M. Nonius und die Weihung des Treverers Attalus an die Fortuna-Nemesis in Isernia*, in "Mitteilungen des deutschen archäologischen Instituts", II, 1949, pp. 45ss.
GABBA E.-VALLET G. (a cura di), *La Sicilia antica* (vol.II della *Storia della Sicilia*), Napoli 1980.
GABBA E.-VALLET G. (a cura di), *La Sicilia antica*, I, Napoli 1980.
GABRICI E., *Per la Storia dell'architettura dorica in Sicilia*, in "MonAnt" XXXV, 1935, pp. 138 ss.
GALLO L., *Alimentazione e demografia nella Grecia antica*, Salerno 1994.
GANDOLFO F., *Gli affreschi di San Saba*, in *Fragmenta picta* (Catalogo della mostra 1989-90, Castel S. Angelo), Roma 1989, pp. 183-187.
GARLAN Y., *Recherches de Poliorcétique grecque*, Paris 1974.
GARRAFFO S., *Il rilievo monetale tra il VI e il IV secolo a.C.*, in *Sikanie*, Milano 1985, pp. 261-276.
GASTALDI P., *Le necropoli protostoriche della Valle del Sarno: Proposta per una suddivisione in fasi*, in "Annali I.U.O. ArchStAnt", I, 1979, pp.13-58.
GENTILI G.V., *Il grande tempio ionico di Siracusa*, in "Palladio", 17, 1967, pp. 61 ss.
GHINATTI F., *Ancora sulla storia della Magna Grecia*, in "Sileno", 20, 1994, pp. 53-69.
GHINATTI F., *Autenticazione e alienazione dei simboli*, in "Sileno", 19, 1993, pp. 57-69.
GIANNELLI G., *Culti e miti della Magna Grecia*, Firenze 1963².
GIARDINO L., *Herakleia e la sua chora*, in *Da Leukania a Lucania*, Roma 1992, pp. 136 ss.
GIGANTE M., *Civiltà teatrale e epigrammatica a Taranto in età ellenistica*, in "Taras", VIII, 1988, pp. 7-33.
GIGANTE M., *Epicarmo*, in *Enciclopedia dello Spettacolo*, IV, Roma 1957, coll. 1513-1518.
GIGANTE M., *Il manifesto poetico di Nosside*, in *Letterature comparate.Studi Paratore*, Bologna 1981, pp. 243-245.
GIGANTE M., *Il nuovo testo orfico di Hipponion*, in *Storia e cultura del Mezzogiorno.Studi U.Caldora*, Milano 1979, pp. 3-7.
GIGANTE M., in *Atti dei Convegni di Studi sulla Magna Grecia*, Taranto 1965 ss.
GIGANTE M., in *Megale Hellas. Storia e civiltà della Magna Grecia*, Milano 1983, pp. 585-640.
GIGANTE M., in *Storia della Calabria antica*, Roma-Reggio Calabria 1987, pp. 527-563.
GIGANTE M., *L'edera di Leonida*, Napoli 1971.
GIGANTE M., *L'epigramma in Magna Grecia*, Salerno 1967.
GIGANTE M., *La civiltà letteraria*, in *I Bizantini in Italia*, Milano 1982, pp.615-651.
GIGANTE M., *Magna Grecia*, III, Milano 1988, pp. 259-284.
GIGANTE M., *Nosside*, in "La Parola del Passato", CLIV-CLV, 1974, pp.22-39.
GIGLIOLI G.Q., *Bronzetti italici ed etruschi di arte popolare*, in "Archeologia Classica", IV, 1952, pp. 174 ss.
GIGLIOLI G.Z., *Arte lucana?*, in "Studi Etruschi", XXIII, 1954, pp. 405ss.
GINOUVÈS R. ET AL., *La Macédoine de Philippe II à la conquête romaine*, Paris 1993.
GIRONE M., *Note su due magistrature di Locri Epizefiri*, in "Annali della Facoltà di Lettere e Filosofia dell'Università di Bari", 35-36, 1992-93, pp.261-269.
GIRONE M., *Sui laucelarchi*, in "Miscellanea greca e romana", 18, 1994, pp. 81-87.
GIUFFRIDA IENTILE M., *La pirateria etrusca. Momenti e fortuna*, Roma 1983.
GIULIANO A., *Arte greca*, Milano 1986-87, pp. 55 ss., 132 ss., 264 ss., 554 ss., 630 ss.
GIULIANO A., *Busti femminili da Palestrina*, in "Römische Mitteilungen", 60-61, 1953-1954, pp. 172ss.
GIULIANO A., *Prima Italia*, in "Xenia", 3, 1982, pp. 3 ss.
Gli Elimi e l'area elima (Atti del seminario di Studi, 1989), Palermo 1990.
GLOTZ G., *La cité grecque*, Paris 1928 (trad. it.Torino 1973).

GODART L., *Auteurs des textes en Linéaire B de Tirynthe*, "Archäologischer Anzeiger", 1988, pp. 245-250.
GODART L., *L'invenzione della scrittura, dal Nilo alla Grecia*, Torino 1992.
GORINI G., *La monetazione incusa della Magna Grecia*, Bellinzona 1975.
GOW A.S.F.-PAGE D.L., *The Greek Anthology Hellenistic Epigrams*, Cambridge 1965.
GRABAR A., *La part byzantine dans l'art du Moyen Age en Italie méridionale*, in *Il passaggio dal dominio bizantino allo stato normanno nell'Italia meridionale*, Atti del IIConvegno int. di studi (Taranto-Mottola 1973), Taranto 1977, pp. 231-247.
GRABAR A., *Les manuscrits grecs enluminès de provenance italienne, IXe-XIe siècles* (Bibl. de Cahiers Archéologiques VIII), Paris 1972.
GRAEVE V. V.-HELLY B., *Recherches récentes sur la peinture grecque*, in "PACT", 17-1.2, 1987, pp. 17-33.
GRAS M., *À propos de la "bataille d'Alalia"*, in "Latomus", XXXI, 1972, pp. 698-716.
GRAS M., *La Méditerranée archaïque*, Paris 1995.
GRAS M., *Les Grecs et la Sardaigne*, in AA.VV., *Il commercio greco nel Tirreno in età arcaica*, Salerno 1981, pp. 83-95.
GRAS M., *Trafics tyrrhéniens archaïques*, Roma 1985.
GRAS M., *Trafics tyrrhéniens archaïques*, Paris 1985.
GRASSI M.T., *I Celti in Italia*, Milano 1991.
GRECO E., *Archeologia della Magna Grecia*, Roma-Bari 1992.
GRECO E., *Archeologia della Magna Grecia*, Roma-Bari 1993², pp. 311-319.
GRECO E., *Dal territorio alla città. Lo sviluppo urbano di Taranto*, in "AION ArchStAnt" 1981, pp. 139-157.
GRECO E., *Dal territorio alla città: lo sviluppo urbano di Taranto*, in "AION ArchStAn", III (1981), pp. 139 ss.
GRECO E., *I santuari*, in *Magna Grecia*, IV, Milano 1990, pp. 159 ss.
GRECO E., *Ippodamo e Thuri*, in *Atene e l'Occidente*, Atti del Convegno di Acquasparta (1994), in stampa.
GRECO E., *L'"impero" di Sibari*, in Atti XXXII Convegno di Taranto (1992), Napoli 1994, pp. 459-485.
GRECO E., *L'"impero" di Sibari. Bilancio archeologico-topografico*, in

Atti Taranto XXXII, 1992, pp. 459-485.
GRECO E., *L'impianto urbano di Neapolis greca: aspetti e problemi*, in *Neapolis*, Atti del XXV Conv.di Taranto (1985), Napoli 1986, pp. 187-219.
GRECO E., *La città e il territorio: problemi di storia topografica*, in *Poseidonia-Paestum*, Atti del XXVII Conv. di Taranto (1987), Napoli 1992.
GRECO E., *La città* in *Un secolo di ricerche in Magna Grecia*, Atti Taranto XXVIII (1988), Napoli 1990, pp. 305-328.
GRECO E., *Magna Grecia*, Roma-Bari 1980.
GRECO E., *Non morire in città: annotazioni sulla necropoli del "Tuffatore" di Poseidonia*, in "AION ArchStAnt", IV, 1982, pp. 51-56.
GRECO E.-LUPPINO S.-SCHNAPP A. (a cura di), *Laos I*, Taranto 1989.
GRECO E.-THEODORESCU D., *Poseidonia-Paestum II. L'agorà*, Roma 1983.
GRECO E.-THEODORESCU D., *Poseidonia-Paestum III*, Roma 1987.
GRECO E.-TORELLI M., *Storia dell'urbanistica.Il mondo greco*, Roma-Bari 1983.
GRECO G.-PONTRANDOLFO A. (a cura di), *Fratte. Un insediamento etrusco-campano*, Modena 1990.
GRECO G.-PONTRANDOLFO A. (a cura di), *Fratte - Un insediamento etrusco-campano*, Modena 1990.
GRUBEN G., *Die Tempel der Griechen*, München 19803.
GUARDUCCI M., *Epigrafia greca*, I-IV, Roma 1967-1978.
GUARDUCCI M., *Una nuova dea a Naxos in Sicilia e gli antichi legami fra la Naxos siceliota e l'omonima isola delle Cicladi*, in "Mélanges de l'École française de Rome.Antiquité", 97, 1985, pp. 7-34.
GUILLOU A., *Aspetti della civiltà bizantina in Italia*, Bari 1976.
GUILLOU A., *Culture et société en Italie byzantine (VIe-XIe siècle)*, Variorum Reprints, London 1978.
GUILLOU A., *L'Italia bizantina dalla caduta di Ravenna all'arrivo dei Normanni*, in *Storia d'Italia*, diretta da GALASSO G., III, Torino 1983, pp.7-128.
GUILLOU A., *La Puglia e Bisanzio*, in *La Puglia fra Bisanzio e l'Occidente*, Milano 1980, pp.5-36.
GULLINI G., *L'architettura*, in *Sikanie*, Milano 1985, pp. 415ss.
GULLINI G., *La cultura architettonica di Locri Epizefiri*, Taranto 1980.
GULLINI G., *Origini dell'architettura greca in Occidente*, in "ASAtene", LIX, 1983, pp. 97-126.
GULLINI G., *Urbanistica e architettura*, in *Megale Hellas*, Milano 1983, pp. 205ss.
GUTHRIE W.C., *The Greeks and their Gods*, London 1950 (trad. it. *I Greci e i loro dei*, Bologna 1987).
GUYOT C.-ROUGEMONT-ROUGEMONT G., *Marseille antique: les textes littéraires grecs et latins*, in BATS M.-BERTUCCHI G.-CONGÈS G.-TRÉZINY H (a cura di), *Marseille grecque et la Gaule*, Actes du Colloque international d'Histoire et d'Archéologie et du Ve Congrès archéologique de Gaule méridionale-Marseille, 18-23 novembre 1990 = "Études massaliètes", 3, Paris 1992.
GUZZO P.G., *I Brettii*, Milano 1989.
GUZZO P.G., MOSCATI S., SUSINI G. (a cura di), *Antiche genti d'Italia*, Roma 1994.
GUZZO P.G., *Un'hydria a Lecce*, in "Bollettino d'Arte", 69, 1976, pp. 60 ss.
HACKENS T., *La métrologie des monnaies étrusques les plus anciennes*, in *Contributi introduttivi allo studio della monetazione etrusca*, Atti del V Convegno del Centro internazionale di studi numismatici (Napoli 1975), 1976, pp. 221-270.
HENCKEN H., *Syracuse, Etruria and the North*, in "AJA", LXII, 1958, pp. 259-272.
HEUBECK A., *Schrift*, vol. III, cap. X della serie "Archaeologia Homerica", Göttingen 1977.
HIESEL G., *Späthelladische Hausarchitektur*, Mainz 1990.
HILL-RICHARDSON E., *The recurrent Geometric in the Sculpture of Central Italy and its bearing on the Problem of the Origin of the Etruscan*, in "Memoirs of the American Academy in Rome", XXVII, 1962, pp. 153ss.
HILLER S.-PANAGL O., *Die frühgriechischen Texte aus mykenischer Zeit*, Darmstadt 1986.
HOEPFNER W.-SCHWANDNER E.L., *Haus und Stadt im Klassischen Griechenland*, München 1986.
HOEPFNER W.-SCHWANDNER E.L., *Haus und Stadt im klassischen Griechenland*, Berlin 19932.
HÜTTL W., *Verfassungsgeschichte von Syrakus*, Prag 1929.
IANNELLI M.T.-RIZZI S., *Kaulonia: indagini ed ipotesi sull'impianto urbano di età ellenistica alla luce delle più recenti campagne di scavo*, in "RivStorCal", n.s. VI (1985), pp.281 ss.
Il dono delle Eliadi. Ambre e oreficerie dei principi etruschi (?) di Verucchio, Rimini 1994.
IMMERWAHR S.A., *Aegean Painting in the Bronze Age*, London 1990.
IMMERWAHR S.A., *The Athenian Agora*, vol. XIII: *The Neolithic and Bronze Ages*, Princeton 1971.
Inscriptiones Graecae XIV (*Inscriptiones Italiae et Siciliae*), Berlin 1890.
ISLER H.I., *Contributi per una storia del teatro antico: il teatro greco di Iatas e il teatro di Segesta*, "Quaderni ticinesi" 10, 1981, pp. 131 ss.
ISLER H.P., *Les nécropoles de Sélinonte*, in *Nécropoles et sociétés antiques* (Cahiers Centre J.Bérard XVIII), Napoli 1994, pp.165-168.
ISLER H.P., *Monte Iato. Guida archeologica*, Palermo 1991.
ISSERLIN B.S.J., *The Transfer of the Alphabet to the Greeks. The State of Documentation*, in *Phoinikeia Grammata* (Colloque de Liège, Novembre 1989), Namur 1991, pp. 283-291.
JACOB C., *Géographie et ethnographie en Grèce ancienne*, Paris 1991.
JACOBSTHAL P., *Early Celtic Art*, Oxford 19692.
JACOPI G., *Le miniature dei codici di Patmos*, in "Clara Rhodos", VI-VII, 3 (1932-33), pp. 580 ss., figg. 1-27, tavv. I-IV.
JANNI P., *La mappa e il periplo.Cartografia antica e spazio odologico*, Roma 1984.
JANTZEN U., *Bronzewerkstätten in Grossgriechenland und Sizilien*, Berlin 1937.
JEFFERY L., *The Local Scripts of Archaic Greece*, Oxford 1961 (rev. ed. by A.Johnston, 1990).
JEHASSE J.-L., *Aléria antique*, Lyon 19822.
JEHASSE L.-JEHASSE J., *La nécropole préromaine d'Aléria*, in "Gallia", XXV suppl., Paris 1973.
JOHANNOWSKY W., *Aggiornamento della I fase di Capua*, in "Annali I.U.O.ArchStAnt", n.s. 3, 1996, in corso di stampa.
JOHANNOWSKY W., *Materiali di età arcaica dalla Campania*, Napoli 1983.
JOHANNOWSKY W., *Relazione preliminare sugli scavi di Teano*, in "Bollettino d'Arte", 1963, pp. 131ss.
JOHANSEN F., *Una trozzella messapica alla Gliptoteca di Copenhagen*, in "Archeologia Classica", XXIV, 1972, pp. 256 ss.
JONES B., *Beginnings and Endings in Cyrenaican Cities*, in BARKER G.-LLOYD J.-REYNOLDS J., *Cyrenaica in Antiquity*, Oxford 1985, pp. 27-41.
JONES R.E.-VAGNETTI L., *Traders and Craftsmen in the Central Mediterranean.Archaeological Evidence and Archaeometric Research*, in GALE N.H. (ed.), *Bronze Age Trade in the Mediterranean*, Goteborg 1991, pp. 127-147.
JUCKER H., *Die Bronzehydria in Pesaro*, in "Antike Kunst", 7, 1964, pp. 3 ss.
KANE S., *Kore's Return. Statuary from the Sanctuary*, University of Pennsylvania Expedition, 34, 1992, pp. 72 ss.
KAPITÄN G., *Sul Lakkion, porto piccolo di Siracusa del periodo greco*, in "Archivio Storico Siracusano" XIII-XIV, 1967-68, pp.167-180.
KARLSSON L., *Some Notes on the Fortifications of Greek Sicily*, in "OpusculaRomana"XVII, 1989, pp.77-89.
KASCHNITZ G. v.-WEINBERG, *Ausgewählte Schriften*, I-III, Berlin 1965.
KASCHNITZ G. v.-WEINBERG, *Italien mit Sardinien und Malta*, in "Handbuch der Archäologie" II, I, München 1950, pp. 311 ss.
KERÉNYI K., *Die Mythologie der Griechen*, Zürich 1951 (trad. it. *Gli dei e gli eroi della Grecia*, Milano 1963).
KOCH H., *Dachterrakotten aus Kampanien*, Berlin 1912.
"Kokalos", 1955 ss.
"Kokalos" XXX-XXXI, 1984-85 (1987), XXXIV-XXXV, 1988-89 (1992) e XXXVIII, 1992(1995).
KOLDEWEY R.-PUCHSTEIN O., *Die griechischen Tempel in Unteritalien und Sizilien*, Berlin 1899.
KOZLOSKAIA N., *Les problèmes de la colonisation grecque de la Méditerranée occidentale: l'activité eubéo-ionienne in Sicile*, in *Le Pont Euxin vu par les Grecs* (Symposium de Vani, Colchide 1987), Paris 1990, pp.37-50.
KRAAY C., *Archaic and Classical Greek Coins*, London 1976.
KRAAY C., *Greek Coins and History*, London 1969.
KRAUSS F., *Die Tempel von Paestum. 1. Der Athenatempel*, Berlin 1959.
KRAUTHEIMER R., *Early Christian and Byzantine Architecture*, Hardmonds 1981 (trad. it. *Architettura paleocristiana e bizantina*, Torino 1986).
KRAUTHEIMER R., *Roma. Profilo di una città, 312-1308*.
KRISCHEN F., *Die Stadtmauern von Pompeji und griechische Festungsbaukunst in Unteritalien und Sizilien*, in *Hellenistische Kunst in*

Pompeji VII, Berlin 1941.
KWAPONG A.A., *Citizenship and Democracy in Fourth-century Cyrene*, in AA.VV., *Africa in Classical Antiquity.Nine Studies*, Ibada 1969, pp. 101-109.
L'Italie méridionale et les premières expériences de la peinture hellénistique, Actes Table Ronde Rome 28 Février 1994, École Française de Rome (in corso di stampa).
LA ROSA V., *Bronzetti indigeni della Sicilia*, in "Cronache di Archeologia e di Storia dell'Arte - Università di Catania", 7, 1968, pp. 7 ss.
LA ROSA V., *Influenze di tipo egeo e paleogreco in Sicilia* (Atti VIII Congresso Internazionale Studi Sicilia Antica, Palermo, aprile 1993), in "Kokalos", XXXIX-XL, 1993-94, I, 1, pp. 9-47.
LA ROSA V., *L'ospitalità dei re di Sicilia: il sicano Kokalos e il siculo Hyblon*, in "Siculorum Gymnasium", XLV, 1992, pp. 103-106.
LA ROSA V., *Le popolazioni della Sicilia: Sicani, Siculi, Elimi*, in *Italia omnium terrarum parens*, Collana "Antica Madre", XII, Milano 1989, pp. 3-110.
La monetazione di Neapolis nella Campania antica, Atti del VII Convegno del Centro Internazionale di Studi Numismatici (Napoli 20-24aprile 1980), Napoli 1986.
La scuola eleatica. La parola del passato, Rivista di Studi Antichi, XLIII, Napoli 1988.
LAFORGIA E., *Nuove osservazioni sul tempio di Marica*, in "A.I.O.N.", XIV, 1992, pp. 69 ss.
LAMBOGLIA N., *La necropoli ligure di Chiavari*, in "Rivista di Studi Liguri", XXVI, 1960, pp. 91 ss.; XXX, 1964, pp. 31 ss.; XXXII, 1966, pp. 251 ss.; XXXVIII, 1972, pp. 103ss.
LANGLOTZ E., *Die Kunst der Westgriechen in Sizilien und Unteritalien*, München 1963.
LANGLOTZ E.-HIRMER M., *L'arte della Magna Grecia* (trad.it.), Roma 1968.
LARONDE A., *Cyrène et la Libye hellénistique*, Paris 1987.
LARONDE A., *Cyrène et la Libye hellénistique.Libykai Historiai de l'époque républicaine au principat d'Auguste*, Paris 1987, pp. 85-128, 249-256, 424-425.
LARONDE A., *Cyrène et la Libye hellénistique.Lybikai historiai*, Paris 1987.
LARONDE A., *Cyrène sous les derniers Battiades*, in GENTILI B. (a cura di), *Cirene.Storia, Mito, Letteratura*, Atti del Convegno S.I.S.A.C. (Urbino, 3 luglio 1988), Urbino 1990, pp. 35-50.
LARSEN J.A.O., *Greek Federal States*, Oxford 1968.
LAUTER H., *Die hellenistischen Theater der Samniten und Latiner in ihrer Beziehung zum Theater der Griechen*, in *Hellenismus in Mittelitalien*, Kolloquium Göttingen 1976, pp. 413ss.
LAUTER H., *Die Architektur des Hellenismus*, Darmstadt 1986.
LAUTER H., *Ein monumentaler Säulenaltar des 5. Jhs. v. Chr. in Selinunt*, "RM" 83, 1976, pp. 233ss.
LAWRENCE A.W., *Greek Aims in Fortification*, Oxford 1979.
LAWRENCE A.W., *Greek Architecture, revised with additions by R.A. Tomlinson*, Harmondsworth 1983.
LEJEUNE M.-POUILLOUX J.-SOLIER Y., *Etrusque et ionien archaïques sur un plomb de Pech Maho*, in "RAN", XXI, 1988, pp. 19ss.
LENTINI M.C.-GARRAFFO S., *Il tesoretto di Naxos (1985) dall'isolato urbano C4, casa 1-2* (Istituto Italiano di Numismatica, Studi e materiali 4), Roma 1995, ivi alle pp.3 ss. bibl. più recente.
LEPORE E., *Colonie greche dell'Occidente antico*, Napoli 1989.
LEPORE E., *Colonie greche dell'Occidente antico*, Roma 1989.
LEPORE E., *La città greca*, in ROSSI P. (a cura di), *Modelli di città*, Torino 1987, pp. 87-108.
LEPORE E., *Napoli greco-romana - La vita politica e sociale*, in *Storia di Napoli*, I, Napoli 1967.
LEPORE E., *Per una fenomenologia storica del rapporto città-territorio in Magna Grecia*, in Atti del VII Convegno Internazionale di Studi sulla Magna Grecia (Taranto 1967), Napoli 1968, pp. 29-66.
LEPORE E., *Problemi dell'organizzazione della chora coloniale*, in FINLEY M.I. (a cura di), *Problèmes de la terre en Grèce ancienne*, Paris-La Haye 1973, pp. 15-47.
LEPORE E., *Strutture della colonizzazione focea in Occidente*, in "La Parola del Passato", 25, 1970, pp.44-48, ristampa in *Colonie greche dell'Occidente antico*, Roma 1989, pp.124-126.
LESCHHORN W., *"Gründer der Stadt".Studien zu einem politisch-religiosen Phänomen der griechischen Geschichte*, Stuttgart 1984.
LESZL W., *Pitagorici ed Eleati*, in *Magna Grecia*, a cura di PUGLIESE CARRATELLI G., III, Milano 1988, pp.197-226.
Lettura ed interpretazione della produzione pittorica dal IV sec. a.C. all'Ellenismo, Incontro di Studio ad Acquasparta, 8-10 aprile 1983, in "DArch", 1983.2 e 1984.1, ripubblicato con il titolo *Ricerche di Pittura Ellenistica*, in "Quaderni dei Dialoghi di Archeologia", I, Roma 1985.
LEVI M.A., *La città antica*, Roma 1981.
LLINARES GARCÍA M., *Mitología e iniciaciones. El problema de los Argonautas*, in "Gerie iniciaciones. El probl LLOYD J., *Some Aspects of Urban Development at Euesperides/Berenice*, in BARKER G.-LLOYD J.-REYNOLDS J., *Cyrenaica in Antiquity*, Oxford 1985, pp. 49-66.
LLOYD-JONES H.-PARSONS P., *Supplementum Hellenisticum*, Berlin-New York 1983.
LO PORTO F.G., in "Xenia" XVI, 1988, p. 15.
LO SCHIAVO F.-MACNAMARA E.-VAGNETTI L., *Late Cypriot imports to Italy and their influence on local Bronzework*, in "Papers of the British School of Rome", 53, 1985, pp. 1-70.
LO SCHIAVO F.-MACNAMARA E.-VAGNETTI L., *Late Cypriot imports to Italy and their influence on local bronzework*, in "Papers of the British School at Rome" 53, 1985, pp. 1-71.
LOMBARDO M., *Lo psephisme di Lumbardo: note critiche e questioni esegetiche*, in "Hesperìa", 3, Roma 1993, pp.161-188.
LURAGHI N., *Fonti e tradizioni dell'Archaiología siciliana*, in "Hesperìa", 2, Roma 1992, pp.41-62.
LURAGHI N., *Tirannidi arcaiche in Sicilia e Magna Grecia*, Firenze 1994.
MADDOLI G. (a cura di), *La civiltà micenea: guida storica e critica*, Roma-Bari 1992².
MADDOLI G., *Il VI e V secolo a.C.*, in GABBA E.-VALLET G. (a cura di), *La Sicilia antica* (vol.II della *Storia della Sicilia*), Napoli 1980, pp. 1-102.
MADDOLI G., *La civiltà micenea, guida storica e critica*, Roma 1977.
MADDOLI G., *Religione e culti*, in *Un secolo di ricerche in Magna Grecia*, Atti del XXVIII Convegno di Studi sulla Magna Grecia (1988), Taranto 1989, pp.277-303.
MADDOLI G.-CAMASSA G., *I culti nell'età delle colonie greche*, in *Storia del Mezzogiorno*, I,1, Napoli 1991, pp. 395-495.
Magna Grecia e mondo miceneo, Atti del XXII Convegno di Studi sulla Magna Grecia (Taranto, ottobre 1982), Taranto 1983.
MAIURI A., *Una metopa del tempio del Foro Triangolare a Pompei*, in "La Parola del Passato", X, 1955, pp. 50 ss.
MALKIN I., *Religion and Colonization in Ancient Greece*, Leiden 1987.
MALKIN I., *Religion and Colonization in Ancient Greece*, Leiden-New York 1987.
MALLWITZ A., *Kritisches zur Architektur Griechenlands im 8. und 7. Jahrhundert*, "AA" 1981, pp. 599ss.
MANGANARO G., in "A.S.N.P.", s. III, XX, 1990, p.427.
MANGANARO G., *Istituzioni pubbliche e culti religiosi*, in BRACCESI L.-DE MIRO E. (a cura di), *Agrigento e la Sicilia greca*, Atti della Settimana di Studio (Agrigento, 2-8 maggio 1988), Roma 1992, pp. 207-218.
MANGANARO G., *La provincia romana*, in GABBA E.-VALLET G. (a cura di), *La Sicilia antica* (vol.II della *Storia della Sicilia*), Napoli 1980, pp.411-462.
MANGANARO G., *Per una storia della chora katanaia*, in *Stuttgarter Kolloquium zur Historischen Geographie des Altertums*, 4, 1990, pp.127-174.
MANGO C., *La culture grecque et l'Occident au VIIIe siècle*, in XX Settimana CISAM 1973, pp. 683-721.
MANGO C., *Lo stile cosiddetto monastico della pittura bizantina*, in *Habitat, strutture, territorio*, Atti del III Convegno int. di studi sulla civiltà rupestre nel Mezzogiorno d'Italia (Taranto-Grottaglie 1973), Galatina 1978, pp. 45-62.
MARAZZI M.-TUSA S.-VAGNETTI L. (a cura di), *Traffici micenei nel Mediterraneo.Problemi storici e documentazione archeologica*, Atti del Convegno tenuto a Palermo (maggio e dicembre 1984), Taranto 1986.
MARCHESE R.J. (ed.), *Aspects of Graeco-Roman Urbanism.Essay on the Classical City*, BAR 188, Oxford 1983.
MARCONI P., *La cultura orientalizzante nel Piceno*, in "Monumenti Antichi Lincei", XXXV, 1935, cc. 274ss.
MARENGO S.M., *Lessico delle iscrizioni greche della Cirenaica*, Roma 1991.
MARINATOS N., *Minoan Religion. Ritual. Image and Symbol*, Columbia (South Carolina) 1993.
MARTIN DE LA CRUZ J.C. ET AL., *Die erste mykenische Keramik von der iberischen Halbinsel*, in "Prähistorische Zeitschrift", 65, 1990, pp. 49-52.

MARTIN DE LA CRUZ J.C. ET AL., *L'Età del Bronzo nel sud della penisola iberica.La sequenza locale e gli influssi esterni*, in "Seminari 1990 dell'Istituto per gli Studi micenei ed egeo-anatolici", Roma 1991, pp. 85-103.

MARTIN R., *L'architecture de Tarente*, in "ACSISMGr." X (1979), pp. 311-341.

MARTIN R., *L'espace civique, religieux et profane dans les cités grecques de l'archaïsme à l'époque hellénistique*, in *Architecture et Société*, Actes du Coll. 1980, École Française de Rome 1983, pp. 9-41.

MARTIN R., *L'Urbanisme dans la Grèce antique*, Paris 1974².

MARTIN R., *Manuel d'architecture grecque I*, Paris 1961.

MARTIN R., *Rapports entre les structures urbaines et les modes de division et d'exploitation du territoire*, in FINLEY M.I. (a cura di), *Problèmes de la terre en Grèce ancienne*, Paris-La Haye 1973, pp. 97-112.

MARTIN R.-VALLET G., *L'architettura domestica*, in *Storia della Sicilia*, I, Napoli 1979, pp. 321 ss.

MARTINI W., *Vom Herdhaus zum Peripteros*, "JdI" 101, 1986, pp. 23 ss.

MARUGGI G., in *L'edilizia domestica in Magna Grecia*, Atti del Seminario organizzato dall'Università di Lecce (giugno 1992), 1996.

MATTHIAE G., *Pittura romana del Medioevo*, 2 voll., Roma 1987-88 (1ª ed. 1965).

MAZZARINO S., *Introduzione alle guerre puniche*, Catania 1947, pp. 8-20.

MAZZEI M., *Arpi. L'ipogeo della Medusa e la necropoli*, Foggia 1995.

MEIGGS R., *The Athenian Empire*, Oxford 1972.

MEILLIER C., *Callimaque et son temps*, Lille 1979.

MELE A., *Aristodemo, Cuma e il Lazio*, in *Etruria e Lazio Arcaico*, Roma 1987, pp. 155-178.

MELE A., *Il commercio greco arcaico. Prexis ed emporie*, Napoli 1979.

MELE A., *Il pitagorismo e le popolazioni anelleniche d'Italia*, in "Annali del seminario di studi del mondo classico. Archeologia e storia antica" (= AION ArchStAnt), III, 1981, pp. 61 ss.

MELLINK M.J., *Mural Painting in Lycian Tombs*, Atti del X Congresso Internazionale di Archeologia Classica, Ankara 1978, pp. 805-809.

MELLINK M.J., *Notes on Anatolian Wall Painting*, in "Mélanges Mansel", 1, 1974, pp. 537-547.

MERTENS D., *Der alte Heratempel in Paestum und die archaische Baukunst in Unteritalien*, Mainz 1993.

MERTENS D., *Der ionische Tempel in Metapont*, "RM" 86, 1979, pp. 103ss.

MERTENS D., *Der Tempel von Segesta und die dorische Tempelbaukunst des griechischen Westens in klassischer Zeit*, Mainz 1984.

MERTENS D., *Die Entstehung des Steintempels in Sizilien*, in "Diskussionen zur archäologischen Bauforschung" 6 (1995).

MERTENS D., *Die Mauern von Selinunt*, in "Römische Mitteilungen", 96, 1989, pp.87-154.

MERTENS D., *L'architettura*, in AA.VV., *Lo stile severo in Sicilia*, Palermo 1990, pp.75 ss.

MERTENS D., *L'architettura*, in *Lo Stile Severo in Sicilia* (1990), pp. 75 ss.

MERTENS D., *Metapont.Ein neuer Plan des Stadtzentrums*, in "AA" 1985, pp. 645-671.

MERTENS D., *Metaponto.Il teatro-ekklesiasterion*, in "Bd'A" 16 (1982), pp. 1-60.

MERTENS D., *Nota sull'edilizia selinuntina del V sec. a.C.*, in *Studi sulla Sicilia occidentale in onore di V.Tusa*, Padova 1993, pp.131-138.

MERTENS D., *Parallellismi strutturali nell'architettura della Magna Grecia e dell'Italia centrale in età arcaica*, in *Scritti in onore di D. Adamesteanu*, Matera 1980, pp. 37 ss.

MERTENS D., *Per l'urbanistica e l'architettura della Magna Grecia*, in *Megale Hellas*, Atti Taranto XXI (1981), Napoli 1982, pp. 97-141.

MERTENS D., *Per l'urbanistica e l'architettura della Magna Grecia*, in *Megale Hellas, nome e immagine*, Atti 21 ConvMGrecia (Taranto 1981) 1982, pp. 97 ss.

MERTENS D., *Zur archaischen Architektur der archaischen Kolonien in Unteritalien*, in "Neue Forschungen in griechischen Heiligtümern", Tübingen 1976, pp. 167 ss.

MERTENS D.-DE SIENA A., *Metaponto, il teatro-ekklesiasterion*, "BdA" n.s. 16, 1983, pp. 1ss.

MERTENS M.-HORN, *Die Löwenkopf-wasserplier des Griechischen Westens im 6. und 5.Jahrhundert v.Chr.*, Mainz 1988.

MEYER E., *Einführung in die antike Staatskunde*5, Darmstadt 1990.

MILLER S.G., *The Tomb of Lyson and Kallikles: A Painted Macedonian Tomb*, Mainz 1993.

MINGAZZINI P., *Il santuario della dea Marica alle foci del Garigliano*, in "Monumenti Antichi Lincei", XXXVII, 1938, cc. 693ss.

MIRANDA E. (a cura di), *Iscrizioni greche d'Italia.Napoli*, Roma, I, 1990, pp. 47-74, e II, 1995, pp. 42-43.

MITENS K., *Teatri greci e teatri ispirati all'architettura greca in Sicilia e nell'Italia meridionale c. 350-50 a.C.*, Roma 1988.

MOGGI M., *I sinecismi interstatali greci*, I, Pisa 1976.

MOGGI M., *Proprietà della terra e cambiamenti costituzionali a Turi*, in AA.Vv., *L'incidenza dell'antico. Studi in memoria di Ettore Lepore*, Atti del Convegno Internazionale (Anacapri 24-28 marzo 1991), Napoli, I, a cura di STORCHI MARINO A., 1995, pp. 391-399.

MONTELIUS O., *La Civilisation Primitive en Italie depuis l'introduction des métaux*, I-IV, Stockholm 1895-1910.

MOREL J.-P., *Marseille et la colonisation phocéenne*, in *Marseille grecque et la Gaule*, "Études Massaliètes", 3, 1992, pp. 15-25.

MORENO P., *La conquista della spazialità pittorica*, in "Storia e civiltà dei Greci", 4, Milano 1979, pp. 631-676.

MORENO P., *La pittura in Macedonia*, in "Storia e civiltà dei Greci", 6, Milano 1979, pp. 703-721.

MORENO P., *La pittura tra classicità ed ellenismo*, in "Storia e civiltà dei Greci", 6, Milano 1979, pp. 458-520.

MORENO P., *Pittura greca da Polignoto ad Apelle*, Milano 1987.

MORENO P., *Pittura greca da Polignoto ad Apelle*, Milano 1987.

MORETTI G., *Il guerriero italico e la necropoli di Capestrano*, in "Bullettino Paletnologia Italiana", n.s. 1936-1937, pp. 94 ss.

MORETTI L., *Ricerche sulle leghe greche*, Roma 1962.

MORRISON J.S.-WILLIAMS R.T., *Greek Oared Ships 900-322 B.C.*, Cambridge 1968.

MOSCATI S., *Fenici e Greci in Sardegna*, "RANL", 1985, pp. 265-271.

MOSSÉ C., *Les institutions grecques à l'époque classique*, Paris 1967 (trad. it.Bologna 1971).

MOUNTJOY P.A., *Mycenaean Pottery.An Introduction*, Oxford 1993.

MOUNTJOY P.A., *Mycenaean Pottery: An Introduction*, Oxford 1993.

MUSTI D., *L'Urbanesimo e la situazione delle campagne nella Grecia classica*, in *Storia e civiltà dei Greci* (a cura di BIANCHI BANDINELLI R.), VI, Milano 1979, pp. 523-568.

MUSTI D., *Linee di sviluppo istituzionale e territoriale tra Miceneo e Alto Arcaismo*, in AA.Vv., *La transizione dal Miceneo all'Alto Arcaismo*, Roma 1991, pp. 15-33.

NAFISSI M., *La nascita del kosmos, studi sulla storia e la società di Sparta*, Napoli 1991.

NAPOLI M., *La tomba del Tuffatore*, Bari 1970.

NAPOLI M., *La tomba del Tuffatore*, Bari 1970.

NAPOLI M., *La tomba del Tuffatore*, Bari 1970.

NAPOLI M., *Testa di divinità sannitica da Triflisco*, in "La Parola del Passato", XI, 1956, pp. 386 ss.

NAVA M.L., *Stele Daunie*, I, Roma 1980.

NAVILLE L., *Les monnaies d'or de la Cyrénaïque, 450-250 a.C.*, Genève 1951.

NEUTSCH B., *Tonball mit Totenkultszenen aus der italischen Nekropole von Sala Consilina*, in "Apollo", 1, 1961, pp. 53 ss.

NICOSIA F., *La Sardegna nel mondo classico*, in AA.Vv., *Ichnussa*, Milano 1981, pp. 421-476.

NIEMEYER H.G., *Die Phönizier und die Mittelmeerwelt im Zeitalter Homers*, in "Jahrbuch des Römisch-Germanischen Zentralmuseums Mainz" 31, 1984, pp. 3-94.

NILSSON M.P., *Geschichte der Griechischen Religion*, München I, 1967³; II, 1961².

NORDHAGEN P.J., *Italo-byzantine Wall Painting*, in *Bisanzio, Roma e l'Italia nell'Alto Medioevo*, XXXIV Settimana CISAM, Spoleto 1988, pp. 593-619.

NORDHAGEN P.J., *The Frescoes of John VII in S. Maria Antiqua in Rome*, in "Acta ad archaeologiam et artium historiam pertinentia", 3, 1968, p. 110.

ONORATO G.O., *La ricerca archeologica in Irpinia*, Avellino 1960.

ORLANDINI P., *Arte indigena e colonizzazione greca in Sicilia*, in "Kokalos", X-XI, 1964-1965, pp. 539 ss.

ORLANDINI P., *Due nuovi vasi figurati di stile orientalizzante dagli scavi dell'Incoronata di Metaponto*, in "Bollettino d'Arte", 73, 1988, pp. 1ss.

ORLANDINI P., *Le arti figurative*, in *Megale Hellas*, a cura di PUGLIESE CARRATELLI G., Milano 1983, pp. 3005-3554.

ORSI P., in "Notizie Scavi" (e specie "Not. Sc." 1891, pp.391 ss.; 1909, pp.338-340; 1925, pp.177, 309, 313 ss., 319 ss.).

OSANNA M., *Chorai coloniali da Taranto a Locri*, Roma 1992.

OSTBY R., *Osservazioni sui templi di Locri Epizefirii*, "ActaAArtHist", 6, 187, pp. 1ss.
PACE B., *Arte e civiltà della Sicilia antica*, I-IV, Città di Castello 1935-1949 (2ª ed. 1vol., 1958).
PACE V., *La pittura bizantina nell'Italia meridionale*, in *I Bizantini in Italia*, Milano 1982, pp. 497-612.
PACE V., *La pittura delle origini in Puglia*, in *La Puglia fra Bisanzio e l'Occidente*, Milano 1980, pp. 317-400.
PALLOTTINO M., *La Sicilia tra l'Africa e l'Etruria: problemi storici e culturali*, in "Kokalos", XVIII-XIX, 1972-73, pp. 48-70.
PALLOTTINO M., *Les relations entre les Étrusques et Carthage du VIIe au IIIe siècle avant J.-C. Nouvelles données et essai de périodisation*, in "CahTun", XI, 1963, pp. 22-28.
PANCUCCI D.-NARO M.C., *Monte Bubbonia. Campagne di scavo 1905, 1906, 1955*, Roma 1992.
PANDOLFINI M.-PROSDOCIMI A.L., *Alfabetari e insegnamento della scrittura in Etruria e nell'Italia antica*, Firenze 1990.
PAPI R., *Dischi - corazze abruzzesi a decorazione geometrica nei musei italiani*, Roma 1990.
PARIBENI E., *Catalogo delle sculture di Cirene. Statue e rilievi di carattere religioso*, Roma 1959.
PARIBENI E., *Volti, teste calve e parrucche*, in Atti e Memorie della Società Magna Grecia, n.s.2, 1958, pp. 63-66.
PARISE BADONI F., *Capua preromana. Ceramica campana a figure nere*, Firenze 1968.
PARISE BADONI F.-RUGGERI GIOVE M., *Alfedena. La necropoli di Campo Consolino*, Chieti 1980.
PARISE N., *Le emissioni monetarie di Magna Grecia tra VI e V secolo a.C.*, in Storia della Calabria Antica, Roma 1987, pp. 307-321.
PARISE N., *Nascita della moneta e forme arcaiche dello scambio*, Roma 1992.
PARISI C.-PRESICCE, *La funzione delle aree sacre nell'organizzazione urbanistica delle colonie greche alla luce delle scoperte di un nuovo santuario periferico di Selinunte*, in "Archeologia classica", XXXVI, 1984 (1987), pp.19-132.
PARKER A.J., *Il relitto romano delle colonne a Camarina*, in "Sicilia archeologica",30, 1976, pp.25 ss.
PASQUALI G., "*De fabulis Cyrenaeis*", *Quaestiones Callimacheae*, Gottingae 1913, in *Scritti filologici*, I, Firenze 1986, pp. 154-301.
PEDLEY J.G., *The archaic Favissa at Cyrene*, in "American Journal of Archaeology", 75, 1971, pp. 39-46.
PELAGATTI P., *Sacelli e nuovi materiali architettonici a Naxos, Monte San Mauro e Camarina*, "Cron Catania", XVI, 1977, pp. 43-65.
PELAGATTI P., *Sul parco archeologico di Camarina*, in "BArte", 61, 1976, pp. 122 ss.
PENSABENE P., *Cippi funerari di Taranto*, in "Römische Mitteilungen", 82, 1975, pp. 263ss.
PENSANDO F., *La casa dei Greci*, Milano 1981.
PERASSI C., *Correnti artistiche nella monetazione romana repubblicana precedente l'introduzione del denario*, in "Athenaeum", n.s. LXVI, 1988, pp. 345ss.
PERONI R.-COLONNA G., *Italica Arte*, in "Enciclopedia dell'Arte Antica Classica e Orientale", IV, Roma 1961, pp. 251ss.
PERTUSI A., *Aspetti organizzativi e culturali dell'ambiente monacale greco dell'Italia meridionale*, in *L'eremitismo in Occidente nei secoli XI e XII*, in Atti della Settimana di studio (Mendola, settembre 1962), Milano 1965, pp. 383-417.
PERTUSI A., *Bisanzio e l'irradiazione della sua civiltà in Occidente nell'Alto Medioevo*, in XI Settimana CISAM (1962), Spoleto 1964, pp. 75-133.
PERTUSI A., *Monaci e Monasteri della Calabria bizantina*, in Calabria bizantina, Reggio Calabria 1974, pp. 17-46.
PETSAS PH., *O Taphos tôn Lefkadiôn*, Atene 1966.
PFEIFFER R., *Callimachus*, Oxford 1949-53.
PICARDI G., *La sculpture grecque I*, Paris 1994, pp. 384 ss.
PISANI V., *Manuale storico della lingua greca*, Brescia 1973.
Pittura Etrusca al Museo di Villa Giulia, Roma, Museo Nazionale Etrusco di Villa Giulia, 7 giugno-31 dicembre 1989, Roma 1989.
POLACCO L.-ANTI C., *Il teatro antico di Siracusa* (1981).
POMEY P., *Mediterranean Sewn Boats in Antiquity*, in MCGRAIL S.-KENTLEY E., *Sewn Plank Boats*, B.A.R., Oxford 1985, pp. 35-47.
POMEY P.-HESNARD A., *Les épaves romaines et grecques*, in *Le temps des découvertes. Marseille de Protis à la reine Jeanne*, Musée d'Histoire de Marseille, 1993, pp. 59-62.
POMEY P.-LONG L., *Les premiers échanges maritimes du midi de la Gaule du VI au VII av. J.-C. à travers les épaves*, in *Marseille grecque et la Gaule*, "Études Massaliètes", 3, 1992, pp. 189-198.
PONTRANDOLFO A., *I Lucani*, Milano 1982.
PONTRANDOLFO A., *La pittura funeraria*, in *Magna Grecia IV, Arte e artigianato* (a cura di PUGLIESE CARRATELLI G.), Milano 1990, pp. 351-390.
PONTRANDOLFO A.-ROUVERET A., *Le tombe dipinte di Paestum*, Modena 1992.
PONTRANDOLFO A.-ROUVERET A., *Le tombe dipinte di Paestum*, Modena 1992.
PONTRANDOLFO A.-ROUVERET A., *Le tombe dipinte di Paestum*, Modena 1992.
PONTRANDOLFO A.-VECCHIO G., *Gli ipogei funerari*, in *Napoli antica* (Catalogo della mostra), Napoli 1985, pp. 283-293.
POWELL J.U., *Collectanea Alexandrina*, Oxford 1925.
PROCELLI E.-ALBANESE R.M., *Ramacca (Catania). Saggi di scavo nelle contrade Castellito e Montagna negli anni 1978, 1981 e 1982*, in "Not. Scavi", 1988-89, I supplemento, Roma 1992.
PUGLIESE CARRATELLI G. (a cura di), *Magna Grecia*, IV, *Arte e artigianato*, Milano 1990.
PUGLIESE CARRATELLI G. (a cura di), *Magna Grecia. Vita religiosa e cultura letteraria, filosofia e scienza*, Milano 1988.
PUGLIESE CARRATELLI G. (a cura di), *Sikanie. Storia e civiltà della Sicilia greca*, Milano 1985.
PUGLIESE CARRATELLI G., *Appunti per la storia dei culti cirenaici*, "Maia", 16, 1964, pp. 99-111.
PUGLIESE CARRATELLI G., *Cadmo: prima e dopo*, in "La Parola del Passato", 1976, pp. 5-15.
PUGLIESE CARRATELLI G., *Dal regno miceneo alla polis*, in *Scritti sul mondo antico*, Napoli 1976, pp. 135-158.
PUGLIESE CARRATELLI G., *I santuari extramurani*, in AA.VV., *Magna Grecia*, III (a cura di PUGLIESE CARRATELLI G.), Milano 1989, pp. 149-158.
PUGLIESE CARRATELLI G., *I santuari panellenici e le "apoikiai" in Occidente*, in "La Parola del Passato", XLVII, 1992, pp.401-410.
PUGLIESE CARRATELLI G., *La democrazia nel mondo greco*, in *Scritti sul mondo antico*, Napoli 1976, pp. 395-411.
PUGLIESE CARRATELLI G., *La scuola medica di Parmenide a Velia*, in *Tra Cadmo e Orfeo*, Bologna 1990, pp. 269-280.
PUGLIESE CARRATELLI G., *La theà di Parmenide*, in "La Parola del Passato", XLIII, 1988, pp.337-346.
PUGLIESE CARRATELLI G., *Le lamine d'oro "orfiche"*, Milano 1993.
PUGLIESE CARRATELLI G., *Le lamine d'oro "orfiche"*, Milano 1993.
PUGLIESE CARRATELLI G., *Primordi della legislazione scritta*, in PUGLIESE CARRATELLI G. (a cura di), *Magna Grecia.Lo sviluppo politico, sociale ed economico*, Milano 1987.
PUGLIESE CARRATELLI G., *Tra Cadmo e Orfeo.Contributi alla storia civile e religiosa dei Greci d'Occidente*, Bologna 1990, pp.421-430.
PUGLIESE CARRATELLI G., *Tra Cadmo e Orfeo.Contributi alla storia civile e religiosa della Magna Grecia*, Bologna 1990.
PUGLIESE CARRATELLI G., Κυρηναικά, in AA.Vv., *Cirene e i Libyi* = "Quaderni di Archeologia della Libia", 12, 1987, pp. 25-28.
PUGLIESE CARRATELLI G.-ADAMESTEANU D.-FORTI L.-FRAJESE A.-GIGANTE M.-GULLINI G.-ORLANDINI P.-ROLLEY C.-STAZIO A.-SZABÒ A.-VAGNETTI L., *Megale Hellas, Storia e civiltà della Magna Grecia*, Milano 1983.
PUGLIESE CARRATELLI G.-AMPOLO C.-BRIQUEL D.-CASSOLA GUIDA P.-D'AGOSTINO B.-DE SIMONE C.- LA REGINA A.-LA ROSA V.-LEJEUNE M.-LOMBARDO M.-NEGRONI CATACCHIO N.-PARISE N.F.-PERONI R.-PROSDOCIMI A.L., *Italia, omnium terrarum parens. La civiltà degli Enotri, Choni, Ausoni, Sanniti, Lucani, Brettii, Sicani, Siculi, Elimi*, Milano 1989.
PUGLIESE CARRATELLI G.-BONACASA N.-DE MIRO E.-DI VITA A.-GARRAFFO S.-GIUDICE F.-GULLINI G.-JOLY E.-MONACO G.-RIZZA G.-STAZIO A.-SZABÒ A.-TUSA V.-VOZA G., *Sikanie, Storia e civiltà della Sicilia greca*, Milano 1985.
PUGLIESE CARRATELLI G.-CHIECO BIANCHI A.M.-COLONNA G.-D'AGOSTINO B.-D'ANDRIA F.-DE JULIIS E.M.-DE MARINIS R.-KRUTA V.-LANDOLFI M.-RONCALLI F. , *Italia, omnium terrarum alumna. La civiltà dei Veneti, Reti, Liguri, Celti, Piceni, Umbri, Latini, Campani, Iapigi*, Milano 1988.
RACCUIA C., *La fondazione di Gela*, in "Kokalos", XXXVIII, 1992, pp.273-302.
RAININI I., *Santuario di Mefite in Valle d'Ansanto*, Roma 1986.
RALLO A., *Nuovi aspetti dell'urbanistica selinuntina*, in "Annuario Atene", LXII, 1984 (1988), pp.81-91.
REINACH A., *Textes grecs et latins relatifs à l'histoire de la peinture*

ancienne, in "Recueil Milliet", 1921, Paris 1985.
RIDGWAY B.S., *The Archaic Style in Greek Sculpture*, Princeton 1977² (Chicago 1933).
RIDGWAY D., *L'alba della Magna Grecia*, Milano 1984.
RIDGWAY D., *L'alba della Magna Grecia*, Milano 1984.
RIDGWAY D., *L'alba della Magna Grecia*, Milano 1984.
RIDGWAY D., *L'alba della Magna Grecia*2, Milano 1992.
RIZZA G., *Motivi unitari nell'arte sicula*, in "Cronache di Archeologia e di Storia dell'Arte - Università di Catania", 4, 1965, pp. 7 ss.
RIZZA G.-DE MIRO E., in *Sikanie, Storia e civiltà della Sicilia greca*, Milano 1985.
ROBERTSON C.M., *A History of Greek Art*, Cambridge 1975.
ROBERTSON M., *The Art of vase-painting in Classical Athens*, Cambridge 1994.
RODENWALDT G., *Römische Reliefs. Vorstufen zur Spätantike*, in "Jahrbuch", LV, 1940, pp. 12 ss.
ROEHL H., *Imagines inscriptionum Graecarum antiquissimarum*, Berlin 1907.
ROEHL H., *Inscriptiones Graecae antiquissimae*, Berlin 1882.
ROMEI I., *Sacelli arcaici senza peristasi nella Sicilia greca*, "Xenia" 77, Roma 1989, pp. 5 ss.
ROSENBAUM E., *Cyrenaican Portrait Sculpture*, London 1960.
ROSTOVZEV M., *Ein spätetruskischer Meierhof*, in "Antike Plastik - Walter Amelung zum sechzigsten Geburtstag", Berlin-Leipzig 1928, p.213 (cfr. anche: *Storia economica e sociale dell'impero romano*, Firenze 1933, tav.III, 5, XII, 2).
ROUGÉ J., *La marine dans l'Antiquité*, Paris 1975.
ROUSSEL D., *Tribu et cité*, Paris 1976.
ROUVERET A., *Histoire et imaginaire de la peinture ancienne (V s. av. J.C.-I s. ap. J.C.)*, BEFAR 274, Roma 1989.
ROUVERET A., *Histoire et imaginaire de la peinture ancienne*, B.E.F.A.R. 274, École Française de Rome, Roma 1989.
SAKELLARIOU M.B., *The polis-state.Definition and origin*, Athens 1989.
SALIS A. v., *Neue Darstellungen griechischer Sagen, II, Picenum*, in "Sitzungsberichte der Heidelberger Akademie der Wissenschaften, Philosophisch-historische Klasse", 1936-1939, 1.
Sammlung griechischer Dialektinschriften, ed. H. Collitz, Göttingen 1884.
SANMARTÍ-GREGO E.,*Massalia et Emporion: une origine commune, deux destins différents*, in BATS M.-BERTUCCHI G.-CONGÈS G.-TRÉZINY H. (a cura di), *Marseille grecque et la Gaule*, Actes du Colloque international d'Histoire et d'Archéologie et du Ve Congrès archéologique de Gaule méridionale-Marseille, 18-23 novembre 1990 = "Études massaliètes", 3, Paris 1992.
SANSTERRE J.-M., *Les moines grecs et orientaux à Rome aux époques byzantine et carolingienne*, voll. 2 (Académie Royale de Belgique, Mémoires Cl. Lettres, t. LXVI, 1), Bruxelles 1983.
SARTORI F., *Problemi di storia costituzionale italiota*, Roma 1953.
SARTORI F., *Storia costituzionale della Sicilia antica*, in "Kokalos", vol. 26-27, 1980-81, pp.263-284.
SASSI M.M., *Antropologia del mondo greco*, Torino 1988.
SASSI M.M., *Parmenide al bivio.Per un'interpretazione del proemio*, in "La Parola del Passato", XLIII, 1988, pp.383-396.
SCARFÌ B.M., *Gioia del Colle (Bari). L'abitato peucetico di Monte Sannace*, in "Notizie Scavi", 1962, pp. 1 ss.
SCARFÌ B.M., *Gioia del Colle. Scavi nella zona di Monte Sannace. Le tombe rinvenute nel 1957*, in "Monumenti Antichi Lincei", XLV, 1960, cc. 145 ss.
SCHEIBLER I., *Griechische Malerei der Antike*, München 1994.
SCHIRÒ G., *Aspetti e eredità della civiltà bizantina in Magna Graecia*, in Atti XVII Convegno di studi sulla Magna Graecia, Napoli 1978, pp. 11-58.
SCHWEITZER B., *Zum Krater des Aristonothos*, in "MDAI(R)", LXII, 1955, pp.78-106.
SCHWYZER E., *Dialectorum Graecarum exempla epigraphica potiora*, Leipzig 1923.
SCHWYZER E., *Griechische Grammatik*, I, München 1939.
SESTIERI P.C., *Salerno.Scoperte archeologiche in località Fratte*, in "Notizie Scavi", 1952, pp.86 ss.
SETTIS S., *Idea dell'arte greca d'Occidente fra Ottocento e Novecento: Germania e Italia*, in Atti del XXVIII Convegno di Taranto 1989, pp. 135-176.
SHERK R.K., *The Eponymous Officials of Greek Cities*, V: The Register.PartVI: Sicily.Part VII: Italy, in "Zeitschrift für Papyrologie und Epigraphik", 96, 1993, pp. 267-276.
Sicilia dal cielo.Le città antiche, Catania 1994.
Siritide e Metapontino. Storia di due territori coloniali, Atti del Convegno (Policoro, 31 ottobre-2 novembre 1991), 1996.
SNODGRASS A.M., *La formazione dello stato greco*, in "Opus" V, 1976, pp. 7-22.
SORDI M., *Il IV e III secolo da Dionigi I a Timoleonte - 336 a.C.*, in GABBA E.-VALLET G. (a cura di), *La Sicilia antica* (vol.II della *Storia della Sicilia*), Napoli 1980, pp. 207-208.
SORDI M., *La lega tessala fino ad Alessandro Magno*, Roma 1958.
SPARKES B.A., *Greek Pottery: An Introduction*, Manchester 1991.
STAZIO A., *Moneta e scambi*, in *Megale Hellas*, Milano 1983, pp. 105-169.
STAZIO A., *Monetazione ed economia monetaria*, in *Sikanie*, Milano 1985, pp.79-122.
STELLA L.A., *La civiltà micenea nei documenti contemporanei*, Roma 1965.
STEWART A., *Greek Sculpture: An Exploration*, New Haven-London 1990.
STOCKTON D., *The Classical Athenian Democracy*, Oxford 1990 (trad. it.Milano 1993).
STRAZZULLA M.J., *Le terrecotte architettoniche della Venezia romana*, Roma 1987.
STUCCHI S. (a cura di), *Da Batto-Aristotele a Ibn el-As*, Introduzione alla mostra, Roma 1987.
STUCCHI S., *Architettura cirenaica*, Roma 1975.
STUCCHI S., *Cirene 1957-1966.Un decennio di attività della Missione Archeologica Italiana a Cirene*, Tripoli 1967.
STUCCHI S., *Il naiskos di Lysanias riconsiderato*, in "Quaderni di Archeologia della Libia", 12, 1987, pp. 191-220.
STUCCHI S., *La sede del rilievo "di Afrodite" nell'agorà di Cirene*, in Studi A.Adriani, III, Roma 1984, pp. 851-857.
STUCCHI S., *Questioni relative al tempio A di Prinias ed al formarsi degli ordini dorico e ionico*, in *Antichità Cretesi*, II, 1978, pp. 86 ss.
SYDOW W. v., *Die hellenistischen Gebälke in Sizilien*, "RM" 91, 1984, pp. 239 ss.
TAGLIENTE M., *Policoro: nuovi scavi nell'area di Siris*, in *Siris-Polieion. Fonti letterarie e nuova documentazione archeologica*, Lecce 1986, pp. 129 ss.
TAUSEND K., *Amphiktyonie und Symmachie*, Stuttgart 1992.
TAYLOUR W., *Mycenaean Pottery in Italy and adjacent areas*, Cambridge 1958.
THALMAN S.K., *The Adyton in the Greek Temples of South Italy and Sicily*, Ann Arbor 1980.
THEODORESCU D., *Chapiteaux ioniques de la Sicile méridionale*, Napoli 1974.
THEODORESCU D., *Éléments d'urbanisme et de topographie.État actuel et perspectives*, in *Poseidonia-Paestum*, Atti del XXVII Conv.di Taranto (1987), Napoli 1992.
THEODORESCU D., *Éléments d'urbanisme et de topographie: état actuel et perspectives*, in Atti Taranto XXVII, 1987 (1988), pp.501-540.
THOMPSON M.-MORKHOLM O. - KRAAY C.M., *Inventory of Greek Coin Hoards*, The American Numismatic Society, New York 1973.
THORN J.C., *Warrington's Discoveries in the Apollo Sanctuary at Cyrene*, in "Libyan Studies", 24, 1993, pp. 57-76.
TIMPANARO M. (a cura di), *Pitagorici. Testimonianze e frammenti*, Firenze 1962.
TINÈ BERTOCCHI F., *La pittura funeraria apula*, Napoli 1964.
TINÈ BERTOCCHI F., *La pittura funeraria apula*, Napoli 1964.
TOCCO SCIARELLI G., *T(omba) 104*, in *Napoli antica* (Catalogo della mostra, Napoli 1985), Napoli 1985, pp. 90-99.
TOD M.N., *Greek Historical Inscriptions*, I, Oxford 1946².
TODISCO L., *Scultura antica e reimpiego in Italia Meridionale*, I, Puglia-Basilicata-Calabria, Bari 1994, passim.
TORELLI M., *"Elogia Tarquiniensia"*, Firenze 1975.
TORELLI M., *Dalle aristocrazie gentilizie alla nascita della plebe*, in SCHIAVONE A-MOMIGLIANO A. (a cura di), *Storia di Roma*, I, Torino, 1988, pp. 241-261.
TORELLI M., *Delitto religioso. Qualche indizio sulla situazione in Etruria*, in SCHEID J. (a cura di), *Le délit religieux dans la cité antique* (Atti Tavola Rotonda - Roma 1978), Roma 1981B, pp. 1-7.
TORELLI M., *I fregi figurati delle regiae latine ed etrusche. Immaginario del potere arcaico*, in "Ostraka", I, 1992, pp.249-274.
TORELLI M., *Ideologia e rappresentazione nelle tombe tarquiniesi dell'Orco I e II*, in "DArch", s. III, I, 1983, 1, pp. 7-17.
TORELLI M., *Il commercio greco in Etruria fra VIII e VI sec. a.C.*, in MELLO M. (a cura di), *Il commercio*

greco nel Tirreno in età arcaica (Studi in memoria di M. Napoli), Salerno, 1982B, pp. 67-82.
TORELLI M., *Il santuario greco di Gravisca*, in "PP", 1977, pp. 398-458.
TORELLI M., *La religione*, in PUGLIESE CARRATELLI G.(a cura di), *Rasenna*, Milano 1986, pp. 159-237.
TORELLI M., *La società etrusca. L'età arcaica, l'età classica*, Roma 1987.
TORELLI M., *Lavinio e Roma*, Roma 1984.
TORELLI M., *Macedonia, Epiro e Magna Grecia. La pittura di età classica e protoellenistica*, in *Magna Grecia, Epiro e Macedonia*, Atti del XXIV Convegno di studi sulla Magna Grecia (Taranto 1984), Napoli 1985, pp. 379-398.
TORELLI M., *Macedonia, Epiro e Magna Grecia: la pittura di età classica e protoellenistica*, in *Magna Grecia, Epiro e Macedonia*, Atti del XXIV Convegno di Studi sulla Magna Grecia (Taranto 1984), Napoli 1990, pp. 399-410.
TORELLI M., *Monumenti funerari romani con fregio dorico*, in "Dialoghi di Archeologia", II, 1968, pp. 32 ss.
TORELLI M., *Per la definizione delle strutture del commercio greco-orientale: il caso di Gravisca*, in "PP", 202, 1982A, pp. 304-325.
TORELLI M., *Storia degli Etruschi*, Roma-Bari 1981A.
TORELLI M., *Terrecotte architettoniche arcaiche da Gravisca e una nota a Plinio*, "N.H.", XXXV, pp. 151-152, in *Studi in onore di F.Magi*, Perugia 1979, pp. 307-312.
TORELLI M., *Un'iscrizione posidoniate nella necropoli etrusca di Pontecagnano*, in "AION ArchStAnt", VI, 1984, pp. 277-280.
TORELLI M.-COMELLA A. (a cura di), *Corpus delle stipi votive in Italia*.
TORR C., *Ancient Ships*, Chicago 1964.
TRAVERSARI G., *Statue iconiche femminili cirenaiche*, Roma 1960.
TRENDALL A.D., *The Red-Figured Vases of Lucania, Campania and Sicily*, Oxford 1967.
TREUIL R.-DARQUE P.-POURSAT J.C.-TOUCHAIS G., *Les civilisations égéennes*, Paris 1989.
TRÉZINY H., *Navires attiques et navires corinthiens à la fin du VIII siècle. À propos d'un cratère géométrique de Mégara Hyblaea*, "MEFRA", 92, 1980-81, pp. 17-34.
TRONCHETTI C., *I Greci e la Sardegna,* "Dd'A", 1985, pp. 17-34.

TRONCHETTI C., *I rapporti fra il mondo greco e la Sardegna: note sulle fonti*, "EVO", 1986, pp. 117-124.
TRONCHETTI C., *I Sardi. Traffici, relazioni, ideologie nella Sardegna arcaica*, Milano 1988.
TRONCHETTI C., *Osservazioni sulla ceramica attica di Sardegna*, in AA.VV., *Sardinia in the Mediterranean: a footprint in the sea*, Sheffield 1992, pp. 364-377.
TRONCHETTI C., *Per la cronologia del tophet di Sant'Antioco*, "RivStFen", 1979, pp. 201-205.
TSAKIRGIS B., *The Domestic Architecture of Morgantina in the Hellenistic and Roman Period*, Ann Arbor-London 1985.
TUSA CUTRONI A., in "Kokalos", XXXIV-XXXV, 1988-89, p.397.
TUSA V., *La scultura in pietra di Selinunte*, Palermo 1983.
ULANO R., *Le strategie autocratiche di Archita*, in "Rendiconti dell'Istituto Lombardo", Classe di Lettere e Scienze Morali e Storiche, 123, 1989, pp.123-129.
UNTERSTEINER M. (a cura di), *Parmenide. Testimonianze e frammenti*, Firenze 1958.
UNTERSTEINER M. (a cura di), *Zenone. Testimonianze e frammenti*, Firenze 1963.
VAGNETTI L. (a cura di), *Magna Grecia e mondo miceneo.Nuovi Documenti* (Catalogo della mostra), Napoli 1982.
VAGNETTI L., *I Micenei in Occidente. Dati acquisiti e prospettive future*, in *Modes de contacts et processus de transformation dans les sociétés anciennes*, Atti Convegno Cortona (1981), Pisa-Roma 1983, pp. 165-185.
VAGNETTI L.-JONES R.E., *Towards the identification of local Mycenaean pottery in Italy*, in FRENCH E.B.-WARDLE K.A. (eds.), *Problems in Greek Prehistory*(Papers presented at the Centenary Conference of the British School of Archaeology at Athens, Manchester 1986), Bristol 1988, pp. 335-348.
VAGNETTI L.-LO SCHIAVO F., *Late Bronze Age long distance trade in the Mediterranean: the role of the Cypriots*, in PELTENBURG E. (ed.), *Early Society in Cyprus*, Edinburgh 1989, pp. 217-243.
VALEVA J., *Hellenistic Tombs in Thrace and Macedonia: their form and decorations*, in *Functional and Spatial Analysis of Wall-Painting* (Atti del V Congresso Internazionale sull'affresco antico, Amsterdam 8-12 settembre 1992), ed. by

MOORMANN E.M., Leiden 1993, pp. 119-126.
VALGIMIGLI M.-ANTI C., *Sulle orme di Callimaco di Cirene*, in "Africa italiana", 2, 1929, pp. 211-230.
VALLET G., *La Cité et son territoire*, in Atti del VII Convegno Internazionale di Studi sulla Magna Grecia (Taranto 1967), Napoli 1968, pp. 67-142.
VALLET G., *Les routes maritimes de la Grande Grèce*, in *Vie di Magna Grecia* (Atti del II Convegno di Studi sulla Magna Grecia), Napoli 1963, pp. 117-135.
VALLET G.-VILLARD F., *Megara Hyblaea 4. Le temple du IV siècle*, Paris 1966.
VALLET G.-VILLARD F., *Mégara Hyblaea 2, La céramique archaïque*, Paris 1964.
VALLET G.-VILLARD F.-AUBERSON P., *Megara Hyblaea I.Le quartier de l'agora archaïque*, Rome 1976.
VALLET G.-VILLARD F.-AUBERSON P., *Megara Hyblaea.Guida agli scavi*, Roma 1983.
VALLET G.-VILLARD F.-AUBERSON P., *Mégara Hyblaea. 1. Le quartier de l'agora archaïque*, Roma 1976.
VANSCHOONWINKEL J., *L'Egée et la Méditerranée orientale à la fin du deuxième millénaire* (*Archaeologica Transatlantica*, IX), Louvain-La Neuve 1991.
VATIN C., *L'offrande de Liparéens à Delphes*, in "Ostraka", II, 1993, pp. 145-167.
VELMANS T., *Le décor de la voûte de l'oratoire Santa Lucia: une iconographie rare des Quarante Martyrs*, in Atti del VIConvegno int. sulla civiltà rupestre nel Mezzogiorno d'Italia, Galatina 1986, pp. 341-354.
VIAN F., *Poésie et géographie.Les retours des Argonautes*, in "CRAI" 1987, pp. 249-262.
VILLARD F., *La céramique polycrome du VIIe siècle en Grèce, en Italie du sud et en Sicile et sa situation par rapport à la céramique protocorinthienne*, in "Ann. Atene", LIX, 1981, pp. 133ss.
VILLARD F., *Pittura e ceramica* in CHARBONNEAUX J.-MARTIN R.-VILLARD F., *Grèce Archaïque*, Paris 1968 (ed. it. *La Grecia arcaica*, Milano 1969); *Grèce Classique*, Paris 1969 (ed. it. *La Grecia classica*, Milano 1970); *Grèce Hellénistique*, Paris 1970 (ed. it. *La Grecia ellenistica*, Milano 1971).
Voci topografiche edite nella B.T.C.G. arrivata al vol.XIII, 1994 (ultima voce *Pisa*).
VOIGT E.M., *Sappho et Alcaeus*, Amsterdam 1971.

VOJATZI M., *Frühe Argonautenbilder*, Würzburg 1982.
VOLLENWEIDER M.L., *Die Porträtgemmen der römischen Republik*, I-II, Mainz 1972-1974.
VOZA G., in "Kokalos", XXX-XXXI, 1984-85, pp.674 ss.
VOZA G., in *La Sicilia antica* II,1, Napoli 1980.
WALBANK F.W., *Were there Greek Federal States?*, in "Scripta classica Israelica" III, 1976-77, pp. 27-51.
WARREN P.-HANKEY V., *Aegean Bronze Age Chronology*, Bristol 1989.
WASOWICZ A., *École d'urbanisme de la Sicile et de la Grande Grèce à l'époque archaïque*, in "Riv. di Topografia antica", II, 1992, pp.9-22.
WASOWICZ A., *Modèles de l'amenagement spatial de la cité grecque dans les colonies d'Occident et d'Orient*, in *Territoires des cités grecques* (Table ronde École Française d'Athènes 31 octobre-3novembre 1991), in corso di stampa.
WEITZMANN K., *Die byzantinische Buchmalerei des 9. und 10. Jahrhunderts*, Berlin 1935, pp.37 ss.
WEITZMANN K., *The miniature of the Sacra Parallela. Parisinus Graecus 923*, Princeton 1979 (Studies in Manuscript Illumination, 8), Roma 1981.
WIKANDER Ö., *Acquarossa VI. The Roof-Tiles, Part 2. Typology and Technical Features* (Skrifter utgivna av Svenska Institutet i Rom, 4°, XXXVIII: VI, 2), Stockholm 1993.
WILLIAMS D., *Greek Vases*, London 1985.
WILLIAMS F., *Callimachus Hymn to Apollo*, Oxford 1978.
WINTER F.E., *Greek Fortifications*, London 1970.
WINTER N.A., *Greek Architectural Terracottas from the Prehistoric to the End of the Archaic Period*, Oxford (1993), pp. 273ss.
WITHE D., *Seven recently discovered Sculptures from Cyrene*, University of Pennsylvania Expedition, 18, 1975-76, 2, pp. 14-32.
WITHE D., *The Cyrene Sphinx, its Capital and its Column*, in "American Journal of Archaeology", 75, 1971, pp. 47-55.
WITHE D., *Two Girls from Cyrene*, in "Opuscula Romana", 9, 1973, pp. 207-215.
YNTEMA D., *Notes on Greek Influence on Iron Age Salento*, in *Studi di Antichità* 3, Galatina 1982, pp. 83-131.
YOUNGER G.J., *Bibliography for Aegean Glyptik in the Bronze Age* (CMS, Beiheft 4), Marburg 1991.

ZANCANI MONTUORO P.-ZANOTTI U.-BIANCO, *Heraion alla Foce del Sele*, Roma 1951-54.
ZANKER P. (a cura di), *Hellenismus in Mittelitalien*, in "Abhandlungen der Akademie der Wissenschaften in Göttingen, Phil.-Hist. Klasse" 97, 1976.
ZHMUD L., *Orphism and Graffiti from Olbia*, in "Hermes", CXX, 1992, pp. 159-168.
ZIFFERERO A., *Miniere e metallurgia estrattiva in Etruria meridionale: per una lettura critica di alcuni dati archeologici e minerari*, in "SE", LVII, 1991, pp. 201-241.
ZIMMER G., *Römische Berufdarstellungen*, Berlin 1982.
ZOPPI C., *L'architettura abitativa in età ellenistica: il modello vitruviano e i documenti superstiti*, in "Rend.Acc.",Napoli, n.s. LXIII, 1991-92 (1992), pp.157-187.
ZUNTZ G., *Persephone.Three Essays on Religion and Thought in Magna Graecia*, Oxford 1971.

Joint Works

AA.VV., *Africa in Classical Antiquity.Nine Studies*, Ibada 1969.
AA.VV., *Cirene e i Libyi*, "Quaderni di Archeologia della Libia" 12, 1987.
AA.VV., *Ichnussa*, Milano 1981.
AA.VV., *Il commercio greco nel Tirreno in età arcaica*, Salerno1981.
AA.VV., *L'incidenza dell'antico.Studi in memoria di Ettore Lepore*, Atti del Convegno Internazionale, Anacapri 24-28 marzo 1991, Napoli, I, a cura di A.Storchi Marino, 1995.
AA.VV., *La transizione dal Miceneo all'Alto Arcaismo*, Roma 1991.
AA.VV., *Sardegna preistorica.Nuraghi a Milano*, Milano 1985.
AA.VV., *Sardinia in the Mediterranean: a foot print in the sea*, Sheffeld 1992.
BARKER G.-LLOYD J.-REYNOLDS J., *Cyrenaica in Antiquity*, Oxford 1985.
BIANCHI BANDINELLI R.(a cura di), *Storia e civiltà dei Greci*, VI, Milano 1979.
BRACCESI L.-DE MIRO E.(a cura di), *Agrigento e la Sicilia greca* (Atti della Settimana di Studio: Agrigento, 2-8 maggio 1988), Roma 1992.
CHARBONNEAUX J.-MARTIN R.-VILLARD F., *Grèce Archaïque*, Paris 1968 (ed. it. *La Grecia arcaica*, Milano 1969).
CHARBONNEAUX J.-MARTIN R.-VILLARD F., *Grèce Classique*, Paris 1969 (ed. it. *La Grecia Classica*, Milano 1970).
CHARBONNEAUX J.-MARTIN R.-VILLARD F., *Grèce Hellenistique*, Paris 1970 (ed. it. *La Grecia ellenistica*, Milano 1971).
COSTABILE F. (a cura di), *Polis ed Olympieion a Locri Epizefiri*, Soveria Mannelli 1992.
DARQUE P.-TREUIL R. (a cura di), *L'habitat égéen préhistorique*, Paris 1990.
DESCOEUDRES J.P. (ed.), *Greek Colonists and Native populations*, Oxford 1990.
FARNOUX A.-DRIESSEN J. (a cura di), *La Crète mycenienne*.Actes de la Table Ronde, Athènes, mars 1991.
FINLEY M.I.(par), *Problèmes de la terre en Grèce ancienne*, Paris-La Haye 1973.
FIRPO L. (a cura di), *Storia delle idee politiche, economiche e sociali*, I, Torino 1982.
FRENCH E.B.-WARDLE K.A. (ed.), *Problems in Greek Prehistory*, Bristol 1988.
GABBA E.-VALLET G. (a cura di), *La Sicilia antica*, I, 1980.
GALE N.H. (ed.), *Bronze Age Trade in the Mediterranean*, Goteberg 1991.
GENTILI B. (a cura di), *Cirene, Storia, Mito, Letteratura*, Atti del Convegno della S.I.S.A.C., Urbino 3 luglio 1988, Urbino 1990.
LAFFINEUR R.-CROWLEY J.L.(ed.), *Eikon.Aegean Bronze Age Iconography: Shaping a Methodology*, "Aegaeum", 8, 1992.
MADDOLI G. (a cura di), *La civiltà micenea.Guida storica e critica*, 2 ediz., Roma-Bari 1992.
MCGRAIL S.-KENTLEY E., *Sewn Plank Boats*, "British Archaeological Reports", Oxford 1985.
POLTENBURG E. (ed.), *Early Society in Cyprus*, Edinburgh 1989.
PRONTERA P.(a cura di), *La Magna Grecia e il mare.Studi di storia marittima*, Taranto 1996.
PUGLIESE CARRATELLI G. (a cura di), *Italia omnium terrarum alumna*, Milano 1988.
PUGLIESE CARRATELLI G. (a cura di), *Magna Grecia IV, Arte e Artigianato*, Milano 1990.
PUGLIESE CARRATELLI G. (a cura di), *Magna Grecia*, III, Milano 1989.
PUGLIESE CARRATELLI G. (a cura di), *Magna Grecia.Lo sviluppo politico, sociale ed economico*, Milano 1987.
PUGLIESE CARRATELLI G. (a cura di), *Sikanie, Storia e civiltà della Sicilia Greca*, Milano 1985.
PUGLIESE CARRATELLI G., *Primordi della legislazione scritta*, in G.Pugliese Carratelli (a cura di), *Magna Grecia.Lo sviluppo politico, sociale ed economico*, Milano 1987.
REMAK P. (ed.), *The Role of the Ruler in the prehistoric Aegean*, "Aegaeum", 11, 1995.
RIZZA G. (a cura di), *Il tempo greco in Sicilia, architettura e culti*, "Cron A Stor Art" 16, Catania 1985.
WELLS B. (ed.), *Agriculture in Ancient Greece*, Stockholm 1992.

Acts

Agrigento e la Sicilia greca.Atti della Settimana di Studio, Agrigento 2-8 maggio 1988, Roma 1992.
Atti del Convegno Internazionale, Anacapori 24-28 marzo 1991, Napoli 1995.
Atti del IICongresso Internazionale di Micenologia, Roma-Napoli, ottobre 1991 (in corso di stampa).
Atti del VIIConvegno Internazionale di Studi sulla Magna Grecia, Taranto 1967, Napoli 1968.
Atti XXXIIConvegno di Taranto 1992, Napoli 1994.
Céramique et peinture grecques: modes d'emploi, Atti del Convegno, Paris 26-28 aprile 1995 (in stampa).
Cirene.Storia, Mito, Letteratura, Atti del Convegno della S.I.S.A.C., Urbino 3 luglio 1988, Urbino 1990.
Fenici e Arabi nel Mediterraneo Convegno in Roma, Ottobre 1982, Roma 1983.
Forme di contatto e processi di trasformazione nelle società antiche, Atti del convegno di Cortona (24-30 maggio 1981), Pisa-Roma 1983.
Functional and Spatial Analysis of Wall-Painting, Atti del VCongresso Internazionale sull'affresco antico, Amsterdam 8-12 settembre 1992, Leiden 1993.
Hellenismus in Mittelitalien, Kolloquium Göttingen 1976.
L'Italie méridionale et les premières expériences de la peinture hellénistique, Atti della tavola rotonda, Roma 28 febbraio 1994, École Française de Rome (in corso di stampa).
La Crète mycenienne.Actes de la Table Ronde, Athènes, mars 1991.
Lo Stretto crocevia di cultura, Atti del XXVIConvegno di studi sulla Magna Grecia, Napoli 1993.
Magna Grecia, Epiro e Macedonia, Atti del XXIV Convegno di Studi sulla Magna Grecia (Taranto 1984), Napoli 1990.
Marseille grecque et la Gaule.Actes du colloque international d'histoire et d'archéologie et du VCongrès archéologique de Gaule méridionale (Marseille 1990), in "Études Massaliètes", 3, Lattes/Aix-en-Provence 1992.
Megale Hellas, nome e immagine, Atti 21 Conc M Grecia, Taranto 1981 (1982).
Momenti precoloniali nel Mediterraneo antico, Convegno in Roma, marzo 1985, Roma 1988.
Mural Painting in Lycian Tombs, Atti del X Congresso Internazionale di Archeologia Classica, Ankara 1978.
Nuragic Sardinia and the Mycenaean World.Atti del Convegno di Roma ç1986), "British Archaeological Reports", Oxford 1987.
Phoinikeia Grammata, Colloque de Liègr, novembre 1989, Namur 1991.
Phönizier im Western, Symposium in Köln, April 1979, Mainz 1982 (=Madrider Beiträge, 8).
Traffici micenei nel Mediterraneo. Problemi storici e documentazione archeologica.Atti del Convegno di Palermo (maggio e dicembre 1984), Taranto 1986.
Vie di Magna Grecia, Atti del II Convegno di Studi sulla Magna Grecia, Napoli 1963.

Bibliography of the Files

A.M. Adam, *Remarques sur une série des casques de bronze*, in Mefra 94 1982, pp. 9-32

D. Adamesteanu, *Coppi con testate dipinte da Gela*, in ArchCl V 1953, pp. 1-9

D. Adamesteanu, *Una tomba arcaica di Siris*, in *Forschungen und Funde, Festschrift Bernard Neutsch*, Innsbruck 1980, pp. 31-36

D. Adamesteanu-H.Dilthey, *Macchia di Rossano. Il santuario della Mefitis*. Rapporto preliminare, Galatina 1992

Ch. Aellen, *Les personnifications dans la céramique italiote*, Lausanne 1992 (tesi di dottorato)

H.L. Allen, *Excavations at Morgantina* (Serra Orlando), 1967-1969. Preliminary Report X, in AJA 74 1970, pp. 359-383

F. Alvarez Ossorio, *Catalogo de los exvotos de bronce ibéricos*, Madrid 1941

P. Amandry, *Plaques d'or de Delphes*, in AM 77 1962, pp. 35-71

B. Andreae, *Laurea coronatur. Der Lorebeerkranz des Asklepios und die Attaliden von Pergamon*, in RM 100 1993, pp. 84-106

G. Andreassi-A. Cocchiaro, *Necropoli d'Egnazia*, Fasano 1987

Aa.Vv., *Antike helme. Handbuch mit Katalog*, Mainz 1988

Aa.Vv., *Archeologia nella Sicilia Sud-Orientale* (Catalogo della Mostra Napoli-Siracusa), Napoli 1973

P.E. Arias, *Euthymos*, in *Siculorum Gymnasium*, I, 1941, pp. 77-85

P.E. Arias, *La fonte sacre di Locri dedicata a Pan ed alle Ninfe*, in Le Arti III, 1941, 5, pp. 177-180

P. E. Arias, *Modelli fittili di fontane in età ellenistica*, in Palladio V, 1941, pp. 193-206

P. E. Arias, *Locri. Scavi archeologici in contrada Caruso-Polisà* (aprile-maggio 1940), in NSc 1946, pp. 138-161

P. E. Arias, *L'arte locrese nelle sue principali manifestazioni artigianali. Terrecotte, bronzi, vasi, arti minori*, in Atti Taranto 1976, pp. 479 ss.

P. E. Arias, *La Menade di Locri*, in Aa.Vv., *Studi in onore di A. Adriani*, Roma 1984, pp. 677-679

P. E. Arias, *Euthymos di Locri*, in AnnPisa XVII, 1987, pp. 1-8

P. E. Arias, *La pittura vascolare*, in Magna Grecia IV. *Arte e artigianato*, Milano 1990, pp. 420-438

Aa.Vv., *Armi. Gli strumenti della guerra in Lucania*, Bari 1993

M.I. Artamonov, *Treasures from Scythian Tombs*, London 1969

J.D. Beazley, *Attic Red-figure Vase-painters*, Oxford 1963

B. Ashmole, *Late Archaic and Early Classical Greek Sculpture in Sicily and South Italy*, in *Proceedings of the British Academy XX*, 1934, pp. 91-122

Aa.Vv., *La statua marmorea di Mozia e la scultura di stile severo in Sicilia* - Atti della giornata di studio, Marsala 1986, Roma 1988

Atti del convegno di studi sulla Magna Grecia, Taranto 1961 ss.

G. Barone, *Gessi del Museo di Sabratha*, Roma 1994

M. Barra Bagnasco, *Apporti esterni ed elaborazione locale nella coroplastica locrese tra il V e il IV sec.a.C.*, in BdA LXIX 1984, pp. 39-52

M. Barra Bagnasco, *Protomi in terracotta da Locri Epizefiri*, Torino 1986

L. Basch, *Le musée imaginaire de la marine antique*, Athenes 1987

B. Basile, *Modellini fittili di imbarcazioni dalla Sicilia orientale*, in Bollettino di Archeologia Subacquea, I, dicembre 1993, p. 84

F.L. Bastet, *Pyxis aus Canosa*, in BABesch 57 1982, pp. 155-158

J.D. Beazley, *A Marble Lamp*, in JHS 60 1940, pp. 22-49

J.D. Beazley, *Panathenaica*, XLVII 1943, pp. 441 ss.

J.D. Beazley, *Attic Red-figure Vase-painters*, Oxford 1963

A. Beazley, *Paralipomena. Addition to Attic Black Figure Vase-Painters and Attic Red Figure Vase-Painters*, Oxford 1971

M. Bell, *Morgantina Studies I. The Terracottas*, Princeton N.J. 1981

R. Belli Pasqua, *Due acroliti del Museo Nazionale di Taranto*, in Taras 11,1, 1991, pp. 7-17

C. Berard-C. Bron, *Il gioco del satiro*, in Aa.Vv., *La città delle immagini. Religione e società nella Grecia antica*, Modena 1986, pp. 119-136

E. Berger (a cura di), *Antike aus Sammlung Ludwig II - Terrakotten und Bronzen*, Basel 1982

L. Bernabò Brea, *Akrai*, Catania 1956

L. Bernabò Brea, *Musei e monumenti in Sicilia*, Novara 1958 (A)

L. Bernabò Brea, *Lipari nel IV secolo a.C.*, in Kokalos IV 1958, pp. 119-144 (A)

L. Bernabò Brea, *Che cosa sappiamo dei centri indigeni della Sicilia che hanno coniato monete prima dell'età di Timoleonte*, in AnnIstNum 20 Suppl. 1975, pp. 3-51

L. Bernabò Brea, *Menandro e il teatro greco nelle terrecotte liparesi*, Genova 1981

L. Bernabò Brea, *Ecuba e Taltibio: maschere delle "Troiane" di Euripide in una tomba liparese del IV sec. a.C.*, in StFilCl XII 1995, pp. 3-9

L. Bernabò Brea-M. Cavalier, *Meligunìs Lipara. II. La necropoli greca e romana nella Contrada Diana*, Palermo 1965

L. Bernabò Brea-M. Cavalier, *Il Castello di Lipari ed il Museo Archeologico Eoliano*, Palermo 1977

L. Bernabò Brea-M. Cavalier, *La ceramica liparese di età ellenistica*, Muggiò 1986

L. Bernabò Brea-M. Cavalier, *Meligunìs Lipara. V. Scavi nella necropoli greca di Lipari*, Roma 1991

L. Bernabò Brea-M. Cavalier, *Meligunìs Lipara*. VII., Roma 1995

H.G. Beyen, *Die Pompejanische Wanddekoration vom zweiten bis zum vierten Stil*, I, The Hague 1938

R. Bianchi Bandinelli-E. Paribeni, *L'arte dell'antichità classica. Grecia*, Torino 1992 (3° ed.)

S. Bianco, *Gioielli della tomba 22 di Policoro*, in Aa.Vv., *Bellezza e lusso. Immagini e documenti dei piaceri della vita*, Catalogo della Mostra, Roma 1992

M. Bieber, *The Sculpture of the Hellenistic Age*, New York 1961

A. Bignasca, *Nuove terrecotte dell'offerente del porcellino e la prima metà del IV secolo a Morgantina*, in AntK 35 1992, pp. 18-53

A.M. Bisi, *Due frammenti di sculture arcaiche selinuntine*, in ArchCl XXI 1969, pp. 34-38

A.M. Bisi, *Influenze italiote e siceliote sull'arte tardo-punica: le stele funerarie di Lilibeo*, in ArchCl XXII 1970, pp. 92-130

H.J. Bloesch, *Antike Kunst in der Schweiz*, Erlenbach-Zurich 1943

C. Blumel, *Griechische Skulpturen des VI und V Jahr. v.Chr.*, I, Berlin-Leipzig 1940

C. Blumel, *Die Archaischen-griechischen Skulpturen der Staatlichen Museen zu Berlin*, Berlin 1963

J. Boardmann, *A Greek Vase from Egypt*, in BSA 78 1958, pp. 4-12

J. Boardmann, *Athenian Black Figure Vases*, London 1974

J. Boardmann, *Athenian Red Figure Vases. The Archaic period*, London 1975

F. Bodenstedt, *Phokaeische Elektron-Geld von 600-326 v.Chr.*, Mainz 1976

P.C. Bol, *Antike Bronzetechnik Kunst und Handwerk antiker Erzbilder*, Munchen 1985

P.C. Bol, *Argivische Schilde* (Olympische Forschungen 17), Berlin-New York 1989

J.D.P. Bolton, *Aristeas of procon-

nesus, Oxford 1962

N. BONACASA, *L'area sacra*, in AA.VV., *Himera I. Campagne di scavo 1963-1965*, Roma 1970, pp. 51-235

N. BONACASA, *L'ellenismo e la tradizione ellenistica*, in *Sikanie*, pp. 277-347

M. BORDA, *La pittura romana*, Milano 1958

M. BORDA, *Arte dedalica a Taranto*, Pordenone 1979

M. BORDA, *La kourotrophos dedalica da Taranto nel Museo Civico di Trieste*, in *Scritti* Arias, I, pp. 85-96

A. BOTTINI, *L'attività archeologica in Basilicata*, in Atti Taranto XXVI 1986, pp.

A. BOTTINI, *Elena in Occidente: una tomba dalla chora di Metaponto*, in BdA VI, 1988, pp. 1-18 (a)

A. BOTTINI, *La religione delle genti indigene*, in Magna Grecia III, Milano 1988, pp. 55-90 (b)

A. BOTTINI, *Il mondo indigeno nel V sec.a.C. Due studi*, in BBasil 5 1989, pp. 161 ss. (a)

A. BOTTINI, *La panoplia lucana del Museo Provinciale di Potenza*, in Mefra 101 1989, 2, pp. 669-715 (b)

A. BOTTINI, *Le ambre intagliate a figura umana del Museo Archeologico Nazionale di Melfi*, in Archeologia Warsaw 41 1990, pp. 57 ss.

A. BOTTINI, *Appunti sulla presenza di Dionysos nel mondo italico*, in "Dionysos. Mito e mistero", Atti del Convegno di Comacchio 1989, Comacchio 1991, pp. 157 ss.

A. BOTTINI, *Archeologia della salvezza. L'escatologia greca nelle testimonianze archeologiche*, Milano 1992

A. BOTTINI-E. SETARI, *Loc. Serra di Vaglio- Contrada Braida. Basileis? I più recenti rinvenimenti: risultati, prospettive e problemi*, in BA 16/18 1992, pp. 207-235 ss.

A. BOTTINI-E. SETARI, *Basileis. Antichi re in Basilicata*, Napoli 1995

A. BOTTINI-M. TAGLIENTE, *Una brocchetta con scena figurata da Ripacandida*, in Aa.Vv., *Scritti in onore di Michele D'Elia*, a cura di C.Gelao, c.s.

J. BOVIO MARCONI, *Guida del Museo di Palermo*, Roma 1969

L. BREGLIA, *Catalogo delle oreficerie del Museo Nazionale di Napoli*, Roma 1941

E. BRUMMER, *Griechische Truhenbehalter*, in JdI 100 1985, pp. 1-168

Bibliografia Topografica della Colonizzazione Greca in Italia e nelle isola tirreniche, a cura di G. Nenci E G. VALLET, Pisa-Roma, I 1977...

G. BUCHNER, *Pithecusa: scavi e scoperte*, in Atti Taranto 1971, pp. 361 ss.

G. BUCHNER-D. RIDGWAY, *Pithekoussai*, I, MonAnt, Serie Monografica 4, Roma 1993

H.A. CAHN, *Die Munzen der sizilischen Stadt Naxos. Ein Beitrag zur Kunstgeschichte der griechischen Westens*, Basel 1944

D. CAHN, *Waffen und Zaumzeug. Katalog Antikenmuseum Basel und Sammlung Ludwig*, Basel 1989

A. CALDERONE, *Una placchetta fittile arcaica da Agrigento*, in QuadMess 6 1991, pp. 43 ss.

F. CANCIANI-F.W. VON HASE, *La tomba Bernardini di Palestrina*, Roma 1979

G. CAPUTO, *Il triskele arcaico di Bitalemi di Gela e di Castellazzo di Palma*, in RendLinc XXVI 1971, pp. 3 ss.

T.H. CARPENTER, *Dionysian Imagery in Archaic Greek Art*, Oxford 1986

J.C. CARTER, *Scavi dell'Università del Texas nel territorio di Metaponto 1976*, in Atti Taranto XVI 1976, pp. 845 ss.

AA.Vv., *The Pantanello Necropolis 1982-1989. An Interim Report*, Austin 1990

I. CARUSO, *Bronzetti di produzione magnogreca dal VI al IV sec.a.C.: la classe degli specchi*, in RM 88 1981, pp. 13-106

R. CASSANO in AA.Vv., *Archeologia di una città. Bari dalle origini al X secolo* (Catalogo della Mostra), Bari 1988, pp. 349 ss.

F. CASTAGNOLI, *Iscrizioni*, in Aa.Vv., *Lavinium II. Le tredici are*, Roma 1975, pp. 441 ss.

F. CASTAGNOLI, *Il culto di Minerva a Lavinio*, Roma 1979

G. CASTELLANA, *Il tempietto votivo fittile di Sabucina e la sua decorazione figurata*, in RdA VII 1983, pp. 5-11

M. CAVALIER, *Attività delle Soprintendenze (1960-1965) - Sicilia*, in BdA LI 1966, p. 89

M. CAVALIER, *Nuveaux documents sur l'art du Peintre de Lipari*, Publications du Centre Jean Berard, 3, Naples 1976

M. CAVALIER, *Appendice II. Le terrecotte liparesi di argomento teatrale e la ceramica. I dati di rinvenimento e la cronologia*, in BERNABÒ BREA 1981, pp. 259-302

M. CAVALIER in Meda 7, 1995

L. CERCHIAI, *Le officine etrusco-corinzie di Pontecagnano*, Napoli 1990

J. CHARBONNEAUX-R. MARTIN-F. VILLARD, *La Grecia arcaica (620-480 a.C.)*, Milano 1978

AA.Vv., *Civiltà degli Etruschi*, Catalogo della Mostra Firenze 1985, a cura di M. Cristofani

F. COARELLI, *La cultura figurativa in Sicilia nei secoli IV-III a.C.*, in AA.Vv., *Storia della Sicilia*, a cura di E.Gabba-G.Vallet, II, 1, Napoli 1980, pp. 155-182

M.B. COMSTOCK-C.C. VERMEULE, Sculpture in Stone. *The Greek, roman and etruscans collections of the Museum of Fine Arts*, Boston 1976

P. CONNOLLY, in AA.Vv., *Italian Iron Age Artifacts in the British Museum - Papers of the Sixth B.M. Classical Colloquium 1982*, London 1986

G. CONSOLI, *Messina. Museo regionale*, Bologna 1980

F. COSTABILE-I. CARUSO, *Scena di Elettra su uno specchio locrese*, in Scritti Arias, I, pp. 361 ss.

F. COSTABILE (a cura di), *I ninfei di Locri Epizefiri. Architettura. Culti erotici. Sacralità delle acque*, Soveria Mannelli (CZ) 1991

F. COSTABILE, *Le statue frontonali del tempio Marasà a Locri Epizefiri*, in RM 102 1995, pp. 5 ss.

P. T. CRADDOCK, *The Composition of the Copper Alloy used by the Greek, Etruscans and Roman Civilizations. 2. The Archaic, Classical and Hellenistic Greeks*, in JASc 4 1977, pp. 103 ss.

F. CROISSANT, *Sybaris: la production artistique*, in Atti Taranto 1992, Napoli 1993, pp. 543 ss.

L. CURTIUS, *Zeus und Hermes*, I Erganzungheft RM 1931, pp. 48 ss.

Corpus Vasorum Antiquorum

M. CYGIELMAN-E. MANGANI, *La Collezione Chigi-Zondadari. Ceramiche figurate, Museo Archeologico Nazionale di Siena*. Monografie, I, Roma 1991

B. D'AGOSTINO, *Il fregio fittile di Pompei*, in AnnAStorAnt IV 1982, pp. 63-93

F. D'ANDRIA, *I materiali del V sec. a.C. nel Ceramico di Metaponto e alcuni risultati delle analisi delle argille*, in *Scritti* Adamesteanu, pp. 117 ss.

F. D'ANDRIA, *Messapi e Peuceti*, in Italia alumna, pp. 653 ss.

CH. DAREMBERG-E. SAGLIO, *Dictionnaire des Antiquitìs Grecques et romaines*, Graz 1962

G. DAUX-E. HANSEN, *Le trésor de Siphnos (Fouilles de delphes II. Topographie et architecture)*, Paris 1987

S. DE CARO, *Una nuova tomba dipinta da Nola*, in RIA s.III, VI-VII 1983-84, pp. 71 ss.

A. DE FRANCISCIS, *Gli acroteri marmorei del tempio Marasà a Locri Epizefiri*, in RM 67 1960, pp. 1 ss.

N. DEGRASSI, *Il Pittore di Policoro e l'officina di ceramica protoitaliota di*

Eraclea Lucana, in BdA 1-2, 1965, pp. 5-37

N. Degrassi, *Lo Zeus stilita di Ugento*, Roma 1981

C. Dehl, *Die Korinthische Keramik des 8. und fruhen 7. Jhs. v.Chr. in Italien. Untersuchungen zu ihrer Chronologie und Ausbreitung*, 11. Beheift AM, Berlin 1994

A. Dell'Aglio-E. Lippolis, *Catalogo del Museo Nazionale Archeologico di Taranto. II, 1. Ginosa e Laterza. La documentazione archeologica dal VII al III sec. a.C.* - Scavi 1900-1980, Taranto s.d.

E. De Miro, *La fondazione di Agrigento e l'ellenizzazione del territorio fra il Salso e il Platano*, in Kokalos VIII, 1962, pp. 122-152

E. De Miro, *Gela protoarcaica. Dati topografici, archeologici e cronologici*, in ASAtene XLV 1983, pp. 53-105

E. De Miro, *La valle dei Templi*, Palermo 1994

M. Denti, *La statuaria in marmo del santuario di Rossano di Vaglio*, Galatina 1992

J.M. Dentzer, *Le motif du banquet couchè dans le Proche-Orient et le mond grec du VII au IV siècle avant J.C.*, Rome 1982

E.M. De Juliis (a cura di), *Il Museo Archeologico di Bari*, Bari 1983

E.M. De Juliis-D. Loiacono, *Taranto. Il Museo Archeologico*, Taranto 1985

M.C. D'Ercole, *La stipe votiva del Belvedere di Lucera*, Roma 1990

A. De Ridder, *Catalogue sommaire des bijoux antiques du Musée du Louvre*, Paris 1924

A. De Siena, *Metaponto e il Metapontino*, in Leukania, pp. 114-135

Ph. Desy, *Recherches sur l'èconomie apulienne au IIe et au Ie siècle avant notre ère*, Bruxelles 1993

W.B. Dinsmoor, *The Architecture of Ancient Greece*, New York 1975

P. Dintsis, *Hellenistische Helme*, Roma 1986

AA.Vv., *Due donne dell'Italia antica. Corredi da Spina e Forentum*, Catalogo della Mostra di Comacchio 1993, Padova 1993 (a cura di D.Baldoni)

E. Dyggve, *Das Laphrion der Tempelbezirk von Kalydon*, Copenaghen 1948

Ch. Dugas, *La céramiques des Cyclades*, Paris 1925

Enciclopedia dell'arte antica, classica e orientale, Roma 1958

M. Egg, *Italische Helme, Romisch-germanisches Zentralmuseum* 11, Magonza 1986

M. Fabbri-A. Trotta, *Una Scuola-Collegio di età augustea. L'insula II di Velia*, Roma 1989

G. Fiorentini, *Ricerche archeologiche nella Sicilia centro-meridionale*, in Kokalos XXVI-XXVII, II, 1, 1980-81, pp. 583-592

G. Fiorentini, *La necropoli indigena di età greca di Valle Oscura (Marianopoli)*, in QuadMess 1 1985-86, pp. 31 ss.

G. Fiorentini, *La nave di Gela e osservazioni sul carico residuo*, in QuadMess 1992, pp. 25-37

T. Fischer-Hansen (a cura di), *Catalogue of Campania, South Italy and Sicily*, Ny carlsberg Glyptotek-Copenaghen 1992

AA.Vv., *Forentum II. L'acropoli in età classica*, Venosa 1991

L. Forti, *Gli unguentari del primo periodo ellenistico*, in RendNap 37 1962, pp. 143 ss.

L. Forti, *La ceramica di Gnathia*, Napoli 1965

L. Forti-A. Stazio, *Vita quotidiana dei Greci d'Italia*, in Megale Hellas, Milano 1983, pp. 643-713

G. Foti, *Attività della Soprintendenza alle antichità della Calabria*, in Klearchos 41-44 1969, pp. 137 ss.

G. Foti, *Il Museo Nazionale di Reggio Calabria*, Cava dei Tirreni 1972

G. Foti-G. Pugliese Carratelli, *Un sepolcro di Hipponion ed un nuovo testo orfico*, in PP 29, 1974, pp. 91-126

G. Foti, *La topografia di Locri Epizefiri*, in Atti Taranto 1976, pp. 343-362

AA.Vv., *Fratte: un insediamento etrusco-campano*, a cura di G.Greco e A. Pontrandolfo, Modena 1990

F.V. Frazzoli-L. Vlad Borrelli-P. Fiorentino, *Indagine XRF su frammenti di statue bronzee sottoposte a corrosione marina*, in AA.Vv., *Applicazione dei metodi nucleari nel campo delle opere d'arte* (Roma-Venezia 1973), Roma 1976, pp. 339 ss.

A. Furumark, *The Mycenean Pottery. Analysis and Classification*, Stockholm 1941

A. Furtwangler, *Beschreibung der Glyptothek*, Berlin 1900

R.M. Gais, *A Crown and Consolation in Rural Southern Italy*, in Archaeology 35 1982, pp. 54-56

W. Gauer, *Die Bronzegefaesse von Olympia, I, Olympische Forschungen* XX Berlin-New York 1991

D. Graepler, *La coroplastica tarantina*, in Cenacolo n.s. 1, 1989, pp. 17-28

C. Greco, *L'ariete di bronzo da Siracusa*, in AA.Vv., *Federico e la Sicilia. Dalla terra alla corona. Archeologia e architettura* (Catalogo della Mostra), Palermo 1995, pp. 418-421

E. Greco, *Serdaioi*, in AnnAStorAnt XII 1990, pp. 39 ss.

G. Greco, *I materiali dai vecchi scavi dell'abitato: 1. Terrecotte architettoniche*, in Fratte

G. Greco, *Serra di Vaglio. La casa dei Pithoi*, Modena 1991

G. Greco, *La ripresa delle indagini allo Heraion*, in AttiMemMagnaGr 1992, pp. 247-258

J.R. Green, *Some Painters of Gnathia Vases*, in BICS 15 1968, pp. 34-50

A. Greifenhagen, *Eine attische Schwartzfigurige Vasengattung und die Darstellung des Komos in VI Jahr.*, Koenigsberg 1929

A. Greifenhagen, *Schmuckarbeiten in Edelmetall, I, Fundgruppen*, Staatlichen Musen Berlin, Antikenabteilung 1971

P. Griffo, *Messina. Necropoli ellenistico-romana agli "Orti Maddalena" e nella zona ad essi adiacente*, in NSc 1942, pp. 66-91

P. Griffo, *Il Museo Archeologico Regionale di Agrigento*, Roma 1987

M. Gualtieri-H. Fracchia, *Roccagloriosa* I, Napoli 1990

M. Guarducci, *Epigrafia greca*, I-III, Roma 1967

M. Guarducci, *Una nuova dea a Naxos in Sicilia e gli antichi legami fra la Naxos siceliota e l'omonima isola delle Cicladi*, in Mefra 97 1985, pp. 7-34

P.G. Guzzo, *Lamina in argento ed oro da Sibari*, in BdA LVIII 1973, pp. 65-74

P.G. Guzzo, *L'archeologia delle colonie arcaiche*, in Storia della Calabria Antica, I, Bari 1987

P. G. Guzzo, *Armi antiche di qua e di là delle Alpi. A proposito di due recenti cataloghi*, in BdA 62-63 1990, pp. 138-145

P. G. Guzzo, *Da Elche a Sardis via Daunia*, in ArchCl 43 1991, p. 961 ss.

P.G. Guzzo, *Oreficerie della Magna Grecia. Ornamenti in oro e argento dall'Italia Meridionale fra l'VIII ed il I secolo*, Taranto 1993

P.G. Guzzo, *Oreficerie della Lucania antica*, in BBasil 10 1994, pp. 25-48 (a)

AA.Vv., *Castores. L'immagine dei Dioscuri a Roma*, Roma 1994 (b)

T. Hadzisteliou-Price, *Kourotrophos-Cults and Representations of the Greek Nursing Deities*, Leiden 1978

H. Herderjurgen, *Untersuchungen zur thronenden Gottin aus Tarent*, Berlin 1968

H. Herderjurgen, *Tarantinischen Terrakotten der Sammlung Schwit-*

ter, in AntK 16 1973, pp. 53-108

R.A. HIGGINS, *Catalogue of the terracottas in the Department of Greek and Roman antiquities of the British Museum*, I. Greek, London 1954

R.A. HIGGINS, *Tarantine Terrakottas*, in Atti Taranto 1970, pp. 267-271

R. HIGGINS, *Magenta Ware*, in BrMusYearbook I 1976, pp. 1-32

A. HUS, *Les bronzes ètrusques*, Coll. Latomus CXXXIX, Bruxelles 1975

G. IACOPI, *Specchio bronzeo da Medma*, in BdA s.IV, XXXV 1950, pp. 193-200

G. IACOPI, *Messina nell'antichità*, in *Messana* III 1954, pp. 3-32

N. DEGRASSI, *Inscriptiones Latinae Liberae rei Publicae*, Firenze 1957

M. IOZZO, *Ceramica "calcidese". Nuovi documenti e problemi riproposti*, in AttiMemMagnaGr s.III 2, 1993, Roma 1994

H.P. ISLER, *Monte Iato: Guida archeologica*, Palermo 1991

AA.VV., *Italia omnium terrarum alumna*, Milano 1988

AA.VV., *Italia omnium terrarum parens*, Milano 1989

AA.VV., *Italici in Magna Grecia. Lingua, insediamenti e strutture*, Venosa 1990

U. JANTZEN, *Bronzewerkstatten in Grossgriechenland und Sizilien*, Berlin 1937

H. JEANMAIRE, *Dionysos. Histoire du culte de Bacchus*, Paris 1991 (5° ed.)

R. JEFFERY, *The Local Scripts of Archaic Greece*, Oxford 1961 (2nd ed. rev.suppl. A.W. JOHNSTON, Oxford 1990)

M. JENTOFT NILSEN, *Two vases of South Italian Shape by an Attic Painter*, in Aa.Vv., *Greek Colonists and Native Populations*, First Australian Congress of Classical Archaeology, Sydney 1990, pp. 243-249

F. JOHANSEN, *Etruskike Bronzereliefer i Glyptotek*, in MeddelGlypt 36 1979, pp. 67 ss.

P. F. JOHNSTON, *Ships and boat-models in ancient Greece*, Annopolis 1985

E. JOLY, *La ceramica: botteghe e Maestri della Sicilia ellenistica*, in Sikanìe, pp. 348-355

C. JONES EISEMAN-B. SISMONDO RIDGWAY, *The Porticello Shipwreck. A Mediterranean Merchant Vessel of 415-385 B.C.*, College Station-Texas 1987

G.A. HANFMANN-J.C. WALDBAUM, in AA.VV., *The Frederick M. Watkins Collection*, Exhibition Catalogue of the Fogg Art Museum, Harvard University-Cambridge 1973, p. 33

W.D. HEILMEYER (a cura di), *Antikenmuseum Berlin*. die ausgestellen Werke, Berlin 1988

V. KARAGEORGHIS, *Excavations in the Necropolis of Salamis*, III (Salamis 5), Haarlem 1974

R. KEARSLEY in J.P. DESCOEUDRES-R. KEARSLEY, *Greek Pottery at Veii: Another Look*, in BSA 78 1983, pp. 9-53

R. KEARSLEY, *The Pendent Semi-Circle Skyphos*, BICS, Suppl. 44, 1989

J. KECK, *Studien zur Rezeption fremder Einflusse in der chalkidischen Keramik. Ein Beitrag zur Lokalisierungsfrage*, in Archaologische Studien 8, Frankfurt-Paris 1988

J.F. KENFIELD, *An East Greek Master Coroplast at Late Archaic Morgantina*, in Hesperia 59, 1990, pp. 265-274

J.F. KENFIELD in *Aja* 96 1992, pp. 771-772

E.C. KEULS, *The Reign of Phallus. Sexual Polities in Ancient Athens*, New York 1985

I. KLEEMANN, *Der Satrapen-Sarkophag aus Sidon*, Berlin 1958

G. KLEINER, *Antiken Terrakotten*, Berlin 1942

H. KOCH, *Zu den Metopen von Thermos*, in AM XXXIV 1914, pp. 237-255

H. KYRIELEIS, *Chios and Samos in The Archaic Period*, in Chios. A Conference at the Homereion in Chios, a cura di J. Boardmann, Oxford 1986, pp. 187-204

E. KUNZE, *Kretische Bronzereliefs*, Stuttgart 1931

E. KUNZE, *Eine Urkunde der Stadt Sybaris*, "Olympische Forschungen" 7 1961, pp. 207-210

E. LANGLOTZ, in *Gnomon* VI 1930, pp. 429-431

E. LANGLOTZ, *Die Ephebenstatue in Agrigento*, in RM LVIII 1943, pp. 204 s.

E. LANGLOTZ-M.HIRMER, *L'arte della Magna Grecia* (trad. di *Die Kunst der Westgriechen*, Munchen 1963), Roma 1968

AA.VV., *Laos II. La tomba a camera di Marcellina*, Taranto 1992

E. LATTANZI (a cura), *Il Museo Nazionale di Reggio Calabria*, Reggio Calabria 1987

E. LATTANZI, *Un'altra testa dal relitto di Porticello*, in VIII Rassegna di Archeologia subacquea, Giardini Naxos 1993, c.s.

C. LAVIOSA, *Le antefisse fittili di Taranto*, in ArchCl 6 1954, pp. 217-250

A.D. TRENDALL, *The red-figured Vases of Lucania, Campania and Sicily*, Oxford 1967 (BICS suppl.I 1970, II 1973, III 1983)

R. LEIGHTON, *Sicily during the Centuries of Darkness*, in CambrAJ 3 1993, pp. 271-283

M.C. LENTINI, *Nuove esplorazioni a Naxos (scavi 1989-1994)*, in Kokalos XXXIX-XL 1993-1994, c.s.

C. LETTA, *Piccola coroplastica metapontina nel Museo Provinciale di Potenza*, Napoli 1971

A. LEVI, *Sorrento - Sculture greche in marmo*, in NSc 1924, pp. 375-384

AA.VV., *Da Leukania a Lucania. La Lucania centro-orientale tra Pirro e i Giulio-Claudii*, Roma 1993

G. LIBERTINI, *Il Museo Biscari*, Roma 1930

Lexicon Iconographicum Mithologiae Classicae, Zurich-Munchen 1981 -

E. LIPPOLIS a cura di, *Catalogo del Museo Nazionale Archeologico di Taranto*, III.1, *Taranto. La necropoli: aspetti e problemi della documentazione archeologica dal VII al I sec.a.C.*, Taranto 1994

E. LIPPOLIS-S. GARRAFFO-M. NAFISSI, *Culti greci in Occidente*. I. Taranto, Taranto 1995, pp. 31 ss.

AA.VV., *Locri Epizefirii*, III, Firenze 1989

F.G. LO PORTO, *Metaponto. Scavi e ricerche archeologiche*, In NSc XX 1966, pp. 136 ss.

F.G. LO PORTO, *Scene teatrali e soggetti caricaturali su nuovi vasi apuli di Taranto*, in BdA 1968, pp. 7-13

F.G. LO PORTO, *Tomba messapica di Ugento*, in AttiMemMagnaGr n.s. XI-XII 1970-71, pp. 99-152

F.G. LO PORTO, *Testimonianza archeologiche di culti metapontini*, in Xenia 16 1988, pp. 22 ss.

F.G. LO PORTO-F. RANALDI, *Le "lastre dei cavalieri" di Serra di Vaglio*, in MonAnt serie misc., III 6 1990, pp. 291-315

F.G. LO PORTO, *Timmari. L'abitato, le necropoli, la stipe votiva*, Spoleto 1991

F. LO SCHIAVO-L. VAGNETTI in AA.VV., *Studies in Sardinian Archaeology III. Proceedings of the Colloquium "Nuragic Sardinia and the Mycenean World"* (Roma 1986), BAR 387, Oxford 1987

R. LULLIES, *Addenda zu "Vergoldete Terrakotta-Appliken aus Tarent"*, in RM 84,1, 1977, pp. 235-260

AA.VV., *Meisterwerke der Antike aus dem Archaeologischen Nationalmuseum Neapel*, Catalogo della Mostra, Bonn 1995

F. MAGI, *La stele greca della Biblioteca Vaticana*, in Mèlanges Eugéne Tisserant, Città del Vaticano 1964, VII

A. Mallwitz-Schiering, *Die Werkstatt des Pheidias in Olympia*, Olympische Forschungen V, Berlin 1964

M.T. Manni Piraino, *Epigrafia selinuntina*, in *Kokalos* XVI 1970, pp. 268-294

M.T. Manni Piraino, *Iscrizioni greche lapidarie del Museo di Palermo*, ΣΙΚΕΛΙΚΑ VI, Palermo 1973

P. Marconi, *Restauro della statua bronzea d'arte greca detta "L'Efebo di Selinunte"*, in BdA VIII 1928, pp. 231-236

P. Marconi, *L'efebo di Selinunte*, Roma 1929 (a)

P. Marconi, *Topografia e arte*, Firenze 1929 (b)

P. Marconi, *Plastica agrigentina*, in Dedalo IX 1929, pp. 579 ss. (c)

P. Marconi, *Note sull'ariete del Museo di Palermo*, in BdA X 1930, pp. 138-142

C. Marconi, *Selinunte. Le metope dell'Heraion*, Modena 1994

F.H. Marshall, *Catalogue of the Jewellery, Greek, Etruscan and Roman, in the Department of Antiquities-British Museum*, London 1911

M. Martelli in AA.Vv., *La ceramica degli Etruschi*, Novara 1987 (a cura di M. Martelli)

G.A. Maruggi, *La necropoli del Regio Arsenale*, in Aa.Vv., *Il Museo di Taranto. Cento anni di archeologia*, Taranto 1988, pp. 17-28

M.A. Mastelloni, *Il vaso plastico*, in AA.Vv., *Le immagini della memoria*, Roma 1993, pp. 39-40

A. Mastrocinque, *L'ambra e l'Eridano (Studi sulla letteratura e sul commercio dell'ambra in età preromana)*, Este 1991

C.C. Mattusch, *Greek Bronze Statuary from the Beginnings through the Fifth Century B.C.*, Ithaca-London 1988

AA.Vv., *Megale Hellas. Storia e civiltà della Magna Grecia*, Milano 1983

M. Mertens Horn, *Beobachtung an dadalischen Tondachern*, in JdI 93 1978, pp. 30-65

M. Mertens-Horn, *Una nuova antefissa a testa femminile da Akrai e alcune considerazioni sulle Ninfe di Sicilia*, in BdA 66 1991, pp. 9-28

M. Mertens Horn, *Die Archaischen Baufriese aus Metapont*, in RM 99 1992, pp. 75-81

M. Mertens Horn, *Resti di due grandi statue di Apollo ritrovati nel santuario di Apollo Aleo di Ciró*, in Catalogo Mostre Soprintendenza Archeologica della Calabria, Crotone c.s.

AA.Vv., *Metaponto I*, in NSc XXIX 1975 (Suppl.)

P. Mingazzini, *Vasi della Collezione Castellani*, Roma 1930

R. Miller, *The terracotta votives from Medma: cult and coroplastic craft in Magna Grecia*, I, II, The University of Michigan 1983

J.P. Morel, *Cèramique Campanienne. Les formes*, Rome 1981

J.M. Moret, *L'Ilioupersis dans la ceramographie italiote*, Geneve 1975

J.M. Moret, *Le jugement de Paris en Grand-Grece: mythe et actualité politique*, in AntK 21 1978, 2, pp. 76 ss.

S. Moscati-C.A. Di Stefano, *Palermo. Museo Archeologico*, Palermo 1991

AA.Vv., *Il Museo archeologico Nazionale di Napoli*, Napoli 1994

AA.Vv., *Museo Nazionale Romano. Le sculture*, I, 1, Roma 1979, a cura di A. Giuliano

AA.Vv., *Il Museo Nazionale della Siritide di Policoro*, a cura di S. Bianco e M. Tagliente, Bari 1985

AA.Vv., *Il Museo Archeologico di Venosa*, Matera 1991

M. Napoli, *Civiltà della Magna Grecia*, Roma 1969

M. Napoli, *La tomba del tuffatore*, Bari 1970

N. Negroni Catacchio, *L'ambra. Produzione e commerci nell'Italia preromana*, in *Italia parens*, pp. 659 ss.

I. Novaco Lofaro, *Arule con Eracle e Acheloo*, in *Klearchos* VIII 1966, pp. 131-140

G. Olbrich, *Archaische Statuetten eines Metapontiner Heiligtums*, Roma 1979

R. Olmos Romera, *El centauro de Royos y el centauro en el mundo ibérico*, in *Homenaje* Almagro Basch 1983, pp. 377 ss.

P. Orlandini, *Nuovi acroteri fittili a forma di cavallo e cavaliere dall'Acropoli di gela*, in *Scritti in onore di G. Libertini*, Firenze 1958, pp. 117-128

P. Orlandini, *Gela. La stipe votiva del Predio Sola*, in MonAnt XLVI 1963, cc. 1-78

P. Orlandini, *Perirrhanterion fittile arcaico con decorazione a rilievo dagli scavi dell'Incoronata*, in *Scritti Adamesteanu*, pp. 175 ss.

P. Orlandini, *Le Arti figurative*, in *Megale Hellas*, pp. 331 ss.

P. Orlandini, *Due nuovi vasi figurati di stile orientalizzante dagli scavi dell'Incoronata di Metaponto*, BdA 49 1988, pp. 6-16

P. Orlandini, *Altri due vasi di stile orientalizzante dagli scavi dell'Incoronata*, in BdA 66 1991, pp. 1 ss.

E.M. De Juliis (a cura di), *Gli ori di Taranto in età ellenistica*, Catalogo della Mostra, Milano 1984

AA.Vv., *L'oro dei Greci*, Novara 1992

P. Orsi, *Gela. Scavi del 1900-1905*, in MonAnt XVII 1906, cc. 5-766

P. Orsi, *Due teste di rilievi attici rinvenuti in Sicilia*, in *Miscellanea dedicata al prof. A. Salinas*, Palermo 1907, pp. 25 ss.

P. Orsi, *Rosarno (Medma). Esplorazione di un grande deposito votivo di terrecotte ieratiche*, in NSc 1913 (a)

P. Orsi, *Piccoli bronzi e marmi inediti del Museo di Siracusa*, in *Ausonia* VIII 1913, pp. 44-75 (b)

P. Orsi, *Templum Apollinis Alei ad Crimisa promontorium*, in Atti-MemMagnaGr 1932, pp. 135-170 Paestum

AA.Vv., *Paestum. La città e il territorio*, Roma 1990

J.M. Pailler, *Bacchanalia. La répression de 186 av.J.Chr. à Rome et en Italie: vestiges, images, tradition*, Rome 1988

M.R. Palumbo, *Le terrecotte figurate di tipo greco in Daunia, Peucezia e Messapia*, Galatina 1986

R. Panvini, *L'attività della Soprintendenza di Agrigento e Caltanissetta nel campo dell'archeologia subacquea*, in Atti della IV Rassegna di archeologia subacquea, Naxos 1989, pp. 193-200

R. Panvini, *La nave arcaica di Gela*, in Archeologia Viva, 1993.

M. Paoletti, *Arule di Medma e tragedie attiche*, in *Scritti* Arias, pp. 371-392

M. Paoletti, *La nave di Porticello: una rotta siciliana*, in *Klearchos* 129-130 1995, pp. 119 ss.

E. Paribeni, *Sculture greche. Catalogo delle sculture del Museo Nazionale Romano*, Roma 1953

E. Paribeni, *Di un gruppo di antefisse siciliane*, in DArch I 1967, pp. 281-287

E. Paribeni, *Commento alla plastica di S. Biagio*, in Atti Taranto XIII 1973, pp. 457 ss.

E. Paribeni, *Le statue bronzee di Porticello*, in BdA 24 1984, pp. 1 ss.

H. Payne, *On Thermon Metopes*, in BSA XXVII 1925-1926, pp. 124-132

H. Payne, *Necrocorinthia*, Oxford 1931

P. Pelagatti, *Antefisse sileniche siceliote*, in CronA IV 1965, pp. 79-98

P. Pelagatti, *Sacelli e nuovi materiali da Naxos, Monte San Mauro e Camarina*, in CronA XVI 1977, pp. 43-65

P. Pelagatti, in AA.Vv., *Storia del-*

la Sicilia, I, Napoli 1980, pp. 619 ss.

P. PELAGATTI, *L'attività della Soprintendenza alle Antichità della Sicilia Orientale*. Parte II, in Kokalos XXVI-XXVII 1980-1981, II 1, pp. 694-731

P. PELAGATTI, *Naxos (Messina). Gli scavi extraurbani oltre il Santa Venera 1973-1975*, in NSc 1984-1985, pp. 253-304 (a)

P. PELAGATTI, *Ricerche nel quartiere orientale di Naxos e nell'agorà di Camarina*, in *Kokalos* XXX-XXXI 1984-1985, pp. 679-694 (b)

P. PELAGATTI, in Btcgi XII, Pisa-Roma 1993, s.v. Nasso, pp. 268-312

Perachora I
H. PAYNE, *Perachora. The Sanctuaries of Hera Akraia and Limenia*, Oxford 1940

T.J. DUNBABIN, *Perachora* II, Oxford 1962

M. PFROMMER, *Studien zu alexandrinischer und grossgriechischer Toreutik fruhhellenistischer Zeit*, Archaologische Forschungen 16, Mainz am Rhein 1987

G. PIANU, *La necropoli meridionale di Eraclea. 1. Le tombe di secolo IV e III a.C.*, Roma 1990

G. PIANU, *Spazi e riti nell'agorà di Eraclea Lucana*, in AA.VV., *L'espace sacrificiel*, Lyon 1991, pp. 201 ss.

G. PISANO, *I gioielli*, in AA.VV., *I Fenici*, Catalogo della Mostra, Milano 1988, pp. 370 ss.

L. POLACCO, *I trionfi dell'amore nei misteri di Venere Acrense*, in NumAntCl 21 1992, pp. 173-202

AA.VV., *Polis e Olympieion a Locri Epizefiri*, Soveria Mannelli (CZ) 1992, a cura di F. Costabile

AA.VV., *Pontecagnano II. Le necropoli del Picentino I. Le tombe della Prima Età del Ferro*, in AnnAStorAnt Quad.5, Napoli 1988

A. PONTRANDOLFO, *La pittura funeraria in Magna Grecia*, in Magna Grecia IV, Milano 1990, pp. 351-390

A. PONTRANDOLFO-A. ROUVERET, *Le tombe dipinte di Paestum*, Modena 1992

AA.VV., *Popoli anellenici in Basilicata* (Catalogo Mostra Potenza), Napoli 1971

AA.VV., *Popoli e civiltà dell'Italia antica*, Roma 1974 -

V. POULSEN, *Iconographic Studies in the Ny Carlsberg Glyptothek*, Copenaghen 1972

AA.VV., *Principi imperatori vescovi. Duemila anni di storia a Canosa*, Catalogo della Mostra, Venezia 1992, a cura di R. CASSANO

H. PRUCKNER, *Die Lokrischen Reliefs*, Mainz am Rhein 1969

G. PUGLIESE CARRATELLI, *Storia civile*, in *Megale Hellas*, pp. 5-102

G. PUGLIESE CARRATELLI, *Storia civile*, in *Sikanie*, pp. 7-78

G. PUGLIESE CARRATELLI, *La scuola medica di Parmenide a Velia. Tra Cadmo e Orfeo. Contributo alla storia civile e religiosa dei Greci d'Occidente*, Bologna 1991

G. PUGLIESE CARRATELLI, *Le lamine d'oro orfiche,* Milano 1993

G. PUGLIESE CARRATELLI-G. FIORENTINO, *Agrigento. Museo Archeologico*, Palermo 1992

A.D. TRENDALL-A. CAMBITOGLOU, *The Red-figured Vases of Apulia*, I Oxford 1978; II 1982 (BICS suppl.I 1983)

G. RIZZA-E. DE MIRO, *Le arti figurative dalle origini al V secolo a.C.*, in *Sikanìe*, pp. 125-242

E. ROHDE, *Psiche. Culto delle anime e fede nell'immortalità presso i Greci*, Bari 1970

C. ROLLEY, *Greek Bronzes*, Freibourg 1986

C. ROLLEY, *Trois bronzes de Métaponte*, in RA I 1989, pp. 115-126

C. ROLLEY, *Les bronzes grecs et romains: recherches récentes*, in RA 1990, pp. 405-422

C. ROLLEY, *Bronzes en Messapie*, in Atti Taranto 1991, pp. 185-207

C. ROLLEY, *La Sculpture grecque*, Paris 1994

C. ROLLEY, *Têtes de marbre de Paestum*, in AA.VV., *Lo stile severo in Grecia e in Occidente*, Roma 1995

E. RONCALLI, *Le lastre dipinte da Cerveteri*, Firenze 1965

AA.VV., *Roma medio-repubblicana* (Catalogo della Mostra, Roma 1973), Roma 1973

R. ROSS HOLLOWAY, *Influences and Styles in the Late Archaic and Early Classical Greek Sculpture of Sicily and Magna Graecia*, Louvain 1975

A. RUMPF, *Chalkidische Vasen*, Berlino-Lipsia 1927

D. RUSSO, *Il tempio di Giove Meilichio a Pompei*, Napoli 1991

C. ABBIONE, *Intorno a una serie di statuette arcaiche locresi*, in *Klearchos* 47-48 1970, pp. 109-156

C. SABBIONE, in AA.VV., *Il Museo Nazionale di Reggio Calabria*, a cura di E.Lattanzi, Roma-Reggio Calabria 1987

F. SALVIAT, *Sur la religion de Marseille grecque*, in "Marseille grecque et la Gaule", Actes du Colloque, Etudes massaliètes, 3, 1992, pp. 141-150

A. SANPIETRO, *La ceramica a figure nere di S.Biagio (Metaponto)*, Galatina 1991

M. SANTANGELO, *Selinunte*, Roma 1953

L.A. SCATOZZA HOERICHT, *Le terrecotte figurate di Cuma*, Roma 1987

J. SCHAEFER, *Studien zu den griechischen Reliefpithoi des 8-6 Jahr.v.Chr. aus Kreta, Rhodos, tenos und Boiotien*, Kallmuenz 1957

K. SCHAUENBURG, *Bendis in Unteritalien?*, in JdI 89 1974, pp. 137-186

K. SCHEFOLD, *Gods and Heroes in Late Archaic Greek Art*, Oxford 1992

W. SCHIERING, *Werkstatten Orientalisierender Keramik*, Berlin 1957

B. SCHLOERB-VIERNEISEL, *Glyptothek Munchen. Katalog der Skulpturen. II. Klassische Skulpturen des 5. und 4. Jahr.v.Chr.*, Munchen 1979

E. SCHMIDT, *Geschichte der Karyatide*, Wurzburg 1982

M. SCHMIDT-A.D. TRENDALL-A. CAMBITOGLOU, *Eine Gruppe Apulischen Grabvasen in Basel*, Mainz 1976

K. SCHUMACHER, *Beschreibung der Sammlung antiker Bronzen*, Karlsruhe 1890

AA.VV., *Attività archeologica in Basilicata 1964-1977. Scritti in onore di Dinu Adamesteanu*, Matera 1980

AA.VV., *AΠAPXAI. Scritti in onore di P. E.Arias*, I-III, Pisa 1982

Supplementum Epigraphicum Graecum

B. SEGALL, *Museum Benaki Athen. Katalog der Goldschmiearbeiten*, Athen 1938

M. SESTIERI BERTARELLI, *Il tempietto e la stipe votiva di Garaguso*, in AttiMemMagnaGr 1958, pp. 67-68

M. SESTIERI BERTARELLI, *Statuette femminili arcaiche e del primo classicismo nelle stipi votive di Poseidonia*, in RIA s.III, XII 1989, pp. 5-47

M. SGUAITAMATTI, *Vases plastiques hellénistiques de Grand Gréce et de Sicile. Remarques préliminaires*, in NumAntCl 20 1991, pp. 117-146

H. SICHTERMANN, *Vasen in Unteritalien aus der Sammlung Jatta*, Tubingen 1966

AA.VV., *La Sicilia greca. Det grekiska Sicilien* (Mostra Malmo 1989), Palermo 1989

J. SIEVEKING, *Die terrakotten der Sammlung Loeb*, Munchen 1916

AA.VV., *Sikanie. Storia e civiltà della Sicilia greca*, Milano 1985

E. SJOQVIST, *Excavations at Serra Orlando (Morgantina) - Preliminary Report II*, in AJA 62 1958, pp. 155-162

U. SPIGO, *La ceramica siceliota a figure rosse: variazioni sul tema*, in BdA 1987, pp. 1-24 (a)
SPIGO 1987b
U. SPIGO, *Crateri del IV secolo a.C. con figurazioni ricollegabili al culto di Dioniso*, in L. BERNABÒ BREA-U. SPIGO, *Da Eschilo a Menandro. Due*

secoli di teatro greco attraverso i reperti archeologici liparesi, (Catalogo della Mostra), Lipari 1987, pp. 31-42 (b)

U. Spigo, *Due rappresentazioni fittili di navi greche*, in Atti IV Rassegna di Archeologia Subacquea, Giardini Naxos 1989, Messina 1991, pp. 71-83

U. Spigo, *Nuovi rinvenimenti di ceramica a figure rosse di fabbrica siceliota ed italiota da Lipari e dalla provincia di Messina*, in MedA 5-6 1993, pp. 42 ss.

K. Staehler, *Klassische Akrotere*, in AA.Vv., Festschrift H.Kenner, II, Wien 1985, pp. 326 ss.

P. Stary in HambBeitrA, 8 1981, pp. 66 ss. (a)

P. Stary, *Zur eisenzeitlichen Bewaffnung und Kampweise in Mittelitalien*, Marburg 1981 (b)

P. Stary, in AA.Vv., *Italian Iron Age Artifacts in the British Museum - Papers of the Sixth B.M. Classical Colloquium 1982*, London 1986

A. Stewart, *Greek Sculpture*, New Haven & London 1990

C.M. Stibbe, *Archaic bronze hydriai*, in BABesch 67 1992, pp. 1-62

AA.Vv., *Lo stile severo in Sicilia*. Catalogo della Mostra, Palermo 1990

H.W. Stoop, *Floreal figurines from South-Italy*, Leiden 1960

M.W. Stoop, *Santuario sul timpone della Motta I. Bronzi*, in AttiMemMagnaGr n.s. XI-XII, 1970-71, pp. 38-50

M.W. Stoop-G. Pugliese Carratelli, *Scavi a Francavilla Marittima. Tabella con iscrizione arcaica*, in AttiMemMagnaGr n.s.VI-VII, pp. 14 ss.

D.E. Strong, *Catalogue of the Carved Amber in the Department of Greek and Roman Antiquities*, London 1966 (a)

D.E. Strong, *Greek and Roman Gold and Silver Plate*, London 1966 (b)

M. Szabò, *Archaic Terracottas of Boeotia*, Roma 1994

W. Taylour, *Mycenean Pottery in Italy*, Cambridge 1958

A.L. Tempesta, *Antefisse fittili da Metaponto*, in BBasil 11 1995, c.s.

G. Tigano, *Modellini fittili di imbarcazioni dalla necropoli ellenistica di Milazzo*, in Atti IV Rassegna di Archeologia Subacquea, Giardini Naxos 1989, Messina 1991, pp. 51-70

G. Tigano, *Ultimi scavi a Milazzo*, in Kalòs. Arte in Sicilia, 6, n. 1-2, gennaio-aprile 1994, p. 34

G. Tocco Sciarelli-J. De La Geniere-G. Greco, in *Atti* Taranto 1987, Napoli 1992, pp. 385-396

M. Torelli, *Il santuario di Hera a Gravisca*, in ParPass 26 1971, pp. 44-

G. Traversari, *Sculture del V-IV sec. a.C. del Museo Archeologico di Venezia*, Padova 1973

A.D. Trendall, *Vasi antichi dipinti del Vaticano. Vasi italioti ed etruschi a figure rosse*, Città del Vaticano 1953

A.D. Trendall, *Phlyax Vases*, Oxford 1967

A.D. Trendall, *The Red Figured Vases of Paestum*, Rome 1987

A.D. Trendall, *Red-figured Vases of South Italy and Sicily*. A handbook, London 1989

A.D. Trendall-A. Cambitoglou, *Second Supplement to the Red-figured Vases of Apulia*, London 1991 (Part I), London 1992 (Part II)

A.D. Trendall-T.B.L. Webster, *Illustrations of Greek Drama*, London 1971

A. Tullio, *La collezione Archeologica del Museo Mandralisca*, Cefalù 1979

A. Tullio, *La collezione archeologica*, in Cefalù. Museo Mandralisca, Palermo 1991

V. Tusa, *La necropoli di Selinunte*, in AA.Vv., *Odeon ed altri monumenti archeologici*, Palermo 1971, pp. 175-326

V. Tusa, *L'attività archeologica della Soprintendenza alle Antichità ella Sicilia occidentale nel quadriennio 1968-1971*, in Kokalos XVIII-XIX 1972-73, pp. 392-410

V. Tusa, *La scultura in pietra di Selinunte*, Palermo 1983

V. Tusa, *La statua di Mozia*, in SicA 66-68 1988, pp. 15-22

V. Tusa, *La Sicilia nella preistoria*, 2ª ed. Palermo 1992

A. Uguzzoni-F .Ghinatti, *Le Tavole di Eraclea*, Roma 1968

J.P. Uhlenbrock, *Concerning some Archaic terracotta protomai from Naxos*, in Xenia 18 1989, pp. 9-26

L. Vagnetti, *Un anello del Museo Archeologico di Firenze e le oreficerie di S. Angelo Muxaro*, in SMEA XV 1972, pp. 189-201

L. Vagnetti, *I contatti precoloniali fra le genti indigene e i paesi mediterranei*, in AA.Vv., *Magna Grecia. Le metropoli e la fondazione delle colonie*, Milano 1985, pp. 127 ss.

G. Vallet, *Rhegion et Zancle*, Paris 1958

G. Vallet-F. Villard, *Mégara Hyblaea VIII.Remarques sur la plastique du VIIe siècle*, in MEFRA LXXVI 1964, pp. 25-42

E.D. Van Buren, *Archaic Fictile Revetments in Sicily and Magna Graecia*, Washington 1973

H. Van Der Meijden, *Terrakottaarulae aus Sizilien und Unteritalien*, Amsterdam 1993

F. Van Keuren, *The Frieze from the Hera I Temple at Foce Sele*, Roma 1989

A. Villa, *La necropoli di Solunto*, in Studi sulla Sicilia occidentale in onore di V. Tusa, Padova 1993, pp. 215-218

F. Villard, *Tripi. Ricerche ad Abacaenum*, in NSc 1954, pp. 46-50

F. Villard, *Sicile grecque*, Paris 1955

F. Villard, *Vases de bronze grecs dans une tombe étrusque du VIIe siècle*, in MonPiot 48 1965

F. Villard, *La céramique polychrome du VII siècle en Grèce, en Italie du Sud et en Sicile et sa situation par rapport à la céramique protocorinthienne*, in ASAtene LIX N.S. XLIII 1981, pp. 133-137

D. Von Bothmer, *Amazons in Greek Art*, Oxford 1957 (a)

D. Von Bothmer, *Greek Vases from the Hearst Collections*, in MMA Bullettin 15, 7, 1957 (b)

G. Voza, *L'attività della Soprintendenza alle Antichità della Sicilia Orientale*, II, in Kokalos 22-23 1976-1977, pp. 551-597

G. Voza, *La necropoli della valle del Marcellino presso Villasmundo*, in CrnAStorArt 17 1978, pp. 104-110

G. Voza, *Problematica archeologica*, in E. Gabba-G. Vallet (Edd.), *La Sicilia antica*, Napoli 1980, I 1, pp. 5-42

G. Voza, *Evidenze archeologiche di VIII e VII sec.a.C. nel territorio di Siracusa: la necropoli di Villasmundo nella valle del Marcellino*, in ASAtene XLIV 1982, pp. 169-171

G. Voza, *I contatti precoloniali col mondo greco*, in Sikanìe, pp. 543-562

E. Walter-Karydi, *Samische Gefasse des 6. Jahrhunderts v.Chr.-Landschaftsstile ostgriechischer Gefaesse*, Samos VI, I, Bonn 1973

H.B. Walters, *Catalogue of the bronzes in the Department of Greek and Roman Antiquities* - British Museum, London 1899

H.B. Walters, *Select bronzes in the British Museum*, London 1951

T.B.L. Webster, *Towards a classification of Apulian Gnathia*, in BICS 15 1968, pp. 1-33

D. Williams, *Three groups of South Italian Jewellery in the British Museum*, in RM 95 1988, pp. 75-95

R.J.A. Wilson, *Sicily under the Roman Empire. The archaeology of a Roman province. 36 B.C.- A.D.535*, Warminster 1990 (a)

R.J.A. WILSON, *Roman Architecture in a Greek World: the Example of Sicily*, in L. HENIG (Ed), *Architecture and Architectural Sculpture in the Roman Empire*, Oxford 1990, pp. 67-90 (b)

N.A. WINTER, *Greek Architectural Terracottas*, Oxford 1993

U. WINTERMEYER, *Die polychrome Reliefkeramik aus Centuripe*, in JdI 90 1975, pp. 136-241

P. ZANCANI MONTUORO-U. ZANOTTI BIANCO, *Heraion alla Foce del Sele. I. Il santuario. Il tempio della dea. Rilievi figurati vari*, Roma 1951

P. ZANCANI MONTUORO, *Lampada arcaica dallo Heraion alla foce del Sele*, in AttiMemMagnaGr XIII 1960, pp. 69-77 (a)

P. ZANCANI MONTUORO, *Il corredo della sposa*, in ArchCl XII 1960, pp. 37-50 (b)

P. ZANCANI MONTUORO, *Hera Hippia*, in ArchCl XIII 1961, pp. 31 ss.

P. ZANCANI MONTUORO, *Heraion alla Foce del Sele. I. Altre metope del Primo thesauròs*, in AttiMemMagnaGr 1964, pp. 76-83 (a)

P. ZANCANI MONTUORO, *Piccola statua di Hera*, in FESTSCHRIFT E. VON MERCKLIN, Waldassen 1964, pp. 174-178 (b)

P. ZANCANI MONTUORO, *Uno scalo navale di Thurii*, in AttiMemMagnaGr n.s. XIII-XIV 1972-73, pp. 75-79

J.L. ZIMMERMANN, *Une cuirasse de Grand Grèce*, in MusHelv 36 1979, pp. 177-184

J.L. ZIMMERMANN, *L'armure en bronze de Malibu*, in GettyMusJ 10 1982, pp. 133-140

K. ZIMMERMANN, *Grachwil*, in AA.VV., *Trésors des princes celtes, Galeries nationales du Grand Palais 1987-1988*, Paris 1987, pp. 244-246

J.L. ZIMMERMANN, *Du thorax à la lorica. Cuirasses figurées et commemoratives d'Italie méridionale*, Genève 1989

Index of Names

Index of Names

A

A-ahmes 90
A-ta-na (Athena) 41
Abdera 165
Achaea 148, 183, 189, 236, 263
Achaean 234, 236, 238, 243, 244, 245, 255, 263, 315, 319, 322, 330, 345, 366, 372, 373, 375, 382, 390
Achaean, colonization 33
Achaioi, Greek, ethnic 34
Acheloos 196
Achilles 149, 319
Achradina 270, 272, 274
Acrae 153, 220, 221, 272, 276, 347
Acragas 115, 154, 160, 162, 163, 164, 166, 168, 170, 176, 189, 198, 199, 217, 220, 221, 228, 254, 286, 288, 293, 294, 295, 296, 299, 300, 322, 327, 331, 332, 333, 334, 336, 339, 345, 346, 354
Acroceraunia 204, 205
Acropolis 36, 55, 58, 61, 63, 67, 69, 70, 81, 85, 92, 336, 375, 385, 390, 391, 394
Acrotatus, King 176
Actium 75
Adeinias 200
Admonitions 33
Adria 205, 290
Adriatic 163, 174
Adriatic Sea 202, 205, 210
Aegae 105, 106, 183
Aegean 147, 202, 309, 320, 330, 369, 398
Aegean Islands 25, 55, 145
Aegean Sea 25, 186, 201, 204
Aegean Thalassocracy 25
Aegina 28, 61, 63, 88, 320, 327
Aegium 148
Aeoliae Insulae (Lipari) 184
Aeolian archipelago 109
Aeolian Islands 109, 145, 160, 162, 351, 378
Aeschylus 140
Aëtion 36
Aetna 164
Aetna/Catana 228
Aetolia 149
Africa 98, 112, 126, 145, 175, 205, 206, 307, 309
Agasias 198
Agatharcus 99
Agathocles 175, 176, 220, 221, 303, 305, 341, 350
Agathon 105
Agnello, S.L. 272

Agoracritus 68
Agrigento (ancient Acragas) 110, 115, 254, 286, 300, 327, 354
Agrigentum, Roman 221
Agrippa 101
Agrius 209, 214
Agyrion 171
Agyris 171, 220
Agyrium 220
Ahhiyawa 33, 34
Aianteioi 152
Aias 151, 152
Aiglanor 200
Akiris, Agri River 248
Akkas 199
Akrai 276
Akrillai 276
Akrotiri in Thera 25, 26, 29, 33
Al Mina 43, 177, 181, 184
Alabon 267
Alaisa (Halaesa) 221
Alalia, modern Aleria 127, 128, 138, 154, 155, 187, 188, 189
Alas 198
Alashiya 34
Alcamenes 68, 220
Alcander 220
Alcinous 47
Alcyoneus, Giant 84
Aleria 127
Alexander the Great 74, 75, 99, 105, 106, 175, 307, 398
Alexander the Molossian 175
Alexandria 101, 107, 108, 137, 305, 307, 351, 378, 396, 398
Almuandria 101 Alpheus River 204, 205
Aluntium (now San Marco d'Alunzo) 221
Amarna, the letters of 34
Amasis 90, 149
Amato 152
Amazon 70, 71
Amazonomachy 71
Ambracia 183
Ameinocles 138
Amendolara 234, 235
Amenhophis III 33
America 209, 346
Amin[ei] 224
Ammistamru II, King 34
Amnisus 36
Among 33, 34, 264, 318, 325
Amphis[tratos?] 98
Amphitrite 69
Amurru 34
Amyclae 151
Anactorium 183
Anaphlystos 96
Anapo 276

Anapos Valley 153
Anathema 81
Anatolia 38, 40, 43, 45, 85, 109, 121, 145, 147
Anavyssos 58
Anaxilas 147, 157, 159, 160, 163, 184, 191, 192, 220, 226
Ancona 205, 232
Andocides 92, 94
Androgenes 89
Andromachus 220
Andronikos, Manolis 105
Andros 180
Antas 130
Antenor 58
Anthili 54
Antibes 193
Antigonids 78
Antigonos 81, 104
Antigori 114, 115
Antiochus 147, 151
Antiochus II 78
Antiparos 25, 200
Antiphemos 199
Antipolis (modern Antibes) 193
Antisthenes 81, 82
Apamea 78
Apelles 99, 104, 193
Aphrodisia 260
Aphrodite 64, 67, 78, 162, 191, 193, 197, 252, 256, 280, 298, 357, 378, 391
Aphrodite Euploia 145
Apollo 46, 54, 56, 58, 63, 65, 72, 145, 146, 148, 149, 156, 186, 196, 200, 210, 215, 224, 309, 310, 324, 370, 380, 394
Apollo Alaios 149, 245, 339
Apollo Archegetes 146, 149, 192, 279
Apollo Hyakinthios 151
Apollodorus 99
Apollonia 183, 313
Apolloniades 220
Apollonius, of Rhodes 34
Apoxyomenus 74
Apulia 107, 112, 210, 226, 396, 397
Ara Maxima 210
Aradus 121
Aramaean 127
Aratus 99
Arcadia 53, 72, 151, 369, 372
Arcadion 198
Arcesilas 145
Archaic age 202, 205
Archaic Greek 239
Archaic period 52, 56, 234, 236, 239, 243, 244, 245, 246, 255, 256, 258, 260, 262, 313, 319,

320, 329, 330, 336, 347, 350, 351, 353, 354, 372, 380, 389, 391
Archaic times 235
Archanes, necropolis 38
Archanes, script 38
Archedamos 198
Archelaus, King 105
Archermus of Chios 56, 58
Archias 181, 200, 270
Archimedes 176
Architas 218
Archives, Mycenaean 37
Archivio Storico Siciliano 202
Archonides I 220
Archonides II 220
Archytas 174
Areopagus 51
Ares 51
Arethusa 228
Arganthonius 154
Argive 272
Argolid 25, 30, 34, 36, 37, 85, 86, 148, 109, 114, 189
Argolis 183
Argonautica 34
Argonauts 26, 209
Argos 30, 47, 65, 114, 181, 236, 320, 376
Ariadne 88, 396
Aricia (now Ariccia) 130, 378, 380
Aristeides 99
Aristion of Paros 58
Aristodemus 157, 163, 218
Aristogeiton 198
Aristophanes 51
Aristoteles 200
Aristotle 53, 99, 106, 139, 145, 148, 152, 153, 222
Aristoxenus 166, 228
Arkalochori 38
Arles 72, 352
Arpi 226
Arrubiu 114
Arsinoe 313
Artemis 61, 151, 243, 362, 363, 366
Artemis Hemera 151
Artemis Limnatis 146
Artemisium 132
Artemisium Zeus 65
Asclepius 71, 81, 82, 176, 228, 339
Ashmolean Museum 37
Asia 25, 189
Asia Minor 25, 56, 58, 102, 105, 109, 127, 145, 147, 148, 151, 154, 157, 163, 187, 189, 223, 224, 233, 238, 262, 289, 298, 299, 300, 320, 327, 330, 370
Asiatic Ionia 189

Assyria 126
Assyrian, archives 39
Assyrians 34
Astacus 183
Asyut (Egypt) 223
Athena 48, 58, 63, 67, 69, 78, 81, 84, 89, 94, 148, 149, 151, 152, 153, 191, 194, 223, 228, 235, 241, 243, 244, 248, 254, 290, 293, 294, 301, 303, 325, 332, 376, 395
Athena Nike 67, 69
Athena Parthenos 68
Athenagoras 102
Athenaion 255
Athenian Acropolis 61, 226
Athenian Cephisodotus 71
Athens 36, 47, 48, 49, 51, 52, 53, 56, 58, 62, 65, 67, 70, 75, 78, 85, 86, 87, 88, 89, 90, 96, 98, 99, 105, 117, 160, 164, 165, 166, 168, 174, 181, 183, 209, 223, 228, 260, 263, 278, 296, 301, 333, 336, 337, 347, 358, 370, 372, 375, 376, 380, 382, 391, 394, 398
Atlantis 34
Atossa 160
Attalids 78
Attalus II 78, 81
Attic 189, 226, 301, 337, 368, 372, 396
Attica 33, 36, 47, 85, 87, 89, 109, 119, 217, 259, 333, 364, 365, 369
Auberson, P. 267
Augusta 266
Augustan Age 205
Auxerre Goddess 56
Ayia Irini in Kea 25

B

Bacchante 189
Bacchiad 181, 183, 270
Bacchylides 34, 151
Baetis (Guadalquivir) 154
Baia di Porto Conte (Alghero) 119
Bakchios 98
Balearic Islands 145
Balkan Peninsula 141
Barca 145, 215
Basento 245, 248
Basilicata 112, 113, 210
Bassae 70, 71
Battiad 215
Battus 145, 309, 310
Belevi 78
Belvedere 260

Bérard, V. 209
Berbati 85
Berenice 314
Berlin 78, 94, 96, 394
Berytus 121
Bible 34, 121, 123
Binliff 30
Bithia 124
Black Sea 26, 147, 209, 364, 366
Blinkenberg 145
Boeotia 44, 45, 58, 88, 89, 96, 109, 119, 177, 369, 372
Bologna 210, 387
Bon-Porté 140
Borne 25
Bosporus 103, 183
Bradano 248
Bradano River 236, 244
Brettii 226
Brindisi 204
British, architect 37
Broglio di Trebisacce 113
Bronze Age 25, 26, 39, 42, 114, 116, 117, 347
Bronze, to the Iron Age 36
Bruttii 141, 174
Bryaxis 71
Bryce 34
Brygos 94
Buchner 239
Bura 148, 183
Byblos 121
Byzantium 183, 352

C

Cacus 210
Cadiz 121, 124, 127, 128, 130
Cadmeia, citadel 34
Cadmus 34, 44, 45, 46, 157, 159, 163
Caere (Cerveteri) 102, 130
Caesarea 137
Cagliari 114
Calabria 109, 112, 113, 177, 189, 226, 347, 395
Calabrian 206
California 29
Callippus 175, 220
Callistratus 71
Camarina 153, 154, 159, 166, 170, 176, 200, 220, 221, 228, 258, 272, 276, 293, 294, 299, 300, 301, 302, 303, 304, 347, 357, 361, 365, 366
Camicus 210
Camirus 53, 184
Campania 88, 90, 103, 119, 130, 141, 146, 166, 177, 189, 209, 215, 218, 226, 239, 243, 244,

319, 347, 352, 378, 380, 396
Campidoglio 78
Canaanites 43
Canicattini Bagni 276
Cannatello 110, 115
Canon 65
Canosa 396
Cantera 267
Cantera River
Canusium 228
Cape Lilybaeum 206
Cape Malea 204
Cape Pachynus (Capo Passero, Sicily) 205
Cape Pachynus 206
Cape Schisò 208
Cape Taormina 208
Capo Colonna 148, 149, 166, 205, 210, 236, 244, 245, 255, 339
Capo del Fiume 245
Capo dell'Armi 208
Capo Graziano 109
Capo Leuca 205
Capo Passero 205, 274
Capo Schisò 146
Capo Spartivento 208
Capo Zefirio 196
Capua 119, 163, 166, 378, 380
Caralis 124
Carians 34
Carias 198
Carta, Rosario 278
Carthage 121, 124, 126, 128, 130, 132, 157, 160, 162, 168, 170, 171, 174, 175, 176
Carthage, Gulf of 206
Caryatids 68
Carystus 104
Casale Nuovo 115
Casmenae 153, 272, 274, 276, 277, 278, 279, 289, 304, 347
Cassander 105
Cassandra 151
Castel dell'Ovo 145
Castello 262
Castor 156
Castro Via 255
Castrum Lucullanum 145
Catalogue of Ships 30
Catalonia 201, 232
Catana 153, 164, 166, 171, 175, 189, 193, 220, 221, 330
Caulonia 152, 166, 171, 183, 217, 224, 226, 252, 330, 347, 351, 357, 359, 360
Cavone 113, 364
Ceglie 226
Cenchreae 180, 204
Cene 241
Centaur 70

Centauromachy 63, 67
Centocamere 255, 256
Centuripae 171, 221
Ceos 26, 39, 85, 180
Cephallenia 204
Cephaloedium 171
Cephisodotus 72, 78
Cerveteri 89, 102, 130
Chabrias 215
Chadwick, John 30, 37
Chairestratos 78
Chalcedon 183
Chalcidian Rhegium 215
Chalcidice 180
Chalcis 120, 141, 149, 154, 177, 180, 183, 184, 191, 226, 239
Chalois 25
Chamezi 33
Charinos 95
Charondas 220
Chateaubriand 137
Cheimaros 197
Chiaramonte Gulfi 276
China 74
Chios 26, 52, 90, 187, 188
Chones 151
Ciasca, A. 126
Cicero 221, 222, 274, 305, 307
Cimon 228
Circe 209, 214
Circle A 30
Claros 148
Classical age 202, 205, 257, 355
Classical era 41, 339
Classical period 236, 252, 259
Cleander 157, 220
Cleandridas 166
Cleisthenes 90, 94, 394
Cleombrotos 235
Cleon 51
Cleonymus 176
Cleophrades 90
Cline 34
Clitias 89
Cnidian Aphrodite 72
Cnidos 72, 184, 274
Cnossos 37, 38, 39, 40, 41, 117
Cocalus 210
Cocalus, King 154
Cohen, Robert 215
Colaeus 137, 154, 202
Colchis 147, 148
Collina del Castello 261
Collina della Batteria 255
Colline Metallifere 119
Colophon 148, 151, 155, 165, 188, 189, 208, 238, 373
Columba, G. 202, 208
Conero 205
Corcyra (Corfu) 147, 159, 165, 181, 183, 204

Cordano 301
Corfu 61, 147, 204, 320, 324
Corfu, Straits of 205
Corinth 48, 49, 85, 88, 89, 96, 101, 155, 159, 164, 165, 166, 168, 177, 180, 181, 183, 186, 200, 204, 209, 223, 224, 263, 270, 272, 282, 299, 300, 320, 322, 343, 370, 372, 373, 383, 385, 390
Corinth, Gulf of (Lechaeum) 180, 183, 184, 204, 205
Corinthia 263
Corsica 127, 128, 138, 145, 155, 187, 188, 189
Cos 26, 29, 157, 176, 189
Cosentia 174, 370
Cothon 288
Cothon River 283
Cratemenes 191
Crathis River 113, 148, 255
Cremissa 195
Cresilas 67
Crete 25, 26, 28, 29, 30, 33, 34, 37, 38, 39, 43, 55, 56, 85, 86, 87, 96, 105, 109, 114, 119, 145, 146, 153, 186, 189, 199, 204, 205, 263, 309, 383
Crimea 147, 366
Crimesus River 175
Crimisa 149, 166, 217, 245
Critius 63, 86, 148
Crito 34
Croesus, Kroisos 90
Croto 246
Croton, (Kroton) 52, 148, 149, 152, 155, 156, 157, 163, 165, 166, 174, 175, 176, 183, 189, 194, 195, 196, 205, 210, 217, 218, 224, 226, 236, 238, 244, 245, 246, 255, 322, 332, 361, 362, 365, 368, 373, 375, 383
Cumae (Kyme) 119, 126, 130, 137, 141, 145, 146, 157, 163, 166, 177, 189, 191, 200, 209, 210, 217, 218, 226, 237, 238, 239, 243, 255, 347, 351
Cusa 288
Cyane 105
Cybele 197
Cyclades 25, 26, 33, 34, 55, 58, 85, 146, 186, 189, 192, 209, 263, 369
Cydonia, (modern Khaniá, Greece) 39
Cylon 174
Cyme 151, 177
Cypro-Minoan 37, 39
Cyprus 26, 33, 34, 37, 39, 42, 43, 85, 87, 109, 114, 118, 119, 120, 124, 184, 376

Cypselus 183
Cyre 200
Cyrenaic 215, 311, 314
Cyrenaica 205, 232, 309, 313, 314
Cyrene 47, 53, 64, 106, 107, 127, 145, 175, 186, 189, 200, 205, 215, 217, 232, 309, 311, 313, 314, 373
Cythera 39, 85, 205
Cythera, Strait of 204

D

D'Aubinac 37
Daedalus 55, 114, 382
Damareta 162, 163
Danaidai, from Egypt 34
Danaoi 122
Danaus 34
Darius 103, 105, 106, 160, 163
Dark Age 47, 117, 243
Dasios 228
Daskon 294
Dead Sea 29
Decimoputzu 114
Deinomenes 157
Deinomenidai 160, 164
Deinomenids 49, 163, 270, 297
Delos 26, 56, 101, 146, 382
Delphi 54, 58, 61, 96, 145, 146, 163, 186, 193, 200, 248, 309, 320
Demarete 228
Demeter 54, 89, 105, 198, 236, 282, 289, 370, 378
Demochares 191
Demonax 145, 215, 311
Demone 193
Demophanes 192
Demosthenes 78, 218
Dendra, Lord of 30
Denham, H. M. 208
Dexilaos 194
Di Grazia 283
Di-we (Zeus) 41
Di-wo-nu-so (Dionysus) 41
Diadumenus 65
Dicaearchia 188, 239
Didyma 58, 60, 327, 390
Dikaios 199
Dinos 96
Diocles 168, 220, 221
Diodorus 34, 128, 149, 156, 157, 170, 260, 280, 288, 296, 297, 302, 337
Diodorus Siculus 220, 221, 260, 350
Diomedes 210, 228
Dion 174, 175

Dione 67
Dionysius 78, 132, 160, 170, 171, 174, 175, 192, 228, 241, 248, 290, 299, 331, 338, 341, 346, 350, 351, 357, 363, 364, 396
Dionysius I 170, 175, 176, 220, 221, 228, 297, 337
Dionysius II 174, 176, 220
Dionysuse Via 272
Dioskouroi or Dioscuri 58, 156, 258, 310, 376, 395
Dipylon Head 58
Dirillo 276
Dirlmeier, Kilian 30
Discobolos 63
Discophorus 65, 70
Diver 103, 106
Dodecanese 86, 157
Dodona 374
Doidalsas 78
Dorico 322
Dorieus 162
Doryphoros 65, 72, 74
Doxenus 228
Drepanum 174
Dresden 84
Dresden Maenad 71
Droyssen 75
Ducetius 164, 299
Dymanes 217, 220

E

Early Archaic period 243
Early Bronze Age 25
Early Classical 65, 67, 71, 372
Early Cycladic grave 25
Early Cycladic II 33
Early Cypriot II 33
Early Helladic II 30
Early Iron Age 119
Early Minoan II 38
Early Minoan IIB 33
Early Minoan, period 30
Echia 145
Echinades Islands 149
Egypt 26, 30, 38, 40, 55, 56, 101, 105, 109, 123, 126, 137, 145, 163, 175, 176, 187, 205, 215, 223, 232, 311, 372
Eisogonos 81
Elba 145
Elder 102
Elders, Council of 215
Elea (Hyele) 217, 226
Elea 155, 156, 166, 176, 189, 217, 226, 245, 249, 255, 259, 262, 315, 347, 351, 351, 352, 354, 358

Electrides Islands 210
Eleusis 89
Elis 205
Elymi 128, 147, 336
Emmenidai 160, 164
Empedocles 221, 295, 340
Emporiae 127
Endoios 58
Enkomi 33
Enna 171, 356
Entella 171, 175, 221
Entymos 199
Epeius 210
Ephebos, Blond 63
Ephesos 58
Ephesus 60, 98, 370
Ephorus 151, 196, 266
Epicharmos 198
Epicurus 78, 82
Epidaurus 71
Epirus 47, 151, 176, 204, 205
Eqwesh 33
Eratosthenes 208
Erbessus 171
Erechtheum 67, 68
Eretria 46, 96, 99, 105, 120, 154, 160, 177, 180, 226, 239, 320
Ergastinai 68
Ergoteles 191
Ergotimos 89, 90
Eros drawing 74
Erythia 210
Erythrae 145
Eryx 162, 174
Esarhaddon 126
Esaro 149
Esaro River 255
Etesian 137
Etna 153, 157
Etna, Mount 206
Etruria (Veii) 120
Etruria 89, 90, 96, 101, 102, 103, 119, 120, 122, 180, 202, 209, 243, 375, 376, 390
Euanthes 196
Euboea (Manika) 33
Euboea 33, 45, 86, 119, 124, 141, 145, 154, 160, 166, 177, 189, 191, 192, 209, 243, 263, 276, 324, 354
Euboean Gulf 25, 183
Eucelados 197
Eucheiros 90
Euclid 228
Eucritos 197
Eudramon 192
Euhesperides 215, 314
Eumelus 181, 209
Eumenes 81, 228
Eumenes II, King 78, 81

Euopidas 197
Euphranor 99
Euphronius 93, 94, 95
Eupompus 99
Euripides 105
Euro-Asiatic continent 121
Europe 25, 26, 98, 264
Eurotas 75
Euryalus 171, 341, 350
Eurydice 106
Euryleon 286
Euthydicus 63
Euthykartides 56
Euthymides 93, 95
Eutychides 75
Euxine Sea (Black Sea) 147
Evander 210
Evans, Sir Arthur 33, 37, 38
Evenetus 228
Execias 90, 93

F

Fabius 108
Farnese 75
Farnese Heracles 74
Fates 105
Fattoria Stefan 365
Fauvel Head in the Louvre 58
Filicudi 109, 110
Final Bronze Age 116, 119
First Intermediate, period 33
Fishing 102
Fleet, The Admiral of the 33
Fondo Paviani 115
Forum Boarium 210
Francavilla 234
Francavilla Marittima 234
France 127, 140
Franchthi Cave 25
French 106, 254, 267, 268, 284, 353
Frettesina 115
Frigillus 228
Fusco 272
Fusco necropolis 270

G

Gades (modern Cadiz) 124
Gargano 109
Gate IV 295
Gate V 295
Gate VI 295
Gaul 193, 352
Gauls 81, 398
Gaza 46
Gela 140, 153, 154, 157, 159, 160, 162, 163, 168, 170, 176184, 189, 197, 199, 220, 221, 228, 270, 276, 279, 280, 294, 295, 299, 301, 322, 325, 332, 334, 351, 354, 361, 362, 368, 387, 391
Geloans (Licata) 176
Gelon 159, 160, 162, 163, 170, 176, 200, 228, 273, 274, 289, 296
Gelon I 220
Gelon II 220
Geneleos Group 58
Genoa, Gulf of 133
Geometric, period 36, 233
Gerace 252
Geron 163
Gerousia 215
Geryon 210
Giardini Margherita 210
Gibraltar 127
Gibraltar, Strait of 121
Giglio 140
Gilgamesh, epic 41
Gla 114
Gla in Boeotia 30
Gods 67, 138
Golden Fleece 209
Gordium 102
Gorgias 166
Gorgon 61
Greece 39, 44, 46, 47, 52, 54, 55, 85, 86, 90, 96, 98, 109, 114, 117, 118, 160, 163, 175, 176, 177, 202, 205, 206, 208, 209, 223, 233, 236, 239, 243, 263, 267, 280, 309, 310, 315, 318, 322, 324, 328, 332, 336, 342, 343, 345, 346, 352, 365, 366, 369, 370, 372, 373, 375, 376, 378, 380, 382, 385, 389, 391, 395, 396, 397, 398
Greek 233, 234, 235, 236, 238, 239, 241, 243, 244, 245, 248, 254, 258, 259, 260, 262, 263, 264, 265, 266, 267, 268, 270, 272, 273, 276, 277, 278, 282, 283, 286, 289, 294, 296, 298, 299, 300, 307, 309, 310, 315, 316, 318, 319, 320, 324, 327, 329, 330, 333, 336, 337, 339, 340, 341, 343, 345, 346, 347, 351, 352, 353, 354, 356, 357, 358, 359, 360, 361, 362, 364, 365, 366, 368, 369, 370, 372, 376, 377, 378, 380, 382, 385, 387, 389, 391, 394, 396
Greek Bronze Age 205
Greek Dark Age 119, 120
Greenland 29
Guadalquivir 123, 154, 202
Guadalquivir Valley 114
Gulf of Kiparissia (Trifilia) 204
Gyges, King 193, 238

H

Hades 105, 107
Hadrian 218
Hagia 197
Hagia Triada 40
Halicarnassus 71, 166, 307
Halykos 154, 174, 299
Hama 87
Hamilcar 163, 168, 175,
Hannibal 168, 170, 290
Harpagus 188
Hasdrubal 175
Hatti (Hittites) 29
Hecataeus 201
Hecate 198
Helen 149
Helenus 176
Helice 148, 183
Helius 210
Hellas 98, 141, 215
Hellenic era 139
Hellenistic periods 236
Hellespont 187
Helorus 272
Helorus River 159
Hephaestus 26
Hera 149, 191, 199, 209, 236, 240, 244, 254, 255, 317, 320, 332, 333, 362
Hera Lacinia 148, 149, 174, 195, 210
Heraclea (Herakleia) 217
Heraclea 162, 164, 166, 174, 176, 197, 217, 218, 226, 240, 261, 354, 359, 363, 364, 378, 396
Heraclea Minoa 154, 299, 361
Heracleides 220
Heracles 84, 149, 192, 196, 198, 209, 210, 226, 244, 302, 303, 320, 334, 377, 380
Heraclidae 36
Heraion 148, 244, 245, 255
Herakleia 240, 260, 354
Herbita 220
Herculaneum 101
Hercules 187, 201, 202
Hermes 105, 107
Hermocrates 168, 170, 288, 290
Hermokles 96
Heroa 260
Herodotus 26, 34, 43, 44, 45, 103, 127, 133, 137, 138, 145, 148, 149, 154, 160, 166, 183, 202, 205, 223, 297, 309, 311
Hesiod 137, 204, 209, 214

Hesperides, Garden of 74
Hicetas 175, 220
Hieron 94, 159, 163, 164, 176, 200, 273, 274, 280, 293, 294, 297, 305, 307, 342
Hieron I 220, 221
Hieron II 176, 220, 221, 299, 303, 307, 341, 342
Hieronymos 163, 220
Hill 51, 274, 276
Hilltop Sanctuaries 38
Himera 132, 154, 162, 163, 168, 189, 191, 199, 220, 228, 258, 259, 264, 278, 279, 280, 289, 290, 291, 293, 294, 296, 327, 331, 332, 347, 354, 360, 361, 365, 375
Himeraeae, Thermae 170, 174
Himilco 170, 171
Hipparinus 220
Hipparis 153, 293, 294, 302, 303
Hippocrates 154, 157, 159, 162, 220, 299
Hippodamus 165, 259, 260, 289, 296, 298, 299, 300, 301, 302, 303, 304
Hippon 175
Hipponion 338
Hipponium 153, 166, 171, 174, 196, 224, 226, 237, 330, 338
Hittite 34
Homer 30, 34, 36, 47, 137, 140, 202
Hunting 102
Huxley 34
Hyacinthus 151
Hybla 147, 157, 276
Hyblaea 252, 264, 266, 267, 268, 270, 272, 273, 274, 277, 279, 280, 282, 284, 289, 294, 315, 316, 318, 325, 329, 339, 347, 351, 353, 355, 359, 360, 362, 370
Hyblon 147, 266
Hyele 155, 255, 315
Hyksos, Kings 34
Hylleis 220
Hyperides 89

I

Ialysus 53, 184
Iapygia 210, 239, 244, 377, 385
Iberia 124, 128, 145, 209, 222, 352
Iberian Peninsula 145
Ibiza 128
Idomeneus 34, 36
Iglesias 130

Iliad 34, 71, 181
Ilioupersis 71
Ilissus 58
Ilium 152
Illyria 180, 387
Imera 154
Incoronata 238, 243
Inessa 164
Iolcus 209
Ionia 224
Ionian 245, 302, 320, 322, 330, 351, 370, 372, 373, 380, 383, 389, 390, 391
Ionian Islands 25, 204, 385
Ionian Sea 177, 183, 205, 208, 322, 345, 377
Ionian, coast 174, 315, 354
Ionio 267
Irene 71
Iris 69
Irminio 276
Iron Age 34, 36, 39, 119, 243, 389
Ischia 109, 117, 137, 177, 189, 191, 239, 243, 272, 354
Ischia, Isle of 124
Ischia, Pithekoussai 88, 145, 163, 166
Isone 200
Israel 44
Issa (Lissa) 221
Issus 232, 397
Isthmia 189, 320
Istria 372
Italian Peninsula 141
Italy 65, 88, 90, 96, 98, 101, 105, 109, 112, 114, 115, 117, 119, 124, 140, 141, 146, 147, 148, 151, 152, 156, 157, 160, 165, 166, 171, 176, 183, 184, 188, 189, 194, 201, 202, 205, 217, 220, 226, 232, 243, 263, 315, 365, 368, 370, 372, 378, 380, 389
Ithaca 47, 180
Jason 148, 209
Jehovah 34
Jeremiah 34
Julius Caesar 222
Justin 123, 128, 130, 132

K

Kale Akte 157, 164
Kallistes 197
Kaprogono 197
Karaburun 102, 103
Kart-Hadasht (Carthage) 126, 128
Kasmenai 276

Kassel 65
Keftiu 33
Kertsch 98
Khaniá 39
Killikyrioi 159
Kition 120
Kittos 98
Kizilbel 102, 103
Kleophon 96
Knapp 33
Knossos 30, 33, 34
Kouros from Athens 58
Kraay 228
Kroisos (Croesus) 90
Kruta, Venceslas 585
Kyllyrioi 159
Kyme 126, 239, 243, 255
Kytion 33

L

La Rocca, Eugenio 607
Lacinio 236
Laconia 85, 90, 96, 109, 184
Laconian 243, 256, 370, 372, 373, 374, 385, 387, 389
Laconians 256
Lade 157, 160, 188
Laffineaur, R. 33
Lamato 152
Lamentinus Sinus (Bay of Sant'Eufemia) 152, 166, 174
Lametos (now Lamato or Amato) 152
Lamis 197, 266, 268
Lampon 165
Lampsacus (modern Lapseki) 187
Languedoc 222
Laos 262
Lapith 70
Lapseki 187
Larache 121
Late Archaic period 256
Late Bronze Age 26, 29, 30, 33, 47, 109, 114, 116, 118, 201
Late Classical 236
Late Cypriot 119
Late Cypriot II 33, 118
Late Cypriot III 118
Late Helladic 39
Late Helladic IIIB 36
Late Helladic, culture 41
Late Imperial period 266
Late Minoan 30
Late Minoan I 33, 39
Late Minoan IA 29
Late Neolithic 25, 366
Latinus 214
Latium 210, 378

Laurion 85
Laus 165, 166, 224
Lazio 115
Leaning Satyr 72
Lebanon 43, 121, 124
Lechaeum 180, 204
Lefkadia 107
Lefkandi 30, 86, 117, 180
Lelantine Plain 154
Lelantine War 180
Lemnos 26
Leochares 71
Leontini 119, 147, 164, 166, 168, 170, 171, 175, 189, 193, 220, 228, 267, 273, 297, 347, 351
Lepore 264
Leptines 171
Lerna (Argolis) 30, 33
Lesbos 26
Leuca, Capo 205
Leucadia 204
Leucas 183
Leucopetra 208
Levant 223
Libone 333
Libya 145, 186, 187, 309, 313, 314
Licata 176
Liguria 232
Lilybaeum 174, 350
Lindioi 153, 280
Lindos 98
Lindus 53, 184, 188, 199
Linear A 37, 38, 39, 40, 41
Linear B 34, 37, 39, 40, 41, 85
Lipara 162, 220, 221
Lipari 109, 110, 119, 184, 378
Lipari Islands 42
Lippolis, E. 260
Livy 124, 239
Lixus (modern Larache) 121
Lizard-Slayer 72
Llanete de los Moros 114
Locri (Lokroi Epizephyrioi) 183, 217
Locri 197, 217, 218, 226, 237, 252, 255, 260, 263, 330, 338, 347, 351, 356, 357, 358, 359, 360, 370, 374, 376, 380, 382, 387, 390, 391, 394, 395
Locri Epizephyrii 152, 156, 171, 189, 196, 210, 226, 373
Locri, (Lokroi) 52, 152, 163, 166, 171, 174, 176
Lokroi Epizephyrioi 249, 338, 356
London 78, 88
Louvre 106
Lucani 141, 174, 378, 380
Lucania 215, 217, 226, 239, 262, 339, 343, 347, 352, 365, 365, 366, 377, 378
Lucius Papirius Cursor 176
Ludovisi 390, 391, 394
Ludovisi, Throne 64
Lycaon 210
Lycia 71, 101, 102, 376
Lyciscos 198
Lycophronidas 198
Lydia 154, 193
Lydian 238
Lydos 89, 90
Lykaios (Lycaeus) 311
Lyons, Gulf of 133
Lysippus 72, 74, 75, 99, 377, 380, 398
Lysoi 151

M

Macedon 223
Macedonian 396, 397
Macomer 123
Macompsisa (modern Macomer) 123
Maddoli, Gianfranco 481
Maeander River 188
Maeandrum 221
Maenaca 127, 187
Magna Graecia 52, 61, 103, 133, 152, 154, 155, 156, 157, 163, 164, 166, 171, 174, 175, 176, 189, 194, 205, 215, 217, 220, 221, 223, 224, 226, 228, 233, 240, 244, 252, 254, 255, 256, 258, 259, 262, 264, 270, 297, 322, 327, 328, 331, 337, 338, 339, 343, 351, 352, 353, 356, 359, 361, 365, 366, 368, 369, 370, 372, 373, 376, 380, 382, 385, 387, 389, 390, 396
Magnesia 188, 221
Mago 130
Mainland 30
Mainland Greece 239, 243, 263, 264, 268, 272, 274, 289, 299, 301, 315, 316, 319, 320, 322, 324, 325, 330, 333, 339, 340, 342, 343, 345, 346, 365, 369, 370, 372, 373, 375, 376, 378, 380, 385, 389, 391, 395, 396, 397
Mainland Greece 29, 34, 38, 39, 55, 61, 189, 196, 200, 223, 224
Mainland Greek 327
Mainland Ugarit (Syria) 39
Malacus 218
Malaga 124, 127
Malaka (Malaga) 124
Malchus 130, 162
Malea, Cape 134
Malée, Cap (Malea) 134
Mallia 38
Malophoros (Demeter) 198
Malophoros 282, 284, 289, 290
Mamercus 175, 220
Mamertines 175
Mandrocles 103, 197
Manes 90
Manika 25
Mannella 360
Manni 270
Mantinea 145, 215, 311
Manuzza 282, 283
Marathon 36, 160
Marcus Claudius Marcellus 176
Mardonius 36
Mare Piccolo 112
Marsa Matruch 112
Marsala 350
Marseilles 127, 128, 137, 154, 187, 189, 193, 352
Marsyas 98, 396
Martin 244, 263, 268
Marylos 197
Massalia (Marseilles) 127, 128, 187, 232, 53, 154, 155
Massalia (modern Marseilles) 137, 189, 193
Massalia 130, 140, 193, 217, 222, 226, 351, 352, 372
Massaliot 222
Mataurus 196
Mazare 188
Medes 63
Medica sativa 248
Mediterranean 109, 112, 114, 122, 126, 128, 133, 134, 137, 138, 140, 177, 187, 201, 202, 204, 222, 224, 226, 232, 266, 294, 309, 398
Mediterranean basin 121, 193, 223, 240, 263
Mediterranean islands 127
Mediterranean Sea 121, 206
Medma 153, 166, 171, 196, 226, 237, 374, 376, 391, 394
Megale 215
Megara 147, 160, 166, 183, 243, 252, 260, 264, 266, 267, 268, 270, 272, 273, 274, 277, 279, 280, 282, 284, 289, 294, 315, 316, 318, 322, 325, 329, 339, 340, 347, 351, 353, 355, 359, 360, 362, 370
Megara Hyblaea 147, 148, 159, 183, 189, 197, 198, 209
Megara Nysea 197
Megarians 189, 266, 267, 319
Megaris 145, 180, 263, 267
Meidias 98

Melanthius 99
Melas 56
Melian 25
Melita (Malta) 220, 221
Melos 25, 26, 33, 39
Melosas 197
Menaenum 164
Menander 78
Mende 69
Menecrates 199
Menekolos 294
Menelaus 78
Menidi 36
Menkheperreseneb 33
Mertens, Dieter 283, 288, 243, 315
Mesembria 183
Meso-Helladic, times 36
Mesolithic 25
Mesopotamia 26, 40
Messana (Messina) 184
Messana 159, 164, 170, 171, 175, 176, 184, 208, 221
Messara 30
Messene 191
Messenia 41, 85, 109, 147, 159, 184, 204, 205, 314
Messina 184, 243
Messina, Strait of 145, 146, 147, 152, 153, 154, 157, 163, 166, 171, 177, 180, 205, 206, 208, 226
Metapontion 359
Metaponto 238
Metapontum 151, 155, 157, 163, 166, 183, 184, 189, 193, 194, 196, 217, 224, 226, 226, 236, 238, 243, 244, 245, 246, 248, 252, 254, 255, 260, 277, 317, 319, 322, 327, 328, 329, 330, 331, 334, 337, 339, 340, 343, 347, 359, 361, 362, 363, 364, 365, 366, 368, 370, 372, 373, 375, 376, 382, 385, 387, 390, 394, 395, 396
Metaurus 237
Mezquitilla-Chorreras 124
Micciades 56
Michelangelo 75
Micon 99
Micythus 163, 220
Midas 90, 95
Middle Ages 372
Middle Bronze Age 26, 29, 33
Middle Helladic 30
Middle Helladic period 113
Middle Minoan I 38
Middle Minoan IA 29, 33
Middle Minoan II 38, 39
Middle Minoan III 39
Midea 30

Miletus 34, 86, 154, 155, 165, 187, 259, 296, 327, 390
Militello, Pietro 37
Miniature Frieze 33
Minnesota Messenia Expedition 30
Minos 26, 34, 146, 151,
Minos, King 210
Minos, Palace of 37, 41
Misenum 239
Mistral 137
Mithridates VI 84
Mnasandridas 198
Mnesiades 92, 93
Mochlos on Crete 29
Moio della Civitella. 245
Molp[a] 224
Monte Casale 276, 277, 347
Monte Finocchito 276
Monte Iato 343, 359
Monte Lauro 277
Montiferro 123
Moralia 284
Morgantina 164, 171, 220, 299, 303, 307, 342, 356, 359, 360, 361
Morocco 121, 130
Mothone 204
Motta di Francavilla Marittima al Mare 245
Motya 64, 124, 128, 132, 171, 198, 282, 347, 351
Mount Taphios 149
Mu Quarter 38
Museo Archeologico, Syracuse 301
Muslim, populations 28
Mycenae 29, 30, 37, 39, 47, 85, 86, 114
Mycenaean 243
Mycenaean age 30
Mycenaeology 37
Mylae 42, 171
Myscos 198
Mysia 145
Myskellos 149
Mytilene 223

N

Naples 81, 224, 257, 258, 259, 260, 262, 352, 377, 396
Naples, Bay of 117, 145, 148, 163, 176, 239
Naryka 152
Naucratis 149
Naucydes 70
Navarino 204
Naxos 25, 26, 56, 146, 147, 149, 159, 164, 166, 171, 177, 180,

183, 189, 192, 208, 228, 258, 259, 279, 280, 289, 293, 294, 296, 297, 298, 299, 315, 331, 347, 351, 353, 358, 359, 360, 372
Neapolis 108, 163, 166, 176, 215, 217, 218, 220, 226, 239, 243, 258, 260, 274, 297, 331, 341, 342
Near East 39, 42, 55, 352
Nearchus 89
Neda, river 204
Neleidai 151
Nemea 226
Nemesis 68
Neo-Atticism 70
Neo-Palatial 33
Neolithic 33
Neptune 328
Nestor 151, 191
New York 58
Nicaea (Nice) 127, 222
Nicaensium 222
Nicander 148
Nice 127
Nicias 96, 99, 106
Nicomachos 196
Nicomachus 99, 105, 106
Nidri 30
Nikandre 56, 382
Nike 56, 226, 228
Nikosthenes 90
Nile Delta 149
Niobe 84
Nisaea 280
Nisaeus 220
Nomai 164
Nora 124
North Africa 121, 154, 232
Nostoi 34
Numana 205
Nunzio Allegro 290
Nuraghe Antigori (Sarroch) 118

O

Oanis 153, 293, 302, 303
Odysseus 34, 209, 214
Odyssey 34, 137, 177, 205, 209
Oenotrus 210
Oiniadas 197
Ôlzbet S.art.ah, (Israel) 44, 46
Olympia 36, 61, 63, 67, 68, 96, 156, 163, 191, 194, 197, 199, 200, 226, 235, 260, 296, 320, 333, 374
Olympiads, (776 b.c.) 44
Olympus 210, 296, 327
Olympus, Mount 209

Olynthus 358
Onesimos 94
Onomastos 191
Ophellas 175
Opicia 141
Opuntii 196
Orchomenos in Boeotia 25
Oristano 118
Orlandini, Piero 243
Orontes 75, 87, 209
Orosei 114
Orroli 114
Orsi 270
Ortygia 147, 170, 171, 174, 228, 256, 270, 272, 274, 305, 338, 347, 350
Ostia 65
Otranto 205
Otranto Channel 133
Otranto, Strait of 204, 205
Oxford 37
Ozolae 196

P

Paeans 34
Paeonius 69
Paestum (Poseidonia) 101, 103, 108, 148, 152, 153, 155, 156, 165, 166, 176, 194, 195, 196, 217, 226, 236, 244, 245, 254, 255, 257, 260, 262, 318, 320, 322, 327, 328, 332, 333, 339, 343, 361, 365, 370, 373, 374, 375, 380, 385, 390, 396
Pagasae-Demetrias 101, 106
Palaepaphos-Skales 39
Palaepolis 239, 258
Palatine, Mount 210
Palestine 26, 43, 46, 122, 123
Palici 164
Palinurus 224
Pamphylia 186
Pamphyloi 217, 220
Pamphylus 99
Panaetius 220, 347
Panarea 110
Panchareos 197
Pandosia 166, 174, 195, 241
Panormus 124, 171
Pantalica 115, 276
Pantanello 244
Pantares 199
Parian master-sculptor 71
Paros 25, 26, 64, 372, 374, 385
Parrhasius 99, 104
Parthenon 67, 68, 69, 70, 78, 81, 333, 395
Parthenope 145, 163, 239, 243, 258

Pasha, Mustafa 108
Pasiadas 199, 200
Pasquier, Alain 63
Patras, Gulf of 204, 205
Pausanias 81
Pausias 99
Peithagoras 286
Pelagatti 270
Peleshet 34, 123
Pella 101
Peloponnese 36, 101, 114, 147, 157, 165, 180, 204, 205, 206, 236, 315, 322, 333, 369, 372, 373, 385, 387, 391, 394
Penelope 36
Pentapolis 215
Pentathlon 128
Pentathlus 162
Penticapaeum 98
Pentikapaion 98
Peplos Kore 58
Pergamum 78, 81, 82, 84, 262, 307, 378, 398
Periander 183
Pericles 51, 52, 67, 71, 96, 165, 218
Perieres 191
Peristeria 85
Persephone 105, 106, 304, 370, 391
Persephone, Sanctuary of 197
Persia 160, 223, 311, 370, 372, 389, 398
Persian 375
Petelia 166, 195, 217
Phaestus 38, 39, 153
Phaestus, Chambers 25 and LI 38
Phaistos Disk 38
Phalanthus 151, 224
Phalaris 154, 199, 220, 221, 294
Pharaoh Merneptah's 30
Pharos 232
Pharsalus 64
Phaselis 186
Pheidileos 191
Phidias 372, 376
Phidias 65, 67, 68
Phileia 58
Philip 99
Philip II 105, 106, 397
Philip II of Macedon 226
Philistine 127
Philistines 26, 34, 122
Philistus 176
Philotectes 210
Philoxenus 99, 105
Phintias 93, 176, 220
Phintylos 197
Phlegraean Islands 109
Phlegraean Plain 210

Phocaea 154, 160, 187, 188, 189, 193, 223, 245, 315
Phocaea, Ionian 222
Phocaean 389
Phocaeans 202
Phocaeans 351, 389
Phoenicia 126
Phoenician 128, 286, 347, 352
Phrygia 102
Phryne 72, 200
Phylakopi in Melos 25
Phyromachos 75, 81, 82
Piazza Duomo 272
Piediluco-Contigliano 116
Pileo-Delphic Amphictyony 54
Pillars 187, 201, 202
Pindar 34, 296, 301, 309, 310, 334
Piraeus 165, 296, 299, 369
Piraeus Apollo 61
Pisistratids 49, 94
Pisistratus 89
Pithekoussai (Ischia) 117, 208
Pithekoussai (modern Ischia) 88, 145
Pithekoussai 119, 120, 124, 126, 137, 177, 189, 191, 239, 243, 272, 354, 358, 360
Pithekoussai-Cumae 189
Pitsà 101
Pixunte 224
Plataea 99, 186, 200, 309
Platani River Valley 110
Plato 82, 107, 174, 175, 176, 223, 224
Platonic Academy 215
Pliny 75, 101, 102, 104, 121
Pliny the Elder 56
Plutarch 205, 223, 284
Plutus 71
Po River 205
Po Valley 115, 210
Po-se-da (Poseidon) 41
Policoro 360, 396
Polieion 151
Poliochni 26
Poliochni in Lemnos 25
Polion 96
Poliouchoi 282
Pollis 220, 221
Pollux 156
Polybius 152, 154, 157, 174, 202, 307
Polyclitus (Polykleitos) 65, 70, 72, 74, 372, 376
Polycrates 156, 160, 188
Polydorus 184
Polyeuctus 78
Polygnotus 96, 99
Polygnotus of Thasos 63
Polyzelus 163, 200, 220

Pomey, Patrice 133
Pompeii 101, 105, 352, 397
Pompeius Trogus 130
Pontecagnano 119, 380
Pontrandolfo, Angela 457
Pontus 84
Pontus Euxinus 177, 183, 187
Populonia 145
Porcos 200
Porta Rosa 262
Porta Settembrini 252
Porticello 65
Portigliola 252
Porto Grande 272
Porto Saturo 256
Poseidon 78, 223, 224
Poseidonia 236, 244, 249, 256, 318, 361, 362, 364, 365, 370
Poseidonia, v.Paestum
Potidaea 183, 196
Pozzuoli 188, 239
Praisos 154
Praxiteles 72, 78
pre-Hellenic 239
Priam 48, 71
Priene 188, 302
pro-Punic 286
Prochyte 145
Procne and Itys 68
Proetus 151
Proklees 95
Prometheus 84
Propontis 183, 187
Protagoras 165
Proto-Palatial 30
Protogenes 99, 104
Provence 137, 201, 232, 352
Psammetichos I, Pharaoh 55
Psiax 92
Ptoan Sanctuary 58
Ptolemaic 206, 313
Ptolemais 215, 313
Ptolemies 78, 232
Ptolemy 215
Ptolemy I 175
Ptolemy I Soter 215
Ptolemy III 313, 314
Ptolemy III 99
Ptolemy III Euergetes 215
Publius Statius 228
Pugliese Carratelli, Giovanni 141
Punta Alice 149, 166
Punta Alice 245
Punta della Campanella 149
Punta di Stilo 152
Puteoli 145
Pylos (Navarino) 204
Pylos 30, 34, 39, 40, 41, 114, 151

Pyrgi 130
Pyrrhos 193
Pyrrhus 175, 176, 218, 220
Pythagoras 156, 163, 188, 375
Pythea 198
Pytho (Delphi) 146
Python 72, 94
Pyxus 155, 166
Qubur el-Walaydah, (south of Gaza) 46

Q

Qurna 33

R

Rallo 283
Rampin Rider 58
Ramses III 30
Raphael 75
Ras Shamra, Syria 37
Reason 72
Red House 33
Reggio Calabria (Chalcidian Rhegium) 217
Rekhmira 33
Renaissance 372
Rhadamanthys 107
Rhamnus 68
Rhegion 177,43
Rhegion, Rhegium 52
Rhegium 243, 351, 373, 375, 390
Rhegium, (Rhegion) 52, 146, 147, 157, 163, 166, 171, 175, 176, 177, 180, 184, 189, 191, 192, 208, 217, 218, 220, 224, 226
Rhodes 26, 34, 43, 53, 109, 127, 181, 184, 186, 189, 199, 206, 223, 263, 294, 296, 299, 307, 322, 377, 389
Rhodes, Islands 184
Rhypes 149
Riace 65
Ridgway, David 117, 239
Ripe 183
Rolley, Claude 369
Roma Via 272
Rome 262, 266, 307, 352
Rome 52, 78, 101, 119, 130, 132, 137, 145, 157, 162, 176, 210, 217, 262, 266, 307, 352
Rosalia Camerata Scovazzo 290
Rouveret, Agnès 99
Russia 101, 107

S

S. Mazzarino 132
Sabelli 166
Sacred Way 61
Sagras River 152, 156
Saint Peter 137
Sakellariou, M.B. 177, 263, 264
Sala Consilina 373
Salamis 163, 196
Salentina Peninsula 204
Salerno, Gulf of 163
Saliagos 25
Salso River 244
Samian 202, 309, 330, 389, 390
Samians 184, 389
Samos 26, 52, 55, 56, 58, 60, 90, 99, 103, 147, 154, 155, 156, 160, 186, 187, 188, 239, 330, 370, 382, 385, 389, 390
Samothrace 26, 82
Samuel 123
San Biagio 151, 243, 244, 319, 362, 363, 368, 390
San Cusmano 266, 267, 272
San Lorenzo 258
San Nicola 295
Sanctuary of Hera 58
Sant'Eufemia, Bay of 152, 166
Sant'Imbenia 119
Santa Maria d'Anglona 238
Santa Venera 280
Santorini 200, 310
Sardinia 114, 115, 118, 119, 120, 121, 122, 123, 124, 126, 128, 128, 130, 145, 157, 226
Saronic Gulf (Cenchreae) 204
Saronic Gulf 165, 180
Sarroch 118
Sartori, Franco 215
Saseno 204
Sassi, Maria Michela 515
Satyrion 151, 256, 385
Sauroctonus 72
Sausgamuwa, king of Amurru 34
Schliemann, Heinrich 37
Schmidt, G. 295
Scidrus 166
Scoglio del Tonno 112
Scopas 71, 72, 397
Scylacium 152, 174, 217
Scylax 205
Scylla 82, 159
Scylla and Charybdis 134, 208
Scylleticus Sinus (Bay of Squillace) 174
Scythes 220
Sea Peoples 26, 30, 33, 34
Second Palaces on Crete 29
Segesta 162, 165, 168, 171, 221,

336, 337, 343
Sele 149, 153, 244, 245, 370, 373, 374, 383, 389, 390, 391
Sele River 148, 209, 236, 244, 320, 322, 380, 390
Seleucus I 77, 82
Selinos 288
Selinunte 358
Selinuntines 162
Selinus 124, 147, 154, 159, 165, 168, 174, 189, 197, 198, 200, 220, 223, 228, 252, 259, 260, 264, 268, 270, 279, 280, 282, 283, 284, 286, 288, 289, 290, 291, 293, 296, 299, 315, 319, 320, 322, 325, 327, 328, 331, 332, 333, 336, 340, 341, 345, 346, 347, 350, 351, 358, 359, 362, 370, 374, 380
Selinus, Thermae 174
Selymbria 183
Semite 34
Senmut 33
Serra, Orlando 356
Serraglio 29
Sexi (modern Almu) 64, 370
Shaft Grave Circles A and B 29
Shaft Grave Circles A and B of Mycenae 30
Sheqelesh 122
Sherdana 122, 123
Siana 89
Sibyl 145
Sicana 198
Sicania 151
Sicel 147, 164, 171, 266, 267, 276
Sicels 171, 175, 270, 274, 276
Sicilian Channel 154, 162
Sicily 33, 42, 105, 109, 110, 115, 117, 119, 120, 121, 122, 123, 124, 132, 137, 140, 141, 145, 146, 147, 149, 151, 153, 154, 157, 160, 162, 163, 164, 166, 168, 170, 171, 174, 175, 176, 177, 183, 184, 189, 197, 199, 201, 202, 205, 206, 208, 209, 210, 217, 220, 221, 222, 223, 224, 228, 233, 243, 259, 263, 264, 266, 270, 272, 274, 276, 278, 279, 280, 286, 294, 296, 297, 298, 299, 300, 322, 324, 325, 327, 330, 333, 334, 337, 338, 339, 341, 343, 345, 347, 350, 351, 352, 353, 354, 355, 356, 357, 359, 361, 365, 365, 369, 370, 376, 380, 385, 387, 390
Sicyon 99
Sid 130
Sidon 101, 121, 130
Sigeum (modern Yenisehir, Turkey) 189
Sikelikon 205
Silarus (Sele) 153
Sinaranu 34
Siphnian Treasury 58, 61
Siphnos 26
Sirens 209
Siris (Sirino) 224
Siris 149, 151, 152, 155, 156, 157, 165, 166,188, 189, 193, 237, 237, 238, 261, 319, 347, 351, 354, 365, 370, 373, 373, 382, 389, 396
Siris River 217, 218
Sleeping Head from Ephesus 60
Smyrna 78, 277
So[ntia] 224
Socrates 71, 82
Soloeis 171
Solon 89, 223
Soluntum 127, 302, 342, 343
Somrotidas 197
Sophilus 89
Sorrento 148, 149
Sotades 95
Sotairos 198
Sounion 56
Spain 121, 123, 124, 128, 130, 132, 187, 193
Sparta 47, 49, 52, 53, 98, 156, 165, 166, 168, 176, 183, 184, 189, 218, 226, 264, 370, 372, 374, 387
Sperlonga 82, 84
Spina 205, 210
Spinazzo 108
Squillace, Gulf of 206
Starr 34
Stefano Vassallo 290
Stone Age Aegean 25
Strabo 95, 134, 151, 157, 189, 205, 208, 218, 220, 222, 243, 274
Stratonicos 81
Sublime Porte 28
Suessa 226
Suessula 224
Sulcis 124
Sybaris 113, 114, 148, 149, 152, 153, 155, 156, 157, 163, 165, 166, 183, 189, 194, 195, 196, 224, 226, 234, 235, 236, 238, 243, 244, 245, 246, 255, 260, 262, 319, 322, 353, 372, 373, 382, 383, 389
Syracuse, (Syrakousai) 49, 53, 61, 101, 108, 110, 132, 138, 147, 148, 151, 154, 159, 160, 163, 164, 165, 166, 168, 170, 171, 174, 175, 176, 180, 181, 183, 189, 192, 196, 197, 199, 200, 205, 206, 209, 220, 221, 228, 243, 249, 256, 260, 267, 270, 272, 273, 274, 276, 280, 294, 296, 297, 298, 303, 305, 307, 315, 322, 324, 325, 327, 328, 330, 331, 332, 333, 337, 338, 340, 341, 342, 343, 345, 346, 350, 351, 353, 360, 377, 382, 389
Syrakousai (modern Syracuse) 138
Syrakousai = Syracuse
Syrakousai 276
Syria 26, 37, 39, 40, 44, 45, 55, 121, 124, 177, 181, 184, 209
Syros 25, 90
Syrtis 145

T

Tamassos 120
Taormina 208, 339
Taranto 106, 112, 262
Taranto, Bay of 193
Taranto, Gulf of 137, 194, 195, 205, 206
Taras 184, 197, 218, 223, 233, 243, 249, 352
Taras, v. Tarentum
Tarentum 53, 64, 108, 151, 156, 157, 166, 174, 176, 184, 189, 194, 196, 197, 218, 223, 224, 226, 233, 234, 243, 244, 245, 256, 260, 261, 270, 345, 352, 370, 372, 373, 376, 376, 377, 378, 380, 382, 383, 385, 387, 390, 394, 395, 396, 397, 398
Tarquinia 102, 106, 389
Tarquinius Superbus 157
Tarquins 157
Tarsis 132
Tarsus 122, 184
Tartessus 123, 127, 154, 187, 202, 209
Tataies 191
Taucheira 215, 313
Tauromenium 171, 220, 221, 222
Tavole Palatine 236
Teanum 378
Tedeschi Via 255
Tegea 72
Tel Abu Hawam 112
Tell Fekheriyeh, (Syria) 44
Tellaro 276

793

Telos 160
Temenos 282
Temesa 195, 224
Temple of Apollo 60, 61
Temple of Olympia 63
Tenea 181
Tenos 26, 180
Teresh 122, 124
Teresh at Tarsus 122
Terillus 163, 220, 293
Terina 152, 153, 166, 174, 195, 217, 226
Termitito 113
Terpone 193
Teuthras 145
Thapsos 110, 115, 147
Tharros 124, 127, 128
Thasos 26, 56, 372, 374, 390
The Archaic Period in
Theano 48
Thebes 33, 34, 36, 39, 47, 53, 98, 99, 101, 104, 105, 114
Themistocles 65, 164, 165, 337
Thenceforth 25
Theocles 192
Theognis 223
Theogony 209
Theokles 266
Theopompus 184
Thera (modern Santorini) 26, 29, 34, 39, 47, 101, 102, 189
Thera (Santorini) 200
Thera 186, 189, 205, 215, 309, 310
Theran 215
Therans 186
Thermos 320
Theron 160, 162, 163, 199, 220, 286, 293, 294, 297
Theseus 88, 146
Thesmophoros 199
Thespiadai 157
Thespiae 99
Thessaly 54, 106, 209
Thorikos 36
Thrace 107, 108, 187, 223
Thrasybulus 220
Thrasydaeus 163, 191, 221
Thucydides 26, 34, 120, 128, 132, 138, 149, 151, 168, 202, 205, 208, 263, 266, 276, 280, 284, 294
Thuria 16, 260
Thurii 96, 164, 165, 166, 171, 174, 176, 197, 218, 221, 226, 257, 260, 261, 262, 296, 299
Thurina 260
Thurioi 165

Tiber 145
Tibios 90
Tiglathpileser III 126
Tiles, House of the 30, 33
Tilos 157
Timaeus 34, 121, 152, 155
Timarchus 78
Timoleon 174, 175, 220, 221, 274, 294, 295, 299, 300, 301, 302, 303, 304, 305, 339, 357, 365
Timotheus 71
Timpone della Motta 234
Tiryns 30, 39, 114
Titus 218
Tjeker 122
Torre Mordillo 113
Torto 154
Toscanos 124
Traeis River 165, 166
Tréziny, Henri 347
Trianda on Rhodes 29
Tribunali Via dei 258
Trifilia 204
Tripolitania 130
Troezen 183
Troy 48, 141, 151, 152, 210
Troy V 29
Tudhaliyas IV 34
Tunis 137
Tunisia 124
Turkey 189, 228
Tusa 288
Tuscany 119
Tyche 77, 274, 297, 305
Tyndarion 220
Tyndaris 171, 221, 299, 342
Tyre 120, 121, 123, 126, 128
Tyrian 126
Tyrrhenian 109, 208, 237, 239, 245, 373
Tyrrhenian Sea 137, 177, 180, 205, 206, 389
Tzepi, A. Kosmas 33
Tzepi, of Marathon 33

U

Ugarit, (modern Ras Shamra, Syria) 34, 37, 116
Ugarit, Mainland (Syria) 39
Ugento 373
Ulysses 36, 47, 48, 137, 177
User-Amon 33
Utica 121, 124

V

Vaglio 217, 377, 380, 396
Vagnetti, Lucia 109
Valerius Maximus 217, 222
Vallet, G. 260, 267, 268
Valona 204
Vari 89
Vasiliki 33
Vasto 377
Veii (Isola Farnese, Rome) 102, 119
Velabrum 210
Velia 155, 245, 354, 389
Velleius Paterculus 121
Venice 48
Ventris, Michael 37, 41
Venus 72
Vergina 105, 106
Vico 37
Victory 69, 70, 228, 290, 332
Vignale 259
Villa Adriana 68
Villabartolomea 115
Villanovan 119
Villard, F. 267, 268
Vitelia or Vitalia 226
Vitruvius 101, 334
Vittoria; Piazza della 274
Vivara 109, 145
Volcei 217
Volos 101
Vounoi 33
Voza 274, 277, 305
Voza digs 270
Vrana-Marathon 30

W

Wadi Khalij 309
Warrior Vase 30
West 30, 42
West House 26
Williams, Dyfri 85
Wolf 37
World War II 233

X

Xanthippe 67
Xanthus 71, 376
Xenocrates 104, 165
Xenophanes 155
Xerxes 160

Y

Yali 33
Yenisehir 189

Z

Zacynthus 204, 205
Zadar 205
Zakros 40, 41
Zaleucus 196, 226
Zancani Montuoro 234, 390
Zancle 145, 146, 157, 159, 164, 166, 177, 180, 184, 188, 189, 191, 220, 223, 224, 228, 280, 298
Zankle 243
Zeno 82
Zeus 34, 65, 67, 81, 156, 191, 195, 199, 200, 243, 254, 296, 311, 312, 324, 327, 329, 333, 354, 373, 377, 378, 385, 390, 398
Zeus Aglaios 151
Zeus Agoraios 254
Zeus Ammon 232
Zeus Meilichios 196, 198
Zeus Olympios 191
Zeus Olympius 191, 197, 217, 218, 221, 226
Zeus, Temple of 67, 68
Zeuxis 99, 104, 105

Palazzo Grassi would like to extend its thanks to the following individuals and organizations for their generous contribution to the preparation of the graphic aspect of the exhibition directed by Pierluigi Cerri, by giving permission to use the photographs for the ATLAS along the walls of Palazzo Grassi:

The British Museum

ARCH. PHOT. PARIS/SPADEM, CNMHS/SPADEM
photos by Philippe Berthé

Ecole Nationale Supérieure des Beaux-Arts, Paris
Photo ENSBA

Wallraf-Richartz-Museum, Köln, Rheinisches Bildarchiv, Köln

Mimmo Jodice, Napoli

Banco di Napoli, for the illustrations from:
"Paestum", Ed. F. Zevi, Napoli, 1990
"Pompei I", Ed. F. Zevi, Napoli, 1991

Soprintendenza Archeologica di Salerno

Reggio Calabaria, Soprintendenza Archeologica della Calabria

"Il teatro antico di Siracusa", "I monumenti dell'arte classica"
edited by Luigi Polacco e Carlo Anti
Maggioni Editore, Rimini, 1981
Plates by Alberto Carlo Scolari

Longanesi & C. Editori in Milan for the illustrations from:
"L'alba della Magna Grecia" by David Ridgway, Milan, 1984

Dieter Mertens, for the illustrations from:
"Il cosiddetto Trono di Boston" in M. Guarducci
from "Bollettino d'Arte", 1987

Roma, Soprintendenza Archeologica per l'Etruria Meridionale
Photos by S.A.E.M. Mauro Benedetti

New York, The Metropolitan Museum of Art, Dodge Fund, 1930

Taranto, Soprintendenza Archeologica della Puglia
Credito Italiano, Milano for the illustrations from:
"Megale Hellas. Storia e civiltà della Magna Grecia", Libri Scheiwiller, Milan, 1983
"Sikanie. Storia e civiltà della Sicilia greca", Garzanti
"Rasenna. storia e civiltà degli Etruschi", Libri Scheiwiller, Milan, 1986

© Photo R.M.N.

The Saint Louis Art Museum

Edizioni SEAT, Torino for the illustrations from:
"Teatri greci e romani - Alle origini del linguaggio rappresentato"
edited by Paola Ciancio Rossetto and Giuseppina Pisani Sartorio

Trapani, Soprintendenza per i Beni Culturali ed Ambientali

Soprintendenza Archeologica di Pompei

Caltanissetta, Soprintendenza per i Beni Culturali ed Ambientali
Photos by G. Castelli
Photos by G. Nicoletti

Napoli, Soprintendenza Archeologica delle Province di Napoli e Caserta

Hirmer Fotoarchiv, München

Ministry of Culture, Athens

National Archaeological Museum, Athens

Ernst Wasmuth Verlag GmbH &

Co. for the illustrations from: "Bildlexikon zur Topographie des antiken Athen" by John Travlos Deutsches Archäologisches Institut, Tübingen, 1971

Staatliches Museum Schwerin
Photos by H. Maertens, Bruges

Martin von Wagner-Museum der Universität Würzburg/Antikenabteilung
Photos by Karl Öhrlein

Musée du Louvre, Paris/Bridgeman Art Library, London

Staatliche Museen zu Berlin - Preussischer Kulturbesitz
Antikensammlung
Photos by Johannes Laurentius
Photod by Ingrid Geske-Heiden

Rob Smeets, Milano

Electa, Milan for the illustrations from:
"Magna Grecia", vol. I-IV, 1985-90

American School of Classical Studies, Athens
Colour illustrations by Piet de Jong

A special thank to:
Jean-Pierre Adam, Giuseppe Andreassi, Klaus Anger, Thomas Aumüller, Giovanna Bacci, Hans-Georg Bankei, Marcella Barra-Bagnasco, Paolo Belli, Heinz Jürgen Beste, Irene Blum, Nicola Bonacasa, Rosalia Camerata Scovazzo, Joe Carter, Marina Cipriani, Federica Cordano, Katharina Dalcher, Francesco D'Andria, Ernesto De Miro, Antonio De Siena, Carmela Angela Di Stefano, Giovanni Di Stefano, Antonino Di Vita, Graziella Fiorentini, Daniela Gaus, Liliana Giardino, Emanuele Greco, Giovanna Greco, Gottfried Gruben, Giorgio Gullini, Erik Hansen, Isabel Haupt, Achim Heiden, Valentina Hinz, Hans Peter Isler, Silvana Jannelli, Gundula Jenewein, John Kenfield, Hermann Kienast, Fritz Krinzinger, Wolf Koenigs, Manolis Korres, Maria Costanza Lentini, Enzo Lippolis, Matthias Lohmann, Silvana Luppino, Michael Maass, Klaus Mathieu, Marina Mazzei, Madeleine Mertens-Horn, Rosalba Panvini, Paola Pelagatti, Patrizio Pensabene, Friedrich Rakob, Frank Rumscheid, Claudio Sabbione, Florian Seiler, Roberto Spadea, Umberto Spigo, Dinu Theodorescu, Maria Trojani, Agata Villa, Paolo Vitti, Giuseppe Voza, Armin Wiegand, Wolfgang Wurster
for the records on urban planning and architecture.

Special thanks to the Soprintendenza archeologica della Basilicata and the Soprintendenze ai BB.CC.AA. della Sicilia, the Società S.A.R.A. Nistri/Roma and l'Istituto Geografico Militare/Firenze.

For the Atlas texts a special thanks to:
Luigi Bernabò Brea (Theatre), Nicola Bonacasa (Hellenistic Art in Sicily), Angelo Bottini (the debatte on the "Troni"), Giovanni Gorini (the coinage), Emanuele Greco (the colonization), Pietro Giovanni Guzzo (Jewellery), Piero Orlandini (Artistic Culture the "Troni": intruductory text), Angela Pontrandolfo (Italic Peoples - Painting - Coroplastics), Giovanni Pugliese Carratelli (History), Elisabetta Setari (Hoplitism - Banquetting - Dionysism - Runerary Rituals)

Trasletors of the Atlas texts:
Malcolm Bell, Sebastiano Brandolini, Catherine Flynn

Photos Credits

Unless otherwise indicated, all the white-and-black illustrations of the objects have been give by the Soprontendenze and Museums

Special thanks to the Credito Italiano for its generous contribution in providing the photographs

Adamesteanu: 260
Archaeological Receipts Fund (TAP Service), Athens: 27, 28, 31, 99, 100, 177 (in alto)
Archivio Alinari, Firenze: 69 (in basso), 74 (in alto, a sinistra), 79 (Anderson)
Archivio RCS Libri & Grandi Opere 29, 32, 34, 36, 37, 38, 48 (in alto), 49 (in alto), 52, 59, 65, 101, 102, 138, 156, 160, 181 (a sinistra), 204, 455, 478 (in basso), 484, 495, 554 (a destra), 557, 558, 559, 625
Piero Baguzzi 74 (in alto a destra), 83, 122 (a destra), 123 (a sinistra), 130, 131, 133, 135, 144, 152 (a sinistra), 184 (in basso), 322, 567, 574 (a destra), 575, 588 (in basso), 590, 608 (in basso)
Alberto Bertoldi 49 (al centro), 72, 121, 122 (a sinistra), 123 (a destra), 124, 126, 127, 129, 132, 150, 298, 425, 466-467, 468, 574 (a sinistra)
Mario Matteucci 42, 45, 152 (a destra), 155, 165, 168, 169, 589 (in alto)
Archivio Scala, Firenze: 65 (in alto), 75
Atelier du Patrimoine, Marseille: 578, 581 (in basso)
Lidiano Bacchielli: 215, 309 (in alto), 313
Andrea Baguzzi, Milano: 40, 50, 51, 53, 64 (a destra), 70, 76, 77 (in alto), 112, 151, 177 (in basso), 181 (a destra), 192, 193, 195, 196, 197, 200, 216, 219, 224, 225, 226, 227 (in alto e al centro), 228, 229 (in basso), 236, 367, 368, 371, 373-377, 379, 381, 382, 383 (a sinistra), 384, 385, 387, 390-393, 394 (in alto), 395 (a destra), 396, 398, 443 (a destra), 444, 445 (a destra), 448, 449 (in alto), 450-452, 454, 457-465, 469, 471-478 (in alto), 480, 481, 486-490 (a destra), 491, 493, 494, 499, 500, 503, 504, 505, 507, 508, 510 (a destra), 512, 516, 518, 534, 542, 543, 545, 546 (in basso), 547, 551, 552, 553, 560, 561, 614, *Cat. 5-7, 9, 10, 13, 15, 16, 21, 22, 26-37, 46-54, 65-70, 76, 79-85, 100, 102-105, 106, 108-112, 114, 115, 117, 118, 120, 127, 128, 133, 134 III-137, 139, 140, 144, 145, 148-151, 159-166, 168-176, 189, 191-198, 201-203, 205-213, 215-222, 224, 225, 228, 234, 235, 243-251, 253, 255-262, 266, 268-285, 287, 289-294, 295-299, 301-313, 315-336, 338-343, 345-349, 351, 397*
Michel Bats: 582 (in alto e al centro)
Copyright © Bildarchiv Preussischer Kulturbesitz, Berlin 1995
 Ingrid Geske: 207, 383, 395 (a sinistra), 449 (in basso) *Cat. 76, 146*
 Jürgen Liepe: 388, *Cat. 122*
P.J. Bomhof, Rijksmuseum van Oudheden, Leiden, *Cat. 344*
Copyright © 1995 The Metropolitan Museum of Art, New York: 57 (a sinistra), 92, 93, 178-179, 446, 485, *Cat. 134 I e II, 288, 337*
Copyright © 1995 / All rights reserved the Museum of Fine Arts, Boston, *Cat. 11, 78, 190*
Copyright © The Nelson Gallery Foundation. All reproduction Rights Reserved, *Cat. 286*
Copyright © Photo RMN, Paris: 441, *Cat. 200, 223, 416*
 M. Chuzeville: 180, 573
 H. Lewandowski: 95, *Cat. 200*
C.N.R.S., Centre Camille Jullian, Aix-en-Provence: 140 (cliché Margot Derain), 352 (in basso), 581 (in alto), 582 (in basso), 583
Marco Crillissi - Soprintendenza Archeologica di Sassari: 115, 117, 118, 119
Lorenzo De Masi, Roma: 610, 611, *Cat. 402*
Didierjean: 352 (in alto)
ENI, per gentile concessione: 238
Ekdotike Athenon S.A., Athens: 104, 105
Werner Forman Archive, London: 588 (in alto)
FotOttica Randazzo: 109
Thomas Goldschmidt Fotograf, Badisches Landesmuseum, Karlsruhe: *Cat. 116, 263*
Hunting Aerofilms Limited, Borehamwoo: 309, 311, 312
Idini, Roma: 81, 621, 622
IGM, per gentile concessione: 257
F. Krinzinger: 261
David Lees: 128 (in alto)
Giuseppe Leone, copertina, 110 (in basso), 128 (in basso), 158, 159, 161, 162, 164, 167, 170, 172-173, 182, 186, 194, 198, 202, 205, 221, 227 (in basso), 229 (in alto e al centro), 230, 287, 301, 306, 400 (in basso), 401-405, 407, 408, 409, 411-420, 422-425 (a destra), 426, 427, 430-436, 456, 482, 490 (a sinistra), 510 (a sinistra), 531 (a destra), *Cat. 1-4, 8, 19, 20, 24, 25, 38-45, 55-64, 72-75, 86-97, 98, 99, 101, 121, 123-126, 129, 142, 147, 152-156, 167, 177-188, 204, 230-233, 236-242, 350, 353-395*
Mairie-dépôt des fouilles de La Cloche, Marignane: 584 (in basso)
Dieter Mertens: 244-245, 246, 319, 321, 323, 326, 328, 331, 332, 333, 335, 336-344
New York University Excavations at Aphrodisias, New York: 517
Claire Niggli - Antikenmuseum Basel und Sammlung Ludwig, Basel: 453, *Cat. 214*
Pedicini, Napoli: 82 (in basso)
Pubbliaerfoto, Milano: 147, 153, 235, 269, 276, 279, 290, 293, 295, 302, 349-350
Pytheas-KFT, Budapest: 589 (in basso)
Stefan Rebsamen - Bernisches Historisches Museum, Bern: 386
M. Sarri, Roma: 91
SRA, Montpellier: 577
Studio Christa Koppermann, Gauting bei München: 96, 397, 620, *Cat. 267*
Henry Tréziny: 347, 351
Vasari, Roma: 80
R. Venturini, Salerno: 536 (a destra), 537 (a destra)
P. Zigrossi: 214, 445 (a sinistra), *Cat. 14, 141*

Translators Andrew Ellis *Map-making* Studio Aguilar
David Stanton
Vanessa Vesey
Carol Rathman
Jeff Jennings
Harriett Graham
John Hunt
Georges Whiteside

Fotocomposizione Grande - Monza

Printed in Italy March 1996
by New Interlito - Italia - Caleppio di Settala (Milan)